Africa's Geography

DYNAMICS OF PLACE, CULTURES, AND ECONOMIES

First Edition

Benjamin Ofori-Amoah
Western Michigan University

SENIOR DIRECTOR	Veronica Visentin
EXCECUTIVE EDITOR	Glenn Wilson
EDITORIAL MANAGER	Judy Howarth
CONTENT MANAGEMENT DIRECTOR	Lisa Wojcik
CONTENT MANAGER	Nichole Urban
SENIOR CONTENT SPECIALIST	Nicole Repasky
PRODUCTION EDITOR	Indirakumari S.
PHOTO EDITOR	Rajalaxmi Rajendrasingh
COVER PHOTO CREDIT	© Pavliha / iStockphoto

This book was set in 10/12 pt ITC New Baskerville Std by SPi Global and printed and bound by Quad Graphics.

Founded in 1807, John Wiley & Sons, Inc. has been a valued source of knowledge and understanding for more than 200 years, helping people around the world meet their needs and fulfill their aspirations. Our company is built on a foundation of principles that include responsibility to the communities we serve and where we live and work. In 2008, we launched a Corporate Citizenship Initiative, a global effort to address the environmental, social, economic, and ethical challenges we face in our business. Among the issues we are addressing are carbon impact, paper specifications and procurement, ethical conduct within our business and among our vendors, and community and charitable support. For more information, please visit our website: www.wiley.com/go/citizenship.

ISBN: 978-0-470- 58358-6 (PBK)

ISBN: 978-1-119- 40153-7 (EVALC)

Library of Congress Cataloging-in-Publication Data:

Names: Ofori-Amoah, Benjamin, author.
Title: Africa's geography : dynamics of place, cultures, and economies /
 Benjamin Ofori-Amoah, Western Michigan University.
Description: First edition. | Hoboken, New Jersey : Wiley, [2020] | Includes
 bibliographical references. |
Identifiers: LCCN 2019003184 (print) | LCCN 2019003909 (ebook) | ISBN
 9781119401575 (Adobe PDF) | ISBN 9781119401605 (ePub) | ISBN 9780470583586
 (pbk.)
Subjects: LCSH: Africa—Geography. | Africa—Historical geography. | Human
 geography—Africa. | Africa—Economic conditions.
Classification: LCC DT12.25 (ebook) | LCC DT12.25 .O46 2020 (print) | DDC
 916—dc23
LC record available at https://lccn.loc.gov/2019003184.

V10009069_032719

To Agnes for all the years . . .

PREFACE

This book has been long in coming. The idea to write a textbook on the Geography of Africa was first conceived in the mid-1990s, in conjunction with my late colleague Samuel Aryeetey-Attoh. We were going to write the book together, but we changed our mind to do it as an edited book. However, after I had helped recruit most of the chapter authors, I had to drop out of the project due to some personal issues. The first edition of that book was published under the title *Geography of Sub-Saharan Africa* in 1996, by Prentice-Hall, and was followed by two more editions in 2002 and 2009. Over the years, however, the desire for this current book grew stronger for several reasons. First, I became increasingly convinced that geography was uniquely placed as a discipline to address the continued misconception and misinterpretation of Africa and its people. This is because of geography's ability to explain spatial expression of events and phenomena from a multidisciplinary points of view. Second, I noticed that until the end of the 1970s, books on geography of Africa covered the entire continent. However, from the 1980s, such books came to be more about sub-Saharan Africa or South of the Sahara than Africa for reasons that I thought were very arbitrary to say the least. Third, existing geography texts I noticed usually had a chapter on Africa's past after which the rest of the topics especially in human geography were treated with little background. Given that much of the current human geography is a result of past developments, I thought this lack of background was an important omission to understanding the geography of Africa.

I wrote this book to incorporate these elements that I found missing in existing texts. For this reason, the book takes misconceptions about Africa and its people very seriously and uses every opportunity to address such misconceptions. The book is also the first one in decades that covers the entire African continent, although certain references are made to sub-Saharan Africa due to past scholarly works. In addition to the chapter on Africa's past, the book also weaves into all appropriate chapters some background knowledge that will provide readers with a deeper understanding of present features and patterns discussed in the chapter. In particular, this provides an understanding of some of the past efforts by African countries to resolve current problems facing them. Of course, as an economic geographer, I am biased about the coverage I give to economic activities, and I even have a chapter on manufacturing, which is curiously missing in most of the existing texts.

Pedagogically, the book adopts an approach that will hopefully enrich and enhance student learning experience. After the introduction of each chapter, readers are asked to do some prereading assignments. At the end of the chapter, they are asked to do a postreading assignment during which they compare the answers of their prereading assignment with what they got out of the chapter. While the topics are traditional, most of the chapters have "problems and issues" sections, which address problems facing Africa and what needs to be done about those issues.

The book is for college students who are interested in learning about Africa first from a geographic perspective. Given the interdisciplinary nature of geography, and given the topics discussed in the book, other social science students and researchers will also find the book useful. Finally, because of the reviews that it provides, the book will also be useful to policy researchers. For my academic colleagues who will use this book, I admit that there are more chapters and topics than can fit into one semester, but it is my hope that you will choose the topics that are most relevant to you. I look forward to your criticisms, suggestions, and recommendations.

Benjamin Ofori-Amoah

Western Michigan University

ACKNOWLEDGMENTS

I am indebted to several groups of people for the publication of this book. The first is the undergraduate students who took my Geography of Africa course at both the University of Wisconsin-Stevens Point and Western Michigan University, whose interactions motivated me to write this book. The second group is my graduate students at Western Michigan University, who helped me with the research, data collection and processing, maps, and other illustrations that are in this book. These graduate students include Stephen Anim-Preko, who researched and pulled down all the relevant publications, which formed the basis of this book; Sokhna Diop and Bandhan Ayon, who drew most of the maps in the book, Rajesh Sigdel, who pulled and processed data for most of the chapters, and Alex La Porte and Dennis Donkor, who helped in updating some of the data.

The third group I want to thank is my office and technical staff at the Department of Geography at Western Michigan University—Mary Lou Brooks for helping me purchase and secure some of the photographs used in the book and Gregory Anderson for the technical expertise in drawing and updating some of the more complicated maps in the book.

I am also grateful to the reviewers of the manuscript—Dave Kneiter, Richard O. Djukpen, William G. Moseley, Richard Grant, Godson Obia, J. Henry Owusu, James Saku, Martin Oteng, and Sumanth Reddy. I am thankful for their very helpful inputs. I also thank my colleague at Western Michigan, Gregory Veeck, who provided feedback on the reviewers' comments and how to respond to them.

The fifth group is my family, Agnes, David, Jonathan, and Abigail. I am most grateful to—Agnes for her patience as the writing became prolonged; David and Abigail for helping me with their technical expertise on the maps.

Last but not the least, is the Wiley team—Ryan Flahive and Jessica Fiorillo—the first two editors who worked with me on the book; and the current team— Veronica Visentin, Glenn Wilson, Lisa Wojcik, Nichole Urban, Nicole Repasky, Judy Howarth, Jennifer Yee, Indirakumari Siva, and Rajalaxmi Rajendrasingh, who kept me on my toes to complete this project. I am grateful. The responsibility of all errors that may be encountered in the book are, however, all mine.

CONTENTS

6   Population   **146**

13 Mineral and Energy Production   449

CHAPTER 1

This is Africa
Images, Perceptions, Myths, and Realities

Africa is the second largest continent in the world by both area and population and the most diverse in terms of human culture. It is widely accepted that it is the original home of human beings. It has contributed its fair share to world civilization by generating great civilizations such as Ancient Egypt, Kush, Meroe, Great Zimbabwe, Ghana, Mali, and Songhai, Oyo and Benin. Its universities predated those of the Western world. Its rich natural and human resources constituted an integral part of the economic development of modern Europe and America. It still has most of the world's strategic minerals as well as its second largest rainforest region. It still produces most of the world's tropical foods and other products.

PREREADING ASSIGNMENT
1. On a piece of paper, list all images and thoughts that come to your mind when you hear the name Africa. Classify them into positive and negative.
2. How did you acquire these images?

In spite of all these, Africa is the most misunderstood and the most misrepresented continent in the world. In the 19th century, when outsiders did not know much about it, they called it the "Dark Continent." When they started to know something about it, they called it a land of savages, who needed civilization. When the shackles of external political control of the continent were finally shaken off, it became the epitome of backwardness and the very essence of being a "Third World" region. In the 1980s, when its efforts at achieving economic development appeared to be going nowhere, it was branded the "dying continent," and many experts began passing death sentences over it by the turn of the 21st century. Today, popular images of Africa are mostly negative, and they include Africa as one small country, a uniform region, a symbol of poverty, a place of roaming wildlife, a place of starving people, and a place of wars, genocide, HIV/AIDS, and Ebola. In view of these, it is only appropriate to start our search for information, knowledge, and understanding of Africa by examining some of these images of Africa. We answer three questions: (1) To what extent are these images true? (2) Where do the negative images about Africa come from? (3) How do we resolve the problem? However, before you start, do the prereading assignment.

Africa—The One Small Country Continent

In 1984, not long after I had arrived in Vancouver, Canada, to pursue my doctoral studies in geography, I had the following conversation with one of my newly found nonstudent friends. "I understand you are from Africa," he said. "Yes" I replied. "I have a brother who lives in Nairobi, do you know him?" he asked. Struggling to hide my bewilderment at the question, I replied, "No, but you see what you are asking me is like asking a person who lives here in Vancouver if he or she knew someone who lives in Toronto." "Oh, I did not know that. Is Africa that big?" he asked. "Yes, it is the second largest continent in the world, second only after Asia," I said. To the geographically informed, this conversation seems elementary, but this encounter is a common one to many Africans, who live outside of the African continent.

It is not the image of Africa as one country that is misplaced. After all, there are countries such as Russia, Canada, the United States, China, and Brazil that are huge in terms of their land area. The problem is the lack of understanding about the sheer size of Africa. As the second largest continent, Africa covers an area 11,667,000 square miles (30,065,000 km²). This is about 22.3% of the world's total land area. It is almost four times the size of continental United States. From its most northern point of Al-Ghiran in Tunisia to its most southern point of Cape Agulhas in South Africa, Africa is about 5,000 miles (8,047 km) long. From its most western point on Cape Verde Islands to its most eastern point of Ras Xaafuun (Cape Hafun) in Somalia, Africa is about 4,600 miles (7,043 km) wide, spanning six time zones. Yet as Stock (2004) has pointed out, the use of Mercator projection on many maps makes Greenland almost as large as Africa (Figure 1.1).

Africa consists of 54 countries (Figure 1.2), including the outlying islands of Madagascar, Mauritius, Seychelles, Comoros, and Cape Verde, and 55, if we count Western Sahara as a separate independent country (Table 1.1). With an area of 919,000 square miles (2.4 million km²), Algeria, the largest of these countries, is about 23% the size of Europe and 24% the size of the United States. Yet, in the news media, one is more likely to hear about Africa than individual African countries.

Africa, the Uniform Region

Closely related to the image of Africa as one country is the image of Africa as a **uniform region**. A uniform region is an area defined on the basis of a single or multiple criteria that are homogenous throughout the area. The criterion may be a physical factor such as climate, topography, and soil, or it may be a human factor such as income, standard of living, education, and ethnicity. Thus, Africa is usually seen as a region of one climate, one culture, one language, people of one complexion, a place of the HIV/AIDS epidemic, and a place of abject poverty. Thus, there are no differences at all on the continent. All Africans look alike, they are all dark-skinned, they all live under a hot climate, they all face chronic food shortages not having enough to eat, and they all speak Swahili.

Nothing can be far from the truth. Yes, Africa is the most tropical of all the continents, and because of that it has some of the hottest climates in the world. However, there are also temperate climates that experience all the four seasons as other temperate areas. Even within the hot climate belts, mild to freezing temperatures are

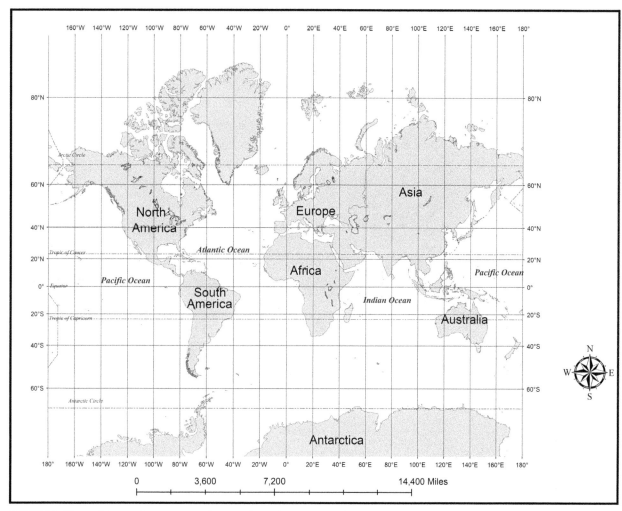

FIGURE 1.1 The world according to Mercator's projection. There are several good qualities about the Mercator's projection. For example, it represents the shapes of small areas very well. In addition, it represents true direction; that is, any straight line on map represents actual compass bearing. Also it preserves true scale along the equator. However, the projection cannot represent the poles. As a result, it distorts greatly toward the poles. This is why Greenland looks either bigger than or almost as big as Africa.
Source: Copyright © 2018 Esri, World Climate Data, United Nations, and the GIS User Community. All rights reserved

recorded and the highest mountains such as Mount Kilimanjaro and Mount Kenya are snow-capped all year round, even though they are not very far from the equator.

The cultural mosaic of Africa is mind-boggling. Often researchers working on sub-Saharan Africa justify the exclusion of North Africa from their work because they claim that North Africa is more like the Middle East and Europe and that many of the people in North Africa do not consider themselves Africans. Indeed, some have even gone to the extent of limiting Africa only to Sub-Saharan Africa (Cornia and Helleiner, 1994; Moss, 2007). For example, Moss (2007, p. 4) writes:

> "Africa" is sometimes used to refer to all the countries on the mainland continent plus six island nations of Cape Verde, Comoros, Madagascar, Mauritius, Sao Tome and Principe, and Seychelles. In much of the literature, however – including this book – the term "Africa" and even "the continent" is instead used synonymously with what more accurately would be called sub-Saharan Africa to mean just the forty-eight African countries,

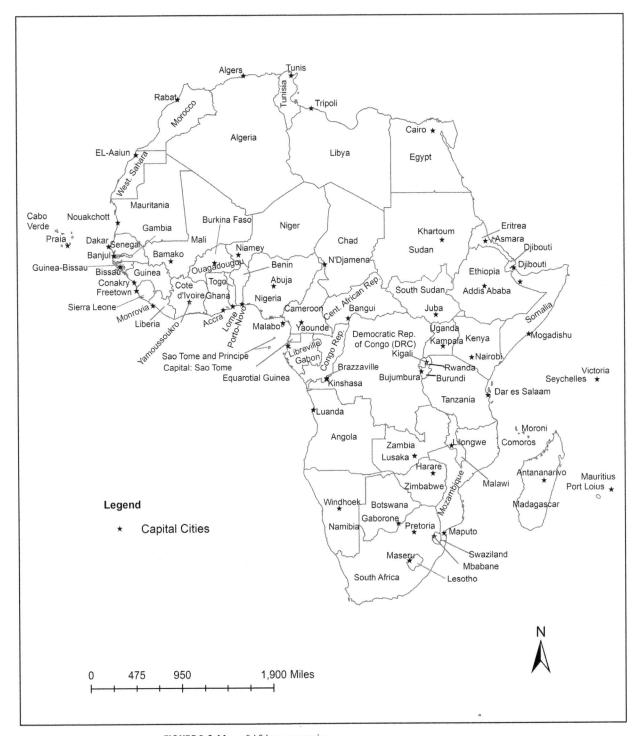

FIGURE 1.2 Map of African countries.
Sources: Copyright © 2018 Esri, World Climate Data, United Nations, and the GIS User Community. All rights reserved

TABLE **1.1**

African Countries—Areas, Capital Cities, 2015

Country	Area (Sq. Mi)	(Sq. Km)	Capital city
Algeria	919,595	2,381,740	Algiers
Angola	481,354	1,246,700	Luanda
Benin	43,450	112,620	Porto Novo
Botswana	224,607	600,370	Gaborone
Burkina Faso	105,946	274,200	Ouagadougou
Burundi	10,740	27,830	Bujumbura
Cameroon	179,714	475,440	Yaounde
Cape Verde	1,557	4,030	Praia
Central African Republic	240,324	622,980	Baungui
Chad	495,755	1,284,000	N'Djamena
Comoros	719	2,170	Moroni
Congo, Dem. Republic	905,446	2,345,410	Kinshasa
Congo Republic	132,047	342,000	Brazzaville
Cote d'Ivoire	123,847	322,460	Yamoussoukro
Djibouti	8,950	22,000	Djibouti
Egypt	385,229	1,001,450	Cairo
Equatorial Guinea	10,831	28,050	Malabo
Eritrea	17,413	121,320	Asmara
Ethiopia	483,123	1,127,127	Addis Ababa
Gabon	103,347	267,670	Libreville
Gambia	4,127	11,300	Banjul
Ghana	92,098	238,540	Accra
Guinea	94,926	245,860	Conakry
Guinea-Bissau	13,948	36,120	Bissau
Kenya	224,961	582,650	Nairobi
Lesotho	11,720	30,350	Maseru
Liberia	38,250	111,370	Monrovia
Libya	678,400	1,759,540	Tripoli
Madagascar	226,658	587,041	Antananarivo
Malawi	45,747	118,480	Lilongwe
Mali	482,077	1,024,000	Bamako
Mauritania	398,000	1,030,700	Nouakchott
Mauritius	788	1,860	Port Louis
Morocco	177,117	446,550	Rabat
Mozambique	313,661	801,590	Maputo
Namibia	317,818	823,144	Windhoek
Niger	458,075	1,186,408	Niamey
Nigeria	356,669	923,768	Abuja

(Continued)

African Countries—Areas, Capital Cities, 2015 (*Continued*)

Country	Area (Sq. Mi)	Area (Sq. Km)	Capital city
Rwanda	10,169	26,338	Kigali
Sao Tome & Principe	386	1,001	Sao Tome
Senegal	75,951	196,712	Dakar
Seychelles	175	71,740	Victoria
Sierra Leone	27,699	71,740	Freetown
Somalia	246,000	637,660	Mogadishu
South Africa	473,290	1,219,912	Pretoria
South Sudan	239,285	619,745	Juba
Sudan	728,215	1,886,068	Khartoum
Swaziland	6,704	17,360	Mbabane
Tanzania	364,017	945,090	Dodoma
Togo	21,925	56,790	Lome
Tunisia	59,664	163,610	Tunis
Uganda	93,070	236,040	Kampala
Western Sahara	97,334	266,000	El Aaiun
Zambia	290,586	752,610	Lusaka
Zimbabwe	150,873	390,580	Harare

Source: United Nations, Department of Economic and Social Affairs, Population Division (2015).
World Population Prospects: The 2015 Revision, custom data acquired via website.

excluding Morocco, Algeria, Tunisia, Libya, and Egypt. Such a distinction is surely arguable, but in the development world the countries of North Africa are typically placed in the Middle East (for example World Bank) because they are in many ways more a part of the cultural and political life of that region.

The irony is that the word "Africa" was first used by the Romans to refer to the region around Carthage (Tunisia) including the coastal areas of Libya, when the area became a Roman province, while the Arab version "Ifriqiya" referred to Tunisia. Etymological studies also indicate that the Greek "aphrike" referred to "land free of cold and horror," while in Ancient Egyptian "af–ruika" meant "birthplace." So, the true origin of the word "Africa" is actually North Africa and not sub-Saharan Africa. Later on, the name came to be applied to the entire continent, until the World Bank popularized the term Sub-Saharan Africa.

The fact is Africans are the most diverse groups of people anywhere in the world. North Africa may be part of the Middle East in terms of culture, but there is nothing among the people and cultures of sub-Saharan Africa that is easily and readily identifiable as a common trait except for the skin color of the majority (see Box 1.1). The total number of ethnic groups in Africa has eluded anthropologists ever since the time of Herskovits, the pioneer of American anthropological study of Africa. With each ethnic group is also a culture. It is thus, more appropriate to talk of African cultures than an African culture. As for Swahili, it is a language spoken only in East Africa. While most African people are dark-skinned, there are also light-skinned

Box 1.1 | North Africa and Sub-Saharan Africa

From a Western point of view, North Africa and sub-Saharan Africa lie in different continents. The northern fringe of Africa lies firmly within the Middle East and is cut off from the bulk of Africa by the Sahara Desert. Yet while the world's greatest desert undoubtedly forms a sizeable obstacle to the movement of people and goods between the north and the south, this Western perception is largely the product of racism borne out of the slave trade.

To the 17th- and 18th-century slave-trading nations of Western Europe, it was not possible for a people considered fit only for slavery to be associated with a people who developed civilization such as ancient Egypt. In fact, today a great deal of evidence points toward the fact that the Ancient Egyptians were Africans who moved from the Sahara into the valley of the Nile as the climate changed and the desert expanded.

This long-standing cultural link is being reinforced today as North African states have begun to recognize the benefits of improving links with the rest of the continent. Thus, after being at loggerheads with the countries in the Nile Basin for a long time, Egypt has over the past three years entered into negotiations with the other Nile Valley states over a new treaty. Algeria and Nigeria are talking about a $7b project of Trans-Saharan Gas Pipeline (TSGP).

Along with South Africa, Senegal, and Nigeria, Algeria was one of the leading nations in the development of the well-publicized New Partnership for African Development (NEPAD). President Abdelaziz Bouteflika appears convinced Algeria's future economic success will be closely allied to the economic growth in Africa as a whole, despite the fact that 78% of Algeria's trade is with the EU. While Egypt and Algeria have targeted stronger links with sub-Saharan Africa on mainly economic grounds, Libya is keen to promote cooperation for both political and economic reasons.

If only one North African state had decided to embark upon a campaign to strengthen ties with sub-Saharan Africa or had planned a major pipeline project with West Africa, it could be dismissed as an isolated development. But the growing links between the Northern African states and the countries to the south cannot be regarded as a mere coincidence. Cultural and linguistic ties between the two regions remain strong, particularly across the western half of the Sahara. One thing is certain, the countries of Africa—north and south—can achieve more together than they could apart.

Extracted from Ford, N. 2003. "Maghreb: Hands across the Sahara the Arab States of North Africa Which in Modern Times Have Traditionally Looked Chiefly towards the West for Trading Partners Are Beginning to Spread Their Nets Somewhat Wider." *The Middle East*, issue 337, August–September.

Africans who are not just descendants of European and Arab immigrants or mixed races, but are indigenous Africans such as the Imazighen (Berbers), the original natives of Northwestern Africa, some Ethiopians, and Khoisan.

There are African Christians and African Muslims, and there are African animists, as well as African atheists too. Africans practiced Christianity in North Africa long before the Protestant Reformation and centuries before the birth of David Livingstone, the Scottish physician and explorer, whose life goal is stated in history books as "to open Africa to Christianity and civilization." There are differences in inheritance, marital, and kingship systems. Some African cultural groups have patrilineal system of inheritance, others have matrilineal system. Polygamy, the practice that allows more than one marriage partner at a time, and polygyny, the practice that allows more than one wife at a time, as well as monogamy, are all practiced.

There are food shortages and other hardships in Africa just as everywhere else. However, like elsewhere, these are not the conditions of all Africans. In most cases, outbreaks of food shortages tend to be limited to regions and localities of a country. In some cases, there may be people living in the same country that may not even know or hear about such incidents.

Africa, the Epitome of Poverty, Backwardness, and the State of being a "Third World"

Africa is the epitome of poverty and the state of being a Third World. Africa does not fare well on many of the most popular development indicators—the **gross national income** (GNI) per capita, commercial energy consumption, rate of GNI growth, infant mortality, life expectancy, literacy rates, and import index. Thus, by international standards, material poverty is undeniably a feature of most parts of Africa. It has most of the world's poorest countries, whatever criteria we use to measure it.

However, economists know that the **GNI per capita**, which is the dollar value of the total goods and services produced by a nation divided by its population, is a very faulty measure. First of all, it is an average measure and an estimate. So it does not really reflect the true picture of income distribution. Second, the measure can only include recorded economic activities and transactions. It does not capture economic activities in the informal sector, which tends to be larger in most African economies. This means that the measure actually underestimates the total goods and services that are generated in a given country in Africa. Third, the GNI per capita does not take into account the basket of goods a dollar can buy in a given African country, but time and time again, this has proven to be very different from what a dollar can buy in the United States or a European country. Finally, the GNI per capita assumes that people in Africa live the same lifestyles as people in the developed economies do, so the usual conclusion people draw about a country with a GNI per capita of say $350 is that the country must be poor.

The use of the imperfect GNI is not the issue because like it or not, we need to have some form measurement for assessment and evaluation and no indicator is perfect. The issue is that somehow there is expectation that majority of African countries should have low GNI per capita. So North African countries and South Africa are usually separated from the rest of the continent. North African countries are considered as part of the Middle East, while South Africa is relatively more developed economically. The remaining countries on the continent are usually lumped together as Sub-Saharan Africa for poverty analysis. During the early 1990s, one expert even went to the extent of considering countries within this amorphous region that had GNI per capita estimates higher than $350 as an anomaly. Thus, the eminent British Geographer, O'Connor (1991 p. 10 and 12) writes:

> For rather more than half the countries in Tropical Africa per capita GNP estimates for the late 1980s were between $250 and $350 ... Just six countries have substantially higher figures that make them all rather special cases ... Gabon, with large oil revenues and a very small population has much higher figure still, possibly over $3,000, though this depends on whether its population is assumed to be under one million or substantially more. This is the case where an average figure is particularly misleading, for many people in Gabon have a standard of living no higher than in most parts of Africa.

The above statement implies that there are some expectations that a country in Sub-Saharan should not have a gross national income of $3,000. So, even though the statistic is clear, O'Connor had to go the extra mile to explain that the number

Box 1.2 | Mackinnon and Chambers Contrasting Economic Fortunes of China and Africa

Source: Skyscrapper - © Travelpix Ltd/Getty Images.

Source: Malnutrition kids - © Harry Dempster/Getty Images.

In their effort to show differences in economic development, Mackinnon and Chambers (2007, p. 9) posed the two photos above with a description of economic development process that has taken place in China and Africa since 1978. While it is true that China has experienced high economic growth since its reform policies in 1978, the selection of the starving children as the only symbolic representation of Africa is very stereotypical of how Africa is pursued in the broader picture of economic development. These contrasting photos assume a lot of things that are completely erroneous and yet contribute to perpetuate the stereotypical images of Africa. For example, it lumps the wide variation of living conditions of the more than China's 1 billion people together and represents it with skyscrapers while the hundreds of millions of Africans are represented by starving children, as if there are no skyscrapers in Africa and no starving children in China. Why did not the authors compare downtown Shanghai with downtown Lagos, Nairobi, Abidjan, or Johannesburg? And why did they not compare poverty in an African country with poverty in China? What is wrong with this picture? You decide.

Source: Mackinnon, D. and Cumbers, A. 2007. *An Introduction to Economic Geography, Globalization, Uneven Development and Place*. Harlow, UK: Pearson Education, p. 9.

was an anomaly. Similarly, MacKinnon and Cumbers (2007) displayed a picture of Shanghai's skyscrapers juxtaposed with two starving children to contrast economic fortunes of China and Africa (see Box 1.2). The message is that while China is building skyscrapers, Africa is still starving to death. Why the authors did not compare the skyscrapers of Shanghai with those of Nairobi, Lagos, or Johannesburg, but with starving children of Africa is another example of how even eminent geographers fall prey to stereotypical and distorted views of Africa.

Once again, there is poverty in Africa. It is real. However, for every celebrity concert that is staged in aid of Africa, there are millions and millions of Africans who go about their lives without proceeds of aid concerts. For every baby adopted by celebrity, there are millions more that are taken care of by African parents or relatives, and for every aid that is announced, there are millions of Africans who keep living without any handout. This is not against the aid industry and philanthropy and their generous donors, but Africa is a big continent of extreme contrasts that cannot be truly portrayed by average statistics such as GNI per capita and its associated measures.

Do You See Lions and Cheetahs in the Streets and on the Way to School?

This is a question that has been asked of some Africans living abroad, including this author, several times. Truly, Africa has the most diverse wildlife of any region in the world, but wildlife is not ubiquitous. For example, there are no zebras in West Africa, and neither are cheetahs. Instead, both animals are found in Eastern and Southern Africa, and in the case of cheetahs a few places in North Africa. Besides, except for those living close to national parks in Africa, the first time many Africans will see any of these animals live will be in a zoo or in a national park. No, Africans do not meet lions, elephants, and giraffes in the streets or on their way to school, or to work. With the exception of those who live near national parks, they do have to make the effort to go and see these wild animals just as is the case for other people around the world.

You Must Have Studied Outside Africa!

The image of Africa as a place without institutions of higher learning and, sometimes even, elementary schools also comes through when people make the statement "You must have studied outside Africa." Yes, there are many Africans who live outside the continent who had their entire education outside Africa. However, institutions of higher learning do exist in Africa. In fact, before the establishment of some of Europe's oldest universities—Oxford and Cambridge—in the 12th century, institutions of higher learning were doing full business in Timbuktu and Jenne, in the present-day country of Mali. Modern high schools and teacher training colleges were established under missionaries and colonial rule during the 19th century, with modern universities following in the first half of the 20th century. By the mid-1970s, many of the universities were offering baccalaureate, masters, and doctoral degrees in a selected number of disciplines.

SOURCES OF NEGATIVE IMAGES AND PERCEPTIONS ABOUT AFRICA

These negative images and perceptions about Africa derive from several sources including ethnocentrism, the nature of the academic research enterprise, the nature of news media, the unintended actions of nongovernmental organizations, and the demonstration effect of past and current behaviors of vested interest groups inside and outside of Africa. We examine each of these in turn.

Ethnocentrism and the Role of Early European Visitors to Africa

At the roots of all the negative images and perceptions that we may have about other people and their cultures is **ethnocentrism**. Ethnocentrism is the tendency to believe in the superiority of our own culture and state of affairs to those of other groups of people. This causes us to interpret other people's way of life through our spectacles and usually with disdain. Ethnocentrism finds expression in different forms. With respect to Africa, these forms include **Eurocentrism**, **Americentrism**, and **Sinocentrism**, whereby Europeans, Americans, and Chinese have, respectively, interpreted Africa through their self-centered images. These ethnocentric attitudes against Africa were further advanced by events such as the slave trade and the reports by early European explorers as well Christian missionary activities. Thus, the Atlantic Slave Trade left the impression that any cultural group that sold some of its own members into slavery could not be held in the same esteem as those that did not. Apart from this, returnees from Africa from the time of the early explorers and missionaries brought back stories that painted negative images about Africa. David Livingstone, for example, was bent on bringing Christianity to the "pagans" and open Africa to "civilization." Similarly, Stanley's (1890) book *In the Darkest Africa* contains several references to darkness, savages, and cannibalism. In the introduction to the book, he writes:

> As I mentally review the many grim episodes and reflect on the marvelously narrow escapes from utter destruction to which we have been subjected during our various journeys to and fro that immense gloomy extent of primeval woods, I felt utterly unable to attribute our salvation to any other cause than to gracious Providence who for some purpose of His own preserved us. All the armies and armaments of Europe could not have lent us any aid in the dire extremity in which we found ourselves in that camp. . .; an army of explorers could not have traced our course to the scene of the last struggle had we fallen, for deep, deep as utter oblivion had we been surely buried under the humus of trackless wilds (Stanley, 1890, p. 4).

Of the Unyoro civilization in East Africa, Samuel Baker also writes:

> The prime utensil of the African savage is the gourd; . . .the most savage tribes content themselves with the productions of nature . . .; but the semi-savage, like those of Unyoro, affords an example of the first step towards manufacturing art; the utter savage makes use of nature – the gourd is his utensil; and the more advanced natives of Unyoro adopt it as the model for their pottery (Richards and Place, 1960, p. 168).

The Nature of News and the Media

Given ethnocentrism, the next most important source of the distorted views about Africa is the nature and characteristics of modern news media (Stock, 2004). Concerns about this have been raised by many professionals and individuals, Africans and non-Africans, alike. There are several aspects to this. One is that nothing is worth reporting unless it is tragic or catastrophic. The result is that the only time people hear about Africa in the news is when there is a disaster such as famine and starving people, flood victims, victims of deadly diseases such as Ebola and HIV/AIDS, civil wars and refugees. It does not take long for the people who are already not very familiar with Africa to form the view that Africa is a land of extreme suffering. As Cheela Chilala of Zambia eloquently puts it:

> A cycle has developed: the western media peddles negative images of Africa to their people, their people in turn expect the western media to peddle such images. That after all is the only Africa they have come to know, anything that departs from the norm becomes suspect in the eyes of the average western mind (Chilala 2005).

Chilala illustrates this with the behavior of a group of American students who went to Zambia in 2001. The students spent all their free time at the shopping malls in Lusaka without taking a single photograph, because they said if they showed those pictures to their folks back in America, no one would believe them that they were in Africa. But when he took the students to one of the shanty compounds, they all pulled out their cameras and took photographs. I had a similar experience in 2008, when I went to Kampala, Uganda, with some US colleagues on an assignment. One particular colleague complained to the group, "I came to Africa to see Africa but instead I have been stuck here in this resort by the Lake Victoria." To this I reminded the group, "This resort too is Africa." It is this same behavior that makes the media show images of poverty in an African country even when an event is taking place in the most beautiful part of the capital city of the country.

The manner in which news about Africa is presented is also problematic. Research indicates that news coverage on Africa since colonial times have tended to preserve the status quo regarding what is known about Africa and been even inflammatory and negative. For example, during the colonial Africa's wars of independence, Africans were presented as irrational and primitive. Similarly, in the Zimbabwean War of Independence, there was a marked difference between how black and white casualties of the war were covered in the news. When the casualties were white, it was reported as brutal murder, but when the casualties were black, they were hardly mentioned in the news. The following excerpts from Melisa Wall's (2007) "Analysis of News Magazine's Coverage on the Rwanda Crises in the United States" are another example.

> "For four centuries, hatred between the minority Tutsi tribe and the majority Hutus has been the curse of Rwanda" – what is happening in Rwanda was only the "latest" tragedy (Masland et al. 1994, p. 33).
>
> We could only expect more of the same; after all, "Rwanda is helpless against its demons" (Hammer et al. 1994).
>
> After all, "Rwanda is a crucible full of explosives" (Gibbs 1994, p. 57) and the entire nation was "like a time bomb" (Gibbs, Crumley et al. 1994, p. 28).

As Wall points out, the implication of all the above is that violence is innate or has always been part of the Rwandan people and it was only a matter of time for it to come out.

As I have already pointed out, the nature of news is to report the negative and the sensational. It is the same everywhere. However, it is the unbalanced nature and consistency with which negative images about Africa are presented, that is the difference. The result is that outsiders are left with only one image of the Africa, the negative one. Dowden (2009, p. 6) writes:

> When we see floods in New Orleans we do not think that all of America is permanently under water, or when we see troops marching in Indonesia we do not think all Asia is at war. We know from other images we see and stories we read that there is a functioning and thriving America and a peaceful and successful Asia. But we have no other ideas of Africa, no sense of ordinary Africa. Persistent images of starving children and men with

guns have accumulated into our narrative of the continent: Africans are gun-toting, mindless warriors or hopeless, helpless victims who can do nothing for themselves, doomed to endless poverty, violence and hunger. Only foreign aid and foreign workers can save them. The endlessly repeated images of guns, oppression, hunger and disease create the impression that this is all that ever happens in Africa.

In effect, this situation cements ethnocentric attitude of outsiders toward Africa.

The Nature of Academic Research Enterprise

Another source of distorted images about Africa can be traced to the nature of social science research, to which we owe much of our knowledge of Africa. In particular, social science research on Africa has suffered from three syndromes (Ofori-Amoah, 1995). The first is the **saturation hypothesis syndrome**. This is the situation whereby social scientists conduct research on topics that may be more relevant to foreign countries, usually the scientists' home base, than to Africa. An example of this may occur in studies that compare an African country with a developed country regarding the status of a social, cultural, political, or environmental issue. Since status reports on such issues are closely associated with the level of economic development, these types of studies end up making the African country "backward," thus confirming the usual stereotypical images about Africa.

The second syndrome of social science research is **extrapolation**. This manifests itself when researchers use experiences and conventions established elsewhere to guide research in Africa. This syndrome rests on the assumption that all countries go through the same path and experience and therefore African countries will have the same experience as developed countries. This assumption does raise expectations and so when those expectations are not met, there is a tendency to think negatively about Africa. For example, in the early postindependence days, economists strongly believed that African countries did not have to reinvent the wheel because all that they needed to learn had been already accomplished by developed countries. As a result, all that they needed to do was to take them and implement them. By the end of the first decade, after most African countries had returned to independence, it became clear that such prescription was seriously flawed. However, instead of examining why the so-called proven strategies failed, the simplistic reason of corruption and mismanagement became the culprit, which, in turn, went to reinforce Africa's image as corrupt and mismanaged continent.

The third and final syndrome of social science research is **overgeneralization**. This is the tendency to overextend research results from a particular locale in Africa to the whole continent or a substantial region of the continent "irrespective of the cultural mosaic, economic variations, different historical experiences of the countries and peoples of Africa" (Ofori-Amoah, 1995). This manifests itself in titles of articles and books that give the impression that their content is about Africa, yet they may only focus on a specific country. On the assumption that Africa is a homogenous region, this syndrome in the end helps to perpetuate the usual stereotypical images about Africa.

These are not limited only to social scientists but can be found among the general population as well. Thus, there is a tendency of people living in affluent societies to extrapolate values of their own saturated development into Africa, trying to force comparisons that are really off base, and when they do not find comparable situations, they automatically ascribe that to ignorance and backwardness.

Nongovernmental Organizations and the Aid Industry

Another source of the negative images of the Africa is the activities of nongovernmental organizations and the aid industry—from the private foundations, through the World Bank and the United Nations. There is a long-standing debate as to whether or not foreign aid helps or hurts Africa. On the one hand, aid agencies provide much needed relief to African societies in terms of material support. However, these efforts have also created unintended consequences both inside and outside Africa. Inside Africa, a culture of aid-dependency has been created, while outside Africa, an image that Africa cannot do anything for itself without foreign aid has been formed.

The role of the aid industry in perpetuating negative images about Africa is also closely intertwined with the news media. As Dowden (2009) points out, the aid industry needs journalists to talk about where disaster is happening, in return they provide journalists with transportation and accommodation. In recent years, the aid industry and even the United Nations have resorted to using celebrities to champion such courses for them. This has worked like magic, because the celebrities draw the media along. So we get into a cyclical situation where one group feeds the other. These NGOs and their celebrity ambassadors may mean well, but because they attract a lot of media, the unintended consequence is to reinforce the notion that Africa cannot do anything for itself.

The Demonstration Effect of Past and Current Behavior of Vested Interest Groups in Africa

It is always easy to point fingers at someone else for one's own problems, but truth be told, part of the consistent negative images of Africa derives from Africa's own actions. The fact is Africa has had a long history of atrocities, which go beyond basic human dignity—corrupt governments that have left countries vulnerable to widespread famine, power struggles that have ended up in meaningless civil wars victimizing thousands of citizens rather than helping, and resource wars that have turned natural resources from blessings to curses in some countries are all events that have continued to paint a rather gloomy picture of Africa in the minds of outsiders. In particular, the fact that these things are happening in this day and age is hard for outsiders to fathom, even though their own countries may have had similar histories in the past. The fact is as long as these negative events continue to occur, and as long as we are only able to interpret current events in terms of our own contemporary histories, it will be difficult for Africa to completely get rid of these negative images. The question now is how do we deal with this.

THE PLAN OF THIS BOOK

The way to correct these negative images and perceptions people have about the continent of Africa is through education. However, such a task cannot be accomplished by one disciplinary and academic persuasion. Instead, it needs a multidisciplinary approach and efforts. This book is a contribution from the field of geography toward this effort. **Geography** is particularly relevant in helping people to understand Africa because it is concerned with understanding the distribution patterns of phenomena, the forces that shaped and continued to shape such patterns, and their implications for now and the future. To this end, geographers study a wide range of topics drawing on a wide range of methods and approaches from both the physical and social sciences as well at the humanities in order to understand the patterns of interest. Given the fact that distribution patterns are constantly changing, geography is also dynamic.

This book presents a select number of topics from Africa's physical and human landscapes that will provide readers an opportunity to examine, ponder, think, and evaluate the various perceptions, notions, and beliefs they have about Africa and its people. These topics are loosely grouped in four parts. Part I consisting of three chapters including this one provides a general introduction to Africa, by reaching into Africa's past. Thus, Chapter 2 traces the historical background of the people of Africa from the dawn of history through the periods where their lives became intertwined with the rest of the world through trade and colonialism. The chapter reveals the rich history of the achievements and shortcomings of the people of Africa from independence, through colonialism and back to independence. Chapter 3 picks up the story of the African people from their return to independence through their struggle to achieve better standards of living. Together, these chapters show that Africa's precolonial, colonial, and postcolonial experiences may provide a useful framework for understanding contemporary Africa. This framework is in fact adopted in this book where appropriate. Part II focuses on Africa's physical geography, which is the physical environmental context with which Africans have to interact. Chapter 4 deals with the geology, relief, and drainage basins, while Chapter 5 discusses the climate and biogeography of the continent. Both chapters show that while Africa's physical environment has many opportunities, it also poses some serious challenges.

Parts III and IV shift the focus to Africa's human geography or the geography of Africa's human landscapes. Part III contains four chapters. Chapter 6 examines the population of Africa; Chapter 7 society and cultures; Chapter 8 cities, towns, and villages; and Chapter 9 politics and governance. These chapters address the population, societal and cultural, as well as the settlement, and the political and governance patterns of Africa and the issues that arise from these patterns. The chapters highlight the root causes of some of the current problems facing the continent.

Part IV provides an insight into the various economic activities by which Africans earn a living. There are seven chapters in this section. Chapter 10 deals with transportation and communication. Chapter 11 deals with agriculture, Chapter 12 fisheries and forestry, Chapter 13 mineral and energy production, Chapter 14 manufacturing, Chapter 15 trade and tourism, and Chapter 16 education and health. The message of all these chapters is that Africans are hardworking people who are engaged in all economic activities as anywhere else in the world. However, these activities face serious challenges that derive from their historical evolution as well as the internal and external physical and the human landscapes that need to be addressed.

Finally, one of the common themes in discussing geography of vast regions such as Africa is to use regional groupings. In geography of Africa, there is a general agreement that these regional groupings are North Africa, West Africa, Central Africa, East Africa, and Southern Africa, but there is no agreement as to which countries fall into which region. Thus, East Africa is usually considered as consisting of Uganda, Kenya, and Tanzania, just as it was in the colonial days, even though in comparison to West Africa, East Africa should, in fact, include Ethiopia, Eritrea, Somalia, and Sudan. The regional groupings used in this book are shown in Table 1.2.

> **TABLE 1.2**
>
> **African Regional Groupings Used in This Book**
>
> | Regional Grouping | Countries |
> | --- | --- |
> | North Africa | Algeria, Egypt, Libya Arab Jamahiriya, Morocco, Tunisia, Western Sahara |
> | West Africa | Benin, Burkina Faso, Cape Verde, Cote d'Ivoire, Gambia, Ghana, Guinea, Guinea-Bissau, Liberia, Mali, Mauritania, Niger, Nigeria, Senegal, Sierra Leone, Togo |
> | Central Africa | Cameroon, Central African Republic, Chad, Congo, Democratic Republic of Congo, Equatorial Guinea, Gabon, Sao Tome and Principe |
> | East Africa | Burundi, Comoros, Djibouti, Eritrea, Ethiopia, Kenya, Rwanda, Seychelles, Somalia, Sudan, South Sudan, Tanzania, Uganda |
> | Southern Africa | Angola, Botswana, Lesotho, Madagascar, Malawi, Mauritius, Mozambique, Namibia, South Africa, Swaziland, Zambia, Zimbabwe |

Postreading Assignment

A. Study the Following Key concepts

Americentrism	**Geography**	**Overgeneralization**	**Sinocentrism**
Ethnocentrism	**GNI per capita**	**syndrome**	**Uniform region**
Eurocentrism	**Gross national**	**Saturation hypothesis**	
Extrapolation syndrome	**income**	**syndrome**	

B. Discussion Questions

1. (a) Discuss the images you had about Africa that you listed down with and identify the sources from where you got those images.

   (b) Check your list to see if you can cross out any negative images or add any positive images.

   (c) Keep checking your list as you go through this book to make note and track any changes.

2. Discuss the assertion that North Africa is really part of the Middle East and therefore Africa should only refer to Sub-Saharan Africa.

3. Find a news article on Africa and critically examine it to see if it contains any evidence of negative images or not.

Web Resources

There are so many resources on the Web for the study of geography of Africa. The following are a few of such resources.

1. For maps of Africa and African countries, visit the following sites:
   http://www.enchantedlearning.com/school/Africa/Africamap.shtml
   http://geography.about.com/library/maps/blafrica.htm

2. For a fun game to test your knowledge about African countries and their capital cities, visit the following website: http://www.lizardpoint.com/fun/geoquiz/afrquiz.html

3. For African daily news, visit the following sites:
   http://allafrica.com
   http://news.bbc.co.uk/2/hi/africa/default.stm
   http://www.newsfromafrica.org

4. For reports and information about Africa, visit the website of the United Nations Economic Commission for Africa (UNECA) at http://www.uneca.org.

References

Chilala, C. 2005. *When Cameras Lie Roses and Thorns. Zambia Daily Mail.* http://www.daily.mail.co.zm/media/news/viewnews.cgi?category=23. Accessed 30 July 2009.

Cornia, G. A., and Helleiner, G. K. 1994. (Eds.) *From Adjustment to Development in Africa: Conflict, Controversy, Convergence, Consensus?* Houndmills, UK: St. Martin's Press.

Dowden, R. 2009. *Africa: Altered States, Ordinary Miracles.* New York: Public Affairs.

Gibbs, N. 1994. "Why? The Killing Fields of Rwanda: Hundreds of Thousands Have Died or Fled as a Result of Tribal Strife. Are These the Wars of the Future?" *Time,* 16 May: 56–63.

Gibbs, N., Crumley, B., Michaels, M., and Purvis, A. 1994. "Cry the Forsaken Country: for More Than 2 Million Refugees, Hunger and Disease Take Up Where a Vicious Civil War Left Off." *Time,* 1 August: 28–37.

Hammer, J., Stanger, T. and Sparkman, R. 1994. "Deeper into the Abyss: an Orgy of Tribal Slaughter Kills Thousands as Most of the Foreigners Flee for their Lives." *Newsweek,* 25 April: 32.

MacKinnon, D., and Cumbers. A. 2007. *An Introduction to Economic Geography: Globalization, Uneven Development and Place.* Harlow: Pearson Education.

Masland, T., Hammer, J., Breslau, K., and Tanaka, J. 1994. "Corpses Everywhere: Once More, Tens of Thousands Massacred." *Newsweek,* 18 April: 33.

Moss, T. J. 2007. *African Development: Making Sense of the Issues and Actors.* Boulder, CO: Lynne Reiner Publishers.

O'Connor, A. M. 1991. *Poverty in Africa: A Geographical Approach.* London: Belhaven Press.

Ofori-Amoah, B. 1995. "Development Research and Africa's Development Crisis." *Review of Human Factor Studies.* 1(1): 26–44.

Richards, C., and Place, J. 1960: *East African Explorers.* London: Oxford University Press.

Stanley, H. M. 1890. *In Darkest Africa or The Quest, Rescue, and Retreat of Emin Governor of Equatoria.* New York: Charles Scribner's Sons.

Stock, R. 2004. *Africa South of the Sahara: A Geographical Interpretation,* 2nd Edition, New York: The Guildford Press.

Wall, M. 2007. "An analysis of news magazine coverage of the Rwanda crisis in the United States." In Thompson, A. (Ed.) *The Media and the Rwanda Genocide.* London, Ann Arbor, Kampala, Ottawa: Pluto Press/Fountain Publishers/IDRC. pp. 261–273.

CHAPTER 2

From Empires in the Sand and Civilizations in the Jungle to Colonies and Freedom

A Portrait of Africa's Past

The present is the product of the past. Thus, any physical or human geographic pattern that is observable at any place and at any time has been shaped to varying degrees by past processes, events, decisions, or policies. Simply put, one cannot fully understand the present geography of a place or area without reference to its past. To this end, we will continue our study of the geography of Africa with a look at Africa's past. In this chapter, we trace in very broad outlines of Africa's history from the earliest times through the return to political independence in the second half of the 20th century. We do this in four broad sections: in the first section, we focus on the peopling of Africa, from the origin of the African people through their expansion on the continent. In the second section, we outline the evolution and development of African civilizations, from Antiquity to the 19th century. In the third section, we focus on interactions between Africa and the outside world, from the Trans-Saharan trade through colonialism. In the final section, we focus on the return to independence. Before we start, do the prereading assignment.

The Origins of the African People

It was Charles Darwin who first suggested that Africa might be the original home of human beings. In his book *Descent of Man and Selection in Relation to Sex*, Darwin (1897, p. 155) wrote:

> "In each great region of the world, the living mammals are closely related to the extinct species of the same region. It is therefore probable that Africa was formerly inhabited by extinct apes closely related to the gorilla and chimpanzee; and as these two species are now man's nearest allies, it is somewhat more probable that our early progenitors lived on the African continent than elsewhere."

Shillington (2005) says that this suggestion provoked great controversy in Europe due in part to religious reasons and in part to ethnocentrism. First, Darwin was challenging the Biblical account of the origin of human beings, and second, Europeans could not accept the slight chance that they might have all originated from Africa. However, studies of fossil remains now indicate that environmental changes at the beginning of the Miocene epoch (the geological time from 23.8 to 5.3 million years ago) were crucial to the beginnings of *hominids*, the early ancestors of *Homo sapiens sapiens* or human beings. According to Newman (1995), lush forest occupied much of Africa, Europe, and Asia at that time. However, by mid-Miocene epoch, (16–15 million years ago), cooler and drier weather had caused a retreat of the dense forest and the emergence of woodland vegetation, which may have played a major role for the emergence of the early ancestors of *Homo sapiens sapiens*.

Researchers now believe that the first of the early ancestors of the *Homo* genus was the *Australopithecus afarensis*, who appeared no later than 3 million years ago in East Africa—in Ethiopia, where the famous Lucy and the First Family were discovered, and in Kenya and Northern Tanzania. Several Australopithecus species followed before the advent of the *Homo* genus (Table 2.1).

The first of the *Homo* genus was the *Homo habilis*, who started living about 2 million years ago. These were the first tool makers. Next came the *Homo erectus*, about 1.8 million years ago. These were believed to be more precise and advanced in tool making, the first to use fire to cook food, and the first hominids to leave Africa for Europe and Asia (Shillington, 2005; Stock, 2004). *Homo sapiens* appeared about 200,000 years ago, and they were followed by *Homo sapiens sapiens*, the immediate ancestors of modern Africans, and for that matter modern human beings, about 120,000–90,000 years ago. By 60,000 years ago, they had spread all over Africa and were moving into Europe and Asia (Shillington, 2005; Stock, 2004). In the process, they began to adapt to environmental differences, which, in Africa, resulted in four genetic groups—the capoid, the pygmoid, the tall negroid, and the caucasoid (Newman, 1995). The capoids occupied south-central, southern, and along the east coast of the continent. The caucasoids occupied the Mediterranean Coast, the Nile Valley, and the northeast coast along the Red Sea and in the Horn of Africa. The tall

TABLE **2.1**

Hominid Evolution and Africa

Hominid	Approximate time/period	Location found
Australopithecus afarensis	No later than 3 m years ago	East Africa, South Africa
Australopithecus africanus	3–2.5 m years ago	South Africa
Australopithecus aethiopicus	2.5 m years ago	Lake Turkana, Kenya
Australopithecus boisei	1.8–1.4 m years ago	Olduvai Gorge, Tanzania
Homo habilis	2 m years ago	East Africa
Homo erectus	1.8–1.3 m years ago	
Homo sapiens	150,000–100,000 years ago	Laetoli, Tanzania; Omo, Ethiopia
Homo sapiens neanderthalensis		Northern Africa
Homo sapiens sapiens	90,000 years ago	
Immediate forerunners of Contemporary Africans	15,000–10,000 years ago	

Source: Compiled from Newman, 1995. *The Peopling of Africa*, pp. 5–21.

negroids occupied the present-day Sahara, the Sahel, and interior of East Africa, while the short negroids occupied the coastal areas of western Africa and central Africa (Figure 2.1).

Evolution and Development of Early Cultures

The only evidence about the evolution and development of the cultures of these early ancestors of modern Africans comes from the tools they created and the paintings and drawings they left behind. The tools indicate that Stone Age culture began in Africa around 2 million years ago, when *Homo habilis* created the first stone tools. These tools also called Oldowan Culture, after Olduvai Gorge where they were discovered, were crude. However, by the Middle to Late Stone Age (between 120,000 and 90,000 years ago), these crude technologies had become more refined, diversified, and sophisticated into the Acheulian culture, named after St. Acheul, France, where it was first discovered. Among the most important tools of this culture were the hand axe, the bow and arrow, and the microlith or "tiny stone." Other tools were also made from animal bones.

From the paintings and drawings in caves found in the Sahara and north of the Drakensberg in South Africa, we can also learn that improvements in these tools were accompanied by more diversified forms of livelihoods and increasing ability of people to live in the ever-changing environment on the continent. Alongside these early developments was the evolution of the four major African parent languages: the Khoisan developed by the capoids, Afro-Asiatic by the caucasoids, Nilo-Saharan by the tall negroid, and the Niger-Congo by the short negroid. We will learn more about these language groups in Chapter 7.

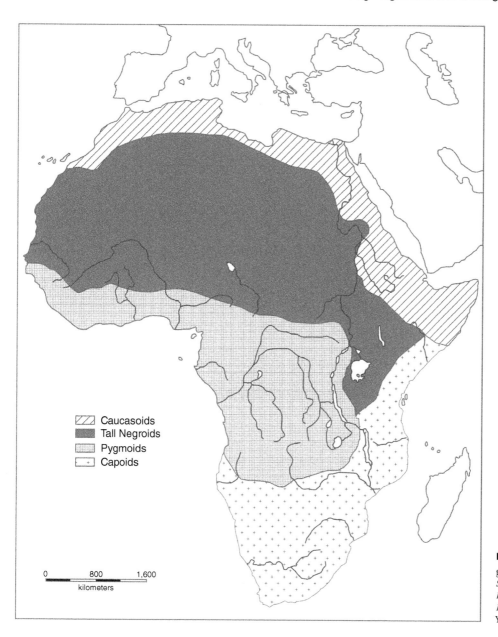

FIGURE 2.1 The four regional genetic populations of Africa. *Source:* Newman, J. 1995. *The Peopling of Africa: A Geographic Interpretation.* New Haven, CT: Yale University Press.

Transformation through Agriculture, Metallurgy, and Expansion

From about 9000 BC, the cultural evolution of the African people underwent major transformations through the establishment of sedentary agriculture, the use of metals, and population expansion.

Establishment of Agriculture

Between 11000 and 6000 BC, Africa experienced alternate periods of very wet and very dry climates, and it was at the beginning of the wet period of 9000 BC that both arable and pastoral farming began. By 2000 BC agriculture had become established over much of the continent (Shillington, 2005). Four areas were particularly important for crop and livestock domestication: (1) The Nile Valley, where sorghum, barley, wheat, and flax were domesticated; (2) The Maghreb (North Africa west of Egypt) and Central Sahara, where sheep and goats were raised; (3) Ethiopian Highlands, where teff, finger millet, mustard, coffee Arabica, cattle, and sheep were domesticated; and (4) West Africa, where millet, African rice, yam, kola nuts, oil palm, cowpeas, and the dwarf goat were domesticated (Iliffe, 1995).

Adaptation to the physical environment resulted in the practice of arable farming in wet areas, pastoral farming in the dry areas, hunting in the drier areas, and transhumance—the practice of raising livestock on upland pastures in the summer and lowland pasture in the winter—in the Maghreb (Shillington, 2005). The ability to grow more food and raise animals enhanced the growth of more settled life in larger communities. This also led to the need for a more effective social organization and the need to work cooperatively, which led to increased specialization and local trade.

The Processing and Use of Metals

The second transformation of early African societies was brought by the discovery and use of metals. The first of these metals was copper, which was used in Ancient Egypt as far back as 4000 BC. The use of bronze and gold also became prominent in North and West Africa. However, it was the use of iron that made the biggest impact because of its superiority in forging tools and weapons and because of its relative abundance. It was initially thought that iron-making was introduced to Egypt in about 650 BC from Western Asia, and from Egypt, it spread to the rest of Africa. However, it is now known that long before iron was introduced to Egypt, between 1000 and 600 BC Africans were smelting iron in the region between Lake Chad and the Great Lakes region of East Africa. By 400 BC, iron-smelting was widespread in the savanna region of West Africa, especially on the Jos Plateau, in Central Nigeria, where an iron culture called the **Nok Culture** developed (Stock, 2004; Yeboah, 2003). Among the artifacts recovered from this culture are sculptures of human heads, clay pots, iron implements, and smelting furnaces. Iron tools enhanced agricultural activities and iron weaponry later on supported empire building plans.

Population Expansion

The third and final transformative force of early African societies was population expansion, and one of the most important of these was the Bantu expansion. The original home of the proto-Bantu (people) was northeastern Cameroon and southeastern Nigeria (Figure 2.2). As farmers, they produced palm oil, nuts, and yams and still used stone tools. According to Ehret (2002), sometime after 4000 BC, a small group of the proto-Bantu started moving from their original home southward along the Atlantic to the Ogowe (Ogooue) River in modern-day Gabon. By 3000 BC, Bantu communities occupied areas in southern Cameroon. Over the next 500 years, they spread southward toward the Congo River, where they split into two. The West Bantu went southward into the grassland of Angola and Namibia. The East Bantu went southeastward to the Zambezi River and South Africa and

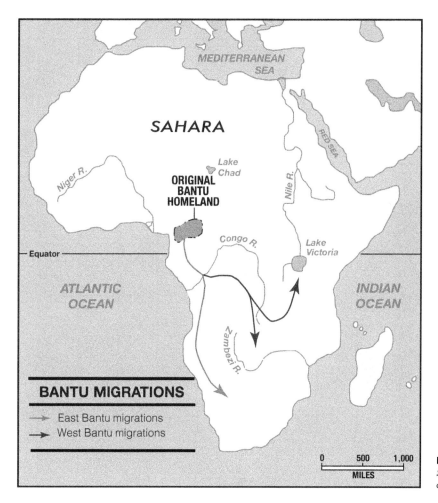

FIGURE 2.2 The Bantu migration.
Source: Adapted from http://www.historyhaven.com/APWH/unit2/bantu_migration

also northward to Kilimanjaro and the Great Lakes region of East Africa. By about 400 AD, Bantu-speaking people were occupying much of the eastern and southern Africa (Iliffe, 1995). The Bantu expansion transformed the lives of the people living in Southern Africa, with their sedentary iron technology, pottery, food preparation, and language, with the exception of the Khoisan.

THE DEVELOPMENT OF AFRICAN CIVILIZATIONS

The transformation that sedentary agriculture brought to early African societies eventually matured into empires, kingdoms, and civilizations that brought prosperity and fame as well as decline to different regions of Africa.

North and East Africa

The first great African civilizations occurred in North and East Africa and include Ancient Egypt, Meroe, Nubia, Axum, Ethiopia, Bunyoro, Buganda, and the city-states of East African coast (Figure 2.3).

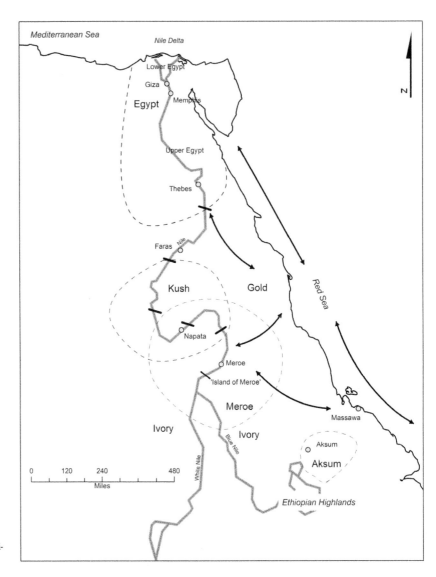

FIGURE 2.3 Ancient Egypt, Kush,
Meroe, and Axum.
Source: Shillington, K. 2005. History of Africa.
Revised 2nd Edition. New York: Palgrave Macmili-
ian, Reproduced with Permission of SNCSC

Ancient Egypt

Ancient Egypt is the most well known of all the African civilizations. With a lifespan from 3100 BC to about 30 BC, Ancient Egypt lasted longer than any other
African civilization. Historians usually divide the long history of Ancient Egypt
into three periods: the Old Kingdom (ca. 2685–2200 BC), the Middle Kingdom
(ca. 2040–1670), and the New Kingdom (ca. 1570–1085 BC), interspersed by two
periods of relative disintegration.

Initially, Europeans claimed that the astonishing civilization of Ancient Egypt
could not have been created by Africans (Diop, 1974). However, we now know that
Ancient Egypt was created by Africans and that the empire started when changing
climates of eastern Saharan pushed people into the fertile Nile Valley to develop
sedentary agriculture and settled communities. By 3500 BC, the settled communities north of the river's first cataract had grown into two clusters—Lower Egypt
around the delta area and Upper Egypt around the first cataract. About 3100 BC,

Narmer, the King of Upper Egypt, conquered Lower Egypt, united the two kingdoms, and established the first dynastic rule of Ancient Egypt.

For the next 3,000 years, amidst high and low points, the civilization of Egypt developed organizational, artistic, architectural, scientific, and other cultural innovations that were unprecedented in the history of the world, and left enormous legacies in the fields of science, mathematics, astronomy, arts, architecture, technology, and industry. Examples of these legacies include mummifications, medicine, surgery, decimal numerals, geometry, 12-month year as well as the 365-day year, the pyramids, stone cutting, metal work, and textiles.

Nubia

Lying to the south of Egypt in the Upper Nile region and with its rich gold reserves was Nubia, a former province of Ancient Egypt, which rose to prominence during the intermediate periods of Ancient Egypt. The Nubians established four kingdoms in succession of each other. The first was the Kingdom of Kerma, which grew powerful enough that it almost conquered Egypt. The second was Kush, which was able to conquer Ancient Egypt in 730 BC. It established the Twenty-fifth Dynasty of Ancient Egypt, and ruled as pharaohs, until the Assyrian conquest of 670 BC. The third kingdom was Meroe (Merowe), which quickly became an important center of trade, linking inner Africa to the south with Egypt to the north and with other links to the east and beyond. In religion, art, and architecture, Meroe was like Ancient Egypt, but its structures were smaller in sizes and more regular (Afolayan, 2000; Davidson, 1966). The fourth kingdom was Christian Nubia, which consisted of three smaller kingdoms. To the north was *Nobatia*, with its capital *Pachoras*, in the middle was *Makuria*, with its capital *Old Dongola*, and to the south was *Alodia*, with its capital *Soba*. Christianity reached these kingdoms through Egypt and Axum. Makuria expanded to dominate the region and was the main force against the southern advance of Islam in the Nile Valley. After several attempts to invade Nubia failed, the Arabs signed a treaty with the Nubians, which lasted for 600 years. Over time slow influx of Arab traders and the persecution of Alexandria Christians by Egyptian rulers cut off the supply of Christian missionaries and Christian Nubia eventually diminished.

Aksum (Axum) and Ethiopia

Up in the highlands region bordering northern Ethiopia, Tigray, and Eritrea grew the Kingdom of Aksum, which was created by the Ge'ez-speaking people, the ancestors of modern Ethiopia. Aksum became very prosperous in the 3rd and 4th centuries. It minted its own currency and its industries included glass crystal, brass, and copper, frankincense and myrrh, which it exported to Egypt, Greece, and the eastern Roman Empire. Aksum was noted for its massive stone temples, palaces, and tombstones for the wealthy class, some of which stood as tall as 108 ft (33 m) and weighing about 700 tons. Aksum also became famous when in the 4th century AD, its king Ezana (320–50 AD) converted to Christianity through Christian scholars from Alexandra. The rise of Islam in the 7th and 8th centuries and subsequent loss of trade further curtailed the influence of Aksum. However, Aksum developed a distinct African Christian culture, which like Christian Nubia, survived the Islamic invasion of North Africa, and remained a bastion of Christianity in Africa until the arrival of Europeans.

The vacuum left by Axum was filled by the Christian Kingdom of Ethiopia, which was organized by about 1000 AD. The kingdom took off when in about 1150 AD the Zagwe dynasty seized the throne from the old Axum ruling family and established

Christianity as a state religion. However, the difficult mountainous terrain, environmental decline, and dwindling resources made it difficult for the king's court to be supported, so the kingdom adopted a system by which the capital was moved sometimes two or three times a year to different parts of the kingdom. In 1529 Ethiopia was attacked by the neighboring Muslim state of Adal, but Adal was defeated with the help of the Portuguese. Ethiopia continued to be a bastion for Christianity throughout the colonial period.

The Almoravid and the Almohad Empires

In the farther Northwest Africa, the Sanhaja branch of the Amazigh (Berbers) established two Islamic empires following their conversion to Islam. The first of these was the Almoravid Empire (1062–1150) and the second was the Almohad Empire (1150–1269). The Almoravid began as a religious movement to purify the practice of Islam among the Gudala clan of the Sanhaja Berbers after one of its chiefs, Yahya ibn Ibrahim, returned from pilgrimage to Mecca. Ibrahim engaged a young and devout Muslim preacher Abdallah ibn Yasin of the Gazzala clan to preach to his people, but he was not successful with the Gudala. Instead, Yasin's message got traction among the Gudala's neighbors, the Lamtuna Berbers, who saw Yasin's message as an opportunity to fulfill their long-standing aim of uniting all the Sanhaja people. Thus, the religious movement became not only political but also militant. Calling itself al-Murabitum (Almoravids), Yasin's converts embarked a series of conquest, which brought the Trans-Saharan and the whole of modern-day Morocco under its control. It founded Marrakesh as its capital. In 1085, the Almoravid entered Al-Andalus (southern Spain) initially on the invitation of the Muslim rulers to help fight Christians, but in 1090 the Almoravid became rulers of Al-Andalus, after overthrowing the Muslim host. At its peak the Almoravid Empire covered modern-day Morocco, Algeria, and Spain and they were also in full control of the Trans-Saharan Trade (Naylor 2015).

The Almohad Empire overthrew the Almoravid also for religious reasons. Its founder, Ibn Tumart of the Masmuda Berber, opposed the laxity of the Almoravid Muslim practices, and decided to establish a more devout Islamic empire. After building followers among his own clan and other nearby ones, he made an unsuccessful attempt to invade the Almoravid Empire in 1130 and died shortly after that. However, Abdl al-Mumin who became the new leader of the Almohad conquered the Maghreb and Al-Andalusian. By 1172, the Almohad Empire stretched from modern-day Morocco to Egypt and southern Spain and Portugal. It established Seville as its capital in Al-Andalus and Marrakesh as its capital in North Africa. The empire's influence in Spain and Portugal ended after it lost a series of wars in 1212, 1236, and 1248 against a coalition of Christian princes of Aragon, Castile, Navarre, and Portugal. In North Africa, the empire collapsed from internal disintegration. Although both empires began with some puritan ethos, they warmed up to new cultural ideas and made contributions to both art and architecture that are still evident today (Naylor, 2015).

The Great Lakes Region and the East African Coast

Further south in the Great Lakes Region of East Africa and East African Coast were several kingdoms and city-states. The kingdoms included the Bunyoro-Kitara, Tooro, Buganda, and Rwanda. The **Bunyoro-Kitara** was the first state system in the Great Lakes Region (Uzoigwe, 2012). At its peak, it covered a considerable area in the region and was well organized. It was a centralized system of government of checks and balances. The kingdom was divided into provinces, which were ruled by governors, who were also members of a parliament. It also had a cabinet, which could override the king in matters of policy, but its decision had to be approved by the king. A series of events including an administrative system that encouraged succession, successive kings that did not seem to care about loss of territory, and the rise of rival states led to the decline of the empire, and in 1894 the empire ended when the British declared a protectorate over Uganda and took action to suppress every resistance (Uziogwe, 2012).

The **Buganda Kingdom** began to gain influence and territorial size in the declining period of the Bunyoro-Kitara Kingdom during the 16th to 18th centuries. Much of the expansion were former territories of the Bunyoro-Kitara. By 1876, it had become the most powerful kingdom in the Great Lakes Region. It was another well-organized kingdom. It was divided into counties, subcounties, parishes, and subparishes, all of which were ruled by chiefs appointed by the king (Kabaka). It had a navy to guard its southern flanks, and it developed an impressive network of public roads, all of which led to the capital. The introduction of foreign religions—Islam and Christianity—into King Mutesa's court in the 1860s and 1880s, respectively, created conflicts inside and outside the court among Muslims, Protestants, and Roman Catholics. Mwanga, Mutesa's son, became king in 1884, but not equipped to deal with this situation as well as mounting pressures from his quasi-cabinet members, saw Christianity as a threat and resorted to murdering 40 Christian missionaries and converts in 1885. This backfired forcing him to go into a temporary exile. The Kingdom's later alliance with the British to defeat its rival neighbor—the Bunyoro—did not preserve its independence, as it became part of the Uganda Protectorate in 1894 (Kiwanuka, 1972).

To the south the pastoralists groups of Ba-Hima and Ba-Tutsi developed two major Tutsi-dominated kingdoms of Rwanda and Burundi. **Rwanda** emerged as a political kingdom in the mid-17th century out of a number of small polities on both sides of the Congo-Nile Divide. The kingdom developed a strong military force because of constant struggle over limited resources in the neighboring kingdoms and also for expansion through incorporation. In 1895, a palace coup following the death of the king set off a series of internal conflict that wakened the kingdom, and when the new king attempted to take on the forces of the Congo Free State, the kingdom's devastated defeat forced it to enter into an alliance with the European colonialists. This effectively ended the kingdom's independence. **Burundi** also emerged as unified kingdom of small polities toward the end of the 18th century. By the late 19th century, a central administrative system of four divisions—a core area under the king, a second area under the king's sons, and a third and fourth areas under appointed chiefs were in place. German and Belgian colonial activities contained the kingdom and also helped its continuation and domination over the local area (Newbury, 2001).

East of the Great Lakes, the center of civilization was along the coast where a number of city-states including Mogadishu, Barawa, and on the offshore islands of Lamu, Zanzibar, and Kilwa were founded. It was initially thought that these city-states were established by the Arabs, but research has shown that they were established before the Arabs arrived. These city-states were port cities that traded in ivory, oriental pottery, and Indian silks.

West Africa

In West Africa, a number of empires, kingdoms, and caliphates grew up in the savanna and the fringes of the desert to the north, as well as the thick jungle to the south. In the savanna zone were the empires of Western Sudan, Kanem-Bornu, the Hausa States, and the Islamic caliphates of Sokoto, Massina, and Tukulor, and the Mandinka Empire. In the forest were Benin, Oyo, Dahomey, and Asante.

The Empires of Western Sudan

The term "**Western Sudan**" was used by Arab scholars to refer to the region between the Sahara Desert and the forest zone of West Africa. Within this region, a number of empires and kingdoms emerged from about 700 AD through the 18th century, of which the earliest and the most important were Ghana, Mali, and Songhai (Figure 2.4).

The Empire of (Old) Ghana It is not certain when old Ghana started. What is certain is that between 500 AD and 1000 AD, the Soninke-speaking people exploited their location in a transition zone between the desert and the savanna as well as between the salt mines of the Sahara and the gold fields of the Upper Senegal region, to build a large empire between the Senegal and the Niger Rivers, called Ghana. The capital of Ghana was Kumbi Selah or Ghana. Ghana became the southern terminal of the **Trans-Saharan trade** with the northern city of Awdaghost as its most important commercial center. Customs duties collected from the trade were an important source of government revenue. Despite its wealth, fame, and apparent strong central government, by the middle of the 12th century, the empire had collapsed. It was initially believed that the fall of Ghana was due to the loss of Awdaghost in 1054 to the Almoravid and later invasion by the Almoravid in 1076, but this has been questioned by other historians (Boahen et al., 1986; Bennison, 2016). At any rate, the empire was finally conquered by Mali in 1235.

The Mali Empire Mali grew from a small Mandingo or Malinke principality called Kangaba, near modern Bamako, Mali, into a large empire comprising Ghana and

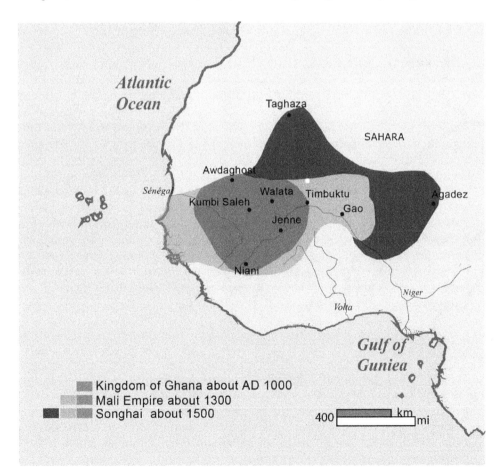

FIGURE 2.4 The empires of Western Sudan (from Adu Boahen et al., 1986, p.18). *Source:* http://fpif.org/wp-content/uploads/2013/01/GHANA-MALI-SONGHAI-EMPIRE.jpe

beyond (Figure 2.4). Mali inherited the same location advantages of Ghana and became the new southern terminal of the Trans-Saharan trade. The capital of the empire was Niani. Unlike Ghana, Mali started as an Islamic state and for that reason benefited a great deal from Islamic scholars and administrators. Mansa (King) Musa, Mali's most famous king, promoted Islamic education and sent a number of his citizens to pursue further studies at the Moroccan University of Fez, who then returned to start their own centers of learning, among which were those at Timbuktu. Mansa Musa was also perhaps one of the richest men who ever lived, and it was his extravagant pilgrimage to Mecca from 1324 to 1325 that put Mali on the world map of the day. It is reported that he spent so lavishly in Cairo and gave so much gold away that not only did he have to borrow to return home, but also the value of gold in Egypt fell for the next 12 years after his pilgrimage. In the end, Mali Empire collapsed due to internal and external factors, and by 1450, its place had been taken over by Songhai (Boahen et al., 1986).

The Songhai Empire Songhai was the largest and the last of the three Western Sudanese empires (Figure 2.4). Like its predecessors, it grew out of the small Kingdom of Gao, which was centered on the middle reaches of Niger River. The empire expanded under one of its most famous kings Sunni (Sonni) Ali in 1468, and by the time of his death in 1492, Songhai had become a huge empire encompassing the former territories of both Ghana and Mali (Boahen et al., 1986). Askiya, The Great, (Mohammed Ture) (1493–1528), Sunni Ali's successor, saw in Islam a unifying force, so two years into his reign, he embarked on a pilgrimage to Mecca. On his return, he promoted Islam as a state religion. Timbuktu was revived as a center of learning, and the status of Gao and Jenne as commercial and religious centers was enhanced. Like Ghana and Mali, tributes, customs duties from the Trans-Saharan trade, and the royal farms were the chief sources of government revenue. The empire was conquered in 1591 by the forces of El-Mansur, the Sultan of Morocco, who wanted to control the salt mines in the Sahara and the legendary gold resources of Songhai. However, when the latter proved false, the Sultan lost interest and Songhai was left to disintegrate as various ethnic groups asserted their independence. The southern termini of the Trans-Saharan trade moved eastward to the relatively peaceful routes with the empire of Kanem-Bornu and the Hausa States as the new southern anchors.

The Kanem-Bornu Empire

Kanem-Bornu grew around the Lake Chad region in the "eastern" end of Western Sudan, around 900 AD. It was established by the Kanuri-speaking people first as Kanem. The empire became Kanem-Bornu when during the 14th century, internal conflict of succession, frequent attacks from vassal and neighboring states, and economic decline forced the king at that time to move to Bornu, a former tributary state. Kanem-Bornu reached its peak during the reign of its most famous king Idris Alooma (about 1569–1600). It became the new center for Islamic learning after the fall of Timbuktu and Jenne. After declining in the mid-18th century, the empire was eventually absorbed into the Sokoto Caliphate of the 19th century, but it kept its independence until the British colonial invasion.

The Hausa States

To the west of Kanem-Bornu in modern-day northern Nigeria is Hausaland, where the Hausa created a number of city-states, between 1000 and 1200 AD, instead of one large empire. The most important of these states were Kano, Katsina, Kebbi, Gobir, Zamfara, and Zaria. All of them were walled city-states located in rich agricultural lands and were nodes on important trade routes. Each state had a king, who was supported by a group of advisers and officials. The main sources of revenue were customs duties, land tax, and artisan's tax. Islam played an important role in all the states, although its perceived lack of rigor coupled with the zeal among adherents contributed to the 19th-century Fulani Jihad that absorbed all the states into one Islamic caliphate, an Islamic state under a *caliph* or a political and religious leader considered to have descended from Prophet Mohammed.

The Islamic Caliphates of Sokoto, Masina, and Tukulor, and the Mandinka Empire

The weak state of Islamic practices, the revival of "radical" Islamic orders, political and social oppression, and the rise of devout leaders who saw the need to reform Islam facilitated three Islamic revolutions or jihads (holy wars) in the 19th-century West Africa (Figure 2.5).

The first jihad, the Fulani or Sokoto Jihad of 1804 led by Usman Dan Fodio against the Hausa States created the **Sokoto Caliphate** (1804–1903), which became the largest empire in West Africa in the 19th century. The second, the Masina Jihad of 1818 led by Seku Ahmadu against the Bambara and other provincial states of the former Songhai Empire created the **Masina Caliphate** (1818–1852). The third, the Futa Jallon Jihad of 1851 led by al-Hajj Umar against the Bambara, the Manlinke, and the Fulani created the **Tukulor Empire** (1852–1864). All three were theocracies that brought political and social stability in their respective areas and helped spread and establish Islam in West Africa. However, by the end of the 19th century, increasing European intrusion into Africa had ended all of them (Webster et al., 1967).

The **Mandinka Empire** (1870–1898) of Samori Toure was Islamic but not a jihadist state. Samori Toure was a member of the Diula subgroup of the Mandinka people, whose goal was to unite all the Mandinka people. The empire was perhaps the best organized of all the 19th-century West African empires (Webster et al., 1967). Samori was very much aware of the European colonial intentions and after seeing the treachery of many French agreements with African leaders in the region, he abrogated his own agreement with the French and mounted the most effective resistance to **colonialism** in the whole of Africa—the Franco-Mandinka War of 1890–1897. During this resistance, Samori relocated his entire empire in a different region in West Africa. The empire ended when Samori was finally captured by the French in 1898 and exiled to Gabon (Webster et al., 1967).

The Empires of the Forest and the Guinea Savanna Zones

The forest region and the transition zone between the forest and the savanna grassland (Guinea Savanna) of West Africa were also home to a number of kingdoms and empires from about 1300 through the advent of colonialism. Among the most noted ones were Benin (ca. 1300–1897), Oyo (1400–1861), Dahomey (1575–1890), and Asante (ca. 1600–1900) (Figure 2.5).

The Kingdom of Benin (ca. 1300–1897) Benin was founded by the Edo people of the south-central Nigeria. It was a well-organized kingdom and was famous for its guilds of artisans, which included bronze cutters, smiths, and cloth weavers. Its main exports included salt, beads, and iron implements, while imports included European goods and slaves. Benin was still in its prime when it was conquered by the British in 1897 (Webster et al., 1967).

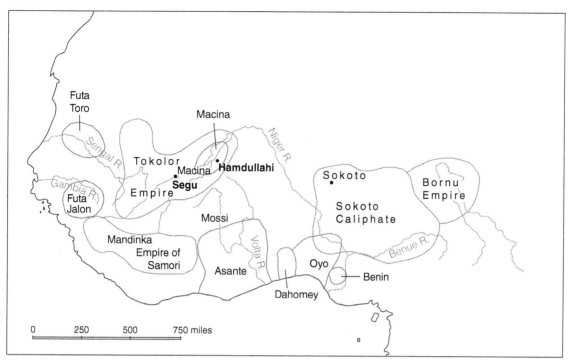

FIGURE 2.5 The savanna and forest states.
Source: Modified from O. 1967. The Growth of African Civilisation: The Revolutionary Years of West Africa since 1800. London: Longman Group Limited, p. 15.

The Oyo Empire (1400–1861) The Oyo Empire of the Yoruba people of Western Nigeria begun at Ife, about 1400. Between 1610 and 1790, Oyo grew to be the largest empire at the edge of the savanna. It developed a very high civilization that manifested itself in rich arts of bronze, ivory, wood, and baked earth. It also developed the most sophisticated governmental system of checks and balances to reduce dictatorship and corruption (Webster et al., 1967). Oyo had a diversified economy that included agriculture (cereal production, kola nuts, oil palm, cotton), manufacturing (iron tools, pottery, cotton textiles, dyed clothing), and trade (exporting pepper, kola nuts, cotton cloth, ivory, and slaves and importing sea salt, European goods, woolen cloth, and gunpowder). Oyo began disintegrating in 1837 and finally ended in 1860 following attacks by the Fulani, Dahomey, and the British.

The Kingdom of Dahomey (1575–1890) Dahomey was founded by the Aja people of the modern country of Benin, around 1620 (Webster et al., 1967). The kingdom emerged around 1708 to 1740 and reached its peak in the 19th century. It developed a unique and effective centralized system of government. Its military was famous for its 2,500-woman battalion of three brigade divisions. This battalion was so fierce in battle that it was branded the Amazons. Like other forest kingdoms, the economy of Dahomey was based on agriculture, manufacturing and trade, especially slave trade. The kingdom ended in 1894 when it was conquered by the French.

The Asante Empire (ca. 1600–1900) The Asante Empire was founded by the Oyoko clan of the Akan people of modern Ghana. The empire originated about the middle of the 17th century under its most famous king Osei Tutu and his successor Opoku Ware. At its peak, the empire covered an area much larger than modern Ghana. Administratively, the Asante Empire had a federal system of government. Like Benin and Oyo, Asante also had a guild of artisans and was famous for its wood work and *kente* cloth. Like the other empires, the economy of Asante was based on agriculture, manufacturing, and trade, and it participated in the slave trade. After several battles with the British, the empire was finally conquered in 1900 in a battle in which the Asante army was led by the Queen Mother, Yaa Asantewaa (Webster et al., 1967).

Central and Southern Africa

Among the most important empires or kingdoms of Central Africa were Luba, Lunda, Kongo, and Loango (Figure 2.6). **The Luba Empire (1300–1889)** was established in the Lualaba Lakes region of modern-day Katanga Province of Congo Democratic Republic, about 1300 AD. From about 1700 to 1860, the empire grew big, reaching the shores of Lake Tanganyika in East Africa through strong military, political leadership and a vibrant trade. The empire started disintegrating after the death of its last great king Ilunga Kabale in 1874.

The Kingdom of Kongo was organized by people living around the mouth of the Congo River, who became united by 1400. At its peak, it stretched from the mouth of the Congo River to modern Angola. The kingdom was well organized.

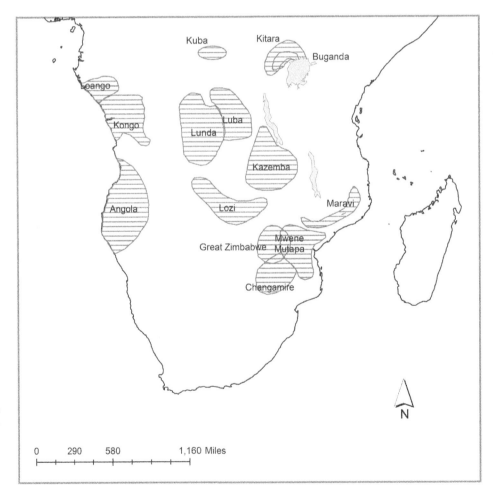

FIGURE 2.6 **Major kingdom of Southern Africa.**
Source: Yeboah, I. E. A. 2003. "Historical Geography of Sub-Saharan Africa: Opportunities and Constraints" In Aryeetey-Attoh, S. (Ed.) *Geography of Sub-Saharan Africa.* Upper Saddle River, NJ: Prentice Hall, pp. 83.

However, introduction of Christianity to the kingdom by the Portuguese in 1480 and the attempt by the Portuguese to support the king in a dynastic dispute destabilized the indigenous communities causing the kingdom to eventually collapse (Hochschild, 1998). **The Loango Kingdom (1300s–1883)** was particularly famous for its cloth, which was made from fibers of raffia palm or wine palm. As a result, palm trees constituted the cornerstone of the economy. However, the introduction of European cloth greatly weakened the indigenous cloth industry. The **Lunda Empire** and its associated satellites of Luba and Kazembe were established around 1600 and were known traders with the Arabs on the Swahili Coast and the Portuguese on the Atlantic coast. The empire collapsed when Portuguese and Belgian colonialists partitioned it in 1884.

In Southern Africa, the most significant empires and civilizations included the Leopard's Kopje, Mapungubwe, Maravi Empire, and Great Zimbabwe. **The Leopard's Kopje** is the site where a cattle-keeping culture that once lived on the Zimbabwean plateau was first identified. What was remarkable about this culture was that they developed an incredible technology for terracing the hillsides for both farming and building houses that goes back to the 1200s. The terraces were retained by stone walls.

The Maravi Empire (1500–1700) was located around the southern end of Lake Malawi. It was a federation of three chiefdoms, the Chinyanja ruled by the Kalonga dynasty, the Manjanga ruled by the Lundu dynasty, and the Chewa by the Undi dynasty. The empire was known for its iron manufactures and exports, and as a source of ivory.

Great Zimbabwe (1200–1450) refers to the ruins of a group of stone buildings in the heart of modern-day Zimbabwe, built by the ancestors of the Shona people, between 1200 and 1450. For a long time, Europeans thought that the Great Zimbabwe was not built by Africans because of the sheer size and complexity of the buildings. The buildings were used as enclosure for the capital city, which was on the hilltop, but it was later extended to the valley. Inside the main enclosure was the king's palace. This wall was later on surrounded by a much thicker and higher wall leaving a very narrow way between them. Great Zimbabwe was abandoned in 1450 for unknown reasons. Other states with stone-building culture were founded after Great Zimbabwe, such as Torwa and Maputa near Great Zimbabwe, but none could match the level of Great Zimbabwe (Davidson, 1966).

Elsewhere in southern Africa, small chiefdoms were merging into larger groups. Among these were the Tswana, the Nguni, and the Khosa. Much later in the 19th century, between 1816 and 1840, a combination of ecological, political, and economic forces led to a revolutionary movement of state formation among the Nguni and Sotho-Tswana groups. The Nguni people referred to this as *Mfecane*, which means the "crashing," while the Sotho-Tswana referred to it as *Difaqane or Lifaqane*, which means "the scattering." Out of these movements emerged the Zulu, Swazi, Gaza, and the Ndebele kingdoms.

With the exception of Islamic and some Christian influences, this section shows that from Antiquity through the 19th century, Africa had its own home grown empires, kingdoms, and civilizations. The question of what would have become of Africa had it been left alone is one that we will never be able to answer, but what we know is that Africa attracted the attention of the outside world precisely because of these same civilizations. This attraction would escalate starting from the 15th century. In the next section, we turn our attention to Africa's interaction with the outside world and how that interaction shaped its future.

AFRICA AND THE OUTSIDE WORLD

The first significant interactions between the outside world and Africa occurred in North Africa, where the various powers of the Ancient World vied for influence. Later on, the scope of this interaction widened to include more people from Europe and Asia and the rest of Africa.

North Africa and the Outside World

Hyksos, Phoenician, Roman, Greek, and Byzantine North Africa,

Hyksos The Hyksos were perhaps the first group of foreigners who had significant interaction with Africa. These foreigners from West Asia invaded Ancient Egypt in 1650 BC, established the 15th dynasty of Ancient Egypt and ruled as Pharaohs for 100 years until they were driven out in 1550 BC.

Phoenicians and Greeks About 1000 BC, during the New Kingdom of Egypt Phoenicians, from the region of Palestine began trading along the Mediterranean Coast of North Africa and Spain. By 700 BC, they had established several trading posts along the North African coast, one of which was **Carthage**, near modern-day Tunis. Intermarriages between the Phoenicians and the local African population produced a new breed of people called Carthaginians. Carthage is usually known in history books for its idol worshipping and human sacrifice practices, but it was also a great center of civilization. From 573 BC, it became the dominant city in the western Mediterranean, and sometimes challenged Rome and later Alexandria.

The Greek era in Africa began when in 332 BC, Alexander The Great conquered Ancient Egypt and immediately laid the foundation of Alexandria as the new capital city of his empire. After Alexander's sudden death, Egypt came under the control of Ptolemy, one of his generals, who established the Ptolemaic dynasty to rule Egypt. Alexandria became the commercial, intellectual, and cultural hub of Hellenism, and its three harbors, famous lighthouse, library, architecture, and street layout became the very best of Greek culture. From Alexandria, Greek culture diffused to the urban centers in Egypt, the Maghreb, and also Europe. Greek gradually replaced Egyptian language and writing, and the Greek terms, Libya and Ethiopia, referring to the original North African people and the dark-skin people, respectively, are examples of that legacy.

Romans, Vandals, and Byzantine Between 264 and 146 BC, Carthage and Rome fought three wars (Punic Wars), over the control of the Mediterranean. The Third Punic War (149–146 BC) ended in complete destruction of Carthage, and its tributary areas became the Roman Province of Africa. The province produced olives, fruits, grains, wine, timber, and wool as well as clay lamps for the empire, but the uncompromising pastoral Africans made it a tough province to govern. In 30 AD, the Romans conquered Egypt, ending the Greek period in Africa and by 44 AD the entire Mediterranean coast of North Africa was under the Romans.

During the waning years of the Western Roman Empire, Germanic Vandals invaded and occupied Roman North Africa in 430 AD, though they were not able to fully control all the native North Africans. In 533 AD Emperor Justinian of the Byzantine Empire exploited a dynastic dispute among the Vandals to invade and restore Roman North Africa as part of the Byzantine Empire, rebuilding Carthage as its capital (Naylor, 2015). The Romans left architectural styles in their African province, which are still visible today especially in Tunisia. They also labeled the original inhabitants of North Africa as "barbarian," meaning people who spoke unintelligible language. This term became corrupted as Berbers by the Arab, which became the name of the original people of North Africa until the 1980s.

Christian North Africa

The growth of Alexandria during the Greek and Roman times in North Africa brought a lot of scholars to the city, and it was through these scholars that Christianity was introduced into North Africa in the 1st century. Christianity found strong support among the poor in Egypt, and by the 2nd century, it had gradually spread westward and then down the Nile Valley to Nubia and Axum as we have already seen. However, during the 3rd and 4th centuries, North African Christians disputed over church doctrines with the Roman Church authorities, which resulted in schism, persecution, and subsequent excommunication of the majority of the Christians in the Maghreb and also in Egypt. In Egypt, this majority formed the Coptic Church of Egypt, while the minority remained with the Roman Christian Church. Some historians believe that this split contributed to the eventual collapse of Christian North Africa to the Muslim invasion (Illife, 1995; Shillington, 2005).

In spite of these schisms, Christian North Africa left some very important legacies for Christianity, including the world's first Christian theological seminary, the monastic movement, and Christian missionary activities. In addition, it produced a number of Christian theologians who helped shape the early Christian faith. From the Maghreb were Tertullian (160–240 AD), the first to articulate the theology of the Trinity, and St. Augustine of Hippo (354–430 AD), who contributed greatly to the theological and doctrinal foundations of the Roman Catholic Church. From the Egypt Christians were St. Anthony, the Doyen of monastic movement, and St. Pachomius, founder of the first monastic community (Afolayan, 2000; Illife, 1995; Shillington, 2005).

Arab and Muslim North Africa

The Arab invasion of Egypt in 640 AD ended the Byzantine Empire in Africa. The Arabs built a new capital at Cairo, and by 711 AD, Islamic army had conquered the Maghreb. However, Arab and Islamic leaders became more interested in Southwest Asia, especially Baghdad, than in Africa, until the Fatimid, a Tunisian-based group claiming direct descent from Fatima, Mohammed's only surviving daughter, captured Egypt in 969 AD and declared it independent of the Baghdad Caliphate. The Fatimid encouraged large numbers of Bedouins, or nomadic Arabs, to move westward from Arabia to Egypt and the Maghreb, spreading the Islamic faith and the Arabic language. It was this action that completed the "Arabization" of North Africa (Shillington, 2005). From there Islamic missionaries went south into Western Sudan to spread the Islamic faith and strengthen nominal Muslims through jihads and trade. The Fatimid also restored agriculture through dam and canal repairs, and they revived the Red Sea trade. However, they also extracted exorbitant taxes on the peasants and imported the Mamluks, or Turkish slave horsemen to staff their military.

After the last Fatimid caliph's death in 1171, Egypt came under Salah-al-Din ibn Ayyub (known in Europe as Saladin) and his dynasty, which strengthened Islam, modernized the army, and returned Egypt to stability and prosperity. In 1250, the Mamluks seized power and ruled Egypt for the next 250 years, during which Cairo became the intellectual center of the Arab world.

Ottoman North Africa

The Mamluks became very unpopular because of their harsh and dictatorial rule as well as the heavy tax burden on the peasants. In 1517, they were driven out by the Ottoman Turks, and Egypt became part of the Ottoman Empire. The Ottomans extended their influence to Algiers in 1518, Tripoli in 1551, and Tunis in 1574, but Egypt remained their most important African colony. The Ottomans restored agricultural system of Egypt and expanded the boundary south and revived trade. However, the viceroys or *pashas* that were initially appointed from Istanbul, the Ottoman capital, eventually became more powerful and corrupt and were really not answerable to anyone. This weakened Ottoman Egypt and it was not able to defend itself against Napoleon's invasion of Egypt (1798–1801) until the British intervened.

After Napoleon was driven out, Mohammed Ali, originally from the Ottoman Province of Albania, became the Pasha of Egypt, and from 1805 to 1849, he transformed Egypt into the most powerful state of the Ottoman Empire. He established a salaried civil service and a professional army. He restored agriculture, extended the irrigation system, and reformed the tax system as well. Mohammed Ali was succeeded by his son Ismail, who continued the modernization of Egypt, taking advantage of the economic boom Egypt had from cotton exports. He invested heavily in extending railroads to the cities in the delta region and also entered into joint venture with France to build the Suez Canal. Unfortunately, these projects in the end bankrupted Egypt and provided the pretext for increasing interference by European nations into the internal affairs of Egypt and its eventual colonization.

The Swahili Coast

Along the East African coast, interaction between Arab traders and Bantu-speaking people produced a new cultural group called the Swahili, (people of the coast) who spoke Kiswahili. By the 10th century, the term Swahili was being used to apply to "a distinctive coastal society that was Islamic in religion and culture, but primarily African in language and personnel" (Shillington, 2005, p. 126). From 1050 to 1200 AD, new Muslim immigrants from the Persian Gulf and Oman brought growth to existing as well as to new towns. In all there were about 40 Swahili towns between Mogadishu to the north and Sofala to the south, of which Mogadishu and Kilwa were the most important (Figure 2.7). The towns grew very wealthy from the brisk trade they conducted—gold, and ivory from the interior and cotton cloth, glass, and shell beads to the interior. However, the society was highly stratified—the Muslim rulers were the wealthiest and they lived in large stone houses. Next were the merchants who were also capable of amassing wealth because of their trade. Below them were the bulk of the towns' inhabitants, who were Muslim artisans, craftsmen, and clerks, and distinctively African. This group lived in modest mud houses.

The Trans-Saharan Trade

The Trans-Saharan trade linked North Africa and Southern Europe, with the Sahara, savanna, and forest states of West Africa. According to Boahen et al. (1986), the trade started sometime between 300 and 400 AD, reached its peak between 1400 and 1600, and declined in the 20th century. Existence of industrious and highly productive states that later on transformed into prosperous empires in both North and West Africa, external demand for goods in the region, introduction of the camel to North Africa, and the spread of Islam were all factors that made the trade possible.

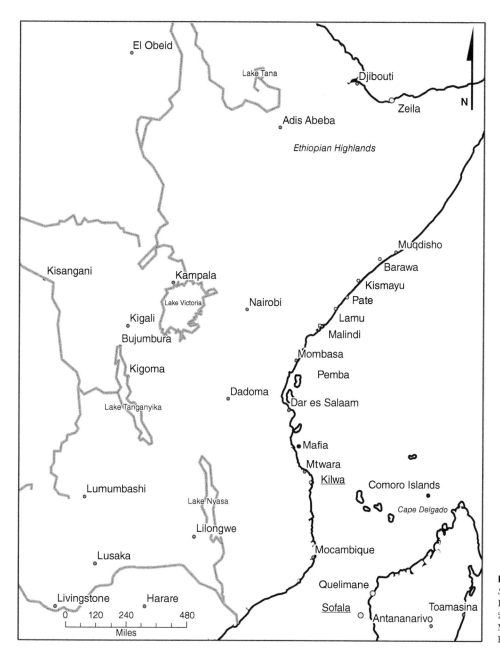

FIGURE 2.7 The Swahili Coast.
Source: Shillington, K. 2005. History of Africa. Revised 2nd Edition. New York: Palgrave Macmiliian, Reproduced with Permission of SNCSC

The trade was organized along seven main north–south caravan routes (Figure 2.8). The importance of these routes at any one time depended on which West African state was controlling the trade. Towns on the trade routes performed particular functions. Some served as rendezvous points, where all the caravans assembled, purchased supplies, and hired guides, while others served as refreshments and trading centers. The caravans usually left North Africa from September to October and West Africa in March or April (Boahen et al., 1986).

A large number of goods were traded. Textiles and garments, brass, copper, silver, tin, and lead came from Europe and the Muslim world. Horses, books, paper, cowries, tea, coffee, sugar, spices, jewelry, perfumes, bracelets, needles, razor, scissors, knives, trinkets, carpets, and beads came from North Africa; salt and copper from the Sahara; millet, sorghum, wheat, Shea butter, ivory, ostrich feathers, gold, and

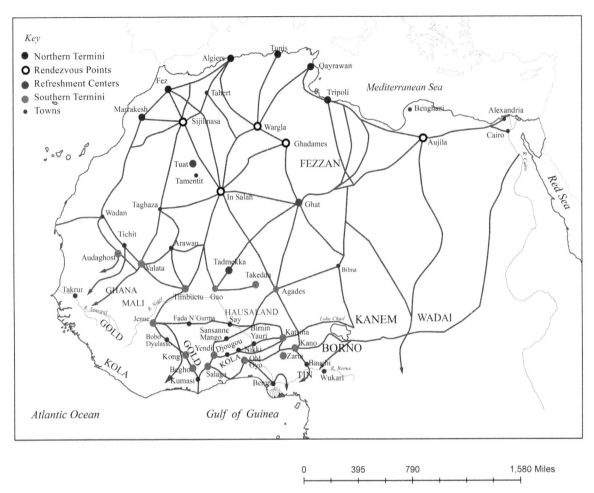

FIGURE 2.8 The Trans-Saharan trade routes (from Adu Boahen et al., 1986, p. 6).
Source: Boahen, A., Ajayi, J. F. A, and Tidy, M. 1986. Topics in West African History. New Edition. Harlow, UK: Longman Limited, p. 6.

slaves from Western Sudan; and gold, kola nuts, and slaves from the forest states. Trading was conducted mainly by barter in which a weight of gold was exchanged for another product. Cowries and later on European currencies were also used.

The Trans-Saharan trade had important political, economic, and social consequences on West Africa. Politically, it helped the development of Western Sudanese empires by bringing wealth, weapons, and good political administration. Economically, it stimulated agriculture and industry and promoted more exploitation of natural resources. Socially, it extended the influence of Islam in West Africa as most of the traders from North Africa were Muslim. It also helped spur urbanization as some of the trading centers grew from small towns to become important urban centers.

The Coming of (Western) Europeans and Early Colonies

As we have already shown, Europe's interest in Africa began in Antiquity. However, this interest declined with the Arab conquest of North Africa until the 15th century. There were several reasons for this. First, Europeans wanted to know more about Africa and beyond. Second, they wanted to find an alternative route to India that was not controlled by Muslims so as to gain control over the spice trade. Third, gold had become important in Europe and through the Trans-Saharan Trade they knew of Africa's gold. Fourth, they wanted to spread their Christian faith, and fifth, they wanted colonies. The Portuguese launched their first voyage in 1417. They reached the mouth of the Senegal River in 1460, the Gold Coast (modern-day Ghana) in 1471, the mouth of the Congo River in 1482, and the Cape of Good Hope in 1488. In 1497, they reached the Swahili Coast and in 1498 India. The Portuguese were soon followed by the Castilians, but they withdrew from Africa when they reached the New World.

The Portuguese built a settlement on the island of Goree off the coast of Senegal, as well a series of forts or castles and colonies along the African coast. The first of the forts was the El Mina castle in the Gold Coast, built in 1482, and the first colony was established on the West African islands of Sao Tome and Principe. They also established diplomatic relations with the Kingdom of Kongo, hoping to get access to gold, copper, silver, and spices. However, as already mentioned, their diplomatic relations contributed to the destabilization and the collapse of the Kongo and Ndongo kingdoms. On East Africa's Swahili Coast, the Portuguese were even more brutal. They bombarded all the towns whose rulers refused to become Portuguese subjects and pay tribute until the rulers agreed. Zanzibar, Kilwa, Mombasa, and Barawa were all subjected to this treatment. Only Malindi was spared because the Sultan agreed to their demands.

The Dutch arrived in Africa in the 1530s but became more interested in Africa only in the 1590s. They established the Dutch East India Company in 1602, and by 1640, they had driven the Portuguese from the West African coast. In 1652, the company sent a fleet of 90 men under Jan van Riebeeck to build a fort, develop a fruit and vegetable garden, and a refreshment station at the Cape of Good Hope for its trading ships. However, after arriving at the Cape, the group decided to colonize the area around the Cape, by allocating large tracts of Khoisan land to themselves, which directly caused the first war with the Khoisan people. The settlement became Cape Town and the colonized area became the Cape Colony. Members of the group that settled around the Cape became traders and innkeepers, while beyond the Cape, they became Boers or seminomadic pastoral farmers.

Other Europeans who interacted with Africa in this early period include the English who arrived in 1518, the French in the 1530s, the Danes in 1642, the Swedes in 1647, and the Prussians in 1682. The Swedes and the Prussians left in 1661 and 1732, respectively. The rest expressed some interest in missionary work, but their priorities soon shifted to the Atlantic slave trade.

The Slave Trades

From Antiquity through the beginning of the Atlantic Slave Trade in the 16th century, slavery had existed in every culture. Most slaves were casualties of wars and conquests. However, the type of slave trade that occurred in Africa from the 16th to 18th centuries was unprecedented in history. The main theater for this trade was the lands bordering the Atlantic Ocean, but there was also a second and a smaller one—the African coast and islands of the Indian Ocean.

The Atlantic Slave Trade

The first African slaves across the Atlantic were actually taken to Portugal and Spain to work on farms. Then after the establishment of the Sao Tome sugar plantations, the island became a destination for African slaves. However, European plans to exploit the rich resources of the New World through establishment of mines and plantations, and the failure of the initial plan to use the New World's native population and convicts for labor created a desperate need for labor from Africa (Shillington, 2005). The first African slaves to the New World were sent across the Atlantic in 1532. For the next 200 years, a great **triangular trade** anchored by Africa, the New World, and Europe and involving Africans, the Dutch, English, Portuguese, the French, and the Americans developed. Slaves went from Africa to the New World, plantation crops—sugar, tobacco, coffee, and cotton—went from the New World to Europe, and manufactured goods (cloth, metal ware, and guns) went from Europe to Africa (Figure 2.9). From the beginning up till the mid-17th century, most of the captives were from the so-called Slave Coast, which was the western Nigeria coast. However, as the trade expanded, it stretched all along the coast of western Africa, from Senegal to Angola (Shillington, 2005). In addition to war captives and criminals, many of the people who became slaves were victims of unwarranted and unprovoked raids.

The Indian Ocean Slave Trade

The Indian Ocean or East African slave trade began when Africans, mostly women, were sent to the Persian Gulf states to serve as concubines and house maids. However, expansion of sugar and spice plantations on French colonies of Mauritius, Reunion, and Seychelles during the second half of the 18th century, labor shortages in Brazil due to the antislavery campaign in the 19th century, and

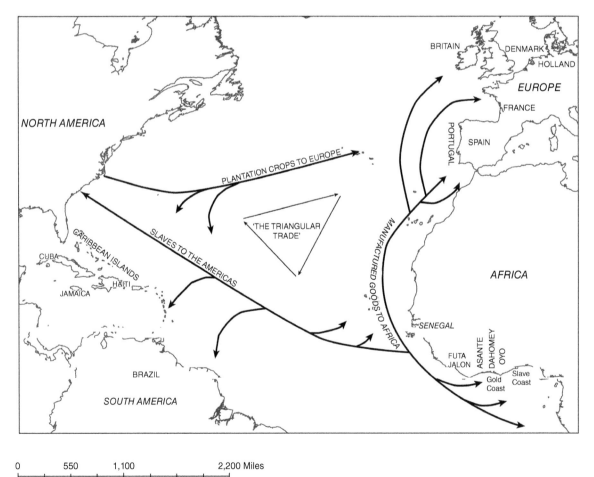

0   550   1,100   2,200 Miles

FIGURE 2.9 The Triangular trade.
Source: Shillington, K. 2005. History of Africa. Revised 2nd Edition. New York: Palgrave Macmiliian, Reproduced with Permission of SNCSC

rapid growth of clove plantations in Zanzibar changed the nature of the slave trade here. It is estimated that from the 1860s about 70,000 slaves a year were exported into these islands. Since the coastal areas could not supply all the slaves needed, many slave raiding groups, Africans and Swahili/Arabs, penetrated into the interior and established bases from where they hunted, captured, and made slaves out of members of weak or less organized kingdoms. The most famous of the Swahili-Arab slave traders was Hamad bin Muhammad, commonly known as Tippu Tip.

Abolition and Effects of the Slave Trade

By the end of the 18th century, Britain had become the single largest exporter of African slaves, yet in a few years later Britain as well as all the European nations abolished the trade. Denmark abolished it in 1805. Britain followed it in 1807; the United States banned it in 1808, Holland 1814, and France 1817. Britain went on to force all nations to stop the trade, even so slavery was not abolished until 1834 in British colonies, 1848 in French colonies, 1865 in the United States, 1873 in Zanzibar, and 1888 in Brazil. By the time it was all over, an estimated 13 million people had been removed from Africa. The humanitarian push by abolitionists such as William Wilberforce and Granville Sharp plus the fact that the trade was no longer a prop to the economies of Europe, especially Britain, were the main reasons for abolishing the slave trade (Boahen et al., 1986).

The effects of the Atlantic Slave Trade on Africa were devastating. It caused a great deal of social upheaval by way of wars and conflicts and disruption of established communities. It depopulated the continent and removed some of its most able-bodied young men and women permanently from the continent. It dehumanized and lowered the self-esteem of Africans (Boahen et al., 1986). It also introduced consumption of European manufactured goods, which truncated indigenous technological progress. It did not create any lasting investment in Africa—only shameful monuments that remind a continent of its ignominious past.

In contrast, European merchants reaped huge profits. Shillington (2005) reports that the slaves in the New World were sold two or three times their cost in Africa. The fact that Africa became a market for manufactured products from Europe also added to the profits. The results of these huge profits went into building cities such as Birmingham, England as well as major European seaports such as Bristol and Liverpool in Britain, Bordeaux and Nantes in France, and Amsterdam in the Netherlands. Ultimately, part of this accumulated wealth helped start the industrial revolution, which completely transformed Europe and America in the 18th and 19th centuries. Finally, the abolition of the slave trade and slavery had far-reaching consequences on Africa. In particular, it renewed interest in Christian missionary activities and the institution of "legitimate" trade, especially in sub-Saharan Africa, which eventually led to colonization of Africa.

Christian Missionaries, "Legitimate" Trade, and the Mapping of Africa

Christian Missionaries

We have already seen how Christianity became established in North Africa during the 1st century but lost ground to Islam in the 7th century, leaving Ethiopia and few places in Nubia as the only enclaves of the faith. Christian missionaries returned to Africa with the European explorers from the 15th century, and several efforts were made including setting up missions and sending some Africans to Europe to study and return as clergymen. However, most of them were not successful. Some of the returned African clergy did not remember all of their own language, some died shortly after their return, while some became marginalized in their own community. Thus, by the end of the 18th century, Christianity's impact in Africa was still very limited (Isichei, 1995). For the abolitionists and the humanitarians, the introduction of Christianity and Western education to Africa was one sure way to atone for the hideous crime of the slave trade. A number of missionary societies were therefore formed. Among them were the London Missionary Society (1795), the Church Missionary Society (1799), the Leeds Methodist Missionary Society (1813), the Basel Mission (1815), the Wesleyan Missionary Society (1818), Societe' des Missions Evangeliques (1822), the Bremen Mission (1824), and the Universities Mission to Central Africa (1859). By 1900, Christian communities had been established in Liberia, modern-day Sierra Leone, Ghana, Benin, Uganda, and Madagascar. Christian missionary activities did not only focus on making converts but also on education and studying of local languages that allowed them to be put into writing.

Legitimate Trade and the Mapping of Africa

Just as Christianity and Western civilization were seen as necessities for Africa, so did the institution of **legitimate trade**—trade in natural resources such as rubber, palm oil, groundnuts, cotton, cocoa, coffee, tea, timber, and mineral resources. However, for this to work, it was essential to know more about Africa's interior. Between 1788 and 1877, many expeditions were financed by European merchants, such as the African Association and European governments into Africa's interior. By the beginning of the 1880s, European knowledge of Africa's interior had dramatically improved, thanks to the unsung African heroes, who led all the European explorers to their so-called discoveries (see Box 2.1). Brisk trade by many European companies soon

Box 2.1 | Samuel White Baker's "Discovery" of the Albert Nyanza (Lake Albert)

For several days our guides had told us that we were very near to the lake, and we were now assured that we should reach it on the morrow. I had a lofty range of mountains at an immense distance west, and I had imagined that the lake lay on the other side of this chain; but I was now informed that . . . the lake actually was within a march of Parkani. . . . The guide Rabonga now appeared and declared that if we started early on the following morning, we should be able to wash in the lake by noon. The sun had not risen when I was spurring my ox after the guide. . . . The day broke beautifully clear, and having crossed a deep valley between the hills, we toiled up the opposite slope. I hurried to the summit. The glory of the prize burst suddenly upon me! There like a sea of quicksilver, lay far beneath the grand expanse of water – a boundless sea horizon on the south and south-west glittering in the noon-day sun; and on the west, at fifty or sixty miles distance, blue mountains rose from the bosom of the lake to a height of about 7,000 feet above its level.

It is impossible to describe the triumph of that moment – here was the reward for all our labour – for the years of tenacity with which we had toiled through Africa. England had won the sources of the Nile! . . . As an imperishable memorial to one loved and mourned by our gracious Queen and deplored by every Englishman, I called this great lake "the Albert N'yanza".

Source: From C. Richards and J. Place 1960. East African Explorers: Samuel White Baker. London: Oxford University Press pp. 172–173.

followed along the coast of West Africa especially with trade in palm oil, timber, and vegetables, and, to some extent, the need to control this trade contributed in part to the colonization of Africa.

African historians are divided over the effect of the legitimate trade on Africa. Some see the trade as the main cause of several wars that occurred in Africa in the 19th century. Others see it as the main cause of Africa's development problems, instead of colonialism, while others claim that the trade became possible only after the revenues from the slave trade declined (Dike, 1956; Hopkins, 1968; Manning 1986). In spite of these different views, the fact is the legitimate trade ushered in the next phase of Europe's African strategy—colonialism.

Colonial Africa

Prelude to Colonialism

Officially, Colonial Africa was born in 1885, but colonialism actually started not long after the European voyages of exploration. We have already seen how the Portuguese established colonies on Sao Tome, in Angola and Mozambique, and on the Swahili Coast. In the Senegal River valley, the French gained control of Goree in 1677 and established other colonial outposts in Saint Louis, Dakar, and Rufisque. In 1787, the British had established Sierra Leone as a colony for freed slaves, and the coastal areas of the Gold Coast and Lagos were also British colonies in 1821 and 1861, respectively. In South Africa, the British captured and occupied the Cape in 1806. In 1811, they joined the Boers to drive away the Xhosa from their land and gave it to 5,000 British settlers (Harsch, 1980). However, the Boers did not like the British laws and other changes so between 1835 and 1843, about 12,000 of them left the Cape Colony, beginning what is known in South African history as the Great Trek. The trekkers settled on Zulu lands in Natal, and this started a series of wars until the Zulu were defeated at Blood River in 1838. However, in 1843, the British declared Natal a British colony, and this forced the Boers to trek again to establish the Transvaal and the Orange Free State. By the 1860s, the native Africans had been forced to become "squatters" on their own land with many of them seeking work on the European farms and plantations.

In North Africa, relations between France and Ottoman Algeria were severed in 1827 because France refused to pay for grain supplies it had received from Algeria. Meanwhile, Turkish pirates based in Algiers, Tunis, and other Mediterranean ports had been attacking and raiding Christian ships in the Mediterranean. In 1830, France invaded Algeria on the pretext of ending the menace caused by the Algiers-based pirates. After capturing Abd al-Qadir, the leader of the Algerian resistance movement, in 1847, French as well as Spanish settlers moved to Algeria and seized olive plantations and vineyards of the Arab-African population. By 1871, there were as many as 130,000 settlers in the Algerian colony (Shillington, 2005).

The Scramble for and the Partition of Africa

The **scramble for Africa** and the **partition of Africa** refer to a time in Africa's history during which European nations rushed to forcibly acquire territories that resulted in arbitrary division of the continent into colonies. The reason for this state of affairs was primarily economic. The English industrial revolution that started in the 1750s had matured and spread to continental Europe and America by the 1880s. Europe needed markets for their goods and sources for raw materials. The long-standing reputation of Africa as a source of gold, and the discovery of large deposits of diamonds in South Africa in the 1860s, made Europeans believe that the vast African interior was rich with abundant natural resources. Apart from this, the possession of colonies was a symbol of power. This was particularly important for France and Europe's newest nations—Italy and Germany, which did not actually exist until 1860 and 1870, respectively. For these two nations, it was all prestige. As the German Chancellor Prince Otto von Bismarck said, Germany also needed "a place in the sun."

As a result of all these, the isolated cases of forcible acquisition of African lands became widespread from the 1870s. For example, in 1870, Italy took possession of parts of Eritrea. Between 1879 and 1884, Henry Morton Stanley went on a secret mission to organize a Congo state for King Leopold II of Belgium. Portugal claimed Angola and the mouth of the Congo. Pierre de Brazza claimed western Congo Basin for France and in the same year France occupied Tunisia. Meanwhile, Egypt's continued debt situation and British interest in the Suez Canal prompted Britain to occupy Egypt as a de facto protectorate in 1882. In South Africa, the British fought two wars against the Xhosa (1877–1878), and the Zulu (1879), to expand the Cape Province and annex Natal. In 1884, France occupied Guinea, and Germany declared protectorate over Togo, Cameroon, and Southwest Africa. It was in this atmosphere that Prince Otto von Bismarck, the German Chancellor, called the Berlin Conference to agree on the rules for partitioning Africa, in November 1884. Fourteen nations and empires including the United States were invited, but the United States did not participate. On February 26, 1885, the Berlin Act was signed (Boahen et al., 1986).

The terms of the Act were implemented soon afterward, through a carefully calibrated strategy of treacherous treaties with African rulers or declaration of protectorates, agreements among the colonial powers, and military conquests of the rulers who resisted (see Box 2.2). By the early part of the 20th century, Africa had become a colony of Europe, with the exception of Ethiopia (Figure 2.10).

Box 2.2 | Colonization of the Rhodesias

The colonization of Northern and Southern Rhodesia Zambia and Zimbabwe, respectively, is an example of the use of treachery as a colonization tool.

Cecil Rhodes whose Consolidated Goldfields was attracted to the Transvaal after gold was discovered in the Witwatersrand (Rand) in 1886 dreamed of endless amounts of goldfields buried under the Zimbabwean plateau that could be turned into a second Rand without having to deal with the Boer government of Transvaal. The only thing standing in the way of this scheme was the kingdom of Ndebele, which controlled the western half of the plateau. In 1888, Rhodes tricked Lobengula, the Ndebele king, to sign his kingdom away, when the British missionary Reverend Helm deliberately misinterpreted the treaty to the king. Rhodes and his cronies moved in and divided up the land for white farmers. Lobengula appealed to the British government, but the British government did nothing to help. Instead, it approved the claims that Cecil Rhodes submitted. When Rhodes and his gang soon found out that there was not as much gold as previously thought they vandalized and destroyed the ancient historical shrines, artifacts, and eventually conquered the Ndebele kingdom in 1893, killing Lobengula. Rhodes claimed the lands north and south of the Zambezi River for the British and named them after himself—Northern Rhodesia (north of the river) and Southern Rhodesia (south of the river).

Source: From Keppel-Jones, A. 1983. *Rhodes and Rhodesia: The White Conquest of Zimbabwe.* Kingston, Ont: McGill-Queens University Press.

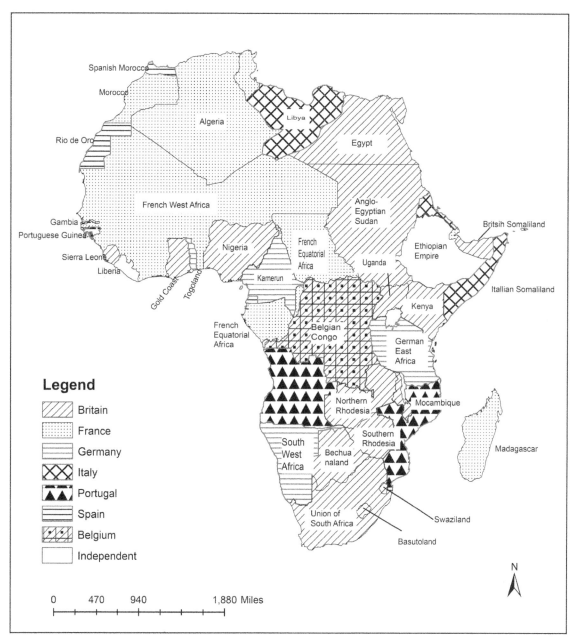

FIGURE 2.10 Africa under colonial rule.
Source: Copyright © 2018 Esri, BucknellGIS

Colonial Administrative Policies and Systems

Theoretically, three administrative policies were adopted by the colonial powers. The British adopted **indirect rule**—a policy of ruling a country or colony through its own traditional chiefs and councils. The French adopted the policy of **assimilation**, which was based on the notion that the French culture had reached the highest levels of superiority that all people must be assimilated into it (Webster et al., 1967).

Assimilated people were to be French-like, and their places of residence were to become overseas extension of France. Once assimilated, the people from the colonies had full legal and political rights of French citizens including the right for representation in the French parliament.

The Belgian and the Portuguese adopted a mixed policy of indirect rule and assimilation. The Portuguese policy was similar to the French. Colonial individuals who adopted the Portuguese language and culture were called *assimilados*. These were exempted from tax and labor obligations. However, they had no voting rights in local and central government.

These policies reflected the colonial administrative systems that were set up. For Britain, each colony had its own administrative system headed by a governor who reported to the Secretary of State for Colonies. Assisting the governor were legislative and executive councils, which made and passed laws for the colonies. For the purposes of local government, each colony was divided into regions, then provinces, then districts, then traditional states. Each region, province, and district was headed by a commissioner. The French, Belgians, and Portuguese had a very centralized and authoritarian colonial administrative system. They all had governor-generals who were in charge of the colonial administration and took their orders directly from their respective home governments. With respect to local government, they also divided their colonies into regions and districts.

In practice, however, the administrative policies were different. The so-called indirect rule of the British actually turned out to be dictatorial. The commissioners dictated to the traditional rulers, and sometimes uncooperative traditional rulers were replaced with those who would cooperate. Similarly, the French policy of assimilation had mixed results. For example, Algeria was ruled as extension of France, while the protectorate of Morocco was ruled through the Sultan. In West Africa, after initial success of granting French citizenship to natives of Dakar, Goree, St. Louis, and Rufisque, the four original French colonies in Senegal, the rights of citizenship for the four settlements was abolished. The French were also bent on dismantling traditional customary law so they did not use it as much as the British did. Like the French, the Portuguese allowed only a small number of Africans to qualify, only 4,400 in Mozambique and 30,000 in Angola as late as 1950 (Abaka, 2002). These Africans became clerks, teachers, and traders, but they were never given the voting rights in local and central government. The Belgians tried a form of assimilation policy in the Congo Free State, but adopted an indirect rule in Rwanda and Burundi.

The Colonial Economy

The colonial economy was based on commercialization with emphasis on agricultural, mineral, and timber production for the primary goal of obtaining raw materials and securing markets for manufactured goods from Europe (Igbozurike, 1976). It pursued this policy using multipronged strategies: introduction of European currencies as the media of exchange, institution of taxes, land grabbing, promotion of cash crops cultivation, construction of railroads and roads, extraction of minerals, flooding of African markets with new manufactured goods, and last but not least, brutal and ruthless suppression of dissenting voices. These were accomplished either through private concessionary companies or the central government or both.

Before World War I Before World War I, colonial governments spent most of their energies constructing railroads and roads and dealing with African resistance movement. Most of the railroads were single lines that ran from the coast to the resource regions of the interior. The resistance movement was against colonial land policies and forced labor, coercion to produce certain products especially cotton. With respect to land policies, the situation was better in several British colonies, where well-organized opposition by educated Africans prevented land takeovers by Europeans. For example, in the Gold Coast members of the Aborigines Rights Protection Society successfully argued in London against the Lands Bill of 1897 that would have threatened traditional land tenure system. In southern Nigeria and Bechuanaland (Botswana), a similar protest succeeded. In Kenya, however, large tracts of rich agricultural land were appropriated for white settlers, causing a lot struggle between 1901 and 1908. Eventually, the Africans, especially the Kikuyu, became squatters on their own lands. In South West Africa (Namibia), when both the Herero and the Nama people revolted against a similar land grab by the German settlers in 1904, they were ruthlessly suppressed. The Herero were almost wiped out to extinction for killing 100 Germans in the revolt, while the Nama were reduced to doing menial jobs.

With respect to coercion to produce particular crops, again the situation was a bit better in British West Africa and in Uganda. In West Africa, forced labor was initially used to collect wild rubber from the forest, but it was stopped after the colonialists saw that African peasants were more efficient producing other crops. Thus, groundnuts (peanuts) and palm oil, which had been precolonial exports, were allowed to continue and, in fact, expanded both in Senegal and in Hausaland of Northern Nigeria. Indeed, the British extended the railroad to Hausaland hoping to persuade the Hausa to grow cotton, but the Hausa decided to grow groundnuts instead. Other successful examples of cash crop production by small-scale peasants were cocoa production in Gold Coast and cotton production in Uganda. In the Gold Coast, for example, the small-scale peasants were so successful that by 1914, the Gold Coast had become the world's largest producer of cocoa.

Elsewhere, matters were different. In the Congo Free State, the concessionary companies forced the Africans to collect wild rubber from the forest. Those who refused either had to flee or risk of being killed, and this caused abandonment of whole towns and villages, until growing African resistance, a fall in the price of rubber, and growing international criticisms caused a change in the practice (Hochschild, 1998). In German East Africa, the push for cotton cultivation caused the *maji maji* uprising that resulted in the death of thousands of Africans.

World War I and the Interwar period Colonial Africa was very much part of World War I as British East, South, and West African troops fought against Germany in the German colonies in Africa (Togo, Cameroon, South West Africa, and German East Africa). In North Africa, troops from British and French colonies fought against the Ottoman Empire, an ally of Germany. About 50,000 West African troops fought in East Africa, while as many as 150,000 fought for France on the Western Front in Europe (Shillington, 2005). After the war, Germany lost her African colonies to the allies: France and Britain shared Togo and Cameroon, South West Africa became a South African protectorate, Belgium got Rwanda and Burundi, and Britain got German East Africa and renamed it Tanganyika.

Colonial Africa reached its peak in the interwar period. European settlements expanded in Rhodesia, Kenya, Tunisia, and Algeria. Coffee production was developed in Cote d'Ivoire, Angola, Tanganyika, Uganda, and Eastern Congo, although in Kenya Africans were banned from *arabica* coffee production. Cotton cultivation was imposed in Ubangui-Chari, Upper Volta (Burkina Faso), and Niger. A number of agricultural investments were made. The most ambitious was the British government's 1925 Gezira Scheme of Sudan. This was a large-scale cotton project on a 1.96-million-acre land between the White Nile and Blue Nile made possible by the Sennar Dam on the Blue Nile. The success of the Gezira Scheme caused France to create its own, the Office du Niger project in the inland delta zone of the Niger in French Soudan (Mali) in 1932. Completed in 1947, the project that was intended for cotton and rice production did not really work due to environmental, social, and economic reasons.

The mining sector also attracted attention. All mineral rights were appropriated by colonial authorities, which were then leased to European companies using cheap African labor. In West Africa, the British took over the gold mines of Asante, Gold Coast, and the tin mines in Jos, Nigeria. However, the richest mining region outside the Witwatersrand was the Copperbelt of the Katanga region of the Congo Free State and the adjacent region in Northern Rhodesia. On the Free State side, the mining activity was in the hands of the Union Miniere Company, while on the Rhodesian side it was controlled by the British South African Company. It was to serve these two adjacent mining regions that the Northern Rhodesian Railroad was built. Other areas of significant mining activity were Sierra Leone (iron ore) and Southern Rhodesia (coal, gold, copper, and asbestos).

Colonial economic policies also created a large pool of cheap migrant labor. The institution of compulsory tax on all African males meant that either people had to produce cash crops or work in the mines or railroad to get cash to pay the tax. This could only mean one thing for African men who neither lived in a cash-crop-producing area nor a mining area—migration. Given the prevailing low wages and limited accommodation offered, this meant that the workers' family had to remain at home or in the rural area. In South Africa, the Natives Land Act of 1913 and subsequent legislation reserved all skilled jobs in mining and agriculture to whites and restricted movements of blacks. Blacks were required to carry a pass to avoid arrest, fines, or imprisonment. In Northern Rhodesia, migrant workers received very short contracts and less pay; they could not be accompanied by spouses and had no opportunity for skill improvement. In contrast, the Union Miniere offered three-year contracts, encouraged wives to stay close to the mines, paid missionaries to provide basic primary education, and provided minimum skill development.

In Portuguese Africa, the large numbers of Portuguese migrants to Africa made it difficult even for the assimilados, and majority were used as contract labor, which was a code word for slaves. Africans became landless per the Decree Law Number 3983 of 1918. *Assimilados* were paid three times less than their Portuguese counterparts (Abaka, 2002).

Education and social development was another area of the economy that saw some improvements. About the 1920s, the colonial governments became more interested in education, due in part to Lugard's (1922) publication of the *Dual Mandate of British Tropical Africa* and the Phelps Stokes Fund of America's Report (Lewis, 1962). Both publications called for the need to educate Africans in the colonies. Mission schools in both British and French colonies began receiving government subsidies. In British colonies, plans were also made to establish high schools in Khartoum, Sudan, in 1902, at Makerere, Uganda, in 1924, and at Achimota, Gold

Coast, in 1927, all of which would eventually transform into universities. However, the biggest problem with all the schools was that the curriculum lacked African content. Apart from reading, writing, and numbers, it was all about the language, culture, and history of the colonial powers.

A sector that was conspicuously missing in the colonial economy was manufacturing. No effort whatsoever was made to establish industries in the colonies since that would have defeated the underlying premise of the whole colonial enterprise of keeping the colonies as producers of raw material and consumers of manufactured goods. Instead, all efforts were made to discourage if not dismantle the indigenous manufacturing and technological base in the colonies, by flooding the market with new manufactured goods from Europe and emphasizing agricultural production and mining. The only exception to this was the mining areas where plants were established to partially process minerals and in the white minority-controlled South Africa and Southern Rhodesia (Burdette, 1990).

World War II and Postwar reforms Colonial Africa once again found itself in the middle of World War II. Indeed, World War II began in Colonial Africa when in 1935 Italy invaded Ethiopia and occupied Addis Ababa in 1936. Several appeals from Haile Selassie, the Emperor of Ethiopia, went unheeded until Italy invaded British Somaliland and Egypt in 1940. In 1941, a coalition of troops from British West and East Africa, Belgian Congo, French Equatorial Africa, and South Africa drove Italy out of Ethiopia and restored Haile Selassie. After that, the African troops fought in North Africa against Italy and Germany, and participated in the invasion of Sicily in 1943. Prior to this, about 80,000 French West African troops had fought against the Germans in France in 1940. Finally, African troops also fought in Southeast Asia against the Japanese.

Africa's importance as a source of raw materials increased during the war as other sources in Asia were cut off, but once again most of the profit went to the colonial powers. The postwar period saw several reforms in the colonies due to increasing demand from African nationalists. For example, in the British colonies, more funds were provided for transportation systems, education, and health care. New hospitals were built in the major cities; new universities were planned or established including Ibadan (Nigeria), Legon (Gold Coast), Makerere (Uganda), and Khartoum (Sudan); and more scholarships were provided for Africans to go and study in British universities. Roads, airports, and seaports were also built, and the number of African representations in both the executive and legislative councils was increased.

In the French colonies, the new constitution of 1946 abolished the *indigenat* labor system, whereby people were forced to work for free for a certain number of days, and French citizenship was restored to qualified Africans. In addition, the colonies were allowed to send 10 delegates to the French National Assembly in Paris. The French did not build universities because they assumed that Africans would attend universities in France.

It was the goal of both France and Britain to introduce reforms gradually toward self-government in their colonies at a pace and context controlled by them. However, the gathering clouds for independence had already reached a saturation point and nothing was going to stop the outpouring of African nationalism that would descend on colonialism. In the end, it was Africans rather than the French and the British who dictated the pace for self-government. Within 10 years after the end of World War II, African colonies began their long-awaited return to independence.

THE RETURN TO INDEPENDENCE

Reasons for the Independence Movement

Three factors explain the independence movement that swept across Africa, especially from the 1950s. The first is the nature of colonialism itself. The second is the rise of African nationalism. The third is the role of World War II.

The Nature of Colonialism

At its core, colonialism was tyrannical, racist, and dehumanizing. It rested on the premise that the colonial power was superior to the colonized and for that matter the former can seize the property and the will of the colonized and use them as pleased. Such forcible acquisition of land would generate vehement reaction in every culture, irrespective of ethnic background, socioeconomic status, creed and belief systems. Yet when Africans rightfully responded, they were brutally murdered, repressed, and dehumanized. Not only that, but the will and wishes of the colonial powers were imposed on Africans and they were forced to comply with those wishes. It can be said that colonialism brought some modernization to African societies, but it was never accepted by Africans. So, it was only a matter of time for it to end, and that time came in the post-World War II era.

The Rise of African Nationalism

As already pointed out, nationalistic reaction to colonialism began right from the beginning and did not really go away. Instead, it found expression through revolts, rebellion, and migration, while in urban areas it was through strikes, looting, and formation of youth associations and political pressure groups (Adu Boahen et al., 1986; Iweriebeor, 2002). Among the pressure groups were the Aborigines Rights Protection Society of Gold Coast (1897), the Wafd of Egypt (1918), the Young Tunisian Party, the Destour (1920), the Etoile Nord-Africaine (1926), the People's Union of Lagos (1908); the Nigerian Democratic Party (1923), the National Congress of British West Africa (1920), and the South African Native National Congress (1912), which transformed into the African National Congress (1923). The activities of these groups were enhanced by Pan-African ideas from the United States and the West Indies, especially the activities of Marcus Garvey and W. E. Du Bois, and the **Negritude** movement, which pressed for acceptance of African culture as part of the assimilation process in French colonies. Several Pan-African congresses were held in Paris in 1919, London, Brussels, and Paris in 1921, Lisbon in 1922, and New York in 1927, which provided a common forum and inspiration for liberation of Africans and the African Diaspora.

The Effects of the Two World Wars

As already pointed out, the two World Wars produced a lot of African ex-servicemen. Many of these men became disappointed when they did not receive anything for their war efforts. This situation got worse when the 1929 World Economic Crisis and subsequent worldwide depression hit African farmers and business people very hard as both demand and prices fell. More importantly, the two World Wars exposed the myth of European superiority. In particular, fighting side by side with white soldiers, the African ex-servicemen saw the full humanity of the white man. In addition, they were also exposed to the full spectrum of European society—its poverty, its brutality, and its working class. These troops returned home with a completely new view of the white man and were set to dismantle the prestige and mystique about them, through actions such as strikes and civil disobedience. Thus, these men became the bulk of the foot soldiers for the independence movement.

Ready to lead the causes of these African ex-servicemen and the general populace was a growing number of educated Africans, a nationalist intelligentsia, which came of age during the 1940s–1950s. Many of these future leaders had attended the sixth Pan-African Congress in London in 1945 and left determined to lead their people to independence. This conviction was affirmed in 1947 when India returned to independence from the British. At that point, there was no turning back.

The March to Independence

In 1950, only four African countries were independent—Ethiopia, Liberia, Egypt, and South Africa. Ethiopia was never colonized. Liberia was recognized as an independent country in 1847. Egypt returned to independence in 1922, South Africa was granted independence in 1910, but it was independence only for the British and the Boers without nonwhite South Africans. However, by the end of the 1960s, only about six countries were not independent (Figure 2.11). In general, this remarkable turn of events was achieved through one of three means: party politics and elections, negotiation between colonial powers and local leaders, and armed struggle. Since these stories are well summarized by Figure 2.11, we only highlight a few examples as case studies.

British Colonies

The British colonies or protectorates in North Africa were the first to return to independence, starting with Egypt in 1922, then Libya in 1951, and then Sudan in 1956. The Gold Coast followed in 1957, changing its name to Ghana at independence. Drawing inspiration from Ghana's independence, the rest of British Africa had a relatively smooth return to independence except Kenya and Southern Rhodesia, where it was through armed struggle and negotiation. In Kenya, the armed struggle manifested itself through the *Mau Mau* uprising, which started in the 1940s as a grassroots reaction to acquisition of native lands. The goal of the uprising was not to fight a large-scale war but to use repeated small raids in the countryside to force white settlers to abandon their property. The attacks became more intense and widespread in 1952 prompting the colonial administration to impose a State of Emergency, imprison a number of political leaders, and bring in reinforcement from Britain. The *Mau Mau* fighters were finally defeated in 1956, but they forced the British government to reconsider the demands of the white settlers in Kenya, and by 1960 the British government had accepted the principle of majority rule, which returned Kenya to independence in 1963.

In Southern Rhodesia, the white settlers and their counterparts in Nyasaland had proposed a Central African Federation comprising Northern and Southern Rhodesia and Nyasaland, with the sole aim of strengthening their hold on the region and preventing any move toward independence. However, the African nationalists opposed the idea, so in 1964, the federation broke up and Northern Rhodesia

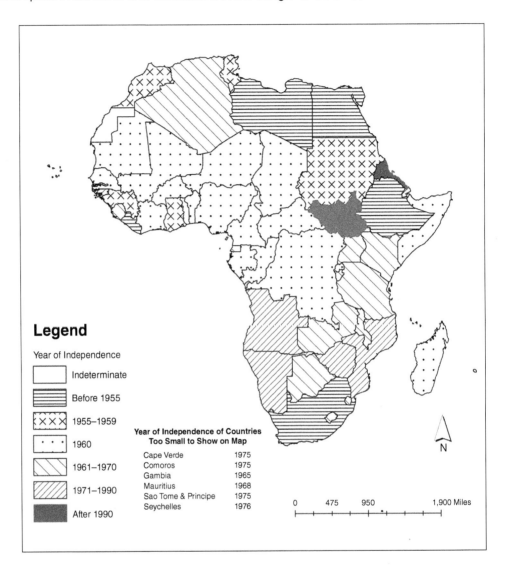

FIGURE 2.11 The return to independence.

regained independence as Zambia and Nyasaland as Malawi. In Southern Rhodesia, however, the white minority regime was still in control. Sensing that Britain would grant independence to the African majority, the white minority government led by Ian Smith unilaterally declared Southern Rhodesia independent from Britain and began imposing apartheid-type policies and governance on the colony. In 1975, Robert Mugabe took over the Zimbabwe African National Union (ZANU) and stepped up ZANU's guerrilla warfare with the help of Mozambique freedom fighters and Zambia. In 1980, Southern Rhodesia finally regained independence under the new name of Zimbabwe.

French Colonies

The French had no inclination of granting independence to her North African colonies especially Algeria because of its considerable French settlement. So, when a peaceful demonstration of Muslim nationalist in May 1945 turned deadly with about

100 Europeans and 8,000 Algerians dead, it became clear that independence could only be won through a full-blown war. On November 1, 1954, the Front de Libera-tion Nationale (FLN) launched the Algerian War of Independence (1954–1962). Both sides suffered heavy casualties—FNL suffered 153,000 dead and 160,000 wounded, while France suffered 25,000 dead and 65,000 wounded. Since France did not want to repeat the experience in the rest of French North Africa, both Morocco and Tunisia regained independence in 1956, even before the end of the Algerian conflict and its independence in 1962.

For the rest of French Africa, the initial proposal was to form two separate federa-tions, one for French West Africa and the other for French Equatorial Africa. How-ever, in 1958, France gave the colonies ultimatum to vote "yes" to stay with France or "no" to be completely independent. All but Guinea voted to stay with France. Guinea paid a very high price for its independence vote, because France removed all the infrastructure it had built in the country and material including government files, and Guinea had to rely on the former Soviet Union and a £10 million gift from Ghana to survive. Two years later in 1960, however, France returned all her remain-ing 13 African colonies to independence.

Belgian Colonies

The independence movement began in 1956, when a small number of nationalist intelligentsia comprising teachers, clerks, and shopkeepers in the Belgian Congo started demanding for equality in the social and economic life of the colony. Several political parties emerged when Belgium agreed to grant this group representation in the local government. The most important were ABAKO (Alliance des Ba-Kongo) led by Joseph Kasavubu, CONAKAT (Confederation des Associations Tribales du Katanga) led by Moise Tshombe, and the MNC (Mouvement National Congolais) led by Patrice Lumumba. Only the MNC tried to be colony-wide in scope. In 1959, after a political rally in Leopoldville resulted in a riot, looting, and destruction of property, Belgium quickly arranged to return the colony to independence on June 30, 1960, as Congo Leopoldville, with Patrice Lumumba as Prime Minister, and Joseph Kasavubu as President. Unfortunately, within six months of independence, Cold War politics and internal power struggle threw the new country into serious crises that culmi-nated in the death of Patrice Lumumba, as well as the second Secretary-General of the United Nations, Dag Hammarskjold, and the institution of a 30-year dictatorship of Mobutu Sese Seko, which was fully supported by Western governments.

Portuguese Colonies

In all the Portuguese colonies, independence came through bitter armed struggle because the Portuguese did not want to grant independence. In Guinea-Bissau and Cape Verde, it took more than 10 years (1963–1974) before Amilcar Cabral's PAIGC (Partido Africano da Independencia de Guine e Cabo Verde) were able to force the Portuguese to withdraw. Similarly, in Mozambique, Eduardo Mond-lano's and Samora Machel's FRELIMO (Frente de Libertacao de Mocambique) war of independence lasted from 1964 until 1975 when the Portuguese were forced out.

In Angola, the struggle against the Portuguese was started by Augostinho Netos' MPLA (Movimento Popular de Libertacao de Angola) in 1961, when the Portuguese brutally repressed a peasant revolt against cotton cultivation. MPLA carried out most of the fight until the Portuguese withdrew in 1975, but then two other groups, backed by Western and South African interests against the socialist-oriented MPLA, decided to fight MPLA for control over Angola. The two parties were Holden Roberto's FNLA (Frente Nacional Libertacao de Angola) backed by the United States and Jonas Savimbi's UNITA (Uniao Nacional para a Independencia Total de Angola) backed by South Africa. However, with the help of 13,000 Cuban troops, Neto was able to repel the attack.

South West Africa and Eritrea

South West Africa had been given to South Africa after World War 1 as a trusteeship of the United Nations, but South Africa wanted to keep it as one of its provinces. In 1960, Sam Nujoma formed the South West Africa People's Organization (SWAPO) and started guerrilla warfare against South Africa. In the mid-1980s, South Africa was forced to end her occupation of South West Africa in return for the release of her troops that had been cut off in Angola, by the Cuban-backed MPLA forces. In 1990, South West Africa returned to independence as Namibia.

The Italian colony of Eritrea also became a British trusteeship in 1941. In 1950, the United Nations arranged for Eritrea to become part of the Ethiopian Federation. However, Ethiopia dissolved the federation in 1961, and annexed Eritrea as one of its 14th provinces in 1962. The Eritreans organized the Eritrean Liberation Front (ELF) and began a 30-year war with Ethiopia. The war ended in 1991, when the Soviet-backed Ethiopian government collapsed. In 1993, Eritrea returned to independence.

The Struggle to End Apartheid

As already stated, the granting of independence from Britain to the Union of South Africa in 1910 did not bring any freedom to the country's African majority. Instead, their situation grew worst as discrimination and segregation laws kept them from full citizenship and participation in the affairs of their own homeland. In 1948, the National Party of South Africa came to power and instituted the "Apartheid" or separate development policy, which reinforced previous segregation and discrimination laws. Thus, the Population Registration Act of 1950 classified the South African population into whites and nonwhites, the latter consisting of coloreds, Indians, and Bantu. In addition, the Group Areas Act (1950) defined where various population groups could live. The white areas were out of bounds to nonwhites. The Bantu Education Act also forced blacks to attend government schools where they learned about racial differences and low-skilled activities. Other wide-sweeping laws segregated public places, buses, schools, and occupation and wages, all meant to keep the African majority at the bottom of the socioeconomic ladder. The African National Congress (ANC) staged several protests including refusal to carry passes, but the South African government imprisoned many of its members. Meanwhile, some members of the ANC who believed in African-only party broke away to form the Pan-African Congress (PAC).

In March 1960, while independence movement was sweeping across Africa, the South African police opened fire on peaceful protesters at Sharpeville, north of Johannesburg, killing 69 people and wounding 180. This event received world-wide condemnation, but South Africa responded by withdrawing from the British Commonwealth of Nations and declaring itself a republic. Both the ANC and PAC realized that it would need armed struggle to get justice. They immediately started organizing for it, but after a few successful sabotage attacks, nine group leaders, including Nelson Mandela, Walter Sisulu, and Govan Mbeki, were arrested, tried, and imprisoned for life in 1964.

However, the protest movements actually intensified in the 1970s. On June 16, 1976, police opened fire again on 15,000 school children in a peaceful demonstration in Soweto, a suburb of Johannesburg, and this caused rioting all over the country. Several student leaders were arrested and beaten to death, among them Steve Biko. The protests continued in the 1980s forcing the President P. W. Botha to declare a "State of Emergency" in some of the townships. Some modifications of apartheid laws were made such as unbanning interracial marriages and relaxing the Group Areas Act. However, the core issue of granting political rights to blacks remained unchanged. International sanctions and reaction were growing and investments started leaving the country, forcing the Rand, the national currency, to fall dramatically. The failed invasion of Namibia added to the troubles of the government, and when F. W. de Klerk became the President in 1989, he was forced to take dramatic measures—he repealed the Population Registration and Group Areas Acts, unbanned the ANC and the PAC, as well as other political parties, and, the most important of all, released longtime political prisoners including Mbeki (1987), Sisulu (1989), and Mandela (1990). Negotiations for a new constitution followed, and after a successful multiracial government election in April, 1994, Nelson Mandela became the first black president of South Africa.

South Sudan

South Sudan's independence came at the end of what was the longest civil war in modern Africa. The war began in 1955 when the black, Christianity, and African religion-dominated southern part of Anglo-Egyptian Sudan pushed for independence from the Arab and Muslim-dominated north just before the country's independence from Britain. The war lasted for 17 years after the severe bombardment and destruction of many southern towns including Juba by the Sudanese army. After a relatively short period of peace, the second civil war erupted again in 1983 till 2005, when a comprehensive peace agreement was signed. Among other things, the agreement provided for a referendum in 2011 on whether or not the people of South Sudan would remain in Sudan. In January 2011, about 98% of South Sudanese voted for separation from Sudan and on July 9, 2011, South Sudan officially declared itself independent of Sudan (North) thus becoming Africa's newest country. Unfortunately, independence did not bring peace to South Sudan because in 2013, a power struggle between the two top political leaders of the country resulted in another civil war between the two largest ethnic groups of the country—the Dinka and the Nuer—until August 24, 2018 when the two leaders agreed to a permanent ceasefire.

The Ongoing Saga of Western Sahara

With apartheid ended and South Sudan a separate country, the only non-self-governing political entity remaining in Africa is Western Sahara (formerly Spanish Sahara), where independence efforts under the United Nations have been thwarted by traditional claims by Morocco and Mauritania. The Polisario Front, the organization leading the independence movement, started fighting the Spanish in 1973. However, after the Spanish pulled out, both Morocco and Mauritania laid claim to the territory. The Polisario Front backed by Algeria fought back and in 1979 Mauritania withdrew. Morocco annexed the territory abandoned by Mauritania. In 1991, a ceasefire agreement was reached, to be followed up by a referendum. However, that has been stalled by Morocco who has vowed not to give up the territory. As recent as 2007, Morocco proposed some form semiautonomous governing entity for Western Sahara but still under Morocco's jurisdiction.

Summary

Africa has a very rich history. From the earliest times, Africans learned to negotiate their environments as best as they could, creating technologies, relationships and interactions of various kinds through conquests, agreements, and negotiations. These led to the rise of empires, kingdoms, which attained varying degrees of civilizations. They created political and social organizations that ranged from simple to complex. They also created economic activities that provided support and sustenance for them. They developed languages, traditions and customs, and religious beliefs, and knowledge systems, some of which benefited both the contemporary and subsequent worlds.

This state of affairs was interrupted by both voluntary and forcible interactions with the outside world. As a result, these interactions produced both positive and negative impacts on Africa. Thus, these interactions brought new cultures and their associated languages, religion, and technologies. They also brought trade that had economic, social, and political consequences. For example, the slave trades removed a large number of able-bodied Africans from the continent. They also created a lot of misery for societies that became victims of the trade. They left an indelible mark on Africa and provided a fertile ground for ethnocentric attitudes against Africa. The legitimate trade tried to make up for the sins of the slave trade, but it ended up laying the foundation for eventual colonization of the continent.

Colonialism ended local and regional conquests and introduced Western forms of education, health care, infrastructure, and lifestyle to Africa. However, colonialism also subjected Africans to hardships, misery, and suffering, with hundreds of thousands paying with their lives. It truncated indigenous capability and self-sufficiency and created a dependency situation that persists today. It brought together different ethnic groups and forced them to live together in artificially defined political units, which has become a source of major political and ethnic strives in modern Africa. Eventually, Africans managed to get free, but the wounds that had been caused would take a long time to heal, as we will see in the rest of the book.

Postreading Assignment

A. Study the Following Concepts

Assimilation Policy
Bantu Migration
Colonialism
Indirect rule

Legitimate Trade
Maghreb
Negritude
Nok Culture

Pan-African Congress
Partition of Africa
Scramble for Africa
The Great Trek

Triangular Trade
Trans-Saharan Trade
Western Sudan

B. Discussion Questions

1. Now that you have filled in the table you constructed before reading the chapter, use it to construct a narrative of Africa's history under the following headings: ancient times, the Dark Ages, the medieval period, and the modern era.

2. Debate the assertion that the civilization of Ancient Egypt and Great Zimbabwe were not created by Africans.

3. Discuss the assertion that the Atlantic Slave trade was good for Africa, because the trade saved people from ritual murder.

4. Was the Atlantic Slave trade abolished because of humanitarian reasons or economic reasons?

5. Discuss the pros and cons of colonialism on Africa. Do you think Africa is better off because of colonialism?

6. Discuss the main factors that led to the return to independence movement.

7. What role did the World Wars play to end colonialism in Africa?

8. Why do you think all the former Portuguese colonies in Africa had to gain their independence through armed struggle?

References

Abaka, E. 2002. "Portuguese Africa." In Falola, T. (Ed.) *Africa: Volume 4: The End of Colonial Rule Nationalism and Decolonization.* Durham, NC: Carolina Academic Press, pp. 379–397.

Afolayan, F. 2000. "Bantu Expansion and Its Consequences." In Falola, T. (Ed.) *Africa: Volume 1: African History Before 1885.* Durham, NC: Carolina Academic Press, pp. 113–136.

Boahen, A., Ajayi, J. F. A., and Tidy, M. 1986. *Topics in West African History.* New Edition. Harlow, UK: Longman Limited.

Burdette, M. M. 1990. "Industrial Development in Zambia, Zimbabwe, and Malawi." In Konczacki, Z. A., Parpart, J. L., and Shaw, T. M. (Eds.) *Studies in the Economic History of Southern Africa Volume I: The Front-Line States.* London: Frank Cass, pp. 75–126.

Davidson, B. 1966. *African Kingdoms.* New York: Time Incorporated.

Darwin, C. 1897. *Descent of Man and Selection in Relation to Sex.* New York: D. Appleton and Company.

Dike, K. O. 1956. *Trade and Politics in the Niger Delta, 1830–1885: An Introduction to the Economy and Political History of Nigeria.* London: Oxford University Press.

Diop, C. A. 1974. *The African Origin of Civilization: Myth or Reality.* Translated from the French by Mercer Cook. New York: L. Hill.

Ehret, C. 2002. *The Civilization of Africa: A History to 1800.* Charlottesville, VA: University Press of Virginia.

Harsch, E. 1980. *South Africa: White Rule Black Revolt.* New York: Monard Press.

Hochschild, A. 1998. *King Leopold's Ghost: A Story of Greed, Terror, and Heroism in Colonial Africa.* Boston, MA: Houghton Mifflin.

Hopkins, A. G. 1968. "Economic Imperialism in West Africa: Lagos 1890–92." *Economic History Review* 21(3): 580–606.

Igbozurike, M. 1976. *Problem Generating Structures in Nigeria's Rural development.* Uppsala: The Nordic Africa Institute.

Iliffe, J. 1995. *Africans: The History of a Continent.* Cambridge: Cambridge University Press.

Isichei, E. 1995. *A History of Christianity in Africa: From Antiquity to the Present.* Grand Rapids, MI: W. B. Eerdmans Publishing Co.

Iweriebeor, E. E. G. 2002. "Trends and Patterns in African Nationalism." In Falola, T. (Ed.) *Africa Volume 4: The End of Colonial Rule Nationalism and Decolonization.* Durham, NC: Carolina Academic Press, pp 3–27.

Keppel-Jones, A. 1983. *Rhodes and Rhodesia: The White Conquest of Zimbabwe.* Kingston, Ont: McGill-Queens University Press.

Kiwanuka, M.S. M, 1972. *A History of Buganda from the Foundation of the Kingdom to 1900* New York: Africana Publishing Corporation.

Lewis, L. J. 1962. *Phelps-Stokes Fund. African Education Commission (1920–1921). Phelps-Stokes Fund. African Education Commission (1923–1924).* London, New York: Oxford University Press, 1962.

Lugard, L. 1922. *The Dual Mandate in British Tropical Africa.* London: Cass.

Manning, P. 1986. 'Slave Trade, "Legitimate" Trade, and Imperialism Revisited: The Control of Wealth in the Bights of Benin and Biafra.' In Curtin, P., Lovejoy, D., and Paul, E. (Eds.) *Africans in Bondage: Studies in Slavery and the Slave Trade: Essays in Honor of Philip D. Curtin on the Occasion of the Twenty-fifth Anniversary of African Studies at the University of Wisconsin*, pp. 203–233.

Naylor, P. C., 2015. *North Africa: A History from Antiquity to Present* Austin: University of Texas Press.

Newbury, D. 2001. "Precolonial Burundi and Rwanda: Local Loyalties, Regional Royalties" *The International Journal of African Historical Studies*, 34(2): 255–314.

Newman, J. 1995. *The Peopling of Africa: A Geographic Interpretation*. New Haven, CT: Yale University Press.

Shillington, K. 2005. *History of Africa*. Revised 2nd Edition. New York: Palgrave Macmillan.

Stock, R. 2004. *Africa South of the Sahara: A Geographical Interpretation*. New York: The Guildford Press.

Uzoigwe, G. N. 2012. "Bunyoro-Kitara Revisited: A Reevaluation of the Decline and Diminishment of an African Kingdom." *Journal of Asian and African Studies*, 48(1): 16–34.

Webster, J. B., Boahen, A. A., and Idowu, H. O. 1967. *The Growth of African Civilisation: The Revolutionary Years of West Africa since 1800*. London: Longman Group Limited.

Yeboah, I. E. A. 2003. "Historical Geography of Sub-Saharan Africa: Opportunities and Constraints." In Aryeetey-Attoh, S. (Ed.) *Geography of Sub-Saharan Africa*. 2nd Edition, Upper Saddle River: Prentice Hall, pp. 78–104.

CHAPTER 3

The Struggle for a Better Standard of Living
The Elusive Goal of Economic Development

The early postcolonial period in Africa was a time of great optimism. The task in front of African countries was clear and that was to lift the living conditions of their people from poverty, backwardness, and tradition into the modern world, as seen in Europe and North America (United States and Canada), as quickly as possible. It was an enormous task, but doable. After all, Africa had huge natural resources, which could presumably be harnessed to generate the revenue needed for development projects. Apart from this, Africa did not have to reinvent the wheel since all that was needed to achieve its goals of development had already been demonstrated by developed countries of the world at that time. Indeed, there were a few theories and models already in place that could be adopted, but even more encouraging was the fact that renowned social scientists of the day from both West and East kept busy developing new theories and models for the so-called development latecomers including African countries to catch up with the standard of living in developed countries. African countries also kept busy crafting and implementing development plans, which incorporated or adapted some of the prevailing theories and models. Now after decades of economic development efforts, it has become apparent that achieving economic independence would be a lot harder than the political one. Thus, instead of closing the gap between them and the developed countries, African countries have seen the gap widening in several areas of living conditions. Instead of moving forward, they have seen several countries in Asia that were behind them in the 1950s and 1960s, bypass them in several areas of development. Instead of being counted among economically progressive countries, many African countries have found themselves among the ranks of world's poorest countries. These trends raise the obvious question of what happened.

In this chapter, we attempt to answer this question to complete our review of Africa's past from the postcolonial period Africa to date. The focus here is not to critically evaluate the economic development efforts, as it is usually done. This will be done in the rest of the chapters of this book. Rather the focus here is to tell the story of Africa's development efforts as they occurred from the time they came out of colonialism to the present. We begin with the economic development theories that were developed either before or after African countries returned to independence. We then look at what African countries actually did in practice and conclude with a brief assessment of the extent and reasons why economic development has been elusive. However, before we do that do the prereading assignment.

ECONOMIC DEVELOPMENT THEORIES AND IDEOLOGIES

At the dawn of independence, African countries had to choose both a development ideology and a development theory. **Ideology** refers to the principles that guide the economic and political policies of a country (Schraeder, 2000), while **development theory** provides the framework for achieving the goals of development, which may be defined here as positive changes or improvements in the living conditions of people. There were two main ideologies—capitalism and socialism—but there were quite a few development theories, and as the independence movement swept through the 1960s, more theories were added. Broadly speaking, the theories could be classified into two: **modernization theories** and **dependency theories**. The modernization theories were more aligned with the **capitalist ideology**, while dependency theories were more aligned with the **socialist ideology** (Cypher and Dietz, 2004).

Capitalist Ideology and Modernization Theories

Capitalist development ideology sees free market system as the great engine for human achievement and progress, and for that reason the best philosophy for economic development. With this ideology, the primary role of the government is to maintain law and order, while resource allocation is accomplished by the free market system. Within this framework, modernization theories saw underdeveloped countries as **dual economies** or societies, with a large traditional sector and a small modern sector, and defined the economic development problem as how these countries could transition from the traditional to the modern sector. To this end, modernization theories focused on removing hindrances to the transition or providing what was needed for the transition (Eisenstadt, 1973; Peet, 1991; Ofori-Amoah, 1995). Several theories, models, or strategies were offered for this.

Rosenstein-Rodan (1943) advanced the **big-push theory**, which stated that the economic development problems facing underdeveloped countries were such that piece-meal or bit-by-bit approaches would not be enough. Instead, it would need a massive investment in a number of sectors to unleash what was considered as the "hidden potentials." This should be facilitated by the government with emphasis on concurrent investment in social overhead capital such as infrastructure, schools, and hospitals.

Nurkse (1952) proposed the **theory of balanced growth**, which argued that there was a vicious cycle of poverty in underdeveloped economies and the only way to break that was by large-scale investments across all sectors of the economy. In contrast, Hirschman (1958) did not believe that underdeveloped economies had the resources required for the big-push and balanced growth. Consequently, Hirschman proposed the **theory of unbalanced growth**, which called for targeting a few sectors that would produce the greatest return on investment, and once this had been attained, growth would **trickle down** to other sectors or areas.

The Nobel Prize Laureate Sir W. Arthur Lewis (1954) attributed the gap between developed and less-developed countries to the low wages in the latter's large traditional sector. In his **development with unlimited supply of labor theory**, Lewis proposed that if less-developed countries focused on labor-intensive industries that paid higher wages, labor would be attracted from agriculture to industry, until industry reached its maximum profit. At some point in time, the surplus labor in agriculture would be eliminated, which will eventually reduce the gap between less-developed and developed nations.

Rostow (1960) proposed **the stages of growth theory** as an alternative to the Marxist theory of development as articulated in the Communist Manifesto of Marx and Engels. The Communist Manifesto described five stages of economic growth through which all human societies will pass: the traditional society, the transitional society, the capitalist society, the socialist society, and finally communism. In his book *The Stages of Economic Growth: A Non-Communist Manifesto,* Rostow proposed five stages of economic growth process, by which all societies would go through. These stages were the traditional society stage, the preparation for take-off stage, the take-off stage, the drive to maturity stage, and the stage of high mass consumption. Other theories emphasized the role of **savings**, and **investment** in capital stock as well as **technological progress** and called on underdeveloped countries to increase all three as a way to develop (Harrod, 1939; Domar, 1946; Solow, 1956).

Marxist or Socialist Ideology and Dependency Theories

Marxist or socialist development ideology originated from the ideas of Karl Marx and his analysis of the capitalist development. Marx saw economic development as a stage process that all human societies go through, and capitalism was one of those stages. This progression occurred through class struggle between the capitalist, who owned and controlled the means of production, and the working class or the proletariat, which was being exploited. This class struggle will eventually overthrow capitalism and replace it with socialist mode of production, or communal ownership of the means production (Willis, 2005).

In this tradition, dependency theories defined **dependency** as a conditioning process that makes one society become dependent on the other (Furtado, 1963; Dos Santos, 1969; Frank, 1969; Sunkel, 1972; Wallerstien, 1974). They hypothesized that development and underdevelopment were interdependent structures within the modern world system. This system is dominated by a core, which grows at the expense of the periphery (Wallerstien, 1974). The problems of underdeveloped countries began when they became articulated into the modern world system through the European voyages of exploration, long-distance trade, and colonialism. This process continues today through neocolonial mechanisms such as foreign investment, foreign aid, foreign trade, and other forms of international relations. Thus, dependency theorists argued that the factors identified by modernization theories as causes of underdevelopment were rather symptoms or characteristics of underdevelopment, but they did not explain why the countries were underdeveloped (Szentes, 1976).

As early as 1937 Raul Prebisch, an Argentine economist pioneered these theories when he became critical of the idea that international trade was beneficial to all parties. In particular, he began to investigate why agricultural markets collapsed and found that it was because of long-term deterioration of terms of trade of agricultural products and raw materials. Prebisch (1950) argued that given the state of affairs in which developed countries exported all manufactured goods and less-developed countries exported only agricultural products and raw materials, all the benefit of trade would go to developed countries. Prebisch's work received a boost from the British development economist, Hans Singer, which led to the **Prebisch–Singer hypothesis** that, as a result of continued technological progress, the prices at which less-developed countries sell on the world market would decline, while what its imports would stay just about the same. As a result, less-developed countries had one of two options: one was to restructure their economies toward domestic markets through **import substitution industrialization**—in which a country could start to industrialize by manufacturing simple and basic products it used to import. The other option was to restructure the economy from exporting raw materials to **exporting processed and manufactured goods**. Although Prebisch had several reservations about this policy, such as possibility of draining the foreign exchange, the possibility of the industries becoming too capital intensive, and the small size of the domestic market, he still promoted it.

Frank (1969) who popularized dependency theories argued that countries in Latin America became better off at periods when their relationship with the center countries was weak and worse off when the relationship was strong. The only way out of this predicament, according to dependency theories, was for the periphery to break the link with the core through a socialist revolution. Dependency theories were introduced and applied to Africa through the work of Amin (1972), Rodney (1974), and Leys (1975).

Three other ideas that leaned toward dependency theories were multilateral or regional economic integration, integrated rural development, and basic needs approach (Aryeetey-Attoh, 2003). A **regional economic integration** is a grouping of sovereign nations for the purposes of economic and ultimately political cooperation. Several reasons were advanced for this cooperation among them increased competition within the grouping, increased investment, expanded market, political clout in dealing with outside world, and political stability within the grouping (Nkrumah, 1964; Perloff, 1969; Axline, 1977).

Integrated rural development (IRD) was a development strategy that sought to address the development disparities between urban and rural areas. This widening gap between the rural and urban areas was causing large rural–urban migration, which, in turn, was creating a lot of problems for the urban areas. To address this issue, IRD was conceived as a series of programs and projects, whose long-run effects were to raise the living conditions of rural people. This called for specifically targeting rural areas for development in an integrated manner that would include not only agricultural development but also infrastructure, health care, and agro-industry. The strategy called for a hierarchy of growth centers for specific investment projects and the use of **appropriate technology**—technology that was suitable to the physical as well as socioeconomic environment of the place (Boudeville, 1966; Kukllinski, 1972; Rondenelli and Ruddle, 1976; Schumacher, 1975).

Closely associated with IRD was the **basic needs approach (BNA)**, which was a reaction to the failure of conventional development strategies to address issues of poverty (Ghai et al., 1977; Streeten, 1981; Ghosh, 1984). The approach argued that it was possible and necessary to meet the basic needs of the poor without raising income. It emphasized "improvement in health, nutrition, and basic education by redirecting public services, such rural water supplies, sanitation facilities, schools" (Ghosh, 1984, p. 4). So, what did African countries do with all these seemingly confusing and contradictory ideas?

AFRICA'S ECONOMIC DEVELOPMENT IN PRACTICE

The economic development plans that African countries developed and implemented in the 1950s and 1960s incorporated several of these theories. From the beginning, it appeared they all started from a common point in terms of which theory or strategy to adopt. From the late 1960s throughout the 1970s, however, the countries became diverged in the theories and models they pursued, only to converge again in the 1980s and 1990s.

The 1950s–1960s: From the Modernization Project to Mixed Development Strategies

African countries began their search for economic development by first choosing an ideology. Of the 10 countries that were independent in the 1950s, only Egypt and Guinea officially leaned toward socialism. The rest, Ethiopia, Liberia, South Africa, Libya, Morocco, Tunisia, Sudan, and Ghana, started in the capitalist camp. However, during the 1960s most of these countries switched sides and as more countries became independent, the ideologies became "Africanized" into what Young (1982) has labeled African capitalism and African, Arab, or populist socialism.

African capitalism welcomed the free market competition and foreign investment of capitalism, but with a strong government role in providing incentives as well as becoming a major shareholder of businesses. Its leading exponents were Jomo Kenyatta of Kenya, Houpheout Boigny of Cote d'Ivoire, and Hastings Banda of Malawi. In contrast, **African populist socialism** believed that African societies were homogenous with no sharply demarcated classes. So, the concept of class struggle was alien to Africa. Instead, the enemy was the external entity of Western Imperialism (Young, 1982, p. 98). The leading exponents of this view were Gamal Nasser of Egypt, Kwame Nkrumah of Ghana, Julius Nyerere of Tanzania, Leopold Senghor of Senegal, and Muamar Gadaafi of Libya.

In terms of economic development theories, however, there was not much of a difference among the countries. They all believed in modernization and saw manufacturing, construction, and services as paths to development and modernity, while agriculture stood for tradition and stagnation. To implement these ideas, all the countries followed strategies that blended elements of both the modernization and dependency theories. Thus, all of them adopted the import substitution model of industrialization. Large-scale industrial projects were established to produce goods that were previously imported for the domestic markets. Among the common ones were textiles, breweries and soft drinks, food processing, sawmills, cement, iron and steel, pharmaceuticals, and oil refineries. This was accomplished through both private and public sector involvement. In South Africa, for example, the government established the South African Coal, Oil, and Gas Corporation (SASOL) in 1950 in addition to the state-owned Iron and Steel Corporation (ISCOR), which had been established in 1928. Ghana also established the Ghana Industrial Holding Corporation (GIHOC), a conglomerate of several manufacturing industries. In Egypt, Algeria, Tunisia, Congo Democratic Republic (DRC), Guinea, and Libya, existing private sector manufacturing companies were nationalized. In Egypt, for example, about £700 million (Egyptian) in shares and assets were transferred into the public sector between 1952 and 1966, to seek a rapid and broad-based industrialization. In socialist

Guinea, three bauxite mines remained joint ventures with private companies in spite of nationalization (Onimode, 1988). In other countries such as Cote d'Ivoire, Kenya, Liberia, Malawi, Botswana, and Swaziland, the state cooperated with foreign agribusiness companies with limited control. Most countries also pursued indigenization or Africanization policies, which aimed at filling positions once held by expatriates with native-born professionals. This also led to full or partial nationalization of commercial banks, insurance companies, and trading firms in countries such as Algeria, Congo Democratic Republic, Egypt, Libya, Somalia, Sudan, and Uganda (Ikiara, 1994).

At independence, the agricultural sector of many African countries consisted of large-scale farms and small-scale peasants. The former included coffee, tea, cotton, rice, peanuts, rubber, olives, grapes, and sisal plantations. African countries followed this tradition by emphasizing large-scale farming, so as to generate enough revenue to fund industrialization. The existing large-scale farms were nationalized in countries that followed the populist socialism ideology—Egypt, Libya, Tunisia, Guinea, Congo Republic, Senegal, and Tanzania—and even in Zambia, which really was not socialist at that time. New state farms were established in all these countries as well as in Ghana, Nigeria, and Ethiopia, which did not really have large-scale plantations before independence. This emphasis on large-scale mechanized farming meant neglect of small-scale farmers, and for that reason, food crop production. In several cases, the agriculture sector featured prominently in economic development plans, but not much actually happened in practice. This was the case in Congo Republic, Ghana, DRC, Malawi, and Zambia, just to name a few.

Next to manufacturing industries, the sector that received the most attention in this early period was infrastructure and social services, particularly education. Many countries instituted fee-free primary and subsidized secondary and tertiary education. At the tertiary level, every African country that was independent, except the former French colonies (Benin, Central African Republics, Chad, Togo, Gabon, and Senegal), during this period moved to establish national universities by building them from scratch or converting existing colonial colleges into full-fledged institutions (Lulat, 2005). Ethiopia established six colleges; Nigeria established five universities, Ghana, Libya, and Morocco built two each; while Sudan, Tunisia, Algeria, Zambia, Malawi, Liberia, and Sierra Leone either established or upgraded at least one existing institution into a full-fledged university. Apartheid South Africa upgraded five of its white-only as well as three of its nonwhite universities during this period.

The effects of these policies were varied. For example, the ISI policy brought impressive gross domestic product (GDP) growth rates to Cote d'Ivoire, Kenya, Egypt, Morocco, and Zambia, while in other countries including Senegal, South Africa, Ghana, Algeria, and Tunisia, the GDP growth rates declined. One thing was becoming apparent and that was all the countries had already started accumulating huge external debt as they resorted to external borrowing to support their projects. By the end of the 1960s, in spite of the short period of time over which it had been implemented, the modernization project had become suspect, as the high hopes of political and economic independence were turning into disappointments, frustration, and growing national debt.

This resulted in either a change of government by way of military coups or a change in ideology or both. Thus, 21 countries or about half of the independent African countries during the period under consideration had a change in government by way of military coup (Table 3.1). Some of these changes in government were followed by changes in development ideology. Among the countries that changed from African capitalism to African socialism after a change in government were Algeria (1965), Libya (1969), and Tunisia (1962). Congo Republic changed from African socialism to African-Marxist ideology in 1969 after a change in government. Ghana changed

TABLE 3.1

Successful Military Coups in Africa, 1950–2015

Year	Country
1952	Egypt
1958	Sudan
1960	Congo-Kinshasa
1963	Togo, Congo-Brazzaville (Congo Rep), Dahomey (Benin)
1964	Gabon
1965	Algeria, Dahomey (Benin), Burundi
1966	Central African Republic, Upper Volta (Burkina Faso), Nigeria, Ghana, Burundi
1967	Sierra Leone, Togo
1968	Sierra Leone, Mali
1969	Sudan, Libya, Somalia
1971	Uganda
1972	Ghana
1973	Rwanda
1974	Ethiopia
1975	Nigeria
1977	Seychelles
1978	Ghana
1979	Ghana
1980	Liberia
1981	Ghana
1984	Guinea
1987	Burundi
1989	Sudan
1990	Chad
1994	Gambia
1997	Sierra Leone, Democratic Republic of Congo
1999	Comoros, Niger, Cote d'Ivoire
2003	Guinea Bissau, Sao Tome & Principe
2005	Mauritania
2008	Guinea, Mauritania
2009	Madagascar
2010	Niger
2012	Guinea Bissau, Mali
2013	Central African Republic, Egypt
2014	Burkina Faso
2015	Burkina Faso

Source: Compiled from Jimmi Wangome (1985) and other news sources.

from African capitalism to African socialism in 1961, due to lessons learned, and so did Zambia in 1968. However, Ghana switched back to African capitalism in 1966 after another change in government. Tanzania became more convinced to follow African socialism ideology and took the bold step to implement a plan to that effect in 1967.

The 1970s: From Mixed Development Experiments to Economic Insolvency

The 1970s–1980s was a period of mixed economic development experiments. However, due to some dramatic ideological shifts from capitalism and populist socialism, **Afro-Marxism** appeared to have been more dominant. First, Egypt abandoned socialism and so did Algeria and Tunisia. At the same time, Somalia joined the Congo Republic as Afro-Marxist countries. In 1975, Madagascar and the former Portuguese colonies of Cape Verde Is, Guinea Bissau, Angola, and Mozambique also became Afro-Marxist countries, with Ethiopia following in 1976 (Figure 3.1).

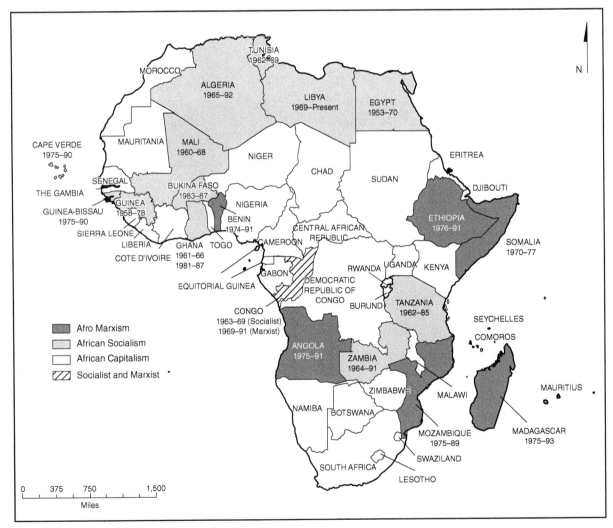

FIGURE 3.1 Ideologies of African countries 1950–1990.
Source: Adapted from Schraeder. P. J. 2000 African Politics and Society A Mosaic in Transformation. Boston and New York: Bedford/St. Martin's Press pp. 170.

These countries began implementing their Marxist agenda, focusing specifically on the rural economy and the rural poor. This new agenda received further boost from the reaction against the ISI model, which was criticized for neglecting the rural areas.

To address this, IRD, with its associated growth center approach and appropriate technology, became the new buzz words in African development, with much support from the World Bank. In Ethiopia, all rural lands were nationalized, and tenancy and hired labor on private farms were abolished. All peasants were given the right to a plot of land not exceeding 25 acres. Peasants associations were formed and charged to undertake redistribution of land and development programs, and to perform local government functions. In 1977, these associations were extended into an All-Ethiopian Peasant Association to provide a more effective link between the rural areas and the central government. In order to provide services to the very sparsely populated rural areas, the government began promoting collectivization in 1977 and "**villagization**" in the 1980s. In spite of these, agriculture development strategy was still focused on state farms. With respect to the urban economy, existing industries, banks, and insurance companies were nationalized. In theory, it was not the intention of the state to do away with private capital. Instead, private capital was to supplement state capital but in practice the rhetoric scared private investment away (Wubneh and Abate, 1988).

Similarly, Mozambique identified agricultural transformation as central to its economic development and saw organization of communal villages with agricultural cooperatives and productive state farms as the two strategies for economic recovery. Accordingly, the government took over close to 2,000 farms abandoned by the Portuguese and combined them into large state farms. Two examples of this were the Limpopo Afro-Industrial Complex, which combined about 1,500 small-scale abandoned Portuguese farms into one state farm, and the EMOCHA farm in North Zambezia that consisted of 22 private tea plantations. Heavy investments were made in mechanization—tractors and harvesters—and in irrigation and related equipment. In the industrial sector, the state in its 1979–1980 plan took over abandoned and sabotaged factories and decided to follow some form of import-substitution, as well decentralization policies that would locate factories appropriately—near the sources of raw material, energy, and transportation. In 1981, the state made plans to continue to import more raw materials for its clothing, shoe, household, utensils, and agricultural equipment industries with long-term goals of establishing a textile plant in each of its 10 provinces, an aluminum smelting plant, paper and wood processing, and iron and steel (Isaacman and Isaacman, 1983).

Angola also saw agriculture as the backbone of her economy and industry as the leading sector for economic development. It allowed for three forms of ownership—state, cooperative, and private. Angola had no intention of doing away with private capital. In fact, its nationalization policy only applied to Portuguese interests (Tvedten, 1997).

Within the capitalist-oriented countries, two strategies were followed. Some countries, such as Kenya, Nigeria, Mauritius, and Senegal, continued the ISI policy during the first half of the 1970s. Others such as Cote d'Ivoire, Egypt, South Africa, Swaziland, and Tunisia began experimenting with export-led industrialization. Later on in the 1980s, more countries adopted the export-led industrialization by establishing export-processing zones (EPZs), which are demarcated geographic areas for firms to locate in and produce for export in return for incentives such as tax breaks and worker training.

Efforts at rural development in these countries also became more deliberate. The **growth center approach** and appropriate technology gained national consideration.

For example, Cote d'Ivoire, Ghana, Kenya, Libya, Niger, Nigeria, and Tanzania were among African countries that either considered seriously or actually implemented the growth center approach in their rural development plans. Ghana adopted the growth center approach in its 1975–1980 plan, Kenya in its 1970–1974 and 1974–1978 plans, and Tanzania in its second five-year plan of 1969–1974. In all these, a series of centers were going to be selected and targeted for development projects with the hope that the effects would trickle down to the surrounding rural areas. At the same time, appropriate technology centers began popping up all across the continent due to the work of Schumacher's Intermediate Technology Group and OXFAM.

However, no rural development program caught the world's attention more than Tanzania's *Ujamaa's* program. The rationale behind this scheme made sense in geographic terms. At independence, 92% of Tanzania's rural population, about 11 million, lived in isolated homesteads. This made distribution of services a very expensive project. In order to deal with this problem, the **Ujamaa project** sought among other things to create a new settlement geography that would reduce the cost of providing essential services to Tanzania's rural dwellers by concentrating the scattered homesteads into fewer villages. The main guidelines of this strategy for agricultural and rural development was announced by President Julius Nyerere in 1967 at Arusha, Tanzania, hence the name Arusha Declaration. The idea was based on three elements of traditional African society: mutual respect, common property, and communal labor. Initially, people were encouraged to move voluntarily. However, when they resisted, government officials resorted to coercion and intimidation. The 1973 villagization scheme was aimed at forcing about 5–6 million rural dwellers to move into *Ujamaa* villages (Ake, 1996). Government statistics indicate that by 1977, 13.5 million rural dwellers had been consolidated in 7,300 villages. However, the project had modest success. The villages were to form cooperatives to manage their own affairs and work communally. However, local party officials originally appointed to work with the local cooperatives usurped the power of the cooperatives and regional party secretaries came to dominate and control all development projects. In the end, people rejected the communal requirement of *Ujamaa* and after 10 years less than 2.5% of GDP came from the communal agricultural activity (Ake, 1996).

In all countries, expansion of social services especially education and health care continued throughout the period emphasizing not only primary and secondary education but also tertiary education. The greatest growth occurred in Nigeria, Ethiopia, Egypt, and Tunisia. Nigeria's higher education institutions exploded as the government sought to upgrade a number of state polytechnic institutes. From 1972 to 1988, 30 new universities were added to the 5 that existed before 1972. Ethiopia added eight universities from 1976 to 1985; Egypt and Tunisia added six each; Libya, Mozambique, and Morocco added three each. In addition to these, African countries sent large numbers of their young men and women abroad to pursue graduate studies in the fields of science, technology, arts, and social sciences on government scholarships (Lulat, 2005).

African countries also began looking at regional economic integration, as a means to forge economic development. About nine regional economic integrations were established during this period all for the purpose of forging new ways to develop their economies through cooperation and trade (Table 3.2). However, nothing really came out of them.

By the end of the 1970s, it was apparent that the socialist experiments were in trouble—the emphasis on large-scale mechanized farming approach to agriculture that was the centerpiece of the socialist and Marxists experiments did not work.

TABLE 3.2

Regional Economic Integration in Africa

Organization	Member states	Goals and objectives
1959: The Equatorial Customs Union (UDE) (1959–1965)	Chad, Central African Republic (CAR), Congo, Gabon	To maintain some form of economic and political integration
1964: The Central African Customs and Economic Union (UDEAC)	Congo, Chad, CAR, Gabon, Cameroon (1966), Equatorial Guinea (1985)	To establish closer union and strengthen regional solidarity; promote gradual and progressive establishment of a Central Africa Common market; remove trade barriers to trade; unite economies by pursuing policies that are of common interest
1966: West African Customs Union (UDEAO)	Burkina Faso, Cote d'Ivoire, Mali, Mauritania, Niger, and Senegal	To stimulate intraregional trade through a 50% tariff reduction on imports from members
1967: East African Community (EAC) (1967–1977)	Kenya, Tanzania, Uganda	To strengthen and regulate industrial, commercial, and other relations among members; removal of trade barriers; establishment of a common tariff and excise duties; free exchange of currency
1969: Southern African Customs Union (SACU)	South Africa, Botswana, Lesotho, Swaziland, Namibia (1990)	To maintain a common external tariff; to share customs revenues; coordinate policies and decision-making on a wide range of trade issues
1973: West Africa Economic Community (CEAO) replaced UDEAO	Burkina Faso, Cote d'Ivoire, Mali, Mauritania, Niger, Senegal	To implement an active cooperation and economic integration policy; to increase trade among members
1975: Economic Community of West African States (ECOWAS)	Benin, Burkina Faso, Cape Verde Is, Cote d'Ivoire, Gambia, Ghana, Guinea, Guinea-Bissau, Liberia, Mali, Mauritania, Niger, Nigeria, Senegal, Sierra Leone, Togo	To eliminate customs duties, abolish quantitative and administrative restrictions on trade; establish a common tariff and a common commercial policy; promote freedom of movement of people, services, and capital; harmonize agricultural, industrial, and monetary policies; and joint development of infrastructure
1980: Southern African Development Coordination Conference (SADCC)	Angola, Botswana, Lesotho, Malawi, Mozambique, Swaziland, Tanzania, Zambia, Zimbabwe, Namibia (1990)	To promote cooperation among members to lessen dependence on South Africa
1982: Preferential Trade Area (PTA)	Angola, Burundi, Djibouti, Kenya, Lesotho, Malawi, Mozambique, Rwanda, Somalia, Sudan, Uganda, Tanzania, Zambia, Zimbabwe	To promote cooperation and integration in all areas of economic activity; raise the standards of living of the people of the region; create a common market by the year 2000; contribute to the progress and development of Africa
1983: Central African Economic Community (CEAC)	Congo, Chad, CAR, Gabon, Cameroon, Equatorial Guinea, DRC, Burundi, Rwanda, Sao Tome	To attain economic community status
1992: Southern African Development Community (SADC) Replaced SADCC	Angola, Botswana, Lesotho, DRC, Malawi, Mauritius, Mozambique, South Africa, Seychelles, Swaziland, Tanzania, Zambia, Zimbabwe	To reduce economic dependence; create a genuine and equitable regional integration; promote national, interstate, and regional policies; secure international cooperation within the framework of the SADC's strategy for economic liberalization

(Continued)

TABLE **3.2**

Regional Economic Integration in Africa (*Continued*)

Organization	Member states	Goals and objectives
1993: The Common Market for Eastern and Southern Africa (COMESA) replaced PTA	Burundi, Comoros, Djibouti, Egypt, Eritrea, Ethiopia, Kenya, Libya, Madagascar, Malawi, Mauritius, Rwanda, Seychelles, Somalia, Sudan, Swaziland, Uganda, Zambia, Zimbabwe	To establish customs union through removal of trade barriers; establish a common tariff and rules of origin; coordinate macroeconomic policy; free movement of services and capital; work toward currency convertibility; cooperate in economic and social development; redistribute benefits from integration
1994: Economic and Monetary Union of West African States (UEMOA) Replaced CEAO	Burkina Faso, Cote d'Ivoire, Mali, Niger, Senegal	To develop a national economic policy; harmonize the legal and regulatory framework for economic activity; harmonize fiscal policy; unify national economic space

Source: Oyejide, T. A., Elbadawi, I., and Collier, P. 1997. Regional Integration and Trade Liberalization in SubSaharan Africa. Houndmills, Basingstoke, Hampshire: Macmillan.

In Ethiopia, Mozambique, and Angola, land reforms and nationalization initially raised agriculture production, but soon it started to decline. In Ethiopia, for example, agriculture production rose by 21.4% in 1975–1976, but declined by 9.5% in 1977–1978. In 1982, Ethiopia became a net importer of food (Wubneh and Abate, 1988). In Mozambique, agricultural production grew by 12% in 1981, yet it did not help Mozambique reduce its food imports (Isaacman and Isaacman, 1983). In Angola, coffee production dropped by 68% between 1973 and 1978, other cash crops production by 80–95%, while industrial production dropped by 72% (Tvedten, 1997). Zambia's rejection of capitalist development and flirtation with self-reliance socialist style of development through nationalization and ISI policy brought remarkable industrial growth about 12.7% initially. However, emphasis on large-scale commercial farms proved disastrous in the 1980s when copper prices fell (Andersson and Kayizzi-Mugerwa, 1993).

Conditions were no better in the other countries that did not experiment with socialism. In Algeria, the government backed away from heavy industry to investment in agriculture and light industry. It also broke up large state-owned companies and promoted joint ventures. However, when the price of oil dropped in 1986, the government found itself unable to provide basic needs to the people (Bouhouche, 1998). In neighboring Morocco, the story was similar. Good phosphate prices in the 1973–1974 brought substantial revenue, which enabled the government to undertake more public investments from 1974 to 1977. In 1976, however, the price of phosphates dropped and the government had to borrow money. This was made worst by poor harvest and war with Western Sahara. By 1980, the country was in severe debt (Denoeux and Maghraoui, 1998). After pursuing ISI policy under its socialist experiment in the1960s, Tunisia pursued liberal economic policies and invited private entrepreneurs back into the economy. From 1972 to 1977, private sector investment exceeded that of the public sector. In addition, increased remittances of Tunisians working in France helped boost state revenue that allowed the state to continue support of social and other development programs. However, a fall in oil prices and a dramatic decrease in remittances due to global recession and subsequent lay-offs in France, in the early 1980s, caused a huge drop in state revenue, and in 1986, Tunisia recorded its first negative growth since independence (King, 1998).

In Nigeria, the oil boom in the 1970s led to the neglect of agriculture to the point where agricultural products such as palm oil, cotton, and groundnuts, which used to account for 75% of exports before the 1970s, virtually disappeared in their contribution to the economy in the mid-1970s. Like in other countries, the oil boom led to expansion in government expenditure and by 1976, expenditure had exceeded revenue. Continuous lavish spending led to a decline in real income and in 1982–1983, the economy registered negative growth (–6.7%) (Ake, 1996).

In Cote d'Ivoire, high rate of agricultural output and good commodity prices enabled increased investments in infrastructure and expansion of the agro-based industrialization, as well as agricultural diversification. During the 1973–1974 oil crisis, however, instead of curbing investment expenditure, Cote d'Ivoire resorted to heavy external borrowing to maintain the high rate of investment. By 1980, it was having difficulty servicing its heavy external debt. In Senegal, good commodity prices helped the government embark on a number of expansionary policies including increase in minimum wage, expansion of the public sector, and increase in external borrowing. However, a series of adverse events including droughts in 1973–1974 and 1978 and collapse of commodity (groundnuts) prices on the world market bankrupted public-owned firms and made it difficult for the government to pay for its 68,000 public servants (Tshibaka, 2003).

This overall pitiful performance as measured by economic growth indicators created a major concern among both African governments and some external interests. First, in 1979, after a series of prolonged meetings between the African Ministers of Planning and the UN Economic Commission of Africa (ECA), African heads of state issued the Monrovia Declaration that called for African countries to rally around a program of mutual support, cooperation, and self-reliance.

The 1980s: From Economic Insolvency to Structural Adjustment Programs

The ECA and the Organization of African Unity (OAU) prepared an extensive document to spell out some strategies for implementing the Monrovian Declaration. In April 1980, the document was adopted at the extraordinary session of the African Heads of State and Government of the OAU in Lagos and it became known as **the Lagos Plan of Action** (LPA) (OAU, 1980). The central message of the LPA was that African development problems were all external and for that reason for Africa to develop it must try to reduce its dependence on external sources through a policy of self-reliance (Browne and Cummings, 1984). Instead of focusing on exporting outside, it should focus on producing for its own consumption. Instead of relying on foreigners, it should rely on its own expertise. It should achieve this through formation of effective regional integrations that would eventually be merged into an African Economic Community.

While the LPA was in the works, African Finance Ministers asked the World Bank to prepare a special paper on economic development problems facing the continent. The World Bank (1981) issued the document *Accelerated Development in Sub-Saharan Africa* or the *Berg Report*, named after its chief author Elliot Berg. In contrast to the LPA, the Berg Report put the greater part of the blame for Africa's problems in the 1970s on Africa's internal policies. In particular, the report charged that the basic reason for the poor economic performance of African countries was due to wrong prices and too much government involvement in the economy. Thus, in contrast to self-reliance, regional cooperation, and a break from the export-led development, the Berg report emphasized structural adjustment policies (SAPs).

These policies include mobilization of domestic resources through currency devaluation and other fiscal and credit policies; public sector reforms through privatization and deregulation through removal of price controls and subsidies; trade liberalization through removal of import quotas and reduction of tariffs; and institutional reforms to support the productive sector. In effect, SAPs were a return to neoclassical economic theory of capitalist development (Demery, 1994; Mengisteab and Logan 1995; Soludo, 2003; Taylor, 2005).

African countries reacted negatively to the Berg Report and charged that it was inconsistent with the Lagos Plan and that it would make Africa more dependent than before, which was in contrast to the self-reliance goal of the LPA. However, given their weak financial resources and their need to depend on external donors, African countries found themselves unable to implement to any greater extent the provisions of the LPA (Campbell and Loxely, 1989). Indeed, donor countries paid very little attention to the LPA (Brown, 1996). Instead, most African countries had to follow the prescription of the Berg Report in various structural adjustment programs throughout the 1980s and 1990s in return for loans (Table 3.3). In the interim, the United Nations introduced its Program of Action for African Economic Recovery and Development (UN-PAARED) 1986–1990 (OAU, 1986), which embodied a promise by the developed countries to provide technical and financial support, but nothing came out of it (Asante, 2003).

The performance record of SAPs in Africa was a checkered one. Initially, the World Bank's own periodic reviews indicated that SAPs were working, while evaluative studies conducted by African and Africanist researchers indicated otherwise

TABLE 3.3

Structural Adjustment Programs in Africa

Year	Country
1979	Malawi
1980	Senegal,[1] Kenya
1981	Madagascar
1982	Mali
1983	Democratic Republic of Congo, Ghana, Niger, Morocco, Senegal, Zambia
1985	Angola, Burundi
1986	Guinea-Bissau, Guinea, Nigeria, Tanzania, Togo, Tunisia, Sierra Leone
1987	Uganda
1988	Lesotho
1989	Benin, Cameroon, Cote d'Ivoire
1990	Central African Republic, Mozambique, Zimbabwe
1991	Burkina Faso, Egypt
1993	Ethiopia
1994	Algeria, Chad, Comoros, Sierra Leone
1997	Guinea[2]
1999	The Gambia

[1]The program was cancelled in 1981 and then renewed in 1983.
[2]Second SAP.

(see, e.g, Campbell and Loxely, 1984; Cornia and Helleiner, 1994; Van der Hoeven and Van der Kraij, 1994; Mengisteab and Logan, 1995). For one thing, there was no agreement about how to evaluate the effects of SAPs (Soludo, 2003), and this made it difficult to get a true assessment as to whether or not the programs were working. Besides, several of the policies were so harsh that some African governments were reluctant to implement them. So, after a while, the bank's own review came to be dependent on how serious the government was. Obviously, countries that were unable to implement the policies due to public opinion were blamed for the policies' failure, while countries that stuck to their guns to implement the program irrespective of public opinion were received rave reviews. In the end, the effects of SAPs were unsatisfactory. Even in most of the so-called success stories, overall growth rates rose in the early years of the program's implementation, only to decline later. Eventually, after a decade of implementation, the World Bank finally admitted that SAPs had not met expectations (Corbo et al., 1992; Hussain and Faruqee, 1994).

It was around this time in 1989 that the OAU and the UNECA produced African *Alternative Framework to Structural Adjustment Programs for Socio-Economic Recovery and Transformation* (AAF-SAP) (OAU, 1989). Based on the Lagos Plan, AAF-SAP argued that Africa's problems are structural and should therefore be dealt with accordingly. It was based on the central principle that economic development should not make people's lives more miserable. Thus, the report charged that instead of helping to improve living conditions of Africans, SAPs rather worsened the situation. What Africa needed was the alleviation of poverty and general improvement in living standards of the people, through increased, expanded, diversified, and self-reliant productive capacities. For policy alternatives, the AAF-SAP proposed similar policies that were in the Lagos Plan. As before, reaction to the AAF-SAP was mixed. It was criticized for being too heavy on philosophy and light on substantive ways of implementation and also for ignoring the role of African governments in creating the problem (Herbst, 1993; Abbott, 1994; Mosley, 1994). However, it was endorsed by the United Nations General Assembly as a framework for "constructive dialogue." In addition, the report also caused the World Bank to issue its 1989 document *Sub-Saharan Africa: From Crisis to Sustainable Growth*, which seemed to agree, to some extent, with the AAF-SAP. In particular, the report argued that both African governments and financiers must share the blame for Africa's development predicament. However, it also argued that sound incentives, good infrastructure, and human resources development were needed to provide the necessary enabling environment for Africa's development. In spite of this, nothing came out of the AAF-SAP plan, and as the 1990s approached, it was clear that African countries would continue the busy work of crafting plans and declarations in their search for development (see Table 3.4).

The 1990s: Poststructural Adjustment Era

The 1990s saw African countries engaged in more economic development partnership programs than ideologies. In 1990, the UNECA called a meeting of African NGOs, African governments, and UN agencies on Popular Participation for Democracy in Africa to discuss the political context of economic development in Africa. The conference issued the African Charter for Popular Participation for Development that demanded freedom of association, democratic institutions, rule of law, social and economic justice, and political accountability at leadership level (Taylor, 2005).

TABLE 3.4

Growth of Output of African Countries, 1990–2015

Country	GDP Average annual % growth		Agriculture[1] Average annual % growth		Industry[2] Average annual % growth		Manufacturing Average annual % growth		Services[3] Average annual % growth	
	1990–2000	2000–2015	1990–2000	2000–2015	1990–2000	2000–2015	1990–2000	2000–2015	1990–2000	2000–2015
Algeria	1.9	3.5	3.6	6.8	1.8	2.8	—	—	2	6.5
Angola	1.6	9.6	—	—	—	—	—	—	—	—
Benin	4.6	4	5.6	3.2	3.8	1.1	5.5	-0.4	4.2	5.4
Botswana	4.9	4.6	0.3	3.1	2.6	0.7	7.8	5.6	8.2	7
Burkina Faso	5.5	5.8	6.3	3.7	5.1	5.7	4.7	0.6	3.7	6.4
Burundi	-2.9	3.6	-1.9	-0.2	-5.2	2.3	—	-0.9	-1.6	7.4
Cape Verde	12.1	5.0	11.5	4.4	9	4	—	—	13.4	3.6
Cameroon	1.8	3.6	5.3	4	-0.6	1.2	1.9	2.1	0	4.8
Cent. African Republic	1.8	0.1	3.5	-1.7	0.1	1.0	-3.2	2.8	0.2	1.4
Chad	2.2	8.4	—	3.2	—	10.2	—	12.0	—	7.6
Comoros	1.6	2.1	2.6	2.7	4	3.1	1.7	3.6	0.2	1.1
Congo Republic	1	4.6	-0.6	5.2	4.5	2.8	-4.3	8.6	-2.2	6.3
Cote d'Ivoire	3.1	2.5	—	—	—	—	—	—	—	—
DRC	-4.9	5.9	1.4	2.4	-8.3	5.8	-8.7	6.7	-4.7	7.6
Djibouti	-2	4.5	—	—	—	—	—	—	—	—
Egypt	4.4	4.4	3.1	3.2	5.1	4.1	6.3	3.9	3.9	5.1
Equatorial Guinea	36.7	10.0	—	3.1	—	0.3	—	8.5	—	9.5
Eritrea	6.5	0.5	—	—	—	—	—	—	—	—
Ethiopia	3.8	9.7	2.6	7.1	4.2	12.1	3.7	9.6	5.8	12.1
Gabon	2.3	2.5	2.0	1.3	1.6	-0.2	3.0	2.8	3.1	5.6
Gambia	3	3.4	2.8	1.3	1.6	3.2	1.3	2.5	4	3.7
Ghana	4.3	6.8	—	4.0	—	11.6	—	3.9	—	8.1
Guinea	4.2	2.5	4.5	3.6	4.7	2.4	3.8	1.6	3.0	2.0
Guinea-Bissau	0.6	2.9	—	3.1	—	2.8	—	—	—	2.9
Kenya	2.2	4.8	1.9	2.7	1.2	5.0	1.3	3.6	3.2	5.3
Lesotho	4.1	4.2	2.0	1.3	8.3	4.7	7	1.8	3.3	4.3
Liberia	4.2	3.7	—	-0.1	—	15.1	—	4.8	—	8.1

Country	GDP Average annual % growth		Agriculture[1] Average annual % growth		Industry[2] Average annual % growth		Manufacturing Average annual % growth		Services[3] Average annual % growth	
	1990–2000	2000–2015	1990–2000	2000–2015	1990–2000	2000–2015	1990–2000	2000–2015	1990–2000	2000–2015
Libya	—	1.3	—	—	—	—	—	—	—	—
Madagascar	2	2.8	1.8	1.6	2.4	4.1	—	—	—	1.1
Malawi	3.7	5.4	8.6	2.2	2	6.8	0.5	6.8	1.6	6
Mauritania	2.9	5.3	1.1	3.3	2.4	6.3	4.1	0.1	6.1	5
Mauritius	5.2	4.3	0	2.3	5.4	2	5.3	1.4	6.3	5.8
Morocco	3	4.6	0.4	5.5	2.9	3.6	2.6	3.3	3.1	4.7
Mozambique	8.6	7.6	5.7	6	10.6	7.3	10.2	4.3	5.1	8.5
Namibia	3.3	5	4.5	-0.9	1.9	5	2.6	3.3	2.9	5.8
Niger	2.4	5	—	5.2	—	10.9	—	9.3	—	3.9
Nigeria	1.9	7.9	3.4	7.5	0.9	3.5	-1.4	10.6	2.6	10.9
Rwanda	-0.2	7.6	2.5	4.9	-3.8	9.5	-5.8	6.6	-0.8	8.1
Sao Tome & Principe	—	5.3	—	3.1	—	4.8	—	4.7	—	6.1
Seychelles	4.4	3.7	0.3	-1.3	11.6	2.8	8.3	0	4.8	3.6
Senegal	3	4	2.4	2.9	3.8	3.8	3.1	2.5	4.5	4.6
Sierra Leone	-3	7	0.1	5.9	-3.3	11.7	-3.3	3.4	-6.2	6.5
Somalia	—	—	—	—	—	—	—	—	—	—
South Africa	2.1	3.2	1	2.4	0.7	1.7	1.6	2.1	2.4	3.8
South Sudan	—	—	—	—	—	—	—	—	—	—
Sudan	5.5	5.3	7.2	2.8	8.9	5.6	7.2	6.7	1.7	7.4
Swaziland	3.2	3.5	0.9	03	3.1	3.8	2.8	4.2	3	3.9
Tanzania	3	6.7	3.2	4.3	3.1	1.6	2.8	7.9	2.6	7.2
Togo	3.5	3.2	4	1.1	1.8	4.1	1.8	3.1	3.9	3.8
Tunisia	4.7	3.6	2.6	2.7	4.4	1.9	5.7	2.6	5.3	4.8
Uganda	7	7.1	3.4	2.2	12.3	8.3	14.2	6.0	8.2	6.3
Zambia	1.6	7.3	3.6	-0.1	-2.2	8.4	1	5.2	3	9.2
Zimbabwe	2.5	-1.3	4.3	-4.8	1.4	-0.3	0.4	-2.4	3	3.6

Source: World Development Indicators, The World Bank.

[1] Agriculture includes cultivation of crops, livestock production, forestry, hunting, and forestry.

[2] Industry includes manufacturing, mining, construction, electricity, water, and gas.

[3] Services include wholesale trade, retail trade (including hotels and restaurants), transport, government, financial, professional and personal services such as education, health care, and real estate.

In 1991, the UN launched its New Agenda for Development of Africa (UNADAF), to revive the UN-PAARED. The UNADAF affirmed that a basic condition for economic development was political and social stability. However, the commitment by developed countries to support this once again failed (Asante, 2003). In the same year, the African Leadership Forum under Chief Olusegun Obasanjo of Nigeria held a series of meetings with participants from the Organization of Economic Cooperation and Development (OECD), UN Economic Commission for Africa (UNECA), and the OAU in Kampala to establish a Conference on Security, Stability, Development and Cooperation in Africa (CSSDCA). The Kampala Document, which was produced by the meetings, set a theoretical framework for measuring achievements of certain shared values (Taylor, 2005). Another initiative that was launched in 1991 was the African Economic Community (AEC) with the sole purpose of promoting economic, social, and cultural development through cooperation and coordination of policies in the use of both human and natural resources. The treaty, which called for a gradual removal of barriers to free movement of people, goods, services and capital among member states, came into force in 1995.

In 1997, the then Deputy President of South Africa Thabo Mbeki started floating the idea of African Renaissance, by which he suggested five areas of engagement for Africa's renewal: encouragement of cultural exchange, emancipation of the African woman from patriarchy, mobilization of youth, broadening, deepening, and sustenance of democracy, and establishment of sustainable economic development (Vale and Maseko, 1998; Taylor, 2005). Among the core elements of this idea were the need to establish and maintain a system of good governance, introduce new economic policies that attract private sector, reduce state intervention in economic activities, establish regional economic arrangements to lessen disadvantages of small markets, and introduce policies that would ensure access to good education, health care, decent housing, clean water, and modern sanitation (Taylor, 2005).

Mbeki's ideas received support from the developed countries, and in 1999, President Mbeki, President Obasanjo of Nigeria, and President Bouteflika of Algeria requested a mandate from the OAU to draft a new development plan for Africa. After soliciting support from some of G7 countries (Nordic countries, the United States, Japan), the three leaders developed a plan called the Millennium Africa Recovery Plan (MAP), which was presented to the Conference of Ministers of UNECA in Algiers in May 2001. At the same conference, the Senegalese President Abdoulaye Wade presented the "Omega Plan for Africa," and the UNECA presented "A Compact for African Recovery" (Melber, 2002). A decision was made to merge the three proposals. In July 2001, the merged proposals called New African Initiative (NAI) was adopted by the summit, but later the name was changed to New Partnership for Africa's Development (**NEPAD**).

Essentially, NEPAD has three main goals: (1) to promote accelerated growth and sustainable development in Africa; (2) to eradicate widespread and severe poverty; and (3) to halt the marginalization of Africa in the globalization process. It recognizes that Africa cannot continue to be the ward of benevolent guardians. Instead, Africa must be the architect of its own destiny. To achieve these objectives, paragraph 49 of the NEPAD document outlines a number of specified tasks, which include the following:

> (1) Strengthen mechanisms for conflict prevention, management and resolution and ensure that they are used to restore and maintain peace; (2) Promote and protect democracy and human rights by developing clear standards of accountability, transparency and participative governance; (3) Restore and maintain macroeconomic stability by developing standards and targets for fiscal and monetary policies and appropriate

institutional frameworks; (4) Institute transparent legal and regulatory frameworks for financial markets and auditing of private companies and the public sector; (5) Revitalize and extend the provision of education, technical training and health services (with priority to HIV/AIDS, malaria and other communicable diseases); (6) Promote the role of women in social and economic development; (7) Build the capacity of the states in Africa to set and enforce the legal framework and maintain law and order; and (8) Promote the development of infrastructure, agriculture and its diversification.

Earlier reviews of Africa's economic development within the new framework of NEPAD were skeptical. For example, Asante (2003) believed the NEPAD framework would fall victim to either the "begging bowl syndrome" or the "broken promises syndrome." The begging bowl syndrome refers to a situation where African countries are quick to adopt the economic development framework or resolution but then expect funding to come from external sources. In contrast, the broken promise syndrome is when after supporting the framework or resolution, African governments fund completely different set of priorities, while funds promised by developed countries fail to come through.

Taylor (2005) also observed that much of what could or could not happen with NEPAD would depend on African leaders and elites themselves. In particular, he argued that African leaders should be honest to the creed of NEPAD and should not, for example, support leaders such as Robert Mugabe of Zimbabwe, as well as other corrupt bureaucracies that make development difficult.

A recent evaluation UNCTAD (2012) reported that under the framework of NEPAD the average annual economic growth rate of African countries has been 5% compared to 2.7% in the decade before NEPAD. In addition, NEPAD's Comprehensive African Agricultural Development Program (CAADP) has provided a framework to increase agricultural productivity. Ten countries have allocated 10% of their annual budgets to agriculture, while nine have achieved the 9% average annual agricultural output required by NEPAD. Another area that has seen improvements is politics and governance. Although political instability is still present on the continent, African countries are now quick to condemn election malpractices and unconstitutional takeover of governments through military coups. In spite of these, the report indicated that Africa is still far away from eliminating poverty, putting itself on sustainable development path and overcoming marginalization in the global economy.

LOOKING BACK

At the return of independence, African countries were all bent on raising the standard of living of their people. Although no clear effort was made to define what it was that they wanted, most of the leaders and elites of the independence movements had lived in Europe and the United States, so they presumably wanted the same things that Europeans and Americans enjoyed for their people: good living wages, better homes, schools, colleges, and universities for the youth, clinics and hospitals for the people, better transportation, clean water, and electricity. Accordingly, African countries went to work to achieve these goals.

After more than 50 years of independence for most of the countries, it is clear that there are more schools, clinics, and hospitals than there were in the 1960s. More Africans have received formal education compared to in the 1960s. Thus, literacy and life expectancy at birth have improved. Better transportation and communication systems as well as better homes and housing have evolved.

However, Africa's hope to catch up or close the gap between itself and Europe and America has not happened.

Table 3.4 compares the average annual growth of the GDP, agriculture, industry, manufacturing, and services of the past two decades, 1990–2000 and 2000–2015. The table shows while 32 countries show increase in their annual GDP growth rate, in 15 countries the average growth rate declined. With respect to agriculture, 17 countries showed improvement in their growth rate, while in 16 countries did worse than the previous decade. For industry, 23 countries showed improvement, while 15 did not. For manufacturing, it was a split between the countries that reported data for both periods—in 18 countries the average growth rate was better in 2000–2015 than in 1990–2000, while in another 15 countries it was the opposite. For the service sector, 37 countries reported data for both periods. Of these, 28 countries had growth rates better than the previous decade, while 9 countries had worse over the same period. Although the majority of countries showed increases in their average growth rates of their economies, as we will see in later chapters, the actual output of African countries to the global economy was very small. Apart from this on several measures used as indicators of development, which we will present in Chapter 6, Africa's scores are low.

Poverty as measured by world standard is pervasive on the continent. Few Africans earn a good living wage. The benefits of good housing, electricity, health care, and clean water have become accessible to urban dwellers, while rural live has not made significant changes in a number of countries. Schools, colleges, and universities exist but not all of them are well equipped with necessary physical infrastructure and human resources needed for effective functioning. The same goes for hospitals. Transportation continues to be a problem in many countries just as it was in the 1960s and in some cases have even deteriorated. Majority of African countries continue to have dependent economies: economies that produce what they do not consume and consume what they do not produce, with foreign aid constituting a substantial chunk of the national budget, just as they were at independence. Some Asian countries that were behind Africa in economic growth in the 1950s and 1960s have now crossed the threshold of developed economies. In contrast, there are a few countries such as Botswana, Rwanda, Mauritius, and South Africa that are reportedly doing well on a number of development indicators. Granted the statistical basis of many of Africa's development indicators are questionable. However, it appears the goal of economic development has been elusive to the majority of African countries. The obvious question is why has economic development been so elusive to attain in Africa.

The answers are very varied, and there are plenty of blames to go around. Some blame the adoption of faulty development theories and policies, incompetence, corrupt government officials, public mismanagement, weak institutions, and lack of democratic institutions. Others blame external forces of colonialism and neocolonial policies of developed countries such as international trade, foreign investment and aid, and structural adjustment policies. We will address these issues in greater detail in later chapters, but suffice it to say here that Africa's development problems derive from both internal and external sources, and there are several examples of each case. For example, the deliberate plan to destabilize the Congo Democratic Republic because of Western interests, and the criminal removal of Patrice Lumumba from power as well as the unflinching support of Mobutu Sésé Seko for 30 years during which he increasingly became dictatorial, oppressive, and corrupt was clearly external. Mobutu's willingness to be used by Western interests against his very young country and his pursuit of policies that crippled the economy and people of a country so rich in natural resources was internal. On the other hand, mismanagement and corrupt practices of people in position of responsibility and lack of accountability and rule of law that make it difficult to address injustice and equitable distribution of resources are all internal.

Similarly, adoption of ill-advised economic development plans from early postindependence era through SAPs, the volatility of primary commodity prices on the world market, and the vehement reaction to anything proposed by ECA and African countries by the West are all examples for external sources of Africa's problems.

At the same time, there is the checkered record of political stability, good governance, and economic development of Ethiopia, a country that was never colonized compared to Botswana, a country that became independent only in 1966, with a high incidence of poverty and other problems, and it yet was able to transition to middle-income status in less than 50 years (see Chapter 9) is another indication that diagnosing the causes and solution to the economic development problems of African countries is not an easy task.

The fact is the process of economic development is very complex. It is also a long process that may not have many shortcuts. Finally, it is also a learning process that manifests itself when a critical mass of essential learning outcomes provides the momentum for right change to occur. We will have more to say about this in the remaining chapters of this book, but for now, this concludes our survey of Africa's past. We are now ready to study the spatial patterns and processes of physical and human landscapes of Africa and as we do this, we will be making references to the historical past that we have surveyed. In particular, where appropriate, we will be referring to three important periods that Africa's history has prescribed: precolonial Africa, colonial Africa, and postcolonial Africa.

Postreading Assignments

A. Study the Following Key Concepts:

African capitalism	Capitalist ideology	Integrated rural development	The Lagos Plan of Action
African populist socialism	Dependency theories		The stages of growth theory
Afro-Marxism	Development theory	Marxist or socialist ideology	
Appropriate technology	Dual economy	Modernization theories	Ujamaa project
Balanced growth	Economic development	NEPAD	Unbalanced growth
Basic needs approach	Growth center approach	Regional economic integration	Unlimited supply of labor
Big-push theory	Ideology		Villagization

B. Discussion Questions

1. Go back to the answers you gave to the questions at the beginning of the chapter. Check if there is any that you want to revise. Give reasons for your revisions.

2. Discuss the view that Africa's economic development problem is due to its colonial past.

3. Discuss the assertion that in spite of numerous efforts at economic development, Africa is still one of the world's poorest regions.

4. Do you agree that Africa's development efforts have not produced the expected results? Why and why not?

5. To what extent does regional economic integration a viable strategy for Africa's development?

6. What are structural adjustment programs (SAPs)? Why did African countries introduce SAPs and what were the overall effects?

7. What prospects do NEPAD hold for Africa? To what extent will it follow the path of previous efforts at integration?

References

Abbott, G. C. 1994. "Two Perspectives on Adjustment in Africa." *Africa Review of Money, Finance and Banking* 1(2): 5–31.

Ake, C. 1996. *Democracy and Development.* Washington, DC: Brookings Institution.

Amin, S. 1972. "Underdevelopment and Dependence in Black Africa." *Journal of Modern African Studies* 10: 503–524.

Andersson, P.-A., and Kayizzi-Mugerwa, S. 1993. "External Shocks and the Search for Diversification in Zambia." In Blomstrom, M., and Lundahl, M. (Eds.) *Economic Crisis in Africa: Perspectives on Policy Responses.* London and New York: Routledge, pp. 143–161.

Aryeetey-Attoh, S. 2003. "Geography and Development in Sub-Saharan Africa." In Aryeetey-Attoh, S. (Ed.) *Geography of Sub-Saharan Africa.* Upper Saddle River, NJ: Prentice Hall, pp. 193–231.

Asante, S. B. K. 2003. "NEPAD: A Partnership of Unequal Partners." *New African.*

Axline, W. A. 1977. "Underdevelopment, Dependence, and Integration: The Politics of Regionalism in the Third World." *International Organization* 31(1): pp. 83–105.

Boudeville, J. R. 1966. *Problems of Regional Economic Planning.* Edinburgh: Edinburgh University Press.

Bouhouche, A. 1998. "The Essence of Reforms in Algeria." In Leyachi, A. (Ed.) *Economic Crises and Political Change in North Africa.* Westport, CT: Praeger Publishers, pp. 7–30.

Brown, M. B. 1996. *Africa's Choices After Thirty Years of the World Bank.* Boulder, CO: Westview Press.

Browne, R. S., and Cummings, R. J. 1984. *The Lagos Plan of Action Vs. The Berg Report: Contemporary Issues in African Economic Development.* Washington, DC: Howard University.

Campbell, B. K., and Loxely, J. 1989. *Structural Adjustment in Africa.* New York: St. Martin's Press.

Corbo, V., Fischer, S., and Webb, S. B. (Eds.) 1992. *Adjustment Lending Revisited: Policies to Restore Growth.* Washington, DC: A World Bank Symposium.

Cornia, G. A., and Helleiner, G. K. (Eds.) 1994. *From Adjustment to Development in Africa: Conflict, Controversy, Convergence, Consensus?* New York: St. Martin's Press.

Cypher, J. M. and Dietz, J. L. 2004. *The Process of Economic Development.* 2nd Edition. London and New York: Routledge.

Demery, L. 1994. "Structural Adjustment: Its Origins, Rationale and Achievements." In Cornia, G. A., and Helleiner, G. K. (Eds.) *From Adjustment to Development in Africa: Conflict, Controversy, Convergence, Consensus?* New York: St. Martin's Press, pp. 25–48.

Denoeux, G. P., and Maghraoui, A. 1998. "The Political Economy of Structural Adjustment in Morocco" In Leyachi, A. (Ed.) *Economic Crises and Political Change in North Africa.* Westport, CT: Praeger Publishers, pp. 55–88.

Domar, E. D. 1946. "Capital Expansion, Rate of Growth and Employment." *Econometrica* 14(2): pp. 137–147.

Dos Santos, T. 1969. "The Crisis of Development Theory and the Problem of Dependency in Latin America." In Berstein, H. (Ed.) *Underdevelopment and Development.* Harmondsworth, England: Penguin.

Eisenstadt, S. N. 1973. "Social Change and Development." In Eisenstadt, S. N. (Ed.) *Readings in Social Evolution and Development.* Oxford: Pergamon Press.

Frank, A. G. 1969. *Capitalism and Underdevelopment in Latin America: Historical Studies of Chile and Brazil.* New York: Monthly Review Press.

Furtado, C. 1963. *The Economic Growth of Brazil.* Berkeley, CA: University of California Press.

Ghai, D. P., Khan, A. R., Lee, E. L. H., and Alfthan, T. 1977. *The Basic-Needs Approach: Some Issues Regarding Concepts and Methodology.* Geneva, Switzerland: International Labor Office.

Ghosh, P. K. (Ed.) 1984. *Third World Development: A Basic Needs Approach.* Westport, CT: Greenwood Press.

Harrod. R. F. 1939. "An Essay in Dynamic Theory." *The Economic Journal* 49(193): 14–33.

Hirschman, A. O. 1958. *The Strategy of Economic Development.* New Haven: Yale University Press.

Hussain, I., and Faruqee, R. 1994. *Adjustment in Africa: Lessons from Country Case Studies.* Washington, DC: The World Bank.

Ikiara, G. K. 1994. "Entrepreneurship, Industrialization & the National Bourgeoisie in Africa." In Himmelstrand, U., Kinyanjui, K., and Mburugu, E. (Eds.) *African Perspectives on Development: Controversies, Dilemmas & Openings.* Nairobi/New York: East African Educational Publishers/St. Martin's Press. pp. 118–127.

Isaacman, B., and Isaacman, A. 1983. *Mozambique: From Colonialism to Revolution, 1900–1982.* Boulder, CO: Westview Press, Inc.

King, R. J. 1998. "The Political Logic of Economic Reforms in Tunisia." In Leyachi, A. (Ed.) *Economic Crises and Political Change in North Africa.* Westport, CT: Praeger Publishers, pp. 107–128.

Kukilinski, A. (Ed.) 1972. *Growth Poles and Growth Centers in Regional Planning.* Paris: Mouton & Co.

Leys, C. 1975. *Underdevelopment in Kenya: The Political Economy of Neocolonialism.* London: Heinemann.

Lewis, W. A. 1954. "Economic Development with Unlimited Supplies of Labour." *Manchester School of Economics and Social Studies* 22: pp. 139–191.

Lulat, Y. G. M. 2005. *A History of Higher Education in Africa from Antiquity to the Present: A Critical Analysis.* Westport, CT: Praeger Publishers.

Melber, H. 2002. "The New Partnership for Africa's Development (NEPAD): Scope and Perspectives." In Melber, H., Cornwell, R., Gathaka, J., and Wanjala, S. (Eds.) *The New Partnership for Africa's*

Development (NEPAD): African Perspectives. Discussion Paper 16. Uppsala, Sweden: Nordic African Institute, pp. 6–13.

Mengisteab, K., and Logan, B. I. 1995. *Beyond Economic Liberalization in Africa: Structural Adjustments and the Alternatives.* London: Atlantic Highlands.

Mosley, P. 1994. "Decomposing the Effects of Structural Adjustment: The Case of Sub-Saharan Africa." In Van Der Hoeven, R., and Van Dr Kiaaij, F. (Eds.) *Structural Adjustment and Beyond in Sub-Saharan Africa.* The Hague, The Netherlands: Ministry of Foreign Affairs, pp. 70–98.

Nkrumah, K. 1964. *Africa Must Unite.* London: Heinemann.

Nurkse, R. 1952. "Some International Aspects of the Problem of Economic Development." *American Economic Review* 42(2): pp. 571–583.

Ofori-Amoah, B. 1995. "The Saturation Hypothesis and Africa's Development Problems: On the Nature of Development Theory and Its Implications for the Human Factor in Africa's Development." In Adjibolosoo, S. B-S. K. (Ed.) *The Significance of the Human Factor in African Economic Development.* Westport, CT: Praeger Publishers.

Onimode, B. 1988. *A Political Economy of the African Crisis.* London: Institute for African Zed Books Ltd.

Organization of African Unity (OAU). 1980. *The Lagos Plan of Action for Economic Development of Africa, 1980–2000.* Addis Ababa, Ethiopia: OAU.

Organization of African Unity (OAU). 1986. Africa's Economic Recovery and Development (UN-PAARED). Addis Ababa, Ethiopia: OAU.

Organization of African Unity (OAU). 1989. The African Alternative Framework to Structural Adjustment Programme for Socio-Economic Recovery and Transformation (AAF-SAP). Addis Ababa, Ethiopia: OAU.

Oyejide, T. A., Elbadawi, I., and Collier, P. 1997. *Regional Integration and Trade Liberalization in Sub-Saharan Africa.* Houndmills, Basingstoke, Hampshire: Macmillan.

Peet, R. 1991. *Global Capitalism: Theories of Societal Development.* London and New York: Routledge.

Perloff, H. S. 1969. *Alliance for Progress: A Social Invention in the Making.* Baltimore, MD: Johns Hopkins Press.

Prebisch, R. 1950. *Economic Development of Latin America and Its Principal Problems.* New York: United Nations.

Rodney, W. 1974. *How Europe Underdeveloped Africa.* London: Bogle-L'Ouverture Publications.

Rondenelli, D. A., and Ruddle, K. 1976. *Urban Functions in Rural Development: An Analysis of Integrated Spatial Development Policy.* Washington, DC: Office of Urban Development, Agency for International Development, US Department of State.

Rosenstein-Rodan, P. N. 1943. "Problems of Industrialization of Eastern and Southern Europe." *Economic Journal* 53: pp. 205–216.

Rostow, W. W. 1960. *The Stages of Economic Growth: A Non-Communist Manifesto.* Cambridge: Cambridge University Press.

Schraeder, P. J. 2000. *African Politics and Society: A Mosaic in Transformation.* Boston: Bedford/St. Martin's.

Schumacher, E. F. 1975. *Small Is Beautiful: Economics as if People Mattered.* New York: Harper and Row.

Solow, R. 1956. "A Contribution to the Theory of Economic Growth." *Quarterly Journal of Economics* 70: pp. 65–94.

Soludo, C. C. 2003. "In Search of an Alternative Analytical, and Methodological Frameworks for an African Economic Development Model." In Mkandawire, T. and Soludo, C. (Eds.). *African Voices on Structural Adjustment: A Companion to Our Continent, Our Future.* Trenton, NJ: Africa World Press and Council for the Development of Social Science Research in Africa, pp. 17–72.

Sunkel, D. 1972. "Big Business and Dependencia." *Foreign Affairs* 50: pp. 517–531.

Szentes, T. 1971. *The Political Economy of Underdevelopment.* Budapest, Hungary: Akad. Kiado.

Taylor, I. 2005. *NEPAD: Towards Africa's Development or Another False Start.* Boulder, CO: Lynne Rienner.

Tshibaka, T. 2003. "Environmental Policy Reforms, External Factors and Domestic Agricultural Terms of Trade in Selected West African Countries." In. Mkandawire, T., and Soludo, C. (Eds.) *African Voices on Structural Adjustment: A Companion to Our Continent, Our Future.* Trenton, NJ: Africa World Press and Council for the Development of Social Science Research in Africa, pp. 275–304.

Tvedten, I. 1997. *Angola Struggle for Peace and Reconstruction.* Boulder, CO: Westview Press.

UNCTAD. 2012. "The New Partnership for Africa's Development: Performance, Challenges, and the Role of UNCTAD." Geneva, Switzerland, 2–5 July.

Vale, P., and Maseko, S. 1998. "South Africa and the African Renaissance." *International Affairs* 74(2): pp. 271–287.

Van Der Hoeven, R., and Van Dr Kiaaij, F. (Eds.) 1994. *Structural Adjustment and Beyond in Sub-Saharan Africa.* The Hague, The Netherlands: Ministry of Foreign Affairs.

Wallerstien, I. 1974. *The Modern World System,* vol. 1. New York: Academic Press.

Wangome, J. 1985. "Military Coups in Africa: The African Neo-colonialism That Is Self-Inflicted." https://www.globalsecurity.org/military/library/report/1985/WJ.htm. Accessed October 11 2018.

Willis, K. 2005. *Theories and Practices of Development.* Abingdon, UK: Routledge Publishers.

World Bank. 1981. *Accelerated Development in Sub-Saharan Africa: An Agenda for Action.* Washington DC: World Bank.

World Bank. 1989. *Sub-Saharan Africa: From Crisis to Sustainable Growth.* Washington DC: World Bank.

Wubneh, M., and Abate, Y. 1988. *Ethiopia: Transition and Development in the Horn of Africa.* Boulder, CO: Westview Press.

Young, C. 1982. *Ideology and Development in Africa.* New Haven, CT: Yale University Press.

Geology, Relief, and Drainage Basins

The previous chapters have mentioned some of the features of Africa's physical landscape as reference points. In this chapter, we focus on these landscapes with particular reference to geology, relief, and drainage basins. Geology is a field of study in its own right just as geography, but our concern here will be limited to the major rock formation processes that shaped Africa's physical structure, when these processes occurred, and their effects. Relief will deal with the lowlands and highlands, while drainage basins will be limited to the geographic areas occupied by major rivers and lakes. However, you must first do the prereading assignment.

THE GEOLOGY OF AFRICA

Geologists study the history of the earth's formation using the geologic time scale. Table 4.1 summarizes the major divisions of the geologic time scale and the major events that occurred in Africa during this time scale.

The Precambrian Time (4.6 b to 570 m years ago)

Over 57% of Africa's lithosphere consists of cratons or very old and stable rocks, which were formed in the Precambrian time, the oldest on the geological time scale. The cratons were formed by voluminous granite intrusive activities and deposition of sedimentary and volcanic rocks in deep basins along continental margins that were severely folded and later uplifted. This makes Africa a very old continent. A significant development during the latter part of this time was the Pan-African episode, during which several long linear belts were formed. Among these are the Mozambique belt of Eastern Africa, the Katanga belt from Namibia to the Democratic Republic of Congo and Zambia, the West Congo belt between Angola and Gabon, the Dahomey-Ahaggar belt between Ghana and Algeria, and the Mauritanide belt from Senegal to Morocco.

TABLE 4.1

Major Events in Africa's Geological History

Era	Major events
Cenozoic	• A succession of dry and humid periods led to the shrinking of glaciers on the top of Mount Kenya and Mount Kilimanjaro and the desertification of both the Sahara and Kalahari. • Alternating wet and dry periods (called Pluvial periods). • Formation of the Ahaggar and Tibesti Mountains and Lake Chad. • Severe fracturing of rocks in Central Sahara and East Africa leading to the formation of the Great Rift Valley and Lake Victoria Basin, and the volcanic mountains of East and Central Africa, and the islands of Sao Tome and Principe. • Volcanic activities in Nigeria, Kenya, and Cameroon and folding in the northwest leading to the formation of the Atlas Mountains. • Retreat of continental seas leading to massive sedimentation north of the Equator.
Mesozoic	• Break-up of Gondwanaland causing the Atlantic and Indian Oceans take present shapes. • Inland extension of the Mediterranean Sea to the Sahara and Gulf of Guinea to the Benue valley. • Intrusive activities leading to formation of kimberlites of the Congo Basin and Southern Africa. • Folding of Cape Mountains and subsidence of the Karroo basin led to the formation of the Drakensberg. • Marine invasion of East African coastlands and separation of Madagascar from mainland Africa. • Marine deposits in North Africa, southern Sahara, and parts of Tanzania and Madagascar.
Paleozoic	• Extensive marine invasion covering thick deposits of sandstone, limestone, and dolomite over the northern half of the continent. • Large-scale deformation causing uplift of the Sahara followed by extensive glaciation and flooding. • Collision of the North American and African plates causing intensive folding of Western part of Africa—including the Mauritania mountain chain in north-west Africa. • Formation of the Karroo System of Southern Africa and the plateaus of Central and Eastern Africa.
Precambrian	• Formation of series of long belts in the Pan African Episode, including the Mozambique, the Katanga, the West Congo, and the Dahomey-Ahaggar Belts. • Formation of ancient cratons.

Source: Simplified from Udo, R. (1982): The Human Geography of Tropical Africa, pp. 4 & 5.

The Paleozoic Era (570 m to 245 m years ago)

During this era, Africa was part of Gondwanaland, a super continent consisting of Madagascar, India, South America, Australia, and Antarctica (Figure 4.1). However, geologists believe that the African continent took its present shape during this era. During this time, thick deposits of sandstone, shale, limestone, and dolomite over much of the northern half of the continent including the Sahara and Western Africa were covered by ancient seas (Udo, 1982; Grove, 1993). Large-scale deformation then raised the Sahara by approximately 5,000 feet (1,524 m), which was followed by glaciation and flooding. Two mountain building activities occurred during the rest of this era. The first occurred when the North American and the African plates collided, and this resulted in the warping and folding of mountain along the West African coast and major **subsidence** in other areas. The second resulted in the formation of the Karroo System of Southern Africa and the plateaus of Central and Eastern Africa (Udo, 1982).

The Mesozoic Era (245 m to 66.4 m years ago)

The Mesozoic era is a time of rise and fall in sea level that led to massive land formations. First, marine deposits covered North Africa, Southern Sahara, parts of Tanzania, and northern Madagascar. Second, terminal folding of the Cape Mountains and the subsidence in the Karroo Basin in South Africa led to the formation of the Drakensberg Range in Southeastern Africa. In addition, marine deposits extended over Western Sahara and Senegal, while the Indian Ocean extended over Somalia and much of Ethiopia, and Madagascar was separated from mainland Africa. Third, the supercontinent, **Gondwana**, broke up causing the Atlantic and the Indian Oceans to take their present shapes (Figure 4.1). In addition to inland extensions of the Mediterranean seas, several intrusive activities also occurred that created the kimberlites (diamond-rich rocks) of the Congo basin and Southern Africa.

The Cenozoic Era (About 66.4 m to the Most Recent)

During the first part of this era (the Tertiary period), retreat of continental seas left massive sedimentation, especially north of the equator. This was followed by many volcanic activities in Nigeria (Jos and Biu Plateaus), Kenya, and Cameroon, with some folding activities in Northwest Africa that led to the formation of the Atlas Mountains (Udo, 1982). Continued volcanic activities and faulting created the Red Sea depression, the severely fractured rocks of the Central Saharan region, the Great Rift Valley of East Africa, the Lake Victoria Basin, and the volcanic mountains of East and Central Africa. The Islands of Sao Tome and Principe were also formed during this period (Udo, 1982).

The second part of this era (the Quaternary period) saw continuous volcanic activity that caused the formation of the Ahaggar and Tibesti Mountains of Central Sahara. Cold humid periods called pluvial, similar to the glacier periods in the northern hemisphere, occurred with thicker glaciers covering the mountains

FIGURE 4.1 A Reconstruction of Gondwanaland (After King). The black areas indicate the present extent of continental deposits laid on the super-continent.
Source: Harrison Church, R. J. Clarke, J. I., Clarke, P. J. H., and Henderson, H. J. R. 1971 Africa and The Islands New York: John Wiley & Sons Inc. p. 21.

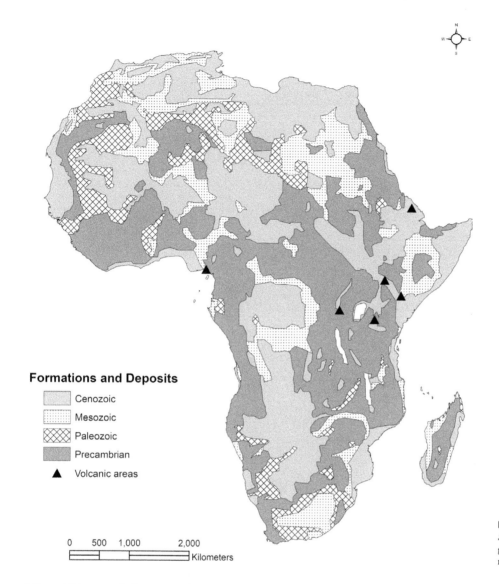

Formations and Deposits

- Cenozoic
- Mesozoic
- Paleozoic
- Precambrian
- ▲ Volcanic areas

FIGURE 4.2 Geology of Africa.
Source: Adapted from http://
go-passport.grolier.com/
map?id=mtlr004&pid=go

of East Africa, and the extensive water resources under the Sahara (Udo, 1982). However, distinct humid periods followed by longer and drier spells caused the sizes of Lake Chad and the glaciers of Mt. Kenya and Mt. Kilimanjaro to shrink. A succession of these alternative longer dry and shorter humid periods, about the last 10,000 years ago, led to the desertification of both the Sahara and the Kalahari.

The result of all this geological history is well summarized in Figure 4.2. From this, we can reiterate that the majority of Africa's basement complex consists of Precambrian formations and deposits. These are followed by the Cenozoic, Paleozoic, and Mesozoic formations and deposits.

THE RELIEF OF AFRICA

From the coastline to its vast interior, Africa's relief features reflect its geologic history. Thus, because a greater portion of Africa's lithosphere consists of very old rocks, the coastline is largely smooth with very little indentations. In addition, much of the vast interior of the continent consists of undulating ancient plateau surfaces,

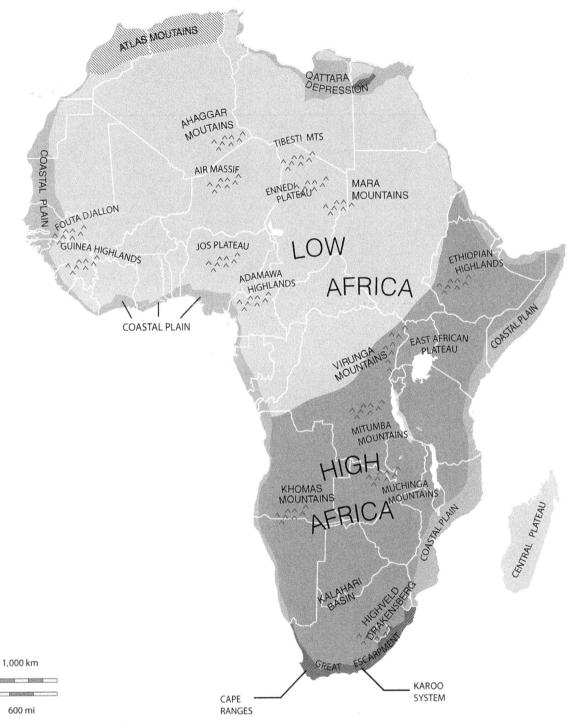

FIGURE 4.3 Relief outline of Africa.
Source: Created by David Ofori-Amoah

leaving a few areas of faulted structures, young folded rocks, and higher lands above the plateau. From the coast to the interior, Africa's relief features may be classified into three regions: the coastal plains, the interior plateaus, basins, and highlands, and the Rift Valley System (Figure 4.3).

The Coastal Plains

The coastal plains comprise the strip of relatively low-lying lands extending from the shoreline to about 805 km (500 miles) inland, at its widest extent, and with an average elevation of 153 m (500 feet) above sea level. They constitute varied relief features that include sandy beaches, deltas, sandbars, and lagoons as well as low and high cliffs. Following Orme (1996), we use a regional approach to examine the main features of these plains.

The Mediterranean Coast

The Mediterranean coast is dominated by sandy plains, delta, shallow lagoons, **barrier beaches**, and cliffs. The general elevation ranges from 1,640 feet (500 m) in the east to 1000 m (3,281 feet) above sea level (Orme, 1996). Sandy plains and shallow lagoons occur from the Sinai Peninsula to the Nile delta. Within this zone, salt marshes, sabkhas (salt flats), and discontinuous barrier beaches host several shallow lagoons. West of the delta to Cape Bon occur several beach dune ridges separated by elongated sabkhas and a cliff coast around Cyrenaica (eastern portion of Libyan coast). West of Cape Bon, the coastal plains disappear into prominent cliffs with an exception of the swampy plains of the Medjerda delta in Tunisia, the lowlands of the Fetzara, Soummam, and La Mocta of Algeria and the Moulouya in Morocco.

The Atlantic Coast

From Morocco to Cape Verde, the coastal plains are dotted with several lagoons, marshes, and sabkhas; low coastal cliffs, fixed parallel dunes, and ridges of Saharan sand; and the Langue de Barbarie (the Berber Tongue), a 373-mile (600 km)-long sandspit, which separates the Senegal River from the Atlantic Ocean (Figure 4.4). Between Cape Verde and Sherbro Islands, Sierra Leone, the plains are broken up by the broad estuaries of the Gambia, the Casamance (Senegal), the Geba (Guinea Bissau), the Konkouré (Guinea), and the Scarcies (Sierra Leone). From here to the Niger delta, a series of elongated lagoons dominate the coastal plains. Among them are the Ébrié and Aby Lagoons (Cote d'Ivoire), the Keta Lagoon (Ghana),

FIGURE 4.4 Langue de Barberi, Senegal
Source: https://media-cdn.tripadvisor.com/media/
photos/02/3f/ec/95/langue-de-barbarie-sur.jpg

Lake Nokoue and Porto Lagoon (Benin), and the Lagos Lagoon (Nigeria). The Niger delta, about 150 miles (240 km) long and 200 miles (320 km) across, forms the Nigerian coast where many of its distributaries are blocked by sandbars, mangrove swamps, and tidal beaches.

From the Niger delta to South Africa, the coastal plains are very narrow, as they are limited inland by cliff and rocky landscapes except around the mouth of the Congo River, where it is broken by a V-shaped canyon by the river. From Angola to South Africa, the narrow coastal strip of 75–124 miles (120–200 km) is dominated by the Namib Desert. A portion of this stretch is the Skeleton Coast so-called because of the many white bones from whaling and seal hunting days and the remains of so many shipwrecks that littered the strip. This area of sand dunes is said to be so inhospitable that the San people called it the "The Land God Made in Anger." South of the Skeleton Coast are rocky plains or **desert pavements**, with many **inselbergs** (Lancaster, 1996, 2009). In South Africa, the coastal plains give way once again to a rugged cliff coast of the Western and Southern Cape (Figure 4.5), interspersed with sandy bays and barrier beaches (Orme, 1996).

The Indian Ocean and the Red Sea Coasts

Along the Indian Ocean, the eastern coast of Madagascar is rugged while broad alluvial lowland occurs along the west coast. On the mainland, the coastal plains reach its widest extent (185 miles/300 km wide) in and around the Mocambo Bay in central Mozambique, the Dar es Salaam Basin in Tanzania, and in Somalia as well as sections along the Red Sea Coast. Elsewhere, the plains disappear under rugged, rocky, and cliff topography.

The Interior Plateaus and Highlands

From the coastal plains, the land rises to the interior plateaus, basins, and highlands, which constitute the bulk of Africa's relief features. It has become customary

FIGURE 4.5 Cape Point, South Africa, the most southwesterly point of Africa. Here the coastal plain is replaced by cliffs.
Source: Photograph by Benjamin Ofori Amoah

among geographers to divide this relief region into two, using an imaginary line from the mouth of the Congo River to Sudan's southern border on the Red Sea. North of the line is usually referred to as **Low Africa**, while south of the line is **High Africa** (Osei and Aryeetey-Attoh, 2009; Stock, 2004) (Figure 4.3).

Low Africa

Most of the land in Low Africa lies between 500 feet (152 m) and 1,000 feet (305 m) above sea level. A greater portion of this landscape is taken up by the Sahara and its varied desert landscapes, which include **sand seas**, **desert pavements**, **dry lakebeds and water courses**, **isolated inselbergs**, **basins** and **depressions**, as well as mountains (Raisz, 1952; de Villers and Hirtle, 2002; Ballantine et al., 2005).

Sand Seas or Ergs
The sand seas of Low Africa feature various shapes and forms of sand dunes all created as a result of interaction between wind and sand. Ergs occupy about 15% of the Sahara, almost 50% of Mauritania and Western Sahara, and substantial portions of Mali, Algeria, Niger, and Libya (de Villers and Hirtle, 2002). Among the most common sand dunes are echo dunes, crescentic dunes or barch-ans, star dunes, longitudinal dunes or seif, and dome dunes (Figure 4.6a-4.6c). These dunes are either anchored or unanchored. **Anchored dunes** form around obstacles such as vegetation or high scarps, while unanchored dunes form on flat surfaces. Unanchored dunes are also mobile and they move by hopping or jumping, a process called **saltation.** As a result, these ergs are ephemeral and they could disappear as quickly as they appear depending on the speed and direction of the winds that create them. Some of these dunes can reach 40 miles (64.4 km) long and 1,600 feet (487.7 m) high, often butting and intersecting in complex patterns, and casting a wide range of colors. In Mali, the dunes along the Niger River, for example, are pink in color. In eastern Niger, the Erg de Teneree is golden, while in northern Chad, they are of dark chocolate in color. Among the largest dunes are the Great Ergs of Algeria and Erg de Murzuq of Libya.

FIGURE 4.6A A Star Dune in the Sahara.
Source: iStock.com/Pavliha

FIGURE 4.6B Barchans—
Sahara.
Source: wrangel/iStockphoto.com

FIGURE 4.6C A Sand Sea—
South Tunisia.
Source: Photograph by Benjamin
Ofori Amoah

Desert pavements Another surface feature of this part of Low Africa is desert pavements, which are vast areas of sheer rock and gravel plains (Figure 4.7a). According to de Villiers and Hirtle (2002), desert pavements are more common than ergs in this part of Low Africa, and it is estimated that they constitute about 70% of the Sahara. Desert pavements have different names depending on the size of the rocks and gravel that compose them. Where they are composed mostly of small rocks and gravel, as in Western and Central Sahara, they are referred to as regs and seirr, respectively. Where they are composed of larger rock fragments and boulders as in Libya, Morocco, and Algeria, they are called hamada. For the most parts, desert pavements are usually flat and featureless; however, in some places, the rocks tend to be polished and colorful (de Villiers and Hirtle, 2002). Several explanations have been offered as to how desert pavements form. Among the most common and acceptable causes are **deflation**, **wash**, and **upward migration** of stones. Deflation is where loose fine grain material is swept away by wind leaving behind the coarse rock material. Wash is the winnowing of fine materials by surface wash, while upward migration of stones is the process by which alternate wetting and drying of fine rock particles eventually causes stones from underneath to move upward (Dixon, 2009).

Depressions, wadis, chotts, and inselbergs Other features of this portion of Low Africa's landscape are depressions, wadis, chotts, and inselbergs. Depressions are sunken lands below their surrounding elevations due to tectonic forces, glaciations, or other forms of erosion. The most important examples of these are the Chad Basin, which encompasses the modern country of Chad, and the Qattara Depression in Egypt. The Qattara Depression (6,489–7,529 square miles/18,100–19,500 km²) is 440 feet (134 m) below sea level and is the second lowest point on the continent of Africa after Lake Tanganyika (Albritton et al., 1990). Wadis are dry watercourses found in mountainous areas, which get filled with water during rains (Figure 4.7b). Chotts are basins of salt flats left over from evaporated moisture (Figure 4.7c), while inselbergs are steep rock hills that rise abruptly from the surrounding areas.

FIGURE 4.7A A Desert Pavement—Sahara.
Source: iStock.com/ HomoCosmicos

FIGURE 4.7B Wadi Foum El Khanga, S. Tunisia. There are numerous wadis in Low Africa like this one on the Algerian-Tunisian border. *Source:* Photograph by Benjamin Ofori-Amoah

FIGURE 4.7C Chott El Djerid—Tunisia. This dry salt lake bed is 110 km/68 mi long and 70 km/43 mi wide. *Source:* Photograph by Benjamin Ofori-Amoah

Highlands Above the general elevation of these landscapes of Low Africa, however, stand a number of prominent highlands, which include the Atlas Mountains of northwest Africa, the mountains and plateaus of Central Sahara, and the highlands and plateaus of West Africa (Table 4.2). The Atlas Mountains of northwest Africa consist of three mountain ranges composed of relatively young folded rocks, which stretch for a distance of 1,500 miles (2,500 km) long from Morocco through Tunisia. The first range, which lies exclusively in Morocco, is the Moroccan Atlas, the second is the Tell Atlas of Algeria and Tunisia, and the third is the Saharan Atlas in Algeria. The highest peaks in the Atlas Mountains are all in the Moroccan Atlas, and they include Mount Toubkal, 13,671 feet (4,167 m); Mount Bou Naceur, 10,958 feet (3,340 m); and Mount Siroua, 10,835 feet (3,304 m). The Tell Atlas is

TABLE **4.2**

Africa's Highest Peaks

Name	Elevation above sea level		Mountain/Range	Country of location
	Feet	Meters		
Mt. Kilimanjaro	19,340	5,895		Tanzania
Mt. Kenya - Batian	17,057	5,198	Mt. Kenya	Kenya
Mt. Kenya - Neilan	17,022	5,198	Mt. Kenya	Kenya
Margherita Peak	16,763	5,109	Rwenzori	Uganda
Mt. Stanley	16,753	5,109	Rwenzori	DRC/Uganda
Mt. Kenya - Lenana	16,355	4,985	Mt. Kenya	Kenya
Mt. Speke	16,043	4,890	Rwenzori	Uganda
Mt. Baker	15,889	4,843	Rwenzori	Uganda
Mt. Luigi di Savoia	15,181	4,627	Rwenzori	Uganda
Mt. Meru	14,978	4,565	Mt. Meru	Tanzania
Ras Dashan	14,872	4,533	Seimen Mountains	Ethiopia
Mt. Karisimbi	14,790	4,507	Virunga Mountains	Rwanda
Tullu Dimtu	14,229	4,337	Bale Mountains	Ethiopia
Mt. Wagagai	14,140	4309	Mt. Elgon	Uganda
Mt. Toubkal	13,435	4,167	High/Grand Atlas	Morocco
Mt. Cameroon	13,435	4,095	Cameroon Highlands	Morocco
Mt. Lesatima	13,120	3,999	Aberdare	Kenya
Thabana Ntlenyana	11,425	3,482	Drakensberg	Lesotho
Mt. Mafadi	11,320	3,450	Drakensberg	South Africa
Emi Koussi	11,204	3,415	Tibesti Mountains	Chad
Mt. Keguer Terbi	11,076	3,376	Tibesti Mountains	Chad
Mt. Bou Naceur	10,958	3,340	Middle Atlas	Morocco
Mt. Tarso Taro	10,909	3,325	Tibesti Mountains	Chad
Mt. Kahuzi	10,853	3,308	Mitumba Mountains	DRC
Mt. Siroua	10,835	3,340	Anti Atlas	Morocco
Mt Pic Tousside	10,712	3,265	Tibesti Mountains	Chad

the lowest of the three ranges while the Saharan Atlas continues to Tunisia as the Aures Mountains, cresting at Mount Chelia (7,638 feet/2,328 m) above sea level.

The highlands and plateaus of Central Sahara include the Ahaggar and the Tassili Plateaus of Southern Algeria, the Air Massif of Niger, the Tibesti Mountains and the Ennedi Plateau of Chad, and the Darfur Dome of Sudan. The Ahaggar or Hoggar is a large plateau that consists of "needles of rocks some reaching over 1,000 feet, (304 m) split by weathering and cooling into prisms and pyramids" (de Villiers and Hirtle, 2002, p. 127). The highest point is Mount Tahat (9,573 feet/2,918 m) in Algeria. The Tassili Plateau houses the more than 15,000 rock paintings in its caves that made UNESCO declare it a World Heritage Site. Its highest point is Adra Afao (7,080 feet/2,158 m). The Air Mountains, or Air Massif, consist of meta-morphosed intrusive granitic rocks that reach above 6,000 feet (2,022 m) in Mount Idoukal-n-Taghes, while the Tibesti Mountains are the largest and highest mountains of the Sahara. Their highest point is Emi Koussi (11,204 feet/3,415 m).

To the southeast of the Tibesti Mountains lies the severely weathered Ennedi Plateau, which crests at 4,756 feet (1,450 m), and the Darfur Dome. The dome is a large volcanic feature dominated by the Marra Mountains and the Deriba Crater, which houses the 3.1-mile (5 km)-wide Deriba Caldera (Figure 4.8). Further south of Central African Republic are the Yade Mountains, which reach 3,750 feet (1,143 m).

The highlands and plateaus of West Africa include the Fouta Djallon (3,000–5,000 feet/914–1,524 m) of Central Guinea, the Guinea Highlands (980–1,600 feet/299–488 m) of southeast Guinea, north Sierra Leone, and northwest Cote d'Ivoire, the Jos Plateau of central Nigeria (4,000–6,600 feet/1,219–2,012 m), the Adamawa-Alantika-Mandara Range (3,300–8,700 feet/1,006–2,652 m) of southeast Nigeria, through north-central Cameroon to Central African Republic, and the Cameroon Highlands, a chain of extinct and active volcanic mountains, which extends southwest to comprise the islands of Sao Tome and Principe' in the Atlantic Ocean. Included in this mountain chain is Mount Cameroon, 13,435 feet (4,095 m), an active volcano as well as the second highest point in Low Africa.

FIGURE 4.8 The Jebel Marra, Darfur, Sudan. Note: The inner and outer craters. The Deriba Caldera is in the inner crater at 9,980 feet (3,042 m). *Source:* Smithsonian Institution

High Africa

High Africa has a general elevation of 1,000 feet (305 m) above sea level. However, its relief consists of two distinct features: extensive areas of highlands and plateaus and the Great Rift Valley. Most of Africa's highest mountains are in this region (Table 4.2).

The highlands and plateaus The highlands and plateaus of High Africa include the Ethiopian (Abyssinia) Highlands, the East African Plateau, the Southern African Plateau, and the Great Escarpment of Southern Africa. The Ethiopian Highlands are rugged volcanic mountains located in Ethiopia, Eritrea, and northern Somalia ranging in elevation from 5,000 feet (1,200 m) to almost 16,000 feet (4,900 m). The highlands are divided into two sections by the Great Rift Valley, with the Semien Mountains to the northwest and the Bale Mountains to the southeast. Ras Dashan (14,872 feet/4,533 m), Ethiopia's highest mountain and Africa's fourth highest, is in the Semien Mountains, while the highest peak in the Bale Mountains is Tullu Demtu (14,229 feet/4,337 m).

South of the Ethiopian Highlands is the East African Plateau, which averages about 8,000 feet (2,438 m) in elevation. Rising above this general elevation are several distinctive mountain ranges and isolated peaks all of which are associated with volcanic activities and the Rift Valley System. In the northwest, flanking the western Rift Valley System lies the snow-capped Rwenzori Mountains. The highest point of this range is the Margherita Peak (16,763 feet/5,109 m). South of the Rwenzori, along the borders of Uganda, Rwanda, and the DRC is the volcanic chain of the Virunga Mountains. The highest point of these mountains is Mount Karisimbi (14,790 feet/4,507 m) on the border of Rwanda and the Congo Democratic Republic (Figure 4.9). Further south of the Virunga Mountains are the Mitumba Mountains of DRC, which crest in Mount Kahuzi (10,853 feet/3,308 m. In the northeastern portion of the East African Plateau along the borders of Uganda and Kenya

FIGURE 4.9 Mount Karisimbi, an active volcano in the Virunga Mountains.
Source: iStock.com/Robert_Ford.

is Mount Elgon (14,140 feet/4,309), a massive extinct volcanic mountain with a 5-mile (8 km) diameter caldera. Southeast of Elgon and lying entirely in Kenya are the Uasin Gishu Plateau, which lies in the Rift Valley, the Mau Escarpment, and the Aberdare Range, which form the eastern rim of the Rift Valley. East of the Aberdare Range is Mount Kenya (17,057 feet/5,198 m), Africa's second highest mountain (Figure 4.10). Further south in Tanzania is Kilimanjaro (19,340 feet/5,895 m), the highest mountain in Africa (Figure 4.11), and Mount Meru (14,978 feet/4,565 m).

South of the East African Plateau is the Southern African Plateau, a vast high plateau block broken up by a few major river valleys and structural basins. The plateau rises from 2,000 to 4,000 feet (610–1,219 m) in Tanzania and reaches 4,000–6,000 feet (1,219–1,829 m) in the Bie and the Huila Plateaus of Angola. From here, the elevation falls to 3,500–5,000 feet (1,067–1,524 m) in Zambia, Zimbabwe, and Namibia, with isolated peaks and ridges. These include the Nyika Plateau (7,000 feet/2,134 m) along Zambia and Malawi border, the Konigstein Peak (8,550 feet/2,606 m) in Namibia, and Mount Nyangani (8,504 feet/2,592 m), and the Great Dyke of Zimbabwe (5,003–5,314 feet/1,525–1,620 m). Eastward from Namibia and westward from Zimbabwe, the high plateau drops in elevation into the Kalahari Basin, an area of 350,000 square miles (906,496 km²), which covers most of Botswana and parts of Namibia and South Africa. The general elevation of the basin is between 2,600 and 3,950 feet (800–1,200 m). However, the relief here transitions into extensive sand seas, large inland deltas, and pans (small dry lakes). The sand sea here is the most extensive on the earth (Thomas and Shaw, 1993). The inland deltas include those of the Okavango, Kwando, and Ciuto rivers of Northwestern Botswana and nearby Namibia and Zambia, while the pans include the Etosha Pan in Namibia and the Makgadikgadi pan in Northeastern Botswana, which serves as a reservoir for spill over water from the Okvango delta (Lancaster, 1996). Northeast of the Kalahari Basin and south of Zimbabwe, the land rises from 2,000 to 3,000 feet (about 600–900 m) in the Transvaal Bushveld to 4,000–6,000 feet (1,200–1,830 m) in the Highveld plateau, over the Witwatersrand, a narrow ridge of 5,577–5,906 feet

FIGURE 4.10 Mount Kenya.
Source: iStock.com/ guenterguni

FIGURE 4.11 Mount Kilimanjaro.
Source: iStock.com/1001slide.

(1,700–1,800 m) well known for its rich gold deposits (Mountjoy and Hilling, 1988). West of the Highveld lies the Upper Karroo (Karroo a derived Khoikhoi word meaning "waterless"), a vast expanse of undulating low plateau region of about 2,000 feet (600 m) above sea level deeply carved by the Orange River.

Further south, the Southern African Plateau rises into the Great Escarpment of Southern Africa, reaching its most prominent elevation in the Drakensberg of Lesotho and South Africa, with Thabana Ntlenyana (11,425 feet/3,482 m) in Lesotho as its highest peak (Figure 4.10). From the Drakensberg, the escarpment continues westward along the southern section of the continent, with a lower elevation of between 5,000 and 8,000 feet (1,524–2,348 m). It assumes different names becoming the Khomas Mountains of Namibia and terminating in the Serra da Chela (7,566 feet/2,306 m) of Angola.

Between the escarpment and the coastal plains in South Africa is the Great Karroo, which lies between 1,476 and 2,461 feet (450–750 m) above sea level, and the relatively lower Little Karroo. To the southwest lie the Cape Ranges, a group of fold mountains that include the Cedarberg, the Olifants Mountains, the Swartberge, the Langeberg, and the Table Mountain (Mountjoy and Hilling, 1988).

The rift valley system As already mentioned, High Africa is also deeply scarred by the world's longest and most spectacular rift valley—the East African Rift Valley or simply called the Great Rift Valley (Figure 4.12). From its northern end, off the

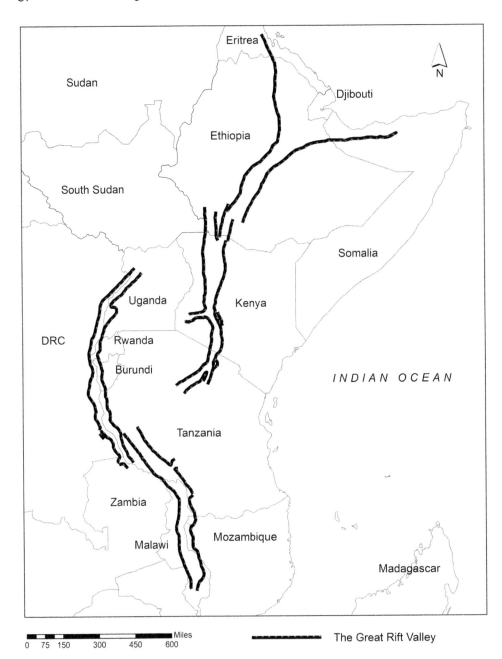

FIGURE 4.12 The Great
Rift Valley.
Source: ESRI Feature class:
https://services7.arcgis.com/
Gw2vEo9WjwgQp6Er/arcgis/
rest/services/East_African_Rift
_System/FeatureServer

coast of Djibouti, to its southern end, beyond Lake Malawi, the rift valley is about
3,107 miles (5,000 km) long (Nyamweru, 1996), and it is considered as the most
striking relief feature of Africa. There are two main branches—the Eastern branch
and the Western branch.

The Eastern branch begins as the Afar Depression, from the borders of Eritrea
and Djibouti and runs through Ethiopia, Kenya, and Northern Tanzania. In the
Afar section, the valley is about 249 miles (400 km) wide with steep walls of 9,843
feet (3,000 m) (Nyamweru, 1996). Further south of Ethiopia, the valley becomes
narrower averaging between 38 and 44 miles (60–70 km) wide, with well-defined
walls of 3,281 feet (1,000 m) above sea level. In Kenya, it becomes the Turkana Rift

Zone, where it is occupied by Lake Turkana, while in Northern Tanzania, it is known as the Gregory Rift Zone. Here it is occupied by Lakes Naivasha and Magadi Basin (Nyamweru, 1996). From Northern Tanzania, the valley becomes less pronounced and disappears, although in recent years, it has been suggested that it continues into the Indian Ocean (Nyamweru, 1996).

The Western branch begins as the Albert Rift Zone, west of Lake Victoria. Flanked by the Rwenzori, this section of the valley contains Lake Albert, Lake Edward, Lake Kivu, and the Virunga Mountains. South of the Virunga Mountains, the valley continues as the Lake Tanganyika Rift Zone, where it houses Lake Tanganyika, (Nyamweru, 1996), the Rukwa Rift Zone, which runs parallel to the Lake Tanganyika Rift Zone, and the Lake Malawi Rift Zone, which contains Lake Malawi and the Shire Valley. Here the valley is 25–56 miles (40–90 km) wide, with fault scarps reaching over 14,764 feet (4,500 m), especially around the lake. From that point, evidence of fault structures continues for about 373 miles (600 km) south and then disappears.

The formation of the rift valley is known to have occurred in the Cenozoic era. However, geologists are still debating about how exactly it was formed. In its simplest form, rift valleys are formed when the block between two fractures in the crust subsides or the blocks outside the fractures are elevated. In the case of the Great Rift Valley, however, geologists believe that the process is more complicated. Essentially, it is believed that the valley is the result of an attempt by the earth's tectonic forces to split the old African plate into two—the Nubian Plate and the Somali Plate—while at the same time the entire African Plate is moving away from the Arabian Plate (Nyamweru, 1996).

DRAINAGE BASINS OF AFRICA

The African continent is endowed with numerous rivers, streams, and lakes, which occupy specific areas of the continent. This section discusses the major river basins, a select number of minor river basins, and major lakes.

River Basins

There are six major drainage basins in Africa. By order of size, they are the Congo, the Nile, the Chad, the Niger, the Zambezi, and the Orange basins (Table 4.3). We will consider each of these in turn in addition to minor basins—the Senegal, the Limpopo, the Okavango, and the Volta (Figure 4.13).

The Congo Basin

The Congo Basin is one of the most distinguished geographic features of Africa. With an area of 1,335,000 square miles (3,457,634 km^2), which includes the entire country of the Democratic Republic of Congo most of Congo Republic, Central African Republic, Eastern Zambia, Northern Angola, and parts of Cameroon and Tanzania, the Congo Basin is the largest river basin in Africa, and second only to the Amazon Basin in the world. With the general elevation of 984–1,400 feet (300–500 m) and flanked at the edges by highlands of between 2,297 and 3,397 feet (700–1,200 m) above sea level, the Congo Basin has a cross section of a true basin.

At 2,900 miles (4,667.1 km) long, the Congo is Africa's second longest river as well as the World's second largest in terms of discharge (1,450,000 cu. ft/41,059 cu.

Major and Selected Minor Drainage Basins of Africa

Basin	Area Sq. Mi.	Area Km²	Principal River	Length Miles	Length Km	Countries in the basin
Congo	1,335,000	3,457,634	Congo	2,900	4,667	DRC, Congo Republic, Central African Republic, Zambia, Angola, Cameroon, and Tanzania
Nile	1,293,000	3,348,855	Nile	4,132	6,650	Burundi, DRC, Egypt, Eritrea, Ethiopia, Kenya, Rwanda, South Sudan, Sudan, Tanzania, and Uganda
Chad	939,773	2,434,000	Chari-Logone	1,211	1,949	Cameroon, Chad, Central African Rep., Nigeria, and Niger
Niger	730,000	1,890,691	Niger	2,600	4.184	Benin, Burkina Faso, Cameroon, Chad, Cote d'Ivoire, Mali, Niger, Nigeria
Zambezi	468,000	1,212,114	Zambezi	2,200	3,541	Angola, Botswana, Malawi, Mozambique, Namibia, Tanzania, Zambia, and Zimbabwe
Orange	330,000	854,696	Orange	1,300	2,092	Botswana, Lesotho, Namibia, South Africa
Senegal	186,187	483,000	Senegal	1,118	1,800	Guinea, Mali, Mauritania, Senegal
Limpopo	160,323	415,000	Limpopo	1,087	1,750	Botswana, Mozambique, South Africa, and Zimbabwe
Volta	151,441	400,000	Volta	1,000	1,609	Benin, Burkina Faso, Cote d'Ivoire, Ghana, Mali, and Togo
Okavango	124,785	323,192	Okavango	1,000	1,609	Angola, Botswana, Namibia

meters of water into the Atlantic Ocean per second). Only the Amazon discharges more cubic feet of water per second into the ocean. With a depth of more than 755 feet (230 m), it is also considered as the deepest river in the world. The Congo begins as the Chambeshi River in Zambia, and after assuming different local names it joins the Lualaba at Ankoro in DRC. Just before Kisangani, the Lualaba pours over the Boyoma Falls (formerly Stanley Falls), a series of seven cataracts or rapids, after which it becomes the Congo. Between Kisangani and Kinshasa, the river cuts a great counterclockwise loop receiving numerous tributaries among which are the Lomami, the Rula, and the Kwa Kasai on the left and the Ubangui and the Sangha on the right. In this section, the river ranges from 3 to 8 miles (5.6–12.9 km) wide. However, at the confluence with the Kasai, the river is forced into the Chenal, a narrow valley of ½ to 1 mile wide. After that the river breaks into two lake-like branches called the Malebo Pool, at the end of which is the Livingstone Falls, a series of rapids, which cause the river to drop 900 feet (270 m) in 220 miles (350 km). At Matadi, which is 83 miles (133.6 km) to the Atlantic Ocean, the river opens an estuary, which continues as a deep underwater canyon under the Atlantic Ocean for about 125 miles (201.2 km) (Figure 4.13).

Keddy et al. (2009) refers to the Congo Basin as the "greatest unknown" because our knowledge of this vast basin is still limited to disappearing forests and exotic apes, and studies that were conducted during the colonial period. However, as they indicate, the Congo Basin is more than that. For example, it contains about 30% of Africa's freshwater reserves as well as Africa's greatest hydroelectricity potential. Also, because the basin stands astride the equator, the tributary rivers north of the equator have peak discharges that alternate with the tributary rivers south of the

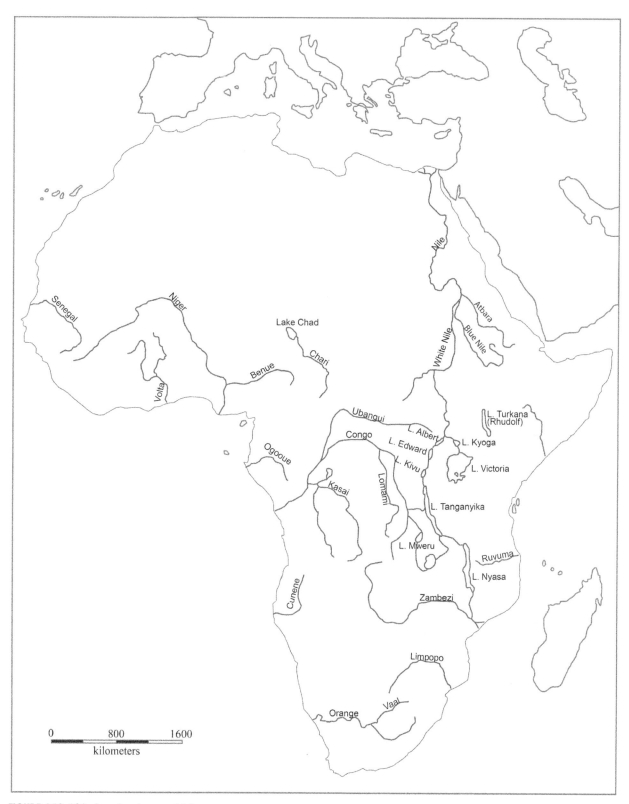

FIGURE 4.13 Africa's major rivers and lakes.
Source: World Wildlife Fund US/HydroSHEDS/ DEG WWF Water Risk Filter.

equator. This allows the Congo to maintain a water level that varies only slightly—about 5.9 feet (1.8 m) during the year—unlike those of many tropical river systems. The basin is also home to the world's second largest rainforest as well as its fourth largest wetland, an estimated area of 73,359 square miles (190,000 km²), of which we know very little (Keddy et al., 2009). Besides, with some 9,000 miles (12,875 km) of navigable waterways, the Congo Basin hosts the world's most extensive inland waterway of any single river system. Recent use of remote sensing imagery has enabled a more accurate mapping of the vegetation in the basin, but whether these will lead to more studies of this relatively unknown vast region remains to be seen.

The Nile Basin

With an area of 1,293,000 square miles (3,348,855 km²), the Nile basin is the second largest drainage basin in Africa (Figure 4.13). It includes the 11 countries of Burundi, Democratic Republic of Congo, Egypt, Eritrea, Ethiopia, Kenya, Rwanda, South Sudan, Sudan, Tanzania, and Uganda.

The Nile (4,132 miles/6,650 km long) is Africa's as well as the World's longest river. Many consider Lake Victoria as the source of Nile. However, if the rivers that flow into Lake Victoria are taken into account, the Kagera River from the highlands of Burundi, which is the single largest river flowing into Lake Victoria, can be considered as the distant source of the Nile. The Nile flows out of Lake Victoria, at Jinja, Uganda, as the Victoria Nile, over the submerged Ripon Falls into Lake Kyoga and then over the Murchison Falls to Lake Albert. From Lake Albert, the Albert Nile enters South Sudan and becomes the Al Jabal River (Bahr el Jabal or Mountain Nile). Below Juba, the river flows through the Sudd region, a vast expanse of very flat clayey swamp plain, after which it is joined by the Al-Ghazal River. The Al Jabal River becomes the White Nile, after it is joined by its first major tributary, the Sobat, from the Ethiopian Highlands. At Khartoum, Sudan, the White Nile becomes the Nile, after it is joined by it most important tributary, the Blue Nile from Lake Tana in the Ethiopian Highlands. From that point, the Nile cuts over hills and rock outcrops, creating six cataracts or rapids, in the process. After receiving its last major tributary, the Atbara, the river flows into Lake Nasser, an artificial lake created by the Aswan High Dam, and enters the sea north of Cairo.

Managing the use of the Nile river system among the 11 countries in the basin has been controversial. The main source of the controversy is the Nile Treaty of 1929, which was signed between Great Britain, Italy, and Egypt. The treaty guaranteed Egypt's use of the Nile at the expense of the rest of the nations in the basin. It forbade any nation south of Egypt from doing anything with the Nile or its feeding tributaries that would reduce Egypt's consumption of water from the Nile, without the consent of Egypt (Okoth-Owiro, 2004). In 1959, the treaty was modified to split the control of the river between Egypt and Sudan, with Egypt still wielding the most control. It allocated 55.5 billion cubic meters of Nile water per year to Egypt and 18.5 billion cubic meters to Sudan.

Since their return to independence, the other countries in the basin have objected to the treaty. In particular, Tanzania and Ethiopia have argued that the treaty signed under the colonial period is not binding on them and therefore the treaty needs to be negotiated. In response, Egypt claims that the treaty is binding and that any effort to break out of the agreement would be considered as "an act of war" (Okoth-Owiro, 2004).

However, given that none of these positions is tenable in the present context, there has been a push for a middle ground position. This position advocates that every state is free to use the waters that flow through its borders provided such utilization does not interfere with a "reasonable utilization" of water by other states. The problem here is defining the "reasonable utilization."

Ultimately, the full use of the waters of the Nile Basin requires a new international institution—the Nile River Basin Administration or Authority. With increasing drought in some of the upper riparian countries such as Ethiopia and Kenya, the Nile Basin Initiative (NBI) was launched in 1999 to provide institutional framework for establishing guidelines for cooperative action. After 10 years of negotiations, a new agreement was ready to be signed in 2010. However, Egypt and Sudan did not attend the meeting and refused to ratify the agreement. In 2011, Ethiopia announced plans for its Renaissance Dam project on the Blue Nile. This immediately drew strong opposition from Egypt. However, in 2015, Egypt and Ethiopia signed an agreement in Khartoum, Sudan, with Sudan as the witness, regarding Ethiopia's dam project. The broader question of sharing the waters of the Nile by all the countries in the basin still remains unsolved, but it is clear that the only way forward is for all the countries to cooperate.

The Chad Basin

With an area of 939,773 square miles (2,434,000 km²), the Chad Basin is the third largest **drainage basin** in Africa. It is also Africa's largest inland drainage basin. It comprises five countries—Cameroon, Chad, Central African Republic, Nigeria, and Niger. The principal feature of the basin is Lake Chad, a shallow lake of about only 3.5 to 4 feet (1.1–1.2 m) deep and covering an area of 5,000 square miles (12,950 km²). In addition to the lake, the basin is drained by a few rivers. From the south are the Chari (590 miles/949 km) and its main tributary, the Logone, which accounts for 95% of the water flow into the lake, and the El Beid, the Yedseram and the Ngadda Rivers. To the north of the basin is the Komadougou Yobe River (Ibrahim, 2009) (Figure 4.13).

Lake Chad presents a classic example of a shrinking lake. Estimates of the extent to which this has occurred vary, but they all point in the same direction. According to Ibrahim (2008) prior to 1960, Lake Chad was the fourth largest lake in Africa and the sixth largest in the world, with a surface area of more than 9,653 square miles (25,000 km²). Between 1967 and 1973, however, the lake began to shrink due to smaller amount of water inflow and small flooding. By 1973, a shallow zone in the lake had emerged breaking the basin into northern and southern pools. From then on water level continued to fall as more areas formerly under water became dry lake bed. By 1997, most of the lake's open water had been replaced by marsh and dry land. By 2001, the lake had been reduced to a surface area of 579 square miles (1,500 km²), only 6% of its 1960 size.

The causes of this state of affairs are several and include both physical and human reasons. Physically, the main source of water in the basin is rainfall. In normal years, annual rainfall amounts vary from 59 in. (1,500 mm) in the south to 4 in. (100 mm) in the north, with most of the rain occurring from May through October. Over the past several decades, however, rainfall has been erratic and scanty and these have resulted in long periods of droughts, which in turn have accelerated the rate of evaporation in the region (Ibrahim, 2008).

Among the human causes of this disaster are "uncontrolled irrigation, tree-cutting for fuel wood, a scramble for fertile land on the lake shores for farming and the construction of dams on tributaries feeding the lake" (VOA Report, 2009). In 1979, after a series of prolonged drought, Cameroon decided to build the Maga Dam on the

Logone River in the Waza-Logone area of its Extreme-North province for rice production, which reduced the flow of the Chari-Logone River. Apart from this, Nigeria also decided to construct 20 reservoir dams on the Hadejia river system, a tributary of the Yobe, which empties into the lake (Goes, 2001). The result is that the dams of the Hadejia river system reduced the contribution of the Komadougou Yobe to 1% of the water inflow to the lake. Finally, as the lake contracted, the availability of water became a major issue among the 30 million or so that live within the basin.

Mechanism for managing the resources of Lake Chad exists but has not been effective. As far back as 1964, the Lake Chad Basin Commission (LBCB) was established among Cameroon, Chad, Central African Republic, Niger, and Nigeria, with Libya joining in 2008. The commission was "to ensure sustainable and equitable management and conservation of the natural resources." However, the group has not taken its task seriously until recently. One of the projects the Commission is hoping to undertake is the construction of a 93-mile (150-km) canal that will direct some of the waters of the Ubangi River into Lake Chad. This plan initially proposed in the 1960s gained renewed interest in 2008, with the consent of both Congo Republic and the Democratic Republic of the Congo (Noury, 2009). The only hold up now is funding. Another initiative is a forestation project, which is being spearheaded by Cameroon.

The Niger Basin

The Niger Basin covers a total area of 730,000 square miles (1,890,691 km²) and includes parts of Guinea, Mali, Cote d'Ivoire, Burkina Faso, Benin, Niger, Chad, Nigeria, and Cameroon (Figure 4.13). It is the fourth largest drainage basin in Africa. The Niger (2,600 miles/4,184.29 km long) is the third longest river in Africa and longest river in West Africa. It rises in the Fouta Djallon highlands of Guinea as the Tembi, only 150 miles (241.40 km) from the Atlantic Ocean, but it treks for more than 2,000 miles (3,219.69 km) in the opposite direction before entering the Atlantic. It receives a number of tributaries in its upper course before it enters Mali, where it receives two major tributaries, the Bagade and the Bani before it enters the "Inland Delta." This is a vast alluvial floodplain, where the river breaks into distributaries and numerous lakes. The Inland Delta serves both as storage and loss of the total water inflow of the river. It is estimated that about 44% of the water inflow of the river is lost here through seepage and evaporation. From here the river flows through Niger and enters Nigeria, where it flows into the Kainji Dam reservoir. Further down at Lokoja, it receives its largest tributary, the Benue River, from the Adamawa Highlands. At Aboh, the river separates into many distributaries to enter the Gulf of Guinea. With a total area of 14,000 square miles (36,259.83 km²), the Niger delta is that largest delta in Africa.

A major problem in the Niger Basin is the silting up of the upper course of the river in Central Guinea, which in turn has had adverse effects on livelihood, particularly fishing activities. Fishermen along the river estimate that in the 1990s, it was possible to catch about 50 kg of fish in the span of an hour. By 2007, an entire night of fishing could not even yield a quarter of the 1990s average catch (Samb, 2007). This has been attributed to deforestation, soil erosion, and climate change, particularly declining rainfall. This situation is threatening the lives of about 110 million people in nine countries who live in the basin.

Collaborative efforts to manage the resources of the Niger basin go back to 1964 when the newly independent countries in the basin formed the Niger River Commission modeled after the Tennessee Valley Authority of the United States. However, the Commission was not effective until 2002, when the Niger Basin heads of state agreed to formulate a shared vision for the development of the basin, through a Sustainable Development Action Program (SDAP) (Andersen et al., 2005). Both the World Bank and the Integrated Water Resource Management of the European Union Water Initiative have supported the efforts in the basin. In 2007, the World Bank approved a loan of $500 million for the program to be administered in two phases over a 12-year period. The overall goal of the project is to achieve sustainable increase of water resources, increase hydropower production, and foster economic growth of the basin. How successful will the NBA be well depend in no small measure on the political will of the countries in the basin to work together cooperatively.

The Zambezi Basin

With an area of about 468,000 square miles (1,212,114 km²), the Zambezi Basin is the fifth largest drainage basin in Africa (Figure 4.13). The basin covers parts of Angola, Botswana, Malawi, Mozambique, Namibia, Tanzania, Zambia, and Zimbabwe. The Zambezi (2,200 miles/3,541 km long) begins in the Kalene Hill of Zambia. It flows through Angola and reenters Zambia, pouring over the Chavuma Falls and into the wide region of flood plains. Here it receives a number of tributaries, goes over a series of waterfalls, and forms part of the boundary between Zambia and Namibia. It then receives the Cuando River, passes through Botswana and forms the boundary between Zambia and Zimbabwe. At Maramba (Livingstone), the river pours over the famous Victoria Falls, which is over 354.3 feet (108 m) drop, and flows into the Kariba Dam Lake. After receiving its two major tributaries, the Kafue and the Luangwa, it enters Mozambique, flows into the Lake Cahora Bassa, and on to the Indian Ocean.

The Zambezi Basin faces a number of problems, including uncoordinated water resource development, poor environmental management approaches, and weak adaptation to climate change. The weak adaptation to climate change is especially important as incidence of flooding and severe drought has been frequent in the basin in recent years. In 2007, for example, over half a million people in Botswana, Malawi, Mozambique, Namibia, Zambia, and Zimbabwe were affected by intense flooding (Semu-Banda, 2008). To address these and other related matters, the eight countries in the basin signed the Zambezi Watercourse Commission (ZAMCOM) in 2004. In 2005, they developed the Integrated Water Resources Management (IWRM) Strategy, which addressed how the waters of the basin would be used to benefit all the countries. Since then, the focus of the annual meeting of the ZAMCOM has been the translation of the strategy into implementation (Semu-Banda, 2008). A secretary general was appointed in 2014, and a full secretariat became operational in 2015.

The Orange Basin

The Orange River, together with its principal tributary the Vaal, forms a drainage basin of about 330,000 square miles (854,696 km²), which includes South Africa, parts of Botswana and Namibia, and Lesotho. This is the smallest of the six major drainage basins of Africa. The river, which is about 1,300 miles (2,092 km) long, rises in the Lesotho Highlands as the Sinqu (Senqu) River and after entering South Africa, it receives the Caledon at the head of the Hendrik Verwoerd Reservoir, and the Vaal its major tributary. The Orange flows through series of deep gorges and rapids, culminating in the Augrabies Falls, after which it forms the boundary between South Africa and Namibia and goes through some of its most rugged sections. It enters the sea at Orangemund through Alexander Bay in Namibia's coastal desert.

Drought is a perennial problem of the Orange basin, and for that reason the number one problem in the basin is water scarcity. To deal with this problem, the countries of the basin formed the Orange-Senqu River Commission (ORASECOM) in 2000 to "advise member states on the shared use of water resources." Since then, the Commission's activities have included development of policies and procedures for the agreement, the development of institutional framework for the agreement, and conducting studies that will inform the decision-making process of member states and application of appropriate management system.

Minor River Basins

In addition to these major drainage basins, Africa has numerous minor drainage basins that have similar environmental and use management issues. We will discuss four of these basins because of their international importance.

The Senegal basin The Senegal River basin covers an area of 186,487 square miles (483,000 km²) and includes portions of Guinea, Mali, Mauritania, and Senegal (Vick, 2006). It is the seventh largest river basin in Africa. The Senegal (1,020 miles/1,641 km long), the second longest river in West Africa, is formed when two rivers, the Bafing and the Bakoye, both originating from the Fouta Djallon of Guinea and southwest Mali, meet at Bafoulabe' in Mali. Further downstream, near Bakel the Senegal is joined by another important tributary, the Faleme, also from the Fouta Djallon.

Like most river basins, the Senegal basin had severe seasonal flooding as well as drought and famine. These problems caused the three countries in the basin Mali, Mauritania, and Senegal to mount a regional river basin development effort, which was unprecedented in Africa and was even considered unique in the world (Vick, 2006). They developed institutional and legal framework to work together to deal with the problems in 1978. For the next 10 years, they conducted studies, secured financing, and began the construction of two dams, one on the Bafing tributary at Manantali in Mali and the other on the Senegal at Diama. The Manantali dam, completed in 1987, was for irrigation, hydroelectric power, and control of navigation, while the Diama dam, completed in 1986, was to stop salt water from flowing up river in the dry season and also control navigation in the dry season. Unfortunately, as Vick (2006) has documented, these well-intentioned projects ended up producing several unintended consequences, including increase in water-borne diseases, dramatic decline in fish production destruction of low-cost recessional farming, and loss of livestock. In the meantime, the actual goals of the projects—hydroelectric power production, irrigation, and the navigation—have not yet been completely achieved (Vick, 2006). In spite of all these, the Senegal River Basin presents an example of a river basin development that can be emulated by other African countries.

The Limpopo basin The Limpopo (1,087 miles/1,750 km long) drains a basin of about 160,323 square miles (415,000 km²), including portions of Botswana, Mozambique, South Africa, and Zimbabwe. The river begins in South Africa as the Crocodile River and becomes Limpopo after it is joined by the Marico River. Flowing in a great arc, the river forms the boundary between South Africa and Botswana and South Africa and Zimbabwe, before it enters Mozambique, where it receives the most important tributary, the Olifants, and enters the sea near the port of Xai-Xai.

The Limpopo Basin has two main drainage issues—droughts and floods. These are caused by several factors. First, the arid or semi-desert environment of much of the basin (including the Kalahari) combined with a highly variable rainfall regime leaves long stretches of the Limpopo and its tributaries in a state of intermittent stream in drier years. Second, both the Limpopo and its major tributaries have very steep gradients—for example, the Limpopo drops from 3,281 feet (1,000 m) above sea level at its headwaters in South Africa to about 656 feet (200 m) just before entering Mozambique and drops again to 329 feet (100 m) for its last 249 miles (400 km) (Silva et al., 2010). The Olifants has even more dramatic drop—from 4,921 feet (1,500 km) in South Africa to about 263 feet (80 m) just before entering Mozambique. These drastic drops in elevation make the lower section of the basin more vulnerable to floods in years of copious rain (Silva et al., 2010). Third, many of the tributaries of the Olifants and the Limpopo have also been dammed in South Africa, and opening these dams during heavy rains has also contributed to the flooding in Mozambique. (Silva et al., 2010). To deal with these issues, Mozambique has embarked on flood management program, which includes educating people about the dangers of living in flood plains, encouraging people in flood plains to have two homes, one in an upland area that will not be affected by flood, and building of elevated houses in areas that are not frequently affected by floods. However, there are several obstacles to these efforts. Some people do not want to move due to cultural beliefs. Others who see livestock as a symbol of wealth do not want to move away from the flood plain due to lack of good pasture elsewhere. Perhaps the strongest resistance comes from those who have survived previous flood events and for that reason think they can survive new ones. Unfortunately, these are the people who are often killed (Patsanza, 2010).

The Volta basin The Volta River basin covers an area of 154,441 square miles (400,000 km²) consisting of the six riparian countries of Burkina Faso, Ghana, Togo, Benin, Mali, and Cote d'Ivoire (Owusu et al., 2008). The Volta (1,000 miles/1,609 km), the principal river of the basin, begins as the Baoule in the Kong Mountains in Burkina Faso. As the Black Volta (Mouhoun) it forms the boundary first between Burkina Faso and Ghana and then between Cote d'Ivoire and Ghana, before entering Ghana, where it is joined by the White Volta, also from Burkina Faso, to form the Volta. The river flows into the Lake Volta, the largest artificial lake in Africa created by the Akosombo Dam, receiving several tributaries including the Afram and the Oti. The river enters the sea near Akuse.

Like other river basins, the Volta basin faces several issues the most pressing being the water level fluctuations of Lake Volta. The hydroelectric power dam is the main source of electricity supply for Ghana. However, fluctuations in the water level of the lake in some years—1983, 1998, and 2007—had severely affected electricity generation capacity (Owusu et al., 2008). In those years, relationship between Ghana and its northern neighbor, Burkina Faso, had been strained with Ghana accusing Burkina Faso for taking too much water from the headwaters of the Volta. To this, Burkina Faso has countered that Ghana's electricity supply was unreliable, so it had no choice but take care of itself. Even so, studies have shown that the main reason for fluctuating levels of water in the basin is declining rainfall (Andreni et al., 2000; Owusu et al., 2008). The problem is unlike many transnational river basins, there are no agreements governing the Volta River basin and as long as this situation prevails, it is going to be difficult to manage the water resources of the basin.

The Okavango basin The Okavango Basin covers a total area of 124,785 square miles (323,192 km²) in Angola, Namibia, and Botswana. The Okavango (1,000 miles/1,600 km long) begins in central Angola as the Kubango. It flows south forming part of the border between Namibia and Angola and goes over the Popa Falls before entering into Botswana, where it empties into an inland delta in the Kalahari basin. With an area of about 5,791.5 square miles (15,000 km²), the Okavango delta is the largest inland delta in the world. Given that the three countries in the basin are dry, the potential for water conflict was very high. However, in 1994, the three countries signed an agreement called the Permanent Okavango Basin Water Commission (OKACOM) to provide advice of the use of the water resources of the basin.

Lakes

Africa has numerous lakes of various sizes. Most of the larger ones are found in East Africa, an area that can be aptly described as the Great Lakes Region of Africa (Figure 4.14). Among these larger lakes are Lake Victoria, Lake Tanganyika, Lake Malawi, Lake Rudolf, and Lake Chad (Table 4.2).

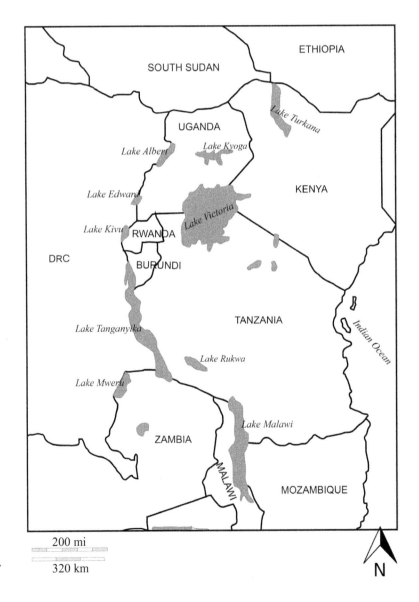

FIGURE 4.14 Africa's Great Lakes Region.
Source: Created by Benjamin Ofori-Amoah

Lake Victoria

With a surface area of 26,828 square miles (69,484 km²), Lake Victoria is the largest lake in Africa, and the second largest freshwater lake in the world. The lake sits at an elevation of 3,724 feet (1,135 m) above sea level. It has an average depth of 131 feet (40 m) and a maximum depth of 276 feet (84 m). Several rivers empty into the lake. They include Sondu Miriu, Nyando, Nzoia, and Yala, all from Kenya; the Mara from Tanzania; and the Kagera, the single longest inflow of the lake, from Burundi, Tanzania, and Rwanda. An estimated 35 million people live around the lake and depend on it for their livelihood, using it for transportation, drinking, and fisheries.

The lake has several environmental and ecological problems. Several rivers that flow into the lake are heavily polluted by high sediment load from agricultural and densely populated areas, and untreated or semi-treated industrial and municipal effluents all of which cause **eutrophication**, which is excessive nutrients that causes plant growth in lakes (Cavalli et al., 2009). In recent years, rapid colonization by water hyacinth has added to these problems. The emergence of water hyacinth in the lake was first reported in 1989. In 1994, when it was first estimated, it had covered 667 acres (270 hectares) of the lake. By the peak of infestation in 1998, it had covered 42,547 acres (17,218 hectares), with the Winam Gulf of Kenya as the most severely affected area. This rapid takeover by water hyacinth had adverse effects of the various uses of the lake—fisheries, transportation, and drinking water (Balirwa, 2007). Uganda used herbicides to control the weed, but after initial success, which led to massive collapse of the weed in 1998, nothing was done to prevent its resurgence and in 2006 the plants reappeared (Balirwa, 2007).

Another problem is the fluctuating water levels of the lake since the 1960s, with the highest occurring in the El-Nino years of the 1960s and 1997-1998 period. Between 2002 and 2006, water level fell below pre-1961 level and current water levels have been estimated to be below normal (LVBC, 2006; Awange et al., 2008). Part of this has been attributed to two hydroelectric power projects both in Uganda and part is also attributed to climatic factors, namely, changes in rainfall amounts in the region (Awange et al., 2008). This drop in water levels has led to drying up of the papyrus wetland at the lake's edges and about 80% collapse of the tilapia fisheries.

The need for collaboration in managing such an extraordinary resource as Lake Victoria has long been recognized. Initial regional efforts collapsed after the breakdown of the East African Community in 1977. In 1994, Kenya, Tanzania, and Uganda entered into an agreement to develop and implement the Lake Victoria Environmental Program (LVEMP). The overall goal of the program is "rehabilitation of the lake ecosystem for the benefit of the people who live in the catchment, the national economies of which they are a part, and the global community." The objectives include fisheries management, pollution and water hyacinth control, and management of wetlands and land use in the lake's catchment area. The overall budget of the program was $79.4 million. Implementation of the program ended in December 2005, but in 2009, the World Bank approved a loan of $90 million for the first phase of Lake Victoria Environmental Management Project II (LVEMP II).

Lake Tanganyika

Lake Tanganyika, average width of 32 miles (50 km) and mean length of 404 miles (650 km), is located in the western branch of the rift valley along the boundaries of Burundi, Democratic Republic of Congo, Tanzania, and Zambia. It is the second largest lake in Africa and in the tropics by surface area. With a surface area of 12,700 square miles, (32,893 km^2) it is less than half the size of Lake Victoria (Nicholson, 1999). However, with a mean depth of 1,871 feet (570 m), and a maximum depth of 4,823 feet (1,470 m), Lake Tanganyika is second among the world's lakes in terms of depth, volume, and biological diversity. Only Lake Baikal in Russia is ahead in all these respects (Verschuren, 2003).

The main environmental concern over the past few years has centered on the lowering aquatic ecosystem productivity of the lake. The cause of this has been attributed to global climate change (Verburg et al., 2003; O'Reilly et al., 2003). These two studies argue that rising air due to global warming over the past century coupled with the naturally deep lake has increased the temperature variation between the surface and deep water layers of the lake. This in turn has reduced the natural mixing process between the surface and deep waters that is so essential for aquatic productivity (Verschuren, 2003). The ultimate result of all this is a decline in fisheries. Like its counterparts of the Great Lakes region of the continent, Lake Tanganyika is an international lake that calls for coordination and cooperation of all the neighboring countries to ensure its proper management. This cooperation needs to be properly informed by more research into all the key factors that affect the dynamics of the lake.

Lake Malawi (Nyasa)

With a surface area of approximately 1,120 square miles (28,800 km^2), Lake Malawi is Africa's third largest lake. As part of the Great Rift Valley lakes, Lake Malawi is a deep lake, especially in the northern end. Like Lake Tanganyika, this depth has created a close to permanent stratified water layer and surface temperatures of between 73.4°F and 77°F (23°C and 25°C) (Song and Chuenpagdee, 2010). It is 360 miles (579.4 km) long and 46 miles (74.03 km) wide. Like all the lakes of the Great Lakes region, Lake Malawi is an important source of fisheries. However, these fisheries almost collapsed due to poor resource management. We will discuss this more in the fisheries chapter.

Lake Albert

Lake Albert is the first of the Western Rift Valley lakes from the north. It lies on the border of Uganda and the Democratic Republic of Congo. It is about 93.21 miles (150 km) long and averages about 22 miles (35 km) wide with a surface area of 2,046.34 square miles (5,300 km^2), and a mean depth of 115 feet (35 m). There are two main water inflows into the lake: one is the Victoria Nile, and the other is the Semliki River. Up until 2006, Lake Albert was perhaps well known for its diverse fisheries and as the original home of the Nile perch (Ford, 2007). However, the discovery of large reserves of hydrocarbon near the lake in 2006 has changed all that. In particular, since Lake Albert lies on the border of Uganda and Democratic Republic of Congo, the geographic location of the oil field has already generated some controversy between the two countries. Rukwanzi, an island in the lake near the oil find, became the main target. In 2007, a Ugandan court ruled that the island belongs to Uganda, which the DRC has accepted (Anonymous, 2008). No one knows yet the extent of the oil reserves in Lake Albert, but the question that is on the mind of many observers is whether Uganda and DRC can avoid the "oil curse."

Lake Turkana (Lake Rudolf)

Measuring about 155 miles (250 km) long and between 10 and 15 miles (16.1–24.14 km) long and a surface area of surface area of 2,705 square miles (7,000 km²), Lake Turkana, located in the eastern arm of the Great Rift Valley, is considered as the largest desert lake in the world. Three rivers feed the lake—the Omo, the Turkwei, and the Kerio, but the last two are largely seasonal. Some of the oldest human fossils have been found along the shores of the lake.

However, what is keeping Lake Turkana in the news these days is Ethiopia's decision to build a dam, the Gibe III Dam, on the Omo River, in 2006. Ethiopia said that it needed the dam to generate electricity, about 1,800 MW, twice the capacity of its current electricity generation (Anyangu-Amu, 2010). The estimated 500,000 people living around the lake and environmentalists disagreed with the Ethiopian government. They saw the dam construction as eventual devastation of their lives. In the meantime, the Kenya government indicated that it will import between 200 and 400 MV of electricity from Ethiopia (Anyangu-Amu, 2010). Others called on the Kenyan government to concentrate and expand the Lake Turkana Wind Power project, which has the potential of supplying one-fifth of Kenya's energy requirements. The Gibe III Dam opened in 2016, and people are already seeing signs of its impact. Experts are predicting Lake Turkana to dwindle and eventually disappear, but before that there will be conflicts over water resources.

Lake Kivu

Lake Kivu (surface area 1,040 square miles/2,700 km²) is located in the western branch of the Rift Valley, on the borders of Uganda and Rwanda, and in an area of very active volcanic activity. Volcanic activity taking place below the lake produces molten matter, which in turn releases carbon dioxide. In addition, bacteria also convert the carbon dioxide into methane (Nayar, 2009). The concentration of the carbon dioxide and methane at the bottom of the lake increases with depth. With depths of about 164–263 feet (50–80 m), the lake is devoid of oxygen. As a result of this, Lake Kivu has been described by some observers as "the lake that could explode" like Lake Nyos, a smaller lake in Cameroon, which emitted large amount of carbon dioxide on August 12, 1986, suffocating 1,700 people and 3,500 livestock to their death. A report by the Swiss Institute of Aquatic Science and Technology authorized by the Rwandan government estimates that Lake Kivu has 300 times more carbon dioxide than Lake Nyos did in 1986. Others have described it as the "killer lake."

Scientists agree that in order to avoid another catastrophe, Lake Kivu's gas pressure must be released, but what to do with the extracted gas is now debatable. The Rwandan government's solution is to convert the gas into electricity, something that has been done before (Nayar, 2009; Sharife, 2009). It is estimated that the amount of electricity that can be generated from the methane gas from the lake is about 10 times the electricity needs of both DRC and Rwanda.

However, some environmentalists think that extracting the gas will disturb the ecosystem and perhaps hasten the imminent explosion of the lake. From 2008, the Rwandan government initiated some pilot projects to generate electricity from the lake, and in 2009, the Rwanda and DRC announced a joint project that would generate an additional 200 MW from the lake (Nayar, 2009). Clearly, the risk of this project could be high but so is the need to improve lives. This is one of the many conundrums of Africa's development.

Other Lakes

Lake Kyoga and Lake Edward are other lakes in Africa's Great Lakes Region. Kyoga is the largest of an inland drainage system that covers about 1,815 square miles (4,700 km²) in Uganda (Mbabazi et al., 2009). It is a shallow lake with an average depth of 13 feet (4 m) and maximum depth of 23 feet (7 m). Lying across the border of Uganda and DRC, Lake Edward is the smallest of the Rift Valley lakes. It measures—and has a maximum depth of 384 feet (117 m). It is connected to Lake George, which is another shallow lake (Russell and Werne, 2009).

Summary

Geologically, about 57% of Africa's bedrock was formed in the oldest geological time period. The result is that the physical structure of the continent is very rigid with few places of relatively young and folded rocks but a lot of extinct volcanoes. As a result of this rigid nature, the relief of Africa consists of a very smooth coastline and a narrow coastal plain and highlands and plateaus in the vast interior. The interior highlands and plateaus tend to be higher in the southern half of the continent than the northern half and this has caused geographers to divide the continent into Low Africa and High Africa. The boundary between these two regions is an imaginary line from the mouth of the Congo River to the Gulf of Aden. However, above the general elevations of each of these two divisions are higher lands or mountains. In Low Africa, these include the Atlas Mountains, the Ahaggar Plateau, the Tibesti Mountains, the Air Massif, the Ennedi Plateau, and the Mara Mountains. In High Africa, they include the Ethiopian Highlands, the East African Plateau, and the Southern African Escarpment. The only other relief feature of significance is the Great Rift Valley of East Africa that runs south from the Gulf of Aden through East Africa from where it splits into two arms—the Eastern and Western Rift Systems.

Africa has six drainage basins that play host to some of the world's longest and most remarkable rivers. Among these are the Nile, the Congo, the Niger, and the Zambezi, the Orange, and the Chad basins. In addition to these rivers, there are also several freshwater lakes, some of which are among the largest and deepest lakes in the world. The enormous sizes of these river basins and lakes and the increasing scarcity of water have made the resources of these basins a source of controversy among riparian countries. However, these same reasons provide opportunities for cooperation and possibilities of river basin developments that cut across political boundaries.

Postreading Assignment

A. Study the following key concepts

Anchored dunes	Desert pavement	Inselberg	Sudd
Barrier beaches	Drainage basin	Mesozoic	Upward migration
Cenozoic	Ergs	Paleozoic	Wash
Chotts	Eutrophication	Pluvials	Wadi
Deflation	Gondwana	Precambrian	
Depressions	High Africa	Subsidence	

B. Discussion Questions

1. Compare the list of your African rivers, mountains, and lakes with your initial list. Compare the differences between the two. What have you learned about Africa?
2. How has Africa's geology influenced its relief?
3. Compare Africa's Mediterranean coastal plains with its Atlantic coastal plains.
4. Discuss the main landforms of Low Africa.
5. What are the main relief features of High Africa?
6. Compare and contrast the main relief features of Low and High Africa.
7. Is the division of Africa's relief into Low and High Africa justified? Why and Why not?
8. Discuss the view that river basin development could be an effective means for regional economic development of Africa.
9. Select one of the river basins discussed in the chapter. Research into recent development and assess the prospects of how the basin can provide a context for development.
10. Why is the Congo Basin referred to as the biggest unknown?

References

Albritton, Jr. C. E., Brooks, J. E., Issawi, B., and Swedan, A. 1990. "Origins of the Qattara Depression, Egypt." *Geological Society of America Bulletin* 102: 152–160.

Andersen, I., Dione, O., Jarosewich-Holder, M., and Olivry, J. C. 2005. *The Niger River Basin: A Vision for Sustainable Management.* Washington, DC: The World Bank.

Andreini, M., van de Giesen, N., van Edig, A., Fosu, M., and Andah, W. 2000 "Volta Basin Water Balance." ZEF Discussion Papers on Development Policy No. 21, Bonn.

Anyangu-Amu, S. 2010. "Kenya: Construction of Dam will Devastate Local Communities." *Global Information Network* March 24 Retrieved May 15, 2011, from Research Library. (Document ID: 1992499651).

Anonymous 2008. "DR Congo-Uganda: Lake Albert Ruling." *Africa Research Bulletin: Political, Social and Cultural Series* 45(9), 17670C-17671A. Retrieved May 15, 2011, from Research Library. (Document ID: 1579131941).

Awange, J., Ogalo, L., Bae, K., Were, P., Omondi, P., Omute, P., and Omullo, M. 2008. "Falling Lake Victoria Water Levels: Is Climate a Contributing Factor?" *Climatic Change* 89(3–4): 281–297.

Ballantine, J-A. C., Okin, G. S., Prentiss, D. E., and Roberts, D. A. 2005. "Mapping North African Landforms Using Continental Scale Unmixing of MODIS Imagery." *Remote Sensing of Environment* 97: 470–483.

Balirwa, J. S. 2007. "Ecological, Environmental and Socioeconomic Aspects of the Lake Victoria's Introduced Nile Perch Fishery in Relation to the Native Fisheries and the Species Culture Potential: Lessons to Learn." *African Journal of Ecology* 45(2): (June 1): 120–129.

Cavalli, R. M., Laneve, G., Fusilli, L., Pignatti, S., Santini, F. 2009. "Remote Sensing Water Observation for Supporting Lake Victoria Weed Management." *Journal of Environmental Management* 90(7): 2119.

de Villiers, M., and Hirtle, S. 2002. *Sahara: A Natural History.* New York: Walker & Company.

Dixon, J. C. 2009. "Aridic Soils, Patterned Ground, and Desert Pavements." In Parsons, A. J. and Abrahams, A. D. (Eds.), *Geomorphology of Desert Environments.* Second Edition. Springer Science + Business Media B.V. pp 101–122.

Ford, N. 2007. UGANDA-DCR: Avoiding the 'Curse' of Oil. *African Business* 337: 72–73.

Goes, B. J. M. 2001. Effects of Damming the Hadejia River in Semiarid Northern Nigeria—Lessons Learnt for Future Management *Regional Management of Water Resources.* Proceedings of a symposium held during the Sixth IAHS Scientific Assembly at Maastricht, The Netherlands, IAHS Publ. no. 268, p. 73.

Grove, A. T. 1993. *The Changing Geography of Africa.* Second Edition. Oxford: Oxford University Press.

Ibrahim, A. T. 2009. "Use of MERIS Data to Detect the Impact of Flood Inundation on Land Cover Changes in the Lake Chad Basin." An Unpublished PhD Dissertation, Hong Kong Polytechnic University.

Keddy, P. A., Fraser, L. H., Solomeshch, Junk, W. J. Campbell, D., Arroyo, M., Alho, C. 2009. "Wet and Wonderful: The World's Largest Wetlands Are Conservation Priorities." *Bioscience* 59(1): 39–51.

LVBC 2006. *Special Report on the Declining Water Levels of Lake Victoria.* Kisumu, Kenya: Lake Victoria Basin Commission (LBVC),

Lancaster, N. 1996. "Desert Environments." In Adams, W. M., Goudie, A. S., and Orme, A. R. (Eds.), *The Physical Geography of Africa.* Oxford: Oxford University Press, pp. 211–237.

Lancaster, N. 2009. Dune Morphology and Dynamics. In Parsons, A. J. and Abrahams, A. D. (Eds.) *Geomorphology of Desert Environments.* Second Edition. Springer Science + Business Media B.V. pp 557–596.

Mbabazi, D., Makanga, B., Orach-Meza, F., Hecky, R., Balirwa, J., Ogutu-Ohwayo, R., Verburg, P., Chapman, L., and Muhumuza, E. 2010. "Intra-lake Stable Isotope Ratio Variation in Selected Fish Species and their Possible Carbon Sources in Lake Kyoga (Uganda): Implications for Aquatic Food Web Studies." *African Journal of Ecology,* 48(3): 667–675.

Mountjoy, A. B., and Hilling, D. 1988. *Africa: Geography and Development*. London: Hutchinson Education.

Nayar, A. 2009. "A Lakeful of Trouble." *Nature*, 460(7253): 321–323.

Noury, V. 2009. "Lake Chad is Dying." *New African* 483: 22.

Nyamweru, C. K. 1996. "The African Rift System." In Adams, W. M., Goudie, A. S., and Orme, A. R. (Eds.), *The Physical Geography of Africa*. Oxford: Oxford University Press, pp. 18–33.

Okoth-Owiro, A. 2004. *The Nile Treaty: State Succession and International Treaty Commitments: A Case Study of The Nile Water Treaties*. Konrad Adenauer Foundation Law and Policy Research Foundation Occasional Papers East Africa 9. Nairobi: Konrad Adenauer Foundation Law and Policy Research Foundation.

O'Reilly, C. M., Alin, S. R., Plisnier, P-D., Cohen, A. S., and McKee, B. A. 2003. "Climate Change Decreases Aquatic Ecosystem Productivity of Lake Tanganyika, Africa." *Nature* 424(6950): 766–768.

Orme, A. R. (1996) "Coastal Environments." In Adams, W. M., Goudie, A. S. and Orme, A. R. (Eds.), *The Physical Geography of Africa*. Oxford: Oxford University Press, pp. 238–266.

Osei, W. Y., and Aryeetey-Attoh, S. 2003. "The Physical Environment." In S. Aryeetey-Attoh (Ed.), *Geography of Sub-Saharan Africa*. Second Edition. Upper Saddle River, NJ: Prentice Hall, pp. 12–47.

Owusu, K., Waylen, P., and Qiu, Y. 2008. "Changing rainfall inputs in the Volta basin: implications for water sharing in Ghana." *GeoJournal* 71:201–210.

Patsanza, M. 2010. "Mozambique: Co-existing with Floods." Global Information Network, April 23. Retrieved February 19, 2011, from Research Library.(Document ID: 2017099881).

Raisz, E. 1952. "Landform Map of North Africa." Environmental Protection Branch, Office of the Quartermaster General.

Russell, J. M., and Werne, J. P. 2009. "Climate Change and Productivity Variations Recorded by Sedimentary Sulfur in Lake Edward, Uganda/D. R. Congo." *Chemical Geology* 64(1–4) (30 June): 337–346.

Samb, S. 2007. "Environment West Africa: Niger River Arteries Clogged." *Global Information Network*. New York: Jan 2.

Semu-Banda, P. 2008. "Development-Southern Africa: Nations Agree on Zambezi Plan." *Global Information Network*, New York: December 3. Retrieved May 15, 2011, from Research Library (Document ID: 1606195851).

Sharife, K. 2009. "Damnation for Africa's Big Dams?" *African Business* 352: 52.

Silva, J. A, Eriksen, S., and Ombe, Z. A. 2010. "Double Exposure in Mozambique's Limpopo River Basin." *The Geographical Journal* 176: 6–24.

Song, A. M., and Chuenpagdee, R. 2010. "Operationalizing Governability: A Case Study of a Lake Malawi Fishery." *Fish and Fisheries*, 11: 235–249.

Stock, R. 2004. *Africa South of the Sahara: A Geographical Interpretation*. Second Edition. New York: The Guildford Press.

Thomas, D. S. G. and Shaw, P. A. 1993. "The Evolution and Characteristics the Kalahari, southern Africa." *Journal of Arid Environments* 25: 97–108.

Udo, R. K. 1982. *The Geography of Tropical Africa*. Ibadan: Heinemann Educational Books (Nigeria) Ltd.

Verburg, P., and Antenucci, J. P. 2003. "Persistent Unstable Atmospheric Boundary Layer Enhances Sensible and Latent Heat Loss in a Tropical Great Lake: Lake Tanganyika." *Journal of Geophysical Research* 115: D11109.

Verschuren, D. 2003. "The Heat on Lake Tanganyika." *Nature* 424 (6950): 731–732.

Vick, M. J. 2006. "The Senegal River Basin: A Retrospective and Prospective Look at the Legal Regime." *Natural Resources Journal* 46(1): 211–243.

CHAPTER 5

Climate, Biogeography, and Soils

Climate, biogeography (distribution of flora and fauna), and soils are the other components of the physical environment that are studied by geographers. However, unlike its geology, relief, and drainage, Africa's climate, biogeography, and soils have sometimes been subjects of misinterpretations or gross overgeneralizations. For example, Africa's climates are considered by some as universally hot, its flora and especially fauna have been portrayed as being on the brink of extinction, and its soils have been long considered as poor and infertile and for that reason a contributing factor to the continent's low agricultural productivity. In fact, Africa's climate and soils are considered by some experts as the part of Africa's economic development problems.

   This chapter describes the main characteristics of Africa's climate, biogeography, and soils, and the opportunities and challenges they present to the continent. The chapter is in four sections. The first section deals with climate, the second biogeography, the third soils, and the fourth opportunities and challenges posed by these elements. However, do the following prereading assignment first.

CLIMATE

In July of 2005, I took two of my colleagues and one student to Kampala, Uganda, for a research project. Although my colleagues were geographers, they did not think they would need jackets in July in Kampala, so they laughed when I told them to take some light jackets along, but they did it anyway. On the second day of our arrival, we were sitting in front of the Makarere University Guest House, where we were staying, waiting for our dinner orders. After 20 minutes, it became chilly enough for all of us to run inside to get our jackets. It was about 70°F (21°C), but the cool breeze from Lake Victoria reaching atop of the Makarere Hill, where we were staying made it feel like low-to-mid 50°F (16°C). Meanwhile, Stevens Point, Wisconsin, our US base, was recording temperatures in the range of 90°F (32.2°C).

PREREADING ASSIGNMENTS

1. List all that comes to mind when you think of Africa's climate and keep the list for future use.

2. List all that comes to mind when you think of Africa's biogeography (vegetation and wildlife) and keep the list for future use.

3. Go the following website: http://www.worldclimate.com/. Enter the name of the city in which you live. If you do not get any climate data try the nearest largest city. Study the climate data. Find the average highest and lowest temperatures.

4. Return to the home page of the site. Enter the name of any African city of your choice. If you do not get any climate data, try another city. Compare the climate data with those of an African city of your choice. What similarities and differences do you see?

Africa's climate is generally hot because of its tropical location. However, due to variation in **air masses**, distances from the sea, and altitude there are areas with moderate temperatures, as well as areas cold enough to have snow all year round. In this section, we begin with the factors affecting Africa's climate, followed by temperature and rainfall conditions and climatic types.

Factors Affecting Africa's Climate

The factors affecting Africa's climate are not different from those affecting climate of other places, and they include position, latitude, and shape, distance from the sea and ocean currents, altitude and air masses and pressure belts.

Position, Latitude, and Shape

As already stated, Africa's position in the tropics makes it the hottest of all the continents because it is in the tropics that the incidence of the sun is felt the most. In addition, the fact that the continent is almost bisected by the equator, coupled with the vast interior plateaus results in very small north–south temperature variations. For example, Cape Town has an average temperature of 62°F (17°C), while Tunis has 64°F (18°C), a difference of only 2°F (1°C), yet the two cities are 4,920 miles (7,917 km) apart. However, east–west temperature variations are more noticeable especially north of the Equator, where the continent is at its greatest extent. For example, Dakar (Latitude 14°N Longitude 17°W) has an average temperature of 76°F (24°C). Zinder, Chad (13°N 8°E) has 83°F (28°C), while Asmara (15°N 38°E) has 61°F (16°C) (Figure 5.1).

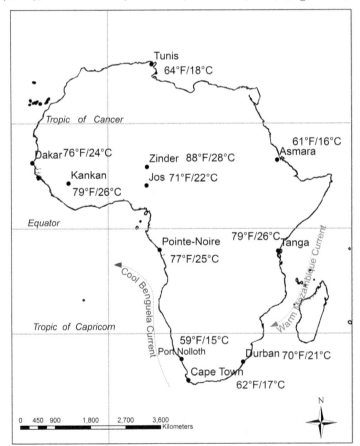

FIGURE 5.1 Effects of latitude, distance from the sea, and ocean currents.
Source: Data from ESRI and World Climate Data.

In contrast, the average temperature for Pointe-Noire, DRC (4°S 11°E) is 77°F (25°C) while that of Tanga, Tanzania (5°S 39°E) is 79°F (26°C).

Distance from the Sea and Ocean Currents

The shape of Africa is only part of the reason for the more noticeable east–west temperature variations north of the Equator. Another reason is the twin factors of distance from the sea and the influence of ocean currents. The daily phenomena of sea breeze by day and land breeze by night make places close to sea experience moderate temperatures compared to places further away. An example of this is the difference in average temperatures of Dakar and Zinder, noted above. Thus, even though the two cities are almost on the same latitude, the fact that Dakar is on the seaside and Zinder is located in the heart of northern Africa accounts for the most of the 7°F (4°C) temperature difference.

Ocean currents also influence climates by either lowering or raising the temperatures and causing rain or **drought** on the adjacent lands. For example, Durban (29°S 30°E) and Port Nolloth (26°S 16°E) in South Africa are almost on the same latitude, yet the average temperature of Durban is 70°F (21°C) while that of Port Nolloth is 59°F (15°C), a difference of about 11°F (6°C). The reason for this is Durban on the southeast coast of Africa is affected by the warm Mozambique Current, while Port Nolloth on the southwest coast is affected by the cold Benguela Currents (Figure 5.1).

Altitude

Another factor influencing the climate of Africa is altitude, which operates through the **lapse rate**. The result is that the extensive high plateaus of Africa's interior, especially in High Africa have moderating influence on the climates of those regions. This explains why several of Africa's highest mountains, which are not very far from the Equator, are snowcapped all year round. In the same vein, Nairobi (1°S 36°E) has a mean temperature of 66°F (16°C) because it is 5,450 feet (1,660 m) above sea level. In contrast, Kindu in DRC (2°S 25°E), at 1,640 feet (500 m) above sea level, has an average temperature of 76°F (24°C). Similarly, Dakar and Asmara are only one degree of latitude apart, but Asmara's average temperature is 61°F (16°C) compared to Dakar's 76°F (26°C) because Asmara is 7,628 feet (2,325 m), while Dakar is only 79 feet (24 m) above sea level (Figure 5.2).

Air Masses

Air masses are portions of the atmosphere whose physical characteristics, particularly temperature and moisture, are horizontally homogenous and at different levels (Trewartha, 1981). There are four main air masses that influence Africa's climate. These are the polar continental (cP), the polar maritime (mP), the tropical maritime (mT), and the tropical continental (cT).

The polar continental (cP) air mass The **polar continental air mass** affects Africa only in the northern hemisphere since in the southern hemisphere Africa is separated from the Antarctic by a very large expanse of ocean. The origin of the cP air mass is in Siberia, and as a result it is very cold and dry. The air mass, however, picks up some moisture across the Mediterranean before reaching North Africa.

The polar maritime (mP) air mass The **polar maritime air mass** originates from both the North and South Atlantic Ocean. It affects both northern and southern

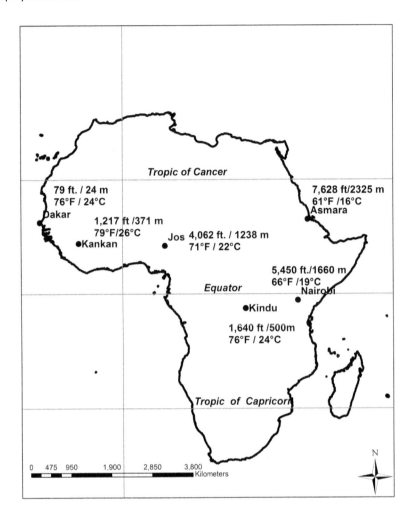

FIGURE 5.2 Effect of altitude.
Source: Data from ESRI and World Climate Data

Africa. Given its origin over water, this air mass is moisture laden and capable of bringing a lot of rains to the areas it affects.

Tropical maritime (mT) air mass Most of the air masses that affect Africa are tropical. One of them is the **tropical maritime air mass**, also called the South East Trades. The mT air mass originates in the Indian Ocean as the South East Trades. After entering the continent through the southeast coast, it moves in the northwesterly direction first crossing the continent and then sweeping across the Atlantic Ocean. On crossing the Equator, it is deflected to the right causing them to flow from south west to the north east and to be known as Southwest Monsoon. The mT air mass is warm and full of moisture and for that reason is responsible for much of the rain along the southeast coast of the continent as well as along West Africa.

The tropical continental (cT) air mass The **tropical continental air mass**, also called the Northeast Trades, originates largely from the Sahara Desert. It is very dry, dusty, and hazy, but the intense heating by day and high radiation by night also makes this air mass cold, a characteristic that is captured by the local name of *Harmatan* in West Africa.

The mT and the cT are the two most dominant air masses in Africa, and influence of either of these air masses is determined by the position of the **Inter-Tropical Convergence Zone** (ITCZ), which is front or transitional zone where the two air masses meet. In turn, the position of the ITCZ is determined by the location of the pressure belts on the continent. Generally speaking, air masses move from high-pressure belts to low-pressure belts. A low-pressure belt develops when moist air in the area rises as a result of intense heating. A high-pressure belt occurs when the opposite happens—where air descends as a result of cooling.

Temperature and Rainfall Conditions

In January, the sun's direct overhead position on the Tropic of Capricorn causes intense heating in the southern part of the continent creating a **low-pressure belt** in the south and **high-pressure belt** in the north. The cT air mass moves further south, pushing the ITCZ south to almost parallel to the west coast of Africa. The whole continent north of 5° except the northwest portion comes under the influence of the cT air mass (Figure 5.3a).

Average temperatures range from 76°F (24°C) from latitude 10°N to 73°F (23°C) south of the Tropic of Capricorn, while north of the Tropic of Cancer they actually fall to 54°F (12°C) (Figure 5.3b). However, given that the cT air mass is cold and dry, very little rain is received in the northern half of the continent. In contrast, parts of section of the continent still under the influence of the mT air mass receive rain. For example, Tamatave (Madagascar) records 16 in. (404 mm), Lusaka 9 in. (213 mm), Calabar 1.6 in. (41 mm), Kano (0.0 in.), and Cairo 0.2 in. (5 mm). This season

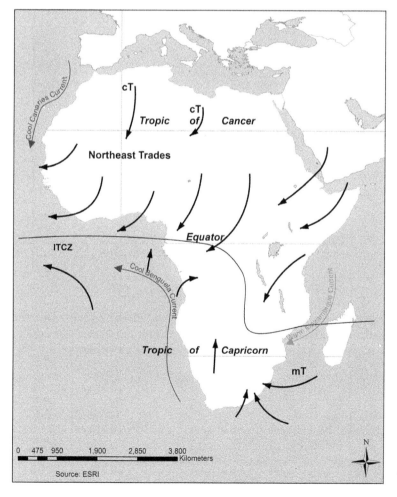

FIGURE 5.3a Air masses—December–January.
Source: Map created from Harrison Church, R. J. Clarke, J. I., Clarke, P. J. H., and Henderson, H. J. R. 1971 Africa and The Islands New York: John Wiley & Sons Inc. p. 32.

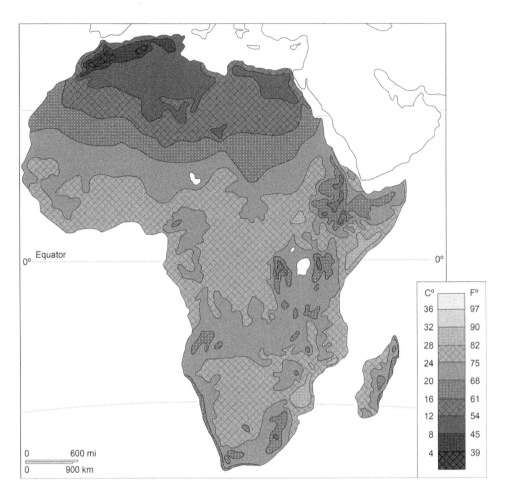

FIGURE 5.3b January temperature conditions. *Source:* Map created from Harrison Church, R. J. Clarke, J. I., Clarke, P. J. H., and Henderson, H. J. R. 1971 Africa and The Islands New York: John Wiley & Sons Inc. p. 32

referred to as the Harmatan in West Africa is characterized by very dry, relatively cold, and hazy as well as dusty conditions, with the dust coming mostly from the Sahara.

In July, the area of intense heating and low-pressure belt lies in the north around the Tropic of Cancer. The mT air mass moves northward pushing the ITCZ to between 18°N and 20°N (Figure 5.4a). A greater portion of the continent comes under the influence of the mT air mass. The average temperature at this time ranges from 91° (33°C) north of the Tropic of Cancer to 55°F (14°C) to south of the Tropic of Capricorn (Figure 5.4b). Much of the northern half of the continent receive a lot of rain. For example, Kano records an average of 8 in. (200 mm) of rain at this time. Calabar 18 in. (445 mm), both Harare and Lusaka record very little or no rain, but Tamatave records 11 in. (267 mm) because of its location in the path of the mT air mass.

Within these general patterns there are several rainfall anomalies on the continent. The two most important anomalies are those of tropical East Africa and the Guinea Coast section of central and eastern Ghana (Trewartha, 1981; Goudie, 1996). The East African case is an anomaly because it is located on the eastside of the continent, two qualifications for receiving copious rainfall. Instead, this region experiences some of Africa's most severe droughts (Camberlin and Philippon, 2002). Among the several explanations given for this anomaly is the fact the prevailing winds are parallel to the coast and the fact that the south east trades lose most of their moisture in the mountains of Madagascar before reaching the coast (Goudie, 1996).

Along the Guinea coast, there is a dry region, centered on Accra, Ghana, which is contrary to the adjacent regions of heavy rains. This has also been attributed to the trend of the coastline, which causes the rain-bearing winds to blow parallel and

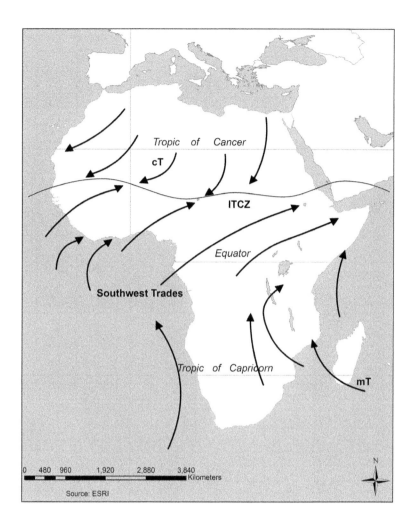

FIGURE 5.4a Air masses
June–July.
Source: Recreated with permission
from Encyclopædia Britannica,
© 2011 by Encyclopædia
Britannica, Inc

thereby unable to affect the land. The presence of cool offshore waters that also chill out the moisture causing much of the rain to fall on the ocean has also been advanced as cause of this phenomenon.

A final word about seasons. With the exception of the northwest and the southwest portions of the continent where temperature variations over the year are significant, seasons in Africa are much more determined by rainfall patterns than temperatures because of the very little variation in temperatures. For much of the continent, then there are no four but two seasons—the wet or rainy season and the dry season. The only other exception to this rule is the equatorial region, which does not experience a clear dry season.

Climatic Types

Combining these average rainfall and temperature conditions, Africa can be divided into three broad climatic types. These are tropical, temperate, and desert climatic types.

Tropical Climates

Four types of tropical climates occur in Africa—the Equatorial, the humid, wet-and-dry, and semi-dry tropical climates (Figure 5.5).

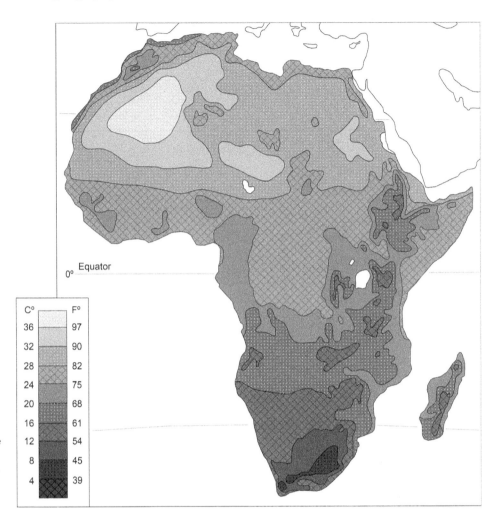

FIGURE 5.4b July temperature conditions.
Source: Recreated with permission from Encyclopædia Britannica, © 2011 by Encyclopædia Britannica, Inc

C°	F°
36	97
32	90
28	82
24	75
20	68
16	61
12	54
8	45
4	39

The Equatorial Climate The **equatorial climate** occurs in a relatively narrow belt, between 5°N and 5°S of the Equator and stretching from much of the Congo basin and along the West Africa coast to Liberia, and along the eastern coast of Madagascar. The characteristics of this climate include high temperatures, heavy rainfall, and high humidity. Average monthly temperatures are high around 77°F (25°C), but these are not the highest tropical temperatures on the continent. However, no monthly average temperature falls below 68°F (20°C). The monthly temperature range of about 5°F (3°C) is smaller than the diurnal temperature range.

Rainfall in excess of 80 in. (2,032 mm) is typical of this climate, with slight variation depending on local conditions. For example, the annual rainfall for Axim, Ghana, is 84 in. (2,133 mm), Calabar, Nigeria, is 116 in. (2,964 mm), while for Tamatave, Madagascar, it is 127 in. (3,236 mm). There is no month that is completely dry. However, rainfall occurs in two peak periods—from April through July and from September through November, with a short break in August and September. Most of the rains are of convectional type and tend to be characterized by thunderstorms. Humidity is high about 80% throughout the year (Table 5.1).

The humid tropical climate Stretching from the Equatorial climatic region to about latitudes 10°N and 10°S to the western flanks of the East African plateau, and along the southeastern coastal strip is the **humid tropical climate** region (Figure 5.6). The average temperatures here are as high as in the Equatorial climatic region,

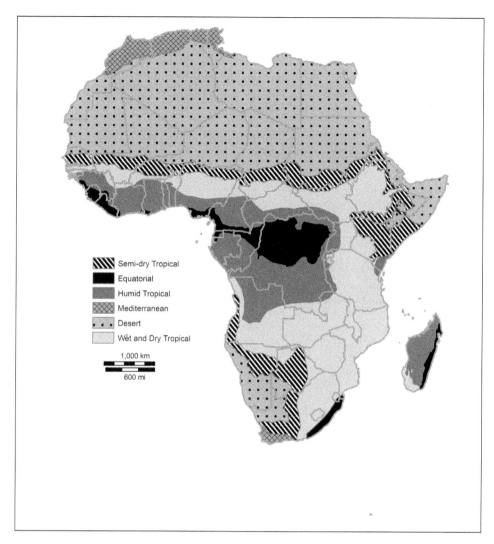

FIGURE 5.5 Africa's climatic zones.
Source: Adapted from https://www.arcgis.com/home/item.html?id=320de51a0e434fe7afb1415b159b894a

hovering between 76°F (26°C) and 82°F (30°C) (Table 5.2). For example, the temperature of Kinshasa (4.5°S) is 76°F (25°C), Enugu (6°N) is 80°F (27°C), Bouake (7°N) is 78°F (26°C), and Kankan (10°N) is 78°F (26°C). However, along the southeast coastal strip, these temperatures are moderated by elevation and distance from the sea. Thus, the average temperature of Durban is 70°F (21°C).

Rainfall amounts are less than those of the Equatorial climate, usually between 39 and 79 in. (1,000 and 2,000 mm). In addition, the double maxima peaks become more distinct with two or so months either completely dry or recording very little rainfall (Table 5.2). The only exception is on the southeastern coastal region where because of the effects of ocean currents, Durban, for example, has no month that is completely dry (Table 5.2).

The wet and dry tropical climate Surrounding the humid tropical climatic region on the north, south and eastern flanks is the wet and dry tropical climatic type. Next to the desert climatic type, the wet and dry tropical climate is the most extensive of Africa's climates. Temperature conditions of this climatic type are also similar to those of the Equatorial and the humid tropical climates, especially in the northern hemisphere. For example, Bamako (13°N) has an average temperature of 82°F (30°C). South of the Equator and on the East African plateau, however, higher elevation moderates the

TABLE 5.1

Average Temperature and Rainfall Data of Selected Stations of the Equatorial Climate

Station			J	F	M	A	M	J	J	A	S	O	N	D	Year
Axim	Temp	°F	78.9	80.5	80.5	80.9	79.8	78.2	77.2	76.0	76.8	78.1	78.8	78.7	78.7
		°C	26.0	27.0	27.2	27.1	26.6	25.7	25.1	24.5	24.9	25.6	26.0	26.3	25.9
	Rain	in.	1.9	2.5	5.2	6.3	15.5	22.5	6.6	2.2	3,2	7.7	6.7	3.7	84.0
		mm	47.4	64.2	132.4	158.8	393.7	570.9	168.4	55.8	80.6	194.5	170.5	94.7	2132.6
Calabar	Temp	°F	79.0	80.4	80.6	80.4	79.9	78.4	77.0	76.6	77.2	77.9	79.0	79.2	78.8
		°C	26.1	26.9	27.0	26.9	26.6	25.8	25.0	24.8	25.1	25.5	26.1	26.2	26.0
	Rain	in.	1.6	2.7	6.2	8.5	11.5	15.5	17.5	16.0	16.1	12.2	6.9	2.0	116.7
		mm	40.6	68.6	157.5	215.9	292.1	393.7	444.5	406.4	408.9	309.9	175.3	50.8	2964.2
Tamatave	Temp	°F	78.6	79.0	77.7	76.3	73.0	69.8	68.4	68.5	70.2	72.5	75.4	77.5	73.8
		°C	25.9	26.1	25.4	24.6	22.8	21.0	20.2	20.3	21.2	22.5	24.1	25.3	23.2
	Rain	in.	15.9	14.6	19.0	12.2	9.3	10.5	10.5	8.1	5.2	4.8	6.0	11.4	127.5
		mm	403.9	370.8	482.6	309.9	236.2	266.7	266.7	205.7	132.1	121.9	152.4	289.6	3236.0

Source: WorldClimate (www.worldclimate.com).

TABLE 5.2

Average Temperature and Rainfall Data Selected Stations with of the Humid Tropics Climate

Station			J	F	M	A	M	J	J	A	S	O	N	D	Year
Enugu, Nigeria	Temp	°F	79.9	82.8	83.8	82.6	80.8	79.0	77.7	77.7	78.1	79.0	79.9	79.0	80.1
		°C	26.5	28.2	28.8	28.1	27.1	26.1	25.4	25.4	25.6	26.1	26.6	26.1	26.7
	Rain	in.	0.7	0.9	3.0	5.6	9.5	10.3	8.4	7.4	12.1	9.1	1.6	0.4	68.9
		mm	17.5	23.4	75.3	141.8	241.6	262.4	212.5	187.6	308.4	230.6	39.9	11.0	1,749.2
Kinshasa, DRC	Temp	°F	77.4	77.1	77.5	77.7	76.6	73.2	70.9	73.2	76.1	77.2	76.8	77.0	76.1
		°C	25.2	25.1	25.3	25.4	24.8	22.9	21.6	22.9	24.5	25.1	24.9	25.0	24.5
	Rain	in.	5.4	5.8	7.2	8.6	5.7	0.2	0.1	0.1	1.6	5.2	9.3	6.1	55.3
		mm	137.2	147.3	182.9	218.4	144.8	5.1	2.5	2.5	40.6	132.1	236.2	154.9	1,404.6
Durban, South Africa	Temp	°F	75.7	76.1	74.7	71.4	67.1	63.5	63.0	64.8	66.9	68.9	71.4	73.9	69.8
		°C	24.3	24.5	23.7	21.9	19.5	17.5	17.2	18.2	19.4	20.5	21.9	23.3	21.0
	Rain	in.	4.7	5.0	5.2	3.3	2.2	1.3	1.4	1.9	2.9	4.3	4.6	4.7	41.6
		mm	119.4	127.0	132.1	83.8	55.9	33.0	35.6	48.3	73.7	109.2	116.8	119.4	1,056.6

Source: WorldClimate (www.worldclimate.com).

temperatures. For example, Kampala, almost on the Equator but at 3,753 feet (1,144 m) above sea level, has an average temperature of 70°F (21°C). Similarly, Lubumbashi at 4,186 feet (1,276 m) has an average temperature of 68°F (20°C) (Table 5.3).

However, once again, it is the rainfall characteristics that set this climate apart from the humid tropics. In general, rainfall amounts range between 20 and 39 in. (500 and 1,000 mm), except for a few areas where relief rainfall occurs. The double maxima rainfall peaks merge into one peak, with at least four months of the year without rain, making the dry season more distinct. For example, Bamako has an annual rainfall of 40 in. (1,018 mm) with each of November through April recording

TABLE **5.3**

Average Temperature and Rainfall Data of Selected Stations of the Wet and Dry Tropical Climate

Station			J	F	M	A	M	J	J	A	S	O	N	D	Year
Bamako, Mali	Temp	°F	77.0	82.2	87.1	90.3	88.7	84.0	79.9	78.4	79.5	81.7	80.2	76.8	82.2
		°C	25.0	27.9	30.6	32.4	31.5	28.9	26.6	25.8	26.4	27.6	26.8	24.9	27.9
	Rain	in.	0.0	0.0	0.1	0.8	2.35	5.2	9.0	12.1	7.8	2.5	0.3	0.0	40.1
		mm	0.4	0.1	3.3	19.2	59.1	131.1	229.2	306.5	198.4	62.8	7.1	0.4	1,018.2
Kampala, Uganda	Temp	°F	77.4	77.1	77.5	77.7	76.6	73.2	70.9	73.2	76.1	77.2	76.8	77.0	76.1
		°C	25.2	25.1	25.3	25.4	24.8	22.9	21.6	22.9	24.5	25.1	24.9	25.0	24.5
	Rain	in.	2.3	2.7	5.0	7.3	5.3	2.8	2.2	3.4	3.9	4.7	5.6	3.7	49.0
		mm	137.2	147.3	182.9	218.4	144.8	5.1	2.5	2.5	40.6	132.1	236.2	154.9	1,404.6
Lubumbashi, DRC	Temp	°F	69.3	68.5	69.1	69.3	65.8	62.4	63.7	66.0	71.6	73.6	70.9	68.7	68.2
		°C	20.7	20.3	20.6	20.7	18.8	16.9	17.6	18.9	22.0	23.1	21.6	20.4	20.1
	Rain	in.	10.0	10.1	8.3	2.0	0.2	0.0	0.0	0.0	0.2	1.2	5.9	10.7	48.2
		mm	253.4	256.4	210.4	50.8	4.2	0.6	0.0	0.3	6.3	30.6	150.0	272.2	1,223.4

Source: WorldClimate (www.worldclimate.com).

less than 1 in. (15 mm). In the southern hemisphere, Lubumbashi has an annual rainfall of 48 in. (1,223 mm) with no rain in June, July, and August (Table 5.3).

The semi-dry tropical climate The **semi-dry tropical climate** lies between the wet and dry tropical and the tropical desert climates and in North Africa between the desert climate and the Mediterranean climatic type. In the northern half of the continent, this climatic type records some of the hottest average monthly temperatures

TABLE **5.4**

Average Temperature and Rainfall Data of Selected Stations of the Semi-Dry Tropical Climate

Station			J	F	M	A	M	J	J	A	S	O	N	D	Year
Gao, Mali	Temp	°F	72.7	77.5	84.4	90.3	95.4	94.8	90.1	87.1	89.1	89.4	91.9	74.3	85.5
		°C	22.6	25.3	29.1	32.4	35.2	34.9	32.3	30.6	31.7	31.9	27.7	23.5	29.7
	Rain	in.	0.0	0.0	0.0	0.1	0.3	0.9	2.8	4.0	1.3	0.2	0.0	0.0	9.5
		mm	0.5	0.0	0.5	1.8	6.4	22.6	70.9	100.5	33.9	4.4	0.1	0.1	241.2
Francistown, Botswana	Temp	°F	77.7	76.3	74.1	69.6	63.5	57.6	57.7	63.0	70.0	75.2	76.5	76.3	69.8
		°C	25.4	24.6	23.4	20.9	17.5	14.2	14.3	17.2	21.1	24.0	24.7	24.6	21.0
	Rain	in.	3.9	3.3	2.4	1.0	0.3	0.1	0.0	0.0	0.3	1.1	2.3	3.6	18.3
		mm	100.0	84.4	60.4	24.2	6.9	2.6	0.4	1.0	6.4	27.0	59.4	91.3	464.7
Windhoek. Namibia	Temp	°F	73.9	71.8	69.8	66.0	60.6	55.8	55.8	60.4	66.6	70.9	72.5	74.1	66.6
		°C	23.3	22.1	21.0	18.9	15.9	13.2	13.2	15.8	19.2	21.6	22.5	23.4	66.6
	Rain	in.	3.1	3.2	3.1	1.5	0.3	0.0	0.0	0.0	0.1	0.5	1.1	1.6	14.4
		mm	78.1	80.3	78.7	37.7	6.6	1.2	0.7	0.9	2.8	11.8	26.9	41.7	365.1

Source: WorldClimate (www.worldclimate.com).

in Africa, with several months exceeding 90°F (32°C). For example, the average temperature of Gao is 86°F (29°C), but from April through July, the average temperatures exceed 90°F (32°C). South of the Equator, elevation and distance from the sea moderate the average monthly temperatures. For example, the average temperature of Francistown, Botswana at 3,284 feet (1001 m) is 70°F (21°C), while that of Windhoek at 5,669 feet (1,728 m) is 67°F (19°C) (Table 5.4).

Annual rainfall of this climatic type ranges from 20 in. (500 mm) or less, with almost all of it occurring in the two to three months. Thus, there are at least six months without rain. For example, Gao that is north of the Equator receives an annual rainfall of 9.5 in. (241 mm), while south of the Equator, Windhoek receives 14 in. (365 mm) (Table 5.4).

Desert Climates

Covering the entire region of the Sahara, the Namib, the Kalahari, and the Horn of Africa, the desert climate is the most extensive climatic type of Africa. Even so, this is not a homogenous climatic type. Instead, there are two subtypes—the tropical or hot desert and moderate or subtropical desert type.

The hot desert climate The hot desert climatic type is characterized by high average temperatures and very little rain, if any. This occurs in the Sahara south of the Tropic of Cancer and in the Horn of Africa. The average temperature of this climate type is 83°F (28°C). However, there are at least two months in which average temperatures reach over 90°F (32°C). For example, the average temperature of Agadez, Niger, is 83°F (28°C) with May and June averages topping 90°F (32°C) each. Faya-Largeau, Chad also has an average temperature of 83°F (28°C) but the average temperatures for each month from May through August exceed 90°F (31°C). The most remarkable feature about the temperatures of the hot desert climate is the large diurnal range. High day temperatures are usually followed by very high nighttime radiation leading to below freezing temperatures at night (Table 5.5).

TABLE **5.5**

Average Temperature and Rainfall Data of Selected Stations of the Tropical Desert Climate

Station			J	F	M	A	M	J	J	A	S	O	N	D	Year
Agadez, Niger	Temp	°F	68.2	72.9	81.0	88.5	93.0	92.5	89.4	87.1	88.9	85.3	76.5	68.8	82.9
		°C	20.1	22.7	27.2	31.4	33.9	33.6	31.9	30.6	31.6	29.6	24.7	21.0	28.3
	Rain	in.	0.0	0.0	0.0	0.1	0.2	0.4	1.6	2.8	0.5	0.0	0.0	0.0	5.6
		mm	0.0	0.0	0.0	1.3	5.6	9.1	41.3	71.9	13.2	0.2	0.0	0.0	143.4
Faya-Largeau Chad	Temp	°F	68.9	72.5	79.2	86.9	92.1	93.4	91.9	90.9	90.7	85.6	76.6	70.2	83.3
		°C	25.4	24.6	23.4	20.9	17.5	14.2	14.3	17.2	21.1	24.0	24.7	24.6	21.0
	Rain	in.	0.0	0.0	0.0	0.0	0.0	0.0	0.2	0.4	0.0	0.0	0.0	0.0	0.7
		mm	0.0	0.0	0.0	0.0	0.0	0.0	5.1	10.2	0.0	0.0	0.0	0.0	17.8
Wadi Halfa, Sudan	Temp	°F	60.6	63.5	71.2	79.9	87.1	89.8	90.0	90.3	87.1	83.1	72.7	63.9	78.3
		°C	15.9	17.5	21.8	26.6	30.6	32.1	32.2	32.4	30.6	28.4	22.6	17.7	25.7
	Rain	in.	0.0	0.0	0.0	0.0	0.0	0.0	0.0	0.0	0.0	0.0	0.0	0.0	0.1
		mm	0.1	0.0	0.0	0.0	0.8	0.0	0.6	0.2	0.0	0.3	0.0	0.1	2.3

Source: WorldClimate (www.worldclimate.com).

TABLE **5.6**

Average Temperature and Rainfall Data of Selected Stations of the Subtropical Desert Climate

Station			J	F	M	A	M	J	J	A	S	O	N	D	Year
Tindouf, Algeria	Temp	°F	55.8	61.0	65.8	69.6	76.1	81.9	93.7	93.0	83.1	74.7	64.9	55.8	73.0
		°C	13.2	16.1	18.8	20.9	24.5	27.7	34.3	33.9	28.4	23.7	18.3	13.2	22.8
	Rain	in.	0.1	0.1	0.1	0.1	0.0	0.0	0.0	0.1	0.3	0.4	0.3	0.3	1.7
		mm	3.3	2.4	3.8	1.7	0.6	0.0	0.1	1.9	7.5	8.9	6.6	7.0	43.9
Cairo, Egypt	Temp	°F	56.8	59.4	63.3	70.5	76.5	81.1	82.2	82.2	79.3	74.7	66.4	59.2	71.1
		°C	13.8	15.2	17.4	21.4	24.7	27.3	27.9	27.9	26.3	23.7	19.1	15.1	21.7
	Rain	in.	0.2	0.1	0.1	0.1	0.0	0.0	0.0	0.0	0.0	0.0	0.1	0.2	1.0
		mm	5.1	3.8	3.7	1.5	1.0	0.2	0.0	0.0	0.0	0.1	2.5	5.7	24.8
Tshane, Botswana	Temp	°F	77.7	78.4	75.4	68.0	60.1	54.1	54.9	60.3	69.4	73.0	76.8	78.8	68.9
		°C	25.4	25.8	24.1	20.0	15.6	12.3	12.7	15.7	20.8	22.8	24.9	26.0	20.5
	Rain	in.	3.4	2.9	2.7	1.4	0.3	0.1	0.0	0.0	0.1	0.6	1.3	1.4	356.9
		mm	85.3	74.2	68.4	34.6	6.9	3.3	1.0	0.5	3.8	16.0	32.1	36.3	14.1

Source: WorldClimate (www.worldclimate.com).

Rainfall in the hot desert climate is very scanty, if any, and rarely exceeds 6 in. (150 mm). For example, Agadez receives an annual rainfall of 7 in. (143 mm), but both Faya-Largeau and Wadi Halfa receive less than 1 in. (3 mm) a year (Table 5.5).

The subtropical desert climate The subtropical desert climate occurs in the Sahara north of the Tropic of Cancer and in the Kalahari and the Namib Deserts of the southern portion of the continent. Average temperatures are lower than the hot desert climate, averaging about 70°F (21°C), and in the Kalahari, there is even a little more rain than the hot desert climate. For example, in the Sahara, the average temperature of Tindouf, Algeria, is 73°F (22°C), while the average temperature of Cairo is 70°F (21°C). In terms of rainfall, Tindouf receives 2 in. (44 mm), while Cairo receives only 1 in. (28 mm). In the Kalahari, Ghanzi's average temperature is 71°F (21°C) and the total rainfall is 17 in. (428 mm) (Table 5.6).

Mediterranean (West Temperate) Climate

Mediterranean or the West Temperate climate occurs in the southwest and northwest sections of the continent. The main characteristic of this climatic type is the hot dry summers and mild wet winters. Average temperatures range from 62°F (17°C) to 64°F (18°C). For example, Cape Town's average temperature is 62°F (17°C), same as Algiers; while Tunis and Rabat have 64°F (18°C). Annual rainfall is usually less than 39 in. (1,000 mm)—for example, Cape Town has 24 in. (612 mm), Algiers 26 in. (660 mm), and Tunis 21 in. (446 mm)—with virtually all of it falling in the winter months, from October through February in the north and May through August in the south (Table 5.7).

TABLE **5.7**

Average Temperature and Rainfall Data of Selected Stations of the Mediterranean Climate

Station			J	F	M	A	M	J	J	A	S	O	N	D	Year
Algiers, Algeria	Temp	°F	50.7	51.8	54.3	58.1	63.1	69.4	74.7	75.9	72.1	65.5	58.3	52.7	62.2
		°C	10.4	11.0	12.4	14.5	17.3	20.8	23.7	24.4	22.3	18.6	14.6	11.5	16.8
	Rain	in.	4.0	3.3	3.0	2.3	1.5	0.6	0.1	0.2	1.3	3.4	4.3	5.1	29.1
		mm	102.8	82.9	76.4	58.5	38.8	15.1	2.4	5.4	32.5	85.5	109.3	129.3	739.4
Tunis, Tunisia	Temp	°F	51.1	52.3	55.2	59.4	65.5	73.0	78.4	79.3	75.2	67.6	59.7	53.2	64.2
		°C	10.6	11.3	12.9	15.2	18.6	22.8	25.8	26.3	24.0	19.8	15.4	11.8	17.9
	Rain	in.	2.4	2.1	1.8	1.5	0.9	0.4	0.1	0.3	1.3	2.2	2.1	2.5	17.6
		mm	61.6	52.4	45.6	38.4	22.2	10.4	3.3	7.2	32.0	54.9	53.5	62.9	446.1
Cape Town, South Africa	Temp	°F	69.8	70.2	68.0	63.3	59.2	55.9	54.5	55.4	57.7	61.2	68.4	67.8	62.2
		°C	21.0	21.2	20.0	17.4	15.1	13.3	12.5	13.0	14.3	16.2	1.6	19.9	16.8
	Rain	in.	0.6	0.6	0.9	1.9	3.6	4.1	3.6	3.3	2.1	1.6	1.0	0.8	24.1
		mm	15.9	15.2	21.6	49.5	91.7	105.4	91.2	82.6	54.3	39.6	24.2	19.3	612.5

Source: WorldClimate (www.worldclimate.com).

BIOGEOGRAPHY

Associated with these climatic types are vegetation, fauna, and soils. Africa's vegetation falls into four broad classes—forests, grasslands, desert, and mountain vegetation. The main types of these classes are the tropical rain forest, warm temperate forest, woodland savanna, dry savanna, semi-desert, temperate grassland, desert, and mountain vegetation (Figure 5.6).

Tropical Rain Forest

This is the vegetation of the Equatorial and the adjacent humid tropical climates—and is found in the Congo Basin, the West African coast, and the Eastern coast of Madagascar. The tropical rain forest has the highest biodiversity of all of Africa's vegetation. Plant stands occur in three layers—upper, middle, and the undergrowth. The upper layer consists of isolated tall trees that reach 164 feet (50 m), many of them with large buttresses that reach 9–13 feet (3–4 m) high. The middle layer consists of trees between 65 and 100 feet (20–30 m) tall with crowns so thick that they form a canopy. The bottom layer consists of scanty undergrowth, which is caused by insufficient light through the middle layer canopy. In addition to these, there is a large number of climbing plants or lianas that festoon the trees of the middle and top layers, while epiphytes such as orchids are also common on the top of the canopy layer (Meadows, 1996; Grainger, 1996). Among the common tree species are the African mahogany, obeche or wawa, sapele, and the oil palm. However, none of these occurs in pure stands.

As with other features, Africa's tropical rain forest is not homogenous but has several variations. Thus, the true rain forest, which is evergreen, is found at the core of the Congo Basin and along the coast of West Africa. North and south of this occurs semi-evergreen or deciduous forest in which trees of the upper layer shed their leaves during the dry season. Along the coast of Gambia, Guinea, Guinea-Bissau, the

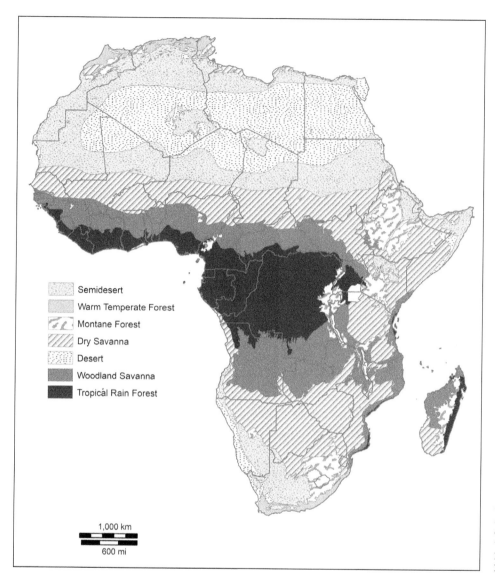

FIGURE 5.6 Vegetation
of Africa.
Source: Created from https://
databasin.org/datasets/68635d7c
77f1475f9b6c1d1dbe0a4c4c
https://www.climond.org/
Koppen.aspx

Niger Delta, Cameroon and Gabon, a tropical wetland forest dominated by mangrove trees is more prevalent. The tropical rain forest is home to numerous game and wildlife. Among the most well-known are the bangos, bonobos, buffaloes, chimpanzees, mountain gorillas, giraffes, elephants, bushbucks, and duikers.

Warm Temperate (Mediterranean) Forest

Warm temperate forest is found in the few areas on the continent that have Mediterranean type of climate. In Southwest Africa, the most extensive of this type of vegetation is the *fynbos*, an Afrikaan term that means fine bush. This vegetation consists of evergreen shrubs and trees that vary in height. On sandy soils, the fynbos is replaced by *strandveldt*, a combination of fynbos and thicket type of vegetation. Trees are of medium height between 50 and 100 feet (15 and 30 m) high. In addition, their leaves have smaller surface areas and tend to be hardy and reflective so that they reflect much of the sunlight during the hot and dry summers. Trees occur in pure stands compared to tropical rainforest and the woodland savanna.

In North Africa, temperate forests are found in the Morocco, Algeria, and Tunisia, mostly in the mountainous regions. In the humid regions, tree species include firs, maritime pines, cedars, and deciduous oaks. In the semi-dry and drier lower slopes, the true temperate forest is replaced by marquis, a type of degraded forest due to a combination of human and natural factors. Trees are smaller and shorter and stand volume is low. Dominant tree species here include Aleppo pines, evergreen oaks, cork oak, and junipers (McGregor et al., 2009; Ellatif, 2005; Nedjahi and Zamoum, 2005).

Tropical Woodland

Tropical woodland savanna is the vegetation associated with the outer fringes of the humid tropics and the tropical **wet and dry climates**. This is the largest vegetation type of Africa. However, it is a transitional vegetation between the rain forest and the savanna or tropical grassland vegetation. As a result, the areas adjacent to the rain forest are dominated by secondary forest—which in many places consists of a mixture of natural trees and planted tree crops. The three-layered structure of the rain forest changes gradually to very few tall trees, open canopy, and for that reason relatively thick and shrubby undergrowth. Many of the trees here are deciduous, shedding their leaves during the long dry season. Trees are usually 50–65 feet (15–20 m) tall.

As distance increases from the rain forest, tree density declines and the undergrowth transitions from shrubs into tall savanna forming wooded savanna vegetation. The most common tree species include the shea butter tree, the baobab, and several species of acacias, such as acacia tortilla (umbrella tree), and the sausage tree. In West Africa, this vegetation is called *Guinea savanna* woodland; in Southern, Central, and Eastern Africa, it is called *miombo* forest, while in South Africa, it is called the *bushveld*.

The tropical woodland and wooded savanna vegetation is home to most of Africa's wildlife reserves and for that reason support a large number of Africa's fauna (Osei and Aryeetey-Attoh, 2003). These include the savanna elephants, baboons, cheetahs, lions, rhinoceros, waterbucks, hyenas, giraffes, hartebeest, impalas, gazelles, zebras, roan antelopes, and wildebeest.

Dry or Sudan Savanna

Dry savanna is the vegetation of the dry and wet climate. The tall grass of the wooded savanna transitions into short grass of dry savanna vegetation. Trees are shorter, smaller, fewer, and much more scattered, usually occurring in bush thickets. In addition, the trees here are accustomed to the long dry periods. Thus, they have thick juicy barks, deep roots, and are deciduous. The few dominant ones include the baobab and various species of acacias. This type of vegetation belt is sometimes referred to as **Sudan savanna** vegetation. The common animals of this vegetation type include the oryx, aardvarks, ostriches, elands, warthogs, steenboks, and cheetahs.

Semi-Desert or Sahel

The semi-desert vegetation is associated with the semi-arid climate. This is also a transitional vegetation between the dry savanna and the desert vegetation. In order to survive the very long dry season, trees here are shorter, thinner, thornier, and less woody. The most dominant plant here is cactus. However, short and hardy grass interspersed more often with sandy or hard baked bare ground dominate the vegetation. This is sometimes referred to as the **Sahel savanna** or Sahel for short. Animals here include eland, cheetahs, suricate, lions, and leopards.

Desert

Vegetation of the desert climate is restricted only to oases, which are fertile or water spots in the desert. The single most important tree vegetation of these areas is the date palm. Mature date palms may reach up to 100 feet (30 m) tall, and they usually occur in concentrations in the oases. In addition to the date palm, other plants that are part of the desert vegetation are African Welwitchsia, cypress, olive, and the African Peyote Cactus. These plants are very hardy and adaptable to the harsh environment of their habitat.

Temperate Grassland

Temperate grassland occurs in the areas of Africa with long hot summer months. The vegetation is predominantly grassland interspersed with various kinds of geophytes or bulbs. The grass may consist of various species such as sweet grass as well as sour grass. The only area of Africa with substantive cover of this vegetation type is the High Veldt of South Africa, an area bordered on the east by the Drakensberg, to the south by the Upper Karroo, to the west by the Kalahari, and to the north by the bushveld.

Mountain Vegetation

Mountain vegetation is essentially mixed vegetation that is differentiated by altitude and is therefore restricted to Africa's high mountains. Hedberg (1957), who did the pioneering work in this area, identified three vegetation zones: the Montane Forest Zone below 9,842 feet (3,000 m), the Ericaceae Zone between 9,842 and 11,811 feet (3,000 and 3,600), and the Alpine or Afroalpine Zone above 11,811 feet (3,600 m). According to Hedberg, the vegetation of the Montane Forest Zone consists of broad-leaved hardwood trees, bamboos and parkland, and East African rosewoods (Taylor, 1996). The vegetation in the Ericaceae Zone consists mostly of low evergreen shrubs, while the Afroalpine zone consists largely of giant lobelias, a type of flowering plant.

SOILS

The soils of Africa have long been subjected to sweeping generalizations and oversimplifications (Areola, 1996). The most pervasive of these overgeneralizations was the classification of all African soils as lateritic and for that matter poor. Research now shows that not all African soils are lateritic.

Identification of major soil types in Africa has been done through several classification systems. The two that are often used by researchers are the Food and Agricultural Organization (FAO)—United Nations Educational and Scientific Organization (UNESCO) system and the Soil Taxonomy System of the United States Department of Agriculture (USDA). According to the US system, Africa has no less than 13 major soil groups, of which the largest are oxisols, alfisols, utisols, aridisols, entisols, and dunes, pans or rocklands (Figure 5.7).

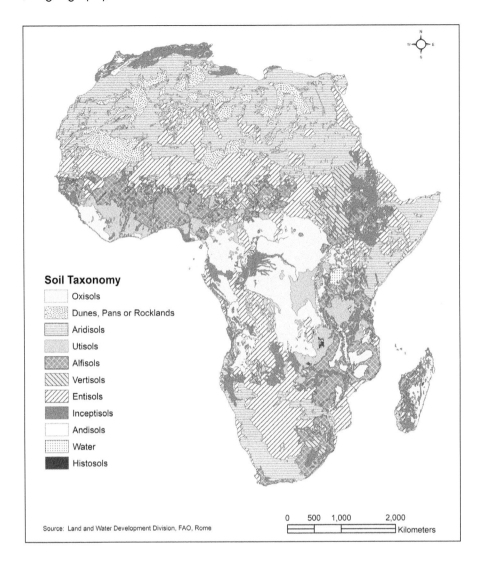

FIGURE 5.7 Major soil types of Africa.
Created from World Soils Resources, International Programs Division, USDA/Natural resources Services/ Office of Agriculture, Global Programs, USAID Distribution of Soil Orders, 1996. https://www.nrcs. usda.gov/Internet/FSE_MEDIA/ nrcs142p2_050338.gif

Soil Taxonomy
- Oxisols
- Dunes, Pans or Rocklands
- Aridisols
- Utisols
- Alfisols
- Vertisols
- Entisols
- Inceptisols
- Andisols
- Water
- Histosols

Source: Land and Water Development Division, FAO, Rome

0   500   1,000   2,000
Kilometers

Oxisols

Oxisols are the soils of Africa's equatorial rain forest region and parts of the humid tropics and savanna woodland. Thus, they occupy most of the Congo Basin, Sierra Leone, Liberia, southwest Ghana, and eastern Madagascar, with isolated pockets in Gabon and Angola. Eswaran et al. (1986) estimated that oxisols occupy about 14.3% of Africa's land area. These soils are red and yellow in color and are heavily weathered and leached. They have high content of clay, iron, and aluminum oxides, but no weatherable minerals. This makes them physically strong but chemically poor (Areola, 1996).

Utisols

Utisols are the soils of the rest of the humid tropical climate and the savanna woodland vegetation zone, including Guinea, much of Cote d'Ivoire, west central Ghana, the Niger-Benue corridor, western portion of Congo Basin, Zambia, and much of Tanzania. In all they cover about 6.2% of Africa according to Eswaran et al. (1986).

Like oxisols, utisols are also heavily weathered and leached soils. They are reddish or yellowish in color due to the presence of iron oxides. As a result of the heavy weathering and leaching, utisols have more concentration of clay and iron oxides in the top horizons and less of primary minerals such as calcium, magnesium, and potassium. For this reason, they are of poor quality without the use of fertilizer.

Alfisols

Taking up 10.5% of Africa are the alfisols, the main soils of the wet and dry tropical climate and the dry savanna vegetation zone. However, in Cote d'Ivoire, Ghana, Togo, Benin, and Nigeria, they also constitute the soils of the humid tropical climate and the woodland savanna vegetation zones. Alfisols are lightly leached soils and as a result, they have a relatively higher concentration of clay, aluminum, and iron in their subsoils. Alfisols are among the richest soils in Africa, although they are still considered deficient in nitrogen and phosphorus compared to those of other regions of the world. Alfisols have five suborders three of which pertain to Africa. The three are udalfs found in the humid tropics, ustalfs, in the wet and dry and semi-arid environments, and xeralfs in the Mediterranean climatic region.

Aridisols

About 26.4% of Africa is covered by aridisols, the main soils of the semi-dry and desert environments—including the Sahara, the Kalahari, and much of the Horn of Africa. Without much vegetation to add organic matter, aridisols are light in color. In relatively moist areas, these may be leached, while over large areas they are covered by sanddunes, pans, and rocklands. These conditions make aridisols not suitable for agriculture (Eswaran et al 1997).

Vertisols

Vertisols have about 50–70% clay content and for that reason are able to expand with moisture and contract in dry conditions. They are found mostly in Southern Sudan and isolated pockets in Southern Africa as well as West Africa. In the Sudan, they underlay much of the Gezira Plain, while in West Africa, they are found in the Lake Chad Basin. There are also considerable concentrations in Zimbabwe, Kenya, Somalia, and on the southern borders of the Sahel. The high clay content of these soils make tilling difficult for local people, even though the use of machinery and irrigation have led to successful farming in some vertisols regions such as Sudan's Gezira Scheme (Eswaran et al 1997).

Other Soils

All these soils have formed and developed over a very long period and so they have well-developed profiles and for that matter, horizons. However, there are other soil orders that are either relatively young or do not have properly developed horizons. Two of these are **entisols** and **inceptisols** (Osei and Aryeetey-Attoh, 2003). Entisols are the largest group of soils in Africa. They are therefore a very diverse group of soils. According to Eswaran et al. (1997), about 50% of entisols are acidic in nature. They cover much of the tropical dry and wet climate and the Sudan savanna vegetation regions. Inceptisols are also young soils that are more developed than entisols, yet lack clearly defined horizon characteristics like the other soils. These soils have no accumulation of clays, iron, aluminum, or organic matter. They are found in the Niger Delta and in the Congo Basin (Osei, 2003).

NATURE'S OPPORTUNITIES AND CHALLENGES

Africa's physical environment presents many opportunities and challenges to human life. Among the opportunities are limited natural hazards, abundance mineral wealth, abundant wildlife habitat, and abundant sunshine and long growing season. Among the challenges are climate change and **desertification**.

Nature's Opportunities

Limited Natural Hazards

In terms of natural hazards such as earthquakes, volcanic eruptions, tornadoes, hurricanes, winter snow storms and blizzards, and summer heat waves, Africa is a blessed continent. The geologic structure of the continent is so strong and stable that it records very little earthquakes and volcanic eruptions. It is true that there are active volcanoes on the continent, but major volcanic eruptions are rare. In terms of weather hazards, severe thunderstorm occurs, but it is not anywhere close to the devastating effects of tornados or tropical cyclones. With the universally warm temperatures, snowfall and all its associated hazardous weather events do not occur in Africa.

Abundance of Mineral Wealth

Africa's geological history has also endowed it with abundant mineral resources. As we will see later in Chapter 10, Africa's mineral wealth has few comparisons in the world today. Thus, after almost two centuries of domestic and foreign exploitation and in some cases plunder, Africa still has the world's largest reserves of chrome, platinum, manganese, tantalite, platinum, cobalt, diamonds, gold, phosphate rocks, and bauxite. It is most likely that more known and unknown mineral deposits and reserves will be either identified or estimated in the future.

Abundant Wildlife Habitat

Africa abounds in wildlife. During the 18th and 19th centuries, this abundant wildlife attracted large hunting parties from outside the continent, and today, it is perhaps the leading attraction of visitors to the continent. Africa's forest and savanna regions are home to some of the world's largest land mammals. Among these are the African elephant, hippopotamus, various species of giraffes, lions, rhinoceros, warthogs, mountain gorillas, wildebeest, cheetahs, and zebras. In addition to these, are a whole host of birds and reptiles. It is the only place in the world where large herds of these animals can be seen roaming in the wild. It is true that a lot of these have been achieved through aggressive wildlife programs, but it takes a conducive habitat to support such large numbers of animals in the wild to accomplish this and for that Africa's physical environment must be credited.

Abundant Sunshine and Long Growing Season

Africa's abundant sunshine has often been seen as negative because of the intense heat associated with it. However, whether this intensity of heat is worse than freezing cold temperatures, winter snow storms and blizzards, slippery roads, and the cost of staying alive is debatable. Besides, with plenty of sunshine and warm temperatures all year round than most parts of the world, the only factor limiting year-round cultivation of crops in Africa is water. There is nowhere in the world that has such an advantage is present on such an extensive area of geographic space. All these features have become problems because Africa is yet to figure out how to turn these physical features into resources.

Nature's Challenges

The challenges Africa's physical environment poses are many. They include uneven distribution of natural resources, climate change, erratic rainfall, drought, desertification, species extinction, and deforestation. We will, however, discuss three of these: unequal distribution of natural resources, climate change, and desertification.

Unequal Distribution of Natural Resources

Africa's rich natural resources are unevenly distributed relative to its current political structure. As we will see in subsequent chapters, a far greater proportion of its known agricultural, energy, forest, and mineral resources are either located in a particular region or dominated by a handful of countries. For example, South Africa dominates the mineral wealth of the continent. While this could be partially blamed on the part of the political structure of the continent, it is at the same a challenge to have overconcentration of certain resources in a small portion of such a huge continent.

Climate Change

The evidence The concern about climate change seems to be a relatively recent development, but as a phenomenon, climate change has been going on for a very long time. As mentioned in Chapter 4, the first significant episode of climate change in Africa that there is some evidence on began in the Cenozoic Era (about 66.4 million years ago). Before this time, the whole world, including Africa, experienced much warmer and more equitable climate, with tropical conditions extending to paleo latitude 45°N. However, temperatures began to fluctuate slowly but steadily from then culminating in the cold humid periods or pluvials that caused glaciers to form on top of the East African and Ethiopian Mountains and the alternate humid and dry periods, which led to the emergence of the Sahara Desert.

Nicholson (1996) suggests that these fluctuations have continued to the relatively recent past. In particular, she suggests that North Africa might have experienced wetter conditions from about the 9th through the 13th centuries. This was followed by several dry periods, especially from 1550 through 1630 after which humid conditions returned until 1710 (Nicholson, 1996; Miller 1982). From 1711 through 1770, much of the continent experienced dry conditions, except the coastal regions of West Africa, Southern Africa, and parts of East Africa. From 1771 through 1860s, declining rainfall caused severe droughts in the Sahel, West Central Africa, and Southern Africa, in some years causing water levels of Lake Malawi, Lake Chilwa, and Lake Ngami to drop. From 1861 through 1890, humid conditions returned throughout the continent except for West Central Africa, where conditions were relatively dry. East Africa also experienced relatively dry conditions between 1880 and 1890, which caused a drop in the level of Lake Rukwa (Nicholson, 1996). From 1891 through 1930, mean rainfall began to decline with West Africa experiencing a severe drought in 1895.

Comparing trends from 1930–1960 to 1961–1990, Hulme (1996) shows that north of the Equator, mean rainfall declined by 30% in the Sahel and increased by 10% in the coastal regions of West Africa, while it declined in south of the Equator. Hulme (1996) also found that rainfall seasonality increased by more than 8% in the southern coastal regions of West Africa, while it decreased elsewhere. Similarly, rainfall variability increased except in Egypt, Eastern Libya, and some parts of Somalia. These rainfall variability patterns have also been observed in Northern and Southern Africa (Hoerling et al., 2006), specific regions as South Africa (Mason et al., 1999), the Lake Victoria Basin (Kizza et al., 2009), and the Sahel (Mahe and Paturel, 2009).

With respect to temperatures, Equatorial, West, and North Africa cooled slightly with 1961–1990 mean temperatures being 0.9°F (0.5°C) less than those of 1931–1960. However, in the Sahel and also in areas south of the Equator temperatures rose 0.9°F (0.5°C) in June, July, and August. The rate of warming per year for the 20th century was 0.9°F (0.5°C), with the six warmest years having all occurred since 1987, and led by 1998 (Hulme et al., 2005). Perhaps, the most important evidence of the warming taking place south of the Equator is the retreat of glaciers on the mountains of East Africa. According to Thompson et al. (2009), from 1912 to 2007, the glacier on Kilimanjaro's Kibo peak, for example, diminished from 4.64 sq. miles to 1 sq. mile (12.06 km² to 2.6 km²) a decrease of 78%. They also show that the annual rate of ice loss increased from about 1.1% a year from 1912 to 1953 to more than 1.4% a year from 1989 to 2007. If these rates continue, they predict that the glacier will be gone by 2020.

Causes of climate change It is tempting to see climate change as a product of only human interaction with the physical environment, but the causes are more complex. Hulme (1996) has grouped these causes into three main categories, namely, causes related to land cover changes, causes related to changing global ocean circulation, and causes related to changing composition of global atmosphere. The land cover changes explanation says that climate change is due to reduction in land cover—especially the tropical rain forest and the dry savanna. These have led to reduced soil moisture and rainfall.

The changing composition of global atmosphere explanation says that climate change is due to changes in the earth's greenhouse effect. The earth receives ultra-violet and visible radiation from the sun and emits infra-red radiation back into the atmosphere (Tuckett, 2009). In order to maintain energy balance, some of the ultra-violet radiation is trapped by molecules in the earth's atmosphere, creating the same effect as a greenhouse. These molecules, which are mostly carbon dioxide (CO_2), water vapor (H_2O), and ozone (O_3), are called *natural* or *primary* greenhouse gasses. Over time, however, human activities—agriculture, industrialization, and transportation—have either increased the amount of greenhouse gases as in the case of CO_2 or introduced new ones as in the cases of methane (CH_4), nitrous oxide (N_2O), and fluorinated gases. All these have altered the natural composition of the earth's atmosphere causing more heat to be retained by the earth's atmosphere and consequently a rise in temperature.

The changing global ocean circulation explanation refers to the El Nino Southern Oscillation (ENSO) and the **Indian Ocean Dipole** phenomena and their influence on Africa's climate. The ENSO phenomenon is a reversal in sea surface temperatures (SSTs) in the tropical zones of Eastern and Western Pacific Ocean.

The phenomenon alternates between two unusual phases, a warmer than normal phase called **El-Nino** and a colder than normal phase called **La-Nina** (Suplee,1999).

Like ENSO, the Indian Ocean Dipole (IOD) is an oscillation of sea-surface temperatures between two phases—a positive phase and a negative phase (Saji et al., 1999; Nielsen, 2008). The positive phase (*p*IOD) is characterized by heavy rains in Western Indian Ocean and drought in Eastern Indian Ocean, while a negative phase (*n*IOD) brings heavy rains to the east and drought to the west.

It has been established that both phenomena have modulating effect on Africa's rainfall, with the strongest effects found in eastern equatorial and south eastern Africa (Ropelewski and Halpert, 1987; Nicholson, 1996; Nicholson and Kim, 1997). For example, in eastern Africa, abnormally high rainfall occurs in some parts during both IOD and ENSO years with below average rainfall in the subsequent year (Lindesay et al., 1986; Nicholson and Entekhabi, 1986; Nicholson, 1996; Indeje et al., 2000; Reason and Jagadheesha, 2005). In Southern Africa, ENSO prevents the ITCZ from reaching its normal southern position, which results in drought (Lindesay et al., 1986; Nicholson and Entekhabi, 1986; Nicholson, 1996; Reason and Jagadheesha, 2005; Toulmin, 2009). In West Africa, Camberlin et al. (2001) studied rainfall patterns from 1951 to 1997 and found that ENSO effect contributed significantly to the variance in rainfall conditions, including drought in the Sahel, although Paeth et al. (2005) found that warm SST of the Gulf of Guinea to be a stronger link.

Projected impacts of climate change The impact of climate change on Africa has been expressed in very dire predictions that encompasses every aspect of life on the continent—temperature, rainfall, water, forests, savannahs, cities, economies, and human relations. For example, Collier et al. (2009) predict that climate change is likely to affect Africa more severely than any other region in the world due to its large size, its tropical location, and weak agriculturally dominated economies. In general, they believe that many regions of Africa will experience more frequent and intense droughts and floods. Other predictions include a rise in sea level, scarcity of fresh water, cyclones, coastal erosion, deforestation, woodland degradation, desertification, spread of malaria, and food insecurity (Toulmin, 2009; Collier et al., 2009). In addition, North Africa, the Sahara, and Southern Africa will become drier because temperatures across the continent will rise by 5.8–6.5°F (3.2–3.6°C), while East Africa will become wetter. This will in turn cause higher rates of evaporation reducing the capacities of Africa's current hydroelectric power facilities. The drought will also reduce the volume of flow of Africa's major rivers, which will in turn become a potential source of "water wars" (Toulmin 2009).

The impact of climate change on African economies is equally dire given that majority of African countries have agricultural economies. Thus, higher temperatures will increase soil aridity because of higher rate of evaporation. Increased rainfall variability will make crop production more precarious. At the same time floods, storms, and below-normal weather patterns can wipe out crops, while rise in sea level has the potential of taking out prime farmlands such as those of the lower Nile Valley and Kenya. Drier conditions will also reduce availability of pasture and will accelerate overgrazing and **land degradation**, while reduction in the levels of inland lakes as well as changes in coastal ecosystems will disrupt fisheries production in some African countries.

Climate change will also affect human settlements in Africa. For example, coastal cities will be affected as a result of rise in sea level. This will increase flooding and inundation of previously settled lands, damage housing and infrastructure and eventually force some people to relocate from coastal areas. Rising temperatures will exacerbate the effects of heat islands and heat waves in large urban areas leading to an increase in demand for drinking water, cooling systems, and raise the threat of fire outbreaks in cities. Most of the people who will suffer from all these of course will be the urban poor (Toulmin 2009; Collier et al., 2009).

Climate change politics and implications for Africa It needs to be recognized that climate change has been a topic of controversy since the United Nations (UN) sponsored the first Earth Summit in Rio de Janeiro in 1992. Although most countries adopted the UN Framework Convention on Climate Change (UNFCC), it took five years of intense negotiation until a protocol to implement the framework, the Kyoto Protocol of 1997, was adopted. Even so it was not until February 16, 2005, that it came into full force, with the United States, Australia, and a few developed countries still having not ratified it. In 2007, the UN's Intergovernmental Panel on Climate Change (IPCC), a group of nearly 3,000 atmospheric scientists, oceanographers, ice scientists, economists, public health and other experts, issued its fourth report, which gave a definitive warning about the imminent danger of greenhouse gasses. To respond to this urgency, the UN convened a climate change summit of world leaders in December 2009 in Copenhagen, Denmark, to discuss and formulate measures to deal with greenhouse gases after the expiration of the Kyoto Protocol.

Unfortunately, the conference was overshadowed by controversies over the work of the IPCC. First, climate change skeptics and critics managed to intercept and leak numerous e-mail conversations among the scientists, which seemed to indicate a cover-up and falsification of data by the scientists to support their position that climate change was indeed occurring. A parliamentary as well as an independent inquiry later on cleared the scientists of this accusation, but the IPCC's credibility was tarnished, and this emboldened climate change skeptics to raise more questions about the IPCC's report. A second and more serious allegation proved true and that was the report falsely predicted that the glaciers on the Himalayas could disappear by 2035. A third issue was that developing countries led by China, India, Brazil, and South Africa did not want any legally-binding commitments on emission standards. They argued that developing countries were historically not responsible for the increase in the earth's greenhouse gasses and therefore they did not want any legally binding commitments that would hinder their development. The Copenhagen Summit was the largest UN Summit on Climate Change, to date and with President Barack Obama as the new US President, there were high hopes that it would be the definite moment to get some concrete agreements for further action. However, these developments almost derailed the Summit, until President Barack Obama negotiated a compromise with China, India, Brazil, and South Africa. The result was that much of the agreements that needed to be ironed out had to wait until the 2010 Climate Change Summit in Cancun, Mexico. Following the Cancun Meeting, a group of developing countries, including small island states that felt more threatened by sea-level rise, led by South Africa saw that the uncompromising position of China, India, and Brazil, regarding legally-binding commitments would prevent a global agreement. As a result, the group broke ranks with China, India, and Brazil at the Durban meeting in 2011 and with the support of the EU and the United States, forced a framework for a such an agreement at the next meeting in Paris in 2015. However, by the time of the Paris meeting, the US had eased its stand on the legally binding commitments because of lack of support in the US Congress. In the end, the Paris Agreement of 2015 called on all nations to work toward keeping the increase in global temperatures below 2°C and to limit temperature increase to 1.5°C above preindustrial levels. However, each nation had to decide how it was going to meet this target. There were no legal commitments to these targets, and the argument developed countries were more historically responsible for the greenhouse effect and therefore had to be held to different standards did not make it into the agreement. Unfortunately, in June 2017, President Donald J. Trump announced his intention to withdraw the United States from the Agreement in November 2020, the earliest date that such an action is possible.

What are the implications of all these for Africa? How one answers this question depends on whether one is a climate change skeptics or climatic change believer. Climate change skeptics point to the difficulty in predicting climate change and whether what is being predicted is not just a natural course of events like the past climate changes. They also believe that the data are imprecise and therefore too difficult to provide a safe and sound forecast. However, supporters of climate change point to events that are already happening on the continent—serious floods, drought, increased rainfall variability, and shrinking glaciers on Mountains Kenya and Kilimanjaro.

In spite of these disagreements, African countries have put climate change on the priority list because they believe that climate change is real. Among the prescriptions that have been advanced to deal with it are the two courses of action—adaptation and mitigation. Adaptation involves making the necessary changes to cope with what will eventually be normal. Mitigation involves taking steps to reduce the effect of climate change. Adaptation strategies are nothing new to Africans since for years Africans living in marginal environments have learned to cope. However, mitigation is a whole different story and requires more commitment on the part of the governments. With limited resources and skepticisms in certain political circles in developed economies, funding for climate change initiatives in Africa is going to be an issue. Thus, only time will tell the extent to which commitments to climate change in African countries are going to play out.

Desertification

Definitions and types Another environmental challenge, which in part is related to Africa's climate change, is desertification. Article 1 of the United Nations Convention to Combat Desertification (UNCCD) in Those Countries Experiencing Serious Drought/Desertification, particularly Africa (United Nations, 1994) defines desertification as "land degradation in arid, semi-arid, and dry subhumid areas resulting from various factors, including climatic variations and human activities." To Warren (1996), however, desertification comprises three interrelated elements, namely, drought, desiccation, and dry-land degradation. **Drought** is a period of below normal precipitation that results in serious hydrological imbalances and ultimately disruptive land productivity (UN, 1994). Drought is traumatic, but it is temporary in the sense that it does not entirely destroy the dry-land ecosystem and the economic system associated with it (Warren, 1996). **Desiccation** is a severe and prolonged dry period that eventually destroys the dry-land ecosystem and the human communities around it. **Dry-land degradation** is the reduction in land productivity to the point where it will either require decades for the land to naturally recover or external capital and technology to accelerate recovery (Warren, 1996).

The causes of desertification Although all three components are evident in Africa, the causes, extent, and impact of desertification are still shrouded in controversy. The reason for this is largely due to the fact that there has not been one consistent definition of the term desertification (Warren, 1996; Osei, 2003; Slegers and Stroosnijder, 2008). Stebbing (1937) attributed desertification to human causes—indigenous land use system, population growth, and overgrazing. Although this was refuted later by an Anglo-French Commission, Stebbing's ideas persisted among others that have attributed the causes to failure of environmental self-regulation, agriculture in marginal lands due to increasing demand for food, as well as big capital and corporations.

A report on drought and desertification in 2008 by the UN Economic Commission for Africa (UNECA) states that desertification's impact on Africa reaches economic growth and poverty reduction, agriculture and food security, biodiversity, energy production, and human migration. The report noted that majority of Africans derive their livelihoods from agriculture. Unfortunately, most of the land, especially those in arid and semi-arid regions, are marginally productive. Consequently, desertification event such as drought or land degradation can be very serious. The UNCCD estimated in 2004 that about six million hectares of productive land had been lost to land degradation every year since 1990. It is estimated that by 2025 about two-thirds of Africa's arable land would be lost to land degradation (United Nations Economic Commission for Africa (UNECA), 2008).

Consequences of desertification One of the most serious and direct consequences of desertification, particularly drought, is famine. For example, the Sahelian drought of 1968–1974 killed hundreds of thousands of people and millions of livestock. The 1983–1984 droughts in Ethiopia and Sudan killed 1 million people. In 2000–2003, an estimated 14.2 million people in the Horn of Africa needed food assistance, because of drought. Similarly, in 2005, many African countries including Ethiopia, Zimbabwe, Malawi, Eritrea, and Zambia faced food shortages.

Desertification's impact on water availability is also obvious. All the countries of North Africa have water deficit, and it is estimated that if rainfall pattern does not improve, Southern Africa would become a water-deficit region as well. It is estimated that about 230 million Africans will be facing water scarcity by 2025 and by 2100 the flow of the Nile will be reduced by 75% (UNECA, 2008). This has already impacted biodiversity and energy consumption in many parts of the continent. Table 5.8 shows the impact on energy generation from some of the continents leading hydroelectric power plants. Finally, desertification has caused massive migrations and major dislocations of millions of Africans, which is seen as a coping mechanism by millions of Africans who live in such marginal lands as the Sahel and the Horn of Africa. The ECA estimates that about 135 million Africans are at risk of being displaced because of desertification.

Action responses to desertification As a result of all these, desertification has generated a number of responses that fall within the framework of the UNCCD and strategies outside the framework. Within the framework of the UNCCD, two broad actions have been taken—the first at the national level and the second at the international or regional level. At the national level, African countries have put in place national action plans (NAPs) (UNECA, 2008). In some countries such as Kenya, Burundi, and Tunisia, NAPs have been adopted into the socioeconomic policies and plans. Some also have established national diversification funds (NDFs) and national coordinating bodies (NCBs). The first is to provide easily accessible sources of funding for NAP priorities, while the latter is to coordinate, guide, and lead cross-sectoral and integrated planning of desertification initiatives. Countries are expected to incorporate these into their national development strategies (NDS) as well as poverty reduction strategies (PRS).

At the international or regional level, two types of actions have been put in place—the subregional action programs (SRAPs) and regional action programs

TABLE **5.8**

Impacts of Drought on Electricity Generation in Selected African Countries

Country	Period	Consequences of drought
Zambia	2015	Drought led to a 560-megawatt power deficit, which is about a quarter of the country's needs.
Ghana	2006–2007	Severe drought reduced the power generation of the Volta Hydroelectric power project by more than half leading to severe power rationing
Uganda	2004/2005	Reduction in water levels at Lake Victoria resulting in reduction in hydro-power generation by 50 MW
Kenya	1992	Failure of rains led to power rationing in April–May 1992
Kenya	1998–2001	Massive drought decreased hydro generation (25 percent in 2000), which had to be replaced by more expensive fuel-based generation. Power rationing in 1999–2001
Lesotho	1992	Hydro operation limited to six months, leading to 20 percent reduction compared to 1991
Malawi	1997–1998	Engineering operations affected by drought. Amount of hydro energy generated was six percent less than in years of normal rainfall.
Mauritius	1999	Massive drought led to 70 percent drop in normal annual production of electricity.
Ghana	1997–1998	Low rainfall led to lowering of the Volta Dam Reservoir that led to power rationing
Tanzania	1997	The Mtera dam reached its lowest ever level resulting in a 17 percent drop in hydro generation, use of thermal generation to meet the shortfall, and power rationing
Zambia	1992	Poor rainfall resulted in a 35 percent reduction in hydro generation in relation to the previous year.
Zimbabwe	1993	Drought led to a drop of over nine percent in energy production compared to 1992

Source: African Energy Policy Research Network (2005) and others.

(RAPs). Both programs aim at managing cross-boundary aspects of the desertification problem. To date, five SRAPs have been established under the auspices of regional institutions. The Permanent Inter-State Committee on Drought Control in the Sahel (CILSS) and the Economic Community of West African States are in charge for the West Africa and Chad subregions; the Arab Maghreb Union (AMU) is in charge of the AMU subregion; the Southern African Development Community (SADC) is in charge for the Southern African subregion, while the Intergovernmental Authority on Development (IGAD) is managing the program for Eastern Africa.

In contrast, strategies outside the UNCCD framework include those related to agriculture and natural resources management (UNECA, 2008). At the national level, many countries have developed several policies, plans, and strategies that focus on specific sectors such as forestry, agriculture, and water. In the forest sector, these national forest programs (NFPs) policies have addressed deforestation problems. In the agriculture sector, emphasis has been placed on sustainable agriculture, in which better land management practices are promoted to deal with land degradation. In the water sector, conservation and water management has been the focus. To support these policies, many countries have implemented several projects and programs. Among these is Operation Acacia—a land restoration project through the replanting of acacias being implemented in six countries, Burkina Faso, Chad, Kenya, Niger, Senegal, and Sudan, by the Food and Agricultural Organization (FAO) with financial support from the Italian government. This project has restored 13,000 ha of degraded land.

Some countries have also adopted innovative community-based approaches that emphasize indigenous knowledge systems of land management. Among these are indigenous terrace farming in Konso District, Ethiopia and Togo, agroforestry system of the Gedio zone of Ethiopia, soil conservation practices in Ghana and the Central Plateau of Burkina Faso, a sand encroachment control in Mauritania, and the Thuo-Boswa Landrace Cattle Project of Northwest Cape Province (UNECA, 2008).

Several regional programs have also been initiated in the area of agriculture and natural resources management. These include New Partnership for Africa Development (NEPAD)'s Comprehensive Africa Agricultural Development Program (CAADP), which aimed at raising Africa's agricultural productivity by 6% by the year 2015 through sustainable water management systems and application of fertilizers. Others include NEPAD Environmental Initiative (EI) that aims at combating desertification, the Green Wall of Sahara Initiative, the African Land Policy, and the Regional Program for the Integrated Development of the Fouta Djallon Highlands (RPID-FDH).

Finally, there are programs aimed at developing and strengthening drought and desertification monitoring systems and drought risk and disaster management. Here too a plethora of national, regional, and international efforts have been or are being undertaken. With respect to monitoring, they include desertification information system, the Long-term Ecological Monitoring and Observatory Network, the Land Degradation Assessment (LADA), Regional Climate Forums, Climate for Development in Africa (ClimDev Africa) Program, the Climate Prediction and Application Center (ICPAC), the African Center of Meteorological Applications for Development (ACMAD), and the African Monitoring of the Environment for Sustainable Development (AMESD). With respect to drought risk and disaster management, they include the African Regional Strategy Disaster Risk management and the Forum on African Drought Risk and Development (ADDF).

In spite of all these efforts, the UNECA (2008) report indicates that the problem of drought and desertification is still a major one due to many problems. For example, poverty continues to be a major obstacle to implementing the strategies and programs. Funding remains inadequate as the bulk of it comes from international development agencies outside the continent. This in turn has made many of these programs unsustainable since funding agencies reprioritize what they want to fund periodically. Also, many of the areas prone to drought and desertification lack basic infrastructure compounding the problem of accessibility. Lack of consistent national policies, weak institutional structures, and lack of indigenous capacity in managing programs and projects have also led to lack of coordination in all these myriads of programs and projects. To be able to make any headway in the future, a lot is going to depend on African governments and their commitment to combating drought, desertification, and land degradation.

Summary

Africa's location in relation to the earth's planetary system determines to a large extent its climate, biogeography, soils as well as its natural opportunities and challenges. As a result of being the only continent crossed by all three major tropical latitudes, Africa has the warmest climates of all continents. Its location astride the equator causes climatic conditions to be repeated north and south of the Equator. Its vast east-west extent north of the Equator versus its narrower extent south of the Equator coupled with its uniformly large interior plateau, areas of relatively higher elevations, tropical air masses, and warm and cold ocean currents that wash its shores cause generally moderate temperatures in the southern and eastern parts. The most important differentiating climatic element, however, is rainfall, which is mostly influenced by the two air masses—the mT and the cT air masses. Combination of the rainfall and temperature conditions leads to different climatic types that include the equatorial, the humid tropics, the tropical wet and dry, the tropical semi-dry, the desert, and the Mediterranean climatic types.

Africa's vegetation types correlate closely with these climatic types, with rainfall, temperature, and sometimes altitude, the same factors that affect climate, playing a role in determining the type of vegetation cover. Thus, rapid plant growth, dense forest, and high and complex biodiversity coincide with areas of highest rainfall, high temperatures, and high humidity, while less-luxuriant forest as well as grassland vegetation occurs in areas of declining rainfall. However, due to the variability within rainfall patterns forest and grassland vegetation is by no means homogenous. Instead they range from the true rain forest, deciduous forest, woodland savanna, temperate grassland, dry savanna, semi desert, and desert vegetation.

Africa's soils types are as varied as its climatic and vegetation types. Like other major regions of the world, Africa has some poor soils as well as rich soils. Contrary to previous notions that most African soils were lateritic, we now know that is not the case. It is true that the high clayey content of most of the soil types as well as high acidic content make tilling and cultivation of the land difficult for farmers with limited resources. However, these problems are not unique to Africa, except that they may be more formidable because resources needed to deal with these problems may be either lacking or very limited.

On the whole, Africa's physical environment presents it with a number of opportunities as well as challenges. Among the opportunities are the limited number of earth movements, abundant sunshine, rich natural resources, including minerals and wildlife, and a longer growing season. Among the challenges are uneven distribution of resources, climate change, and drought and desertification.

Postreading Assignments

A. Study the Following Key Concepts:

Air mass	High-pressure belt	Lapse rate	Sudan Savanna
Desertification	Humid Tropical Climate	Low-pressure belt	Tropical continental air mass
Drought	Indian Ocean Dipole	Mediterranean Climate	Tropical maritime air mass
El-Nino	Inter-Tropical Convergence	Polar continental air mass	Wet and Dry Climates
Equatorial climate	Zone	Polar maritime air mass	
Guinea Savanna	Land degradation	Sahel Savanna	
Harmatan	Land desiccation	Semi-Dry Tropical Climate	

B. Discussion Questions

1. What have you learned from this chapter that you did not know? Have you changed any notions you had a about Africa's climate, biography, and soils?

2. What are the main factors that affect Africa's climate?

3. Discuss the main climatic types of Africa.

4. Describe the essential characteristics of the Africa's major vegetation types and indicate how they are related to climate.

5. What are the main soil types of Africa?

6. Discuss the assertion that Africa's physical environment is a major cause for its economic underdevelopment.

7. Examine the evidence of global warming within the African context.

8. What are African countries doing to combat desertification? To what extent are these efforts going to succeed?

References

Areola, O. 1996. "Soils." In Adams, W. M., Goudie, A. S., and Orme, A. R. (Eds.) *The Physical Geography of Africa*. Oxford: Oxford University Press, pp. 134–147.

Camberlin, P., and Philippon, N. 2002. "The East African March–May Rainy Season: Associated Atmospheric Dynamics and Predictability Over the 1968–97 Period." *Journal of Climate* 15(9): 1002–1019.

Camberlin, P., Janicot, S., and Poccard, I. 2001. "Seasonality and Atmospheric Dynamics of the Teleconnection between African Rainfall and Tropical Sea-Surface Temperature: Atlantic Vs. ENSO." *International Journal of Climatology* 21: 973–1005.

Collier, P., Conway, G., and Venables, T. 2009. "Climate Change and Africa." In Helm, D., and Hepburn, C. (Eds.) *The Economics and Politics of Climate Change*. Oxford: University of Oxford Press.

Ellatif, M. 2005. "Morocco." In Merlo, M., and Croituru, L. (Eds.) *Valuing Mediterranean Forests: Towards Total Economic Value*. Wallingford, Oxfordshire, GBR: CABI Publishing, pp. 69–88.

Eswaran, H., Ikawa, H., and Kimble, J. M. 1986. Oxisols of the World. *Proc. Symp. on Red Soils*. Beijing, Amsterdam: Elsevier, pp. 90–123.

Eswaran, H., Almaraz, R., van den Berg, E., and Reich, P. 1997. "An Assessment of Soil Resources in Africa in Relation to Productivity." *Geoderma* 77: 1–18.

Goudie, A. S. 1996. "Climate: Past and Present." In Adams, W. M., Goudie, A. S., and Orme, A. R. (Eds.) *The Physical Geography of Africa*. Oxford: Oxford University Press, pp. 34–59.

Grainger, A. 1996. "Forest Environments." In Adams, W. M., Goudie, A. S., and Orme, A. R. (Eds.) *The Physical Geography of Africa*. Oxford: Oxford University Press, pp. 173–195.

Hedberg, O. 1951. "Vegetation Belts of East African Mountains." *Svensk Botanisk Tidskrift* 45(1): 140–202.

Hoerling, M., Hurrrell, J., Eischeid, J., and Phillips, A. 2006. "Detection and Attribution of Twentieth-Century Northern and Southern African Rainfall Change." *Journal of Climate* 19(16): 3989–4008.

Hulme, M. 1996. "Climate Change within the Period of Meteorological Records." In Adams, W. M., Goudie, A. S., and Orme, A. R. (Eds.) *The Physical Geography of Africa*. Oxford: Oxford University Press, pp. 103–121.

Hulme, M., Doherty, R., Ngara, T., and New, M. 2005. "Global Warming and African Climate Change: A Reassessment." In Low, P. S. (Ed.) *Climate Change and Africa*. Cambridge: Cambridge University Press.

Indeje, M., Semazzi, H. M., and Ogallo, L. J. 2000. "ENSO Signals in East African Rainfall Seasons." *International Journal of Climatology* 20: 19–46.

Kizza, M., Rodhe, A., Xu, C.-Y., Ntale, H. K., and Halldin, S. 2009. "Temporal Rainfall Variability in the Lake Victoria Basin in East Africa during the Twentieth Century." *Theoretical and Applied Climatology* 98: 119–135.

Lindesay, J. A., Harrison, M., and Haffner, T. 1986. "The Southern Oscillation and South African Rainfall." *South African Journal of Science* 82: 196–198.

Mahe, G., and Paturel, J.-E. 2009. "1896–2006 Sahelian Annual Rainfall Variability and Runoff Increase of Sahelian Rivers." *Geoscience* 341: 538–546.

Mason, S. J., Waylen, P. R., Mimmack, G. M., Rajaratnam, B., and Harrison, J. M. 1999. "Changes in Extreme Rainfall Events in South Africa." *Climate Change* 41: 249–257.

McGregor, H. V., Duponta, L., Stuut, J.-B. W., Kuhlmann, H. 2009. "Vegetation Change, Goats, and Religion: A 2000-Year History of Land Use in Southern Morocco." *Quaternary Science Reviews* 28: 1434–1448.

Meadows, M. E. 1996. "Biogeography." In Adams, W. M., Goudie, A. S., and Orme, A. R. (Eds.) *The Physical Geography of Africa*. Oxford: Oxford University Press, pp. 161–172.

Miller, J. C. 1982. "The Significance of Drought, Disease and Famine in the Agriculturally Marginal Zones of West-Central Africa." *The Journal of African History*, 23(1): 17–61.

Nedjahi, A., and Zamoum, M. 2005. "Algeria." *Valuing Mediterranean Forests: Towards Total Economic Value*. Wallingford, Oxfordshire, GBR: CABI Publishing, pp. 89–103.

Nicholson, S. E. 1996. "Environmental Change within the Historical Record." In Adams, W. M., Goudie, A. S., and Orme, A. R. (Eds.) *The Physical Geography of Africa*. Oxford: Oxford University Press, pp. 60–87.

Nicholson, S. E. and Entekhabi, D. 1986. 'The Quasi-periodic Behavior of Rainfall Variability in Africa and its Relationship to the Southern Oscillation.' *Journal of Climatology and Applied Meteorology.* 34: 331–348.

Nicholson, S. E., and Kim, J. 1997. The Relationship of the EL Nino-Southern Oscillation to African Rainfall." *International Journal of Climatology* 17: 117–135.

Nielsen, O. 2008. "Indian Ocean Dipole." http://my.opera.com/nielsol/blog/2008/12/08/indian-ocean-dipole (accessed 26 August, 2010).

Osei, W. Y. 2003. "Human-Environment Impacts: Forest Degradation and Desertification." In Aryeetey-Attoh, S. (Ed.) *Geography of Sub-Saharan Africa.* Upper Saddle River: Prentice Hall, pp. 48–77.

Osei, W. Y., and Aryeetey-Attoh, S. 2003. "The Physical Environment." In Aryeetey-Attoh, S. (Ed.) *Geography of Sub-Saharan Africa.* Upper Saddle River: Prentice Hall, pp. 12–47.

Paeth, H., Born K., Girmes, R., Podzun, R., and Jacob. D. 2009. "Regional Climate Change in Tropical and Northern Africa due to Greenhouse Forcing and Land Use Changes." *Journal of Climate* 22(1): 114–132.

Reason, C. J. C., and Jagadheesha, D. 2005. "A Model Investigation of Recent ENSO Impacts over Southern Africa." *Meteorology and Atmospheric Physics* 89: 181–205.

Ropelewski, C. F., and Halpert, M. S. 1987. "Global and Regional Scale Precipitation and Temperature Patterns Associated with El Nino/Southern Oscillation Relationship." *Monthly Weather Review* 115: 1606–1626.

Saji, N. H., Goswami, B. N., Vinayachandran, P. N., and Yamagata, T. 1999. "A Dipole Mode in the Tropical Indian Ocean." *Nature* 401: 360–363.

Slegers, M., and Stroosnijder, L. 2008. "Beyond the Desertification Narrative: A Framework for Agricultural Drought in Semi-Arid East Africa." *Ambio* 37(5): 372–380.

Stebbing, E. P. 1937. "The Threat of the Sahara." *Journal of Royal African Society* 36: 3–35.

Suplee, C. 1999. "El Nino/La Nina: Nature's Vicious Cycle." *National Geographic* 195(3): 72–95.

Taylor, D. 1996. "Mountains." In Adams, W. M., Goudie, A. S., and Orme, A. R. (Eds.) *The Physical Geography of Africa.* Oxford: Oxford University Press, pp. 287–306.

Trewartha, G. T. 1981. *The Earth's Problem Climates.* Madison: University of Wisconsin Press.

Thompson, L. G., Brecher, H. H., Mosley-Thompson, E., Hardy, D. R., and Mark, B. J. 2009. "Glacier Loss on Kilimanjaro Continues Unabated." Proceedings of the National Academy of Sciences 106(47): 19770–19775.

Toulmin, C. 2009. *Climate Change in Africa.* London: Zed Books.

Tuckett, R. P. 2009. "The Role of Atmospheric Gases in Global Warming." In Letcher, T. M. (Ed.) *Climate Change: Observed Impacts on Planet Earth.* Amsterdam: Elsevier, pp. 3–19.

United Nations. 1994. *United Nations Convention to Combat Drought and Desertification.* Paris.

United Nations Economic Commission for Africa. 2008. *Africa Review Report on Drought and Desertification.* Addis Ababa: United Nations Commission for Africa.

Warren, A. 1996. "Desertification." In Adams, W. M., Goudie, A. S., and Orme, A. R. (Eds.) *The Physical Geography of Africa.* Oxford: Oxford University Press, pp. 342–355.

Population

In the preceding five chapters, we have learned about the history of the African people from the earliest time to the present. We have also learned about the physical environment they live in and the opportunities and challenges it presents. In this chapter, we continue to learn more about the African people in contemporary terms. The chapter answers the following questions: What is the population of Africa? Where on the continent do they live and why? What are the main characteristics of the population in terms of age and sex composition, socioeconomic indicators, and processes and rates of change? To what extent do these characteristics affect economic development? The chapter consists of three sections. The first section is population size and distribution, the second is population characteristics, and the third is population issues and development.

Since the answers to these questions involve the use of statistical data, it is important to state some important facts about population statistics of Africa. First, there has never been a census of all Africans at the same time (Zuberi et al., 2003). As a result, the population data on Africa are estimates that were obtained from questionable primary data. Second, as we learned in Chapter 2, the majority of the present-day African countries did not exist before the 1960s. This makes country level population data in the 1950s and 1960s a bit more suspicious. The result of all these is that all the population data that are used in this chapter are estimates, which may either be more or less than actual numbers. With this in mind, do the prereading assignment.

POPULATION SIZE AND DISTRIBUTION

With a total land area of 11,667,000 square miles (30,065,000 square kilometers), which is 22.3% of the world's land area, Africa was home to 1,185,073,000 people, in 2015, according to the United Nations population estimates. This was about 16% of world's total population. Where did these people live?

Distribution by Density

Population Density

Based on the 2015 United Nations population estimates, the **population density** of Africa was 101 persons per square mile or 39 persons per square kilometer. A visual representation of this distribution is given by Figure 6.1, while the detailed distribution by country is given in Table 6.1. From the map, we can identify both the most densely populated regions as well as the most sparsely populated regions on the continent. In these regions, densities were either much higher or much lower than the average for the continent. The most densely populated regions were (1) The Mediterranean Coast of Morocco, Algeria, and Tunisia; (2). The Lower Nile Valley; (3) The West African Coast; (4) The Northern Interior of Ghana and Nigeria; (5) The Great Lakes Region of Eastern Africa; (6) Southeastern Coastal Region of

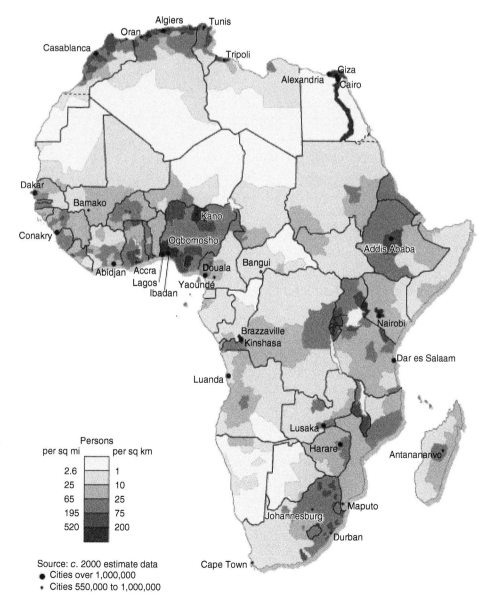

FIGURE 6.1 Population distribution of Africa.
Source: Recreated with permission from Encyclopædia Britannica, © 2011 by Encyclopædia Britannica, Inc

TABLE **6.1**

Africa's Population Distribution by Size, Density, and Urban Dwelling, 2015 Estimates

Country	Area (Sq. Mi)	Area (km²)	Population	Population density Sq. Mi	Population density km²	% of Urban population
Africa	**11,726,394**	**30,371,221**	**1,185,073,000**	**101**	**39**	**40.0**
Algeria	919,595	2,381,740	39,667,000	43	17	66.5
Angola	481,354	1,246,700	25,072,000	52	20	58.5
Benin	43,450	112,620	10,880,000	250	97	42.0
Botswana	224,607	600,370	2,262,000	10	4	61.1
Burkina Faso	105,946	274,200	18,106,000	171	66	25.7
Burundi	10,740	27,830	11,179,000	1,041	435	11.0
Cameroon	179,714	475,440	23,344,000	130	49	58.4
Cape Verde	1,557	4,030	521,000	335	129	61.1
Central African Rep.	240,324	622,980	4,900,000	20	8	38.9
Chad	495,755	1,284,000	14,037,000	28	11	27.6
Comoros	719	2,170	788,000	1,096	424	28.2
Congo Republic	132,047	342,000	4,620,000	35	14	62.1
Cote d'Ivoire	123,847	322,460	22,702,000	183	71	50.6
Dem. Rep. of Congo	905,446	2,345,410	77,267,000	85	34	35.2
Djibouti	8,950	22,000	888,000	99	38	76.8
Egypt	385,229	1,001,450	91,508,000	238	92	43.4
Equatorial Guinea	10,831	28,050	845,000	78	30	39.7
Eritrea	48,528	121,320	5,228,000	108	52	21.6
Ethiopia	483,123	1,127,127	99,391,000	206	99	16.7
Gabon	103,347	267,670	1,725,000	17	7	86.0
Gambia	4,127	11,300	1,991,000	482	197	58.1
Ghana	92,098	238,540	27,410,000	298	121	51.2
Guinea	94,926	245,860	12,609,000	133	51	35.4
Guinea-Bissau	13,948	36,120	1,844,000	132	66	30.0
Kenya	224,961	582,650	46,050,000	205	90	22.2
Lesotho	11,720	30,350	2,135,000	182	70	26.9
Liberia	38,250	111,370	4,503,000	118	47	47.8
Libya	678,400	1,759,540	6,278,000	9	4	77.9
Madagascar	226,658	587,041	24,235,000	107	42	30.2
Malawi	47,392	118,480	17,215,000	363	183	19.8
Mali	482,077	1,024,000	17,600,000	37	14	35.9
Mauritania	398,000	1,030,700	4,068,000	10	4	41.4
Mauritius	788	1,860	1,273,000	1,615	627	41.8
Morocco	177,117	446,550	34,378,000	194	77	58.2
Mozambique	313,661	801,590	27,978,000	89	29	38.4
Namibia	317,818	823,144	2,459,000	8	3	38.0
Niger	458,075	1,186,408	19,899,000	43	16	17.1

(*Continued*)

TABLE 6.1

Africa's Population Distribution by Size, Density, and Urban Dwelling, 2015 Estimates (*Continued*)

Country	Area (Sq. Mi)	Area (km²)	Population	Population density Sq. Mi	km²	% of Urban population
Nigeria	356,669	923,768	182,202,000	511	200	49.8
Rwanda	10,169	26,338	11,610,000	1,142	471	18.9
Sao Tome and Principe	386	1,001	190,000	492	198	62.2
Senegal	75,951	196,712	15,129,000	199	79	42.4
Seychelles	175	71,740	96,000	549	210	55.3
Sierra Leone	27,699	71,740	6,453,000	233	89	38.4
Somalia	246,000	637,660	10,787,000	44	17	37.4
South Africa	473,290	1,219,912	54,490,000	115	45	61.7
South Sudan	239,285	619,745	12,340,000	52	20	18.9
Sudan	718,723	1,861,484	40,235,000	56	22	40.1
Swaziland	6,704	17,360	1,287,000	192	75	21.4
Tanzania	364,017	945,090	53,470,000	147	60	26.4
Togo	21,925	56,790	7,305,000	333	134	43.4
Tunisia	59,664	163,610	11,254,000	189	72	67.3
Uganda	93,070	236,040	39,032,000	419	195	13.3
Western Sahara	97,334	266,000	530,000	5	2	81.8
Zambia	290,586	752,610	16,212,000	56	22	35.7
Zimbabwe	150,873	390,580	15,603,000	103	40	38.3

Source: United Nations, Department of Economic and Social Affairs Population Division (2015). *World Population Prospects: 2015 Revision*, custom data acquired via website.

South Africa; and (7) Eastern Madagascar and the small island nations of Mauritius and Comoros, Cape Verde, and Sao Tome and Principe. In contrast, the most sparsely populated regions were (1) The Sahara Region; (2) Large parts of central Africa, between Chad and Angola; and (3) Namibia and Botswana and western South Africa.

From Table 6.1, Mauritius was the most densely populated country in Africa with 1,615 persons per square mile (627 persons per km²), while Western Sahara, with a density of five, persons to the square mile (2 persons per km²), was the most sparsely populated political unit in 2015. The 10 most densely populated countries on the continent accounted for only 4.1% of continent's land area, but 22% of its population. In contrast, the 10 most sparsely populated countries on the continent accounted for 30% of its land area, but only 6% of its population. This means that with 15% of Africa's population, Nigeria, the continent's most populous country had more people on just 3.1% of Africa's land area compared to the 10 most sparsely populated countries combined. Indeed, in 2015, the about 61% of Africans lived in only 10 countries—Nigeria, Ethiopia, Egypt, DRC, South Africa, Tanzania, Sudan, Kenya, Algeria, and Uganda. These accounted for 42% of Africa's land area.

Rural-Urban Distribution

Africa's population is predominantly rural, even though what constitutes urban and rural is debatable. According to the UN latest estimates, only 40% of Africa's population is urban (Table 6.1). Three countries—Libya, Djibouti, and Gabon and the territory of Western Sahara—were between 70% and 90% urbanized, primarily due to smaller proportion of habitable land or their small land areas. Six other countries—Algeria, Botswana, Cape Verde, Congo Republic, Sao Tome and Principe, and Tunisia—are 60–70% urbanized. Eight other countries were 50–60% urbanized and these included Angola, Cameroon, Cote d'Ivoire, Gambia, Ghana, Morocco, Nigeria, and Seychelles. The remaining 36 countries were all less than 50% urbanized. This makes Africa the least urbanized of all the continents. What factors affect or explain the population distribution of Africa?

Factors Affecting Population Distribution

Two main factors affect population distribution of Africa. They are physical and human factors. Some geographers add a third factor, usually referred to as historical factors, which may be either physical or human factors that influenced events in the past.

Physical Environmental Factors

To a greater degree, the physical environment exerts a powerful influence on where people can and want to live and where they cannot and do not want to live on the African continent. This influence is expressed through conditions of climate, topography, drainage, and soil.

Climate Of all the physical environmental factors that influence Africa's population distribution, climate is the most important, and the most direct effect of climate on population distribution of Africa is the amount and distribution of rainfall. As Udo (1982) points out, all sparsely populated areas on the continent receive less than 30 in. (750 mm) of rain per year, while densely populated areas receive more. The only exceptions to these are the Lower Nile Valley, which receives less rain but is densely populated, and the Congo Forest, which receives a lot of rain but it is sparsely populated.

Several studies continue to show the influence of rainfall variability on Africa's demography, and directly or indirectly on its population numbers and distribution. For example, Camberlin (2010) shows that between 1990 and 2000, regions with high rainfall variability tended to have lower demographic growth rates. Similarly, a connection between rainfall variability and outmigration has been established in Ethiopia (Ezra, 2001) and Burkina Faso (Henry et al., 2003). Rainfall variability also caused drought, which in turn has caused considerable mortality (Kidane, 1989), civil conflict (Hendrix and Glaser, 2007), and a decrease in fertility (Pedersen, 1995).

As we learned in Chapter 5, except in the high altitudes, the Mediterranean and the southern Atlantic coasts, temperatures are generally high everywhere in Africa so the influence of temperatures on population distribution is not as strong as rainfall. However, when high temperatures combine with high rainfall and high humidity, conditions are not only enervating for human habitat, but they tend to be conducive to many dangerous disease-carrying vectors. This is part of the reason of why the Congo Basin and its immediate areas of the humid tropics are among some of the most sparsely populated areas on the continent.

Availability of water, soil quality, and topography Rainfall is also the single most important determinant of availability of water in Africa, which in turn makes it possible for people to live in dry desert conditions. Examples of this are the oases of North African countries and also in the Nile Valley of Egypt and the Sudan, where almost all the population lives along the Nile.

Udo (1982) observes that the relationship between soils and population distribution is not direct. However, places with fertile soils are the most preferred sites for human habitat in Africa, unless there are strong countervailing forces. Where availability of water combines with fertile soils, population concentration tends to be higher. This explains why the Nile Valley, the Great Lakes Region, and the coastal interiors of West Africa are among the most densely populated regions of the continent. As Scott (2004) also points out, the relationship between soil fertility and population densities could be a two-way affair since farming practices can either decrease or increase the ability of soils to support high population densities. Examples of the latter are the pockets of high population densities of the northeast and northwest Ghana and the Kano Region of northern Nigeria. In these areas, permanent agricultural systems based on heavy application of manure sustain population densities of 1,026 per square mile or 400 persons per km².

Topography is another physical environmental factor that affects the population distribution of Africa. Generally, flat lands and rolling hills are the most preferred places for human settlement if other physical environmental factors such as climate and soil conditions are favorable. A good example of this is the East African Plateau, which is among the most densely populated regions of the continent. In contrast, very rugged topographies are generally uninhabitable.

Predominance of diseases vectors and pests Finally, predominance of diseases, disease vectors, and pests also prevent human settlements and associated activities such as livestock farming in certain parts of the continent. The most important of the disease vectors is the tsetse fly, which transmits *trypanosomiasis* among cattle and sleeping sickness among human beings (Udo, 1982). The effect of this disease on depopulation of certain portions of the African continent was first noted during the latter period of colonial Africa. For example, Fitzegerald (1957) and Harrison Church (1957) commented on vast areas of West Africa, Gabon, and the DRC that had been depopulated by the disease. Similarly, Blacker (1962) found that the worst tsetse-infested areas also had some of the lowest population densities. According to Oluwafemi (2009), the problem of tsetse fly is still prevalent in Africa, except North Africa and Madagascar, and it is classified as severe in 37 African countries, from Senegal in the north to South Africa in the south. In an interesting twist of events, however, other researchers indicate that population growth is actually eradicating the fly because of clearance of the fly's habitat (Reid et al., 2000).

Other diseases that are known to exert influence on Africa's population's distribution include river blindness, malaria, and HIV/AIDS. For example, before the World Health Organization (WHO) mounted a successful 30-year campaign in 1974 to eliminate it, river blindness was identified as the cause of depopulation of the Red and White Volta valleys of northern Ghana and neighboring Burkina Faso (Hunter, 2010), as well as considerable areas of the savanna belt stretching from Senegal to Uganda (Udo, 1982). Webb (2005) concluded that malaria's constraint on tropical Africa's population growth predates even the establishment of permanently settled communities. The devastating impact of HIV/AIDS on population of many parts of Africa has well been documented (e.g., Boerma et al., 1998;

Garenne et al., 1996; Kalipeni et al., 2004; Nunn et al., 1997; Sewankambo et al., 2000; Timæus and Jasseh, 2004; Urassa et al., 2001). While no study has yet focused on establishing a direct relationship between the disease and population distribution, one can infer such a relationship from the fact that the disease has raised mortality rates in a number of African countries, especially those in the southern part and for that reason could be seen as affecting population distribution.

Human Factors

Human-related or human-induced factors that affect population distribution in Africa include political instability, wars and social unrest, and the economy.

Political instability, wars, and social unrest Everyone wants peace and tranquility, a place where life can at least be predictable in the sense of day-to-day living. Thus, when political instability, wars, social unrest, and the like become the daily state of affairs, people eventually flee. Unfortunately, Africa has had more than its share of these events both in historical times and in relatively recent past. For example, Mason (1969) gives an account of how slave raiding depopulated the Middle Belt of Nigeria. Rodney (1973) also estimated the Africa's population loss due to the slave in millions. Postcolonial civil wars and social unrest in several countries have created millions of internally displaced people and **refugees** on the continent. For example, it is estimated that Angola's 26-year-long war affected about 3.7 million people, of which some 90,000 were either killed or permanently maimed and 1.7 million became refugees (Ahmad, 2000). The Rwandan genocide decimated over a million people, about a third of the country's population. Similarly, Bah (2011) estimates that at its height in 1999, the Sierra Leone Civil War displaced about half a million people. As recent as the end of 2015, the United Nations High Commission for Refugees (UNHCR) estimated that 11,197,751 in 13 African countries were internally displaced. Majority of them were in Sudan (29%), Nigeria (19%), South Sudan (15%), DRC (10%), Somalia (10%), Libya (3%), and Cote D'Ivoire (3%). The rest were in Burundi, Cameroon, Central African Republic, Chad, Mali, and Niger.

Political decisions and government policies Sometimes political decisions and other government policies have also forced redistribution of population. This was the case in Kenya and Zimbabwe, where colonial policy that allocated the most agriculturally productive lands to white minority groups confined large numbers of native populations to less productive areas and creating artificially high population densities in those areas. It was also the case of South Africa during the Apartheid policy, which restricted the majority population to the so-called homelands. Another political factor that has affected population distribution in Africa is creation of national parks, wildlife sanctuary, and nature reserves even though as Udo (1982) points out, the areas set aside were relatively small.

Economy Closely related to political and social instability is the economy. In particular, economic disparities between and within regions influence the distribution of population since in general people want to live in areas where they can be gainfully employed. In most cases, the effect of this may be only temporary, as it is the case of certain short-term migrant workers. However, over the years, this has become more and more permanent.

POPULATION CHARACTERISTICS

Population characteristics refer to distinctive features that usually describe a given population. For our purpose, we will look at age and sex composition, and income, education attainment, and life expectancy as measured by the **human development index** (HDI) and growth characteristics.

Age and Sex Composition

Age

In general terms, Africa's population is very young. According to the 2015 estimates, about 42% of the population was under the age of 15 with only about 5% above the age of 60 (Table 6.6). In 33 countries, the percentage of population under 15 was between 40% and 50%, although Niger was actually the only country with 50% of its population under age 15. In terms of the upper age group, only Mauritius, Seychelles, and Tunisia, had 10% or more of their population at 60 years or more. For the rest of continent, the percentage of population over 60 years old was all in single digits (Table 6.2).

TABLE **6.2**

Age and Sex Composition of Africa's Population (2015 Estimates)

Country	Population	Sex composition			Age composition percentage	
		Male (1,000s)	Female (1,000s)	Sex ratio	Under 15	60+
Africa	**1,186,000,000**	593,455,000	592,724,000	100	42	5
Algeria	35,423,000	19,958	19,709	101.3	29	9
Angola	18,993,000	12,516	12,606	98.5	48	4
Benin	9,212,000	5,426	5,454	99.5	42	5
Botswana	1,978,000	1,130	1,132	99.9	32	6
Burkina Faso	16,287,000	8,984	9,121	98.5	46	4
Burundi	8,519,000	5,524	5,655	97.7	45	4
Cameroon	19,958,000	11672	11,672	100.0	43	5
Cape Verde	513,000	257	264	97.4	30	7
Central African Rep.	4,506,000	2,415	2,485	97.2	39	6
Chad	11,506,000	7,028	7,010	100.3	48	4
Comoros	691,000	398	391	101.8	40	5
Congo Republic	3,759,000	2,311	2,309	100.1	43	6
Cote d'Ivoire	21,571,000	11,546	11,155	103.5	43	5
Dem. Rep. of Congo	67,827,000	38,533	38,734	99.5	46	5
Djibouti	879,000	446	412	100.9	33	6
Egypt	84,474,000	46,240	45,268	102.1	33	8
Equatorial Guinea	693,000	433	412	105.1	39	5
Eritrea	5,224,000	2,619	2,609	100.4	43	4
Ethiopia	84,976,000	49,608	49,783	99.6	41	5

(*Continued*)

TABLE **6.2**

Age and Sex Composition of Africa's Population (2015 Estimates) (*Continued*)

Country	Population	Sex composition Male (1,000s)	Female (1,000s)	Sex ratio	Age composition percentage Under 15	60+
Gabon	1,501,000	872	853	102.3	37	7
Gambia	1,751,000	986	1005	98.0	46	4
Ghana	24,333,000	13,635	13,774	99.0	39	5
Guinea	10,324,000	6,322	6,286	100.6	43	5
Guinea-Bissau	1,647,000	916	929	98.6	41	5
Kenya	40,863,000	23,017	23,033	99.9	42	5
Lesotho	2,084,000	1,057	1,078	98.0	36	6
Liberia	4,102,000	2,270	2,234	101.6	42	5
Libya	6,546,000	3,157	3,122	101.1	30	7
Madagascar	20,146,000	12,082	12,153	99.4	42	5
Malawi	15,692,000	8,593	8,622	99.7	45	5
Mali	13,323,000	8,885	8,715	101.9	48	4
Mauritania	3,366,000	2,047	2,021	101.3	40	5
Mauritius	1,297,000	629	644	97.6	19	15
Morocco	32,381,000	16,989	17,388	97.7	27	10
Mozambique	23,406,000	13,666	14,312	95.5	45	5
Namibia	2,212,000	1,197	1,262	94.8	38	6
Niger	15,891,000	10,029	9,870	101.6	51	4
Nigeria	158,259,000	92,789	89,413	103.8	44	5
Rwanda	10,277,000	5,560	6,050	91.9	41	5
Sao Tome and Principe	165,000	95	96	99.1	43	4
Senegal	12,861,000	7,429	7,701	96.5	44	5
Seychelles	87,000	49	48	102.6	23	11
Sierra Leone	5,836,000	3,193	3,260	98.0	42	4
Somalia	9,359,000	5,368	5,419	99.1	47	5
South Africa	50,492,000	26,797	27,693	96.8	29	8
South Sudan	12,340,000	6,179	6,161	100.3	42	5
Sudan	43,192,000	20,197	20,038	100.8	41	5
Swaziland	1,202,000	636	651	97.8	37	6
Tanzania	45,040,000	26,574	26,896	98.8	45	5
Togo	6,780,000	3,609	3,695	97.7	42	5
Tunisia	10,374,000	5,561	5,692	97.7	23	12
Uganda	33,796,000	19,507	19,525	99.9	48	4
Western Sahara	530,000	300	273	110.1	26	6
Zambia	13,257,000	8,094	8,118	99.7	46	4
Zimbabwe	12,644,000	7688	7915	97.1	42	4

Source: United Nations, Department of Economic and Social Affairs Population Division (2015). *World Population Prospects: 2015 Revision,* custom data acquired via website.

Sex

In 2015, Africa's **sex ratio** was 100, which meant there were equal number of males to females. However, 16 African countries had sex ratios above 100, which indicates they had more males than females. These included Algeria, Comoros, Cote d'Ivoire, Egypt, Equatorial Guinea, Gabón, Libya, Liberia, Mali, Mauritania, Níger, Nigeria, Seychelles, Sudan, and Western Sahara. Four countries—Cameroon, Chad, Congo Republic, and Eritrea—had sex ratios of 100 each. The rest had below 100 (Table 6.2).

Population Pyramids

Population pyramids show sex and age composition of a given population. In 2015, Africa's population pyramid had a broad base and a narrow top (Figure 6.2a). This pyramid depicts a young population and a rapid growth rate, and it is typical of developing countries in general, and for that matter African countries. However, there were two interesting variations of this general trend. The first was a population pyramid with narrower base and a larger middle-aged population (Figure 6.2b), mostly typical of developed countries. Countries represented by this pyramid included Algeria, Mauritius, Namibia, Seychelles, South Africa, and Tunisia. The second was a population pyramid that was equally broad at its base as well as its middle section depicting a population that is transitioning into a middle-age population (Figure 6.2c). Countries represented by this population pyramid included Cape Verde, Djibouti, Egypt, Libya, Morocco, and Namibia.

Income, Education Attainment, and Life Expectancy at Birth

The leading measure of income, education attainment, and life expectancy at birth is the HDI. This index is a composite ratio based on the three components. The income is measured by GNI per capita purchasing power parity. The purchasing power parity is the gross domestic product per capita adjusted for the relative cost of living. The education attainment is measured by literacy or years of schooling. The index is categorized into four levels—very high (0.800 and above), high (0.700–0.799), medium (0.550–0.699), and low (below 0.550). Trend data on the HDI and its components show that over all African countries have been improving. However, in 2015, no African country scored in the very high category (Figure 6.3a). Only five—Seychelles, Mauritius, Algeria, Tunisia, and Libya—were in the high HDI category. These were also the only countries that scored above the World average of 0.717. For the remaining countries, 14 fell in the medium range, while 35 countries fell in the low HDI (Figure 6.3b). More than half the continent (32 countries) had purchasing power parity of $500–$5,000 (Figure 6.3b). Only two countries had over US$20,000—Seychelles ($23,886) and Equatorial Guinea ($21,157); and only six countries had incomes above the world average of $14,447. These were Seychelles, Equatorial Guinea, Mauritius, Libya, Botswana, and Gabon. The mean average years of schooling of the world in 2015 was 8.3 years. Only four African countries—Seychelles, Mauritius, Botswana, and South Africa scored above this average. In 14 countries, the mean years of schooling was under 5 years (Figure 6.3c). In terms of life expectancy, only eight countries, Algeria, Egypt, Morocco, Libya, Tunisia, Seychelles, Mauritius, and Cape Verde, were above the world average of 71.6. Twenty-three countries had life expectancy

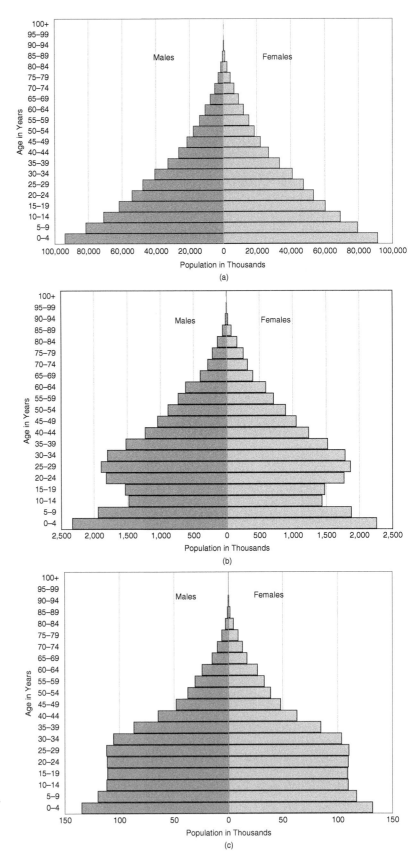

FIGURE 6.2 Population pyramids of African
countries: (a) Africa, (b) Algeria, (c) Botswana.
Source: Data from United Nations Department of
Economic and Social Population *World Population
Prospects: 2015 Revision,* custom data acquired via
website.

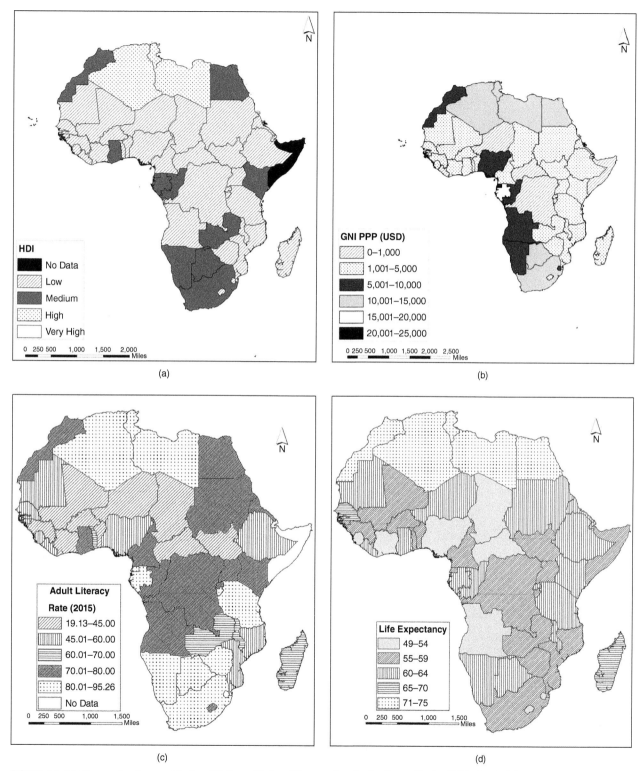

(a)

(b)

(c)

(d)

FIGURE 6.3 (a) Human development index; (b) Gross National Income Purchasing Power Parity, 2015; (c) adult literacy; (d) life expectancy.

Source: (a, b, c) UNESCO, UNDP and World Bank (d) Data from United Nations Department of Economic and Social Population Division (2015). World Population Prospects: The 2015 Revision Custom Data, acquired via website

at birth below 60 years (Figure 6.3d). Compared to developing countries' average, Africa showed only slight improvements—nine African countries scored above the developing countries' average HDI of 0.668; eight countries had life expectancy higher than developing countries' average of 70.8 years; 10 countries had higher mean average years of schooling than the average of 7.2 years, and 11 countries had GNI (PPP) above the developing countries' average of $9,257.

Population Growth

According to UN population estimates, Africa's population grew from 227,270,000 in 1950 to 1,186,178,000 in 2015 (Table 6.3). This represented a change of 354% over the 60-year period and 5.9% every year. From the table, the largest percentage changes occurred between 1975 and 1980, and 1980 and 1985, which was 15% in each of the two periods. Annual population growth rates followed a similar pattern. From 1950 to 1955, it was estimated to be 2.1% per annum. It reached a peak of 2.8% per annum from 1980 to 1985 and started declining after that. In 2010–2015, it was 2.5%. In 2010–2015, only 12 countries had rates of 3.00–3.99, and only two countries South Sudan and Niger had 4% annual population growth rate (Figure 6.4).

These growth rates show a general declining trend, but compared to other developing regions of the world, they seem to be quite high. For example, in 1975–1980, Africa's population growth rate of 2.77% was the highest of all the world's major regions followed by Latin America and the Caribbean (2.29%), and Asia (1.95%). By 2010–2015, Africa was the only region with a population growth rate of above 2.0% (2.50%). Latin America and the Caribbean had (1.12%) and Asia (1.04%).

TABLE **6.3**

Population Growth Rates of Africa 1950–2015

Year	Population (1,000s)	Change (%)	Growth rate (%)
1950	227,270		
1955	253,397	11.50	2.1
1960	285,049	12.49	2.5
1965	322,309	13.07	2.4
1970	366,792	13.80	2.5
1975	418,765	14.17	2.6
1980	482,236	15.16	2.8
1985	556,131	15.32	2.8
1990	638,729	14.85	2.7
1995	726,285	13.71	2.5
2000	819,462	12.83	2.36
2005	921,073	12.40	2.4
2010	1,033,043	12.16	2.3
2015	1,186,178	13.6	2.5

Source: United Nations, Department of Economic and Social Affairs Population Division (2015). *World Population Prospects: 2015 Revision,* custom data acquired via website.

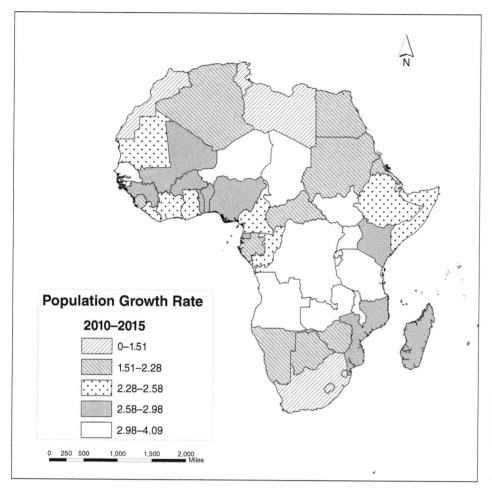

FIGURE 6.4 Population growth rates of African countries, 2005–2010.
Source: Data from United Nations Department of Economic and Social Population Division (2015). *World Population Prospects: 2015 Revision,* custom data acquired via website.

Natural Increase

Population growth has two components—natural increase and net migration. Over 99% of Africa's population growth is due to natural increase, which is the difference between births and deaths (Figure 6.5). The rate of natural increase in Africa was 26.0 per 1000 population in 2010–2015, down from the peak of 28.4 in 1980–1985. The highest rate of natural increase recorded in 2010–2015 was Niger's 40 per 1,000 population, while the lowest recorded was Mauritius' 4 per 1,000 population. The majority of the countries (40) saw decline in the rate of natural increase, while 15 countries recorded an increase of their 1980–1985 rates. Only two countries recorded below rates below 10, one was South Africa (8.6), while the other was Mauritius (4.0). The majority of the countries recorded rates of 20–29.5 in 2010–2015.

Fertility rates The decline in the rate of natural increase is in turn due to declines in both **fertility rates** and **mortality** rates. Two common measures of fertility rates are the crude birth rates and total fertility rates. The **crude birth rate** is the number of births by 1,000 population, while the **total fertility rate** is the expected number of children a woman will have by going through the child-bearing years. The statistics for both measures are given in Table 6.4, which shows that Africa's crude birth rate has been declining since 1975. Nevertheless, form 2010–2015 only four countries had crude birth rates of 10–20.

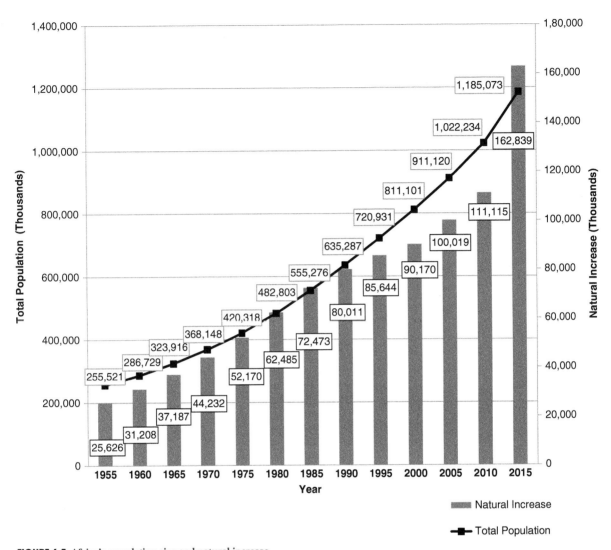

FIGURE 6.5 Africa's population size and natural increase.
Source: Data from United Nations Department of Economic and Social Population Division (2015). *World Population Prospects: 2015 Revision,* custom data acquired via website.

Africa's total fertility rate in 2010–2015 was 4.71, down from 6.62 from 1975 to 1980. The highest rate was 7.63 in Niger, while Mauritius' 1.50 was once again the lowest. Majority of African countries—39 of them—had total fertility rates of 4 and above. Indeed, eight of these countries had total fertility rates of 6 or more. Among these were Malawi, DRC, Chad, Zambia, Somalia, Mali, and Niger.

The declining fertility rates show two broad transitions. In about 50% of the countries, the rates stalled, before declining while in the remaining 50% the rates went up before declining. Countries that saw stalling rates include Algeria, Angola, Benin, DRC, Kenya, Madagascar, Nigeria, and Sierra Leone. Countries that saw a rise in fertility rates before a decline include Central African Republics, Congo, Gabon, Malawi, Mauritania, and Senegal (Table 6.4).

Explanation of fertility transitions Fertility transitions in Africa have attracted a great deal of research. Some have focused on the continent as whole (e.g., Kalipeni, 1995; Yousif, 2009), some have focused on subregions (e.g., Caldwell, 1997; Dorius, 2008; Garenne, 2008; Jones, 2006; Kirk and Pillet, 1998), while others have

TABLE 6.4

Trends in Fertility and Mortality Measures 1975–2015

Country	Crude birth rate (births per 1,000 population)				Total fertility rate (children per woman)				Crude death rate (deaths per 1,000 population)				Infant mortality rate (Infant deaths per 1,000 live births)			
	1975–1980	1995–2000	2005–2010	2010–2015	1975–1980	1995–2000	2005–2010	2010–2015	1975–1980	1995–2000	2005–2010	2010–2015	1975–1980	1995–2000	2005–2010	2010–2015
Africa	45.6	38.8	36.9	35.8	6.62	5.35	4.89	4.71	17.2	13.7	11.3	9.8	121	93	69	59
Algeria	45.0	21.6	23.1	25.1	7.18	2.88	2.72	2.93	13.3	5.3	5.1	5.1	105	42	34	30
Angola	53.5	51.6	48.7	46.2	7.35	7.00	6.60	6.20	24.9	21.1	15.8	14.2	161	38	104	96
Benin	47.2	43.6	39.1	36.6	7.00	6.16	5.31	4.89	20.0	12.9	10.3	9.6	134	92	74	69
Botswana	45.0	28.9	25.3	25.6	6.37	3.70	2.90	2.90	9.9	12.5	8.4	7.5	75	65	39	32
Burkina Faso	48.8	46.7	43.7	40.8	7.02	6.73	6.08	5.65	21.5	16.2	11.5	10.0	133	100	78	67
Burundi	49.9	43.6	44.3	44.2	7.48	7.18	6.52	6.08	19.2	14.9	12.9	11.7	125	103	86	78
Cape Verde	40.6	31.4	22.8	21.8	6.62	4.14	2.62	2.37	11.2	6.2	5.4	5.5	76	33	21	20
Cameroon	45.3	41.6	39.6	37.5	6.47	5.77	5.21	4.81	16.6	13.7	13.2	11.9	108	88	82	74
CAR	42.2	39.9	35.6	34.3	5.95	5.54	4.85	4.41	18.2	18.5	17.5	15.2	119	114	106	93
Chad	49.4	51.2	48.5	45.9	6.87	7.41	6.85	6.31	21.5	18.0	16.4	14.5	138	114	106	96
Comoros	46.7	38.4	36.0	34.6	7.05	5.60	4.90	4.60	16.8	9.6	8.6	7.7	127	74	67	58
Congo	43.1	38.7	38.5	37.3	6.35	5.12	5.05	4.95	13.0	14.5	11.4	9.0	84	85	64	51
Côte d'Ivoire	49.9	41.5	38.4	37.4	7.81	6.05	5.36	5.10	16.6	16.5	15.2	13.9	125	99	85	73
DRC	46.3	47.4	44.8	42.6	6.46	7.10	6.60	6.15	19.1	16.9	12.3	10.7	129	113	84	73
Djibouti	42.0	32.9	27.6	25.7	6.64	4.81	3.70	3.30	12.1	10.4	9.6	8.7	96	72	63	55
Egypt	39.0	25.5	25.2	28.5	5.60	3.40	2.98	3.38	13.1	6.8	6.4	6.2	133	37	23	19
Eq. Guinea	32.9	40.9	36.9	35.5	5.68	5.87	5.36	4.97	22.1	15.4	12.5	11.0	149	100	80	70
Eritrea	46.5	36.8	37.9	35.0	6.62	5.60	4.80	4.40	19.2	10.4	8.2	6.9	125	73	54	46
Ethiopia	48.5	45.5	36.4	33.2	7.18	6.83	5.26	4.59	20.8	15.2	9.6	7.8	137	97	60	50
Gabon	37.8	34.3	31.5	30.8	5.57	4.77	4.15	4.00	16.2	11.0	10.3	9.0	95	60	53	43
Gambia	51.6	45.8	43.7	42.8	6.34	5.99	5.79	5.78	20.8	12.7	9.7	9.0	101	70	51	47
Ghana	44.0	35.1	33.5	33.5	6.69	4.81	4.29	4.25	14.3	10.6	9.6	9.2	99	67	55	51
Guinea	46.9	43.8	39.7	37.6	6.45	6.24	5.54	5.13	24.3	15.4	12.7	10.4	171	112	81	59
G. Bissau	45.1	41.9	39.0	37.7	6.25	6.05	5.23	4.95	20.7	15.5	13.6	12.4	143	115	102	92
Kenya	49.9	38.1	37.9	35.4	7.64	5.07	4.80	4.44	12.5	12.7	10.6	8.7	80	74	59	52
Lesotho	41.9	33.1	28.4	28.9	5.69	4.37	3.37	3.26	15.1	13.5	17.3	14.9	110	79	76	60
Liberia	49.0	43.5	38.6	35.7	6.93	6.05	5.23	4.83	20.3	14.4	10.3	9.0	164	129	72	61
Libya	43.7	22.4	22.9	21.7	7.67	3.25	2.66	2.53	8.5	4.8	4.8	5.3	67	30	24	24

TABLE 6.4

Trends in Fertility and Mortality Measures 1975–2015 (Continued)

Country	Crude birth rate (births per 1,000 population)				Total fertility rate (children per woman)				Crude death rate (deaths per 1,000 population)				Infant mortality rate (Infant deaths per 1,000 live births)			
	1975–1980	1995–2000	2005–2010	2010–2015	1975–1980	1995–2000	2005–2010	2010–2015	1975–1980	1995–2000	2005–2010	2010–2015	1975–1980	1995–2000	2005–2010	2010–2015
Madagascar	47.4	42.9	36.3	34.8	7.00	5.80	4.83	4.50	18.0	11.4	7.9	6.9	122	78	46	37
Malawi	53.4	45.5	42.5	39.6	7.60	6.40	5.80	5.25	21.9	18.7	12.5	8.6	159	121	80	60
Mali	49.9	48.4	47.1	44.4	7.15	6.95	6.70	6.35	26.9	18.5	13.1	11.0	163	118	89	84
Mauritania	43.9	38.8	36.0	34.0	6.57	5.55	4.97	4.69	13.9	9.7	8.9	8.1	99	76	73	67
Mauritius	26.5	17.9	13.3	11.4	3.10	2.03	1.70	1.50	6.2	6.6	7.1	7.3	38	20	13	12
Morocco	38.6	23.2	20.8	21.3	5.90	2.97	2.49	2.56	12.1	6.5	6.1	5.7	102	44	32	26
Mozambique	47.9	45.4	42.0	40.0	6.52	5.85	5.65	5.45	22.1	17.2	13.5	11.8	148	111	74	64
Namibia	43.8	33.1	29.5	30.2	6.60	4.29	3.60	3.60	12.1	9.7	8.9	7.3	87	58	43	34
Niger	55.5	54.0	50.8	49.8	7.63	7.75	7.68	7.63	26.4	18.3	12.7	9.6	139	103	64	60
Nigeria	47.1	43.1	41.7	40.3	6.76	6.17	5.91	5.74	20.1	17.9	14.8	13.3	134	119	90	76
Rwanda	53.4	42.2	37.6	32.9	8.43	5.90	4.85	4.05	19.6	16.4	9.4	7.5	128	116	59	49
S. T. & Princ.	40.9	39.3	36.5	34.9	6.50	5.41	4.90	4.67	10.4	9.3	7.7	7.1	65	55	46	44
Senegal	49.5	40.5	38.9	38.9	7.45	5.78	5.15	5.18	18.8	11.2	8.3	6.6	97	68	54	44
Seychelles	29.3	19.0	19.4	18.0	4.27	2.18	2.30	2.33	7.4	7.4	7.4	7.6	28	11	10	10
Sierra Leone	46.4	45.1	41.3	36.9	6.25	6.41	5.51	4.79	24.5	26.3	17.5	14.1	162	149	117	94
Somalia	45.6	49.7	46.2	43.9	7.00	7.70	7.10	6.61	20.7	16.5	13.7	12.4	137	105	90	79
South Africa	35.8	24.9	22.1	21.0	5.00	2.95	2.55	2.40	11.6	9.6	14.7	12.5	71	53	52	38
South Sudan	48.8	44.6	39.4	37.3	6.92	6.42	5.60	5.15	25.0	17.0	13.6	12.0	169	114	89	78
Sudan	46.1	40.3	36.1	33.7	6.92	5.63	4.83	4.46	13.4	11.0	8.9	7.9	89	74	60	53
Swaziland	48.4	34.1	31.4	30.2	6.73	4.49	3.75	3.36	14.3	12.0	15.0	14.1	108	80	76	65
Tunisia	36.5	18.7	17.0	18.4	5.65	2.34	2.02	2.16	10.3	5.5	6.0	6.6	97	29	19	19
Togo	47.7	39.8	38.7	36.3	7.28	5.54	5.04	4.69	15.7	12.7	11.2	9.3	101	80	64	50
Uganda	48.9	48.8	46.1	43.7	7.10	6.95	6.38	5.91	16.6	18.1	11.9	10.2	111	98	70	61
Tanzania	47.3	42.0	42.0	39.7	6.73	5.75	5.58	5.24	15.9	15.1	9.7	7.3	109	92	52	37
W. Sahara	44.1	25.9	21.5	19.1	6.23	3.18	2.44	2.20	17.3	7.6	5.8	5.6	134	64	44	37
Zambia	49.1	44.4	43.1	40.6	7.38	6.15	5.90	5.45	15.0	19.2	12.3	9.7	101	106	70	55
Zimbabwe	47.6	33.1	35.6	36.1	7.30	4.20	4.02	4.02	11.3	16.3	16.3	11.1	74	67	62	48

Source: United Nations, Department of Economic and Social Affairs, Population Division (2015). *World Population Prospects: 2015 Revision*, custom data acquired via website.

focused on individual countries such as Ghana (Addai, 1999), Namibia (Garenne and Zwang, 2006), Nigeria (Ibisomi, 2008), and Kenya (Opiyo and Levin, 2008). With respect to fertility stalls, three main reasons have been identified in the general literature. Garenne (2008, p. 2) summarizes these as follows:

> "Firstly, a change in demographic factors, such as the tempo in fertility (earlier births or a stop in the increase of mean age at birth), or shorter birth intervals (due to mortality change, or to better health status). Secondly, a change in proximate determinants of fertility such as less contraceptive use, less abortion, earlier abortion, earlier marriages or premarital fertility, less infertility, less separation between spouses, and more sexual intercourse. Thirdly, a change in the socioeconomic context, such as a halt in urbanization, a decline income per capita, less education or a stall in trends of level education, increasing poverty, or a decrease in labor force participation."

Others have attributed the causes of the stall to slow economic growth and the HIV/AIDS epidemic (Doskoch, 2008). The argument here is that fertility generally declines when countries are experiencing economic growth. In Africa, however, most of the continent's economies stopped growing for the most part of the 1990s, while mortality increased due to HIV/AIDS.

Explanations of fertility decline With respect to overall decline, the causes have been attributed to cultural, social, and economic factors. These factors include the child value system, education, and improved health care, level of economic development, and standard of living.

The child-value system defines how society values children and whether children are seen as assets or liabilities. In traditional African societies, children were generally seen as assets because they serve as social security for their parents. It was imperative for people to have children to provide labor and to take care of them in their old age. Such a system had a built-in bias toward having many children, especially when high infant mortality was common because of poor health care. While this child-value system still exists in varying degrees on the continent, improvements in health care, education, and overall level of economic development have weakened its effects on fertility rates on the continent.

Improved health care and support for family has played a major role in the declining fertility in African countries (Caldwell and Caldwell, 2002; Kirk and Pillet, 1998; Mbacke, 1994; National Research Council, 1993; Ross et al., 2007; Short and Kiros, 2002; Zuberi et al., 2003). For example, a United Nation's (2007) study on government population policies reported that in 1976, only 21 African countries provided direct support for use of contraceptives, seven others provided some indirect support, while 13 provided no support at all. In 2007, all but nine countries provided direct support for contraceptives. Of the nine remaining countries, six provided indirect support with only three providing no support (UN 2007). In addition, the report showed a dramatic shift in how governments viewed the issue of high fertility. For example, in 1976, 22 African governments thought the fertility rates of their respective countries were satisfactory, five thought they were too low, while only 15 thought that the rates were too high. In 2007, as many as 34 governments thought the fertility rates in their respective countries were too high, only nine thought the rates of their countries were satisfactory, and only one thought its rate was low (UN, 2007). This has helped reduce the rate of infant mortality and rapid advance epidemics such as HIV/AIDS.

Education has also played multiple roles in Africa's declining fertility. First, education has raised the cost of childbearing and removed children from farms

(Caldwell, 1980). Second, educated women have lower desire to have many children because of the high opportunity cost of childbearing, because they live in a nucleated family environment rather than a farming environment and are less likely to experience high infant mortality (Kirk and Pillet, 1998; Kravdal, 2002). Third, education and the use of contraceptives are also breaking the stronghold of religion on fertility levels in Africa. For example, in a cross-country study of the role of religion on fertility, which included 22 African countries, Heaton (2011) established the use of contraceptives among religious groups even though on the average, Christians were more than twice as likely to use contraceptives as Muslims.

The HIV/AIDS epidemic has also contributed to fertility decline in a way that was not expected. In particular, several researchers predicted decades ago that the HIV/AIDS will lead to increased fertility (see Hosegood, 2008; Gregson, 1994). However, as Hosegood (2008) reports, HIV/AIDS has rather caused fertility to either stall or decline, especially among infected people and to a lesser extent among the general population. Among the main reasons for this are the biological effects on fecundity of women with HIV/AIDS, reductions in sexual activity and new partners, a desire to avoid pregnancy, the use of condoms, and the negative impact of HIV/AIDS on the quality and stability of relationship (Ahdieh, 2001; Feldblum et al., 2007; Gregson et al., 1997; Hosegood, 2008; VanDevanter et al., 1999).

Finally, the declining fertility rates may also be attributed to increasing levels of economic development (Ibisom, 2008; Kalipeni 1995; Kirk and Pillet, 1998). For example, Kalipeni (1995) found a link between higher human development indices and low fertility rates and concluded that improvements in social, economic, and demographic conditions are crucial to achieving irreversible and sustainable fertility transition in Africa. Kirk and Pillet (1998) also found a progression from higher fertility to lower fertility rates with socioeconomic variables while establishing that the more impressive fertility declines were in those African countries that had implemented strong family planning programs. In Nigeria, Ibisomi (2008) showed that while the number of children desired by couples is still high because of religion and culture, the number of children couples actually have is greatly influenced by socioeconomic factors.

Mortality rate Mortality refers to deaths occurring in a population. Mortality rate is measured by **crude death rate**, **infant mortality rate**, and **life expectancy at birth**. Crude death rate is the number of deaths per 1,000 population. Infant mortality rate is the number of infant (less than 1 year old) deaths per 1,000 live births, while life expectancy at birth is how long a person born today is expected to live. Like fertility rates, all these rates have been improving in Africa. From 1975 to 1980, Africa's crude death rate was estimated as 17.2 per 1,000 population. In 2010–2015, it was 9.8 (Table 6.4). From 2010 to 2015, Algeria had the lowest crude death rate of 5.1, while Central African Republic had the highest rate of 15.2. In general, crude death rates show a declining trend in almost every country. However, in 11 countries, crude death rates rose, especially in the 1990–2000 period after declining in the preceding decade. These countries are Botswana, Central African Republic, Congo, Cote d'Ivoire, Lesotho, Namibia, Rwanda, South Africa, Swaziland, Zambia, and Zimbabwe. This is most likely due to the rise of HIV/AIDS in those countries. In nine countries, the crude death rates appear to have stalled at the lower end over the last three decades. These include Cabo Verde, Mauritius, Sao Tome and Principe, Seychelles, and all the North African countries.

With respect to infant mortality, between 1975 and 2015, the rate dropped from 121 to 59 per 1,000 live births, a drop of 51%. With the exception of seven, all countries on the continent saw a steady drop in their infant mortality rates. For the seven countries that deviated from this trend infant mortality rates rose during the period of 1990–2000 after the rates had fallen in the prior decade. The countries are Botswana, Burundi, Central African Republic, Congo, DRC, Kenya, and Zimbabwe. Seychelles had the lowest infant mortality rate (10 per 1,000 live births), while Chad had the highest being (96). However, only 22 countries had infant mortality rates of 50 or less per 1000.

Infant mortality in Africa is affected by biosocial or sociodemographic and household factors. For example, in Cote d'Ivoire, Andoh et al. (2007) found that infant mortality was higher among male children, children born in less than 24 months of preceding sibling, children of less educated mothers, and children in rural areas. These findings have been confirmed in Nigeria (Jones et al., 2003). A study of 11 African countries by Ayamele (2009) also found that infant mortality rate was higher in rural areas than urban areas, and that higher literacy levels was strongly associated with lower infant mortality except for three countries—Chad, Ethiopia, and Niger, where there was no association. In addition, higher wealth was positively associated with lower mortality in six of the countries (Benin, DRC, Mali, Malawi, Madagascar, and Nigeria), while in Cameroon, Ethiopia, Niger, and Rwanda, there was no association.

Trend data show that Africa's conditions have improved in terms of all these measures of demographic characteristics from even a decade ago. However, Africa still trails behind all the other major regions in comparison. Table 6.5 provides comparative estimates of the various measures for Africa and other major regions of the world, from which we can see that relatively speaking, Africa still has the highest crude birth rates, highest crude death rates, lowest life expectancy at birth, and highest infant mortality.

These trends seem to be consistent with the **Demographic Transition Model** (Figure 6.6), which shows that both fertility and mortality rates decline from high to low as societies go through modernization (Davis, 1945; Notestein, 1944). Although the model has since been criticized for ignoring cultural and other factors (see e.g., Caldwell, 1996; Kirk, 1996; McCann, 2009), it has remained a very powerful generalization partly due to its assertion that the transition will occur in every society (Coale, 1973), and partly due to the fact that economic factors particularly improved standard of living do influence fertility (Bongaarts and Watkins, 1996; Kalipeni, 1995).

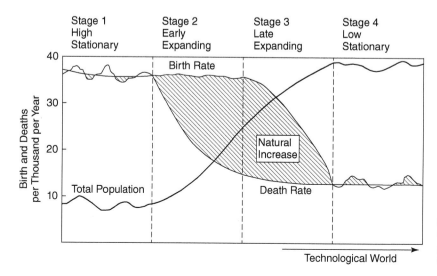

FIGURE 6.6 The Demographic Transition Model. *Source:* Created by David Ofori-Amoah.

TABLE 6.5

Comparative Data with World Major Regions

Country	Crude Birth Rate (Births per 1,000 population)				Crude Death Rates (Deaths per 1,000 population)				Life Expectancy (at Birth)				Infant Mortality Rate (Infant Deaths per 1,000 live births)			
	1980–1985	1990–1995	2000–2005	2010–2015	1980–1985	1990–1995	2000–2005	2010–2015	1980–1985	1990–1995	2000–2005	2010–2015	1980–1985	1990–1995	2000–2005	2010–2015
World	28	24	21	20	10	9	8	8	62	65	67	70	76	63	49	36
Africa	45	41	38	36	16	14	13	10	51	52	53	60	111	102	81	59
Asia	29	25	20	18	9	8	7	7	61	65	69	72	78	62	46	31
Europe	14	12	10	11	11	11	12	11	72	73	74	77	18	13	8	5
L. America	31	25	21	18	8	7	6	6	65	68	72	75	60	39	25	20
N. America	15	15	14	12	9	9	8	8	74	76	77	79	11	9	7	6
Oceania	20	20	18	17	8	8	7	7	70	73	75	77	33	28	25	20

Source: United Nations, Department of Economic and Social Affairs, Population Division (2015). *World Population Prospects: 2015 Revision,* custom data acquired via website.

Net Migration

Net migration, the difference between immigration and emigration, is the second component of population growth. Lack of readily available data makes it difficult to ascertain the actual contribution of net migration to Africa's population. However, United Nations estimates show that the contribution of net migration to Africa's population is not only negligible but also negative. A negative net migration means that more people leave permanently than those who come in permanently. For example, in 1975, Africa's net migration was –1,915,000, which was only (–0.46%) of its total population. In 2015, it was –2,900,000 (–0.24%). With the exception of three countries, almost every African country's net migration has been negative since the 1970s. The three countries are South Africa, Botswana, and Gabon. A few other countries had positive net migrations through the 1970s, but these became negative later due to political instability and other factors. These countries include Eritrea, Somalia, and Uganda, which had positive net migrations until 1980s; Djibouti until the 1990s, and Libya and Core d'Ivoire until the 2000s. As a component of population growth, net migration originates from two sources—intranational or international. However, since intranational migration affects population growth at subnational level only the discussion here will focus on international migration.

Mabogunje (1970) defined a **migration system** as a set of places linked by flows and counter flows of people, goods, services, and information, which tend to facilitate further exchange, between the places. From this definition, we can identify two systems of international migration in Africa: international migration within Africa and international migration outside Africa. The first, which is by far the largest, is migration among African countries and the second is migration between African and overseas countries.

Migration inside Africa According to United Nations revised estimates on international migration, in 2015, there were 20,649,557 international immigrants in Africa. This was about 1.7% of the total population of Africa and a decrease from 2.5% in 1990. Of these, 20,444,752 or 99% were from inside of Africa itself. There were five countries that had more than 1 million international immigrants. These were led by South Africa and followed by Cote d'Ivoire, Nigeria, Kenya, and Ethiopia. These five countries housed 42% of the total African immigrants on the continent. For the majority of African countries, the percentage of international migrants to total population is very small. However, for a few countries that percentage has been consistently around 10% or more since 1990. These countries are Cote d'Ivoire, Djibouti, Gabon, Gambia, Seychelles, and Libya. Approximately 59% of these immigrants in 2015 originated from 11 countries, led by Burkina Faso, Somalia, DRC, and Sudan. These four countries contributed more than 1 million immigrants, while the remaining seven countries had more than 500,000 each. Within this large system, much focus has been given to three international migration subsystems in Africa: the Southern African, the West African, and the North Africa migration subsystems (Adepoju, 2000; Agadjanian, 2008; Arthur, 1991; Betts, 2006; Baldwin-Edwards, 2006; Crush, 2000; De Haas, 2006; SAMP, 2008). To these we may add the East and Central African subsystems.

Anchored by South Africa, the **Southern African migration subsystem**, dates back to the late 19th century when a large pool of cheap labor was needed to work the new gold and diamond mining industry of South Africa. To meet this need, migrant workers were recruited from neighboring areas of present-day Lesotho, Mozambique, and Malawi (Zuberi and Sibanda, 2004). These workers were recruited through the Employment Bureau of Africa (TEBA), which at its peak had over

500,000 contract laborers a year, from Botswana, Lesotho, Malawi, Mozambique, Swaziland, Zambia, and Zimbabwe, working in the mines, as well as on commercial farms and plantations (Black et al., 2006; Zuberi and Sibanda, 2004). During the Apartheid era, several laws were passed that restricted movements of Africans within the country. Economic downturn in the 1990s hit the South African mining industry very hard, which led to large layoffs of more local workers than foreign workers, a policy which benefitted workers from Mozambique the most (Black et al., 2006). Following the fall of apartheid government in 1994, South Africa passed new immigration laws, which still placed emphasis on employment as the key reason for immigration. Recent studies report of a dramatic shift in labor recruitment and a surge in anti-foreigner sentiments in the country (Crush and James, 1995; Chirwa, 1998). In addition to South Africa, another country that started attracting migrants was Botswana, which served primarily as transit for people who wanted to go to South Africa. However, the rise of HIV/IDS epidemic in that country seems to have curtailed the flow of migrants. United Nations data estimates show that as a region, Southern Africa was home to 2,960,849 African immigrants. Of these 68.4% were domiciled in South Africa. Most of the rest were in Zimbabwe, Malawi, Mozambique, Botswana, and Zambia. About 85% of the migrants originated within the region led by Zimbabwe (23.3%), and followed by Mozambique (20.7%), Lesotho (15.9%), Namibia (6.1%), Swaziland (4.1%), and Malawi (3.7%). About 3%, however, originated from DRC, while another 2% came from Ethiopia.

In contrast, the **West African migration subsystem** has had several anchors depending on the circumstances in the region. In the early postindependence era, a booming cocoa production industry made Ghana and Cote d'Ivoire preferred destinations for migrant labor from neighboring countries (Agadjanian, 2008). The collapse of the world cocoa market and the oil boom in the 1970s, redirected migrant flow from Ghana to Nigeria, while political stability kept Cote d'Ivoire a good destination. However, recent wars and instability turned prospective migrants away from Cote D'Ivoire. The origins of most of the migrants within this subsystem have been consistent—they have come from the northern landlocked countries of Burkina Faso, Mali, Niger, and Chad (Adepoju, 2006; Agadjanian, 2008). One of the factors that has promoted the movement of people within this migration system is the Economic Community of West African States (ECOWAS), which guarantees freedom of movement among member states. In 2015, the region was home to 5,882,320 African immigrants. Cote d'Ivoire was the top destination with 35.6% followed by Nigeria (18.2%), Burkina Faso (11.2%), and Ghana (5.1%). Almost all (93.9%) of these immigrants originated from the region. The largest contributors were Burkina Faso (24.2%), Mali (14%), Cote d'Ivoire (11.4%), Benin (9.1%), and Ghana (6.6%).

Like the other two subsystems, the **North African migration subsystem** also predates colonial times, during which large groups of nomadic herdsmen roamed the region. The arrival of colonialism in Algeria (1830), Tunisia (1881), Egypt (1882), and Morocco (1912) directed the migratory patterns toward Europe (de Haas, 2006). In the early postcolonial period, particularly from the 1950s to 1973, North African countries followed the same migration policies except for Egypt, which imposed strict controls on emigration. In 1973, as a result of the Arab Oil Embargo, Libya, with its vast oil resources emerged as a dominant country in North Africa and started a guest-worker program to attract primarily unskilled workers from Egypt and Tunisia. Between 1992 and 2000, Libyan leader Muammar Gaddafi decided to pursue a new international policy that was much more oriented to the rest of Africa. As part of this, Gaddafi encouraged people from sub-Saharan Africa to go and work in Libya. An important feature of the North Africa subsystem of migration is that the anchor countries have increasingly become transit countries for migrants who want to reach Europe rather than the migrants' final destinations. However, once they reach North Africa, most of them become stranded and start living in very poor conditions (Baldwin-Edwards, 2006). Recent UN estimates support these trends. Thus, in 2015, there was an estimated 423,577 African migrants in North Africa, of which 40.4% were in Libya, 28% in Algeria, 17.2% in Egypt, 7.2% in Tunisia, and 6.1% in Morocco. The leading countries of origin were Somalia (35%), Western Sahara (21.5%), and Sudan (16.5%). A much smaller proportion came from the countries in the region—Algeria (6.8%), Egypt (5.7%), Libya (4.7%), and Morocco (2.8%).

The **Central and East African migration subsystems**, though dates back to colonial period, have not been a focus of attention compared to other regions—especially Southern, West and North African subsystems. Like other regions, the dynamics of these regional migrations have shifted with internal stability and economic prospects. In 2015, Central Africa had about 1,956,714 African migrants in the region. About 25.7% of these were in Chad, 21.5% in DRC, 19.1% in Cameroon, 18.6% in Congo Republic, and 12.5% in Gabon. Most of the migrants were from Central African Republic (19.8%), Sudan (19.2%), DRC (11.9%), Angola (11.3%), Rwanda (6.1%), Nigeria (5%), and Cameroon (4%). With respect to the East African subsystem, there were about 5,082,665 migrants in the region in 2015. The majority were distributed as follows: Kenya (20.1%), Ethiopia (19.7%), South Sudan (18%), Uganda (13.6%), Sudan (9.4%), and Rwanda (8.5%). The majority of these immigrants were from within the region—Somalia (19.7%), DRC (16.3%), Sudan (14.9%), Uganda (10.7%), and South Sudan (8.7%). The reasons behind these migration systems are basically the same and include such physical, economic, social, and political factors as drought, poverty, unemployment, civil war, political instability, the need to support family, and the desire to better one's prospects (Betts, 2006).

Migration outside Africa United Nations estimates of international migration outside Africa show that in 2015, there were 161,167,068 migrants of African origin living outside Africa, of which 56.8% were living in Europe, 25.6% in Asia, and 13.4% in North America (United States and Canada). This migration began slowly in the early postcolonial period, but gathered momentum from the 1990s (Table 6.6).

About 73% of Africans living in **Europe** in 2015, originated from 10 African countries with Morocco alone accounting for 27% while the remaining nine countries accounted for the 45% (Table 6.7). About 96.1% of the migrants lived in 10 European countries and 40.1% of which lived in France. Other top resident countries were the United Kingdom, Italy, Spain, and Germany (Table 6.8). While the

---

TABLE **6.6**

African Migrants in the Major Regions of the World, 1990–2015

Region	1990	1995	2000	2005	2010	2015	%
Asia	1,777,604		2,163,034	2,397,548	3,389,501	4,134,932	25.6
Europe	4,431,130	4,901,043	5,586,170	7,454,084	8,603,174	9,195,990	56.9
North America	548,697	806,390	1,095,908	1,492,748	1,926,698	2,281,390	14.1
Latin America	19,325	19,558	20,250	28,158	39,463	52,289	0.3
Oceania	126,717	137,693	228,407	326,629	435,286	502,467	3.1
Total	6,903,473	5,864,684	9,093,769	11,699,167	14,394,122	16,167,068	100.0

Source: United Nations, Department of Economic and Social Affairs Population Division (2015). *World Population Prospects: 2015 Revision*, custom data acquired via website.

TABLE 6.7

Top Ten Countries of Origin of African Migrants in Europe 1990–2015

Year	Morocco	Algeria	Tunisia	Angola	Egypt	Senegal	Kenya	S. Africa	Ghana	Nigeria	Somalia	Africa Total
1990	1,375,064	842,314	397,891	162,918	134,389	128,798	119,096	99,487	97,254	88,170	+	4,431,130
1995	1,498,505	882,932	409,117	180,878	152,927	134,121	129,609	143,472	117,452	123,700	+	4,901,043
2000	1,692,575	929,043	420,537	206,050	173,014	143,444	142,386	191,499	138,573	163,640	+	5,586,170
2005	2,106,495	1,469,307	517,824	217,960	219,893	204,202	+	232,565	176,292	266,214	153,434	7,454,084
2010	2,472,372	1,484,565	545,781	196,238	267,470	264,415	98,112	281,761	217,300	370,476	222,694	8,603,174
2015	2,507,560	1,597,319	584,359	213,459	282,923	269,394	+	311,879	232,623	398,476	279,948	9,195,990

*This does not mean that there were no migrants from this country. There were but mot among the top 10.

TABLE 6.8

Top Ten Countries of Destination of African Migration to Europe 1990–2015

Year	France	UK	Italy	Portugal	Germany	Belgium	Spain	Netherlands	Switzerland	Sweden	Africa Total
1990	2,318,463	475,203	424,074	267,582	211,583	183,049	170,018	167,087	59,645	42,287	4,431,130
1995	2,353,523	622,737	517,812	301,226	241,206	165,394	212,592	210,431	72,491	51,307	4,901,043
2000	2,468,540	781,671	612,818	347,174	271,891	143,450	362,707	261,236	87,731	55,122	5,586,170
2005	3,340,074	993,964	839,615	362,137	340,445	130,690	727,788	304,489	99,248	69,108	7,454,084
2010	3,462,867	1,287,218	1,066,386	316,997	408,978	155,661	1,070,619	310,773	112,745	114,836	8,603,174
2015	3,745,759	1,446,053	1,066,565	347,188	423,071	213,283	969,710	327,188	132,468	168,163	9,195,990

Source: United Nations, Department of Economic and Social Affairs, Population Division (2015). *World Population Prospects: 2015 Revision*, custom data acquired via website.

overwhelming majority of immigrants from Francophone Africa lived in France, those from Anglophone Africa did not live only in the United Kingdom but in other European countries as well including Germany, Italy, and Spain.

About 99.9% of 2,281,390 African migrants living in North America in 2015 were in the **United States and Canada**. Of these, 1,418,357 or 74% were in the United States while 567,774 or 26% were in Canada. Of those in the United States, 73% came from 10 countries led by Nigeria, Ethiopia, Egypt, Somalia, and Ghana. In Canada, 67% of the African migrants came from 10 countries led by Morocco, Algeria, Egypt, and South Africa.

The Brain Drain A distinctive feature about Africa's international migration is the **brain drain**, which is the migration of substantial proportions of the total skilled workforce of African countries. Estimates of the size and extent of this brain drain are varied and a bit difficult to come by. Table 6.7 shows African-born 25 years and older living in nine developed countries in 2010 (the latest year for which comparative data were available) classified by skill level. The table shows that of the 3,338,617 men who were living in the nine countries in 2010, 36% were of low skill, 23% medium, and 40.4% were high skilled. On the women side, 41.4% of the 2,979,496 women were low skill, 22.2% were medium, while 36.4% were high skill. Of particular note is the extremely high proportion of skilled African men and women living in Australia, Canada, the United Kingdom, and the United States compared to France, Germany, Portugal, Spain, and the Netherlands. Based on past reports, most of this skilled workforce is in health and education (see, e.g., Abdellatif, 2010; Baldwin-Edwards, 2006; World Bank, 2006).

Brain drain has been occurring since the 1960s, when African countries sent their promising young men and women to study abroad as part of massive human capital development programs (Abdellatif, 2010). At that time, majority of these young men and women returned home as they were supposed to. However, as deteriorating economic and political conditions in African countries worsened productivity incentives and workplace satisfaction through the 1970s and 1980s, majority of the students decided to not return after their studies. The situation worsened when education and health care professionals, who had trained and were working in their respective countries, also emigrated. By the 1990s, emigration of skilled Africans had become a major problem. Several efforts have been made in the past to stem this flow, but these have failed because of the complex nature of the reasons why young professionals leave. Essentially, it is a combination of economic, social, and political environments of Africa, and unless African economies become viable with the certainty and the political stability that assures African professionals a decent life, it will be difficult to stop the flow.

Refugees and asylum seekers in Africa Another group of international migrants are refugees and asylum seekers. **Refugees** are people who have been forced to leave their places of origin for another place or country due to natural or human disaster or both. According to United Nations estimates, the number of refugees has been growing since 1960 (UNHCR, 2009). Thus, in 1960, there were an estimated 75,000 refugees in Africa. At the end of 2015, there were 5,313,282 refugees in Africa, which was 34%% of the total refugee population in the world. About 79% of these refugees originated from seven countries: Somalia (21%), South Sudan (14.7%), Sudan (11.7%), DRC (10.2%), Central African Republic (8.9%), Eritrea (7.1) %), and Burundi (5.5%). Every African country, with the exception of Cape Verde, Comoros, Equatorial Guinea, Mauritius, Sao Tome and Principe, and Seychelles, hosted some refugees. However, eight countries hosted about 72% of the total refugee population. These were Ethiopia (15%), Kenya (12%), Uganda (10%), Chad (8%), DRC (8%), Sudan (7%), and South Sudan (8%).

Asylum seekers are people who are awaiting decisions on their refugee applications. At the end of 2015, there were 558,437 asylum seekers in Africa. Of these 548,005 or 98% were of African origin, and the majority were from Ethiopia (13%), DRC (13%), Eritrea (10%), Zimbabwe (10%), Somalia (9%), Nigeria (8%), and Sudan (7%). The remaining 2% foreign citizens were from Bangladesh, India, China, Pakistan, and Iraq. South Africa was the most preferred asylum country, accounting for 26.5% of all the asylum applications. The rest applied to Germany (11.3%), Kenya (6.7%), Italy (6.2%), Uganda (6.1%), France (4.4%), and the United States (3.6%). South Africa continues to be a favorable place for asylum seekers because of its generous treatment of both refugees and asylum seekers, less cumbersome application process, and also its relatively stronger economy. Zimbabwe was the leading country of origin of refugees and asylum seekers to South Africa. In 2015, it accounted for 36% of all application for asylum in South Africa.

Irregular or undocumented migration Irregular, illegal, or undocumented migration is when a noncitizen enters a country without the appropriate travel documents—a passport and a visa. It also includes situations when a migrant who is a noncitizen enters a country with appropriate travel documents but overstays the duration he or she is allowed by law, without seeking permission to do so. The origins of this type of migration in Africa can be traced back to precolonial days, when people moved relatively freely from one place to another to engage in various kinds of economic activities including agriculture, fisheries, and mineral production. The imposition of colonial boundaries and the reinforcement of those boundaries during the postcolonial period introduced the phenomena of irregular migration in Africa. People who could previously enter a country without any problems found themselves having to meet all kinds of requirements. Those who could meet these formal requirements had to find creative ways of entering the country and remaining in it for purposes of employment.

An important feature in irregular migration is the **transit country**, which is a country used as entry point by migrants to reach their ultimate destination. In Southern Africa, Botswana serves as the most important transit country for getting into South Africa, Zambia, Zimbabwe, and Tanzania, while all the North African countries serve as transit points for irregular migrants to enter France, Spain, the Netherlands, Italy, Belgium, and Germany. The main sources of these irregular migrants are Nigeria, Ghana, and Senegal in West Africa, and Morocco, Tunisia, and Algeria in North Africa (Campbell, 2010).

Causes of International Migration

The general causes of international migration inside and outside of Africa have been discussed in the simplistic model of "push-pull" factors. The **push factors** are all the factors that make people's places of origin no longer attractive causing them to leave for other places. The **pull factors** are those factors that make places more attractive causing people to want to move and settle there permanently. Specifically, however, pull and factors can be economic, political, environmental, and sociocultural factors.

Economic factors Economically, imbalances among individual African countries and between African countries and developed countries have been identified as one of the main reasons behind international migration both within and outside Africa. This imbalance caused in part by unfavorable trade policies of Africa's major trading partners particularly the EU and in part by the chronic slow economic growth, manifests itself in many features of African economies. They include severe unemployment and underemployment of educated young people, and low wages, poor working conditions, little promotion prospects, heavy workload, and limited access of modern technology in work place, for the employed. All these serve to push people away into migration.

In contrast, there is promise of work and better working conditions in recipient countries backed up by deliberate and aggressive recruiting by both governments and private agencies. These are the reasons cited by the numerous health care workers as well as other skilled personnel that have left and continue to leave their countries and the continent (see, e.g., Adepojou, 2004; Agadjanian, 2008; Betts, 2006; Buchan and Sochalski, 2004; Connell et al., 2007; Kohnert, 2007; Ulicki and Crush, 2002). In addition, space-cost convergence brought about by improved transportation and communication has made it possible for people who could previously not afford to travel to do so.

Political factors Politically, regional organizations, government immigration policies, and political instability have been identified as the reasons behind international migration. In the case of regional organizations, the roles played by the Southern African Development Community (SADC), established in 1992, and the Economic Community of West African States (ECOWAS), established in 1975, have been particularly important. The SADC's overall goal is to promote integration and cooperation among all member states, while ECOWAS' goal is to promote free movement of goods, capital, and people and to make it possible for citizens of member states to enter and reside in any member state (Adepoju, 2000; Agadjanian, 2008; Black et al., 2006).

Immigration policies of both African and overseas countries also affect international migrations. According Black et al. (2006), most African governments' position on immigration is either neutral or hostile. As a result, there are only few countries in Africa that have enacted policies to encourage emigration, and almost all of them are in North Africa. For example, Morocco has been consistent in promoting emigration as a way of controlling unemployment levels in the country (Baldwin-Edwards, 2006). Even Algeria and Egypt, which have had some "hostile" immigration policies at some point, enacted policies that encouraged emigration. For example, in 1968, Algeria signed agreements with France that restricted emigration of Algerians to France to 35,000 a year. Similarly, Egypt adopted an open door immigration policy after 1973, which allowed emigration of large numbers of Egyptians to go to the Gulf States and also to Libya (de Haas, 2006). Other government policies that have encouraged immigration include work-visa programs of apartheid South Africa and Libya, immigrant-friendly policies of Botswana, and less cumbersome policies for refugees and asylum-seekers such as those of South Africa.

In contrast, most of the destination countries of African immigrants have pursued aggressive immigration policies to get skilled Africans. For example, most of the citizens from North Africa who went to Europe through agreements signed between North African governments and European countries ended up becoming permanent residents of European countries because of aggressive legalization campaigns in the Netherlands (1975), Belgium (1975), and in France (1981–1982) (de Haas, 2006). In the case of Morocco, Baldwin-Edwards (2006) reports that massive family reunion in the 1970s and 1980s increased the number of Moroccans in France, Belgium, Germany, and the Netherlands from 400,000 in 1975 to more than one million in 1992. By 1998, there were 1.6 million Moroccans in Europe, of which 430,000 were granted EU nationality even though Moroccan government strongly opposed the action (de Haas, 2006). Another example of recipient country policies is the decision by many Organization for Economic Co-operation and Development (OECD) countries to ease their restrictions on visa requirements for highly skilled professionals (Buchan, 2007). At the same time, researchers continue to find that efforts to enforce strict immigration laws result in the increase in irregular migration (Kohnert, 2007; Baldwin-Edwards, 2006; Betts, 2006).

Sociocultural and environmental factors Associated with political instability are other sociocultural factors such as unrest, incidence of conflicts, civil wars, food insecurity, and HIV/AIDS pandemic, which have also contributed to international migration (Bascom; 1995; Connell et al., 2007; Findley, 1994; IOM, 2003; Lucas, 2006). Grote and Warner (2010) address the role of environmental factors on migration in Africa. They argue that migration could be a possible coping mechanism people use to reduce their vulnerability to environmental shocks such as floods, drought, desertification, or soil degradation. In addition, these events may cause migration once the tipping point has been reached. However, they also admit that not all environmental factors may lead to migration.

POPULATION ISSUES

Africa's population size, distribution and characteristics have generated several issues all of which focus on the relationship between population and economic development. During the 1970s and 1980s, it was about whether or not Africa's rapid population growth is detrimental to its economic development. Over the past decade or so, it has focused more on international migration and economic development. In this section, we will review these concerns outlining the salient points of the debates and their implications for African countries.

Population Growth (Natural Increase) and Economic Development

The question of whether Africa's population size and growth is detrimental to its economic development is firmly rooted in the old debate of population and development that dates back to Antiquity. The history of this debate is one of controversy (Ofori-Amoah and Adjibolosoo, 1998).

The pessimists take their cue from Malthus (1798) who synthesized all the prior ideas about the negative effects of population in his population theory that said unchecked population growth could have disastrous effects on the well-being of people. In the 20th century, Malthus' ideas received a boost through the work of Hardin (1968), Ehrlich (1968), and other nongovernmental agencies. This **neo-Malthusian view** argued that rapid population growth was the main cause of poverty and environmental degradation. To eliminate poverty and environmental degradation, population growth must be curbed through birth control and mutual coercion.

The optimists follow the ideas of people such as Godwin, Sadler, Carey, Chalmers, and Marx and Engels, who were Malthus' contemporaries (Hutchinson, 1967). For example, Godwin argued that poverty exist not because of overpopulation but maldistribution and unavoidable underproduction. Both Engels (1844) and Marx (1867) also argued that Malthus' views would only occur under capitalism, which did not only condemn the poor to starve to death but also ignored the power the fact that

that labor could be mobilized for improved production. During the 20th century, these views were revived by the ideas of Boserup (1970) and Simon (1981). Boserup (1970) argued that rapid population growth is actually needed to bring improvements in agricultural, while Simon (1981) argued that population is the ultimate resource of any country. As a result, even though an additional mouth to an existing population would appear to be an additional burden through the growing years, that person is also a boon, since that person will also contribute to the economy eventually. The purpose of this broad outline of the population debate is to show that after more than two centuries there appears to be no clear agreement about the population-development debate (Ofori-Amoah and Adjibolosoo, 1998; Hutchinson, 1957). However, the question of whether or not rapid population growth and large population size are detrimental to Africa's economic development still remain.

Rapid Population Growth and Africa's Economic Development

The issue as to whether rapid population growth is detrimental to economic development appears to be a no-brainer on the surface. This is because rapid population can lead to large population size, and a large population size is more difficult to support than a small population size. Second, rapid population growth diverts resources from productive investments into feeding a growing population, since it is easier to feed a family of one than a family of two. Third, rapid population growth creates imbalance in the age structure and distribution of the population, which in turn increases the dependency ratio. The pressure to feed and take care of the basic needs of a growing population also makes it difficult for the government to provide essential services, especially education, thus leading to poor quality of the population. Finally, rapid population growth is the main cause of environmental degradation. The increasing mouths to feed lead to the need for more agricultural land. This in turn destroys land cover and degrades soil conditions.

However, rapid population growth is a problematic concept since what constitutes "rapid" is all relative and so is population size. Growth rates are affected by the base on which they are calculated. A small base can exaggerate growth rate while a large base can shrink growth rate. Second, population size per se may or may not affect economic development. As you observed from prereading assignments, there are cities in developed countries that have populations larger than African countries. Also the number of children a family will have to feed may not be the real issue as whether or not that family has the ability to do so. If they do not, even taking care of a single child may be a difficult task.

Third, rapid population growth can stretch out existing services, but that is assuming that nothing is being done to provide more services and to upgrade them, which is the case in many African countries. Here one may argue that governments' inability to extend existing services or provide new ones to meet the needs of the population may not be necessarily due to rapid population growth, but due to a host of other factors including inept planning and allocation of resources, corrupt practices, mismanagement of public funds, and lack of maintenance management, as well as unfavorable international political and economic order. In these circumstances, continuous provision of adequate facilities and services would be difficult even when there is zero population growth.

As for environmental degradation, there is some evidence that rapid population growth can have a negative impact on the environment but most of that impact depends on the technology of production and consumption. Thus, if most people living in Africa do not have to use the shifting cultivation and the bush fallow techniques of farming, the so-called "destruction" of the rain forest and other environmental degradation would be reduced.

In the final analysis, we may surmise rapid population and economic development are interdependent but may not be causally related. It is important to control population growth rate but rapid population growth rate is not the cause of poverty in the developing countries as it is often claimed by some. There is nothing inherent in curbing population growth that can bring economic development and for that matter alleviate poverty unless a conscious effort is also made to increase the productive capacities and abilities of the poor people. This is because the causes of poverty are too complex for one factor to be singled out as the cause. It is reasonable, however, to see the control of rapid population growth as part of the economic development strategy of Africa but not the only one.

Migration and Development

Another population issue that has become a major concern in recent years is the impact of international migration on economic development of Africa. There are two main views in this debate. On the one hand, international migration is seen as a positive factor in development. On the other hand, it is seen as a negative factor. Both views have centered on the role of four main elements: brain drain, remittances, the **diaspora**, and the returned migrants (Oucho, 2008).

Migration as a Positive Factor in Africa's Development

Proponents of migration as a positive factor say that although African migrants' remittances are relatively small compared to other regions of the world, they nevertheless have increasingly become a big part of the economies of many African countries. Estimates of remittances are variable but the fact is they have become a dominant fixture in boosting incomes of households in the migrants' home countries. For example, Kohnert (2007) estimates that in 2004, African migrants transferred about $14 billion, while Seymour (2011) estimates that they total about $21billion a year. In North Africa, where data on remittances seem to be a bit better, "remittances have constituted the highest ratio to GDP of any given region in the world" over the past two decades (Baldwin-Edwards, 2006, p. 315). In 2004, for example, remittances exceeded tourism in its contribution to Morocco's GDP. In Tunisia, remittances and tourism were the two major sources of foreign currency, while remittances were also one of the largest sources of foreign exchange in Egypt and Algeria (de Haas, 2006; Hassan, 2009). In other parts of Africa, remittances represented 3% of the GDPs of Nigeria and Kenya, 7% of those of Ethiopia, Senegal, and Sudan, 11% of that of Ghana, 23% of that of Cape Verde, and about 40% that of Lesotho (Kohnert, 2007).

In addition to serving as substantial export earnings for some countries, remittances also help sustain and support livelihood of the poor, raise income levels, pay for essential services as siblings' education, investment in real estate and other infrastructure, enhancing agricultural production, and establishment of numerous small-scale business enterprises, especially in the retail sector (e.g., Azam and Gubert, 2006; de Haas, 2006; Lucas, 2006; Oucho, 2010). For example, in Morocco, de Haas (2006) found distinct differences between incomes of households receiving international remittances and those without. In Ghana, Adams and Cuecuecha (2013) found that household receiving international remittances had the highest per capita expenditure than those without. In Mali, Azzam and Guber (2006) found that the average remittances received per households was roughly equivalent to annual consumption expenditure required to keep three people from above the poverty line, which is $1 or CFA F700 a day. In addition, households with migrants abroad had about 56% more income per capita than households without migrants abroad. In Somalia, remittances have become an invaluable foundation for the households most of whom live in refugee camps, while in Zimbabwe, most people would not be able to survive without international remittances (Oucho, 2010).

Proponents of migration's positive role to Africa's development also cite the role of Africans in the diaspora in their home countries. This factor, which has been referred to as **brain gain** in contrast to brain drain, shows itself in several ways, including transfer of knowledge and new ideas and establishment of foreign trade. The return migrants become leaders in politics and innovation in industry and service. Examples are the leaders of Africa's independence movements in the 1950s and 1960s. Apart from this, the diaspora can become agents of trade promotion, technology transfer, and productive investments. As Mercer et al. (2008, p. 68) succinctly put it

> "They identify, fund and construct public infrastructural projects such as roads, water and electricity supplies; support public institutions such as schools, hospitals, libraries, market places, town halls and post offices; and contribute to the beautification of the homeplace."

They also have the potential for encouraging the expansion of education in their home countries and putting pressure on African governments to be serious about fixing their economies (Seymour, 2011). In Tunisia, Abdellatif (2010) notes that investment in real estate by Tunisian migrants did not only improve the quality of life but also spurned out job creation in the local building sector and the formation of building companies, building material stores, and carpentry and ironmongery businesses. Similarly, the agricultural sector benefitted in the expansion of acreages and modernization of production methods. Examples of such business ventures have been found in many African countries including Ghana, Cameroon, Nigeria, Somalia, Tanzania, and Zimbabwe (Mercer et al., 2008).

Migration as a Negative Factor to Africa's Development

Opponents of migration as a positive factor counter the above arguments on several grounds. First, they argue that the emigration of highly skilled people from African countries introduces various forms of external costs to the countries. Such costs include the role of the highly skilled on productivity of others; the influence of the highly skilled on economic growth, the role the highly skilled play in the delivery of specific services, the loss of tax revenue, and the loss of the public money spent in educating the highly skilled (Lucas, 2006).

Second, migration from Africa is transfer of cash resources from Africa (Landau and Vigneswaran, 2007). For example, an IOM (2006) study showed that South Africa spent US$1 billion in training health workers only to lose them to other countries. While it is true that these migrants may send remittances, the fact that most of the remittances end up in private hands does not compensate for the heavy public investments the government makes in both education and health care.

Third, remittances may also worsen inequality since in general most migrants tend to come from relatively well-to-do backgrounds (Landau and Vigneswaran, 2007; Lucas, 2006). It is therefore possible for remittances to bypass the people who need it the most. Remittances also undermine the political pressures on corrupt governments since they relieve pressure on people and make them less demanding of their respective governments for help. Apart from this, migration may also have a number of social impacts, such as removal of role models for the youth and lack of educated class and qualified future leaders.

Fourth, advocates for migration and development often call for negotiation between sending countries and receiving countries. However, opponents argue that this will likely prove ineffective for three reasons (Landau and Vigneswaran, 2007). First, the migrants themselves may not have strong or adequate legal standing to participate in such negotiations or dialogs. Second, few African countries have clearly articulated immigration policies compared to such receiving regions as Europe, which though may be internally divided in immigration matters usually present a common front externally when it comes to dealing with non-EU members. Finally, in the case of the receiving developed countries, there is more concern about security than about how they can help African countries develop. In conclusion, Landau and Vigneswaran (2007) argue that African countries would do better by focusing on migration among themselves through the development of improved data and understanding of migration within Africa.

Fifth, migration may have a positive impact on development through remittances and the work of the diaspora. However, this impact is usually not even across space. Besides, the effectiveness of remittances is hindered by a number of structural and human constraints to development including inadequate infrastructure, excessive red tape and corruption, and general lack of trust in government (de Haas, 2006).

In conclusion, the relationship between migration and development is a complex one. On the one hand, migration may be seen as safety valve for skilled people who may not find employment in their places of origin. Remittances and the role of the diaspora and returned migrants provide avenues for family support, provision of services, investment, and innovation adoption. However, migration of highly skilled people can impede long-term economic development (Baldwin-Edwards, 2006). The fact that poor countries spend hard-earned cash to train some of their citizens only to lose them to relatively rich countries is a disturbing trend. Besides, could it be also that remittances are having the same effect as the foreign-aid syndrome? Could remittances also create and reinforce a dependent population that is always looking for handout because they have someone living in the "rich-man's" land who will always provide? These are questions that demand further investigations.

Summary

With a population of 1,032,005,000 people per 2010 UN population estimates, Africa is home to 15% of the world's population. While this population size results in population density of 88 persons to square mile or 34 per square kilometer, about 20% of the population is housed in 10 countries, which only constitute 4.1% of Africa's land area, while about 62.5% is housed in 10 countries, which accounts for 44% of its land area. Thus, Africa shows a very uneven population distribution with relatively few pockets of very high densities and a much larger area of very low densities or virtual emptiness. This pattern of population distribution is caused by both physical and human factors including topography, altitude, latitude, distance from the sea, economy, and social and political unrest.

The demographic and socioeconomic characteristics of Africa's population place it either at the top or at the bottom when compared to similar indicators of other major regions of the world. Therefore, while fertility is declining overall and in fact has declined in a number of African countries, the highest fertility rates are still recorded in Africa. The same goes for the highest mortality and infant mortality rates, and for that matter, the lowest life expectancy at birth in the world. Over 99% of Africa's population growth is from **natural increase**, which in turn is affected by several factors including cultural, economic, and social factors. Although the contribution of migration to Africa's population growth is miniscule, it has dominated population issues in Africa so much so that it can hardly be ignored. In this regard, there are two main types of migration—**internal migration** and **external migration**. The first type includes migration within same country and **internally displaced people**, while the second is migration between African countries and outside the continent, including those who are refugees as well as those seeking asylum. The causes of all these forms of migration may be explained by the "traditional pull-push factors," be they could be economic, social, political, or cultural.

Africa's population has generated a great deal of debate as to whether its rapid growth is detrimental or helpful to the continent's economic growth. Some believe that rapid population growth is the main cause of poverty in Africa, while others believe that the causes of poverty lie somewhere else. Apart from this, there is also a major debate going on as to whether migration can be an agent for development. Proponents of this position cite remittances, which are currently estimated to be $29 billion, and the role of the diaspora of how migration could be turned into a development asset. Opponents cite the brain drain and limited impact of remittances on overall development as problematic. In the end, it appears that African countries need to seriously consider creating a more welcoming environment for the skilled segment of their population to remain at home—a very complicated matter that underpins the whole problem of development in a globalizing world. We will have more opportunities to revisit this in subsequent chapters.

Postreading Assignment

A. Study the Following Concepts

Asylum seeker	External migration	Malthusian population	Population pyramid
Brain drain	Fertility rate	theory	Pull factors
Brain gain	Human development	Migration system	Push factors
Crude birth rate	index	Mortality	Refugee
Crude death rate	Infant mortality rate	Natural increase	Sex ratio
Demographic characteristics	Internally displaced	Neo-Malthusian view	Total fertility rate
Demographic Transition	People	Net migration	Transit country
Model	Internal migration	Population density	
Diaspora	Life expectancy at birth	Population growth	

B. Discussion Questions

1. What factors affect population distribution of Africa?

2. Discuss the concept of fertility transition within the context of Africa. Is Africa going through fertility transition? Why and Why not?

3. What do you understand by the concept of fertility stall? What do you think are the main reasons for this in Africa?

4. Discuss the relevance of the demographic transition theory to African countries.

5. Distinguish between the **Malthusian Population Theory** and the Neo-Malthusian population view. Are these theories still relevant for African countries? Why and why not?

6. Discuss the statement that Africa's number one problem is its rapid population growth.

7. Distinguish between refugees and asylum seekers. Why are these special populations growing in Africa?

8. Why are many African countries losing their highly skilled workers to developed countries? What do you think are the long-term implications for these?

9. Can migration play a positive role in Africa's economic development? Why and why not?

References

Abdellatif, B. H. 2010. "African Skilled Labor Migration: Dimensions and Impact." In Adepoju, A. (Ed.) *International Migration Within, to and From Africa in a Globalised World.* Accra: Sub-Saharan Publishers, pp. 97–118.

Adams, R. H., and Cuecuecha, A. 2013. "The Impact of Remittances on Investment and Poverty in Ghana." *World Development* 50: 24–40.

Addai, I. 1999. "Does Religion Matter in Contraceptive Use Among Ghanaian Women?" *Review of Religious Research* 40: 259–277.

Adepoju, A. 2000. "Issues and Recent Trends in International Migration in Sub-Saharan Africa." *International Social Science Journal* 52(165): 383–394.

Adepoju, A. 2006. "Internal and International Migration within Africa." In Kok. P., Oucho, J., Gelderbloom, D., and Van Zyl, J. (Eds.) *Migration in South and Southern Africa: Dynamics and Determinants.* Cape Town, South Africa: Human Sciences Research Council, pp. 26–46.

Agadjanian, V. 2008. "Research on International Migration within Sub-Saharan Africa: Foci, Approaches and Challenges." *The Sociological Quarterly* 49: 407–421.

Ahdieh, L. 2001. "Pregnancy and Infection with Human Immunodeficiency Virus." *Clinical Obstetrics and Gynecology* 44(2): 154–166.

Ahmad, K. 2000 "Starving citizens are Real Victims of Angola's War." *The Lancet* 355(9200): 297.

Andoh, S. Y., Umezaki, M., Nakamura, K., Kizuki, M., and Takano, T. 2007. "Association of Household Demographic Variables with Child Mortality in Cote D'Ivoire." *Journal of Biosocial Science* 39: 257–265.

Arthur, J. A. 1991. "International Labor Migration Patterns in West Africa." *African Studies Review* 34(3): 5–87.

Ayamele, O. D. 2009. "Urban and Rural Differences Across Countries in Child Mortality in Sub-Saharan Africa." *Journal of Health Care for the Poor and the Underserved* 20: 90–98.

Azam, J.-P., and Gubert, F. 2006. "Migrants' Remittances and the Household in Africa: A Review of Evidence." *Journal of African Economies* 15 (AERC Supplement 2): 426–462.

Bah, A. B. 2011. "State Decay and Civil War: A Discourse on Power in Sierra Leone." *Critical Sociology* 37(2): 199–216.

Baldwin-Edwards, M. 2006. "Between a Rock & a Hard Place': North Africa as a Region of Emigration, Immigration & Transit Migration." *Review of African Political Economy* 33 (No. 108, North Africa: Power, Politics & Promise): 311–324.

Bascom, J. 1995 "The New Nomads. An Overview of Involuntary Migration in Africa," In Baker, J., and Aina, T.A. (Eds.): *The Migration Experience in Africa, Nordiska Afrikainstitutet,* Uppsala, pp. 197–219.

Betts, A. 2006. "Towards a Mediterranean Solution? Implications for the Region of Origin" HeinOnline (http://heinonline.org) 18 *International Journal of Refugee.* 2011(Wed Jul 6 12:07:33).

Black, R., Crush, J., Peberdy, S., Ammassari, S., Hilker, L. M., Moullesseaux, S., Pooley, C., and Rajkotia, R. 2006. *Migration & Development in Africa: An Overview.* Cape Town: Southern African Migration Project (SAMP).

Blacker, J. G. C. 1962. "The Demography of East Africa." In Russell, E. W. (Ed.). *The Natural Resources of East Africa.* Nairobi: East African Literature Bureau, p. 23.

Boerma, J., Nunn, A., and Whitworth, J. 1998. "Mortality Impact of the AIDS Epidemic: Evidence from Community Studies in Less Developed Countries." *AIDS* 12(Suppl. 1): S3–S14.

Bongaarts, J., and Watkins, S. C. 1996. "Social Interactions and Contemporary Fertility Transitions." *Population and Development, Review* 22(4): 639–682.

Boserup, E. 1970. *Conditions of Agricultural Change.* Chicago: Aldine.

Buchan, J., and Sochalski, J., 2004. "The Migration of Nurses: Trends and Policies." *Bulletin of the World Health Organization* 82: 587–594.

Caldwell, J. C. 1976. "Toward A Restatement of Demographic Transition." *Theory Population and Development Review* 2(3/4 Sep.–Dec.): 321–366.

Caldwell, J. C. 1980. "Mass Education as a Determinant of the Timing of Fertility Decline." *Population and Development Review* 6: 225–255.

Caldwell, J. C. 1996. "The Demographic Implications of West African Family Systems." *Journal of Comparative Family Studies* 27(2): 331–352.

Caldwell, J. C. 1997. "The Global Fertility Transition: The Need for a Unifying Theory." *Population and Development Review* 23(4): 803–812.

Caldwell, J. C., and Caldwell, P. 2002. "Africa: The New Family Planning Frontier." *Studies in Family Planning* 33(1): 76–86.

Camberlin, P. 2010. "More Variable Tropical Climatea Have a Slower Demographic Growth" Paper Submitted to Climate Research, Université de Bourgogne, Dijon, France

Campbell, E. K. 2010. "Irregular Migration within and to the Republic of South Africa and from the African Continent to the European Union: Tapping the Latent Energy of the Youth." In Adepoju, A. (Ed.) *International Migration Within, to and From Africa in a Globalised World.* Accra: Sub-Saharan Publishers, pp. 169–207.

Chirwa, W. C. 1998. "Aliens and AIDS in Southern Africa: The Malawi-South Africa Debate." *African Affairs* 97(386): 53–79.

Coale, A. J. 1973, "The Demographic Transition Reconsidered." *International Population Conference*, Liege, I, pp. 53–72.

Connell, J., Zurn, P., Stilwell, B., Awases, M., and Braichet, J-M. 2007. "Sub-Saharan Africa: Beyond the Health Worker Migration Crisis?" *Social Science & Medicine* 64:1876–1891.

Crush, J. 2000. "Migration Past: An Historical Overview of Cross-Border Movement in Southern Africa." In McDonald, D. A. (Ed.) *On Borders: Perspectives on International Migration in Southern Africa.* New York: St. Martin's Press, Southern African Migration Project, pp. 12–24.

Crush, J., and James, W. (Eds). 1995. *Crossing Boundaries: Mine Migrancy in a Democratic South Africa.* Cape Town, South Africa and Ottawa, Canada: IDRC.

De Haas, H. 2006. "North African Migration Systems: Evolution, Transformations, and Development Linkages." *Migracion Y Desarrollo*, pp. 65–95.

Dorius, S. F. 2008. "Global Demographic Convergence? A Reconsideration of Changing Intercountry Inequality in Fertility." *Population and Development Review* 34(3): 519–537.

Doskoch, P. 2008. "Fertility Declines Have Stalled in Many Countries In Sub-Saharan Africa." *International Family Planning Perspectives* 34(3): 149–150.

Ehrlich, P. 1968. *The Population Bomb.* Cutchogue, NY: Buccaneer Books.

Ezra, M. 2001. "Demographic Responses to Environmental Stress in the Drought- and Famine-Proneareas of Northern Ethiopia. *International Journal Population Geography* 7(4): 259–279.

Feldblum, P. J., Nasution, M. D., Hoke, T. H., Van Damme, K., Turner, A.N., and Gmach, R. 2007. Pregnancy Among Sex Workers Participating in a Condom Intervention Trial Highlights the Need for Dual Protection." *Contraception*, 76(2): 105–110.

Findley, S. E. 1994 "Does Drought Increase Migration? A Study of Migration from Rural Maliduring the 1983–1985 Drought." *International Migration Review* (28): 539–553.

Fitzgerald, W. 1957. *Africa: Social, Economic, and Political Geography of its Major Regions.* London: Methuen & Co.

Garenne, M. 2008. "Situations of Fertility Stall in Sub-Saharan Africa." *African Population Studies* 23(N°2/Etude de la Population Africaine* Vol. 23 N*2).

Garenne, M., and Zwang, J. 2006. Premarital Fertility in Namibia: Trends, Factors, and Consequences." *Journal of Biosocial Science* 38: 145–167.

Garenne, M. L, Madison, M, Tarantola, D., Zanou, B., Aka, J., and Dogore, R. 1996. "Mortality Impact of AIDS in Abidjan, 1986-1992." *AIDS* 10(11): 1279–1286.

Gregson, S. 1994. "Will HIV Become a Major Determinant of Fertility in Sub-Saharan Africa?" *Journal of Development Studies* 30(3): 650679.

Gregson, S., Zhuwau, T., Anderson, R. M., and Chandiwana, S. K. 1997. "HIV and Fertility Change in Rural Zimbabwe." *Health Transition Review* 7(Suppl. 2): 89112.

Grote, U., and Warner, K. 2010. "Environmental Change and Migration in Sub-Saharan Africa." *International Journal of Global Warming* 2(1): 17–47.

Hardin, G. 1968. "The Tragedy of the Commons." *Science* 162(3859): 1243–1248.

Harrison Church, R. J. 1957. *West Africa: A Study of the Environment and of Man's Use of It.* 1st Edition. Longman: London.

Heaton T.B. 2011. "Does Religion Influence Fertility in Developing Countries." *Population Research and Policy Review.* 30(3): 449–465.

Hendrix, C., and Glaser, S. M. 2007. "Trends and Triggers: Climate, Climate Change and Civil Conflict in Sub-Saharan Africa." *Political Geography* 26(6): 695–715.

Henry S., Boyle, P., and Lambin, E. 2003. "Modelling the Influence of the Natural Environment on Interprovincial Migration in Burkina Faso, West Africa. *Applied Geography* 23: 115–136.

Hosegood, V. 2008. *Demographic Evidence of Family and Household Changes in Response to the Effects of HIV/AIDS in Southern Africa: Implications for Efforts to Strengthen Families.* Joint Learning Initiative on Children and HIV/AIDS.

Hunter, J. M. 2010. "River Blindness Revisited." *The Geographical Review* 100(4): 559–582.

Hutchinson, E. P. 1967. *The Population Debate: The Development of Conflicting Theories up to 1960.* Boston: Houghton-Mifflin.

Ibisomi, L. D. G. 2008. "Fertility Transition in Nigeria: Exploring the Role of Desired Number of Children." *African Population Studies*, Vol. 23 (N°2/Etude de la Population Africaine* Vol. 23 N*2).

International Organization for Migration (IOM) 2006. *World Migration 2005: Costs and Benefits of International Migration,* Geneva: International Organization for Migration.

Jones, G. 2006. "A Demographic Perspective on the Muslim world." *Journal of Population Research* 23(2): 243–265.

Jones, G., Steketee, R. W., Black, B. E., Bhutta, Z. A. & Morris, S. S. (2003) The Bellagio Child Survival Study Group. How many Child Deaths can we Prevent this Year? *Lancet* (362): 65–71.

Kalipeni, E. 1995. "The Fertility Transition in Africa." *Geographical Review*, 85(3): 286–300.

Kalipeni, E., Craddock, S., Oppong, J. R., and Ghosh, J. (Eds.) 2004. *HIV & AIDS in Africa: Beyond Epidemiology.* Malden, MA: Blackwell

Publishing. See especially Chapter 1 (Craddock), Chapter 3 (Oppong and Kalipeni), Chapter 5 (Oppong and Agyei –Mensah), Chapter 21 (Brown) and Chapter 22 (Ghosh and Kalipeni).

Kidane, A. 1989. "Demographic Consequences of the 1984-1985 Ethiopian famine." *Demography* 26(3): 515–522.

Kirk, D. 1996. Demographic Transition Theory. *Population Studies* 50(3): pp. 361–387.

Kirk, D., and Pillet, B., 1998. "Fertility Levels, Trends, and Differentials in Sub-Saharan Africa in the 1980s and 1990" *Studies in Family Planning* 29(1): pp. 1–22.

Kohnert, D. 2007. *African Migration to Europe: Obscured Responsibilities and Common Misconceptions. CIGA Working Papers.* http://www.giga-hamburg.de/workingpapers.

Kravdal, O. 2002. "Education and Fertility in sub-Saharan Africa: Individual and Community Effects." *Demography* 39(2): 233–250.

Landau, L. B., and Vigneswaran, D. 2007. "Shifting the Focus of Migration Back Home: Perspectives from Southern Africa." *Development* 50(4): 82–87.

Lucas, R. E. B. 2006. "Migration and Economic Development in Africa: A Review of Evidence." *Journal of African Economies.* 15(AERC Supplement 2): 337–395.

Mabogunje, A. L. 1970. "Systems Approach to a Theory of Rural–Urban Migration", *Geographical Analysis,* 2(1).

Malthus, T. R. 1798. *An Essay on the Principle of Population, as it Affects the Future Improvement of Society with Remarks on the Speculations of Mr. Godwin, M. Condorcet, and Other Writers.* London: J. J. Johnson.

Mason, M. 1969. "Population Density and "Slave Raiding"—The Case of the Middle Belt of Nigeria." *Journal of African History* 10: 235–260.

Mbacke, C. 1994. "Family Planning Programs and Fertility Transition in sub-Saharan Africa." *Review of Population and Development Review* 20 (1): 188.

McCann, C. R. 2009. "Malthusian Men and Demographic Transitions: A Case Study of Hegemonic Masculinity in Mid-Twentieth-Century Population Theory." *Frontiers* 30(1): 142–171.

Mercer, C., Page, B., and Evans, M. 2008. *Development and the African Diaspora. Place and the Politics of Home.* London & New York: Zed Books.

National Research Council 1993. *Factors Affecting Contraceptive Use in Sub-Saharan Africa.* Washington, DC: National Academy Press.

Notestein, F. W. 1944. "Population: The Long View." In Schultz, T. W. (Ed.) *Food for the World.* Chicago: University of Chicago Press, pp. 36–57.

Nunn, A. J., Mulder, D. W., Kamali, A., Ruberantwari, A., Kengeya-Kayondo, J. F., and Whitworth, J. (1997). "Mortality Associated with HIV-1 Infection Over Five Years in a Rural Uganda Population:Cohort Study. *British Medical Journal* 7111: 767–771.

Ofori-Amoah, B., and Adjibolosoo, S. B-S. K. 1998. "Population as a Cause of Africa's Economic Underdevelopment: Myth or Reality." In Adjibolosoo, S. B.-S. K., and Ofori-Amoah, B. (Eds.). *Addressing Misconceptions About Africa's Economic Development:*

Seeing Beyond the Veil. Lewiston, New York: The Edwin Mellen Press, pp. 11–37.

Oluwafemi, R. A. 2009. "The Impact of African Animal Trypanosomosis and Tsetse Fly on the Livelihood and Well-Being of Cattle and Their Owners in the BICOT Study Area of Nigeria." *The Internet Journal of Veterinary Medicine 5.2.* Academic OneFile (accessed June 4, 2011).

Opiyo, C. O., and Levin, M. J. 2008. "Fertility Levels, Trends and Differentials in Kenya: How Does the Own children Method Add to Our Knowledge of the Transition?" *African Population Studies* 23 (N°2/*Etude de la Population Africaine* Vol. 23 N*2).

Oucho, J. O. 2010. "African Diaspora and Remittance Flows: Leveraging Poverty?" In Adepoju, A. (Ed.) *International Migration Within, to and From Africa in a Globalised World.* Accra: Sub-Saharan Publishers, pp. 137–168.

Pedersen, J. 1995. "Drought, Migration and Population Growth in the Sahel: the Case of the MalianGourma: 1900-1991." *Population Studies* 49(1): 111–126.

Reid, R. S., Kruska, R. L., Deichmann, U., Thorton, P. K., Leak, S. G. A. 2000. "Human Population Growth and the Extinction of the Tsetse Fly." *Agriculture, Ecosystems and Environment* 77: 227–236.

Rodney, W. 1973. *How Europe Underdeveloped Africa.* London and Dares Salaam: Bogle-L'Ouverture Publications and Tanzanian Publishing House.

Ross, J., Stover, J., and Adelaja, D. 2007. "Family Planning Programs in 2004: New Assessments in a Changing Environment." *International Family Planning Perspectives* 33,(1): 22–30.

SAMP [The South African Migration Project] 2008. The South African Migration Project WebSite. Retrieved May 2008 (http://www.queensu.ca/samp/).

Scott, R. 2004. *Africa South of the Sahara: A Geographical Interpretation.* 2nd Edition. New York: The Guildford Press.

Sewankambo, N., Gray, R., Ahmad, S., Serwadda, D., and Wabwire-Mangen, F. (2000). "Mortality Associated with HIV Infection in Rural Rakai district." *Uganda. AIDS,* 14(15): 2391–2400.

Simon, J. 1981. *The Ultimate Resource.* Princeton, NJ: Princeton University Press.

Short, S. E., and Kiros, G-E. 2002. "Husbands, Wives, Sons, and Daughters: Fertility Preferences and the Demand for Contraception in Ethiopia." *Population Research and Policy Review* 21: 377–402.

Timæus, I. M., and Jasseh, M. 2004. "Adult Mortality in Sub-Saharan Africa: Evidence from Demographic and Health Surveys." *Demography* 41(4): 757–772.

Udo, R. K. 1982. *The Human Geography of Tropical Africa.* Ibadan: Heinemann Educational Books (Nigeria) Ltd.

Ulicki, T., and Crush, J. 2002. "Gender, Farm Work, and Women's Migration from Lesotho to the New South Africa." In Crush, J., and McDonald, D. (Eds.) *Transnationalism and New African Immigration to South Africa,* Toronto, Canada: South African Migration Project (SAMP) and the Canadian Association of African Studies, pp. 64–79.

UNCHR. 2009. *Global Report.* Geneva: United Nations

United Nations Department of Economic and Social Affairs. 2007. *World Population Policies.*

Urassa, M., Boerma, J., Isingo, R., Ngalula, J., and Ng'weshemi, J. 2001." The Impact of HIV/AIDS on Mortality and Household Mobility in Rural Tanzania." *AIDS* 15(15): 2017–2023.

VanDevanter, N., Thacker, A. S., Bass, G., and Arnold, M. 1999. Heterosexual Couples Confronting the Challenges of HIV Infection. *AIDS Care* 11(2): 181–193.

Webb, Jr. J. L. A. 2005. Malaria and the Peopling of Early Tropical Africa*. *Journal of World History* 16 (3): 269-I (Retrieved 28 May 2011).

World Bank 2006. *International Migration, Remittances and the Brain Drain.* Washington, DC: The World Bank.

Yousif H. M. 2009. "How Demography Matters for Measuring Development Progress in Africa?" *The African Statistical Journal* (8): 12–27.

Zuberi, T., Sibanda, A., Bawah, A., and Noumbissi, A. 2003. "Population and African society." *Annual Review of Sociology,* 29: 465–486.

Zuberi, T., and Sibanda, A. 2004. "How Do Migrants Fare in a Post-Apartheid South African Labor Market?" *The International Migration Review* 38(4): 1462–1491.

CHAPTER 7

Unity in Diversity
Africa's Societies and Cultures

Africans are the most culturally diverse people in the world yet they are more often treated as one homogenous group. In this chapter, we focus on the **societies** and **cultures** of Africa. Society and culture are terms of many meanings. However, a common trend through all the many definitions is that society is an organized group of people with a shared goal (Hanson, 2005), while culture is the total sum of learned behavior, habits, and capabilities as a member of society (Tylor, 1874). This chapter is about the diversity of Africa's societies and cultures, as well as the common elements among them. The chapter is divided into three sections. The first section discusses the factors that have influenced Africa's societies and cultures. The second section describes a sample of major elements of Africa's cultures, including race and ethnicity, worldviews and religions, language, family and kinship, age and gender, art and symbolism, cuisines, and dress and adornment. The third section discusses some of Africa's cultural issues and challenges but first, do the prereading assignments.

FACTORS AFFECTING AFRICA'S SOCIETIES AND CULTURES

In Chapter 2, we learned that African societies and cultures have been influenced by both internal and external forces right from the beginning. These forces, including migration, trade, war, conquest, empire building, and other forms of social interactions, have in turn manifested themselves through ethnocentrism, Islam, Christianity, colonialism, postcolonial policies and realities, and globalization.

Ethnocentrism

As discussed in Chapter 1, ethnocentrism is part of every culture and can play a very important role in cultural evolution through actions as simple as labeling the people of other cultures with derogatory terms to feeling too superior to even embark on cultural imperialism. African societies and cultures have been subjected to this act of ethnocentrism from both within and from outside. For example, the term *San*, meaning people different from ourselves, was given to the original inhabitants of Southern Africa by their neighbors who called themselves *Khoikhoi*, which means "real people." A similar case is how the name *Berber* came to be applied to the indigenous inhabitants of North Africa by the Romans and the Arabs (Chapter 3). The Portuguese and Spaniards called the people of sub-Saharan Africa *negro* for their dark complexion. Foreign anthropologists labeled the short-statured people of central Africa *pygmies*, while the San and the Khoikhoi people were labeled as the *Bushmen* and *Hottentots*, respectively, by Europeans. As these examples show, over time these labels become the very identities of societies and cultures. Within the continent, ethnocentrism worked through a feeling of cultural superiority and played a strong role in the building of empires and kingdoms. This cultural superiority is still present in many African countries and has been a source of many conflicts.

Christianity and Islam

As discussed in Chapter 3, Christianity and Islam are two foreign religions that have had more profound effects on African societies and cultures than the labeling exercise of ethnocentrism. The imposition of these foreign religions, the requirements of converts to live according to principles of the Bible and the Koran, and the introduction of Western and Arab cultures that accompanied them brought profound changes to the worldviews, belief systems, values, names, marital and kinship systems, and other cultural practices of Africans (Goodman, 2005).

Colonialism

The European colonial enterprise imposed a further set of societal and cultural changing structures, especially in language, politics, economy, law, and governance. The colonial administrative systems were alien to Africa. Even the so-called indirect rule of the British was a caricature of the traditional administrative systems, since the chiefs were given new powers that derived not from the people but from the colonial administration, and since in some cases, the rightful chiefs were replaced by people outside the royal chieftains, who would cooperate. European languages became the languages of government business. Colonialism combined with Christianity and Islam on a "civilizing" mission of Africa condemning all aspects of African religion as paganism and fetishism, and making it possible for Christianity and Islam to spread. Africa was also exposed to a new economy of crop, mineral, and other raw material production to supply European industries, while becoming consumers of a wide range of European goods. While some elements of Africa's material culture, especially production technologies, were left untouched, others such as transportation and communication technologies, as well as urban morphology were transformed.

In Northern, Eastern, and Southern Africa, where there was a substantial number of European settlers, large appropriation of lands by the colonial governments changed the land tenure system. In addition, racial and ethnic divisions became accentuated with segregated settlements. In some places, deliberate efforts were made to raise some local ethnic groups over and above the rest. In Rwanda, the Belgians elevated the Tutsi over the Hutus and appointed them as administrators and perhaps helped develop the mythology of Tutsi superiority to Hutu inferiority. In Algeria, the French sought to do the same thing with the Kabyle, a section of the native Algerians. This was also the case for the Barotse in Zambia, the Baganda in Uganda, the Fulbe or Fulani in Northern Nigeria, and the coastal Swahili in German East Africa (Tanzania).

Postcolonial Policies and Realities

The return to independence movement that swept across the continent after World War II was, to a large extent, a reaction to all this cultural domination, which ironically had been considered by the early African elites as "progress" until they realized the real intentions of the colonial enterprise (Falola, 2003). Efforts at undoing some of the imposed structures after independence, however, have been half-hearted. For example, while many countries embarked on indigenization strategies, most of these efforts were very shallow; at best, they replaced expatriate personnel with Africans, while the institutional structures were left intact.

Similarly, expansion of Western education reached its greatest extent without much attention paid to the content of the curriculum. In the process, educated Africans became more and more alienated from their own societies and cultures, learning more about the history, geography, politics, and sociology of the colonial countries than their own. The newly independent countries saw Europe as the model and thought the only way to be like Europe was to adopt and expand the structures that the colonial masters had left behind. Thus, the majority of the small African elites saw themselves as the custodian of the colonial culture and made sure it continued.

In politics and governance, there was a considerable effort to create something uniquely African by combining a traditional African political system with the European parliamentary political systems. A number of states did away with party politics and opted for a one-party system arguing that traditional African societies were naturally socialistic. Unfortunately, this experiment did not follow the traditional democratic principle of consensus building that was truly African. Instead, it created an autocratic system of intolerance that stamped out any freedom of expression.

Apart from these, any efforts at turning back the cultural clock were hindered by the realities of the rules of engagement in international trade and politics that the newly independent African countries found themselves in. As a result, African societies and cultures became more and more dependent on outside interests and this covertly continued to modify African societies and cultures.

Globalization

Truly speaking, the "globalization" of Africa was completed during the colonial period, when Africa became fully integrated into the World economy. However, the rapid advances in modern communication technologies since the 1990s—the Internet, electronic mail, cellular phones, Google Earth, and social media—have taken the integration of Africa into the global economy into a new level that one can arguably identify globalization as one of the forces that is currently influencing African societies and cultures. These advances have accelerated the rate of cultural diffusion and encouraged voluntary adoption of outside cultural traits. Thus, the very basis of authority, the respect for the elderly and the extended family system are all important African cultural traits that are being questioned as young people call for more freedom, accountability, and responsibility from those in position of authority.

As a result of these factors, contemporary African societies and cultures are neither truly African nor truly foreign, but a blend of what used to be authentically African and authentically foreign. Of course as the saying goes "tradition dies hard," so while many cultural attributes and practices have changed and are being changed, there are others that have resisted all these influences. It is important to bear this in mind as we look at a sample of these cultural attributes in the rest of this chapter.

A SAMPLE OF AFRICA'S CULTURAL ATTRIBUTES

African cultures are so numerous and complex that we can only discuss a sample of them and in broad outlines here. The sample we have chosen to discuss here are race and ethnicity, worldviews and religion, language, literature, visual art and symbolism, family and kinship, age and gender roles, and general social life.

Race and Ethnicity

The terms **race** and **ethnicity** are used to describe physical, social, and cultural characteristics of people. Race is usually used to refer to a group of people with common characteristics such as skin color and physical appearance (phenotype). Ethnicity refers to languages, values, and institutions, patterns of behavior, personal experiences, aspirations, and worldviews that set us apart from each other (Deng, 1997). The first person to have used race to classify human groups was the biologists Carolus Linnaeus in 1735 (Ahluwalia, 2006). Linnaeus and others who followed him such as the German philosopher Immanuel Kant used the classification to indicate that whites were superior to blacks. Capitalism, slavery, Christian missionary activities, and colonialism all reinforced this notion. However, during the first part of the 20th century, the work of W. E. B. Dubois and the Pan African movement, the independence movement in Africa, as well as the civil rights movement in the United States of America challenged this notion.

In relatively recent times, a number of African scholars have convincingly argued that the idea of race and ethnicity were created by European missionary and colonial enterprises (Bayart, 1993; Mudimbe, 1988; Vail, 1989). Vail (1989), for example, argued that ethnicity is not a natural entity but rather an ideological creation to meet the needs of missionaries and colonial administration. However, to accept this claim will be attributing all the differences in languages, beliefs, and other cultural practices we see in Africa today to colonialism, which will not be accurate. At the same time, it needs to be emphasized that our consideration of race and ethnicity in this chapter has nothing to do with the superiority or inferiority of any group. Neither should it be construed as a perpetuation of colonial legacy. Instead, it is based on the simple fact that the people of Africa are diverse in physical outlook, appearance, skin color, culture, values, and belief systems and how they interact and impact the physical landscape. Such diversity of people and cultures across space is central to geography of any place and that needs to be recognized.

Racial Groups

From Chapter 3, we learned that environmental adaptation of the earliest African ancestors had resulted in the four genetic groups: the Capoid, who occupied south-central, southern, and along the east coast of the continent; the Caucasoid, who occupied the Mediterranean coast, the Nile Valley, and the northeast coast along the Red Sea and in the Horn of Africa; the tall Negroid, who occupied the present-day Sahara, the Sahel, and interior of East Africa; and the short Negroid, who occupied the coastal areas of West Africa and Central Africa. While these groups still exist, the same forces that shaped their evolution and development have continued causing some continuity as well as change among modern-day Africans.

The dominant racial group of Africa is the Negro (dark or brown-skinned people) (Udo, 1982). This group consists of three subgroups: the Sudanese Negro of West Africa; the Bantu Negro of Eastern, Central, and Southern Africa; and the Hamitic Negro also of East Africa. This latter subgroup is a crossbreed of Hamitic and Negro groups and includes the Dinka of South Sudan and the Maasai of Kenya and Tanzania. Next in size is the Caucasoid (light and brown-skinned people), which also falls into three subgroups—the Semitic, the Hamitic, and people of European stock. The Semitic group consists largely of Arabs of North Africa and Sudan. The Hamitic group includes the Amazigh (*pl.* Imazighen) (Berbers) of North Africa, the Fulani of West Africa, the people of Ethiopia and the Horn of Africa, and the descendants of Europeans settlers (Dutch, British, Portuguese, and French). The San and the Khoikhoi people are perhaps the only groups remaining from the original Capoid group. However, there is now a new racial group, the Mongloid or Asiatic group, which consists largely of Indians in Eastern and South Africa and the Merina people of Madagascar.

Within these broad racial groups are ethnic groups with distinct cultures. These ethnic identities are so strong that with the exception of a few countries where race was politicized as in Apartheid South Africa and former Sudan, most Africans would identify themselves by their ethnicity rather than by race.

Ethnic groups

Every African country is multiethnic and in some countries, the exact number of groups may not be known. Table 7.1 gives the major ethnic groups in each African

TABLE 7.1

Major Ethnic Groups of African Countries

Country	Major ethnic group
Algeria	Arab, Amazigh (Berber), European
Angola	Ovimbundu, Kimbundu, Bakongo, Mestico (Mixed European and African) Chokwe, Kongo, Lingala, Herero, San
Benin	Fon, Adja, Yoruba, Bariba, Fulani, Ottamari, Ewe
Botswana	Tswana, Kalanga, Basarwa, Herero, San, Chewa
Burkina Faso	Mossi, Gurunsi, Senufo, Lobi, Bobo, Mande, Fulani
Burundi	Hutu, Tutsi, Twa, Europeans, South Asians
Cameroon	Basaa, Baka, Efik, Eket, Beti-Pahuin, Fulani, Hausa, Igbo, Meta, Tiv
Cape Verde	Creole, African, European
Central African Rep.	Baya, Banda, Majia, Sara, Mboum, Lingala, Aka, Zande, Fulani
Chad	Sara, Arab, Mayo-Kebbi, Kanem-Bornu, Ouaddai, Hadjerai, Tandjile, Gorane, Fitri-Batha Fulani, Hausa, Mandinka
Comoros	Antalote, Cafre, Makua, Oimatsaha, Sakalava
Congo, Dem. Rep.	Luba, Kongo, Mongo, Mangbetu-Azande, Lingala, Zande, Chokwe, Efe, Sua, Alur, Hutu
Congo Republic	Kongo, Sangha, M'bochi, Teke, Lingala, Tutsi, Aka, Twa, Beti-Pahuin
Cote d'Ivoire	Akan, Mande, Gur, Krous, Fulani, Hausa, Mandinka
Djibouti	Somali, Afar
Egypt	Egyptian, Arab, Beja, Nubian

(*Continued*)

> **TABLE 7.1**

Major Ethnic Groups of African Countries (*Continued*)

Country	Major ethnic group
Equatorial Guinea	Fang, Bubi, Mdowe, Beti-Pahuin
Eritrea	Tigrinya, Tigre, Kunama, Afar, Agnaw, Beja, Saho
Ethiopia	Oromo, Amhara, Tigraway, Somali, Gurage, Sidama, Welaita Kwama, Afar, Agnaw, Saho
Gabon	Fang, Bapounou, Nzebi, Obamba, French
Gambia	Mandinka, Fula, Wolof, Jola, Serahuli
Ghana	Akan, Mole-Dagbon, Ewe, Ga-Adangbe, Guan, Gruma, Grusi, Mande-Busanga, Hausa, Yoruba
Guinea	Fulani, Mandinka (Malinke), Soussou
Guinea-Bissau	Balanta, Fulani, Manjaca, Mandinka, Papel, Jola
Kenya	Kikuyu, Luhya, Luo, Kalenjin, Kamba, Kisii, Meru, Maasai, Oromo, Somali
Lesotho	Sotho, San
Liberia	Kpelle, Bassa, Gio, Kru, Grebo, Mano, Gola, Gbandi, Loma, Kissi, Vai, Mandinka (Mandingo), Mende, Americo-Liberians
Libya	Amazigh, Arab, Greek, Maltese, Italians, Egyptians
Madagascar	Merina, Cotiers, French, Indian, Creole
Malawi	Chewa Nyanja, Tumbuka, Yao, Lonwe, Sena, Tonga, Ngoni, Ngonde, Asian, European
Mali	Mandinka (Mande), Fulani (Peul), Voltaic, Songhai, Tuareg, Moor, Marka
Mauritania	Moor, Fulani, Mandinka, Wolof
Mauritius	Indo-Mauritian, Creole, Sino-Mauritian, Franco-Mauritian
Morocco	Amazigh (Berber), Arab, Jewish, French
Mozambique	Makhuwa, Tsonga, Lomwe, Sena, Chewa, Makonde, San, Makua
Namibia	Ovambo, Kavango, Herero, Damara, Nama, Caprivian, San, Chewa, Ambo, Himba, Gwari
Niger	Hausa, Djerma Sonrai, Tuareg, Fulani (Peuhl), Kanouri Manga, Mandinka
Nigeria	Hausa, Fulani, Yoruba, Igbo, Ijaw, Kanuri, Ibibio, Tiv, Esan, Efik, Eket
Rwanda	Hutu, Tutsi, Twa
Sao Tome & Principe	Mestico, Forros, Servicais, Tongas, Portuguese, Beti-Pahuin
Senegal	Wolof, Fulani, Sere, Jola, Mandinka, Soninke
Seychelles	Mixed French, African, Indian, Chinese, Arabs
Sierra Leone	Tenne, Mandinka, Creole, Fulani
Somalia	Somali, Arabs
South Africa	Zulu, Xhosa, Afrikaner, San, Khoikhoi, Ndebele, Swazi, Venda
Sudan	Arab, Nubian, Kwama, Beja, Tigre, Fulani, Hausa
South Sudan	Dinka, Baka, Zande
Swaziland	Swazi, San
Tanzania	Chewa, Maasai, Makonde, Makua
Togo	Ewe, Mina, Kabre, Fulani, Ga, Yoruba
Tunisia	Arab, Amazigh, Jewish
Uganda	Baganda, Banyakole, Basoga, Bakiga, Iteso, Langi, Acholi, Bagisu, Lugbara, Bunyoro, Alur, Ganda, Twa
Western Sahara	
Zambia	Bemba, Chewa, Lozi, Nsenga, Tumbuka, Ngoni, Lala, Kaonde, Lunda. Europeans, Asians, Chokwe
Zimbabwe	Shona, Ndebele, Europeans, Asians, Chewa, Venda

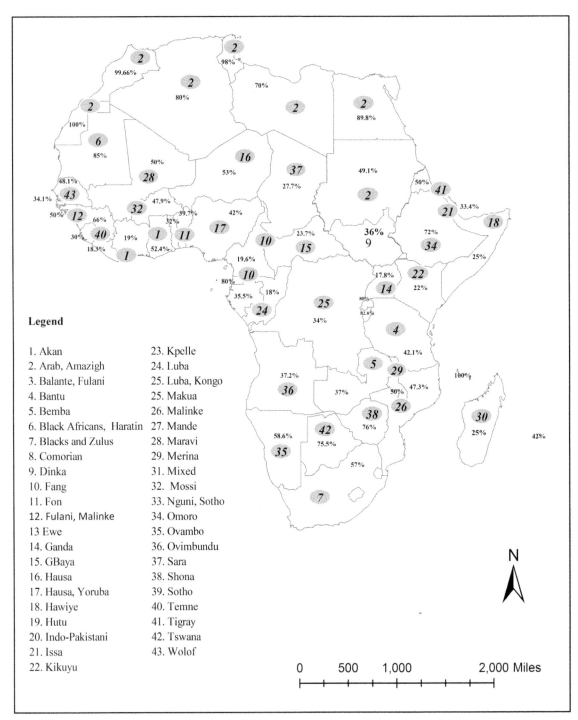

FIGURE 7.1 Major ethnic groups by country.
Source: Created by Sokhna Diop

country, while Figure 7.1 shows the most dominant group of each country. Nigeria, Africa's most populous country, tops the list with over 250 ethnic groups, followed by DRC with over 200 and Tanzania with more than 130. Each ethnic group in turn has several subgroups that exhibit variations in dialects and minor cultural traits. For example, the Yoruba of Nigeria are further divided into Egba, Ekiti, Ijebu, Ijesa, Ondo, and Oyo (Falola, 2001). Similarly, in Morocco, the Amazigh (*pl.* Imazighen) ethnic group consists of the Ruffians, the Chleuhs, and the Soussi (McDougall, 2010).

Most ethnic groups are small numbering only a few thousands to a couple of millions people. However, there are about 16 ethnic groups that number at least 10 million each (Table 7.2). According to estimates, the largest of these ethnic groups is the African Arab, who also constitutes the majority of the world's Arab population. Following the Arab are the Amazigh, the Hausa, the Yoruba, the Oromo, and the Igbo. Estimates show that each of these numbers at least 30 million.

Several of these largest ethnic groups are found in more than one country. The most widespread of these are the Fulani, who are found in 18 countries, almost all of them in West Africa, the Mandinka in 13 countries, the Hausa in 7 countries, the Amazigh and the Arab in six countries each, and the Somali in four countries (Table 7.2). As Hameso (1997) points out, Africa's ethnic groups have collective community living; they occupy a specific geographic area; and they have distinct languages, worldviews and religious beliefs, as well as distinct social and political organizations.

Religions and Worldviews

Generally speaking, Africans adhere to three major types of religions and their associated worldviews. They are indigenous or traditional African religion, Christianity, and Islam.

TABLE 7.2

Top 16 Ethnic Groups of Africa

Ethnic group	Country
Akan	Cote d'Ivoire, Ghana
Amazigh (Berber)	Algeria, Libya, Mauritania, Morocco, Sudan, Tunisia,
Amhara	Ethiopia
Arab	Algeria, Egypt, Morocco, Libya, Tunisia, Sudan
Fulani	Guinea, Nigeria, Cameroon, Senegal, Mali, Sierra Leone, Central African Rep., Burkina Faso, Benin, Niger, Gambia, Guinea Bissau, Ghana, Chad, Sudan, Togo, Cote d'Ivoire
Hausa	Cameroon, Chad, Cote d'Ivoire, Ghana, Niger, Nigeria, Sudan
Hutu	Rwanda, Burundi, DRC
Igbo	Nigeria, Cameroon
Ijaw	Nigeria
Kongo	DRC, Angola, Congo Republic
Mandinka	Gambia, Guinea, Mali, Sierra Leone, Cote d'Ivoire, Senegal, Burkina Faso, Liberia, Guinea Bissau, Niger, Mauritania, Chad
Oromo	Ethiopia
Shona	Zimbabwe, Mozambique
Somali	Somalia, Djibouti, Ethiopia, Kenya
Yoruba	Benin, Nigeria
Zulu	South Africa

Indigenous African Religions and Worldviews

The eminent Kenyan theologian and philosopher, John Mbiti (1969) wrote that the African is not religiously illiterate but in fact notoriously religious. This statement, which was in defense of indigenous African religions and worldview, implies that before Christianity and Islam arrived in Africa, African societies had their own religious beliefs and worldviews. These practices and worldviews varied across the various ethnic groups on the continent. However, they all believed in the power of supernatural forces in the affairs of the living and, for that matter, demanded a certain code of conduct. In order of importance and power, these forces are the supreme being, spirits, ancestors, and witchcrafts and diviners.

Supreme being All indigenous African religions believe in the existence of the Supreme Being, God the Creator, who knows everything, sees everything, and is everywhere. The conception of God the creator, however, varies across ethnic groups even within the same country. For example, in Central Africa, the Biaka believe that the Supreme God has the same weaknesses as humans, while the Banda and the Manda believe the Supreme God is a distant god who is not interested in his creation and yet controls its ultimate destiny (Woodfork, 2006). Most indigenous religions also believe in a range of intermediaries between the Supreme God and humans, and these include the spirits, ancestors, deities or witchcraft, and diviners or priests. These intermediaries help in executing punishment for social crimes such as murder, stealing, bearing false witness, incest, and adultery as well as other taboos.

Spirits The conception of the spirits again varies across ethnic groups. For example, the Yoruba of Nigeria have a hierarchy of spirits or gods, under the Supreme God, for various things of life such as Sango, the god of thunder, and Ogun, the god of iron (Falola, 2001). Most groups do not have such a hierarchy. All throughout the continent, however, spiritual worship is practiced through **animism**. Thus, the spirits reside in all kinds of places including trees, water bodies, mountains, boulders, caves, as well as other human-made shrines (Njoku, 2006). There are good spirits as well as treacherous ones. Perhaps a common example of the latter is the water spirits, affectionately called *Aisa Qandiasa* by the Amazigh of Morocco and *Mamiwata*, by many ethnic groups in the rest of Africa (Njoku, 2006; Woodfork, 2006). It is believed that these spirits live in water bodies with their families and can lure bathers, fishermen, people fetching water, or people traveling by water because they have light skin and look like beautiful European women. In some cases, the water spirit is a white male whose mischievous activities include capsizing canoes and sleeping with women who are alone to produce albinos, or they are fat black snakes which swallow their victims, making it impossible to find them. The chief of all the evil spirits is Satan.

Ancestors The ancestors are still part of the family, and they continue to wield a lot of influence over the living. If the living treats them nicely, they will be protected else, they will be punished. As a result, at traditional gatherings, festivals, and special occasions, the ancestors are called upon in prayers and in the pouring of libation. This fear and respect for the ancestors serve as a moral check on the living, since any immoral act is seen as an affront to the ancestors. The belief in ancestors also implies the belief in life after death. However, death is feared and is generally seen as a very sad event, especially when a young person dies.

Witchcrafts The most pervasive belief in indigenous African religions is the existence of witchcrafts or evil *djinns* as they are called in North Africa. So pervasive is this belief that it is even found among African Christians and Muslims. Generally speaking, there are two types of witchcraft—white or good witchcraft and black or bad witchcraft—but it is believed that both operate in darkness (Igwe, 2004; Mukenge, 2002). It is also believed that witches are able to change themselves into other creatures to kill their victims. Practically, black witchcraft seems to be the explanation of anything that happens in society that is negative, abnormal, and hard to explain. For example, an accidental event, the death of a young person, and infertility of a married couple are all attributed to witchcraft. The fear of witchcrafts causes people to find spiritual and physical protection in all kinds of objects including drinking of concoction, fetishism, and wearing of amulets.

Diviners Indigenous African religions also believe in diviners, who are people with the ability to understand the present and the future. It is believed that diviners can actually identify culprits of a misfortune and can kill those people through spiritual means if the victim so desires. So, diviners are consulted to find out the real causes of misfortunes such as the death of a baby, accidental or untimely death of a young person, infertility of a married couple, or disease affliction (Mukenge, 2002). Diviners use a variety of ways including throwing and reading cowries on the ground and reading a shadow from a cooking pot. Some diviners are also herbalists who serve as traditional healers.

Traditional African religions are the original religious beliefs and practices of Africans. While most of the beliefs and practices have been completely transformed by the foreign religions, they have been very resilient among both Christians and Muslims as it is not uncommon to see Christians and Muslims still haunted by the fear of witchcraft and other spirits (Figure 7.2).

Christianity

Christianity believes in the existence of a Triune God comprising the Father, the Son, and the Holy Ghost, who created the world and all things in it with human being as the crown jewel of the creation to be in charge and to worship him. However, humans became separated from God because of sin and they can only be reconciled back to God by belief in Jesus Christ as savior. Thus, unlike traditional African religions, Christianity has only one intermediary between humans and God and that is Jesus Christ. The Holy Bible is the source of the Christian faith. Christians believe that it was written by the inspiration of God, and it contains all that people need to live as God intended. Key elements of the teachings of the Bible have been codified in a set of statements or beliefs, among which are the Ten Commandments, the Greatest Commandment, the Great Commission, and the Apostles Creed. These affirm among other things the belief in the Triune God, love for God, love your neighbor as yourself, forgiveness of sin through Jesus Christ, resurrection of the body, communion of all believers, the Second Coming of Christ, judgment, and everlasting life to be spent either in Heaven or Hell.

The African independent churches (AICs) Christianity made major inroads in Africa, especially in the 20th century through Catholic, Anglican, Methodist, Presbyterian, Baptist, and other missionary activities, as well as the activities of African converts such as William Wade Harris (Box 7.1), and Simon Kimbangu (Box 7.2). Along these also came a major transformation, which many theologians have called the African Reformation (Anderson, 2001) that resulted in a proliferation of Christian Churches known as African Independent Churches, African Indigenous Churches, African Initiated Churches or AICs for short. According to Anderson (2001), there

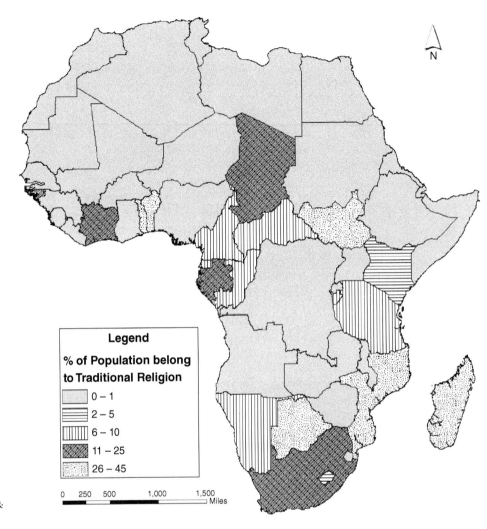

FIGURE 7.2 Traditional
religion.
Source: Created by Sokhna Diop &
Bandhan Ayon

Box 7.1 | William Wade Harris: An African Prophet

William Wade Harris (1865–1929) was one of the most remarkable preachers in the history of Christianity. Harris was born in Liberia. He was from the Kru subgroup of the Grebo ethnic group. He was raised as a Methodist by his maternal uncle who was a Methodist minister and worked in various occupations including seaman, bricklayer, Episcopalian teacher, and a government interpreter. He became an activist against the Americo-Liberians who were ruling the country and suggested that Liberia should become a British colony instead of being ruled by Black Americans. He was jailed after being accused of leading a Grebo uprising, and it was at the

jail in 1910 that Harris received a call to become an African prophet. After he was released from jail, Harris traded Western cloths for a long white robe, with black bands around his chest, a white turban and no shoes. He carried a Bible, a staff shaped as a cross, a gourd rattle and a bowl, and had two female assistants.

Finding no place in his own country, Harris crossed into Ivory Coast (Cote d'Ivoire) in 1913 and within 17 months he had reached out to 200,000 people in Ivory Coast and Ghana, and converted about 100,000 people. Harris' approach and message were simple. He would approach a town with his assistants, singing and playing the gourd rattle. People in the town would soon gather around and then he would preach to them. His message was straightforward—he preached about the power of God to save and called upon his listeners to get rid of their fetishes or bring them to him, which he would burn. He called on his listeners to turn away from the fire from heaven which would burn them in their sin and he would immediately baptize all those who believed. He would place the Bible on the heads of new converts, and it is said that some of those people would go into some ecstatic manifestations. Sometimes people possessed by evil spirits would be invited to touch the prophet's clothes and they would be set free. Harris never intended to establish a church. He always sent new converts to established mainline churches—Methodist and Catholic Churches.

In Ghana, Harris confronted and confounded traditional African religion, and it is said that about 1000 new people came to hear him every day. However, opposition from the Catholic Missionaries forced him to return to Cote d'Ivoire. Back in Ivory Coast, Harris continued to draw large crowds, but there too the French administration and Catholic missionaries accused him of fraud. They arrested him, beat him, and expelled him from Ivory Coast at the end of the 1914. Over the next 10 or so years, Harris' believers were systematically suppressed and prayer houses destroyed. Harris returned to his country where he remained until his death in 1929. Within a two-year period, 1913–1915, William Wade Harris had set off what is still the greatest Christian mass movement on the west coast of Africa. Although Harris never intended to establish a church, thousands of his followers soon found themselves at odds with the Methodist churches—over finances, banning of polygyny, and introduction of foreign liturgical services. So just before Harris died, his followers organized themselves into the Harrist Church, apparently with the blessing of Harris.

Sources: Anderson, A. H. (2001) *African Reformation: African Initiated Christianity in the 20th Century.* Trenton, NJ: Africa World Press, Inc., pp. 70–76.

Sundkler, B. and Steed, C. 2000. *A History of the Church in Africa.* Cambridge: Cambridge University Press. pp. 197–201.

Box 7.2 | Simon Kimbangu: African Envoy of Jesus Christ

Simon Kimbangu (1887–1951) was born in the village of Nkamba, western Belgian Congo (DRC). He was baptized in the Baptist Church and was a lay preacher. In 1918, during the influenza epidemic, Kimbangu received a call from God to a special service in a dream. For the next three years, Kimbangu did nothing about this. Instead, he went to Leopoldville (Kinshasa) to look for work because the Baptist Missionary would not allow him to become an evangelist due to his inability to read well enough. On April 6, 1921, Kimbangu returned to Nkamba where he is reported to have prayed and healed a woman who was paralyzed, a blind man, a deaf man, and a crippled girl. Immediately, the word spread like wildfire and thousands flocked to Nkamba to receive healing and experience the revival. Many believed that a new Pentecost had descended in Africa and that Kimbangu was the chosen vessel. Kimbangu preached against fetishism and proclaimed trust in God, moral chastity, monogamy, and obedience to governmental authority. He declared many people who professed to be prophets at the time as false prophets. Protestant Churches began to fill. In spite of his peaceful message, the Colonial Administration found Kimbangu as a threat. People had stopped working on the farms and in the mines because they all went to Nkamba, while Catholic Churches were being deserted. Kimbangu was declared anticolonial, and he was arrested. Nkamba was plundered by soldiers and many of Kimbangu's supporters were imprisoned. It is said that Kimbangu escaped, but three months later, he was arrested again and on October 3, 1921, he was tried and found guilty of sedition and hostility against Whites. He was sentenced to 120 lashes and death, but appeals from the Baptist Missionaries to the King of Belgium commuted his death sentence to life. After receiving 120 lashes in Leopoldville, Kimbangu was sent to a prison in Elizabethville (Lubumbashi) 2,000 km away from his home, He was never released; his family was never allowed to see him till he died in prison 30 years later in 1951.

After his death, Kimbangu's wife Muile Marie continued the underground movement until she died in 1959. Thousands of Kimbangu's followers were deported after his death and this rather helped to spread the message of Kimbangu. In 1955, the group held a protest in Leopoldville against the persecution, and in 1956, it appealed to the United Nations and organized itself into a church called the Church of Jesus Christ on Earth by His Special Envoy Simon Kimbangu (EJCSK) or Kimbanguist Church. In 1959, 6 months before DRC's independence, EJCSK was officially recognized, and in 1969, it was admitted to the World Council of Churches. The Church grew rapidly under the successive

leadership of Kimbangu's three sons during which time they purged it out of some excesses. However, they could not unite all the different factions within the group so several secessions occurred in the 1960s and 1970s. In spite of this, EJCSK kept growing, building an extensive network of schools, hospitals, and other social programs. Critics point out that EKCSK was a strong supporter of Mobutu Sese Seko's long and dictatorial rule of DRC. They also point out that Church members worship Kimbangu and see him as the Jesus Christ for Africa, an allegation that Church leaders deny.

In spite of these, one cannot help but to admire the remarkable story of Simon Kimbangu. He had not started a church and his public ministry lasted only five months, three of which was spent underground yet he ended up creating a church that is now the largest independent church in Africa with estimated membership of between 1 and 3 million.

Source: Anderson, A. H. 2001. *African Reformation: African Initiated Christianity in the 20th Century.* Trenton, NJ: African World Press Inc. pp. 125–133

are three types of AICs, namely, African/Ethiopian Churches, Prophet Healing/Spiritual Churches, and Pentecostal/Charismatic Churches (PCC).

The African or Ethiopian-type Churches are churches that broke away from the European Mission churches, but maintained and practiced the same church rituals. *The Prophet Healing/Spiritual Churches* derive from the Pentecostal movement and thus emphasize spiritual power. They do not have any written theology as European mission churches. They emphasize healing, through the use of several objects such as holy water, ropes, and ashes. In addition, they adhere to several food taboos and they wear prescribed uniforms to church (Anderson, 2001). These churches constitute the largest and the most significant segment of AICs. The largest of these are the Kimbanguist and the Christ Apostolic Churches in Central Africa, the Christ Apostolic, the Aladura, and the Harris Churches in West Africa, and the Zion Christian Church and the Amanazaretha in Southern Africa (Anderson, 2001).

The Pentecostal/Charismatic Churches (PCC) also emphasize the power of the Holy Spirit. They also tend to have young and charismatic leaders such as the late Benson Idahosa of Nigeria, Nicolas Duncan-Williams and Mensah Otabil of Ghana, T. B. Joshua of Nigeria, and Nevers Mumba of Zambia (Meyer, 2004). They preach "prosperity gospel," which emphasizes prosperity as a God-given blessing and rejects mainline churches' legitimization of poverty. They also tend to be "global" in orientation and most often have the word "International" added to their names even though they may be the only branch in the world. They ban alcohol and drinking and wearing of uniforms. Unlike mainline churches that see belief in demons as superstitions, PCCs devote a lot of attention to casting out demons from their membership (Anderson, 2001; Meyer 2004). In spite of their relatively recent origins, some of these churches are not only large but are also the fastest growing churches in Africa.

The rise of AICs has been attributed to several reasons. First, African Christians wanted to be independent and have a place of their own given the discriminatory and paternalistic attitudes of mainline Churches in Eastern and Southern Africa. Second, AIC was a reaction to European mission churches for their lack of sensitivity to a number of African cultural traits such as polygyny and reverence to ancestors, which though were in the Bible, yet were vigorously condemned by the European churches. Third, was the inability of European mission churches to present the gospel in a way that was culturally acceptable to African Christians. Finally, there were also personal reasons such as a charismatic individual who disagreed with or refused the discipline of established Church authorities (Anderson, 2001; Comaroff, 1985; Hastings, 1994; Sundkler, 1961; Turner, 1979). Today, Christianity is the dominant religion in 14 African countries, where at least 75% of the population is Christian, and in 13 other countries where at least 26% of the population is Christian (Figure 7.3).

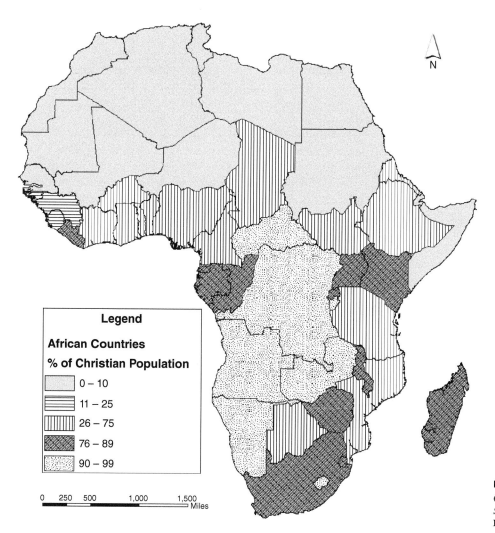

FIGURE 7.3 Percentage of Christians by country.
Source: Created by Sokhna Diop & Bandhan Ayon

Islam

Islam, like Christianity, believes in one God (Allah) whose last and the most out-standing messenger or prophet was Mohamed. The main purpose of life is to please Allah. The Islamic faith and behavior rest on five foundations or what is referred to as the five pillars of Islam. First, all Muslims must embrace the Islamic testimony or *tawhid*, which affirms the basic belief in the unity and supremacy of Allah over all things—there is no god but Allah. Second, all Muslims are required to pray five times a day—at dawn, midday, midafternoon, sunset, and nightfall (Njoku, 2006). Third, all Muslims are required to fast sometime during the year, except the young, the sick, travelers, and pregnant women. Fourth, all Muslims are required to give about 2–3% of their assets to the less fortunate in the community and as an exercise of faith. Fifth, all Muslims who are able and can afford are required to go on a pilgrimage (hajj) to the Muslim Holy City of Mecca in Saudi Arabia, once in their lifetime.

The Quran (Koran) is the holy scriptures of Islam and contains the Hadith, or the recorded sayings and activities of Mohamed, which were revealed to him by Allah, as well as a set of ethical teachings which form the foundations of Sharia or Islamic law (Asante, 2002). The Quran also teaches about existence of angles, resurrection of life after death, and heaven and hell, and it forbids imprisoning a fellow Muslim, lust, homosexuality, immodest attire for women, drinking of alcohol, gambling, and eating pork, and other animals that are not killed with proper Muslim rites (Njoku, 2006).

An important feature of Islam is the existence of tariqahs or "ways" commonly known as Sufi orders or brotherhoods. These originated from the desire of certain Muslims to gain a deeper understanding and forge closer relationship with Allah and the supernatural through devotion and self-discipline that went beyond the required practices of the average believer (Ross, 2008; Vikør, 2000).

During the early post-independence period, many Islamic reformist activities resulted in political responses from the various governments making it clear that extreme religious views would not be tolerated in politics. This was the case in Mali, Guinea, Cote d'Ivoire, Kenya, Nigeria, and Tanzania. Since the 1980s, a new genera-tion of young Muslim intellectuals who reject accommodation of pre-Islamic ele-ments in Islamic faith of Africa has been calling for reform of Islam and institution of Sharia law in Africa's Islamic countries. African countries, which adopt Islam as the state religion such as Algeria, Morocco, Mali, Mauritania, and Niger, also adopt Sharia except that its implementation is limited. Perhaps the most contentious case is that of Nigeria, where since 2000 the northern states, which are all Muslim, have adopted Sharia law over the objection of the federal government.

Several factors aided the spread of Islam in Africa. First, massive Arab migration across the continent as well as activities of Muslim nomads provided an important link between Muslim clerics who were looking to spread and reform Islam and the people they were seeking to convert. Second, many ruling classes of Africa adopted Islam as a state religion to avoid conquest, and as a unifying force for establishing firm control over their subjects. Third, the mingling of long distant Muslim traders across the continent with non-Muslim communities, and the activities of African Muslim clerics such as Usuman dan Fodio (Box 7.3) (see also Chapter 3) helped spread the faith. Finally, Islam was culturally more accommodating to certain Afri-can cultural practices than Christianity. For example, prayer rituals, polygyny, belief in spirits and holy men with special powers, and the use of tombs of founders of Sufi orders as shrines all had their parallels in traditional African reli-gions. Today, Islam is the dominant religion in about 23 countries of Africa, where it accounts for 60–100% of the population (Figure 7.4). Majority of Africa's Muslims are Sunni, while a small minority are Shia (Oppong, 2003). The roots of these two main sects

Box 7.3 | Shehu Usuman dan Fodio—Commander of the Faithful

Usuman dan Fodio (1754–1817) was born in 1754 in Maralta in Gobir, one of the Hausa States of modern-day Northern Nigeria to a family of the Toronkawa Fulani. He studied theology, law, and Arabic under various scholars including Alfa Nuhu who initiated him into the Qadiriyya brotherhood. At the early age of 20, dan Fodio started his career as Shehu (Hausa for Sheik meaning teacher, writer, or preacher) in Degel. He embarked on numerous missionary tours throughout Hausaland preaching against the vices of Muslims in Hausaland including corruption, oppression, and illegal taxes. He advocated for education of women and called for strict adherence of spiritual and moral values of Islam. A prolific writer, dan Fodio wrote about all these not only in Arabic but also in Fulani and Hausa and this gave him a large number of followers. Many of his followers believed that he was the Mahdi, the expected one though dan Fodio saw himself as the forerunner of the true Mahdi. Dan Fodio's influence enabled him to strike an agreement with Sultan Bawa of Gobir, who granted dan Fodio and his followers, freedom of religion, exemption from unIslamic taxes, release of Muslim prisoners, and freedom for Muslim men to wear turbans and women to wear veils. Sultan Bawa died in 1790, but his successor Nafta was alarmed by the influence of dan Fodio and set out to curb this influence. Nafta ordered that only dan Fodio could preach and that new conversions to Islam must end and those who were not born Muslim must return to their former religion. Nafta died in 1802, but his successor Sultan Yunfa was even more determined to stop dan Fodio. It is believed that Yunfa invited dan Fodio to his courts and tried to murder him by poison. When that failed Yunfa attacked and arrested some of his followers in Degel. When dan Fodio's other followers forced the release of the prisoners, and dan Fodio refused to hand them over, Yunfa threatened to attack Degel. This caused dan Fodio to flee from Degel

to Gudu on February 21, 1804, a day that is still celebrated in Northern Nigeria. At Gudu, dan Fodio called for an attack on the nearby towns of Gobir. After being proclaimed the Commander of the Faithful, dan Fodio called for a full-scale jihad or holy war on the rulers of the Hausa States. Thousands of his fellow Fulani heeded the call and participated in the jihad. Within 10 years, dan Fodio's forces had conquered all of Hausaland and over the next two decades would conquer other areas to create the largest empire in 19th Century Africa—the Sokoto Caliphate. Usuman Dan Fodio died in 1817 leaving the consolidation and administration of the empire to his brother, Abdullahi, and son, Mohammed Bello.

Usuman dan Fodio's jihad had far reaching consequences for Western Sudan. Politically, it replaced the Hausa states with the Sokoto or Fulani Empire. It triggered two more jihads in Western Sudan, the jihads of Seku Ahmadu and al-hajj Umar. It led to the decline of the Oyo Empire of the Yoruba and converted the northern part to an Islamic emirate. Economically, the Fulani Empire brought some sort of stability in the region that helped to boost agricultural and other economic activities, which now became centered on Kano as Katsina was destroyed in the war. Socially, the jihad established Islam on solid foundation in Hausaland. The numerous writings of dan Fodio as well as his brother Abdullahi and son Mohammed Bello left a great deal of guidelines for subsequent leaders. As Boahen et al. (1986, pp. 49–50) states "If today Islam is a force to reckon with in Nigeria, and indeed in the Sudanese states of Senegal, Mali, Niger, and even Guinea—it was because of the revolutionary Islamic movements of the late eighteenth and nineteenth centuries in general, and of Usuman dan Fodio in particular."

From: Boahen, A. Ade Ajayi, J. F. and Tidy, M. 1986. *Topics in West African History*. Second Edition. Edinburgh Gate, Harlow: Addison Wesley Longman Limited.

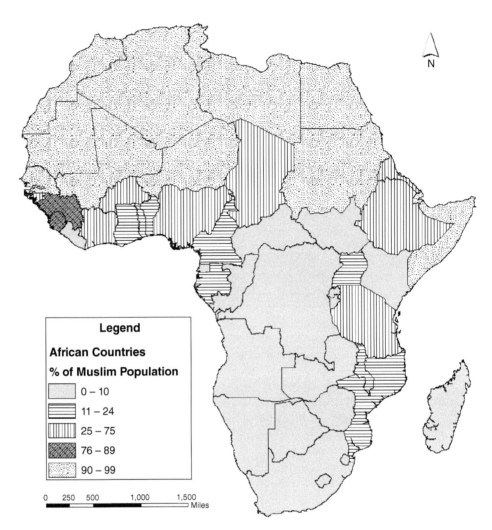

FIGURE 7.4 Percentage of muslims by country.
Source: Created by Sokhna Diop & Bandhan Ayon

go back to the early days of Islam after Mohammed's death. The Sunni wanted the next leader or caliph to be Abu Bakr, Mohammed's friend, counsellor, and fellow tribesman, while the Shia wanted Shia Ali, Mohammed's cousin and son-in-law or blood descendant. Today, Sunni and Shia have many common beliefs, but they have differences as well. A difference that is often referred to is that Sunni believe in the power of God in the material world, while Shia believe in sacrifice and martyrdom (Harney, 2016). Ahmadiyya is a smaller sect that claim that its founder Ahmad was the long-awaited Messiah (Otiso, 2013).

Languages

It is estimated that Africa has about 2,000 (33%) of the world's 6,000 languages. Each of these languages has sublanguages or dialects. Classifying that many languages has not been without controversy (see Heine and Nurse, 2000). Following the latest information as compiled by Heine and Nurse (2000) and Childs (2003) Africa's languages fall under four broad language phyla or families: Niger-Congo, Nilo-Saharan, Khoisan, and the Afro-Asiatic or Semi-Hamitic. A fifth and relatively small language family in Autronesian (Figure 7.5).

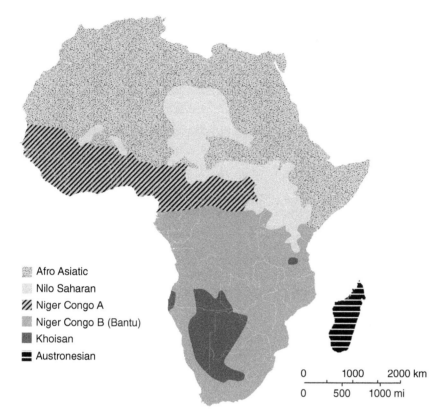

FIGURE 7.5 Africa's major language groups.
Source: https://upload.wikimedia.org/ wikipedia/commons/thumb/3/35/African_ language_families.png/300px-African_language_ families.png

Legend:
Afro Asiatic
Nilo Saharan
Niger Congo A
Niger Congo B (Bantu)
Khoisan
Austronesian

The Niger-Congo Family

With about 1,436 languages by latest estimates, the Niger-Congo is the largest **language family** in Africa and in the world (Williamson and Blench, 2000). It includes all the languages spoken in West Africa, below the Sahara, Central Africa, and Southern Africa. It consists of five major subfamilies: Kordofanian, West Atlantic, Mande, North Volta-Congo, and the South Volta-Congo, each of which is further divided into many languages (Heine and Nurse, 2000).

Kordofanian and West Atlantic The Kordofanian is a group of small languages that were originally spoken in the area of the Nuba Mountains of Sudan. The West Atlantic languages are spoken in the region from the mouth of the Senegal River to Liberia. They include Wolof (Senegal and Gambia), Temne (Sierra Leone), Diola and Serer (Senegal), and Fulani (from Senegal to Chad).

Mande The Mande languages are spoken over greater part of West Africa. They include Mende (Sierra Leone and Liberia), Mandinka (Mali, Senegal, Gambia, Guinea, Sierra Leone, Cote d'Ivoire, and Burkina Faso), Soninke (Mali, Senegal, Cote d'Ivoire, Gambia, and Mauritania), Bambara (Mali), Dyula (Burkina Faso, Cote d'Ivoire, and Mali), Susu (Guinea), and Vai (Liberia and Sierra Leone).

North Volta-Congo This consists of three families—Kru, Gur, and Adamawa-Ubangi. Kru is spoken in Liberia and parts of Cote d'Ivoire. The Gur languages are spoken in an area extending from Mali through northern Cote d'Ivoire, Burkina Faso, Ghana, and Togo. They include Mossi (Burkina Faso) and Dagomba,

Mamprusi, and Grunsi (Ghana). The Adamawa languages include about 80 small languages spoken in northeastern Nigeria and Cameroon. The largest of these are Mumuye and Tupuri. The Ubangi languages are spoken in northern Cameroon, southern Chad, Central African Republic, South Sudan, Congo Republic, and northern DRC. They include Banda, Zande, Gabaya, and Sango, which is a lingua-franca in Central African Republic and the DRC.

South Volta-Congo This family includes the Kwa and the Benue-Congo languages. The Kwa languages are spoken along the coastal belt of Western Africa, stretching from southeastern Cote d'Ivoire to southwestern Nigeria. They include Akan (Ghana and Cote d'Ivoire), Ewe (Ghana, Togo, Benin, and Nigeria), Fon (Benin), Avatime and Kebu (Ghana and Togo), Ebrie (Ghana and Cote d'Ivoire), Guan and Ga-Dangbe (Ghana), and Ega (Cote d'Ivoire).

The Benue-Congo family of languages occupies the southern half of the continent from southern Nigeria, Cameroon, and Central African Republic through South Africa. It is the largest of the Niger-Congo family of languages. It includes Yoruba, Edo, Igbo, Nupe, Bini, Cross River (Nigeria), and over 500 Bantu languages that are spoken from the Congo Basin down to South Africa. These include Swahili, (Eastern Africa), Zulu and Xhosa (South Africa), Sotho (Lesotho), Setswana (Botswana), Mukua and Thonga (Mozambique), Bemba (Zambia and DRC), Shona (Zimbabwe and Mozambique), Kikuyu (Kenya), Ganda (Uganda), Ruanda (Rwanda, Uganda, and DRC), Rundi (Burundi and DRC), Mbundu (Angola), Luba (DRC), Kongo (Congo Republic, DRC, and Angola), and Lingala (DRC).

The Afro-Asiatic Family

The second largest group of African languages is the Afro-Asiatic family, which includes the languages of North Africa, the Horn of Africa, and parts of East Africa. They are usually divided into six groups: Tamazight (Berber), Chadic, Cushitic, Egyptian, Omotic, and Semitic.

Tamazight (Berber) Tamazight (Berber) is the language of the Imazighen, the indigenous people of North Africa. The language is currently spoken by a large number of people in Morocco and Algeria and to lesser extent in Tunisia, Libya, the Siwa Oasis in Egypt, eastern Mali, western and northern Niger, and Mauritania (Hayward, 2000). In Morocco, Algeria, Tunisia, and Libya, they include several dialects such as Tamazight, Tashelit, Tarifit, and Kabyle. In other parts, they include Tamajeq spoken by the Tuareg and Zenaga, which is spoken in Mauritania.

Chadic This family language is spoken by people living around Lake Chad and parts of Nigeria, Cameroon, Central African Republic, and Niger. The largest and the most well-known of these languages is Hausa. The rest are spoken by small populations.

Egyptian and semitic Egyptian is the language of Ancient Egypt. It is also the language with the longest history of written records. However, today it has very few speakers. The most important of the Semitic languages is Arabic, which is spoken in various forms in North Africa, from Egypt to Morocco. Others are Tigre, Tigrinya, and Amharic, which are spoken in Eritrea and Ethiopia.

Cushitic Cushitic languages are spoken in parts of Ethiopia, Kenya, Djibouti, and the Horn of Africa. They include Beja (Sudan, Egypt, and Eritrea), Kwara and Omotic (Ethiopia), Sidamo and Afar (Djibouti, Eritrea, and Ethiopia), and Somali.

The Nilo-Saharan Family

This family includes pockets of languages spoken along the northern belt of West Africa through Sudan and the rest of East Africa. According to Bender (2000), this is the least widely accepted family. The most important of the Saharan languages are Songhai (Niger, Mali, Nigeria, Burkina Faso, Benin) and Kanuri (Nigeria, Niger, Chad, and Cameroon), while the most important Nilo languages include Luo (Kenya and Tanzania), Dinka (South Sudan), Teso (Uganda and Kenya), and Kalenjin (Kenya).

The Khoisan Family

The Khoisan family of languages is the smallest of the four African language phyla (Guldermann and Vossen, 2000). Much of this language family has become extinct. According to one estimate, there were as many as 100 languages in this phylum, but it is believed that only 30 remain right now, much of which is spoken in Botswana and Namibia, and in a few pockets in Southern Angola, Western Zimbabwe, and northern South Africa. This is the language of the San and the Khoikhoi people, which is affectionately referred to as the "click" language. The only Austronesian family of languages in Africa is Malagasy which is spoken in Madagascar.

European Languages and Lingua Franca

Given the multilingual nature of most African countries, it was problematic to agree on a **lingua franca** (a common language) in many countries. To select one language over the rest would have been a political minefield since it would have implied that the other languages were not important. As a result, most African countries adopted the languages of their former colonial masters as official language or the language of government business. These include English, French, and Portuguese. In North Africa, however, Arabic is the official language for all the countries. Other official languages include Tamazight in Morocco and Algeria, French in all the countries, Italian in Libya, and English in Egypt. Similarly, in Kenya and Tanzania, Swahili and English are the official languages (Figure 7.6). In addition, in some countries, a number of local languages have either become the lingua franca or are in the process of becoming as more people learn to speak them. Among these are Malay-Polynesian in Madagascar, the Akan in Ghana, Luganda in Uganda, Pidgin English in Anglophone West Africa, and Hausa in West Africa (Oppong 2003).

Literature

When Europeans and people of European origin talk about literature, they are usually referring to written letters. To the African, literature also includes oral forms (Julien, 1995).

Oral Literature

Oral literature is the oldest and the most enduring form of literature in African societies. It consists mainly of folklores in the form of oral history, legends, and myths with moral lessons, proverbs, as well as musical and dancing expressions. The subject matter usually covers the whole gamut of virtues and vices of everyday life including love, kindness, patience, peace, hatred, wickedness, deceit, craftiness,

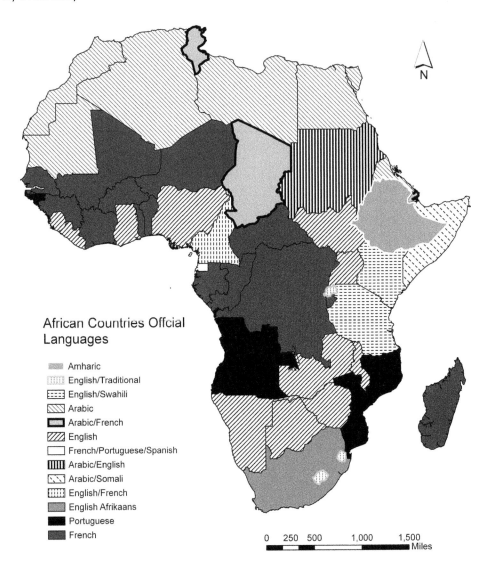

FIGURE 7.6 Africa's official languages.
Source: Created by Abigail Ofori-Amoah

envy, jealousy, tragedy, and triumph. Some are woven around trickster characters, whose adventures can teach life lessons (Ebewo, 2004). Most of the time, the trickster is an animal character, but the type of animal varies across the continent. In West Africa, it is the spider or the tortoise. In East, Central, and Southern Africa, it is the rabbit or the hare. In North Africa, it is the ass, the jackal, the fox, or the hyena. Sometimes, the story is about people. Most often, there are lessons at the end of the stories that may be why some animals or people look or behave the way they do. Sometimes, the lessons may be explanation of a proverb or a wise saying, or for better or worse the consequences of being a trickster. Though almost anyone can tell a story, there are only a relatively few that can make it into an art. These people are orators who can hold attention of their listeners for a long time. As a result, some of them become professional storytellers in the urban areas, where they tell stories for a living.

Written Literature

Written literature in Africa predates the Western literature, as evidenced in Ancient Egypt, and the cave paintings in Central Sahara and Southern Africa. During the 3rd and 4th centuries, for example, African scholars such as Anthony of Egypt,

Augustine of Hippo (in Algeria), and Cyprian of Carthage helped shape Christian theology and practice through their works. In addition, the 13th and 14th century African Arab scholars such as Ibn Khaldun (Tunisia), and Ibn Ajarrum Ab'ul Hassan and Ibn Battuta (Morocco), and the authors of the *Timbuktu Manuscripts*, contributed to history, geography, and government of the known world. By the 19th century, there were many scholars in the Islamic realm of Africa. The book *Ethiopian Unbound: Studies in Race Emancipation* published in 1911 by J. E. Casely-Hayford of Gold Coast (Ghana) is considered to be the first English novel written by an African (Afolayan, 2004). Modern African plays, poetry, and novels began to take root from the 1920s through the early 1950s with authors such as Herbert I. E. Dhlomo and Alan Paton of South Africa, Agostinho Neto of Angola, Leopold Sedar Senghor and Ousmane Sembene of Senegal, Camara Laye of Guinea, Cyprian Ekwensi, Amos Tutuola, Chinua Achebe of Nigeria, Mouloud Feraoun and Mouloud Mammeri of Algeria, and Albert Memmi of Tunisia.

The establishment of the African Writers Series in 1962 by the Heinemann Education Books of London led to an explosion of written literature in Africa as a new breed of writers sought to challenge and correct the assumptions of colonialism, neocolonialism, and the new realities of Africa in their novels. From the 1970s through the end of the 20th century, the number of African novelists and poets grew, with more women representation. This literature focused on the disillusionment with the African state after the hype of independence, the critique of oppressive governments, and the revisions of previous representations (Julien, 1995).

By the 1980s, Africa's written literature had reached such a high quality that in 1986 Wole Soyinka of Nigeria received the Nobel Prize for literature, the first African to receive that honor. He was followed by Naguib Mahfouz of Egypt in 1988, Nadine Gordimer of South Africa in 1991, and John M. Coetzee also of South Africa in 2003.

Visual Art and Symbolism

Visual art expressed in woodwork, beadwork, stonework, metalwork, weaving, pottery, as well as body decorations and adornment, is central to African societies and cultures (Blauer, 1999). It does not only represent an important sector of the traditional African economy but it also conveys a lot of symbolism or representation of meaningful expression of the cultures, which make it.

Woodwork

Africa's wood-based art includes masks, stools, headrests, and ritual, household, and funeral objects. Wooden masks usually worn at festivals can take different types of shape. The most famous examples of these are facemasks of the Dogon people of Mali (Figure 7.7a), the stools of the Akan of Ghana, Figure 7.7b), the headrests of the Karamojong of Uganda, the Turkana of Kenya, and the Zulu, and the twin images of the Yoruba of Nigeria (Figure 7.8). Other wooden objects include household utensils, baby dolls, board games, and musical instruments (Figure 7.9a and Figure 7.9b). Some of this traditional wood-based art have undergone transformation to become a vibrant industry. Perhaps the most extreme of such transformations is the casket-making industry of Ghana, where a combination of ingenuity, imagination, and talent of Ghana's wood workers backed by customers' willingness to pay has given rise to what has been referred to as "fantasy coffins." These coffins take various shapes such as a fish, a coke bottle, a vehicle, an airplane, and a canoe or sailing boat, as determined by either the owner's occupation or death wishes (Figure 7.10).

FIGURE 7.7A Dogon wooden mask.
Source: Copyright Viscorp | Dreamstime.com http://www.dreamstime.com/
viscorp_info

FIGURE 7.7B Wooden stools.
Source: Ann Porteus, Sidewalk
Tribal Gallery on VisualHunt.

FIGURE 7.8 Ritual
wooden objects.
Source: https://static.lib.virginia.
edu/artsandmedia/artmuseum/
africanart/Exhibitionhtml.
Source: Copyright Worldshots |
Dreamstime.com

(a) Yoruba Twins

(b) Fertility Dolls

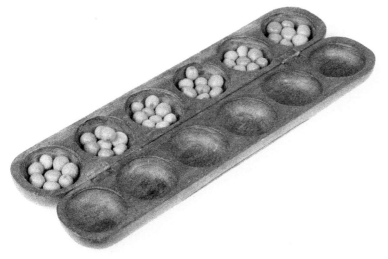

FIGURE 7.9A Oware—The most popular wooden/board game in Africa.
Source: Copyright Bidouze Stéphane | Dreamstime.com

FIGURE 7.9B Traditional drums.
Source: Copyright Prillfoto | Dreamstime.com

Stonework

Stonework was dominant in the Nile Valley from Egypt down to the Ethiopia as evidenced by the pyramids and some of Ethiopia's church buildings. For the rest of Africa, the only other prominent evidence to date is the Great Zimbabwe. Modern stonework in Africa includes the Shona sculpture, made of serpentine stone, which began in the late 1950s by sculptors from Zimbabwe, Malawi, Mozambique, Angola and Zambia, and the Kisii stonework based on soapstone of Kenya.

Beadwork

The use of beads for physical adornment is found in all African societies and cultures. However, the most elaborate beadwork is found among the Maasai of Kenya and Tanzania; the Samburu of Kenya; the Ndebele, Zulu, and Xhosa of South Africa; and the Yoruba and the Wodaabe of West Africa (Figure 7.11). Among these groups, the beadwork worn reflects individual status symbol except among

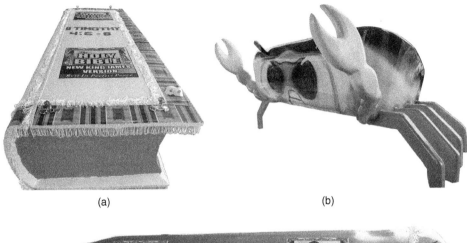

(a)   (b)

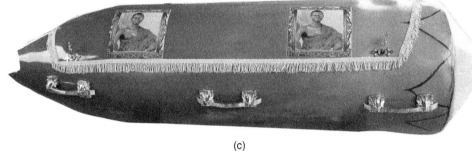

(c)

FIGURE 7.10 A sample of fantasy coffins of Ghana: Coffins shaped as (a) the Bible, (b) a crab, and (c) an okra.
Source: Created by David Ofori-Amoah

FIGURE 7.11 A Samburu woman with traditional African beadwork.
Source: Anna Om/ Shutterstock.com

the Yoruba, where beadwork is reserved for only for the royalty and the very rich. The colors of the bead are also symbolic. For the Maasai, for example, blue represents the sky, green represents the grass, while red and white represents life-sustaining elements the blood and milk of the cattle (Blauer 1999).

Rock and Wall Painting and Body Decorations

Rock paintings are found throughout the African continent from Morocco to South Africa and from Mali to Ethiopia, with some dating as far as 30,000 years ago. Most of them tell stories of old like the rock paintings of the Sahara, which indicate that the Sahara used to be a forest region thousands of years ago. Modern wall paintings are however very limited. According to Blauer (1999), it is only done in South Africa, where the Ndebele women have been doing it since the 19th century. The most remarkable thing about this artwork is that the women who do it do it freehand with no help and yet they are able to create perfect paintings with complex designs.

Body decorations are another common element in traditional African societies and cultures. They are part of the adornment and sometimes they are done to cover the entire body; at other times, they are applied to the face. They are also associated with celebrations, festivals, or certain rites of passage. Some of the decorations are for esthetic reasons. They include painting faces or parts of the body or dying and tattooing parts of the body of both women and men. The young men of the nomadic Wodaabe people, for example, paint their faces and wear special costume to put up a show to attract a female partner. Amazigh women also adorn their bodies with tattoos and dyes (Becker, 2006).

Metalwork

Metalwork by traditional African artisans has declined due to establishment of modern mining industry during colonial and the postcolonial period. However, evidence of metalwork in traditional African societies can be seen in the display of metal bracelets, necklaces, totem poles, royal crowns, and stools as well as other sculptures.

Weaving and Textile Printing

From north to south and from east to west, traditional African societies and cultures produced woven cloths, blankets, and tapestry and stenciled and printed textile, with distinct regional characteristics and symbolism, which still go on today (Figure 7.12). The most famous of the cloths are the woolen strip weave of Morocco, the Kente cloth of Ghana, the Asoke cloth of Nigeria, the Mud cloth of Mali, and the Kuba cloth of DRC (Blauer, 1999; Gillow, 2003).

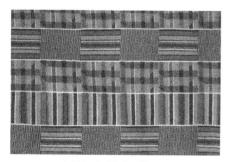
(a) Kente Cloth, Ghana

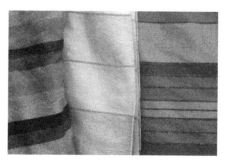
(b) Amazigh Silk, Morocco

(c) Kuba Cloth, DRC

FIGURE 7.12 A sample of traditional African woven textiles.
Source: Worldshots | Dreamstime.com
Source: Rayela Art on Visualhunt.com
Source: Piccaya | Dreamstime.com

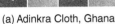

(a) Adinkra Cloth, Ghana

(b) Dogon Mud Cloth, Mali

FIGURE 7.13 A sample of African tie & dye, stenciled and printed textile.
Source: Copyright Galina Agarkova |Dreamstime.com.
Source: Ann Porteus, Sidewalk Tribal Gallery on VisualHunt.com

There are two major types of textile printing in Africa. One is tie and dye and the other is textile stenciling and stamping. West Africa is again the center of this art form and the Yoruba of Nigeria again are experts in the tie and dye cloth. Tie and dye cloth is also produced in Tunisia and Morocco, where woolen fabric is used (Gillow, 2003). The two most famous products of Africa's traditional textile stenciling and stamping are the Adinkra cloth of the Akan of Ghana and the Mud cloth of Mali (Figure 7.13). There are over 80 Adinkra symbols (Table 7.3), each with its own interpretation, which are used to stamp the cloth after dyeing, washed, and dried (Blauer, 1999).

TABLE 7.3

A Selection of African Symbols: Amazigh, Dogon, and Akan

A selection of Amazigh symbols		A selection of Adinkra symbols of the Akan			
	Diamond—Femininity, Womanhood		Chief of Adinkra Symbols: Greatness, leadership, and charisma		No one should bite the other—peace and harmony
	Sun: Life, power, but also evil force because it drains water and can destroy crops		War Horn—vigilance and wariness		Independence:- Independence, freedom, emancipation; also cooperation
	Arrow: Male energy and fertility		Sword of War: Courage, valor, and heroism		Crocodile—adaptability
	Wheat: Life and death		The leg of a hen: Nurturing and discipline		Handcuffs: Law and justice, slavery, and captivity
	Weaving Comb: balance, tidiness and cohesion		The Heart: Patience and tolerance		Compound House: Security and safety

(Continued)

TABLE **7.3**

A Selection of African Symbols: Amazigh, Dogon, and Akan (*Continued*)

A selection of Amazigh symbols		A selection of Adinkra symbols of the Akan	
Ship: water and means of strength, blessing, wisdom	Linked Hearts: Understanding and agreement	Siamese Crocodiles: Democracy and unity
Anchor: Solidity, continuity, faithfulness, balance, lucidity	Spider's Web: Wisdom, Creativity, and complexities of life	Except for God: Supremacy of God
A Selection of Dogon Symbols	Twisting: Initiative, dynamism, and creativity	God is King: Majesty and Supremacy of God
Kanaga: Primordal energy of the universe	By God's Grace: Faith and trust in God	By God's Grace All will be well: Hope, faith, and providence
Creativity	Return and Get It: Importance of learning from the past	Seed of Wawa Tree: Hardiness, toughness, and perseverance
Sirus	Moon and Star: Love, faithfulness, and harmony	Change your character: Life transformation

Source: Nana Yaw http://ccpc2008.blogspot.com/2010/09/adinkra-symbol.html

Family and Kinship

The African family system is complex. The conjugal family, consisting of one man and one woman or one man and many women and children, is a subset of the much larger extended family system, which consists of brothers, sisters, aunts, uncles, nephews, and nieces and grandparents. As a result, married couples are not only obligated to their spouses and children but also to their extended families. In many ethnic groups, terms such as cousins, uncles, or aunts do not exist since they are all either brothers and sisters or fathers and mothers. Within most ethnic groups, all these relations will be living in the same compound or in close proximity to each other. For these reasons, African households and families tend to be large.

Marriage

There are two main types of marital systems in Africa—**monogamy**, marriage of one spouse and **polygamy**, marriage of multiple spouses. There are two types of polygamy. One is **polygyny**, which is the marriage of one man to more than one woman at the same time and the other is **polyandry**, which is the marriage of one woman to more than one man at the same time. Of these, the most widespread is polygyny, because it is not only sanctioned by the traditions of most ethnic groups of Africa but it is also sanctioned by Islam.

Initially, polygyny was an economic necessity for the agrarian societies of Africa since it provided labor. Also among some cultures, it was prohibited for a breast-feeding mother to have sexual intercourse because of the belief that the woman's breast milk might be contaminated thereby hurting the child. So, breastfeeding mothers would stay with their relatives until they weaned their children. Polygyny was thus necessary since most families were agrarian. Other researchers such as Nnam (2007) argue that polygyny became established in Africa because the Atlantic Slave Trade changed the sex ratio of Africa's population toward more females, making it necessary for men to marry more than one woman.

Marriage practices Whether monogamy or polygamy, there are strict rules in most ethnic groups as to the choice of marriage partners. Most African societies practice **clan exogamy**, which forbids marrying from one's own clan. A few such as the Sotho-Tswana practice **clan endogamy**, which permits marrying from one's own clan (Afolayan, 2004). Either way preparation to enter marriage used to begin in an early age, especially for females, depending on the ethnic group. This was accomplished through a betrothal system, at the birth of a baby girl. There were also arranged marriages that occurred between the parents. These practices are becoming rare these days even though they still occur in some ethnic groups. In general, readiness for marriage is not only determined by physical maturity but also by financial ability. A young man must be capable of taking care of the wife-to-be. In addition, marriage is not just an agreement between lovers. It is an agreement between the two families so the families investigate each other to make sure that nothing jeopardizes the marriage, before they give their consent. For these reasons, in many cultural groups, impregnating a girl without marriage comes with very heavy fines and a forcible marriage. For example, among the Karamojong of Uganda, the fine could be as heavy as 30 cows on the boy or man (Otiso, 2006).

There are as many marriage rituals as there are ethnic groups, but in most ethnic groups, the marriage is sealed when there is transfer of bridewealth and dowry between the families. In Morocco, for example, the groom provides both the bridewealth and the dowry. The bridewealth is for the bride's family, while the dowry is for the bride alone. In turn, the bride's family also provides a kind of dowry for the bride to take into the marriage (Njoku, 2006). In the DRC, the groom pays the bridewealth to the bride's family, while the bride provides the groom's family with the dowry (Mukenge, 2002). In Senegal, the groom provides the dowry and also pays for the wedding (Ross, 2008). In Central African Republic, both the groom's and the bride's families exchange bridewealth, even though the groom's family provides more (Woodfork, 2006). However, among the Bunyoro of Uganda, the bridewealth is paid later because of high divorce rate (Otiso, 2006). The size of the bridewealth varies from group to group, and it can be very small as in the case of the Yoruba of Nigeria or as much as one's annual salary as in Senegal (Falola, 2001; Ross 2008). Although bridewealth among some cultures is still paid in terms of cattle, sheep, goats, and metals, these days most of it is paid in cash. The purpose of the bridewealth is not to "purchase" the bride but to legitimize the marriage and its offspring and ensure stability of the relationship (Mbaku, 2005). In all cases, the bride's family accepts the bridewealth only after the bride has given her consent.

Celebration of the marriage following exchanges of bridewealth can range from a simple event as the bride going to the husband's house to an elaborate event of a weeklong eating, drinking, and dancing. However, among the educated the traditional ceremony is usually followed by Western-styled wedding in a Church, for Christians, and in some public place such as the Court or hotel for non-Christians.

There is also diversity regarding where newly married make their home. Some ethnic groups are **patrilocal**, which means the bride moves into the husband's village, household, or place. Among these are the Buganda of Uganda, the Akan of Ghana, the Fulani and Yoruba of Nigeria, the Imazighen and Arabs of North Africa except among the Tuaregs. Other ethnic groups are **matrilocal**, that is the groom moves to the wife's town or household. Examples of this are the Chewa, the Bemba and Tonga of Zambia (Oppong, 2003). In the traditional African setting, marriage is supposed to be a lifelong bond. As Falola (2001) points out, a bad marriage was usually deemed better than divorce. Thus, both families worked hard to avoid divorce. However, among many ethnic groups divorce was permitted in such circumstance as adultery, abandonment, and criminal behavior that often brought shame to the family.

Today, the traditional marriage is being transformed by increasing Westernization and currents of global nature. For example, in many urban areas, it is common to find couples living together and even having children without marriage. In addition, educated women are increasingly rebelling against polygyny even in Islamic countries and arranged marriages. Divorce is also becoming more permissible these days especially in urban areas, and even among Christians.

Children

All across Africa, children are seen as assets and social security rather than liability. Childlessness in traditional African societies carries a lot of stigma and can bring a lot of ridicule or pressure on couples. Among some cultures such as the Nguni of South Africa, an impotent husband can ask his brother or another male relative from the family to father a child with his wife to bear children for him, while a barren wife can ask her sister or another female relative from her family to do the same thing for her. In either case, the children will belong not to the biological mother or father, but to the couple who is unable to have children (Afolayan, 2004). In cultures that do not practice the above, childless marriage is one of the top reasons for divorce or polygyny. Pregnancy brings joy to the family and a lot of preparation is made to receive the newborn. Childbirth is usually followed by naming ceremony and celebration.

In most African cultures, women do the raising and socialization of children. At very early age, children learn to do household chores as well as participate in household economic activities. In rural areas, this involves taking care of crops or livestock, while in the urban areas, it may be going out to sell some items and keeping the household store. Also in rural areas child socialization is done by the whole village. There are many rites of passage for a growing child in an African society, which include circumcision, puberty, and adulthood.

African children go through formal education like children elsewhere. In most countries, primary education is free. However, parents have to provide food, clothes, and school supplies, which may be difficult for the poorest in society. Here the extended family plays a crucial role because children from poor households are usually sent to live with their relatively able relatives to go to school. There are also cases where through arrangements by other members of the extended family, children may be sent to live with unrelated families to serve as housemaids in exchange for formal education or learning some trade. Even so, some children may still drop out from school, due to poverty, difficult household circumstances, or learning disability, which for the most part is rather ridiculed by society as moronic, stupid, or weak intellect.

In rural areas, children usually leave the village for the major urban areas after high school or some college in the hope of finding a job, and they start contributing to the family they left behind at home, soon after they start working. In contrast, children from affluent families may leave home early attending boarding schools and continuing through high school to the university. In urban areas, children usually live with their parents until they find work that pays well enough to be independent. In addition, children of affluent families usually are protected from doing household chores because of most of those chores are done by housemaids.

Kinship

Kinship has many meanings, but its use here refers to the system of relationship among people as well as the line of descent by which inheritance is passed on from one person to another within a given ethnic group. Within the extended family systems, most African ethnic groups are also organized into lineages and clans. A lineage is a group of families that trace their descent to one ancestor. A clan is a collection of lineages that also claim to have one common ancestor. Clans usually have a totemic animal as the symbol and they serve as broad support systems for its members especially during the time of celebration or need. Although clans were originally for the inhabitants of particular villages, new settlers may be eventually accepted into a particular clan after they have proven to be good neighbors over time.

There are three main systems by which Africans trace their relationships and line of descent. These are matrilineal, patrilineal, and duolineal or bilineal systems. In **matrilineal system**, the relationships and line of descent are traced through the mother side. Examples are the Makua, Yao, Lugulu, Makonde, and the Mwera of Tanzania (Otiso, 2013) and the Akan of Ghana. Children belong to the mother's clan, so in polygynous families within this system, for example, family relationship tends to be stronger on the mother side than on the father side. Since children belong to their mother's clan, the relationship between children and their maternal uncles (mothers' brothers) tend to be stronger than the relationship with their paternal uncles (fathers' brothers). Among some Akan groups of Ghana (Asante), maternal uncles are obligated to take care of their nephews and nieces as their own children.

In the **patrilineal system**, children belong to the father's clan and relationships are stronger on the father's side among polygynous families than on the mother side. Examples are the Yoruba and Igbos of Nigeria, the Oromo of Ethiopia, the Zulu of South Africa, and the Mandinka of West Africa. In **bilineal system**, inheritance can go either way. Examples are the Zaramo and Ngulu of Tanzania (Otiso, 2013), the Hausa of Nigeria, and the Tuareg of the Sahara. In reality, however, these are more complex systems than explained above.

Some African historians claim that next to Mesopotamia, Africa has the oldest matriarchy in the world, but the system was ended by colonialism, through "**disafricanization**," a process by which Africans exchanged their traditional cultural values for Western values (Nnam, 2007). Today, most African societies are patrilineal.

Age, Sex, and Gender

Age

Throughout traditional African societies respect for the elderly is preeminent and an essential component of the socialization process. Children are brought up to respect the older members of society. The manifestation of this varies across ethnic groups, but they involve addressing, greeting, and caring or helping the elderly with chores and other physical activities. For example, the Akan of Ghana greet and address people who are old enough to be their father or mother as father and mother. Similarly, in Nigeria, young Yoruba men prostrate or bow very low to greet the elderly while young women kneel (Falola, 2001). Children and the youth will give up their seat to older people whether at home or in public setting. In the rural areas, it is also common to see young people offering to relieve older members of society of luggage or items they may be carrying. As a result of the extended family system, children also learn to take care of the elderly since they may share the same house. The elderly are also future ancestors so it is important to treat them with respect. Among many African societies, the elderly is always right in matters of dispute.

However, rapid economic changes and pressures of the modern economy are all taking their toll on traditional African societies. Thus, respect and care of the elderly appears to be weakening. Western education has brought the questioning of authority and for that matter the elderly into African societies. Changing economic conditions, rise of career families in urban areas, as well as children spending more time in school are all eroding the time for eldercare. Unfortunately, in many countries, the extended family system is still taken for granted, and gerontology, the study of aging is still in its infancy. It is therefore not easy to estimate the current state of eldercare on the continent, and this needs urgent attention.

Sex and Gender Roles

Contemporary African society is patriarchal and the better treatment men receive over women both explicitly and implicitly is evident on many fronts. For example, Boserup (1970) addressed the fact that women's contribution in development was not being recognized. Similarly, Ewelukwa (2002) recounts several instances of poor treatment of widows ranging from accusation of having killed their husbands, stripping widows of belongings and sometimes their children, being kicked out of their matrimonial homes, and being subjected to outmoded rituals and humiliation, which sometimes result in chronic illness. In Central African Republic, women also are supposed to be stoic, absorb pain, as well as tolerate their husband's infidelity. If a woman commits adultery, the husband has the right to demand his bridewealth, and even murder her and her lover if caught red-handed. However, if the man commits the same offence, nothing happens to the man because his infidelity is expected (Woodfork, 2006). In South Sudan, the Dinka blame women for barrenness in marriage and this gives the right of the husband's parents to force their son to marry another woman (Essien and Falola, 2008). This situation is in fact common among many ethnic groups.

Also, while African society cherishes children, sons are more preferred in patrilineal African societies than girls and a wife could be divorced for not having a son or sons. In matrilineal societies, however, there is more preference for daughters than sons but a woman's inability to have a daughter may not threaten her marriage. Similarly, education of girls in many African countries lagged behind that of boys, until relatively recent. Researchers have attributed this unequal treatment of men and women to introduction of foreign cultural elements, particularly Islam, Christianity, and colonialism, that replaced the matriarchal nature of African societies with patriarchy (Johnston-Anumonwo, 2003; Nnam, 2007). The question, however, is that why has Africa not been able to turn the clock back?

Gender division of labor Njoku (2006), cautions that the domination of women by men in African society, however, is neither simplistic nor universally practiced as assumed, but it is a complex web of interrelations. In all African societies and cultures, there is a clear gender division of labor, which sees the primary functions of women as taking care of the family and men as providing the resources needed to take care of the family. As Njoku (2006) reports in Moroccan societies, it is the role of the women to shop, cook, and feed the family, while the husband is at work. Similarly, in Central Africa Republic, Woodfork (2006) reports that women are supposed to obey and be faithful to their husbands, farm, raise the children, and do housework. In Nigeria, both Yoruba and Hausa men are farmers, while the women help with harvest (Falola, 2001). Nomadic Fulani men maintain livestock, while the women maintain the animal shed and sell dairy products. Fulani boys and girls across West Africa do the same house and farm work growing up until they become teenagers, at which time the boys tend the cattle while the girls milk and prepare butter and cheese (Falola, 2001; Mbaku 2005). In the DRC, Mukenge (2002) reports that while men do big game hunting, women collect herbs and insects. Both men and women fish, but in pastoral groups, men tend cattle and goats, while women raise chickens. In arable farming, men cut the trees, both men and women till the land but women do the harvesting. Across the country, house building is a man's job, but women help with the cutting and transporting of the thatch for roofing, and also filling the building frame with mud. At home, women cook and clean, while men do the repairs. These are the same in Sudan and South Sudan and many cultural groups in West and East Africa (Essien and Falola, 2008). Finally, there are also some mutual responsibilities that are shared by both men and women in raising the family. While mothers spend most time with children, fathers are not completely out of the scene since for the most part mothers defer disciplinary actions to fathers.

In all these, women are not powerless and passive participants in African societies as it is sometimes portrayed in research and popular media. They do have influence in both private and public matters. In Morocco, as in other African countries, older women command a lot of respect and are often supported by their children and for that reason can influence decision-making (Njoku, 2006). In the same vein, uneducated men perform traditional forms of labor including house help compared to their educated female counterparts. Igbo and Yoruba women of Nigeria as well as the Makola women of Ghana are avid traders, some of them having been so successful to earn the name "cash queens." These women exert considerable power and influence that have in the past even brought down national governments.

Women issues have made major inroads over the past several decades in African countries. Education of girls that lagged behind that of boys is picking up and women are represented in most works of life in every African country. There are women doctors, lawyers, dentists, pilots, teachers, and professors. They are still few in certain professions such as engineering, but they are making inroads. They have been very successful in popular culture and the control of the informal economy. Educated women have more freedom than the uneducated and rural women. The increasing numbers of women organizations in African countries and government legislations have contributed to this changing perceptions and roles of women in African societies, but there is a long road ahead. Men still dominate most of the powerful positions in society. There is still the perception that a woman's place is in the kitchen, and there is the contentious issue of female genital mutilation (FGM) among some ethnic groups.

The Problem of Female Genital Mutilation (FGM)

The World Health Organization (2008) defines FGM as all procedures involving partial or total removal of the external female genitalia or other injury to the female genital organs for nonmedical reasons. Increasing concern about this practice in recent decades often gives the impression that FGM is both widespread in Africa and it is often sanctioned by religion. However, in a comprehensive study of FGM in Africa Ericksen (1989) showed that most of the cultures that engage in the practice are in West and East Africa and the Nile Valley, while cultures in the rest of North Africa, the Saharan region, and Southern Africa do not. Andro and Lesclingand (2007) also affirmed that FGM is practiced in 28 African countries, and that the percentage of women who undergo the practice in those countries varied from 1.4% in Cameroon to 96% in Guinea. In addition, they established that FGM has less to do with religion and more to do with other cultural traditions. For example, about 75% of Ethiopian women go through the practice yet there are only few Muslims. In contrast, the practice is nonexistent in Morocco, Algeria, and Tunisia. In the same vein, only about 2% women in Niger, a predominantly Muslim country, go through it, while over 90% of women are subjected to the practice in Mali, Niger's western and fellow Muslim neighbor.

The origin of FGM has been traced to Ancient Egypt, where it was used as a measure of fertility control (Ball, 2008; Momoh, 1999). Later on Western medicine recommended clitoridectomy as a cure for hysteria, melancholy, lesbianism, epilepsy, masturbation, and to control sexual desire (Ball, 2008; Dawson, 1915). Today, most of the reasons for the practice are sociocultural—including coming of age rituals, promotion of cleanliness, as well as a show of femininity. Thus, those who continue with the practice defend it on the basis culture and for that matter as identity, which cannot be destroyed. In contrast, those who oppose it see it as another form of male domination and suppression of sexual pleasure for women and a very painful and sometimes fatal practice to subject girls as young as 3–4-year olds to (Falola, 2003).

As a result of increasing concern since 1990, some progress has been made toward banning FGM. In 2003, African governments signed official agreement to condemn and combat the practice. Now there are laws in many countries to that effect, but the enforcement is another matter (Ssenyonjo, 2007). There is evidence to show that much of the effort to combat FGM lies with the government and education, because in countries with substantial African diaspora population, where FGM is practiced such as France and the United Kingdom, stricter enforcement of laws banning FGM has proven successful (Andro and Lesclingand, 2007).

Gender inequality is a major problem in Africa. Some people believe that the solution lies in education and the government action. Others believe that the solution lies with the African woman herself as she discards imitation for originality, dependence for independence, and ignorance for knowledge she will begin to realize her full potential at which point real gender equality can be achieved (Bwakali, 2001). However, women alone cannot solve the problem. The roots of the problem lie deep within the African culture, which will require a concerted effort of the entire society.

Cuisines

Food in African societies and cultures is more than a means of survival. It is also a social mechanism to bond, celebrate, and mourn. Food is used to entertain friends as well as strangers. Certain foods are only eaten on special occasions, while people will abstain from eaten during the period of bereavement.

The present food geography of the continent is a combination of a complex set of factors that include the physical geographic environment, external influences, and cultural ingenuity of adaptation. Societies and cultures living in the humid tropic and subhumid tropic zones derive most of their foods from roots or tubers such as cassava, yam, and cocoyam, fruits and tropical herbaceous plants such as banana and plantain, rice, and corn. In contrast, cultures in savanna regions derive most of their food from grains such as millet, guinea corn, sorghum, and wheat. Of course, there are a few crops that grow widely in several climatic belts such as corn, cassava, and vegetables.

In every African country, there is at least one popular dish that may be tied to one or more of the ethnic groups of the country. In North Africa, bread is the basic staple and forms the foundation of all meals. In addition, *ful mudammas* (cooked, creamy fava beans) is a national dish in Egypt, while *couscous* is a staple in Algeria, Morocco, and Tunisia. In West and Central Africa, it is *fufu* or *foufou*. The ingredient used in both the *fufu* and the soup or sauce vary across the region. In Ghana, *fufu* is made out of pounded plantain and cassava and eaten with light, palm nut, or peanut butter soup, while in Nigeria, it is made out of pounded yam and eaten with *egusi* sauce. Another staple in many countries in sub-Saharan African countries is a variant of *fufu* made out of cornmeal or *gari* (cassava meal) with soup, tomato, or hot pepper sauce. It is called *banku* in Ghana, *eba* in Nigeria, *nshima* in DRC and Zambia, *posho* in Uganda, *ugali* in Kenya and Tanzania, *nsima* in Malawi, *sadza* in Zimbabwe, *phaletshe* in Botswana, and *pap* in South Africa. The sauces and soups that go along with these foods usually contain meat—beef, goat, lamb, chicken, or fish. Stews and sauces are usually made with palm oil in the humid tropical environments, shea butter and peanut oils in the savanna regions, and olive oil in North Africa. Protein-based foods include meat products such as beef, goat, lamb, chicken, and fish.

Mealtime rituals and practices also vary across the continent. In North Africa, for example, lunch is the most important meal of the day. In addition, a meal consists of several courses, and it is usually served in large portions and all members of the household sit around and eat it. In most of sub-Saharan Africa, supper is the most important meal of the day and consists of one main course. Generally speaking, however, most Africans eat without silverware.

Beverages feature prominently in the diet of Africans. Tea and coffee are favorite drinks. Local drinks made out of fruit and ginger as well as locally brewed and imported alcoholic beverages are also common. Wine is prevalent and used to be very dominant in South Africa and North Africa. However, Islamic culture has led to a drastic decline of wine consumption in North Africa. In West Central and East Africa, palm wine in both its fresh and distilled forms is very popular.

As with other cultural elements, the daily diet of Africans is also changing due to education, changes in the social structure, and globalization. For example, educated and middle class households in urban areas eat just like their counterparts in the West—a mix of traditional as well as imported foods. They eat separately sitting at dining tables and using silverware even with some of the traditional staples. Even in sub-Saharan Africa, where traditional meals used to be served with no appetizers and desserts, it is common to see educated and middle class households eating salads and desserts as part of their meals these days.

Another diet fixture that is catching on in a number of African countries is the foreign-styled fast-foods, such as fried chicken and French fries, and fried rice and chicken. Ironically, eating these foods is considered as a sign of upward mobility. New staples are also entering the diet of Africans and in some cases replacing traditional staples. In Ghana, for example, rice is quickly threatening to unseat plantain as the leading staple food especially in the south, yet decades ago, a typical Akan person would eat rice only during the time of grieving a lost relative, because rice was not considered as real food.

Dress and Adornment

African societies and cultures generally have two types of attire—African or traditional and Western attire. African dress is the more indigenous dress which either originated with the ethnic groups or if introduced from outside has been modified, adapted, or transformed over such a long period of time that it has become part and parcel of the indigenous culture. African traditional dresses used to be great identifiers of one's ethnic group, geographic origin, social status, lifecycle, lifestyle, and emotional state. This is no longer the case because of the blending of traditional dresses across various ethnic groups.

In North Africa, indigenous and Islamic traditions have forged some form of uniformity in both women and men clothing across the region. Thus, traditional women clothing consists generally of large long flowing dresses that cover full bodies with variation in style according to locality and also social status. They include *gallibaya* and *tob sebleh* of Egypt *Sifsari, fouta* and *blouza* of Tunisia *karakou; blousa* the *djerba fergani* of Algeria; and the *djellaba*, the *burnoose* and the *kaftan*, of Morocco (Figure 7.14). Traditional men's clothing in North Africa is similar to women clothing with slight variations in style (Figure 7.14).

Throughout the rest of Africa, the most common traditional women dress is the wrapper, a rectangular piece of cloth that is wrapped around the waist to ankle length, and a top (Figure 7.15). This traditional dress is often worn with a head gear that may be as simple as a head scarf as among the Akan of Ghana to very elaborate sizes as among the Igbo, Yoruba, and Hausa of Nigeria. Sometimes, the main wrapper may also be formed into a long skirt called slit or short skirt, in which case a third wrapper may be used over the skirt or as a shoulder wear. Other traditional women dress includes various forms of long dresses similar to those of North Africa. They include the *boubou and the boubou riga* of West Africa, the *basuti* of Uganda, the *mishanna* of Rwanda, the *shuka* of Kenya, the *dirac* of Djibouti, and the Victorian-style long dress of the Herero women of Namibia. Traditional men's wear in the rest of Africa include the men's wrapper in West Africa and East Africa, the *boubou* and *boubou-riga* of West Africa, the *kanzu* of East Africa, the *musisi* of Zambia, and the *kikhoi* of Tanzania.

FIGURE 7.14 Traditional dresses of North Africa.
Source: Sun_Shine /Shutterstock.com

FIGURE 7.15 Traditional dresses of West, East, and Central Africa.
Source: Atfie Sahid /Shutterstock.com

Beyond these traditional dresses, most cultures on the continent have adopted Western-style of dressing for both men and women. Pants or trousers, shirts, blouses, jeans, T-shirts, as well as suits are very common. In Tunis, for example, it is common to see women dressed up in Western-style clothing without any veils. African women like women elsewhere love jewelry and various forms of adornments, including earrings, necklaces, and bracelets. Various styles of hairdo are very common in the sub-Saharan section of the continent, while in the Muslim countries, most women use hair cover.

Social Relations and Lifestyle

Across the continent, hospitality to strangers is a very high priority for most ethnic groups. It is common in the rural areas especially for people to welcome strangers into their homes with the best treatment they can give. In urban areas, however, increasing crime and anonymity is making this less and less of a common practice.

Lifecycle Celebrations

Lifecycle changes are celebrated to varying degrees. As already mentioned, marriage and childbirth are universally celebrated among all ethnic groups with religion and social status determining how elaborate it could be. In addition, there are many rites of passage rituals as there are ethnic groups that are celebrated across the continent, some of which are very active, while others are becoming extinct due to changing times. Funeral is generally the most solemn occasion in all African societies. However, if a very old person dies, it is a time of joyful celebration. Among Islamic societies and cultures, the dead is given a simple and quick burial. In contrast, in some countries and among certain ethnic groups, burial can be delayed as long as even a year all the while the body is being kept in the morgue. This is very common in Ghana and Nigeria. The reason is that funeral is a community affair, and if the person was a prominent member of society the funeral will draw a lot of people all of whom have to be fed. Funerals in these circumstances can be very elaborate and expensive. The bereaved family therefore needs time to prepare and that usually takes time. A unique and expensive funeral celebration is the *famadihana* or "turning the bones" of the Merina and the Betsileo of the Central Highlands of Madagascar. In this celebration, family members from all over the island gather at their family crypt once every 2 to 7 years to exhume the bodies of their dead relatives, clean the bones, spray them with perfume and replace their old silk shrouds with expensive new ones and rebury them, amidst celebration of food, drink, and dancing for two days (Bearak, 2010). In recent decades, this celebration has been declining partly due to opposition from the protestant churches and partly due to the cost. Other celebrations include numerous religious and national holidays and festivals.

Music, Entertainment, and Sports

Music, dance, plays, and sports are essential parts of the African societies and cultures. There are as many traditional African music and dances as there are ethnic groups and languages, with each group emphasizing on a particular aspects of music. Among many groups in West, East, and Central Africa traditional music was accompanied by instruments such as drums, rattles, and the xylophone. However, in South Africa, the Nguni people emphasized vocal singing.

European-styled music was introduced to Africa by either Christian missionaries or colonial officers. Thus, the early African musicians who tried to modernize traditional African music did so through church or religious music. Among the early pioneers were John Knox Bokwe of South Africa, who in the 1890s developed the *makwaya* or (Choir) music, and Enoch Sontonga, the teacher who composed the now famous *Nkosi sikele-Afrika* (God Bless Africa) in 1897.

By the late colonial period, other African musicians had also begun adapting modern instruments to playing traditional African music, which eventually developed into a number of distinct music genres and dance. Among these were Mustafa Loumghari and *rai* music in Algeria and Morocco; E. T. Mensah and *highlife* in Ghana; Eboa Lotin and *makossa* in Cameroon; Tunde King and I. K. Dairo and *Juju music* in Nigeria; the African Jazz and O. K. Jazz and *rumba, samba, tango, and cha-cha-cha* music in DRC; and Youssou N'Dior and *mbalax* in Senegal. In Southern Africa, *makaya* continued to dominate early independence period, but other new music styles were added including the *isicatamiya* (a Zulu word for stalking approach) of Solomon Linda and the Ladysmith Black Mambazo and the *sefela* music of Basuto migrants from Lesotho (Afolayan, 2004). Later on these were joined by Margaret Singana and Miriam Makeba of South Africa, Sonny Okusen of Nigeria and the *ozzidi* music, and Fela Anikulapo-Kuti' of Nigeria and *Afro-Beat*. African music has since evolved into a wide range of musical types. Today, Africans play and enjoy rock, reggae, rap, popular, religious, and other Western-styled music.

Sports and other forms of entertainment is also part and parcel of daily life in Africa. Africans also enjoy track and field, boxing, basketball, cricket, field hockey, tennis, and wrestling. In the Northwest Africa, winter sports such as skiing is also enjoyed. However, the most popular sport on the continent is soccer. The increasing number of African soccer players in European premier soccer leagues has created a situation where Africans now pay more attention to European leagues than domestic ones, which is another signs of changing times.

AFRICA'S SOCIAL AND CULTURAL ISSUES

Africa's cultural mosaic presents some issues and challenges to its economic development. Among these are language and development, oral literature and corruption, ethnicity and conflicts, and **religious fundamentalism** and extremism.

Language and Development

Two main concerns have been raised about the language situation of African countries. The first is the place of African languages in the development of Africa, and the second is the problem of dying languages (Djite, 1993, 2008; Robinson, 1996; Trudell, 2009). These authors argue that the use of European languages in Africa is a hindrance to progress. They argue that development is about people, and it is impossible to place people at the center if their own language is ignored. This is because to be effective both the people's needs and development goals must be effectively communicated. There is evidence to show that the use of foreign language is a hindrance to literacy of both adult learners and some children even in the formal school system. Development concepts are often conceived in technocratic terms that are often difficult for even the technocrats themselves to translate into their own mother tongues, let alone to be understood by those who are less educated in European languages. This view thus is not arguing for a lingua franca, but rather arguing for the need to pay attention to national languages as part of the development discourse and in particular literacy in these national languages as part of the development process.

The second concern relates to the death of African languages and sidelining of existing ones (Brenzinger et al., 1991; Gabsi, 2011; Lupke, 2009; Omotoso, 2004). Brenzinger et al. (1991) are concerned that minority languages are in particular dying at a faster rate due to neglect, as well as "indigenization" of European languages. While this may be seen as a way to unite people, these authors argue that such unity is only superficial and therefore calls on the need to protect minority languages. In addition, language is part of culture and adopting a language without any conscious effort to translate it into one's own culture results in adopting the culture of the language. Among other things these authors argue for the need to pay attention to African languages and including minority languages political support and then language documentation, comparative studies, and positive language attitudes.

Oral Literature and Corruption

Ebewo (2004) argues that despite their positive functions in African societies and cultures folktales also contribute negatively to the current sociopolitical problems of Africa. Ebewo (2004, p. 50) writes "the emphasis on telling, teaching, and enjoyment of tales involving tricksters and their nefarious activities might be a contributory factor of the current corruption and indiscipline in present African societies because of the psychic effects of those stories may have on the young individuals." This argument is something that needs a serious and closer scrutiny because in most of those stories the moral lesson that one draws is that being crafty or a trickster actually is more beneficial than playing by the rules. This obviously is the wrong message to pass on to the younger generation that will be tomorrow's leaders.

Ethnicity and Conflicts

The cultural element that has generated the most concern of both researchers and policy makers is ethnicity, and the particular issue that has been at the forefront of this is ethnic conflicts. This has led many African observers and researchers to identify ethnicity as one of the most difficult challenges facing Africa (Deng, 1996; Kimenyi, 1998; Tarimo, 2010; Zerfu et al., 2008). Several researchers have drawn a link between Africa's development and its ethnic complexity. They argue that Africa is poor because it is unstable, which in turn is due to its ethnic complexity (Bates, 2000; Collier and Hoeffler, 1998; Easterly and Levine, 1997; Kaplan, 1994). Some identify ethnicity as a basis on which several other factors including colonial policies, greed, and corruption combined to cause the civil wars of the DRC, Nigeria, Liberia, and the Rwanda genocide (Bates, 2000). However, others argue that ethnic groups rather promote development through the many ways they help in capital formation and extended family support, and through the fact that ethnic diversity does not necessarily imply violence and instability (Bates, 2000). Explanations as to why these tend to be the case and suggestions to resolve these problems are many, but since they all relate to politics and governance process, we will discuss the details of this debate in Chapter 9.

Religious Fundamentalism and Extremism

Two concerns that have risen from religion and worldviews of Africa are religious fundamentalism and extremism. There is no agreement of the definition of religious fundamentalism. According to Emerson and Hartman (2006), the term is sometimes used to refer to taking religion seriously. Sometimes it refers to doing things out of religious conviction or groups or the belief that religion trumps everything in public life. **Religious extremism** is distortion of the basic teachings of religion and using it to cause harm.

The concern about religious fundamentalism in Africa is about its impact on economic development, while the concern about religious extremism is with peace, security, and terrorism. In a comprehensive review article, Gifford (1991) raised a number of trends in Africa in which Christian fundamentalism with its emphasis on dispensationalism, faith and prosperity gospel, as well as a particular conceptualization of the world sends the wrong signal and message for personal and public responsibility to the achievement of development. For example, dispensationalism presents the belief that we are living in the end times during which hardships of all kinds are supposed to occur. In addition, Christian fundamentalism projects that the World is evil and that Christians should not desire anything that is of the world since it is more important to think of the afterlife. Critics say that such beliefs make African Christians willing to accept whatever hardships they have to go through because it is something ordained by God and thus is bound to happen. In addition, this diverts attention from dehumanizing social and economic conditions and any effort at planning and working to eliminate them.

Similarly, faith and prosperity gospel preaches that people's material needs will be provided by a wonder-working God and that all that it takes is faith in God, evangelism, and giving to the work of God through paying tithes. As a result, Christians spend an enormous amount of time in all-night as well as weekday prayer meetings irrespective of the time and day of the week, expecting a miracle to happen. Critics charge that this also has the potential of ignoring all the social, economic, and political causes of poverty in Africa. Finally, the practice of blaming witches for every social evil and the emphasis on prayer as the sole solution of everything diverts attention from seeking solutions to problems ranging from the prevalence of diseases that may arise from poor environmental conditions to broken down infrastructure due irresponsible governance structures and institutions.

Concerns about religious extremism relate more to Islamists groups that are increasingly becoming linked with Al-Qaeda as well as the Islamic State (ISIS) and their terrorist acts. According to Krech (2011), there are four regional Al-Qaeda organizations in Africa: the Egyptian Islamic Jihad (EIJ), the Libyan Islamic Fighting Group (LIFG), Al-Qaeda in the Islamic Maghreb (AQIM), and Al-Shabab in Somalia. AQIM originated from the bloody Algerian civil wars in the 1990s, but merged into a full Al-Qaeda branch after Osama bin Laden's death. The group now has operations in Algeria, Burkina Faso, Libya, Mali, Mauritania, Morocco, Niger, Nigeria, and Tunisia (Krech, 2011).

Al-Shabab, a Somalia militia emerged in 2004 and 2005. It joined Al-Qaeda in 2010 and by 2011 it had become the strongest of Islamist militia controlling the entire south of Somalia, including many of the suburbs of Mogadishu, Somali's capital. Al-Sahbab has been responsible for many attacks including the 2010 World Cup Finals bomb in Kampala in which 64 people were killed (Krech, 2011) and the 2013 Westgate Shopping Mall attack in Nairobi, Kenya, where 67 people dead and 175 wounded. Their goal is to establish an Al-Qaeda state in the Horn of Africa. In Nigeria, there is another group that recently declared allegiance to ISIS, and that is officially known as People Committed to the Propagation of the Prophet's Teachings and Jihad, but commonly known by its Hausa name of Boko Haram, which literally means "No Western education." This group founded in 2002 in Maiduguri, Nigeria, by Ustaz Mohammed Yusuf is an extremely conservative, fundamentalist group that opposes Western lifestyle and ideals including elections and Western education (Adesoji, 2010). This group has been responsible for several atrocities in Nigeria and neighboring countries including suicide bombings in Abuja, Nigeria's capital in 2011 and the kidnapping of 200 school girls from Chibok town in Nigeria in 2014, on the police headquarters and UN headquarters, respectively, in Abuja, Nigeria's capital. A regional coalition of Nigeria, Cameroon, Chad, and Niger formed to combat the group appears to be succeeding. In March 2015, it drove Boko Haram from all the towns it had occupied, and in October, 2016, Boko Haram released 21 of the school girls it had captured. There is still a long way to go in rooting out the group since it usually resorts to guerrilla tactics from the nearby forested region.

Summary

Contemporary African societies and cultures are a product of forces internal as well as external to the continent. These forces include ethnocentrism, Christianity, Islam, colonialism, postcolonial policies, and globalization. Given these forces and the processes of cultural change, contemporary African societies and cultures are neither truly African nor foreign. Instead, they are a blend of traditional African and foreign cultural attributes. Thus, while religion and worldviews, family and kinship systems, literature, visual art and symbolism, cuisine, and dress and adornment have a large dose of traditional African features, one can see traces of foreign attributes that have been borrowed to modify the traditional ways or to coexist with the traditional attributes. There is also a great deal of similarities and overlaps of the various cultural practices, while there are also distinctive differences. In the final analysis, some of these attributes generate concerns that may or may not hinder the development process. Among these are the role of language in development, oral literature and corruption, ethnicity and conflicts, and religious fundamentalism and extremism. We will discuss some of these topics in the appropriate chapters of the book.

Postreading Assignments

A. Study the Following Concepts

Animism	Language family	Patrilocal	Religious fundamentalism
Clan endogamy	Lingua franca	Polyandry	Society
Clan exogamy	Matrilineal	Polygamy	
Culture	Matrilocal	Polygyny	
Disafricanization	Monogamy	Race	
Ethnicity	Patrilineal	Religious extremism	

B. Discussion Questions

1. Take a look at the answers your wrote down at the beginning of the chapter and see if you would like to change any of them. Consider why you want to make changes if any.
2. Discuss the factors affecting African societies and cultures.
3. Is the concept of race and ethnicity relevant in studying the cultural geography of Africa? Why and why not?
4. What are the main characteristics features traditional African religions?
5. Account for the growth of AICs in Africa?
6. What factors helped spread Islam in Africa?
7. Discuss the main language groups of Africa.
8. Compare and contrast the matrilineal and patrilineal kinship systems of Africa.
9. Discuss the role of symbolism in African cultures.
10. Discuss the role of age and gender in African societies? What do you need to be done to restore gender equality in African societies?
11. "There is no one African culture but many." Discuss this statement in relation to dress, adornment, and cuisines.
12. Discuss some of the problems facing African countries as a result of their multicultural characteristics.

References

Adesoji, A. 2010, "The Boco Haram Uprising and Islamic Revivalism in Nigeria". *Africa Spectrum*, 45 (2): 95–108.

Afolayan, F. 2004. *Culture and Customs of South Africa*. Westport, CT: Greenwood Press.

Ahluwalia, P. 2006. "Race." *Theory, Culture & Society* (23): 538–545.

Anderson, A. 2001. *African Reformation: African Initiated Christianity in the 20th Century*. Trenton, NJ: Africa World Press.

Andro, A., and Lesclingand, M. 2007. "Female genital mutilation: The situation in Africa and in France." *Population & Societies* 438:1–4.

Ball, T. 2008. "Female Genital Mutilation." *Nursing Standards* 23(5): 43–47.

Bates, R. H. 2000. "Ethnicity and Development in Africa: A Reappraisal." *The American Economic Review* 90(2): 131–134.

Bayart, J. F. 1993. *The State in Africa: The Politics of the Belly*. London: Longman.

Bearak, B. 2010. "Dead Join the Living in Family Celebration." *New York Times*, September 5. http://www.nytimes.com/2010/09/06/world/africa/06madagascar.html?pagewanted=1&_r=2 (accessed 21 February 2017).

Becker, C. 2006. "Amazigh Textiles and Dress in Morocco: Metaphors of Motherhood." *African Arts*. Autumn 42–96.

Bender, M. L. 2000. "Nilo-Saharan." In Heine, B., and Nurse, D. (Eds.) *African Languages: An Introduction*. Cambridge: Cambridge University Press, pp. 43–73.

Blauer, E. 1999. *African Elegance*. New York, NY: Rizzoli International Publications Inc.

Boserup, E. 1970. *Women's Role in Economic Development.* London and Baltimore: Allen and Unwin.

Brenzinger, M., Heine, B., and Sommer, G. 1991 "Language Death in Africa." *Diogenes* 1991(39): 19. http://dio.sagepub.com/content/39/153/19.refs.html

Bwakali, D. J. 2001. "Gender Inequality in Africa." *Contemporary Review* 270–272.

Childs, G. T. 2003. *An Introduction to African Languages.* Philadelphia, PA: John Benjamins Publishing Company

Collier, P., and Hoeffler, A. 1998. "On Economic Causes of Civil War." *Oxford Economic Papers* 50(4): 563–730.

Comaroff, J. 1985. *Body of Power, Spirit of Resistance: The Culture and History of a South African People.* Chicago & London: University of Chicago Press.

Dawson, B. E. 1915. "Circumcision in the Female: Its Necessity, and How to Perform it." *American Journal of Clinical Medicine.* 22(6): 520–523.

Deng, F. M. 1996. "Identity in Africa's Internal Conflicts." *The American Behavioral Scientist.* 40(1): 46–65.

Deng, F. M. 1997. "Ethnicity: An African Predicament." *The Brookings Review* 15(3): 28–31.

Djite', P. G. 1993. "Language and Development in Africa." *International Journal of the Sociology of Language.* 100/101: 149–166.

Djite', P.G. 2008. *The Sociolinguistics of Development in Africa.* Clevedon: Multilingual Matters Ltd.

Easterly, W., and Levine, R. 1997. "Africa's Growth Tragedy: Policies and Ethnic Divisions." *Quarterly Journal of Economics* 112 (4): 1203–1250.

Ebewo, P. 2004. "Heroes of African Folktales: Agents of Contemporary Corruption?" *Lwati: A Journal of Contemporary Research* (1): 50–58.

Emerson, M. O., and Hartman, D. 2006. "The Rise of Religious Fundamentalism." *Annual Review of Sociology* 32:127–144.

Ericksen, K. P. 1989. "Female Genital Mutilations in Africa." *Cross-Cultural Research* 23: 182–204.

Essien, K., and Falola, T. 2008. *Culture and Customs of Sudan.* Westport, CT: Greenwood.

Ewelukwa, U. U. 2002. "Post-Colonialism, Gender, Customary Injustice: Widows in African Societies." *Human Rights Quarterly* 24(2): 424–486.

Falola, T. 2001. *Culture and Custom of Nigeria.* Westport, CT: Greenwood Press.

Falola, T. 2003. *The Power of African Cultures.* Rochester, NY: University of Rochester Press.

Gabsi, Z. 2011. "Attrition and Maintenance of the Berber Language in Tunisia." *International Journal of Soc. Lang.* 211: 135–164.

Gifford, P. 1991. "Christian Fundamentalism and Development." *Review of African Political Economy, Fundamentalism in Africa: Religion and Politics* 52: 9–20.

Gillow, J. 2003. *African Textiles.* San Francisco: Chronicle Books.

Goodman, J. 2005. *Berber Culture on the World Stage: From Village to Video.* Bloomington: Indiana University Press.

Guldermann, T., and Vossen, R. 2000. "Khoisan." In Heine, B., and Nurse, D. (Eds.) *African Languages: An Introduction.* Cambridge: Cambridge University Press, pp. 99–122.

Hameso, S. Y. 1995. *Ethnicity and Nationalism in Africa.* Commack, NY: Nova Science Publishers.

Hanson, F. A. 2005. "Culture Against Society." *Society* 65–68

Hastings, A. 1994. *The Church in Africa 1450-1930.* Oxford: Clarendon.

Harney, J. 2016. "How Do Sunni and Shia Islam Differ?" *New York Times* January 3. https://www.nytimes.com/2016/01/04/world/middleeast/q-and-a-how-do-sunni-and-shia-islam-differ.html?_r=0 (accessed 21 February 2017).

Hayward, R. J. 2000. "Afroasiatic" In Heine, B., and Nurse, D. (Eds.) *African Languages: An Introduction.* Cambridge: Cambridge University Press, pp. 74–98.

Heine, B., and Nurse, D. (Eds.) 2000. *African Languages: An Introduction.* Cambridge: Cambridge University Press, pp. 99–122.

Igwe, L. 2004. "A Skeptical Look at African Witchcraft and Religion." *Skeptic* 11 (1): 72–74.

Johnston-Anumonwo, I. 2003. "Geography, Gender, and Development in Sub-Saharan Africa." In Aryeetey-Attoh, S. (Ed.) *Geography of Sub-Saharan Africa.* 2nd edition. Upper Saddle River, NJ: Prentice Hall, pp. 298–323.

Julien, E. 1995. "African Literature" In Martin, P. M., and O'Meara, P. (Eds.) *Africa.* 3rd edition. Bloomington: Indian University Press, pp. 295–312.

Kaplan, R. 1994. "The Coming Anarchy." *Atlantic Monthly* 273 (2): 44–76.

Kimenyi, M. S. 1998. "Harmonizing ethnic claims in Africa: A proposal for ethnic-based Federalism." *Cato Journal;* Spring 18: 1.

Krech, H. 2011. "The Growing Influence of Al-Qaeda on the African Continent." *African Spectrum* 46(2): 125–137.

Lupke, F. 2009. "At the Margin-African Endangered Languages in the Context of Global Enadangerment Discourses." *African Research & Documentation.* 109: 15–41.

Mbaku, J. M. 2005. *Culture and Customs of Cameroon.* Westport, CT: Greenwood.

Mbiti, J. S. 1969. *African Religions & Philosophy.* New York, NY: Praeger.

McDougall, J. 2010. "Histories of Heresy and Salvation: Arabs, Berbers, Community, and the State." In Hoffman, K. E., and Miller, S. G. (Eds.). *Berbers and Others: Beyond Tribe and Nation in the Maghrib.* Bloomington and Indianapolis: Indiana University Press, pp. 15–38.

Meyer, B. 2004. "Christianity in Africa: From African Independent to Pentecostal-Charismatic Churches." *Annual Review of Anthropology* 33: 447–74.

Momoh, C. 1999. "Female Genital Mutilation: The Struggle Continues." *Practicing Nursing.* 10(2): 31–33.

Mudimbe, V. Y. 1988. *The Invention of Africa: Gnosis, Philosophy, and the Order of Knowledge.* Bloomington: Indiana University Press.

Mukenge, T. 2002. *Culture and Customs of the Congo.* Westport, CT: Greenwood Press.

Nnam, N. 2007. *Colonial Mentality in Africa.* Lanham, MD: Hamilton Books.

Njoku, R. C. 2006. *Culture and Custom of Morocco.* Westport, CT: Greenwood Press.

Omotoso, K. 2004. "Africa Lost Without Translation" *New African* 52–53.

Oppong, J. R. 2003. "Culture, Conflict, and Change in Sub-Saharan Africa." In Aryeetey-Attoh, S. (Ed.) *Geography of Sub-Saharan Africa.* 2nd edition. Upper Saddle River, NJ: Prentice Hall, pp. 134–164.

Otiso, K. M. 2013. *Culture and Customs of Tanzania.* Westport, CT: Greenwood.

Otiso, K. M. 2006. *Culture and Customs of Uganda* Westport, CT: Greenwood.

Robinson, C., 1996. *Language Use in Rural Development: An African Perspective.* Berlin: Mouton de Gruyter.

Ross, E. S. 2008. *Culture and Customs lf Senegal.* Westport, CT: Greenwood Press.

Ssenyonjo, M. 2007. "Culture and the Human Rights of Women in Africa: Between Light and Shadow." *Journal of African Law* 51(1): 39–67.

Sundkler, B. G. M. 1961. *Bantu Prophets in South Africa.* Oxford: Oxford University Press.

Tarimo, S. J. A. 2010. "Politicization of Ethnic Identities: The Case of Contemporary Africa." *Journal of Asian and African Studies* 45(3): 297–308.

Trudell, B. 2009. "Local-language literacy and sustainable development in Africa" *International Journal of Educational Development* 29: 73–79.

Turner, H. W. 1979. *Religious Innovation in Africa.* Boston: G. K. Hall.

Tylor, E. B. 1874. *Primitive Culture.* New York, NY: Henry Holt & Co.

Udo, R. K. 1982. *The Human Geography of Tropical Africa.* Ibadan: Heinemann Educational Books (Nigeria) Ltd.

Vail, L. 1989. "Introduction: Ethnicity in Southern African History." In Vail, L. (Ed.) *The Creation of Tribalism in Southern Africa.* Berkeley: University of California Press, pp. 1–18.

Vikør, K. S. 2000. "Sufi Brotherhoods in Africa." In Levtzion, N., and Pouwels, R. L. (Eds.) *The History of Islam in Africa.* Athens: Ohio University Press, pp. 440–476.

Williamson, K., and Blench, R. 2000. "Niger-Congo." In Heine, B., and Nurse, D. (Eds.) *African Languages: An Introduction.* Cambridge: Cambridge University Press, pp. 11–42.

Woodfork, J. C. 2006. *Culture and Custom of Central African Republic.* Westport, CT: Greenwood Press.

WHO 2008. *Eliminating Female Genital Mutilation. An interagency Statement. Geneva:* WHO.

Zerfu, D., Zikhali, P., and Kabenga, I. 2008. "Does Ethnicity Matter for Trust? Evidence from Africa" *Journal of African Economies* 18(1): 153–175.

Cities, Towns, and Villages

1. If you have visited an Africa city, town or village before,
   a. What is the name of the city and which country was it in?
   b. What did you expect to see before you arrived?
   c. What did you actually see when you arrived?
   d. Were there any things that surprised you? Why and Why not?
   e. Did you find any similarities and differences between your own city and what you found in Africa?
2. If you have not visited any African city, town, or village before,
   a. Write down all that comes to mind regarding the idea of a city, town and village in Africa.
   b. Are these negative, positive, or mixed?

In 2008, I had an opportunity to hear a report from an American student who had just returned from Nigeria, and the first thing she said was: "I went to Nigeria expecting to see poverty, jungle, and little huts here and there, but when I arrived in Lagos, I saw skyscrapers and a modern city." Have you ever wondered if Africans live in cities, towns or little huts? This chapter will address some your curiosity. Specifically, the chapter focuses on the **human settlement** system of Africa, which is hierarchically differentiated as cities, towns, and villages. The chapter is divided into four main sections. The first section clarifies some basic concepts that will be important to the rest of the chapter. The second section focuses on African cities. The third section discusses Africa's small towns and villages, while the fourth discusses the linkages and interactions between the two parts of the system. Let us begin with some prereading assignments.

SOME CONCEPTS AND DEFINITIONS

At its first conference on human settlement in 1976, United Nations defined human settlement as consisting of the totality of human community—whether **city**, town, or village—with all the social material, organizational, spiritual, and cultural elements that sustain it (UN, 1976). These include shelter or buildings that house the people who live there, infrastructure, which is the complex networks required to deliver and remove goods and services that are required for proper functioning of the place.

In Africa, cities are usually distinguished by their enormous size, heterogeneity in terms of its population, and the nonagricultural nature of their economy. Towns are smaller than cities and have fewer services than cities. Villages are the smallest in size and in general have agrarian economies. In practical terms, what constitute a city, town, or village depends on government definitions. Common terminologies that are used in academic and policy discussions regarding cities, towns, and villages are **urban** and **rural** areas. Unfortunately, there is no agreement as to what these two concepts mean among African countries and globally as well. Efforts at defining urban and rural terms have used various criteria including population size, administrative purposes, urban functions, and lifestyle. On the assumption that an urban area should be large in size, population size has been used as a proxy for defining urban areas. However, as it is the case elsewhere, different African countries use different populations threshold to define what is urban (Table 8.1). For example, in Botswana, an urban area is an agglomeration of 5,000 or more people where 75% of economic activity is nonagricultural. In Senegal, urban refers to all agglomerations of 10,000 people or more, while in Ethiopia it is localities of 2,000 or more inhabitants (UN, 2005). Other countries define urban areas administratively. In Egypt for example, urban areas include governorates of Cairo, Alexandra, Port Said, Ismailia, Suez, frontier governorates, and capitals of governorates and districts. In Tunisia, urban refers to people living in communes. In Malawi, urban areas include all townships and town planning areas and all district centers, while in South Africa it refers to all places with some form of local authority (Table 8.1).

Elsewhere in developed countries, other criteria such as urban functions and lifestyle have been used, but these do not fit very well in the African context. What is clear from this brief discussion is that although the term "urban" seems to be understood by people it is not easy to define it. In developed countries, long-term changes brought about by economic development and the revolution in telecommunication

TABLE **8.1**

Some Urban Definitions Used in Africa

Country	Urban definition
Botswana	Agglomeration of 5,000 or more where 75% of economic activity is nonagricultural
Burundi	Commune of Bujumbura
Comoros	Administrative centers of prefectures and localities of 5,000 or more inhabitants
Egypt	Governorates of Cairo, Alexandria, Port Said, Ismailia, Suez, frontier governorates or capitals of other governorates, as well as district capitals (Markaz)
Equatorial Guinea	District centers and localities with 300 dwellings and/or 1,500 inhabitants or more
Ethiopia	Localities of 2,000 or more inhabitants
Liberia	Localities of 2,000 or more inhabitants
Malawi	All townships and town planning areas and all district centers
Mauritius	Towns with proclaimed legal rights
Niger	Capital city, capitals of the departments and districts
Senegal	Agglomerations of 10,000 or more inhabitants
South Africa	Places with some form of local authority
Sudan	Localities of administrative and/or commercial importance or with population of 5,000 or more inhabitants
Swaziland	Localities proclaimed as urban
Tunisia	Population living in communes
Tanzania	16 gazetted townships
Zambia	Localities of 5,000 or more inhabitants, the majority of whom all depend on the nonagricultural activities

Source: United Nations Demographic Year Book, 2005.

technology have caused some people to argue for the abandonment of rural and urban differences. In Africa, people have been talking about the rural–urban continuum since the 1970s. However, the division between urban and rural areas is still real and profound depending on the country, but it is also complex. First, in every African country there are marked differences in the economic activities, physical layout, physical infrastructure, social amenities, and the general living conditions between areas considered as urban compared to areas considered as rural. For example, the economic activities in most rural areas consist largely of agriculture. The architectural layout of nice walled modern self-contained houses, and green lawns and paved roads of urban areas contrasts with traditional mud-built houses with no plumbing and sewer, unpaved and heavily gullied streets, and unkempt environments of the rural area. At the same time, the differences are more complex when one considers the fact that there are some areas within urban areas that look like rural landscapes, a situation that has given rise to the term "ruralization" of the urban landscape.

In view of all these, we will use the term **urban areas** to refer to settlements (cities, municipalities, and towns) that are regarded by their respective national governments as urban. Similarly, **rural** will refer to all nonurban settlements. The term **peri-urban** will refer to the transitional zone between urban and rural areas. The term **urban system** will refer to a hierarchical and stratified system of urban areas.

URBAN AREAS: CITIES AND LARGE TOWNS

The focus of this section is to learn about Africa's urban system—its cities and large towns. It does this in two steps. First, it traces the evolution and development of Africa's cities and large towns. Second, it explores the contemporary African city with respect to its internal structure and some of the current problem and issues of Africa's contemporary cities and large towns.

Evolution and Development of Africa's Urban System

The common methodology for studying evolution and development of the urban system is to divide the period under consideration into subperiods and examining what cities grew in each period and the factors that influenced the growth of the cities. For Africa, this methodology has led to the use of different periods and classification of cities. Winters (1983) classified precolonial African cities as political and commercial cities. O'Connor (1983) adopted the indigenous, Islamic, colonial, and postcolonial periods, Coquery-Vidrovitch (1991) used precapitalist, capitalist, and colonial periods, while Grant and Nijman (2002) as well as Otiso and Owusu (2008) adopt precolonial, colonial, national, and global phases. Each of these methodologies is only a way to manage the analysis and presentation of a complex subject. Therefore, for our purpose, we consider the evolution and development of Africa's urban system in three broad periods: precolonial period (before 1850), colonial period (1850–1950s), and postcolonial period (since 1960s).

Precolonial Period (before 1850)

According to Newman (1998), most settlements in Africa originated from living floors, which were places that people gathered temporarily during the day and retreated to safer places at night. Over time, these living floors and caves transformed into camps, where social interaction and exchange among 30–50 people could take place (Newman, 1998). However, as African societies became more organized political, economic, and social factors led to the transformation of some of these small towns into cities and the creation of new ones. We will examine this transformation over three subperiods—Ancient Africa (before 500 AD), the medieval and mercantilist African period (500–1500 AD), and the European mercantilist period (1500–1850).

Ancient Africa (before 500 AD) Historical records show that the first cities in Africa occurred with the emergence of the first major kingdoms and empires on the continent, due to the need to control the political, cultural, and religious ceremonies of conquered jurisdictions. This in turn provided a need for capital cities, most of which were established from the scratch. These early cities grew in three main areas: (1) the Lower Nile Valley, (2) the Upper Nile Valley, and (3) the Mediterranean Coast (Figure 8.1).

The cities of the Lower Nile included Abydos, Memphis, Thebes, Avaris, and Alexandria, all of which became the capital of the ancient Egypt at some point (Chandler, 1994a). Memphis and Avaris each had 100,000 people, while Thebes had about 60,000. Avaris was also the first walled city in the Nile Valley (Chandler, 1994a). Alexandria became a major city of commerce, culture, and learning, and the center of the Greek civilization in Africa. With a population of about 300,000 at its peak, Alexandria vied with Patna, India as the world's largest city throughout the 3rd century. The cities of the Upper Nile included Kerma, Nepata, Meroe, Adulis, and Aksum. Meroe, in particular, had a very favorable location and for that reason grew to become a very successful commercial center. On the Mediterranean coast, the most important city was Carthage, which was a city of about 200,000 people with an urban area of 700,000, at its peak (see Chapter 3).

Much of the information about the internal structure of these ancient or classical African cities has been obtained through archaeological excavations, which makes it difficult to gain a full knowledge of how these cities were actually laid out. Kerma, for example, is said to have been centered on the royal palace with a large royal audience courtyard, interspersed with gardens and animal enclosure. It is estimated that there were about 2,000 people living in this central part of the city. However, most people lived outside the city walls (Goodwin, 2006; O'Connor, 1983).

In the case of Alexandria, the city was dissected into four main quarters by two major arterial streets—the east–west Canopic Street along which most of the cities' monumental buildings were located and the north–south Street of the Soma. Among the monumental buildings were palaces, temples, theaters, agoras or marketplaces, lighthouse docks, warehouses, courtyards, and the world's largest library and museum (Goodwin, 2006). Alexandria's residential areas were segregated. To the west was the original village of Rhakotis occupied by Egyptians; to the northeast were the Jewish quarters, near to which were the royal palace and the royal harbor. The rest was the Greek city. Alexandria was a walled city except the Jewish quarters, with ethnic cemeteries located outside the wall. The social structure was hierarchical. Greeks had citizenship, while Egyptians and Jews did not. Meroe, another **classical African city** is said to have straight intersecting street with well-built Roman-styled houses, palaces, audience chambers, stores, baths, domestic and staff quarters, and a precinct surrounded by a stonewall.

The medieval and mercantilist African period (from 500 to 1500) Three major events during this period affected the growth of cities in Africa. The first was the rise of medieval empires across the continent (Chapter 2). The second was the Arab invasion of Africa and the subsequent Arabization and Islamization of North

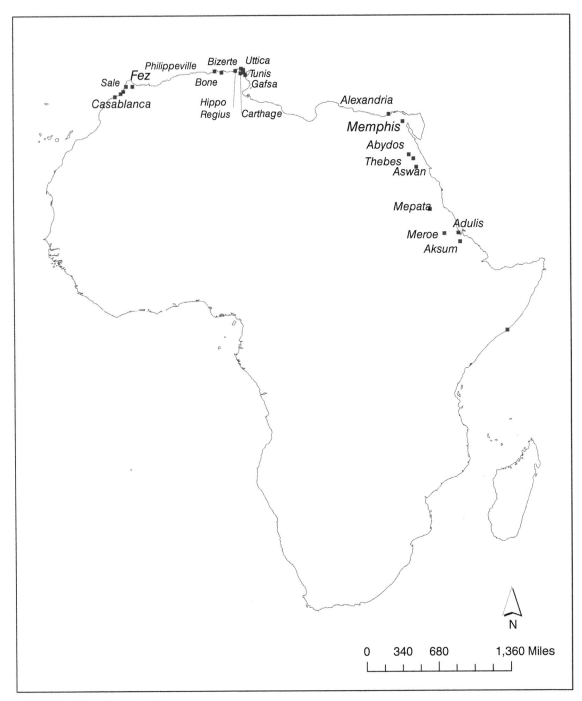

FIGURE 8.1 Cities of ancient Africa.
Source: Map based on Freund, B. 2007. *The African City: A History.* Cambridge: Cambridge University Press, p. 3.

Africa, Western Sudan, and the Swahili Coast. The third was the lucrative Trans Saharan Trade and the Swahili Coast trade, the control of which transformed small principalities and towns into large empires and cities, respectively. These events concentrated urban growth once again in the Lower Nile Valley and the Maghreb, the Niger Basin and West Africa, and the Swahili Coast (Figure 8.2).

In the Lower Nile Valley and North Africa, the old cities such as Alexandria continued to be important, but new cities emerged including Fostat and Cairo in

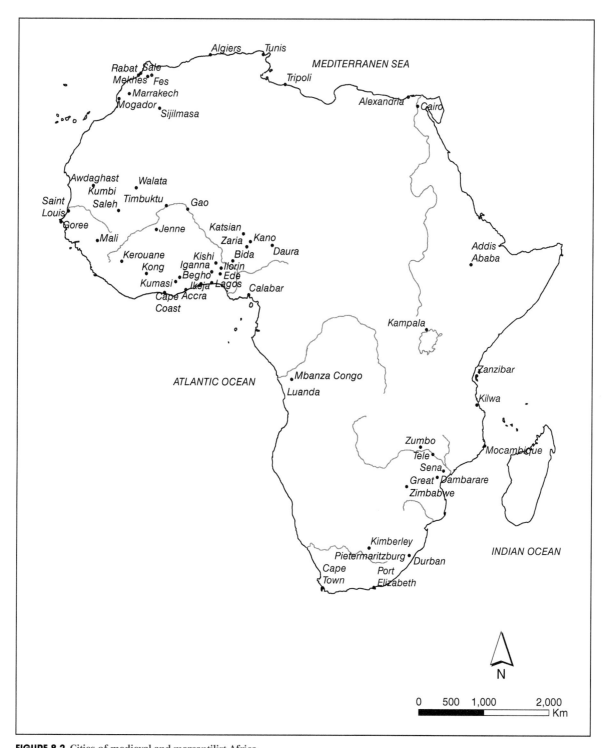

FIGURE 8.2 Cities of medieval and mercantilist Africa.

Source: Map created in part from Freund, B. 2007. *The African City: A History.* Cambridge: Cambridge University Press, p. 39.

Egypt, and Qairawan (Kairouan) in Tunisia. Founded in 969 AD, by the Fatimid, Cairo reached its peak as a medieval city, between 1293 and 1341, with 500,000 people, 35 major market places, and 494 mosques. It was the world's largest city (Chandler, 1994b). In the Maghreb, new cities emerged including Fez, Meknes,

Marrakesh, and Sijilmasa all in modern Morocco, and Tunis, in modern Tunisia all because of the Trans Saharan Trade.

In the Niger Basin, the Trans Saharan Trade influenced the growth of a number of cities, which included Kumbi Saleh, Walata, Awdoghast, Gao, Mali, Jenne, and Timbuktu. Kumbi Saleh, Mali, and Gao grew also because they were the capital cities of the Ghana, Mali, and Songhai Empires, respectively (Figure 8.2).

About 999 AD, on the northern Nigerian plain, the Hausa-speaking people created seven city-states, namely Biram, Daura, Gobir, Kano, Katsina, Rano, and Zaria. At their peak, Kano was about 11 miles in circumference, while Katsina was about 13 miles. (Chandler, 1994b) Further south in the forest belt of Nigeria, were Ile-Ife, Oyo, Igana, Ikoyi, Kishi, Ilorin, Ede, and Idode (Mabogunje, 1968). In East Africa a number of coastal towns emerged during the 8th and the 9th centuries, including Lamu, Kilwa, Malindi, Sofala, Dar es Salaam, and Mogadishu (Aryeetey-Attoh, 2003; Otiso and Owusu, 2008), while in Southern Africa, it was the city of Great Zimbabwe.

The forces that influenced the development of the cities created three main forms of city structure. The first was the **indigenous African city**, which consisted of two main sections, the royal section and the people's section. The royal section containing the palace was highly fortified depending on the city, by walls and a series of security checks and gates that made it difficult for even the city's inhabitants to see the king perform normal human functions such as eating and sleeping (Hull, 1976; O'Connor, 1983). In some of the cities such as Mbanza-Kongo, the capital of the Kongo Kingdom, the king's court had separate sections for men and women (Coquery-Vidrovitch, 2005). In addition, the royal section also housed the main market center that served both as social and trading center. Beyond this inner wall were the residents of the city, who were in turn separated by other series of walls with gates, again depending on the type of society. In Hausa cities, for example, the inner gates served as a source of revenue as people had to pay toll to enter into different sections of the city. At the outer edge of the city was the main city wall that served as a defense mechanism against outside invaders. The indigenous African city was a compact and relatively unplanned city with mostly one-story mud houses.

The second form was the **mercantilist African city**, which also consisted of two broad sections—the fortress and the commercial city. In Cairo, the old city consisted of high-density residential neighborhoods with seven-floor apartments, and small and winding streets, while the commercial city hosted libraries, museums, and beautiful mosques, hotels, and medical/university districts (Freund, 2007). In Kumbi Saleh and Hausa land, the fortress continued as the royal residence and original inhabitants, while the merchants mostly occupied the commercial city or new town. Since most of the merchants were Muslim, the commercial area, mosques dominated the commercial area making it more Islamic.

The third form of the medieval African city was the **Islamic African city**. The Islamic Africa city was similar to the mercantilist African city, with two exceptions. First, the Islamic African city had three nuclei of influence—the Emir's palace, the Grand Mosque, and the central market. The section with Emir's palace also housed the army and other state institutions. The Grand Mosque and the central market were located in the commercial section of the city, which also housed artisans including leather and metal works. Second, the residential area consisted largely of two sections, the Muslim and the non-Muslim sections depending upon the city. Fez, for example, had indigenous Africans, Arabs, and Jewish quarters. In any case, the Muslim section served as the base for Muslim clerics dominated by other smaller mosques as well as schools. It is reported that Agadez, for example, had about 70 mosques; virtually every quarter had a mosque (Coquery-Vidrovitch, 2005).

The European mercantilist period (from 1500 to 1850s) This era began with the European voyages of exploration and ended with colonialism. In between these two major events, the preoccupation of European nations to amass wealth on a world scale led to the establishment of a network of world trade and exploitation for precious metals, and agricultural raw materials, the Atlantic Slave Trade, the exploration of Africa's interior, and the institution of the so-called legitimate trade. Given that most of these new activities were sea-bound rather than land-bound, the focus of urban development shifted from the interior to the coastal areas, and places that could participate in these events. At the same time, the decay of empires and struggle for control over Africa's interior added to the decline of the earlier cities. In the Nile Valley and North Africa, Cairo, Marrakesh, and Fez, all declined. In the Niger Basin, the Moroccan Invasion of Songhai in 1591 led to the fall of Gao, Mali, and Timbuktu. The Fulani jihads ransacked Kano and Katsina, caused the decline of the Oyo and its nearby cities, and replaced them with much smaller Sokoto. In East Africa, Kilwa and Mombasa fell successively to the Portuguese, the Turks, and the Arabs.

In contrast, small coastal settlements were transformed as slave ports or centers of early colonial activities. Among the most important were Algiers (Algeria), Elmina (Ghana), Whydah (Benin), Mbanza Kongo and Luanda (Angola), Cape Town (South Africa), and Zanzibar (Tanzania). Chandler (1994b) reports that Algiers was the greatest slave port of all times. From a tiny fishing village before 1500, Algiers had grown to a city of 75,000 by 1600 with about 15,000 slaves. By 1634, the city's population had reached 100,000 of which 25,000 were slaves. Cape Town and Zanzibar also grew to become important slave ports.

The internal structure of these **European mercantilist cities** consisted of European quarters organized around forts or castles and African quarters around the palace of the local king or chief. The Atlantic Slave Trade brought both Europeans and Africans to the forts and castles along the African coast, but while the Africans settled among the Africans, Europeans set up different quarters for themselves—Dutch, Portuguese, Danish, English, and French quarters (Coquery-Vidrovitch, 2005). The social structure of these new towns and cities also changed due to two developments. First, intermarriages between Africans and Europeans created a creole culture, and a mulatto population with European family names. Members of this group became leading merchants, major employers, and estate owners, adopting aristocratic style among the people. Second, the arrival of freed Afro-Brazilians, especially along the Benin to Nigerian coast, ironically became leading and wealthy merchants of the slave trade adopting aristocratic lifestyles and introducing the Brazilian-style home (Coquery-Vidrovitch, 2005). There were some cities such as Kilwa that were rebuilt by the Europeans with European layout and architecture. Such cities had a series of warehouses and businesses along the coast and high-class residence on the facing hillside. In between was the city center with administrative offices, boutiques, and ordinary people residences.

Colonial Period (1850s–1950s)

Three major factors influenced the growth of cities and large towns during the colonial period. These were transportation and communication nodes, resource areas (especially places of mineral wealth), and the seats of colonial administration.

Among the cities that owed their origins to transportation development during colonial period were Cape Town, Port Elizabeth, Durban, and East London (South Africa), Nairobi (Kenya), Dar es Salaam (Tanzania), Mombasa (Kenya), Maputo (Mozambique), Lagos and Port Harcourt (Nigeria), Takoradi (Ghana), Freetown (Sierra Leone), and Dakar (Senegal) (Figure 8.3).

FIGURE 8.3 Cities of colonial Africa.
Source: Map created in part from Freund, B. 2007. *The African City: A History.* Cambridge: Cambridge University Press, p. 67.

Cities and towns that grew because of mineral wealth include Kimberly (South Africa), and Akwatia and Oda, (Ghana) due to diamonds; Johannesburg, Benoni, Boksburg, Brakpan (South Africa); Obuasi, Konongo, Dunkwa, Prestea,

Tarkwa (Ghana); KweKwe (Zimbabwe) all due to gold; and Ndola, Kitwe, Kabwe, Mufilira (Zambia), Lubumbashi, and Kolwezi (DRC), due to copper, zinc, and cobalt.

Existing settlements that grew because they were selected to become seats of colonial administration included Rabat, Cairo, Dakar, Brazzaville, Accra, Lagos, Ouagadougou, and Bobo-Dioulasso, while new settlements that were established as seats for colonial administration included Nairobi, Lusaka, and Zomba (Freund, 2007). Apart from these, there were some towns that grew during the colonial period not because of any of the three factors, but because people flocked into them to seek what they perceived as economic opportunities. Examples of such cities were Casablanca in Morocco, Ibadan in Nigeria, and Kampala in Uganda.

The internal structure of the **colonial city** was very much determined by the policy of the colonizer (Winters, 1982). In the British colonies that had few British settlers, the precolonial city was pretty much left intact with new quarters added to accommodate European settlers. Therefore, while the city saw growth in population, sanitary and environmental conditions did not change (Mabogunje, 1962). However, where large European settlers were present such as Harare, Lusaka, and Nairobi, the city was built to the taste of the settler population. The European integrity of the city was strictly controlled by laws that prohibited **rural–urban migration**. In contrast, the French and Portuguese rebuilt most of their colonial city to conform to European standards. The city had a grid street pattern, central business district, and other public buildings that took after European architecture.

The colonial city was a segregated city. Thus, there were European, Asian, and African quarters of the city. This segregation was based on both theories of racial superiority and concerns over epidemic outbreaks. Colonial Europe believed that segregation was a good urban policy to safeguard the health and security of Europeans living in Africa. In Francophone Africa, Winters (1982) reports that the European areas were separated from the African areas by a no-man's land, a swamp, or a cliff. The French residents always took the higher grounds to avoid being downwind from Africans. In Kenya, for example, Africans and Asians were considered unhygienic and laws (The Public Health Law of 1930 and the vagrancy Acts of 1922 and 1949) were passed to ensure implementation of this belief (Otiso, 2005). In South Africa, Freund (2007, p. 110) writes:

> . . .The idea of planning for an integrated urban environment in which Africans could be assimilated as citizens was unthinkable. . . . Black people were associated with all the vices of slum life, with poor sanitation, and hygiene, and their homes were seen as the source of epidemics of plague, cholera, and malaria. Clean-ups after such epidemics were often the excuse for shutting down spaces where Africans congregated.

In Ghana, the colonial administration contemplated clearing the native area of Accra for building after an epidemic outbreak (Freund, 2007). In Nairobi, the African or native quarters was added to the city center as an afterthought, while in Lourenco Marques (Maputo) "the shacks, mud and garbage" were added to the outskirts (Freund, 2007, p. 80).

The economic functions in the city were equally segregated. The central business district catered to Europeans. There was then a secondary market controlled by the Asian merchants, who served as middlemen between the Africans and Europeans, and the market place for the Africans. The colonial city, however, could not completely escape the process of urbanization. Even when African quarters were included as part of the plan, these neighborhoods were never sufficient to keep up with that lure of rural–urban migration, and as the economies grew, shack settlement began to appear beyond the planned perimeters of cities such as Algiers and Casablanca as early as the late 1920s (Freund, 2007).

Postcolonial Period (since 1960s)

Accelerated urban growth The postcolonial era has been a period of accelerated urban growth in Africa. In 1950 only 32 million (or 15%) Africans were living
in cities. By 2000 the number had jumped to 323.2 million (38%), and by 2015
urban residents had reached 472 million (UN-Population Division 2016), with the
majority of the populations of South Africa, Morocco, Algeria, Tunisia, Libya, and
Egypt, living in urban areas. In 1950, only three urban agglomerations in Africa,
Cairo, and Alexandria, both in Egypt and in Johannesburg, South Africa had population of 1 million or more. In 2015, there were 58 urban agglomerations with
population of 1 million or more, with an estimated total population of 174 million (UN Habitat, 2014) (Figure 8.4). Cairo, Africa's largest urban agglomeration
had 18.7 million, followed closely by Lagos with 13 million. It is estimated that by
2025 close to 60% of Africans will be living in large cities. Most of this growth initially occurred in the capital cities, where population increase was around 430%.
However, there were some of them that were outside the capital cities. Among
these noncapital cities are Johannesburg (South Africa), Douala (Cameroon),
Lubumbashi (DRC), and Mombasa (Kenya). What factors have accounted for this
tremendous growth?

Explanations of the accelerated urban growth The single most important factor of
the accelerated urban growth in Africa is population increase, which as we have seen
in Chapter 6 stems from two sources—natural increase and migration. During the
early postindependence period, much of the urban growth was due to rural–urban
migration, which in turn was due to freedom of movement and urban-bias political and economic development policies of the period. With respect to freedom of
movement, Africa's rural population had been virtually immobile during the colonial period. In East and Southern Africa, Africans were forbidden to live permanently in cities. With independence, the restriction was no more, so the movement
to the cities increased rapidly. Against this background, the European quarters
that dominated the colonial city began hollowing out as Europeans departed soon
after independence. In Algiers, for example, about half of the city's population, all
Europeans, departed soon after independence. The same thing occurred in former
colonial cities such as Lourenco Marques (Maputo) (Mozambique) and Luanda
(Angola) (Freund, 2007). This in turn created more room for the people from the
countryside. As early migrants settled, family networks, information flow, and tales
of "bright city lights" created a self-sustaining engine for more people to migrate to
the cities (Adepoju, 1992; Byerlee, 1974; Gugler, 1969).

Political and economic development policies had a built-in urban bias that aided
this massive movement to the existing urban centers during the period. Politically,
all the newly independent African countries had to choose a seat of government.
Some countries chose the same cities used by colonial administration. In the French
colonies where there were only two colonial capitals—Dakar for French West Africa
and Brazzaville for French Equatorial Africa, new national capitals had to be established from either existing cities and towns or from scratch. For example, Gaborone
in Botswana, Kigali in Rwanda, and Nouakchott in Mauritania were all established
as new capitals (Freund, 2007). The capital cities became the preoccupation of their
respective governments in an effort to turn the cities into symbols of national pride.
This was further aided by the economic development policies, which concentrated
investments in the capital cities or places that already had some infrastructure base
to support those investments (Chapter 3). The cities became the new centers of

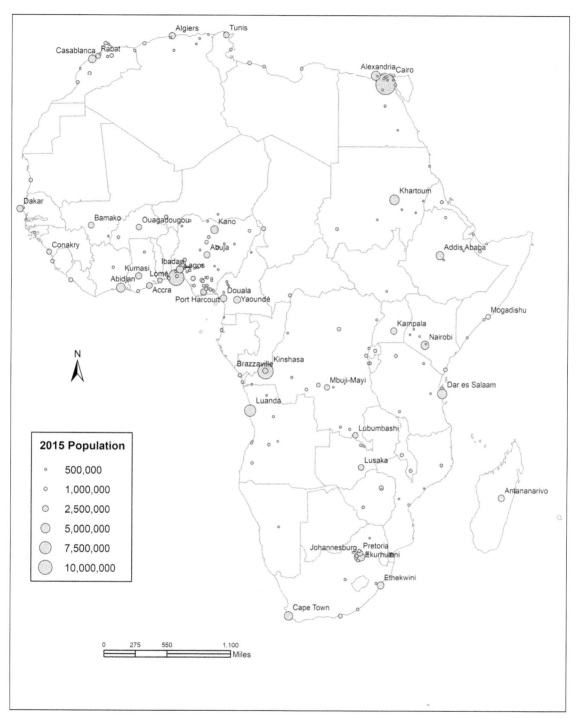

FIGURE 8.4 Africa's postcolonial cities.
Source: Created by Greg Anderson

employment and better-paid jobs, while very little attention was given to the development of agricultural sector and rural areas. In some countries, the rural situation was made worse by drought, soil depletion, crop failure, and overgrazing. With their livelihoods disappearing, rural dwellers had no choice but to move to the urban

TABLE **8.2**

Top 20 Largest Urban Agglomerations in Africa

City	Country	Estimated urban area population (millions)
Cairo	Egypt	18,772
Lagos	Nigeria	13,123
Kinshasa	DRC	11,587
Johannesburg	South Africa	9,399
Luanda	Angola	5,506
Khartoum	Sudan	5,129
Dar es Salaam	Tanzania	5,116
Abidjan	Cote d'Ivoire	4,860
Alexandria	Egypt	4,778
Nairobi	Kenya	3,915
Cape Town	South Africa	3,660
Kano	Nigeria	3,587
Dakar	Senegal	3,520
Dar-el-Beida (Casablanca)	Morocco	3,515
Addis Ababa	Addis Ababa	3,238
Ibadan	Ibadan	3,160
Yaoundé	Cameroon	3,066
Doula	Cameroon	2,943
Durban	South Africa	2,901

Source: United Nations, Department of Economic and Social Affairs, Population Division (2014) World Urbanization Prospects 2014 Revision. CD-ROM Edition.

centers in droves hoping to find jobs. However, once they arrived in the cities and did not find jobs, most migrants found it difficult to return to the rural areas, where they lived before because of the hope of finding a job that will improve their conditions than in the rural areas (Todaro, 1969).

Since mid-1980s globalization forces have become more important and have in fact played a greater role in the acceleration of urban growth on the continent (see, e.g., Grant, 2006; Grant and Nijman 2002; Grant and Yankson, 2003; Otiso and Owusu, 2005; Yeboah, 2000). These forces include the structural adjustment policies that forced the majority of African countries to enact trade liberalization and other economic policies and governance reforms such as privatization, deregulation, currency exchange, establishment of export processing zones, institution of mortgage programs, and landownership by foreigners. In many African countries, these reforms opened to the door to private investment from both inside and outside of the countries. The outside investment came mainly from two sources—foreign companies and development organizations, and Africans living abroad, while the domestic investments came from people who were able to cease the opportunities that became available because of the liberalization policies. Much of the capital inflow from Africans living abroad went to establishment of businesses and house building. The result was rapid growth of both domestic and foreign companies as well as in the housing sector.

At the same time, the retrenchment that accompanied the structural adjustments programs resulted in large unemployed urban dwellers. This not only exacerbated the existing socioeconomic differentiation, but many of the newly unemployed entered the **informal sector** as a way of survival, and thereby extending the **informal areas** of the city geographically (Grant and Yankson, 2003). Finally, competition among African cities and pressure to improve image have also led to aggressive marketing on the part of these cities with visionary marketing and other promotional plans. Example is Johannesburg's Vision 2030 as world class African City (Sihlongonyane, 2016). The combination of these forces has transformed the spatial and the social structures of Africa's postcolonial or contemporary city so much so that it is important to devote more time to examine these features.

The Internal Structure of Africa's Cities

Spatial Structure

There is no one model of the spatial structure of Africa's **postcolonial city**. However, if we use major land use as proxy, we can discuss the spatial structure of the postcolonial city in terms of its commercial, government, industrial, residential, transportation, and open land areas.

Commercial areas These areas include the expansion of the old commercial core (CBD) of the colonial city with expatriate department stores and the central markets of the traditional type, as well as the new CBDs made possible by liberalization policies and foreign direct investments. In Accra (Ghana), for example, Grant and Yankson (2003) reported the emergence of three CBDs. The first is the local CBD, which is the old colonial core, which now caters to the local population. The second is the national CBD that extends from the old core, which caters to the national economy, and the third is the global CBD, which anchors the offices of foreign companies and caters to the global market. Otiso and Owusu (2008) reported of a second CBD development in Nairobi, Kenya.

Commercial activities however, are not restricted only to these cores, but they are also found along all the major arterial roads and streets leading to the main residential areas of the city, merging into local open markets of such areas, and spilling over to even residential areas. In recent years, a number of large supermarkets (Shoprite) and modern malls have been added to these commercial areas. The predominant activity in these areas is retailing and street vending, which is almost ubiquitous. Others include corporate head offices, hotels, guesthouses and restaurants, banks, insurance, and offices of doctors, accountants, and lawyers.

Government business areas Adjacent to the old commercial core is usually the government business area, which houses the buildings of the executive (various ministries or departments of government), legislative, and judicial branches of governments. These areas together with the new commercial areas discussed above still represent some of the nicest sections of the postcolonial city and are comparable to many central business districts of Western cities (Figures 8.5A–8.5D).

Industrial areas These areas include substantial industrial districts or estates established as part of the industrialization efforts of the early postcolonial period. However, some of these estates with their factory buildings have not recovered from

FIGURE 8.5A City
Center, Cairo.
Source: iStock.com/efesenko

FIGURE 8.5B City Center,
Nairobi, Kenya.
Source: iStock.com/derejeb

the deterioration that resulted of economic down turn of the late 1970s through the
1990s, and many of them have been closed down. In Accra, Ghana, some of these
areas have been converted to other uses including mega church buildings. Since
the liberalization policies these areas have a boost from the establishment of many
export processing zones.

Residential areas With the exception of South Africa, residential segregation
sanctioned by racial laws of the colonial city gave way to spatial segregation based

FIGURE 8.5C City Center, Johannesburg, South Africa.
Source: iStock.com/thissatan

FIGURE 8.5D City Center, Largos, Nigeria.
Source: iStock.com/John Carnemolla

on ethnicity and income. However, given the multiethnic nature of Africa, it is a lot easier to characterize these areas of the postcolonial city on the basis of income than ethnicity. There are four such residential areas—high-income, middle-income, low-income, and mixed-income areas.

High-income areas These areas include the former European neighborhoods and high-end government housing that are now occupied by a racially mixed group of expatriates, top government officials, and affluent professionals. Residences here are usually those of the members of the diplomatic corps, as well as the homes of wealthy merchants and business owners who show off their wealth in mansions and mini castles of all shapes. They also include relatively new developments of real estate companies built for people in the highest income brackets of Africa including certain members of the diaspora population, who as highly qualified professionals in overseas countries, have amassed considerable wealth and have decided or planning to return to their home countries. Since the 1990s, many of these areas have been built as **gated communities** or privately enclosed residential areas that restrict access (Grant, 2005; Morange et al., 2012). These areas are usually well serviced with all amenities of a modern society, including portable water, covered sewage, and electricity built by large real estate developers often with ties abroad. Yet, due to unreliability of public utilities, many of the houses in these areas have wells or large water tanks to store water and personal generators to supply their own power in case of power outages. These communities are usually located in areas with rich natural amenities—oceanfront, rolling hills, islands, riverfronts, or beautiful valleys. Examples include Cairo's Maadi, Sixth of October, and New Cairo; Casablanca's Californie, L'Oasis, and Racine; Nairobi's Gigiri, Spring Valley, Runda and Muthiaga; Accra's Trassaco Valley, Lagos' Ikeja and Abidjan's Cocody. Some of the houses in these areas cost over US$1 million.

Middle-income areas These areas constitute the residences of a small but growing middle class of middle management personnel in the public and private sectors, and self-made small- to medium-scale business owners, as well as middle-level professionals of the diaspora. Some of these areas were also part of the former European neighborhoods that have since gone through population turnover from very rich native population to present-day middle-income occupants. Heliopolis in Cairo is an example of such areas. Other areas were part of the public housing projects in the early postindependence era that were specifically built for middle management government personnel. However, the bulk of the housing in these areas has been built by individuals and real estate development companies, some of which are built as gated communities (Morange et al., 2012). Unlike the high-income areas, most of the self-built houses have their own utilities. In addition, streets are mostly unpaved and riddled with potholes of various sizes that require extraordinary driving skills to negotiate around them, while sewers are mostly open and sometimes clogged with all kinds of debris.

Low-income areas Low-income areas consist of government sponsored housing for low-income people, and privately owned housing of the low-income people and the urban poor (Yeboah, 2005). Both the government-sponsored and privately built low-income areas have been variously referred to as the informal, squatter, and slum settlements.

The meanings of these forms of residential areas have generated a lot of debate among researchers (Myers, 2011; UN-Habitat, 2003). As used here, the term an **informal settlement** or residential area refers to an area in which the land was acquired legally but buildings were constructed without permit and for that matter without following the existing subdivision regulations. Residents in these areas have secure ownership rights but are out of compliance with existing building codes and subdivision regulations. In contrast, a **squatter settlement** is an illegal occupancy of public or private lands. Squatters, as residents of these areas are often called, do not have any legal rights to ownership. While informal settlements and squatters are primarily distinguished by ownership rights to land, slums are mostly distinguished by the living conditions or what UN-Habitat refers to as deprivations. Thus, **slums** are areas with "inadequate access to safe drinking water, inadequate access to sanitation and other infrastructure, poor structural quality of housing, overcrowding, and insecure residential status" (UN-Habitat, 2003, p. 12). Since informal settlements do not fully comply with subdivision regulations, it is easy for them to develop slum conditions and the same can be said of squatter settlements. In Nairobi, for example, Nyairo (2006) reports how even government sponsored housing projects, Umoja and Kayole, deviated from their original medium-density planned units and developed slum and informal conditions because of many unplanned extensions and incompatible land uses.

Together, these informal, squatter, and slum areas constitute the largest residential zone in the postcolonial city. They serve as the homes of people with diverse cultural, social, and occupational backgrounds including skilled workers, clericals, traders, technicians, and laborers many of whom migrated from the rural areas hoping to improve their living conditions by acquiring better jobs in the urban areas. Faced with the reality of limited job opportunities these new urban arrivals could not afford better residences and ended up either creating or renting shelters for themselves. Among the most famous are City of the Dead in Cairo, Makoko in Lagos, Khayelitsha in Cape Town, and Kibera in Nairobi.

In terms of location, these areas are also among some of the less attractive, cheaper or unclaimed parts of the city, such as down sections of the African quarters of the colonial city, former garbage dumps, ravines, liable to flood areas or outskirts of the city (see, e.g., Gerlach, 2009; Grant, 2006; Myers, 2011). In recent decades, however, those at the outskirts have been outflanked by new suburban developments. Most of the housing in these areas is built with discarded materials such as paperboards, wood, and galvanized steel. Most lack basic amenities such as plumbing and electricity, while open sewer, blocked drainage, large garbage accumulations in the streets, and indiscriminate disposal of solid waste including human excreta are common sights. These areas also constitute the hub of the so-called informal activities in the city. As a result, most of the dwellings here have also become warehouses of second-hand clothes, small appliances, and foodstuffs, while the streets teem with vendors of various items (Pitcher and Graham, 2007).

Mixed-income residential areas While conditions in informal areas could deteriorate into slums, it is also important to point out that many informal areas of the postcolonial city can best be described as mixed residential areas. This is because it is common to find houses that belong to all three income classes next to each other in many of the informal areas. Pitcher and Graham (2007, p. 179) vividly captures this feature in the following observation about Luanda:

> By the twenty-first century then, Luanda reflected all of the contradictions, conflicts, mistakes, and choices of preceding years. . . . Well-appointed, furnished apartments costing as much as $15,000 a month to rent stood next to buildings that should be condemned. Raw sewage ran alongside brand new Volvo SUVs and Toyota Prados. Hawkers lined congested streets and sidewalks, selling everything from sunglasses to the kitchen sink, and government soldiers-turned-private security personnel closely guarded the freshly painted buildings occupied by the ruling elite.

Social Structure

As already pointed out, the social structure of the postcolonial city is very complex. All of Africa's cities and large towns are cosmopolitan in nature, even though most of them may have started as ethnic towns. As a result, residents may be broadly classified as African and non-African or nationals and immigrants. Each of these broad classes may be further classified by factors such as ethnicity, age, education, sex, and income. For our purpose, we use income as a proxy for socioeconomic status, to divide the social structure of the postcolonial city into three income classes: upper or high class, middle class, and lower class residents.

The upper class The World Bank defines members of the global rich class as all individuals with per capita income above $17,000 in 2005 purchasing power parity (PPP) as members of the global rich class. Given the general classification of most African countries as low-income countries, it may be an oxymoron to talk about high-income or upper-class residents in Africa's postcolonial cities. However, there surely are people in Africa's postcolonial city that fall into this class. In 2010, this group accounted for 4.8% of Africa's population (African Development Bank, 2011). These consist of high-level government officials, people who have direct connections to the highest offices of the state and corporate executives, and owners of large business enterprises. Indeed, the upper echelon of this class consists of the "super rich," who are defined as individuals with at least $1 million to invest. According to a 2007 survey by Meryl Lynch, there were about 100,000 individuals across the continent who belonged to this "super-rich" group (Redfern, 2007). Members of the rich class prefer to live away from the poverty of the city behind the security and comfort of gated communities with mansions (Mekawy and Yousry, 2011). In Luanda, for example, Pitcher and Graham (2007) reports that members of this class have lifestyles comparable to the upper middle class of the United States; they live in gated communities that resemble those in Florida; they wear clothes purchased at smart boutiques in Paris and Milan, and drive luxury sedans and four-wheel drive vehicles. This type of lifestyle can be found in every one of Africa's top postcolonial cities.

The middle class Defining and estimating the middle class is even harder than the upper class. Again, the World Bank defines the global middle class as all individuals with a per capita income above $4,000 in 2005 PPP. In Africa, the African Development Bank (AfDB) defines the middle class as individuals with per capita daily consumption of $2–20 in 2005 PPP (African Development Bank, 2011). Juma (2011, p. 8) notes:

> It is not an easy task to define what middle class means or how many people fall in that category across . . . Africa. But the group we are referring to falls somewhere between Africa's large poor population (defined as those living on less than $2 a day) and the small, rich elite. These people are not middle class in developed country terms, or even by the standards of emerging markets, but in African terms they have disposable income and are demanding an increasing amount of goods and services that contribute to the overall well-being of society. Their average income is between $1,460 and $7,300 a year.

AfDB estimates that in 2010 there were nearly 326 million people or 34.3% of Africa's population who were in this group. According to the Leke et al. (2010), in 2000 about 59 million households had $5,000 or more in annual income. Defining the middle-class households as those with income of $20,000 or more, Leke et al. (2010) indicate that Africa already has more middle-class households than India. Members of this class are generally young, technical, and entrepreneurs who have been identified as one of the sources of economic growth that is going on the continent. They are better educated, mostly employed in salaried jobs or have their own small businesses. They have fewer children and spend more on nutrition and the education of their children (African Development Bank, 2011).

The lower class The lower class constitutes more than 60% of all residents of the postcolonial city. There is no comprehensive study on socioeconomic characteristics of the members of this class. However, scattered studies at the local or regional scale indicate that the majority of members of this group belong to the urban poor, which Yeboah (2005, p. 150) defined as people "with very little or no formal education, economic capital, assets, housing, power, and even social networks and capital . . . They may be employed in the informal sector and have skills that they can sell. Yet, their employment insecurity makes them vulnerable, and they move in and out of poverty."

The daily life and conditions of the members of this class has, however, been well documented (e.g., Grant, 2009; Kipper and Fischer, 2009; Myers, 2011; Ndijo, 2006; Oldewage-Theron and Slabbert, 2010; Omasombo, 2005; Simon, 1997; Sims, 2003; UN Habitat, 2008; Yeboah 2005). Thus, for this class, life is an everyday struggle and a state of emergency, but also an incredible expression of ingenuity and courage. They engage in all kinds of activities that will earn them some money to buy food and clothes, and pay for school fees and health care. Most of these activities require physical strength such as carrying heavy luggage over the head or on push carts over considerable distances, and peddling few items along the streets all day. The major means of transportation of this class is walking, and motorbike taxis—such as the *boda boda* in Kampala (Uganda), *beskin* in Doula (Cameroon), *okada* in Lagos (Nigeria), *toleka* in Kisangani (DRC), and *tuk tuk* in Cairo, as well as public transportation. Most of these people have no access to water, schools, health clinics, but they have a lot of drug pushers as well as street violence.

Economy Composition

The conventional view is that the postcolonial city's economy consists of two sectors—the formal and the informal sectors. However, the meaning and contributions of the informal sector has been debated ever since Hart (1973) first used the term "informal" to describe the economy of Ghana (e.g., Grant, 2013; ILO, 1972; Mbembe and Nuttail, 2008; Myers, 2011; Yeboah, 2003). Generally speaking, the **formal sector** consists of all economic activities that are regulated by the government to the extent that its ownership, size of operation, gross revenue or income, and profits or losses are reported as required by the government. As a result, these activities are countable.

In contrast, the informal sector consists of all economic activities that are not regulated to the extent that the government does not have information regarding ownership, size of operation, annual proceeds, and profits or losses. This sector is dominated by a large number of small-scale entrepreneurs and self-starters across the gamut of economic activities. Some researchers and government officials see the informal sector as an illegal and underground economy. Others laud it as symbol of ingenuity and entrepreneurship of urban residents, and an essential coping mechanism. No matter how one sees it, the fact is by all accounts the informal sector is the larger of the so-called two-sector economy of the postcolonial city, and for that matter the largest employer in the majority of Africa's postcolonial city. Simply put, this so-called informal sector is the private sector of the economy of African cities as well as the continent as a whole. However, because of the inability of African governments to regulate it, the sector has been seen as "parasitic" on the formal economy, and its operators are ignored by most governments and sometimes even harassed by them.

The activities in these sectors are discussed in detail in Chapters 10 through 16, but suffice it to say here that African cities dominate the nonfarm economic production of their respective countries. They are the seats of most important public and private companies as well the sites of their most production facilities. Like cities elsewhere, they are also the centers of finance, trade, and commerce, as well as gateways to the rest of the world—hosting not only most of the international airports and seaports but also the head offices of the global business.

Problems and Issues of Africa's Postcolonial City

Like cities elsewhere, Africa's postcolonial city faces a number of problems and issues that have been extensively researched over the past several decades (Aryeetey-Attoh, 2003; Boadi et al., 2005; Rakodi, 1997; Stren, 1991; Stock, 2004; UN-Habitat, 2003, 2008, 2010). This section discusses a select number of these issues—including rapid urbanization and primacy, urban governance and management, infrastructure, housing, transportation and mobility, sanitation and environmental health, criminal violence, poverty, and unemployment.

Rapid Urbanization and Urban Primacy

One of the effects of rapid urbanization in postcolonial Africa has been the development of **urban primacy**, which is the extent to which a country's investment becomes concentrated in a few cities and subsequent emergence of an urban system dominated by a primate city. According to Jefferson (1939), a **primate city** is a city that is supereminent not only in size but also in national influence compared to all the other cities in the same country. With the exception of Morocco, Nigeria, and South Africa, every African country has this type of urban system. For example, Algeria's capital and largest city Algiers (2,851,000) is almost four times the size of Oran (776,000) the second largest city. In Angola, Luanda (4,790,000) is three times the size of the Huambo (1,039,000), the second largest city. Conakry (1,767,200) Guinea's largest city is 13 times the size of Nzerekore (132,728), its second largest city. Addis Ababa (2,979,100) Ethiopia's largest city is 11 times the size of Mekele (261,200), its second largest city.

This type of urban primacy is a problem because as we have already mentioned, it neglects other areas, and makes the primate cities the main attraction for rural dwellers. Indeed, this neglect is evident in the focus of urban research, almost all of which is on primate city. So just as most urban researchers of Africa flock to the primate cities, so do most rural dwellers flock to the cities hoping to find opportunities that may not be available. This in turn creates subsequent problems for both the urban as well as the rural areas.

Past efforts to deal with this problem through decentralization efforts have mostly been on paper only. In recent years, the idea of building satellite towns and renewed emphasis on deconcentration through multiple CBDs have gained attention (Grant, 2015; van Hoorloos, 2018; Versi, 2011; Watson, 2014). The building of satellite towns has been adopted in African countries including Egypt and Nigeria, with mixed results. In recent years, the idea has become popular and is being adopted in South Africa for Wescape near Cape Town, in Kenya for Tatu City and Konza Techno City, near Nairobi, in Ghana for King City and Hope City, in Nigeria for Eko-Atlantic, and in Morocco for King Mohammed VI Green City (Grant, 2015; van Hoorloos 2018). In addition, Grant (2015) reported that that this surge of interest in satellite cities had led to the purchase of agricultural land around Nairobi, Accra, Lubumbabshi, and Lusaka, while developers were negotiating to buy large tracts of land around Dar es Salaam, Harare, Kigali, Kampala, and Luanda.

Proponents hope that this will become a template for solving the problems of urban Africa, but the question is will this really be a solution to the problems facing Africa's cities. The skeptics of these projects are many. Myers (2011) cautions against the tendency to rush and impose Western-conceived ideas upon African cities instead of understanding the character of Africa's cities and finding solutions that build on those characteristics. Watson (2014) raises several concerns about these projects including affordability of housing units even by Africa's growing middle class, all of which will lead further spatial and social separation between the rich and poor. Grant (2015) recognizes the predicament that African cities find themselves—they need foreign direct investment to build new infrastructure, office buildings, and housing in order to connect with the global economy. At the same time, the urban visions in the existing satellite cities will only accentuate the marginalization of the urban poor, who constitute the majority of urban dwellers. He therefore calls on African policy makers to consider inclusive urbanization, whereby prioritization of projects will lead to reduction inequality in the cities. For this, some have called for indigenous urban form, which was more sustainable in the past (Asomani-Boateng, 2011). The fact is creating satellites to the megacities of Africa provide no solution to the problems facing the city. It shifts a small percentage of the population away from the city, but it does not provide any solutions to the problems of the existing megacities. Besides, there is nothing to prevent people from moving into the satellites. Eventually, the satellites may end up becoming clogged with the same problems of the old city with informal housing. However, a recent report on the State of African Cities (UN-Habitat, 2014) seems to indicate that the movement into Africa's top cities is slowing down and giving way to the second-tier cities. This could be a welcome relief, but conscious efforts should be made to implement decentralization policies, which have been on paper and name only, in many countries.

Urban Governance and Management

Governing and managing Africa's postcolonial city have attracted a lot of attention (Aina, 1997; Myers, 2011; Rakodi, 1997; UN Habitat, 2010). The rapid growth of many of Africa's urban areas has not kept pace with the structures and instruments of governing and management. To some extent, African countries are trying to administer and manage a contemporary city that is cosmopolitan, heterogeneous, and chaotic with models inherited from colonialism. All across the continent local authorities are relatively weak and although many countries, especially those of the sub-Saharan section, have implemented decentralization policies over the past few decades, most have not been effective. Local authorities still lack the power and autonomy to tax, to enact and enforce local ordinances, and to reform outdated rules and regulations.

The layers of governmental authority in urban Africa are also complex. There is the state, local authorities, and civil society represented by a wide range of nongovernmental organizations. According to UN Habitat (2010) often these levels of authorities work at cross purposes, which in turn becomes a barrier to implementing meaningful projects. To resolve this, UN-Habitat (2010) suggests four approaches of regional governance based on the examples of success stories elsewhere, to African countries. These include autonomous local authorities, confederate regional government, mixed system of regional governance, and finally unified regional governance. These systems may hold promise for regional governance in Africa but each of them will require changing the way government business is done completely in urban Africa. In the final analysis, externally imposed governance structures are always more difficult to succeed than those from within.

Political awareness is definitely growing in African countries and increasingly the old practice of holding positions of authority for life is dying off as democratic movement sweeps across the continent. However, there is much more that needs to be accomplished. The political system is still ridden with high levels of corruption. To a large extent, political elites in Africa see politics as a path to wealth accumulation at the expense of the people. The obsession with security and longevity in power results in many people in the political arena playing the ethnic, economic, and religious games with the people (Aina, 1997). In many sectors of the urban economy bribery and corruption have become institutionalized. Bureaucratic red tape and deliberate "roadblocks" in getting simple things such as building permits, property registration, and developing a private property can take months and may require paying bribe to officials who are in charge. There is virtually no accountability on the part of authorities. The practice of mismanagement of funds has created a populace who want to evade taxes even if they can afford them because they do not think the taxes they pay will benefit them. Unless there are real efforts at boosting the revenue of urban areas for upgrading basic infrastructure of transportation, water, sewer, and deal with garbage, all the regional governance systems will not accomplish much for African cities.

Housing

The problem of housing in the postcolonial city is a multifaceted one. Based on existing definitions, it is widely accepted that majority of Africa's urban residents live in informal, squatter, or slum areas (UN-Habitat, 2010). The diagnoses and prognoses of this problem and issue are diverse (Boudereaux, 2008). On the one hand, professional planners and government authorities blame residents for not following the law. On the other hand, residents and their researcher advocates blame the government on many grounds. First, they charge that government involvement in the housing production industry is a cause of the housing problem since governments do not have the resources to provide adequate housing. Second, onerous governmental regulations and bureaucracies that breed corruption and high interest rate make it too difficult for full private sector participation in the urban housing market. Third, multilayered land tenure systems and nationalization of private lands by governments in some countries threaten private ownership and for that matter private housing development.

These positions have resulted in several strategies in how to deal with slums and provide affordable housing. Traditionally, governments have tried eviction of residents from informal and slum areas, due to the ability of residents to organize to block such actions or the tendency of residents to just move to another area. Governments have also used the new or satellite town strategy by which new towns are planned and built in order to redistribute the population. However, as we have seen, these areas are not affordable to those who need housing the most. Even when they are, they tend to revert back to slum conditions due to a complex host of factors including lack of regulation enforcement and inability of the planners or designers to design neighborhoods that are suitable to the cultural needs of intended residents (see, e.g, Ayotamuno et al., 2010). Others advocate for accepting the informal and slum areas as what they are but with governmental empowerment so that the local people can provide for their basic needs. Others point to a number local grassroots movements that have by themselves improved the living conditions in the areas they live through local self-help initiatives. In the final analysis, the housing market is a complex problem that requires the cooperation of both government and private sectors. Governments should realize that their appropriate role in the housing market will be to develop policies and programs that will provide enough incentives for the private sector to enter into the housing market. Such programs may include streamlining the building provision process from land acquisition through development, reducing interest rates, loan schemes for low-income housing, and revising subdivision rules and regulations including building codes and actually enforcing them.

Transportation and Mobility

Transportation and mobility are major issues in Africa's postcolonial cities. These issues relate to accessibility, connectivity, and capacity of the network, and affordability of the mode. **Accessibility** refers to the ability of getting from one place to another in a transportation network. **Connectivity** is the ease of getting from one node to another in the transportation network, while **capacity** is the maximum volume of vehicles a given network can carry. On all these measures, transportation in African cities perform very badly. First, the dominant mode of transportation is surface transportation in the form of road and walkways. At the time of writing, only two cities on the entire continent, Cairo and Algiers had subways or underground transportation. In terms of road, the network is inadequate, Dakar, Kinshasa, Lagos, and Nairobi have small-scale suburban rail network, but it is very limited and serves about 2% of the market (Kumar and Barrett, 2008). Most of the roads were constructed several decades ago at a time when the cities were much smaller and had only one city center, and when car ownership was quite low. These road networks have lagged behind the increased traffic volume that has resulted in the enormous growth of the cities. Where new roads have been constructed, most of them are unidirectional—going either north–south or east–west, and most of them are two lanes. There are very few multiple lanes and there are virtually no circumferential beltways or bypasses that take through traffic out of the city roads and streets. These have created a problem of network capacity.

The problem of network capacity is compounded by the physical quality of the road. A recent study of public transportation in nine African cities (Abidjan, Accra, Addis Ababa, Dakar, Dar es Salaam, Johannesburg, Lagos, and Nairobi) reported that Lagos and Johannesburg had the highest percentage of paved roads with 93% and 85% respectively. These were followed by Dakar (65%), Addis Ababa (63%), Accra (61%), Abidjan (59%), Nairobi (48%), Dar es Salaam (39%), and Douala (25%) (UITP and UATP, 2010). The surface quality of road network is also marred by myriads of potholes, which need to be negotiated. These in turn slow down travel while raising the wear and tear on vehicles, especially during the rainy season.

On top of these are problems of accessibility and affordability, which in turn are functions of the transportation provision market. From the early postindependence period through the 1980s, state-owned companies operated metropolitan transit systems consisting of large buses in all cities. The fares were regulated and controlled by governments to make them affordable. However, continued losses forced many of these services into bankruptcy or to privatize during the structural adjustment programs (Kumar and Barrett, 2008). The result is that the bulk of public transportation is now provided by the private sector, which is inadequate because of the small capacity sizes of the vehicles and also because of safety concerns (UITP and UATP, 2010).

Affordability of transportation is a function of income and the fare to pay, which in turn depends on the mode and distance to travel. So affordability is very much a problem faced by the low-income people, and for them it is a combination of how much fare they have to pay and the distance between their residences and travel destinations. However, in the private sector, there is some uncertainty surrounding when fares will go up. Sometimes all that it may take is bad weather; sometimes it is the price of fuel going up. As a result, many low-income residents resort to providing their own transportation—namely walking or use motorbike taxis, which are highly prone to accidents and severe injuries.

A final problem related to transportation in the postcolonial city is environmental pollution caused by vehicle emissions. Several cities have announced major transportation improvements. Algiers plans to extend its subway–tramway links with two additional lines, which will be completed by 2020. Cairo is constructing a third subway line to the Cairo Airport, with three additional lines planned to be completed by 2022 (Amoroso et al., 2011). However, urban transportation and mobility is a crippling problem for Africa's postcolonial city that calls for better transportation planning. This should include improved efforts at forging closer relationship between land use and transportation, improvement in the physical infrastructure including alternative modes of transportation, and improvement in transportation management including enforcement of existing laws.

Sanitation and Environmental Health

African cities have major sanitation and environmental problems. These derive mostly from disposal of solid and human waste. There is the apparent lack of respect for public space in most cities. Public space is seen as a place to dispose of all kinds of solid waste including human waste. One reason for this attitude is that the infrastructural base for keeping citywide cleanliness is either very weak or nonexistent in most cities. Boadi et al. (2005) estimated that between 20% and 80% of solid waste in African cities were dumped in open spaces. The percentage is lower in cities in North Africa than the rest of the continent. For example, UN Habitat (2008) reports that in 2005, 19% and 11% of slum dwellers in Cairo and Alexandria respectively, and 3% of nonslum dwellers disposed their trash in open lots or on the streets. In Casablanca it was 12% while in Rabat it was 2% of slum dwellers and 4% of nonslum dwellers. In cities where garbage disposal outlets exist, they seem to be overwhelmed because they are either too small or they are not properly used. The result is that in many cities, especially in sub-Saharan section of the continent, open sewers and blocked drains are common. For cities such as Dakar, Accra, and Kinshasa, these clogged drains contribute to flooding during times of heavy rains (Misilu et al., 2010).

In terms of disposal of human waste, a study of the state of sanitation in sub-Saharan Africa reported that in 2007 about 40% of urban population in sub-Saharan Africa had access to improved sanitation with septic tanks being much more common than improved latrines, while fewer than 10% still practice open defecation (Morella et al., 2008). Apart from this, the practice of many households sharing water and sanitation facilities is also common in African cities. For example, Morella et al. (2008) found that in urban households with formal service provision more than 40% shared toilet facilities with other households. In Benin, Burkina Faso, Congo Republic, Ghana, Guinea, and Madagascar the percentage was over 50%. The health risks associated with such shared facilities are higher due to poor maintenance of such facilities. Once again, the percentage of urban dwellers with access to improved sanitation as well as household connection for North Africa was better—averaging 93.2% and 70.2% respectively (UN Habitat, 2008).

The need for African countries to deal with this issue cannot be overemphasized. There are of course many different views, some focusing on the causes of the problem. One such view ascribes the causes of this to the low user fees of these services, which in turn does not generate enough revenue to upgrade and expand the services. This is ultimately attributed to weak urban management due to overburden bureaucracy and corrupt practices of government officials. In the final analysis, user fees need to be instituted to provide additional revenue stream that will sustain the system. In addition, there needs to be real education about basic hygiene, sanitation, and the value of public space and the indiscriminate use of such spaces to dump human waste. The health consequences of such practices needs to be elevated in a public education and laws should be passed and enforced to stop such behavior.

Criminal Violence and Urban Youth

The daily pressure of life and the breakdown of governance and the feeling of despair and helplessness have made many urban residents turn to several devices of their own including vigilante "law enforcement." Thus, in many of African cities criminal behavior is summarily dealt with in the most brutal and inhumane way possible. These actions led Ndijo (2006) to refer to Douala, Cameroon's largest city and commercial capital as an African necropolis.

However, nowhere on the continent has urban violence received much publicity than in South Africa and Nigeria. In South Africa, Abrahams (2010) provides a synopsis of the various types of crimes that have occurred in the country before and after apartheid. In particular, he focuses on the gang violence and xenophobia in South African cities—Johannesburg, Cape Town, and Durban. Abraham asserts that under apartheid system, the state actually supported a lot of the gang violence among Johannesburg's mining communities since it was seen as a "black-on-black" violence. Gang violence increased between February 1990 and April 1994, when the apartheid system ended especially due to the numerous clashes between supporters of the Inkatha Freedom Party, the United Democratic Front, and the African National Congress. Crime statistics stabilized after 1994, and certain crimes declined but others such as public violence increased. This was especially the case with the crime of xenophobia. Abrahams reported that beginning from 1995 the crime against foreigners increased culminating in the even on May 11, 2008 when migrants from Mozambique, Zimbabwe, and Malawi were attacked and killed or injured in Alexandria township north of Johannesburg. Similar attacks occurred in Durban and Cape Town. In 2009, another 3,000 foreigners were driven out of their shacks from De Dooms Township in Cape Town. The causes of this violence are complex and include poverty, income disparity between the rich and the poor, poor service delivery, lack of housing, and widespread unemployment (Abrahams, 2010).

In addition to these factors, protracted wars, civil unrest, and criminal violence devastated a number of these cities, causing people to flee from them and worsening the situation with breakdown of infrastructure and essential services. Among these cities, which Myers (2011) refers to as wounded cities, are Algiers, Monrovia, Freetown, Abidjan, Bissau, Abidjan, Ndjamena, Kinshasa, Kigali, Nairobi, Brazzaville, Maputo, Luanda, Mogadishu, and cities of apartheid South Africa.

A segment of the urban population that is usually associated with a lot of such criminal violence is the urban youth. The conventional argument is that the high unemployment rate among the urban youth causes them to channel their anger and frustration into various forms of violence (El-Kenz, 1996; Kaplan, 1996; USAID, 2005). Sommers (2010) refers to this notion as "youth bulge and instability thesis." Perhaps because of this many African governments have in the past embarked on forced removal of the youth from large urban areas. However, all such efforts have failed since the youth just board the next bus or train back to the city. Sommers (2010) argues that such notion of youth and violence is erroneous, not because such a relationship cannot be statistically proven, but rather that the lives of many urban youths are dominated either by work or by finding work. However, because the overwhelming majority of urban jobs in Africa are in the informal sector, it is impossible to account for much of what the youth does. This may fall under the rubric of underemployment, but it is not the same as unemployment. In the same vein, Katumanga (2005) argues that many of the so-called angry unemployed youth were goaded by a government with devious aspirations.

The fact is that the youth have to employ several strategies to survive in the city. One is to become affiliated with religious or nonreligious groups, some of which may have violence as part of their agenda. Besides, the youth also undergo a lot of pressure that vary according to gender. Male youth, for example, have to prove or establish their manhood by being able to get married and building a house, and while the city might be able to help them do that if they find a job, the city can also offer them a way for escaping such responsibility. For female youth the options are much more limited, since they are sometimes either forced into prostitution or pregnancy with the hope of having a more settled life even though their boyfriends may be equally poor (Sommers, 2010). Finally, the specific programs that target the most vulnerable urban youth do not seem to exist. Such programs should target the need of the poor among the urban youth based on the participation of such groups from input solicitation through analysis and policy formulation so that the final policy outcomes will be successful when implemented.

RURAL AREAS: SMALL TOWNS AND VILLAGES

Africa is rapidly urbanizing, but the bulk of Africans in the majority of African countries still live in rural areas—in small towns and villages. Unfortunately, because of the dominant focus of research on Africa's primate cities and a few dominant commercial centers, there is a dearth of information about the geography of rural areas—particularly the evolution and development and spatial and social structure. Most of the existing work is on small towns in South Africa (see Hoogendorn and Visser, 2015 for a review). In this section, we focus on the evolution and development, spatial and social structure, problems and issues, and how they relate to urban areas.

Evolution and Development of Rural Settlements

From the evolution and development of the large cities, we could infer that Africa's small towns and villages are part of its settlement system that have remained relatively small for a variety of reasons. For example, it could be that these small towns and villages did not have advantages that other settlements had to make them grow to become cities. It could also be that some had advantages and were perhaps ahead of some of present-day large cities but were not able to sustain their position due to conquest or other factors, and for that reason declined. It could also be that these towns and even villages grew initially, but stopped growing at some point due to changes in their fortune.

In the postcolonial period, however, the situation of the rural areas was worsened by development policies that bypassed the rural areas (see Chapter 3). In addition, when environmental conditions such as drought combined with collapse of prices of primary commodities, the mainstay of rural economies, in the 1960s and 1970s, rural life became difficult, setting off a massive wave of migration to the urban as well as other rural areas (Caldwell, 1969). By the early 1970s, African countries that had returned to political independence in the 1950s and early 1960s realized what had gone wrong and began to address the problem through rural development policies and programs. However, as we learned in Chapter 3, the implementation of rural development programs did not work for a host of reasons. For example, countries such as Ghana, Kenya, and Tanzania, which adopted the growth center approach for rural development, had problems with implementation. In Kenya, more investments projects still went to Nairobi and Mombasa than all the rural areas combined. In Tanzania, it became too expensive, and Ghana never implemented the approach because of a change in government (Gaile, 1979; Ofori-Amoah, 1998). With respect to Tanzania's famous *Ujamaa* program, rural dwellers resented the idea of collective farming, and the overemphasis on transportation in selecting the new villages shortchanged other important factors such as availability of water, fertile soil, and avoidance of insect-infected areas. In the end, the program ran out of money (Ergas, 1980; Moore, 1979; Silberfein, 1998a). In Angola and Mozambique, the program failed because the government did not have the resources to provide the seeds, fertilizers, farm equipment, and other supporting infrastructure that were promised (Silberfein, 1998a). In Ethiopia, relocation of people without regard to their sociocultural and environmental backgrounds and distance from their original home, shortage of wood and water supplies, and inability of the government to deliver on promises led to the dismantling of cooperatives and new villages in 1991.

While the above examples mirror most of African countries' rural development efforts, it is important to note that some countries have since done better by providing basic infrastructure such as improved water, electricity, good roads, and schools to their rural areas. These include Algeria, Botswana, Egypt, Morocco, Tunisia, and South Africa. However, on most development indicators, the gap is still wide between urban and rural areas. The result is that Africa's rural areas are still beset with problems of inadequate public amenities, limited economic opportunity, and upward social mobility, isolation, and outmigration.

Internal Structure of Rural Settlements

Spatial Structure

According to Udo (1982, p. 48), the basic unit of rural settlement is the compound, which he defines as "a cluster of houses or huts usually referred to by the name of its head occupied." The actual form of a compound varies across the continent. It could be separate huts surrounded by a wall or it could be in the shape of a quadrangle with a common courtyard. Rural settlements "therefore consists of a wide range of groupings of compounds which vary from very closely nucleated or compact villages and hamlets to widely dispersed and scattered compounds" (Udo, 1982, p. 54).

From this, we can identify two main types of rural settlements: **nucleated** and **dispersed** towns and villages. Nucleated towns and villages are the most common type of rural settlement in Africa. This type of settlement may take a compact and concentrated form or a linear form. A linear settlement may be either along the main road, a river, or in a dry valley. In contrast, dispersed towns and villages consist of individual farmsteads that are scattered over a wide area, which may be connected with tracks or paths.

In either case, the spatial form of especially the nucleated settlements consist of several activity nodes—market, stores, schools, religious and government administrative buildings, and hospitals and clinics. The number and scale of these activity nodes depends on the size and functions of the town (see, e.g., Owusu, 2005, 2008). For example, some towns serve as district or county administrative seats. Where traditional chiefs are still active, some towns also serve as seats of paramount or district chiefs. Others serve as market centers, where buyers and sellers from the district or county, and beyond, meet on established days of the week to do business. Still some towns serve as religious centers for adherents of certain religious groups, which trace their origins to the town.

Beyond these activity nodes, the rest of the land use consists of residential, transportation, and farmland. Traditionally, most of the houses in these towns and villages were built of mud, thatch, sticks, or a combination of mud and sticks, whereby the sticks are used to raise the super frame and filled in with mud. The houses might also be rounded or rectangular and the roofing material may be mud, thatch, bamboo, or corrugated iron sheets, and without indoor plumbing and toilet facilities. The only exceptions were the houses of a few wealthy individuals, which could boast of modern building materials. However, these traditional types of houses are being replaced by modern houses built of cement and equipped with all modern amenities. These houses belong to native sons and daughters or their relatives. These natives often live in the urban areas or abroad. An example of this is the Kwahu area of Ghana, where these modern mansions have converted a handful of rural towns into enclaves of modernity beyond the urban periphery. Apart from these mansions, other buildings that might stand out in form, style, and size include the market place, churches, mosques, the chief's palace, district or county administrative buildings, schools, and health clinics, where applicable.

Social Structure and Economy Composition

Unlike their large cities and towns counterpart, Africa's rural areas are almost homogenous on ethnic basis. This is because, as it was pointed out in Chapter 7, ethnic groups occupy particular geographic areas of their respective countries, so by default, small towns and villages in most African countries are clustered by their ethnicity. This also means that where a substantial number of minority ethnic group exists, they tend to live in a section of the town for obvious reasons. Since agriculture or fishing may be the predominant occupation, and because almost all the educated members of the community leave the community, income appears to be the only important differentiating socioeconomic factor. This well-to-do group is usually very small and includes a few wealthy farmers, important property owners, successful small-scale business men and women, and parents or relatives of well-established professionals in the urban areas, as well as the diaspora, whose remittances have made those relatives appear wealthy in the eyes of the community. Generally speaking, agriculture is the primary economic activity except for coastal and some large river or lake towns, where fishing takes over. In some cases, rural crafts also tend to be important and may be pottery, woodwork, beads-making, and traditional textiles, that we learned about in Chapter 7.

RURAL–URBAN LINKAGES AND INTERACTIONS

Rural–urban interaction is one aspect of rural geography that has generated most research interest, and this research shows that the two spatial entities of Africa's human settlement system are not isolated. Instead, they are linked together by interactions that are social, economic, and political (Unwin, 1989).

Social Linkages and Interaction

These consist mostly of movement of people on a temporary and permanent basis. Temporary movements involve the numerous daily, weekly, or monthly flows of people between small towns and cities and large towns for social and economic reasons. Some of these are work-related, others to family and other personal reasons. However, the more permanent movement has been the focus of most research and three main forms have been identified—rural to urban migration, rural to rural migration, and urban to rural migration. We have already seen how rural–urban migration contributed to the rapid urban growth and urbanization of Africa's leading cities. However, several studies have found that rural–urban migration is decreasing (e.g., Beauchemin and Bocquier 2004; Chen et al., 1998; Potts, 1995, 2005). This trend is making other forms of rural–urban interaction more important to the dynamics of Africa's settlement system.

Rural–rural migration is the movement from a rural area to another rural area in the same country (Beauchemin and Bocquier, 2004; Cross, 2006; Cross et al., 1998;Fay, 2011; Ito, 2010). Studies of this type of migration in South Africa and Zambia indicate that both economic and noneconomic factors are behind this type of migration. These include better economic opportunity, access to agricultural land, life cycle events, evictions, and proximity to family ties and social network (Cross, 2006; Fay, 2011; Ito, 2010; Wittemyer et al., 2008).

While rural–urban migration has attracted the most attention in migration studies in Africa, **urban–rural migration**, the movement of people from urban areas back to rural areas in the same country has not. Studies conducted on urban–rural migration in Nigeria, Zambia, Uganda, Tanzania, and Francophone West Africa show that this type of migration is occurring due to a number of reasons. These include (1) availability of land to subsist; (2) economic recession and retrenchment that resulted in massive job losses in the early 1980s; (3) government policy of decentralization that resulted in the creation of new States and Local Government Areas as well as many public and private sector jobs, in rural areas; (4) old age and retirement; (5) cost of living; (6) city congestion and safety; (7) socioeconomic disposition and house ownership; (8) family and continuing family support; and (9) quality of life (see, e.g., Adewale, 2005; Andraes, 1992; Beauchemin, 2009; Beauchemin and Bocquier, 2004; Ferguson, 1990; Onyebueke, 2008; Onyeonoru, 1994, 2008; Potts, 1995, 2005). Whether this trend will become widespread is too early to tell, but given the observation that rural–urban migration peaked in the 1970s and 1980s, the potential of urban–rural migration to cause a polarization reversal cannot be overemphasized.

Economic Linkages and Interactions

The movement of young people into urban and other rural areas results in labor for the receiving areas, which may or may not be needed. When this labor becomes wage earners, they turn around to send remittances, money to their relatives in the rural areas. These remittances supplement or constitute the main support of the family back in the countryside.

Urban areas also depend on rural areas for food and industrial raw material, while rural dwellers receive income for their produce and depend on urban areas for manufactured or imported goods. This creates intraregional trade, transportation, and marketing between the rural and urban areas.

Another linkage that creates interaction between urban and rural areas is the strong ties that many urban dwellers have with their hometowns. These ties oblige them to build a house for their relatives as well as themselves in their hometowns. Where there are substantial numbers from a particular town, village, or district in large cities these members usually form Hometown Associations, which go back to their hometowns on special occasions to help with community development projects such as provision of school, building of clinics, portable and electricity projects.

Political Linkages and Interactions

For most African countries, the rural areas contribute the bulk or a substantial source of government revenue through the sale of their agricultural produce and the implicit tax that they pay. Some of that revenue goes back to the rural areas as government allocation albeit relatively small, and also as part of infrastructures—for example, roads, water, education, and health. Given that most Africans live in small towns and villages, in most African countries these small towns and villages have become a political voting force for better or for worse. On the one hand, in countries where political awareness is maturing, as in Ghana, these rural dwellers can no longer be bought by politicians who appeal to ethnic affiliations, but ignore the pressing issues facing the country. On the other hand, where such political awareness is lacking, rural dwellers can keep an ineffective government in power based on last minute favors they receive and ethnic affiliations of politicians.

Summary

Cities, towns, and villages are the main components of the human settlement system of Africa. Although there is no common agreement of the definitions of these concepts, it is generally agreed that cities occupy the top of the systems followed by towns and then villages. As a cradle of civilization, Africa was the site of some of the world's earliest cities. Since then Africa saw a slow but steady urban growth with the greatest growth occurring in the postcolonial period. Among the factors that have influenced the urban growth in Africa are empire building, trade, religion, colonialism, and postcolonial policies. These factors also shaped the internal structure of the city. Thus, the early cities were centered on the royal palace. As cities became more open to trade, a commercial section emerged dominated by the central market place. Islamic influences on many of these commercial cities added a third geographic focus to the city, the central mosque. The city also became segregated between Muslims and non-Muslims. European trading activities along the coast transformed some villages and isolated forts into large towns and cities, with yet another form of social and spatial segregation—European quarters around the fort and the African section around the palace. This form of city expanded later under colonialism. The postcolonial city has tried to undo the segregation based on race and ethnicity but it has substituted it with segregation based on income. Thus in addition to commercial, industrial, government, and other institutional areas, there are upper class, middle class, and lower class residential areas.

The rapid growth of urban areas in the postcolonial period has brought alongside it many problems among which are urban primacy, sanitation and environmental health, transportation and mobility, housing, urban governance and management, and criminal violence. Perhaps the biggest losers in all this growth have been the rural areas—towns and villages where the majority of Africans still live. The neglect of these areas has left them with problems of outmigration, isolation, poor amenities, which in turn have led to low quality of life in these areas. However, there are many interactions between urban and rural areas through the flow of people, goods, services, and ideas that benefit both urban and rural dwellers and occasionally change the order of arrangements within the settlement system. Whether or not these interactions will help to eliminate the gap between them is still unknown.

Postreading Assignments

A. Study the Following Concepts

City	Human settlement	Mercantilist African city	Rural–rural migration
Classical African city	Indigenous African city	Peri-urban	Rural–urban migration
Colonial city	Informal areas	Postcolonial city	Urban
European mercantilist city	Informal sector	Primate city	Urban–rural migration
Formal sector	Islamic African city	Rural	Urban primacy

B. Discussion Questions

1. Compare the list of positive and negative things you wrote down about Africa's cities at the beginning of the chapter. Has anything changed? Is the change for better or worse?

2. What factors have influenced the evolution and development of cities in Africa?

3. Discuss the transformation of the internal structures of African cities from the precolonial and the colonial period. What factors helped shape these structures?

4. What have been the dominant factors of urban growth in postcolonial Africa?

5. Distinguish among informal, squatter, and slum settlements? Which of these dominate the contemporary African cities and why?

6. Discuss the major land use types in contemporary African cities.

7. Attempt a characterization of the social structure of African cities.

8. Discuss some of the major problems facing Africa's cities and recommend how these problems may be resolved.

9. What is a primate city urban system? Explain why Africa's urban system may be described as a primate city urban system?

10. Discuss how Africa's rural areas may be developed.

11. Discuss the main interactions between Africa's cities, towns, and villages and how they influence the dynamics of the urban system.

References

Abrahams, D. 2010. "A Synopsis of Urban Violence in South Africa." *International Review of the Red Cross* 92(878): 495–520.

Adepoju, A. 1992. "Migrant Africa." *The UNESCO Courier* 1: 36–39.

Adewale, G. J. 2005. "Socio-Economic Factors Associated with Urban–Rural Migration in Nigeria: A Case Study of Oyo State, Nigeria." *Journal of Human Ecology* 17(1): 13–16.

African Development Bank 2011. "*The Middle of the Pyramid: Dynamics of the Middle Class in Africa.*" AfDB Market Brief April www.afdb.org.

Aina, T. A. 1997. "The State and Civil Society: Politics, Government, and Social Organization in African Cities." In Rakodi, C. (Ed.) *The Urban Challenge in Africa: Growth and Management of its Large Cities.* Tokyo and New York: United Nations University Press, pp. 411–446.

Amoroso, S., Salvo, G., and Zito, P. 2011. "Sustainable Urban Public Transport: A Comparison Between European and North African Cities." *Managing Sustainability Proceedings of the 12th Management International Conference.* Portoroz, Slovenia, November 23–26, pp. 437–450.

Andraes, G. 1992. "Urban Workers as Farmers: Agro-Links of Nigerian Textile Workers in the Crisis of the 1980s." In Baker, J., and Pedersen, P.O. (Eds.) *The Rural–Urban Interface in Africa: Expansion and Adaptation.* Uppsala: Scandinavian Institute of African Studies, *Seminar Proceedings* 27, pp. 200–222.

Aryeetey-Attoh, S. 2003. "Urban Geography of Sub-Saharan Africa." In Aryeetey-Attoh, S. (Ed.) *Geography of Sub-Saharan Africa.* 2nd Edition. Upper Saddle River: Prentice Hall, pp. 254–297.

Ayotamuno, A., Gobo, A. E., and Owei, O. B., 2010. "The Impact of Land Use Conversion on a Residential District in Port Harcourt, Nigeria." *Environment & Urbanization* 22(1): 259–265.

Asomani-Boateng, R. (2011). "Borrowing from the Past to Sustain the Present and the Future: Indigenous African Urban Forms, Architecture, and Sustainable Urban Development in Contemporary Africa. *Journal of Urbanism* 4: 239–262.

Beauchemin, C. 2009. "Rural–Urban Migration in West Africa: Towards a Reversal? Migration Trends and Economic Situation in Burkina Faso and Cote d'Ivoire." *Population, Space, and Place* 17: 47–72.

Beauchemin, C., and Bocquier, P. 2004. "Migration and Urbanization in Francophone West Africa: An Overview of the Recent Empirical Evidence." *Urban Studies* 41(11): 2245–2272.

Boadi, K., Kuitunen, M., Raheem, K., and Hanninen, K. 2005. "Urbanisation Without Development: Environmental and Health Implications in African Cities." *Environment, Development and Sustainability* 7: 465–500.

Boudereaux, K. 2008. "Urbanisation and Informality in Africa's Housing Markets." *Economic Affairs* 28(2): 17–24.

Bryceson, D. F. 2006. "African Urban Economies: Searching for Sources of Sustainability." In Bryceson, D. F., and Potts, D. (Eds.) *African Urban Economies: Viability, Vitality or Vitiation?* Basingstoke, UK: Palgrave Macmillan, pp. 39–66.

Burgess, E. W. 1925. "The Growth of the City." In Park, R. E., Burgess, E. W., and McKenzie, R. D. (Eds.) *The City*. Chicago: University of Chicago Press, pp. 47–62.

Byerlee, D. 1974. "Rural–Urban Migration in Africa: Theory, Policy and Research Implications." *International Migration Review* 8(4): 543–566.

Caldwell, J. C. 1969. *African Rural–Urban Migration: The Movement to Ghana's Towns*. New York: Columbia University Press.

Chandler, T. 1994b. "Urbanization in Ancient Africa." In Tarver, J. D. (Ed.) *Urbanization in Africa: A Handbook*. Westport, CT: Greenwood Press, pp. 3–14.

Chandler, T. 1994a. "Urbanization in Medieval and Early Modern Africa." In Tarver, J. D. (Ed.) *Urbanization in Africa: A Handbook*. Westport, CT: Greenwood Press, pp. 15–32.

Chen, N., Valente, P., and Zlotnik, H. 1998. "What Do We Know About Recent Trends in Urbanization?" In Bilsborrow, R. E. (Ed.) *Migration, Urbanization, and Development: New Directions and Issues*. New York: UNFPA—Kluwer Academic Publishers, pp. 59–88.

Coquery-Vidrovitch, C. 1991. "The Process of Urbanization in Africa: From the Origins to the Beginning of Independence." *African Studies Review* 34(1): 1–98.

Coquery-Vidrovitch, C. 2005. *The History of African Cities South of the Sahara: From the Origins to Colonization*. Translated by Mary Baker. Princeton, NJ: Markus Wiener.

Cross, C. 2006. "Migrant Motivations and Capacities in Relation to Key Migration Streams." In Kok, P., Gelderblom, D., Oucho, J., and van Zyl, J. (Eds.) *Migration in South and Southern Africa: Dynamics and Determinants*. Pretoria: Human Sciences Research Council, pp. 205–226.

Cross, C., Mngadi, T., and Mbhele, T. 1998. "Constructing Migration: Infrastructure, Poverty and Development in KwaZulu-Natal." *Development Southern Africa* 15(4): 635–659.

Davis, K. 1965. "The Urbanization of the Human Population." *Scientific American* (September).

Dubresson, A. 1997. "Abidjan: From the Public Making of a Modern City to Urban Management of a Metropolis." In Rakodi, C. (Ed.) *The Urban Challenge in Africa: Growth and Management of its Large Cities*. Tokyo and New York: United Nations University Press, pp. 252–291.

El-Kenz, A. 1996. "Youth and Violence." In Ellis, S. (Ed.) *Africa Now: People, Policies and Institutions*. London and Portsmouth, NH: James Carey and Heinemann. p. 16.

Ergas, Z. 1980. "Why Did the Ujamaa Policy Fail? Towards a Global Analysis." *The Journal of Modern African Studies* 18: 387–410.

Fay, D. A. 2011. "Post-Apartheid Transformation and Population Change Around Dwesa-Cwebe Nature Reserve, South Africa." *Observation and Society* 9(1): 8–15.

Florin, B. 2005. "Urban Policies in Cairo from Speeches on New Cities to the Adjustment Practices of Ordinary City Dwellers." In Simone, A., and Abouhani, A. (Eds.) *Urban Africa: Changing Contours of Survival in the City*. Dakar: CODESRIA Books, pp. 29–67.

Freund, B. 2007. *The African City: A History*. Cambridge: Cambridge University Press.

Ferguson, J. 1990. "Mobile Workers, Modernist Narratives: A Critique of the Historiography of Transition on the Zambian Copperbelt [part one]." *Journal of Southern African Studies* 16(3): 385–412.

Gaile, G. L. 1979. "Distance and Development." In Obudho, R. A., and Taylor, D. R. F. (Eds.) *The Spatial Structure of Development*. Boulder, CO: Westview Press, pp. 210–222.

Gerlach, J. 2009. "Three Areas: Manshiet Nasser, the City of the Dead, Boulaq al Dakrour." In Kipper, R., and Fischer, M. (Eds.) *Cairo's Informal Areas Between Urban Challenges and Hidden Potentials*. Cairo: GTZ, pp. 49–51.

Goodwin, S. 2006. *Africa's Legacies of Urbanization: Unfolding Saga of a Continent*. Lanham, MD: Lexington Books.

Grant, R. 2005. "The Emergence of Gated Communities in a West African Context: Evidence From Greater Accra, Ghana." *Urban Geography* 26(8): 661–683.

Grant, R. 2006. "Out of Place? Global Citizens in Local Spaces: A Study of the Informal Settlements in the Korle Lagoon Environs in Accra, Ghana." *Urban Forum* 17(1): 1–24.

Grant, R. 2009. *Globalizing City: The Urban and Economic Transformation of Accra, Ghana*. Syracuse, NY: Syracuse University Press.

Grant, R. 2013. "Gendered Spaces of Informal Entrepreneurship in Soweto, South Africa." *Urban Geography* 34(1): 86–108.

Grant, R. 2015. "Sustainable African Urban Futures: Stocktaking and Critical Reflection on Proposed Urban Projects." *American Behavioral Scientist* 59(3): 294–310.

Grant, R., and Nijman, J. 2002. "Globalization and the Corporate Geography of Cities in the Less-Developed World." *Annals of the Association of American Geographers* 92(2): 320–340.

Grant, R., and Yankson, P. 2003. "City Profile: Accra." *Cities* 20(1): 65–74.

Gugler, J. 1969. "On the Theory of Rural–Urban Migration: The Case of Sub-Saharan Africa." In Jackson, J. A. (Ed.) *Migration*. Cambridge: Cambridge University Press.

Hart, K. 1973. "Informal Income Opportunities and Urban Employment in Ghana." *Journal of Modern African Studies* 11(1): 61–89.

Hoyt, H. 1939. *The Structure and Growth of Residential Neighborhoods in American Cities*. Washington DC: Federal Housing Administration.

Hull, R. W. 1976. *African Cities and Towns Before the European Conquest.* New York: W. W. Norton.

ILO (International Labour Office) 1972. *Employment, Incomes and Equality: A Strategy for Increasing Productive Employment in Kenya.* Geneva: ILO.

Ito, C. 2010. "The Role of Labor Migration to Neighboring Small Towns in Rural Livelihoods: A Case Study in Southern Province, Zambia." *African Studies Quarterly* 12(1): 45–73.

Jamal, V., and Weeks, J. 1993. *Africa Misunderstood or Whatever Happened to the Rural–Urban Divide.* Basingstoke: Macmillan.

Jefferson, M. 1939. "The Law of the Primate City." *Geographical Review* 29(2): 226–232.

Juma, C. 2011. "Africa's New Engine." *Finance & Development* 48(4): 6–11.

Kaplan, R. D. 1996. *The Ends of the Earth: A Journey at the Dawn of the 21st Century.* New York: Random House.

Katumanga, M. 2005. "A City Under Siege: Banditry and Modes of Accumulation in Nairobi, 1991–2004." *Review of African Political Economy* 32(106): 505–520.

Kipper, R., and Fischer, M. (Eds.) 2009. *Cairo's Informal Areas between Challenges and Hidden Potentials.* Cairo: German Technical Cooperation (GTZ).

Kuepe, M., Nordman, C. J., and Roubaud, F. 2008. "Education and Earnings in Urban West Africa." *Journal of Comparative Economics* 37: 491–515.

Kumar, A., and Barett, F. 2008. *Stuck in Traffic: Urban Transport in Africa.* Draft Final Report.

Lampard, E. E. 1965. "Historical Aspects of Urbanization." In Hauser, P. M., and Schnore, L. F. (Eds.) *The Study of Urbanization.* London: John Wiley, pp. 519–554.

Leke, A., Lund, S., Roxburg, C., and van Wamelen, A. 2010. "*What is Driving Africa's Growth?*" McKinsey Global Institute.

Lewis, W. A. 1954. "Economic Development with Unlimited Supplies of Labor." *The Manchester School of Economic and Social Studies* 22(2): 139–191.

Mabogunje, A. L. 1968. "*Urbanization in Nigeria.*" London: University of London Press.

Mabogunje, A. L. 1962. "*Yoruba Towns.*" Ibadan: Ibadan University Press.

McKinsey Global Institute. 2010. "*Lions on the Move: The Progress and Potential of African Economies.*" Seoul, San Francisco, London, Washington: McKinsey & Company.

Mekawy, H. S., and Yousry, A. M. 2011. "*Cairo: The Predicament of a Fragmented Metropolis.*" http://www.i3.makcdn.com/wp-content/blogs.dir/231013/files/2012/03/cairo-informal-gc-final-august-2011.pdf. Accessed September 22, 2012.

Meier, R. L. 1962. "*A Communication Theory of Urban Growth.*" Cambridge, MA: MIT Press.

Mbembe, A., and Nuttall, S. 2008. "Introduction: Afropolis." In Nutall, S., and Mbembe, A. (Eds.) *Johannesburg: The Elusive Metropolis.* Durham, NC: Duke University Press, pp. 1–33.

Misilu, M. N. E., Chen, S., and Zhang, L. Q. 2010. "Sustainable Urbanization's Challenge in Democratic Republic of Congo." *Journal of Sustainable Development* 3(2): 242–254.

Moore, J. 1979. "The Villagization Process and Rural Development in the Mwanza Region of Tanzania." *Geografiska Annaler* 61B: 65–80.

Morange, M., Folio, F., Peyroux, E., and Vivet, J. 2012. "The Spread of a Transnational Model: 'Gated Communities' in Three Southern African Cities (Cape Town, Maputo and Windhoek)." *International Journal of Urban and Regional Research* 36(5): 890–914.

Morella, E., Foster, V., and Baerjee, S. G. 2008. "*Climbing the Ladder: The State of Sanitation in Sub-Saharan Africa. Africa Infrastructure Country Diagnostic (AICD) Background Paper 13.*" Washington, DC: The International Bank for Reconstruction and Development/The World Bank.

Myers, G. 2011. *African Cities: Alternative Visions of Urban Theory and Practice.* London and New York: Zed Books.

Ndijo, B. 2006. "Doula: Inventing Life in an African Necropolis." In Murray, M. J., and Myers, G. A. (Eds.) *Cities in Contemporary Africa.* New York: Palgrave Macmillan, pp. 103–118.

Newman, J. L. 1998. "The Origins of African Rural Settlement." In Silberfein, M. (Ed.) *Rural Settlement Structure and African Development.* Boulder, CO: Westview Press, pp. 35–46.

Nyairo, J. 2006. "(Re)Configuring the City: The Mapping of Places and People in Contemporary Kenyan Popular Song Texts." In Murray, M. J., and Myers, G. A. (Eds.) *Cities in Contemporary Africa.* New York: Palgrave Macmillan, pp. 71–94.

O'Connor, A. M. 1983. "*The African City.*" New York: Africana Publishing Company.

Ofori-Amoah, B. 1998. "Growth Centers and Regional Development in Africa: Failure or Another Missed Opportunity?" In Adjibolosoo, S. B.-S. K., and Ofori-Amoah, B. (Eds.) *Addressing Misconceptions About Africa's Development. Seeing Beyod the Veil.* Lewiston, NY: Edwin Mellen Press, pp. 151–173.

Oldewage-Theron, W., and Slabbert, T. J. C. 2010. "Depth of Poverty in an Informal Settlement in the Vaal Region, South Africa." *Health SA Gesondheid* 15(1): Art. #456, 6 pages. DOI: 10.4102/hsag.v15i1.456.

Omasombo, J. 2005. "Kisangani: A City at Its Lowest Ebb." In Simone, A., and Abouhani, A. (Eds.) *Urban Africa: Changing Contours of Survival in the City.* Dakar: CODESRIA Books, pp. 96–119.

Onyebueke, U. V. 2008. "Ageing and Urban–Rural Drift in Nigeria: Coping or Dispensing with City Accommodation in Retirement." *Ageing Research Reviews* 7: 275–280.

Onyeonoru, I. P. 1994. "Labour Migration and Rural Transformation in Nigeria." *International Sociology* 9(2): 217–221.

Otiso, K. 2005. "Colonial Urbanization and Urban Management in Kenya." In Salm, S. J., and Falola, T. (Eds.) *African Urban Spaces in Historical Perspective.* Rochester, NY: University of Rochester Press, pp. 73–97.

Otiso, K. M., and Owusu, G. 2008. "Comparative Urbanization in Ghana and Kenya." *GeoJournal* 71: 143–171.

Owusu, G. 2005. "The Role of District Capitals in Regional Development: Linking Small Towns, Rural-Urban Linkages and Decentralisation in Ghana." *International Development Planning Review* 27(1): 59–89.

Owusu, G. 2008. "The Role of Small Towns in Regional Development and Poverty Reduction in Ghana." *International Journal of Urban and Regional Research* 32(2): 453–472.

Pitcher, M. A., and Graham, A. 2007. "Cars Are Killing Luanda: Crynism, Consumerism, and Other Assaults on Angola's Postwar, Capital City." In Murray, M. J., and Myers, G. A. (Eds.) *Cities in Contemporary Africa*. New York: Palgrave Macmillan, pp. 173–194.

Potts, D. 2005. "Counter-Urbanisation on the Zambian Copperbelt? Interpretations and Implications." *Urban Studies* 42(4): 583–609.

Potts, D. 1995. "Shall We Go Home? Increasing Urban Poverty in African Cities and Migration Processes." *Geographical Journal* 161(3): 245–264.

Rakodi, C. (Ed.) 1997. *The Urban Challenge in Africa: Growth and Management of Its Large Cities*. Tokyo and New York: United Nations University Press.

Redfern, P. 2007. "Africa's Super-Rich Grow Richer." East African. https://allafrica.com/stories/200707030847.html. Accessed November 5, 2018.

Silberfein, M. 1998b (Ed.). *Rural Settlement Structure and African Development*. Boulder, CO: Westview Press.

Silberfein, M. 1998a. "Cyclical Change in African Settlement and Modern Resettlement Programs." In Silberfein, M. (Ed.) *Rural Settlement Structure and African Development*. Boulder, CO: Westview Press, pp. 47–72.

Siddle, D. J. 1970. "Location Theory and Subsistence Economy: The Spacing of Rural Settlements in Sierra Leone." *Journal of Tropical Geography* 31: 79–90.

Sims, D. 2003. "*The Case of Cairo, Egypt. Understanding Slums: Case Studies for the Global Report on Human Settlements*." London: University College London/DPU.

Simon, D. A. 1997. "Urbanization, Globalization, and Economic Crisis in Africa." In Rakodi, C. (Ed.) *The Urban Challenge in Africa: Growth and Management of Its Large Cities*. Tokyo and New York: United Nations University Press, pp. 74–108.

Sihlongonyane, M. F. 2016. "The Global, the Local and the Hybrid in the Making of Johannesburg as a world class African city." *Third World Quarterly* 37(9): 1607–1627

Sommers, M. 2010. "Urban Youth in Africa." *Environment and Urbanization* 22(2): 317–332.

Stock, R. 2004. *Africa South of the Sahara. A Geographical Interpretation.* New York: The Guilford Press.

Stren, R. E. 1991. "Helping African Cities." *Public Administration and Development* 11: 275–279.

Todaro, M. P. 1969. "A Model of Labor Migration and Urban Employment in Less Developed Countries." *The American Economic Review* 59(1): 138–148.

Udo, R. K. 1982. "*The Human Geography of Tropical Africa.*" Ibadan: Heinemann Educational Books (Nigeria) Ltd.

UN-HABITAT. 2010. "*The State of African Cities: Governance, Inequality and Urban Land Markets.*" Nairobi: United Nations Human Settlements Programme (UN-HABITAT).

UN-HABITAT. 2008. "*The State of African Cities: A Framework for Addressing Urban Challenges in Africa.*" Nairobi: United Nations Human Settlements Programme (UN-HABITAT).

UN. 2005. *Demographic Yearbook Table 6 "Urban Definitions."*

UN-Habitat. 2003. "*The Challenge of Slums: Global Report on Human Settlements.*" New York: Earthscan Publications.

UN-Habitat 2014. *The State of African Cities. Re-imagining Sustainable Urban Transitions.* Nairobi: United Nations Human Settlement Programme.

United Nations. 1976. "The Vancouver Declaration on Human Settlements." *Habitat: United Nations Conference on Human Settlement.* Vancouver, Canada, May 31–June 11.

UITP and UATP. 2010. *Report on Statistical Indicators of Public Transport Performance in Africa.*

USAID. 2005. "*Youth and Conflict: A Toolkit for Intervention.*" Washington, DC: Office of Conflict Management and Migration, United States Agency for International Development.

van Hooloos, F., and Kloosterboer, M. 2018. "Africa's New cities: The Contested Future of Urbanisation." *Urban Studies* 55(6): 1223–1241.

Versi, A. 2011. "Tatu City—The Future Face of Africa?" *African Business* (May 37–39).

Watson, V. 2014. "African Urban Fantasies: Dreams or Nightmares?" *Environment & Urbanization* 26(1): 215–231.

Winters, C. 1983. "The Classification of Traditional African Cities." *Journal of Urban History* 10(1): 3–31.

Winters, C. 1982. "Urban Morphogenesis in Francophone Black Africa." *Geographical Review* 72(2): 139–154.

Yeboah, I. E. A. 2000. "Structural Adjustment and Emerging Urban Form in Accra, Ghana." *Africa Today* 47(2):61–89.

Yeboah, I. 2003. "Demographic and Housing Aspects of Structural Adjustment and Emerging Urban Form in Accra, Ghana." *Africa Today* 10: 107–119.

Yeboah, I. E. A. 2005. "Housing the Urban Poor in Twenty-First Century Sub-Saharan Africa: Policy Mismatch and a Way Forward for Ghana." *GeoJournal* 62: 147–161

Wittemyer, G., Elsen, P., Bean, W. T., Burton, A. C. O., and Brashares, J. S. 2008. "Reply to J. Igoe et al. and L.P. Shoo's E-Letters." *Science.* http://www.sciencemag.org/content/321/5885/123/reply#sci_el_11823.

CHAPTER 9

Politics and Governance

When the sudden death of President John Atta Mills of Ghana was announced on July 24, 2012, political observers around the world began sitting on needle and pins watching and waiting to see what will happen to Ghana. Mr. Thomas Fessy, the BBC correspondent of West Africa wrote: "This is the first time that a president has died while in office in Ghana. In a country hailed as a solid democracy, John Atta Mills' sudden death should not spark a political crisis but will certainly test the country's democratic institutions." A day later, a Reuter report stated: "In line with Ghana's constitution, Vice-President John Dramani Mahama, who is 53, took the oath of office as head of state before a somber parliament hours after the announcement of Mills' death. Mahama will serve as caretaker president until the elections at the end of the year. Analysts hailed this as a sign that the country's political institutions were solid and working smoothly." The report went on to say that "Ghana has seen democratic elections decide its leadership no fewer than four times since the last military coup in 1981, a rare feat in a region where power is still just as often determined by the bullet as by the ballot."

PREREADING ASSIGNMENTS

1. What types of governments do you think African countries have?
2. List as many African countries as you know that have multiparty elections.
3. List as many African countries as you know that have democratic governments.
4. Which African countries do you know have had civil wars?
5. How many women presidents are there in Africa and of which countries do they serve as presidents?

The implication of this story is that something negative was expected to happen, and rightly so, from the sudden death of Ghana's president because of Africa's political history. After all, this is a continent that began experiencing political instability within a decade of achieving its freedom from colonialism. Not only that, it is also a continent on which institutionalized dictatorship through one-party system and president-for-life became so firmly rooted that peaceful transition of power was very rare indeed. However, the story also shows a mismatch between the slow but steady changes occurring in Africa and what people have come to expect from the continent. The purpose of the chapter is to highlight Africa's political and governance landscape, with particular reference to the systems and structures of government and their effectiveness in executing their functions for the benefit of the African people. The chapter is in three sections. The first section deals with the evolution and development of the political landscape, the second section examines the contemporary governance and politics indicators, while the third section discusses some of the issues and challenges of politics and governance on the continent.

Throughout the chapter we consider **politics** as the process by which the government performs its duties and **governance** as rules and procedures by which the government carries out its duties effectively (Hyden et al., 2004).

EVOLUTION AND DEVELOPMENT OF POLITICAL AND GOVERNANCE SYSTEMS IN AFRICA

Precolonial Africa

Precolonial Africa developed several political and governance systems along with the empires and kingdoms discussed in Chapter 2. Following Schraeder (2000), these systems were of two main types—centralized and decentralized or segmented political systems.

Centralized Political System

In this system, political authority resided in a central government whose policies applied uniformly throughout the territory of jurisdiction. The people in this political system owed their allegiance to the central authority. Drawing on Potholm's (1979) work, Schraeder (2000) identifies three types of this political system, namely pyramidal, associational, and centralized monarchy.

The **pyramidal monarchy** was the most common of the centralized political systems (Potholm, 1979; Schraeder, 2000). In this system, the central authority resided in the king who had the authority to enforce his will throughout the kingdom. However, this form of monarchy was also a federal system in which provincial or state chiefs or subchiefs appointed by the king had autonomy. In addition, this political system had bureaucratic checks-and-balances that ensured that no person in authority abused power. Examples of the federal system were the Songhai Empire and the Asante Empire, while the most elaborate of the checks-and-balances system was that of the Oyo Empire of modern-day western Nigeria.

The **associational monarchy** was similar to the pyramidal monarchy except that there were "associational groups" that undertook various duties on behalf of the king (Schraeder, 2000). These duties included collection of taxes, administering justice, settling of land disputes, control of trade, and exploitation of natural resources. Perhaps the most important of such groups, especially in West Africa, were the secret societies, referred to as the *Po* for men and *Sandy* for women (Schraeder, 2000).

The **centralized monarchy** was the most authoritarian of all the political systems in precolonial Africa (Schraeder, 2000) and it was best exemplified by the Kingdom of Dahomey (in modern-day Benin). The kings were absolute monarchs, with very little checks and balances. All political appointees served at the kings' pleasure. The most powerful group in the kingdom was the Council of Ministers, the king's advisory council. This council was appointed by the king from the commoners group, who could not threaten the ruling monarch's position (Webster, Boahen, and Idowu 1967). Monitoring the activities of officials were the Naye, often called the king's wives, who were always present when officials reported to the kings. However, conquered people had no political rights, and had to work as slaves for the king in exchange for protection.

Decentralized Political Systems

The decentralized or segmented political systems had no recognizable central government, but political authority and power was diffused throughout the society. This system included band organization, clan, age groups, oracle-led and the absolute village systems (Potholm, 1979; Schraeder, 2000).

Band organization was the oldest as well as the most decentralized political system of precolonial Africa. A band usually consisted of members of an extended family, with no clear structure of political authority. Decisions were usually made face-to-face and by consensus. This type of organization has almost disappeared except among a few groups where hunting and gathering is still a major source of living such as the San people.

The **clan system** was based on divisions in ethnic groups that traced their descent to a common ancestor. While each clan had its own political organization, there was no central authority that oversaw all the clans within the ethnic group. Inherent in this system was competition rather than cooperation among the clans. Loyalty to clan was stronger than loyalty to the larger ethnic group and sometimes clans would make alliances for self-interest and preservation, which in turn led to alternating times of peaceful coexistence and clan warfare.

The **age group system** transcended clans and other affiliations. One's age group served as a source of mutual help. It also predetermined the individual's responsibility to society including service in the military, doing community work or serving in other capacity in society. This system was well practiced among the Maasai ethnic group, and the Riverian, the Akwa, and the Ogoja Ibo in Nigeria (Webster and Boahen, 1967). The **oracle-led system** was slightly different from the clan system in that while there was no central authority, the various clans or groups were brought together under a spiritual leader or the oracle that was revered by all the groups. The Shilluk people of South Sudan, the Cross River Ibo and the Ibibio of Nigeria, had a system like that. This heavy use of oracle consultation to settle disputes helped to strengthen the Ibo political system, because of their perceived impartiality (Webster and Boahen, 1967). Finally, **the autonomous village system** consisted of villages that resembled city states in the Western sense. The individual villages though connected by common language, custom, and belief systems were rather independent of each other instead of coming under one central authority. Some of the villages had a system that was close to a centralized system while others did not. Examples of this system were the Swahili cities and the Owerri Ibo of Nigeria.

Colonial Africa

The political and governance systems of Colonial Africa were discussed in Chapter 2—indirect rule in the British realm and assimilation in the French, Belgian, and Portuguese realms. Therefore, instead of repeating the story here, we focus on one element of the colonial state that was not discussed in Chapter 2 and that is the contradiction of the colonial state and its impact on the Africa.

On the one hand, the colonial state was based on the European nation–state system. This system originated from 17th century Europe when the Treaty of Westphalia at the end of Europe's Thirty Years' War (1618–1648) initiated a new political system that recognized the rights of sovereign political units to exercise control over people residing in officially marked territories. These political units consisted of people with same language, ethnic background, and customs. The contradiction is that European colonialists brought the idea of the nation–state to Africa without consideration of Africa's ethnic mosaic. The result is that none of the colonial territories that eventually became the present-day African countries was a nation–state. Rather, the colonial state divided many African nations into several states. The worst case was the Somali people, who were divided across the French Territory of the Afars and Issas (modern-day Djibouti), Italian and British Somaliland, and the western Ogaden region of the Ethiopian Empire (Kromm, 1967). In West Africa, the Ewe people were divided among the British, French, and the German colonies. In East Africa, the Hutus and Tutsis were split between the Belgian and the French colonies. Ethnic groups that were previously independent of each other were brought together under one colonial power, which then became one country after independence. This has resulted in a number of issues, including questions of language, boundary, national identities, irredentism, and secession, to postcolonial Africa.

The politics and governance of the Colonial Africa also weakened the precolonial political institutions. First, the replacement of traditional authorities in the French, Belgian, and Portuguese colonies by new colonial powers did away with the checks and balances that regulated precolonial political systems (Schraeder, 2000). Second, even in the British colonies, where the policy of indirect rule relied on chieftaincy institution, it was only the chiefs who pledged loyalty to the colonial power that were supported. Chiefs who refused to cooperate were forcibly replaced. Moreover, the overemphasis on chieftaincy without any support of other related institutions that governed the life of the people led to abuse of power (Matthews, 1937). Oftentimes, when demands from the colonial power ran counter to local interests, local rulers had to choose between siding with the colonial power and maintaining their position, and siding with their people and losing their favor with the colonial power. This tactics of divide-and-rule created distrust between the indigenous privileged classes and the people, thereby eroding all sources of accountability.

As already mentioned in Chapter 2, colonialism also created artificial order of superiority among ethnic groups. The most cited example is the Hutu and Tutsi in Rwanda and Burundi, where French colonialists made an elitist class out of the Tutsi. In Algeria, the French again singled out the Kabyle, a subgroup of the Imazighen for special attention. They claimed that Kabyle had Roman origins and were much closer to the French than other Arab and Amazigh groups. As a result, the Kabyle could be more easily assimilated into the French culture including Christianity and the French political system, although the Kabyle were devout Muslims (Goodman, 2005).

Finally, colonialism was a repressive enterprise that could only succeed through coercion. The tool for this coercion was the colonial police and military forces, which were often recruited from different ethnic groups or colonies. According to Schraeder (2000), the British were fond of stationing troops from South Asia in their African colonies. The idea here was that the troops would not have any inhibitions in executing their jobs. Thus, revolts, rebellions, or demonstrations were brutally repressed, until it got to a point where it was no longer economically and politically feasible. The legacy of this top-down authoritarian political system would manifest itself in many diverse ways in postcolonial Africa.

Postcolonial Africa

Postcolonial Africa faced a daunting political and governance task. Per their constitutions, the majority of African countries emerged from colonialism as republics with a very small minority—Morocco, Libya, Burundi, Lesotho, and Swaziland—as kingdoms. Their constitutions established all the three branches of government—the legislature concerned with enacting and passing laws, the executive concerned with executing the laws, and the judiciary branch in charge of interpreting the constitution and enforcing the law of the land. Some countries adopted a parliamentary system while others adopted a presidential system. In the **presidential** system the three branches of government, the executive, legislature, and judiciary, are independent. There are checks and balances to make sure that no one of these can be controlled by the other. In the **parliamentary** system the relationship between the executive and legislative branches are fused. The prime minister, who is the leader of the majority party is also the head of government, and appoints the cabinet. There is a ceremonial head of state, who may either be a monarch or a president, in whose name executive action is taken. Of the kingdoms, Morocco, Libya, Burundi, and Lesotho, were constitutional monarchies, while Swaziland was an absolute monarchy, not accountable to anyone. The legislative branches also differed. Some countries had **unicameral**, which consisted of only one house, while others followed a **bicameral** system of a lower house and an upper house.

These structures and institutions looked good on paper but running them effectively presented a major hurdle. First, almost all of the countries were mechanical units of ethnic groups of different languages, customs, beliefs, and traditions that had been hastily put together. Second, the human and financial resources needed to effectively run these units were nonexistent. Africans had not been prepared to govern their new political units. Third, the new leaders most of them untested in international politics had to operate in the complex and antagonistic world of Cold War politics (Mutua, 2008). There was a great deal of political optimism, but the road was going to be bumpy.

From Multiparty Rule to Single-Party Rule

The first major move by Africa's political leaders toward getting matters under control was the establishment of a single-party political system. African leaders justified this move on several grounds. First, one-party system was consistent with precolonial Africa's political and governance systems, during which time there was no multiparty system, but instead decisions were based on consensus building. Second, multiparty politics could hinder rapid economic development and could lead to a "waste of scarce resources" due to competition for resources. Third, one-party systems would enable the government to guide and protect the people.

No matter how one sees it, as Schraeder (2000) points out, the single-party political system was the most significant political act undertaken by African leaders in the postcolonial era because of its effects on politics and governance. First, it did away with existing political parties except for the ruling party removing all forms of checks and balances in the system. Second, it concentrated the power of the state into the hands of top and inner circle sole-party operatives, which directly or indirectly led to the growth of parastatals, or state-owned organizations and a rapid expansion of government bureaucracies. Third, general elections became mere referenda and rubber-stamping of what the leaders wanted. Fourth, all voices of opposition were silenced and those outspoken were thrown into prison or chased into exile. Finally, it helped to solidify the positions of African leaders as leaders for life.

Without any opposition parties to check on the actions of presidents and ruling parties, many presidents became engaged in excesses of power and authority, as many declared themselves presidents for life. Many presidents built a network of special security forces, as well as a group of loyalists who frequently received political and economic rewards from the president. In many cases, these circles of network were filled largely with members of the presidents' ethnic group.

For example, Francisco Marcias Nguema declared himself president-for-life of Equatorial Guinea in 1972 and embarked on the elimination of anyone who opposed him. When the Catholic Church opposed his demand for putting his picture on every altar in churches, he started a program of persecution that claimed an estimated 50,000 people's life by the time he was overthrown in 1979 (Ayitey, 1992). In Morocco, King Mohammed V served as his own Prime Minister; while King Hassan II, his successor, became his own Prime Minister, as well as Minister of Interior, Defense, and Agriculture. In Algeria, Ahmed Ben Bella within a short time became personally in charge of the Ministries of Interior, Finance, and Information, while serving as President of the Republic, head of government, and secretary-general of the ruling party (Willis, 2012).

In Ghana, all anti-government newspaper campaigns, strikes, and boycotts, which were guaranteed by the constitution, became illegal. In Tanzania, President Nyerere declared that the Western form of democracy was not suited to the African situation, and arrested people who opposed the idea. In Zambia, a permanent state of emergency was imposed. In Cameroon and Malawi, newspaper editors had to get clearance from the government to publish their stories, while in Tunisia President Bourguiba incarcerated many of his political opponents (Ayitey, 1992). In Morocco, King Hassan used the parliamentary deadlock between the opposition and royalist parties and a subsequent riot in Casablanca to declare a state of emergency, suspend the 1962 constitution and the parliament, and began ruling by decrees. It was not until 1975 that he introduced a new constitution, which only formalized the state of emergency that had been in place (Willis, 2012).

There were also economic and fiscal policy excesses. For example, President Felix Houphouet-Boigny spent $360 million to build the world's largest Roman Catholic basilica in his hometown, Yamoussoukro, in Cote d'Ivoire. Some of the financial excesses also went to private pockets of the ruling class. In Cameroon, for example, the ruling class handpicked by President Ahidjo himself and top civil servants became extremely wealthy as they saw the state as a means of accumulating wealth for themselves and their families (Mbaku, 2007). Other examples include the many deficit-financed projects across the continent that threw many of the newly independent countries into financial insolvency.

As a result of all these, within 10 years of independence many African states had developed symptoms of what would later be labeled as neopatrimonialism—a combination of modern bureaucratic structures and personalized, unaccountable, and autocratic rule. According to Diamond (2010, p. 55):

> The fundamental purpose of neopatrimonial governments is not to produce public goods—roads, bridges, markets, irrigation, education, health care, public sanitation, clean drinking water, and effective legal system—that increase productivity, improve human capital, stimulate investment, and generate development. The point of neopatrimonialism rather, is to produce private goods for those with access to power. Contracts are granted not based on who can deliver the best service for the lowest price, but rather who will pay the biggest bribe. . . . Government funds disappear into the overseas accounts of officeholders. Public payrolls are swollen with the ranks of phantom workers and soldiers, whose pay goes into the pockets of the higher-ups.

Due to this and other factors that will be discussed later, by the mid-1980s only four of all the civilian heads of state of Africa since independence had willingly relinquished political power. These were Ahmadou Ahidjo of Cameroon (in 1982 after 22 years in power), Leopold Sedar Senghor of Senegal (in 1982 after 20 years), Siaka Stevens of Sierra Leone (in 1985 after 14 years), and Julius Nyerere of

Tanzania (in 1985 after 23 years). Most of the rest stayed until they were removed from power by military coups, while a handful were removed by popular uprising.

The Military Interregnum 1950s–1990s

Military intervention in politics and governance of postcolonial Africa began in Egypt when, on July 23, 1952, members of the so-called "Free Officers' Club" of the Egyptian army led by Mohammed Naguib and Gamal Nasser overthrew the government of King Farouk, ending the Mohammed Ali dynasty in Egypt. The next coup occurred in Sudan in 1958, just two years after its independence, but it was in the 1960s and 1970s that the number of successful military coups in Africa reached its peak. From 1960 to 1969, military coups successfully overthrew democratically elected governments in 14 countries. In three of those countries, Togo, Burundi, and Sierra Leone, this occurred twice. From 1971 to 1979, eight successful coups occurred with three of them in Ghana alone (see Chapter 3). The obvious question is why did the military become so involved in politics in Africa?

Reasons for military intervention in politics There are two main perspectives on the answer to this question: the military's own justification for the coups and the perspectives of outsiders. The military's own reasons as contained in the first public statements of coup leaders were political, economic, and social. Politically, previous governments were accused of incompetence, not ruling in the interest of the people, and stifling democratic rule by too much centralization of power and banning freedom of speech and other forms of opposition (Onwudiwe, 2004; Wiking 1983). Economically, previous governments were accused of gross mismanagement of the economy resulting in rising cost living, heavy borrowing, and rising unemployment. Socially, previous governments were corrupt and engaged in the politics of self-aggrandizement.

From the perspectives of outsiders (political observers and researchers), the reasons for the military intervention were personal, corporate, and foreign interests (Onwudiwe, 2004). At the personal level, it is argued that coup leaders usually had personal motives for their actions that bordered on either fear of political reprisal or professional advancement due to the political nature of promotions in the military. As a result, coup leaders took advantage of the least opportunity they had for self-protection. At the corporate level, it is argued that military coups occurred as a form of protecting the military's own interest as an institution. This became necessary especially when the integrity and interests of the military were threatened by its relationship with the government. Thus, meddling in the internal affairs of the military by a civilian government, or establishing a parallel military organization by the government became a pretext for staging coups. Finally, the military had, in some cases, overrated its "professionalism" and discipline and had assumed that it was better equipped than anyone else to rule their respective countries. With respect to foreign interests, military coups were fully or partially attributed to the Cold War politics when both the West and East bought allies among African soldiers with weaponry and promised support and rewards to overthrow leaders that were of different ideological persuasions.

Military rule in action The performances of military governments have become the subject of a major debate. In general, there are two views. An earlier view was that because of the military's discipline, command structure, nationalism, and sacrifice, it could mobilize people into action, and would not only do a better job modernizing Africa, but would speed up development of Africa (Agbekaku, 2000; Gutteridge, 1968).

However, this earlier view has now been replaced by the view that military intervention in African politics was the worst thing that happened to postcolonial Africa for several reasons. First, military governments promised more than they could deliver. For example, Chukwuma Nzeogwu, who led Nigeria's first coup in January 1966, asserted that "every law-abiding citizen would henceforth have freedom from fear and all forms of oppression, freedom from general inefficiency, and freedom to live and strive in every field of human endeavor" (Agbese, 2005, p. 65). Siad Barre assured Somalis of transformation of the economy from an import-based consumer economy to one in which Somalis would live better lives, develop their potentials, and fulfill their aspirations. Ignatius Acheampong promised Ghanaians real benefits, a new sense of meaning and purpose to their lives in 1972, while in Liberia, Samuel Doe promised that his government will level the playing field—bringing equal economic and social opportunity for all (Agbese, 2005).

However, Nzeogwu's promise heightened ethnic tensions that led to subsequent coups and counter coups, and eventually plunging Nigeria into civil war (1967–1970). Similarly, Acheampong's promise to Ghana failed as his effort to introduce a new form of government, meant to solidify his hold on the country eventually, paved the way for more military interventions and the almost collapse of the Ghanaian economy. In Liberia, Doe replaced the Americo-Liberian oligarchy with a new one dominated by members of his minority Krahn ethnic group and left a legacy of an 11-year brutal civil war, while Siad Barre's Somalia deteriorated into a failed state.

Second, military governments committed the same offenses they had accused their predecessors of committing. Among these were gross mismanagement of the economy, abuse of human rights, suppression of democratic principles, and corruption. Gross mismanagement of the economy was evident in all the countries that were under military rule because at the time the rule ended, per capita incomes had declined, unemployment rates and inflation were both high, and national debt had increased (Deng, 1998). Some of these conditions resulted from projects that defied common sense. For example, in Central African Republic (CAR), General Jean-Bedel Bokassa declared himself Emperor Bokassa I of the Central African Empire in 1976, and spent more than $20 million, about a quarter of the country's annual revenue, on his coronation. In the DRC, Mobutu converted his hometown—Gbadolite—into the "Versailles of the Jungle" and acquired mansions abroad with state funds. In Liberia, Doe and his officials acquired wealth and land just as the Americo-Liberian government that preceded them. By the end of their regime they had stolen an estimated $300 million of public funds (Adebajo, 2002).

With respect to corruption, military governments either equaled or exceeded their civilian predecessors. The most extreme cases of this occurred in DRC and Nigeria. In DRC, it was widely reported that Mobutu's personal wealth of between $6–10 billion at the time of his death was all acquired at the expense of DRC's economy. According to Reno (1999), the President's share of government expenditure kept increasing from 28% in 1972 to 95% in 1992. At the same time agriculture went from 29.3% in 1972 to 4% in 1992, while social service dropped from 17.5% in 1972 to 0% in 1992 (Acemoglu et al., 2002). In Nigeria, Mbaku (2007, p. 39) asserts that "military rule has contributed more than any single factor to making corruption endemic in Nigeria." The irony is that several efforts were made by the military to curb corruption, the most serious of which was the Operation Purge the Nation initiated by General Murtala Mohammed who overthrew a previous military government in 1975. About 50 heads of government departments were forced to retire and 11,000 civil servants were also purged. Unfortunately, General Mohammed was assassinated only after 201 days in office and with that also died the hope that perhaps military rule would have, for once, stamped out corruption in Nigeria. Indeed the level of corruption in Nigeria reached its peak under the last military government of General Sani Abacha from 1993 to 1998, who reportedly stole about $5 billion during his time in office (Mbaku, 2007).

Third, military governments often ruled by decrees so there were no avenues for civil society to express its views. Abuse of human rights and suppression of democratic principles were common. The excesses of these varied from country to country, but in many instances, political opponents were hunted down, silenced, or forced into exile; people were arrested and imprisoned without cause, and civilians were often brutalized and subjected to "military" discipline. The Press was persecuted and made to tow the official line of the government. Intimidation, disappearances, and summary executions were common in some of the countries. Some military leaders surrounded themselves with secret police service who worked as a network of informants for people who would say any negative things about the government. All these imposed a culture of fear and silence on the public. General Idi Amin of Uganda, General Bokassa of Central African Republic, Mobutu Sese Seko of DRC, and Samuel Doe of Liberia were notorious among military leaders for these acts. In the case of Amin and Mobutu, their intolerance was even extended to threatening the lives and families of women who refused their amorous advances (Onwumechili, 1998).

Military regimes also continued the single-party system of the civilian government since most of them did not actually allow political parties. In addition, they continued the political ideologies particularly socialism that had started under some of the civilian regimes. As a result of all these policies, military regimes also created an atmosphere for the majority of Africa's civil wars in the postcolonial era: Nigeria (1967–1970), DRC (1996–2003), Rwanda (1990–1994), Burundi (1993–2005), Chad (1965–1982; 1998–2002; 2005–2010), Sudan (1955–1972; 1983–2005), Darfur (2003–2010), Liberia (1989–1996; 1999–2003), Sierra Leone (1991–2002), and Cote d'Ivoire (2002–2004; 2011).

By the middle of the 1990s, however, both military and autocratic civilian rules were losing ground due to a combination of both internal and external factors. First, the collapse of the single-party system of the Soviet Union and Eastern Europe in 1989 effectively ended the Cold War. Suddenly, the rationale that African leaders had used to promote their brand of one-party system crumbled. Similarly, autocratic African leaders could no longer use the Cold War to get Western or Eastern support to suppress democratic voices and movements in their respective countries. Second, the economies of the majority of African countries were in shambles and the imposition of structural adjustment policies among other things required democratization and trade liberation as conditionality by Western interests in return for foreign assistance. Third, the rise and empowerment of civil society and internal demands for political and economic reforms resulted in a number of public demonstrations, which peaked in 1991 with 86 demonstrations in 30 African countries (Adejumobi, 2000; Schraeder, 2000).

Return to Multiparty Politics

The return to multiparty politics in Africa took different forms including multiparty elections, national conferences, co-opted transitions, guided democratization (Adejumobi, 2000; Martin, 1993; Schraeder, 2000), and citizen revolution. Multiparty elections occurred in countries with strong civil society to force overhaul of electoral laws and infrastructure to ensure among other things free and fair competitive elections, and press freedom. Among these countries were Benin Republic, Zambia, Malawi, Congo, and Cape Verde.

Coopted transition occurred in countries in which civil society initiated political reforms but were later coopted or hijacked by the ruling regime. The result is that previous electoral laws and controls remained intact with the opposition either weakened or fragmented that election results hardly changed from before the onset of the democratic movement. Among these countries were Kenya, Togo, DRC, Tanzania, and Tunisia, Morocco, and Egypt, before the Arab Spring.

Guided democracy occurred in countries in which the state actually undertook reforms under a managed form of democratic systems that ensured competitive multiparty elections, press freedom, but still could be manipulated. Among these countries were Ghana, Nigeria, Cote d'Ivoire, Senegal, Gambia, Cameroon, and Algeria. Finally, citizen revolution occurred where a strong civil awakening caused the collapse of autocratic regimes, and new constitutions that allowed for multiparty democratic elections. This occurred in Egypt, Libya, and Tunisia.

The democratic movements began in the late 1980s in North Africa, where serious economic downturn caused countrywide unrest in Tunisia from 1978 to 1981 and in Algeria and Morocco in 1988. In Tunisia, President Bourguiba unwillingly agreed to some limited form of party politics registering only three opposition parties, to ensure that the president's party would be favored in elections. The opposition's ability to organize against the government under Ben Ali's government was further diffused by the fear against the growing Islamist party (Willis, 2005).

In Algeria, the 1988 countrywide unrest in which 500 people died, forced President Chadli Benjedid to call for multiparty elections. A new constitution was promulgated in 1989 that allowed the creation of political parties and multiparty elections. However, the increasing popularity of the Islamist party *Front Islamique du Salut* (FIS) whose radical views threatened to move the country to the far left created some unease among the top military officers. When the FIS won very narrowly in the first round of the presidential election in 1991, the army became convinced that FIS would win the second-round election. On January 11, 1992, the military cancelled the election and banned the FIS (Willis, 2012). As we will see later, this action began a 10-year civil war between various Islamist groups and the Algerian government.

In Morocco, King Hassan began making several overtures to political parties in the early 1990s that resulted in the Kutla Alliance under King Mohammed VI. This was an alliance of *Istiqlal*, the largest and oldest political party in Morocco, and other political parties that agreed to join the government. However, the alliance did not control any cabinet department since they all remained in the hands of royal appointees (Willis, 2012).

The multiparty democratic movement may have begun in North Africa but it was in Sub-Saharan Africa that it got real traction. In the West African country of Benin, a hopelessly broken economic and political situation led to a national conference on civic, religious, and other interests in February 1990 that managed to wrestle power from the 17-year rule of Mathieu Kerekou to pave the way for democratic elections (Joseph, 2010). In March 1990, the Zambian parliament rejected a bill to strengthen Zambia as a one-party state. In 1991, a multiparty elections transferred power from the ruling party since 1964 to a new party. Around the same time, the South African Parliament voted to unban the African National Congress (ANC) and released Nelson Mandela from prison after 27 years. This was followed by the abolition of the apartheid policy in June 1991, and the first truly democratic election in the history of South Africa that elected Nelson Mandela as President, in 1994.

In addition to the call for democracy, more than half of African countries enacted new constitutions, most of them with a two-term limit on the presidency (Table 9.1). In addition, African presidents began to step down as required by the constitutions of their respective countries, even though their supporters urged them to seek constitutional amendments.

Somalia, which had become the poster child of a failed state in Africa, even did not completely escape the democratic movement that was sweeping across Africa. In 1991, following the fall of Siad Barre's regime, two clans declared themselves semiautonomous in the northern part of the country. To the northeast, the Haarti group declared their region as Puntland, while to the northwest the Isaaq clan called their territory Somaliland, with its capital at Hargeysa. From that time the people of Somaliland went ahead to promulgate a new constitution, organized two presidential elections, rebuilt their capital city, three universities, hospitals, and schools that were completely destroyed by Siad Barre, with the help of Somalis in the diaspora, while the rest of the country continued to struggle with terrorism. Owing to these efforts, however, some people called upon the international community to recognize Somaliland (e.g. Kaplan, 2010) but that did not happen. Instead, in 2017, Somalia was finally able to elect a new president, and it is the hope that a federal system of government will eventually be the best way to bring Somaliland into Somalia.

It must be noted that not all efforts at democratic movement were initially successful. For example, in Rwanda, the initial democratization efforts announced in 1990 eventually deteriorated into the largest genocide in the history of modern Africa in

TABLE 9.1

Presidential Term Amendments in Africa since 1990

Constitution does not contain a two-term only provisions (8 countries)	Constitution contains a two-term limit on the presidency (30 countries)			
		Two-term limit was reached (19 countries)		
	Two terms not served by any president (11 countries)	Constitution amendment not attempted (9 countries)	Constitution amendment attempted (10 countries)	
Cote d'Ivoire	Angola	Benin	Without success (3 countries)	With success (10 countries)
Equat. Guinea	Burkina Faso*	Cape Verde	Malawi	Algeria – 2008
Gambia	Burundi	Ghana	Nigeria	Cameroon – 2008
Guinea-Bissau	Cen. African Rep	Kenya	Zambia	Chad – 2005
Mauritania	Congo Rep.	Mali		Djibouti – 2010
Sudan	DRC	Mozambique		Gabon
Seychelles	Liberia	Sao Tome & Principe		Guinea
Zimbabwe	Madagascar	Tanzania		Namibia
	Niger	Senegal		Togo
	Rwanda			Tunisia – 2002
	Sierra Leone+			Uganda

*In 2002 Burkina Faso reduced presidential term to five-year terms but has not been applied to incumbent president.
+Current president began his second term on November 17, 2012.
Source: Posner and Young, 2010; Africa Progress Panel 2011.

1994 due to a combination of political and sociocultural factors (Reyntjens, 1996). Also in some countries, the same ruling parties have remained in power since transitioning to multiparty politics. For example, in Tanzania, the ruling party (CCM) has been in power since the country transitioned into multiparty politics, because of the weak opposition parties vis-à-vis the ability of the ruling CCM to use the constitution and the legal framework to its advantage. The same can be said of Botswana (Hoffman and Robinson, 2010). In addition, in 12 countries the ruling parties sought constitutional amendments to remove term limits on the presidency (Table 9.2). All but three succeeded in doing so, except Namibia where the amendment applied only to Sam Nujoma, the country's first president. In addition to removing the term limits, Guinea and Gabon extended the presidential term from 5 to 7 years, while Tunisia raised the age limit of the president from 70 to 75 years. Even so, by 2010 almost all presidential elections held on the continent were contested.

After its initial tinkering with democratic reforms, North Africa seemed to have escaped the political changes that had been sweeping the continent since 1990. However, beneath the apparent calmness was a volcano, fed by regimes of intolerance and "hereditary republics," and economies choked by high unemployment, waiting to explode. On December 17, 2010, Mohammed al-Bou'azizi, an unemployed university graduate-turned street vendor in Sidi Bouzid, a small Tunisian town, set himself on fire to protest injustice and impunity of public officials in administering the rule of law. Within days, this lone event triggered off what became the **Arab Spring**—a massive public uprising in North Africa that called for political, economic, and social reforms. On January 14, 2011, after 29 days of public demonstration, the 23-year old regime of President Zine El Abidine Ben 'Ali ended with the president fleeing his country. On January 25, 2011, Egyptians took to the street in open defiance of Hosni Mubarak 30-year rule, causing the government to fall on February 11, 2011. The revolution then spread to Libya, on February 16, 2011 in Benghazi, and on October 20, 2011 Muammar Gadhafi's 42-year old rule of Libya ended (Dabashi, 2012; McCaffrey, 2012a, 2012b, 2012c).

There were demonstrations in Morocco and Algeria as well, but they did not have the same impact as those of Tunisia, Egypt, and Libya. This has been explained by the

TABLE 9.2

African Presidents and Presidential Term Limits since the 1990s

President who stepped down after serving term without seeking constitutional amendment		President who tried and failed to amend constitution after serving term		President who tried and succeeded to amend constitution after serving term	
President	Country	President	Country	President	Country
Mathieu Kerekou	Benin	Bakili Muluzi	Malawi	Abdelaziz Bouteflika	Algeria
Antonio Montiero	Cape Verde	Olusegun Obasanjo	Nigeria	Paul Biya	Cameroon
John Jerry Rawlings	Ghana	Frederick Chiluba	Zambia	Idriss Deby	Chad
Daniel arap Moi	Kenya			Omar Bongo	Gabon
Alpha Konare	Mali			Lansana Conte	Guinea
Joaquim Chissano	Mozambique			Samuel Nujoma	Namibia
Miguel Trovoada	Sao Tome & Principe			Gnassingbe Eyadema	Togo
France A. Rene	Seychelles			Zine El Abidine Ben Ali	Tunisia
Benjamin Mpaka	Tanzania			Yoweri Museveni	Uganda

fact that the parties that staged the demonstrations were mostly marginal to the political center in the two countries. In the case of Morocco, the situation was further diffused when King Mohamed, amended the constitution to give more power to parliament. In the case of Algeria, the bitter experience with the Islamist movement in the early 1990s made people wary of what might happen after going through a similar uprising.

Multiparty elections in Tunisia, Egypt, and Libya, returned democratic governments to power; however, it is only Tunisia that, at this time of writing, appears to have stabilized. Egypt's democratically elected Muslim Brotherhood government was overthrown from power by the military on the grounds of saving the country from chaos, and the country seems to have gone back to pre-Arab Spring days. Libya is still struggling to unite its warring factions. Given the long suppression of democratic institutions and practices in the all these countries, it will take time for people to unlearn living under autocracy to learn to live in a democracy.

POLITICS AND GOVERNANCE INDICATORS OF AFRICA

After five decades of experimenting with constitutional government, most of the features of the governmental systems in early postcolonial times remain. The majority of African countries describe themselves as republics, with all three branches of government represented. About 31 of the countries have a unicameral legislature, while 22 have bicameral. On paper and in practice, all presidents are elected by popular votes, and in the countries that follow the parliamentary system, the president then appoints the Prime Minister to be the head of government. A few things have changed. There are only three kingdoms left—Morocco, Lesotho, and Swaziland. Most of the countries with parliamentary systems of governments now have executive presidents as well. Finally, presidential terms range from 4 to 7 years, with the majority of them limited by two terms. The question is how are African countries doing in terms of politics and governance? Writing at the end of the 1990s, Samatar and Samatar (2002, p. 9) defined five types of the African state with respect to effectiveness. The first, an **integral** state, is the one that delivers the public goods as it is expected, and functions to make life more positively predictable. The second, a **developmental** state, is committed to enhancing human capital, productive forces, and national accumulation but at the expense of other civic and basic liberties. The third a **prebendal** state, is preoccupied with the well-being of the regime and its associates, resulting in personal enrichment of the members of the regime and their associates at the expense of the larger majority in the state. The fourth, a **predatory** state, is the one that has lost its capacity and stability such that scavenging over dwindling public resources becomes so vicious that individual survival becomes the order of the day. The fifth, a **cadaverous** state, is the one that has lost every quality of being a state. It is clear that the democratic movement have placed most African countries from the cadaverous and predatory categories.

However, majority of African countries may fall in the prebendal state.

A number of indicators have been developed in the past decade or so to help answer this question in spite of the loose and fluid meanings of governance. McFerson (2010) classifies these measures into three main groups: (1) comprehensive surveys of governance and corruption; (2) measures of human rights and civil liberties; and (3) specialized surveys. The three major comprehensive surveys are the World Bank's Worldwide Governance Indicators (WGI), the Transparency International (TI)'s survey of corruption perception, and the Ibrahim Index of African Governance (IIAG). To this, we may add Freedom House's Freedom in the World index, which is based on two broad measures of political rights and civil liberties. Political rights include the right to vote freely, participate in public office, and join political parties or organizations of your choice. Civil liberties include freedom of expression and beliefs, associational rights, rule of law, and personal autonomy. All these measures have their shortcomings. The WGI measures governance attributes of voice and accountability, political stability and violence, government effectiveness, regulatory quality, rule of law, and control of corruption. These measures are based on the relative rankings of countries and for that reason are not able to assess country-specific improvements. The TI survey is a measure of corruption perception and for that reason has been criticized since perception cannot be exactly measured. The Ibrahim Index of African Governance (IIAG) is compiled from 88 indicators that are then grouped into 14 subcategories that are in turn related to four overarching categories of safety and law, participation and human rights, sustainable economic opportunity, and human development. The scores in each of these four categories are then averaged to obtain a composite index. However, the IIAG has also been criticized for being based on measures that are weakly related to governance (McFerson, 2010). In spite of their shortcomings, these measures do provide some idea about where African countries are in terms of politics- and governance-related issues, but only measures from the WGI and the IIAGI are presented here. Table 9.3 shows the performance of African countries in terms of the WGI's voice and accountability, political stability and violence, and government

TABLE **9.3**

Governance Measures of African Countries: Voice & Accountability, Political Stability, and Government Effectiveness, 2000–2015

Country/Territory	Voice and accountability			Political stability and violence			Government effectiveness		
	2000	2008	2015	2000	2008	2015	2000	2008	2015
Algeria	12.98	19.71	24.63	9.18	14.90	13.33	14.15	32.52	35.10
Angola	8.65	16.35	15.76	1.93	31.73	25.24	3.41	13.11	15.38
Benin	59.62	57.21	58.13	70.53	55.77	48.10	45.37	40.78	30.29
Botswana	66.83	61.54	62.56	78.74	81.25	86.67	70.73	71.36	72.12
Burkina Faso	38.94	36.54	40.89	43.48	48.08	23.33	29.76	39.81	31.73
Burundi	4.33	28.37	13.79	1.45	9.13	6.67	4.88	12.62	12.02
Cameroon	15.38	16.83	21.67	28.02	27.40	14.29	26.83	20.87	21.63
Cape Verde	71.63	75.48	74.88	86.96	74.52	71.90	64.88	57.28	59.62
Central African Rep	27.40	19.23	11.82	12.56	6.73	5.24	5.37	5.34	1.44
Chad	19.23	8.65	10.34	13.04	4.33	14.76	23.90	2.43	6.73
Comoros	14.42	35.10	37.44	39.61	15.87	40.48	7.32	0.97	5.77
Congo Demo. Rep	2.40	9.62	12.81	0.00	2.88	3.81	0.98	1.46	3.85
Congo Rep.	7.69	15.87	21.18	16.91	21.63	28.57	6.34	9.22	14.90
Cote d'Ivoire	17.79	12.50	32.51	12.08	7.21	20.48	16.10	9.71	28.37
Djibouti	24.04	14.90	9.36	32.37	54.33	30.95	10.73	17.48	16.35
Egypt Arab Rep.	24.52	15.38	18.23	44.44	28.37	8.57	49.76	43.69	22.12
Equatorial Guinea	4.81	2.88	1.97	37.68	51.92	38.10	2.93	1.94	7.21
Eritrea	10.10	0.96	0.99	18.84	22.12	18.10	12.20	7.77	4.81
Ethiopia	19.71	11.54	14.29	17.39	8.65	8.10	15.61	41.75	28.85

(*Continued*)

TABLE **9.3**

Governance Measures of African Countries: Voice & Accountability, Political Stability, and Government Effectiveness, 2000-2015 (*Continued*)

Country/Territory	Voice and accountability			Political stability and violence			Government effectiveness		
	2000	2008	2015	2000	2008	2015	2000	2008	2015
Gabon	33.17	23.56	22.17	65.22	53.37	50.48	29.27	20.39	23.56
Gambia	15.87	24.04	8.37	63.77	47.12	49.05	36.59	26.21	18.75
Ghana	49.52	58.65	65.52	31.40	44.23	50.00	57.56	56.31	44.71
Guinea	13.46	9.13	24.14	3.86	2.40	31.43	19.51	10.19	12.5
Guinea-Bissau	26.44	25.48	25.62	29.95	23.08	31.90	11.71	13.59	4.33
Kenya	21.63	39.42	41.87	14.98	10.58	9.05	34.63	34.47	43.75
Lesotho	39.42	45.19	50.25	42.51	36.54	41.90	48.78	42.23	26.92
Liberia	13.94	41.35	38.92	2.90	12.50	21.43	2.44	6.80	7.69
Libya	5.29	3.37	9.85	32.85	73.56	3.33	10.24	11.17	1.92
Madagascar	50.96	36.06	34.48	46.86	29.33	32.86	28.78	30.10	8.65
Malawi	47.12	40.87	48.28	30.92	41.83	45.24	41.46	35.92	26.44
Mali	48.08	54.33	39.90	51.21	50.48	7.62	16.59	23.79	17.79
Mauritania	23.08	20.19	23.15	55.07	24.52	22.86	48.29	16.50	13.94
Mauritius	78.85	72.60	72.41	71.01	76.44	79.52	69.76	77.18	80.77
Morocco	33.65	26.44	28.08	38.16	25.96	34.76	54.63	48.54	50.48
Mozambique	44.71	46.15	37.93	38.65	56.25	26.19	39.51	37.86	23.08
Namibia	57.21	59.62	67.49	33.33	92.79	66.67	60.98	60.68	64.42
Niger	45.67	32.21	39.41	44.93	24.04	15.24	11.22	26.70	30.77
Nigeria	30.29	27.40	33.00	8.70	5.29	5.71	14.63	15.53	16.83
Rwanda	7.21	10.58	17.24	5.31	33.65	44.29	27.80	50.00	51.44
S.Tome & Principe	60.58	52.88	57.64	82.61	51.44	53.81	36.10	29.13	22.60
Senegal	51.44	40.38	57.14	25.12	38.94	40.00	51.71	50.97	38.94
Seychelles	52.88	48.56	49.75	88.89	71.63	68.10	55.12	57.77	68.75
Sierra Leone	6.25	43.27	36.95	4.35	37.50	43.33	4.39	10.68	9.62
Somalia	1.92	2.40	1.48	2.42	0.00	1.90	0.49	0.00	0.00
South Africa	70.19	63.94	68.97	35.75	45.67	38.57	75.61	69.42	64.90
South Sudan	#N/A	#N/A	6.40	#N/A	#N/A	2.38	#N/A	#N/A	0.48
Sudan	3.37	6.25	3.45	0.97	1.92	4.29	9.27	8.25	6.25
Swaziland	9.62	12.98	11.33	40.58	40.87	29.52	26.34	24.76	34.13
Tanzania	32.21	43.75	40.39	22.71	37.98	30.48	40.49	38.35	31.25
Togo	12.50	17.31	39.52	31.88	38.46	39.52	7.80	3.40	11.06
Tunisia	27.88	11.06	19.05	56.52	49.04	19.05	71.22	66.02	49.04
Uganda	18.75	32.69	20.00	11.59	17.31	20.00	40.98	34.95	37.02
Zambia	32.69	42.31	51.43	41.55	60.10	51.43	17.07	25.73	33.17
Zimbabwe	17.31	7.21	25.71	10.63	13.46	25.71	22.93	4.37	11.54

Source: The Worldwide Governance Indicators 2018 Update

effectiveness. The numbers are worldwide percentile rankings. For example, a ranking of 35 says that only 35% of all the countries in the world performed worse than the country on that indicator. From the table, Mauritius, Botswana, Cape Verde, and Namibia are top performers on all three indicators. South Africa has also been performing well in terms of voice and accountability and government effectiveness, but poorly on political stability and violence, while Seychelles has also ranked high in political stability and violence and government effectiveness but low on voice and accountability. However, the majority of African countries fall in the lower percentile group. With respect to WGI's regulatory quality, rule of law, and control of corruption, African countries were worse off, with the exception of Botswana and Mauritius and to some extent South Africa and Cape Verde (Table 9.4). Countries within the 50th percentile range with respect to regulatory quality included Ghana, Namibia, and Rwanda. With respect to rule of law, they were Cape Verde, Ghana, Morocco, Namibia, Rwanda, and Lesotho. In terms of control of corruption, the 60th percentile group included Rwanda, Seychelles, Namibia, Senegal, Tunisia, Ghana, Sao Tome & Principe, and Morocco. Table 9.5 shows the IIAG in rank order. The index ranges from a low of 1 to a high of 100. Once again, the top countries in 2015 were Mauritius, Botswana, Cape Verde, Seychelles, Namibia, and South Africa. The table also shows a 6-year change, with some countries changing for the better and others for the worse. These indicators show that while African countries have made progress, they are still confronted with some major political and governance issues. The next section addresses a selection of these issues, bearing in mind that the extent and severity of these issues vary across the continent.

TABLE **9.4**

Governance Measures of African Countries: Regulatory Quality, Rule of Law, and Control of Corruption, 2000–2015

Country	Regulatory quality			Rule of law			Control of corruption		
	2000	**2008**	**2015**	**2000**	**2008**	**2015**	**2000**	**2008**	**2015**
Algeria	23.04	21.36	10.58	12.44	27.88	20.67	14.15	33.98	28.37
Angola	3.92	16.02	17.79	1.91	6.73	12.02	2.44	4.85	3.85
Benin	40.69	34.95	30.77	43.06	35.58	32.21	37.56	36.89	30.77
Botswana	71.57	64.56	68.27	64.59	70.19	73.08	75.12	80.10	77.40
Burkina Faso	46.57	49.51	41.83	31.10	44.71	34.13	54.63	45.15	47.12
Burundi	12.25	9.22	27.40	2.87	14.90	11.54	9.76	13.59	10.10
Cameroon	26.47	20.39	19.23	11.00	13.46	15.87	8.78	17.48	12.98
Cape Verde	53.92	52.91	45.19	69.86	66.35	70.67	62.93	75.24	78.85
Central African Rep	17.16	9.71	5.29	3.83	4.81	1.44	5.37	16.02	6.25
Chad	20.10	12.14	9.62	17.22	2.40	10.10	22.93	3.40	6.73
Comoros	10.29	3.88	12.98	7.18	13.94	20.19	6.34	24.27	30.29
Congo Demo. Rep	1.96	7.77	6.25	0.96	2.88	3.37	1.46	7.28	9.13
Congo Rep.	11.27	8.25	10.10	4.78	10.58	13.46	12.20	8.74	9.62
Cote d'Ivoire	28.92	18.45	32.69	11.96	4.33	30.29	27.32	10.19	42.31
Djibouti	21.57	27.67	28.37	24.40	35.10	18.27	14.63	52.91	33.65
Egypt	35.78	49.03	24.52	51.20	52.88	35.58	43.90	27.67	35.10
Equatorial Guinea	6.37	7.28	5.77	10.05	8.17	5.29	1.95	2.43	0.00

(*Continued*)

TABLE **9.4**

Governance Measures of African Countries: Regulatory Quality, Rule of Law, and Control of Corruption, 2000–2015 (*Continued*)

Country	Regulatory quality			Rule of law			Control of corruption		
	2000	2008	2015	2000	2008	2015	2000	2008	2015
Eritrea	15.69	1.46	1.44	36.36	9.13	4.81	73.66	46.60	5.29
Ethiopia	12.75	19.90	14.42	25.36	30.77	38.46	38.05	29.61	42.79
Gabon	43.63	28.16	24.04	46.89	32.69	33.65	36.10	14.08	28.85
Gambia	37.75	40.29	34.62	48.33	43.75	29.33	40.98	25.24	21.63
Ghana	49.02	53.40	53.37	54.55	52.40	60.58	58.05	57.28	53.37
Guinea	25.98	10.68	20.67	6.22	3.37	9.13	25.85	7.77	15.38
Guinea-Bissau	11.76	10.19	9.13	6.70	5.29	6.73	11.71	10.68	3.37
Kenya	36.76	47.57	43.27	22.97	15.87	36.54	14.15	13.11	13.46
Lesotho	34.31	28.64	39.42	53.11	49.04	50.96	56.59	60.19	60.10
Liberia	4.90	6.31	19.71	0.48	9.62	19.23	3.90	28.16	31.25
Libya	4.41	18.93	0.48	26.32	28.37	1.92	26.34	19.42	0.96
Madagascar	32.35	44.17	25.96	43.54	38.46	28.85	55.61	55.34	24.04
Malawi	40.20	35.44	23.08	34.45	51.92	44.23	52.20	41.26	23.08
Mali	49.51	39.32	30.29	37.32	45.67	25.00	29.27	40.78	29.81
Mauritania	33.33	29.13	21.15	41.15	11.54	21.15	50.24	26.70	16.35
Mauritius	69.61	74.27	82.21	79.90	83.17	77.40	72.20	73.79	67.79
Morocco	52.45	48.54	49.04	55.98	47.60	54.81	59.02	43.20	50.48
Mozambique	42.16	36.89	34.13	27.75	33.65	19.71	42.93	39.32	20.67
Namibia	61.27	56.31	50.96	57.89	60.58	61.54	70.24	73.30	65.38
Niger	25.49	37.86	26.44	21.53	25.48	30.77	16.10	23.79	33.17
Nigeria	20.59	21.84	21.63	14.83	14.42	12.98	5.85	21.36	11.06
Rwanda	13.73	33.98	60.58	7.66	37.98	60.10	30.73	62.14	75.00
Sao Tome & Principe	19.61	24.76	25.48	49.76	37.02	21.63	57.56	37.38	52.40
Senegal	46.08	44.66	48.56	52.15	47.12	51.92	57.07	36.41	59.13
Seychelles	16.18	25.24	50.48	66.99	59.13	62.02	69.76	63.59	77.88
Sierra Leone	8.82	16.50	20.19	4.31	19.71	17.79	17.07	16.50	21.15
Somalia	0.00	0.00	0.96	0.00	0.00	0.00	0.98	0.00	1.44
South Africa	64.71	65.53	63.94	55.02	54.81	59.13	73.17	62.62	58.17
South Sudan	#N/A	#N/A	2.88	#N/A	#N/A	0.96	#N/A	#N/A	0.48
Sudan	8.33	4.85	4.81	3.35	5.77	8.17	24.39	2.91	2.40
Swaziland	32.84	31.07	33.17	30.62	32.21	46.63	50.24	53.88	45.08
Tanzania	39.71	34.47	41.35	39.71	44.23	39.42	14.15	41.75	25.48
Togo	24.02	16.99	22.60	29.19	21.15	23.08	29.27	15.53	25.96
Tunisia	51.96	54.85	38.94	47.37	57.69	56.25	59.02	53.40	55.29
Uganda	55.39	47.09	46.15	26.79	41.83	43.27	20.98	20.87	12.02
Zambia	39.22	36.41	37.98	33.97	38.94	47.12	20.98	39.81	43.27
Zimbabwe	7.84	1.94	3.85	9.09	1.44	6.25	15.12	4.37	7.21

Source: The Worldwide Governance Indicators 2018 Update

TABLE **9.5**

2015 Ibrahim Index for African Governance

Rank	Country	Score	6-Year change	Rank	Country	Score	6-Year change
1	Mauritius	79.9	2.3	28	Liberia	50	8.7
2	Botswana	73.7	−0.5	29	Swaziland	49.7	1
3	Cabo Verde	73	1.9	30	Sierra Leone	49.4	3.8
4	Seychelles	72.6	4.0	31	Ethiopia	49.1	7
5	Namibia	69.8	3.6	32	Gabon	48.8	1.5
5	South Africa	69.4	−1.9	33	Madagascar	48.5	−7.6
7	Tunisia	65.4	3.4	34	Togo	48.5	9.7
8	Ghana	63.9	−2.1	35	Gambia	46.6	−3.9
9	Rwanda	62.3	8.4	36	Djibouti	46.5	2.3
10	Senegal	60.8	3.7	37	Nigeria	46.5	2.5
11	São Tomé & Príncipe	60.5	2.9	38	Cameroon	45.7	−0.1
12	Kenya	58.9	5.1	39	Zimbabwe	44.3	9.7
13	Zambia	58.8	4.3	40	Mauritania	43.5	−2.7
14	Morocco	58.3	5.7	41	Guinea	43.3	1.9
15	Lesotho	57.8	0.3	42	Congo	43	2.6
16	Benin	57.5	0.7	43	Burundi	41.9	−2.1
17	Malawi	56.6	1.1	44	Guinea-Bissau	41.3	4
18	Tanzania	56.5	−0.6	45	Angola	39.2	5
19	Uganda	56.2	3.4	46	DRC	35.8	2.7
20	Algeria	53.8	−0.6	47	Equatorial Guinea	35.4	2
21	Côte d'Ivoire	52.3	13.1	48	Chad	34.8	2.3
22	Mozambique	52.3	−1.8	49	Sudan	30.4	−0.6
23	Burkina Faso	51.8	1	50	Eritrea	30	−5.6
24	Egypt	51.0	3.5	51	Libya	29	−18
25	Mali	50.6	−4.7	52	CAR	25.7	−4.9
26	Comoros	50.3	3.7	53	South Sudan	18.6	—
27	Niger	50.2	5.9	54	Somalia	10.6	0.3

Source: 2015 Ibrahim Index of African Governance.

POLITICAL AND GOVERNANCE ISSUES IN AFRICA

Boundary Disputes

The arbitrary nature of Africa's political boundaries has posed problems for many countries since their return to independence. Consisting mainly of what Ajala (1983) calls straight lines, rivers, and watersheds, and based not on consideration of Africa's multiethnic nature but on agreement among colonial powers, these boundaries split ethnic groups between and sometimes among countries.

African leaders began addressing the issue very early in 1958, when most of the countries were still under colonial rule. At an All African People's Congress in Accra,

Ghana, a resolution denouncing the colonial boundaries, and calling for an abolition of the boundaries as well as an Independent States of Africa as a permanent solution to the problem was adopted. However, as more African countries became independent, the matter was exhaustively discussed at the Organization of African Unity (OAU)'s first meeting in May 1963, in Addis Ababa (Ajala, 1983).

Essentially, there were two views: the principle of **uti possidetis** and the **principle of self-determination**. The *principle of uti possidetis* advocated for by Nigeria and supported by Mali, Ethiopia, Kenya, and Malagasy (Madagascar) called on states to accept the borders as they were at the time of independence since any attempt to change the boundaries would create a second "Scramble of Africa" and cause too many unnecessary conflicts. In contrast, *the principle of self-determination*, championed by Ghana, and supported by Morocco and Somalia, argued that people should be free to determine their political, economic, and social future. A compromise solution was for all parties to resolve border disputes by peaceful means.

In the early postcolonial period, these principles helped to peacefully resolve border disputes between Guinea and Liberia in 1960, Liberia and Cote d'Ivoire in 1961, Mali and Mauritania in 1963, Niger and Upper Volta (Burkina Faso) in 1964, and Ghana and Upper Volta (Burkina Faso) in 1964. However, this peaceful trend was broken in 1964 by the Sand War between Morocco and Algeria over Morocco's claim of the two Algerian provinces of Tindouf and Bechar, and the Somali claim for the Ogaden and Haud regions of Ethiopia and the Northern Frontier District (FND) of Kenya (Kendie, 2003). Ethiopia and Eritrea also went to war in 1998 over the border town of Badme, which was eventually given to Eritrea, even though Ethiopia did not agree.

However, most of the subsequent boundary disputes have been peacefully resolved at the International Court of Justice (ICJ). These include: (1) the Cameroon and Nigeria border dispute over the Bakassi Peninsula, a group of oil rich islands in the Atlantic Ocean, which was ruled in favor of Cameroon (McHugh, 2005). (2) The dispute between Mali and Burkina Faso over a 100-mile strip of land in 1983. (3) The dispute over the Aouzou strip between Libya and Chad in 1990 ruled in favor of Chad. (4) Botswana and Namibia over the Kasikili/Sedudu Island (3–3.5 km²) in the Chobe River in 1996 settled in favor of Botswana in 1999, and over a second river island in the southeastern Caprivi Strip in 1997, also ruled in favor of Botswana in 2003 (Le Roux 1998, 1999). (5) Benin and Niger boundary along the Niger and the Mekrou Rivers in 2001, which was settled in 2005. (6) The boundary between the Sudan and South Sudan, even though the agreement was not reached until a long and protracted war. Current boundary disputes include the Lemi Triangle between Sudan and Kenya, the Nadapal between Kenya and South Sudan, and the Lake Malawi dispute between Tanzania and Malawi. Boundary disputes will always be present in Africa given the nature of its boundaries. However, it appears that resolving such disputes before the International Court of Justice is the best way to go.

The Land Question

The predominant customary tenure system in precolonial Africa was the communal land system. In that system, all land was vested in the village or town chief. In the societies that had no chiefs such as the Tiv of Nigeria, land allocation was made by a compound elder (Venatus, 2010). Land was not a saleable property since it belonged to the community. However, once a family had cultivated a particular piece of land, that property would reside in the family or clan and could be passed down to descendants. New households would receive their land allocation from the family or clan reserves. Unallocated land belonged to the community and was accessible to all for grazing, hunting, and forestry (Kalabamu, 2000). In some ethnic groups such as the Akan of Ghana, the Mossi of Burkina Faso, the Yoruba of Nigeria, and the Buganda of Uganda, there were also stool or skin lands. These lands were given to individuals to work on in return for payment of royalties or homage (Oppong, 2003).

Colonialism changed these customary arrangements. Through a series of so-called "agreements," proclamations, and conquests, colonial powers appropriated Africa's lands. This was particularly extensive in Southern Africa (South Africa, Zimbabwe, Namibia, Mozambique, and Angola), Kenya, Cote d'Ivoire, and in North Africa (Egypt, Algeria, and Libya) (African Union 2010; Moyo, 2008). Land became divided into European land and native reserves with Africans becoming tenants on their own land (Kalabamu 2000; Moyo, 2008; Silungwe, 2009). The European lands were allocated to individual European settlers while the rest were declared government land. In the native reserves of North, East, and Southern Africa, and across British West Africa, the policy of indirect rule modified the customary system into a quasi-ownership and control system in which the land was still administered by the existing or imposed chiefs, but on behalf of the colonial power instead of the community. The concept of land ownership to the extent that land could be transferred through market mechanism was introduced into Africa.

The result is that at the return to independence African countries had two broad land tenure systems: the traditional customary system and the so-called modern land tenure system. The **traditional land tenure systems** included the family, communal, and stool or skin lands already discussed. The modern land tenure systems included the private and public lands. The public lands were vested in the state, while private lands were vested in individuals, who had purchased the land and may have freehold rights, outright ownership, or lease rights, which usually spanned from 49 to 99 years (Oppong, 2003). African countries have since struggled with land reforms trying to strike a balance between the customary and modern tenure systems. These efforts have followed three main approaches, namely land redistribution, land restitution, and tenure reforms (Kalabamu, 2000). **Land redistribution** provides land rights to disadvantaged people to enable them gain access to land. **Land restitution** gives land back to communities that were deprived of their land rights, while **tenure reforms** revise, change, or modify the rules of access, use, ownership, and transfer of land rights (Bruce, 1998; Carey-Miller, 1998; Kalabamu, 2000).

In Egypt, Algeria, Libya, Tanzania, Zambia, Mozambique, and Angola, land redistribution took the form nationalization of settler and foreign corporate lands. Kenya, Swaziland, Botswana, and Zimbabwe followed land acquisitions through market-based compensation. Other countries have pursued various land reform efforts including titling or appropriation for cash crop production (African Union et al., 2010). In spite of these, land remains one of the main sources of tension in many African countries. In former settler colonies such as Kenya, Zimbabwe, and South Africa, the inability to resolve historic claims in the colonial era and the continued unequal redistribution of land after independence is a major source of conflict (see the case of Zimbabwe in Box 9.1). In mineral-rich countries such as DRC, South Sudan, Sierra Leone, and Liberia, control over land motivated by global commercial interests have become a major source of tension resulting in protracted wars and untold human suffering, including large numbers of internally displaced populations, who then could not get access to land.

In recognition of this and other roles that land plays in the economies and livelihoods of African countries, the African Union organized a workshop on land

Box 9.1 | Zimbabwe's Land Question

The Zimbabwe land question began in 1888 when the British imperialist and empire builder, Cecil Rhodes obtained mining rights from King Lobengula of the Ndebele people. When Lobengula found that he had been duped, he repudiated the concession, but Rhodes used it to justify his sending a Pioneer Column protected by soldiers of his British South African Company (BASC) into Matabeleland in 1890. When the mineral wealth failed to meet expectations, the venture became a land grabbing and speculation project. Rhodes and his BASC seized 1.5 million acres of the best land and allocated them to the white settlers, leaving the marginal lands to the surviving Africans (Pomeroy, 2000). After defeating the Ndebele people in 1893–1894, and again in 1897, the BASC became owners of territory and named it Rhodesia.

In 1918, in a case of over land ownership, the Privy Council of Britain affirmed the titles of land ownership given by the BASC and ruled that the African natives had lost their land rights through conquest (Chavunduka and Bromley, 2010). In 1930, the division of land between the colony's two races was formalized by the Land Apportionment Act, which divided into white areas and African areas. It allocated 51% of the total land area to the 50,000 whites and only 29.8% to over a million Africans (Mlambo, 2008). To perpetuate this state of affairs, the white minority group led by Ian Smith, unilaterally declared Southern Rhodesia independent in 1963, when they sensed that Britain was going to grant independence to the colony. During the 1960s and 1970s, also large numbers of African families were removed from the central districts of the country in order to create ranches for white farmers, without any compensation. The long-armed struggle that followed between the white minority regime and the black majority was all about keeping their land for the white and gaining back the land for the blacks. Even so, the negotiation for independence in 1980 made sure that white-owned lands would not change hands unless it was through purchase at a high price for the first 10 years (Pomeroy, 2000).

During the first decade of the country's independence, the program of buying land from white farmers with funds from international donors, particularly Britain, worked. However, in 1997, the program ran into difficulties because of the British government's reluctance to bear the responsibility for the program and allegations of misuse of the funds by other donors. By 1999, the promise of land for the rural poor had not been fulfilled while 11 million hectares of rich agricultural land were still in the hands of 4,500 mostly white commercial farmers. This led to large-scale land occupations in 1997 and 1998, organized by the Zimbabwe War Veteran Association (WVA). Increasing pressure by the WVA forced the government to promise a Z$50,000 one-time pay-off for each veteran and on Z$2,000 per month pension for life, while it was not clear how the government was going to meet these obligations.

The situation became worse when the economy turned sour due to the failure of structural adjustment programs causing high unemployment and massive inflation. Demand for economic and political reforms by civil society generated a national debate resulting in the formation of a new political party, the Movement of National Democratic Change (MDC) in 1999. MDV promised "people-driven land reform" and promised to purchase 6–7 million hectares of underutilized, derelict, and multiple owned lands for resettlement.

The government responded by reviving the call for rapid land redistribution thereby sanctioning a new wave of land occupations across the country, changing part of the constitution to give itself more powers to enforce land-related laws, and by attacking MDV members. In 2000, the government officially announced the Land Reform Fast Track (LRFT) program with the aim to compulsory acquisition of about 8.3 million hectares commercial farms for redistribution. Further laws were passed to legalize occupations that did not follow proper procedures and set aside court orders for eviction. In addition, they made transfer of land immediate and served a 90-day notice to the previous owner with up to two years of imprisonment if the owner failed to comply. Zimbabwe's commercial farmers union (CFU) reacted by challenging the law and policies in court, some of which were successful, but that did not stop the process. It also negotiated with the government and transferred 562 farms to the government but that did not stop fast-track land occupations. By 2002, about 1,000 commercial farms had closed. Initial evaluation of the program was largely negative. However, recent reviews have been positive.

Zimbabwe's land reform activities have generated a lot of debate among scholars and in the international community. There are many who have criticized and vilified Robert Mugabe, the former Zimbabwean president, for breaking international law of property rights and human dignity and for destroying the country. There are others who support him saying that the Europeans stole the land in the first place, so it is right for them to return the land to the rightful owners. Whichever way, Zimbabwe must find a way to resolve the land question if it is going to see improvements in the living conditions of its people. What do you think?

Source: Pomeroy, W. 2000. "Colonial Land Question Still Haunts Zimbabwe." *People's Weekly World* April 15.

Mlambo, A. S. 2010. "This Is Our Land": The Racialization of Land in the Context of the Current Zimbabwe Crisis." *Journal of Developing Societies* 26(1): 39–69.

Fast Track Land Reform in Zimbabwe www.hrw.org/reports/2002/**zimbabwe**/ (accessed 10 June 2013).

policy framework in 2006 and developed a Framework and Guidelines on Land Policy in Africa, which was accepted at by the African Heads of State and their 2009 Summit. The document offers a basis for commitment by African countries to formulate sound land policies based on popular participation that address current and emerging land issues for sustainable human development (African Union et al., 2010). There is not much that one can disagree with the document but whether this has brought about any change at all is hard to tell.

Democratic Multiparty Elections

Democratic multiparty elections have been advancing in more African countries since the 1990s. However, free and fair elections remain an issue in many African countries. The powerful presidential role guaranteed by the constitutions of African countries still threatens true democratic elections in Africa, because presidents can use their power to manipulate elections. For example, in Nigeria's 2007 elections, the outgoing President Olusegun Obasanjo first tried to amend the constitution to enable him run for a third time, but when that failed, he sought to manipulate the election outcome to his advantage and that of his People's Democratic Party (PDP). He replaced his closet rival in the party leadership, Vice President Abubakar Atiku, with his own hand-picked loyalist Yar' Adua as PDP's nominee (Suberu, 2010). He appointed his favorites to the Independent National Election Committee (INEC) as well as the Economic and Financial Crimes Commission (EFCC). The INEC failed its constitutional duties of conducting voter education and regulating campaign financing. It also failed to provide biometric Direct Data Capture (DDC) machines on time, which disenfranchised many people due to delays in registration and verification (Suberu, 2010). The elections were fraught with major problems. In opposition party strongholds voter lists were poorly matched, polling officials and materials were late or did not arrive at all; and ballots were fewer than registered voters. In addition, there were fewer results sheets, not enough ink for thumb printing, lighting, and a lack of security to ensure transparency in the counting, recording, transmitting, and announcing the results. Some ballot boxes disappeared, while others were stuffed with premarked ballots. In many areas, the process was so bad that the opposition party virtually boycotted the elections. Violence broke out in many states leading to loss of about 200 lives including 39 police officers. The opposition party won a number of gubernatorial seats but overall the election dashed the hope of many Nigerians that their country was finally getting back on track in democratic elections.

In Zambia's 2001 elections, President Chiluba instituted programs to sell government-owned houses to tenants at very favorable prices and to find new homes for traditional chiefs. He also bribed the former president as well as traditional chiefs, with cars, bicycles, and clothing. The 2008 elections were similarly plagued with fraud and manipulation, which among other things, disenfranchised 500,000 new Zambian voters (Baldwin, 2010).

Sometimes manipulation and rigging of democratic elections have also resulted in open conflict and violence. For example, in 1991, the Algerian military cancelled the country's parliamentary elections and banned the leading party for fear that the party (Islamist) would win the presidential elections. This triggered a 10-year civil war between militant Islamists and government security forces (Willis, 2012). In 2007, Kenya's elections turned violent when Kibaki, the incumbent president, was hurriedly sworn in without resolving allegations of election fraud and rigging. The opposition Orange Democratic Party (ODM) reacted swiftly targeting the Kikuyu, Kibaki's ethnic group, living in the Rift Valley, and murdering hundreds of them as well as destroying their properties. The Kikuyu in Nairobi fought back against the supporters of ODM, which included the Luo, Lahya, and the Kalenjin ethnic groups, leading to more than 1,000 people dead and 30,000 displaced (Chege 2010; Kiai, 2010). In Cote d'Ivoire, the refusal of the incumbent President Laurent Gbagbo to accept the results of the November 2010 elections in favor of his opponent Alassane Quattara, led to explosion of violence from December 2010 through May 2011.

In contrast to these bad cases of elections, several African countries have established good records for multiparty democratic elections. Among these are Botswana, Ghana (see Box 9.2), South Africa, Mauritius, Senegal, and Madagascar. In these countries, contested elections have resulted in peaceful transitions although in the case of Botswana there has been actually no transition because the same party has ruled the country since independence. The record of these countries, as well as the removal of Robert Mugabe from power by Zimbabweans in 2017 and Jacob Zuma by South Africans in 2018, gives some hope for the future of the democratic movement on the continent. Yet, there is a danger of democratic movements becoming what Roque (2010) has referred to as "merely ornamental—the trappings of democracy without substance; a political system that is still authoritarian, exclusive, and hegemonic but with a veneer of democracy."

For democratic movement to take hold in Africa, multiparty elections must be free and fair. This requires an objective and independent media that will inform the public about the choices before them. The public needs to be educated about the fact that national elections transcend ethnic affiliations; they are about policy platforms. A free and fair election also requires an independent and objective electoral commissioner to reduce the incidence of manipulation and rigging. Constitutions must allow the courts sufficient time to investigate allegations of manipulation, fraud, and rigging before swearing in a new government. Finally, it requires politicians and their supporters to accept the results of elections as the people's verdict, and gracefully accept defeat in elections.

Box 9.2 | Ghana's 2008 Election

Having won its independence in 1957, the small West African country of Ghana was a trail blazer of the African independence movement that swept the sub-Saharan section of the continent in the 1960s. However, within nine years the model country to show that the black man was capable of taking care of his own affairs was in trouble and the government was overthrown by a military coup. From 1966 to 1992, Ghana was under military rule except for six years of civilian government from 1969 to 1972, and 1979 to 1981. In 1992, however, Ghana entered its Fourth Republic with a democratic election. By 2008, three successful parliamentary and presidential elections in 1996, 2000, and 2004 each associated with smooth transitions of government had established Ghana as a beacon among Africa's new democracies. However, given the troubled elections in Nigeria, Kenya, Zimbabwe, Cote d'Ivoire, and Senegal, the stakes were still high for Ghana's scheduled elections in 2008.

A total of seven parties contested the election but essentially, the election was a contest between the two leading parties—the ruling New Patriotic Party (NPP) led by Nana Akufo-Addo and the leading opposing National Democratic Congress (NDC), led by John Atta Mills. According to Gyimah-Boadi (2010), the two leading parties had both positive and negative records so the campaign was quite intense. The publications of party manifestos made the election more of an issue based, and except for a few glitches such as limited time to resolve irregularities and local disputes, leading to sporadic violence in the north of the country; everything went smoothly on Election Day—December 7, 2008. NPP won 49.1% while NDC won 47.8% of the votes, and since no party secured a majority of the vote (i.e. more than 50%) required by the constitution, a run-off was required.

The atmosphere on the election run-off day was tense with several reports of intimidation and harassment on both sides. The initial results announced by the Electoral Commissioner was a deadlock since no party had won enough votes to be the winner. As a result, the whole country had to wait for one constituency—Tain in the Brong Ahafo Region—which had not been able

to take part in the run-off due to logistic reasons. In the meantime, both parties petitioned the Electoral Commissioner to investigate reports of irregularities, with the NPP filing an injunction to stop the polling in Tain district and announcement of final results until the irregularities in the Volta Region, NDCs stronghold had been fully investigated. When the results came in, NDC had won by only 40,586 votes out of the 9,001,478 votes cast (0.6%). Nana Akuffo-Addo conceded defeat, and on January 7, 2009, John Atta Mills was sworn in as President, with no postelection violence as it had occurred in Kenya, and the postelection tug-of-war of Zimbabwe.

Gyimah-Boadi (2010) attributes this rare peaceful transition to a number of factors. The first was the professionalism and strength displayed by the Electoral Commission and the law courts of Ghana. The Electoral Commission stood firm in the face of tremendous and furious attacks. The courts expeditiously did their job. The second was the role of the outgoing President John Kuffour. Although his party won the first round of elections but lost the second round, he refused to declare a state of emergency in the face of looming violence, when others were calling for that. He instead urged all the presidential candidates not to take to the streets but accept the election results as authentic. The third was the role played by Ghana's civil society including religious, secular, and professional organizations. For example, they helped voter education through sponsoring of televised presidential and vice presidential debates and provided a forum for parliamentary candidates to meet with their constituencies. The media also helped to inform voters of various party platforms and kept the public informed as the results started coming in. The fourth was the support from international community including foreign diplomats in Ghana, UNDP, and international election observers. Ghana's example shows that even contentious election results need not result in violence.

Source: Gyimah-Boadi, E. 2010 "Another Step for Ghana." In Diamond, L., and Plattner, M. F. (Eds.) *Democratization in Africa: Progress and Retreat.* 2nd edition. Baltimore: The Johns Hopkins University Press, pp. 137–151.

Civil Society, Citizen Representation, and Accountability

The role of civil society in politics and governance cannot be overemphasized (Nwachukwu, 2009). The stronger the civil society, the better it will be able to prevent government attempts to restrict democratic principles (Peterson, 2010). While civil society has played a major role in the democratic movement in many African countries, civil society is not always free in every African country. For example, in Tanzania, the activities of NGOs are restricted to economic development—that is, activities aimed at raising standard of or eradication of poverty (Hoffman and Robinson, 2010). Similarly, in Angola, civil society cannot work independently but only in agreement with the government. Many existing legislations allow African governments to scrutinize activities of NGOs and impose fines or suspension if the organization is found to be deviating from its original charter. Such actions may be needed because in some cases NGOs have been accused of representing external interests more than internal matters of the countries since the organizations derive much of their funding from external sources (Kaldor 2003; Mkandawire, 2010).

In many African countries, the legislature has been accused of serving themselves, passing legislation to increase and protect their interests irrespective of the conditions of their constituents. In Kenya, Kiai (2010, p. 214) reports of legislators perks that include:

> an almost nontaxable salary of $150,000 a year, interest-free mortgages; subsidies to buy $50,000-cars; . . . lifetime pensions of $4,000 a month after serving five years; and a gratuity payment of $22,000 at the end of each five year term (perhaps to help fund their election campaigns) . . . Let us not forget that Kenya has a GNP of about $600 per person per year, and more than 40% of all Kenyans live on less than a dollar a day. Kenya ranks in the bottom 25 countries in the Development Index of the United Nations Development Programme (UNDP) while its legislators' perks ranks among the top five countries in the world.

This behavior of elected officials is encouraged by lack of governmental accountability to the citizens who voted for them. The legislature, whose duty is to hold presidents accountable, often does not have the constitutional power to do so. Sometimes the power of the legislature is weakened by presidential and party benefits, which are especially very attractive at the cabinet level.

There are various explanations for the lack of accountability in Africa. For example, the taxation theory of accountability says that there is a relationship between taxation and accountability. The theory describes two types of economies—the "rentier economy" and the "merchant economy." The former is an economy that derives much of its revenue from the extraction of a limited number of natural resources, while the latter refers to an economy that derives its revenue from a large array of economic activities and segments of its citizens (Mkandawire, 2010). Since governments in rentier economies often do not have to rely on citizens for revenue, there is often a mismatch between the regime and the citizens in terms of accountability. In contrast, because the merchant economies rely more on citizens, there is more accountability. Extending this theory to African economies, it is argued that because the majority of African economies rely on foreign aid to make their budget expenditures, they are more accountable to such external entities as The World Bank and the IMF than to their own citizens (Adibe, 2010 and Mkandawire, 2010).

The problem of accountability is further complicated by the meaning of leadership in Africa and the attitude of the public. Agulanna (2006) argues that leaders do not only lead, they also serve, and this aspect of leadership appears to be missing in many African leaders. Instead, they adopt the patronizing and colonial mentality as overlords in dealing with their people. Leaders should put the welfare of the people they serve first. Instead, Africa has had its fair share of selfish leaders whose main reason for getting into political leadership position was to amass wealth for themselves and family at the expense of the people.

This goes on because of the attitude of the public. As Mwenda (2010) also notes in the case of Uganda, both the lower and the middle classes in many African countries have failed in their civic duties. With respect to the lower class, the general attitude has been to ignore the government and do whatever it needs to survive. For example, if prices of their cash crops are hit by higher taxes, they withdraw production and resort to subsistence farming, rather than complain to the government. Similarly, the middle class of Africa has failed in forming a political pressure group. In most cases, they have resorted to one of several options—(1) ignore the government and go about their own affairs; (2) join a local branch of an international NGO; and (3) leave the country for greener pastures, or become part of the problem. Both Adibe (2010) and Mkandawire (2010) have called on the international community to use its influence to help establish the culture of accountability in Africa, but ultimately if African politicians are going to be accountable, it must come from within. The people of Africa must demand it.

Rule of Law and Access to Justice

Rule of law, the protection of individual freedom and rights against the state, the right to impartial trial, and to be presumed innocent until proven guilty before a properly constituted court, in postcolonial Africa are still problematic. This is despite the fact that all African countries guarantee these rights in their constitutions and charges the judiciary to ensure them. Taiwo (2011) attributes this to the fear of the judiciary to hold the executive and legislative branches of government accountable against citizens and an executive branch that is not willing to uphold the rule of law and submit itself to it. He argues that for the most part the judiciary has been found complicit in subverting citizens rather than protecting them from the government. Rarely do African governments lose cases against citizens, and when they do so they resort to intimidation of judges including dismissal, or efforts to corral and silence judges. The need for the judiciary to rely on the executive branch to enforce its rulings and the lack of financial independence have added to the courts ineffectiveness and loss of moral authority.

Like the land question, the roots of much of this problem have been traced into colonialism. Precolonial Africa had two sets of laws—Islamic law or Sharia in North Africa and other Islamic domain and customary law for the rest of the continent. Colonialism imposed European laws, which to all intents and purposes were applied selectively (McKinnon, 2006). The rule of law and human rights applied only when offenses were against the colonial powers and citizens, but not the other way around. This is borne out by how colonial powers treated Africans in their respective colonies. It was only on the eve of independence that the rule of law and respect for human rights were hurriedly added to the constitutions (McKinnon, 2006). Most African countries thus had to operate a judiciary system that was alien at its core and required expertise that they did not have. In addition, the learning process of the system was curtailed by the one-party system and the military rule that dominated the politics of the majority of the countries from the mid-1960s through the 1980s.

Another face of the state as far as the rule of law and individual rights and protections are concerned is the law enforcement—the police. African countries have had a record of police brutality and corruption to a point that the public has lost confidence in them (Francis, 2012). So rather than reporting crimes and offenses to them, people either do not go to the police or take matters into their hands in dealing with crime.

Access to justice also continues to be unequal in African countries. From the hands of autocratic and authoritarian civilian and military regimes and the tyranny of civil wars and ethnic conflict, the weak, the vulnerable, and the poor among Africa's societies have been subjected to some of the most unspeakable acts of abuses in the contemporary world. Detention without trial and sometimes disappearance of political opponents, the brutalization by government security forces of people who stand up to speak against government excesses, and the intimidation of the working poor, the amputation of children and adults limbs, and senseless genocide are a few examples of these abuses that have occurred in some African countries. Even in situations where Special Courts are established to deal with people who have committed hideous crimes against the state, the pace had been very slow especially where the accused were prominent people or their relatives. In Sierra Leone for example, it took four years for the Special Court to hand down its first verdict about the perpetrators of the civil war that maimed thousands of children. As Wyrod (2010) reports, in some cases trials had outlasted the indicted—such as Foday Sankoh and Sam Bockarie. Things are no better with regular courts and enforcement of customary laws. Court officials and local chiefs are equally corrupt denying justice to many people especially the poor.

In Kenya, for example, Human Rights Watch (2012) reported that the planners and perpetrators of the 2007 and 2008 postelection violence, especially those attributed to security forces had not been punished. The few cases that were tried did not involve the people who had been believed to have caused most of the killings and rapes. The government continued to deny the extrajudicial killings, torture, and disappearances that occurred in the period.

The only time the rule of law seems to work is when it involves a prominent member of the opposition party. Unfortunately, in some cases the charges are false. In Ethiopia, for example, Human Rights Watch (2012) reported the arrest of more than 200 members and supporters of the Oromo Federal Democratic Movement (OFDM) and the Oromo People's Congress (OPC), in 2011. All of them were accused of aligning with the Oromo Liberation Front (OLF), which the Ethiopian government has labeled as a terrorist group. Leaders of other political parties such as the Vice Chairman of the party Unity for Democracy and Justice (UDI) were arrested on similar charges. In Swaziland, Human Rights Watch (2012) reported a case where the Chief Justice dismissed another judge for insubordination and for insulting the king. Before his dismissal, the judge was summoned before a six-member Judicial Services Commission, which was appointed by the king.

Neopatrimonialism, Venality, and Corruption

As already defined, neopatrimonialism is a practice whereby formal institutions are bent to work for interests of government officials (Hyden, 2000). Venality is lack of integrity or honesty that makes one susceptible to bribery, while corruption is misuse of public office to benefit oneself. It includes all forms of behavior from extortion of bribes from people seeking government services, misappropriation of public funds, nepotism, and illegal taxation of private exchange (Mbaku, 2007). Neopatrimonialism breeds venality and corruption, because people who do not have contacts and insiders in the establishment cannot get anything done unless they are willing to cough out something.

The need for bureaucratic reform cannot be overemphasized here. African governments need to reform some of the bureaucratic structures that seem to serve the interest of the people in power and their networks of families and friends more than the public at large. As Olowu (2000) points out, the two sets of public sector reforms that had taken place in Africa in the 1990s, namely indigenization and structural adjustment program, were both wrong-headed. None of them focused on building the capacity of the public sector to be professional, efficient, and effective in terms of serving the people rather than the political elite and the executive branch of government. Reforms that are needed are those that make the public sector more accountable to the public; a legislature that is a bit more independent from the executive branch, a more decentralized public service, and a reaffirmation of ethical practices of the public sector. In particular, there is an urgent need to establish a professional public service that is meritorious in its hiring personnel practices, nonpartisan, anonymous, and representative of all the various segments of the people it is supposed to serve (Olowu, 2000).

Corruption researchers distinguish among different types of corruption. The one that is relevant to Africa is the distinction between systemic and opportunistic or individualized corruption (Meagher and Thomas, 2004). **Systemic corruption** is when corruption is so pervasive that government institutions including the police, judiciary, legislature, and the electoral system have all been compromised. **Individualized** or **opportunistic** corruption is the opposite. The corruption in most African countries tends to be more systemic than opportunistic. The frightening thing is that bribery and corruption have become institutionalized in the majority of African countries because the public that is subjected to this treatment has accepted them as the normal way of doing business.

The causes of corruption in Africa are varied. Some attribute it to soft state, incompetence and inefficiency, chronic poverty and material deprivation, and cultural attributes. Others classify the causes into—structural and individual—the former relating to state and its institutions and the latter relating to incentive structures for state or public officials including discretionary authority, temptation or salaries, monitoring and supervision, sanctions, and rent-seeking behavior.

Solving the corruption problem has followed four main approaches—namely societal, legal, market, and political strategies (Gillespie and Okruhlik, 1991). The societal approach involves defining an acceptable moral standard, educating the public, and calling on civil society to be vigilant to report corrupt behavior. The legal approach involves passing legislation on corruption and corrupt behavior, expecting civil society to report corrupt cases, the police to investigate and bring charges, and the judiciary to prosecute and impose appropriate penalties if convicted. The market approach involves reducing government regulation of the market in order to reduce barriers or obstacles that usually force private businesses and individuals to pay bribes. The political approach involves decentralizing power and making public sector more transparent.

Mbaku (2007, p. 143) argues that these traditional approaches to dealing with corruption are fraught with problems because, to be successful, "each strategy depends on the effectiveness and professionalism of the country's counteracting institutions (e.g., the police, judiciary, and the mass media)." However, that is not the case. First, many African countries do not have a strong private media that can investigate and expose corrupt practices. Second, the judiciary systems are not completely independent from the executive branch. Third, all governmental institutions were colonial handovers and were not designed to serve the needs of the public. Finally, all existing institutions are themselves corrupt and therefore are not in a position to do self-cleaning. As a result, Mbaku (2007) offers a public choice approach that argues that public officials have self-interested behavior that results in corrupt practices. What is required are new institutions and new rules that move this self-interest behavior of public officials toward public-interest behavior. These include "an independent judiciary, a well-constrained police force, a professional and neutral military, an independent central bank, and a free press (Mbaku, 2007, p. 144).

The call for bureaucratic reforms and new institutions as well as new rules is in order. The problem, however, is bureaucracies, institutions, and new rules do not operate themselves. They require people to make them work and if society's attitude to corruption does not change, an independent judiciary, a well-constrained police force, and an independent central bank will only exist on paper. This is the central argument of what Adjibolosoo (1993) refers to as the human factor perspective. This perspective defines the human factor as the set of personality characteristics and other dimensions of human performance that allows political, economic, and social institutions to function and remain functional over time. For Adjibolosoo, the human factor characteristics go beyond human capital, which is knowledge and skills obtained through education and training. Instead, the human factor includes dedication, honesty, accountability, and responsibility and ability to sustain the rule of law, a just legal system, and respect for human dignity. Unless, people operating Africa's institutions not only possess but also practice these virtues, no amount of institutional reforms will get the job done. Two cases that illustrate these points are Kenya's 2017 elections and the removal of South African president Jacob Zuma from power. After its 2007 election crises, Kenya promulgated a new constitution that most Kenyans believed would prevent such crises from happening again. Yet, the 2017 elections and the political circus that followed proved that constitutions are mere pieces of paper without the backing of the will of the citizens to make it work. In contrast, the removal of Jacob Zuma as the President of South African due to charges of corruption and violation of the constitution in 2018 proves the power of the institutions when backed by the will of the people.

Civil Wars

We have noted the increasing number of civil wars in Africa over the past few decades in previous sections of this book, albeit such incidents have been limited to a relatively few countries. The causes of these wars have been attributed to such factors as political ideology, personal rivalries, ethnicity control over resources, external influences, all of which can be related to governance issues.

Political Ideology and Personal Rivalries

Ideological differences and personal rivalries among political leaders of countries have been a cause of disagreement in African countries, since the late colonial and early postcolonial period. When personal egos make such differences irreconcilable, the result has been civil wars. Examples include Tunisia, Algeria, Congo DRC, Angola, Chad, and Liberia.

In Tunisia, Habib Bourguiba the Neo-Destour party president, and Sala Ben Youssef, the party secretary disagreed on the terms of Tunisian independence in the mid-1950s (Willis, 2012). Bourguiba, accepted a French plan in 1955 that granted autonomy as a step toward Tunisia's full independence, but Salah Ben Youssef, denounced the agreement and criticized Bourguiba in public. The disagreement resulted in Youssef's expulsion from the party to which Youssef responded by declaring war on Bourguiba, which was ended with French intervention and Youssef's exile.

In Algeria, the *Fronte de Liberation Nationale* (FLN), the movement that had fought for Algerian independence, consisted of several subgroups: a Provisional Government group (GPRA) that had been formed in exile; six regional military commands that had fought the war inside the country; a liberation army (ALN) formed by Algerians in exile in Morocco and Tunisia, and a Federation for National Liberation (FFFNL). An umbrella organization, the National Council for Algerian Revolution (CNRA) was formed to set up political institutions for the new country. However, at a conference in Tripoli, the GPRA asserted itself as the right body to rule the country and dismissed Houare Boumediene, the Chief of Staff of the ALN. When the other subgroups opposed the move, war broke out between the ALN and pro-GPRA forces, in August 1962, claiming over 1,000 lives before GPRA was defeated in September 1962.

In Angola, the Alvor Agreement that set up the coalition government of the three parties that had pushed for independence and transition timetable fell apart in November 1975, when Agostinho Neto's Popular Movement for the Liberation of Angola (MPLA) declared Angola independence. Jonas Savimbi's Union for Total Independence of Angola (UNITA) responded with his own declaration of independence—the Social Democratic Republic of Angola with Huambo as its capital. Holden Roberto's National Front for the Liberation of Angola (FNLA) followed suit with its Democratic Republic of Angola with Ambriz as its capital. In 1976, with most of the country under MPLA, the Organization of African Unity recognized Neto and the MPLA as the legitimate government of Angola. However, UNITA and FNLA refused to recognize the government. This began a 27-year long civil war that ended in February 2002, with the death of Savimbi and his other top leaders. An estimated 500,000 people died in the war (Roque, 2010).

In Chad, the National Liberation Front (FROLINAT), an opposition group to President Tombalbye's regime spilt into several factions, including the *Forces Armees du Nord* (FAN) led by Hissein Habre and *Forces Armees Popularies* (FAP) led by Gukuni Wedei, after the assassination of the President. By 1979, these factions plus Libya's geopolitical ambitions had split Chad into four almost autonomous territories (Azevedo and Nnadozie, 1998; Azevedo, 1998; Burr and Collins, 2006). After efforts to broker an agreement through the establishment of a Traditional Government of National Union (GUNT) failed, disagreements between Wedei and Habre exploded into an open war in Ndjamena from March 16 to December 16, 1980, which ended in Habre's defeat and exile. However, the war continued for the next nine years until the former commander of Habre's forces—Idriss Deby overthrew his former boss and gained control of the country in 1989 (Burr and Collins, 2006).

In Liberia, the National Patriotic Front of Liberia (NPLF) that had been formed in 1989 by Charles Taylor and Yomie Johnson to oppose the brutal rule of Samuel Doe became engaged in a power struggle after Doe's death. Johnson declared himself Acting President, but the Economic Community of West African States Monitoring Group (ECOMOG) replaced him with a unity government led by Amos Sawyer. Civil war among the various factions of the NPLF and against the government continued until 1996 when Taylor overran Monrovia ending the Sawyer regime and eventually becoming president in 1997 (Badru, 2010).

In Sierra Leone, the power struggle and subsequent civil war began in 1991, when Foday Sankoh's the Revolutionary United Front (RUF), a group of Sierra Leoneans trained in Libya and supported by Charles Taylor invaded Sierra Leone, with the goal of bringing about economic and political change in the country (Bah, 2011). The RUF continued to fight the military government and overthrew the subsequent civilian Sierra Leone's People Party (SLPP) government of Ahmad Kabbah that followed. Although the international community's refusal to recognize the RUF government brought back the Kabbah government, the civil war continued until 2002.

As indicated in Chapter 2, South Sudan represents the most recent example of how personality conflicts among leaders of African countries can degenerate into an open civil war. Thus, South Sudan leaders fought for more than 50 years to get their separate country only to plunge it back into civil war because of lack of trust between the president and the vice president.

Ethnicity

Many researchers have identified the multiethnic nature of African countries as a major cause of Africa's civil wars. In the Nigerian Civil War of 1967–1970, the Igbo and other marginalized ethnic groups of the southeastern Nigeria felt that the Nigerian state had privileged the Hausa and Yoruba ethnic groups against them. They did not see any way out but to secede from the Nigerian state.

In Liberia, we have already seen how the cleavage between the Americo-Liberians and the indigenous people, and the latter's feeling of being left out of both the political and social class of the country, among other things, led to the toppling of the Tolbert regime by Master Sargent Samuel Doe. Doe's regime in turn replaced the Americo-Liberian oligarchy with a new one consisting of the Krahn, his own ethnic group, and courted the Mandingo, while marginalizing the Gio and Mano (supporters of Charles Taylor) (Peterson, 2010).

In Sierra Leone, postcolonial politics was controlled by the Sierra Leone People's Party (SLPP) and the All People's Congress (APC). These two parties were initially dominated by the three biggest ethnic groups—Mende, Temne, and Limba. However the SLPP eventually became a Mende party, the APC the Temne and Limba party, while the smaller ethnic such as Kisi, Creole, Fula, Loko, and Soso were marginalized (Bah, 2011). By the time of the outbreak of the civil war, the power struggle between the SLPP and the ACP had translated into patronage politics in which the country was ruled by the president and small group of confidants selected from the president's ethnic group.

In Chad, there was a long tradition of atrocities against the southern ethnic groups, most notably the Sara that date back to precolonial times. In particular, the Sara was subjected to frequent raids by the northern ethnic groups such as the Fulani, the Tubu, and the Arab who kept or sold them as slaves. The Fulani, for example, preferred Sara women as concubines and to discourage this, the Sara decided to elongate their women's lips to make them less attractive. During the colonial period, the unassimilated Sara again bore the brunt of forced manual labor, porterage, military service, and construction of railroads. So, when Francois Tombalbye, a Sara, led Chad back to independence and became the first president, the Northern groups found that unacceptable, while the Sara saw it as an opportunity to settle some old scores. This tension was exacerbated by insensitive government actions. For example, the government appointed the Sara to civil service positions for which they were not qualified or culturally prepared. Southern government officials disregarded northern cultural traditions. The government also tried to institute a radical form of Africanization policy that involved imposition of Sara traditional initiation customs as a condition for civil service jobs. These provided the background for the desire of northerners to rule the country and the subsequent struggle between Gukuni Wedei and Hissien Habre, two northern leaders from the same Tubu ethnic group but different clans, each of whom wanted to be president. After Habre had won the long struggle against his fellow Tubu rival Gukuni Wedei he alienated the Zaghawa ethnic group from which he had drawn his top military commanders—Idriss Deby and Hassan Djamous, by embracing the Chadian Arabs. The Zaghawa saw this as a betrayal; so after failing to overthrow Habre, about 2,000 of them defected to join Deby, who later on overthrew Habre, his former boss from power.

In the Sudan, black Africans (the Fur) and Arab Africans, who had lived together for a long time in the Darfur became irreconcilable enemies when the Sudanese government and its ally former Libyan leader Muammar Gaddafi promoted Arab supremacy policies in the Darfur. These started with a movement called Arab Gathering (Burr and Collins, 2006). The group distributed seditious material against black Africans in the Darfur in the 1980s and threatened violence if it did not get fair representation in the government. With the backing of Gaddafi, this group calling themselves Janjaweed (ruffians) attacked the Fur from March 1988 until May 1989. The Sudanese government exacerbated the ethnic tension when in 1994 it started promoting Arabization of the Darfur by gerrymandering the administrative divisions of the Darfur province in such a way that the Fur, the largest non-Arab ethnic group in the province, became minority in each of the four new administrative regions (Burr and Collins, 2006). The Sudanese government appointed Arab governors for each of these regions and deposed the hereditary Sultan and traditional rulers of the non-Arab Masalit. At the same time, Sudanese government agents continued recruiting members to join the Janjaweed and arming them, while disarming all the non-Arab groups in the region. In 2001, the non-Arab groups decided to work together to oppose the Arabization policy. They formed two rebel groups, the Justice and Equality Movement (JEM) and the Sudanese Liberation Army (SLA), and in 2003 the groups mounted an attack on government installations in Darfur for the years of neglect and abuse. The Sudanese government responded by mounting a campaign of genocide using the Janjaweed militia backed by aerial bombardment of non-Arab villages. Since then the level of violence has been on and off amidst several ceasefire and peace agreements.

A final example of how ethnicity has fueled civil wars in Africa is the Rwanda tragedy of 1994 between the Hutu majority and the Tutsi minority. Many have attributed the roots of this conflict to the Belgian colonialists who elevated the Tutsi minority over the Hutu majority. In 1959, a Hutu revolt forced many Tutsis to flee the country including the then King. In 1973, a military coup brought into power Major-General Habyarimana, a moderate Hutu. In 1990, Rwandese Patriotic Front (RPF) consisting mostly of Tutsi refugees in Uganda invaded Rwanda and forced a constitutional amendment for shared government. A ceasefire agreement calling for a transitional and shared government was signed in Tanzania in 1993, which did not please the Hutu extremists. On April 6, 1994, the presidents of Rwanda and Burundi died, when their plane was shot down over Kigali. Hutu extremists blamed the Tutsi rebels for this and within hours, the Rwanda presidential guard, the armed forces and Hutu militias set up roadblocks and began killing Tutsis. The killing spread to the countryside and within three months, about 800,000 people were murdered. The killing ended when the RFP gained control over the country, in July 1994. It must be noted that although ethnicity has become an easy factor to explain many of Africa's civil wars, for the most part ethnicity has merely provided a cover for deep political, economic, and personal reasons of conflict perpetrators.

Economic and Political Decay

Economic and political decay often found expression in the state's inability to ensure equitable distribution of resources over time and space, equal access to justice and fairness, and addressing repression and marginalization of social and ethnic groups within the country.

In Chad, the government's inability to deal with the severe Sahel droughts of the 1970s that killed both humans and animals provided another impetus for the civil war. Instead of addressing these matters, the Tombalbye administration was more concerned with an "Africanization" policy that alienated the northern ethnic groups. Similarly, the Darfur, lying more than 700 miles (1127 km) away from Khartoum, had historically been a difficult region to govern. In particular, the modern state of Sudan had failed to integrate the region and its people—the Zaghawa, the Bedeyiat, the Massalit, and Arab Baqqart. The failure of the government to do anything about the repeated droughts left the people on their own, and as resources became more scarce tensions increased. Traditional ways of resolving disputes through a council of elders that had sustained the various groups from time immemorial went by the wayside, and were replaced by the power of AK47s, which were now very abundant (Burr and Collins, 2006).

In Sierra Leone, the government of Siaka Stevens was more consumed with personal rule. After 10 years in power, he declared Sierra Leone a one-party state in 1978. Distribution of diamond dealer licenses was made on political grounds, favoring Lebanese and Afro-Lebanese, who were less threatening (Harris, 2012). He built a large network of loyalty through personal favors and political appointments, while silencing his rivals through arraignment before Commissions of Enquiry. Smuggling of diamonds and other exports and imports were common. The army became a moneymaker for the country's northern ethnic groups, and economic decline resulted in deterioration in education, transportation, health care, and high proportion of unemployed youth. All these created a large pool of disgruntled youth, which became ready volunteers and recruits for the RUF (Harris, 2012).

Control Over Resources

Control over resources has played a role in civil wars in Africa since the early postindependence period. It was central to the civil war in DRC, when the highly mineralized province of Katanga announced its secession, and has been prominent in subsequent wars. In the Nigerian Civil War, control over oil resources provided another layer to the ethnic tension that was mostly seen as the cause of the war. The southeastern part of the country that wanted to secede also had Nigeria's oil reserves, control over which would have been a boon to breakaway Biafra but a disaster for Nigeria. Similarly, the Angolan Civil War was also in part about who would control the country's mineral resources, while the Rwandan genocide has also been attributed to resource control (Daley, 2006). Perhaps, the most widely documented case of how resource control caused or motivated prolonged civil war is the control of diamonds in Sierra Leone's civil war. Thus, both rebel (RUF) and government soldiers were reported to be involved in the diamond trade (Bah, 2000, 2011).

External Influences

External influences on Africa's internal affairs are not new and Africa's civil wars are no exceptions. These external influences have taken the form of geopolitical visions of countries and individuals, inaction or untimely intervention on the part of external entities, as well as proximity and adjacency effects. For Liberia, the role of external influence goes back to the very foundation of the country with the arrival of the Americo-Liberian population that dominated the political, economic, and social echelons of the country for so long until the Samuel Doe's revolution. For Nigeria, it goes back to colonialism that created an almost ungovernable country because of its large number of diverse ethnic groups that had very little in common with each other. Colonialism also played a major role in Rwanda and Burundi, by fostering a false superiority of Tutsi minority over the Hutu majority setting the stage for conflicts that eventually exploded in a genocide (Daley, 2006; Mamdani, 2001).

The Cold War set the gold standard of how external influences could add more fuel to civil wars in Africa. Angola's civil war became protracted because the Soviet Union and Cuba were backing the MPLA, while the US and apartheid South Africa were backing UNITA. Post-Cold War era has seen both a rush to arm countries because of their stands against terrorism or inaction or slow intervention to stop wars. The civil wars in Rwanda, Liberia, Sierra Leone, Chad, and the Darfur are examples of how the rush to arm warring factions on the one hand and the slow intervention or nonintervention on the other hand helped prolong the wars. In the case of Chad, Egypt, the US, Sudan, and France supported Habre, while Gaddafi supported Gukuni, and later on Deby.

At the individual level, perhaps the most telling example was the geopolitical vision of Libya's Muammar Gaddafi. Dreaming of Pan-Arab Empire, Gaddafi initially made overtures for a union with Egypt and then Sudan. However, after being rebuffed by both countries, he turned his attention to a Pan-Arab Empire that would stretch from the Mediterranean to the heart of Africa through the annexation of Chad. The occupation of the Aozzou Strip was the first step in this grand design. Using the large oil wealth of his country and playing on the personal dislike among the leaders of Chad, Gaddafi armed, supported, and funded every leader of the Chadian Civil War from Gukuni Wedei, Hissiene Habre, to Idriss Deby. Even though he sometimes fought against these leaders, none of that mattered as long as he could annex Chad as part of Libya, in the end. When all that failed and a new friendly Islamist government appeared in Sudan, Gaddafi gladly accepted Sudan's overtures and helped the "Arabization" policy in West Sudan, especially the Darfur with arms and funds.

The proximity and adjacency effects are manifest in spillovers of civil wars into neighboring countries or regions. Examples of these are the Sierra Leone and Darfur civil wars. In Sierra Leone the spillover came from Liberia while in the Darfur, it was from Chad. The long civil war in Chad had made the Darfur a haven from where dissident groups marched on Ndjamena. The arming of these groups created a proliferation of weapons among the various ethnic groups to first protect themselves and second to settle disputes over dwindling resources brought about by drought and famine and no government help.

Ethnic and Minority Issues

If ethnic issues loom large in civil wars in Africa, then it is imperative that African countries pay attention to them. Ethnicity theoreticians such as Horowitz (1985) classify states into those with ranked ethnicity and those with unranked or parallel ethnicity. Ranked ethnic states are those with a clear stratification of ethnic groups in a pecking order of importance, while unranked are those without. Apart from this, states may also be classified based on whether their ethnic groups are geographically concentrated or geographically intermixed. Based on these classifications, countries with unranked ethnic structure and geographically concentrated ethnic groups might be better off than those with ranked ethnic structure and intermixed ethnic groups. However, it is not as simple as that because much of the ethnic-based problems are a result of bad ethnic management, which is expressed in the relationship between the state and its ethnic groups.

Drawing on the work of Rothchild's (1985, 1986, 1991) Suberu (2000) identifies three models by which the African state has managed ethnic issues. The first is **hegemonic**

repression, the second is **hegemonic exchange**, and the third is **polyarchical** or **non-hegemonic exchange**. In the hegemonic repression, the hegemonic ethnic group represses certain ethnic groups because they oppose the policies of the hegemonic group. Eventually the repressed groups push back against their oppressors with several explosive consequences, including civil wars. In the hegemonic exchange, policies and practices are designed to accommodate or incorporate diverse ethnic segments of the population. Such policies and practices include proportionality in allocation of and filling of political positions, recruitment of civil service personnel, and allocation of state expenditures. In the polyarchical exchange, ethnic management and its institutions are enshrined in the constitution and are actually implemented.

Suberu (2000) associates the hegemonic exchange model of ethnic management with the long reigns of Jomo Kenyatta of Kenya and Felix Houphouet-Boigny of Cote d'Ivoire. Both leaders established one-party systems in their respective countries, but both went to considerable efforts to make sure that no ethnic group was permanently left out. They incorporated all major ethnic groups into their cabinets, and other branches of government, and considerable reciprocity of state–ethnic relationships. However, much of the success of this model in both countries appeared to have depended on the dominant personalities of the two leaders and their abilities to manipulate their respective political systems. Thus, once both leaders were gone their successors were not able to maintain the system. The result is that in both countries ethnic tensions began to simmer again resulting in a civil war in Cote d'Ivoire and postelection conflicts in Kenya.

In spite of this, there is evidence to show that if hegemonic exchange is based on sound policy that is seen as beneficial to all ethnic groups, there is a chance that this form of ethnic management can be successful. An example of this is Ghana's less-known "geographic affirmative action policy" that was instituted in the early years of independence. The differences between the southern and the northern regions in living conditions were quite stark. Education was seen as the key to bridge the gap between the two regions of the country, but because of the relatively higher incidence of poverty in the North, the government established scholarships for the education of the children in the North from kindergarten through university. However, in order to attract teachers and other government workers to move to the North, the scholarship was given a geographic twist: the scholarship was also available to children of anyone from the South who was willing to relocate to the North for work. This made the policy attractive to southerners as well. As a result, the policy has survived both the military and civilian regimes since the return to independence, and has to date educated thousands of Ghanaians from both the North and the South.

Many students of African politics believe that only two countries in postcolonial Africa have used the polyarchichal exchange model of ethnic-management, namely Mauritius and Botswana. However, for Botswana it depends on who is doing the evaluation, because some people see the San people as an oppressed minority (e.g., Good, 2010). Algeria and Morocco have also used this model to manage the Imazighen issue (see Box 9.3).

Unfortunately, other ethnic minorities are still subjected to discrimination and abuses. In the DRC, for example, the Mbororo nomadic cattle herders who move across the borders of DRC and Central African Republic has been accused of being allies with the Lord Resistance Army (LRA), a rebel group in Northern Uganda. Consequently, DRC government security forces fighting in the area frequently kill Mbororo men and rape Mbororo women and girls (Human Rights Watch 2012). The plight of Ogoniland people in Nigeria, the Tuareg of Northern Mali, the San of Botswana, are still lingering. In the final analysis, African countries need to implement antidiscrimination laws based on ethnicity that are enshrined in their constitutions.

Box 9.3 | The Amazigh (Berber) Spring

The Amazigh, the original inhabitants of northern portion of Africa from the Siwa Oasis in modern Egypt to the east to the Canary Islands to the west, and from the Mediterranean Sea to just below the Sahara Desert, had been subjected to several waves of influence of immigrants from outside Africa. The most important of these include the Romans (146 BC–439 AD), the Byzantines (533–647); the Arabs (7th–8th centuries); the Turks (1515–1830), and the French (1830–1962). These outsiders called them the Berbers.

During the French colonial rule of Algeria, a divide-and-rule tactics raised the Kabyle group of these natives above other groups. However, when Algerian nationalism began in the 1930s and 1940s, even the Kabyles became marginalized since the movement centered on three articles of faith: "Islam is our religion, Algeria is our country, and Arabic is our language." Postcolonial Algeria further alienated the Amazigh when it chose Arabic as the national language, and launched an Arabization program in Algerian schools and public space (Goodman 2005). In spite of this, Kabyle leaders organized to draw the point home that the countries of the Maghreb region of today had been formed out a vast region that used to be "Berber" land. They coined the term Imazighen or "free men" (singular Amazigh) to refer to themselves and Tamazight to the group of languages they spoke. During the 1960s and 1970s the Kabyle in the diaspora, especially Paris, formed several organizations to advocate for the cause of the Amazigh identity through publication of journal and promotion of Amazigh studies. Kabyle consciousness was further enhanced by the teaching of Kabyle language by Mouloud Mammeri, the Algerian novelist at the University of Algiers in 1965, the Kabyle radio station, Kabyle music artists, and the establishment of the University of Tizi-Ouzou in Tizi-Ouzou the capital city of Kabyle in 1978 (Goodman, 2005; Aitel, 2013).

The pent-up discontent against repression of the Amazigh culture was released when on March 10, 1980 Mouloud Mammeri's lecture on ancient Kabyle poetry at the University of Tizi-Ouzou was cancelled by the government because it would lead to public disorder. Demonstrations, which became known as the **Berber Spring,** reached a head when at 4:15 A.M. on April 20, 1980 police stormed the university campus and arrested students, professors, doctors, and other workers. The following day the whole region erupted with confrontations against the police and more arrests. After a month-long citizen debate, the Berber Spring submitted a document outlining social and political claims and demand. The Berber Spring spread to Morocco, but it took more than 10 years for both Algeria and Morocco to address the marginalization of the Amazigh.

In Algeria, a constitutional amendment officially recognized Amazigh and Tamazight as components of Algeria's national identity just as Arab and Islam. On June 14, 1994, and in 2003, a unified version of Amazigh was introduced in schools. In 2011, in the wake of the Arab Spring, Tamazight was recognized as an official language in the new constitution. This has helped to advance the cause of the Amazigh across the whole of North Africa. There is no doubt that more needs to be done even in Algeria because after recognizing Tamazight as official language, President Abdelaziz Bouteflika backtracked in 2005 saying that only Arabic can be an official language in Algeria. Apart from this the fate of the Amazigh in Libya is still being sorted out, but this is a good case of minority issues in Africa.

Source: Goodman, J. E. 2005. *Berber Culture on the World Stage: From Village to Video.* Bloomington and Indianapolis: Indian University Press.

Willis, M. J. 2012. *Politics and Power in the Maghreb: Algeria, Tunisia, and Morocco from Independence to the Arab Spring.* New York: Columbia University Press.

Women Issues

The status and role of women constitute another governance issue in Africa. Since Boserup's (1970) pioneering work on the role of women in development, research has consistently established the need to incorporate women in all areas of development yet progress on this front has been slow. Every African country now has women organizations and there have been several pronouncements as to how to bring women into the decision-making arena. The critical question is what it is that prevents these pronouncements from becoming concrete actions in African societies?

The answer lies in the very depth of certain traditional beliefs about women in many African cultures. Bluntly put, the majority of African cultures do not hold women to be equal to men when it comes to decision making, leadership, and positions of authority. Even in matrilineal societies, the traditional roles that women had, had been eroded and the system is only effective for tracing kinship ties. Men still dominate leadership roles and decision making. As we have seen, some of this has been traced to colonialism, but the "bad-mannered" colonialists have been gone for some 50 or so years. Besides, back in their respective countries, they have changed and have since given more recognition to their women. Yet, Africa still holds on to retrogressive beliefs and traditions about women as caregivers but not as breadwinners and important decision makers. It is such beliefs that make families value education of boys over girls, or discourage girls and young women from pursuing higher education, make young women look down on themselves that they cannot reach for their best because they are females. Such beliefs and attitudes are not only pervasive among the less educated but even the educated elite and, for that matter, among institutions of government as well. Therefore, for full recognition of women in leadership and decision-making positions, there will be a real need for education of women and men as well as enactment and enforcement of sexual harassment and discrimination laws. A conscious effort to increase women representation in the hiring practices of public service will also help.

The Media and Press Freedom

The media performs two primary roles in good governance. First, it acts as "watchdogs" of governments in performing their historical and social responsibilities. Second, it calls for new rules that will lead to good governance (Olokotun, 2000). The extent to which the media can fully accomplish these roles depends on its integrity and its relationship with the state.

According to Siebert et al. (1956), there are generally four models of state–media relations—the authoritarian, libertarian, social responsibility, and social-centrist models. The authoritarian and the social-centrist models require the media to publicize the activities of the government. The libertarian guarantees free speech while the social responsibility calls on journalists to be politically and socially sensitive in reporting news, and how that will impact the national development program. This also mandates the government to regulate the press in relation to nation building and development program agenda. Olokotun (2000) reports that many African countries operate with this model. What is needed is to move beyond this to the libertarian model. To do this, African governments must not only pay lip service to press freedom and protection of free speech, but they must also implement existing laws.

Freedom of Information is still limited in many countries, yet African countries have been participants or supporters of numerous declarations on freedom of information beginning with Article 19 of the Universal Declaration of Human Rights, which states:

> Everyone has the right to freedom of opinion and expression; this right includes freedom to hold opinions without interference and to seek, receive and impart information and ideas through any media and regardless of frontiers.

In 1981, African countries affirmed the importance of freedom of information in Article 9 of the African (Banjul) Charter on Human and Peoples' Rights adopted by the OAU. In May 1991, African newspaper journalists at a seminar sponsored by the United Nations Educational, Scientific, and Cultural Organization (UNESCO) in Windhoek, Namibia, created the Declaration of Windhoek, which called for "free, independent, pluralistic media worldwide, characterizing free press as essential to democracy and as fundamental right." To commemorate the 20-year anniversary of the Declaration of Windhoek, a Windhoek +20 Working Group planned a conference on freedom of information in Africa in 2011 in Cape Town South Africa, to evaluate the progress made since the Windhoek Declaration, 20 years ago. Unfortunately, the conference found that only nine countries had passed legislation guaranteeing freedom of information: South Africa (2000), Angola (2002), Zimbabwe (2003/2007), Uganda (2005) Ethiopia (2008), Liberia (2010), Guinea (2010), Nigeria (2011), and Niger (2011). Yet even in these countries, the implementation of the laws had not materialized. For example, in an editorial on Nigeria's freedom of information law, the Daily Trust (2012) stated that the act has been in name only.

Arrests, trials, and imprisonment of journalists are still common. Sometimes governments have passed legislations that give the presidents extraordinary powers to revoke licenses or imprison their critics in the press (Fomunyoh, 2005; Wyrod, 2010). In Burundi, for example, the journalist Jean Claude Kavumbugu spent 10 months in a pretrial jail for questioning the ability of the Burundian army to defend the country against the al-Shabaab terrorist group. In the DRC, police attacked a cameraman who was filming empty seats at a government rally in the Katanga Province. Another journalist, Dede Ilunga, was detained for 17 days for criticizing the president's development program. In Equatorial Guinea, journalists working for the state-owned media are not allowed to criticize the government. In Malawi, critics of the government on human rights record have become the object of intimidation, harassment, and sometimes mysterious death. Any publication, news coverage, or discussion that implicates the government may result in the editor of the newspaper or reporter or program host being summoned for questioning or arrest by the police and sometimes radio or program shut down.

For Africa to continue to make progress on the democratic front, freedom of press, speech, and assembly, as well as freedom of information must be guaranteed not only on paper in the constitution, but also in reality. African governments must learn to receive and accept criticism and not see it as the end of their political careers and agenda. In turn, the media also has to aspire for professionalism in its work, guaranteeing objectivity and authenticity (Olokotun, 2000). There is no democracy if people are not free to speak their minds and question the actions of elected officials.

The Problem of Local Government Reforms

Every African country has some form of local government that was inherited from the colonial system. These systems were essentially extensions of the colonial central administration rather than representation of the people in the colonial government.

In the famous indirect rule of the British system, these were in the form of chiefs who were overseen by a district commissioner who then reported to a regional or provincial commissioner.

Since independence, African countries have embarked on various local government reforms including deconcentration, delegation, and devolution. **Deconcentration** is shifting some administrative workload from the central government to the local level. **Delegation** is passing certain decision-making powers from the central government to the local level, while **devolution** is the transfer of power to a local unit with some autonomy and independent and indirect supervision from the central government (Enemuo, 2000; Rondenelli, 1981).

In spite of all these, in most countries decentralization has remained only on paper. In some countries such as Nigeria and Tanzania, it has also become another way for political elites to accumulate wealth and power at the expense of the local people. Most of these officials are government appointees rather than locally elected officials. Enemuo (2000) summarizes three reasons why decentralization has not been effective. The first is that the multiethnic nature of African countries makes central governments nervous of committing fully to devolution of power because that could lead to secession movements. The second is that limited human and financial resources make it difficult to implement a full-blown devolution of power, while the third says devolution will slow down the pace of economic development, which needs to proceed rapidly. Clearly, none of these reasons has been vindicated given the political and economic development history of Africa.

The fact is good governance requires participation of the people at the grassroots that goes beyond voting in general elections. The idea of a central government tucked away in the capital city may still be alien in some African countries depending on the geographic size of the country. In this case, proximity of the government to the people becomes extremely important. Thus, while there can be no one-size-fits all, each African country must decide what type of decentralization will be appropriate— whether deconcentration, devolution, or delegation. Whatever form of decentralization is selected must be supported by an information and communication sharing systems to facilitate decision making. In addition, there will be the need to strengthen the weak financial bases of local governments. The traditional way in Africa has been central or federal government transfers, which for the most part constitutes the bulk of funding for local governments. However, local governments must be empowered to generate their own local revenue sources. This is not an alien idea in many African communities whereby communal labor supported by local taxes has built a number of local development projects. Unfortunately, this system has broken down in many areas due to increasing misunderstanding to relate taxes to services instead of property and lack of transparency as well as cases of misappropriation of funds.

Regional Groupings and Changing Geopolitics

The formation of regional groupings by African countries for purposes of political and economic integration or cooperation in the mid-1960s through the mid-1970s was discussed in Chapter 3. These include the OAU established in 1963, the Economic Community of West African States (ECOWAS) established in 1973, the Southern African Development Coordinator Conference (SADCC), established in 1989, and the Arab Maghreb Union (AMU) also established in 1989. The OAU was preoccupied with completing the liberation of African countries and was not very effective in dealing with conflict, corruption, and good governance of member countries. However, with the end of the Cold War in 1989 and the end of apartheid in 1994, the OAU became woefully inadequate to deal with the new geopolitics. First, there was a retreat from Africa in the early post-Cold War period as the breakdown of the Soviet Union and the increasing development of Asian countries offered more promise for Western and Eastern investments. Second, the failure of the development prescriptions of the World Bank, IMF, and their related African Development Bank and Economic Commission of Africa (ECA) in lifting Africa's development problems drove home the need for African countries to forge closer, stronger, and more serious cooperation than they had done in the past. Third, the end of apartheid in South Africa and the return to civilian rule in Nigeria rearranged the internal geopolitics of the continent. South Africa's position as the strongest economy on the continent, and Nigeria's position as the most populous country on the continent, as well as the largest oil producer in Africa became the new "powers" on the continent. The two countries used their newly found position to play crucial roles in the formation of the African Union (AU) as well as NEPAD in 2002 (see Chapter 3). While South Africa also became dominant in the SADCC, Nigeria also began assuming more leadership role in ECOWAS especially in its ECOMOG.

Externally, Africa's changing geopolitical situation as a potential haven for terrorists on the one hand and increasing importance as a producer of natural resources (oil, strategic minerals, and timber) revived Africa's relations with US, and India and China, respectively. Emboldened by their newly found wealth, both China and India backed their new engagement with real investment as they sought more of Africa's natural resources. The first Forum on China-Africa Cooperation (FOCAC) was held in Beijing in 2000 and in January 2006, the Chinese government issued its first African Policy paper. This of course caused the EU to also reevaluate its African policy. Thus, once more Africa was on the world's geopolitical stage.

These raise two-fold concern. The first is with Africa's ability to deal with general emergencies such as armed conflicts, and other disaster management. Past AU and ECOMOG intervention efforts are commendable but mobilization of forces has always depended on external help. In the case of Liberia and Sierra Leone, it was not until help came from the West that the forces were able to accomplish their task. In the recent case of Mali, French troops arrived long before AU and ECOMOG troops did. Since it has become clear that Africa has to confront its own problems, it is time for Africa to take up the challenge and equip itself to deal with these problems. In the early postcolonial era, Kwame Nkrumah of Ghana proposed the need to establish an African High Command, an elite force that could be deployed to resolve conflict issues and restore peace, but no one paid attention. Bolarinwa (2010) reports that in the mid-1990s, the US Government proposed the creation of an African Crisis Response Force (ACRF), a standing force of about 5,000 African troops, trained and equipped by Western countries that could be deployed quickly for peacekeeping operations. However, both Britain and France did not support the idea, and neither did South Africa nor Nigeria, the two countries that President Clinton had hoped would support the idea. It seems that this might be a good idea now.

The second concern is whether the African countries that have become targets of the new Asian investments can avoid going down the same path that European exploitation took them. The key question is: will Africa standup to extract bargains that will bring long-term sustainable development by way of not only infrastructure but a productive economy? Or will Africa return to a beggar economy again after all its resources have been extracted?

Summary

Precolonial Africa had two main political and governance systems—centralized and decentralized systems. The centralized system included pyramidal, associated, and centralized monarchies. The decentralized systems included the band, the clan, the age group, the ritual, and the autonomous village systems. Each of these systems had its own rules of citizen participation, as well as checks and balances to ensure such participation. Colonialism superimposed the European concept of nation–state upon these systems, which among other things divided African nations among several states, incorporated several African nations into one state, weakened or destroyed precolonial political institutions, and introduced an authoritarian political legacy. Postcolonial Africa faced the daunting tasks of governing political units that had been mechanically created without the resources and expertise to administer such units. After a few years of experimenting with multiparty politics, the majority of African countries reverted to a one-party political system, giving enormous power to the presidency or whoever was the head of government. With all the checks and balances removed, presidential rule in most countries transitioned into personal rule during which all voices of opposition were silenced, economies were mismanaged, and state funds were misappropriated by government officials and their network of families and friends. For personal and corporate reasons, Africa's military exploited this state of affairs, seized the reins of government by the gun, and promised to make things better. From the mid-1960s through the 1980s, military regimes became the order of the day in the majority of African countries. Unfortunately, political, economic, as well as social conditions became worse under military regimes, some of them leading to devastating civil wars. Eventually, the end of the Cold War in the late 1980s, worsening economic and political conditions, and the rise of civil society demanding political and economic reforms broke the stranglehold of the military and one-party systems on Africa and paved the way to multiparty democratic elections.

Since then African countries have made great strides in their political and governance systems, but they have a lot more work to do to establish true democracy. Areas of concerns include free and fair multiparty elections, true citizen representation and government accountability, neopatrimonialism, venality and corruption, freedom of the press, information, and association, rule of law, land tenure systems, and dealing with ethnic and other minorities issues. To be successful in dealing with these issues will require transformation of people's world views, attitudes, beliefs, mentality, on what kind of societies they want to create for now and posterity.

Postreading Assignments

A. Study the Following Concepts

Age group system	Delegation	Modern land	Presidential system
Arab Spring	Developmental state	tenure system	Pyramidal monarchy
Associational monarchy	Devolution	Nonhegemonic exchange	Self-determination
Autonomous village	Hegemonic exchange	Opportunistic corruption	Systemic corruption
Band organization	Hegemonic repression	Oracle-led system	Tenure reforms
Cadaverous state	Individualized corruption	Parliamentary system	Unicameral
Centralized monarchy	Integral state	Polyarchical exchange	and Bicameral
Clan system	Land redistribution	Prebendal state	Uti possidetis
Deconcentration	Land restitution	Predatory state	

B. Answer the Following Questions

1. Compare the answers you wrote down at the beginning of the chapter with what you know now. Are there any changes you want to make? If so what are they?

2. Discuss the assertion that precolonial Africa had no systems of government.

3. In what way did colonialism impact politics and governance system in Africa?

4. Distinguish between the concepts of politics, governance, and government.

5. Why did African countries adopt the one-party system in the early postcolonial period?

6. Why did the military become involved in politics and governance in Africa?

7. What were the main effects of military regime on African countries?

8. What were the main factors that led to the multiparty democratic elections in Africa?

9. What is neopatrimonialism? Do you consider neopatrimonialism a problem in Africa? Why and why not?

10. Distinction between venality and corruption. Why has corruption become institutionalized in Africa and what do you think can be done to end it?

11. What are the main obstacles facing freedom of the press and movement in Africa?

12. What are some of the ethnic and minority issues facing African countries, and how can these issues be solved?

13. Assess the causes of civil wars in Africa and recommend solutions for reducing the incidence of civil wars on the continent.

14. Discuss the future of democratic multiparty elections in Africa.

15. Evaluate the philosophical perspectives debated by African countries to address boundary disputes?

16. What is geopolitics? Illustrate how changing geopolitics within and outside Africa have influenced politics and governance in Africa.

17. Why have many local government reforms in Africa not worked?

References

Acemoglu, D., Verdier, T., and Robinson, J. A. 2002. "Kleptocracy and Divide-and-Rule: A Model of Personal Rule." *Journal of European Economic Association* 2 (2–3): 162–192.

Adebajo, A. 2002. *Liberia's Civil War: Nigeria, ECOMOG, and Regional Security in West Africa.* Boulder, CO: Lynne Rienner Publishers.

Adibe, C. E. 2010. "Accountability in Africa and the International Community." *Social Research* 77(4): 1241–1280.

Adjibolosoo, S. B-S. K. 1993. "The Human Factor in Development." *The Scandinavian Journal of Development Alternatives* XII (4): 139–149.

African Union, African Development Bank, and Economic Commission of Africa 2010. *Framework and Guidelines on Land Policy in Africa.* Addis Ababa: AUC-ECA-AfDB Consortium.

Agbese, P. O. 2005. "Soldiers as Rulers: Military Performance." In Kieh, J. R. G. K., and Agbese, P. O. (Eds.) *The Military and Politics in Africa: From Engagement to Democratic and Constitutional Control.* Aldershot, UK: Ashgate, pp. 58–90.

Agulanna, C. 2006. "Democracy and the Crisis of Leadership in Africa." *The Journal of Social, Political, and Economic Studies* 31(3): 255–264.

Aitel, F. 2013. "Between Algeria and France: The Origins of the Berber Movement." *French Cultural Studies* 24(1): 63–76.

Ajala, A. 1983. "The Nature of African Boundaries." *African Spectrum* 18(2): 177–189.

Ayitey, G. B. N. 1992. *Africa Betrayed.* New York: St. Martin's Press.

Azevedo, M. J. 1998. *Roots of Violence: A History of War in Chad.* Amsterdam: Gordon and Breach.

Azevedo, J. M., and Nnadozie, E. U. 1998. *Chad: A Nation in Search of its Future.* Boulder, CO: Westview.

Badru, P. 2010. "Ethnic Conflict and State Formation in Post-Colonial Africa: A Comparative Study of Ethnic Genocide in Congo, Liberia, Nigeria, and Rwanda-Burundi." *Journal of Third World Studies* 27(2): 149–169.

Bah, M. S. 2000. "Exploring the Dynamics of the Sierra Leone Conflict." *Peacekeeping & International Relations* 29 (1/2): 1–6.

Bah, A. B. 2011. "State Decay and Civil War: A Discourse on Power in Sierra Leone." *Critical Sociology* 37(2): 199–216.

Bolarinwa, 2010. "Africa's Regional Powers, Priorities and the New Geopolitical Realities." *Africa Review* 2(2): 175–200.

Bruce, J. 1998. "Learning from the Comparative Experience with Agrarian Reform." In: Barry (Ed.) *Proceedings of the International Conference on Land tenure in the Developing World.* South Africa: University of Cape Town.

Burr, J. M., and Collins, R. O. 2006. *Darfur : The Long Road to Disaster.* Princeton, NJ: Markus Wiener.

Carey-Miller, D. L. 1998. "Revision of Priorities in South African Land Law." In: Barry (Ed.) *Proceedings of the International Conference on Land tenure in the Developing.* South Africa: World. University of Cape Town.

Chavunduka, C., and Bromley, D. W. 2010. "Beyond the Crisis in Zimbabwe: Sorting out the Land Question." *Development Southern Africa* 27(3): 363–379.

Chege, M. 2010. "Kenya Back from the Brink." In Diamond, L., and Plattner, M. F. (Eds.) *Democratization in Africa: Progress and Retreat.* 2nd edition. Baltimore: The Johns Hopkins University Press, pp. 197–211.

Dabashi, H. 2012. *The Arab Spring: The End of Postcolonialism.* London and New York: Zed Books.

Daley, P. 2006. "Ethnicity and Political Violence in Africa: The Challenge to the Burundi state." *Political Geography* 25: 657–679.

Daily Trust, 2012. "Nigeria: Reality of the Freedom of Information Act." September 17, 2012. http://allafrica.com/stories/2012 09170161.html (accessed 16 January 16 2013).

Diamond, L. 2010. "The Rule of Law Versus the Big Man." In Diamond, L., and Plattner, M. F. (Eds.) *Democratization in Africa: Progress and Retreat.* 2nd edition. Baltimore: The Johns Hopkins University Press, pp. 47–58.

Deng, F. 1998. "African Policy Agenda: A Framework for Global Partnerships." In Deng F. M., and Lyons, T. (Eds.) *African Reckoning: A Quest for Good Governance.* Washington, DC: Brookings Institution, pp. 136–175.

Dunne, M., and Hamzawy, A. 2008. "The Ups and Downs of Political Reform in Egypt." In Ottaway, M., and Choucair-Vizoso, J. (Eds.) *Beyond the Façade: Political Reform in the Arab World.* Washington DC: Carnegie Endowment for International Peace, pp. 17–43.

Enemuo, F. C. 2000. "Problems and Prospects of Local Governance." In Hyden, G., Olowu, D., and Ogendo, H. (Eds.). *African Perspectives on Governance.* Trenton, NJ: Africa World Press, pp. 181–204.

Fomunyoh, C. 2005. "Africa's Democratic Deficit." *Georgetown Journal of International Affairs* 6(2): 13–19.

Gillespie, K., and Okruhlik, G. 1991. "The Political Dimension of Corruption Cleanups: A Framework for Analysis." *Comparative Politics* 24(1): 77–95.

Good, K. 2010. "The Illusion of Democracy in Botswana." In Diamond, L., and Plattner, M. F. (Eds.) *Democratization in Africa: Progress and Retreat.* 2nd edition. Baltimore: The Johns Hopkins University Press, pp. 280–294.

Goodman, J. E. 2005. *Berber Culture on the World Stage: From Village to Video.* Bloomington and Indianapolis: Indian University Press.

Gutteridge, W. 1968. *The Military in African Politics.* London: Methuen.

Gyimah-Boadi, E. 2010. "Another Step for Ghana." In Diamond, L., and Plattner, M. F. (Eds.) *Democratization in Africa: Progress and Retreat.* 2nd edition. Baltimore, MD: The Johns Hopkins University Press, pp. 137–151.

Harris, D. 2012. *Civil War and Democracy in West Africa: Conflict Resolution, Elections and Justice in Sierra Leone and Liberia.* New York: I .B. Tauris.

Hoffman, B., and Robinson, L. 2010. "Tanzania's Missing Opposition." In Diamond, L., and Plattner, M. F. (Eds.) *Democratization in Africa: Progress and Retreat.* 2nd edition. Baltimore: The Johns Hopkins University Press, pp. 219–232.

Horowitz, D. 1985. *Ethic Groups in Conflict.* Berkeley: University of California Press.

Human Rights Watch 2012. World Report: Events in 2011.

Hyden, G. 1992. "The Study of Governance." In Hyden, G., and Bratton, M. (Eds.) *Governance and Politics in Africa.* Boulder:CO: Lynne Reinner Publishers.

Hyden, G. 2000. "The Governance Challenge in Africa." In Hyden, G., Oluwu, G., and Okoth-Ogendo, H. W. O, (Eds.) *African Perspectives on Governance.* Trenton, NJ: Africa World Press, pp. 5–32.

Hyden, G., Court, J., and Mease, K. 2004. *Making Sense of Governance: Empirical Evidence from Sixteen Developing Countries.* Boulder, CO: Lynne Reinner Publishers.

Kakwenzire, J. 2000. "Human Rights and Governance." In Hyden, G., Oluwu, G., and Okoth-Ogendo, H. W. O. (Eds.) *African Perspectives on Governance.* Trenton, NJ: Africa World Press, pp. 61–90.

Kalabamu, F. 2000. "Land Tenure and Management Reforms in East and Southern Africa – The Case of Botswana." *Land Use Policy* 17: 305–319.

Kaldor, M. 2003. "The Idea of Global Civil Society" *International Affairs* 79(3): 583–593.

Kaplan, S. 2010. "The Remarkable Story of Somaliland." In Diamond, L., and Plattner, M. F. (Eds.) *Democratization in Africa: Progress and Retreat.* 2nd edition. Baltimore: The Johns Hopkins University Press, pp. 249–262.

Kendie, D. D. 2003. "Towards Northeast Africa Cooperation: Resolving the Ethiopian Somalia Disputes." *Northeast African Studies (New Series)* 10(2): 67–109.

Kiai, M. 2010. "The Crisis in Kenya." In Diamond, L., and Plattner, M. F. (Eds.) *Democratization in Africa: Progress and Retreat.* 2nd edition. Baltimore, MD: The Johns Hopkins University Press, pp. 212–218.

Kromm, D. E. 1967. "Irredentism in Africa: The Somali-Kenya Boundary Dispute." *Transactions of the Kansas Academy of Science* 70(3): 359–365.

Le Roux, C. J. B. 1999. "The Botswana-Namibian Boundary Dispute in the Caprivi: To what extent does Botswana's Arms Procurement Program represent a drift towards Military Confrontation in the Region?" *South African Journal of Military Studies* 29: 53–70.

Le Roux, C. J. B. 1998. "The Botswana – Namibia Boundary Dispute: Towards a Diplomatic Solution or Military Confrontation?" *New Contree* 80–93.

Mamdani, M. 2001. *When Victims Become Killers: Colonialism, Nativism, and the Genocide in Rwanda.* Oxford, UK: James Currey.

Matthews, Z. K. 1937. "An African View of Indirect Rule in Africa." *Journal of the Royal African Society*, 36(145): 433–437.

Mbaku, J. M. 2007. *Corruption in Africa: Causes, Consequences, and Cleanups*. Lanham, MD: Lexington Books.

McCaffrey, P. 2012a. "Why Tunisia?" In McCaffrey, P. (Ed.) *The Arab Spring*. Ipswich, MA: H.W. Wilson, pp. 41–43.

McCaffrey, P. 2012b. "Egyptian Politics: Nasserism and the Muslim Brotherhood." In McCaffrey, P. (Ed.) *The Arab Spring*. Ipswich, MA: H.W. Wilson, pp. 65–69.

McCaffrey, P. 2012c. "The Strange Odyssey of Muammar Qaddafi." In McCaffrey, P. (Ed.) *The Arab Spring*. Ipswich, MA: H.W. Wilson, pp. 87–91.

McFerson, H. 2010. "Developments in African Governance since the Cold War: Beyond Cassandra and Pollyanna." *African Studies Review* 53(2): 49–78.

McHugh, A. M. 2005. "Resolving International Boundary Disputes in Africa: A case for the International Court of Justice." *Howard Law Journal* 49(1): 209–239.

Mckinnon, D. 2006. "The Rule of law in Today's Africa." *Commonwealth Law Bulletin* 32(4): 649–655,

Mkandawire, T. 2010. "Aid, Accountability, and Democracy in Africa." *Social Research* 77(4): 1149–1182.

Moyo, S. 2008. *African Land Questions, Agrarian Transitions and the State: Contradictions of Neo-liberal Land Reforms*. Dakar: Council for Development of Social Science Research in Africa (CODESRIA).

Mwenda, A. M. 2010. "Personalizing Power in Uganda." In Diamond, L., and Plattner, M. F. (Eds.) *Democratization in Africa: Progress and Retreat*. 2nd edition. Baltimore, MD: The Johns Hopkins University Press, pp. 233–247.

Mutua, M. 2008. "Human Rights in Africa: The Limited Promise of Liberalism." *African Studies Review* 51(1): 17–39.

Nwachukwu, O. 2009, "Civil Society, Democracy and Good Governance in Africa." *CEU Political Science Journal* 4(1): 76–101.

Olokotun, A. 2000. "Governance and the Media." In Hyden, G., Oluwu, G., and Okoth-Ogendo, H. W. O. (Eds.) *African Perspectives on Governance*. Trenton, NJ: Africa World Press, pp. 91–121.

Olowu, D. 2000. "Bureaucracy and Democratic Reform." In Hyden, G., Oluwu, G., and Okoth-Ogendo, H. W. O. (Eds.) *African Perspectives on Governance*. Trenton, NJ: Africa World Press, pp. 153–179.

Onwudiwe, E. 2004. "Military Coups in Africa: A Framework for Research." In Kieh, J. R. G. K., and Agbese, P. O. (Eds.) *The Military and Politics in Africa: From Engagement to Democratic and Constitutional Control*. Aldershot, UK: Ashgate, pp 17–35.

Onwumechili, C. 1998. *African Democratisation and Military Coups*. Westport, CT: Praeger.

Oppong, J. R. 2003. "Culture, Conflict, and Change in Sub-Saharan Africa." In Aryeetey-Attoh, S. (Ed.) *Geography of Sub-Saharan Africa*. 2nd edition. Upper Saddle River, NJ: Prentice Hall, pp. 134–164.

Peterson, D. 2010. "Liberia Starts Over." In Diamond, L., and Plattner, M. F. (Eds.) *Democratization in Africa: Progress and Retreat*. 2nd edition. Baltimore, MD: The Johns Hopkins University Press, pp. 178–193.

Posner, D. N., and Young, D. J. 2010. "The Institutionalization of Political Power in Africa." In Diamond, L., and Plattner, M. F. (Eds.) *Democratization in Africa: Progress and Retreat*. 2nd edition. Baltimore, MD: The Johns Hopkins University Press, pp. 59–72.

Potholm, C. P. 1979. *The Theory and Practice of African Politics*. Englewood Cliffs, NJ: Prentice-Hall.

Reno, W. 1999. *Warlord Politics*. Boulder, CO: Lynne Reinner.

Rondenelli, D. 1981. "Government Decentralization in Comparative Perspectives: Theory and Practice in Developing Nations." *International Review of Administrative Science XLVII* (2): 318–336.

Roque, P. C. 2010. "Angola's Façade Democracy." In Diamond, L., and Plattner, M. F. (Eds.) *Democratization in Africa: Progress and Retreat*. 2nd edition. Baltimore, MD: The Johns Hopkins University Press, pp. 325–337.

Rothchild, D. 1985. "State and Ethnic Relations in Middle Africa." In Carter, G. W., and O'Meara, P. (Eds.) *African Independence: The First Twenty-Five Years*. Bloomington, IN: Indiana University Press, pp. 71–96.

Rothchild, D. 1986. "Inter-Ethnic Conflict and Policy Analysis in Africa." *Ethnic and Racial Studies* 9(1): 66–86.

Rothchild, D. 1991. "An Interactive Model for State-Ethnic Relations." In Deng, F. M., and Zartman, I. W. (Eds.) *Conflict Resolution in Africa*. Washington DC: Brookings Institution, pp. 190–218.

Samatar, A. I. 2002. "Somalia: Statelessness as Homelessness." In Samatar, A. I., and Samatar, A. I. (Eds.) *The African State: Reconsiderations*. Portsmouth, NH: Heinemann, pp. 217–251.

Schraeder, P. J. 2000. *African Politics and Society: A Mosaic in Transformation*. Boston, MA: Bedford/St. Martin's.

Siebert, F. S., Peterson, T., and Schramm, W. 1956. *Four Theories of the Press: The Authoritarian, Libertarian, Social Responsibility and Soviet Communist Concepts of what the Press should be and Do?*. Urbana-Champaign, IL: The University of Illinois Press.

Silungwe, C. M. 2009. "Customary Land Tenure Reform and Development: a Critique of Customary Land Tenure Reform Under Malawi's National Land Policy." *Law, Social Justice and Global Development Journal* (*LegalTrac*. Web. 8 May 2012).

Suberu, R. T. 2010 "Nigeria's Muddled Elections" In Diamond, L., and Plattner, M. F. (Eds.) Democratization in Africa: Progress and Retreat. 2nd edition. Baltimore, MD: The Johns Hopkins University Press, pp. 121–136.

Suberu, R. 2000. "Governance and the Ethnic Factor." In Hyden, G., Oluwu, G., and Okoth-Ogendo, H. W. O. (Eds.) *African Perspectives on Governance*. Trenton, NJ: Africa World Press, pp. 123–151.

Taiwo, O. 2011. *How Colonialism Preempted Modernity in Africa.* Bloomington and Indianapolis: Indiana University Press.

The Carter Center 2010. *African Regional Findings and Plan of Action for the Advancement of the Right of Access to Information.* Accra, Ghana: The Carter Center and African Regional Conference on the Right of Access to Information.

United Nations Economic Commission for Asia and the Pacific (N.D) "What is Good Governance?." http://www.unescap.org/pdd/prs/ProjectActivities/Ongoing/gg/governance.pdf (accessed 26 January 2013).

Venatus, V. K. 2010. "Changing Customary Land Tenure System in Tivland: Understanding the Drivers of Change." *Canadian Social Science* 6(6): 146–150.

Webster, J. B., Boahen, A. A., and Idowu, H. O. 1967. *The Growth of African Civilisation: The Revolutionary Years of West Africa since 1800.* London: Longman Group Limited.

Willis, M. J. 2012. *Politics and Power in the Maghreb: Algeria, Tunisia, and Morocco from Independence to the Arab Spring.* New York: Columbia University Press.

Wiking, S. 1983. *Military Coups in Sub-Saharan Africa: How to Justify the Illegal Assumption of Power.* Uppsala: Scandinavian Institute of African Studies.

Wyrod, C. 2010. "Sierra Leone: A Vote for Better Governance." In Diamond, L., and Plattner, M. F. (Eds.) *Democratization in Africa: Progress and Retreat.* 2nd edition. Baltimore, MD: The Johns Hopkins University Press, pp. 166–178.

CHAPTER 10

Transportation and Communication

PREREADING ASSIGNMENT

Before we start, do the following prereading assignment.

1. What comes to mind when you think of transportation in Africa?

2. Make a list of all the modes/ forms of transportation by which the people of Africa travel in the countries they live in.

3. Of this list indicate which mode you think is the most widely used.

4. List all the main forms of communication used in Africa. Which of these forms do you think is the most widely used?

5. What do you foresee as the main problems of transportation and communication in Africa?

Transportation, the movement of people, goods, and services from one place to another, and communication, the mechanism of exchanging information between individuals and places, are indispensable to understanding the geography of places because of the physical, economic, political, and social roles they play in shaping places and regions. Physically, transportation and communication remove geographic isolation by overcoming the friction of distance. Economically, transportation and communication play the dual roles of being factors of production and distribution and sources of employment. As factors of production, transportation and communication allow locations to specialize. Without transportation and communication, every city, town, or village would have to be self-sufficient in what it needs to survive. However, by allowing locations to specialize transportation and communication help raise the productivity of people and places. By the same token, transportation and communication also add value to commodities, by imparting place utility and time utility. **Place utility** is the value a commodity gains by moving it from where it is least needed to where it is most needed. **Time utility** is the value a commodity gains by moving it to a place when it is needed. In these roles, transportation and communication contribute to the standard of living that we enjoy. As factors of distribution, transportation and communication networks also serve as the blood vessels of economies. Without them economies cannot function effectively.

Politically and socially, transportation and communication provide integration and cohesion of political units such as countries. Throughout history, changes in transportation and communication technologies have advanced major changes in human condition. Thus, worldwide exploration, industrialization, urbanization, trade and colonization, internationalization, and current globalization have all been made possible due to improvements in transportation and communication.

This chapter focuses on Africa's transportation and communication sectors. The chapter is divided into two sections and a summary. The first section deals with transportation, while the second section deals with communication. Each of these sections will focus on concepts, evolution, and development of the sector, contemporary organization, and problems and issues facing the sector. Before you continue, do the prereading assignment.

TRANSPORTATION

In 1922, Lord Lugard, the British colonialist and architect of the indirect rule stated: "the material development of Africa may be summed up in the word 'transport.'" After almost a century, transportation may not be the key but still a necessary requirement for material development of Africa. This is because Africa's transportation network is the least developed in the world. In this section, we consider the transportation system of Africa. We do this by looking at each of the major modes of transportation—road, rail, water, and air— with respect to their evolution and development, contemporary systems and organization, and problems and issues facing them.

Road Transportation

Precolonial Trails and Roads

The most dominant mode of transportation in precolonial Africa was land-based transportation, which consisted of trail and human porterage. These trails constituted the main mode of transportation for the first economies of hunting and gathering on the continent. As settlements grew and became more established a network of trails began to emerge. Trails also provided the migration routes that occurred on the continent, and later on helped support the emergence and subsequent expansion of empires and trade. In the Nile Valley and the Mediterranean region of the continent, these trails were upgraded into paved roads during the Egyptian and Roman civilizations. The oldest of these roads was discovered in Egypt in 1994. According to Wilford (1994), the road had an average width of six-and-a-half feet; it was paved with sandstone and limestone slabs and was dated between 2,600 and 2,200 BC. Over time, the vehicles on these trails and road transitioned from the donkey, the horse, and the camel to the wheeled vehicles. For the rest of the continent, however, trails continued to dominate both overland trade and travel with human porterage and animals such as donkeys, horses, and camels as the main vehicles.

Colonial Roads

Road transportation did not initially receive much attention during the colonial period because the focus was on waterways and railroads. However, due to the limited number of navigable rivers, and the expense of railroad construction, animal-wagons were the main means of transportation in many parts of Africa, particularly the north and south of the continent (Christopher, 1984). The first major road construction projects occurred in South Africa and Algeria during the first half of the 19th century. For the rest of the continent, roads were not properly cared for and often disappeared beyond the towns into mere tracks (Mlambo, 1994). This also made travel very slow, about 12.4–18.6 miles (20–30 km) a day and the animals suffered from diseases.

From the early 1920s, however, modern road transportation began to appear with the arrival of the first Ford vehicles from the United States, and this helped accelerate road building on the continent. Most of the roads were short and they took off from either water ports or railroad stations. Since the initial idea was for these roads to feed the railroad and river transportation networks, they were called **feeder roads** (Van Der Laan, 1981). In French Africa, these were constructed to carry cotton to the rail in Mali and Burkina Faso, banana in Guinea, and groundnuts (peanuts) in Senegal. Later on, these were extended to link the seats of colonial administration. However, further plans for developing road transportation never materialized.

Postcolonial Roads

By the early 1960s, only few African countries—South Africa and the North African countries—had paved roads. According to Debrie (2010), Mali, for example, had only 155.3 miles (250 km) of paved roads, while both of Niger and Burkina Faso had only 31 miles (50 km) of paved roads. In these and other Francophone African countries in West Africa, colonial transportation investment had concentrated on the western side to the isolation of their eastern regions. To address these and other deficiencies in the transportation networks, African countries embarked on massive road building projects. Mali, for example, concentrated first on the southern and the most populous region as well as most productive part of the country in terms of cotton, its main export. It did this by constructing a triangle of road network anchored to the west by Bamako, to the northeast by Segou and to the south by Sikasso. It then extended the link from Segou to Gao as part of serving its neglected eastern region. Niger built a west-east "Unity Road" corridor from Niamey to Lake Chad. It then constructed a number of roads perpendicular to the corridor to serve other areas including the northern "Uranium Road" to Agadez and beyond to Airlit. Senegal built Dieri Road from Dakar to Matam, while Mauritania built its "Road of Hope" from Nouakchott to Nema. Within two decades of independence, about 932 miles (1,500 km) of paved roads had been completed in Mali, and between 1979 and 1986 Niger built over 745.6 miles (1,200 km) of roads (Debrie, 2010). Similar road-building projects were undertaken across the continent.

After having concentrated on their interior regions, African countries then turned their attention to connecting with their neighbors as the next phase of development of road transport. For landlocked countries in particular, this was also necessary to gain access to seaports. Thus Mali, Burkina Faso, Niger, and Chad all constructed paved roads to the neighboring countries. In 1971, this individualized action was formalized when the United Nations Economic Commission for Africa (UNECA) proposed the building of a **Trans-African Highway (TAH) network**. Construction has continued since.

The Contemporary Road Network

Road transportation is now the most dominant mode of transportation in Africa. It is estimated that there are about 653,682, miles (1,052,000 km) of classified roads (main and secondary roads) and about 305,715 miles (492,000 km) of unclassified roads in the network (Figure 10.1). Geographically, this network consists of three groups—international, national, and rural or local networks.

The international network consists of roads that cross national boundaries to serve a number of countries. Given that there are 17 landlocked countries in Africa, these roads emanate from the coastal countries to the landlocked countries. For Central Africa, they include the two roads from Douala, Cameroon to Chad and Central African Republic. For East Africa, they include two roads: one from Mombasa, Kenya to Uganda, Rwanda, Burundi, and DRC, and other is from Dar es Salaam to DRC and Zambia. For southern Africa, the main route is from Durban to Zambia

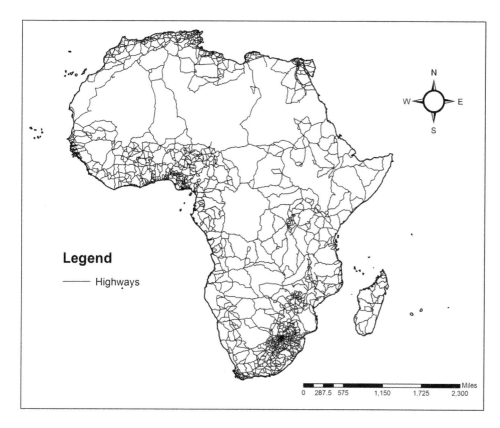

FIGURE 10.1 Africa
road network.
Source: ESRI, Garmin

and southern DRC. Others include those from Beira, Walvis Bay, and Dar es Salaam.
For West Africa, there are several routes from Nigeria, Benin, Togo, Ghana, and
Cote d'Ivoire to Burkina Faso, Mali, and Niger, while from North Africa they are
from Egypt, Libya, and Algeria to Sudan, Chad, and Niger. It was to augment these
international networks that the TAH network was proposed. This network consists of
nine TAH corridors anchored by all the major cities on the continent (Figure 10.2).

The national network consists of classified roads of individual countries. Generally,
these networks show a wide range of density and connectivity. These are usually classified as primary, secondary, and tertiary roads. Primary and secondary roads are
paved while tertiary roads are not. The road density per 1,000 people varies from
0.3 mile (0.5 km) per 1,000 people in Burundi to 7 miles (21.0 km) in Namibia.
The percentage of roads paved also varies among countries. Richer countries such
as South Africa and Botswana have higher proportion of roads paved, while poorer
countries such as Central African Republic, Chad, and DRC have less that 20% of
their roads paved. Rural networks consist largely of unclassified or unpaved roads in
most countries.

Organization of Road Transport Service

Road transportation service in Africa may be classified in two ways—by geography
or area of operation and by ownership. By geography, they are urban transportation and rural transportation. Urban transportation can be further classified into
intraurban and **interurban**. The first refers to within cities and the second between
cities or within the urban system and across national boundaries or international.

FIGURE 10.2 Trans-African Highway.
Source: African Development Bank 2010.

By ownership, road transportation consists of public and private. Intraurban transportation was discussed in Chapter 8, so this section will be limited to interurban and rural transportation.

Interurban private road transportation is the dominant sector of the road transportation service. This consists primarily of medium-sized (minibuses) and large-sized passenger buses that ply between cities and by default through some of the rural areas, and trucks that carry largely cargo. The medium-sized passenger buses operate over short-to-medium distances while the large buses operate over medium-to-long distances and across national borders. Each vehicle usually specializes in servicing a particular route with the frequency of service depending on route length. Over short distances the service may be several times in a day; over medium distances it may be once a day, while over longer distances it may be a couple of days or even once a week.

Service begins at terminals or stations that are usually scattered over the city depending on the routes of operations. There are usually two types of service. The first is a local service that stops at every town or village between origins and destinations. The second is an express service, which operates as a nonstop or limited stop service between origins and destinations. In countries, where these private operators are unionized, the union sets the fares and the freight rates, and manages the terminals or stations regarding the order in which the vehicles are loaded. Fares are set using various methods. Sometimes, it is discriminatory in that a flat fare is charged irrespective of the distance the person is traveling.

Interurban public road transportation service consists of government-operated service between cities and to rural areas. This type of government service used to be more predominant in the early postindependence period through the 1980s. Thus, a fleet of buses operated by a state-owned transportation corporation usually radiated from the capital city and regional or provincial capitals to various parts of the country. This was seen as a necessary service to the people. However, management problems, frequent breakdowns due to bad roads, and lack of spare parts for proper maintenance plunged many of these services into insolvency. During the period of the structural adjustment programs (SAPs) many of these services were either discontinued or privatized due to the divestiture. Today very few countries have such state-operated buses.

Another interurban road transportation is the rental car service, which operates as extension of the city taxi service. This service caters largely to tourists and natives living abroad who return home for short vacations, and expatriates and researchers or who may occasionally need transportation to project sites in the absence of project vehicles. The providers of this service may be tour companies or single operators and they usually provide not only the vehicles but also the drivers.

Problems and Issues in Road Transportation

Quality   By international standards, Africa's road network has a lower spatial density mostly because of the sparse population distribution of the continent. Apart from this, the quality of roads varies widely. Gwilliam (2011) estimates that about 43% of the main networks are in good condition; 31% are fair, while 27% are poor. After more than 40 years of construction, the TAH network is yet to come to fruition. At a mid-2008 review of progress of the network, the African Development Bank (AfDB) reported that almost 50% of the roads in the over 50,000 km network were in poor conditions, and about 25% either had an earth surface or were completely nonexistent. Sadly, at its 15th Forum in Yaoundé, Cameroon, in 2013, the Association of African Road Managers and Practitioners (AGEPAR) noted again that in spite of continuous efforts to integrate the continent with good roads the results have been disappointing (Bainkong, 2013). Africa's road density still remains the lowest in the world—being 7 km (4.5 mi) per 100 square km (39 square mi) compared to 12 km (7.5 mi) in Latin America and 18 km (11 mi) in Asia. The network remains scattered, unusable, and in some places nonexistent; most of the missing links were in Central Africa (Table 10.1).

TABLE **10.1**

Status of the Trans-African Highway Network

Route	Terminals	Length Km	Mi.	Current status
TAH 1	Cairo – Dakar	8,636	5,366	Substantially complete. Major sections in Tunisia, Algeria, and Morocco under upgrading to motorways. Missing link is a short desert route on the Morocco–Mauritania border.
TAH 2	Algiers – Lagos	4,504	2,799	Substantially complete: 200 km of desert track in Niger. Border and security restricts usage.
TAH 3	Tripoli – Windhoek – Cape Town	10,808	6,716	Paved national roads in Libya, Cameroon, Angola, Namibia, and South Africa. Missing links are in Chad, Central African Republic, Congo Republic, and DRC. Also missing is the bridge over the Congo between Congo Republic and DRC.
TAH 4	Cairo – Gaborone – Cape Town	10,228	6,355	Southern portion from Cape Town to Kenya is complete. Missing link in Tanzania through Dodoma is gravel road while the earth road from Kenya to Ethiopia is under construction. Crossing from Sudan to Egypt is by ferry.
TAH 5	Dakar – Ndjamena	4,496	2,794	100% complete from Dakar to Fotokol.
TAH 6	Ndjamena – Djibouti	4,219	2,622	Mostly earth road between Chad and Sudan.
TAH 7	Dakar – Lagos	4,560	2,834	About 80% complete (100% paved in Nigeria, Benin, Togo, Ghana, Cote d'Ivoire, and Senegal. Missing links (765 km) in Liberia, Sierra Leone, Guinea, Guinea Bissau. Varying conditions—9% good, 59% fair, and 32% poor.
TAH 8	Lagos – Mombasa	6,259	3,899	Easter link from Kenya to Uganda is complete. Western links in Central African Rep, Cameroon, and Nigeria mostly complete. Missing links in DRC and parts of Central African Republic.
TAH 9	Beira – Lobito	3,523	2,189	Substantially complete but the western portion through Angola and DRC must be reconstructed. Alternative route exists in the Trans-Kalahari Highway from Maputo to Walvis Bay.

Source: Robert M. Okello 2010. Infrastructure and Intra-African Trade.

At the national level, the AfDB (2010) report noted that the countries with most of their national road networks in good condition were South Africa, Mauritius, Burkina Faso, Botswana, and Central African Republic in that order. In contrast, the countries with most of their national road network in poor conditions were Congo Republic, Togo, Guinea, and DRC. For rural network, it was Mauritius, Burkina Faso, Ghana, Kenya, and Malawi that had most of their rural networks in good condition, while Rwanda, Madagascar, and Angola had the highest percentage of their road network in poor conditions. Rural accessibility is particularly a problem, as roads are generally unpaved and become unusable especially in the rainy season.

Safety Road safety is also a major problem in Africa. It is estimated that with only 4% of the world's vehicle fleets, Africa accounts for about 10% of the world's road fatalities. The causes of these are complex and include poor quality of roads, speeding, drunk driving, overloading, and poor vehicle and road maintenance. A number of countries including Ghana and South Africa have established National Safety Councils to deal with the safety problems.

Funding and maintenance management The roots of the poor conditions of most of Africa's road network lie in funding and maintenance. According to Gwilliam (2011), about 50% of African countries do not devote enough funds to maintenance of road networks, and about 25% do not allocate enough funds for even routine maintenance tasks. This is because most of the road construction and maintenance rely on external funding. There are policies in place to generate domestic funds for road building and maintenance through user fees and fuel taxes. However, these are not properly administered. In some cases, the fuel taxes are set much below the cost of maintenance for political reasons. The result is that not enough revenue is generated for even maintenance. Besides, there is also the problem of collection of fees and taxes and the corrupt practices of evasion of such taxes, tolls, and transfer of funds from the collection agencies to road funds. In addition, board members overseeing the road funds are usually political appointees, and are therefore not independent from the government. Owing to lack of domestic funds, regular maintenance does not occur leaving the physical conditions of roads to deteriorate till they become really expensive to fix them.

Road network administration There are two types of road administration in African countries—the first type is where the agency is part of the ministry of transportation and the second type is when it is established as independent agency. Research indicates that paved roads fare better under independent agency. However, both types of road administration are plagued with similar problems. First is the ability to recruit and retain qualified technical staff especially engineers and transportation planners. This has led to a situation where much of the work of monitoring performance and asset management is contracted out to consultants. Without a transparency process of awarding these contracts, this practice has become another recipe for corruption and inefficiencies.

Administration of rural roads is even more problematic due to a number of reasons. First, local government structures are very weak in many African countries because of half-hearted decentralization policies. For this reason, local governments have very limited means of generating revenues, and thus have to depend on transfer payments from central governments, which in turn do not allocate enough funds to cover road infrastructure. In cases where road administration is centralized, main trunk ways as well as major urban roads always take precedence. Community self-help and hometown associations have in some cases contributed toward building of rural roads but after that, the maintenance of such roads has fallen through the cracks. Gwilliam (2011) cites a case in Zambia where a nongovernmental organization built 1,000 km (621.3 mi) of roads but because no institution became responsible for maintenance, the roads have all deteriorated.

Road funding and spending Gwilliam (2011) also draws a distinction between road funding and road spending. The first refers to allocation of budget to roads, while the second refers to actual execution of activities. It is estimated that African countries spend about 1.8% of their GDP on roads, compared to Brazil, India, Korea, and Russia who spend 2–3% of their GDP on roads. Road spending varies widely across the continent and is mediated by several factors including country size, physical geography, income level, and existence or nonexistence of road institutions. For example, large, landlocked, and low-income countries as well as countries with rolling terrain, humid conditions, and road institutions tend to spend more on roads than countries that do not have such characteristics and institutions. Apart from this, because there is a general lack of maintenance, a greater proportion of the capital spending goes into rehabilitation of existing roads and a lesser proportion to upgrades and new roads.

Inflation and cost of road work Related to the problem of funding and spending on road networks in Africa is inflation, which leads to rising cost of roadwork. Gwilliam (2011) cites data to show that average maintenance cost of road in Africa is $2,160 per km compared to $2,024 per km in South and East Asia. He also reports that the unit cost of recently completed road projects in Africa were two to three times higher than those in the World Bank's road cost database (ROCKS). He attributes the causes of these to lack of effective competition for road projects in Africa, recent rising cost in key road-building inputs such as bitumen, cement, and steel, and delays in implementation of projects. The result of all these has been substantial cost overruns of road projects, which are becoming problems for donor agencies.

Overengineering and underengineering Generally speaking, a minimum of 300 vehicles per day on a nonrural road is considered as the threshold to make paving the road economically viable. If the number of vehicles per day on a paved main road is below 300, the road is said to be overengineered, while an unpaved road with more than 300 vehicles per day is said to be underengineered. Gwilliam (2011) estimates that on the average about 30% of Africa's main road network appears to be overengineered, while about 10% is underengineered. Both **overengineering** and **underengineering** can increase cost of roadwork; overengineering can add to cost overrun, while underengineering can accelerate the deterioration of the road.

Water Transportation—Inland Waterways and Ocean Transportation

Precolonial Period

Water transportation emerged concurrently with trail along Africa's coastal regions as well as in the interior regions with navigable rivers and lakes. The Dafuna Canoe found in 1987 near the Yobe River in Nigeria, and dated as over 8,000 years old, is an indicator of how far back water transportation has been in Africa. Transportation by inland waterways was prevalent in Ancient Egypt as well as other parts of the continent, where navigable reaches permitted. These navigable reaches included those on the Nile, the Senegal, the Gambia, the Middle and Lower Niger, the Benue, and the Lower Volta (Van Der Laan, 1981; Law, 2011), as well as the Congo, and the Ogooue in Gabon (Law, 2011). These rivers provided the main artery of transportation in their respective valleys. They also created river communities that came to control various sections of the rivers, and served as middlemen in the long-distance trade between the interior and the coast in precolonial Africa. Inland waterways became very important from the late 1700s through the 1880s, when Europeans tried to reach Africa's interior.

Ocean transportation was widely used in Ancient Africa, especially along the Mediterranean Coasts where several seaports were established by the Ancient Egyptians, Greeks, Phoenicians, and Romans. One of these was Mersa Gawasis, on the Red Sea, which after its excavation in 2011 is now considered to be the world's oldest seaport. Some of these ports such as Alexandria, Tunis, Algiers, and Tripoli, solidified their positions through the Medieval Period under Arab and Ottoman colonization of North Africa, while others declined. Elsewhere on the continent ocean transportation was also used by fishermen and other coastal residents. Along the eastern coast of Africa, Arab and Persian trade with Africans led to the growth of coastal towns such as Mombasa, Kilwa, and Mogadishu. The European voyages of exploration from the 15th century converted many fishing villages along the coast of Africa into ports or landing sites as well as establishment of new ones.

Colonial Period

Four major developments advanced water transportation in Africa during the colonial period. The first was the technological development in water vessels. The second was the building of the Suez Canal, the third was the use of rail to augment inland waterways, and the fourth was the development of modern seaports. The main technological developments in water vessels were the steady increase in the size of the vessels and the emergence of the steamer. The increase in vessel size allowed more tonnage of cargo and later passengers, while the steamships cut the travel time between places, and allowed scheduled services (Christopher, 1984).

The site of the Suez Canal had been on the crossroads of transportation, communication, and commerce since ancient times. However, initially it was all about connecting the Nile either to the Red Sea or to the Mediterranean Sea, by canals. Historical records show that at least three canals were constructed in Ancient Egypt to accomplish this (Hallberg, 1931). From the 16th century, various European powers, especially France, kept an on-and-off interest in the canal for imperialistic reasons, but it was not until the 19th century during the reign of Mohammed Ali in Egypt that the canal was seriously considered. After a couple of setbacks, construction began in 1859 from Port Said (named after the Viceroy) to Suez. The canal was opened in 1869 in Suez, and instantly it reduced the voyage from Western Europe (England) to East and Southeast Asia (Calcutta), from 20,922 km (13,000 mi) to 12,875 km (8,000 mi).

The use of rail to augment inland waterways became necessary for dealing with the physical obstacles in most of Africa's large rivers, namely, rapids and waterfalls—which impeded river transportation. The most significant example of this occurred in the Belgian Congo, where waterfalls and rapids interrupted the continuous use of the Congo River System (Figure 10.3). To deal with these, three railroads were built along three waterfall segments of the Congo River. The first was from Kolongo to Kindu to go around a series of rapids. The second was from Ponthierville (Kindu) to Stanleyville (Kisangani), to go around the Stanley Falls. The third was from Leopoldville (Kinshasa) to Matadi to go around another series of rapids.

The development of modern seaports in Africa was driven by political and economic reasons of colonialism and changing technologies of ocean transportation that made the trading posts that dotted the coast of Africa inadequate or obsolete. The first of these modern seaports appears to have been built in Algiers in 1594 when Algiers was a Regency of the Ottoman Empire. This was for both economic and defense reasons. However, it was in the 19th and early 20th centuries that modern port development accelerated. By the eve of the independence movement, most of the existing modern seaports of Africa had been built.

Postcolonial Period

Given that majority of the seaports were built in the late 19th and 20th centuries, the early postcolonial period saw modernization and extensions of many of those seaports. At the same time, the seaports had to catch up with containerization. In Nigeria, for example, increasing trade due to new oil exports put pressure on the government to acquire three private ports in the Niger Delta region—Warri, Burutu, and Calabar (Akinwale and Aremo, 2010). In Southern Africa, Fraser and Notteboom (2012) report of several seaports increasing their container

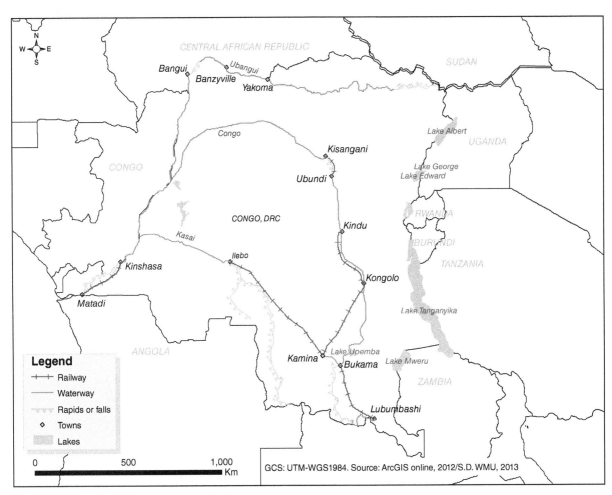

FIGURE 10.3 The Congo River waterway and rail system.
Source: Created by Benjamin Ofori-Amoah

trade and share of container trade market during this period. In South Africa, container trade grew from 4% in 1985–1989; and 11% from 1990 to 1999, with much of that growth occurring at Cape Town, Durban, and Port Elizabeth. Port Louis, Mauritius, increased its container throughput from 4% in 1985 to 10% in 2010; Toamasina, Madagascar, increased its market share from 2% in 1985 to 3% in 2010, while Walvis Bay, Namibia went from 1% in 2000 to 6% in 2010.

However, the economic downturn in the 1980s affected water transportation severely. With the exception of oil production, export trade dropped sharply thus affecting the volume of goods that were shipped from Africa's seaports (AfDB, 2010). Some of the seaports fell behind in upgrading their infrastructure and technologies to keep up with global trends. Inland waterways such as the vast network of the Congo River system fell into disrepair with outmoded equipment and technology and improper channel markings, and nonphysical barriers. The same occurred in West Africa's inland waterways.

Improvements in Africa's trade in the last decade revealed another problem of Africa's seaports, namely congestion and inefficiencies. Many countries, including Nigeria, Ghana, Madagascar, Tanzania, and Mozambique, adopted the **concession approach** to privatization of their seaport activities. A **concession** is a contractual agreement between a government and a private entity by which the private entity takes over the management and operations of a public facility with the responsibility to financing the infrastructure and upgrading of the facilities' equipment, for an agreed fee and over an agreed period. This of course generated a lot of tension with labor unions who among things charged that the concessions were a form of re-colonization. Apart from this privatization also increased competition among the seaports. In Southern Africa, for example, Fraser and Notteboom (2012) reported about the competitive advantage the port of Maputo had over Durban in terms of its proximity to the industrial district of Gauteng, South Africa. This led to growth in volume of traffic in Maputo of about 15% during the recession of 2008–2009, while Durban saw a 4% decline. A similar competition has been occurring on the west coast of southern Africa between Cape Town, South Africa and Walvis Bay, Namibia. Cape Town gets the competitive edge over Walvis Bay regarding the Gauteng industrial district. However, Walvis Bay is in a better position in relation to the landlocked countries of Botswana, and parts of Zimbabwe and Zambia.

Contemporary Water Transportation Network

Inland waterways Inland waterways were very important means of transportation in the 20th century in all of Africa's riparian regions. As it was mentioned in Chapter 4, the Congo Basin has the largest network of inland waterways in Africa. This has been the most important means for moving people in the DRC, but political and economic instability that have characterized the DRC have also retarded the growth and improvements of this vast network. In the Nile Basin, 9 of the 11 countries in the basin had navigable reaches that combined well with other modes of transportation to serve the people in the basin. River ports were common especially in Egypt and Uganda. However, most of these have declined partly due to civil wars in the Sudan that especially created safety concerns that caused people to switch over to road transport. Egypt today has the most developed inland water transportation system. In 2007, it launched a program to increase traffic on the Nile by 2017 and eventually phase out trailer-trucks. On its part, Lake Victoria transportation is beset with several problems including poor connectivity with other transportation modes, poor navigation facilities including lighthouses, antiquated water vessels, and low ridership (Nile Basin Initiative, 2012). The Niger, the Zambezi, the Senegal, and the Gambia have also served as important inland water transportation arteries but faced the same problems, in addition to natural obstacles such as rapids and waterfalls. In recent years, governments of countries in these basins have made pronouncements about the importance of these waterways and initiated plans to harness their potential. There has been some talk about linking Africa's major rivers and lakes with canals just as Europe and the United States did in the early periods of their development to form Trans-African Waterway System. Whether this will happen requires political will, cooperation, and commitment on the part of African countries.

Ocean transportation There were about 78 major seaports in Africa in 2015 (Table 10.2). The locations of most of these are shown in Figure 10.4. Ports are usually classified according to their functions and the goods they handle. Using these two criteria, Africa's ports are of seven different types. They include general cargo, feeder, hub, bulk, and river ports, as well as transshipments and dedicated oil terminals (Table 10.3). Data from the United Nations Conference on Trade and Development (UNCTAD) in 2014 also showed that 34 African countries owned 840 ships, which was only 1.7% of the total world fleet. Nigeria had the largest number of ships (31.5%) followed by Egypt (26.3%), South Africa (7.2), and Angola (6.3%). By ship deadweight or mass, Angola accounted for 25.6%, Nigeria 21%, and Egypt 15% (Table 10.4). About 25% of the number of ships were registered in the top 25 ship

TABLE **10.2**

Modern Major Seaports of Africa

Country	Seaport	Country	Seaport
Algeria	Algiers, Annaba, Ghazaouet, Oran	Libya	Tripoli, Benghazi, Tobruk, Marsa el Brega
Angola	Luanda, Lobito, Nambibe	Madagascar	Toamasina, Mahajanga, Antsiranana
Benin	Cotonou	Mauritania	Nouakchott, Nouadhibou
Cameroon	Doula	Morocco	Casablanca, Agadir, Tangier
Congo Rep	Pointe Noire	Mozambique	Maputo, Beira, Nacala
Congo D. R.	Matadi, Boma, Banana	Namibia	Walvis Bay, Luderitz
Djibouti	Djibouti	Nigeria	Lagos (Apapa), Port Harcourt
Egypt	Alexandria, Port Said, Suez, Damietta	Senegal	Dakar, Kaolack
Eqt. Guinea	Malabo, Bata	Sierra Leone	Freetown
Gabon	Libreville, Port Gentil	Somalia	Mogadishu, Barbera, Merca
Gambia	Banjul	South Africa	Durban, Cape Town, Port Elizabeth, East London
Ghana	Tema, Takoradi	Sudan	Port Sudan, Suikan
Guinea	Conakry, Kamsar	Tanzania	Dar es Salaam
G. Bissau	Bissau	Togo	Lome
Cote d'Ivoire	Abidjan, San Pedro	Tunisia	Tunis, Bizerta, Sfax, La Goelette
Kenya	Mombasa, Lamu	West. Sahara	Ad Dakhla, Laayoune (El Aaiun)
Liberia	Monrovia, Buchanan, Cape Palmas, Grenville		

registries led by Panama, Bahamas, Liberia, Singapore, and Malta. By deadweight, however, 51% of the ships were registered in the top 25 registries led by Singapore, The Bahamas, Panama, and Liberia (Table 10.5).

International Containerization data shows that in 2014, Africa handled 4.1% of the world's container traffic (TEU). Ocean transportation today is mostly for goods transportation in container ships that are measured in twenty-foot equivalent units or TEUs. In 2014, Egypt accounted for 31.4% of Africa's container traffic followed by South Africa (17.2) and Morocco (10.9) (Figure 10.5). The busiest seaports in terms of container traffic handled in 2015 reflect on the top leading countries with a few exceptions. Port Said (Egypt) was followed by Tanger-Med (Morocco) and Durban (South Africa) (Figure 10.6).

Problems and Issues of Africa's Water Transportation

Seaport infrastructure and capacity There are two types of seaport infrastructure, physical and soft infrastructure (AfDB, 2010). The physical infrastructure includes deep-water facilities and berths, and the superstructure facilities for loading and unloading ships, movement of cargo, as well as fuel, water, and cleaning and repair services. The soft infrastructure includes the administration of shipment, custom services, taxation, and the paperwork that go with the physical movement of goods. These two determine the capacity and efficiency of the port.

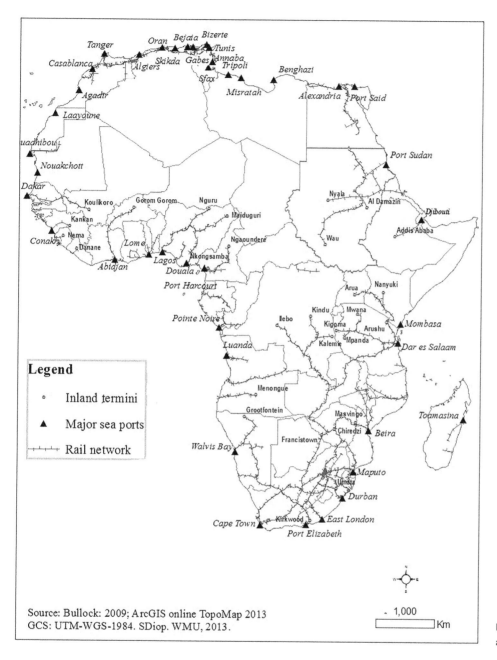

FIGURE 10.4 African seaports and railways.

Compared to the rest of the world, African ports are generally small in terms of size and cargo handled. Port statistics based on tonnage is difficult to compare because of differences in tonnage measurement. However, available data from Containerization Yearbook 2016 and other sources show that by metric tons of cargo, only three African seaports made it to the top 100 seaports in the world in 2015. They were Richards Bay (South Africa) ranked 38, Saldanha Bay (South Africa) ranked 58, and Alexandria/El-Dekheila (Egypt) ranked 87; by container traffic, there were four in the 2015 top 100 seaports—Port Said (East) ranked 43, Tanger ranked 44, Durban ranked 46, and Alexandria/El-Dekheila ranked 77, while the World Shipping Council ranked only Port Said (41) among the top 50 container ports. Together, Egypt and

TABLE **10.3**

Port Types by Functions

Port type	Description
General cargo	Medium-sized ports with volume ranging from 2 to 10 million tons per year and 100,000–500,000 TEUs per year. E.g Port Elizabeth and Walvis Bay.
Hub	Large regional ports that serve large hinterlands, which in turn have small ports. E. g. Port Said and Durban.
Feeder	Smaller ports with depth and number and size of vessels restrictions. Less that 100,000 TEUs per year.
Bulk	Dedicated to handling large volumes of bulk material and accommodating vessels with depth of 18–25 m. In general they have no container terminals. E.g. Richards Bay (coal) and Saldanha (iron ore) in South Africa; Port Saco (iron ore) in Angola, and Buchanan (iron ore) in Liberia.
Transshipment	A large container terminal where cargo is transferred from one carrier to another. E.g. Algiers, Durban, Mombasa, and Djibouti. They handle very large container vessels above 6,000 TEUs, very few African ports meet this requirement.
Oil	These are dedicated to handle crude oil, which is most often transported by Capesize vessels of 120,000 to 150,000 dwt. These require greater depth than any African port can provide at this time. Very few African ports have dedicated oil terminals, e. g. Cape Town. Oil tankers are mostly handled offshore with links to landside storage tanks through submarine pipelines.
River	Small and isolated ports on rivers that do not serve ocean-going vessels. The only exception in Africa is Matadi in DRC, which is a river port but serves ocean-going vessels.

Source: African Development Report 2010.

TABLE **10.4**

Ship Ownership in Africa, 2014

Ownership by count			Ownership by deadweight		
Country	**Number**	**%**	**Country**	**Tons**	**%**
Nigeria	258	31.5	Angola	5,629.7	25.6
Egypt	216	26.3	Nigeria	4,602.6	21.0
South Africa	59	7.2	Egypt	3,299.8	15.0
Angola	52	6.3	Libya	2,440.3	11.1
Algeria	49	6.0	South Africa	2,196.9	10.0
Libya	32	3.9	Algeria	1,427.6	6.5
Morocco	26	3.2	Ethiopia	433.8	2.0
Ethiopia	17	2.1	Cameroon	428.7	2.0
Tunisia	13	1.6	Congo	364.2	1.7
Ghana	10	1.2	Tunisia	329.9	1.5
Seychelles	10	1.2	Seychelles	212.9	1.0
Tanzania	10	1.2	Mauritius	147.7	0.7
Rest of Africa	68	8.3	Rest of Africa	601.9	2.7
Total of Africa	840	100.0	Total of Africa	21,968.4	100.0

Source: Data from UNCTAD.

TABLE 10.5

Registered Countries or Flag Nations of Ships Owned by African Countries

Registration by count			Registration by deadweight		
Top 25 registries	Number	%	Top 25 registries	Tons	%
Panama	61	7.4	Singapore	15.6	15.6
Bahamas	35	4.3	Bahamas	10.9	10.9
Liberia	26	3.2	Panama	5.8	5.8
Singapore	19	2.3	Liberia	3.7	3.7
Malta	17	2.1	Isle of Man	3.4	3.4
Bermuda	13	1.6	Bermuda	3.3	3.3
China, Hong Kong SAR	11	1.3	Marshall Islands	3.1	3.1
Cyprus	7	0.9	Malta	2.7	2.7
Isle of Man	7	0.9	China, Hong Kong SAR	1.4	1.4
Marshall Islands	6	0.7	Cyprus	0.5	0.5
Norway	2	0.2	UK	0.4	0.4
UK	1	0.1	Indonesia	0.3	0.3
Top 25 registries	205	25	Top 25 registries	19,703.2	51.1
Other registries	615	75	Other registries	18,862.01	48.9

Source: Data from UNCTAD.

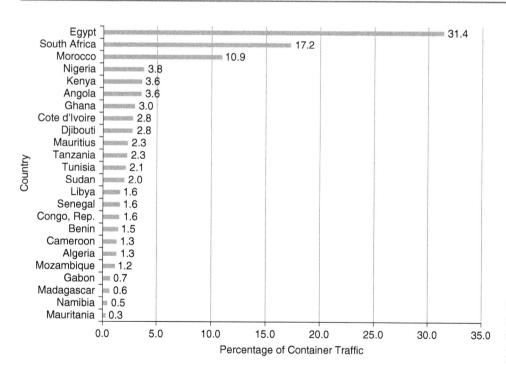

FIGURE 10.5 Container traffic (percent TEU) in Africa in 2014. *Source:* Containerization International Yearbook.

South Africa, as well as Morocco, have the largest seaport capacities as well as some of the most sophisticated seaports in Africa. Apart from these, the majority of the seaports are small, congested, and have outdated equipment. The AfDB (2010) port development report noted that only nine ports could accommodate the post and

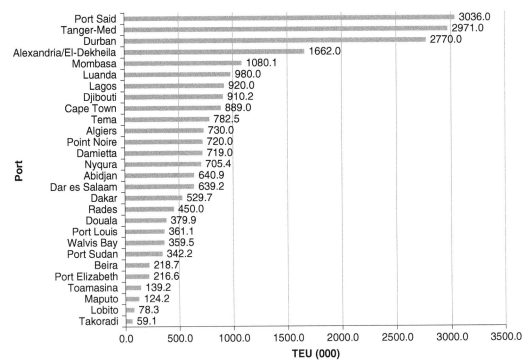

FIGURE 10.6 Busiest seaports in Africa by container traffic handled in 2015.
Source: Containerization International Yearbook, 2017

super **Panamax** ships, which are the largest ships that can pass through the Panama Canal after it was expanded. Four of these were in Egypt, three in South Africa, and one each in Mauritius and Morocco. Thus, in spite of the growth of container traffic in Africa by developing countries standard, African countries are not competitive. African seaports return a greater part of the containers empty than anywhere else does in the world. The capacity situation is better in North and Southern Africa, where Egypt and South Africa have larger capacities, and worse in West, Central, and East Africa, especially in Tanzania and Mozambique.

AfDB (2010) attributed the cause of congestion to several factors including poor physical infrastructure, malfunctioning regulatory systems, and poor management. Part of the poor physical infrastructure is due to the negligible role Africa plays in seaborne trade. For this reason, Africa's merchant fleets are very small and consist largely of old vessels. A major obstacle here is financing the physical infrastructure at the port.

Efficiency Seaport efficiency is measured in various ways among which are **turnaround time**, **dwell time**, and Liner Shipping Connectivity Index (LSCI). The turnaround time is the duration that cargo stays in port before or after shipment. When total turnaround is divided by the number of ships, an average turnaround time is obtained. The turnaround time usually consists of two parts, time at berth and time off berth. The ratio between the time off berth (waiting time to berth) to the time at berth is the waiting rate, which is a good indicator of congestion. A high ratio indicates high congestion.

A measure of port efficiency that is of more concern to exporters and importers is the dwell time, which is the number of days a ton of cargo remains at port (AfDB, 2010). African ports are notorious for their dwell time. With the exception of Durban's 4 days and Mombasa's 5–7 days, majority of the seaports have more than 10 days of dwell time. The worst are the West African ports—Doula, Cameroon, (19 days), Tema, Ghana (20 days), and Lagos-Apapa, Nigeria, (19–25 days). These are about four times higher than in East Asia. Low efficiency also contributes to high cost since the time spent at the port translates into loss of business. Thus, low efficiency in turn is one of the determining factors of shipping lines to call at a port.

Port efficiency also depends on how much integration the port has with world trade. This is measured in terms of several factors including number of ships, the ships' container-carrying capacity, maximum ship size, number of services, and the number of companies that send ships to serve the port. Africa's low participation in global trade (Chapter 15) also constitutes a drag on the efficiency of its ports since it leads to low connectivity with the rest of the world.

Port management and administration Generally speaking, there are three models of port management—the **landlord port**, the **tool port**, and the **service port** models. With the landlord port, the public authority (PA) owns the facilities and rents them out or awards concessions to private companies to operate the port. With the tool port, the PA owns the superstructure and equipment while private sector operates the facilities. For service port, the PA owns the superstructure and manages all services.

Until 1980, African ports were all government controlled. From the 1980s, however, several factors combined to gradually push African countries toward private involvements in port management and administration. First was the realization that governments should limit their roles to provision of public goods. Second, the period of SAPs and divestiture forced African governments to outsource many of the port services. In recent years, there has been a shift toward the landlord model of port management. This has been in the form of awarding concessions of various types. Some countries especially in West Africa have also followed public–private partnership. The highest rate of private sector involvement is found in North, East and Southern Africa, with West Africa being the least even though Ghana and Nigeria have actually adopted the landlord model. Even so, in many African countries the control of ports seems to be still under central governments' control due to the apparent unwillingness on the part of governments to let go. Given that studies have shown that privatization actually lowers cost for the government, this situation is striking.

Regulatory environment Privatization has several advantages for Africa's port systems but that alone cannot resolve all the problems of inefficiency. World Bank (2009) reports the case of Apapa port of Lagos where the award of a concession to private company to manage the port in 2006 drastically reduced congestion at the port initially to the point that liners dropped their waiting charges from €525 to €75 per TEU. By 2009, acquisition of new equipment actually tripled the capacity of the port, but then a new problem emerged in the form of unclaimed containers. By the end of January 2009, there were 851 unclaimed containers even though all clearance charges had been paid. This caused the Nigerian Port Authority to shut down the port in February to mid-April to clear the backlog. This shows that privatization efforts need the backing of strong regulatory reforms. For the most part, there are no independent governing bodies for Africa's ports with authority to prevent this case from happening, except in South Africa.

Fleet size and cost Fleet size and the cost of acquiring new ships to replace the old ones constitute another set of problems for Africa. Thus, the number of companies operating shipping business in Africa fell between 2004 and 2009. In Egypt, for example, it fell from 61 in 2004 to 47 in 2009 while in South Africa it fell from 38 in 2004 to 30 in 2009 (AfDB, 2010). This makes it difficult to achieve economies of scale and efficiency.

Customs procedures Africa has unnecessarily long and cumbersome customs procedures. For example, it takes 7 days to export and 8 days to import goods in developed economies compared to 34 and 40 days in Africa. It is even longer for Central Africa and Africa's landlocked countries—where it is 55 and 56 days, respectively, to clear imported goods (AfDB, 2010). Part of these long delays is the extensive amount of paperwork required by African countries. The average is eight documents for export and nine for import as compared to four and five, respectively, in North America. The most required in Africa for export is 12 in Angola and Malawi, and 18 for imports in CAR. Such excessive paperwork breeds opportunities for corruption, extortion, and unnecessary delays, as well as increasing cost for exporters and importers. A number of African countries have instituted several reforms including the adoption of new software that have helped reduce customs. This includes *Transports Internationaux Routiers* (TIR) and the World Customs Organization (WCO) Columbus program. The first allows goods to cross international borders with limited customs interference while the second aims at reducing custom clearance time as well as corruption.

Connectivity and accessibility problems Seaports are as efficient as their connectivity to the nodes in the area they serve, and for that reason other modes of transportation, namely road, rail, and inland waterways. Unfortunately, due to what AfDB (2010) calls the vicious cycle of underinvestment, dilapidated facilities, and little trade participation, intermodal connectivity of Africa's seaports is rather poor. Road transport, the most dominant mode of transportation in Africa has very weak connectivity as we have already seen, with major unconnected links in the TAH network. As we will see below, rail transport, which is the cheapest land-based mode of transportation for hauling bulk goods over medium to longer distances, was neglected in many countries from the 1970s through 1980s. Thus, with the exception of North African countries and South Africa, the rail–seaport connectivity is very weak. Indeed, about 19 seaports do not even have rail terminal at the ports. This means that everything has to be hauled to and from these ports by road and trucks that are poorly maintained. The implication of this for port efficiency and productivity cannot be overemphasized.

The role of inland waterways and seaports in Africa cannot be overemphasized. Seaports are anchors in the global trade and Africa needs to find innovative ways to be more integrated into this system. Given the expense that is involved in developing and maintaining seaports, one strategy will be to forge regional cooperation to develop regional hubs. This will be a difficult move politically, but the advantage of that will far more outweigh the current situation where every country is trying to develop its own seaport without the resources to do so.

Over the past few years, however, several countries have begun major seaport expansion projects mostly due to Chinese investments. Most of these projects are in the West and East African region. The East African projects are coupled with modern railroad lines. Some of the projects have already been put on hold but most of them are moving ahead. One that has been completed is the port of Djibouti, which is now considered as the most technologically advanced seaport in Africa. Other reforms have also cut down of the dwell time by digitizing the whole port procedures. For example at the Port of Tema, Ghana the dwell time is now down to two days. It is the hope that if all these come on line, Africa will be able to overcome its current isolation due to its old and dilapidated port infrastructure.

Rail Transportation

Colonial Rail

Rail transportation was introduced to Africa during the colonial period. It began in 1833, when Mohammed Ali, the Pasha of Egypt, considered building a railroad between Cairo and Suez, in order to improve transportation between Europe and India. However, after purchasing the rails, he had to abandon the project because of pressure from other European interests to build a canal instead. Ali's successor, Abbas I contracted Robert Stephenson, son of George Stephenson, and in 1854, the first railroad in Africa was completed between Alexandria and Kafir el-Zayyat, a town on the Rosetta branch of the Nile Delta. From there Ottoman Egypt moved quickly to expand its railroad network. Other developments in this early period included about 3-km (1.86 mi) rail linking Cape Town to the interior by 1860s and the Wadi Halfa–Sarras rail built by the British in Sudan.

From the late 1880s through the turn of the 19th century, however, Britain, France, and Germany all began to finance railroad construction in their colonies. Italy joined in the fray in the 1930s when it took control of Libya. Almost all of these lines started from seaports on the coast and reached for the interior, and were built first for the administration of the colonies, and second to exploit either mineral or agricultural resources efficiently. The seaports made it easier to bring the railroad material and subsequent transportation of raw material from the interior. The seaports were also chosen since most of them were the sites of the new submarine cables that connected West Africa to Europe.

The most remarkable development occurred in South Africa, where the discovery of diamonds in Griqualand in 1867 and Kimberley in 1870, and gold in the Witwatersrand in 1886 brought the most rapid development of rail network in colonial Africa. According to Boahen (1990, p. 184), "the length of railway lines rose from 110 km (68 mi) in 1869 to 4,190 km (2,603 mi) by 1905." In central Africa, discoveries of substantial minerals in the Katanga province of Belgian Congo (DRC) and the British colony of Northern Rhodesia (Zambia) led to development of several railroad links. Among these were a line from Broken Hill (Kabwe, Zambia) through Elizabethville (Lubumbashi, DRC) to Bukama, the head of navigation on the Congo River in DRC, and the Benguela Railroad from Lobito, Angola to the Katanga Railroad at Chilongo (Warthin, 1928). Construction of new lines stopped during World War I and World War II but resumed soon after in the 1920s and 1950s, respectively. The level of investment varied with the colonial power. Ajayi and Crowder (1985) noted that over half of the investment in rail occurred in South Africa, with the rest going to British, Belgian, French, and German Africa. The French in particular did not want to invest public funds in building infrastructure in their colonies and by 1901 had passed a law that required the end of subsidies to the colonies (Debrie, 2010).

Postcolonial Developments

At the return to independence, the modern transportation system in Africa was dominated by rail, with most of the lines able to support themselves. However, in most countries the rail network was a stark reminder of colonial economic policies. Most of the lines linked the interior or resource regions to the coast, or the capital city, where there was no coastline. There were no connected networks—no connections between places that were off the main exploitation grid. In West African countries, for example, the railroad had either a north–south orientation with very little east–west connections or west–east connections depending on the alignment of the coast. In East and Southwestern Africa, the railroads had east–west and west–east orientation, respectively, for the same reason.

However, from the mid-1960s to the late 1960s many of these railroads began to decline due to rising cost, declining profits, and a change from profits to deficits, which in turn could be attributed to the rise of road transportation and other political factors (Due, 1979). In the decades that followed, many of the lines fell into so much disrepair that they were abandoned. In Angola, Mozambique, Sierra Leone, and Liberia, most of the lines were destroyed by prolonged civil wars. Railroad data in Africa are very spotty but for most of the countries with relatively reasonable data, Table 10.6 shows that the length of the network has been decreasing since 1980.

Over the past decade or so, a number of factors have brought renewed interests in the railroad in Africa. First is the harsh reality of climatic impact on Africa's roads. The torrential African rainfall even in less humid areas can be harsh on the numerous unpaved roads that crisscross the continent. During such outburst of rainfall, many of these roads are washed out and rendered impassable, cutting off whole regions and even some landlocked countries such as Burundi and Rwanda from the rest of the world (Ford, 2004a). Second, all things being equal, road transport has

TABLE **10.6**

Railroad Routes (in Km/Mi) Based in African Countries Reporting Data

Country	1980		1990		2000		2014	
	Km	Mi.	Km	Mi.	Km	Mi.	Km	Mi.
Algeria	3,907	2,428	4,293	2,668	3,973	2,469	3,800	2,361
Cameroon	1,143	710	1,104	686	1,006	625	976	606
DRC.	4,511	2,803	4,511	2,803	3,641	2,262	3,641	2,262
Congo Rep	519	322	—	—	900	559	—	—
Cote d'Ivoire	1,180	733	709	441	639	397	639	397
Egypt	4,437	2,757	4,751	2,952	5,024	3,122	5,195	3,228
Gabon	341	212	683	424	814	506	810	503
Kenya	2,101	1,306	2,065	1,283	2,634	1,637	—	—
Malawi	789	490	789	490	710	441	—	—
Morocco	1,756	1,091	1,893	1,176	1.907	1,185	2,109	1,310
Mozambique	—	—	—	—	—	—	3,116	1,936
Nigeria	3,512	2,182	—	—	3,557	2,210	—	—
South Africa	23,596	14,662	21,613	13,430	22,657	14,078	20,500	12,738
Sudan	4,786	2,974	4,784	2,973	4,599	2,858	4,313	2,680
Tanzania	4,444	2,761	4,444	2,761	4.582	2,847	—	—
Tunisia	2,047	1,272	2,270	1,411	2.260	1,404	2,244	1,394
Uganda	1,232	766	1,232	766	261	162	—	—
Zambia	—	—	1,273	791	1,273	791	—	—
Zimbabwe	3,394	2,109	2,759	1,714	—	—	—	—

Source: World Bank Data Set.

the highest line-haul cost over longer distances. This makes shipment of goods over longer distances such as those from landlocked countries of Africa very expensive both in time and in cost. In contrast, rail has the lowest line-haul cost after water transportation, over longer distances. Thus, for the 17 land-locked countries, in particular, as well as the big countries with dispersed populations, it makes more economic sense to ship goods, services, and even people by rail than by road. Third, in Africa's major conurbations, as we saw in Chapter 7, mass transportation of people has become a nightmare as a result of serious traffic jams that cripple effective urban mobility, with its associated productivity loss and psycho-social stress. As shown by the experience of developed countries, adding more roads to solve such problems actually makes the situation worse. Finally, there were funds available through major donor agencies such as the World Bank and International Monetary Fund (IMF), and China for such projects. Among some of the major railroad projects that have been initiated due to these factors include (1) the Asmara-Massawa Railway in 2002; (2) the opening of the GauTrain, Africa's first high-speed train link from Johannesburg to Pretoria, South Africa in 2010; (3) the South Africa's rail corridors; (4) the reconstruction and reopening of the Benguela Railway by Angola in 2011; and (5) the upgrading of the Nacala Railway from Nacala, Mozambique to Malawi in 2014. The rest include the Djibouti-Addis Ababa Railroad, the Mombasa-Nairobi line, and the Mombasa-Malaba line.

Contemporary Rail Network

Africa has about 52,240 mi (84,072 km) of railroad network of which about 44,800 mi (72,100 km) or 85.7% is in use. Globally, this is very small, about 3% of the total rail network worldwide. Of these, 40.8% is in South Africa, 23.8% in North Africa, while the rest of the continent accounts for the remaining 35.5% (World Bank, 2013). The entire network is still a mirror image of its colonial past—a network that is sparse, low density, and unconnected. Few countries have network in the real meaning of the word when compared to population distributions. Among these are South Africa, Nigeria, Egypt, Tunisia, and Algeria. A very small portion of the lines are electrified and the majority of these lines are in South Africa (9,000 km/5,592 mi or 42% of its total lines). The rest are found in DRC (858 km/533 mi), Zimbabwe (313 km/195 mi), Egypt (63 km/39 mi), Algeria (283 km/176 mi), and Tunisia (65 km/40 mi). Similarly, except for some sections of the South Africa's network that is double track, the entire network is single track. There is no trans-continental rail line in the true sense of the term, and there are a few international lines, among which are the South Africa to Zambia and DRC, the Kenya to Uganda, Tanzania–Zambia, DRC–Angola, Cote d'Ivoire–Burkina Faso, and Senegal–Mali lines.

There are three main railroad gauges in Africa. The first is the Cape gauge, which is used in the South Africa to DRC network as well as in the former British colonies of Ghana, Nigeria, and Sudan. The second is the meter gauge used in former French colonies, as well as Kenya, Uganda, northern Tanzania, Ethiopia, and Djibouti. The third is the standard gauge used substantially in North Africa, and in isolated mining lines of Mauritania, Guinea, and Gabon (Bullock, 2009; Gwilliam, 2011). Most of the tracks are old and in some cases have never been upgraded since the colonial times—over 100 years old. Mechanical signals and train orders are still used on numerous tracks of the network. In addition, chronic under maintenance has rendered many sections of tracks inoperable. Several proposals have been made to fix these tracks, but as we will see later, it has not been easy to implement the proposals.

Organization of Rail Service in Africa

The organizational history of rail service in African countries followed the same pattern as water transportation. Thus, until the 1990s, the government owned and managed most rail services. A litany of difficulties, inefficiencies, corruption, and mismanagement wrecked the service in many countries. As privatization and liberalization of African economies took hold in the 1990s, African governments changed strategies toward privatization. First, they adopted the use of **management contracts** in which governments contracted private specialist agencies to manage the rail service. Examples of countries, which tried this approach, are Zambia, Botswana, Nigeria, Togo, and DRC (Gwilliam, 2011). The main weakness of this approach was that the government was still in charge of the financing and the maintenance of the physical infrastructure, and this did not work well. So a second approach in the form of railway concessions was adopted. This practice particularly accelerated from 1990 to 2000. Today, apart from South Africa, over 70% of the railways in African countries are managed by private agencies (World Bank, 2013). The concessions are of different types. In Mozambique and Tanzania, for example, the state ownership in concessions is still high—about 49%; in Madagascar, the state has 25% stake in some concessions (Madarail) and 10–20% in others (Sitarail, Transrail, and Camrail). However, there is a small number of companies that hold these concessions, among which are Sheltham from South Africa, NLPI from Mauritius, and RITES from India. The World Bank estimates that since 1996 the International Development Agency (IDA) has provided about $1billion for these concessions.

Like elsewhere, rail is used in Africa for two types of services—passenger and cargo. The passenger rail service is of two categories—regional and intercity long-distance service and city-suburban service. The regional and intercity long-distance services link the capital cities with regional cities and the rural areas in between. In some countries, these provide the only means of transportation especially in areas where there are no competing roads or the roads are unpaved and difficult to use. The service carries two categories of passengers—first class and second class—or second-class and third-class trains without air conditioning. The majority of the passengers travel third class and especially in the rural areas with no access roads. These consist largely of traders who travel between the villages and market centers with their merchandise on a more frequent basis. Overnight trains usually include sleeper trains.

Suburban train service is limited across the continent. The main ones are found in the major cities of South Africa (Cape Town, Durban, Johannesburg, and Pretoria), Egypt (Cairo and Alexandra), Algeria (Algiers, Constantine, and Oran), Tunisia (Tunis), Morocco (Casablanca and Rabat), and in Senegal (Dakar-Rufisque). Other minor services operating one or two lines only in morning and evening rush hours are found in Kenya (Nairobi), Nigeria (Lagos), Ghana (Accra), Zimbabwe (Harare and Bulawayo), Angola (Luanda), Mozambique (Maputo), and Kinshasa (DRC). Apart from Luanda, where the service runs six times a day, the rest are all two times a day—morning and evening. Once again, data on the number of passengers carried is very sparse, but Table 10.7 shows that the number seems to be increasing in countries for which data are available. Cargo or freight train service provides bulk and semibulk hauling of commodities from source to port, and from port to source. From source, the commodities consist largely of raw materials—minerals (coal, copper, gold, manganese, phosphates, and tin) and agricultural produce (cereals, cocoa, coffee, and cotton). From port, the commodities are largely manufactured products. Once again, from countries with available data on this, the trend in the tonnage of goods carried by the rail is downward with the exception of South Africa (Table 10.7). However, cargo train faces stiff competition from truck and is therefore not able to return with full load.

TABLE **10.7**								

Railroad Passengers and Goods Carried in Countries Reporting Data

Country	Passengers carried (millions)				Goods carried (million tons)			
	1980	1990	2000	2014	1980	1990	2000	2014
Algeria	2,070	2,991	1,142	1,186	2,457	2,680	1,980	928
Cameroon	244	457	327	494	578	757	1,048	1,056
Congo Rep	337	410	84	—	538	421	85	—
Cote d'Ivoire	1,252	205	126	20	602	289	537	—
DRC.	430	260	94	37	1,727	1,341	362	148
Egypt	11,164	34,876	34,960	40.837	2,190	2,828	3,980	1,592
Gabon	10	54	88	109	25	—	1,611	2,447
Kenya	704	716	350	—	2,281	1,919	1,492	—
Malawi	80	116	27	—	234	65	88	—
Mali	130	197	204	—	—	—	—	—
Morocco	936	2,237	1,956	5,449	3,788	4,903	4,576	5,384
Nigeria	1,533	1,269	363	—	822	178	—	—
Senegal	100	184	138	—	307	564	371	—
South Africa	20,201	10,641	11,890	14,689	99,556	101,746	106,605	113,342
Sudan	1,100	—	205	—	1,970	—	1,164	—
Tanzania	314	584	946	—	1,106	1,408	1,990	—
Tunisia	862	1,019	1,257	1,298	1,698	1,820	2,282	2,024
Uganda	—	351	—	—	—	159	210	—
Zambia	308	267	—	—	6,864	5,590	—	—

Countries were selected based on data availability. The last year that data was most available was 2014.
Source: World Bank Data Set.

Problems and Issues of Rail Transportation

Low connectivity It appears that many African countries have not been able to overcome the legacy of the orientation of colonial transportation networks. The result is that very few new rails have been built in the postcolonial period. This has created not only a huge connectivity problem of rail networks in many countries but also a complete lack of intermodal connectivity. For this reason, the full potential of railroads has not been realized.

Low traffic volume Railroads in Africa carry less traffic volume than they do in other regions of the world. For example, World Bank data shows that the highest growth in railroad traffic from 2008 to 2009 occurred in Asia, where freight volume increased by 74% and passenger by 64%. In Europe and America, freight rate was 40% and 25%, respectively, while Africa recorded a modest 7%. Indeed, the data show that Africa's contribution to global freight by train was negative 2%, while passenger volume by train was 2%.

Within Africa, South Africa accounted 79.42% of the freight volume, North Africa 8.95%, and the rest of Africa 11.64% in 2009. Of the passenger traffic, Egypt and North Africa accounted for 76.2%, South Africa 22.1%, and the rest of

Africa, 1.7% (World Bank, 2013). This generally low traffic volume and density is uncompetitive and make it difficult for railroads to achieve financial sustainability.

Low labor productivity African railroads also have low labor productivity except for South Africa. Compared to African average of 100%, South Africa's labor productivity was 270%, North Africa's was 54.7%, while the rest of Africa was 37.1% (World Bank, 2013). However, Gwilliam (2011) documents that concession-run railroads have higher labor productivity than state-run railways partly because concessions are able to cut staff and discard old rolling stocks.

Quality of service The quality of service of Africa's railroads is a major concern. This includes adequate capacity, frequency, speed, reliability, security, and safety of the service. Safety is particularly major as the number of derailment and fatal accidents in Africa is relatively high, given the small size of its rail network. For example, most African railroads report about 100 derailments a year compared to 2,000 reported by the United States and its extensive network (Gwilliam, 2011).

Competition and institutional arrangements African railroads are unable to compete against road transportation due to the inherent inability of rail to offer door-to-door service, poor service quality, and institutional arrangements. The very characteristic of rail's infrastructural rigidity coupled with its sparse network in Africa imposes extra shipping cost to and from train stations. Added to this is the quality of service concerns that we have already mentioned. However, Gwilliam (2011) attributes the main obstacle to competitive railroads in Africa to institutional arrangements. He argues that there is a lack of trade facilitation and cross-border coordination, which translates to unnecessary long transit time. He cites the example of the main train service from South Africa to DRC, which takes 38 days, but only 9 days are used in the actual travel while 29 days are used for interchange and border crossing. By contrast, the same trip by road takes only 8 days out of which 4 days are used for border crossing. Unregulated and lower truck fees also give trucks advantage over trains, which are required to fully fund the maintenance of their tracks. In West and East Africa, landlocked countries especially have alternative routes to reach the ports by road.

With respect to institutional arrangements, there are two broad types: state-managed railroads and railroad concessions. State-managed railroads are still found in Morocco, Algeria, Tunisia, Egypt, Angola, Namibia, Botswana, and South Africa. In these countries, public agencies managing the railroads are usually granted autonomy as private agencies. However, oversight is generally weak and oftentimes governments and politicians interfere with efficient management.

As already mentioned, railroad concessions have been very popular across the continent, but they have not been without their own problems. First, concessions require appropriate oversight, which can sometimes be a rare commodity in Africa, and this can lead to market abuse. Second, some of the concessions are struggling financially. Third, governments and concessionaries had overoptimistic expectations and potential for growth when they went into the concessions. However, the poor quality of the physical infrastructure and low traffic volume prevented the expectations from becoming a reality. Fourth, there was also underestimation of how much investments would be needed to realize financial viability. Unfortunately, not only did the investment prove larger, but governments also overestimated private sector interest in investing in railroads. Fifth, concessions have not been interested in passenger traffic due to many reasons including government fare controls and not willing to pay compensation. The result is that not much has been invested in promoting passenger traffic, and for that reason it has remained low and in some cases even deteriorated. A World Bank (2013) study reviewing concessions in Africa, reports that 7 out of 12 (58%) of concessions have negative cash flow and high debt load.

In spite of these difficulties facing railroad concessions, the World Bank insists that privatization through concessions is the only way to revitalize Africa's railroad system. This is despite the fact that the most successful railroad services in Africa are in South Africa and the North African countries, which are all state-owned and state-managed. Instead, the World Bank argues that the problems facing Africa's railroads are the same as elsewhere and can be solved by the same solutions. To this end, it proposes a new approach, which incidentally includes an active role of the government in railroads. Thus, the new approach calls for the need for (1) states to remain involved in the ownership and financing of railway; (2) states to define appropriate financing system for each concession, including learning from the EU to cover total costs of railroad infrastructure through public financing and charges for usage of infrastructure, and to be transparent and engaged in constant dialogue with railroad operators; and (3) states to understand the role and scope of concessions.

Air Transportation

Colonial Air Transport

Air transportation began to attract the attention of colonial governments alongside road transportation during World War I. Before the war, worldwide view was that air transportation was going to be accomplished through lighter-than-air dirigibles or airships. However, World War I changed that as a result of the use of heavier-than-air planes in the war. For the colonial powers, and particularly Britain and France, the possibility of traveling to their colonies in much shorter time was very attractive. As a result, the idea of extending air transportation to the colonies including Africa was conceived with the organization of the British and French civil aviation. As early as 1917, the first of three studies on civil aviation by the Department of Civil Aviation in the War Ministry of Britain was commissioned. Two other reports on imperial air routes and government assistance on development of civil aviation followed in 1920. In the report on imperial air routes, the connection to Cape Town was ranked second only to a connection to India (McCormack, 1989). In 1924, a number of small private companies that had converted airplanes used in World War I for air service were combined to form the Imperial Airways, with support from the British government, and in 1927, it was mandated to develop routes that would bring air transportation to every corner of the empire.

In the period between the commissioning of the British reports and the release of their findings, however, there were other developments. In 1919, the French airline company, *Compagnie Generale Aeropostale* (CGA), organized the first air service to Africa from Toulouse to Casablanca. In 1920, Belgian Congo colonialists formed an airline company, *Ligne Aerienne du Roi* Albert (LARA) to operate a hydroplane along the Congo River from Leopoldville (Kinshasa) to Stanleyville (Kisangani). The company failed in 1922 but in 1923 the colonialists provided partial funding for the creation of the *Societé Anonyme Belge d'Exploitation de la Navigation Aérienne* (SABENA). Sabena made its first flight from Brussels to Leopoldville in 1925. In the same year, the French CGA extended its service to Dakar.

The first British air service to Africa occurred in 1931 from London to Nairobi. In 1932, the service was extended to Cape Town, and in 1936 a second service to West Africa from Khartoum through Kano to Lagos was established. This service was extended to Accra in 1937 and Takoradi in the Gold Coast (Ghana) in 1939. Imperial Airways also partnered with Wilson Airways in Kenya, the Southern Rhodesia (Zimbabwe) and Nyasaland (Malawi) Airways (RANA), and the Elder Dempster Shipping Lines' Colonial Airways in West Africa. However, the British government had no interest at that time in supporting any regional or local air service in its African colonies, and held that such services should be paid for by the colonies themselves (McCormack, 1989). In South Africa, domestic air service was organized by the Union Airways, but when Imperial turned down an invitation to take over the service, the South African Airways (SAA) was organized in 1933. By 1939, SAA had become a strong competitor to Imperial Airways.

By the eve of World War II, Imperial Airways operated services to 85 airports and airfields, but only four of them were in West Africa (McCormack, 1989). French air companies were preparing to connect with French West Africa, but the United States under Pan-American Airlines (PANAM) was operating in West Africa. Italy was also operating some air services in North and East Africa, while Belgium had an air service to the Congo (H. O. M., 1942).

As it occurred in other parts of the world, the outbreak of World War II became a game changer for air transportation in Africa. In 1940, Imperial was reorganized into the British Overseas Airways Corporation (BOAC), partly due to competition from Air France, Sabena, and Lufthansa, which were doing well in West Africa. Even so, BOAC was initially plagued with lack of suitable equipment and facilities. For example, there were no airfields in the Gambia and Sierra Leone to accommodate the Eastern route – England – Bathurst (Banjul) – Freetown – Takoradi route. In addition, some of the distances to be covered were beyond the range of any of its planes. The American Douglas Company's DC-3, the plane that broke through the barrier and made passenger air transport possible, was out at that time, but the BOAC could not use it because of the buy British policy that was in place at that time. This gave advantage to such competitors as SAA and PANAM and throughout the war, the two airlines dominated Africa's domestic air transport to support the war effort.

The war also opened up air transportation in West Africa, as it became the anchor in the long-distance flight from the US to North Africa, particularly Egypt, and beyond. With the German U-boats in the North Atlantic and the Mediterranean, the only safe route to supply the Allied army in Egypt was a southern route. Takoradi, a seaport in the Gold Coast (Ghana) was converted to a naval base from which warplanes could fly to Egypt. This route, which became known as the Takoradi Route or Trans-African air route played a decisive role in getting supplies to the besieged British Army in Egypt that led to the final defeat of Germany in North Africa (Ray, 1975). The employment of thousands of local staff by BOAC and PANAM on the Takoradi Route, and the American carrier fleet base in Accra introduced many West Africans to airport operations. In 1946, three regional air transportation authorities and subsequently corporations replaced BOAC in Africa. They were the West African Airways Corporation (WAAC) (McCormack, 1989), the Central African Airways Corporation (CAAC), and the East African Airways Corporation (EAAC).

Postcolonial Developments

Postcolonial Africa continued to develop its air transportation by establishing national airlines, renovating, expanding, or building new airports, and acquiring new aircraft fleet. In the former British colonies, the regional airlines collapsed within a decade or so after independence, because every country wanted to establish its own national airline. Thus, the West African Airways Corporation collapsed in 1958, the Central African Airways in 1967, and the East African Airways Corporation in 1977. In contrast, Francophone countries in West Africa organized the Air Afrique Airline Company, which had substantial initial success.

In the meantime, Africa's air transportation faced a number of problems including national rules and regulations that hindered free international air travel as well as safety issues. Connectivity was also an issue. It used to be that Africans had to fly to Europe in order to go to another African country. To address these matters, the ministers of state responsible for civil aviation met in 1988 in Yamoussoukro, Cote d'Ivoire, to create a new civil aviation policy for Africa. The policy that became known as the **Yamoussoukro Declaration** aimed "to create a conducive environment for the development of intra-African and international air services." Among its several objectives were gradual liberalization of entry into the African airline market, abolition of capacity and frequency limits of international air service in Africa, protection of universal tariffs up to the **fifth freedom**, and freedom of operators to set fares. The fifth freedom of traffic right is the right of a licensed airline company in a member country of the agreement to operate in other countries that are also part of the agreement. In 1999, the Yamoussoukro Decision (YD) was adopted to commit the 44 signatory countries to take steps to deregulate air transportation and promote regional air markets for international air transportation in Africa. In 2000, the decision was endorsed by African Heads of State and in 2002, it became binding on all signatories. The YD process also led to the creation of regional air transportation grouping of the Banjul Accord Group (BAG) of West Africa in 2004, and agreements among existing regional groupings including Economic Community of Central African States (CEMAC) Common Market for Eastern and Southern Africa (COMESA), East African Community (EAC), Southern African Development Community, and West African Economic and Monetary Union (WEAMU).

While these efforts were going on, many of the existing African airlines were filling for bankruptcy due to mismanagement, corruption, and growing debt. For example, Ugandan Airways collapsed in 1989, Air Afrique in 2002, and Nigerian Airways in 2003; Ghana Airways in 2004; Air Gabon in 2006; and Cameroon Airways in 2008. Only a few out of the remaining countries had substantial operations. Among these were South African Airlines, Air Mauritius, Ethiopian Airlines, Egypt Air, Air Algerie, and Royal Air Maroc (Royal Moroccan Airline). The collapse of the national airlines affected West and Central Africa the most, since they were left with no major domestic carrier. In contrast, East and Southern Africa still had three dominant airlines—South Africa Airlines, Kenyan Airlines, and Ethiopian Airlines. Thus, from 2001 through 2007, domestic flight in West and Central Africa declined, while those in North, East, and Southern Africa grew, with North Africa showing the strongest growth.

The collapse of these national airlines helped swing the trend toward public–private partnerships. Kenyan Airways, which was on the brink of collapse, was one of the first major national airlines to set the trend (see Massey, 2010). However, there were other state-owned airlines that managed to stay in business and appear to be doing well. Ethiopian Airlines is one such airline. In 2002, while other African national airlines were becoming defunct Ethiopian Airlines ordered four Boeing aircrafts and leased six others. In 2003, it completed a new terminal building at its home base—Addis Ababa and a 3,800-m runway to accommodate Boeing 747s and Airbus A-340s (Ford, 2004b). Others are South African Airlines, Egypt Air, Royal Air Maroc, and Air Algerie.

In recent years, improved economic growth has made Africa a player in the world of civil aviation. Air transportation in Africa grew about 6.2% between 2004 and 2007. Southern Africa, East Africa, and North Africa had higher growth in passenger traffic compared to West and Central Africa, where passenger traffic actually declined. In 2011, the International Air Transport Association (IATA) identified Africa as the second fastest growth region in commercial air transport and would see a 7.7% growth in passenger volume over the next three years. In the same vein major aircraft manufacturers projected Africa would purchase more aircrafts in the future. Airbus projected 929 new aircraft by 2028; Boeing 710 between 2010 and 2029, while Embraer projected 220 aircrafts (Anonymous, 2011). Similarly, the Airport Company of South Africa (ACSA) in 2016 projected a 5.1% growth in air traffic in Africa by 2031, the highest in the world (Chinghoso, 2016).

Organization and Performance of Air Transportation Service

Today Africa has over 2,500 airports of which the most important ones are shown in Figure 10.7. These airports provide two types of air transportation service in Africa: domestic and international services. The international air service consists of two parts—intracontinental or intra-African and intercontinental services. The first is within Africa, and the second is outside Africa. These services are provided by both African and non-African airlines.

The performance of airline services is usually measured in several ways including revenue passenger kilometer or mile (RPK or RPM) and available seat kilometer or mile (ASK or ASM), which respectively measure airline traffic volume and capacity. There is also revenue ton-mile/kilometers, (RTM or RTK), which measures the amount of goods that are transported by airlines. By the RPK measure, the African Airlines Association (AFRAA) (2016) reported that the global airline industry carried 3.6 billion passengers in 2015, of which Africa accounted for 79.5 million passengers. This was only 2.2% of the global air travel compared to Asia Pacific (32.1%), Europe (26.9%), North America (24.4%), and Latin America (5.8%). About 92.6% of the total air travel in Africa in 2015 were due to five countries—South Africa (28.3%), Egypt (25.3%), Morocco (17.8%), Nigeria (10.7%), and Algeria (10.5%). Of the 79.5 million, 48.2 million (60.7%) were international passengers, while 31.2 million (39.2%) were domestic (AFRAA, 2016). These services were provided by both African and non-African airlines. African airlines reporting data on passengers accounted for 49.8 million (62%) of total passengers carried. About 88.4% of these were carried by the top 10 largest African airlines led by Egypt Air, Ethiopian Airlines, South African Airways, Royal Air Maroc, and Air Algerie (Table 10.8). By ASKs and RPL measures, however, the top five African airlines in 2015 were Ethiopian Airlines, South African Airlines, Egypt Air, and Kenyan Airways.

The intercontinental air service is the largest sector of Africa's air transportation market. This sector grew by 43.6% between 2001 and 2007 at an annual rate of 6.2% (Gwilliam, 2011), and at a rate of 5.3% since 2012. This sector is dominated by foreign airlines although there are a few African airlines that compete well (Table 10.9). About 24 African airlines reporting data to AFRA carried some 23.7 million (47.6%) of Africa's intercontinental air traffic. These included the Ethiopian Airlines, South African Airways, Kenyan Airways, Egypt Air, Royal Air

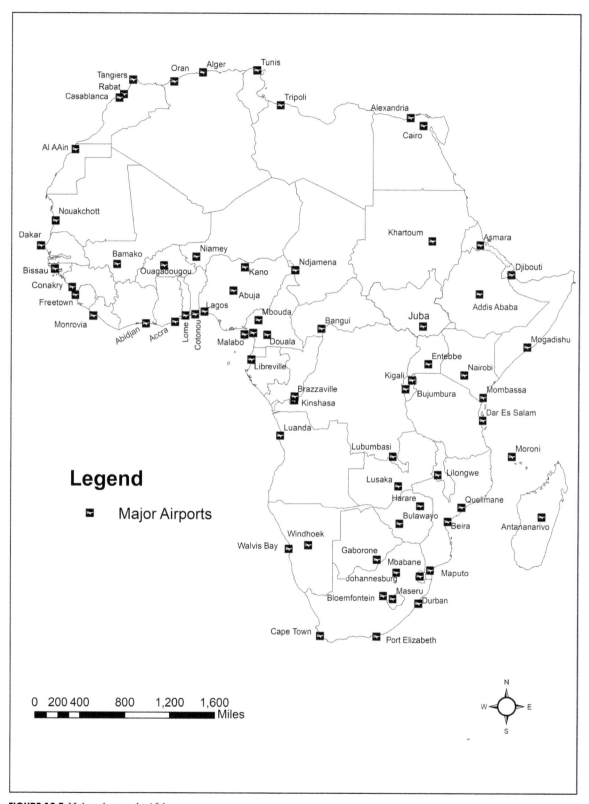

FIGURE 10.7 Major airports in Africa.

Source: ESRI and Garmin International Inc (formerly DeLorme Publishing Company, Inc)

> TABLE **10.8**

Top African Airlines by Passenger Carried in 2015

Country	Domestic passengers (000)	Intra-African passengers (000)	Intercontinental passengers (000)	Total passengers carried (000)	Percentage
Egypt Air	1,813	832	6,191	8,836	17.8
Ethiopian Airlines	1,047	3,004	2,951	7,002	14.1
South African Airways	3,153	1,980	1,503	6,636	13.3
Royal Air Maroc	855	1,429	3,913	6,197	12.5
Air Algérie	1,719	368	3,451	5,538	11.1
Kenya Airways	682	1,946	1,008	3,636	7.3
Tunis Air	—	370	2,374	2,744	5.5
Air Mauritius	155	550	765	1,470	3.0
TAAG Angola	611	227	424	1,262	2.5
Tassili	652	37	—	689	1.4
Lam Mozambique	497	190	1	688	1.4
Nile Air	—	4	602	606	1.2
Air Namibia	92	357	112	561	1.1
TACV	339	210	—	549	1.1
RwandAir	13	470	59	542	1.1
Air Seychelles	193	129	186	508	1.0
ASKY	482	—	—	482	1.0
Air Madagascar	235	80	101	416	0.8
Precision Air	219	155	—	375	0.8
Starbow	252	—	—	252	0.5
Badr	143	81	14	237	0.5
Air Botswana	76	150	—	227	0.5
Air Zimbabwe	115	79	—	194	0.4
Air Burkina	4	115	—	119	0.2
Total	13,347	12,764	23,654	49,766	100.0

Source: AFRAA/ACI-Africa.

Maroc, Air Algerie, TAAG Angola, and Air Mauritius. Table 10.9 also shows that while seat capacities of some airlines such as British Airways and South African Airways have declined, others such as Emirates and Ethiopian Airlines have increased since 2001. Most of the intercontinental air transportation service passed through one of four hubs—Cairo, Johannesburg, Nairobi, and Addis Ababa, and the most heavily traveled route in 2015 was Cairo-Jeddah route followed by Johannesburg to London-Heathrow (AFRAA, 2016; Bofinger, 2017).

Intracontinental or intra-African travel grew at an annual rate of 3% between 2001 and 2004 and at an annual rate of 9% between 2004 and 2007. Bofinger (2017) estimates that the average growth of this market from 2001 to 2015 was 12.3%. Much of this growth occurred in the service between North Africa and the rest of the continent. An example was the expansion of Royal Air Maroc to 10 countries in West and Central Africa. However, by volume of traffic more intracontinental travel

TABLE 10.9

Top Intercontinental Airlines in Africa, 2015

Airline	Estimated seat KMs (billions) 2001	Estimated seat KMs (billions) 2015	Market share % 2015
Emirates	2.14	38.62	10.73
Air France	16.29	26.58	7.38
Ethiopian Airlines	2.89	24.24	6.73
Egypt Air	12.32	22.13	6.15
South African	23.52	18	5.00
British Airways	16.75	15.10	4.20
Turkish Airlines	0.84	12.45	3.46
Royal Air Maroc	6.19	12.07	3.35
Qatar Airways	0.34	11.39	3.16
KLM	5.85	10.7	2.97
Kenya Airways	3.04	9	2.50
Delta Airlines	0	8.01	2.23
Lufthansa	2.87	7.28	2.02
Air Algerie	3.33	6.8	1.89
Saudia (Saudi Arabian Airlines)	1.84	6.42	
Top 15 Total	98.21	228.79	63.56
Others	68.73	131.16	36.44
Total	166.94	359.95	100.00

Source: Bofinger, H. C. 2017. *Air Transport in Africa: A Portrait of Capacity and Competition in Various Market Segments.* WIDER Working Paper 2017/36. Washington, DC: The World Bank. p. 10.

occurred within sub-Saharan Africa. Owing to the collapse of some of the national airlines, connectivity declined especially in West and Central Africa in that period. This, of course, gave advantage to the African airlines in East and Southern Africa to capitalize on. Thus, in 2015, about 23.3% of the intracontinental travel was by Ethiopian Airlines, followed by South African Airways (14.5%) and Kenyan Airways (10.7%) (Table 10.10). However, for travel between North Africa and the rest of Africa, about 77% of the total flight in 2015 were carried by two airlines—Royal Air Maroc (45.9%) and Egypt Air (31.4%) (Table 10.10).

Domestic air transportation is the service within African countries. According to AFRAA (2016) in 2015, there were about 600 regional and city-pairs air transportation services in Africa. However, a little over half (51.4%) served less than 5 flights a week; 12.5% had 1 flight a week, while only 3.2% had more than 50 flights per week. South Africa had the largest share of this market (49.3%) followed by Nigeria (17.6%) and Kenya (5.4%). As a result, about 42% of these travels originated from South African Airports. The leading airlines in this sector were Comair Ltd (23.0%), South African Airways (15.5%), and Mango Airlines (12.9%). Owing to all these traffic patterns, the top 10 busiest airports in Africa in terms of passenger traffic in 2015 were located in seven countries—South Africa, Egypt, Nigeria, Morocco, Algeria, Kenya, and Tunisia (Table 10.11 and Figure 10.8).

TABLE 10.10

Top Intra-African Airlines in Africa, 2015

Airline	Estimated seat KMs (billions) 2001	Estimated seat KMs (billions) 2015	Market share % 2015
Ethiopian Airlines	0.98	10.87	28.5
South African Airways	4	6.76	17.7
Kenya Airways	1.66	5.02	13.2
Arik Air		1.2	3.2
Air Mauritius	0.5	1.06	2.8
TUIfly		0.94	2.5
Egypt Air	0.38	0.93	2.4
SA Airlink		0.84	2.2
Royal Air Maroc	0.41	0.75	2.0
TAAG-Angola	0.36	0.7	1.8
Air Namibia	0.31	0.69	1.8
Air Austral	0.4	0.62	1.6
Tunis Air	0.33	0.56	1.5
ASKY		0.54	1.4
Comair Ltd		0.48	1.3
Top 15 total	9.33	31.95	83.9
Others	8.10	6.13	16.1
Total	17.43	38.08	100.0

Source: Bofinger, H. C. 2017. *Air Transport in Africa: A Portrait of Capacity and Competition in Various Market Segments.* WIDER Working Paper 2017/36. Washington, DC: The World Bank. p. 13.

In terms of ownership, air transportation service in Africa is a mixed bag of private, public, and private–public companies. All the international airlines are privately owned. The leading African providers are either fully or partly government-owned. South African Airlines, Ethiopian Airlines, Egypt Air, and Royal Air Maroc are fully owned by the government. Kenyan Airways and Air Mauritius are private–public partnerships. All the foreign-based airlines that do business in Africa are private except Emirates, which is government-owned.

Problems and Issues of Air Transportation

Physical capacity In studies of challenges to growth of air transport in Africa both Bofinger (2008) and Gwilliam (2011) noted two problems related to physical capacity, one on the landside and the other on the airside. On the landside, both studies claim that Africa has enough capacity in the number of airports and runways, but there are not enough parallel taxiways to leave and enter runways, not enough number of apron ways for parking, and not enough space for processing passengers. Both studies report that there are two massive gateways into Africa—Egypt in the north and South Africa in the south. These are supported by six intermediate

TABLE 10.11

Top 20 Busiest Airports in Africa, 2015

City	Country	Airport	Domestic 2015	International 2015	Total 2015
Johannesburg	South Africa	OR Tambo	10,384,653	9,583,760	19,968,413
Cairo	Egypt	Cairo	2,211,177	13,009,578	15,220,755
Cape Town	South Africa	Cape Town	7,682,509	1,713,047	9,395,556
Casablanca	Morocco	Mohammed V	795,760	7,379,899	8,175,659
Addis Ababa	Ethiopia	Bole	1,096,981	6,644,555	7,741,536
Algiers	Algeria	Houari Boumédiène	1,883,565	4,996,065	6,879,630
Lagos	Nigeria	Murtala Muhammed	3,778,086	3,023,478	6,801,564
Hurghada	Egypt	Hurghada	540,230	6,226,114	6,766,344
Sharm El Sheikh	Egypt	Sharm El Sheikh	845,762	4,918,576	5,764,338
Nairobi	Kenya	Jomo Kenyatta	1,403,009	3,913,778	5,316,787
Tunis	Tunisia	Tunis Carthage	254,957	4,326,316	4,581,273
Marrakech	Morocco	Ménara	177,407	3,764,979	3,942,386
Khartoum	Sudan	Khartoum	513,986	2,602,157	3,116,143
PlaineMagnien	Mauritius	SSR	159,265	2,939,601	3,098,866
Borg El Arab	Egypt	Borg El Arabt	135,268	2,652,233	2,787,501
Accra	Ghana	Kotoka	565,166	1,666,780	2,231,946
Dakar	Senegal	Léopold Sédar Senghor		1,696,767	1,696,767
Abidjan	Côte D'Ivoire	Félix Houphouët Boigny	41,357	1,427,287	1,468,644
Entebbe	Uganda	Entebbe	14,934	1,375,144	1,390,078

Source: AFRAA/ACI-Africa.

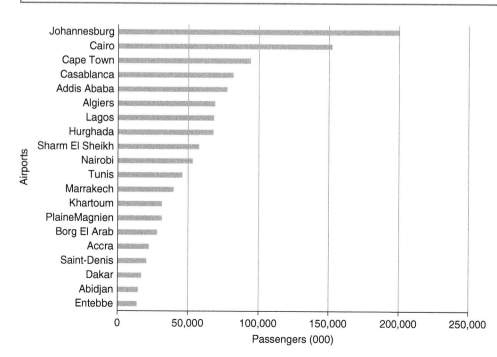

FIGURE 10.8 Africa's Busiest Airport by Passenger Traffic in 2015s.
Source: AFRAA/ACI-Africa

entry points (Morocco, Algeria, Tunisia, Senegal, Ethiopia, and Kenya). Of these only North African countries have invested adequately in the taxiways and aprons, and processing space for passengers. The rest of Africa has not. On the airside, air navigation systems and traffic control are strong around the major airport hubs but either inadequate or nonexistent outside the hubs. The result is air navigation service providers (ANSP) face the challenge of improving their infrastructure and technology to accommodate current and future demand. This will involve use of satellite, radar, and automation technologies (Vogel, 2013).

Expensive air fares and high airport charges Flying to Africa and within Africa are generally more expensive than flying elsewhere. Within Africa, it is estimated that flights per mile or kilometer tend to be more expensive than elsewhere. This is due to several reasons including safety and reliable issues. African airport charges are high compared to developed countries. According to Gwilliam (2011) only North African airports have comparable charges. For the rest of Africa, the charges tend to be 30–40% higher, and are even much higher in Cote d'Ivoire, Cameroon, and Ghana. Gwilliam (2011) attributes these high charges to the fact that the majority of African airports do not have any other sources of revenue such as car rental, hotel services, and extensive duty-free shopping facilities. As a result, high airport charges have become the main source of revenue.

Increasing competition The competition facing African airlines is in the intercontinental air service. Here African airlines do not have the capacity to compete. As of 2015, African airlines accounted for 47.6% compared to non-African airlines capacity of 52.4%. These competitors are largely European and Middle Eastern, and in recent years North American and Asian airlines. This leaves the domestic air service as the one in which African airlines have the most potential to grow. State-owned African airlines are not only facing competition from foreign airlines; they also have to contend with competition from privately owned African airlines. These private airlines include Coma Air, Arik Air, Safair, SA Link in South Africa, and Fly 540 Ltd. In a way, the competition is forcing the major African airlines to develop strategies. For example, South African Airlines is expanding its service to China, India, and other parts of Asia. It has signed a codeshare agreement with Etihad of United Arab Emirates to share 22 service routes including Shanghai, Singapore, and Istanbul. Ethiopian Airlines is following a similar strategy seeking to expand its service into India. On its part, Kenya Airways has reduced its intercontinental service to Europe, while expanding its intercontinental and international as well as domestic services in Asia and Africa, respectively (New African, 2013).

Management, administration, and safety issues In spite of the efforts to privatize the airline business, there are still companies that are either fully owned or partially owned by the government. Safety has been a major concern of African airline operations. In 2007, for example, Africa accounted 25% of all fatal air transport operations though it had only 4.5% of total air traffic. In 2009, Africa had the world's highest loss of Western-built jets as well as accidents for all aircrafts. The rate was 9.94 per 1 million flights of Western-built jets and 12.24 accidents per 1 million of all flights (Thomas, 2010). Since then air travel safety on the continent has improved. This has been attributed to many reasons. For example, the African Airline Association attributes it to old fleet of aircrafts—particularly Soviet-built crafts—with average age of 20 years. The IATA attributes it to poor regulatory oversight and inadequate safety management systems (Gwilliam, 2011). In simple terms, inadequate maintenance of aging aircrafts is seen as the main culprit in this unfortunate situation. Owing to this safety issue, the European Commission in 2006 started a blacklist that "effectively banned carriers with poor safety records and air-lines from certain countries from operating in EU countries (Dunn, 2011). By 2011, there were 100 African Airlines and 14 African countries on the list. The African Airline Association has reacted to this ban as "unfair" since many of the airlines on the blacklist had no planes let alone fly to Europe (Dunn, 2011).

To address these concerns, donors, international development institutions, and governments have instituted programs through a regional approach. In this approach, support from developed countries has facilitated the creation of regional safety over-sight bodies to pool resources to focus on air travel safety issues. The oldest of these regional organizations is the *Agence pour la Securite de la Navigation Aerienne en Afrique et a Madagascar* (ASECNA), which was created in 1959 by France and its former colonies in sub-Saharan Africa. The organization was formed to forge cooperation of air spaces and improve safety of air transportation among member countries. It is now based in Dakar, Senegal, and consists of 17 countries including France. Another program is the US Department of Transportation's Safe Skies for Africa Program, which pro-vided support to East Africa to establish a new oversight unit. The International Civil Aviation Organization (ICAO) has also been working with various regional organiza-tions such as BAG, WAEMU, and CEMAC to improve safety. In 2012, African Union's Ministerial Meeting on Aviation Safety adopted the **Abuja Declaration** that aimed at bringing the accident rate in African aviation in line with global average by 2015. In addition, the declaration included plans to establish and equip civil aviation authori-ties with resources and autonomy needed to operate; implement safety management systems; certify all aerodromes; and request IATA operational safety audit (IOSA) of all African airlines. Indications are that the Abuja Declaration appears to have had some positive impact. For example, the AFRAA (2016) reported that there were 24 fatal airline accidents worldwide in 2014, of which 9 (29%) occurred in Africa. In 2015, there were 19 fatal airline accidents worldwide of which 2 (10.5%) occurred in Africa. In addition, 45 African airlines were on the IOSA registry in 2015. Still given the relatively small number of flights in Africa, safety is still a concern. AFRAA (2016) report called on all its member airlines to also get the IATA Safety Audit of Ground Operations (ISAOG) to ensure quality, safety, and security.

In view of all these, it is clear that Africa's air transportation needs a total overhaul. There is the need to (1) improve safety; (2) invest in maintenance, expansion, and modernization of existing airports to bring them up to par with international stand-ards rather than building new airports; (3) implement the YD process to achieve full privatization, which would also eliminate the need to support unprofitable routes; (4) remove outmoded regulations; and (5) reduce the high airport fees.

There is also the need to forge regional cooperation and pull resources together under improved management. The days of going it alone have passed. With limited resources and growing global competition, African countries have to be serious in working together through more cooperation, meaningful mergers, and partner-ships. There is a tendency of some observers to discourage this under the pretext of open skies arguments, but African countries need to realize that these were the same arguments made during the deregulation of airline industries in developed countries in the 1970s. At that time, the main argument for deregulation was based on the theory of contestable markets that said that competition was good for the consumer so there should be easy entry and exit into the airline industry. Initially many small airline businesses emerged but within a decade or so, they were gone due to either bankruptcy or purchase by the big players. Today the domestic US airline industry has even fewer airlines than the regulation period—with Delta, American, and United Airlines—taking the lion's share of the domestic as well as the intercontinental market. At the moment the main competition facing African airlines seems to be the intercontinental; but as demand for international air travel improves, international air travel will become more competitive and at that time size will be important.

COMMUNICATION

Print communication and the press were discussed in Chapters 7 and 9, respectively. The discussion in this section will therefore focus on telecommunication, which is communicating over distance by way of transmission of electrical waves or impulses. It includes telegraph, telephone (fixed lines and mobile), radio, television, and the Internet.

Telecommunication in Precolonial and Colonial Periods

Precolonial Africa devised various methods of telecommunication, to bring people back to the village, and over distances, especially during the era of kingdoms and empire building. These included market place exchanges, fire and smoke, talking drums, and messengers. Modern telecommunication in Africa began with the telegraph, the first line of which was between Cairo and Alexandria in Ottoman Egypt in 1823. In 1835, the line was extended to Suez. Two years later in 1837, a telegraph line was established between Algiers and Blida, and in 1842, the telegraph was introduced to South Africa, with the Fort Beaufort-Grahamstown-Fort Peddie line. By 1854, all of Algeria's major towns had telegraph services (Huurdeman, 2003).

The first telephone in Africa was introduced in Senegal in 1879. Senegal was followed by South Africa in 1880, Egypt in 1881, Mauritius in 1882, Ghana in 1890, Tunisia in 1891, Tanzania in 1892, Benin and Togo in 1894, Lesotho 1895, Ethiopia in 1897, and Congo Republic in 1899. To improve both the telegraph and telephone service submarine cables, which had been invented in the 1820s, were needed in Africa.

In 1884, the first submarine cable was extended from Madeira (Canary Islands) to Saint Louis, Senegal, by the French. Competitive rivalry among the colonial powers hastened the pace of submarine cables in Africa. By 1898, there were two large African cable systems in operation—the Aden-Zanzibar-Mozambique-Durban in Eastern Africa, and the Lisbon-Madeira-Accra-Cape Town system in western Africa. Spanish colonial policies thwarted the developments in northwest Africa. However, by 1903, France had completed the main western line of telecommunication (Quevedo, 2010). The expansion of the railroad in Africa during the late colonial period extended the use of the telegraph and subsequently the telephone to other parts of the continent.

During the 1920s, telecommunication service in Africa was boosted by the arrival of radio, which debuted in Egypt in 1922, South Africa in 1924, and Kenya in 1927. Throughout the 1930s, radio diffused rapidly across the continent—reaching Zimbabwe in 1932, Mozambique in 1933, Sierra Leone in 1934, Congo Republic in 1935, Ghana in 1935, and Nigeria in 1936 (Damone, 2012; Mytton, ND). In Egypt, the radio was initially established by private interests. However, growth became so rapid that in 1926 a decree was established to regulate the ownership. In 1931, private ownership was banned and the radio was placed under the central government. In other parts of the continent, radio was initially introduced for the relatively few expatriates and by religious groups (Damone, 2012). However, as colonialism became established radio became the technology for communication between the colonial powers and their subjects.

World War II provided a major impetus for expansion of broadcasting in Africa. Britain adopted a policy of using radio to educate and inform African listeners. BBC staff members were sent across the continent to help establish, advice, and improve on the service. The BBC model of independent radio was tried but was not very successful even though broadcasting in African languages proved successful. In contrast, the French adopted a different policy—based on the policy of assimilation; all broadcasting originated from France and was highly centralized for all French colonies in Africa (Mytton, ND). During the 1950s, just on the eve of the independence movement of the majority of African countries, television was added to the telecommunication systems of Africa when the first television service began in Nigeria in 1959.

Postcolonial Developments

At the return to independence, the telecommunication service of Africa included the telegraph, the telephone, radio, and television. For the most part these services were controlled by a single provider, namely the government. These government-run telecommunication companies were inefficient and money-losing. The phones, which were all, fixed or landlines had many problems with them, and the coverage was poor since in most countries, majority of the population had no access to them because of their expense. Intercountry links were very limited, and intra-African communication had to be transmitted through communication transit centers outside of Africa. Most radio services were on short wave, which caused a lot of delays and interferences, and television was very much limited to the few rich people who could afford. Likewise, most of the television services were from abroad since most countries did not have the financial resources and expertise to develop their own programs (Mytton, ND). Thus, there was a great deal of interest in linking the continent through telecommunication technology even in the early postcolonial period. As a result, major efforts were directed at development of telecommunication infrastructure.

Infrastructure Development

The first major step taken toward the achievement of this interest was the creation of the Pan-African Telecommunication Network (**PANAFTEL**), which emerged from a meeting of telecommunication experts in Dakar, Senegal, in 1962. Further steps toward the creation of the network were taken in 1967 at the meeting in Addis Ababa, Ethiopia. A feasibility study under the auspices of the International Telecommunication Union (ITU) was initiated in 1968 and completed in 1969, except West Africa. Implementation began in 1975, after the West African survey had been completed. The network consisted of intercountry land-based microwave links. In West and North Africa the network was supported by submarine cables and A and B standard satellites, with a few links to other continents (ITU, 2003). From 1982 to 1992 massive investments were made in many African countries with loans from the African Development Bank, European Investment Bank, and the World Bank, However, more than half of this investment went to only three countries—Algeria, Morocco, and Nigeria.

A full inventory taken in 1990 showed that PANAFTEL had created 24,233 mi (39,000 km) of radio relay links, 4,971 mi (8,000 km) of submarine cable, 39 international switching centers, and 42 of the 45 member states had international satellite stations (Nuruddin, 1999). The size of the network had more than doubled; the Northern zone was relatively complete; the Eastern African zone had a working system; and the Southern African zone was almost complete. The West African zone, however, was having difficulty due largely to maintenance and operational difficulty, while the Central African zone had the weakest network primarily due to lack of political commitment to implement it. PANAFTEL had many problems among which were environmental (torrential rains and extreme temperatures), human capital (lack of skilled personnel), inadequate maintenance, low demand for intra-African communication, as well as the perception that the political will needed to install the missing link especially in Central Africa could not be overcome. International funding was terminated in 1992 (Nuruddin, 1999).

Although PANAFTEL was a bold undertaking, it was widely believed that intra-African communication system would have to be further augmented by an African satellite system to make it more efficient and economical. Feasibility study for this was first requested in 1975 by the Conference of African Telecommunications Administrators. From 1980 through 1990, many feasibility studies were conducted on various aspects of the project, including final study by ITU, which involved 50 African countries and 600 experts from 1987 to 1990. Among other things, the study recommended that a communication satellite adopted on the continental scale would be the best option for achieving efficient and economical telecommunication. The recommendation was adopted by the African Heads of State in 1991 in Abuja, Nigeria, and in 1993 the Regional African Satellite Communication System for the Development of Africa (**RASCOM**) was created in Abidjan, Cote d'Ivoire. RASCOM was established to be cooperatively owned by countries buying minimum investment shares of $50,000. By March 1994, 35 countries had signed up, out of which 30 had paid their initial shares. RASCOM was tasked with launching two satellite systems, but it had a late start and was plagued by similar problems as PANAFTEL; therefore, it was not until 2007 that it was able to launch its first satellite, Rascom-QAF1 into orbit. In December 2010, the satellite was replaced by another one due to a fuel leak. In the meantime, other regional competitors such as INTELSAT and INMARSAT began to chip away the potential market of RASCOM.

Other projects conceived but not successful were the Africa One, which was considered to be one of the most ambitious in Africa's infrastructural history, and the Global Mobile Personal Communication by Satellite (GMPCS). The Africa One project was an American Telephone & Telegraph (AT&T) telecommunication project that was conceived to end the isolation of Africa from the global undersea network. Thus, it was proposed to be a regional undersea network around the continent of Africa to provide a bridge between the individual domestic networks of African countries into the global network (Marra and Schesser, 1996). The network consisted of "40,000 km of undersea fiber-optic cable, encircling the second largest continent in the world, and with landings in approximately 40 different countries." The idea was born in 1995 and it was supposed to be completed in 1999, but the project did not get off the ground because of a number of reasons. First SAT-3 was activated before Africa One. Second, South Africa a key African player did not want to participate. Finally, the collapse of the troubled global telecommunication industry in 2001, in which many telecommunication giants such as British Telecom, Lucent, and Cisco faced severe financial difficulties, made the project financially impossible.

According to Terabit Consulting (2013) things began to change from the mid-2000 due to three factors. First, the rapid adoption of mobile phones exceeded expectations. Second, international financial institutions including the World Bank and the African Development Bank—and other private financiers—became interested in funding telecommunication infrastructure again. Third, submarine suppliers also began to focus attention on Africa. Thus, while total investment in telecommunication infrastructure in sub-Saharan Africa from 1988 to 2008 was $953 million, the total investment from 2009 to 2012 alone was $2.927 billion. These investments included three intercontinental cables on the east coast, four along the west coast, and additional investments in regional systems. Tables 10.12 and 10.13

TABLE 10.12

Africa's Intercontinental Submarine Cables, 1993–2013

Ready-for-service date	System	Owners
Western Africa		
1993	SAT-2	Consortium
2002	SAT-3/SAFE	Consortium
2010	Glo-1	Globacom
2010	Main One	Main Street Technologies
2012	Africa Coast to Europe (ACE)	Consortium
2012	West Africa Cable System (WACS)	Consortium
Eastern Africa		
2009	East Africa Marine System (TEAMS)	TEAMS Ltd./Etisalat
2009	Seacom	IPS (Aga Khan Fund)/ Remgro/Herakles Telecom/ Convergence Partners/ Shanduka Group
2010	East African Submarine Cable System (EASSy)	Consortium/West Indian Ocean Cable Company (WIOCC)

Source: Submarine Telecoms Industry Report 2013.

TABLE 10.13

Proposed New Systems

System	Owners
Atlantic Cable System-Africa (ACSea-AFR) (Possible integration of project with SACS)	Telebras/Odebrecht
BRICS Cable	Imphandze Subtel Services (South Africa)
South Atlantic Express (SAEx)	eFive Telecoms
WASACE South	WASACE Cable Worldwide/Aterios Capital

Source: Submarine Telecoms Industry Report 2013.

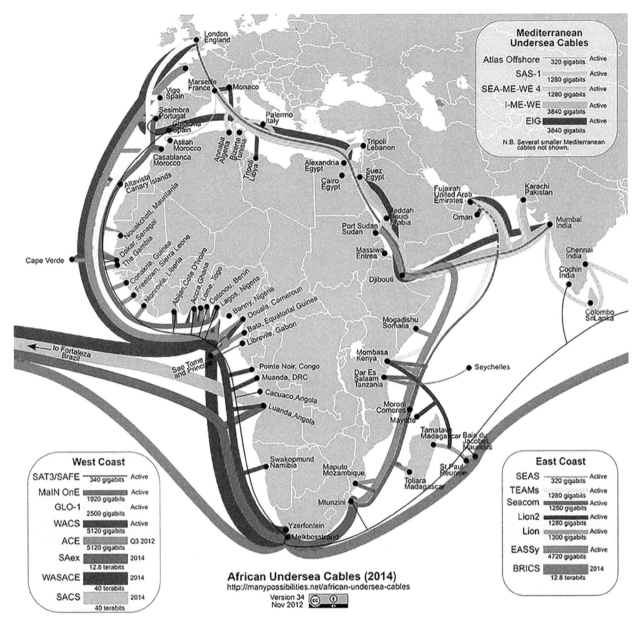

FIGURE 10.9 Africa's Undersea Cables by 2014.

show the completed systems and future systems, respectively. The East African Submarine Cable System (EASSy) sponsored by 25 telecom operators, most of whom were African, is particularly important. The agreement to undertake the project was signed among 28 leading telecommunication operators, most of them African, in 2003. However, the construction did not begin until 2007. It was completed and came alive in 2010. With that, EASSy provided the last submarine fiber-optic link around Africa, connecting South Africa to Sudan with landing sites in Madagascar, Mozambique, the Comoros, Tanzania, Kenya, Somalia, and Djibouti. Figure 10.9 is a map of undersea cables around Africa by 2014.

Another related infrastructural development is the Pan-African e-Network project, which is a brain-child of the former president of India, Dr. A. P. J. Kalam. The project was conceived in 2007 to assist Africa in capacity building through tele-education and telemedicine. The tele-education would provide quality education to about 10,000 students from top-notched Indian Universities in various fields over a five-year period. Regarding telemedicine, the project aimed at providing medical consultations to medical practitioners in Africa. The first phase was inaugurated in 2009 in 11 countries—Benin, Burkina Faso, Gabon, The Gambia, Ghana, Ethiopia, Mauritius, Nigeria, Rwanda, Senegal, and Seychelles. The second phase was inaugurated in 2010 in 12 countries—Botswana, Burundi, Cote d'Ivoire, Djibouti, Egypt, Eritrea, Libya, Malawi, Mozambique, Somalia, Uganda, and Zambia. By the beginning of 2013, the project had been commissioned in 47 of the 48 countries that had signed the agreement.

Privatization

The liberalization of telecommunication was accompanied by foreign investment and establishment of regulatory system. In spite of these accomplishments, Djifack-Zbaze and Keck (2009) found that while the effects of competition had reduced prices and improved availability of services, prices were still higher in Africa compared to the world average. To reduce prices they called for more competition in the mobile phone market and better regulation in the landline sector. In terms of penetration, Africa seems to be closing the telecommunication divide that used to exist between it and the rest of the world, particularly in the mobile phone sector. For multilateral commitments the results have been mixed with inconsistencies as to whether the terms of the commitments will be met or not.

In South Africa, for example, Gillwald (2005, p. 471) states that while reforms in the telecommunication sector have made economic gains, the two "national objectives of accelerated sector development and affordable access to communication services have not been met." As in many areas of social services, South Africa's case was unique in the sense that prior to 1994, the tele density of South Africa varied between the white minority and the nonwhite majority. For the former group it was high as any developed country but for the latter, it was about 1%, just like the rest of Africa. As a result, reform of the telecommunication sector followed a partial approach that on one hand sought to privatize but on the other hand provided some subsidies for the poor. A universal service fund (USF) was established to provide this need but the oversight of the agency was removed from the core functions of the regulating body. Before privatization, South Africa Telkom subsidies kept its local rates on the back of high long-distance service. After privatization, the companies switched by charging lower for long-distance service and higher for local service—cost-based tariff approach. This is seen as a key factor in the drop of 600,000 subscribers of Telkom's service.

In 1995, almost all landline telephones in Africa were state monopolies. By 2004, only 44% of African countries had their telecommunication as state monopolies. In the mobile phone sector the percentage of state monopolies dropped from 70% to less than 10% during the same period (Djifack-Zebaze and Keck, 2009).

Regulatory Efforts

Alongside the infrastructural development and privatization were several efforts to streamline regulations among countries and foster transparency that would attract foreign investments into the telecommunication sector. In 1975, the OAU created the Pan African Telecommunication Union (PATU) as its specialized telecommunication agency. It was charged with advising the membership "on all aspects of telecommunication development including policy and technological choice, regulatory matters, capacity development etc." (ITU, 2003, p. 7-E). However, the quibbling over the location of headquarters and lack of contribution from members rendered PATU ineffective.

In 1999, African Telecommunications Union (ATU) was created by the African Union (AU) to succeed PATU. ATU was created on the conviction that sustainable development cannot be effectively achieved without ensuring fundamental rights to communication, especially by the people who live in rural Africa. ATU sees development of the telecommunication sector as a key to address the rural–urban divide. Its emphasis is on public–private partnerships in policies and operations. The private partners are considered associate members of the union. ATU also assists member states with policy formulations and regulatory mechanisms (McCormick, 2005). However, ATU is financially weak since it depends on member state contributions.

Most of the regulatory activities have however occurred at the regional level. Among these are SADC's Telecommunications Regulators Association of Southern Africa (TRASA) in 1998; ECOWAS' West Africa Telecommunication Regulators Association (WATRA) in 2002; and COMESA's Association of Regulation of Information and Communication of Eastern and Southern Africa (ARICEA) in 2003. While these were going on the various existing telecommunication services—telephone, radio, television—expanded alongside with new modes of communication—the Internet, mobile phone, and social media.

Contemporary Telecommunication Services in Africa

Fixed Telephones In spite of the progress made under PANAFTEL in radio relay stations, international telephone switching centers, and submarine cable laid, by 1990, only few African countries—Egypt, Botswana, and South Africa—had substantial telephone coverage. Subscriptions to fixed telephone lines grew steadily throughout the 1990s and 2000s reaching a peak of 32.3 million (33 subscriptions per 1,000 population) in 2008. From there subscriptions began to fall, and by 2015 there were 24.1 million (24 subscriptions per 1,000 population) (Figure 10.10). As we will see later, this decline of fixed line subscribers was due to the growth of mobile phone market. Nigeria is the most competitive fixed lines country in Africa, but the largest fixed line broadband market is South Africa, followed by Egypt, Morocco, Algeria, and Tunisia (Roa, 2011).

Radio Data on radio set ownership are very spotty. The World Bank database provides continuous data from 1975 to 2001 only. The data show that in 1975 the number of radio sets per 1,000 people in Africa was 2,273,301. By 1984, the number had doubled 4,744,516. By 2001, the number of radio sets per 1,000 people had more than doubled again to 10,857,578. Radio underwent major transformation in Africa in 1987, when efforts to end state control in the majority of African countries began. In December 1987, a private entrepreneur in Ouagadougou, Burkina Faso, launched the Horizon FM as a private station that was going to be devoted to music, commercials, but no politics. The government tried to shut it down, but failed. This began the privatization movement and competition with the state-controlled radio stations. The majority of these independent stations operated on medium-wave transmissions. According to Mytton (ND), these stations are of five types. The first is the fully commercial station, which wants to make profits through heavy advertising and sale of airtime. The second is the

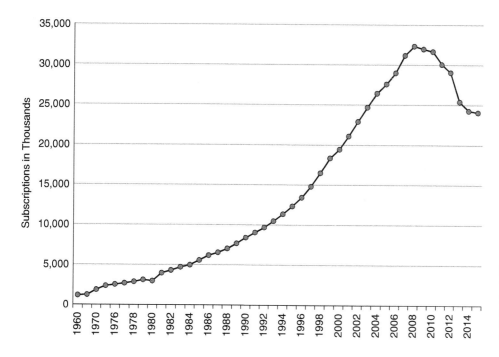

FIGURE 10.10 Fixed
Telephone Subscriptions,
1960–2015.
Source: Data from World Bank
2016, International telecommunication Union (ITU).

religious station, which uses the radio to spread religious faith with limited commercial and is mostly supported by listeners. The third is the community radio
station that broadcasts in local languages and ran mostly on volunteers from the
local community. The fourth is the factional radio station that caters to political or
ethnic sentiments, some of which border on hate, and have been found in the past
for instigating ethnic conflict such as the Rwanda genocide. The fifth type of radio
station is the humanitarian station that exists mainly to counter the effects of the
ethnic stations. The freedom of expression is still mixed in African countries. On
the one extreme are countries such as Ghana, where the former government-
controlled radio station, the Ghana Broadcasting Corporation, has been dwarfed
by independent radio stations. Yet, there are other countries in which freedom of
expression is still limited.

Mobile Communication Data from the World Bank database indicate that
although mobile phone subscriptions began in 1987, growth of subscription was
very slow for the next 10 years (Figure 10.11). According to Minges and Kelly (1994),
until 1992 cell phones were available in only six African countries—Egypt, Tunisia,
Algeria, Morocco, Mauritius, and South Africa. After 1992, cell phone operations
became available in four more countries—Gambia, Ghana, Kenya, and Nigeria. The
first signs of take-off in subscription appeared between 1998 and 2002 when the
number of cell phone subscribers grew from 4,156,952 to 36,901,047, an increase
of 788% over a period of four years. From 2003, cell phone subscribers grew rapidly
at an average rate of 141% per year and by 2015 there were more than 955 million
subscribers in Africa (Figure 10.11). At this rate, it is likely that mobile phone subscription in Africa will reach 1 billion by 2020.

   This rapid growth began to affect landline or fixed line subscriptions. Uganda
became the first country in Africa to have more mobile phone subscribers than
landlines, placing it third in the world after Finland and Cambodia (ITU, 2003).
The four biggest mobile phone subscriber countries in 2015 were Nigeria,
Egypt, South Africa, and Algeria. Among the major investor companies are

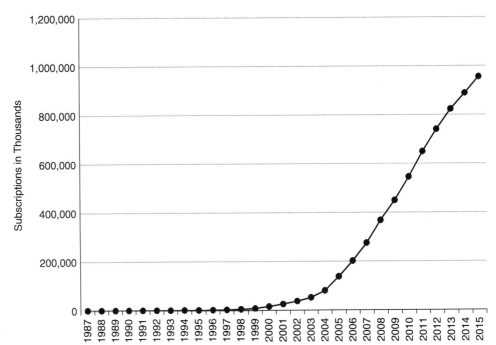

South Africa's Mobile Telephone Network (MTN), India's Bharti Airtel, France Telecom, Britain's Vodafone, Egypt's ORASCOM, and Luxembourg's Millicom (Rao, 2011).

The rapid growth of cell phone in Africa could be attributed to cell phone providers from South Africa. In 1993, the South African government decided to award contracts to two cell phone companies. The contract was for 15 years at the basic fee of R100 million plus 5% of the net income charge. To prevent small companies from applying, the application fee was fixed at R50,000. Out of the 80 applicants, the contract was awarded to Telkom and MTN. Telkom was government-owned provider of phone services in South Africa. MTN was a consortium of M-Net (a South African TV service provider), NAFTEL (a black business group), Transtel, and UK-based Cable and Wireless. Telkom signed a partnership agreement with the UK-based Vodafone and South-African-based Rembrandt group to form Vodacom, a new company. From 1994, South Africa's cell phone market grew slowly but from 2001, the momentum began to register, and by 2007 about 72.9% of South Africa's population owned cell phones (Vodazone.co.za).

The pay-as-you-use system adopted by the cell phone companies in lieu of expensive plans in the United States, for example, is perhaps the single most important factor in the rapid diffusion of cell phones in Africa because it became cheaper than landlines. Most cell phone users use it for sending text, followed by taking photographs or videos. In Kenya, however, most of the cell phone owners use it to transfer money.

The use of cell phones has spurred a few remarkable innovations that need to be mentioned. In 2007, the M-Pesa money transfer system was introduced in Kenya. Registered users deposit money with an agent. The agent deposits the money in a cyber-wallet protected by a pin. The money can be used to make payments. Since its introduction, transfer of money has become the number one use of cell phones in Kenya. In Ghana, the Mobile Technology for Community Health is another innovation by which nurses use cell phone application to collect data from pregnant mothers and upload them unto a central data bank that allow them to monitor the progress of the mothers. In Nigeria, SMS technology and small battery-operated printers are being used to send HIV/AIDS test results to hospitals at a shorter time than before. In South Africa, Ghana, and Malawi young people are using mobile phones to get all kinds of medical and therapeutic help (Hampshire et al., 2015).

The Internet Like mobile phones, the growth of Internet users began slowly in 1996 according to data available from the World Bank. At that time, there were only 427,471 Internet users of which 83% were in South Africa, 9% in Egypt, and 2% in Nigeria. Fourteen countries did not have data on Internet users. Internet usage began to pick up in 2002 with the number of users reaching 9,673,166. Between 2002 and 2008, the number of Internet users rose from 9.7 million to 74.6 million, an 87% increase. By 2015, there were estimated 300 million Internet users in Africa, an increase of 302% from 2008, or an average rate of 43% per year (Figure 10.12). Although these high percentage growth rates are obviously affected by the small number of Internet users to start with, there are no indications that the growth of Internet over the near future is going to decline. The distribution of users by countries has also shifted. The largest group of users was no longer living in South Africa but in Nigeria, which accounted for 29% of Internet users. Next was Egypt with 12%, South Africa with 10%, Kenya and Morocco with 7% each.

Much of this growth has come from some large-scale Internet providers on the continent, mostly based in South Africa. In a recent study, Luiz and Stephan (2012) found that the South African companies were motivated by market size, regulatory environment, and government policy and potential for growth and profits compared to the saturation in their home markets were the main factors that have led to this expansion. It started with cyber cafes. Mutula (2003) reported that cyber cafes in a few countries, including Senegal, Ghana, Malawi, Tanzania, Kenya, and Mozambique, were too many for the demand. Investment by governments in South Africa, Botswana, Namibia, Uganda, and Zimbabwe in the early 2000s helped the growth Internet in these countries. In spite of the rapid growth of Internet use, in Africa, only 25% of Africa's total population use the Internet, according to the 2015 data. This means more needs to be done by African countries to have full Internet coverage.

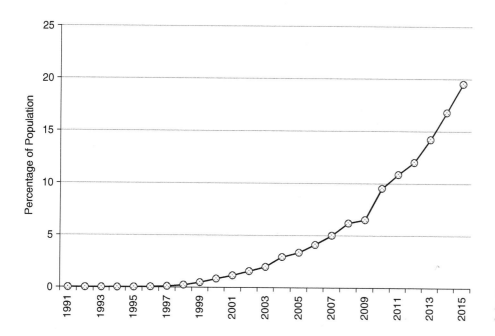

FIGURE 10.12 Internet users.
Source: World Bank World Development Indicators

Social Media: Google, Twitter, Facebook on Mobile The use of social media is limited right now but it is growing. Google is reporting increasing use of in-searches in Africa. Google has set up offices in a number of African countries—including Senegal, Ghana, and Nigeria. Facebook is the leading social media platform in Africa followed by YouTube. In 2014, it was estimated that 100 million Africa were using Facebook every month. About 80% of them did so through mobile devices. Majority of these people were living in Nigeria (15 million), South Africa (12 million), and Kenya (4.5 million). Twitter has announced codes for Nigeria, (40404:Zain, 20644:Glo Mobile), Kenya (8988:Safaricom), and Madagascar (40404:VIP), and is working on expanding to other countries on the continent. Rao (2011) reports that Twitter played a major role in the Arab Spring in Egypt. Unfortunately, some African governments are becoming concerned about the use of social media especially during political elections. For example, in 2016, Cameroon, Chad, DRC, Gabon, Gambia, Congo Republic, and Uganda blocked the use of social media during elections.

Telecommunication and Development of Africa

The emergence of new telecommunication technologies and especially the new information and communication technologies (ICTs)—Internet and smart cell phones, have focused interest on the role of ICT in the development of Africa. One view sees ICTs as key to the development of Africa (Barr, 1998; Richardson, 1998; African Partnership Forum, 2008). Citing examples from Asia and other parts of the world, these proponents argue that ICTs can break the isolation of the rural areas of Africa, and for that matter bring Africa into the 21st century. ICTs can thus make Africa an active participant in the global economy. ICTs, such as the Internet can inform farmers and small business owners about global markets, and commodity prices; inform communities about successful development strategies; and disseminate news among developing countries. Smart phones can provide information to people who live in remote areas regarding access to credit and healthcare-related matters. The 10th Meeting of the African Partnership Forum in Tokyo, Japan in 2008 noted that ICT contribute to economic growth by "(1) increasing productivity across all sectors; (2) facilitating market expansion beyond borders to harvest economies of scale; (3) lowering costs of and facilitating access to services, notably in administration, education, health and banking; (4) providing access to research; (5) development of ICT products and services; (6) contributing to better governance, a prerequisite to growth, through increased participation, accountability and transparency."

However, there is counterview to the idea that ICTs hold the panacea for Africa's development problems (Heeks, 1999; Melkote and Steeves, 2004). These people argue that there is too much hype about what ICT can deliver to the poverty that exists in Africa. They point out that a lot of the benefits of ICT cannot be realized in Africa because a number of preconditions that would allow the benefits of ICT to be realized are nonexistent in Africa right now. For example, the majority of rural dwellers is illiterate and therefore cannot access the Internet. Apart from this, access to knowledge about market prices per se is of no good to a farmer who does not have any means to move his or her product to the market because of poor transportation. Similarly, ICTs cannot make African countries active participants of the global economy unless they produce what the market wants and needs in reasonable quantities to affect the demand and supply conditions. As we will see in Chapter 15, Africa's contribution to global trade now is very negligible because of its low productivity. Unless efforts are made by African countries to change the situation, it will continue to be marginalized in the global economy.

Summary

Transportation and communication networks play essential roles in the economic development of countries, although the causal relationship between them has not always been easy to establish. This is because on the one hand it is intuitive that a country needs good transportation and communication networks to be able to produce and distribute goods and services efficiently for the benefit of its citizens. On the other hand, transportation and telecommunication networks are not cheap. Instead, they both require heavy investments that may be financially impossible for poor countries. At the same time, our discussion in this chapter has shown that although progress has been made, the current state of transportation and telecommunication infrastructure in the majority of African countries is woefully inadequate, and the future of Africa's economic life and its participation in the global economy will be severely hampered if the current state is not improved. Given the many equally important demands on the governments of Africa, to fix the transportation and telecommunication infrastructure will require serious consideration of revenue generation and in strategic investment spending. Part of this strategic package must be a maintenance program that will stem the physical infrastructure from complete deterioration before they are fixed. Apart from these, African countries need to cooperate more than just paying lip service and develop regional hubs for telecommunication technologies. Such regional cooperation must also have a common policy and plan framework that can direct further activities of both private and nongovernmental organizations so as to remove unnecessary duplication and layers of activities that in the end work at cross purposes with each other.

Postreading Assignment

A. Study the Following Concepts

Abuja Declaration	Intraurban transport	Place utility	Trans-African Highway
Dwell time	landlord port	RASCOM	network
Feeder roads	Overengineering	Service port	Turnaround time
Fifth freedom	PANAFTEL	Time utility	Underengineering
Interurban Transport	Panamax	Tool port	Yamoussoukro Process

B. Discuss the Following Questions

1. Look at the list you drew up before reading the text and see if there any of your notions about Africa's transportation system has changed? If so, has the change been positive or negative?

2. Is Lord Lugard's assertion that the material development of African can be summed up in one word "transportation" still valid in contemporary Africa?

3. Discuss and assess the impact of colonialism on Africa's transportation network?

4. What do you see as the main problems facing road transportation in Africa?

5. Discuss the rise and fall of the railroad as a mode of transportation in Africa. What prospects does the railway have in improving transportation in Africa?

6. Why is inland waterway the least of all the modes of transportation in Africa?

7. Discuss the main problems facing air transportation in Africa. What do you think can be done to solve these problems?

8. In what ways do Africa's seaports account for the marginalization of Africa in global trade?

9. What is the dominant form of telecommunication in Africa? What factors have contributed to the growth of this technology?

10. Discuss the evolution and development of telecommunication in Africa.

11. What role has privatization played in transportation and telecommunication in Africa?

12. Discuss the view that ICTs is key to Africa's economic development.

References

African Airlines Association (AFRAA). 2016. *Annual Report.* Nairobi, Kenya: Camerapix Magazines Limited.

African Development Bank (AfDB). 2010. *Ports, Logistics, and Trade in Africa.* Oxford: Oxford University Press.

African Partnership Forum 2008. *ICT in Africa: Boosting Economic Growth and Poverty Reduction 10 Meeting of African Partnership Forum.* Tokyo, Japan, April 7–8.

Akinwale, A. O., and Aremo, M. O. 2010. "Concession as a Catalyst for Crisis Management in Nigerian Ports." *The African Symposium* 10(2): 117–126.

Anonymous. 2011. "Clear Skies for African Airlines." *African Business* Special Report 378: 43.

Bainkong, G. 2013. "Stakeholders Discuss Trans-African Road Infrastructure." *Cameroon Tribune* [Yaounde, Cameroon] 17 April 2013. *Business Insights: Global.* Web. 25 July 2013.

Barr, D. F. 1998. "Integrated Rural Development through Telecommunications." In Richardson, D., and Paisley, L. (Eds.) *The First Mile of Connectivity.* Rome: FAO, pp. 152–167.

Boahen, A. A. (Ed.) 1990. *General History of Africa VII Africa Under Colonial Domination 1880–1935.* Paris: UNESCO.

Bofinger, H. C. 2017. *Air Transport in Africa: A Portrait of Capacity and Competition in Various Market Segments.* WIDER Working Paper 2017/36. Washington, DC: The World Bank.

Bofinger, H. C. 2008. *Africa Infrastructure Country Diagnostic: Air Transport: Challenges and Growth.* Washington, DC: World Bank and SSATP.

Bullock, R. 2009. *Off Track: Sub-Saharan African Railways.* Africa Infrastructure Country Diagnostic (AICD) Background Paper 17. Washington, DC: The International Bank for Reconstruction and Development/World Bank.

Christopher, A. J. 1984. *Colonial Africa.* London: Croom Helm.

Debrie, J. 2010. "From Colonization to National Territories in Continental West Africa: the Historical Geography of a Transport Infrastructure Network." *Journal of Transport Geography* 18: 292–300.

Due, J. F. 1979. "The Problem of Rail Transport in Tropical Africa." *The Journal of Developing Areas* 13(4): 375–393.

Dunn, G. 2011. "Blacklist Infuriates African Operators." *Flight International* 180(5301): 13.

Ford, N. 2004a. "Africa's Rail Renaissance." *African Business* (June) 22–23.

Ford, N. 2004b. "Happy Landing for Ethiopia Airlines." *African Business* (July) 32–33.

Fraser, D., and Notteboom, T. 2012. "Gateway and Hinterland Dynamics: The Case of the Southern African Container Seaport System." *African Journal of Business Management* 6(44): 10807–10825.

Ghingosho, E. 2016. "Air Transport Catalyst for Economic Growth across African Continent," Creamer's Media Engineering News, January.

Gillwald, A. 2005. *Good intentions, poor outcomes: Telecommunications reform in South Africa* 29: 469–491.

Ginghosho, E. 2011. "Air Transport Market Trends in Africa." *Paper Presented at the Airline Business Seminar* (July 19–21).

Gwilliam, K. M. 2011. *Africa's Transport Infrastructure: Mainstreaming Maintenance and Management.* Washington, DC: The World Bank.

H. O. M. 1942. "Air Transport and the Future." *Bulletin of International News* 19(26): 1173–1178.

Hallberg, C. W. 1931. *The Suez Canal: Its History and Diplomatic Importance.* New York: Columbia University Press.

Hampshire, K., Porter, G., Owusu, S. A., Mariwah, S., Abane, A. Robson, E., Munthali, A., DeLannoy, A., Bango, A., Gunguluza, N., and Milner, J. 2015. "Informal m-health: How Are Young People Using Mobile Phones to Bridge Healthcare Gaps in Sub-Saharan Africa?" *Social Science & Medicine* 142: 90–99.

Heeks, R. 1999. "Information and Communication Technologies, Poverty, and Development." *Development Informatics.* Working Paper Series No. 5 Manchester.

Huurdeman, A. A. 2003. *The Worldwide History of Telecommunications.* Hoboken, NJ: John Wiley & Sons.

International Telecommunication Union (ITU). 2003. *Assessment of Telecommunication and ICT Infrastructure in Africa.* ITU Symposium: African ICT Roadmap to Achieve NEPAD Objectives. Arusha, Tanzania: ITU.

Law, R. 2011. "West Africa's Discovery of the Atlantic." *International Journal of African Historical Studies* 44 (1): 1–25.

Lugard, F. D. 1922. *The Dual Mandate in British Tropical Africa.* Edinburg and London: William Blackwell and Sons.

Luiz, J. M., and Stephan, H. 2012. "The Multinationalisation of South African Telecommunications Firms in Africa." *Telecommunications Policy* 36: 621–635.

Massey, A. 2010. "Lessons from Africa: New Public Management and the Privatization of Kenyan Airways." *Public Policy and Administration* 25: 194–215.

McCormack, R. 1989. "War and Change: Air Transport in British Africa, 1939–1946." *Canadian Journal of History/Annales Canadiennes d'histoire* 24(3): 341–359.

McCormick, P. K. 2005. "The African Telecommunications Union: A Pan-African Approach to Telecommunications Reform." *Technology Policy* 29: 529–548.

Melkote, S. R., and Steeves, H. L. 2004. "Information and Communication Technologies for Rural Development." In Okigbo, C. C., and Eribo, F. (Eds.) *Development and Communication in Africa.* Lanham: Rowman & Littlefield Publishers, Inc., pp. 165–173.

Minges, M., and Kelly, T. 1994. "The Paradoxes of African Telecommunication." In Kiplagat, B. A., and Werner. M. C. M. (Eds.) *Telecommunications and Development in Africa.* Amsterdam: IOS Press.

Mlambo, A. S. 1994. From Dirt Tracks to Modern Highways: Towards a History of Roads and Road Transportation in Colonial Zimbabwe, 1890 – World War II.

Mytton, G. No Date. "A Brief History of Radio Broadcasting in Africa."

New African 2013. "Major African Airlines." *African Business* (June).

Notteboom, T. 2012. "Gateway and hinterland dynamics: The Case of the Southern African Container Seaport System." *African Journal of Business Management* 6(44):10807–10825.

Nuruddin, M. M. 1999. "Models for Development of Regional Telecommunications Networks in Africa." In Noam, E. M. (Ed.) *Telecommunication in Africa.* Oxford and New York: Oxford University Press, pp. 257–278.

Quevedo, J. M. 2010. "Telecommunications and Colonial Rivalry: European Telegraph Cables to the Canary Islands and Northwest Africa 1883-1914." *Historical Social Science Research* 35(1): 108–124.

Rao, M. 2011 Mobile Africa Report: Regional Hubs of Excellence and Innovation Mobile Monday

Ray, D. W. 1975. "The Takoradi Route: Roosevelt's Prewar Venture beyond the Western Hemisphere." *The Journal of American History* 62(2): 340–358.

Richardson, D. 1998. "The Internet and Rural Development." In Richardson, D., and Paisley, L. (Eds.) *The First Mile of Connectivity.* Rome: FAO, pp. 170–181.

Thomas, G. 2010 "Africa's Travel Travail." *Air Transport World* 47(10): 35–38.

Van Der Laan, H. L. 1981. "Modern Inland Transport and the European Trading Firms in Colonial West Africa (Transports modernes et firmes commerciales européennes dans les colonies d'Afriqueoccidentale)." *Cahiers d'Études Africaines* 21(84): 547–575.

Vogel, B. 2013. "Africa adopts continental co-operation." *Jane's Airport Review* 25(7).

Warthin, M. 1928. "Transportation Developments in Central Africa." *Geographical Review* 18(2): 307–309.

Wilford, J. N. 1994. "World's Oldest Paved Road Found in Egypt." *New York Times*, May 8. http://www.nytimes.com/1994/05/08/world/world-s-oldest-paved-road-found-in-egypt.html (accessed 30 June 2013).

World Bank. 2009. *Africa's Infrastructure: A Time for Transformation, Part 2 – Sectoral Snapshots*, Chapter 12. "Ports and Shipping: Landlords Needed." Washington, DC: AICD, World Bank Group.

CHAPTER 11

Agriculture

PREREADING ASSIGNMENT

1. When you think of agriculture in Africa, what comes to your mind?

2. List all the crops you know of that Africa leads the world production or ranks among the world's top producers.

3. Identify the particular countries you think are related to the production of these crops or livestock.

4. What technologies of farming do you think African farmers use?

5. What in your view do you think are some of the major problems facing African agriculture?

6. What solutions will you recommend for these problems?

Africa is a continent of farmers. Most Africans depend on agriculture for their livelihoods more than on any other sector. In terms of gross domestic product (GDP), agriculture is the largest sector in most African countries. For example, it accounts for 10–20% of the GDP of 10 African countries, 21–30% of another 11, and over 30% of the GDP of additional 13 countries (Table 11.1). Agricultural products also feature strongly in the export trade of African countries. Indeed, almost every African country exports some agricultural products, and for close to half (24) of the countries agricultural products are their number one export commodity. In terms of employment, agriculture is the leading employer in Africa. It accounts for more than 50% of employment in 25 countries that reported data, and for 21 of these countries, agriculture employs over 60% of the labor force (Table 11.1).

This chapter focuses on agriculture. It is divided into three sections. The first section examines the evolution and development of agriculture as an economic activity in Africa. The second focuses on the contemporary agricultural production systems, and the third deals with problems and issues in Africa's agriculture.

EVOLUTION AND DEVELOPMENT OF AGRICULTURE IN AFRICA

Precolonial Africa

In Chapter 2, we learned that agriculture was one of the transforming forces of early African societies and cultures. By the beginning of the 15th century, agriculture had become firmly established in terms of innovative adaptation to the environment and its products. In the Maghreb and the plateaus of Central Sahara, Africans were practicing **transhumance** and livestock raising. In the savannah regions of West Africa,

TABLE 11.1

Contribution of Agriculture to GDP and Employment in African Countries in 2015

Country Name	GDP (%)	employment (%)	Country name (%)	GDP (%)	employment (%)
Algeria	12.6	11.4	Madagascar	25.6	74.5
Angola		4.2	Malawi	29.7	69.9
Benin	25.3	43.6	Mali	42.0	57.3
Botswana	2.4	26.4	Mauritania	27.7	40.6
Burkina Faso	33.7	80.3	Mauritius	3.6	7.5
Cabo Verde	10.2	28.2	Morocco	14.3	33.5
Burundi	40.4	91.2	Mozambique	25.2	75.3
Cameroon	16.1	62.4	Namibia	6.5	30.4
Cent. African Republic	42.4	72.6	Niger	39.4	62.4
Chad	52.4	76.5	Nigeria	20.9	27.2
Comoros	..	62.0	Rwanda	30.2	75.6
Congo Republic	7.2	41.2	S T & Principe	12.6	23.0
Cote d'Ivoire	25.5	57.2	Senegal	16.9	52.6
Djibouti	..	26.6	Seychelles		
DRC	20.4	65.6	Sierra Leone	60.5	68.4
Egypt	11.3	25.8	Somalia		72.1
Equatorial Guinea	2.0	17.6	South Africa	2.3	6.2
Eritrea		57.3	South Sudan		
Ethiopia	39.2	71.4	Sudan	39.3	33.3
Gabon	4.7	16.6	Swaziland	10.2	22.1
Gambia	18.3	30.2	Tanzania	31.5	67.7
Ghana	21.0	43.4	Togo	40.7	63.1
Guinea	20.8	69.6	Tunisia	11.0	11.9
Kenya	33.3	62.6	Uganda	26.1	72.7
Lesotho	5.5	40.6	Zambia	5.3	54.9
Liberia	34.4	45.5	Zimbabwe	11.6	67.1
Libya		20.2			

Source: Data from Database World Development Indicators. Last Updated 3/01/2018.

nucleated settlements surrounded by concentric circles of permanent cultivated fields and common woodlands and wilderness beyond became a feature of the landscape (Iliffe, 1995). In the forest regions, the tedious nature of clearing the forest made the practice of moving to a new land every year impracticable. The Congo Forest, for example, was completely left to the Baka people, while agricultural communities moved to the forest-savanna transition zones. In East and Southern Africa, intensive cultivation involving transfer of fertile soils to less fertile soils occurred around the Great Lakes Region and in the Kenyan Highlands as well as the Zambezi Valley. In areas of modern-day Burundi and Rwanda, the use of manure, terracing, and hillside irrigation systems were developed. Further south in the Zambezi and Okavango valleys, a system of floodplain irrigation whereby farmers would leave the valley during floods and return to cultivate the land after the floods was adopted. In the dry woodlands and grasslands, however, extensive agriculture involving the use of fire to clear the bush and frequent moves to new locations was practiced (Iliffe, 1995).

The arrival of Europeans from the 15th century brought several changes to Africa's agriculture. First, the Portuguese, for example, introduced new crops such as maize, cassava, beans, cocoa, and sweet potatoes from the Americas, all of which African farmers were able to adapt and cultivate. Second, the Portuguese settlement on the islands of Sao Tome and Principe and Dutch settlement around the Table Bay in South Africa in the 17th century (Chapter 2) introduced the plantation and other European farming systems to Africa. These farms were large and averaged about 6,000 acres or more and depended largely on slave labor from the San people, other African natives, and people from India and Sri Lanka. Third, growing European demand for agricultural products in Africa such as hides, skins, red peppers, gums, and cotton boosted commercial production of these items. There were also some European efforts to establish commercial farms in certain areas of the continent, such as the case of the Danish cotton and coffee plantations in the Gold Coast. The volume of trade in agricultural products fell between 1650 and 1850 due to the slave trade, but it revived in the 19th century following the abolition of the slave trade and the institution of the so-called legitimate trade. Olives, viticulture, and wine as well as cotton became major exports of North Africa; rubber, palm oil, groundnuts, kola nuts, and cotton of West Africa (Naylor, 2009); maize, cassava, rice, and livestock of East and Southern Africa (Iliffe, 1995).

Colonial Africa

Four major developments occurred in Africa's agriculture during the colonial era. The first was the expansion of European farming systems in Africa. The second was the institution of cash crop agriculture. The third was the institution of agricultural research, and the fourth was the decline of food crop production systems.

The Expansion of European Farming System

The period between 1800 and 1884 saw the expansion of European farms in South Africa and in other parts of Africa. In South Africa, the expansion came after the Dutch East India Company went bankrupt in 1794 and the British captured the Cape Colony in 1806. Arrival of more British settlers in 1820 meant more land for settlement and farms. Harsch (1980) reports that 4,000 acres of farm land were seized from the Xhosa and parceled to the settlers. The Great Trek of 1835–1843 during which about 12,000 Boers left the Cape Colony in search for new lands extended these expansions into large sugar and wattle tree plantations, maize farms, and cattle ranches (Christopher, 1984).

In East Africa, all lands in the East African Protectorate were made (British) Crown lands in 1901 and by 1929, the best agricultural land in Kenya in particular had become a land of large farms and ranches of European farms just as they had occurred in South Africa (Ward and White, 1971). A similar development occurred in British Central Africa and French North Africa, where large European farms were established in Northern and Southern Rhodesia, Algeria, Tunisia, and Morocco. The only area where such European farms did not take root was in British West Africa, where efforts to take control of land through legislation (Lands Bill of 1897 in the Gold Coast and Lands Bill of 1910 in Nigeria) failed due to opposition from a coalition of local elites and chiefs.

The Expansion and Institution of Commercial Agriculture

The colonial period was also one of expansion and institution of cash crop or commercial agriculture in Africa. Despite the differences in policies, all the colonial powers either introduced or encouraged the cultivation of cash crops for European markets. Initially, this began with granting of concessions to trading companies in the colonies. However, as these proved unprofitable for such products as rubber and palm oil, the companies resorted to planting their own crops (Christopher, 1984).

Cotton cultivation was initially encouraged but later imposed across the continent because European textile industries could no longer depend upon the United States, which produced about 80% of the world's cotton. European cotton trade groups such as the British Cotton Growing Association (BCGA) founded in 1902, and the French Colonial Cotton Association supplied seeds, established buying centers, built and operated ginneries, and bought all the cotton grown in the colonies at guaranteed prices (Nyambara, 2000; Bassett, 2001). Other crops encouraged were olives and grapes in North Africa; groundnuts (peanuts), cocoa, coffee, rubber, and oil palm in West Africa; and tea, coffee, sisal, rubber, and oil palm in East, Central, and Southern Africa; although in East Africa, Africans were initially prevented from cultivating tea and coffee as cash crops (Austin, 2009; Makana, 2009).

The promotion of commercial agriculture in Africa sometimes involved large-scale projects such as the Gezira Scheme of Sudan, the Office Du Niger of French Soudan (Mali), and the Groundnut Scheme of East Africa. The Gezira Scheme was a commercial cotton production enterprise that the British government established in the Gezira (meaning an island), a portion of the clay plain between the Blue and White Niles in Sudan (Figure 11.1) in the 1920s. Before the Scheme, the area was occupied by semi-pastoral population, who cultivated low-yield drought-resistant grains in a very difficult climatic environment. The Scheme was established to provide revenue to administer the colony and also to provide raw materials for the Lancashire cotton industry (Barnett, 1977). The British government provided a loan of £3 million ($14.6 million) to fund the scheme. The project was approved in 1913 but was not completed until after the completion of the Sennar Dam on the Blue Nile in 1925. The Scheme was administered as cooperative endeavor among European management, the Sudan Plantations Syndicate (SPS), the Kassala Cotton Company (KCC), and African cultivators. Barnett (1977, p. 9) describes how this cooperative worked from 1925 as follows:

> Under the irrigation regime from 1925 onward, inhabitants of the area became "tenants" allocated a holding of land under the direction of the S. P. S. The tenancies were allocated first of all to those who had proprietary rights. But as they were not allowed to occupy more than they could work with their families, few men received more than two thirty feddan units. Each of these was to be cultivated each year, 10 feddans under cotton, 2½ feddans under lubia (animal fodder), 2½ under dura (staple food), and 15 left fallow (1 feddan = 1.038 acres).

The Gezira quickly became the mainstay of the economy of the colony. By 1950, when the administration of the project was turned over to the Sudan Gezira Board, the acreage had reached 207,000 with a net value of £E47, 745,000 ($131.9 million) (Beer, 1955). It had become the most successful project of its kind in Colonial Africa.

As mentioned in Chapter 2, the Office Du Niger also originated from the need for cotton for the French textile industry in the 1920s. The target location for the project was the inland delta region of River Niger in French Soudan (Mali) (Figure 11.2).

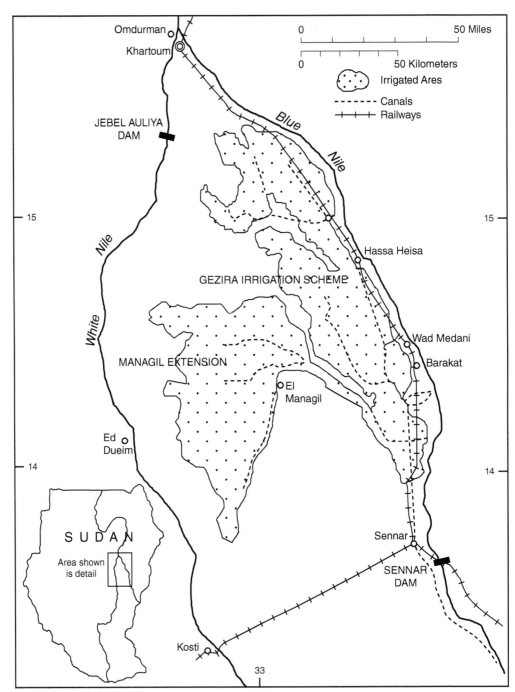

FIGURE 11.1 The
Gezira Scheme.
Source: Hance, W.A. (1975)
A Geography of Modern
Africa. New York: Columbia
University Press p. 162

The project consisted of two dams, one at Sansanding (Markala) and the other at
Sotuba. These would be linked by canals to irrigate a total of 1,480,000 hectares of
which 460,000 hectares would be devoted to cotton and the rest to foodstuffs, all in
a sparsely populated area of nomadic herders and traders who had very little interest
in crop farming (Filipovich, 2001). The project started with the construction of the
Sotuba dam in 1925 and establishment of two farming centers. In 1932, the Office
Du Niger was created as an autonomous body to oversee the construction of the

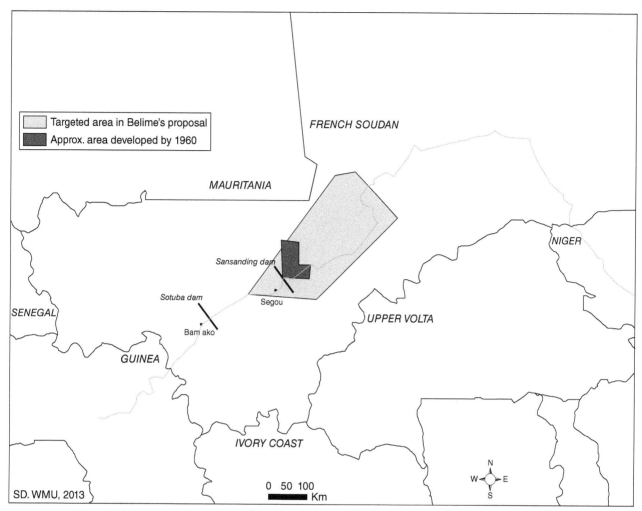

FIGURE 11.2 Office Du Niger.

16-foot high dam at Sansanding, which was completed in 1947. However, as mentioned in Chapter 2, the original goal that this would become another "Gezira" was never realized. Cotton proved unsuitable to the area, and the project was unable to settle the 2.5–3.5 million people needed to farm the land. By 1949, 15,350 (45%) of the 34,000 settlers had left, and only a small portion about 20,460 hectares had been irrigated, and much of that was under rice instead of cotton (Eichenberg and Filipovich, 1986; van Buesekom, 1997).

The Groundnut Scheme of Tanganyika (Tanzania) was another ambitious scheme to introduce large-scale groundnut (peanuts) growing to East Africa during the colonial period. The scheme originated from the fear that shortage of edible oil during World War II would continue after the War (Johnston, 1983). In particular, the United African Company (UAC), a subsidiary of the Unilever Company, a multinational producer of margarine and soap, was in search of alternative sources of vegetable oils and was instrumental in the project. A hurried three-person expert mission to Kenya, Tanganyika (Tanzania), and Northern Rhodesia (Zambia), in 1946, recommended enthusiastically a large-scale groundnut and sunflower cultivation (Rizzo, 2006). A total of 1.3 million hectares was envisaged, most of it in

Tanganyika with the rest in Northern Rhodesia, and Kenya. Annual production was projected to grow from 600,000 tons in the first year to 800,000 tons in the fifth year at a planned cost of £24 million ($95 million). However, the project failed miserably. The machines assembled for clearing and plowing proved inadequate as they broke down and the hard pan of iron or lateritic soils made the first plows useless. As a result, only a small area was cleared. In addition, the harvest was very poor, while the infrastructure requirements proved too expensive causing the project cost to surpass its budget. In 1951, the scheme was abandoned at a loss of almost £36.5 million ($104 million). Other schemes announced or undertaken during the colonial period included the Swaziland Irrigation Scheme and the Zambezi Valley Sugar Scheme of Mozambique.

The Establishment of Agricultural Research

The successful commercialization of industrial crops and the need to combat diseases and pests that hampered productivity created the need for agricultural research (Jeffries, 1964; Roseboom et al., 1998). A number of commodity research or experimental stations were established especially after World War I among which were groundnuts at Bambey, Senegal in 1921; cocoa at Tafo, Gold Coast in 1937; coffee, sisal, cinchona, and insect pests at Amani, Tanganyika in 1927; cotton in Egypt and Sudan, oil palm in Benin, Nigeria in 1939; and coffee in Kenya and Tanganyika. In Belgian Congo, the Institut National pour l'Etude Agronmique du Congo Belge (INEAC) established a central station at Yangambi with an extensive network of 36 stations in Congo, Burundi, and Rwanda (Roseboom et al., 1998).

For purposes of efficiency and better staffing, all the colonial powers encouraged a regional approach. The Gold Coast Cocoa Research Station became the West African Cocoa Research Institute in 1944, the oil palm research station in Nigeria became West African Institute for Oil Palm Research in 1951, the Groundnuts Experiment Station at Bambey became Federal French West Africa Agronomic Research Center in 1950, the Amani Research Station in Tanganyika was relocated in Kenya as East African Agriculture and Forestry Research Organization in 1951. Other new research institutes include the Pyrethrum Research Station in Kenya opened in 1944, the Institute for Research in Cotton and Exotic Textile in French Soudan, Cote d'Ivoire, and Togo in 1946; the Tea Research Institute of East Africa in 1951, and the West African Rice Research Station in Sierra Leone in 1951. Most of these institutes were focused on diseases and pests that affected crop yields. Others such as the Adiopdoume Center in Cote D'Ivoire was a training center for French West Africa (Thompson and Adloff, 1957; Bassett, 2001).

The Decline of Food Production

The overemphasis on commercial agriculture was done at the expense of staple food production. With the exception of a few areas such as Nigeria, the production of staple foods declined. Thus, from self-sufficiency in food production in the precolonial period, most Colonial African societies began experiencing food shortages during the colonial era. Granted, some of the colonies like the Gold Coast (Ghana) grew rich through export crops but those colonies had to spend the money earned on importation of rice and other foods from elsewhere. In addition, not every colony was fortunate to develop cash crop farming due to the unfavorable climatic conditions. In those areas, young men and women had to leave in search for work in cash crop agriculture in other countries. This exacerbated the already declining staple food production.

Postcolonial Africa

At the return to independence, Africa was predominantly an agricultural continent, featuring both arable or crop farming and pastoral or livestock farming. The arable farming clearly had two subsectors—the staple crop farming for domestic consumption and commercial crop farming for export. Similarly, the livestock farming was for both domestic and export markets. With the exception of the few areas that had successful irrigation schemes as the Gezira, much of agriculture was rainfed and employed very rudimentary tools—the machete, the cutlass, the hoe, and the axe. Human power was the prime source of energy with animal plows used in limited areas, and with the exception of European commercial estates majority of the farms were small holdings, characterized by low productivity.

African countries found this state of agriculture totally inadequate and unacceptable and were determined to change it. However, the economic policies that were enacted did not seem to jive with that goal. For one thing, agriculture was seen as a symbol of tradition and stagnation, while industrialization was a symbol of progress and modernity. As a result (as discussed in Chapter 3), much of the agricultural development efforts during that period were either part or derivative of the industrialization strategy. Thus, in addition to the expansion of export crop production to generate more revenue to support the industrialization strategy, economic development plans emphasized large-scale agriculture, planned resettlement schemes, and irrigation projects (Stock, 2004; Obia, 2003).

Large-scale Agriculture

Large-scale industrial agriculture was seen as a way to modernize agriculture. African countries that tinkered with the socialist ideology chose to do this through establishment of state farms (Chapter 2). These farms were based on the socialist mode of production of the former Soviet Union and its Eastern European satellite countries. They were first implemented in Ghana and Guinea in the 1960s. During the 1970s, several other African countries followed suit including Mozambique, Ethiopia, Angola, Tanzania, and Zambia (Obia, 2003; Stock, 2004). African countries which followed the nonsocialist path such as Cote d'Ivoire, Nigeria, and Botswana, also chose large-scale capitalist agriculture of the plantation type. These farms were either domestically or foreign controlled. Large tracts of land were committed to agricultural production but due to inexperience in managing such large projects, shortages of machinery and equipment parts, poor maintenance, and short-term expectations, these projects were not successful and many were abandoned.

Irrigation Schemes

A number of large-scale irrigation schemes were undertaken in the early Postcolonial Africa (see the section under Drainage Basins in Chapter 4). In Sudan, the Gezira Scheme was expanded by the Menagil Extension, which added 800,000 feddans (1.038 feddan = 1 acre) to the original scheme, with the completion of the Roseires Dam, also on the Blue Nile, in 1962. During the drought years of the early 1970s, other schemes such as the Senegal River Basin Authority (Mauritania, Senegal, and Mali), the Kano River (Nigeria), and the Aswan High Dam (Egypt) projects were completed. However, these schemes were hampered by both environmental and human problems. First, unpredictable rainfall amounts and dry conditions affected the water level of these projects making it difficult for the projects to function efficiently. Second, silting of the dams increased the maintenance cost. Third, inundation of rich agricultural land in some cases led to the need to use of marginal land for cultivation. Fourth, mismanagement skewed the benefits toward a few wealthy and influential individuals.

In the Office Du Niger, supervision of farmers and control of farming continued as before however due to lack of maintenance, several of the canals deteriorated, while farmers also constructed illegal canals to tap water to their farms (Hertzog et al., 2012). In the 1980s, following some aid from donors, the Malian government announced new forms of ownership contracts in 1989. According to Hertzog et al. (2012), there were contracts to state-owned companies, long-term leases (30–40 years), one-year leases, and permanent contracts. In 1994, the office was restructured to focus more on water management than crop production. Growing pressure from donors caused the Malian government to pass a new set of agricultural laws that emphasized private and foreign investment as the way for developing agriculture. This new law brought a lot of investors to the office, but some of the contracts did not go through proper channels. The outcry against this caused some of them to be cancelled. Apart from this, most of the contracts were also given without paying attention to the hydrologic consequences of whether there was sufficient water available. In 2011, the new ministry was formed to deal with these problems (Hertzog et al., 2012).

Planned Resettlement Schemes

Planned resettlement schemes were also part of the agricultural development effort in the early Postcolonial period, and two types were implemented. The first was large-scale hydroelectric power projects with some component of agricultural resettlement schemes. Examples of these were the Kariba Dam Resettlement Scheme of Zambia and Zimbabwe (1952), the Volta River resettlement scheme of Ghana (1962–1965), the Kainji Dam resettlement scheme of Nigeria (1967–1968), the Aswan High Dam resettlement scheme of Egypt (1963–1969), and the Manantali resettlement scheme of Mali (1986–1987). Unfortunately, not all of these schemes were successful. For example, in the case of the Volta Dam, about 80,000 people from some 740 villages had to be relocated to 52 rural townships. The agricultural component of the scheme consisted of two phases. In Phase I, each settler was supposed to receive 2–4 acres of land to be devoted to subsistence farming under a lease of 99 years. In Phase II, each settler was to receive 12 acres of land devoted to commercial farming through cooperatives (Lumsden, 1973). However, 20% of the settlers started leaving within the first year of the project, and by the end of the fourth year, only 26,000 were in the area, largely due to inadequate farmland. Only a small portion of the total land required had been cleared (Hart, 1978).

The Aswan High Dam also had significant agricultural component. According to Hassan (2007, p. 75), this included (1) conversion of basin irrigation into perennial irrigation with a total area of 983,000 feddans (1 feddan = 1.038 acres), (2) increasing the area of arable land from 5.8 million feddans to 7.4 million feddans, and (3) increasing the crop area from 3.8 million feddans in 1952 to about 14 million feddans in 1993. However, the impact of the dam on Nubians was negative as they found the housing provided by the Egyptian government inadequate and for that reason many of them were forced to relocate. The Kainji Dam also had to resettle about 40,000 people from 239 existing settlements into 141 new ones (Mills-Tettey, 1989). The scheme was relatively successful in its agricultural settlement compared to the Volta River Scheme.

The second type of planned resettlement scheme with agricultural component was land reforms. Examples of this include Kenya's Million-Acre Scheme, Algeria's Agrarian Reform Cooperatives, Tanzania's Ujamaa Program, Ethiopia's scheme, and Zimbabwe's land reform, which is discussed in Chapter 9). In Kenya's Million-Acre Scheme of 1962–1966, the Kenyan government purchased European farms and divided them initially among the middle-class farmers, who could afford to invest in the relatively large farm. Later on as the landless peasants heard of the program, they all descended on the designated farm areas, so the program was expanded to include the group to reduce frustration. In Algeria's Agrarian Reform Cooperatives of 1971–1979, large absentee private farms were appropriated by the government and redistributed to poor and landless peasants (Laoubi and Yamao, 2009). However, as noted in Chapter 3, Tanzania's Ujamaa program and Ethiopia's resettlement efforts were not successful.

Focus on Small Farmers and Integrated Rural Development

From the mid-1970s through the early 1980s, growing criticism of development projects in general and agricultural development in particular called for new strategies. The large-scale agriculture and resettlement projects were criticized for ignoring the small farmer as well as the food-producing sector. Radical development theorists charged that the **Green Revolution** in Asia had not worked because it was hijacked by large agribusiness interests and suggested that African countries should not adopt it. Even though in every country there were brief moments when the government encouraged people to take to the land and cultivate staple food, these were for the most part very short-lived. A new deal in the form of integrated rural development was crafted by development agencies led by the World Bank (see Chapter 2). This shift coincided with growing concepts and ideas of intermediate and appropriate technologies (Schumacher, 1973) and development from below (Stohr and Taylor, 1981). These ideas that focused on small farmers and rural development were incorporated in development plans of many African countries, but the strategy soon became too expensive and externally dependent, and when economic conditions in many African countries deteriorated in the early 1980s, the strategy became unsustainable.

Structural Adjustments and Agricultural Liberalization

By the late 1970s through the early 1980s, a number of factors including deteriorating environmental conditions (erratic rainfall) and inappropriate agricultural policies in the face of rapid population growth rates had turned every African country from being self-sufficient in food production into a net importer of staple foods. To make the imported food affordable, many African governments had to subsidize prices, which in turn dramatically increased the national debt. In Ethiopia, the situation deteriorated into one of the most severe famines in Africa (see Box 11.1). As we have seen in some of the preceding chapters, the looming

Box 11.1 | The Ethiopian Famine of 1982

Famine is not new to Africa. In all the areas in which there is a marked dry season, there has always been a period usually referred to the "lean season." However, the famine that occurred in Ethiopia was like no other in modern history. In 1972–1974, a severe drought caused a serious famine in the country that culminated in the fall of Emperor Haile Selassie's regime. International calls following this disaster led to the establishment of the Relief and Rehabilitation Commission (RRC). The purpose of this organization was to help deal with future crisis.

In June 1978, the Ethiopian radio broadcast an alert that some 1.5 million people in the northern provinces, including Tigre and Wollo, would face starvation unless some 400,000 tons of food aid was sent. By November 1978, the RRC was claiming that some 2 million peasants were at risk in Wollo. In March 1982, the World Food Council forecasted an impending food crisis and the United Nations' Food and Agricultural Organization (FAO) predicted a cereal deficit. The RRC continued to issue series of alerts. By the fall of 1982, food supplies had run out in Wollo and the Catholic Relief Services had made urgent pleas to the US government through the United States Agency for International Development (USAID). By March 1983, some 28,000 hungry Ethiopians were already gathered in a destitute make-shift camp in Korem and feeding stations run by NGOs were setting up along the roads between Addis Ababa and Asmara. In the most seriously affected regions, Tigre and Eritrea, peasants had resorted to eating cactus fruit and wild grass seeds for survival. In November 1983, the CRS ran low on food and sent an urgent plea to Washington, DC for 16,000 metric tons of grain, but it was not until May 1984, 6 months later that the US government promised only 8,000 tons. The remaining half was not approved until July, 9 months later. By the end of 1984, an estimated 300,000 Ethiopians had starved to death. In October 1984, the BBC television film on the crisis was aired generating a world-wide outpouring of aid. By January 1985, the US government had pledged $590 million in food aid with $151.5 million going to Ethiopia. But it was too late for the estimated 300,000 Ethiopians that had starved to death.

Why did this catastrophe happen? A number of reasons were offered to explain the catastrophe. One reason was the problem of statistical data that led to inaccurate estimation of the magnitude of the problem. Another reason was the fact the Ethiopian government felt that the RRC was exaggerating the crisis and this infuriated the government into inaction. However, the most important reason was politics. First, the Ethiopian government was accused of selling donated food to buy Soviet arms for the civil war in the northern provinces and in Eritrea. Second, the Reagan Administration officials complained about the food aid to the Communist/Marxist— regime of the Ethiopian government. As already pointed, out during the famine of 1972–1974, the silence of Haile Selassie about the crisis and apparent inaction about it led to the overthrow of the longest monarchy in Africa. A series of power struggles followed culminating in the emergence and rise of Lieutenant Colonel Mengistu Haile Mariam and a Marxist regime. Mengistu tried to reorganize Ethiopian society, agriculture, and economy along Soviet lines, while fighting two wars—one in the north and one against Eritrea. In those days, Ethiopia became the most outspoken Marxist country in Africa. Thus, when the calls for food aid came, the Regan administration did not see any rush to relieve a communist regime. Finally, there was also the Civil War. The war created a lot of destruction and difficulty for food distribution. Ethiopian government forces attacked food aid to the rebels and the rebels did the same. Voluntary relief workers could not get through into large sections of Tigre and Eritrea because of the rebels, and they were afraid to go to the government centers because of fear of being conscripted to fight. This increased the effect of the famine. Thus, internally, the Ethiopian government was more concerned with keeping itself in power than addressing the needs of the country. Externally, Ethiopia was caught up in Cold War politics. The result was a disaster of untold proportions. What were the lessons learned from this?

economic crises provided a premise for the structural adjustment and trade liberalization programs (SAPs) of the 1980s and 1990s, which had far severe repercussions on Africa's fragile agriculture. For example, the withdrawal of **agricultural subsidies** and agricultural credit, an important component of the program, made things more difficult for farmers. The private investment that was supposed to go into agriculture following the removal of the subsidies and credit did not materialize. Liberalization of trade, which was the other piece of the program, made matters worse for Africa's agricultural products as cheaper and heavily subsidized agricultural products from outside were dumped on African markets (Bello, 2008). Efforts to shift emphasis from staple food production to export crop production led to a glut on the market and collapse of market prices of such crops as cocoa and coffee. For example, in Ghana, the expansion in cocoa production led to a 46% drop in the price of cocoa, while in Ethiopia, collapse of coffee prices created another food crisis (Bello, 2008). In Malawi, the government's initiative of giving free starter packs to farmers was ended causing drastic decline in food production and a subsequent famine in 2001–2002 (Bello, 2008).

Havnevik et al. (2007) report that in Tanzania, the removal of fertilizer subsidy resulted in sharp prices that caused 80% reduction in real return to maize producers. This was also the case in Ghana, Uganda, and Zambia as well as the many countries in Africa that were forced to adopt these policies (Bertow and Schultheis, 2007). In Morocco, Algeria, and Tunisia, governments found ways around this to push through adjustment policies, which boosted wheat production, in spite of food riots caused by removal of subsidies. Yet in the end, the unpredictable weather and increasing population growth rendered the reforms ineffective. Only Morocco managed to achieve some substantial growth in wheat production. In the end, all three countries had to rely on imports to meet their consumption needs, contrary to what they had planned to achieve. In addition, the push to increase production brought agriculturally marginal lands under cultivation, which were eventually lost due to harsh environmental deterioration (Swearingen, 1996). In Egypt, withdrawal of subsidies from cotton cultivation raised cost of production causing a collapse and a subsequent shift to rice, wheat, maize, and vegetables by farmers (Nassar and Mansour, 2003).

In the meantime, aid from both multilateral and bilateral agencies to African agriculture declined between 1981 and 2001. For the World Bank, for example, it declined from $419 million in 1991 to $123 million in 2000. Indeed, the Bank's own data show that agriculture accounted for only 8% of its total lending to Africa from 1991 to 2006. Apart from this, the validity of the projects supported by these funds was questionable. For example, the World Bank's own Independent Evaluation Group's review of the Bank's support for agriculture in Africa established that

> Bank-supported agriculture activities in Africa have largely responded more to dealing with acute food insecurity when it occurs than to helping countries develop long-term approach to address the factors that create food insecurity (World Bank Independent Evaluation Group, 2007, p. 48).

A case in point is how little aid funding went to support irrigation projects although it is widely known that availability of water is the most critical factor in agricultural production over much of Africa, In Ethiopia, the establishment of Early Warning Systems after the famine of 1983, for example, had very little subsequent funding for irrigation.

Decline of Agricultural Research

The research infrastructure inherited from the colonial period faced many difficulties (Roseboom et al., 1998). The regional research institutes were dismantled as every country sought to develop its own research infrastructure. In British Africa, the links between the research institutes and British expertise slowly declined as funding dried up. In contrast in French Africa, the French kept closer ties with the former colonies and continued to direct and control affairs from Paris (Roseboom et al., 1998). In some countries such as DRC, political instability caused the research infrastructure to quickly disintegrate. In most countries, however, limited funding and brain drain made it difficult for research institutes to function properly, and as the economies deteriorated agricultural research dropped from the top priorities of most African governments and was only kept minimally alive by philanthropic foundations that had agriculture as part of their agenda.

The State of Africa's Agriculture by the Beginning of the 21st century

By the beginning of the 21st century, Africa's performance in agricultural production over the postcolonial period had been a checkered one. With respect to staple food production, only cassava appeared to have experienced a slow but increasing growth rate (Figure 11.3). For the rest of Africa's major staple foods, such as banana, maize, millet, plantain, rice, and sorghum, production rates were negative, flat, or very slow (Table 11.2).

In the industrial or export crop sector, the story was no different (Figure 11.4). Production growth rates for every major export slowed from 1970s through the late 1990s, with all crops but tea registering at least one negative growth rate at some point during the period under consideration (Table 11.3). Livestock production also experienced high levels of unstable growth rates (Figure 11.5), even though the data did not show any negative growths. In all African countries, the share of agriculture in the total investments declined from double-digit percentages to single-digit

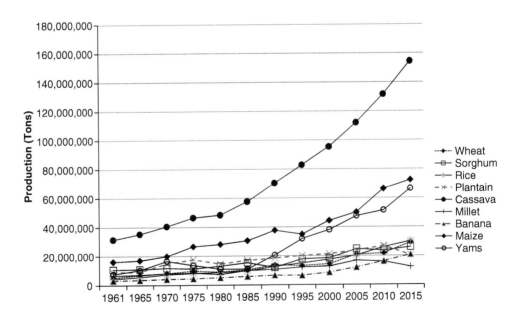

FIGURE 11.3 Major food crop production 1961–2015.
Source: FAO Food Production Statistics

TABLE 11.2

Production Growth (%) of Major Food Crops 1961–2015

Year	Banana	Cassava	Maize	Millet	Plantain	Rice	Sorghum	Wheat
1961–1965	2.5	3.0	1.2	1.7	0.3	6.7	0.4	8.1
1965–1970	3.6	3.0	3.5	2.8	12.6	6.6	1.6	3.9
1970–1975	1.3	2.9	6.8	0.6	3.8	2.2	−0.9	4.0
1975–1980	3.0	0.8	1.1	−2.2	−3.5	1.3	3.2	−1.6
1980–1985	2.9	3.8	1.8	7.3	3.5	2.3	3.5	3.4
1985–1990	2.6	4.4	4.6	1.5	1.6	6.4	−4.3	6.3
1990–1995	−0.5	3.6	−1.5	2.7	1.8	3.5	9.7	−0.8
1995–2000	6.4	3.0	5.3	1.0	1.3	3.4	0.7	1.8
2000–2005	8.2	3.5	2.6	6.2	2.4	3.2	6.9	9.3
2005–2010	7.1	3.5	5.9	−1.0	2.4	5.5	−0.9	0.7
2010–2015	5.7	3.5	1.8	−4.5	−4.7	3.2	2.0	7.0

Source: Data from FAO Crop Production Statistics.

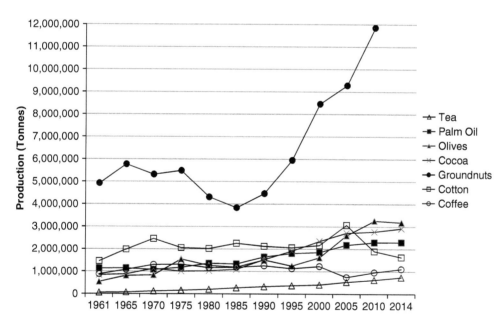

FIGURE 11.4 Major agricultural exports production, 1961–2014.
Source: FAO Food Production Statistics. 2015. Data for Cotton Lint and Palm Oil were not available.

percentages (El-Ghonemy, 2003). Two major efforts that stepped in to deal with this chronic problem were the New Partnership for African Development (NEPAD) and renewed call for Green Revolution in Africa.

The New Partnership for Africa's Development (NEPAD)'s agricultural program

As mentioned in Chapter 3, NEPAD was formed in 2001 with three goals in mind—(1) to promote accelerated growth and sustainable development in Africa; (2) to eradicate widespread and severe poverty; and (3) to halt the marginalization of

TABLE 11.3

Production Growth (%) of Major Export Crops 1961–2014

Year	Cocoa	Coffee	Cotton	Groundnuts	Olives	Palm Oil	Tea
1961–1965	1.1	5.9	9.1	4.3	13.0	0.2	7.3
1965–1970	5.7	4.1	4.9	−1.6	0.6	−1.1	13.5
1970–1975	−2.1	0.3	−3.3	0.6	17.1	1.8	5.8
1975–1980	0.4	−2.3	−0.4	−4.3	−3.7	3.1	5.6
1980–1985	1.3	0.3	2.4	−2.2	−1.1	−0.4	7.0
1985–1990	7.9	1.2	−1.2	3.3	5.4	4.7	4.1
1990–1995	5.1	−2.0	−0.6	6.7	−3.5	1.9	2.8
1995–2000	4.6	1.8	1.0	8.4	6.0	0.6	2.2
2000–2005	3.1	−7.8	8.3	1.9	12.3	3.6	5.9
2005–2010	0.4	5.7	−7.6	5.5	5.0	1.1	3.6
2010–2014	1.2	0.6	8.8	2.4	−0.6	0.0	2.9

Source: FAO Crop Production Statistics—2015 data was unavailable for Cotton lint and Palm Oil.

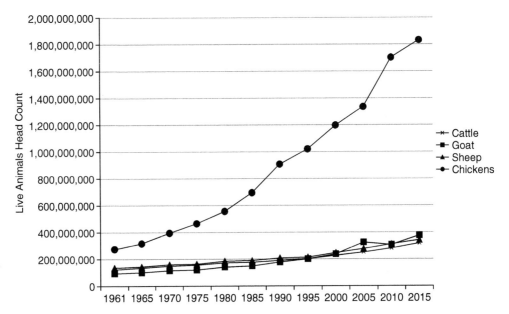

FIGURE 11.5 Major livestock production 1961–2015. *Source:* FAO Live Animals Production

Africa in the globalization process. In 2003, NEPAD established the **Comprehensive Africa Agricultural Development Program (CAADP)**, with the following aims:

- To eliminate hunger and reduce poverty through agriculture
- To bring together key players at the continental, regional, and national levels, to improve coordination, share knowledge, successes and failures, to encourage one another, and to promote joint and separate efforts to achieve the CAAP goals

African leaders agreed to devote at least 10% of their national budgets to agriculture compared to less than 1% before. They also targeted that by 2015 they hope to see

- Dynamic agricultural markets within and between countries and regions in Africa;
- Farmers being active in the market economy and the continent becoming a net exporter of agricultural products;
- A more equitable distribution of wealth for rural populations;
- Africa as a strategic player in agricultural science and technology; and
- Environmentally sound agricultural production and a culture of sustainable management of natural resources in Africa (http://www.nepad.org/foodsecurity/agriculture/about)

In 2007, the EU Commission of European Communities issued a document titled Advancing African Agriculture, which established key principles to partner with African Union on the CAADP, although the partnership was later on criticized for ignoring the small-scale African farmer. However, at the time of writing no evidence existed as to whether or not these 2015 targets have been achieved. In spite of this, a new commitment to end hunger in Africa by 2025, called the Malabo Declaration, was adopted in 2014 by the African Heads of State. The goal is to end hunger through sharing of information, technologies, and best practices in agricultural capacity building policy planning and implementation.

Renewed calls for a Green Revolution in Africa

Since 2004, there has been renewed calls for a Green Revolution in Africa. It started with the then UN Secretary-General Kofi Annan's call for an increased public–private partnership to create a Green Revolution in Africa like the one that helped increased food production in Asia, Middle East, and Latin America. In 2006, the Norwegian fertilizer company Yara International initiated and co-hosted three conferences on Green Revolution for Africa in Oslo, Norway, which ended in 2008. The 2007 conference recommended the establishment of a global fund to help finance investment in agriculture and help farmers to purchase fertilizer and high-yielding seeds and improved delivery systems (Olsen, 2008).

Also in 2006, the Bill and Melinda Gates Foundation and the Rockefeller Foundation established the Alliance for a Green Revolution in Africa to help poor African farmers lift themselves out of poverty, with an initial grant of $150 million. The Alliance has since initiated a number of projects in its five focus areas: (1) getting better seeds to farmers, (2) improving soil health, (3) providing better access to markets, (4) building partnerships to change policies, and (5) strengthening farmer organizations capacities. One of the better seed projects is a $47 million grant that was given to the African Agricultural Technology Foundation, a British nonprofit company to work with International Maize and Wheat Improvement Center and Monsanto Company, to develop harder varieties of maize over 10 years (McLymont, 2008).

Other calls have come from World Food Program (WFP), Food and Agricultural Organization (FAO), the International Fund for Agricultural Development (IFAD), the African Union, as well as academic research (e.g., Ajakaiye and de Janvry, 2010; Breisinger et al., 2011; de Janvry and Sadoulet, 2010; Diao et al., 2008). Moseley (2017) is critical about all these renewed calls for a New Green Revolution. He argues that the New Green Revolution is no different from the first Green Revolution because it ignores the broader political, economic, and social contexts of hunger, malnutrition and food security, and for that reason it might succeed in increasing food productivity but will not address the problem of food security.

AGRICULTURAL PRODUCTION SYSTEMS IN AFRICA

Generally speaking, the concept of a production system refers to a group of interacting firms producing and supplying a set of related goods. As used in this chapter, **agricultural production system** refers to the numerous individual family and corporate units engaged in the production and supply of agricultural produce for both food and industrial raw materials, and how these firms operate in terms of organization and technology. By product characteristics, we may identify two main types of production systems—crop and livestock production systems.

Crop Production Systems

By technology and mode of operation, there are two crop production systems in Africa—traditional and modern crop production systems. The traditional system uses home grown methods of farming and farm management that are rooted in Africa's indigenous production culture. They include **shifting cultivation, rotational bush fallow,** permanent cultivation, and **floodland cultivation,** while the modern systems are adoption and adaptation of Western-style of farming.

Traditional Crop Production Systems

Shifting cultivation Shifting cultivation is the oldest crop production system technology and organization in Africa. It is a method that developed as an adaptation to the environment and human resource capacity of African farmers. Land is cleared by the slash-and-burn method. Crops are then cultivated without any manure or fertilizers. Consequently, every two to three years the farm is abandoned, to allow the land to regain its fertility through natural processes. When the distance between the settlement and farms reaches a point where it is no longer feasible for farmers to do the daily commute, the farmers move the settlement closer to the new farms and start the process all over again. This crop production system used to be very widespread. However, increasing population and other social changes have restricted it to the most sparsely populated regions and the remotest parts of Africa such as the Congo Basin, southwest of Cote d'Ivoire, and parts of Nigeria.

Rotational bush fallow Rotational bush fallow is very similar to shifting cultivation except that the farms are rotated around a fixed settlement. Thus, after two to three years of cultivation, the farmer moves on to a new farm. The old farm is not completely abandoned but eventually, it is left to fallow. The fallow period used to be as long as 20 years but with population growth, this has been reduced to between four and seven years. This is the most widespread of Africa's traditional farming systems.

Permanent cultivation Permanent cultivation—a crop farming system without a fallow period is practiced in areas with high population density and pressure on limited agricultural land. As a result, they tend to be very intensive since population pressure forces the farmers to use every bit of space. They occur in such areas as the rich volcanic soils of southern Uganda, Rwanda, and Burundi, the Igboland of southeastern Nigeria, the Hausaland of northern Nigeria, in the northeast and northwest corners of Ghana, and North Africa. They also occur around all the major urban centers of Africa where market gardening is practiced. The use of manure is high, and in many ways this type of farming can best be described as mixed farming, because it includes livestock farming.

Floodland cultivation Floodland cultivation is practiced in flood plains, where water is provided by floodwater at certain parts of the year. Usually, artificial devices made from local items are used to lift water to irrigate the land during the farming season. They occur in a few areas including the Oyo State in western Nigeria, the Kano and Zaria districts in northern Nigeria, the coastal regions of Guinea and Sierra Leone, and in the Barotseland of Zambia. One common characteristic of all traditional system is that they all employ rudimentary technologies, namely, the machete, the hoe, and the stick. They mostly rely on human energy with some use of animal power in plowing where appropriate. Some also use tractors for plowing while the rest of the work is done manually.

Modern Crop Production System

This system differs from the traditional system with respect to technologies it employs and the size of the farming operation. In terms of technology, tractors and tiling machines replace the machete and the hoe and for that matter fossil fuel rather than human or animal power is the primary source of energy. Irrigation systems where applicable are mechanized while fertilizer usage is relatively higher.

Major Crops

Conventionally, crops produced in Africa used to be classified into two broad divisions—food crops and cash crops. The food crops were the staple foods consumed by the farming family, while the cash crops were exported for cash. Over the years, however, staple foods have increasingly entered the local, national, as well as international markets, such that they have also become cash crops. Thus, as Obia (2003) points out the idea that Africa's agriculture is largely subsistence is mythical. Consequently, the terms staple food crops and industrial crops will be used.

Major staple food crops Following Udo (1982), the main staple crops of Africa may be classified into three main groups—grains, roots, and fruits and vegetables. Figure 11.6 shows where the most important crops under these categories grow.

Grains Grains constitute the most important group of staple foods in Africa, and the most important of these are maize, guinea corn (sorghum), millet, rice, and wheat.

Maize in Africa has the distinction of being consumed almost 100% by humans compared to maize in other parts of the world, where it is mostly used as animal feed or industrial raw material (McCann, 2001). It is an important staple in West Africa, but even more important in Central, East, and Southern Africa. In southern Africa, it accounts for more than 50% of staple food calories. Maize grows in almost every country in Africa—52 out of 55. However, about 78% of Africa's total output came from 10 countries in 2015, of which 50% came from four countries—Nigeria (14.6%), South Africa (13.8%), Ethiopia (10.9%), and Egypt (10.8%) (Table 11.4). Maize constitutes 70% of all grains in South Africa and covers more than 60% of cropped area. New varieties such as the "Obatanpa Gh" maize developed in Ghana in 1992 have helped boost production in Ghana and have been released in West, Central, and Southern African countries (Badu-Apraku et al., 2006).

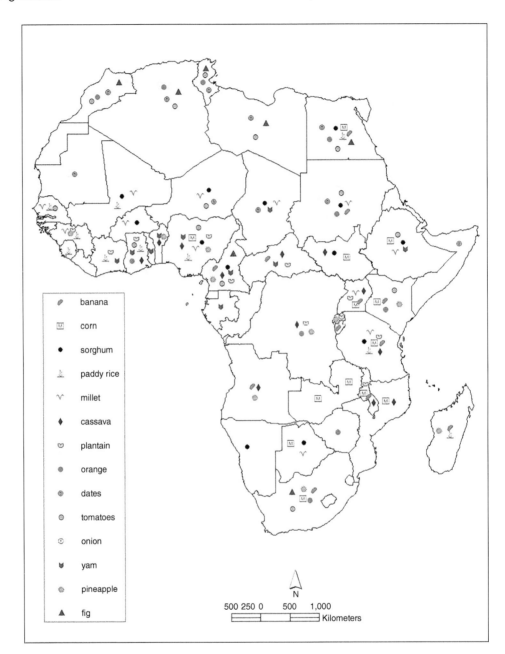

FIGURE 11.6 Distribution of major food crops.
Source: FAOSTAT 2015

Sorghum is the most widely produced grain in Africa after maize. It is consumed both by people and livestock. It is used to make a wide range of traditional foods as well as in beer making. It is a versatile crop that grows both in semiarid and arid environments. Thus, it grows in more than 40 African countries. In 2015, Africa produced 42% of the world's output 60% of which came from Nigeria, Sudan, and Ethiopia (Table 11.4). Most of this production comes from small peasant farmers, who consume most of what they produce and sell the rest. However, the generally low-yielding capacity of African sorghum has generated interest from Foundations and research universities—Bill and Melinda Gates Foundation, Africa Harvest Biotech Foundation International, University of California, as well several NGOs, to develop more nutritious and easily digestible varieties a project that has attracted close to $500 million (Botha and Viljoen, 2007).

TABLE 11.4

Major Grain Staples Production, 2015

	Maize				Sorghum				Rice				Wheat	
Country	Production ('000 MT)	%	Country	Production ('000 MT)	%	Country	Production ('000 MT)	%	Country	Production ('000 MT)	%
S. Africa	14,982	19.3	Nigeria	6,741	23.3	Nigeria	6,734	21.6	Egypt	9,280	35.6
Nigeria	10,791	13.9	Sudan	6,281	21.7	Egypt	6,000	19.2	Morocco	5,116	19.6
Ethiopia	7,235	9.3	Ethiopia	4,339	15.0	Madagascar	3,978	12.8	Ethiopia	4,232	16.2
Tanzania	6,737	8.7	B. Faso	1,708	5.9	Tanzania	2,621	8.4	Algeria	2,436	9.3
Egypt	5,800	7.5	Niger	1,426	4.9	Mali	2,167	6.9	S. Africa	1,750	6.7
Malawi	3,929	5.1	Mali	1,272	4.4	Côte d'Ivoire	2,054	6.6	Tunisia	1,513	5.8
Kenya	3,513	4.5	Cameroon	1,150	4.0	Guinea	1,971	6.3	Sudan	473	1.8
Zambia	3,351	4.3	S. Sudan	990	3.4	Sierra Leone	1,155	3.7	Kenya	329	1.3
Uganda	2,763	3.6	Chad	897	3.1	Ghana	604	1.9	Zambia	202	0.8
Ghana	1,762	2.3	Tanzania	840	2.9	Senegal	559	1.8	Libya	200	0.8
Top 10	60,863	78.4	Top 10	25,644	88.5	Top 10	27,842	89.3	Top 10	25,697	98.0
Others	16,761	21.6	Others	3,342	11.5	Others	3,351	10.7	Others	362	2.0
Total	77,624	100.0	Total	28,985	100.0	Total	31,194	100.0	Total	26,059	100

Source: FAO Crop Production Statistics.

Rice has long been a staple food in West Africa and Madagascar. However, over the decade from 1996 to 2006, Africa as a whole became an important rice consumer, accounting for 32% of the global rice imports (Sumado et al., ND). One result of this has been increasing rice production on the continent. For example, between 2001 and 2005, rice production grew at the rate of 3–4% per annum, and today rice is grown in almost every country on the continent under upland, rainfed lowland, deep water and mangrove swamp, and irrigated lowland conditions. Nigeria has the largest rainfed lowland rice area followed by Tanzania, Madagascar, Guinea, Mozambique, Cote d'Ivoire, and Sierra Leone. The deep water and mangrove swamp rice cultivation is concentrated in the floodplains of Niger River, and the inland basins of Chad, Mali, Guinea, Niger, and Nigeria as well as the mangrove swamps of Guinea Bissau, Guinea, and Gambia. Irrigated wetland rice areas include Egypt, Madagascar, Nigeria, Mali, Guinea, Senegal, and Cote d'Ivoire, while upland rice areas are found in Central and East Africa (Balasubramanian et al., 2007). Research indicates that there is a high probability for Africa to become the center of world rice production, but there are several constraints such as reliance on rainfed cultivation and its vulnerability to the vagaries of the weather; development of high-yielding rice variety that will be both drought and disease-resistant; identification, branding, and promotion of a local variety that will meet national, regional, and international demand. This will require commitment to research and development through public and private partnerships (Balasubramanian et al., 2007). This potential of Africa as a major rice producer has generated many rice projects mostly funded by China and Japan. In Uganda, for example, where 10% of the land area is wetland, Japan International Cooperation Agency (JICA) started a project to increase production by "introducing rice cultivation practices widely adopted in Asia" (Kijima et al., 2011, p. 171). The study showed that Green Revolution is possible in Eastern Uganda through the use of "improved practices such as bunding, leveling, and straight row planting" (Kijima et al., 2011, p. 184). In 2015, the leading producers were Nigeria (21.6%), Egypt (19.2%), and Madagascar (12.8%) (Table 11.4).

Other grains Other important grains are wheat, barley, millet, and teff. Wheat and barley are grown in Egypt, Algeria, Morocco, and Tunisia, where they are staple foods. They are also grown in South Africa and the highlands of Kenya, Tanzania, and Zimbabwe. Millet is much more confined in the Guinea savannah zone of West Africa, while teff grows largely in Ethiopia.

Roots Roots constitute the second most important group of staple foods in Africa, and the most important of this group are cassava, yams, cocoyam, and sweet potatoes. Cassava is the most widely cultivated root crop in Africa, because of its ability to thrive in both tropical and subtropical environments. Next to maize, cassava is also the largest source of calories in Africa. Cassava production in Africa has long been concentrated in West Africa, where the crop has evolved from a reserve food during severe farming through staple food for rural dwellers, cash crop for urban consumption, to an input for animal feed and industrial processing. The introduction of new high-yielding drought-resistant variety by the International Institute of Tropical Agriculture (IITA) in Nigeria boosted expansion in cassava production not only in West Africa but also in East and Southern Africa, into territories that maize was the main source of calories, namely, Zambia, Malawi, and Mozambique.

Two varieties are grown in Africa—the high-yielding bitter variety and the sweet variety. In Central and Southern Africa, the bitter variety accounts for between 70%

and 90% of the production. Nigeria is Africa's largest cassava producer accounting for 37.3% of the total output in 2015. It is also the world's largest producer. The Nigerian government's mandate to include high quality cassava flour (HQCF) in wheat flour for bread making is one the factors that has led to production growth in that country (Kolawole et al., 2010). Other important producers in 2015 were Ghana, DRC, Mozambique, and Angola (Table 11.5). Over 75% of Nigeria's production is processed into *gari*, a precooked staple food which has a much longer shelf life. In East and Southern Africa, however, much of the crop is consumed fresh (Haggblade et al., 2012; Kolawole et al., 2010).

While cassava is the most widely consumed root crop in Africa, yam is the most prestigious root crop in terms of affordability. In addition, it is much more a West African native crop. As a result, more than 90% of the world's yams are grown in the "Yam Belt of West Africa," which includes Nigeria, Benin, Togo, Ghana, and Cote d'Ivoire (Africa Research Bulletin, 2012a; Anonymous, 2010). In 2015, Nigeria, Ghana, and Cote d'Ivoire accounted for about 89% of all the yams produced in Africa (Table 11.5).

Fruits and vegetables All African countries grow a wide variety of fruits and vegetables. Some are grown as staple foods, while others are for export. The fruits include tropical, subtropical, and temperate varieties. The most important in terms of staple food are plantains and bananas. Plantain is cultivated in 18 countries in East, Central, and West Africa, where they constitute an important staple food. Tomekpe et al. (2011) report that introduction of new high-yielding suckers since 1989 by the Cameroon-based African Research Center on Banana and Plantain (CARBAP) through research funded by European Union has greatly boosted production in Nigeria, Ghana, Cameroon, and Central African Republic. In 2015, the top producers were Uganda, Cameroon, Ghana, and Nigeria (Table 11.5).

Banana, including the cooking, sweet, and beer varieties, is more widespread and grown in 39 African countries. However, like plantain the production is concentrated in West, Central, and East Africa. Beer banana is more important in Burundi and Rwanda than the rest of East Africa. The major producers of bananas in 2015 were Angola, Tanzania, Rwanda, Cameroon, and Kenya (Table 11.5).

In 2015, Africa produced 13% of the world's **citrus fruits**, which included oranges, lemons and lime, and tangerines. The most important of these were oranges, which were grown in 33 African countries. These were produced on small-scale orchards in the tropical areas, and on large orchards in the sheltered river valleys of South Africa. Egypt produced 36% of Africa's oranges in 2015 and was followed by South Africa (18.9%), Algeria (11%), and Morocco (9%).

In 2015, Africa also produced 45% of the world's dates, 44% of its figs, 18% of its pineapples, 15% of its apricots, 13% of its avocados, 13% of its mangoes and guavas, 10% of its grapefruit, and 12% of its papaya. Dates, figs, apples, and apricots are fruits that do well in temperate climates—so their production in Africa is much more confined to areas with Mediterranean climate—North Africa and South Africa. In contrast, avocados, mangoes and guavas, grapefruit, pineapples, and papayas are tropical and subtropical fruits so they are produced in many more African countries. Egypt and Algeria produced most of Africa's dates in 2015, while Sudan and Morocco were also important for dates and figs, respectively. Most of Africa's avocados were produced in Kenya, Rwanda, South Africa, and Cameroon, while most of the pineapples were produced in Nigeria, Ghana, and Angola.

Vegetable production Every African country grows some vegetables and this is partly because vegetables constitute a very important component of the diets of

TABLE 11.5

Major Roots and Fruit Staples Production, 2015

	Cassava			Yam			Banana			Plantain		
Country	Area	Production ('000 MT)	%	Area	Production ('000 MT)	%	Area	Production ('000 MT)	%	Area	Production ('000 MT)	%
Nigeria	Nigeria	57,643	37.3	Nigeria	45,677	68.8	Angola	3,595	17.4	Uganda	4,456	21.9
Ghana	Ghana	17,212	11.1	Ghana	7,296	11.0	Tanzania	3,584	17.3	Cameroon	4,076	20.0
DRC	Cote d'Ivoire	14,709	9.5	Cote d'Ivoire	5,945	9.0	Rwanda	2,980	14.4	Ghana	3,952	19.4
Mozambique	Benin	8,103	5.2	Benin	2,650	4.0	Egypt	1,314	6.3	Nigeria	3,040	14.9
Angola	Ethiopia	7,727	5.0	Ethiopia	1,575	2.4	Kenya	1,290	6.2	C. d'Ivoire	1,591	7.8
Tanzania	Togo	5,886	3.8	Cameroon	781	1.2	Cameroon	1,082	5.2	DRC	1,115	5.5
Cameroon	Cameroon	5,198	3.4	Sudan	602	0.9	Tanzania	910	4.4	Tanzania	573	2.8
Malawi	Chad	4,996	3.2	Burundi	475	0.7	Guinea	865	4.2	Guinea	468	2.3
Sierra Leone	C. African Rep.	4,783	3.1	Mozambique	474	0.7	Malawi	670	3.2	Malawi	402	2.0
Benin	Gabon	4,193	2.7	Uganda	216	0.3	Gabon	583	2.8	Gabon	272	1.3
Top 10	Top 10	130,454	84.5	Top 10	65,696	99.0	Top 10	16,876	81.5	Top 10	19,950	98.1
Others	Others	23,965	15.5	Others	679	1.0	Others	3,842	18.5	Others	388	1.9
Total	Total	154,419	100.0	Total	66,375	100.0	Total	20,718	100.0	Total	20,338	100.0

Source: FAO Crop Production Statistics.

most Africans, and partly because of an increasing export trade. FAOSTAT lists about 27 varieties of vegetables that are grown in Africa, of which about 25% were unclassified in 2015. Of the classified vegetables, the largest group was tomatoes (24.2%), followed by dry onions (13.3%), and chilies and green peppers (3.5%). In 2015, Africa produced 11% of the world's tomatoes and 11% of dry onions. It also produced 33% of leguminous vegetables other than beans, 20% of artichokes, and 11% of okra. Much of Africa's vegetable is grown under irrigation and also around the large urban areas.

In the past several years, vegetable production in a number of African countries such as Kenya and Senegal has attracted a great deal of attention (Asfaw et al., 2009, 2011; Mausch and Mithofer, 2011). According to Asfaw et al. (2009), vegetable export in Kenya has surpassed coffee, the traditional export. Mausch and Mithofer (2011) identify three types of vegetable growers—large-scale exporter-owned farms, large-scale contracted farms, and small holder farms. Exporter-owned farm may be as large as 101 hectares in area, large-scale contract farm about 14.2 hectares, while the small holding farm may be 0.31 hectares. In terms of crops, the exporter-owned farm may grow as many as six vegetable crops, the large-scale contract farm five, while the small holder may have three. The major crop is beans; however, small holders grow two additional crops—kale and tomatoes for the domestic market. Other crops are peas, karalla, chilies, aubergines, and okra, while flowers such as roses, carnations, statice, and sunflowers are also cultivated (Asfaw, 2011).

In Senegal, farmers began to diversify into vegetable growing for export after the production of groundnuts became unsustainable due to soil depletion. The two main crops are green beans and tomatoes, but cucumbers, onions, mushrooms, lettuce, and chili peppers are also grown. However, as a result of increasing cost of meeting stringent conditions in the export markets, vegetable growing has seen more consolidation and concentration of vertically integrated large-scale farms. Thus, in 1999, small holders accounted for 95% of the sources of vegetable grown for export; by 2005, they accounted for only 52%. Most of the farmers have become field and processing workers for the exporting companies. Maertens et al. (2011) show that small farmers who could still hold contracts with exporting firms fared better in terms of income and other socioeconomic indicators than those who became employees on the exporter-owned farms.

Major industrial crops Africa is well known for producing a wide range of industrial crops, which are crops that serve as raw material input for manufacturing industries. The most important among these crops are cocoa, coffee, cotton, groundnuts (peanuts), palm products, tea, rubber, and sugarcane (Figure 11.7).

Cocoa Africa accounts for 66% of the world's cocoa production, of which 95% comes from four countries—Cote d'Ivoire, Ghana, Cameroon, and Nigeria. Cocoa was introduced to Africa from South America by Spanish and Portuguese explorers who brought the crop to the islands of Fernando Po (now Bloko), Equatorial Guinea, and Sao Tome and Principe at the beginning of the 19th century, from where it was introduced into mainland West Africa. In 2015, Cote d'Ivoire, accounted for about 50% of Africa's cocoa production, followed by Ghana, Cameroon, and Nigeria (Table 11.6). Cocoa growing is an example of what African entrepreneurship can achieve, given the right conditions. All the crops are virtually grown by Africans and on smallholdings rather than plantations.

After coffee and sugar, cocoa is the most important agricultural export commodity in international trade. However, a major problem facing cocoa growing is the fluctuation of market prices. Negotiations to secure a permanent agreement

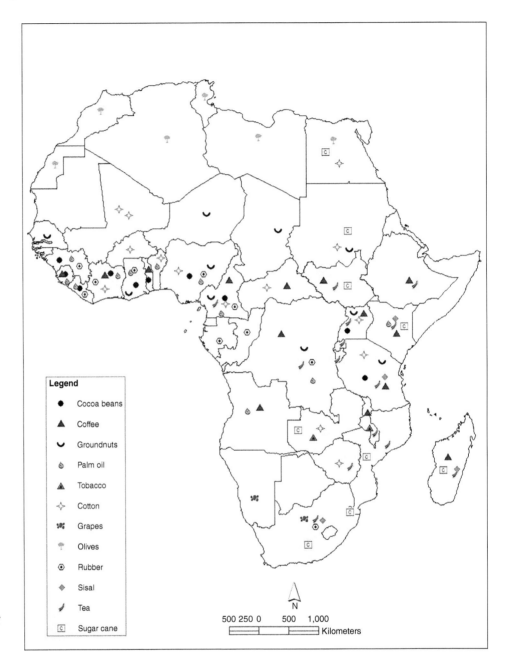

FIGURE 11.7 Distribution of major industrial crops.
Source: FAOSTATS 2015

between producers and consumers of the crop that began in 1956 has not been successful. Conferences under the auspices of the UN in 1963, 1966, and 1967 all failed. The sticking issue was how to set a minimum price. Since then, a series of ad hoc measures in the form of International Cocoa Agreements that require periodic renegotiation have been pursued, sometimes without any agreement.

Coffee Coffee is the most important agricultural export commodity in international trade and Africa produces a little over 13% of the world's coffee, making it the second largest producer and exporter in the world. The crop is indigenous to Africa and was first discovered in Ethiopia. Today, several varieties of coffee still grow in 27 African countries, in an area between Latitude 8°N and S of the Equator, and

TABLE 11.6

Major Industrial (Export) Crops

	Cocoa			Coffee			Cotton			Tea		
Country	Production ('000 MT)	%	Country	Production ('000 MT)	%	Country	Production ('000 MT)	%	Country	Production ('000 MT)	%
Cote d'Ivoire	1,484	50.2	Ethiopia	457	40.9	B. Faso	845	20.4	Kenya	399	56.7
Ghana	858	29.0	Uganda	207	18.6	Mali	514	12.4	Uganda	61	8.7
Cameroon	272	9.2	Cote d'Ivoire	105	9.4	Cote d'Ivoire	416	10.1	Burundi	53	7.6
Nigeria	195	6.6	Madagascar	47	4.3	Egypt	320	7.7	Malawi	47	6.8
Togo	54	1.9	Tanzania	42	3.8	Nigeria	278	6.7	Tanzania	35	5.1
Uganda	23	0.8	Kenya	42	3.8	Benin	269	6.5	Mozambique	32	4.5
Sierra Leone	14	0.5	Cameroon	35	3.1	Cameroon	246	5.9	Zimbabwe	25	3.6
Guinea	13	0.5	DRC	29	2.7	Tanzania	203	4.9	Rwanda	25	3.6
Madagascar	11	0.4	S. Leone	28	2.6	Sudan	131	3.2	Ethiopia	10	1.5
Tanzania	8	0.3	Rwanda	21	2.0	Chad	120	2.9	Cameroon	5	0.8
Top 10	2,937	99.3	Top 10	1,017	91.1	Top 10	3,341	80.8	Top 10	695	98.9
Others	19	0.7	Others	99	8.9	Others	796	19.2	Others	7	1.1
Total	2,956	100	Total	1,116	100.0	Total	4,137	100.0	Total	702	100.0

B. Faso = Burkina Faso.
Source: Data from FAOSTAT Crop Production.

TABLE 11.6

Major Industrial (Export) Crops (Continued)

Groundnuts			Palm Oil			Sugarcane			Rubber		
Country	Production ('000 MT)	%	Country	Production ('000 MT)	%	Country	Production ('000 MT)	%	Country	Production ('000 MT)	%
Nigeria	3,413	27.9	Nigeria	910	39.5	South Africa	17,756	18.6	Cote d'Ivoire	312	46.5
Sudan	1,767	14.3	C. d'Ivoire	370	16.1	Egypt	16,055	16.8	Nigeria	151	22.5
Senegal	669	5.3	DRC	305	13.2	Kenya	6,478	6.8	Liberia	75	11.2
Tanzania	657	5.2	Cameroon	253	11.0	Sudan	5,808	6.1	Cameroon	56	8.3
Cameroon	614	4.9	Ghana	121	5.2	Swaziland	5,554	5.8	Gabon	23	3.5
Mali	538	4.3	S. Leone	61	2.6	Mauritius	4,044	4.2	Ghana	22	3.3
Ghana	426	3.4	Benin	58	2.5	Zambia	4,043	4.2	Guinea	16	2.4
Chad	414	3.3	Guinea	50	2.2	Zimbabwe	3,856	4.0	DRC	12	1.7
Niger	403	3.2	Liberia	44	1.9	Mozambique	3,620	3.8	Congo	2	0.3
DRC	369	2.9	Angola	42	1.8	Uganda	3,405	3.6	C. Afr. Rep.	2	0.2
Top 10	9,271	73.6	Top 10	2214	96.1	Top 10	706,718	73.9	Top 10	671	100
Others	3,325	26.4	Other	91	3.9	Others	24,913	26.1	Others	0	0
Total	12,596	100	Total	2,305	100	Total	95531	100	Total	611	100

C. Afr. Rep = Central African Republic.
Source: Data from FAOSTAT Production.

also in Madagascar. Within this region, however, coffee growing is concentrated in three regions—the Coffee Belt of East Africa and Madagascar, West Africa, and Central Africa. The **Coffee Belt of East Africa** stretches from eastern Ethiopia through Uganda, Kenya, Tanzania, and Malawi. Both *arabica* and *robusta* coffee are grown in this region. However, the *arabica* variety is grown mostly in Ethiopia, Kenya, and Tanzania, while the *robusta* variety is grown mostly in Uganda and Kenya. Production is highly concentrated in the Baganda region of Uganda, the Kilimanjaro, and Bukoba regions of Tanzania, and in the Kisii Highland region of Kenya. Production has declined in the traditional growing areas of Central Kenya—Kiambu and Thika, and is now concentrated in the Rift Valley areas of Nakuru, Kericho, Trans Nozia, Uasin Gishu, and Baringo counties (Africa Research Bulletin, 2012b)

In West Africa, coffee is grown in eight countries—Cameroon, Cote d'Ivoire, Ghana, Guinea, Liberia, Nigeria, Sierra Leone, and Togo, of which Cote d'Ivoire is the most important. Most of the crop here is of the *robusta* variety, and the most important growing areas are Dimbokro, Daloa, Abidjan, Gagnoa, Agboville, Abengwa, and Man. In Central Africa, the most important growing countries are DRC and Angola. In the DRC, much of the growing occurs in the Kasai Valley, the Kisangani region, and along the borders with Uganda, the Bunia district and along the shores of Lake Tanganyika, near Kalami.

Up until 2002, Cote d'Ivoire produced about 30% of Africa's coffee. However, political strife in the country from 1998 through 2010 caused drastic decline in coffee production. As a result, in 2015, Africa's leading coffee producer countries were Ethiopia, Uganda, Cote d'Ivoire, and Madagascar (Table 11.6).

Cotton In 2015, Africa produced only 6% of the world's cotton. However, the bulk of this constituted the most of the world's long staple type of cotton, which is any cotton with fibers longer than 1-3/8 in. This makes Africa's cotton more valuable than cotton grown elsewhere. Cotton growing in Africa is concentrated in three main areas: (1) The Nile Valley, (2) East Africa, and (3) West Africa (Table 11.6).

Cotton growing in the Nile Valley is concentrated in Egypt and the Sudan. In Egypt, cotton occupies between 12.5% and 25% of cropped land, and two varieties of cotton are grown—long-staple cotton (over 1-3/8 in.) and long/medium staple (1-1/8 to 1-3/8 in.). The long/medium staple is grown mainly in Lower Egypt (the delta area), while the long staple is found in the Middle Egypt, especially between Minya and Asyut. Traditionally, cotton growing in Egypt employed various indigenous systems of irrigation such as the shaduf, a traditional irrigation system, and basin irrigation, by which carefully prepared basins was flooded by the Nile every year. However, as already mentioned, the Aswan High Dam converted 700,000 acres from basin to perennial and mechanized irrigation practices.

The major problems facing cotton growing include loss of moisture through evaporation, greater seepage than was anticipated, reduction in amount of silt due to the huge reservoir, and environmental effects of increased application of organic and inorganic fertilizers. Apart from these, the area under cotton cultivation has also shrunk since 1990 due to (1) the introduction of economic reform policies removed government subsidies raised the cost of production while at the same time farmers were allowed to grow crops according to market trends; (2) increasing competition from China and India; and (3) the ending of bilateral agreements between Egypt and the former Soviet Union, which led to a decline in the demand for cotton. These have caused farmers to shift to growing more profitable crops such as vegetables and medicinal and ornamental plants (Nassar and Mansour, 2003).

In Sudan, cotton is the most important cash crop and it is still produced in the Gezira Scheme. The Scheme underwent a major management overhaul in 2008–2009, under the Gezira Act of 2005, which privatized the Scheme. The responsibility for irrigation and planting decisions were transferred to land owners and farmers, respectively (Government of Sudan, 2011). Each tenant holds about 40 feddans in four fields. A four-course rotation over 8 years is practiced in which cotton is grown once every four years, while in the Menagil Extension, a three-year rotation is practiced. Another change that has occurred in recent years is that increased food insecurity and depressing prices of cotton have led to a major diversion of irrigated lands from cotton growing to cereal growing—particularly wheat and sorghum. Cereals now cover half of the cultivated area and this has brought some food self-sufficiency to the region.

In East Africa, cotton is an important export crop, ranking second on the list of export of both Uganda and Tanzania. In Uganda, cotton production is much widespread, but it is more concentrated in the Bugeso, Teso, Bukedi, and parts of the Lango and Acholi regions, where rainfall is not high enough for coffee. In Tanzania, the center of cotton production is the Mwanza Region.

In West Africa, as already discussed, cotton proved too difficult for the Office Du Niger project region and was finally abandoned in 1970, in lieu of rice. However, cotton still remains the most important export crop of Mali, Burkina Faso, and Chad. In Mali, the most important growing areas include Sikasso, Koulikoro, Segou, and Kayes. In Burkina Faso, where cotton is referred to as "white gold" the most important areas are around Bobo Dioulasso and Diebugu in the West, Ouagadougou in the center and Tenkodogo and Kaya in the East. In Chad, production is concentrated in the Sudan savannah zone of the south. Nigeria, Cote d'Ivoire, and Cameroon are other important producing countries in West Africa. Nigeria used to be a very important cotton producer especially in the regions of Southern Katsina, southeastern Sokoto, and northern Zaria. However, since Nigeria became an important oil producer in the 1970s, cotton production like most other crops, in these regions has slackened.

A major problem facing cotton production was pests, which were becoming more resistant to the already high use of pesticides. However, commercial planting of Bollgard II, a genetically engineered cotton crop in 2008, has since increased production and has reduced the use of insecticides in Burkina Faso and other cotton growing areas (Vitale et al., 2011). The leading producers in 2015 were Burkina Faso, Mali, Cote d'Ivoire, Egypt, Nigeria, and Benin (Table 11.6).

Groundnuts (peanuts) Africa produced about 31% of the world's groundnuts (peanuts), in 2015, which came from 46 different countries. Originally introduced into Senegal by French colonialists in the 1820s, groundnut cultivation got a big boost during World War II when groundnuts oil was used as a substitute for diesel oil. Groundnuts growing became established in West Africa in a belt extending from Senegal and Gambia on the west through Mali, northern Nigeria, and Niger to the east. Nigeria became the leading producer of groundnuts in Africa and in the world with the most intensive cultivation occurring in what used to be called the Groundnut Triangle, a 2.5 million acres located in Northern Nigeria, and centered on the city of Kano. Here, pyramids of groundnut sacks used to dominate the landscape. However, drought, rosette virus, neglect of agriculture due to oil boom, lack of organized input and marketing, and dissolution of groundnut marketing board caused many farmers to suffer heavy financial losses. As a result, many of the farmers decided to switch over to cowpeas, sorghum, and pearl millet, and groundnut production have never returned to the pre-1970 levels.

In Senegal and Gambia, groundnuts production has equally declined due to soil depletion, declining world prices, and weakening of farmers' support. Production hit low peaks in 2002–2003 and also 2007–2008. Since 2009, production has however increased due to good rainfall and also vigorous promotion activities. Outside of West Africa other important growing countries include Sudan, Tanzania, Uganda, and DRC. Of the 48 countries that produced groundnuts in 2015, the top 10 countries accounted for 72% of the total production. The most important producers were Nigeria, Sudan, Senegal, Tanzania, Cameroon, and Mali (Table 11.6).

Palm oil The oil palm that produces palm fruit, the source of palm oil, is native to Africa. Its main use originally was for cooking. However, it was its role as the basic raw material for soap-making that transformed the oil palm into a major export crop. Initial prospecting of palm fruit began with wild oil palm products, in West Africa, during the colonial period. Extensive plantations were established in Ghana and Cote d'Ivoire in the 1960s to increase palm oil production and by 1972 some 30,000 acres had been set up. It was these plantations that provided the seedlings for the Southeast Asian plantations that now dominate the world's palm oil production. Due to its high temperature and rainfall requirements, production has continued to be concentrated in the region between Latitudes 5°N and S of the Equator, with most of the producing countries in West Africa and Central Africa. Production has, however, declined. In 2015, Africa produced only 4% of the world's total output. The most important producers were Nigeria, Cote d'Ivoire, DRC, Cameroon, and Ghana.

Tea Africa accounts for 13% of the world's tea output, 60% of which came from Kenya alone. Tea was first introduced to Nyasaland (Malawi) in the late 19th century but conditions were not appropriate for a large operation, so the British focused their attention on British East Africa, specifically Kenya, where tea had been grown on an experimental basis since 1903 (Boateng, 2005). Tea plantation expanded near Kericho, in western Kenya, where elevations of 6000–8000 feet above sea level and good annual rainfall of 71 in. (1,803 mm) provide ideal conditions for tea cultivation. The independence of India and Sri Lanka from Britain in 1947 and 1948, respectively, provided further impetus for tea growing in Africa. The establishment of the Kenya Tea Development Authority (KTA) in the postcolonial period to promote smallholding tea cultivation provided more opportunity for expansion and by 1988 the bulk of Kenya's tea production was in the hands of small holders (Boateng, 2005). Kericho is still the center of tea growing in Kenya, but other areas now include the Nandi Hills and Limura near Nairobi and the Nyambeni Hills, northeast of Mt. Kenya. In addition to Kenya, 16 other African countries grow tea, most of them in Central, East, and Southern Africa. In 2015, these included Uganda, Burundi, Malawi, Tanzania (5%), and Mozambique (Table 11.6). Most of the tea is black tea. Tea producing countries have organizations that look after the interest of tea growers but the chief among these is the East Africa Tea Association, which manages the Mombasa Tea Auction, the largest black tea auction in the world (Boateng, 2005).

Rubber Africa produced only 5% of the world's rubber in 2015. The rubber economy began with the collection of latex from wild native rubber, *Funtumia elastica*, which in the Belgian Congo (DRC) was done under very brutal conditions, including forced labor, torture, and murder of millions of Africans (Loadman, 2005). Rubber plantations were established in the colonial period in Nigeria in 1903, German East Africa (Tanzania) in 1906, and in Liberia in 1907. In 1924, an agent of the Firestone Rubber Company rehabilitated the plantation in Liberia, which had been abandoned, and after obtaining further concession of up to 1 million acres, the company established a rubber estate on the Farmington River near Harbel, Liberia, which became the largest rubber plantation in the world (Munro, 1983).

Rubber production in the postcolonial Africa stagnated due to competition from Southeast Asia as well as synthetic rubber, price fluctuations, and in some cases pure neglect. Nigeria, for example, neglected its rubber production when it hit the oil boom. In contrast, Cote d'Ivoire expanded rubber plantation with its village plantations policy, which was launched in the 1980s. Today, rubber production like palm oil is concentrated in only a few countries in West and Central Africa. Cote d'Ivoire is the leading producer in Africa, accounting for 46% of Africa's total rubber output in 2015. Over the past decade, better and stable prices have pushed many farmers in Cote d'Ivoire to shift from cassava cultivation to rubber production, and some observers even say that rubber will soon overtake cocoa as the leading export crop in the country. Other producers include Nigeria, Liberia, and Cameroon (Table 11.6).

Projections about decline of rubber production in Malaysia and Thailand due to land constraints have generated renewed interest in rubber production in several African countries including Cote d'Ivoire, Nigeria, Gabon, and DRC. For example, in March 2012, Gabon and the Olam Group of Singapore announced plans to establish a 28,000 ha of rubber plantation and a factory in Bitam, northern Gabon. Planting started in 2013 with first harvest expected in 2017 (African Research Bulletin, 2012).

Sugarcane In 2015, Africa produced about 5% of the world's sugarcane and although 39 countries reported production statistics, the most significant producers were South Africa, Egypt, Kenya, Sudan, and Swaziland (Table 11.6).

In South Africa, sugarcane production began between 1847 and 1851, when the crop became the most successful of all the tropical crops introduced to Natal (Kwazulu-Natal) at that time. From 1860 to 1900, production was boosted by the arrival of 152,000 indentured workers from India and the building of sugar mills. More expansion occurred in 1905, and by 1965, sugarcane cultivation had reached northwestern Natal and Eastern Transvaal (Mpumalanga), under irrigation. Today, sugarcane production occurs in a region stretching from Eastern Cape through KwaZulu-Natal to Mpumalanga. However, in Kwazulu-Natal, after cultivated area reached a peak in 2001–2002, it began to decline and so did the production. In contrast, in Mpumalanga, the cultivated area continued to expand, until severe drought in recent years caused both cultivated areas and output to shrink. The share of small-scale producers has also declined in recent years, thus leaving the large-scale producers accounting for about 75% of the total output.

In Egypt, sugarcane growing dates back to 710 AD following the Arab invasion. In the 9th and 10th centuries, Egyptians became the first people to produce refined sugar (Hassan and Nasr, 2008). Importation of high productivity variety of sugarcane from the Far East in 1850 coupled with establishment of sugar mills boosted sugarcane production. From the 1950s through 1980s, sugarcane production continued in Upper and Middle Egypt, especially in the Qena and Aswan governorates using irrigated water. However, increasing drought and limited water resources have prompted the decision to start growing sugarbeet in order to support the sugar industry (Hassan and Nasr, 2008).

Elsewhere on the continent, however, the need for more biofuels has generated more interest in sugarcane production. Some countries such as South Africa and Swaziland have already announced plans to expand sugarcane production and others are expected to follow soon. The greatest potential appears to be in West and East Africa (Hassan, 2008).

Olives Olive production has had a very long history in North Africa, where it is believed to have been introduced by the Phoenicians. Production expanded under the Romans, declined under the Turks, but revived under the Arabs. Production greatly expanded in the 19th and 20th centuries but drought, outmoded technologies, poor marketing support, and high cost of olive oil made African producers noncompetitive (Amara and Abdennebi, 2007; Vossen, 2007). Heavy investments and modernization, especially in Tunisia, seem to have turned things around. Today, all of Africa's olive oil production is found in North Africa, and a little bit in South Africa. In 2015, Africa accounted for 23% of the world's olive oil most of which came from Tunisia (39%), Morocco (26%), Egypt (16%), Algeria (15%), and Libya (4%).

Livestock Production Systems

Livestock production, the rearing of animals for subsistence and commercial reasons, is a major component of Africa's agriculture. Just as crop farming, there are different systems and products of livestock production. In this section, we will examine each of these in turn.

There are two livestock production systems in Africa—the nomadic system and the **permanent system**. The nomadic system consists of **pastoral nomadism** and transhumance, while the permanent system consists of **ranching**, integrated livestock and crop farming, and combined livestock and crop farming.

Nomadic System

Pastoral nomadism Pastoral nomadism is the largest and most widespread nomadic system of livestock production. This system involves constant movement for pasture because of difficult climatic conditions, including areas, where the annual rainfall is less than 40 in. (1,000 mm) and very unpredictable. Pastoral nomadism, therefore, is a clear adaptation to the physical environment. Pastoral nomads depend upon their animals for survival. Animals provide milk, cheese, and meat for food; fiber and skin for clothing and shelter; excrement for fuel; bones for tools; and vehicle and power for transportation. This type of livestock production system includes the Cattle Fulani of West Africa and the Maasai and the Turkana of East Africa.

In addition to these true nomads, there are also a number of semi-nomadic livestock production systems in Africa. These include the Nuer of South Sudan, the Karamojong of northeast Uganda, and the Baggara Arabs of Sudan. The Nuer people live along the Nile Valley where they feed their cattle during the flooding season. In the dry season, the men migrate with the cattle to go and look for pasture, while the women and children stay behind to cultivate crops such as maize, millet, and tobacco (Udo, 1982).

Transhumance Transhumance is a livestock production system that involves movement up and down highlands in search of pasture. During the rainy season, pastoralists move uphill with their stock where there is pasture. During the dry season, they move downhill to the valleys where there is still water and pasture for their stock. The Amazigh of the Atlas Mountain region and the Turkana of Kenya practice this system of livestock production. In addition to cattle, these pastoralists also keep other animals. Both the Maasai and the Turkana keep donkeys, sheep, and goats, with the Turkana keeping camels as well. The donkeys and camels are used to transport belongings during the movement. There used to be a general belief that the members of this livestock production were simple subsistence farmers who held cattle as sign of social standing and did not have any commercial motives or will only sell animals in very rare occasions. In West Africa, however, as a result of the work of several geographers, most notably Bassett (1994) and Turner (2003 and 2009), we now know that such notions were too simplistic and erroneous. What these geographers show rather is a complex system of livestock ownership in which owners, who may be town or city dwellers contract herders, through several arrangements including seasonal charges per livestock, monthly salary paid to the herder or noncash remuneration (Turner, 2009).

Even so, traditional African pastoralists (pastoral nomads) have increasingly found their lives disrupted by the emergence of political boundaries in postcolonial Africa and by government policies that have required travel documents and other efforts to settle or get them to change their ways of life. However, the most formidable foe yet is the old "enemy" of the environment, which forced them to adopt the nomadic way of life, in the first place. With worsening environmental conditions, it is becoming increasingly clear that just moving to another place may no longer be sufficient. In Ethiopia, Africa's leading pastoral country, human encroachment on pastoral lands and security issues in remote areas have brought additional pressure, causing some pastoral groups to lose their territories.

Permanent System

The permanent livestock production system consists of cattle ranching, the integrated livestock and food crop, and the combined livestock and food crop systems.

Cattle ranching Large-scale cattle ranching was traditionally confined to parts of Africa with history of European farming systems, such as Southern Africa and East Africa. However, ranching has gradually spread to other parts of the continent over the years, and now there are a number of private as well as government controlled ranching in several African countries. These include the extensive cattle ranches of South Africa, Botswana, Angola, Zimbabwe, Kenya, and Mozambique. In South Africa, ranching is concentrated in the Cape Province. West Africa has traditionally not been a good cattle ranching area. However, there have been some attempts to establish ranches in Nigeria.

The integrated food crop and livestock production system The integrated food crop and livestock production system is devoted to growing crops for human consumption and raising livestock for food and nonfood functions. This type of farming occurs in areas with a long history of European settlements, as well in areas where high population density, dictates that farmers use every available land to produce enough food for their survival. In areas with strong European history, farms are usually fenced in and, where topography allows, mechanized. However, in areas without that history such as in West Africa, and particularly the northwest and the northeast regions of Ghana and the Hausaland of Northern Nigeria, the farms are usually within or close to the walls of the compound dwelling and for that reason they have been referred to as compound farming. They are also found around major and secondary cities in Africa (Amadou et al., 2012). The system may also be referred to as mixed farming because crop cultivation relies heavily on manure obtained from droppings of livestock, such as goats, sheep, and cattle, while the stock is fed on postharvest remnants. The main crops are millet, guinea corn, and vegetables.

Combined crop and livestock production system   This farming system is very common in Africa. It is practiced largely by settled cultivators, who keep livestock at the same time, for food and cash when needed. However, the animals are not integrated into the crop farming because in most cases they are kept at homes that are further away from the farms. The livestock are thus kept either or free range on open city spaces. Animals kept include cattle, sheep, goats, and chickens.

Major Stock

Livestock in Africa is kept primarily for two main purposes—for their meat and milk production. A few are kept for wool and hair and such byproducts such as skins and hides. In terms of meat production, the most important animals are cattle, chicken, sheep, pigs, and goat, while in terms of milk production, the most important are cattle, buffaloes, and goats. Figures 11.8A–11.8C provide the geographic distribution of livestock on the continent.

Cattle   Cattle is the most important livestock in Africa. According to FAO statistics, there were 317,656,687 heads of cattle in Africa in 2015. These constituted 21%

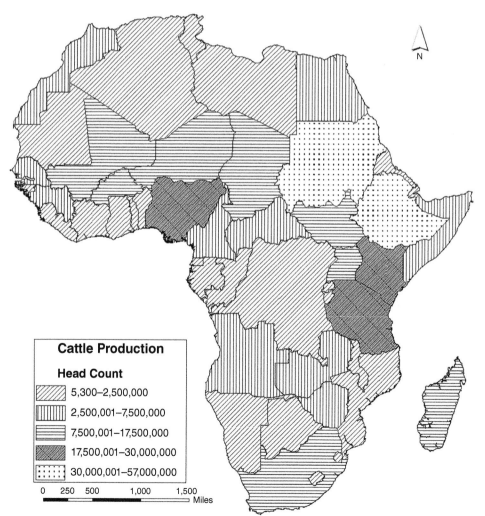

Cattle Production

Head Count

- 5,300–2,500,000
- 2,500,001–7,500,000
- 7,500,001–17,500,000
- 17,500,001–30,000,000
- 30,000,001–57,000,000

0   250   500   1,000   1,500
Miles

FIGURE 11.8A Cattle production, 2015.
Source: FAOSTATS 2015

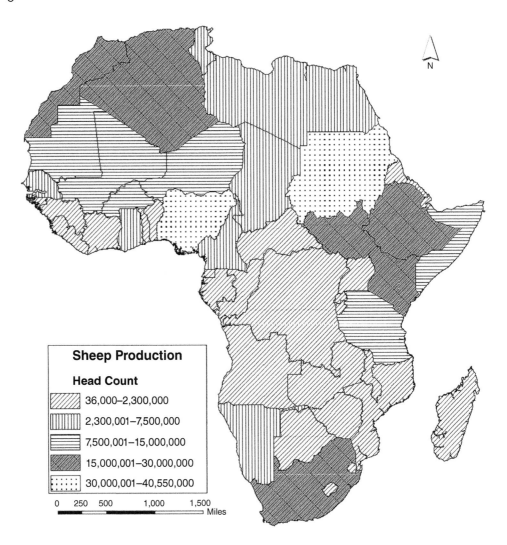

Sheep Production

Head Count

	36,000–2,300,000
	2,300,001–7,500,000
	7,500,001–15,000,000
	15,000,001–30,000,000
	30,000,001–40,550,000

0   250   500   1,000   1,500
Miles

FIGURE 11.8B Sheep
production, 2015.
Source: FAOSTATS 2015

of the world's total stock. In general, the forest regions of West Africa and Central Africa are not suitable for cattle due to the presence of the tsetse fly, which gives the cattle the trypanosomiasis disease. The bulk of Africa's cattle are therefore reared in the Sudan and the Sahel savanna zones of West Africa and the grassland regions of North, Central, East, and Southern Africa. Three main breeds of cattle are reared in Africa. These are the long-horned Mediterranean breed, found mainly in North Africa, the humped-back zebu of East, Central, West, and Southern Africa, and the small shorthorn breed also found in West Africa. The countries with the most heads of cattle in 2015 in Africa were Ethiopia, Sudan, Tanzania, Nigeria, and Kenya.

About 22% of Africa's cattle in 2015 were dairy cattle, while the remaining were beef cattle. Ethiopia, Sudan, South Sudan, Tanzania, Kenya, and Uganda had the most dairy cattle, accounting for about 64%. However, the highest proportions dairy cattle to total cattle population were in Tunisia (94.5%), South Sudan (62.4%), Libya (59.4%), Algeria (53.3%), and Morocco (52.5%). Dairy cattle accounted for 77% of all milk production on the continent in 2015, with Kenya, Algeria, Ethiopia, and South Africa as the top producers. For the rest of the continent, beef cattle

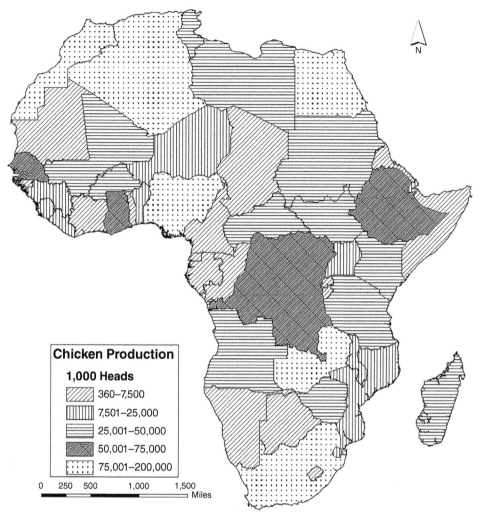

FIGURE 11.8C Chicken production, 2015.
Source: Data from Food and Agriculture Organization FAOSTAT.

were dominant, accounting for 33% of the continent's meat production. The most significant beef producers in 2015 were South Africa (17.2% of the total production), Kenya (8%), Egypt (7%), Ethiopia (6.3%), Nigeria (6.2%), Sudan (6%), and Tanzania (5%).

Chicken Chicken is produced in every African country, and in variety of environments. These environments include large-scale poultry farms as well as the ubiquitous backyard system in which the chickens scavenge mostly for themselves. Since 2000, poultry has seen strong growth, especially since 2005. The animals are kept for both egg production and meat. In 2015, it was the second largest source of meat in Africa, after beef, accounting for 31% of Africa's meat production. In 2015, Africa had 1.8 billion stocks of chickens, about 8% of the world's total stock. The most important producers were Morocco, South Africa, Egypt, Nigeria, and Algeria (Table 11.7).

Sheep, goats, and pigs FAO estimates show that in 2015, Africa had 342.5 million heads of sheep, 376.3 million goats, and 34.3 million pigs. These constituted 28.5% of the world's sheep, 37% of its goats, but only 4% of its pigs.

TABLE 11.7

Major Livestock Production, 2015

	Cattle			Sheep			Goats			Chickens		
Country	Country	Thousand Heads	%	Country	Thousand Heads	%	Country	Thousand Heads	%	Country	Thousand Heads	%
Ethiopia	Ethiopia	57,829	18.2	Nigeria	41,632	12.2	Nigeria	72,527	19.3	Morocco	191	10.5
Sudan	Sudan	30,376	9.6	Sudan	40,210	11.7	Sudan	31,227	8.3	South Africa	162	8.9
Tanzania	Ethiopia	26,713	8.4	Ethiopia	28,892	8.4	Ethiopia	29,704	7.9	Egypt	144	8.0
Nigeria	Algeria	20,184	6.4	Algeria	28,111	8.2	Kenya	25,094	6.7	Nigeria	142	7.9
Kenya	South Africa	18,728	5.9	South Africa	23,937	7.0	Mali	20,083	5.3	Algeria	133	7.4
Uganda	Morocco	14,204	4.5	Morocco	18,509	5.4	Tanzania	18,026	4.8	Tunisia	89	4.9
South Africa	S. Sudan	13,694	4.3	Niger	17,248	5.0	Niger	15,478	4.1	Ghana	71	3.9
Niger	Kenya	12,059	3.8	B. Faso	16,795	4.9	B. Faso	14,308	3.8	C. d'Ivoire	64	3.6
S. Sudan	Mali	11,823	3.7	Uganda	14,422	4.2	Uganda	14,006	3.7	Ethiopia	60	3.3
Mali	Somalia	10,313	3.2	S. Sudan	12,351	3.6	S. Sudan	13,551	3.6	Cameroon	51	2.9
Madagascar	Niger	10,280	3.2	Somalia	11,496	3.4	Somalia	11,650	3.1	Senegal	47	2.6
Top 11	Top 11	226,203	71.2	Top 11	253,603	74.1	Top 11	265,654	70.6	Top 11	1,154	63.9
Others	Others	91,447	28.8	Others	100,358	25.9	Others	122,309	29.4	Others	655	36.1
Total	Total	317,650	100.0	Total	353,961	100.0	Total	387,963	100.0	Total	1,809	100.0

S. Sudan = South Sudan; S. Africa = South Africa; B. Faso = Burkina Faso; C. d'Ivoire = Cote d'Ivoire.
Source: FAO Live Animals Production Statistics.

Sheep and goats are ubiquitous in Africa, while pigs are more prevalent in the non-Muslim realms of the continent. The prevalence of sheep and goats in Africa is due to the fact that they are hardier than cattle and can be reared in both the savanna and forest regions. In addition, because all three animals are easier to keep and their meat is more affordable, they make a greater contribution to the diet of ordinary Africans than cattle. Different types of sheep and goats are reared in Africa. However, they do fall in two breeds, namely, the dwarf and the long-legged breeds. The dwarf breed is found mainly in the forest belts, while the long-legged is found in the savanna regions. Most of the sheep and goats are raised by free-range method. In the grassland areas, the two animals are kept together and usually left to graze around homesteads except during the night and during the rainy season, when they are restricted to their pens to prevent them from eating cultivated crops (Udo, 1982). However, there are large-scale sheep farms in South Africa, Kenya, and North Africa.

Most of the sheep and goats are reared for their meat, and these two are the third and the fourth most important sources of meat on the continent. In the Middle Niger Valley of Mali and Niger, and also in South Africa and North Africa, sheep is also kept for their wool. Also in South Africa, the Angora goat is kept for its mohair. Nigeria, Sudan, and Ethiopia had the most sheep and goats (Table 11.7). South Africa and Algeria were also important sheep raising countries while Kenya and Mali were also important in goats. Algeria, Sudan, South Africa, Morocco, Nigeria, and South Sudan were important sheep meat producers, while goat meat production was dominated by Nigeria (20%) with Sudan, Mali, Kenya, Egypt, and South Sudan as the other significant producers.

Pigs are reared by farmers in all countries even though pig farming is very limited in the Muslim realm of the continent. The stock sizes of African farmers are usually small and they are usually kept on free range to fend for themselves. The most important countries in 2015 were Nigeria (21%), Malawi (9%), Angola (9%), Uganda (7%), and Burkina Faso (7%). Nigeria also produced the most pork (19%), with South Africa (17%), Malawi (9%), Mozambique (9%), Uganda (9%), and Angola (8%) as the other important producers.

PROBLEMS AND ISSUES IN AFRICA'S AGRICULTURE

The problems and issues facing Africa's agriculture have been addressed by numerous research and conferences for so long that there is hardly anything new that one can add. In a recent report on agriculture and food security and its implications for Africa, Scherr et al. (2010) summarize the discourse on drivers, causes, and proposed solutions of hunger and examples that could be adapted to represent the discourse on problems and issues in Africa's agriculture. Following their schema, we can group what has been identified as problems of Africa's agriculture into three— low productivity, lack or poor market organization and access, and disempowered farmers and communities.

Low Productivity

Studies after studies have pointed to the low productivity of Africa's agriculture, compared to other regions of the world, even when compared to other developing countries. This in turn has been attributed to lack of agricultural input, land and ecosystem degradation, and expansion of farming to unsuitable land for farming (Scherr et al., 2010). African agriculture has the least usage of fertilizers and high-yielding seeds of all major regions of the world, even when compared only to other developing regions. In terms of the use of tractors and other farm machinery, perennial irrigation systems, Africa ranks at the bottom. In a publication on agricultural mechanization in Africa, the FAO (2008) noted that there were about 470,000 tractors in Africa; yet, no one knew the conditions of these tractors. It also stated that the total number of working tractors will have to increase to 3.5 million for Africa to catch up with other regions. In terms of farm power sources, the publication pointed out that 65% of sources of farm power in Sub-Saharan Africa was by hand compared to 25% in other developing regions of Asia, Latin America, the Caribbean, and North Africa and the Middle East. In contrast, 50% of farm power sources in these regions derived from engines compared to only 10% in Sub-Saharan Africa. Simply put, Africa's agricultural technology has been in a state of inertia for many decades, with very little or isolated pockets of progress.

The FAO (2008) estimates that only about 5% of Africa's arable land is irrigated compared to 40% of India and about 30% of other developing regions. In the absence of effective irrigation system in most countries, Africa's agriculture has been left at the mercy of precarious natural forces, chief among them being rainfall (see, e.g., Schilling et al., 2012). Thus, agricultural production rises and falls with performance of rainfall. As rainfall patterns have changed due to broader changes in the earth's climate, drought has increased and this in turn has caused degradation of land through soil erosion and farming practices that are no longer useful. Again without any effective means of increasing productivity, the only other option to keep production in the face of growing population has been expanding the existing land under crops. This in turn has pushed cultivation into marginally fertile lands.

Many researchers have also documented the inadequate focus on major Africa crops by the research and development enterprise (Diouf, 1989; Obia, 2003; Odhiambo, (2007). Diouf (1989), for example, shows that for a greater portion of the postcolonial period, no African major food crop was subject to sustained research and development. The research budget of many African countries was inadequate, compared to other parts of the developing world. Apart from this, this research has also shown that in many African countries, the link between universities and research institutes and the general public was either loose or nonexistent. The result is that Africa did not develop any high-yielding and environmental-resistant variety of its crops or livestock. Twenty years later, Odhiambo (2007) showed that not much had changed especially with the underinvestment in Africa's agricultural sector by both African governments and external entities. He noted that between 1980 and 2002, the share of agriculture in the official development assistance fell from 17% to only 3%. With respect to African governments, he noted that although agriculture contributed between 20% and 50% of GDP of African countries, many African governments devoted less than 10% of their budget to agriculture. Other causes of Africa's low agriculture productivity identified include adverse effects of the environment, low population density in a massive land area, land lockedness, and remoteness which all increase transaction costs, as well as debilitating diseases such as malaria, and HIV/AIDS, and land that is unsuitable for agriculture (Bloom and Sachs, 1998).

The Problem of Institutions and Markets

Bingswander and Townsend (2000) attribute Africa's agricultural problems to adverse institutions and policies that have plagued the continent for centuries. They cite the slave trade that deprived Africa of its human resources, colonialism which established institutions of exploitation and the postcolonial period that perpetuated these institutions with poor policies in the form of urban bias and strong centralized governments which ignored rural areas.

Another institutional problem that has long plagued Africa's agriculture is that of unstable markets. The traditional industrial crops have faced wide price fluctuations that have made it difficult for famers to have consistent income. In the early post independence period, many African countries continued the commodity marketing boards that had been established under the colonial period. Among other things, these boards were charged with stabilizing prices through the mechanism of buffer stock by which the boards withheld a portion of the market price of the commodity from farmers, put that portion in a fund, and use it to cushion price fluctuations. As Jones (1987) points out, the funds could not be left idle so the boards began to initially invest it in so-called agricultural-related projects. However, mismanagement, inefficiencies, and misuse of funds defeated the purpose and exposed the farmers to the vagaries of the market.

In addition, the failure to get a common commodity agreement has resulted in numerous ad-hoc commodity agreements that need to be negotiated periodically. An extremely difficult problem with some of these agreements is getting developed countries to level the playing field even under World Trade Organization rules. A case in point is the Cotton Initiative of Doha Development Agenda Round in 2003. The Cotton Initiative, proposed by Benin, Burkina Faso, Mali, and Chad, called for immediate removal of all subsidies to cotton production and exports by all major cotton producers including the United States and China. However, the petition was resisted by the United States with the backing of the European Union and WTO (Kennedy, 2007–2008). By 2008, the whole Doha Rounds had stalled.

While the traditional exports have marketing boards, food crops and newer export crops do not, and this has made it more difficult for farmers in the food crop business since they have to meet very strict regulations of the Global Good Agricultural Practice (GlobalGAP) Certification in order to export to international markets. GlobalGAP was established by Euro-Retailer Produce Working group in 1997 as a quality assurance for consumers about food safety (Asfaw, 2011). It was initially established for fruits and vegetables but was later extended to farms as well as flowers and ornaments. There are four key elements—food safety, environmental protection, occupational health and safety, and animal welfare. Under each of these elements, there are three levels of compliance— "major musts," minor must," and recommendations. "Major musts" require 100% compliance, "minor musts" require 95% (Asfaw, 2011). Farmers must be certified on all these before they can export to GlobalGAP countries. Certification can be obtained through four options—option 1—individual application; option 2—group application, options 3 and 4 can be applied for by both individual and a group of farmers.

Domestically, poor transportation network reduces access to markets since the food producing areas are often in the rural areas and are removed from the urban markets. Access to land is another institutional road block to many African farmers due to the complex land tenure systems that exist in Africa (see Chapter 7). All these act as disincentives to current and future farmers to increase production.

Disempowered Farmers and Communities

A lot of research has also established that the African farmer has been generally disempowered especially when it comes to those who actually do the production— women (Johnston-Anumonwo, 2003). This disempowerment includes lack of land due to the land tenure systems, lack of involvement due to the patriarchal nature of

African societies, and the tendency for agricultural development projects in the past to focus on male heads of the households. The majority of agricultural development projects that were undertaken during the postcolonial period have generally focused on men as heads of households. Farmers and their rural communities have also been disempowered by the urban-bias development policies that have characterized most of the postcolonial period and the failure of decentralization policies to address the imbalance. Deprived of basic rural infrastructure such as good transportation system, electricity, portable drinking water, and sanitary facilities, and good schools, farming communities have become isolated, missing out on economic incentives and support mechanism needed to make a reasonable living in rural areas. The result has been the continuous rural–urban migration of young people.

A Note on Food Insecurity

The question of food insecurity is not necessarily related to agriculture production since there are many countries in the world that do not produce all their food yet they have food security. However, Africa has a food insecurity problem and a greater part of that can be attributed to agriculture production, and past and present policies. In that regard, many of the problems facing Africa's agricultural production have also contributed to the food security problem.

In general, low productivity of staple foods leads to less food for consumption and the need to supplement with food imports and aid. However, a more important problem is lack of storage facilities (Obia, 2003). People who are familiar with food producing regions of Africa know very well about the abundant or surplus production during the harvest season and acute shortage in a couple of months after harvest. The main reason is that except for cassava, which can be processed into gari, none of the major staples of Africa can be stored or preserved for more than three months. Maize, sorghum, plantain and cooking banana, yam, cocoyam, and a host of vegetables all get infested or rotten within a very short time after harvest. Even raw cassava cannot stay longer than a few days after harvest. Yet, no consistent research effort into these foods has been carried or converted to marketable innovations. Third, as already mentioned, availability of water is the most important determinant of food production given the general temperature conditions in Africa. The places with most severe or acute food insecurity problems are also the areas with unpredictable rainfall and water availability. Yet, very little irrigation is used in Africa's agriculture.

Policy Options

The policy options for dealing with problems of Africa's agriculture have been well articulated and documented since the early postcolonial period. They include raising agricultural productivity and providing the necessary support mechanisms—agricultural research, rural infrastructure, and institutional reforms—that will help raise the living standards of farmers and rural dwellers.

Raising Agricultural Productivity

Generally speaking, there are two strategies of raising agricultural productivity in Africa. One is expansion into new agricultural land and the other is intensification of production on existing agricultural land.

Expansion into new agricultural land FAO (2013) estimates that in 2009, agricultural land accounted for 39% of Africa's total land area. The rest was taken up by forest (23%) and other land cover (39%). Of the agricultural land, 3% was under permanent tree crops, 28% for other crop farming, while 69% was meadows and pastureland. With this, it is possible to bring more land under cultivation, and in fact as we have seen already that has been happening in the majority of African countries since the postcolonial period. This strategy, however, does not solve the environmentally related problems such as erratic rainfall pattern and incidence of drought. Thus if drought occurs, more land becomes degraded under this policy option. Apart from this, there is the tendency of expanding agriculture into marginal agricultural lands, which in turn can lead to more land degradation. Finally, the strategy can run roughshod on conservation and preservation of land resources. So unless this option is accompanied by other needs such as agricultural inputs, and proper land use planning this option can compound the problem instead of solving it.

Intensification of production on existing agricultural land This approach emphasizes raising productivity of existing agricultural land through the use of better agricultural inputs and technology. These include increasing use of fertilizers and improved seeds that are either drought resistant or high yielding. The activities of the Alliance for Green Revolution for Africa we discussed earlier are examples of this strategy.

Agricultural Research, Rural Infrastructure, and Institutional Reforms

None of the above strategies to raise agricultural productivity can be achieved and sustained without supporting infrastructure and institutions. Among these are agriculture research and extension, strengthening rural infrastructure for backward and forward linkages to the agriculture sector, and institutional reforms. Once again these have been documented extensively in many publications (see, e.g., Diouf, 1989; Eicher, 1995; Obia, 2003; Odhiambo, 2007; Scherr et al., 2010; World Bank, 1981, 1982, 2008). These studies have called for rural infrastructure to support farming, land reforms to provide more access to farming households, better funding for research and development that focuses on major African staples, and better plans for extension services that will translate research findings to farmers, as well as education of farmers in the use of farming inputs and better farming practices. They have also called for market reforms at both domestic and international level including opening of more intracontinental trade. They have called for integrated rural development with a focus on agro-industries to provide incentives for farmers to produce and for rural dwellers to find alternative sources of employment. Above all, they have called on African governments to politically commit to agricultural development and not necessarily relying on external funding for agricultural development projects. As indicated earlier, Africa's agricultural problems and solutions have been known and widely documented for a long time. The question is why are we still talking about these and when will we stop talking about them? Rather than academically debate this question, I will rather end this chapter with a personal life experience to illustrate what I see as the need for an **agricultural revolution**.

The Need for Agricultural Revolution

I was born in colonial Gold Coast, three years before it became modern Ghana, to a farming family that grew cocoa for cash and a variety of staples—plantain, cassava, cocoyam, yam, and maize—for both food and petty cash. At an early age of 7, I was taught how to wield the machete and the hoe to clear tropical brush. As I got older, I learned how to cut down the big trees with an axe, get the land ready for burning, cleaning, and eventually planting staple foods and cocoa. To keep the weeds away, we used the machete and the hoe. To avoid the African midday to early afternoon heat, my father would usually leave home at dawn for the farm on foot to get some work done before it got hot. On Saturdays, when there was no school as well as on public holidays and vacation, I would join my parents on the farm.

I also learned to harvest plantain, cassava, cocoyam, and yam the staple foods of my ethnic group with the machete and the hoe and hauled them home by carrying them on my head. On the cocoa farm, we used the machete to clear the under-growth and harvest the pods on the tree stems; and a long curved knife fixed at the end of a raffia pole to pluck the pods in the branches, a neck-stiffening task. We would then carry all the pods to one spot, split them open with the machete, and scoop the beans out with our hands into basket. We would pile the fresh beans on to a mat of fresh plantain or banana plant leaves, make the beans into a small hill, and cover them up with more plantain leaves for fermentation. After 5–6 days, we would carry the beans in baskets on our heads to the drying mats, where they would be sun dried and subsequently sold to the cocoa marketing board. The harvest time for staple foods in August was a time of abundance—but we had no proper way of preserving any of the harvest. For maize, we would store the cobs in a traditional silo, under which we would make a fire so that smoke from the fire would help keep weevils away. However, this was not effective and within about 3 months, we would be forced to take the rest of the corn out to avoid losing all of it. Plantain deterio-rated quickly either after harvest at home or on the farm so did cassava, cocoyam, and yam.

My parents who taught me all these had learned it from their parents and so had generations of my ancestors. Nothing had changed except the use of a small machine to spray the cocoa trees against the capsid insect. This was tedious work with relatively very little reward, but my parents had no choice. I can still hear the echo of their frustration, despair, and fears in their constant reminder that "We are sending you to school so that you would not end up like us." So, I thought I was going to see changes that my parents did not see because as I was learning the traditional way of farming, I also started learning about all the wonderful ideas that my new country Ghana was doing and planning to do with agriculture: improved seeds, experimental farms, mechanization, irrigation, agro-industry, and agricul-tural research and development.

Unfortunately, I was wrong because more than six decades later not a single thing has changed. The farming, harvesting, processing, and preservation technologies and the tools are still the same, and we are expecting productivity to increase. We are still talking about improved seeds, drought-resistant varieties and introduction of other crops that are not staples, but still with the machete, the hoe, and the dig-ging stick, and rainfed agriculture.

The modern world has known how to increase agriculture productivity since the English agricultural revolution but for some reason that type of revolution is not suitable for Africa, because there is some uneasiness about how that will impact the numerous small-scale farmers in Africa, and also on the environment. So instead, we should develop new seed varieties, convince Africans to switch from their traditional diets to some new foods, make land more accessible to those who actually do the farming, and create an early warning system to monitor the environment to warn the farmers and governments about impending danger. Reminiscent of the early post-colonial period, we have experts from around the world including some Asian countries that were behind African countries in the 1960s now crisscrossing Africa teaching African farmers about growing crops in places that such crops were not grown. Meanwhile, Africa continues to be marginalized on the global scene because its contribution to the global economy is negligible. The conditions of African farmers continue to be the darling of statistical analysis of world poverty groups.

My point is Africa needs to take steps to improve the living conditions of its people by eliminating poverty, as poverty itself is a hindrance to maintaining environmental quality and sensible use of resources. Africa will never get anywhere in this process if it has to evaluate impact on every single step it takes on places and individuals, or if it is searching for the so-called alternative development. The modern idea of development is Western, whether we like it or not; how a particular group choose to achieve it may differ in its specific details but the outcomes are broadly the same—improvement in living conditions with freedom from servitude to nature and human groups. There is nothing that prescribes or commits African farmers, whether or not they are overwhelmingly women, to the tedious nature of work on the land without any help of modern technology; and there is no law of nature that says majority of Africans have to be farmers, forever. If a true agricultural development is to occur in Africa, it will definitely throw a lot of people off the land but if that process is bungled with home grown improvements in production, processing, and distribution technologies of agricultural products, and long-term policy commitments African economies will expand and will be able to absorb the surplus population. The commitment is important because oftentimes African countries and funding agencies are slow to start a new project but quick to call it off without giving it enough time to work. Africa needs not just a Green Revolution but an agricultural revolution. This is Africa's time for action.

Postreading Assignment

A. Study the Following Concepts

Agriculture production system	Combined crop and livestock system	Integrated food crop and livestock system	Ranching
Agricultural revolution	Floodland cultivation	NEPAD's CAADP	Rotational bush fallow
Agricultural subsidies	Green Revolution	Pastoral nomadism	Shifting cultivation
		Permanent system	Transhumance

B. Discuss the Following Questions

1. Compare and contrast your knowledge of African agriculture before and after reading the chapter.

2. Are there any changes that you would like to make? If so what are they?

3. Discuss the impact of colonialism on agricultural production systems of Africa.

4. To what extent is the current state of Africa's agricultural production systems due to failed policies of postcolonial Africa?

5. Discuss the main features of agricultural production systems of Africa as they relate to crop farming

6. What are the main types of livestock production systems of Africa?

7. What do you see as the main problems facing Africa's agriculture? What recommendations can you make for improving the situation?

8. Discuss the assertion that the classification of Africa's agriculture into subsistence and cash crop farming is longer valid in present day Africa?

9. What do you understand by the term Green Revolution? What do you see as the problems and prospects of the green revolution effort that is currently underway in Africa?

10. Identify some of the major changes occurring in industrial crop farming in Africa? What are the reasons behind these changes?

References

Africa Research Bulletin. 2012a. Commodities; Yam *Economic, Financial, and Technical Series* 49(1) 19426.

African Research Bulletin. 2012b Commodities: Coffee. *Economic, Financial, and Technical Series* 49(3): 19497C.

Ajakaiye, O., and de Janvry, A. 2010. "Agricultural Sector Performance and a Green Revolution in Africa: An Overview." *Journal of African Economies* 19(AERC Supplement 2): 113–116.

Amadou, H., Dossa, L. H., Lompo, D. J., Abdulkadir, A., and Schlecht, E. 2012. "A Comparison between Urban Livestock Production Strategies in Burkina Faso, Mali and Nigeria in West Africa." *Tropical Animal Health Production* 44: 1631–1642.

Amara, T., and Abdennebi, Z. 2007. "North Africa Shaes up Olive Oil Industry." IOL News February 7.

Anonymous. 2010. "Yams Receive a Boost." *Appropriate Technology* 37(4): 48–49.

Asfaw, S., Mithofer, D., and Waibel, H. 2009. EU Food Safety Standards, Pesticide Use and Farm-level Productivity: The Case of High-value Crops in Kenya." *Journal of Agricultural Economic.* 60(3): 645–667.

Asfaw, S. 2011. "The Impact of Food Safety Standards on Rural Welfare." In Mithofer, D., and Waibel, H. (Eds.), *Vegetable Production and Marketing in Africa. Socio-economic Research.* Wallingford, UK: CAB International, pp. 44–65.

Austin, G. 2009. Cash Crops and Freedom: Export Agriculture and the Decline of Slavery in Colonial West Africa." *IRSH Internationaal Instituut voor Sociale Geschiedenis* 54, 1–37.

Badu-Apraku, B., Twumasi-Afriyie, S., Sallah, P. Y. K., and Haag, W. 2006. "Registration of 'Obatanpa GH' Maize." *Crop Science* 46(3): 1393.

Balasubramanian, V., Sie, M., Hijmans, R. J, and Otsuka, K. 2007. "Increasing Rice Production in Sub-Saharan Africa: Challenges and Opportunities." *Advances in Agronomy,* 94: 55–133.

Barnett, T. (1977). *The Gezira Scheme: An Illusion of Development.* London: Frank Cass and Company Limited.

Bassett, T. J. 1994. Hired Herders and Herd Management in Fulani Pastoralism (Northern Côte d'Ivoire). *Cahiers d'Études Africaines* 34, 147–173.

Bassett, T. J. 2001. *The Peasant Cotton Revolution in West Africa; Cote d'Ivoire, 1880–1995.* Cambridge: Cambridge University Press.

Beer, C. W. 1955. "Social Development in the Gezira Scheme." *African Affairs* 54(214): 42–51.

Bello, W. 2008. "Destroying African Agriculture." *Foreign Policy in Focus.* June 3.

Bertow, K., and Schultheis, A. 2007. *Impact of EU's Agricultural Trade Policy on Smallholders in Africa.* Bonn: Germanwatch e.V.

Binswanger, H. P and Townsend, R. F. 2000. "The Growth Performance of Agriculture in Sub-Saharan Africa." *American Journal of Agricultural Economics* 82(5): 1075–1086.

Bloom, D. E., and Sachs, J. D. 1998. "Geography, Demography, and Economic Growth in Africa." *Brookings Papers on Economic Activity* 2: 207–295.

Boateng, O. 2005. "How Africa Came to Grow Tea." *New African* 436(2): 52.

Botha, G., and Vijoen, C. D. 2007. "Can GM Sorghum Impact Africa?." *Trends in Biotechnology* 26(2): 64–69.

Breisinger, C., Diao, X., Thurlow, J., and Al Hassan, R. M. 2011. "Potential Impacts of a Green Revolution in Africa—The Case of Ghana." *Journal of International Development* 23: 82–102.

van Beusekom, M. M. 1997. "Colonisation Indigène: French Rural Development Ideology at the Office du Niger, 1920-1940." *The International Journal of African Historical Studies* 30(2): 299–323.

Christopher, A. J. (1984). *Colonial Africa.* London: Croom Helm.

De Janvry, A., and Sadoulet, E. 2010. "Agriculture for Development in Africa: Business-as-Usual or New Departures? *Journal of African Economies* 19 AERC Supplement 2): ii7 ii39.

Diao, X., Heady, D., and Johnson, M. 2008. "Toward a Green Revolution in Africa: What Would it Achieve, and What Would it Require?" *Agricultural Economics* 39(Supplement): 539–550.

Douf, J. 1989. "The Challenge of Agricultural Development in Africa." *Sir John Crawford Memorial Lecture* November 2, Washington, DC.: Consultative Group on International Agricultural Research, CIGIAR.

Eichenberg, M., and Filipovich, J. 1986. "African Military Labour and the Building of the Office du Niger Installations, 1925-1950." *The Journal of African History* 27(3): 533–551.

Eicher, C. K. 1995. "Zimbabwe's Maize-based Green Revolution; Preconditions for Replication." *World Development,* 23(5): 805–818.

El-Ghonemy, M. R. 2003. "Development Strategies, 1950-2001: Progress and Challenges for the Twenty-First Century." In El-Ghonemy, M. R. (Ed.), *Egypt in the Twenty-First Century: Challenges for Development.* London: Routledge Cuzon, pp. 73–110.

Filipovich, J. 2001. "Destined to Fail: Forced Settlement at the Office du Niger, 1926-45." *The Journal of African History* 42(2): 239–260.

Food and Agricultural Organization of the United Nations. 1999. *The State of Food Insecurity in the World.* Rome: FAO.

Food And Agricultural Organization of the United Nations. 2000. *FAOSTAT Database.* Rome: FAO.

Funnel, D. C., and Binns, J. A. 1989. "Irrigation and Rural Development in Morocco." *Land Policy* 6(1): 43–52.

Government of Sudan and FAO/WFP Crop and Food Security. 2011. Special Report.

Haggblade, S. et al. 2012. "Cassava commercialization in Southeastern Africa." *Journal of Agribusiness in Developing and Emerging Economies* 2(1): 4–40.

Harsch E. 1980. *South Africa: White Rule Black Revolt.* New York: Monard Press.

Hart, D. 1978. "The Political Economy of a Development Scheme: The Volta River Project." *International Relations* 6: 245–256.

Hassan, F. A. 2007. "The Aswan High Dam and the International Rescue Nubia Campaign." *African Archaeological Review* 24: 73–94.

Hassan, F. A. 2008. "Development of Sugar Industry in Africa." *Sugar Tech* 10(3): 197–203.

Hassan, S. F., and Nasr, M. I. 2008. "Sugar Industry of Egypt." *Sugar Tech* 10(3): 204–209.

Havnevik, K., Bryceson, D., Birgegard, L.-E., Matondi, P., and Beyene, A. 2007. "African Agriculture and the World Bank: Development or Impoverishment." *Policy Dialogue No. 1 Report based on Workshop Organized by the Nordic African Institute.* Uppsala: Nordic African Institute.

Hertzog, T., Adamczewski, A., Molle, F., Poussin, J.-C., and Jamin, J.-Y. 2012. "Ostrich-like Strategies in Sahelian Sands? Land and Water Grabbing in the Office du Niger, Mali." *Water Alternatives* 5(2): 304–321.

Iliffe, J. 1995. *Africans: The History of a Continent.* Cambridge: Cambridge University Press.

Jeffries, C. 1964. *A Review of Colonial Research 1940–1960.* London: Her Majesty's Stationery Office.

Jones, W. O. 1987. "Food-Crop Marketing Boards in Tropical Aftrica." *The Journal of Modern African Studies* 25(3): 375–402.

Johnston-Anumonwo, I 2004. "Geography, Gender, and Development in Sub-Saharan Africa." In Aryeetey-Attoh, S. (Ed.) *Geography of Sub-Saharan Africa.* 2nd Edition. Upper Saddle River, NJ: Prentice Hall pp. 298–323.

Johnston, P. 1983. "The Groundnut Scheme—A Personal Memoir." *HABITATINTL* 7(112): 5–16.1.

Kennedy, K. C. 2007–2008. "The Doha Round Negotiations on Agricultural Subsidies." *Denver Journal International Law & Policy* 36(3/4): 335–348.

Kijima, Y., Ito, Y., and Otsuka, K. 2011. "On the Possibility of a Lowland Rice Green Revolution in Sub-Saharan Africa: Evidence from Eastern Uganda." In Yamano, T., Otsuka, K., and Place, F. (Eds.), *Emerging Development of Agriculture in East Africa: 169 Markets, Soil, and Innovations.* Dordrecht: Springer Science+Business Media B.V., pp. 169–184.

Kolawole, P. O., Agbetoye, L., and Ogunlowo, S. A. 2010. "Sustaining World Food Security with Improved Cassava Processing Technology: The Nigeria Experience." *Sustainability* 2, 3681–3694.

Laoubi, K., and Yamao, M. 2009. "A Typology of Irrigated Farms as a Tool for Sustainable Agricultural Development in Irrigation Schemes: The Case of the East Mitidja Scheme, Algeria." *International Journal of Social Economics* 38(8): 813–831.

Loadman, J. 2005. *Tears of the Tree: The Story of Rubber A Modern Marvel.* Oxford: Oxford University Press.

Lumsden, D. P. 1973. "The Volta River Project: Village Resettlement and Attempted Rural Animation." *Canadian Journal of African Studies* 7(1): 115–132.

Maertens, M., Colen, L., and Swinnen, J. 2011. "Export Vegetable Supply Chains and Rural Households in Senegal." In Mithofer, D., and Waibel, H. (Eds.). *Vegetable Production and Marketing in Africa. Socio-economic Research.* Wallingford, UK: CAB International, pp. 111–126.

Makana, N. E. 2009. "Metropolitan Concern, Colonial State Policy, and the Embargo on Cultivation of Coffee by Africans in Colonial Kenya: The Example of Bungoma District, 1930-1960." *History in Africa* 36: 315–329.

Marshall, F., and Hildebrand, E. 2002. "Cattle Before Crops: The Beginnings of Food Production in Africa." *Journal of World History* 16(2): 99–142.

Mausch, K., and Mithofer, D. 2011. "The Impact of Compliance with GlobalGAP Standards on Small and Large Kenyan Export Vegetable-producing Farms." In Mithofer, D., and Waibel, H. (Eds.), *Vegetable Production and Marketing in Africa. Socio-economic Research* Wallingford, UK: CAB International, pp. 67–83.

McCann, J. 2001. "Maize and Grace: History, Corn, and Africa's New Landscapes, 1500-1999." *Comparative Studies in Society and History* 43(2): 246–272.

McLymont, R. 2008. "Green Africa Revolution." *Network Journal* 15(6): 23.

Mills-Tettey, R. 1989. "African Resettlement Housing: A Revisit to the Volta and Kainji Schemes." *Habitat International* 13(4): 71–81.

Moseley, W. G. 2017. "The New Green Revolution for Africa: A Political Ecology Critique." *Brown Journal of World Affairs* XXIII (II): 177–190.

Munro, J. F. 1983. "British Rubber Companies in East Africa before the First World War." *The Journal of African History* 24(3): 369–379.

Nassar, S., and Mansour, M. 2003. "Agriculture: An Assessment of Past Performance and the Task Ahead." In El-Ghonemy, M. R. (Ed.), *Egypt in the Twenty-First Century: Challenges for Development.* London: Routledge Cuzon, pp. 141–159.

Naylor, P. C. 2009. *North Africa: A History from Antiquity to Present.* Austin: University of Texas Press.

Nyambara, P. S. 2000. "Colonial Policy and Peasant Cotton Agriculture in Southern Rhodesia, 1904-1953." *The International Journal of African Historical Studies* 33(1): 81–111.

Obia, G. C. 2003. "Agricultural Development in Sub-Saharan Africa." In Aryeetey-Attoh, S. (Ed.), *Geography of Sub-Saharan Africa.* Upper Saddle River: Prentice Hall, pp. 363–405.

Odhiambo, W. 2007. "Financing African Agriculture: Issues and Challenges." *Paper Presented at the Second African Economic Conference at the United Nations Conference Center (UNCC)* Addis Ababa, Ethiopia 15–17 November.

Olsen, T. K. 2008. *"Norway: Farming Experts Call for 'Green Revolution' in Africa."* New York: Global Information Network, 19 September.

Roseboom, J., Pardey, P. G., and Beintema, N. K. 1998. He Changing Organizational Basis of African Agricultural Research." *EPTD Discussion Paper No. 17.*

Scherr, S. J., Wallace, C., and Buck, L. 2010. "Agricultural Innovation for Food Security and Poverty Reduction in the 21st Century: Issues for Africa and the World." Issues Paper for *State of the World 2011: Innovations that Nourish the Planet* Washington, DC: Ecoagriculture Partners.

Schilling, J., Freier, K. P., Hertig, E., and Scheffran, J. 2012. "Climate Change, Vulnerability and Adaptation in North Africa with focus on Morocco." *Agriculture, Ecosystems and Environment* 156: 12–26.

Schumacher, E. F. 1973. *Small Is Beautiful: Economics as if People Mattered.* London: Blond & Briggs Ltd.

Somado, E. A., Guei, R. G., and Nguyen, N. (ND). "Overview: Rice in Africa." http://www.africarice.org/publications/nerica-comp/module%201_Low.pdf. Accessed 9/14/2018.

Stock, R. 2004. *Africa South of the Sahara: A Geographical Interpretation.* Second Edition. New York: The Guildford Press.

Stohr, W. B., and Taylor, D. R. F. (Eds.) 1981. *Development from Above or Below: The Dialectics of Regional Planning in Developing Countries.* Chichester, England, New York: Wiley.

Swearingen, W. D. 1996. "Agricultural Reform in North Africa: Economic Necessity and Environmental Dilemmas." In Vandewalle, D. (Ed.), *North Africa: Development and Reform in a Changing Global Economy.* New York: St. Martin's Press, pp. 67–92.

Rizzo, M. 2006. "What Was Left of the Groundnut Scheme? Development Disaster and Labour Market in Southern Tanganyika 1946–1952." *Journal of Agrarian Change* 6(2): 205–238.

Thompson, V., and Adloff, R. 1957. *French West Africa.* Stanford: Stanford University Press.

Tomekpe, K., Kwa, M., Dzomeku, B. M., and Ganry, J. 2011. "CARBAP and Innovation on the Plantain Banana in Western and Central Africa." *International Journal of Agricultural Sustainability* 9(1): 264–273.

Turner, M. D. 2009. "Capital on the Move: The Changing Relation Between Livestock and Labor in Mali, West Africa." *Geoforum* 40, 746–755.

Turner, M. D. 2003. Environmental Science and Social Causation in the Analysis of Sahelian Pastoralism. In: Zimmerer, K. S., Bassett, T. J. (Eds.), *Political Ecology: An Integrative Approach to Geography and Environment–Development Studies.* New York: Guilford Press, pp. 159–178.

Udo, R. K. 1982. *Human Geography of Tropical Africa.* Ibadan: Hienemann Educational Books (Nigeria) Ltd.

Vandersypen, K., Keita, A. C. T., Coulibaly, B., Raes, D., and Jamin, J.-Y. 2007. "Drainage Problems in the Rice Schemes of the Office du Niger (Mali) in Relation to Water Management." *Agricultural and Water Management* 89: 153–160.

Vitale, J., Ouattarra, M., and Vognan, G. 2011. "Enhancing Sustainability of Cotton Production Systems in West Africa: A Summary of Empirical Evidence from Burkina Faso." *Sustainability* 3, 1136–1169.

Voice of America Nes 2007. "Un Agencies Call for "Green Revolution" in Africa," July.

Vossen, P. 2007. "Olive Oil: History, Production, and Characteristics of the World's Classic Oils." *HortScience* 45(2): 1093–1100.

Ward, W. E. F., and White, L. W. 1971. *East Africa: A Century of Change 1870–1970.* London: George Allen & Unwin Ltd.

World Bank. 1981. *Accelerated Development in Sub-Saharan Africa: An Agenda for Action.* Washington DC: World Bank.

World Bank. 1982. *International Development Trends and Agriculture and Economic Development.* Washington DC: World Bank.

World Bank World Bank 1989. *Sub-Saharan Africa: From Crisis to Sustainable Growth.* Washington DC: World Bank.

World Bank Independent Evaluation Group. 2007. *World Bank Assistance to Agriculture in Sub-Saharan Africa.* Washington, DC. International Bank for Reconstruction and Development.

World Bank. 2008. *Agriculture for Development.* Washington DC: World Bank.

CHAPTER 12

Fisheries and Forestry

Africans are not only farmers. They also make a living from extractive activities, which involve exploitation of resources from the physical environment. In this chapter, we focus on two of these activities—fisheries and forestry. The chapter is divided into two broad sections. The first section deals with fisheries and the second section forestry. For each of these activities, the chapter addresses three aspects: the activity's evolution and development in Africa, its contemporary characteristics and features, and its problems and issues. Before this attempt the prereading assignment.

FISHERIES

Fishing is the hunting or gathering of food and other valuable resources from aquatic environments. The term fishery is commonly used to refer to fishing as an organized human activity or the location of fishing or both. No matter how it is used, fisheries constitute an important economic activity in Africa. Not only do they provide fish, an important source of protein for both humans and animals, they also provide employment as well as contribute to the gross domestic product. Employment statistics on fisheries are not easily available since they are usually lumped together with agriculture and forestry. However, a Food and Agriculture Organization (FAO) (2014) report on the value of fisheries to Africa indicates that fisheries employed about 12.3 million Africans as full-time fishers or full-time and part-time processors in 2011. The report also estimated the value added of the entire fisheries to be $24 billion or 1.26% of Africa's total GDP in 2011. The focus of this section is on Africa's fisheries. First, it defines some key aspects of the fisheries sector. Second, it outlines the evolution and development of fisheries as an economic activity in Africa. Third, it describes the contemporary fisheries activities with respect to distribution patterns. Fourth, it discusses problems and issues facing the industry.

PREREADING ASSIGNMENTS

1. Identify all areas of Africa that you think have viable fisheries operations.
2. Why do you think those areas have important fisheries operations?
3. Are you aware of any important fish species that are caught in Africa? If so name them and where they are caught.
4. What problems do you think face fisheries operations in Africa? And what do you think can remedy these problems?
5. Do you think forestry is an important economic activity in Africa? If so why and if not why?
6. On the basis of your answer try and identify all African countries for which you think forestry will be a viable economic activity.
7. What other forest products from Africa do you know of?
8. What do you anticipate as the main problems facing Africa's forest products industry and what do you think are the solutions?

Classification of Fisheries, Fishing Vessels and Methods, and Fisheries Data

Classification of Fisheries

Like elsewhere fisheries in Africa can be classified according to location, technological sophistication, and environment. By location they are ocean or marine fisheries and inland fisheries. Ocean or marine fisheries consist of open seas, while inland fisheries consist of rivers, lakes, landlocked seas, and lagoons. By technological sophistication, they are artisanal or traditional and industrial or modern fisheries. Artisanal fisheries use simple equipment and technologies—canoes propelled to a larger extent by human power and to a lesser extent by motor. Industrial or modern fisheries use advanced equipment and technologies—boats propelled by gas or electric engines and sophisticated fishing gear. By environment or source, fisheries consist of capture and culture fisheries. **Capture fisheries** refer to the harvesting and hunting of natural aquatic resources, while **culture fisheries** refer to fish farming or aquaculture.

Fishing Methods and Vessels

Generally speaking, there are three main methods of fishing, each of which gives rise to its own fishing vessel and gear. The three methods are—trawling, seining, and lining. Trawling involves the hauling of a funnel-shaped net called a trawl net by a fishing vessel. Seining involves the use of seine or surrounding nets. Seine nets, and particularly purse seines, surround the school of fish and close at the bottom first as the line is being drawn, thereby trapping the fish. Lining involves the use of natural or artificial baits to catch the fish. The line may have a few or several baits, which are all fitted at the ends of hooks. Within the context of industrial fisheries, these fishing methods in turn define three types of fishing vessels. Trawlers are vessels that employ trawling method; seiners are those that do seining, and liners are those that use the line method.

Fisheries Data

The most comprehensive source of fisheries data on Africa is the FAO of the United Nations Organization's fisheries database (FishStatJ). However, these data are not complete. In most cases, they are estimates and there is also a lot of missing data. As a result, the data must be interpreted with that caveat. Apart from this, the database uses different systems to classify the fish. This section uses the International Standard Statistical Classification of Aquatic Animals and Plant (ISSCAAP). This system classifies marine capture fish into marine fishes, freshwater fishes, diadromous fishes, crustaceans, aquatic plants, mammals, mollusks, and miscellaneous aquatic animals (Table 12.1). Marine fishes are broadly classified as demersals and pelagics. **Demersals** live at or near the bottom and include cod, haddock, hake, pollock, and the flatfish family. **Pelagics** live near the surface and include herrings and tuna, and their related family. Diadromous migrate between salt water and freshwater in the course of their lives. Crustaceans include lobsters, spiny lobsters, crabs, shrimps, prawns, and crayfish; mollusks (oysters, scallops, mussels, snails, squids, octopuses); mammals (whales, porpoise); reptiles (serpents, crocodile), amphibians (frogs), and worms (coral and jellyfish).

TABLE **12.1**

The International Standard Statistical Classification of Aquatic Animals and Plants

Code	Division	Group species
1	Freshwater fishes	11 Carps, barbels, and other cyprinids
		12 Tilapias and other cichlids
		13 Miscellaneous freshwater fishes
2	Diadromous fishes	21 Sturgeons, paddlefishes
		22 River eels
		23 Salmons, trouts, smelts
		24 Shads
		25 Miscellaneous
3	Marine fishes	31 Flounders, halibuts, soles
		32 Cods, hakes, haddocks
		33 Miscellaneous coastal fishes
		34 Miscellaneous demersal fishes
		35 Herrings, sardines, anchovies
		36 Tunas, bonitos, billfishes
		37 Miscellaneous pelagic fishes
		38 Sharks, rays, chimaeras
		39 Marine fish not identified
4	Crustaceans	41 Freshwater crustaceans
		42 Crabs, sea-spiders
		43 Lobsters, spiny-rock lobsters
		44 Shrimps and prawns
		45 Krill, planktonic crustaceans
		46 Miscellaneous marine crustaceans
5	Molluscs	51 Freshwater molluscs
		52 Abalones, windless, conchs
		53 Oysters
		54 Mussels
		55 Scallops, pectens
		56 Clams, cockdes, arkshells
		57 Squids, cuttlefishes, octopuses
		58 Miscellaneous marine molluscs
6	Whales, seals, and other aquatic mammals	61 Blue-whales, fin-whales
		62 Sperm-whales, pilot-whales
		63 Eared seals, hair seals, walruses
		64 Miscellaneous aquatic mammals
7	Miscellaneous aquatic animals	71 Frogs and other amphibians
		72 Turtles
		73 Crocodiles and alligators

(*Continued*)

	TABLE **12.1**	

The International Standard Statistical Classification of Aquatic Animals and Plants (*Continued*)

Code	Division	Group species
		74 Sea-squirts and other tunicates
		75 Horseshoe crabs and other arachnoids
		76 Sea-urchins and other echinoderms
		77 Miscellaneous aquatic invertebrates
8	Miscellaneous aquatic animal products	81 Pearls, mother-of-pearl, shells
		82 Corals
		83 Sponges
9	Aquatic plants	91 Brown seaweeds
		92 Red seaweeds
		93 Green seaweeds
		94 Miscellaneous aquatic plants

Source: FAO 2000.

Evolution and Development of African Fisheries

Precolonial Period

There is ample evidence that fisheries were an important component of the precolonial African economy. For example, ancient carvings in Egypt show vibrant fishing activities in the Nile Valley (Nieland et al., 2005). An integrated farming and fishing culture dating as far back as 2,000 years ago has also been found in the Lake Chad Basin. In the Africa's Great Lakes Region, it has been found that early hunting and gathering including fisheries economy began about 3000 BC, while in Southern Africa, Plug et al. (2010) present evidence of extensive fishing activity by the late Holocene hunters-gatherers. In Southeast Africa, rock paintings found in modern-day Mozambique show several fishing scenes including spearing fish from small river boats. Similarly, a 400-km long stone fish traps along the coast of south western Cape Peninsula in South Africa has been dated back to be 2,000–3,000 years ago (Gribble, ND).

Over the centuries, increasing need for more fish products drove technological improvements in fishing methods and equipment as well as processing of fish products. Along these developments, some ethnic groups developed economies built around fisheries. Among these were the Imraguen of Mauritania, the Lebou and Nhominka of Senegal, the Bijagos of Guinea Bissau, the Lebou of Cape Verde, the Somono (or fishermen) of the Middle Niger, the Fanti of Ghana, the Nunu of DRC, and the Mang'anja of Malawi (Atta-Mills et al., 2004; Campredon and Cuq, 2001; Roberts, 1981).

These groups developed different fishing gears and methods. For example, Campredon and Cuq (2001, p. 94) reports that the Imraguen technique "consisted of wading into the sea with nets made from plant fiber to scoop the fish and dry them on the beach for long term storage." Roberts (1981) also reports that in the Middle Niger Basin, the Somono of the militarized state of Segou had a contract to fish for the state. In return, they were given exclusive rights to fish on the river and new recruits to learn their fish trade. Roberts (1981, p. 181) writes:

> Somono fishing was based on a mixed use of small and large nets. Individuals fished with small nets from shore or a canoe. Large nets, some stretching as far as 300 meters or more, were cooperative ventures.

The Nunu of the Middle Congo also developed pond fishing in the forest section of the flood plain. In this technique, a pond was built to trap receding flood waters after which the water would be scooped out to catch the fish. In the flooded grassland, south of the flood plain low earthen dams were used. The dams were low enough for fish to swim over them during flooding season. However, the receding flood waters were deliberately directed through holes in the dams that housed fish traps to catch all the fish. Fish that still remained behind the dam were picked up as the water level dropped below fish survival level (Harms, 1989).

In East Africa, the Luo of Kenya developed several methods of fishing including the use of basket traps and "herding" for lake fishing and more sophisticated stockades and weirs for fishing in rivers and shallow areas of Lake Victoria. In the basket traps and herding technique, basket traps were set with their entrance facing the open waters of Lake Victoria. Women would then form a semicircle and begin closing in on the traps as they disturbed the water with great splashing (Geheb, 1997).

During the 16th century foreign fishermen, mainly Europeans, entered Africa's marine fisheries off the coast of Morocco. Increasing interaction with Europeans and introduction of improved canoes raised the profile of marine fisheries. African fishermen, especially in West Africa, introduced a number of technological innovations that had major impact on marine fisheries in that part of the continent. Akyeampong (2007) reports on three of such innovations. The first was the beach-seine net, which was introduced between 1850 and 1860 by an Anlo woman fish trader to help the Anlo fishermen of the Gold Coast (Ghana) to undertake marine fishing. This was a drag net disengaged at sea by a few fishermen and dragged ashore by more fishermen. The second was the drift net or the *Ali* net, first used in Nigeria, and the third was the purse-seine net commonly known as *watsa*, which was introduced by a Ga fisherman of the Gold Coast.

Trade in fish was very important during this period. The Nunu, for example, traded dried fish, salt, and pottery for cassava from people who lived beyond the flood plain. However, the rise of the slave trade turned many fishermen into transporters of slaves from the interior to the coast along the Congo River (Harms, 1989). In South-east Africa, records of Portuguese explorers in 1589 show that fishing villages along the Sofala River in modern-day Mozambique engaged in silent barter with people who lived further from the river (Clark, 1960). Further interior, McCracken (1987) also reports that Mang'anja people of the south shores of Lake Malawi, and the upper Shire River Valley, traded some of their dried fish for maize and beans from the farmers in the agricultural highland regions.

In all the fisheries societies, fishing was a man's job but fish trade was conducted by both men and women depending on the society. Among the Fanti of Ghana, however, women also owned fishing equipment and hired male fishers to do the fishing (Walker, 2002). By the time of the colonial period, Africans were already engaged in active fisheries. In the inland areas fishers combined their fishing activities with farming, while in the coastal areas they engaged in fish trade exchanging some of their catch for food and other needs.

Colonial Period

Fisheries were not a colonial priority compared to agriculture and mining, none-theless the colonial period had significant impacts on Africa's fisheries. First, the European doctrine of "open access" did away with the traditional notions of "ter-ritorial waters" that governed marine fisheries. After some protests by African chiefs and fishermen, the doctrine was relaxed for inshore fisheries, but not for deep sea fisheries.

Second, colonialism facilitated European entry into African fisheries. This included the Dutch and the British in South Africa, the Norwegians in the Lake Vic-toria Basin (Graham, 1973; Geheb, 1997), the Greeks in the Lake Malawi fisheries in the 1930s (McCracken, 1987), and the Italians in Sierra Leone in 1955 (Thorpe et al., 2009).

Third, colonialism also brought technological improvements that had profound impact on fisheries. The first of these was improved boat technology, which allowed river boats to handle the rough seas and surfs along the coastal areas and the launch-ing of widespread commercial fishing (Atta-Mills et al. 2004). For the first time it became possible to recruit fishermen to go out to sea on contract. Once again, the Fanti were instrumental in this along the West African Coast. By the 1930s, the Fanti and the Anlo-Ewe were operating in modern-day Cote d'Ivoire, Liberia, and Nigeria (Akyeampong, 2007). The second technological development that affected fisher-ies was the motor car, which allowed traders to buy and sell both fresh and dried fish to distant towns and cities (McCracken, 1987). While only European fishermen were able to own cars, in modern-day Malawi for example, many African fishermen adopted the use of bicycles to distribute their fish products, which in turn led to the development of many cycle repair shops.

Fourth, developments in other sectors of the colonial economy created demand for more fish products and decline of some aquatic creatures. For example, the opening of copper mining in Belgian Congo (DRC) and Northern Rhodesia (Zam-bia) attracted European entrepreneurs—Italians and Greeks—to exploit the fishery resources of Belgian Congo, but there was a problem with crocodiles. In 1944, the mining company in Katanga waged war on the crocodile and by 1946 about 5,000 crocodiles and 60,000 crocodile eggs had been decimated (Gordon, 2003). The decline of crocodile population paved the way for overfishing, and within three years after decimating the crocodile population, the stock of the most valuable catch from the Luapula—the mpumbu—collapsed. Similarly, the Luapula salmon and the green-headed bream of Lake Mweru were depleted due to European fish-ing activities (va Zweiten et al., 2003), while the native species of Lake Victoria also declined (Payne, 1976).

Direct involvement of colonial administration in Africa's fisheries varied from place to place. In the Gold Coast (Ghana), most of the early colonial involvement was about settling conflicts over the harmful effects of the *Ali* nets (Walker, 2002). In the Lake Malawi region, the colonial government introduced brown trout to the Mulunguzi River for sports fishing (McCracken, 1987). Colonial attitudes toward fisheries, however, began to change due to pressing economic, political, and social needs. In the British colonies, it began with the outbreak of World War I when the need to feed South African and Imperial troops in Blantyre and Zomba (in modern-day Malawi) gave a boost to commercial fishing in Lake Malawi, and a number of local fish entrepreneurs took advantage of the situation. Demand for improved nutrition needs of workers on European tea estates eventually led to a ban on fish exports in Malawi. In Nigeria, a Fisheries Office was added to the Ministry of Agri-culture in 1914 (Anko and Eyo, 1984). In the Great Lakes Region, the colonial government enacted a law setting the minimum mesh for gill nets at 127 mm in 1933 to stem the depletion of the lake fisheries by the widespread use of the gill net (Kudhogania et al., 1992). In spite of this law, the catch of indigenous species continued to decline and by 1956 Lake Victoria was experiencing about 10.5% decline of its indigenous species, due to an increase in the number of fishers, especially after World War II. The collapse of the native species caused the colonial administration to introduce four species of tilapia to the lake from 1952 to 1963, and the Nile perch in 1954 (Crean and Geheb, 2001). Tilapia was also introduced into Lake Kariba between 1959 and 1962 (Kolding et al., 2003), and in Morocco oysters were introduced in Oualidia Lagoon south of Casablanca in the 1950s (FAO, 2004).

Other formal actions taken by the colonial government included the establishment of some fisheries institutions and commissioning of several fisheries studies. Among these were the Lake Victoria Fisheries Service (LVFS) of 1947, created to patrol the Lake against the use of illegal nets, the West African Fisheries Research Institute (WAFRI) established in 1952 in Freetown, Sierra Leone, to conduct fisheries research for the four British colonies in West Africa, and its counterpart in Zanzibar for the East African colonies.

During the latter colonial period, attempts were also made to introduce new species and aquaculture into some of Africa's most prominent fisheries. This included the introduction of fish species in some of the rivers in Kenya and Malawi, and the establishment of scientific fish farms in Kenya in 1924, Morocco in 1927, in Egypt in 1934, and in DRC in 1937. More fish farms were established in modern-day Zambia (1942), Malawi (1946), Cameroon (1948), Congo Republic (1949), Zimbabwe (1950), Uganda (1953), Nigeria (1951 and 1954), and Zambia (1958–1960). Most of these were research stations that investigated indigenous tilapia, African catfish, the African boney tongue, and alien carp (Anko and Eyo, 1984; Baddyr and Guenette, 2001; Brummett and Williams, 2000; Dadzie, 1992).

Postcolonial Period

At the return to independence, Africa's fisheries consisted of a large sector of capture fisheries and a small but promising sector of culture fisheries. Although there was some considerable commercialization, a greater portion of the activity was semi-industrial in terms of technology, equipment, and product processing.

Developments in marine capture fisheries   In West Africa, the marine capture fisheries in some of the newly independent countries was dominated by immigrant fishers, mostly from Ghana. The strong nationalistic sentiment at the time coupled with the desire to quickly transition into an industrial economy provided the premise for change. First, the immigrant fishers were expelled. Second, many coastal countries invested heavily in industrial fisheries in the early 1970s, which in most cases translated into the establishment of large-scale state-owned fishery corporations. The regional fisheries institutes established by the colonial governments were dismantled and many countries established their own fishery research institutes.

Artisanal fisheries also benefited from the changes in the large-scale industrial fisheries. Of particular importance was the introduction of outboard motors and cold-storage facilities. Prior to these, artisanal fisheries used canoes, oars, traditional nets, and sheer human power. They relied on indigenous astronomy to determine when to go out to sea and when not to go. After launching the canoe, they would paddle into deep sea, cast the net, and pull it to see if they caught something.

Alternatively, they would drop the net and hold the line to bring it ashore. They would then tie the rope around a coconut palm and pull the net ashore. In the 1970s, these methods became modified. Fishers purchased outboard motors and attached them to their canoes. These took the burden of paddling the oars. There were other changes. In Mauritania, for example, the traditional Imraguen improved their fishing with new sailing boats. In Guinea-Bissau, the Nhominka of Senegal used to migrate to the Bijagos Islands in the dry season where they would live in camps and fish; and return to Senegal to grow rice in the rainy season. From the mid-1980s, however, these camps did not only become more numerous but also more permanent (Campredon and Cuq, 2001).

Africa's marine capture fisheries peaked in the 1970s, after which they began to face a number of problems from both internal and external developments. Competition between local and migrant fishers increased, which led to more conflicts between the two groups. The most formidable of the outside groups were the powerful long distant-fishing fleets from Japan, China, and Europe. The conflicts however reached the world stage when the West African sardine collapsed along with other species such as the Northeast Atlantic herring, the Northwest Atlantic cod, and the South Atlantic pilchard, as a result of overfishing. In addition, the 1973–1974 oil crises forced many small fishing companies and livelihoods out of business. Countries became more protective of their territorial waters.

In 1982, the United Nations' series of meetings to engage the issue concluded with the UN Convention on the Law of the Sea. The Law extended the territorial sea limit of coastal countries to 12 nautical miles from the shore and established an exclusive economic zone (EEZ) of 200 nautical miles. Within the EEZ, coastal states had sovereign rights over the use and management of natural resources and jurisdiction, marine science research and environmental protection. Domestic fishermen had priority within the zone after which coastal states must sell rights to any surplus fish resources that it could not use if another country was interested (some allocation may be made to foreign fishermen). Among other things, the Law also addressed marine and scientific research and settlement of disputes. The Law came into full force in 1994. This and the growing awareness of environmental impact of fishing activities led to the establishment of fisheries management in many countries, and enforcement of their exclusive economic zones. However, this did not stop the powerful fleets of distant-fishing companies from Japan, China, and Europe from fishing in even the EEZs of African countries, including the six-mile exclusive zones reserved for artisanal fisheries (Campredon and Cuq, 2001).

In South Africa, the apartheid regime ignored subsistence fishing activities even though the so-called African homelands inhabitants were heavily involved in fisheries, given the lack of land and other restrictive conditions placed on the Black majority. At the end of the apartheid in 1994, whites owned 93% of all commercial vessels, 96% of all commercial fishing licenses and 99.25% of total allowable catch (TAC) (Isaacs and Hara, 2007). In 1998, the South African government passed the Marine Living Resources Act (MLRA) in which subsistence fishing and fishers were formally recognized by the government and given the right equivalent to commercial fishers. The implementation of the act has however not been easy (Anonymous, 2002; Isaacs and Hara, 2007).

Marine Fisheries however had to deal with many problems, including poor macroeconomic environment of the 1980s and 1990s; decline of fish stock, uncertain ecosystem environment, deterioration in water quality due to increased land-based human activities, habitat destruction, or modification due to coastal erosion and modification of coastline and seabed (Ukwe et al., 2006). As a result, marine capture fisheries in the majority of Africa's coastal state collapsed leaving a few survivors. Among the latter group of countries were South Africa and Morocco, which saw a rather rapid expansion from 1973 to 1996.

Developments in inland capture fisheries Inland fisheries also faced a number of problems that have been well documented by Ogutu-Ohwayo and Balirwa (2006) and Njiru et al. (2005). First, the introduction of new species such as the Nile perch and tilapia into Lake Victoria, for example, boosted production initially, and even converted some artisanal fisheries into commercial ones thereby boosting incomes. However, the new species also led to decline and sometimes total disappearance of native species, and reduction of aquatic biodiversity. In Lake Victoria, for example, the Nile perch caused about 60% decline in the stocks of haplochromines, which used to account for 80% of the fish stock of the lake (Ogutu-Ohwayo and Balirwa, 2006). Second, increasing population around the inland fisheries, especially in the Great Lakes Region, led to increased demand for fish, which in turn was supported by the use of new fishing boats and more destructive fishing nets. Third, increased human activities and inappropriate land-use practices around the fisheries led to pollution, eutrophication, and increased sedimentation of the fisheries. Fourth, many of Africa's lakes and river systems were invaded by aquatic plants, the most serious being the water hyacinths, which invaded Lakes Victoria, Malawi, and Navaisha, and the Shire River.

Fifth, the completion of large-scale hydroelectric power projects such as the Aswan High Dam (Egypt), the Volta River Dam (Ghana), the Kainji Dam (Nigeria), and the Diama Dam (Senegal) caused a decline of the Nile, the Volta, the Niger, and the Senegal fisheries.

Developments in culture fisheries Culture fisheries followed a similar pattern. It grew initially spreading to many of the continent's new countries, hitting a peak in the 1960s after which it began to decline throughout most of the 1970s. However, as Brummett and Williams (2000) have described, the decline was followed by a second wave of growth from the late 1970s through the 1980s, which focused on small- and large-scale fish farms in Cote d'Ivoire, Kenya, Egypt, and Zambia; and shellfish farming in Tunisia, South Africa, Morocco, Senegal, Zambia, Malawi, and Mauritius (Brummett and Williams, 2000). Much of this second wave was stimulated by the infusion of foreign aid that saw small-scale commercial fish farms as important components of rural development. Thus, from 1978 to 1989, these projects attracted about 90% of the estimated $145.62 million of aquaculture investment designated for Africa (Brummett and Williams, 2000; Lazard et al., 1991). Brummett and Williams (2000) note that much of this aid went to extension, training, and building and rehabilitation of state farms and hatcheries. However, when these projects produced disappointing results, the role of small-scale projects in rural development was questioned and the aid community became reluctant to fund further projects.

From 1987 to 2004, the FAO organized a series of meetings on aquaculture in Africa with senior government officials that resulted in replacing donor priorities of poverty alleviation and cheap food for low income and urban areas, with local needs of commercialization (Brummett et al., 2008). The New Partnership for Africa's Development (NEPAD) opened a new avenue for cooperation in the fisheries sector. In 2005, it organized a "Fish for All" Summit in Abuja, Nigeria—the first summit of African Heads of State on fisheries. However, the summit called for international community to provide the financial and technical support for the development of Africa's fisheries.

Toward regional and international fisheries management African countries engaged in a number of regional and international efforts and collaboration in managing their fisheries and dealing with some of these challenges. With respect to inland fisheries, the largest of these collaborations was in the Great Lakes Region, where the Lake Victoria Environmental Management Project (LVEMP) was launched in 1997 with funding from the Global Environmental Facility (GEF) and the International Development Association (IDA). The program's objectives were (1) to maximize sustainable benefits with respect to food, income, and safe water, and reduction of diseases; (2) to conserve biodiversity and genetic resources; and (3) harmonize national management programs and stem degradation. These objectives were to be achieved through national programs. In 2001, the Lake Victoria Basin Commission (LVBC) was formed by the East African Community countries to oversee the harmonization of national management programs, conservation and environmental management including eradication of water hyacinth, management of fisheries, and economic development around the lake.

Other efforts include the Zambezi River Authority (ZRA), the beach management units (BMU) of East Africa, which engage in "coordination, joint planning and implementation, and participation in governmental planning and budgeting" (Nunan et al., 2012, p. 209), the Abidjan Convention for Cooperation in the Protection, Management, and Development of West and Central African (WACAF) Region, and the World Bank's Profish program of 2005. The Protocol of the Abidjan Convention provides a legal framework for the 16 countries in the region to cooperate in the protection of coastal and marine environment (Ukwe et al., 2006), while the World Bank's Profish program was launched to help African countries identify the most critical fishery issues and how to combat them (Nevin, 2005).

Fishery access agreements Rising demand of fish consumption worldwide since the 1980s, made Africa's fishery resources important as Europe and Asia sought new fishing grounds. This led to a number of fishery access agreements between African countries and foreign governments, private companies, and intergovernmental organizations, notably the EU. Unfortunately, these access agreements have been blamed for overfishing since they allow too many fishing boats in the fisheries. More seriously, the lack of transparency of these agreements as to how much revenue they generate and where such revenue goes have raised suspicion of corruption. Corruption has also been found in illegal fishing and among marine inspectors and port official who are charged with enforcing the governing laws of the fisheries (Standing, 2008).

Rebound in culture fisheries and safety concerns Culture fisheries have also rebounded. Part of this is due to increasing world demand for fish products that could no longer be met by the traditional fisheries. African governments have begun to promote aquaculture as the alternative sources. Numerous studies have highlighted Africa's potential for aquaculture. The challenge is whether African countries will be able to capitalize on this opportunity and produce fish that is of world quality standard. The EU banned fish imports from a number of African countries during 1997–2000 including Uganda, Kenya, and Tanzania for reasons of food safety, until proper regulations were put in place. Any efforts in the development of culture fisheries need to keep this in mind (Bagumire et al., 2009).

Fisheries Production

Historically, most of Africa's fish production has come from capture fisheries (Figure 12.1). Indeed in 1984 when FAO began recording data for Africa's culture fisheries, capture fisheries accounted for 99% of Africa's total fish production. Over the past decades, however, the growth of culture fisheries has reduced the contribution of capture fisheries and in 2015, it accounted for 86% (Figure 12.1).

Marine Capture Fisheries

Capture fisheries fall into two main categories—marine capture fisheries and inland capture fisheries. Marine capture fisheries are ocean fisheries, while inland capture fisheries include rivers and lakes. Marine capture fisheries are the most important of Africa's fisheries sector. From the 1960s through the 1970s, they accounted for over 70% of Africa's fish production. Since the 1980s they have consistently accounted for over 60% of the total fish production. In 2015, they accounted for 65% of the total fisheries production (Figure 12.2).

Although fish can be caught from any ocean, the geography of fisheries production shows that some areas of the oceans are more productive than others. Indeed about two-thirds of the Africa's total fish catch comes from four limited areas of its vast ocean surroundings. The reason for this is that there are certain factors that make some parts of the ocean more productive in fish than others. What are these factors?

Factors Affecting the Location of Marine Capture Fisheries in Africa There are two broad factors that affect marine capture fisheries. The first is physical environmental and the second is human environmental factors.

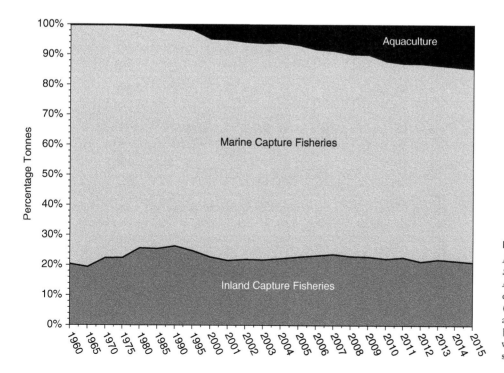

FIGURE 12.1 Sources of Africa's fisheries, 1960–2015. *Source:* FAO. 2017. Fishery and Aquaculture Statistics. Global capture production 1950–2015 (FishstatJ). In: FAO Fisheries and Aquaculture Department [online]. Rome. Updated 2017. www.fao.org/fishery/statistics/software/fishstatj/en

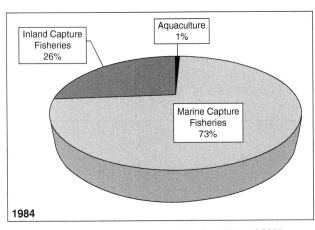
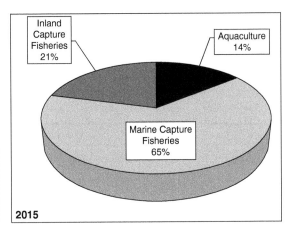

FIGURE 12.2 Composition of Africa's fisheries 1984 and 2015.
Source: FAO. 2017. Fishery and Aquaculture Statistics. Global capture production 1950–2015 (FishstatJ). In: FAO Fisheries and Aquaculture Department [online]. Rome. Updated 2017. www.fao.org/fishery/statistics/software/fishstatj/en

Physical environmental factors All fisheries derive their productivity from one single source, namely the abundance of plankton, the microscopic organisms that form the bulk of fish food. The abundance of plankton is in turn determined by the existence of two natural factors—continental shelves and convergence zones of ocean currents. A continental shelf is the part of the ocean adjacent to land that slopes gently before the ocean floor drops into the ocean deeps. The shallow nature of continental shelves allows sunlight to reach the bottom thereby encouraging photosynthesis. In addition, the close proximity of shelves to the continental landmass makes them rich depositaries of minerals, which in turn attract abundance of plankton.

A second physical environmental factor that creates ideal conditions for plankton to abound is the convergence zones of warm and cold ocean currents. The intermingling of cold and warm currents causes upwelling, which in turn causes plankton to become concentrated in the surface thus attracting fish toward them.

Africa's geological stability provides it with fewer extensive continental shelves compared to other continents. However, there are three areas along its coast where convergence of cold and warm currents provide ideal fishing conditions. One is off the Northwest coast of Africa where the cold Canary Currents meet with the warm Guinea Currents. The second area is along the South West Africa and West Africa coasts, where the cool Benguela Currents meet the warm Guinea Currents and the third area is in the southeast and south where the warm Agulhas Currents meet the cool Benguela Currents and cold waters of the Southern Ocean. As we shall see later, these areas are also part of Africa's productive fisheries.

Human environmental factors By themselves, these physical environmental conditions will not make productive fisheries. They need activation and appropriation from the human environment. In particular, there should be demand for fish and fish products. Second, the technology and capital for conducting fisheries operations should be available. Third, there should be proper management policies to ensure wise use of the fishery resources.

A combination of these factors has given Africa four main fisheries: the Southeast Atlantic comprising Angola, Namibia, and South Africa; the East Central Atlantic, from Gabon to Morocco, the Mediterranean from Egypt to Morocco, and the Southwest Indian Ocean, from Egypt to Mozambique (Figure 12.3). For

FIGURE 12.3 Africa's ocean fisheries.
Source: Based on FAO Major Fishing Areas The boundaries are for illustration only

both Southeast Atlantic and East Central Atlantic, it is the deep upwelling caused by the mingling of the cold Benguela Currents and the warm tropical waters off the coast of Namibia and Angola, and the Guinea Current off the West African coast, and also continental shelf especially for the East Central Atlantic. In contrast, for both Southwestern Indian Ocean and the Mediterranean, it is mostly the continental shelf.

Marine Fisheries Operations Both modern and artisanal methods of fishing are used in Africa's marine capture fisheries. The modern fishing methods use sophisticated technologies including large and high-powered fishing vessels that include trawlers, liners, and seiners. All these fishing vessels have facilities for storage and some processing on board. Most of these fleets belong to corporations that are vertically integrated in the sense that they control the full process of harvesting, processing, and marketing of the fish (Branch and Clark, 2006). South Africa is the only country in Africa that has a long-established large modern fishing fleet, but other smaller modern fishing fleets also exist in Morocco, Senegal, Mauritania, Egypt, Libya, Nigeria, Ghana, and Cote d'Ivoire.

The artisanal fishing methods are the dominant methods of fishing in Africa given that artisanal fisheries constitute the larger portion of Africa's fisheries. These are largely small-scale operations that, as already mentioned, employ low technology, low capital investment, and low output. The main vessels here are wooden canoes or pirogues, a few of which have outboard motors affixed to them. Fish caught are still preserved by traditional methods—namely salting, drying, and smoking. Although most of artisanal fisheries are small scale, they are commercial—most fishermen sell their fish to women or middlemen (Degan et al., 2010). With limited facilities such as coolers and refrigerators, most of the fish is sold fresh.

A complex system of arrangements exists within the artisanal fisheries. Fish traders often enter into some informal contracts with the fishermen for long-time supplies. In return, the fishermen receive financial support, and fishing gear and equipment. In 2014, Africa had 15% of the world's fishing fleet, the second largest after Asia, but the largest percentage of nonmotorized vessels, about 63% of its total fishing fleet (FAO, 2016). The 37% that were motorized constituted only 6% of the world's motorized fishing fleet. Along the eastern coast of Africa, artisanal methods still account for 70% of the marine fisheries catch, while along the western coast it is a little over 50% (FAO, 2010).

Production Trends The most dominant catch of marine capture fisheries in 2015 were herrings, sardines, and anchovies (43%) followed by miscellaneous pelagic fishes (16%), miscellaneous coastal fishes (9%), and marine fishes not identified (9%), and tuna, bonitos, and billfishes (6%) (Figure 12.4). Production trends in Figure 12.5 show that there have been two spurts of growth in marine capture fisheries since the 1960s. The first spurt peaked in 1975 and ended in 1980. The second spurt began after 1980, peaked in 2005, and declined afterward. With reference to specific fish species, Figure 12.6 shows a dramatic decline in herring production after reaching a peak harvest in 1975. For the next two decades, herring production struggled to recover, and it was only in the 1990s that production growth became steady. The production trends of the other fish species have been similar even though the scale of variations has been small. The total catch is distributed over four main fisheries: the East Central Atlantic, South Eastern Atlantic, Western Indian Ocean, and the Mediterranean.

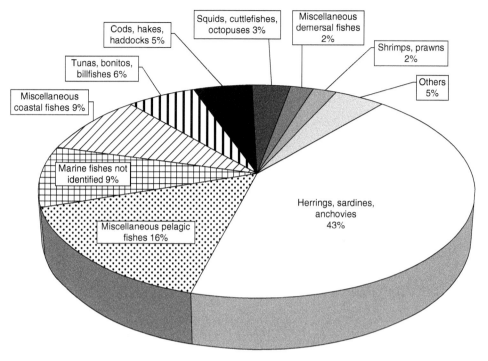

FIGURE 12.4 Composition of Africa's marine capture fisheries, 2015.
Source: FAO. 2017. Fishery and Aquaculture Statistics. Global capture production 1950–2015 (FishstatJ). In: FAO Fisheries and Aquaculture Department [online]. Rome. Updated 2017. www.fao.org/fishery/statistics/software/fishstatj/en

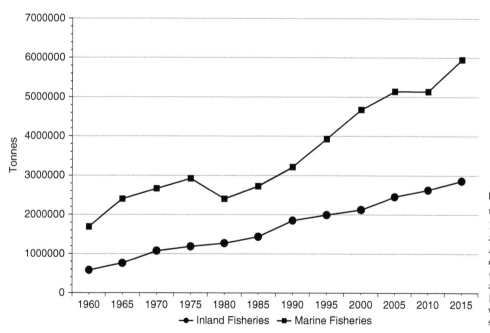

FIGURE 12.5 Production trends of capture fisheries, 1960–2015.
Source: FAO. 2017. Fishery and Aquaculture Statistics. Global capture production 1950–2015 (FishstatJ). In: FAO Fisheries and Aquaculture Department [online]. Rome. Updated 2017. www.fao.org/fishery/statistics/software/fishstatj/en

East Central Atlantic fisheries This is a vast region that stretches from Angola to Morocco. The section from Angola to Guinea-Bissau consisting of EEZs of 16 countries is usually called the Guinea Current Large Marine Ecosystem (GCLME), while the section from Guinea-Bissau to Morocco is called the Canary Current Large Marine Ecosystem (CCLME). The region has grown in importance in fisheries

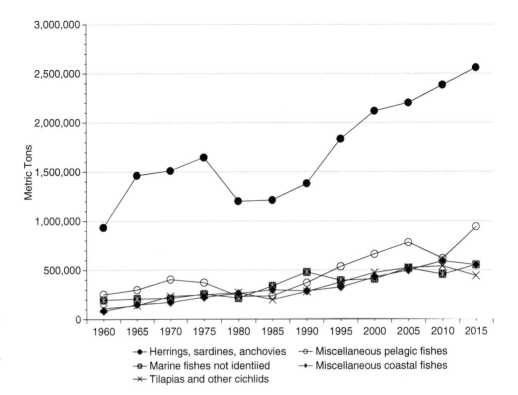

FIGURE 12.6 Production trends of major catch of marine capture fisheries, 1960–2015.
Source: FAO. 2017. Fishery and Aquaculture Statistics. Global capture production 1950–2015 (FishstatJ). In: FAO Fisheries and Aquaculture Department [online]. Rome. Updated 2017. www.fao.org/fishery/statistics/software/fishstatj/en

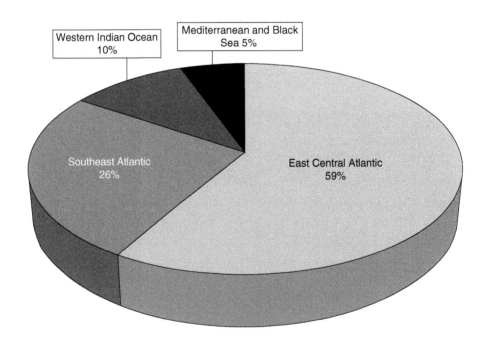

FIGURE 12.7 Sources of Africa's marine capture fisheries.
Source: FAO. 2017. Fishery and Aquaculture Statistics. Global capture production 1950–2015 (FishstatJ). In: FAO Fisheries and Aquaculture Department [online]. Rome. Updated 2017. www.fao.org/fishery/statistics/software/fishstatj/en

production and it is now the most productive of Africa's marine capture fisheries. It accounted for 22% of Africa's marine capture fisheries in 1960 and 59% in 2015 (Figure 12.7). The most important catch by quantity are herrings, sardines, and anchovies. These constituted about 52% of the total catch in 2015. Others were miscellaneous; pelagic and coastal fishes, tunas, bonitos, and billfishes. The production of all these have shown wide fluctuations. Morocco was the leading fishing country of the eastern Central Atlantic fisheries in 2015, accounting for 38% of its total catch. Other important producers were Senegal (11%), Mauritania (11%), Nigeria (10.7%), and Ghana (7.4%).

The Southeast Atlantic fisheries This region includes South Africa, Namibia, and Angola. This region has declined in fish production since late 1960s when it produced 66% of Africa's total marine capture fisheries output. The most dominant catch, the Southern African anchovy, declined sharply after 1968 and has never recovered. In contrast, the whitehead herring made a comeback in 1988 but has since declined. The cape hake has held steady, showing less fluctuation than the other fish species. It was the most important catch in 2015. Other important species include the South African pilchard, Southern African anchovy, round herrings, and Cunene horse mackerel. However, according to FAO (2012) both the Southern African pilchard and Cunene horse mackerel, especially off the coast of Namibia and Angola, have been overexploited. South Africa is the most important fish producer in the Southeast Atlantic fisheries although its total production has declined over the years. In 2015, it accounted for only 37% of the total catch of the region followed closely by Namibia (33%) and Angola (30%). Industrial fishing is more concentrated on the west coast, while recreational and small-scale fisheries are concentrated in the south and east (Branch and Clark, 2006).

The Western Indian Ocean fisheries The Western Indian Ocean fisheries include Egypt, Sudan, Eritrea, Djibouti, Somalia, Kenya, Tanzania, Mozambique, Madagascar, Comoros, Seychelles, and Mauritius. Fish production in this region has increased over the past decades accounting for 8–10% of Africa's total marine capture. This makes the region the third most important fisheries after the East Central Atlantic and the Southeast Atlantic fisheries. Marine fishes not exactly identified constitute the bulk of the catch from this region. However, tunas, bonitos, and billfishes, miscellaneous coastal and pelagic fishes are also important. According to FAO database, Tanzania used to be the dominant fish-producing country of this region. However, since 1993 other countries in the region have seen increased fish production, starting with Egypt, then Seychelles, and in recent years Mozambique. In 2015, Mozambique accounted for 32% of the total fish production from the region, followed by Seychelles (17%), Tanzania (16%), Madagascar (15%), and Egypt (8%). Most of the fisheries here are artisanal.

The Mediterranean fisheries The Mediterranean fisheries extend from Egypt to Morocco. What makes these fisheries productive is not so much of convergence zone of cold and warm currents but rather an extensive continental shelf, a people with long tradition in ocean fisheries, increasing demand for fish products due to population growth and consumption, all of which are supported by modern fishing fleets. In terms of fish production, this region is the smallest of Africa's marine capture fisheries, accounting for 4–8% of the total fish production of Africa (Figure 12.7). The most dominant catch from these fisheries in 2015 were herrings, sardines, and anchovies. They accounted for 39% of the total fish production from the region followed by sardinella (13.5%), marine fishes (10.9%), and jack and horse mackerel (8.5%). The leading fishing country is Algeria, followed by Tunisia, Egypt, and Morocco.

Inland Capture Fisheries

As already indicated, inland capture fisheries account for 32.5% of Africa's total capture fisheries and 21% of its total fisheries production. In 2010, Africa had the largest collection of inland fisheries fleet in the world (42%) (FAO, 2012). Like the marine capture fisheries production trends have risen and fallen over the years—since 1960s—partly as a function of incomplete data, but partly due to several problems that we have already recounted. In 2015, the largest group of fish by tonnage was miscellaneous freshwater fishes, which accounted for 65%. This group was followed by carp, barbels, and other cyprinids (18%), and tilapia and other cichlid (15%).

Africa's Great Lakes Region accounted for about 35% of the inland capture fisheries, in 2015, led by Lake Victoria, which is the most productive freshwater fishery in the world (Ogutu-Ohwayo and Balirwa, 2006). Other lakes of importance are Lake Tanganyika and Lake Malawi. Apart from the lakes, Africa's longest rivers, led by the Nile, the Congo, and the Niger provide the rest of Africa's inland fisheries. Not surprisingly, therefore, the leading inland fisheries countries in 2015 were Uganda (14%), Nigeria (12%), Tanzania (11%), Egypt (8%), DRC (8%), Kenya (6%), and Malawi (5%).

Culture Fisheries or Aquaculture

Culture fisheries or aquaculture is relatively new to Africa compared to Asia where it has been practiced for over 2,000 years. However, it has attracted a great deal of interest over the past two decades. This interest has been largely motivated by the realization that aquaculture holds prospects of making up for food deficiencies, raising income, and changing consumer preferences for aquatic products.

Types of Aquaculture There are different types of aquaculture, depending on the location, environment, design features, and feeding system (Allsopp, 1997). By location, there is **marine-based** or **mariculture** and **land-based** culture. The first may be plastic-lined ponds on the shoreline fed by pumping seawater or in the ocean, while the second is on land. By environment, aquaculture may be **freshwater**, **brackish water**, or **seawater**. By design features aquaculture can be done in ponds, reservoirs, or cages. Aquaculture may also be semi-extensive, semi-intensive, and intensive, by feeding system. **Extensive** aquaculture relies mainly on the natural organisms in the aquatic food chain; **semi-intensive** aquaculture uses supplemental feed, while **intensive** aquaculture is totally dependent on artificial feed (Allsopp, 1997).

Factors Affecting the Location of Aquaculture It would seem as if aquaculture can occur anywhere, but poor location has generally been identified as one of the major reasons why aquaculture enterprises fail (Pillay, 1994). The factors that affect the location of aquaculture include cost factors—climate, land and water resources, site characteristics, and demand factors—market and culture.

Climate, land and water resources Warmer climates are generally considered to be more efficient for growth of aquaculture organisms than cooler climates, which require heating. Availability of unutilized or underutilized land that can be converted to aquaculture as well as water resources is also important. Underestimating these can affect the productivity of aquaculture.

Site characteristics Sheltered or semi-enclosed environments in both marine and inland waters are the most preferred locations for aquaculture. In addition, lack of adequate flow of water in the area can lead to rapid accumulation of waste material, which can eventually create environmental hazards. The physical and chemical properties of the soil do not only determine the soil's water-holding capacity and production of food organisms, the organic content and acid conditions of the soil can also make an aquaculture site expensive (Pillay, 1994).

Climate, land and water resources, and site characteristics can raise the cost of aquaculture substantially. Substantial cost in turn makes it difficult for places that are short on capital to engage in aquaculture.

Market and culture Market for aquaculture products also determines the location of aquaculture. Improvement in transportation technology has now extended the range of markets for aquaculture products. However, the bulk of the world's aquaculture is located in close proximity to where the demand for aquaculture products is also the highest. Closely related to this is the cultural heritage of the people, regarding aquaculture production, which in turn generates availability of experienced and skilled labor in aquaculture. This again is the difference between African countries and Asian countries, where aquaculture has been part of the heritage for thousands of years.

Aquaculture Operations
Most of Africa's aquaculture is earthen ponds although the adoption of tanks made of concrete, blocks, and fiberglass is becoming important (Anetekhai et al., 2004). In 2015, about 51% of Africa's total aquaculture fisheries production occurred in brackish water environment, 39% in freshwater, while only 20% came from marine environment. Only few countries are involved in mariculture—Egypt, South Africa, Madagascar, Mozambique, Namibia, Senegal, and Tanzania (Fakoya et al., 2009). Most of the fish farms are small-scale rural enterprises that depend to a large extent on feed obtained from external sources. These make aquaculture expensive, and inefficient. Intensive, semi-extensive, extensive systems are practiced. However, freshwater pond-based aquaculture using the extensive system of feeding is the most widespread form of aquaculture in Africa. This system is most preferred by small-scale farmers while the small- and large-scale commercial farmers prefer the semi-extensive system. Here farmers use fertilization and supplemental feed in contrast to the extensive that relies on natural feed, including unconventional feed (Gabriel et al., 2007).

Production Trends
Africa's culture fisheries are relatively small compared to Asia and the rest of the world's major regions. In 2015, the global aquaculture production was 106 million metric tons (FAO, 2017). Of this total, Africa accounted for only 2% compared to Asia's (92%), Europe's (3%), and America's (3%). Only Oceania (0.2%) produced less than Africa.

The largest group of species is tilapia, which accounted for 56% of the total culture fisheries production in 2015. Other important species included catfish (14.5%), snappers not exactly identified (8.7%), unidentified mullets (8.2%), and unidentified cyprinids (4.9%). The dominant species of these groups are the Nile tilapia; the North African catfish, the flathead grey mullet, and the common carp. As indicated by Table 12.2, while some of the fish stock have declined or been unsteady, others have become increasingly important. For example, tilapias have been the dominant species since 1984, but their total contribution dipped to 29.6% before bouncing back again to 56% in 2015. Similarly, the common carp has also fluctuated from being the second most important fish from 1980s through 1990s to almost disappearing in 2005 to only 1.8% in 2015. In contrast, the rainbow trout is an example of fish species that has declined completely. Other fish species such as the flathead grey mullet and catfish have become more important (Table 12.2).

TABLE **12.2**

Percentage of Major Fish Species of Africa's Aquaculture 1984-2015

Species	1984	1990	1995	2000	2005	2010	2015
Tilapias	44.2	35.8	30.8	31.9	29.6	46.1	56.2
Carp	23.0	32.5	16.7	14.8	0.6	2.6	1.8
Rainbow trout	11.6	3.9	2.0	0.7	0.4	0.1	0.1
Catfish	9.2	2.5	7.8	1.6	11.7	15.1	14.5
Snappers nei	0.1	0.4	5.4	6.4	2.2	8.9	8.7
European seabass	0.1	1.0	4.9	7.5	2.3	1.3	0.9
Giant tiger prawn	1.1	0.6	4.6	2.9	3.8	0.4	0.2
African bonytongue	3.1	0.3	0.3	0.3	0.2	0.2	0.3
Ballan wrasse	2.6	0.5	2.6	0.0	0.0	0.0	0.0
Mullets nei	1.4	13.5	15.7	28.8	27.4	8.3	8.2
Cyprinids nei	0.6	0.54	0.7	0.1	11.1	12.4	4.9
Other fishes	3.0	8.5	8.5	5.0	10.7	6.6	5.9
Total	100.0	100.0	100.0	100.0	100.0	100.0	100.0

Source: FAO. 2017. Fishery and Aquaculture Statistics. Global capture production 1950–2015 (FishstatJ). In: FAO Fisheries and Aquaculture Department [online]. Rome. Updated 2017. www.fao.org/fishery/statistics/software/fishstatj/en

Egypt dominated culture fisheries production in Africa in 2015 with 65.3% of Africa's total production (Table 12.3). Other important producers were Nigeria with 17.6%, Uganda (6.5%), Ghana (2.5%), Zambia (1.3%), and Madagascar (1.3%).

TABLE **12.3**

Top 10 Culture Fisheries Producers by Percentage Share of Quantity Produced 1984-2015

Country	1984	1990	1995	2000	2005	2010	2015
Egypt	73.3	75.5	64.5	84.8	82.6	70.8	65.3
Nigeria	17.7	9.0	14.9	6.4	8.6	15.4	17.6
Uganda	0.1	0.1	0.2	0.2	1.7	7.3	6.5
Ghana	1.2	0.4	0.5	1.2	0.2	0.8	2.5
Zambia	0.9	1.8	3.7	1.1	0.8	0.8	1.3
Madagascar	0.5	0.3	4.2	2.0	1.6	0.8	1.3
Kenya	0.6	1.5	1.2	0.1	0.2	0.9	1.0
Tunisia	0.3	1.2	0.9	0.4	0.4	0.4	0.8
Tanzania	0.0	1.7	1.1	0.3	0.5	0.6	0.6
Zimbabwe	0.4	0.2	0.1	0.5	0.4	0.2	0.6
Top 10	95.1	91.7	91.3	97.0	96.8	98.1	97.5
Rest of Africa	4.9	8.3	8.7	3.0	3.2	1.9	2.5
Total	100.0	100.0	100.0	100.0	100.0	—	100.0

Source: FAO. 2017. Fishery and Aquaculture Statistics. Global capture production 1950–2015 (FishstatJ). In: FAO Fisheries and Aquaculture Department [online]. Rome. Updated 2017. www.fao.org/fishery/statistics/software/fishstatj/en

Problems and Issues in Fisheries

Africa's fisheries have many problems and issues that hamper their effectiveness. Some of these are natural, others are human-made. The problems also tend to be a little different for capture and cultural fisheries. As such we will look at these problems and issues from the two perspectives.

Problems and Issues of Capture Fisheries

Fisheries decline Africa's fisheries are declining due to economic and ecological factors. Economic factors include overexploitation or excessive fishing and fishing subsidies that allow fishing fleets to make profits (Nevin, 2005). Ecological factors include changes in upwelling regimes that in turn lead to fluctuations in the fisheries production (Ukwe et al., 2006). Increasing use of industrial trawling has also been blamed as a cause of the decline.

Ecosystem degradation and alterations Physical changes brought about by human-induced activities on adjacent lands and direct human involvement with coastal habitats lead to destruction and loss of spawning and breeding grounds for fishes (Ukwe et al., 2006). An example of this is the loss of mangrove forest along the coast of West Africa due to human activities. Also, pollution from human activities such as industrial and agricultural waste and erosion from adjacent lands contribute toward eutrophication and aquatic weeds (Ukwe et al., 2006). Also most of Africa's large coastal cities discharge voluminous amounts of untreated effluents, organic biodegradable material into "sewers, canals, and rivers." These pollute or contaminate marine areas, which in turn affect fish.

Lack of capacity Some African countries lack the capacity to exploit the resources of the EEZs. As a result some African countries sign agreements with other countries to exploit their fisheries resources. While these agreements bring in revenue to the coastal states, in the long run they may not be in the interest of the coastal states since these foreign fleets have been identified as sources of overfishing and over exploitation. This also makes it difficult for coastal countries to address issues of sustainability and building their own capacity in fisheries, since the final destination of revenue from the agreements has also been questioned (Trouillet et al., 2011).

Competition with foreign industrial fleets African fishers have to compete with foreign industrial fisheries fleets in their own fisheries. A large part of this is due to illegal, unregulated, and unreported (IUU) fishing. It is estimated that this costs about $1 billion a year. According to Ndiaye (2011, p. 376), IUU vessels "remain at sea for years without calling at port, while they transship their catch to other vessels and rotate their crew at sea." He goes on to report that these are very well organized fleets that conduct activities at sea with impunity because the coastal countries do not have what it takes to stop or arrest them.

Conflicts at sea One result of the increasing competition at sea is escalation of conflicts at sea. In a recent study of the problem in Senegal, DuBois and Zografos (2012) identify four manifestations of these conflicts—destruction of artisanal fishing equipment; gunwale to gunwale violence; on-board nonviolent conflict, and on-board violent conflict. In the first case, fishing equipment may be damaged and lost completely following an encounter. In the second case, fishermen may throw bottles, stones, and other objects from deck at each other, or spray high-pressure water at each other. In the third case, artisanal fishermen may board industrial fishing vessels and refuse to leave; or industrial fishermen may prevent artisanal fishermen from returning to their vessels. On-board violent conflicts include attempts to set vessels on fire; threats to throw a fisherman overboard, and threats with weapons such as knives and guns. Senegal seems to have most of these conflicts, and it has been reported that between January 2006 and May 2010 about 96 incidents totaling about €153,283 were reported.

According to Dubois and Zografos (2010), these conflicts are in turn triggered by a number of events. For example, both artisanal and industrial fishing vessels may converge on the same fishing grounds. Sometimes, artisanal fishing vessels may follow industrial vessels because the latter has better fish-detecting technologies. In other cases, industrial fishing vessels may seek areas where artisanal vessels have congregated on the assumption that the place is rich in fish. Illegal entry of industrial fishing vessels into the exclusive zones for artisanal fisheries is another source of conflict. The by-catch of industrial fishers is also another source of conflict since it usually attracts artisanal fishers causing them to steer dangerously close to industrial fishers. Traditional mechanisms for resolving some of these disputes exist, but again as Bois and Zagrafos (2010) have shown, these are breaking down because of dishonesty. At the same time, formal dispute resolution through the court system does not work well especially for the artisanal fishers against the industrial fishers.

Governance of fisheries The competition and illegal fishing has generated a lot of governance problems for Africa's fisheries (Standing, 2008). In particular, one of the ways to regulate the competition and illegal fishing has been fisheries access agreements, which grant access to foreign fishing fleets for a fee. Theoretically, a portion of the fees collected is supposed to go into programs that will benefit the local community, but in practice these agreements have become a real source of contention. On the one hand, they have been blamed for causing over-fishing and depletion of the fisheries. On the other, the use of the fees has been called into question. Specifically, the terms of some of the agreements and lack of transparency as to the final destination of collected fees have raised questions of corruption. Thus, conflicts of interests in which influential politicians are also owners or part-owners of fishing fleets make it difficult for objective evaluation of access agreements and enforcement of the terms. Similarly, embezzlement of fees and direct bribe payment for illegal fishing have all also become common. In 2008, for example, Standing (2008) reported that an audit into such fees in Guinea revealed loss of millions of euros due to fraud and theft. Bribe payments between illegal fishing fleet and government officials or between boat owners and government officials have often slowed and sometimes completely thwarted legal actions.

An important group that is often missed out in governance at the local level is the middleman, yet as Crona et al. (2010) have shown in their study of artisanal fisheries in East Africa, these middlemen perform two critical roles. First, middlemen could provide a means of regulating the local fisheries. Middlemen can use their close links with local fishermen to communicate management strategies to local fishermen better than any other group. Second, the credit systems provided by middlemen could offer a way for more government support. Yet, such group is most often ignored when it comes to fisheries governance matters. Other challenges of fisheries governance include compartmentalization of fisheries management whereby there is no coordination between artisanal and industrial fisheries, for example.

Problems and Issues of Culture Fisheries

Lack of facilities and limited attention Africa's culture fisheries have several problems and issues, which vary across the continent. However, the most common is lack of available suitable-sized seed stock (deSilva, 2003). Part of the problem is lack of facilities to cultivate the seed or fish fry (newly hatched fish). Another problem is limited harvest time, even where successful culture fisheries exist. This in turn could be due to lack or dearth of capital expenditure for improvement, and lack of proper marketing strategy (de Silva, 2003).

Sometimes natural factors do contribute to the poor nature of facilities. In Nigeria, for example, the shoreline is not favorable to marine culture fisheries because the shelf is too shallow. There is very high wave action along the coast that offers no protection (Anetekhai et al., 2004). Where conditions favor potential sites, those sites tend to be oil well and other operations sites. Apart from this, the coastal areas tend to be polluted due to concentration of industries in the area.

In many countries aquaculture has been an appendage of capture fisheries, with no clear legislative and strategic framework. The result is that not much attention has been given to the sector as a viable economic activity.

The role of aid In a review of international aid for fisheries in Africa, Cunningham and Neiland (2010) show that in spite of the substantial aid African fisheries had received from 1973 to 2001 many African fisheries have performed poorly. They attribute this in part to the fact that most of the aid had been toward fisheries policy instead of development, and in part to the inability of these projects to build on sound theoretical foundations of fisheries economics. The result is there has been more focus on production but less focus on improving the value of fish resources. While this may be the case and while it is true that Africa cannot depend on foreign aid to develop its fisheries, the truth is the proportion of international aid given to Africa pales in comparison to other regions during the same period. Indeed, the data on which Cunningham and Neiland et al (2005) based their analysis show that China, and five other Asian countries (Indonesia, Bangladesh, Philippines, India, and Sri Lanka) received a total of $5.363 billion in fisheries development aid compared to the $4.6 billion received by the whole of Africa over the same period.

Summary

As an economic activity, fisheries predate colonial Africa. However, like all economic activities in Africa, colonialism impacted the activity both positively and negatively. On the negative side, it introduced new doctrine of open access that set aside the local methods of conservation of fishery resources and introduced some new species that led to the extinction of some native species. On the positive side, colonialism brought improvements in technology and the institution of scientific studies of fisheries. The early postcolonial period saw efforts by many coastal states to establish large-scale fishing industries. However, management problems, and broad macroeconomic problems thwarted these efforts and during the difficult times of the 1980s and 1990s, many of these efforts collapsed. Since that time, there have been new attempts to revive the industry and expand its scope to include culture fisheries from both African governments and international organizations. Today, about 5.7 million Africans directly derive their livelihood from fisheries while indirectly the number is estimated to be about 10 million. These people are engaged in both capture and culture fisheries, with majority in the latter. The existence of continental shelves and the convergence zones of cold and warm currents have created natural conditions for some rich fisheries around the continent. Leading in this area is the East Central Atlantic Ocean, which accounts for 54% of the total fisheries production of Africa. This region is followed by the South Eastern Atlantic Ocean, the Southwest Indian Ocean, and the Mediterranean fisheries. Inland capture fisheries are also important especially in the Nile and Great Lakes Region.

Culture fisheries are relatively small but they are growing. Most of the farms are in brackish and freshwater environments and are dominated by small-scale farms that use extensive and semi-extensive system of feeding. Only about 3% of culture fisheries occur in marine environments.

Africa's fisheries face a number of problems. Marine capture fisheries face problems of depletion, capacity, conflicts, and management, while culture fisheries' problems include lack of facilities, lack of attention, and lack of funding. There are several ongoing efforts to deal with these problems but these will need more commitment than mere lip service.

FORESTRY

Forestry, in its broad use, involves the growing, harvesting, and management of woodlands and their associated resources for the benefit of society. This benefit includes environmental, social, cultural, and economic. Environmentally, forests protect watersheds, regulate streamflow, reclaim degraded land, conserve biological diversity, and they also help maintain the global atmospheric carbon balance. In the social sense forests also serve as laboratories for many educational and scientific activities, and recreation outlets. Economically, forests provide a wide range of products including food, medicine, fuelwood, building materials, furniture, decorations, tools, weapons, and industrial raw materials that can also be traded for foreign exchange. In turn all these products create jobs.

In this section, we consider forestry as a primary economic activity. We begin with the evolution and development of forestry in Africa. This is followed by Africa's contemporary forestry. The final section focuses on problems and issues in Africa's forestry.

Evolution and Development of African Forestry

Precolonial Period

There is very little research on forestry in precolonial Africa. However, from historical accounts we can surmise that Africans learned to use wood for such things as fire, construction, and tools several thousands of years ago. These accounts also indicate that the harvesting of trees, either on a small or large scale, was either a derived or joint demand but not an end in itself. Thus, tree harvesting was undertaken to clear the land for agriculture, or a building after which the wood was used for fuel or in the building structure. There was very little in terms of replanting but more of management. This was seen in the system of farming especially in the shifting cultivation system that allowed vegetation to recover through natural processes. Another evidence of forest management was the existence of numerous sacred groves, or nature preserves, which in many areas were considered as shrines of deity.

Among some ethnic groups such as the Zaramo of Tanzania, forests were also feared places since they were considered to be the abode of both ancestral and malevolent spirits who had healing powers for the people (Sinseri, 2003). Trees in the sacred groves or forests were protected. Extraordinary large trees and trees with hollows and huge buttresses were considered sacred and abodes of spirits and were not to be cut. In some parts such as Zimbabwe, fruit trees were also sacred and required the chief's permission before cutting such trees and commercial exploitation of such trees was also prohibited (Mapedza, 2007).

However, sacred groves were not the only method of conservation. In Southern Africa, some of the local chiefs also preserved what in modern terms can be seen as national parks. These restrictions however did not prevent people from using the forest and woodlands. Forests and woodlands provided useful raw materials for building, fuel, tools, weapons, food, meat, clothing, and traded goods. The use of fire to clear the land for agricultural purposes was practiced by all ethnic groups on the continent. However, in North Africa the use of fire was prohibited in the range lands as well as the oases (Davis, 2007).

The two forces that have influenced land cover from time immemorial played an important role in the state and condition of forestry in precolonial Africa. The first was population growth and increasing human activities and the second was natural changes in climatic factors. Population growth brought more land under settlements and agricultural activities, while climatic changes caused desiccation and drove people away to more livable areas in some cases. In other cases, people were forced to make changes in the use of land intensively or extensively by becoming nomads. Exploitation of natural resources and for that matter forest had to be approved by local authorities. Forested areas were mostly under government with many traditional usage rights.

Colonial Period

Colonial forestry policies were primarily initiated to serve European needs. However, the policies were justified by a narrative that blamed native Africans for causing deforestation and desertification because of their primitive and wasteful ways of agricultural practices. In North Africa, the French, in 1830, blamed the native Africans and Arab nomads for turning what was the "grand granary" of the Roman Empire, into a desolate land (Davis, 2007). In South Africa, Wilson (1865) asserted that the Orange River previously contained more water flow than was being observed. Basing himself on the accounts of drought by missionaries, Wilson (1865, p. 117) wrote:

> Is there a cause besides the interior position of the country and the natural aridity of the soil, which occasions the advance of drought? We assert that there is, and that the

effects of that originating cause are controllable, and indeed to a large extent preventable. . . . . The natives have for ages been accustomed to burn the plains and to destroy the timber and ancient forests.

This story was repeated in East Africa and West Africa. The colonialists' responses to these beliefs were predictable. The French wanted to return Algeria and their other North African protectorates to the "grand granary." For the British and the Germans, the solution was to adopt policies that had been successful in other colonies, especially India, and in Europe, respectively. Laws appropriating land from the natives, and limiting or criminalizing traditional uses of the land for forestry and grazing were passed. Among these were the Algerian forest laws of 1831, 1838, 1885, and 1903 all of which were extended to Tunisia and Morocco; the Forest Act of South Africa in 1888; the forest laws of German East Africa in 1893; the East Africa Forestry Regulations of 1902, the East African Forestry Ordinance of 1905, and the Zimbabwe Forest Acts of 1929, 1930, 1936, and 1949 (Mapedza, 2007).

These laws had varying degrees of severity. For example, the 1903 forest law in Algeria established collective punishment and sequestration of property for forest crimes; prohibited pastoralists from grazing their animals on their migratory journeys to the Tell region; and provided for the establishment of reforestation areas in the name of public good. In South Africa, the act converted an area of 478,867 acres or a third of the Cape Colony into state reserved forests, and gave the government the authority to swap public land for private land in the interest of the public good. From 1895 to 1965, new areas came under protection at the average rate of one a year. In Algeria, Morocco, and Tunisia, all forests were placed under the colony and no communal forests were allowed. In German East Africa, these laws were so provocative that when in 1904 and 1905 two new reserves at Nminangu, and near Kilwa were established, the natives took up arms in the Maji Maji rebellion (Sinseri, 2003; see Chapter 2). The passing of these laws either came with or were followed by establishment of forest service departments. Among these were the forest service departments of Algeria established in 1838, Tunisia in 1889, Southern Nigeria in 1909, South Africa in 1910, Ghana and Sierra Leone 1911, and Morocco in 1913.

The colonial governments also embarked on reforestation projects, especially to make up for the forests that had been "destroyed" by the natives of the continent. These began long before the official colonial period in Africa. The most famous of these projects were the eucalyptus projects of Algeria and South Africa. In South Africa, the species *eucalyptus globulus* or the blue gum was first planted around 1828 and by mid-19th century the species had spread all over South Africa as European migration to South Africa grew. It was the hope that the tree would provide timbers and poles for housing, trade, railroads, and mining (Bennett, 2010). Moreover, Europeans hope to turn South Africa into an image of Europe—a region of farms dotted with trees and forests. However, most of the trees died of drought and fungus and had to be replaced by plantations of other species in the late 19th century in the Cape Colony (Bennett, 2010). During the early 1900s, eucalyptus plantations spread throughout Kwa-Zulu Natal, the Transvaal, and the protectorates of Lesotho and Swaziland. Following the Native Land and the Forest Act of 1913 large plantations of eucalyptus came to occupy former grazing lands of native Africans, and often employed displaced Africans as plantation workers at meager wages.

The French effort to reforest Algeria with eucalyptus between the 1860s and 1870s was not successful. The plant was highly promoted by both private and public agencies as a solution to the dry environment of Algeria. It would not only provide windbreaks for other crops, but also wood for construction and fuel, and a source of income. Thousands of hectares of eucalyptus were planted. However, by the late 1870s, it was becoming clear that the high hopes of eucalyptus would not be realized. In particular, it was found that the tree splintered easily making it hard to cut and mill. It also soaked so much water that it ended up drying up the soil causing stunted growth of other plants. By the 1890s, the euphoria about eucalyptus was all gone.

The appropriation of forest land however did not stop exploitation of the forest, which occurred in two forms—logging for timber wood and conversion to industrial or cash crop agriculture. In North Africa, exploitation of the forest began concurrently with the French occupation since the army of occupation greatly needed wood. Commercial timber concessions however began in 1846 and by 1861 102,000 ha were under business concessions with another 145,000 ha in requisition (Davis, 2007). By the end of World War I, settlers controlled 2,123,288 ha of land, out of which 194,159 were forests (Davis, 2007).

In West Africa, rapid growth of cocoa, coffee, tea, and palm oil cultivation required mass clearance of the rain forest since it was impossible to grow these crops efficiently under the forest (Oliphant, 1940). Apart from this, the complex land tenure system made it necessary to appoint chiefs as indigenous forest conservators sharing power with the forest departments. In Nigeria, as well as the Congo Basin, the growth of the automobile industry led to the demand for tires, which in turn led to demand for latex. At that time the best source of latex was the *Funtumia elastica,* which was native to West Africa. This of course led to massive scale of exploitation of the rubber tree with devastating consequences. Early efforts to control the situation by encouraging replanting proved futile. However, it was only after the emergence of the Para rubber tree in South America as the main source of latex producer that the Forest Ordinance of 1908 made conservation more effective. In Ghana, colonial forestry resulted in a string of forest reserves till 1939. However, from 1940 to 1953, World War II and the independence movement opened the door to timber exploitation. Thus, with all the regulations to establish forest reserves, by 1940, foresters had become concerned about the depletion of such valuable timber species as mahogany from both West and East Africa (Oliphants, 1940). In Tunisia, millions of olives in the Sfax area were cultivated under the pretext of reforestation. By independence in 1956, there were more than 6,000,000 olive trees and 2.3 million fruit trees in the Sfax area compared to about 350,000 in 1881 (Davis, 2007). Similarly, in Southern Rhodesia (Zimbabwe), timber exploitation for mining, railway and commercial tobacco growing was already taking place. However, it was only when the construction of the Bulawayo-Victoria Falls Railway (1902–1904) exposed the ineffective and uneconomic ways of logging, that the colonial government appointed the Simms Commission to make recommendations on the exploitation and management of forest resources in the colony (Mapedza, 2007).

Last but not the least colonial governments also began some forestry research. In West Africa, the French conquest in the 1890s coincided with the beginning of drier conditions, locust attacks, and a devastating famine over large areas of the Sahel from 1900 to 1903. These events made the French question "whether they were part of a long-term trend and desert expansion or not?" (Van Beusekom, 1999). There were two views. One view blamed natural forces—wind, heavy rain, and erosion; the other view held mostly by foresters blamed human action—"irresponsible and unthoughtful behavior of herders who were burning large expanses and then letting their cattle consume newly sprouted fresh grasses before the vegetation had the chance to mature" (van Beusekom, 1999, p 203). This prompted a second mission to French West Africa in 1924, which attributed the deforestation to four human-related factors—land clearance by farmers; brush firing by farmers, herders, and hunters; cattle grazing; and wood cutting by public services. The report noted that deforestation could be repaired and it was time to act since it posed a threat to agriculture. It was this report that eventually led to the establishment of the Office Du Niger (see Chapter 11).

During the mid-1930s, the desiccation and desertification debate intensified in all the colonies due to several factors including the Dust Bowl event in the United States and severe soil erosion in southern and eastern Africa. One of the leading experts in this debate was E. P. Stebbing, a British forester who drew attention to the threat of an advancing Sahara Desert. Stebbing's alarm prompted a joint Anglo-French mission to Northern Nigeria and Niger in 1936–1937, but Stebbing's views of invading sand was not supported though the mission agreed that deforestation had human causes (van Beusekom, 1999).

Postcolonial Period

Reforestation project in apartheid South Africa
Postcolonial Africa inherited the colonial forest conservation laws as well as the conflicts they entailed. In South Africa, reforestation by state plantations expanded rapidly during the 1940s and provided a legal basis for the Nationalist government of 1948 to institute its apartheid policy. More Africans were thus removed from their land to be replaced by state and privately owned eucalyptus plantations (Bennett, 2010). However, just as it had happened in Algeria, the ecological problems with eucalyptus began to reveal themselves. In particular, environmentalists charged that instead of encouraging rain and promoting stream flow, eucalyptus had rather increased aridity of the land. Farmers also became concerned about the plant's desiccation effects on the land. Continued criticisms forced the South African government to authorize more research into the hydrological effects of eucalyptus plantations. Opposition to eucalyptus plantation grew stronger from the 1950s. In neighboring Lesotho, foresters stopped planting eucalyptus in the 1960s. In South Africa, the move to stop growing the tree came to conflict with the expanding trade in pulpwood in the 1970s and 1980s. In postapartheid South Africa, eucalyptus plantation has been a controversial subject: some people see it as a colonial legacy, while others see it as a source of employment for Africans (Bennett, 2010),

Exploitation and deforestation
Other African countries had tensions as well but of a different kind. Many African countries inherited substantial tracts of lands under government protection as forest reserves and national parks from colonial administration. The tension was whether or not these reserves should be opened up for commercial exploitation to aid economic development. African countries opted for exploitation to boost export earnings. Foresters were trained to staff the forest institutes that had been left by the colonial administration while new forestry institutions were created. In Anglophone Africa, these training came through forestry

departments in Monrovia established in 1959, University of Ibadan, Nigeria (1963), Makerere University, Uganda (1970), and the University of Dar es Salaam, Tanzania (1973). In Francophone Africa, most of the training was done in Belgium, France, and Canada until 1975 when forestry programs were established in both Cameroon and Cote d'Ivoire (Temu et al., 2006). Much of the training was geared toward the use of forest as an economic resource so the curricular was much more akin to those in developed countries and emphasized the four areas of silviculture, inventory, harvesting, and wood technology (Temu et al., 2006).

In 1976, 14 African countries accounting for over 75% of Africa's tropical natural forests, felt the need to cooperate in forestry matters by forming the African Timber Organization (ATO). African countries also participated in the UN-led efforts to provide a structure for tropical timber trade that started its formal meetings also in 1976. Subsequent meetings following the international group culminated in the first International Tropical Timber Agreement (ITTA) in 1983. The agreement came into full force in 1985. Among other things, the agreement established forests as strategic resource for development, provided for the expansion of international trade in tropical timber and established the International Tropical Timber Organization (ITTO) to oversee related matters (Flejzor, 2005).

The profitability of many of the timber concessions were hindered by high transportation cost, poor management, and fluctuating world prices, but governments held on since they needed the concession fees and stumpage (Giles-Vernick, 1999). The deterioration of the economies of many countries in late 1970s through the 1980s placed severe strains on the forest sector. In particular, forest products became the target of the stabilization program of the structural adjustment programs (SAPs) to generate revenue. Much pressure was brought to bear on governments to put in a new investment code and welcome new foreign logging companies (Owusu, 1998.). Apart from this, the retrenchment in government employment that resulted from SAPs increased informal activity in the sector, namely artisanal logging, particularly chainsaw milling (Wit and van Dam, 2010).

At the same time, logging practices and rapid growth of the international environmental movement raised serious concerns about the rain forest of which Africa had the second largest area. Alarmed at the rate of "destruction" of the forest, activists pointed to the potential ecological disaster that could befall humanity if the tropical rain forest disappeared. FAO (1993) estimated that from 1980 to 1990, Africa lost 4.1 million ha or 0.7% of forest cover per year due to logging and agriculture.

From deforestation to sustainable management The 1980s also brought the global concerns about the environment in general and tropical forests, in particular, to a head. The concerns had started with the UN Conference on Human Environment in Stockholm in 1972. While the conference focused on whether economic development was detrimental to the environment, there were many other issues that would later on morph into major concerns. In 1978, the FAO noted an absence of inventory of worldwide tropical forests and as a result launched a tropical forestry inventory project. The project exposed high levels of loss of tropical forests worldwide including, of course, those in Africa (Auld, 2014). In a joint report issued on World Conservation Strategy in 1980, the International Union of Conservation of Nature (IUCN), the World Wildlife Fund (WWF), and the UN Development Program (UNDP) elaborated the problems with conservation of tropical forests and called for international action to solve the problems. In 1983, FAO created an action program for management of tropical forests (Auld, 2014). A year later in 1984, a UN Commission on the Environment and Development was created to look into pressure from population growth, modern technology, and resource consumptions, under the Chair of Gro Harlem Brundtland, then Prime Minister of Norway. In 1985, a report called *Tropical Forests: A Call to Action* was released by a joint task force of World Resources Institute, the World Bank, and the UNDP. The need to stop deforestation was gaining more momentum with a great deal of interest from international governmental and nongovernmental agencies and these began to initiate several forest programs for African countries. One of these programs was the Tropical Forests Action Program (TFAP), which was initiated in 1985 to stop deforestation, while meeting local and national forest needs, with funding from the World Bank and the FAO. The program worked through the development of National Forestry Action Programs (NFAPs). African countries adopted several strategies including agroforestry to boost fuelwood production and replanting. Agroforestry was particularly stressed in the Sahelian countries, while replanting was widely promoted throughout the continent.

However, the results of this program and the ones before it were mixed. The FAO estimated that by 1997 about 6 million ha of forest had been planted of which 1.5 million ha were in North Africa, and 1.2 million ha were in South Africa (FAO, 1997). At the same time, Tutu and Akol (2009) reported that TFAP was more about forest development than curbing deforestation. In addition, it did not stress enough the needs and rights of local people, and nothing was being done about the growing population that was also occurring in those countries (Tutu and Akol, 2009). With respect to SAPs targeting the forests, the removal of all government subsidies and devaluation of currencies that were required by SAPs eroded the purchasing power of the poorest population segments in the countries undertaking the program. The increasing outcry against the failure and devastating effects of the SAP eventually forced the World Bank to abandon the program (FAO, 1997).

In the meantime, the drumbeat about the state of tropical forests continued in the release of the Brundtland Report or *Our Common Future*—in 1987, which lamented the slow reaction of governments around the world to the precarious situation of the world's natural environment, and outlined a series of strategies to address the problem, including the concept of sustainable development. By the time the United Nations Conference on Environment and Development (UNCED) convened in 1992, in Rio de Janeiro, Brazil, exclusive focus on the conservation of tropical forests by foreign governments, organizations, and activists was creating tension between the advocates for conservation and the countries that had the resources including those of Africa. These countries argued that it was their sovereign rights to exploit the resources within their national boundaries for development just as developed countries had done to build up their economies.

Capacity building for forest management The UN Conference on the Environment and Development in Rio de Janeiro in 1992 had significant impacts on Africa's forestry, especially in the regions that had substantial forest resources—namely Central Africa. According to Eba'a Atyi et al (2013) the only Ministry of Forestry in Central Africa was in Gabon. In the other countries, forest-related matters were dispersed under various government departments of agriculture. The role of forests as a strategic resource for development was taken for granted; existing laws made no regards for local community; and concession management was very rare.

All that changed after the Earth Summit in Rio de Janeiro in 1992. Ministries of Forestry were established in all the countries and these new departments began to take forest matters seriously.

One of the earliest needs for conservation and sustainable management efforts was to build capacity in forestry research, information sharing, and management of forest resources. According to Temu et al. (2006), Eastern and Southern African countries had established an Advisory Committee on Forestry Education in 1970 but the initiative died in 1988. Two networks that stepped up to fill this gap were the African Forest Research Network (AFORNET) and the Forestry Research Network for Sub-Saharan Africa (FORNESSA). AFORNET is a joint project between the African Academy of Sciences (AAS) and the Swedish Development Cooperation Agency, Department of Research (Sida/SAREC). The AAS in 1991 established Capacity Building in Forestry Research in Africa (CBFR) with the financial support from SAREC. The purpose was to build critical mass of young forest scientists who could make significant contribution to sustainable forest management in Africa (IUFRO-SPDC, 1998). In a subsequent symposium held in 1994 by the AAS and several international organizations, the idea of African Forest Network was floated and after several meetings the network was established in 1999.

FORNESSA was launched in 2000 as a nonprofit, nongovernmental scientific organization open to forestry professionals. It has three subregional networks—the Association of the Forestry Research Institutions of Eastern Africa (AFREA) with 10-member countries, the Forest Research Network of the Conference Responsible for African Agricultural Research (CORAF) with 20 member countries and the Southern African Development Community (SADC) with 14 member countries. The main goal is "to support and strengthen forestry research in order to contribute to the conservation, sustainable management and utilization of forest resources in Sub-Saharan Africa" (http://fornis.net/about). An evaluation of the CBFR program in 2007 indicated that while the program had been successful in training a number of African scientists, it was not enough, and that more support was needed from the international community.

Community-based forest management (CBFM) Community management of forest was enshrined in traditional African society before colonialism. Governance systems under colonial and postcolonial period almost took that away in many African societies. Another effect of the Rio 1992 conference was to restore this through its community-based forest management, which was part of Agenda 21 and Forest Principles. African countries began taking steps toward this. Essentially, this approach to forest management involves decentralization and devolution of authority to manage forests from the Central government to the local level, as well as all the institutional support needed to be successful. Its goal is sustainable development—which is conservation of forests, while meeting economic development needs of the local community. For Africa, the case for this was theoretically sound and it included (1) recognition of local rights, (2) benefit to the local community, (3) use of indigenous knowledge of forest management, (4) better integration of local expertise, interests, and well-being, (5) promotion of ideals of democratic governance, (6) income generation for the local community, (7) elimination of gender discrimination, and (8) proper stewardship of the environment (FAO, 2012).

CBFM began to spread across the continent in various forms throughout the 1990s. In most of the countries, they were just pilot projects but in Tanzania, Namibia, and Gambia there were more serious efforts. For example, Tanzania moved about 4.1 million ha of forest to CBFM. Namibia had 465,000 ha of woodland managed by 13 community groups with another 6 million ha of forestland waiting legalization by 52 community groups, by 2011. In Gambia, 10% of the forest land was under CBFM by 2008.

In 1999, the FAO in collaboration with the Gambia held the first CBFM conference in Africa, in Banjul. Two FAO publications followed in 2011 and 2012. The first one focused on market analysis and development (FAO, 2011) and the second one on institutional structures, policies, and legislation need for successful community-based forestry (FAO, 2012). The FAO (2012) report, which also contained a review of CBFM, however, stated that none of the CBFM projects in Africa have been properly monitored long enough to yield any meaningful learning experiences. On the positive side the claim is that some CBFM have stopped deforestation, increased reforestation, empowered previously vulnerable people, and improved livelihoods of local residents. At the same time, CBFM has been a source of conflict between and among communities; they have also increased deforestation due to weak local institutions and conflicts with government over cost and revenue sharing (FAO, 2012; USAID, 2013).

The Brazzaville Process, the Yaoundé Declaration, and the Liberian Timber Ban
Several collaborative efforts supported by international funding were also initiated. The Conference on the Central African Moist Forest Ecosystems (CEFD-HAC) also known as the **Brazzaville Process** was launched in 1996 to provide a forum for consultation, information sharing, and strengthening of regional cooperation in Central African forest matters. Member countries included Burundi, Cameroon, Gabon, Equatorial Guinea, Central African Republic, Congo Republic, DRC, Rwanda, and Sao Tome and Principe. It was initially supported by the World Conservation Union (IUCN). At its third meeting in 2000, the organization focused on joint management, strategic plan for conservation and sustainability of the Congo Basin, and a timber certification system based on ITTO indicators (FAO, 2001).

Also in 1997, the SADC launched a Forestry Sector Policy and Development Strategy to address a six-point program focusing on training and education, resources and assessment, research, management, industries, marketing, and protection.

Another initiative that was adopted by the Heads of State of Cameroon, Chad, Congo Republic, Equatorial Guinea, and Gabon at their 1999 Summit on the Conservation and Sustainable Management of Tropical Forests in Yaoundé, Cameroon, was the **Yaoundé Declaration**. This declaration called for harmonized national policies; participation of rural population and the private sector in forest decisions; antipoaching and unsustainable exploitation measures; funding for sustainable forest management; and international cooperation. To translate the declaration into action, the group established *la Commission des Forêts d'Afrique Centrale* (COMIFAC) (Koyo, 2006).

Following the Johannesburg UN Conference on Environment and Development in 2002 (Rio +20), the Congo Basin Forest Partnership (CBFP) was created under the leadership of the United States by 29 governmental and nongovernmental organizations. The purpose of this partnership is to work for improvements of communication and coordination of programs, projects, and policies on sustainable management of the Congo Basin. The US led the group from 2003 to 2005 after which France took over. Another group that was set up in 2005 was the network of Central African forest—environment training institutions (RIFFEAC) with support from France the EU (Koyo, 2006).

In Liberia, however, warring factions used the forest and other natural resources to finance their long-protracted civil war. In 2003, the United Nations Security Council took the unprecedented action to impose sanctions on Liberian timber as a way to stop the 14-year-long civil war. The Security Council lifted the ban in 2006.

Timber Certification In 1993, the Forest Stewardship Council (FSC) was founded to promote "environmentally, socially, and economically sustainable management of world forests by identifying good forest practices and certifying actors that follow such practices" (Grant et al., 2013). In addition, the FSC established a chain-of-custody (CoC) procedure that tracks a product from its original source through its production and handling to final purchase by the consumer. The certification is based on whether forest owners and management are following FSC's 10 principles. These include law compliance, workers' rights, indigenous people's rights, community relations, community relations, environmental values and impacts, monitoring and assessment, high conservation values, and implementation of management activities (Grant et al., 2013). The first company certification in Africa was issued to Wajima Cameroun in 2006, and the first community management certification was issued in 2009 to Mpingo Conservation and Development Initiative, a Tanzanian NGO. By mid-2013, certification of 7,508,343 ha of forest in 11 African countries had been completed; and a total of 47 forest-management CoC had been issued (Grant et al., 2013). The FSC has made several efforts to improve the certification process including a special protocol for small and medium forestry enterprises that face greater obstacles in achieving certification. It has also made efforts to recognize the concerns of indigenous communities.

In 2003, the EU launched its timber procurement policies using the Forest Law, Governance and Trade's Voluntary Partnership Agreement (FLEGT/VPA). These laws are similar to the FSC process but with one major difference. The FLEGT/VPA emphasizes not only legality as to how the timber was obtained but whether the timber was obtained in sustainable manner. The Congo Republic was the first country to sign a VPA agreement with the EU in 2009. Other countries that have followed suit are Cameroon, Central African Republic, DRC, and Gabon.

In spite of these, timber certification in Africa has been very slow. Data from the Forest Stewardship Council (FSC) website Africa indicates that in Africa had only 3.5% of global certified forest (FSC Africa 2018). In a study of Ghana's timber industry, Carlsen et al (2012) report that the reasons for this slow uptake include perceived high cost of compliance, unpredictable business environment due to weak state-led governance, the tendency to see certification as another form of colonialism, the perception of certification as another form of regulatory interference and not feeling responsible for forest maintenance.

The 2008–2009 Recession and Africa's Timber Market All these agreements have not sheltered Africa's forest products from the vulnerability of world market changes. The 2008–2009 recession hit Africa's timber market hard, largely as a result of the collapse of the housing market in Southern Europe and lack of foresight to engage in long-range planning. This sent ripple effects through the timber industry beginning with inability to maintain prices, which in turn led to a drop in purchases, and subsequently large layoffs in the industry. In Cameroon 3,300 workers were laid off; in Central African Republic, it was 428 workers, in Cote d'Ivoire 6,000 workers were laid off with another 6,000 temporarily unemployed, while in the DRC the number is unknown (Karsenty et al., 2010). This forced many governments that depended on timber tax to review their policies. In Gabon, for example, the government was contemplating a ban on log exports by 2010. As a result, companies decided to rush log exports toward the end of 2009 no matter the price.

Africa has about 16% of the world's forest. The main threat to this forest is the loss of forested areas. About 59% of this was attributed to conversion of closed forest into small-scale permanent agriculture, followed by large-scale permanent agriculture (12%). Apart from this, the natural forest still remains the main source of wood on the continent. The estimates of the size of this loss have varied over the years. However, the FAO (2010) reported a decline in loss from 4.0 million ha in 1990–2000 to 3.4 million ha during 2000–2010.

Since 1992, the international and local concerns about this resource have produced new forestry laws and codes, decentralization, and national forest program facilities, and institutions in African countries. As we have seen, Central Africa in particular has become home to so many institutions concerned directly and indirectly with forest management, including Conservation of Central Africa's Forest Ecosystems (ECOFAC), Central African Regional Program for the Environment (CARPE), Forest Policy Network for Central Africa (REPOFBAC), and the Conference of Minsters in Charge of Forests in Central Africa (COMIFAC). In addition, the Inter-State Committee for drought Control in the Sahel (CILSS) the ATO and NEPAD all have forest-related programs. Yet, as Kowero et al. (2006) reported these have produced far less commensurate results relative to the efforts. The reasons for these will be discussed in a later section.

Production of Forest Products

Types of Forest Products

Generally speaking, there are two types of forest products—wood forest products (WFP) and nonwood forest products (NWFP). WFP can be classified as raw or semiprocessed forest and processed wood products. Raw or semiprocessed wood products consist largely of roundwood, which refers to all wood removed for use as fuel wood (wood fuel) or industrial purposes (industrial roundwood). According to FAO, wood fuel includes all wood removed and used for cooking, heating, and power generation as well in charcoal production. Industrial roundwood includes sawlogs, veneer, pulpwood, and other industrial roundwood, which is wood used for poles, pilings, posts, fencing, pit props, tanning, distillation, and match blocks. Processed wood products consist of pulp and paper products and charcoal. In contrast, nonwood forest products (NWFP) include food (bush meat, mushrooms, fruits, nuts, animal fodder), construction materials and fiber (bamboo, rattan, palm leaves), and medicines and other healthcare products (herbs, tree barks).

The main resource base of forest products is forest. In Africa this can be further categorized as tropical and subtropical or temperate forests. These are respectively referred to as nonconiferous and coniferous in the FAO database. Majority of Africa's forest products are however derived from the nonconiferous.

In 2015, about 90% of the 737.7 million cubic meters of roundwood produced in Africa were from nonconiferous wood. We limit our discussion in the rest of this chapter to WFP with particular reference to roundwood production. Charcoal production will be discussed in Chapter 13 as part of energy production, while pulp and paper products will be discussed as part of manufacturing in Chapter 14.

Forest Products Operations

The primary forest products operation is logging and two types of logging activities occur in Africa—industrial logging and artisanal logging. Industrial logging uses increasingly sophisticated logging machines that require fewer and fewer labor. The latest of these machines can cut whole logs from the ground twist the tree horizontally, strip it of all its branches while cutting it into logs of required or appropriate lengths. This is usually how large logging corporations operate. The logs are then loaded off onto trucks and sent to saw mills where they are semi-processed into sawn wood and lumber, plywood, and veneer, or logs, and sent to ports for export.

In contrast, artisanal logging is a small-scale operation using less-sophisticated technologies. Traditionally, this type of logging involved the use of axe and pit saw mills. The loggers used axe to fell the trees and haul them onto trucks for shipment. To make boards out of the logs, pit saw mills were used, by which logs were laid on a pit and two men one standing on top of the long and the other in the pit, pull a long saw up and down sawing the long into boards. During the 1980 and 1990s, however, chain saw was introduced in many African countries first to cut down big trees on farms, but later they became more useful for artisanal logging. Environmental concerns of logging led to a ban of artisanal logging in some countries such as Ghana or more restrictions as in the DRC. However, the enforcement of these policies have been very weak, and artisanal logging is very strong—accounting for about 70% of the total log exports in Africa (Wit and van Dam, 2010).

Production Trends

Total roundwood In 1961, Africa's total roundwood production was approximately 277 million cubic meters. This was about 11% of world production. In 2015, the FAO estimated the world's total roundwood production to be about 3.7 billion cubic meters. Of these, Africa produced about 737.7 million cubic meters or 20%. Out of the total African production, 96% was from the nonconiferous species while the remaining 4% were from coniferous species. By sector, 90% of the total was wood fuel, while the remaining 10% was industrial roundwood. Between the two time periods, the percentage increase in production fluctuated between a high of 0.4 and 4.4% (Figure 12.8). The largest and smallest percentage gains were both recorded in the 1960s—from 1963 to 1964, and from 1965 to 1966, respectively. With the exception of 1982 and 1986, the 1980s recorded the most consistent percentage increases—an average of 2% or more. In contrast, since 2000, the average percentage increase has been 0.7%. Since 1970s, no less than 61% of total roundwood production has come from 10 countries. Table 12.4 shows Africa's top 10 countries in total roundwood production in 2015, which included Ethiopia, DRC, Nigeria, Uganda, and Ghana.

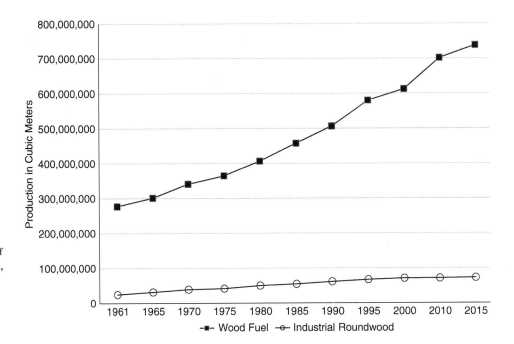

FIGURE 12.8 Composition of total roundwood production, 1961–2015.
Source: FAO 2017 FAOSTAT Forestry Production and Trade. www.fao.org/faostat/en/#data/FOWood Fuel Production

In 1961, an estimated 252.2 million cubic meters of wood fuel were produced in Africa. This accounted for 16.8% of world total production. In 2015, an estimated 665.5 million cubic meters of wood fuel were produced in Africa. This accounted for 35.7% of the world's total wood fuel production. Between the two time periods, wood fuel production has steadily increased with the highest rates of increase, more 3% per annum, occurring from 1982 to 1994. From 1996, the rate of production increase fell below 2%. Africa has accounted for about 24.2% of the world's wood fuel production from 1970 to 2015. The top 10 producing countries in 2015 accounted for 67% of Africa's total wood fuel production (Table 12.4). They included Ethiopia, DRC, Nigeria, Ghana, and Uganda.

Industrial Roundwood Industrial roundwood consists of sawlogs and veneer logs, pulpwood, and other industrial woods or woods that are used for purposes other than fuel. In 1961, the FAO estimated that Africa produced 24.6 million cubic meters of industrial roundwood, which was 8.9% of Africa's total roundwood production. As already mentioned in 2015, Africa produced a total of 72.2 million cubic meters, but this was only 4% of the world total production. Africa's industrial roundwood production did not only grow slowly between 1961 and 2015, but fluctuated substantially. Production increased at an average rate of 2.1 in the 1970s and 2.4% in the 1980s, while the 1990s and 2000s recorded the lowest rates—1.3% and 0.23% respectively. About 68% of the total production in 2015 came from 10 countries including South Africa, Nigeria, DRC, and Uganda.

Trend data on sawlogs and veneer production in Africa is spotty and must be used with caution. In 1961, Africa's total sawlogs and veneer production was estimated as 11.2 million cubic meters. In 2015, total production reached 33.3 million cubic meters. Once again, Nigeria and South Africa dominate Africa's sawlogs and veneer production accounting for 35% of the total production in 2015 (Table 12.4). Other important producers were Cameroon, Cote d'Ivoire, Uganda, Gabon and Ghana. Production of other industrial roundwood is again concentrated in about

| TABLE **12.4** | | | | | | | | |

Roundwood Production in 2015

Total roundwood			Wood fuel			Industrial roundwood		
Country	Production (000 m³)	%	Country	Production (000 m³)	%	Country	Production (000 m³)	%
Ethiopia	111,109	13.4	Ethiopia	108,174	16.3	S. Africa	13,528	18.7
DRC	87,137	12.4	DRC	82,526	12.4	Nigeria	10,022	13.9
Nigeria	75,310	7.6	Nigeria	65,288	9.8	DRC	4,611	6.4
Uganda	46,771	5.8	Ghana	44,018	6.6	Uganda	4,333	6.0
Ghana	46,628	4.7	Uganda	42,438	6.4	Cameroon	3,571	4.9
Kenya	27,432	4.6	Kenya	26,400	4.0	Ethiopia	2,935	4.1
Tanzania	26,957	3.6	Tanzania	24,119	3.6	Tanzania	2,838	3.9
South Africa	25,557	3.2	Egypt	17,740	2.7	Ghana	2,610	3.6
Mozambique	18,708	3.2	Mozambique	16,724	2.5	Cote d'Ivoire	2,356	3.3
Egypt	18,008	3.1	Sudan	15,211	2.3	Gabon	2,200	3.0
Top 10	483,618	65.6	Top 10	442,639	66.5	Top 10	49,004	67.9
Rest of Africa	254,099	34.4	Rest of Africa	222,904	33.5	Rest of Africa	23,270	32.1
Total	737,717	100.0	Total	665,543	100.0	Total	72,174	100.0

Sawlogs and veneer			Other industrial roundwood		
Country	Production (000 m³)	%	Country	Production (000 m³)	%
Nigeria	7,600	22.6	DRC	4,282	15.4
South Africa	4,677	13.9	Ethiopia	2,917	10.5
Cameroon	3,071	9.1	Nigeria	2,400	8.6
Cote d'Ivoire	2,356	7.0	Uganda	2,120	7.6
Uganda	2,213	6.6	Tanzania	1,844	6.6
Gabon	2,200	6.5	Mozambique	1,504	5.4
Ghana	1,860	5.5	Malawi	1,200	4.3
Congo	1,537	4.6	Burkina Faso	1,098	3.9
Rwanda	962	2.9	Zambia	1,080	3.9
Tanzania	785	2.3	Angola	1,050	3.8
Top 10	27,261	81.0	Top 10	19,495	70.0
Rest of Africa	6,059	19.0	Rest of Africa	8,307	30.0
Total	33,320	100.0	Total	27,801	100.0

Source: FAO 2017 FAOSTATS Forestry Production and Trade http://www.fao.org/faostat/en/#data/FO

10 countries. Since 1970s, these countries have produced between 60 and 70% of Africa's total output. In 2015, the most important countries included DRC, Ethiopia, Nigeria, and Uganda (Table 12.4).

Most of Africa's industrial roundwood is produced as sawlogs and veneer logs, while the rest are pulpwood and other industrial roundwood. In 2015, sawlogs and veneer logs accounted for 46%, pulpwood accounted for 16%, while other

TABLE **12.5**

Industrial Roundwood Production in 2015 by Sector and Tree Species

Sector	Coniferous	Nonconiferous	Total	sector (%)	Nonconiferous content (%)
	Cubic meters	Cubic meters	Cubic meters		
Sawlogs + Veneer logs	7,566,388	26,054,105	33,620,493	45.8	77.5
Pulpwood	4,146,344	7,913,855	12,060,199	16.4	65.6
Other industrial roundwood	580,820	27,221,020	27,801,840	37.8	97.9
Total	12,293,552	61,188,980	73,482,532	100	83.3

Source: FAO 2017 FAOSTATS Forestry Production and Trade http://www.fao.org/faostat/en/#data/FO

industrial roundwood accounted for 38% (Table 12.5). By tree species, tropical trees accounted for 83.3% of the total production, 98% of other industrial round-wood, 66% of pulpwood, and 78% of sawlogs and veneer (Table 12.5).

Problems and Issues in Africa's Forestry

Problems and issues facing Africa's forestry have been well documented by many research works (e.g., Bourguignon, 2006; Koweri et al., 2006). What we present here is a summary of these problems. Among these are dry forest threats, low government priority, overreliance on foreign aid, low value addition, weak governance, illegal logging and corruption, forest conflicts, climate change, and the role of NGS.

Population Growth, Urbanization, and the Dry Forest

Population growth and rapid urbanization still pose threats to Africa's forests. The situation is made worse by the fact that most of the foci of the population growth and urbanization are occurring in the dry forest zone, which constitutes about 29.2% of the Africa's total forests. Given the fragile environmental conditions of this zone, population growth and rapid urbanization are putting pressure for more land for buildings as well as agricultural activities.

Low Government Priority and Overreliance on Foreign Capital

All areas of African forestry seem to depend too much on foreign capital. A report by FAO (2003) on 24 African countries showed that in 1999 the average public expenditure in those countries was $0.82 per hectare. Of these about 45% was from external sources. Thus from domestic sources the average funding was only $0.45 per hectare. The report also showed that most countries had low public expenditures on forestry but high levels of international funding. Apart from this, the report also identified that fee charges were low, and that in some cases it was deliberate policy by governments to subsidize wood consumption. Some countries had forest funds but they were not of much help. This meant that much of the funding for forestry had to come from outside. This situation has not changed and this makes the sector too dependent on external sources. It also deprives the abilities of the countries to develop a home-grown forest products industry. It appears that every project or program that has been initiated and has been funded from external sources, each of which comes with its own agenda. The result is that there seems to be no coherent strategy or direction as to what kind of forest product economy to create.

Low Value Addition

Related to the low domestic capital is the dearth of value addition in the range of forest products that Africa produces. Until about the 1980s, the majority of Africa's forest products were in the form of raw logs. A few countries such as Ghana, Nigeria, and South Africa had saw mills and plywood factories but these were all state-owned, and with respect to Ghana and Nigeria they were poorly managed and became victim of mismanagement. This does not only lead low foreign earnings but it also makes Africa's forest products industry very vulnerable to external shocks.

Weak Governance

As we have already seen, there have been numerous attempts to improve governance in forestry, with the key eye on community-based forestry. However, many African countries are yet to fully implement this. As we saw earlier, the system is still fraught with incomplete devolution of power and lack of supporting mechanism for the grassroots. Weak governance continues to plague African countries. This makes it difficult to enforce forest protection laws, illegality, and detrimental activism. Other related problems are poor salary of civil servants that breed environment for bribery and corruption; unstable fiscal policies and legislation—tax policies and other cumbersome governmental regulations that present major obstacles to potential investors.

Illegal Logging and Corruption

An off-shoot of the weak governance is the problem of illegal logging activities and corruption. Activists' organizations such as Greenpeace, Global Witness, and Independent Observer of Forest Control (REM) have documented illegal activities and corrupt practices of natural resources logging activities particularly in DRC. These practices include companies going over the amount of concession granted, multiple companies using the same license, companies whose activities do not show up in official government documents, and those operating under different names. In other cases, government officials come out stating that certain companies have been banned without any follow-up documentation. In other cases, supposedly seized logs tend to disappear (Greenpeace, 2013).

Similarly, Global Witness (2013) reported on the abuse of provision of the EU in four timber-producing countries—Cameroon, DRC, Ghana, and Liberia. Given the focus of the EU's FLEGT Action Plan on large corporations, and the stringent nature of the requirements, both logging companies and African governments have resorted to the use of permits that were originally reserved for artisanal or small-scale logging companies—to give them access to timber on lands identified for development projects. In Cameroon, these permits are called small titles permit; in DRC they are artisanal logging permits; in Ghana they are salvage permits, while in Liberia they are called private use permits (Global Witness, 2013). The report shows that in each of these countries, these permits have become "shadow permits" by which corrupt government elites and officials secretly grant the permits to large logging corporations to enable them gain access to larger areas of forests. Specifically, the report says that in Cameroon the Minister of Forestry granted many of the permits to large companies while pretending that he was regulating them. In DRC, dozens of artisanal logging permits were given to foreign companies from 2010–2012. In Ghana, the Forest Services Commission issued about 400 permits to large companies while assuring the EU and civil society that the matter was under control. In Liberia, large companies have used these permits to buy up about 25% of the country's forests (Global Witness, 2013).

Forest Conflicts

Another off-shoot of weak governance is forest conflicts. Ejigu (2006) identifies these conflicts as state–state, state–community; community–community; timber-induced conflicts, and conflicts arising from forests as rebel havens. State–state conflicts arise by virtue of the fact that African forests tend to have transnational boundaries. An example of this occurred between DRC and Uganda in 2003 (Ejigu, 2006).

State–community conflicts occur when state policies prevents communities from gaining access to forest resources they used to have. Examples are when communities are removed from forest areas in order to protect the forest or communities are left in the middle of a protected forest area. The most outrageous of these conflicts is when state actions tend to benefit logging interest of private companies. An example of this was when timber militias were employed alongside the police and the army to intimidate communities in Liberia in 2003 (Ejigu, 2006).

Community–community conflicts arise when competing access to limited forest resources leads to or contribute to explosive conflicts among them. Sometimes this may occur along ethnic lines. Part of the causes of the Rwanda genocide has been attributed to this kind of conflict between the Hutus and the Tutsis (Ejigu, 2006).

Another conflict that occurs and has become common in Africa is community–wildlife conflict, where communities living near forest reserves, nature preserves, or national parks often struggle with wildlife to keep their farms as well as young ones safe. Conflicts arising from logging mostly derive from illegal logging that have been already discussed. A final source of conflict is where forests are used as safe havens for rebel groups. An example of this occurred in Northern Uganda where the use of the forest as a haven by the rebel group, the Lord Resistance Army, caused the Ugandan Army to clear substantial portions of the forest (Ejigu, 2006). These conflicts create problems for effective management, proper use of forests to generate economic activity, and negatively impact the forest ecosystem.

Climate Change and the Role of NGOs

The IPCC WGII Fourth Assessment Report (2007) shows Africa as the continent that is most vulnerable to climate variability and change. The report predicts that by 2020 about 75–250 million people in Africa would face severe water problems; agricultural production would decline due to decrease in cropland area, crop productivity, and cropping season all as a result of climate change (Kowero, 2011).

Some observers see the role of some NGOs as one of the problems facing forestry in Africa. In particular, Bourguignon (2006) faults NGO campaigns against companies regarding environmental issues. He says that they have been very successful in EU and North American markets against companies that deal with those markets, to the disadvantage of companies that deal in Chinese and Indian markets, where environmental issues are low priority. The idea of buying wood from Africa leads to deforestation is gathering momentum, but it is devastating to Africa and hurting the very people that they are supposed to protect. It is also hypocritical in the sense that deforestation of Africa if anything at all is not new. It began during the colonial period where Africa's forests were exploited for raw material and cultivation of cash crops that still feed Western demands and needs.

Summary

Forestry is a small but an important industry in Africa. It was part of Africa's precolonial economy. The value of forests was manifested in various forest management strategies including sacred groves and the shifting cultivation and bush fallow systems of agriculture. During the colonial period, the role of forestry in the economy was promoted in several activities including reforestation and passing of forest legislations that appropriated all forest lands to the colonial powers and in many places blocked African access to the forest. At the same time, some foundations of the modern forestry industry—logging for commercial gain were established. Direct logging for timber as well as expansion of agriculture into the so-called cash crops led to massive deforestation across the continent. Finally, the colonial period also brought some scientific study of the forest and several regional research institute devoted to silviculture, tree harvesting, and wood technology were established across the continent. The countries that had considerable forest resources sought to exploit the resource for economic development during the early postcolonial period. They also began training forestry professionals, some of them in their own higher education institutions and others in institutions outside. The focus of much of this training was more toward exploitation of forest resources than conservation and development. Unsuccessful efforts to get a better deal for timber trade at the United Nations in 1976 led a number of African countries to form the ATO. However, the global concern about the environment and especially about tropical rain forest during the late 1970s through the early 1990s brought many changes to forestry in Africa. For the first time, forest matters went beyond just logging but it also emphasized sustainability and community involvement. Numerous programs for forest management, community forestry, capacity building, training and networking, and sustainability were established. Many of them focused on Central Africa, and many of them with overlapping goals, duplication, and redundancy.

All these were supposed to enhance the forest products industry. However, the industry has still remained essentially the producer of primary products—namely roundwood, which largely consists of industrial roundwood. There is very little in the value-added sector of the industry especially a complete absence of pulp and paper products.

In addition to the low value addition in the industry, there are a host of other problems that face the sector. These include threats of deforestation due to population growth, rapid urbanization, and climate change, weak governance, low government priority, too much dependence on foreign capital, illegal activities and corruption, conflicts, and too much interference from donors and NGOs. These problems are not insurmountable but it is clear that corruption of government officials needs to be fixed first before any policies and programs can work.

Postreading Assignment

A. Study the Following Concepts

brackish water	Demersals	land-based aquaculture	semi-intensive aquaculture
Brazzaville Process	extensive aquaculture	mariculture	Yaoundé Declaration
Capture fisheries	freshwater aquaculture	marine-based aquaculture	
culture fisheries	intensive aquaculture	Pelagics	

B. Discussion Questions

1. Compare the areas you thought had viable fisheries ground with what you learned from this chapter. Do you see any difference? What have you learned?

2. Compare the reasons you gave as to why those areas had important fisheries operations with what you learned from this chapter. What difference do you see?

3. Are you aware of any important fish species that are caught in Africa? If so name them and where they are caught. Compare your answer now with what you wrote down before reading the chapter.

4. What problems do you think face fisheries operations in Africa? And what do you think can remedy these problems? Compare your answer now to the same question before you read the chapter.

5. Do you think forestry is an important economic activity in Africa? If so why and if not why? Compare your answer to the one you had before. What did you learn?

6. On the basis of your answer try and identify all African countries for which you think forestry will be a viable economic activity. Compare your answer now with the one before. What did you learn?

7. Debate the view that the activities of environmental and donor organizations in Africa's forestry sector are causing more harm than good.

References

Allsopp, W. H. 1997. "World Aquaculture Review: Performance and Perspectives." In Pikitch, E. K., Huppert, D. D., and Sissenwine, M. P. (Eds.) *Global Trends: Fisheries Management.* Bethesda, MD: American Fisheries Society, pp. 153–165.

Akyeampong, E. 2007. "Indigenous Knowledge and Maritime Fishing in West Africa: The Case of Ghana." In Bon, E. K. and Hens, L. (Eds.) *Indigenous Knowledge Systems and Sustainable Development-Relevance for Africa.* Tribes and Tribals Special Volume 1 New Delhi: Kamla-Raj Enterprises, pp. 173–182.

Anonymous, 2002. "Subsistence Fishing in South Africa: Implementation of the Marine Living Resource –(Act)." *The International Law of Coastal Management.*

Anetekhai, M. A., Akin-Oriola, G. A., Aderinola, O. J., and Akintola, S. L. 2004. "Steps Ahead for Aquaculture Development in Sub-Saharan Africa—The Case of Nigeria." *Aquaculture* 239: 237–248.

Anko, E. O., and Eyo, A. 1984. Fisheries Development in Nigeria with Special Reference to Cross River State. In: 16th Annual Conference of the Fisheries Society of Nigeria (FISON), 4-9 November 2001 ,Maiduguri, Nigeria, pp. 303–312.

Atta-Mills, J., Alder, J., and Sumaila, U. R. 2004. "The Decline of a Regional Fishing Nation: The Case of Ghana and West Africa." *Natural Resources Forum* 28: 13–21.

Auld, G. 2014. *"Constructing Private Governance: The Rise and Evolution of Forest, Coffee, and Fisheries Certification".* New Haven, CT: Yale University Press.

Baddyr, M, and Guenette, S. 2001 "The Fisheries of the Atlantic Coast of Morocco 1950-1997." In Guenette, S., Christensen, V., and Pauly, D. (Eds.) *Fisheries Center Research Reports* 9 (4): 191–205.

Bennett, B. M. 2010. "The El Dorado of Forestry: The Eucalyptus in India, South Africa, and Thailand, 1850–2000." *International Review of Social History.* 55 (S18): 27–50.

Branch, G. M., and Clark, B. M. 2006. "Fish Stocks and Their Management: The Changing Face of Fisheries in South Africa." *Marine Policy* 30: 3–17.

Bagumire, A., Todd, E. C. D., Muyanja, C., and Nasinyama, G. W. 2009. "National Food Safety Control Systems in Sub-Saharan Africa: Does Uganda's Aquaculture Control System Meet International Requirements?" *Food Policy* 34: 458–467.

Bourguignon, H. 2006. "Enhancing the Role of Forests in the Socio-Economic Development of Forested African Countries." *International Forestry Review* 8(1): 126–129.

Brummett, R. E., and Williams, M. J. 2000. "The Evolution of Aquaculture in African Rural and Economic Development." *Ecological Economics* 33: 193–203.

Brummett, R. E., Lazard, J, and Moehl, J. 2008 "African aquaculture: Realizing the Potential." *Food Policy* 33: 371–385.

Carlsen, K., Hansen, C. P., and Lund, J. F. 2012. "Factors Affecting Certification Uptake—Perspectives from the Timber Industry in Ghana." *Forest Policy and Economics* 25: 83–92.

Campredon, P., and Cuq, F. 2001. "Artisanal Fishing and Coastal Conservation in West Africa" *Journal of Coastal Conservation*, 7(1): 91–100.

Clark, J. D. 1960. "A Note on Early River-Craft and Fishing-Practices in South-East Africa" *The South African Archaeological Bulletin*. 15(59): 77–79.

Crean, K., and Geheb, K. 2001. "Sustaining Appearances–Sustainable Development and the Fisheries of Lake Victoria." *Natural Resources Forum*. 25(2001): 215–224.

Crona, B., Nystrom, M., Folke, C., and Jiddawi, N. 2010. "Middlemen, a Critical Social- Ecological Linking Coastal Communities of Kenya and Zanzibar." *Marine Policy* 34: 761–771.

Cunningham, S., and Neiland, A. E. 2010. "African Fisheries Development Aid." In Lead, D. R. (Ed.) *The Political Economy of Natural Resource Use: Lessons for Fisheries Reform*. Washington, DC: The International Bank for Reconstruction and Development / The World Bank, pp. 21–44.

Dadzie, S. 1992. "An Overview of Aquaculture in Eastern Africa." *Hydrobiologia* 232: 99–110.

Davis, D. K. 2007. *Resurrecting the Granary of Rome: Environmental History and French Colonial Expansion in North Africa*. Athens, Ohio: Ohio University Press.

Degan, A. A., Hoorweg, J., and Wangila, B. C. C. 2010. "Fish Traders in Artisanal Fisheries on the Kenyan Coast." *Journal of Enterprising Communities: People and Places in the Global Economy* 4(4): 296–311.

De Silva, S. S. 2003. "Culture-based Fisheries: An Underutilised Opportunity in Aquaculture Development." *Aquaculture* 221: 221–243.

DuBois, C., and Zografos, C. 2012. "Conflicts at Sea between Artisanal and Industrial Fishers: Inter-sectoral Interactions and Dispute Resolution in Senegal." *Marine Policy* 36: 1211–1220.

Ejigu, M. 2006 "Land, Forests, Insecurity, and Conflicts" *International Forestry Review* 8(1): 72–77.

Eba'a Atyi, R., Assembe-Mvondo, S., Lescuyer, G., and Cerutti, P. 2013. "Impacts of International Timber Procurement Policies on Central Africa's Forestry Sector: The Case of Cameroon." *Forest Policy and Economics* 32: 40–48.

Fakoya, K. A., Sukefun, O. B., Owodeinde, F. G., Akintola, S. L., and Adewolu, M. A. 2009. "Emerging Research Priorities for the Aquaculture Sector in Sub-Saharan Africa – A Case Study of Nigeria." *Aquaculture, Aquarium, Conservation & Legislation International Journal of the Bioflux Society* 407–424.

Flejzor, L. 2005. "Reforming the International Tropical Timber Agreement." *RECIEL* 14(1): 19–27.

Food and Agriculture Organization 2012. *Guidelines for Institutionalizing and Implementing Community-based Forest Management in Africa*. Accra: Food and Agriculture Organization of the United Nations Regional Office for Africa.

Food and Agricultural Organization 1997. *State of the World's Forests 1997*. Rome: FAO.

Food and Agriculture Organization 1993. *Forest Resources Assessment 1990: Tropical Countries*. Rome: FAO.

Forest Steward Council Africa 2018. "Forest For All Facts and Figures." https://africa.fsc.org/en-cd Accessed October 14, 2018.

Gabriel, U. U., Akinrotimi, O. A., Bekibele, D. O., Onunkwo, D. N., Anyanwu, P. E. 2007. "Locally Produced Fish Feed: Potentials for Aquaculture Development in Sub-Saharan Africa." *African Journal of Agricultural Research* 2(7): 287–295.

Geheb, K. 1997. *The Regulators and the Regulated: Fisheries Management, Options, and Dynamics in Kenya's Lake Victoria Fishery: A Thesis submitted to the University of Sussex in partial fulfilment of the requirements for the Degree of Doctor of Philosophy*.

Giles-Vernick, T. 1999. "We Wander Like Birds: Migration, Indigeneity, and the Fabrication of Frontiers in the Sangha River Basin of Equatorial Africa." *Environmental History* 4(2): 168–197.

Global Witness 2013. *Logging in the Shadows: How Vested Interest Abuse Shadow Permits to Evade Forest Sector Reforms*. London: Global Witness.

Gordon, D. 2003. "Technological Change and Economies of Scale in the History of Mweru-Luapula's Fishery." In Jul-Larsen, E., et al. (Eds) *Management, Co-Management or No Management? Major Dilemmas in Southern African Freshwater Fisheries 2. Case Studies*. Rome: FAO, pp. 165–179.

Graham, M. 1973. *A Natural Ecology*. Manchester: Manchester University Press.

Grant, J. A., Balraj, D., and Mavropoulos-Vagelis, G. 2013. "Reflections on Network Governance in Africa's Forestry Sector." *Natural Resources Forum* 37: 269–279.

Greenpeace 2013. "Cut it Out: Illegal Logging in the Democratic Republic of Congo (DRC)."

Gribble, J. ND. "Pre-Colonial Fish Traps on the South Western Cape Coast, South Africa."

Harms, R. 1989. "Fishing and Systems of Production: The Precolonial Nunu of the Middle Zaire." *Cahiers des Sciences Humaines* 25 (1–2): 147–158.

Isaacs, M., and Hara, M. 2007. "Transformation in the South African Fishing Industry and Its Ability to Redistribute Fishing Rights." *American Fisheries Society Symposium* 49: 507–603.

IUFRO-SPDC Coordinator's Report. 1998. "IUFRO-SPDC in its 15th Year: New Challenges." *IUFRO News* 27 (1): 16-17.

Karsenty, A., Bayol, N., Cerutti, P., Ezzine des Blas, D., and Forni, E. 2010 "The 2008–2009 Timber Sector Crises in Africa and Some Lessons for the Forest Tax Regime." *International Forestry Regime* 12(2): 172–176.

Kowero, G. 2011 "The Dry Forests of sub-Saharan Africa: Making the Case." In Geldenhuys, C. J., Ham, C., and Ham, H. (Eds.) *Sustainable Forest Management in Africa: Some Solutions to Natural Forest Management Problems in Africa*, pp. 2–21.

Kowero, G., Kufakwandi, F., and Chipeta, M. 2006. "Africa's Capacity to Manage Its Forests: An Overview." *International Forestry Review* 8(1): 110–117.

Koyo, J. P. 2006. "Partnership and Forest Dialogue in Central Africa." *International Forestry Review* 8(1): 138–141.

Kudhongania, A. W., Twongo, T., and Ogutu-Ohwayo, G. 1992. "Impact of the Nile Perch on Fisheries of Lakes Victoria and Kyoga." *Hydrobiologia* 232: 1–10.

Lazard, J., Lecomte, Y., Stomal, B., Weigel, J.-Y. 1991. Pisciculture en Afrique subsaharienne: situations et projets dans des pays francophones,propositions d'action, Ministere de la Coope´ration et du Developpement, Paris.

Mapedza, E. 2007 "Forestry Policy in Colonial and Postcolonial Zimbabwe: Continuity and Change." *Journal of Historical Geography* 33: 833–851.

McCracken, J. 1987. "Fishing and the Colonial Economy: The Case of Malawi." *The Journal of African History* 28(3): 413–429.

Ndiaye, T. M. 2011. "Illegal, Unreported and Unregulated Fishing: Responses in General and in West Africa." *Chinese Journal of International Law* 373–405.

Neiland, A. E., Chimatiro, S., Khalifa, U., Ladu, B. M. B., and Nyeko, D. 2005. "Inland Fisheries in Africa: Key Issues and Future Investment Opportunities for Sustainable Development." *A Technical Review Paper for NEPAD Fish For All Summit*, Abuja, Nigeria.

NEPAD Inland Fisheries http://www.nepad.org/foodsecurity/fisheries/inland-fisharies (accessed 10 February 2014).

Nevin, T. 2005. "Africa's Fishing Industry Faces Crises." *African Business* (November) 28–30.

Nunan, F., Luomba, J., Lwenya, C.,Yongo, E., Odongkara, K., and Ntambi, B. 2012. "Finding Space for Participation: Fisherfolk Mobility and Co-Management of Lake Victoria Fisheries." *Environmental Management* 50: 204–216.

Ogutu-Ohwayo, R., and Balirwa, J. S. 2006. "Management Challenges of Freshwater Fisheries in Africa." *Lakes & Reservoirs: Research and Management* 11: 215–226.

Oliphant, J. N. 1940. "The Future of Forestry in Tropical Africa." *Journal of the Royal African Society* 39(156): 428–263.

Owusu, J. H. 1998 "Current Convenience; Desperate Deforestation: Ghana's Adjustment Program and the Forestry Sector." *The Professional Geographer* 50(4): 418–436.

Payne, A. L. 1976. "The Exploitation of African Fisheries." *Oikos* 27: 356–366.

Plug, I., Mitchell, P., Bailey, G. 2010. "Late Holocene Fishing Strategies in Southern Africa as seen from Likoaeng, Highland, Lesotho." *Journal of Archaeological Science* 37: 3111–3123.

Pillay, T. V. R. 1994. *Aquaculture Development.* Oxford, UK: Fishing News Books.

Roberts, R. 1981. "Fishing for the State: The Political Economy of the Middle Niger Valley." In Crummey, D., and Stewart, C. C. (Eds.) *Modes of Production in Africa: The Precolonial Era.* Beverly Hills: Sage Publications, pp. 175–203.

Sinseri, T. 2003. "Reinterpreting a Colonial Rebellion: Forestry and Social Control in German East Africa, 1874–1915." *Environmental History* 8(3): 430–451.

Standing, A. 2008. "Corruption and Commercial Fisheries in Africa." U4 Brief No. 23.

Temu, A. B., Okali, D., and Bishaw, B. 2006. "Forestry Education, Training and Professional Development in Africa" *International Forestry Review* 8(1): 118–125.

Thorpe, A., Whitmarsh, D., Ndomahina, E., Baio, A., and Kemokazi, M. 2009. "Fisheries and Failing States: The Case of Sierra Leone." *Marine Policy* 33: 383–400.

Trouillet, B., Guineberteau, T., Bernardon, M., and LeRoux, S. 2011. "Key Challenges for Maritime Governance in West Africa: Fishery-based Lessons from Guinea and Mauritania." *Marine Policy* 35: 55–162.

Tutu, K., and Akol, C. 2009 "Reversing Africa's Deforestation for Sustainable Development." In Yanful, E. K. (Ed.) *Appropriate Technologies for Environmental Protection in the Developing World.* Springer Science and Business Media, pp. 25–33.

Ukwe, C. N., Ibeb, C. A., and Sherman, K. 2006. "A Sixteen-country Mobilization for Sustainable Fisheries in the Guinea Current Large Marine Ecosystem." *Ocean & Coastal Management* 49: 385–412.

Van Beusekom, M. M. 1999. "From Underpopulation to Overpopulation: French Perceptions of Population, Environment and Agricultural Development in French Soudan (Mali), 1900–1960." *Environmental History,* 4(2): 198–219.

Walker, L. E. 2002. "Engendering Ghana's Seascape: Fanti Fish Traders and Marine Property in Colonial History." *Society and Natural Resources,* 15: 389–407.

Wilson, J. F. 1865. "Water Supply in the Basin of the River Orange or Gariep, South Africa." *The Journal of Royal Geographical Society of London.* 35: 106–129.

Wit, M., and van Dam, J. (Eds.) 2010. *Chainsaw Milling: Supplier to Local Markets.* Wageningen: Tropenbos International.

CHAPTER 13

Mineral and Energy Production

Minerals and energy are two other important sectors of Africa's extractive economy. For its part, mineral production is important in Africa's economy because it does not only provide employment for millions of people, but it also features prominently in Africa's trade with the rest of the world. For that reason, mineral production also brings to Africa important foreign exchange earnings. Energy production also serves as a source of employment for thousands of Africans, and a source of foreign exchange for those tradable energy resources. In addition, both mineral and energy are important inputs to manufacturing industries, and therefore, have the potential of promoting industrialization.

In this chapter, the focus is on the mineral and energy production sectors of Africa's economy. Specifically, the chapter highlights the evolution and development of mineral and energy production in Africa, the factors that affect them as economic activities, recent and current production trends, and problems and issues facing the sectors as well as what is being done about them. The chapter is divided into two broad sections. The first section deals with mineral production and the second with energy production. However, we begin with some prereading assignments.

PREREADING ASSIGNMENTS

1. Make a list of all minerals that are produced in Africa along with at least one country that produces the most of each mineral.

2. What role do you think minerals and energy production played in the colonization of Africa?

3. In what ways do you think colonial governments promoted mineral and energy production in Africa?

4. What do you think are some of the main issues facing mineral and energy production in Africa?

5. How can these problems be solved?

MINERAL PRODUCTION

If Africa is mostly seen as the world's economic development backwater, in the area of mineral wealth, and particularly strategic minerals, it stands either on top of the world or among the leaders. Thus, after almost two centuries of domestic and foreign exploitation and in some cases complete plunder, Africa still has 99% of the world's chromite reserves, 85% of its platinum, 81% of its phosphates, 70% of its tantalite, 68% of its cobalt, 54% of its gold, 50% of its vanadium, and 32% of its bauxite. Africa produces 70% of the world's platinum, 60% of its diamonds, 54% of its cobalt, 28% of its palladium, and 16% of its bauxite. It has the largest reserves of manganese as well as considerable quantities of petroleum, zinc, and lead (USGS, 2011).

Minerals rank first on the list of export of 28 countries, second in 13 countries, and third in 12 countries (Table 13.1). Minerals account for more than 50% of the value of exports of Algeria, Angola, Botswana, Chad, Congo Republic, Democratic Republic of Congo, Equatorial Guinea, Eritrea, Gabon, Ghana, Guinea, Mauritania, Namibia, Niger, Nigeria, and Zambia. Mineral production is the leading foreign exchange earner for about eight African countries—Angola, Botswana, DRC, Namibia, South Africa, Tanzania, Zambia, and Zimbabwe. Mineral production also provides substantial numbers of employment although this has declined over the years due to

TABLE 13.1

The Role of Mineral Production in African Economies

Country with mineral as number one export	Country with mineral as number two export	Country with mineral as number three export
Algeria	Algeria	Algeria
Angola	Angola	Angola
Botswana	Botswana	Botswana
Burkina Faso	DRC	DRC
Cameroon	Ghana	Gabon
Central African Republic	Guinea	Guinea
Chad	Libya	Liberia
DRC	Mali	Libya
Congo	Namibia	Namibia
Egypt	Sierra Leone	Senegal
Equatorial Guinea	South Africa	South Africa
Eritrea	Sudan	Togo
Gabon	Zambia	—
Ghana	—	—
Guinea	—	—
Libya	—	—
Mauritania	—	—
Mozambique	—	—
Namibia	—	—
Niger	—	—
Nigeria	—	—
Sierra Leone	—	—
South Africa	—	—
Sudan	—	—
Tanzania	—	—
Western Sahara	—	—
Zambia	—	—
Zimbabwe	—	—

Source: World Trade Organization and CIA World Fact book.

technological improvements and reforms. The highest employment numbers are found in the Southern African Development Community (SADC) region, where mineral production accounts for 5% of the total employment (Twerefou, 2009).

Evolution and Development of Mineral Production in Africa

Precolonial Period

Mineral production in Africa predates the colonial period. From the time of Ancient Egypt to the eve of the colonial invasion, various groups of Africans learned to look for and use minerals. Indeed, the growth of some of Africa's most important civilizations, such as the Western Sudanese Empires and the forest states of West Africa, was made possible in part because of their mineral wealth. Gold was also very prominent in the Asante Empire of modern Ghana, Great Zimbabwe Kingdom (Ofosu-Mensah, 2011; Hammel et al., 1999) and in Ethiopia. Africans also exploited iron ore and developed very sophisticated forms of products. The people of North Africa were among the earliest users of iron. From here, and through traders, iron use spread and reached West Africa by the 7th century BC. Iron ore mining was also widespread in Southern Africa (Hammel et al., 1999). Precolonial Africans also mined and used copper in the areas where they abounded. The most important of these areas was modern-day Zambia and DRC, which still hosts the world's largest copper belt. Other minerals that Africans were already mining before colonialism were tin in Nigeria and the DRC, diamonds in Ghana, and Sierra Leone, as well as salt especially in the Western Sudanese empires of the Sahel and Sahara. The prevailing mining technology limited most of the activities to alluvial deposits and underground deposits that were not too deep. Thus, mining methods included diving and scavenging river beds, open mining and underground mining (Hammel, 1999). Mineral products obtained through these methods were traded widely across the continent and beyond.

The arrival of Europeans from the 15th century onward initially did not change mining operations in Africa. While Europeans were fortunate to find some minerals such as gold along the coast, most of the mineral production was in fact hidden from them deliberately. The chiefs who were custodians of this wealth did not want Europeans to know the source of their wealth. Even so, Africans traded some of their gold with Europeans. Christopher (1984) estimated that during the early 1700s, the British, Dutch, and the Danes secured about 250,000 pounds of gold a year from the West African coast. However, European exploration of Africa's interior soon after the slave trade changed things. In particular, European intrusion into the strongholds of African kingdoms led to a series of wars that eventually exposed the sources of the mineral wealth, setting the stage for the colonial period.

Colonial Period

The colonial period established European control over mineral production in Africa. Developments in South Africa set the standard for colonial mining enterprise for the rest of the continent. Colonial mining activities began in South Africa with the exploitation of copper deposits in the Namaqualand about the 1850s (Christopher, 1984). However, it was diamonds and gold that raised the profile of colonial mining in South Africa. Thus, the discovery of alluvial diamonds along the Vaal River in 1867 and in the intrusive kimberlite pipes to the south of it in 1870 brought over 30,000 individual prospectors to South Africa to seek their fortune. Big Hole, the center of this rush, was renamed Kimberley after the British Secretary of State for the Colonies (Christopher, 1984). The thousands of prospectors staking claims as in the previous mineral rushes elsewhere became problematic partly because of uncontrolled digging and partly because the geologic formation that contained the diamonds required more sophisticated technologies and more capital, which were beyond the individual prospector. This required consolidation of resources, and through the efforts of Cecil Rhodes, one of the many British prospectors, the thousands of claims consolidated to about 98, by mid-1870, and to two companies by 1889. The two were DeBeers headed by Rhodes, himself, and Kimberley Mines, headed by his rival Barney Barnato (Kesler, 1994). Eventually, De Beers bought out Kimberley Mines and went on to become the most powerful name in the diamond industry.

The significance of this development was that it introduced two types of mining to Africa. The mining system of precolonial Africa became **artisanal**, while the corporate-based mining system became **industrial or large-scale mining**. It also introduced the company compound or town (Christopher, 1984), a segregated housing unit aimed at confining the mines' black workers, who were suspected of smuggling the diamonds out of the mines. Other diamond discoveries include those of Jagersfontein and Koffiefontein in the 1870s and Cullinan near Pretoria in 1902, and South West Africa (Namibia) in 1908. In 1905, the Premier Mine near Pretoria. produced the Cullinan, the largest diamond (3,025 carats) (Christopher, 1984).

Gold mining had begun in 1873 around Pilgrim Rest and Baberton in the Boer Republic of Transvaal but it was not lucrative and the activity was short-lived. In 1886, however, gold was discovered in the Witwatersrand (the Rand), a ridge in southern Transvaal, and this produced another major rush of individual prospectors to the area. To avoid the haphazard development that had occurred around diamond mining, the Transvaal government stepped in to plan for the potential population influx. A series of towns were laid out from Krugersdorp to Gemiston, with Johannesburg as their center and most important (Christopher, 1984). The difficult geological formations in which the gold occurred also led to the introduction of shafts and the use of cyanide to extract the fine particles of gold in the 1890s. In addition, high cost over the mines' lifetime required large concessions as well as large numbers of workers who were not available from the European prospectors. These required formation of mining companies and recruitment of cheap labor from both inside and outside South Africa, particularly Mozambique (Christopher, 1984). Depletion of the central Witwatersrand mines led to the opening of new mines east and west of Johannesburg, in 1910 and 1940s, respectively, all accompanied by new layouts of mining towns. Other minerals discovered in South Africa included coal and iron ore.

The political geography of the Witwatersrand motivated colonial mining in Central Africa. As already mentioned, at the time of the discovery of gold, the Rand was not part of the Cape Colony. It was in the Boer Republic of Transvaal, which constituted a major problem to British imperial interests. The desire to find a "Second Witwatersrand" north of the Limpopo was the driving force behind Cecil Rhodes' British South African Company's charter to exploit the goldfields of Mashonaland (in modern Zimbabwe) in 1889. However, when it did not find any gold, the company moved on to occupy Matabeleland in 1893. The gold deposits found there were not as huge as those of the Rand but other minerals such as asbestos, chrome, and high-grade coal were discovered. Coal production began at Wankie (Hwange) and grew from 349,000 tons in 1914 to 1.2 million in the late 1920s and to 3.5 million tons in the late 1950s (Christopher, 1984).

Further north in Central Africa across the border between Northern Rhodesia (Zambia) and Belgian Congo (DRC) emerged another center of colonial mining.

Here the targets were rich deposits of copper, cobalt, and zinc of the present day Copper Belt of Zambia and DRC. The Belgian colonialists knew about these deposits but that they thought they were not rich enough for exploitation. The extension of the railway from South Africa to the area brought renewed interest. In 1906, Belgian colonialists established the Union Meniere du Haut Katanga (UMHK) to exploit the deposits on the Congo-side of the border. They established Elisabethville (Lubumbashi) as the main center of the copper mining activity in the area. Copper production grew rapidly reaching annual total of 200,000 tons from 1952 through 1960. More copper was found on the Northern Rhodesian side of the border in 1909 and exploitation began in 1923. The two main companies that operated the mines from this period through the 1930s were the Rhoanglo, a subsidiary of Anglo-American Corporation of South Africa and the Rhodesian Selection Trust (RST) (Burdette, 1988). Production reached 253,000 tons in 1940 and 300,000 tons in 1951. As in other areas, new towns were laid out from to Luanshya in the east to Bancroft (Chililabombwe) in the west, centered on Kitwe. These towns grew very rapidly and by 1961, they had 325,000 people of which 42,000 were Europeans all living in segregated sections of the towns.

Elsewhere on the continent, Europeans found more mineral deposits during the late 1800s and early1900s, which led to the development of modern mining activities. Among these were gold in the Gold Coast (Ghana) in 1880; diamonds in South West Africa (Namibia) in 1908, Angola in 1912, Gold Coast in1919, and Sierra Leone in 1932; and bauxite in the Gold Coast in 1914 and French Guinea in 1938. However, only few of these were developed.

The end of World War II revived colonial interest in mineral development as well as prospecting for new minerals. More substantial mineral discoveries occurred in the 1950s including iron ore in Mauritania in 1952 and in Angola; petroleum in Angola in 1952–1955, Algeria and Nigeria in 1956 and Libya in 1959; uranium in Niger, and manganese in Niger and Gabon. With the exception of the petroleum production in Angola and Algeria, most of these minerals were only developed in the postcolonial period.

In spite of these, by the eve of independence, Africa's mineral production had greatly expanded not only in copper, cobalt, and gold but also into manganese, phosphates, iron ore, and petroleum. In addition, some of the colonies had become completely mineral-dependent economies. In Northern Rhodesia, 40% of its GDP, 93% of its export trade, and 68% of its public revenue was due to copper. In Belgian Congo, minerals contributed 67% of exports, 45% of public revenue, and 18% of GDP (UNECA, 2011). In Angola, where independence did not come until mid-1970s the mineral sector grew to dominate its export sector—with oil accounting for 55.4%, diamonds 9.1%, and iron ore 4.5% (Seleti, 1990).

Postcolonial Period

At the return to independence, Africa's mining sector bore the features of a branch plant economy—an economy dominated by foreign subsidiary firms whose activities had very little linkage and benefits to the domestic economy. These firms were only interested in exploiting and exporting raw materials (minerals) to their parent firm economies and retaining the profits from the exports to benefit them. In addition, the sector offered fewer and low-skilled jobs to Africans because of its capital-intensive nature as well as its racist division of labor practices. In Zambia, for example, copper mining accounted for only 15% of employment, while in DRC, the mining sector accounted for only 2% of total employment (UNECA, 2011).

From nationalization to economic and political downturn Against this background, many of the new African governments adopted a philosophy of development based on the idea of sovereignty and the belief that state control was the way to achieve economic development. As a result, most of the existing and new mining operations on the continent were nationalized. Unfortunately, these efforts did not yield the desired effects because of a host of problems including depressed commodity prices, political interference with business decisions, managerial incompetence, corrupt public officials, financial mismanagement, low reinvestments, external debt burden, obsolete technologies, and the rise of synthetic substitutes. By the end of the1980s, many of the state-owned mining operations had stagnated or experienced considerable production decline (see Box 13.1). In Ghana, for example,

Box 13.1 | The Rise and Fall of State-Owned Mining Operations: The Experience of Africa's Copperbelt

In the early postcolonial period, the Zambian government nationalized the Copperbelt operations under the Zambian Consolidated Copper Mines (ZCCM), which was jointly owned by the Zambian Government (60%) and Anglo American (27%). The company adopted a welfare state philosophy, subsidizing unprofitable mines with profitable mines and keeping thousands of people employed (Arndt, 2010). However, as already mentioned from the mid-1970s a number of problems including wide swings in world copper prices, mismanagement, and lack of capital for reinvestment caused production to decline by about 90%. During the 1990s, the World Bank and the IMF forced the government to privatize ZCCM under its SAP. In 1997 the company was privatized. The most profitable mines were bought by international investors while the nonprofitable ones were targeted for closure. Thousands of people lost their jobs. The 2008 recession worsened conditions in the Copperbelt in some of the oldest towns such as Luanshya, but recent Chinese investment seems to be revitalizing the old copper economy backed by rising prices.

As already pointed out, across the Zambian border in the DRC is the continuation of the Zambian Copperbelt, which is known as the Katanga Copperbelt. The center of the mining industry here is Lubumbashi, which as we have already seen grew out of the copper mining activities.

Other centers include Shitwu, Luila, and Kolwezi. In 1967, the Upper Katanga Mining Union (UMHK) that had controlled mining in the province was nationalized by the Mobutu government to become the Societe Generale des Garrieres et des Mines (Gecamines). Similar to its counterpart in Zambia, Gecamines adopted a policy of providing a decent standard of living for its workers, at all cost. Thus, both Gecamines and its predecessor provided basic social services and developed the economic and social structures in their areas of operations (Mazalto, 2009). Then just as it occurred in Zambia, the crisis in copper prices led to declining production, which eventually plunged the economy of the province into deep recession. In 2003, the government agreed to restructure Gecamines in order to avoid bankruptcy. Under the SAP 10,000 of the 25,000 employees were laid off with modest compensation (Mazalto, 2009). Copper has become one of the main commodities of international interest. An impressive 300% increase in price from between 2000 and 2010 coupled with low global inventories present a good outlook with respect to the future. New copper projects in both the Copperbelt and elsewhere are being planned.

Source: Mazalto, M. 2009. "Governance, Human Rights and Mining in the Democratic Republic of Congo." In: Campbell, B. (Ed.) *Mining in Africa: Regulation and Development.* London: Pluto Press, pp. 187–242.

gold production declined from 900,000 ounces in 1960 to 700,000 ounces in 1973 and to an all-time low of 280,000 ounces in 1983. Similarly, manganese production declined from 600,000 tons to 240,000 tons in 1983; bauxite declined from 200,000 to 50,000, while diamonds declined from 3.4 million carats in 1967 to 400,000 carats in 1983 (Barning, ND). In some of the mineral-rich countries, there were even more severe problems as belligerent groups vied for control over the rich mineral deposits as a means to finance their wars of domination or against injustice. This was the case of oil in the Nigerian Civil War in 1970–1973; the case of diamonds in the civil wars of Liberia (1989–1996; 1999–2003) and Sierra Leone (1991–2002), diamonds and oil in the Angolan Civil War (1974–2002), and diamonds, tin, titanium, tungsten in the DRC (1997–2003). These events gave rise to new concepts such as *conflict* or *blood* diamonds (minerals) and new hypotheses about Africa's development problems such as the resource curse or the paradox of the plenty became a fixture among scholars. The term **conflict minerals** came to refer to "the extraction of minerals from conflict-affected areas where human rights abuses take place" (International Peace Information Service, 2012, p. 10). The resource curse hypothesis describes a situation in which the abundance of natural resources translates to less economic growth and less economic development compared to a situation with fewer or no natural resources.

Structural adjustments and their impact At any rate, the declining situation in the mining sector forced many African governments to adopt the World Bank-International Monetary Fund's structural adjustment programs (SAPs). Many governments undertook radical reforms and developed incentive packages, including complete deregulation and privatization of mining operations and generous tax breaks, all aimed at attracting foreign investors into the mining sector (Hilson and McQuilken, 2014). One of the immediate effects of these reforms was that thousands of mineworkers lost their jobs. This was particularly severe in Southern Africa. In Zambia, for example, about 40,000 mineworkers lost their jobs (UNEA, 2011). Many of these workers ended up in the artisanal sector of the industry, while others became casual workers, leading to a huge growth of the sector. Aided by improved commodity prices, these reforms brought substantial new investments and technology into the large-scale mining sector. Twerefou (2009) reported that the total foreign direct investment (FDI) inflow to the continent in 1970 was $11 billion. By the 1990s, it was $100 billion. More than 50% of this investment flow went into the mining industry. This also led to new direct and indirect jobs in the large-scale mining sector, even though not to the same degree as before.

However, by the late1990s, many of these reforms were being criticized for being single-targeted at only attracting foreign investment and promoting export of no value-added mineral products. There was no consideration of the impact of the measures on local development. The reforms also gave too many incentives to the companies compared to local communities and were too much government-centered. At the same time, they weakened the position of the state to a point that it could not formulate policies or negotiate terms that would benefit the country (Campbell, 2009).

Several cases and incidents illustrate these criticisms. For example, an important sector that missed out was the artisanal and small-scale mining (ASM) sector.

This sector had always existed in many African communities. As already pointed out, it was the mining industry before the colonialists brought the modern mining system, and despite all efforts during the colonial era to stamp it out completely, ASM survived. However, from late 1970s as a result of economic collapse, political instability, inability of agriculture to provide basic life support and lack of any alternative rural employment, ASM began to grow in almost all the mineral economies of Africa. Ironically, this growth was accelerated by the numerous laid-off workers in the industrial mining sector due to the SAPs. By the end of the 1980s, ASM was employing millions of people across the continent. In countries such as DRC, Sierra Leone, and Liberia, where industrial mining collapsed in the 1990s due to depressed world markets, government failure, and civil wars, ASM became the only means of mineral production. In DRC, it is reported that in the 1990s ASM actually accounted for 60–90% of cobalt production, which was half of the world's total production (Tsurukawa et al., 2011). In Ghana, Akabzaa (2009) reported that it contributed about 10% of the gold production and 60% of diamonds production. Yet, the sector was treated as peripheral to the large-scale mining sector, and for that reason was not properly planned for even when it was considered.

Examples from Ghana and Zimbabwe, two countries that tried to address the needs of their respective ASMs illustrate this. In both countries, the focus was to build assaying facilities for the miners. As it turned out, the facility in Zimbabwe was not large enough to meet the demands of the miners (Hilson and McQuilken, 2014). This meant that the miners had to wait for weeks before receiving the service and "unable to wait most returned to the riverside, where they resumed environmentally destructive panning activities" (Hilson and McQuilken, 2014). In the case of Ghana, not enough ethnographic study was conducted so by the time the assaying facility was ready for use it was found that the miners were more of the "dig and cash" type that were only interested in making quick cash and had no knowledge or interest in using such advanced technique (Hilson and McQuilken, 2014).

In Mali, a government investigation into how the country could benefit more from its extractive industries revealed that mining companies had accelerated their production schedule to shorten the mine's lifespan, and also to avoid paying taxes to the government since the agreement contained a tax-exempt clause for the first five years. For the Sadiola mine, the production volume was 41.6% more than the company had projected for the first five years of operation; it produced seven years of projected output within the first five years. At the Morila mine, another study conducted after the feasibility study revealed that the gold reserves and the rate of production had been underestimated. As well articulated by Belem (2009, p. 142):

> For a country to see economic growth based on exploitation of mines, it is necessary to control the distortions caused by the country's dependence on exporting mining resources and to integrate this industry into the national economy.

Similarly in the DRC, a new mining code introduced in 2002 ensured profitability of mining companies, restricted the state's room to maneuver and gave private investors more power and rights (Mazalto, 2009) (see Box 13.2).

Box 13.2 | Mineral Sector Reforms in the Democratic Republic of Congo

In the DRC, the mining sector reforms were to, among other things, reorganize the role of the state as a facilitator of foreign investment and regulator of mining activities. However, the new mining code introduced in 2002 ensured profitability of mining companies, restricted the state's room to maneuver, and gave private investors with power and rights (Mazalto, 2009). The reforms were also supposed to lead to improvement in human rights, yet how those rights could be achieved was not directly indicated. Instead of ensuring decentralization, the reforms ended up centralizing a wide range of functions under one new agency, the Steering Committee on the Reform of Public Enterprise (COPIREP). The committee was charged with overseeing investment code introduced by the National Agency for Promotion of Investments (ANAPI), and also the Mining Code, land registry, the Forest Code and export agencies, as well as improving mining administration among public enterprise. In turn, ANAPI was charged with fighting against antiterrorism and money laundering, and providing care for the most vulnerable populations (Mazalto, 2009). The Mining Registry Service, created to provide security for mining property, issues, licenses, and if necessary terminate licenses, has had a crisis in leadership since its establishment in 2003 and as a result has not been able to function properly.

As if these were not enough, three reports issued after the reforms revealed a sector fraught with inadequate accounting system, lack of transparency, and numerous human rights violations by the members of the country's armed forces. The Kalala Report, for example,

highlighted how adopted mining policies were violated with impunity by the very people who were supposed to implement those policies. For example, it was revealed that the majority of the belligerent groups diverted mining revenues for their personal gain and to finance their war activities. The Latundula Report of 2006 showed that many contracts had been signed since 1990 that were not in the interest of the country. In addition, many joint ventures were arbitrarily given tax exemptions over periods extending from 15 to 30 years, while corrupt government officials have sought to enrich themselves. The UN Expert Group report exposed 54 political and business leaders from DRC, Rwanda, Uganda, and Zimbabwe for engaging in illegal trading of high-valued minerals. In 2007, the Minister of Mines was prompted to issue a moratorium on all new mining contracts until the contracts signed between 1996 and 2003 had been re-examined. Yet many observers were skeptical as to what would come out of all these given the entrenched political culture of the country. The Ituri region has become the most dangerous area in Africa. This has been attributed to the fight over resources. However, the real reason is the breakdown of a central authority over this area. Without any capacity of the government to even pay the soldiers that are in this area, the soldiers in turn have to find a way to survive. They do this by violating citizens, terrorizing them and fighting over control of resources with other factions.

Source: Mazalto, M. 2009. "Governance, Human Rights and Mining in the Democratic Republic of Congo." In Campbell, B. (Ed.) *Mining in Africa: Regulation and Development.* London: Pluto Press, pp. 187–242.

Environmental activism also brought forth policies of environmental impact assessment in many countries in the 1990s. These policies are well laid out on paper but the implementation was very weak. The legislative framework backing the policies were either weak or in some cases nonexistent. Institutional skills needed to execute the full process were often lacking, local participation was very minimal, and political will to back up the process was often not there. In addition, coordination among the many institutions that govern land at the local level had not been easy.

In 2001, the World Bank initiated a comprehensive review of its mandate in the mining sector, in what it called Extractive Industry Review (EIR). Among other things, the report, which was published in 2003, urged the Bank to (1) do a better job in tracking the poverty reduction impact of the projects it financed; (2) pay more attention to greater disclosure of revenue management; (3) improve governance issues in host countries; (4) ensure broad participation of stake holders in local areas; and (5) consider environmental and social impacts of projects (EIR, 2003). In recent years, these criticisms have brought pressure on mining companies to care not only about their profits but also about the communities and physical environments in which they operate.

African mining vision (AVM) In 2008, African countries discussed a mining vision, the African Mining Vision (AMV), which was endorsed by the African Union Summit in February 2009. The AMV articulates a policy of "transparent, equitable and optimal exploitation of mineral resources to underpin broadbased sustainable growth and socio-economic development" (Africa Union, 2009, p. 3). It aims at how to use mineral wealth as a catalyst for development. Specifically, the vision seeks (1) to use resource rents to improve physical infrastructure and human resources; (2) to use high-rent resource infrastructure as collateral to open up other places that lack resources; (3) to use locational advantage to develop downward value-added mineral products that could help develop industries; (4) to use relatively large resources to develop upstream value-added products—capital goods industries and services; (5) to promote investment in human resources and research and development that will lead to technological developments.

As a follow-up to the AMV, a number of international organizational and regional initiatives were launched to translate the AMV into reality. The International Study Group (ISG) was charged to explore the extent to which mineral production could contribute to sustainable development. The group consisting of partners from the AU and the African Development Bank, and African civil society organizations submitted its report in 2010 to the African Ministers Responsible for Mineral Resources Development and to the Heads of State in 2011. The next step is to draft policies that would make the AMV a reality (Bijlsma, 2011).

In spite of these mixed developments, reports indicate that the share of the mineral sector in the GDP of African countries, especially the nonoil-producing countries, continues to grow. This was particularly the case in DRC, where it rose from 10.4% in 2000 to 14.7% in 2010; in Zimbabwe, where it rose from 4.7% in 1995 to 12.6% in 2010; and in Cote d'Ivoire, where it was 0.2% in 1995 to 1.6% in 2010 (Table 13.2). The prospects are very good that mineral production will play a major role in the economies of many more African countries in the nearest foreseeable future. In the next sections, the contemporary mineral production is examined.

TABLE 13.2

Increasing Role of Mining in African Economies

Country	Mining as a percentage of GDP						
	1995	1998	2000	2002	2004	2008	2010
Increase							
DRC	—	—	10.4	—	—	—	14.7
Cote d'Ivoire	0.2	—	—	—	—	—	1.6
Liberia	—	—	0.3	—	—	—	1.6
Zimbabwe	4.7	—	—	—	—	—	12.6
The Gambia	—	—	—	—	1.6	—	2.8
Mali	1.9	—	—	—	—	—	6.4
Tanzania	—	1.5	—	—	—	—	2.4
Lesotho	0.1	—	—	—	—	—	4.9
Zambia	—	—	6.8	—	—	—	10.3
Equatorial Guinea	32.3	—	—	—	—	—	55.6
Decrease							
Angola	—	—	47.8	—	—	—	41.3
Congo Rep	—	—	—	37.8	—	28.3	—
Nigeria	48.5	—	—	—	—	—	26.4
Gabon	38.1	—	—	—	—	—	21.2
Cameroon	—	—	11.7	—	—	—	5.2

Source: USGS 2011 Mineral Yearbook Africa.

Mineral Production Operations

As already indicated, there are two types mineral production operations in Africa. The industrial or large-scale mining operations and artisanal or small-scale mineral production.

Industrial or Large-Scale Mineral Production (IMP)

Industrial or large-scale mineral production (IMP) uses sophisticated scientific methods to explore for minerals. Once there is evidence of mineral deposit, the next phase is to evaluate the deposit. This is done by a detailed study of a sample of rock fragments. This is the most expensive phase of the mineral exploration process (Kennedy, 1983). If the content shows that deposits are present, the reserve base is estimated and feasibility analyses on possible extraction are conducted. This primarily involves comparing the estimated cost of extraction with the estimated value of the deposit. If the estimated cost is reasonably less than the estimated value, development will go ahead. If not, the project will be abandoned or put on hold for reconsideration at another time. An important distinction that needs to be made is the difference between a reserve base and reserves. According the United States Geological Survey (USGS), the **reserve base** refers to the part of an identified mineral resource that meets the specified minimum physical and chemical criteria regarding current mining and production practices. **Reserves** or ore deposits refer to the portion of the reserve base that can be economically extracted or produced at a profit at the time of determination. IMP uses two methods of mineral extraction—mining and pumping and well systems (Kesler, 1994). **Mining**, the removal of rock from the ground, can be done by **bulk extraction** or **selective extraction** method. Bulk extraction removes mixtures of ore and worthless rocks. Selective extraction directly targets and removes the mineral. Bulk or selective extraction can be either **open-pit** or **underground** mining. Open-pit mining removes the ore and other worthless rocks. **Strip mining**, which involves stripping the topsoil in order to reach the ore, is used when the ore is shallow and lies flat. **Dredging** is used when unconsolidated material is covered by water that is too much to be economically pumped out. A third type is **hydraulic fracking**, in which a jet of water is used to disaggregate and wash the rock into a processing facility (Kesler, 1994). Underground mining typically uses a vertical shaft or a horizontal adit to reach the ores. **Pumping** and **well** systems are used to extract groundwater, crude oil, and natural gas (Kesler, 1994). There are two main types of these systems—onshore and offshore. Onshore systems usually include wells, pumping, and storage facilities, and a network of pipelines, trucks, and trains that carry the mineral to the refinery. Offshore systems consist of platforms and islands.

IMP has developed advanced methods for processing minerals. For metals, there are two steps. The first step called **beneficiation**, involves crushing and grinding of ore to separate grains of mineral from waste material in the ore by physical examination or chemical processing, depending on the type of mineral. The second step is **smelting**, which separates liquid metal from slag or liquid waste elements. With some metals, a third step, **refining**, may be required for purification. Processing of crude oil involves separation of hydrocarbon molecules and their modification to produce a wide range of products.

Artisanal Mineral Production (AMP)

Given its limited resources, artisanal mineral production (AMP) does not use any of the above scientific methods to look for minerals. In most cases, AMP uses prospecting or random exploration in these environments. Prospecting is based on mere hope and determination, while random exploration involves drilling sufficient number of holes in the ground to see if anything is there at all. They also look for places with potential signs such as existence of gold nuggets, presence of fern vegetation, and diving and exploiting riverbeds (Ofosu-Mensah, 2011). Like their large-scale counterparts, AMP occurs in three types of mines—open-pit, underground, and alluvial mines. Open-pits and underground mines may be abandoned mines, mine tailings, or concessions that belong to large-scale mining companies (International Peace Information Service 2012). However, without sophisticated technologies, artisanal mining usually focuses more on alluvial deposits. Where new shafts are dug they may be not more than 16.4 ft (5 m) deep. In recent years, some artisanal miners have been able to hire machinery to do the initial clearing excavation of top soil for them after which the rest is accomplished by manual labor. In processing the ores, AMP again falls short of the high technology used by IMP. Instead, it uses mostly washing and other chemicals such as mercury to extract the mineral. Unlike large-scale mining, which requires large investment money; artisanal mining relies on personal, family, and small individual investors that provide funding.

As already pointed out, AMP is a big subsector in most of Africa's mineral-dependent economies, but most of these countries struggle to keep the subsector in check. Part of the problem is that there is no official mechanism in place such as registration that will provide the governments with information needed. Even where registration is required, the infrastructure to enforce such requirement is lacking. The result is that most of the operators in the informal sector, primarily evade taxes. This also results in smuggling and subsequent sale of substantial amount of minerals outside the country.

Distribution and Production of Major Minerals

Figure 13.1 is the distribution map of Africa's known mineral deposits. The map shows a continent of great mineral wealth but mineral wealth that is unevenly distributed, with the greatest concentration in the subequatorial region, especially South Africa (Figure 13.2). This mineral wealth includes ferroalloy metals, nonferrous metals, energy minerals, and industrial minerals. **Ferroalloy metals** are combined with other metals especially steel to make it applicable for a wide variety of uses. **Nonferrous metals** consist of all the remaining metals that are not associated with steel. **Energy minerals** or **fossil fuels** are those minerals that have been formed from remains of organic matter—either plants or animals. **Industrial minerals** are all the minerals that are neither energy minerals nor metals (Table 13.3). Africa's most important metals and industrial minerals are discussed below, while its energy minerals are discussed under energy production.

Ferroalloy metals Ferroalloy metals that are produced in Africa include iron ore, chromium, cobalt, manganese, and vanadium.

Iron ore Historically, making steel was a symbol of industrialization, and possession of iron ore was one of the major prerequisites for an industrial revolution. Unfortunately, Africa's iron ore deposits are very small. In 2014, it produced only 5% of the world's output of iron ore. About 69% of that came from South Africa, followed by Mauritania (12%), Sierra Leone (10%), and Liberia with 5%. For a long time, wars and conflicts in Sierra Leone and Liberia, and undeveloped reserves in Guinea other areas of the continent made South Africa the only important source of iron ore in Africa. However, new projects in recent years raised the specter causing Gravelle (2012) to observe that Africa could be the new hotspot for iron ore. These included projects in Congo Republic and Tanzania, Sierra Leone, Liberia, Guinea Kenya, and South Africa (2015 and 2016), and Gabon and Mozambique (2016). One of the main obstacles to the development of many of Africa's rich iron ore deposits is infrastructure—especially good transportation network.

Chromium Chromium is used to make stainless steel, which is then used to make household utensils, food and chemical containers, and automobile parts. In 2014, Africa produced 33% of the world's chromium, 31% of which came from South Africa. South Africa has the second largest reserves of chromium after Kazakhstan. However, in 2014, it was the world-leading producer accounting for 31% of the total world output. The rest of Africa's chromium production came from Zimbabwe and Madagascar.

Cobalt Cobalt is used largely to make steel corrosion and abrasion resistant and also in magnets. Cobalt usually occurs as a byproduct of nickel. However, the largest concentration of cobalt deposits in Africa is found in the Copperbelt, which

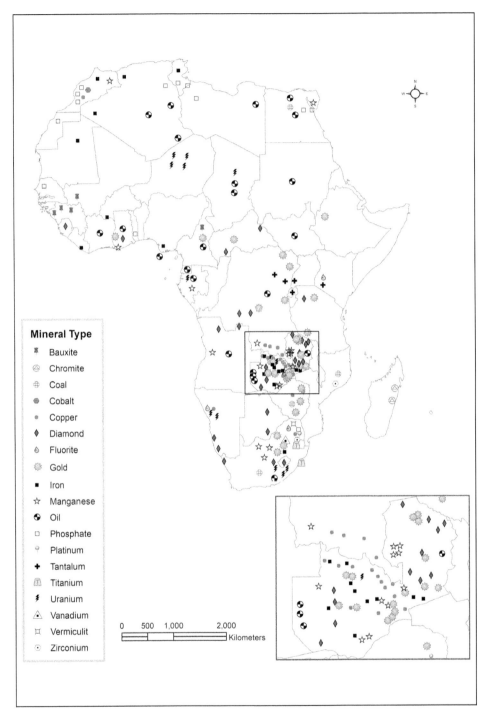

FIGURE 13.1 Mineral resources of Africa.
Source: World Trade Organization and CIA World Fact book

extends from the Katanga Province of the Democratic Republic of Congo to the Copperbelt Province of Zambia. As the name implies, copper is the leading product of these deposits, however, the Copperbelt has 51% of the world's cobalt reserves of which 44% is in the DRC section with the remaining 7% in the Zambian section (Figure 13.3). In 2015, Africa produced 62% of the world's cobalt. This came from seven countries led by DRC, with 81% of the total African and 50% of the total world

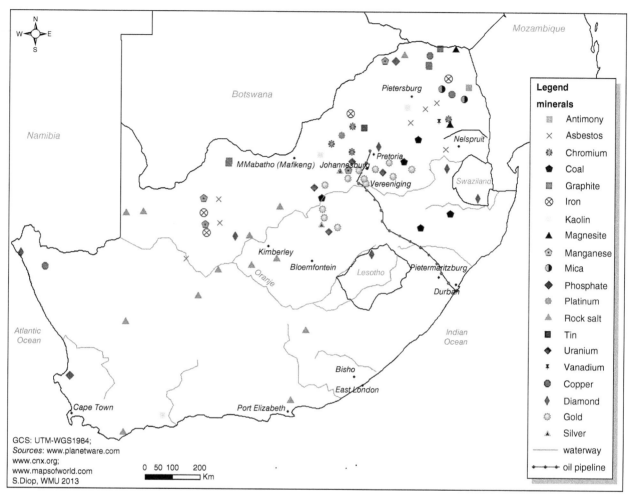

FIGURE 13.2 Mineral resources of South Africa.

output. In the DRC, most of cobalt deposits are found between the cities of Kolwezi and Likasi. Zambia followed DRC with 6% of Africa's output and 4% of the world's. The rest of the seven countries were South Africa, Morocco, Zimbabwe, Madagascar, and Botswana.

Manganese Manganese is used to purify iron or neutralize them in cast iron and steel. Manganese deposits are similar to those of iron ore and are mined usually by open-pit methods. Given that most of the world's leading steel producers lack domestic manganese deposits, Africa's manganese is very important to the global steel industry. In 2014, Africa had more than 29% of the world's manganese reserve, 75% of which were located in South Africa alone. Africa produced 35% of the world total output, 25% of which was due to South Africa. Other important producers were Gabon (22%) and Ghana (8%). Other minor producers included Sudan, Morocco, Burkina Faso, Namibia, and Cote d'Ivoire.

Vanadium Vanadium is another rare mineral that is used to make steel stronger for frameworks of high-rise buildings, offshore oil-drilling platforms, and pipe outlines. It is also used to strengthen titanium and aluminum. The most important deposit is in the Bushveld Complex of South Africa, which holds

TABLE **13.3**

Classification of Minerals

Class	Mineral
Energy minerals	
Fossil fuel	Coal, Petroleum, Natural Gas,
Other	Uranium, Geothermal energy
Metals	
Ferroalloy metals	Iron ore, Chromium, Manganese, Nickel silicon, Cobalt, Molybdenum, Vanadium, Tungsten, Columbium, and Tertullian
Nonferrous metals	
Light metals	Aluminum, Magnesium, Titanium, and Beryllium
Base metals	Copper, Lead, Zinc, and tin
Precious metals	Gold, Silver, and the Platinum-group elements (platinum, palladium, rhodium, ruthenium, iridium and osmium), Gem diamonds, Gem beryl, and Emeralds
Industrial metals	Antimony, Arsenic, Bismuth, Cadmium, Germanium, Hafnium, Thallium, Zinc
Industrial minerals	
Chemicals	Limestone, Dolomite, Lime, Phosphates, Potash, Salt, Sulfur, Nitrogen compounds, Sodium sulfate, Bromine, Iodine, and Fluorspar
Construction/Manufacturing	Cement, Asbestos, Dimension stone, Gypsum, Clays, Diatomite Talc, Mica, Barite, Quartz san, Soda ash, Boron, Feldspar, Lithium, Strontium, Industrial diamond, Graphite, Kyanite

Source: Compiled from Kesler, S.E., 1994, Mineral resources, economics and the environment: New York, Macmillan, 396 p.

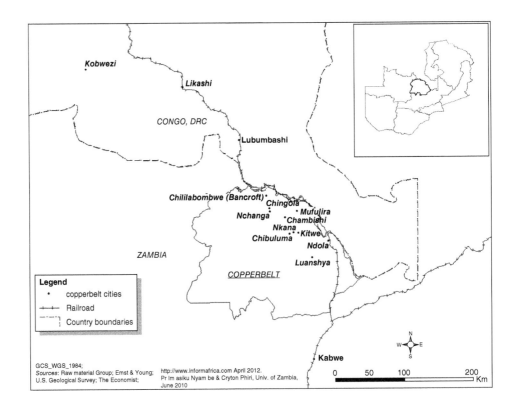

FIGURE 13.3 The African Copperbelt.

about 50% of the world's reserves. Vanadium mining is carried out largely by open-pit methods. In 2015, Africa produced 18% of its total output, all of which came from South Africa.

Nonferrous metals The most important nonferrous metals produced in Africa include bauxite and alumina, copper, lead, and zinc.

Bauxite Bauxite is the primary ore from which aluminum metal is produced, and due to its low ratio weight to strength, aluminum is highly used in the transportation sector, especially in automobile and aircrafts manufacturing. Aluminum is also replacing copper in the transmission of high-voltage electricity. Finally, it is used to make cans, home utensils, and a range of aluminum oxide abrasives and chemical compounds. Once mined, bauxite conversion to aluminum occurs in two stages. The first phase converts the ore into alumina, while the second phase converts the alumina into aluminum. According to USGS, Africa had 32% of the world's bauxite resources in 2015, but produced only 6% of its output. Almost all of that came from three countries in West Africa–Guinea (87%), Sierra Leone (7%), and Ghana (6%). Guinea has 26.2% of the world's bauxite reserves but in 2015, it was the sixth largest producer accounting for 5.5% of the total world production. Ghana also has huge deposits of bauxite, which in fact led to the development Volta River Hydroelectric Power Project in the 1960s. However, the agreement signed with the Kaiser Engineers of US ridiculously evaded the use of Ghana's bauxite. Thus, even though an aluminum plant, the Volta Aluminum Company (VALCO), was built to use alumina to produce final products, the plant had to import alumina from Kaiser's plant in Jamaica. The result is that only one mine at Awaso is operating, while the other huge deposits at Yenahin and Kibi are still untapped. More on this in Chapter 14.

Copper Copper has had many uses over its long history but today most of the world's copper is used for conducting heat and electricity, resisting corrosion, and making roofing, decorative trim and plumbing supplies. In 2015, Africa produced 10% of the world's copper, of which 53.4% came from DRC, 37.3% from Zambia, and 4% from South Africa. The remaining 2% came from Mauritania, Morocco, Namibia, Botswana, and Zimbabwe (Table 13.4). As already mentioned, copper production in DRC and Zambia is concentrated in the Copperbelt, an area lying on the watershed of the Congo and the Zambezi rivers, measuring 280 mi (450 km) long, and up to 160 mi (260 km), and separated by an "imaginary" political boundary between Zambia and the DRC. North of the boundary is the Katanga Copperbelt of DRC, and south of it is the Zambian Copperbelt.

About 10% of the world's copper reserves are located here, placing the two countries among the top 10 copper producers in the world. Today, the chief mines are located at Nchanga, Nkana, Mufilira, and Luanshya. Newer mines are located at Chibuluma, Chililabombwe Chambishi, and Chingola. The remoteness of the Copperbelt and the landlocked position of Zambia led to the establishment of copper-processing plants and smelters and concentrators of other minerals in the Zambian Copperbelt that is second only to the Witwatersrand gold industry on the continent. Thus, Ndola, the regional capital, Kitwe, Mufilira, and Nchanga all have processing plants. On the DRC side, important mining centers include Lonshi, Mufulira, Kinsenda, Kipushi, Kinsevere, Luishia, Tenke-Fungurume, Kolwezi, Likasi, and Lubumbashi, the regional center (Figure 13.3).

TABLE **13.4**

Africa's Copper Production (Metric Tons) 2007-2015

Country	2007	2008	2009	2010	2015 Quantity	2015 African production (%)	2015 World production (%)
Botswana	24,000	29,000	27,700	31,000	9100	0.47	0.04
DRC	149,000	230,000	345,000	430,000	1,020,000	53.41	5.34
Mauritania	31,956	33,073	35,000	37,000	45,000	2.35	0.23
Morocco	5,572	5,600	11,800	11,200	23,900	1.25	0.12
Namibia	6,580	7,471	—	—	14,000	0.73	0.07
South Africa	97,000	108,700	107,600	102,600	77,400	4.05	0.40
Zambia	509,000	534,000	698,000	686,000	712,000	37.28	3.72
Zimbabwe	2,861	2,827	3,572	5,000	8,200	0.42	0.04
Africa	825,969	950,671	1,228,672	1,302,800	1,909,600	100.0	9.99
World	15,500,000	15,600,000	16,000,000	16,100,000	16,100,000	—	100.0

Source: USGS Mineral Yearbooks.

Lead and zinc Lead and Zinc often occur together. Lead is mostly used in electric storage batteries for cars and trucks. Lead is also used for sheathing cables and ammunition. However, some previous uses such as antiknock additives in gasoline, interior paint, glass, ceramics, some chemicals, and plumbing have almost ceased due to health concerns, substitution of plastics, and competition from aluminum, tin, and iron. On its part, zinc is used to make galvanized steel to prevent corrosion and it is used with brass, bronze, and other zinc alloy to make ammunition shell casings. In 2014, Africa produced just about 1.4% of the world's lead output and 1% of its zinc. The bulk of the lead produced came from three countries—South Africa with 42%, Morocco with 41%, and Namibia with 17.4%. About 44% of the zinc production came from Namibia. Other important producers were Burkina Faso (22%), Morocco (16%), South Africa (10.3%), DRC (5%), and Nigeria (3%).

Precious metals and gemstones

Gold Africa has 54% of the world's gold reserves and in 2015, it produced just about 21% of the world's gold. Of this, South Africa accounted for 21.5%, Ghana 19.4%, Sudan 12.3%, Mali and DRC 7% each, and Tanzania 6% (Table 13.5). South Africa has the largest gold reserves in the world and it is the world's leading producer. Gold mining is still in the *Witwatersrand*, even though mining operations have migrated away from the Central Rand around Johannesburg, to the *East Rand*, around Springs–Hiedelburg; the *West Rand* around Randfontein and the *Far West Rand*, around Klerksdorp and Welkom. Since 2000, South Africa's gold production has declined due to a number of reasons, including physical deterioration of deposits due to their depth, increasing cost of labor, and the need to maintain labor safety. All these have combined to raise the production cost.

Ghana is the second largest producer of gold in Africa, after South Africa and the fifth largest in the world. Both alluvial and deep mine gold exist. The most important

TABLE **13.5**

Africa's Gold Production (Kilograms) 2007-2015

Country	2007	2008	2009	2010	2015 Quantity	2015 African production (%)	2015 World production (%)
Algeria	236	647	998	723	106	0.02	0.00
Botswana	2,722	3,176	1626	1,774	757	0.11	0.02
Burkina Faso	2,250	7,633	13181	22,926	36,540	5.44	1.16
Burundi	2,423	2,170	980	293	549	0.08	0.02
Cameroon	600	600	600	600	1,000	0.15	0.03
Chad	150	100	100	100	0	0.00	0.00
Congo Rep	100	100	100	150	150	0.02	0.01
DRC	5,100	3,300	2000	3,500	43,000	6.40	1.37
Cote d'Ivoire	1,243	4,205	6,947	5,316	23,000	3.42	0.73
Egypt	0	0	0	4675	13,657	2.03	0.43
Eqt. Guinea	200	200	200	200	0	0.00	0.00
Eritrea	87	32	30	30	753	0.11	0.02
Ethiopia	4,368	3,465	6,521	5,936	9,370	1.40	0.30
Gabon	300	300	300	300	1,356	0.20	0.04
Ghana	83,558	80,503	91,143	92,380	130,000	19.35	4.13
Guinea	15,628	19,945	18,091	15,217	21,464	3.20	0.68
Kenya	3,023	340	1,055	2,035	300	0.05	0.01
Liberia	311	624	524	666	828	0.12	0.03
Madagascar	-	-	-	-	3,000	0.45	0.10
Mali	52,753	41,160	42,364	38,524	46,500	6.92	1.48
Mauritania	2,332	5,528	7,838	8,326	8,804	1.31	0.28
Morocco	771	587	470	650	448	0.07	0.01
Mozambique	97	298	511	106	242	0.04	0.01
Namibia	2,488	2,115	2,057	2,683	6,285	0.94	0.20
Niger	3,427	2,314	2,067	1,929	1,220	0.18	0.04
Nigeria	180	2,890	1,350	3,718	6,300	0.94	0.20
Rwanda	-	-	-	-	336	0.05	0.01
Senegal	600	600	5,655	5,354	5,670	0.84	0.18
Sierra Leone	212	196	157	270	87	0.01	0.00
South Africa	252,345	212,744	197,628	188,702	144,515	21.51	4.59
Sudan	2,701	2,251	1,922	2,129	82,400	12.27	2.62
Tanzania	40,193	36,434	39,113	39,448	43,293	6.44	1.37
Togo	10,159	11,835	12,955	10,452	15,568	2.32	0.49
Uganda	2,543	2,055	931	918	-		
Zambia	1,269	1,693	3,108	3,410	4,238	0.63	0.14
Zimbabwe	7,018	3,579	4,966	9,620	20,023	2.98	0.64
Africa	501,387	453,619	467,488	473,060	671,759	100	21.33
World Total	2,350,000	2,290,000	2,490,000	2,590,000	3,150,000		

Source: International Trade Center Trade Map data

mines include Obuasi, Bogosu/Prestea, Tarkwa, and Teberebie/Iduapriem. The opening of two new mines—the Nzema Mine in 2011and the Akyem Mine in 2013, and the reopening of the Konongo Mine in 2012 have all helped to boost production.

In Mali, gold has displaced cotton as the leading contributor to gross domestic product (GDP) since 1997 and in recent years, Mali has risen to become the fourth largest gold producer in Africa, after South Africa, Ghana, and Tanzania. Important mines include the Sadiola, Morila, Kalana, Loulo, Tabakato, and the Yatela mines. The Syama mine that was closed in 2001 has also reopened. In Tanzania, the Golden Plateau and Luika Mines opened in 2011 and the Golden Ridge Mine opened in 2013.

These new gold mining operations have compensated for South Africa's declining gold production. Indeed, gold has now become one of the most widely produced minerals in Africa due to increased prospecting and reactivation of old mines. Thus, several African countries that used to have only artisanal gold mines have now opened large-scale gold mining or are planning to open one. Among these are DRC, Central African Republic, and Sierra Leone. USGS projects that Africa's gold production will increase by an average rate of 5% till 2018, and most of this will come from West Africa, particularly Burkina Faso, Cote d'Ivoire, Guinea, Liberia, Mali, Senegal, Sierra Leone, and Togo. The rest will come from Central Africa Republic, DRC, Egypt, Mauritania, Namibia, Sudan, and Tanzania.

Diamonds Africa produces two types of diamonds: gem and industrial diamonds. Gem diamonds are used for jewelry, and decoration in other products. Industrial diamonds are used as abrasives, and for cutting in industry. Both gem and industrial diamonds are cut according to their size, into various shapes to enhance their appearance. For example, the 3,026 carat Cullinan Diamond, the largest diamond ever found in the world, from the Premier Mine of South Africa in 1906, was cut into 96 small brilliants, nine polished fragments, and nine major stones (A carat weighs 0.2 g).

In 2015, Africa produced 47% of the world's natural diamonds, most of which came from five countries: Botswana (35%), DRC (27%), Angola (15%), South Africa (12%), and Zimbabwe (6%). These diamonds consisted of both industrial and gem diamonds. The production of gem diamonds was dominated by Botswana and Angola, which respectively accounted for 21% and 11% of the world output (Table 13.6). In Botswana, diamond mining boomed with the opening of the Debswana diamond mine at Orapa in 1971. Further mines were opened at Letlwakane in 1979 and Jwaneng in 1982. The Jwaneng mine is considered to be the most important discovery anywhere since the one at Kimberley (South Africa) in 1870. With a recovery rate of 94% compared with the world average of 22%, this field is considered the most important single source of quality gem diamonds in the world.

In contrast, most of the industrial diamonds came from DRC, which accounted for 23% of world production, Botswana (11%) and Zimbabwe (6%) (Table 13.7). Most of DRC's diamonds come from two main alluvial sources in the *Kasai River* valley: the *Tshikapa-Luebo* area in Kasai West, Kisangani, and the *Mbuji-Mayi* area in Kasai East. This latter region is the center of the country's diamonds industry. Operations in these areas suffered a lot of crisis in the 1960s and in recent years from inefficiencies.

Diamond production declined during the 1990s due to civil wars in several of the diamonds producing countries. By the end of 2011, many African countries had signed on to the **Kimberley Process**, which was a certification process that was introduced to avoid the so-called "blood diamonds" from Angola, and later Liberia and Sierra Leone. Production has since increased due to reopening, expansion, and rehabilitating of existing mines. Among these are the Damtshaa Mine in Botswana, the Tshibwe and Sankuru Mines in DRC, the Marange fields of Zimbabwe, the Cullinan,

TABLE **13.6**

Africa's Production of Gem Diamonds (Thousand Carats) 2007-2015

Country	2007	2008	2009	2010	2015 Quantity	Africa production (%)	world production (%)
Angola	8,732	8,016	12,445	7,600	8,120	23.0	11.4
Botswana	25,000	25,000	24,000	25,000	14,500	41.2	20.5
Central Afri. Rep	370	302	249	240	0	0	0
DRC	5,700	4,200	3,700	3,400	3,200	9.1	4.5
Ghana	671	478	301	267	174	0.5	0.2
Guinea	815	2,500	557	280	134	0.4	0.2
Lesotho	454	450	450	460	304	0.9	0.4
Liberia	0	0	0	0	41	0.1	0.1
Namibia	2,266	2,435	1,192	1,693	2,053	5.8	2.9
Sierra Leone	362	223	241	306	400	1.1	0.6
South Africa	6,100	5,200	2,500	3,500	5,780	16.4	8.2
Tanzania	239	202	155	77	184	0.5	0.2
Zimbabwe	100	100	100	900	349	1.0	0.5
Africa	52,816	51,114	47,899	45,733	35,239	100	49.7
Worldv	92,300	86,700	75,300	73,900	70,900		

Source: International Trade Center Trade Map data

TABLE **13.7**

Africa's Production of Industrial Diamonds, (Thousand Carats) 2007-2015

Country	2007	2008	2009	2010	2015 Quantity	Africa production (%)	world production (%)
Angola	970	900	1,383	900	902	3.7	1.6
Botswana	8,000	8,000	7,000	7,000	6,230	25.9	11.0
Cent. Afr. Rep	93	74	62	62	0	0.0	0.0
DRC	22,600	16,700	14,600	13,400	12,800	51.8	22.7
Ghana	168	120	75	67	0	0.0	0.0
Guinea	200	600	139	94	33	0.1	0.1
Liberia	0	0	0	0	27	0.0	0.0
Sierra Leone	241	149	160	131	100	0.4	0.2
South Africa	9,100	7,700	3,600	5,400	1,440	5.8	2.5
Tanzania	44	36	27	14	33	0.1	0.1
Zimbabwe	600	700	850	7,500	3,140	12.7	5.6
Africa	44,023	36,987	29,905	36,578	24,705	100.0	43.8
World	77,700	67,200	55,400	61,400	56,500		

Source: International Trade Center Trade Map data

the Finsch, the Kimberley, and the Koffiefontein Mines of South Africa; and the Williamson Mine in Tanzania, as well as other mines in Angola, Ghana, and Namibia.

Gemstones other than diamonds Africa produces other gemstones including ruby, tanzanite, emerald, blue sapphire, rubelite tourmaline, aquamarine, rose quartz, and topaz. The countries in which these gemstones are produced are listed in Table 13.8.

Platinum group of metals (PGMs) This group of metals includes platinum, palladium, rhodium, ruthenium, iridium, and osmium. The main market for these metals is industry. Specifically, they are used as catalytic converters in the exhaust systems of automobiles. In addition, the PGMs are also used in diesel-powered vehicles, the electricity and electronic industries, and dental and medical appliances. In 2015, Africa possessed more than 95% of the world's PGM reserves, almost all of which were in South Africa, with the rest in Zimbabwe. In South Africa, these reserves are found in what is called the **Merensky Reef**. From these reserves, Africa produced 41% of the world's palladium, 78% of its platinum, and 87% of its other PGMs in 2015. South Africa accounted for 88% of Africa's palladium production, 92% of its platinum, and 83% of other PGMs. The most important mines include Pilanesburg, Zondereinde, Booysendal, Roodepoort, and the Western Bushveld Mines. The rest of Africa's production came from Zimbabwe—12% of palladium, 8% of platinum, and 17% of other PGMs (USGS, 2017). In Zimbabwe, the main mines are Unki and Zimplats Mines. New mines at Wesizwe and Bokoni were expected to open in 2018.

TABLE 13.8

Africa's Gemstone Producers

Gemstone	Country
Alexandrite	Tanzania, Zimbabwe
Amethyst	Kenya, Madagascar, Mozambique, Nigeria
Aquamarine	Kenya, Zimbabwe, Namibia, Nigeria
Beryl	Zimbabwe, Madagascar
Emeralds	Zimbabwe, Mozambique
Garnet	Madagascar, Namibia, Nigeria
Goshenite	Nigeria
Iolite	Kenya
Morganite	Mozambique, Nigeria
Rose Quartz	Madagascar, Mozambique
Rubellite	Nigeria
Ruby	Kenya, Tanzania
Sapphire	Tanzania, Madagascar, Nigeria
Tanzanite	Tanzania
Topaz	Namibia, Nigeria
Tourmaline	Zimbabwe, Nigeria
Tsavorite	Tanzania

Source: Compiled from Nevin (2008) "*Africa—Home to World's Most Wanted Minerals*" African Business.

TABLE **13.9**

Africa's Production of Phosphates (Thousand Metric Tons) 2007-2015

Country	2007	2008	2009	2010	Quantity ('000 MT)	2015 Africa production (%)	World production (%)
Algeria	1,800.0	1,805.0	1,017.0	1,525.0	1,289.0	3.19	0.48
Burkina Faso	2.4	2.4	2.4	2.4	1.0	0.00	0.0
Egypt	2,290.3	2,356.5	6,227.4	3,021.3	5,500.0	13.61	2.05
Malawi					12.4	0.03	0.00
Mali					10.0	0.02	0.00
Morocco	27,834.0	24,861.0	18,307.0	26,603.0	26,264.0	65.01	9.80
Senegal	691.3	645.0	948.6	976.2	1,062.0	2.63	0.40
South Africa	2,556.0	2,287.0	2,237.1	2,494.0	1,852.4	4.59	0.69
Tanzania	8.3	28.7	18.0	17.1	23.0	0.06	0.01
Togo	750.1	842.5	725.5	695.1	1,150.2	2.85	0.43
Tunisia	8,002.0	7,691.7	7,409.0	8,148.5	3,228,3	7.99	1.20
Zimbabwe	46.1	21.1	32.1	56.7	6.2	0.02	0.00
Africa	43,430.5	40,540.7	36,924.2	43,539.5	40,398.50	100	15.07
World	159,000.0	165,000.0	162,000.0	182,000.0	268,000.0		

Source: World Mineral Production, British Geological Survey, and US Geological Survey

Industrial minerals

Phosphates Phosphates have a wide range of uses, including bath soap, toothpaste, mouthwash, skin and cosmetic care. They are also used in making fertilizers, fire extinguishers, cement, ceramics, car wash detergent, metal cleaning, water softening, and a wide range of processed foods such as cereals and canned foods. In 2015, Africa had more than 81% of the world's known reserves, of which 75% were located in Morocco and Western Sahara. Most of the remaining deposits were in Algeria, South Africa, Senegal, Egypt, and Togo (Table 13.9). In 2015, Africa produced 15% of the world's phosphates. Morocco was Africa's leading producer accounting for 65% of Africa's production and 10% of the world's total. Other important producers included Tunisia, Egypt, South Africa, Algeria, Senegal, and Togo.

ENERGY PRODUCTION

The Evolution and Development of Energy Production in Africa

Precolonial Period

Energy production has been part of the evolution of humans on the African continent. Like all humans elsewhere, precolonial Africans first drew on their individual human power to accomplish most of their basic day-to-day activities and tasks. The limitation of this source of energy relative to increasing range of needs to be met, as well as tasks and activities to be accomplished led to slow but steady development of different sources of energy over time. Among these were the use of slave labor for a wide variety of household and menial tasks; biomass (wood) for heating, cleaning, cooking, smelting, and manufacturing; animals for farm work and transportation; rivers and wind for transportation; and the sun for drying and heating. Most of these were not on a commercial scale but there was some commercialization with wood and charcoal. By the eve of colonialism, all these sources of energy production, except slave labor, had become well established, with biomass being the most dominant.

Colonial Period

Colonialism introduced modern energy production to Africa for three reasons. The first was an amenity for European settlers; the second was for mining; and the third was to stimulate industrial development (Showers, 2011). Initially, power production occurred in small-scale stand-alone thermal plants with stream-driven turbines. In North Africa, energy was provided by gas, in East and Central Africa it was by wood, in West Africa by imported diesel fuel, while in Southern Africa it was by coal (Showers, 2011). Over time, these were replaced by utility companies when electricity arrived on the continent in the 1880s. According to Eberhard (2007), the first electric light was installed at the Cape Town Railway Station in South Africa in 1881. The use of electricity spread rapidly throughout South Africa due to the gold mining industry. After the Union in 1910, the country's coal and iron and steel industrialization policy made the generation of cheap and abundant energy a top priority and in 1922, the Electricity Act established the Electricity Supply Commission (ESCOM) to generate and supply electricity at the lowest possible cost. ESCOM took advantage of the huge coal deposits of the Witbank Coalfield and by 1930, its electricity was considered to be among the cheapest in the world.

Given the limited coal reserves elsewhere on the continent energy production from coal was not widespread, and the only other place where this was done was in Southern Rhodesia, with the discovery of the Wankie (Hwange) Coalfields in 1893. In North Africa, electricity was first introduced to Egypt (before colonization) in 1893 and to the French Protectorate of Tunisia in 1902 (Showers, 2011). In British West Africa, electricity production also accompanied railway developments and street lighting in 1896 in Nigeria and 1914 in the Gold Coast (Ghana), but only in the European or government quarters. In East Africa, Dar-es-Salaam got streetlight powered from the hydroelectric power in German East Africa (Tanzania) in the early 20th century, and so did Ethiopia. Colonial governments were not only interested in electricity generated by coal-fired plants, but also from other sources, especially water. Before World War I, a number of small hydroelectric power (HEP) projects had been developed. For some of these, the turbines were installed in reservoirs, but most of them were installed in free-flowing rivers, without any dams (Showers, 2011). Colonial interest in HEP in Africa soared after World War I largely due to the publication of *Water and Power of the World* in 1921 by the US Geological Survey (USGS). In particular, the publication highlighted Africa's huge but untapped HEP potential, which at that time was estimated to be 50% of the world's total potential with the Congo River alone accounting for more than 25%. Colonial governments ordered a number of HEP surveys on African rivers, and this was followed by the building of a number of small dams in the 1920s and 1930s particularly in the mining areas. Examples of these were the Mulungushi River Project for the lead–zinc mining at Broken Hill (Kabwe), Northern Rhodesia (Zambia), the Meso Hydro Project in Kenya, and the Kagera River project for tin mining in Uganda (Showers, 2011).

The need for rearmament and the growth of energy-intensive industries such as the aluminum industry after World War II provided another opportunity for electricity generation in Colonial Africa, and this time it was to be done through large hydroelectric power projects and transmission over long distances. A number of large-scale projects were conceived among which were the Grand Inga Project on the Congo, the Volta River project in Gold Coast, and the Kariba Dam Project on the Zambezi in the Federation of Rhodesia and Nyasaland (Zambia, Zimbabwe, and Malawi). Of these, only the Kariba Dam project was completed before the peak of the Independence Era, but its success especially in long-distance transmission of electricity became a template for future large and remote HEP projects in postcolonial Africa. Other major HEP projects that were initiated during the colonial period were the Zambezi River's Cahora Bassa Dam Scheme in Mozambique and Cunene River Basin Scheme in Angola. The former was completed in 1969, but the latter was caught up in the Angolan Civil Wars from 1974 to 1988. Data compiled by Showers (2011) from FAO show that from the 1920s through the 1950s Africa's colonial governments built about 265 dams in their colonies. However, only 37 (about 14%) of these were directly for hydroelectric power generation.

Postcolonial Period

Postcolonial Africa saw the most rapid development of energy production, especially from the 1960s through the 1980s. The emphasis was on hydroelectricity and among the earlier ones were the Volta Dam at Akosombo, Ghana, which opened in 1965, the Aswan High Dam in Egypt in 1970, and the Inga I on the Congo in DRC in 1972. By the 2000s, over 814 dams had been built in Africa of which 79 or 10% were directly for electricity generation (Showers, 2011). The exploitation of energy minerals, particularly petroleum and uranium, in the 1970s boosted Africa's energy production and consumption. A few countries such as Ghana, South Africa, Guinea, and Egypt also pursued nuclear energy during this period.

In all countries, state-owned vertically integrated companies were in charge of energy production. Among these were the Volta River Authority (VRA) of Ghana, *Energie du Mali* (EDM) of Mali, NamPower of Namibia, Eskom of South Africa, Tanzania Electric Supply Company (TANESCO) of Tanzania, and the Uganda Electricity Board (UEB) of Uganda. However, by the 1990s, most of these companies were insolvent. In addition, lack of new investments had eroded their technical capacity, performance, and reliability. The only exceptions were the state-owned companies of Namibia and South Africa (Clark et al., 2005). The result was that not only were the vast majority of Africans off the energy grid, but the small minority that were lucky to be on the grid experienced frequent power outages. The situation became worse when severe drought in 1980s and 1990s caused the water levels of many of the large hydroelectric power projects to drop dramatically, thereby affecting electricity output.

In order to deal with these problems, many African countries began reforming their energy production sectors beginning in the mid-1990s. These reforms involved a two-step approach. The first was some form of commercialization of the state-owned companies and the "unbundling and the introduction of competition and private sector participation" (Clark et al., 2005, p. 4). However, Clark et al. (2005) pointed out that out of the six countries in their study, only Uganda had been able to accomplish both stages. The rest—Ghana, Mali, Namibia, South Africa, and Tanzania—had all paid lip service to the second stage of unbundling and introduction of competition and private sector participation, a situation common to most African countries. Clark et al. (2005) attribute this to the view held by African governments that energy is so crucial to Africa's development that reliability of supply is more important than market competition. In spite of these, significant progress has been made with other forms of privatization including management contracts and invitation, attraction of investment, and for that reason participation of the private sector. Many African countries also sought to increase their energy production through such programs as rural or national electrification projects as well as price and tariff reforms.

Another interest that emerged toward the end of the 1990s was regional infrastructural projects. In 2002, NEPAD published a short-term action plan (STAP) in which over 100 activities and 40 investment projects were identified. The final assessment of these projects in 2010 identified 27 energy sector projects, 12 of which were deemed as investment projects. However, many of the projects were abandoned due to political, financial, technical, and project management problems (ECA, 2011). Politically, there was no single entity that could make regional investment decisions. Financially, the projects did not have clear objectives, cash flow, and returns that would attract investors. Technically, there were no cross-border operating framework and regional standards, and in terms of project management, there were no implementation plans, milestones, and assignment of responsibilities (ECA, 2011).

In spite of all these, it seems a regional approach still has some hope but it will take national governments to be the driving force. In the meantime, a "Declaration of Intent" to integrate the Maghreb electricity market to the EU was signed in 2003 with the Maghreb countries—Algeria, Morocco, Libya, and Tunisia. In 2006, an undersea cable between Morocco and Spain was commissioned and several similar connections between Algeria and Spain, Libya–Italy, Algeria–Italy, and Tunisia–Italy were discussed (Showers, 2011).

A considerable amount of discussion has also focused on **public–private partnership** (PPP). Proponents of PPP distinguish it from the traditional forms of governmental contract by the risk sharing agreement of the project. To them:

> The PPP contract allocates risks and rewards associated with the delivery of these public services between the private entity and the public owner or sponsor of the project.
>
> (ECA, 2011, p. 23)

This could take several forms such as concessions or management and lease contracts. As already pointed out concessions may be brownfield or greenfield. In **brownfield concession**, a private company takes over an existing government-owned facility to extend, complete, or rehabilitate it, and transfer the facility at the end of the contract. In **greenfield concession**, the private company builds a new facility for a period indicated by the contract. A particular type of greenfield concession is the **independent power producer** (IPP) project, in which a private company develops a new power generating facility and "sells the power on a wholesale basis to the government utilities that distribute it to individual customers" (ECA, 2011, p. 24). Finally, another type of PPP that relates to infrastructure is **private partnership in infrastructure** (PPI), which could be divestiture or privatization, or merchant projects. A divestiture becomes a PPP project if the sale of the government facility is accompanied by a contract that requires the private company to sell services back to customers through the government. A merchant project is a project undertaken solely by the private company without any service buying commitment by the government (ECA, 2011). To date, there are two main problems with the PPI projects in Africa. First, all of them are concentrated in South Africa and Nigeria. Second, only about 10% of PPI in Africa has gone to the energy sector. The rest have all gone into ICT and transportation.

Successful use of PPP will require much from African governments. Among other things, ECA (2011) recommends the need for African governments to (1) stay focused on energy infrastructure, (2) strengthen the business climate, (3) set priorities, (4) reduce private sector risks; (5) employ the best and qualified personnel in feasibility and project design stages, and (6) use government and donor funds to substitute private sources.

Distribution of Major Energy Resources and Production

Primary Energy Resources and Production

There are several classifications of energy resources. The classification used in this section is **primary and secondary energy**. Primary energy is energy contained in natural resources such as coal, oil, natural gas, uranium, wood, wind, waterpower, and sunlight. Secondary energy is primary energy converted into more usable form such as electricity and refined fuels. By life span, primary energy may be classified into **renewable** and **nonrenewable** energy. Renewable energy includes solar, wind, water, and biomass. Nonrenewable energy includes coal, natural gas, oil, and uranium.

Official primary energy production data usually include only coal, crude oil, and natural gas, while energy derived from uranium, water, biofuels, geothermal, solar, and wind is solely assigned to secondary energy production. Wood is usually not included in primary energy production but it is included in the discussion in this section. Africa's primary energy production is small compared to other major regions of the world. Since 1980, Africa has ranked second from the bottom of the seven regions of the world with very little variation (Figure 13.4). Thus, in 1980 and 1990, Africa produced only 6% of the world's primary energy. In 2015, it produced 36.4 quadrillion British thermal units (Btu) of primary energy, which was just 7% of the world's total production. **Btu** is defined as the amount of thermal energy that will raise a pound of water by 1°F. About 82% of this production came from five countries—Nigeria, Algeria, Angola, Egypt, and South Africa. This low production reflects in part the limited nature of some of Africa's primary energy resources and in part its inability to

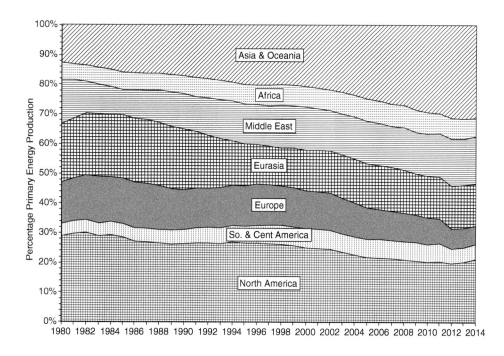

FIGURE 13.4 World primary energy production, 1980–2014.
Source: US Energy Information Administration

harness those that are abundant. These resources include coal, crude oil, natural gas, uranium, water, wood, biogas, and biofuels, and geothermal, solar, and wind.

Coal Coal accounted for 15.7% of Africa's primary energy production in 2015, but Africa's coal resources are very limited. In 2015, Africa produced only 3.4% of the world's coal production, and about 94% of that came from South Africa's Witbank coalfield. Other minor coal producers include Zimbabwe, Botswana, Niger, Egypt, Tanzania, and Mozambique (Table 13.10). However, as a result new coal projects in South Africa, Mozambique, and Botswana, USGS (2012) projected that Africa's coal production will grow by an annual rate of 5% through 2018.

Crude oil or petroleum Crude oil is the single largest source of Africa's primary energy production. In 2015, it accounted of 45.8% of total primary energy production. Africa had 8.3% of the World's proven crude oil reserves in 2015. Of these 37.6% were in Libya, 30.1% in Nigeria, 9.9% in Algeria, and 7.7% in Angola. The remaining deposits were in Egypt, Chad, Congo Republic, Equatorial Guinea Benin, and Cameroon. From these reserves, Africa produced about 10% of the world's crude oil production in 2015. Nigeria, Africa's leading producer accounted for 28% of the total production, and was followed by Angola with 23%, Algeria 17%, and Egypt with 9% (Table 13.11). Recent new oil deposits found in Ghana, Uganda, and Kenya could boost Africa's crude oil production.

Natural gas Natural gas accounted for about 6.7% of Africa's primary energy production in 2015. Africa had about 8.7% of the world's proven reserves of natural gas in 2015 out of which it produced 9% of the world's total output. Most of the reserves

TABLE **13.10**

Coal Production (Thousand Metric Tons) in 2007-2015

Country	2007	2008	2009	2010	2015 Quantity	2015 Africa production (%)
Botswana	828.2	909.5	737.8	988.2	2,065.8	0.8
DRC	126.1	128.8	133.4	133.4	4.4	0.0
Egypt	146.8	0	0	109.9	300	0.1
Ethiopia	0	0	15	20	34	0.0
Malawi	58.6	57.5	59.2	79.2	58.7	0.0
Mozambique	23.6	37.7	25.9	35.7	8,600	3.2
Niger	171.3	182.9	225.1	246.6	221	0.1
Nigeria	20	30	40	44.1	121.6	0.0
South Africa	247,600.2	252,213.4	250,581.7	257,205.8	252,076	94.0
Tanzania	27.2	15.2	16.5	179.5	255.9	0.1
Zambia	14.1	14	14	0	0	0.0
Zimbabwe	2,080.2	1,509.1	1,667.3	2,668.2	4,336.1	1.6
Africa	251,096.3	255,098.1	253,515.9	261,710.6	268,073.50	100.0
World	6,585,000	6,811,000	6,876,000	7,235,000	7,925,000.00	—

Source: International Trade Center Trade Map data

TABLE **13.11**

Petroleum Production (Thousand Metric Tons) in 2007-2015

Country	2007	2008	2009	2010	2015 Quantity	2015 Africa production (%)
Algeria	86,500	85,600	77,800	75,500	67,200	17.0
Angola	82,500	93,500	89,100	92,000	88,700	22.5
Cameroon	4,343.40	4,300	3,700	3,200	4,896.3	1.2
Chad	7,500.00	6,700	6,200	6,400	3,800	1.0
Congo	11,091.80	11,768.30	14,200	15,100.90	13,518	3.4
Cote d'Ivoire	2,423.00	2,964	2,897	2,197	1,704	0.4
DRC	1,105	995	1,100	1,050	1,132.1	0.3
Egypt	34,100	34,600	35,300	35,000	35,400	9.0
Equat. Guinea	17,300	17,200	15,200	13,600	13,500	3.4
Gabon	12,100	11,800	11,829	12,431	11,500	2.9
Ghana	301	301	301	360	5,161	1.3
Libya	85,000.00	85,300	77,100	77,500	19,996	5.1
Mauritania	739.5	592.7	550.1	412	258.9	0.1
Morocco	11.1	9	9.3	10.4	5	0.0
Niger	0	0	0	0	995	0.3
Nigeria	114,100	105,300	101,500	117,200	112,000	28.4
Senegal	42.9	13.4	33.6	53.8	22.9	0.0
South Africa	502	403	270	316	71	0.0
South Sudan	0	0	0	0	7,300	1.8
Sudan	23,100	23,700	23,400	22,900	5,200	1.3
Tunisia	4,546	4,146	3,902	3,731.40	2,547	0.6
Africa	487,306	489,192	464,392	478,963	394,907	100.0
World	3,904,000	3,798,000	3,840,000	3,932,000	4,353,000	—

Source: International Trade Center Trade Map data

were in Nigeria (30%), Algeria (26%), Mozambique (16.5%), Egypt (13%), and Libya (9%). However, about 86% of production came from four countries–Algeria (34%), Nigeria (27.5%), Egypt (17.5%), and Tanzania (14.6%) (Table 13.12).

Uranium Uranium is the primary source of nuclear fuel. The mineral can be extracted by underground, open pit, or by leaching and pumping it to the surface. In 2014, Africa had 18% of the world's known uranium reserves, distributed among South Africa (6%), Niger (5%), Namibia (5%), and Botswana and Tanzania with 1% each. Out of these reserves, Africa produced about 12.4% of the world's uranium output, about 54% of which came from Niger. The other producers were Namibia (39%) and South Africa (6%). In addition to recent projects in Namibia, uranium has also been found in 16 African countries, including Zambia, Botswana, Malawi, Tanzania, Uganda, DRC, and Burundi. However, they remain unexploited.

TABLE **13.12**

Production of Natural Gas (Metric Tons) 2007–2015

Country	2007	2008	2009	2010	2015 Quantity	2015 Africa production (%)
Algeria	84,800	85,800	79,600	80,400	84,600	33.8
Angola	830	680	690	733	650	0.3
Cameroon					369	0.1
Congo	7,276	7,351	7,980	8,438	1,501	0.6
Cote d'Ivoire	1,574	1,300	1,300	1,352	2,177	0.9
Egypt	55,700	59,000	62,700	61,300	44,300	17.7
Equatorial Guinea	2,920	6,670	5,900	6,136	8,405	3.4
Gabon	167	170	170	170	378	0.2
Libya	15,300	15,900	15,900	16,800	11,800	4.7
Morocco	61	50	41	50	82	0.0
Mozambique	2,800	3,100	3,600	3,744	5,695	2.3
Nigeria	35,000	35,000	24,800	36,600	50,100	20.2
South Africa	1,600	1,500	1,200	1,600	1,333	0.5
Tanzania					36,568	14.6
Tunisia	2,285	2,596	3,056	3,402	2,479	1.0
Africa	210,313	219,117	206,937	220,725	250,437	100.0
World	3,070,000	3,181,000	3,101,000	3,318,000	3,696,000	—

Source: British Geological Society, 2013; Brown et al, 2018.

Water Water is the primary source of hydroelectric power, which is generated by the force of falling water on hydraulic turbines. This is usually facilitated by building dams across rivers to raise the height of the water, which means that the higher the dam, the greater the force. In this regard, Africa's rivers constitute potential water energy resources. Indeed, it has been estimated that Africa's hydroelectric power potential is enough to supply all its electricity needs (Blyden and Akiwumi, 2008). However, for a long time, most of this potential remained untapped since a few large dams were completed in the 1960s and 1970s (Table 13.13). As late as 2011, it was estimated that 93% of this hydropower, about a tenth of the world's total, was still unexploited (Eberhard et al., 2011). Much of Africa's HEP potential is locked up in the Congo River. As mentioned in Chapter 4, below Kinshasa, the mighty river tumbles over the Inga Falls, a series of rapids that drop the river 328 ft (100 m) over a distance of 9.3 mi (15 km). Since the colonial period, it has been known that this is one of the best natural sources of electricity in the world, and when fully tapped (Pearce, 2013), it can supply electricity to half of Africa.

Over the past several years, this situation appears to be changing due to both completed and proposed projects. These include the 250-MW Bujagali Dam project on the Nile in Uganda; the 300-MW Takeze Canyon project on the Nile in Ethiopia; the 1,800-MW Gibe II Dam on the Omo River also in Ethiopia; the 120-MW

TABLE **13.13**

Major Hydroelectric Power Projects in Africa

Name	Country	River	Year opened	Capacity (MW)
Inga I	DRC	Congo	1972	351
Inga II	DRC	Congo	1082	1,424
Gilgel Gibbe III	Ethiopia	Omo	2015	1,870
Aswan	Egypt	Nile	1970	2,100
Roseires	Sudan	Blue Nile	2013	1,800
Merowe	Sudan	Nile	2009	1,250
Akosombo	Ghana	Volta	1965	1,020
Kainji	Nigeria	Niger	1968	800
Cahora Bassa	Mozambique-Zambia	Zambezi	1976	2,075
Ruacana	Namibia	Cunene	1978	330
Drakensberg Pumped Storage	South Africa	Tugela-Vaal	1981	1,000
Kafue Gorge	Zambia	Kafue	1973	990
Kariba	Zimbabwe/Zambia	Zambezi	1077	750
Capanda	Angola	Kwanza	2007	520
Spmg Loulou	Cameroon	Sanaga	1981	384
Garleep*	South Africa	Orange	1971	360
Palmiet Pumped Storage	South Africa	Palmiet	1988	400

Djibloho Dam on the Welle River in Equatorial Guinea; and the 1,250-MW project on the Nile at Merowe, Sudan. In addition, there are some large dam projects currently going on including Ethiopia's 6000-MW Grand Renaissance Power project on the Blue Nile; the 1,600-MW Batoka Gorge project on the Zambezi in Zambia and Zimbabwe; and the 1,500-MW Mphaanda-Nkuwa project also on the Zambezi in Mozambique.

The most ambitious of all the projects is the Grand Inga or Inga III power project on the Congo. Plans to tap this enormous resource began in 1970s but only two small HEP projects were completed—the Inga I built in 1972 and the Inga II in 1982. Both were developed mainly for the Katanga Copperbelt. In May 2013, the World Bank approved a loan of $73.1 million for the Inga III or the Grand Inga project, which is estimated to cost $80 billion. When completed, the Grand Inga is estimated to generate 40,000 MW of electricity, which is double that of the Three Gorges Dam of China, currently the World's largest HEP project (Donaldson, 2014). Critics have noted that much of the energy will be transmitted to South Africa, which is a financial partner of the project, and this has raised concerns that the people of DRC may not benefit from the project when completed.

Wood, biogas, and biofuels Wood is the second largest source of primary energy in Africa after crude oil. In 2014, it generated 9.1 quadrillion Btu of energy, which was 25% of the total primary energy production of Africa. For much of rural Africa, wood is the chief source of energy for heating, cooking, and for processing in small scale and traditional manufacturing. Wood provides two sources of primary energy—wood fuel and wood charcoal. Statistics of Africa's wood fuel production were presented in Chapter 12, which showed that Africa accounted for about 24% of the world's total wood fuel production. Wood fuel accounts for 90% of Africa's wood energy, while the remaining 10% comes from wood charcoal. Africa's share in the world production of both wood fuel and wood charcoal has been rising to global dominance as the rest of world has become increasingly dependent on other energy resources. Data on this dominance with respect to wood fuel were presented in Chapter 12. Figure 13.5 shows Africa's share of world wood charcoal production. The leading countries include Nigeria, Ethiopia, DRC, Tanzania, Ghana, and Madagascar Figure 13.6).

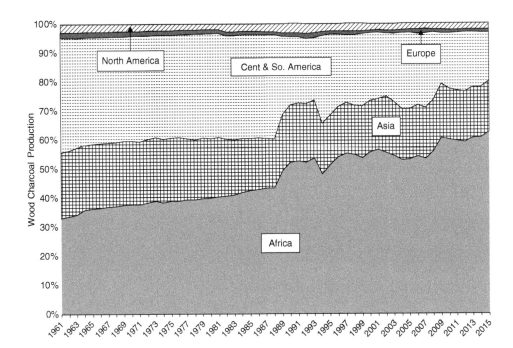

FIGURE 13.5 Percentage wood charcoal production of major world regions 1961–2015.
Source: FAOSTATS, 2015

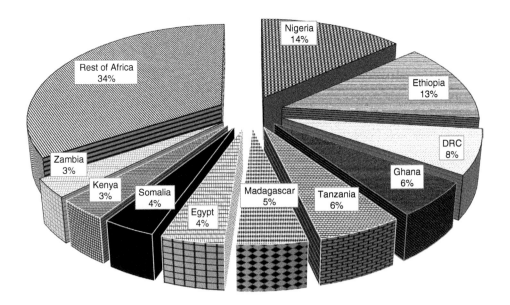

FIGURE 13.6 Top producers of wood charcoal in Africa, 2015.
Source: FAOSTATS, 2015

Biofuels are liquid, solid, and gaseous fuels derived from biomass. They consist largely of biodiesel and ethanol. In contrast, biogas is energy derived from agricultural residues, and municipal and industrial wastes. There is high level of awareness of these sources of energy, and there are several small projects all over the continent aimed at these sources of energy. However, efforts to generate energy from these sources will have to overcome political, economic, sociocultural, and technical constraints (Parawira, 2009; Sulle and Nelson, 2009).

Geothermal, solar, and wind Geothermal, solar, and wind are the other sources of renewable energy in Africa, in addition to wood, biomass, and water. However, lack of data on these sources of energy makes it difficult to provide a comprehensive overview. According to the US Department of Energy, geothermal energy resources are heat from the earth or "reservoirs of hot water that exist in varying temperatures below the Earth's surface." When this reservoir is brought to the surface, it can be used among other things to generate electricity for heating and cooling purposes. There are three ways to bring the reservoir to the surface. The first is to draw the steam generated by the heat of the earth into a plant that is then used to turn turbines to generate electricity. This is called **dry steam** energy generation. The second is to use a reservoir of underground hot water to generate electricity. The hot water is forced to flow upward. This causes its pressure to fall at which point it begins to boil to generate steam, which is then used to turn turbines to generate electricity. The third way is to use hot water of a lower temperature; use the heat from the water to boil a working fluid, vaporize the fluid in a heat exchanger, which is then used to drive turbines to generate electricity (Renewable Energy.com 2014). The distribution of geothermal energy resources is determined by geological formations of places. Experts believe that Africa's greatest geothermal potential is in the Great Rift Valley region.

Solar energy is the most abundant of all primary energy resources in the world. It has been variously estimated that the amount of sunbeam reaching the earth in one hour can supply all the energy needs of the world in one year, and more importantly, all of that is renewable. Therefore, the idea of solar energy is to capture this energy to generate electricity. There are different ways of doing this but the most common is the use of photovoltaic or PV cells that converts sunlight into electricity. Another way is to trap the sunlight using long U-shaped mirrors and use the heat to generate steam, which is then used to turn turbines to generate electricity. For years now, researchers have talked about solar energy in Africa because sunshine is one the most abundant ubiquities in Africa, except for a few hours of cloudy periods. Yet, the vast potential of Africa's solar energy is yet to be harnessed.

Another primary energy source that is ubiquitous in Africa is wind. Generating energy from wind is an old technology that had been used in Europe and other parts of the world. What is new about wind energy technology is that the old wind mill has been replaced by the modern wind turbine, which is a three-turbine rotor mounted to a shaft about 100 ft (30.5 m) high about the ground. Like solar energy, this is another abundant primary energy resource that is ubiquitous, however, because of the minimum wind speed required there are certain parts of the continent that have greater potential than others. According to the International Renewable Energy Agency (IRENA) (2013), 21 African countries have completed both solar and wind energy assessments and at least 14 countries have also completed their geothermal assessments. What is left now is to start developing these resources.

Secondary Energy Production

As already pointed out, secondary energy is mostly electricity, which is generated from solids (e.g., coal and uranium), gas (natural gas), and liquids (oil and water), and wind and the sun. Secondary energy also includes refined fuel that is used to run machines. In 2014, electricity accounted for only 6% of Africa's energy production. This was only 3% the world's electricity production, the lowest of all of the major regions of the world. About 80% of this electricity was generated from fossil fuels, 17% from hydroelectricity, and 2% from nuclear energy. The remaining 1% comes from solar, wind, and geothermal. Electricity production is dominated once again by a handful of countries. About 85% of the total electricity production in 2014 is by 10 countries. Within this group, South Africa produced 33%, Egypt 23%, while the remaining 44% was due to Algeria, Libya, Nigeria, Morocco, Tunisia, Mozambique, Zambia, and Ghana.

In Egypt, Algeria, and Libya, most of electricity generation was from gas-fired plants; in Nigeria it was from oil, while in South Africa it was from coal. In most African countries, electricity generation is based on a combination of hydro and imported coal. Thus, electricity generation from other primary renewable resources on the continent is spotty, isolated, and in most cases anecdotal. For example, only Kenya appears to be tapping into the geothermal resources of the rift valley, which is still very small, less than 10% (Eberhard et al., 2011; Otieno and Awange, 2006). Both Uganda and Tanzania have the potential but have not made any concrete efforts to develop them yet. Similarly, the harnessing of solar energy has been a scattered, isolated, individual, or corporate activity. The only countries that have made some efforts at this are Egypt and South Africa. In North Africa, there is the proposed Mediterranean Solar Plan (MSP), which is estimated to generate 20,000 MW of solar capacity by 2020, and its subsequent integration into a new transnational and trans-Mediterranean grid. The vision is for this to form the backbone of a Euro-Mediterranean Super grid. However, institutional constraints, disagreements of how the benefits will be shared, and lack of any international structure to manage the project are still standing in the way of making this a reality (Razavi et al., 2012). With respect to wind energy, only few countries have taken concrete actions in establishing wind farms. They are South Africa, Morocco, Egypt, Ethiopia, Kenya, and Tunisia in order of electricity generated (Monforti, 2011; Tryou, 2016).

Problems and Issues in Mineral and Energy Production

Africa's mineral and energy production has brought forth a host of problems and issues some of which relate to the physical and human impact of resource exploitation, and some of which relate to the role of mineral and energy production in national economic development.

Physical and Human Impact of Mineral and Energy Production

Mineral production has adverse physical environmental impacts. Not only does it lead to destruction of vegetation, but it also pollutes rivers, streams, groundwater, and the air, all of which poses danger to both humans and wildlife. Evidence of these kinds of pollution have been documented across the continent. Examples include, removal of top soil, construction of access roads and railways, dumping of mine waste, and degradation of forest and deforestation. In 2001, thousands of cubic meters of mine wastewater contaminated with cyanide and heavy metals spilled into the Asuman River in the Wassa West District of Ghana after a tailing dam failed, decimating all form of life in the river (Anane, 2001). In 2009, heavy metal and cyanide concentration from the North Mara gold mine in Tanzania were found to be higher than WHO, USEAP, and Tanzania government levels (Bitala et al., 2009). In Kenya, the Kerio River has an iron content that is three times higher than World Health Organization's recommended level. In Zambia, the Copper Belt effluent ends up in the Kafue River, which is the source of drinking water for 40% of the country's population (Twerefou, 2009), while in Mufilira and Kitwe, sulfur dioxide plume covers about 12,000 ha of land. In the Niger Delta, a recent report released by the UN Environmental Program (UNEP) (2011) indicates extensive pollution in land areas, sediments, and swamp areas, as well as destruction of fisheries and rendering root crops such as cassava inedible. In addition, the report found contaminated water in 28 wells in 10 communities, and that many people in Ogoniland had lived with chronic oil pollution throughout their lives. In South Africa, large volumes of mine water pumped from the gold mines to get access to the mines to the surface are left to evaporate, with some seeping into shallow aquifers. This and other run-offs in turn have contributed to the salination of the Sand River (Usher and Vermeulen, 2006).

The use of heavy metals such as mercury in mining activities also causes chemical pollution in the environment and damaging effects on the brain, kidney, lungs, and other vital organs. In this regard, the particularly high mercury emission in all the mineral regions of Central, North, Southern, and West Africa, with the highest concentrations in South Africa, Zimbabwe, DRC, Nigeria, Ghana, and Algeria is particularly worrisome. Other toxic substances that have been found in mineral production zones are arsenic, cadmium, lead, and sulfuric acid (Twerefuo, 2009).

Energy production also has its own environmental problems. Air pollution from the use of coal and oil contributes toward acid rain, and the weakening of the carbon storage capacity of the biosphere. Hydroelectricity creates flooding, inundation of vast areas of the ecosystem, and loss of human cultures and livelihoods. The social impact of mineral production includes health, conflicts, drug abuse, alcoholism, robbery, and divorce. All the air, water, and chemical pollution in turn have significant impact of the health of not only the miners but also of the communities in which the mines are located. Dust particles from mining activities pose major health hazard for lung and other respiratory diseases. In particular, the use of mercury by AMPs are particularly dangerous to the miners and the people who live in the communities.

Conflicts over mineral production areas have been widespread. Some have been confined to actual areas of production, such as the Niger Delta, while others have exploded into protracted country-wide wars such as in the DRC, Sierra Leone, Liberia, and Angola. According to Twerefuo (2009), much of these conflicts have derived from distribution of royalties, land use, and resettlements. In particular, royalty distribution either goes to local elites, district assemblies, or local chiefs who either treat these as personal or district-wide assets. The result is that the people who actually are adversely impacted by the mining activity feel cheated.

Land use in mineral production areas also causes conflict in situation where large mining concessions prevent or limit local people from using the land. In most cases, the land owners are not properly compensated for but they are expected to cooperate with the new company. Moreover, the concession is usually a large tract of land of which a relatively smaller portion is used for the actual mining operation, with rest of the land used for dumping waste (Akabzaa, 2009).

In some cases, large-scale resettlement schemes have been undertaken which involves disruption of people's lives. For example, from 1990 to1998, about 30,000 people living in 14 communities in the Tarkwa area of Ghana were relocated or resettled. Other social impact include increasing prostitution fueled by migrant expatriates into the area, drug use, reduction in agricultural activities, and noise pollution caused by widespread use of explosives and excavation machines.

All these show that economic and material development has a cost. As Africa strives to improve its living conditions through mineral and energy production, it must also be cognizance of the harmful environmental and social impacts that could occur and plan for them. Environmental activists are standing by to oppose many of these projects especially with large hydroelectric power projects electricity generation, and rightly so, but Africa needs to walk the tight rope of balancing between the needs of its people and environmental concerns. After all, much of the opposition to such projects often comes from countries that have met their basic needs and can now take better care of the environment.

Mineral Production, Conflict, and Development

A second set of issues in mineral and energy production centers around the relationship between mineral reserves and production, and economic development. The role that mineral production played in the economic development in the past, led to a development theory that was solely based on possession of mineral wealth. Hewett (1929) argued that the development of a nation's economic activities depended on availability of domestic minerals. At the initial stages of development, these minerals are exploited and sold outside to generate revenue, which is then used to provide the much-needed infrastructure for further development. These help support the development of a goods exporting sector. Thus, as domestic minerals dwindle, the country is able to support the goods manufacturing sector with imports. While this theory seems to have been demonstrated to some extent by the development of Canada, USA, and Australia, it has not been the case in the majority of mineral-rich African countries. In fact, in some of African countries such as Nigeria, Angola, Liberia, Sierra Leone, and the DRC, minerals have rather become a source of protracted warfare and bloodshed as well as untold suffering, not in the distant past. The obvious question that arises is why were developed countries able to use their mineral wealth to develop and African countries that are well endowed with mineral wealth (except South Africa) have not? This is not an easy question to answer and several perspectives have been shared as to why this is the case. Obi (2009) summarizes these under five perspectives: the new political economy/war economies, neo-patrimonialism; the resource curse; environmental scarcities; and horizontal inequality-conflict perspectives.

The **new political perspective** represented by the work of Collier and Hoeffler (2001) and the World Bank sees wars as incentives for African political elites to amass wealth for themselves. As a result, existence of natural resources becomes a catalyst for the political elites to engage in conflicts, which then gives them opportunities to amass wealth for themselves. The key to end this is to turn that incentive to disincentive. The **neopatrimonialism** perspective attributes the conflict and lack of development to predatory activities of political leaders that translate into high levels of corruption, and patrimonial politics that weaken the state, concentrates access to power and resources in the hands a few, and thereby disenfranchises large groups of people from benefitting from state resources. This breeds a lot of resentment and a feeling of injustice on the part of the disenfranchised, who then see armed struggle and violence as their only way of recourse.

The **resource curse thesis** attributes conflict situation and troubled development in Africa to resource wealth. It argues that mineral wealth provides a platform for corruption, mismanagement, human rights abuses, and eventually violent conflicts. This in turn stops economic development. So rather than enhancing development, possession of high amounts of mineral or natural resources becomes detrimental to development (Ross, 2001, 2004; Obi, 2009; Johannes et al., 2015). On its part, the **environmental scarcities perspective** sees conflict as a result of dwindling resources vis-à-vis increasing population and increasing demand and competition for resources. This breeds ground for conflict. Indeed, this was how some people explained the conflicts in Rwanda, Liberia, and Sierra Leone. Finally, the **horizontal inequality-conflict perspective** as articulated by Stewart (2000) attributes conflict to the tendency of political leaders to solicit the power of horizontal or sociocultural inequalities for their personal political gains. By tying the inequalities to distribution of existing resources, the leaders are able to construct group identities and drive a wedge among the groups pitting one against the other toward conflict situations.

The question is which one of these perspectives is right? Once again, the answer is a complex one. For purpose of further discussion and contribution to the debate, it is important to recognize that there are two issues here that need to be separated from each other: there is the conflict issue and there is the development issue. The conflict issue raises the question of why possession of mineral wealth generates conflict, while the development issue deals with why most African countries have not been able to turn their possession of mineral and energy production into long-lasting economic development.

With respect to the conflict issue, we need to remind ourselves that history is replete with conflicts and wars over resources whether one calls it empire building, colonial conquest, or manifest destiny. Individuals or groups of people have, throughout history, fought for control over other people so as to gain control of their lands and other associated natural resources such as rich mineral resources, fishing grounds, forest resources, or an important trade route. In the same vein, individuals and groups of people have resisted domination and perceived injustice or inequity over distribution of common or shared resources. The so-called resource-curse of modern-day Africa is no different from this pattern of past human history. For some it is due to the long marginalization from equally benefitting from the resource revenue due to greed and neopatrimonialistic politics, expressed in outright corruption and one-sided misappropriation of mineral revenue by those who happened to be in control. For others it is the need to finance an ongoing war by establishing control over mineral resources. In all these cases, the problem is not with the mineral resources, but with people's attitude and behavior. The fundamental question is "Why would a few people try to control the resources that belong to the whole country for the benefit of themselves and those close to them just because they happen to hold political power, or have the power to do so?" This lends support to the neopatrimonialism thesis that it is the decay in Africa's human factor or the human or organic composition of the institutions and management of the use of natural resources revenue that is the problem. The manifestation of this decay of the organic composition of institutions is widespread corruption and mismanagement that have pervaded the continent whereby substantial portions of mineral revenue tend to be squandered by some public officials, and unfortunately sometimes with foreign collaborators.

With respect to the development issue, the obvious question that arises from this situation is why is that developed countries were able to use their mineral wealth to develop and African countries that are well endowed with mineral wealth (except South Africa) have not? This is also not an easy question to answer. However, we can identify certain factors that seem to plague African countries today that were not the same at the time that developed countries were coming up through the same process.

First, African mining activities depended largely on colonial capital. This capital was invested by colonial interests. After colonialism, most of this capital was withdrawn. Indigenous capital that could have stepped in was lacking so in most countries, they had to still depend on foreign capital. This weakened the bargaining position of the countries which in many cases had to settle for agreements that did not bring them any value (see for example, Campbell, 2009; Akabzaa, 2009).

Second, by virtue of its dependence on foreign capital and weak bargaining agreements, mineral production in African countries did not generate any linkages in the local economies. In the main, the producing countries remained primary producers—produced the minerals for export without any effort to develop value-added activities that were linked to the mining operations.

Third, the fluctuating nature of market prices of most of these minerals, partly due to over production, technological changes, or development of substitute materials have for a long period left Africa's mineral economies vulnerable. With the exception of South Africa, whose mineral wealth is very diverse, this fluctuation in prices on the world market further worsens the fortunes of countries that depend on one or two minerals for the bulk of their foreign earnings. These fluctuations lead to a decline in government revenue and subsequent inability on the part of the government to meet its debt obligations. This then leads to search for loans from either the IMF or World Bank, which then comes with devaluation of currency causing the prices of the country's product, and for that matter minerals, to become cheaper on the world market. The result is a further decline of mineral prices and revenue. This has happened too many times to mineral-dependent African countries.

Fourth, in countries that have one or two major minerals, a boom in prices created a feeling of relying solely on the mineral revenue to pay every bill. Thus, rather than reinvesting back the surplus from the boom into other productive areas such as agriculture and industry, those areas were rather neglected completely. This resulted in the development of a vicious circle of decline: neglect of agriculture lead to low production of food and industrial raw material. This leads to the need to use the revenue to fund imports, including food as well as conspicuous consumption, rather than productive sectors in the local economy. So why has South Africa and Botswana so far been successful? South Africa's mining activities right from the beginning relied on indigenous capital. The European investors were settlers who had gone to South Africa to stay. So they had vested interest in seeing that their investments were successful. Second, the profits from the mining activities were invested into industrial activities that were tied to the mining activities. In fact, in the field of mining South Africa developed some of the innovative ways of mining because of the difficulty of reaching some of its minerals. These led to establishment of capital goods industries. Third, South Africa's mineral wealth is diverse and as a result has an advantage that the other countries did not have. To some extent, South Africa was also fortunate to have the only substantial reserves of coal in Africa and so developed a technology that was more dependent on coal than other sources of energy. Indeed this became handy for the country even during the economic sanctions of the Apartheid era. Botswana's case was discussed in Chapter 7.

In spite of these, mineral-rich African countries still have a future. However, it seems that to be successful in turning mining into a development asset, the ideal situation will be African countries to have home-grown investments into their mining sectors. In the absence of that, the only alternative for African countries is to seek foreign direct investments. However, this behooves upon African countries to present stronger terms with potential investors to avoid the one-sided gains to potential investors in the past arrangements. After all, life was going on without the extraction of the given mineral so if the terms are not suitable, there should be no need to rush and accept an agreement that will not benefit the country. As part of this, African countries should look at long-term implications of these investments, in particular the ones that will generate value addition or linkages within the domestic economy rather than just exchanging the export of minerals for building of road or other kinds of infrastructure. In effect, African countries need to think about how they will fix or maintain that infrastructure in 10 to 15 years later when the mineral wealth is exhausted. Finally, African countries need to use the revenue from mineral production and export to diversify their economies to ensure equitable distribution of the benefits from mineral and energy production—and not neglect the rest of the economy. The new African Mining Vision (AMV) articulates these sentiments very well. The question is whether African countries will have the guts to follow through on them.

Summary

Africa is still a hotbed for minerals and has vast untapped resources for energy production, even after it had undergone a long period of colonial and postcolonial exploitation. Yet, much of this wealth had not produced significant results for most of the mineral-rich countries, while the vast energy resources still remain untapped. Over the past few years, African countries have doubled their efforts at correcting this situation. A new vision has been articulated to move beyond just exporting of raw materials to value added products and also to be more mindful of the environment and distribution of benefits. On the energy front, efforts have focused new hydroelectric power projects and general mention about other sources of renewable energy.

The question that still remains is whether African countries would follow up the vision and policies with action. Much of the test is going to be in how they negotiate with potential investors and whether they have the courage to stand firm in the face of institutionalized coercion. Secondly, given the uneven distribution of both mineral and energy resources, one would think that a regional approach in harnessing these resources would be more sensible, practical, and doable. Finally, African countries need to think outside the box especially in the area of other energy resources, seriously look into how their vast resources of renewable energy could be harnessed cheaply to their benefit. For example, rather than continuing to support Institutes of Nuclear and Atomic Energy in many of its universities, African countries should divert those resources into research institutes of solar, wind, and geothermal energy.

Postreading Assignment

A. Study the Following Concepts

artisanal

Beneficiation

Brownfield concession

Btu

Bulk extraction

Cobalt

conflict minerals

Dredging

Dry steam

Energy minerals

Environmental scarcity
  perspective

Ferroalloy metals

Fossil fuels

Greenfield concession

Horizontal inequality-
  conflict perspective

Hydraulic fracking

Independent power
  producer

Industrial

Industrial minerals

Kimberley Process

Large-scale mining

Merensky Reef

Mining

Neo-patrimonialism

New political perspective

Nonferrous metals

Nonrenewable

Open-pit mining

Primary and secondary
  energy

Private partnership in
  infrastructure

Public private partnership

Pumping

Refining

Renewable

reserve base

Reserves

Resource-curse thesis

Selective extraction

Smelting

Strip mining

Underground

B. Do the Following

1. Go back to the answers to the questions to your knowledge of mineral and energy production of Africa now.

2. Try and answer the same questions and compare your answers now with what you had before.

3. Debate the validity of the resource-curse thesis in the light of Africa's situation.

4. Why do you think most of the African countries endowed with minerals have not been able to use their resources to develop as other developed countries did before?

References

African Union. 2009. *The African Mining Vision.*

Addis Ababa Hewett, D. F. 1929. "Cycles in Metal Production." *American Institute of Mining and Metallurgical Engineers Transactions,* 85: 65–92.

Akabzaa, T. 2009. "Mining in Ghana: Implications for National Economic Development and Poverty Reduction." In Campbell, B. (Ed.) *Mining in Africa: Regulation and Development.* London: Pluto Press, pp. 25–65.

Arndt, C. 2010. "High Hopes for Zambia's Copperbelt Ghost Town." *Mail & Guardian* 11: 16.

Belem, G. 2009. "Mining, Poverty Reduction, the Protection of the Environment, and the World Bank Group in Mali." In Campbell, B. (Ed.) *Mining in Africa: Regulation and Development.* London: Pluto Press, pp. 119–149.

Bijlsma, B. 2011. *Governing Mining in Africa: African Perspectives, State Initiatives and International Standards.* Amsterdam: Niza/ActionAid.

Bitala, M. F., Kweyunga, C., and Manoko, M. L. K. 2009. "Levels of Heavy Metals and Cyanide in Soil, Sediments, and Water from the Vicinity of North Mara Gold Mine in Tarime District, Tanzania." *A Report Presented to CCT.*

Blyden, B. K., and Akiwumi, F. A. 2008. "Unrealized Potential in Africa." *IEEE Power & Energy Magazine* (July/August): 52–58.

British Geological Survey, 2013 *World Mineral Production, 2007–2011.* Keyworth, Nottingham: British Geological Survey.

Brown, T. J., Idione, N. E., Raycraft, E. R., Shaw, R. A., Hobbs, S. F., Everett, P., Deady, E. A., and Bide, T. 2018 *World Mineral Production, 2012–2016* Keyworth, Nottingham: British Geological Survey

Burdette, M. M. 1988. *Zambia Between Two World.* Boulder, CO: Westview Press.

Campbell, B. 2009. "Guinea and Bauxite-Aluminium: The Challenges of Development and Poverty Reduction." In Campbell, B. (Ed.) *Mining in Africa: Regulation and Development.* London: Pluto Press, pp. 66–118.

Christopher, A. J. (1984). Colonial Africa. London: Croom Helm

Collier, P. and Hoeffler, A., 2001. "Greed and Grievance in Civil War," http://www.worldbank.org/research/conflict/papers/greedgrievance.htm, The World Bank.

Cuesta, I. ND. "Researching African States: Thoughts about the Spatial Reach of African States South of the Sahara." http://africanstates.wordpress.com/2013/02/01/the-history-of-electricity-production-in-africa/ (accessed 25 July 2014).

Donaldson, D. B. 2014. "World's Biggest Hydro Power Project—Bigger than China's Three Gorges—in Africa Given Go-ahead by World Bank." http://guardianlv.com/2014/04/worlds-biggest-hydro-power-project-bigger-than-chinas-three-gorges-in-africa-given-go-ahead-by-world-bank/#MpGhJbAeEDJziBEp.99. *USGS: Mineral Surveys: Various Years* (accessed 1 August 2014).

Eberhard, A. 2007. "The Political Economy of Power Sector Reform in South Africa." In Victor, D. G., and Heller, T. C. (Eds.) *The Political Economy of Power Sector Reform: The Experiences of Five Major Developing Countries.* Cambridge: Cambridge University Press, pp. 215–253.

Eberhard, A., Rosnes, O., Shikaratan, M., and Vennemo, H. 2011. *Africa's Power Infrastructure: Investment, Integration, Efficiency.* Washington, DC: The World Bank.

EIR. 2003. *Striking a Better Balance – The World Bank Group and Extractive Industries: The Final Report of the Extractive Industries Review.*

Gravelle, J. 2012. "Spotlight on Mining in Africa." *Canadian Journal of Mining* 134 (4): 58.

Hammel, A., White, C., Pfeiffer, S., and Miller, D. 1999. "Pre-colonial mining in southern Africa." *The Journal of the South African Institute of Mining and Metallurgy* January/February: 49–56.

Hilson, G., and McQuilken, J. 2014. "Four Decades of Support for Artisanal and Small-scale Mining in sub-Saharan Africa: A Critical Review." *The Extractive Industries and Society* 1: 104–118.

International Peace Information Service. 2012. *The Formalisation of Artisanal Mining in the Democratic Republic of the Congo and Rwanda.* Bogor, Indonesia: Center for International Forestry Research.

International Renewable Energy Agency (IRENA). 2013. "Africa's Renewable Future: The Path to Sustainable Growth." Abu Dhabi: IRENA.

Johannes, E., Zulu, L., and Kalipeni, E. 2015. "Oil Discovery in Turkana County, Kenya: A Source of Conflict or Development?" *African Geographical Review* 34 (2): 142–164.

Kesler, S. E. (1994) *Mineral Resources, Economics and the Environment.* New York: Macmillan College Publishing Company, Inc.

Mazalto, M. 2009. "Governance, Human Rights and Mining in the Democratic Republic of Congo." In Campbell, B. (Ed.) *Mining in Africa: Regulation and Development.* London: Pluto Press, pp. 187–242.

Monforti, F. 2011. *Renewable Energies in Africa.* Luxembourg: European Union.

Obi, C. 2009. "Nigeria's Niger Delta: Understanding the Complex Drivers of Violent Oil-related Conflict." *Africa Development* XXXIV (2): 103–128.

Ofosu-Mensah, E. A. 2011. "Historical overview of traditional and modern gold mining in Ghana" *International Research Journal of Library, Information and Archival Studies* 1(1): 6–22

Otieno, H. O., and Awange, J. L. 2006. *Energy Resources in East Africa: Opportunities and Challenges.* Heidelberg: Springer-Verlag.

Parawira, W. 2009. "Biogas Technology in Sub-Saharan Africa: Status, Prospects and Constraints." *Reviews in Environmental Science and Biotechnology* 1 8: 187–200.

Pearce, F. 2013. "Will Huge New Hydro Projects Bring Power to Africa's People?" http://e360.yale.edu/feature/will_huge_new_hydro_projects_bring_power_to_africas_people/2656/ (accessed August 1, 2014).

Razavi, H., Nzabanita, E., and Santi, E. 2012. "Energy Sector." In Santi, E., Romdhane, S. B., and Shaw, W. (Eds.). *Unlocking North Africa's Potential through Regional Integration: Challenges and Opportunities.* Tunis-Belvedere: African Development Bank, pp. 26–54.

Ross, M., 2004b. "How Do Natural Resources Influence Civil War? Evidence from Thirteen Cases." *International Organizations,* 58 (1): 35–67.

Ross, M., 2001. "Does Oil Hinder Democracy." *World Politics,* 53 (3): 325–361.

Showers, K. B. 2011. "Electrifying Africa: An Environmental History with Policy Implications." *Geografiska Annaler: Series B, Human Geography* 93 (3): 193–221.

Stewart, F., 2000. "Crisis Prevention: Tackling Horizontal Inequalities." *Oxford Development Studies,* 28 (3): 245–262.

Sulle, E., and Nelson, F. 2009. *Biofuels, Land Access and Rural Livelihoods in Tanzania.* London: IIED.

Tryou, T. 2016. "The Five Biggest Wind Energy Markets in Africa." http://www.renewableenergyfocus.com/view/44926/the-five-biggest-wind-energy-markets-in-africa/ (Acessed October 15, 2018).

Twerefou, D. K. 2009. *Mineral Exploitation, Environmental Sustainability and Sustainable Development in EAC, SADC and ECOWAS Regions.* Africa Trade Policy Center Work in Progress No. 79 Economic Commission of Africa.

United Nations Economic Commission for Africa (UNECA) 2011. *Minerals and Africa's Development: The International Study Group Report on Africa's Mineral Regimes.* Addis Ababa: UNECA.

United Nations Environmental Program (UNEP) 2011. *Environmental Assessment of Ogoniland.* Nairobi: United Nations Environmental Program.

US Department of Energy "Geothermal Basics." http://energy.gov/eere/geothermal/geothermal-basics/ (accessed August 4, 2014).

Usher, B. H., and Vermeulen, P. D. 2006. "The Impacts of Coal and Gold Mining on the Associated Water Resources in South Africa." In XU, Y., and Usher, B. (Eds.) *Ground water Pollution in Africa.* London, UK: Taylor & Francis Group, pp. 301–314.

Manufacturing Activities

The role of manufacturing activities in transforming living conditions of people has been recognized since the European industrial revolution began in England. Not only do manufacturing activities provide jobs for large numbers of people, but their value added to products generate more revenue than raw materials. This translates to higher incomes and better-paying jobs than most other economic activities. Manufacturing activities also provide several linkages within the local economy, which in turn create more jobs in other sectors. For example, it creates demand for raw materials and services, which in turn lead to creation of more jobs in the local economy. Manufacturing jobs are not immune to upswings and downswings of the general economy but they are by and large more stable than the seasonality that characterizes such sectors as agriculture, mineral production, and tourism. Yet, the manufacturing sector is in fact the weakest link in Africa's economy.

In April 2000, the then UN Secretary General, Mr. Kofi Annan, characterized Africa's low-level industrialization as follows: (1) Only a handful of African countries have manufacturing as a share of GDP (gross domestic product) exceeding 25%, which is the benchmark for considering a country as having achieved the threshold of industrial "take-off." (2) The export composition of African countries continues to be dominated by primary products rather than processed or semifinished products. (3) Africa's contribution to global industrial production is just 0.3%. He noted that if Africa is to cross the threshold of chronic poverty, it must see growth in its manufacturing sector (Annan, 2000). Sadly, not much has changed since then. In this chapter, we examine the story of Africa's manufacturing efforts, the structure of its current manufactures, and the problems and prospects of the sector.

EVOLUTION AND DEVELOPMENT OF MANUFACTURING ACTIVITIES IN AFRICA

Precolonial Africa

The state of manufacturing in Africa was not always like it is today for two reasons. First, the word "manufacture" means to make by hands and in that sense Africans were among the pioneers of manufacturing as economic activities. Indeed, Bairoch (1982, 1993) shows that on the eve of the English industrial revolution, a greater proportion (over 60%) of the world's manufactured products were from the present-day developing countries. Of these Africa featured prominently. Thus, precolonial Africa was replete with industrial activities and industrial districts that displayed a high level of specialization and innovativeness based on the prevailing technology of the time. These industries included textile, metallurgy, home utensils and appliances, weaponry, and tools of all kinds. Most of these industries grew to become integral part of the economies of kingdoms and empires that emerged on the continent. Modern industry in precolonial Africa made its debut on the continent in Egypt during the reign of Mohammed Ali (1805–1849). Mohammed Ali established modern arms industry in his goal to transform Egypt into an independent military power. After closing down many traditional industries in Egypt, many of the workers were forced to work in the new factories—textiles, food, and arms. Many of these industries collapsed toward the end of Mohammed Ali's rule but some were revived under Khedive Ismail, who emphasized textiles, sugar, and weapons (Ibrahim and Ibrahim, 2003).

Colonial Africa

Manufacturing activities in Africa declined during the colonial period, except for a few areas such as South Africa and Egypt. There were two reasons for this. The first is African industries were not able to innovate and develop new technologies that could compete with the enormous success that resulted from the emergence of the factory system in Europe. The second reason is that colonial economic policy emphasized commercialization of African economies through production and export of agricultural products and other staples. No efforts were made to encourage manufacturing industries in Africa since that would have been counterproductive to the whole colonial enterprise. Instead, African markets were flushed with manufactured goods from Europe, which looked both modern and superior to African goods.

The only exceptions to this case were enclaves of European settlements such as Dakar, Leopoldville (Kinshasa), and Nairobi, where due to substantial European settlers some manufacturing was allowed to take place (Mabogunje, 1973). The result was that manufacturing industries that had thrived in Africa before colonialism gradually declined, stagnated, or completely collapsed. Indeed it was only during the late colonial period, specifically after World War II that efforts at manufacturing were made but this was limited to semiprocessing of bulky raw materials mostly minerals to reduce the transportation cost from the interior. Among these were cotton lint ginneries, palm oil and groundnut oil mills, fruit and vegetable canneries, leather tanneries, and metal beneficiation factories (Mabogunje, 1973).

Postcolonial Africa

Postcolonial Africa reacted to the colonial economic development in the 1960s in a dramatic way by pursuing a number of industrialization policies including import-substitution and export-led industrialization.

Import-Substitution Industrialization (ISI) Policy

Developments in South Africa, which achieved its independence in 1910, set a template for this reaction. According to Schneider (2000), the development of the manufacturing sector in South Africa began in earnest when successive South African administration after 1924 extracted agreements with the mining companies to benefit the state in exchange for "exploitation of black labor, low tariffs on mining inputs, and cheap electricity" (Schneider, 2000, p. 415). In 1924, the South African government decided to pursue an import-substitution policy of industrialization. This policy aimed at producing domestically to substitute for imports (import-substitution). The cornerstone of this policy according to Schneider (2000) was the Tariff Act of 1925. This made it more profitable to produce domestically than elsewhere. The result was that many American and European firms located in South Africa to get around the tariff and also to take advantage of the growing domestic market. The government granted protected markets to manufacturers and farmers, and sought to maintain industrial peace by negotiating with white unions while brutally suppressing their black counterparts. In addition, capital goods were imported duty free. In 1927, the state-owned Iron and Steel Industrial Corporation (Iscor) was established to take advantage of the abundance of local coal, iron ore deposits, and cheap power, and to produce steel for the local mining industry. Other government policies included deliberate racists division of labor policies that required state enterprises to hire more white workers with higher wages and private firms were given protection if they did likewise (Schneider, 2000). Also the government instituted several inward-looking policies to deal with balance of payments problems and difficulties in capital flows. These included the Board of Trade and Industries' assurances to business people who would establish certain companies; banking laws to restrict capital flow out of the country; and the establishment of the state-owned Industrial Development Corporation (IDC) to provide funds for new and expanding business (Schneider, 2000). These measures led to high growth in manufacturing in South Africa from 1955 through 1981. Manufacturing replaced mining as the leading economic sector, and South Africa became the most industrialized country on the continent.

Like South Africa, the majority of African countries adopted the import-substitution policy of industrialization. Theoretically it was a three-stage policy. First was to establish manufacturing plants to produce for imports. Second was to reduce the volume of foreign inputs, and the third was to use mostly domestic inputs (Nzau, 2010). Manufacturing industries including textiles, garment and apparel, footwear, building materials, vehicle assembly, iron and steel, and oil refineries, were established rapidly, as the first phase. However, as a result of a number of problems, the next two phases were never implemented. First, most of the industries relied on importing not only the capital goods but also the raw material needed for manufacturing. This required substantial hard currency, which did not exist in the first place in most African countries. This resulted in substantial borrowing and massive external debt for the countries. Second, the haste with which some of these industries were established did not allow proper planning and this resulted in grave mistakes in some of the factories, such as the use of faulty material and installation of dilapidated equipment that never worked (Krassowski, 1974; Rugumamu, 1989). Third, the location of the industries also had a built-in urban bias (Chapter 3). The fact that most of the inputs had to be imported meant that the industries had to be located either near seaports or in the capital cities that had relatively better infrastructure for manufacturing activities. This did not only lead to a massive rural–urban migration for jobs that were nonexistent but also a spatial mismatch with distribution of industrial resources on the continent.

Mabogunje, the eminent Nigerian geographer, succinctly captured this situation in 1973 when he observed:

> Many of these problems result from the relative overconcentration of much of the total industrial capacity in African countries in port or capital cities. Yet the most striking fact about the present locational pattern of manufacturing is its marginal location of resources on the continent. . . . Iron ore in Tropical Africa comes mainly from three countries – Liberia, Sierra Leone, Guinea, and Mauritania. . . . Yet, nowhere in tropical Africa is there a clear prospect for the development of a viable iron and steel industry. The three countries with most of the reserves are too small to provide a market of an appropriate size; larger countries such as Nigeria or Ethiopia . . . do not have any notable iron ore deposits. The result is that Africa remains an exporter of iron ore rather than a producer of steel products. The same factors basically underscore the pattern of utilization of other metallic ores. . . . When one reviews the situation in regard to the other natural resources, one is confronted with an industrialization process which goes on largely unmindful of local raw materials resources.
>
> (Mabogunje, 1973, pp. 12–13)

Fourth, most of these industries were state-owned and for that reason were more subject to political manipulation than sound economic principles. In particular, ruling governments used them as political leverage over the opposition by offering jobs and other rewards to the general public (Nzau, 2010). This opened the door to corruption, financial mismanagement, nepotism, and neopatrimonialism, all of which helped drive the companies into financial insolvency. Fifth, since the implementation of the policy could not be extended beyond phase one, most of the industries had no linkages within the local economy. As a result of all these, most of the factories either became mere white elephants or operated under capacity.

These problems of the ISI policy were exacerbated in many African countries by a wave of socialist and nationalist ideologies that led to either nationalization or indigenization of African economies including the manufacturing sector. These policies resulted in government take-over of manufacturing establishments that were privately owned. This ownership came with the responsibility of assuming the risk of investment and for that matter freed the former owners. In some cases, management consultancy and former owners were contacted to manage the newly state-owned firms as it was in the case of Tanzania (Rugumamu, 1989).

On a somewhat positive note, the ISI policy brought awareness to the need to expand the minimum size of the market in order to produce intermediate goods. As a result, the United Nations Economic Commission of Africa (ECA) encouraged African countries to organize themselves into industrial groups as early as the 1960s. The ECA undertook several feasibility studies on various industrial groups and even convened a conference of industrialists and financiers in Addis Ababa in 1967.

The Central African Monetary Union (UDEAC) was established in 1964, while the East Africa Economic Community was established in 1967. More of these organizations followed in the 1970s, all of them with agenda and programs for manufacturing. However, not much came out of these groupings and their activities.

Throughout the 1970s severe economic decline, due largely to the oil crisis and political instability, coupled with corruption and gross mismanagement in high places, and inability to secure the infusion of capital wreaked havoc on state enterprises. Still, majority of African countries held on to the poorly managed state-owned manufacturing companies on the rationale that the state could do a better job to equitably distribute resources than the private sector.

By the 1980s, industrial production in most African countries was either stagnant or in the negative. Even South Africa, the continent's most industrialized country was not immune to this decline, albeit the reasons were different from those of other African countries. Drawing again on the work of Schneider (2000) South Africa's problems were largely due to lack of technological innovation and its racist policies. Thus, the long-standing inward-looking policy without any technological innovations had left South African firms uncompetitive on the global scale. In addition, its long-standing racist policies had excluded the majority of the country's population from effectively participating in the domestic market to a point where the effective domestic market was too small to support the industrialization policy. As international opposition against the apartheid policy grew, the South African government spent more time and resources defending apartheid than making South African companies globally competitive through such investments as technological innovations and autonomy. Thus, substantial funds were spent to relocate manufacturing firms close to the so-called African homelands to prevent blacks from going to white areas, while self-sufficiency and survival goals trumped economic viability of manufacturing activities. Furthermore, international boycott against the apartheid policy was beginning to bite hard and this made it difficult for South Africa to even pursue export-base industrialization as other countries had done (Schneider, 2000).

Structural Adjustment Programs (SAPs) and Export-Led Industrialization

The events leading to the adoption of SAPs were discussed in Chapter 3. The privatization of the state enterprises, liberalization of trade, devaluation of the currencies, and removal of subsidies, that SAPs entailed created massive unemployment and severe economic hardships. Statistics on productivity in the targeted industries such as forest products improved, but their impact on the wider economies was far less clear.

Encouraged by the example of Asian countries, African countries tried to switch industrialization strategy to **export-led industrialization policy**. This policy aimed at producing for export rather than the domestic market. It usually began by way of establishing an Export Processing Zone (EPZ), a large demarcated area of land usually fenced and to which manufacturing firms are invited to locate for incentives. Among these incentives were waiver of export and import duties, subsidized infrastructure, utilities, factory space and warehousing, granting of tax holidays usually for five years, and abundant cheap labor. Mauritius adopted this policy in 1970 but it was in the 1990s that most African countries embraced EPZs as a strategy for industrialization. The results of this strategy however left much to be desired. Weak infrastructure, inadequate entrepreneurial capacity, institutions, political instability, and investor ignorance eroded the benefits of the EPZs that were established.

By the late 1990s, the World Bank and the International Monetary Fund (IMF) both admitted that SAPs had failed even in Ghana, the country that had been hailed as the star pupil of SAPs. In the end, African countries went full circle. The introduction of the heavily indebted poor countries (HIPIC) program in 1996 did not do much to encourage industrialization. HIPIC aimed at providing debt relief to poor African countries, with a condition that the relief was reinvested in education and health care (UNIDO, 2011).

In 2001, the newly formed African Union sought to revive the importance of manufacturing industries in the New Partnership for African Development (NEPAD). However, donor attention was much more focused on a revised HIPIC, which still emphasized social services more than manufacturing. In recent years, there has been renewed interest in EPZs and some countries such as Kenya has seen more firms interested in locating in the EPZs.

The UNIDO and UNCTAD Report on African Industrialization

In 2011, the United Nations Industrial Development Organization (UNIDO) and the United Nations Conference on Trade and Development (UNCTAD) issued a report on the state of industrialization in Africa. In the light of what has expired over Africa's industrialization history, it was not surprising that the report showed that the share of **manufacturing value added (MVA)** in Africa's GDP fell from 12.8% in 2000 to 10.5% in 2008. At the same time, Latin America's MVA share in GDP fell from 17% to 16%, while Asia's rose from 22% to 35%. MVA is the total manufacturing output less total intermediate inputs, which include raw materials, energy, semi-finished goods and services purchased to produce the output. Over the same period the share of manufactures in Africa's exports fell from 43% in 2000 to 39% in 2008 (UNIDO/UNCTAD, 2011). The report also showed that in terms of manufacturing growth 23 African countries had negative MVA per capita growth from 1990 to 2010. With less than 2% of global manufacturing, Africa was not only being marginalized in the world of manufacturing, it was losing ground. Finally, the report noted that Africa's manufacturing strength was in resource-based manufactures about 49% compared to low-technology manufacturing (20%) and medium high-tech manufacturing (31%). In addition, the sector was dominated by small-scale firms, the majority of whom operate in the informal sector (UNIDO/UNCTAD, 2011).

The report used measures to group African countries. The first was the level of industrialization measured by MVA with threshold of twice the regional average, and the second was industrial growth performance measured by the compound annual growth rate of MVA per capita with threshold of 2.5%. On the basis of these the report identified five groups of African countries—forerunners, achievers, catching up, falling behind, and infant stage. The forerunners are countries on a long-term sustained growth with industrialization level that is twice the average of the continent and an industrial growth performance of at least 2.5% per annum. The achievers are countries that attained a high level of industrialization but with industrial performance growth of below the 2.5%. The catching-up are countries on a promising fast growth industrialization path that have potential to achieve higher industrialization level over a relatively short period of time. The falling behind are countries with relatively low level of industrialization and have

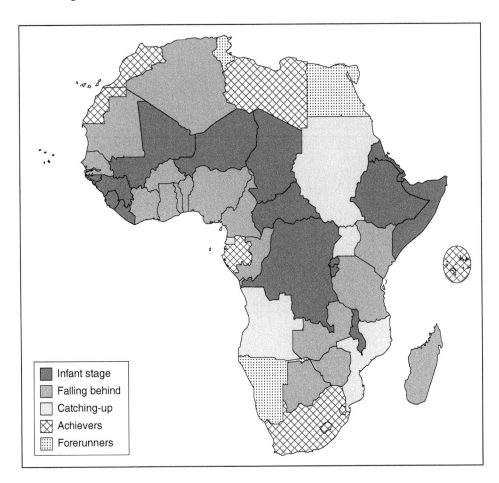

FIGURE 14.1 Industrialization progress in African countries. *Source:* UNCTAD/UNIDO 2011.

Legend:
- Infant stage
- Falling behind
- Catching-up
- Achievers
- Forerunners

not been able to improve their level of industrialization. The infant group is countries with very low industrialization and very poor industrial growth performance (UNIDO/UNCTAD, 2011). Figure 14.1 is a map showing the countries that fall in each of these categories.

UNIDO's Competitive Industrial Performance (CIP) data throw additional light on Africa's industrialization performance. The CIP index shows a country's industrial performance. It is based on four industrial performance measures: manufacturing value added per capita (MVApc), manufactured exports per capita (MXpc), industrialization intensity (which is the average of the share of MVA in GDP and the share of medium- and high-technology activities in MVA) (INDint_index), and industrial export quality index (MXQual_index) (Table 14.1). Only countries with data on all four measures are included in the calculation of the CIP. Based on this measure countries are classified into CIP quintiles—top, upper middle, middle, lower middle, and bottom. In 2015, only 32 African countries were included in the global database of 148 countries. Of these, 15 were in the bottom quintile, 8 in the lower middle, 8 in the middle, and only 1 (South Africa) in the upper middle (Table 14.1). Globally, South Africa ranked 47, while the last four ranked countries were all African—Central African Republic, Burundi, Eritrea, and Ethiopia. The obvious question is why has industrialization been a difficult venture for Africa? For the rest of the chapter, we answer this question by studying specific examples of Africa's industrialization efforts. We begin with a broad examination of Africa's manufacturing production systems, and how these systems have operated in a select number of manufacturing sectors.

TABLE 14.1

Competitive Industrial Performance (CIP) of African Countries

Country	CIP	CIP rank	Quintile	INDint_index	MVApc	MXpc	MXQual_index
South Africa	0.07	47	Upper Middle	0.32	952.18	876.52	0.61
Tunisia	0.04	62	Middle	0.34	683.28	1,125.17	0.71
Morocco	0.04	64	Middle	0.36	474.45	511.80	0.68
Egypt	0.04	70	Middle	0.31	436.64	163.97	0.52
Swaziland	0.03	81	Middle	0.51	1,441.30	888.90	0.63
Nigeria	0.03	82	Middle	0.34	254.37	91.08	0.18
Botswana	0.02	84	Middle	0.18	454.19	2,683.52	0.52
Namibia	0.02	86	Middle	0.18	603.34	1,759.44	0.54
Mauritius	0.02	87	Middle	0.24	1,291.74	1,260.02	0.50
Algeria	0.02	92	Lower Middle	0.12	263.73	272.17	0.18
Kenya	0.01	102	Lower Middle	0.22	118.58	58.93	0.36
Côte d'Ivoire	0.01	104	Lower Middle	0.23	152.58	93.24	0.22
Gabon	0.01	109	Lower Middle	0.09	471.55	647.68	0.14
Congo	0.01	110	Lower Middle	0.06	136.75	560.28	0.70
Senegal	0.01	111	Lower Middle	0.29	120.78	104.52	0.39
Cameroon	0.01	116	Lower Middle	0.23	183.53	45.57	0.21
Zambia	0.01	118	Lower Middle	0.23	126.20	66.62	0.24
Tanzania	0.01	120	Bottom	0.13	54.91	47.28	0.33
Ghana	0.01	121	Bottom	0.07	90.57	79.01	0.26
Madagascar	0.01	124	Bottom	0.20	55.39	38.66	0.25
Uganda	0.00	126	Bottom	0.18	54.96	16.10	0.27
Mozambique	0.00	127	Bottom	0.17	43.26	25.07	0.20
Malawi	0.00	130	Bottom	0.20	46.66	16.45	0.32
Niger	0.00	131	Bottom	0.22	23.98	34.67	0.49
Angola	0.00	132	Bottom	0.08	206.38	20.41	0.00
Cabo Verde	0.00	134	Bottom	0.23	195.45	71.21	0.28
Rwanda	0.00	139	Bottom	0.10	34.08	17.71	0.33
Central African Rep.	0.00	143	Bottom	0.30	52.73	3.71	0.45
Burundi	0.00	144	Bottom	0.13	21.75	3.74	0.31
Eritrea	0.00	145	Bottom	0.12	29.58	0.50	0.25
Ethiopia	0.00	146	Bottom	0.15	19.50	3.60	0.22
Gambia	0.00	147	Bottom	0.08	26.09	0.42	0.08

Source: Data from UNIDO.

Manufacturing Production Systems (MPS) of Africa

A **manufacturing production system (MPS)** is "a population of interacting firms in producing and supplying related sets of goods" (Hayter, 1997). In this case, manufacturing production system may be seen as a group of interacting firms in an industry.

It exhibits a wide range of geographic structures. It could be dispersed but globally integrated and it could be in dense agglomeration forming industrial district or cluster. Generally speaking, MPS is classified by firm size that dominates them. Africa's MPS may be classified by firm size as well as technology, and it includes indigenous or traditional, small-scale, and large-sale manufacturing production systems.

Indigenous Manufacturing Production System

The indigenous MPS consists of the remnants of the manufacturing industries of precolonial Africa. The firms are mainly craft-based that provide a wide range of traditional products. They are small in scale and are characterized by technological inertia in the sense that their methods of production have remained the same from time immemorial with very little change. Most of the workers in this system have little formal education. This means that the system has low infrastructure cost and less need for office space (Abegunde, 2011). Although a vast majority of Africans depend on this system, its products are still crude, not standardized, and are not based on sound scientific principles (Aworh, 2008). This system mostly relies on locally fabricated equipment, and oftentimes maintenance or equipment replacement is a problem. However, over their long period of existence, some of the methods of production have served the system well. A good example of this is gari-making. Cassava, which is the basic raw material contains high levels of cyanide that could be toxic if not properly removed. Without the benefit of modern science, traditional methods of gari-making sought to remove cyanide through peeling of the cassava, washing, grating, fermenting, pressing, sifting, roasting, and sieving to obtain gari, the final product. Traditional manufacturing production systems are also in most cases specialties of particular ethnic groups and therefore tend to occur in regional clusters of small towns and villages and in specific districts in large cities. This clustering allows them to network among themselves and with outside brokers in both purchasing of inputs and selling their products. A few members however sell directly to the market, without going through brokers.

Small-Scale Manufacturing Production System

Small-scale MPS consists of firms that have upgraded their traditional technologies of production through adaptation or use a mixture of modern and indigenous technologies in small-scale manufacturing activities. An example of the former is the upgraded gari-making in Nigeria and Ghana, and of the latter are the metal works and leather works in Gauteng, South Africa, in Suame, Ghana, Jua Kali in Kenya, and Katwe in Uganda (Rogerson, 1998). In the case of the mechanized gari manufacturing, the manual grating, pressing, sifting have all been mechanized, while the frying over open fire is accomplished on sheltered fryers and chimneys to reduce exposure of workers to heat. Since this system combines traditional and modern methods, it may also be referred to as hybrid MPS.

Majority of Africa's manufacturing activities belong to this group. It accounts for two-thirds of the manufacturing employment in Africa and between 24 and 64% of the total manufacturing value added. It also accounts for between 3 and 8% of the GDP of Africa. Like traditional MPS, the firms in the small-scale MPS have small capital most of which comes from personal resources, relatives, or from members of the extensive network in which the firms operate. In the small-scale palm oil industry in Ghana, for example, Osei-Amponsah et al. (2012) identified a network of more than 12 actors including market buyers of crude palm oil from Togo, buying agents from Nigeria, oil palm growers, formal and informal creditors, transporters,

Box 14.1 | The Small-Scale Palm Oil Industry in Ghana

The palm oil industry is one of the most important small-scale industries in Ghana. On the average a small-scale palm oil processing firm may employ about 25 people and may process an average of 4 metric tons of fresh fruit per month (Osei-Amponsah et al., 2012). The fruits are usually brought to the mill by trucks. The fruit bunches are sliced into parts and left on the floor with covering for 3–5 days to help loosen the fruits. The fruits are then carried to the cooking place where they are cooked in large metal containers overnight over fire provided by spent car tires, empty fruit bunches, and fiber sources (Osei-Amponsah et al., 2012). The cooked fruit is transferred into a mechanized digester for pounding, after which the oil is extracted through pressing. The remaining sludge is boiled again for more oil extraction. The oil is finally boiled over low heat for 1–2 hours after which the clean oil rises to the surface for final collection. Among the problems facing this industry are environmental and occupational health, poor quality, and so on. The energy used in processing comes from spent car tires that causes pollution and can thus be harmful to the workers. The disposal of effluents from processors into nearby streams and farms also pollute streams and the environment. Also, packaging materials come from containers that have been discarded from other products that are not properly sanitized and may contain other toxic residues. Also, in order to attract customers, artificial dye—Sudan dye—is added to the oil for additional red color. While this has been banned in Ghana and in many other countries it is still practiced. Also, quality standards are very poor. Without help from regulation there is no way of telling the quality standards of this product—free fatty acids concentrations in the oil are therefore much higher than acceptable limits (Osei-Amponsah et al., 2012).

mill owners, processors, domestic soap makers, and local market buyers, as well as palm oil research scientists (Box 14.1). Small-scale MPS varies in location. In the rural areas, it is quite dispersed, but in large cities, it tends to cluster in particular areas for reasons of economies of scale.

Large-Scale Manufacturing Production Systems

Large-scale MPS consists of relatively large-scale firms that use modern manufacturing technologies whether they are labor-intensive or not. Most of the firms are located in industrial districts or export processing zones in well-established premises, and they require relatively larger capital input and modern technology and machinery where applicable. A substantial number of these systems originated from the manufacturing establishments of the import-substitution era in the early post-independence period that were privatized during the SAP programs. As a result, most of them are now owned by foreign companies, but there are still a few that are domestically owned either privately or by the state, or by both.

Major Manufacturing Industries

It is impossible to cover the entire range of manufacturing activities in Africa in less than a chapter of a book. As a result, only a small select group of industries is discussed here. They are aluminum, automotive, chemicals, computer and electronics, food and beverage processing, forest products, leather works, metallurgy, petroleum refinery, pharmaceuticals, and textiles and garment. The distribution of these industries is given in Figure 14.2.

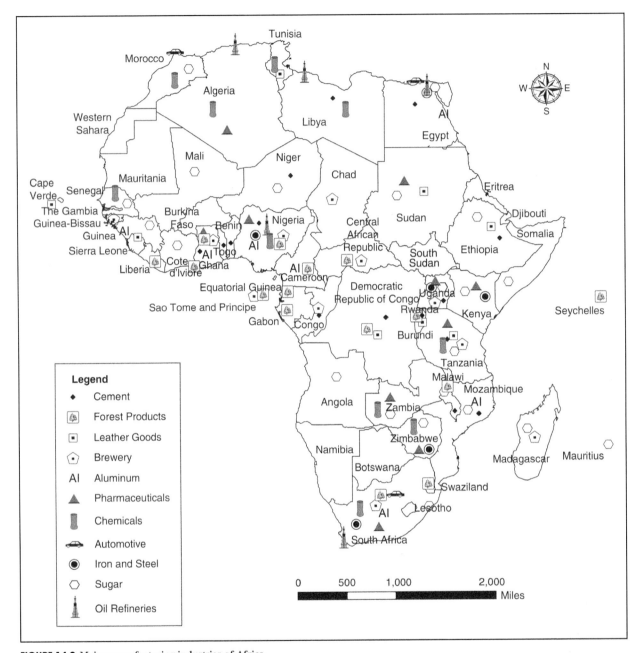

FIGURE 14.2 Major manufacturing industries of Africa.

The Aluminum Industry

Aluminum production begins with bauxite, the main raw material, and progresses through primary aluminum production, production of ingots or semis, and finally pure aluminum production. The industry in Africa is largely confined to the first and second phases of production of alumina and primary aluminum. The result is that Africa's contribution to the global industry is very small. For example, in 2013 Africa's primary aluminum production was only 3.6% of the world's total, even though the prospects for the industry in Africa are good. The reason for this low performance may be two folds. First, Africa's bauxite deposits are limited to very few countries—almost all of it is in Guinea with the rest of it in Ghana, and Sierra Leone. Deposits in Cameroon are of uncertain qualities (Chapter 13). Second, the smelting of alumina to primary aluminum is the most energy-intensive subsector of all major industries and the few African countries that built aluminum smelters because of what was then available, cheap sources of energy have not been able to sustain the energy needs due to increase in demand. This has been the case of Ghana, Cameroon, Nigeria, and Guinea. The experiences of these countries and others that have ventured into this industry are discussed below.

Ghana Ghana's primary aluminum production began with the establishment of the Volta Aluminum Company (VALCO) in 1967. The company was established as a joint venture of two American companies, Kaiser Aluminum and Chemical Company, which owned 90%, and Reynolds, which owned 10%. Reynolds sold its share to the Aluminum Company of America (ALCOA) before VALCO started operations in 1967 (Husband et al., 2009). To make VALCO possible, Ghana had to build a large dam on its longest river, the Volta, at Akosombo to generate cheap hydroelectric power (Figure 14.3). This project was funded by Ghana (50%) and the World Bank and the IMF (50%). VALCO received a number of concessions among which

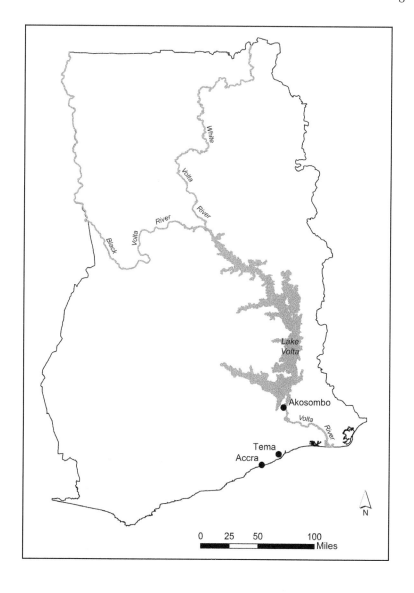

FIGURE 14.3 Ghana's aluminum industry.
Source: Created by Greg Anderson

were low-cost electricity for 30 years at a fixed price of 2.265 mills per kilowatt-hour and several other tax incentives. As indicated in Chapter 13, the agreement did not use Ghana's bauxite but rather alumina from Kaiser's plant in Jamaica, even though Ghana had and still has large bauxite deposits.

The plant operated well albeit under capacity and exported aluminum ingots and semis until the late 1990s when a number of events made it difficult for the plant to operate. First, as a result of growing demand for electricity in the country, the Volta River Authority (VRA) had wanted to extend electricity to the rest of the country but at VALCO's insistence, Ghana had to generate additional electricity from imported oils and coal. Second, extended periods of drought caused a decline in the water level of the dam thus affecting the amount of electricity that could be generated. VRA wanted VALCO to supplement its power needs from other sources just as Ghana was doing but VALCO insisted on getting the same quota of electricity from the VRA as before. However, this could not be met due to the fluctuations in the water level in the Volta. Matters reached a crisis stage when in 1997 the initial 30-year agreement expired and the VRA wanted to renegotiate and charge VALCO the full cost of electricity, which had reached 22.5 mills per kilowatt-hour in 1981 nonsocialist countries (Peter et al., 1995). From 1999 to 2002, VALCO unilaterally continued to pay for its energy use at a discounted rate. Eventually, Kaiser closed the plant in 2003 as part of a bankruptcy proceeding, and in 2004, it sold its interests, obligations, and responsibilities in VALCO to the Ghana government. In 2005, the Ghana government and ALCOA, which still held its 10% share in VALCO signed an agreement to establish an integrated aluminum industry that would use Ghana's bauxite if feasibility studies proved the project viable, but in 2008, ALCOA sold its 10% to the Ghana Government, making it the sole owner of the company. Smelting operations resumed in 2011 with only one of the five production lines. The new government has promised to rebuild the industry.

Cameroon Cameroon's aluminum industry began with the establishment of *Compagine Camerounaise de Al* (Alucam)'s aluminum smelter in Edea in 1957 (Figure 14.4). The company was 58% owned by the French company Pechiney and 42% by the Cameroon Government. The company was powered by the Edea Hydroelectric Dam on the Sanaga River, which was built in 1953, with power guarantees throughout the year. Alucam operated without any major problems until 1988 when increasing power demand and drought led to power shortage at the plant. In 2003, most of Pechiney's share in Alucam was purchased by Aluminum Company of Canada (Alcan), which was in turn purchased by the Australian-based Rio Tinto in 2007. The government still held its share of 46.7%.

In 2009, Alucam had to shut down its plant due to power shortage. It had merged with Rio Tinto-Alcan but power consumption required 50% of Cameroon's total capacity of electricity supply. It was estimated that for the company to triple its output, Cameroon needed to construct another hydroelectric power dam at Lom Pangar in the eastern part of the country (Tumanjong, 2009). Cameroon agreed to supply additional power to Alucam from a gas-fired power plant, which started operation in 2013, while progress was being made toward the Lom Pangar project with funds from the World Bank, the African Development Bank, and Central African States Development Bank (AfDB, 2011). However, continuing energy shortages caused a drastic drop in the output of Alucam in spite of plans to increase output. So, in October 2014, Rio Tinto announced that it would leave Alucam by the end of the year because Alucam no longer fit its new global model. However, skeptics think that the decision was in retaliation to the agreement between the Cameroon and the French Electric Company (EDF) to build a new hydroelectric power project at Nachtigal, a project Rio Tinto was interested in.

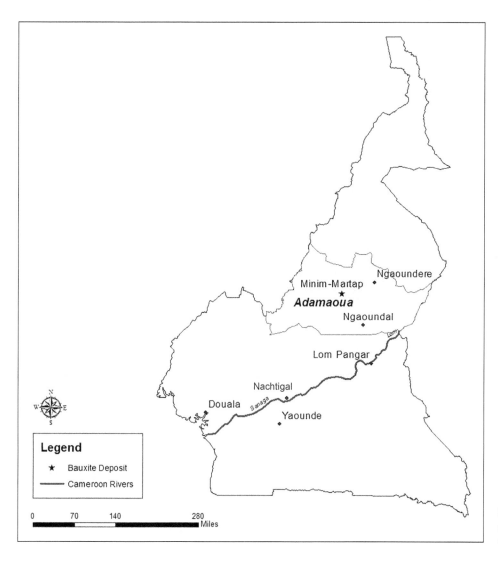

FIGURE 14.4 Cameroon's aluminum industry.
Source: Created by Sokhna Diop

In another development, the Cameroon Alumina Limited, a joint venture of Dubai Alumina Company, Hindalco Industries Limited, and the US-based Hydromine Incorporated signed an agreement in 2012 with the Cameroon government to build another hydroelectric power plant on the Sanaga River. The project would use bauxite reserves of the Minim-Martap and Ngaoundal deposits in the Adamawa region of northern Cameroon to produce 3 metric tons of alumina a year, starting in 2018 (Newman, 2012).

Guinea Guinea has all the factors that are needed to become a powerhouse of Africa's aluminum industry, and a major player globally. It has large bauxite deposits, good hydroelectric power potential relative to low domestic demand, and it has an aluminum smelter with a second one under construction. Yet, the issue of cheap electricity still plagues Guinea. The aluminum industry began in 1959 when bauxite was refined at the Fria Bauxite Aluminum Production Company. In 1973, the company became Friguia, a joint venture between Guinea (51%) and the French Pechiney (49%). In 1997, Pechiney sold its share to Guinea for $1. In 2002, the plant was signed as concession management to Rusal of Russia, which eventually purchased it for $19 million in 2006. However, in 2009 under a new government, a Guinean court ruled that the purchase was illegal since the previous government sold the plant for only $19 million instead of its appraised value of $257 million. In 2012, the Guinea government sent a letter to Rusal to return the plant to Guinea, because the transaction was invalid, and filed for loss revenue to the tune of $1 billion. However, in July 2014 the International Chamber of Commerce court in Paris ruled in favor of Rusal.

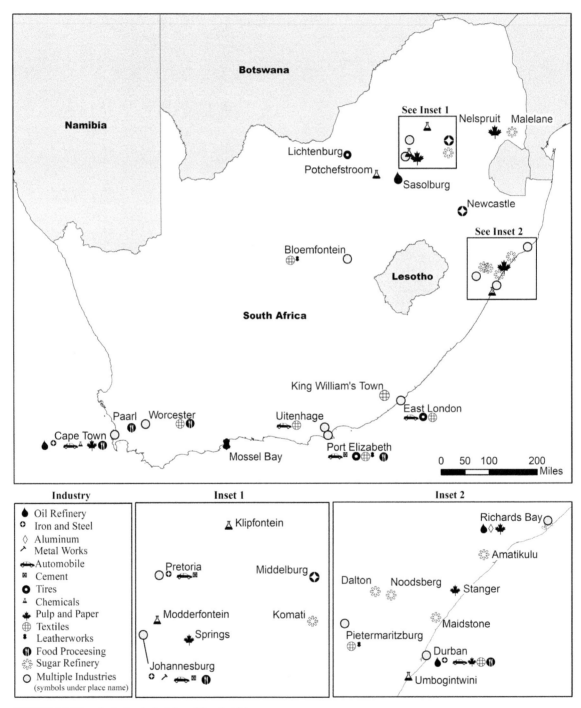

FIGURE 14.5 Manufacturing industries of South Africa.
Source: Created by Greg Anderson

Rusal had also signed an agreement in 2001 to develop the world's largest bauxite deposits at Dian-Dian, which included a feasibility study for an aluminum smelter by 2013. However, in 2012, the smelter was dropped out of the agreement for a refinery. The Guinea government's effort to negotiate for a better portion from mining-related business in the country scared many foreign investors. At the same time, the industry was rocked by a worker's strike over Rusal's refusal to pay the national minimum wage of $324 that resulted in a plant shut down for one year. The main reason was the cost of power. In July 2014, Rusal announced that work on the Dian-Dian project would start with the first stage to be completed by 2016, but the project was delayed until end of 2017 with subsequent phases including an alumina refinery to be completed by 2021.

South Africa South Africa's aluminum industry began in 1971 when the state-owned IDC decided to exploit the surplus electricity that had been generated by the state-owned Electricity Supply Commission (ESCOM or Eskom). An aluminum smelter was built at Bayside, in Richards Bay, and began operation in 1971 with a capacity of 55,000 tons per year, specializing in the production of rolling ingot, extrusion billet, and redrawn rod (Figure 14.5). Hillside Aluminum opened for production in 1995 with an initial capacity of 535,000 tons per annum. After some extension work in 2003, the capacity rose to 700,000 tons per annum, making it the largest aluminum smelter in Africa and in the southern hemisphere. In 2006, Eskom and the Canadian-based Alcan signed a 25-year agreement for 1,355 MW of electricity for an aluminum smelter. The project was slated to start in 2010, however, following Rio Tinto's purchase of Alcan in 2007, the project was delayed and eventually terminated in 2009 due to Eskom's inability to guarantee power for the project. In June 2014, BHP Billiton closed the Bayside plant and demerged its Hillside plant with a new global metals and mining company NewCo. BHP Billiton explained its actions as part of restructuring, but critics saw this as a disinvestment in South Africa, perhaps due to the country's notorious labor problems.

Egypt Egypt's aluminum industry began in 1975 when alumina was first smelted at the aluminum smelter of the Aluminum Company of Egypt (EGYPTALUM) at Naj Hammadi in Upper Egypt (Figure 14.6). The main force behind the industry was to use the cheap hydroelectricity from the Aswan High Dam. The plant reached its design capacity of 100,000 tons per year in 1977 but by 1983 the capacity had been expanded to 180,000. Over the period, the product mix changed from more primary aluminum products to more fabricated aluminum products. During the 1990s, economic reforms and structural adjustment policies resulted in increase in the cost of energy, devaluation of the Egyptian pound, and liberation of output prices, as well as interest rates. Also these measures helped the industry to increase exports, but the drop in aluminum prices made it to shift more toward domestic than export markets.

The Egyptian Revolution of 2011 and its aftermath raised concerns about the business environment of Egypt. Efforts to recover some previous land sales and the confrontation between the Muslim Brotherhood government and the large corporation of Orascom Construction Industries (OCI) made matters worse. While the major player of the industry in Egypt continues to be the state, some concerns have been raised that Egypt might lose its aluminum industry due to the unrest in the country since the 2011 revolution. Recently however, concerns have been raised on the large number of children employed by the industry in unhealthy factory environments.

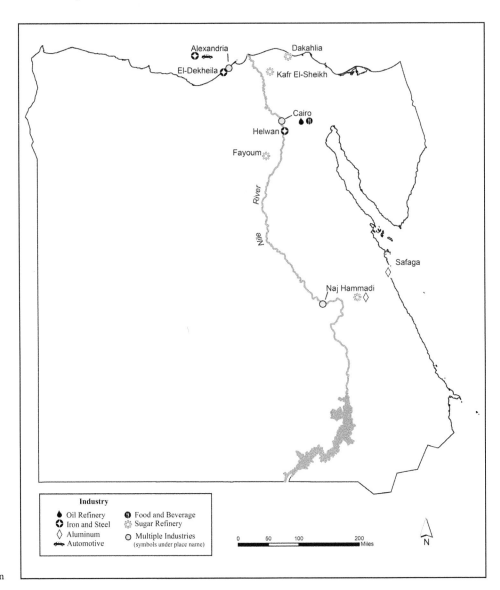

FIGURE 14.6 Manufacturing industries of Egypt.
Source: Created by Greg Anderson

Other countries Other countries with potential for aluminum industry are Nigeria, Mozambique, and DRC, in terms of power-related matters. The aluminum industry in **Nigeria** consists of an aluminum smelter and a number of finished goods producers (Husband et al., 2009). The smelter of the Aluminum Smelter Company of Nigeria (Alscon) is located at Ikot Abasi in the Akwa Ibom State in southeastern Nigeria. The smelter was completed in 1997 at a cost $2.5 billion and operated on an experimental basis for three years, before it was shut down in 2000, having only produced 40,000 metric tons of aluminum. The plant was originally owned by Nigeria (70%), Ferrostaal AG of Germany (20%), and Reynolds Aluminum (10%). Alcoa, which bought Reynolds sold its share to the Nigerian government in 2004, and as a result of further investment made the Nigerian government ended up owning 92.5% with only 7.5% for Ferrostaal. In 2006, Nigeria sold 77.5% of its shares to Rusal, which began massive investment into the plant soon afterward (Husband et al., 2009). However, controversy over how Nigeria government sold its shares to Rusal has brought a series of lawsuits by the US-based Nigerian consortium, Bancorp

Financial Investment Group Divino Corporation (BFIG), that was disqualified from the bid. In 2016, the Nigerian Supreme Court ruled in favor of BFIG but the ownership of the Alscon remains unresolved.

Mozambique's aluminum industry consists of an aluminum smelter (Mozal), which is located near the capital, Maputo (Hathaway, 2007). The industry started in 2000 as a joint venture among four parties—BHP Billiton (47%), South Africa's IDC (24%), Mitsubishi of Japan (25%), and the Government of Mozambique (4%). The smelter doubled its capacity in 2003 raising its electricity requirement to 900 MW, which is supplied from a consortium of electricity companies—MOTRACO—of Mozambique, South Africa, and Swaziland. The second expansion would bring the electricity requirement to 1,350 MW, and this would require a new dam downstream from the Cahora Bassa dam in Mozambique.

Finally, the enormous potential of hydroelectric power projects in both Inga I and Inga II that are being rehabilitated as well as Inga III hold lots of promise for the aluminum industry in DRC. The development of these projects has been accompanied by feasibility studies for an aluminum smelter that will require 2,000 MW of power.

The above show that Africa's aluminum industry is small but has great potential. Yet the fact that African countries have to rely on foreign investments, which always require not only cheap but also below-market priced energy, and the tendency for these foreign investments to cut and run anytime price on the world market dip presents a very formidable challenge to African countries. The irony is that aluminum is increasingly replacing other metals in manufacturing, yet the world's leading aluminum manufacturers insist of cheap electricity for their operations.

The Automotive Industry

The automotive industry made its debut in Africa during the late colonial period when the French Renault and the American Ford and GM Companies established vehicle assembly plants in Morocco and South Africa, respectively. However, the industry did not spread to other parts of the continent until the early post-independence period when several foreign companies established assembly plants in some countries as part of the ISI strategy. Throughout the late 1970s and early 1980s, however, many of these failed leaving a few survivors such as those of South Africa, Egypt, and Morocco.

South Africa South Africa is the largest producer of vehicles in Africa. The industry began when Ford and General Motors established production plants near Port Elizabeth in the 1920s. The industry grew rapidly and by the 1960s it was producing about 120,000 vehicles a year (Nitschke, 2011). Over time, the industry became concentrated in three regions, namely the Gauteng, Eastern Cape, and KwaZulu-Natal. In the Gauteng were Volkswagen, BMW, Daimler, Ford, Nissan, and Fiat, all around Pretoria and Johannesburg. In the Eastern Cape were Daimler Chrysler in East London, Volkswagen in Port Elizabeth, and Delta Motor Corporation in Uitenhage. In KwaZulu-Natal, was Toyota in Durban and Pietermaritzburg with supplier firms in Richards Bay, Ladysmith, and Stanger (Figure 14.5). In 1961, the South African government introduced the first of several local content requirements, which asked for domestic sourcing of 11 peripheral items (Nitschke, 2011). Others were introduced in 1977 and 1989.

The entire industry was highly protected against foreign competition, with government subsidies, imposed import quotas, and repressed labor unions (Lorentzen et al., 2007). This allowed the industry to operate at lower productivity levels than international best practice. Following the political changes in the 1990s, the government pursued trade liberalization policies including abolition of quotas, adjustments of tariffs, and reorientation of the industry toward export markets. It also put in place a program to encourage domestic-based original equipment manufacturers to reduce the range of domestically produced models in order to obtain credits to expand exports.

In recent years, both the government and automobile manufacturers have stepped up their commitment to a more vibrant automotive industry. For example, Ford Motor Company South Africa has increased its production at the Silverton Assembly Plant, near Pretoria, and the Struandale Engine Plant to increase production of its Ford Rangers. From 2009 to 2012, BMW South Africa also invested $26 million in its Rosslyn plant, near Pretoria, and in 2012, it was able to export its first cars—the F30 BMW 3 Series—to China. Also in 2012, Volkswagen received a contract from China to export 12,000 engines from its plant at Uitenhage. Finally, in 2016, the Beijing International Automotive Corp (BAIC) announced to build a $759 million automotive plant in partnership with South Africa's IDC, in the Port Elizabeth area, with start-up production in 2018. At full capacity by 2027 the plant will produce 100,000 units for exports to the rest of Africa.

However, the industry has to contend with a number of issues. One is the cost of manufacturing, which has been estimated to be 20% higher than a car manufactured in Western Europe because of low local content. Other problems include inadequate transportation and supply infrastructure for export, high energy cost, and water scarcity. On top of these are also labor issues. In 2013, for example, a seven-week strike rocked the industry, and in July 2014, both Toyota and Ford stopped production due to strikes in the metals industry.

Egypt Egypt's automotive industry began in 1951 when the Ford Motor Company established an assembly plant in Alexandria. In 1960, the government established the Al Nasr Company and its huge automotive manufacturing complex in the Helwan desert region to assemble Fiat cars. With large infusion of capital over the next decade, the Al Nasr Company became one of the leading firms in Egypt. The dream at that time was to one day produce a national car for Egypt. However, after the 1967 Arab–Israeli War, much of the national resources were diverted into rebuilding the military. Throughout the 1970s the Al-Nasr Company saw declining investment in its physical plant forcing it to operate with obsolete machinery and production lines, while maintaining a large number of employees. As many foreign companies entered the industry in the 1980s under government protection, Al Nasr continued to be a major player with licensed brands including Chrysler, Kia, and Peugeot.

The economic reforms and the SAPs on the 1990s opened the Egyptian market to more foreign companies while restricting public investment. In 2000, Al Nasr was split into four companies and sold to the private sector. Three of the companies became assembly lines, while the fourth assumed all the debts of the former company and therefore had a difficult time to grow (Hamza and Zaher, 2012). An agreement was signed with the EU aimed at reducing all tariffs on automotive products by 2019. However, the 2011 Revolution and its aftermath put a hold on Egypt's goal of becoming a competitive car producer in the Middle East and North Africa (MENA).

Morocco Morocco's automotive industry dates back to 1928 when the French Company Renault started assembling cars in the colony. However, it was not until the postcolonial period that the government took major steps toward a domestic automotive industry. It began in 1962 when *Societe'Maroccaine de Constructions Auto-mobiles* (SOMACA) was set up as a joint venture with 40% owned by the state, 20% by the Fiat Company, 20% by Chrysler France, and 20% by Moroccan private interests. The company produced four main models—Renault, Fiat, Simca, and Peugeot, all at its Casablanca plant. SOMACA also assembled light trucks, while six other firms assembled trucks, buses, jeeps, and land rovers. However, the company was not profitable because it had too many makes and models (23 in all). Production reached its peak in 1976 after which it started to decline due to economic downturn caused by the 1973 oil crisis, decline in phosphates demand, severe drought, and the war in Western Sahara (Rinehart, 1985).

The government was forced to abandon its industrialization plan for austerity measures from 1978 to 1980 in return for $1 billion loan (Estefan, 1985; Rhinehart, 1985). From 1983 to 1993, Morocco accepted the IMF's structural adjustment program. Trade was liberalized, subsidies were removed, and the industrialization policy changed from import-substitution to export promotion. To further stimulate the auto industry, the government introduced the economy car program in 1994. Among other things, the program offered lower taxes on locally assembled Fiat to boost volumes and economies of scale in exchange for significant export of cars, and locally assembled vans and trucks. The government also created the Tanger (Tangier) Med Port and zones, which included an automotive city, and a free trade zone. These were to draw activities away from Casablanca and capitalize on the excellent location of Tanger. In 1998, the US-based Delphi opened a production unit in the Tanger Free Trade Zone/Industrial Zone to manufacture cables. In 1999 Yazaki, a Japanese automotive company also located in the Tanger Free Zone, and in 2010, it opened a second production plant. Other companies that have located in free trade zone include Sumitomo in 2009, a car cable manufacturer and SNOP, a metal stamping firm in 2011. Perhaps the biggest boost yet came in 2012, when Renault, the dominant automotive firm in the country, inaugurated the first phase of its 340,000 unit-car production facility in the Tanger Free Trade Zone. When completed, it will be the largest car factory in Africa (Murtada, 2014). Forthcoming expansion is projected to make Morocco the 19th largest vehicle producer in the world by 2017. With this in mind, the country is also ramping up its human resources development as well as its trade network. For example, the government plans called for training 1,500 managers, 7,000 engineers, 29,000 technicians, and 32,500 operators from 2009 to 2015. With the respect to trade networks, it has already been granted advanced status into the European Union, signed a free trade agreement with Egypt, Tunisia, Jordan, Turkey, Mauritania, and the United States; and it is pushing for similar agreements with the Economic Community of West African States (ECOWAS), Mexico, and Canada.

It is clear that Morocco is capitalizing on the difficulties facing its closest rivals—Egypt, Libya, and Tunisia, as well as its proximity to European and West African markets, and relatively better infrastructure to position itself as second to South Africa in the automotive industry in Africa, a goal it may have already attained. Thus, in 2012, it produced 108,743 vehicles making it the largest car maker in North Africa, surpassing Egypt the traditional leader, and by the same token making it the second largest car producer in Africa after South Africa.

Other countries Many other African countries including Ethiopia, Kenya, and Nigeria are considering the automotive industry. Ethiopia, for example, is making progress with the Belayab Car Assembly and its own local car, the Holland. However, a viable automotive industry has to overcome several constraints. In Nigeria, for example, progress has been slowed down by government vacillations. Importation of foreign cars continues unabated, and the number of worn-out imported vehicles for low-income Nigerians continues to rise, even though these have been banned. The government has also been inconsistent in its policies, and chronic power black-outs make it difficult for continuous plant operations. Limited domestic market, lack of adequate road infrastructure, and financing have also been identified as some of the factors hindering the industry in Kenya as well as in Ethiopia (Jacobs, 2012).

The Chemical Industry

Compared to the global chemical industry Africa's chemical industry is very small. The entire sector of petro-chemicals was neglected although many petroleum refineries exist on the continent. For example, only one of Nigeria's four oil refineries, the Eleme Petrochemical Company Ltd (EPCL) has the ability to produce polyethylene, polypropylene, and polyvinyl, but even that is under capacity (Poymerupdate, 2014).

The industry is concentrated in three regions: North Africa—Egypt, Libya, Tunisia, Algeria, and Morocco—Nigeria, and South Africa. However, South Africa and Egypt have been the only major exporters of basic chemical products in Africa. South Africa has the largest chemical industry on the continent. Facing competition, South Africa chemical manufacturers have moved into other African countries. Other important countries are Algeria, Libya, and Morocco.

Chemical manufacturing in Africa is largely for domestic needs than for export. The output includes a wide range of products such as plastics, fertilizers, solvents, ammonia, explosives, and carbon-tar products. South Africa, Egypt, and Algeria are the most important plastics producers. Algeria, Egypt, and Libya are important nitrogen fertilizer producers; Morocco and Tunisia are important for phosphate-based fertilizers; Nigeria for oil-based fertilizers, while coal and synthetic-based fertilizers are produced in South Africa. Other countries with fertilizer production are Zimbabwe, Zambia, and Tanzania.

The current industry consists of the modern production system with firms of different structures, sizes, and origins. Thus, there are small private indigenous (African) firms; there are also state-owned companies, semiprivate companies, medium-size companies as well as large multinational companies. The small private companies are usually based in a single country and are sometimes within a region. The medium-size companies tend to be international and they include a number of South African companies such as Sasol, AECI, Dow-Sentrachem, and Protea, all of which have subsidiaries in a number of sub-Saharan African countries. Among the state-owned companies are Sonatrach (the Algerian National Oil Company), the Egyptian Petrochemical industries (EGP), the Nigerian National Petroleum Corporation (NNPC), the National Petrochemical Company (Napecto) of Libya; the Office Cherifien des Phosphates (OCP) of Morocco, the National Fertilizer Company in Nigeria, and the Groupe Chimique Tunisien (Tunisia). The last three are mainly engaged in fertilizer production (Mazumdar, 2014).

The multinational companies that are active in Africa include many of the world's major chemical companies such as Hoechst, Du Pont, Bayer, Shell, TotalFinaElf, and ExxonMobil. Other offshore companies with subsidiaries on the continent include Akzo Nobel Chemicals, BASF, Albemarle Corporation, Bayer, Ethyl Petroleum Additives, Monsanto, Rhone Poulenc, ICI, Union Carbide, and Röhm and Haas. The following suppliers of additives are also represented: Ambrosius, GmbH, Mikrochem, Salm Oleochemicals, Sud Chemie Rheologicals, Warner Jenkinson, and Witcom Corporation (Mazumdar, 2014).

The prospects for growth is high due to increasing demand which in turn derives from growing population, increasing agriculture production, and insect-borne diseases that affect humans, plants, and animals (Mazumdar, 2014). In most of the countries, this increasing demand for more chemical products is at the moment being met largely by imports. This has increased Africa's trade deficit in chemicals from $3.2 billion in 2007 to US$6 billion in 2011 (Mazumdar, 2014). As a result, a number of new projects have been announced to boost the petrochemical industry. In Nigeria, for example, there is a proposal to boost petrochemical production at the Elema Petrochemical plant. In Algeria, a new joint project by Sonatrach, Algeria, Total of France, and Qatar Petroleum in Arzew, Algeria will produce 1.1 million metric tons a year of ethylene and other by-products. However, corruption and inadequate capacities that tend to characterize projects of these kinds still complicate an already complex problem of international competition.

The Forest Products Industry

The production of roundwood, the primary item of forest products, was considered in Chapter 12. In this section, we use forest products to refer to three groups of items, processed wood (veneer and plywood), pulp and paper, and other wood products (carvings, manufacturing building materials such as doors and windows, and furniture). With the exception of the other wood products subsector, this industry is one of Africa's least developed industries. This is mainly because of the capital-intensive nature of such subsector as pulp and paper. Only few countries have significant veneer and plywood manufacturing. In 2015, four countries accounted for 54.3% of Africa's total production. These were Ghana (20.6%), Cote d'Ivoire (13.3%), Gabon (10.9%), and South Africa (9.4%) (Table 14.2).

Pulp and paper manufacturing is even more limited than veneer and plywood making. Wood pulp, the main raw material for papermaking, is of two types, namely

---

TABLE 14.2

Plywood Production in Africa, 2015

Country	Cubic meters	Percentage
Ghana	180,000	20.6
Cote d" Ivoire	116,000	13.3
Gabon	95,000	10.9
South Africa	82,091	9.4
Kenya	66,000	7.6
Nigeria	56,000	6.4
Guinea	39,600	4.5
Mali	37,000	4.2
Egypt	28,000	3.2
Congo	26,000	3.0
Total	725,691	83.2
Rest of Africa	146,279	16.8
Total of Africa	871970	100.0

Source: FAO Forest Products.

mechanical pulp and chemical pulp. Mechanical pulp is produced by grinding wood while chemical pulp is produced by cooking wood with chemicals. None of this is prominent in Africa even though a few more countries produce chemical pulp compared to mechanical pulp. In 2015, only three countries reported data on production of mechanical pulp—Madagascar, South Africa, and Tanzania—with 94% coming from South Africa. Similarly, only five countries recorded production of chemical pulp—Angola, Egypt, Nigeria, South Africa, and Tanzania, with South Africa producing 89.4%. Paper products are usually classified into three broad groups—newsprint, printing and writing paper, and other paper and paperboard. Relatively speaking, South Africa is the only country that manufactures these products in any significant quantities. These are produced by two companies the Mondi and the South African Pulp and Paper Industries (Sappi), both headquartered in Johannesburg, but with operating mills elsewhere in the country (Figure 14.5). Sappi operates five mills located in Cape Town (Cape Kraft Mill), Springs (Eratra Mill), Nelspruit (Ngodwana Mill), and Kwadukuza (Stanger Mill). The Mondi Company operates two mills, one in Durban and the other in Richards Bay. In 2015, South Africa produced 93% of Africa's newsprint, 63% of its printing and writing paper, and 60% of its other paper and paperboard.

Other newsprint producers were Ethiopia (6%) and Algeria (1%). For printing and writing paper, they were Egypt (22%), Ethiopia (6%), and Morocco (5%). For other paper and paperboard, South Africa was followed by Egypt (19%), Tunisia (6.5%), and Morocco (4.5%). Pulp and paper manufacturing is a vertically integrated operation so the well-established companies own forestland. In spite of this, wood fiber supply continues to be a problem for the industry in South Africa, while elsewhere it is more of undercapitalization.

While plywood, and pulp and paper manufacturing are dominated by modern production systems with sophisticated technologies, the woodcarving and wood furniture subsectors are dominated by hybrid and indigenous production systems. The wood carving subsector is a carryover from precolonial era during which various localities specialized in them. Today, they consist of small firms that usually cluster together forming their own industrial districts either spontaneously or through some government action. Examples of these include the Mwenge Handicraft district in Dar es Salaam, and the Ahwia Wood Center near Kumasi, Ghana. This subsector produces a wide range of wood products from stools and sculptures through art works that are usually used for interior decorations.

The wood furniture industry uses sawn timber, metals, plastic, and cloth as its main inputs. However, as a result of cost structure of these inputs especially sawn timber and past policies of just exporting raw lumber, the subsector is less developed. The result is that many African countries export sawn lumber and import furniture. For example, Dinh et al (2012) reports that even though Ethiopia has a large amount of unexploited forest, urban households buy imported furniture. This is because the local price of timber (US$667 per cubic meter) does not allow local furniture makers to be competitive with cheap imported ones from China and Vietnam, where timber price is US$344 and US$146–246, respectively. However, the domestic furniture market is dominated by a large number of small-scale and traditional manufacturing systems. The location patterns of these firms vary from single isolated roadside to wholesale furniture districts, some of which date back to precolonial times. Most of these furniture districts are found in Africa's large urban centers (Pogue, 2008). Some of these are well organized and have formed association to take care of their business. In some cases, as in South Africa, there are opportunities for these firms to benefit from research and development such as the Furniture Technology Center Trust of South Africa.

The Iron and Steel Industry

The iron and steel industry of Africa is very small. In 2015, it produced about 1% of the world's crude steel. The industry is dominated by the large-scale manufacturing production system, and is limited to a few countries—South Africa, Egypt, Algeria, Morocco, Libya, and Nigeria.

South Africa South Africa is the leading crude steel producer in Africa. In 2015, it produced 47% of Africa's crude steel and ranked 23rd in world crude steel production. The industry began in 1911 when the Union Steel Corporation was founded in the Transvaal. By 1926, the corporation was operating blast furnaces in Pretoria, Vereeniging (Transvaal), and Newcastle (Natal) (Scott, 1951). In 1928, the South African government established the South African Iron and Steel Corporation (ISCOR or Iscor) in Pretoria to produce steel for the domestic market. In 1937, Iscor established a subsidiary company—the African Metals Corporation (Amcor) to operate a Newcastle blast furnace. World War II, availability of high-grade iron ore deposits at Thabazimbi, the development of ferroalloy manufacturing, local deposits of high-grade ferroalloy metals such as manganese, chromium, and tungsten led to further growth of the industry (Scott, 1951). By the 1950s, the industry was solidly established in Pretoria, Vereeniging, the Witwatersrand, and Newcastle (Figure 14.5) (Coupe, 1995). Additional plants were established in the 1960s and 1970s—Columbus Steel plant in Middleburg in Transvaal in 1966; the Highveld Steel and Vanadium plant near Witbank in 1968; and the Davsteel Division in 1975. The industry had the opportunity to grow to become very competitive on the world stage during this time but government protectionism and the racist labor policies of the apartheid regime stifled productivity growth in the industry (Coupe, 1995). Projected demand in the mid-1970s led to significant investment in capacity but demand shrank in the 1980s and much of the 1990s causing overcapacity in the industry (Roberts, 2005). During the 1980s, the industry underwent restructuring. Iscor closed down its two oldest blast furnaces in Pretoria, and it was privatized in 1989. This involved closure of about 2.5 million metric tons of capacity and rationalization—cutting down on the number of grades produced. In 2004, Iscor became fully owned by LNM Holdings, N.V, which was in turn acquired by Mittal Steel South Africa. In 2006, Mittal Steel merged with Arcelor to form ArcelorMittal South Africa (AMSA) with operations in Vanderbiljpark (Gauteng), Newcastle (KwaZulu-Natal), Vereeniging (Gauteng), and Sadanha (Western Cape) (Kumba Iron Ore, 2011). South Africa's other steel companies include Scraw Metals with facilities at Union Junction (Gemiston), DAV Steel with facilities in Vanderbiljpark, CISCO in Kuilsriver (Western Cape), and Evraz Highveld Steel and Vanadium, with facilities in Witbank (Mpumalanga). In 2014, China's Hebei Iron and Steel Group announced that it would build its largest steel mill in South Africa scheduled to open in 2017. However, at the time of writing the project had not started yet.

South Africa's steel industry meets all its domestic needs and exports the rest—making it the third largest exporter of steel relative to production, after Ukraine and Russia (Kumba Iron Ore, 2011). However, the industry faces a number of challenges. Perhaps the most important of these challenges is transportation cost. The one input that South African iron and steel industry lacks is coking coal, most of which is sourced from Australia and Canada. With most of its steel plants located inland, this makes it expensive. Second, transportation cost of steel is so high that even though South Africa is able to supply its domestic markets it is not competitive in the sea-borne export markets. One scenario the industry is looking at is the possibility of development of new steel-making technologies that eliminates the blast furnace and for that matter coking coal.

Egypt Egypt is second to South Africa in steel production in Africa. In 2015, it produced 40% of Africa's crude steel and ranked 25th in the world crude steel production. The modern industry began in 1954 when the Egyptian Iron and Steel Company (HADISLOB) was established at Helwan near Cairo by the state as part of the ISI policy (Figure 14.6). It was set up as a vertically integrated steel company, mining its own pig iron initially from its Aswan Mines and later from the Bahariya oases, transporting it to the plant and processing the raw material into both long and flat products for the domestic market, all under government protection. It started operation in 1958. As with the rest of Africa, the industry's goal was more toward social profitability than economic profitability—offer jobs and produce for the domestic market. Throughout the 1970s, the company produced under capacity (Abdel-Khalek, 2001). In spite of this, the company began accumulating unsold finished stocks due to increased production and energy cost, and foreign competition. In the meantime, the government with the support of Japan established another iron and steel manufacturing company, the Alexandria National Iron and Steel Company (ANSDK) plant in El-Dekheila/Alexandria, which began production in 1985 using imported iron and gas-coke from local natural gas to produce mostly reinforced steel. By the early 1990s it was producing 745,000 tons of steel (Ibrahim and Ibrahim, 2003).

The liberalization and privatization wave of the 1990s opened the industry to private investments. ANSDK became Ezz-Dekheila, when Ezz Steel Rebars (ESR) bought 28% of its shares. Massive real estate boom in Egypt and nearby regions from 2004 to 2008 led to the greatest expansion of the industry. By 2008, there were 27 firms in the industry of which Al Ezz Steel Rebars Company, the largest, controlled about 62% of the long products market in Egypt. Other firms of importance are Beshay and Misr National Steel (Hasan et al., 2009). The high level of concentration, the limited alternatives to rebars in the construction industry in Egypt, the high capital intensity, and the fact that the owner of the Ezz Steel was a member of the National Democratic Party and the head of the Planning and Budget Committee in the Egyptian Parliament, all provided grounds for public anger against the industry accusing it of being a cartel. However, government investigation to calm down the anger found no wrongdoing.

One of the main challenges of the industry is that due to low iron content of domestic iron ore deposits, Egypt has to import iron ore and other input materials. The other problem is lower prices of steel elsewhere. This has led to increasing imports of steel since 2004. Dumping of cheaper steel in the Egyptian market is also a problem. In fact, in 2009 the government imposed a 10% tariff on some categories of flat steel for a brief period as an antidumping measure. At the same time, several licenses were issued to companies such as the Ezz Company, ArcelorMittal Company, and the Al Kharafi Group of Kuwait to expand steel production (Hasan et al., 2009).

The Arab Spring/Egyptian Revolution of 2010–2011 had negative impacts on investors as uncertainty set in and many government contracts came under scrutiny. For example, in 2011, the chairman of the EZZ Company was sentenced to a 10-year jail term for graft charges and the company was ordered to pay $111 million and lose the licenses. In 2013, the new Islamist government again fined the former chairman $3.8 billion and sentenced him to 44 years in jail including 37 years for improper acquisition of ANSDK, although the license was reinstated later on and the former chairman of the company was released from jail. In the meantime, sales in the iron and steel and other sectors of the metallurgical industry fell although local demand held steady. The industry is bouncing back. In 2016, the Egypt Iron and Steel Company (HADISLOB), which is still state-owned, announced that it was considering an upgrade proposal from Russian companies. However, uncertainty still remains in the foreseeable future.

Nigeria While both South Africa and Egypt demonstrate the potential of the iron and steel industry in Africa, Nigeria illustrates the outcome of poor planning and lack of commitment. The idea of establishing an iron and steel industry in Nigeria began in 1958. However, it was not until after the discovery of better iron ore deposits in Kwara State that more concrete steps were taken. The government established the Nigerian Steel Development Authority (NSDA) in 1971 and charged it to plan, construct, and operate steel plants in Nigeria, and also to send people overseas to train in the management of iron and steel operations (Agbu, 2007). Two steel plants, the Ajaokuta Steel Company (ASC) and the Delta Steel Company (DSC) at Aladja, and three rolling mills one each at Jos, Oshogbo, and Katsina were proposed (Figure 14.7). Other related companies established at the same time were the National Iron Ore Mining Company (NIOMCO) at Itakpe, the National Raw Steel Materials Exploration Agency at Kaduna, the National Metallurgical Development Center at Jos, and the Metallurgical Training Institute at Onitsha (Agbu, 2007; Ohimain, 2013). Only the DSC and the three steel rolling mills were completed. Some of the trainees came back to find that many of the units they were supposed to work in were not ready. In the end, poor remuneration and job satisfaction caused about 75% of the trained workers to leave (Agbu, 2007).

Interest in the project waned from mid-1990 until 1999 when Nigeria returned to democratic rule. By that time, the plant had been idle for 15 years and most of the facilities had deteriorated. A technical evaluation in 2000 estimated that it would cost about $460 million to complete, rehabilitate, and commission the first phase of the project. The government's efforts at privatizing the industry in 2004–2005 were not very successful because the large number of employees had resulted in huge pension liabilities, which scared many potential investors. Summarizing the situation of Nigeria's iron and steel industry, Ohimain (2013, p. 232) observed that

> Despite the huge investments [about $7 billion] in the sector, the Ajaokuta Steel Company (ASC) failed to take off while Delta Steel Company (DSC) and the three-government-owned inland/satellite rolling mills in Oshogbo, Jos, and Katsina are moribund, working under low capacity utilization.

The result is that Nigeria produced only 0.8% of Africa's crude steel in 2015, and still depends on imported steel for its own needs. Poor planning, contracting strategy, design, funding, political location of most of the plants, and political instability have been identified as some of the many factors that caused the industry to fail (Ohimain, 2013). Other crude steel producers in 2015 were Algeria, which produced 5% of Africa's crude steel, Morocco (4%), and Libya (3%).

The Metallurgical Industry

With its rich mineral wealth and vibrant mining activities, one would think that mineral processing and metal works would be one of leading industries in most African countries. However, with the exception of South Africa, the picture here is

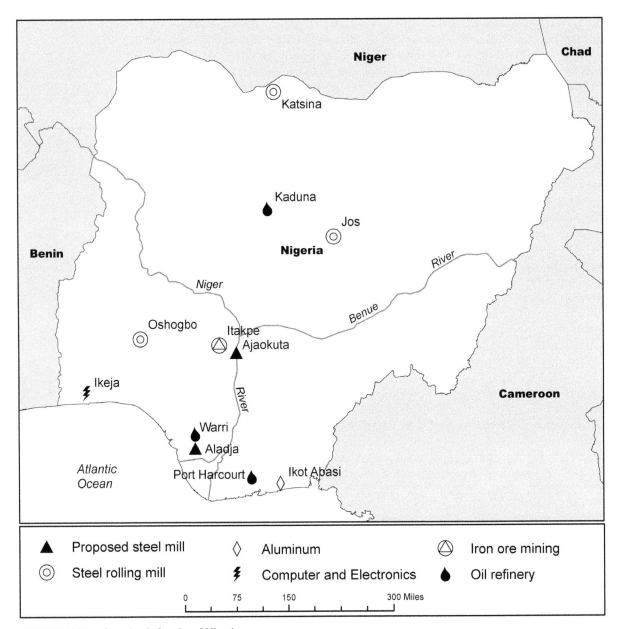

FIGURE 14.7 Manufacturing industries of Nigeria.
Source: Created by Greg Anderson

no different from the other industries that have been discussed. Most of the minerals are exported in raw form. At best the value chain in all the countries including South Africa do not go beyond beneficiation, which is the breaking down of the ore to extract the minerals. For higher value addition, this process needs to be followed by smelting and refining in some cases.

The prospects for Africa to industrialize its mineral production are great as the cost of mining in developed countries is causing the closure of several investments projects. The result is that multinational mineral production firms from developed countries and China are scrambling over Africa once again. The African Development Bank (2012) reported that the world's biggest mining multinationals such as BHP Billiton, Rio Tinto, Anglo American, and Xstrata, and over 200 Australian companies were operating in Africa. As we learned in Chapter 13, African countries have articulated a new vision in the African Mining Vision (AMV). How successful they will be will depend on how well they are able to implement this vision.

If value-added modern mineral processing is in its infancy in most African countries, metal works dominated by small-scale production systems are widespread, and in many African countries these have formed industrial districts of their own. These districts specialize in a wide range of metal products such as automobile parts, small machinery, metal doors, windows, and gates, brick-making machines, molds, and metallic chairs, tables, and beds. They also specialize in automobile repairs. Most of the operators here have little education but go through apprenticeship training under established experts. Among the most well known are the Suame Magazine industrial district of Kumasi, Ghana; the Kamukunji Jua Kali and Zwani industrial districts of Kenya; Katwe in Kampala, Uganda; and the Gerezani, in Tanzania.

Petroleum refinery

Petroleum or oil refinery is the most widespread large-scale manufacturing industry in Africa. Owing to their size, technological sophistication, and large capital investment required, oil refinery is dominated by large-scale production systems, that are either state- or foreign-owned or joint ventures. The largest concentrations are in Egypt, which has nine refineries, and South Africa, Nigeria, and Algeria, with four refineries each. Egypt's refineries are mostly around Cairo, Alexandra, and Suez; South Africa has one in Cape Town, two in Durban, and one in Sasolburg; Nigeria has one in Kaduna, one in Warri, and two in Port Harcourt, while Algeria's refineries are located in Algiers, Arzew, Skikda, and Hassi Messaoud. The Skikda refinery, operated by the state-owned Sonatrach, is the single largest refinery in Africa.

Over the past decade, more crude oil has been discovered on the continent due to increasing exploration, even as the domestic demand for oil has increased. However, the existing oil refinery capacity on the continent is too small to meet this increasing demand due to past policies that had neglected this sector of the industry. For example, Nigeria, the continent's leading oil producer and the 13th largest in the world can only refine less than 20% of its total output (Rettig et al., 2013).

In recent years, however, African countries have realized the need to add value and move away from the colonial legacy of exporting just raw materials in exchange for manufactured goods. A number of countries including Angola, Senegal, Cameroon, and Kenya initiated plans to fix or expand existing refineries, and build new ones. However, these efforts are already meeting many headwinds from global competition. First, due to increasing demand African countries are importing more oil from the United States, Europe, or the Middle East, which makes it financially difficult to develop the domestic resources. Second, Farge (2013) reports that investors are either withdrawing or shifting their interest away from building refineries to building storage facilities. This is happening because investors find it cheaper to import fuel from refineries in the United States and India or even China than produce it from refineries in Africa that are old and unreliable. For this reason, it is estimated that most of the planned refinery projects would not be built. So once again, Africa finds itself in a bind where it wants more refineries to add value but those who control the wallet are using economic reasons to prevent Africa from doing so. How this plays out will depend on whether or not African countries have the courage to use their natural resource advantage to force the companies that are exploiting the crude oil into value-addition ventures.

The Pharmaceutical Industry

The pharmaceutical industry of Africa constitutes just a small percentage of the global market; recently estimated as between US$8 billion and US$10 billion according to African Union (2012). Estimates for the largest markets range from US$2.5 billion in Nigeria in 2011 to US$8.4 billion in South Africa in 2014. The structure of Africa's pharmaceutical industry is complex. Broadly speaking, it consists of all the three types of manufacturing production systems—the indigenous, small-scale, and large-scale production systems.

The indigenous and small-scale production systems largely dominate the pharmaceutics of millions of people on the continent. These systems produce the traditional herbal medicines that were declared fetish during the colonial period, but has remained vibrant for reasons of affordability, accessibility, and cultural beliefs. These traditional medicines still provide a wide range of cure to millions of Africans and have become the last resort when modern medicine fails. In many countries, these were neglected and disparaged even after the postcolonial period (Oppong, 2003). However, over the past decade or so a number of African countries have tried to bring these medicines into the modern system by instituting policies that would help improve sanitation and safety concerns. Unfortunately, most of these policies have only been on paper.

The large-scale pharmaceutical production system consists of both global and domestic companies. The global companies include both innovators such as Pfizer, Sanofi, and GSK, and generic drug makers such as Ranbaxy, Aspen, Mylan, and Cipla. On the domestic front, the majority of the companies are small privately owned companies that serve national markets. A few of these such as South Africa's Aspen are large enough to be comparable to international generic firms. Finally, there are state-owned companies such as Saidal in Algeria and Saphad in Tunisia.

African Union (2012) estimated that there were 38 African countries with pharmaceutical manufacturing activities with varying sizes. For example, Nigeria had 200 registered pharmaceutical manufacturers, South Africa had 30, Ghana and Kenya had 20 and 40, each. Others such as Uganda, Tanzania, Zambia, and Zimbabwe had 5 to 10 manufactures while Cameroon, Namibia, Swaziland, Lesotho, and Malawi had one or two active firms (African Union, 2012). In addition to these, there are also joint ventures between some of the global generic firms and local firms.

The range of products varies with the nature of the industry. In South Africa and the North African countries where the pharmaceutical industry is most developed, the majority of the firms produce "nutraceuticals, cough and cold formulas, simple analgesics and sedatives, anti-malarias, older generation antibiotics, anti-helminthics and first generation anti-hypertensives, anti-diabetics and neuropsychiatric drugs" (African Union, 2012, pp. 30–31).

The industry is beset with a number of problems. First, due to quality concerns manufacturing of drugs for Africa's top two public health concerns, namely HIV/AIDS and malaria, is limited on the continent. Indeed, HIV/AIDS drugs are controlled mostly by the donor community, while only one company is certified to produce malaria drugs on the continent (African Union, 2012). In general, products made in South Africa and North African countries are considered to be close to international standards. For the rest of the continent, certification is on case-by case basis. Among the companies that have gained certification are LaGray in Ghana and Cosmos in Kenya. Other firms are in the process of obtaining certification.

Second, African pharmaceutical manufacturers depend on imports for all their production inputs as well as their machinery, equipment, and other materials they use. With the exception of starches and sugars in a few countries, there are virtually no local inputs at all to the industry. In fact, about 95% of even the active pharmaceutical ingredients (API) come from outside. This obviously has cost as well as development implications.

Third, regulatory mechanisms for manufacturing, importing, exporting, and distributing medicines are also lacking. Most African countries do not have the minimum institutional structures to ensure safety, efficacy, and proper licensing of medicines. Inspection and control of informal markets for drugs are mostly nonexistent and continuous monitoring and evaluation of medicines in the formal market is weak. In most cases, these problems result from understaffed and underfunded regulatory agencies. Other problems include limited pool of trained scientists for the industry, access to capital, limited intraregional trade, limited research and development, and increasing global competition.

To address these issues, some African countries including Ghana, Nigeria, Algeria, and Tunisia have used some protectionist tools such as import restrictions on certain medicines to support their domestic pharmaceutical industries. In a much more comprehensive way to deal with the industry's problems, the African Union (2012) published a **pharmaceutical manufacturing plan for Africa** (PMPA). The plan outlines an approach that would provide technical assistance to African countries in key areas of the industry. These include human resources development, technical manufacturing, regulatory and policy skills, and the development of business skills for the pharmaceutical industry. The implementation of this plan calls for collaborative efforts between African and international development partners in funding, the establishment of mutual trust and legal basis, the development of a detailed shared work plan with roles and responsibilities, governance and reporting structures, and a lead role by the African Union Central Commission (African Union, 2012). The United Nations Industrial Development Organization (UNIDO) has been tapped as the main partner in the plan.

Food and Beverage Processing

Food and beverage processing is the largest manufacturing industry in Africa, and it includes meat processing, dairy products, fruit and vegetable canning, grain milling, sugar refinery; and ready-made meals. Over the past several years, this industry has become increasingly important due to the realization of value added in processed food compared to raw food. Market reports attribute this shift in the African food market to three factors. First is the growth of supermarket chains such as South Africa's Shoprite and Pick n Pay and France's Carrefour, which are expanding aggressively in urban areas across the continent. Second is the change in consumer taste due to increasing ability of the growing African middle class to demand and purchase high-quality brand-name processed foods. Third is the emergence of reliable food conglomerate with distribution networks to service the market. Among these are the Fan Milk International of Ghana and Zambeef of Zambia.

The industry structure consists of large-scale multinationals from both inside and outside of Africa and state-owned companies, as well as small-scale and indigenous production systems. The non-African multinationals companies include Nestle, Unilever, Del Monte, Cargill, and Coca Cola. There are however a large number of African multinational companies such as the JSE and Tiger Brands of South Africa; BIDCO the Nairobi-Kenya-based edible oil processing company with operations in East and Central Africa; the Kenyan-based East African Breweries; Cheetah Malawi, an indigenous spice processing company; and FreshPikt Zambia, a fruit and vegetable processing company with operations in Zambia, Malawi, and Mozambique. In West Africa, they include Blue Skies of Ghana, specializing in processed food and packaged fruits; Ghana Agro Food Company in tuna canning, wheat milling, and feed milling, and Darko Farms for poultry; and Burkina Faso's ETALON, which specializes in flour milling.

However, depending on the subsector and the country, the indigenous and small-scale production systems tend to dominate this industry. This could be due to two reasons. First, most of the subsectors of the industry do not have fully developed value addition. Second, where such fully developed value-addition chains exist they are most likely to be in South Africa and in a handful of other countries.

Food processing Sugar refinery is typical of the large-scale manufacturing production system of the food processing subsector. The industry is represented in more than a dozen countries in southern Africa, East Africa, West, and North Africa. Yet it is dominated by two countries—South Africa and Egypt. In South Africa, sugar mills are concentrated in the KwaZulu-Natal (Figure 14.8) near the source of sugar cane, its main raw material, and not far from Durban, where the sugar is refined for export (Castel-Branco, 2012). Most of Egypt's sugar production is from sugar beet and the refineries are located in Kafr El-Sheikh (Hamul City), Dakahalia, Fayoum, Naga Hamadi (Figure 14.6) (Hassan, 2008). Other countries with substantial sugar manufacturing include Swaziland, Zimbabwe, Zambia, Malawi, Mozambique, and Angola, Sudan, Mauritius, Kenya, Ethiopia, Somalia, Tanzania, Uganda, Cote D'Ivoire, Senegal, Mali, Guinea, Niger, and Morocco (Hassan, 2008).

In contrast, subsectors such as meat processing, fruit and vegetables, and ready-made meals are dominated by indigenous production systems, except in South Africa. With respect to meat processing, the main problem is that many of the large livestock-producing countries such as Ethiopia, Nigeria, Tanzania, and Mali do not have fully developed abattoirs or slaughterhouses and supporting infrastructure such as reliable power supply and efficient transportation facilities. As a result, these countries find it more profitable to export live animals to neighboring countries than seeking value-added products such as red meat export. This in turn has opened the domestic markets to a large number of small-scale firms that use simple implements, operating in shanty and unhygienic slaughterhouses. In most cases, there are no standardized meat processing procedures for these firms to follow and as a result, quality and safety are the top two problems of this subsector of the industry. However, recent emergence of firms such as Kenya's Farmer's Choice and Uganda's Fresh Cuts is beginning to change the industry. In 2014, Allanasons of India announced a $20 million food processing industry in Ethiopia. Large South African food processing companies also announced plans in 2013 to expand into the rest of the continent with some acquisitions.

Many African countries have great potential in tropical fruits and vegetable processing but they are faced with the problem of postharvest losses. In Egypt for example, Selim (2009) estimates that this postharvest loss was as high as 60%. The main causes of this postharvest loss include lack of storage and modern processing facilities, poor packaging, and multiple labor handling.

Before turning to beverages, there is one more subsector of food processing that needs mention and that is the ready-made meals subsector. This is the most widespread sector of the food processing industry. There are many different varieties, usually differentiated by price and service. At the very top are the high-end

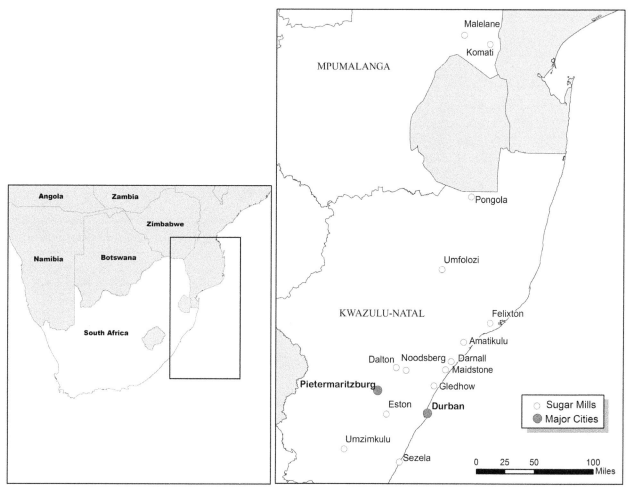

FIGURE 14.8 Sugar mills of South Africa.
Source: Created by Greg Anderson

restaurants that are either stand-alone, or are affiliated with multinational hotel chains such as Marriott, Hyatt Regency, Four Seasons, Holiday Inn, Novotel, and other top hotels in the national capitals and in tourist resorts. However, the majority of the firms in this subsector are very small one-person enterprises usually operated by women who cook and sell ready-made local food from small restaurants/shops or from particular spots on the streets. The firms with established shops operate like small-scale restaurants where customers go in to purchase and eat the food while the street vendors operate more on takeaway basis. In some cases, the providers may organize themselves into a food vending district where they compete for customers. Once again, these are unregulated and quality and safety are the main problems.

Beverage processing As we indicated in Chapter 11 Africa leads the world in cocoa production and ranks second in tea and coffee production, yet only a small proportion of these outputs are converted to value-added products. This leaves the beverage industry to alcoholic and nonalcoholic drinks. Brewery is strongly represented in Africa and beer companies are among the largest manufacturing companies on the continent. Large multinational companies such as SAB Miller of South Africa, Diageo of Britain, Castel of France, Guinness of Ireland, and Heineken of the Netherlands have significant subsidiaries in many African countries. Apart from these, there are national beer brands that are produced by local firms in many African countries. One of the largest is East African Breweries Limited, which consists of a group of seven companies including the Kenyan Brewery Limited and the Ugandan Brewery Limited. Examples of these local beers are the Tusker of Kenya, the Nile of Uganda, the Safari of Tanzania, the Nova Cua of Angola, the Three Horses of Madagascar, and the Star and Club beers of Nigeria and Ghana. The wine subsector is also very active with the most famous and world-known being those of South Africa and Morocco. In addition, there are a wide range of locally brewed wine and spirits from various sources, the most famous being the palm wine, and its associated spirit, *akpeteshie* of West Africa.

Soft drinks have also had a long presence in Africa and they are represented in all African countries. The industry is dominated by the two American soft drink giants—Coca Cola and Pepsi Cola. For a long time, the soft drink market was greatly advanced by the bad drinking water in most African countries. In recent decades, bottled water production has become very important as rising incomes have enabled many people to turn away from bad drinking water. This has cut into the market of the soft drinks.

The Computer and Electronics Industry

The computer and electronic industry consists of assembly of computers, computer peripherals, and communication equipment. The industry is prominent in some African countries, the most important being South Africa, Nigeria, Kenya, and Egypt.

South Africa Once again, the industry leader is South Africa, especially in the information and communication technologies subsector. The industry originally developed to provide telecommunication systems, and supply military systems and other related components for economic development. Owing to structural changes in the economy in the late 1980s to 1990s, the composition and orientation of the industry changed especially from defense to general consumer market (Coote and Coetzee, ND). The industry has gained worldwide reputation in software development especially in the areas of prepayment, revenue management, and fraud protection. Part of this was due to the country's highly developed network infrastructure and government backing in the form of tax incentives and financial assistance through the IDC. Some of the world leaders in information technology sector including IBM, Unisys, Microsoft, Intel Systems Application Protocol (ISAP), Dell, Novell, and Compaq have subsidiaries in South Africa. The industry is centered in the Gauteng, Western Cape, and KwaZulu-Natal.

Nigeria In Nigeria, the industry cluster is the Otigba Computer Hardware Village or the Ikeja Computer Village in Lagos, Nigeria. According to Oyelaran-Oyeyinka (2007), the village began in the early 1990s when a few sales and repairs outlets of office stationery and equipment located along Otigba and Pepple Streets in the residential area of Ikeja, in Lagos State. As computer demand grew, more computer-related firms located in the area. Soon space became a problem and through private efforts, more office buildings were constructed. As the area began to attract national attention, it transitioned into a computer hardware assembly district, and by 2003, there were about 2,500 sales and repair outlets (Oyelaran-Oyeyinka, 2007). The area attracted new talents of computer science, engineering, and electronics graduates who ventured into building computer clones. Retail began to focus on importation of computer parts, components, and accessories. By the end of 2004, the area spreading across eight streets had become a hub of information communication technology (ICT) attracting people from other African countries. An important characteristic of this cluster is the level of interfirm relations, which is attributed to the educational backgrounds of the entrepreneurs. The growth of the district has attracted a number of banks into the area. Recent competition from China and other Asian countries has forced the firms in the district to respond in several ways, which include forming links with the firms in those countries and increasing their promotion in the local market more aggressively. In a 2005 study of the district, Oyelaran-Oyeyinka (2007) reported that both foreign-branded and locally branded computers were assembled and only 10% of the firms interviewed were foreign-owned.

Egypt Egypt's electronics industry began in the 1980s with the establishment of the consumer electronics and appliances industry by the Olympia and Baghat Groups. Most of the software used were supplied by equipment manufacturers with much of the local development limited to applications—especially the large users such as Al-Ahram, Cairo University, and the Central Agency for Public Agency Public Mobilization and Statistics (CAPMAS). Equipment manufacture was dominated by US-based companies' branch offices of IBM, Texas Instruments, and Hewlett-Packard (US Department of Commerce, 1983), while local companies focused on speech and language software.

In 2000, a government decree established Egypt's Smart Village located in Sixth of October, about 20 minutes west of downtown Cairo and near the Pyramids and the Sphinx of Giza. The village is a 600-acre industrial park, created to attract global giants in ICT—80% privately owned. It is the home of Egypt's Ministry of Communications and Information Technology (MCIT) and the National Telecommunication Regulatory Authority (NTRA). Other tenants include mobile phone providers, Oracle, HP, Alcatel-Lucent (Nokia), Ericsson, and Microsoft Egypt. Nile University is also located here—specializing in ICT courses. In 2013, the government announced a strategy aimed at creating 30,000 jobs in the electronics industry by 2020. IBM also announced an agreement with the Egyptian Information Technology Industry Development Agency (ITIDA) in 2014 to provide cloud computing services to 100 Egyptian Software Companies.

Other major players are Chinese, Japanese, and Korean electronics companies. The problem facing the industry is global competition. For example, the Hong Kong-based computer manufacturer, Lenovo, and Hisense, Japan's Sony, Casio, Sharp, and Fuji, as well as Korea's Samsung are all making big inroads into the African market that is going to be difficult for African companies to compete.

The Leather Goods Industry

The leather goods industry of Africa is another industry that has not progressed deep into its value chain. This value chain consists of livestock (cattle, sheep, and goats), hides and skin recovery, tanning, manufacturing of leather goods, and marketing. The result is that while Africa has about 15% of the world's cattle, and 25%

of its sheep and goats, it produces only 9% of the world's cattle hides, and 5.1% of its sheep and goatskins (FAOSTAT, 2013). Even more surprising is the fact that leather and leather products account for less than 4% of Africa's exports. This is because Africa's leather industry has remained unorganized for a long time. For example, only a few countries have mechanized abattoirs, where animals could be slaughtered and processed for their hides and skins under regulations. Majority of the slaughter occurs in rural and urban areas under very poor unregulated conditions, where the slaughterhouse consists of slabs. While most tanneries are in the modern production systems, they have had two problems. First, many of them were established as part of the export-led industrialization with the goal of exporting semi-processed leather rather than processing leather for the manufacturing of final leather goods. Second, many of them have not received much reinvestment. They are therefore either in bad shape or have deteriorated. Tanneries also generate a lot of solid waste into the environment and this has led to the need for several regulations in a number of African countries including Egypt, Ethiopia, Kenya, Namibia, Tunisia, Zambia, and Zimbabwe. In some cases, such as in Egypt and Morocco this has involved relocation of the industry from Old Cairo, and Fez and Casablanca, respectively, to industrial districts equipped with waste treatment facilities.

Manufacture of leather products has potential in many African countries because of the availability of the raw material and other input base, and because of abundance of cheap labor. However, the subsector faces a lot of competition from Asia, Europe, and North America. Africa's cheap labor is mostly unskilled and there are not enough training centers or institutes in tanning, footwear design, machine operations, as well as managerial skills on the continent. Apart from these, there is not enough production of other goods such as leather bags and garments.

In the past few years however, global demand for leather and particularly from India, has focused on Africa. By virtue of its large livestock population, Ethiopia has been the target. In 2011, two Indian development institutes—the Central Leather Research Institute (CLRI) and the Footwear Design Development Institute (FDDI)—committed to using technology to make Ethiopia's leather industry globally competitive by 2016. In 2012 the Ethiopian government supported a partnership with the Chinese Huajian International Shoe PLC in a $2 billion investment in the Ethiopian leather industry (Fry, 2012). Clearly, it appears that African countries need to move up the value chain of their leather industry to accrue to itself the benefits of value-added manufacturing. Whether or not this could be achieved by these Chinese and Indian investments is too early to tell.

The Textile and Garment Industry

Textiles Africa's textile industry displays all three forms of manufacturing production systems—the indigenous, the small-scale, and the modern or large-scale firms. The indigenous textile production systems consist of small-scale firms that are still engaged in making precolonial textile and clothing products. The small-scale production systems produce traditional textiles combining modern raw material input with traditional equipment and vice versa. What keeps these two systems going is the uniqueness of their products in terms of their design, purpose, and cultural values attached to them. The most famous of these are the *kente* and *adinkra* cloths of Ghana, the *Asoke* cloth of Nigeria, the *derma* cloth of Niger, the *mud* cloth of Mali, and others discussed in Chapter 7. In some cases, these products dominate a whole submarket of the clothing sector. An example of this is the *adinkra* cloth of Ghana, which dominates the mourning and funeral wear submarket of Ghana.

Most Africans, however, depend on large-scale modern textile manufacturing system for most of their everyday clothing needs. This subsector was one of the very first industries established either in the late colonial or early postcolonial Africa. This was due in part to the historic role textiles have played as vanguards of industrialization and in part due to its suitability to the ISI model of industrialization. The local demand for clothing placed textiles and garments among the largest manufacturing activities and there was a correlation between population size and plant size. So the largest plants were in the countries with the largest population. Today, the modern manufacturing systems include privately owned domestic and foreign firms as well as state-owned firms that survived the privatization movement of the SAP period.

Since the mid-1970s, the fortunes of the Africa's textile industry have risen and fallen with changing global trends, perhaps more than any of its manufacturing industries. In 1974, as a result of increasing competition from developing countries of Asia, especially, the United States, Canada, and (Western) European countries decided to protect their domestic textile and clothing industries by imposing a quota on textile and clothing exports from other countries (Mutume, 2006). This quota system became known as the **multifiber arrangement** (MFA). The initial effect of this arrangement was actually beneficial to small textile exporting countries in Africa since the textile producers in the MFA countries could not meet the high level of domestic demand. Apart from this, Asian multinationals located branch plants in African countries to get around the quota system.

However, as trade liberalization became popular in the 1980s, textile producers in Asia and large textile retailers in developed countries began to press for more free trade. The idea received further support during the Uruguay Round of 1986 to 1994. In 1994, a new Agreement on Textiles and Clothing was established by the World Trade Organization (WTO) to phase out the old quota system by 2004 (Mutume, 2006). In the interim, the African textile industry received a boost from the US government's African Growth and Opportunity Act (AGOA) of 2000, which provided "a duty-free entry of some products from African countries into the US market that adopted market-based economic policies" (Mutume, 2006 p. 18). The WTO agreement was initially welcome by textile producers from developing countries including those in Africa, but as the initial deadline of 2008 approached, it became clear that the beneficiaries were going to be those countries with very efficient textile industries. Thus, between 2004 and 2008, African exports to the United States drastically declined. Not only that but its respective domestic markets were flooded by cheap imports from China (Xiaoyang, 2014). By 2011, exports from Asian countries—China, India, and Pakistan, exceeded $2.3 billion, $211 million, and $150 million, respectively. For China, this represented an increase in 67% since 2004 (Xiaoyang, 2014).

According to Mutume (2006) the African textile industry shed over 250,000 jobs, most of which occurred in Lesotho, South Africa, Swaziland, Nigeria, Ghana, Mauritius, Zambia, Madagascar, Tanzania, Malawi, Namibia, and Kenya. In Lesotho, for example, textile manufacturing was the main stay of the economy before the end of MFA; it was the largest public sector employer and it accounted for 75% of the export earnings. Some of the firms were subsidiaries of large Asian textile companies that had established there to get around the old quota system and to take advantage of the AGOA. However, after the quota system ended, six of the 50 textiles and clothing firms closed down and left 6,600 workers unemployed. Another 10,000 workers were placed on short-term schedules by the remaining firms as they faced competition in the market (Mutume, 2006).

After retreating from Southeast African textile industry in anticipation of the end of AGOA and the MFA, Chinese investments have returned over the past few years to establish cotton ginneries in places such as Mozambique and Tanzania. Part of this is to get around a quota system imposed by the Chinese government on the importation of cotton to protect the cotton farmers in China. According to Xiaoyang (2014) this policy has been criticized in China and there are indications that the policy would be reversed soon. The question is when this happens, will Chinese investment remain or not? However, given that AGOA has been extended to 2025, it is most likely that Chinese investment will remain.

Government policies also appear to be part of the problem, in what appears to be privatization run amok. For example, Xiaoyang (2014) reports that although the governments in Southeast Africa emphasize value addition, most do not have a functioning textile sector to do so. The only country with a significant textile sector is Tanzania, which has been facing a cotton shortage since 2010. In particular, local ginners prefer to sell to foreign buyers rather than to domestic mills, because domestic buyers lack the letters of credit to guarantee buying whole year stocks compared to foreign buyers who have deep pockets to do so. Xiaoyang (2014) writes:

> The Tanzania Cotton Board, a government body established to regulate and promote the cotton sector, understands the problem, but it is not willing to interfere. The market determines the sales direction and, according to the director of the cotton board, the government cannot regulate the sales direction, even when it hopes to get more added value on cotton. This attitude regarding the cotton sector is common among authorities in the region. An official in Zambia's Ministry of Agriculture said that cotton is mainly in the hands of the private sector. . . . The government solely stipulates guiding policies and coordinates investment.

Obviously these governments have not or are not aware of the huge support the US, EU, and Chinese governments give to their farmers in terms of farm subsidies, and many different ways these governments get involved in their respective manufacturing sectors. They apparently never heard of the owners of the Airbus Company and the huge bailout that the US government gave to the US automobile industry and the financial sector during the 2008 recession.

Given China's strategy to become the world's largest textile producer and exporter, the options for Africa's textile and clothing industry are limited. It has been suggested that African countries can invoke "anti-dumping" measures to restrict Chinese textile and clothing imports over a period, during which Africa can improve efficiency and competitiveness of its industry. Mutume (2006) reports that a number of African countries including Kenya adopted that policy before the old quota system expired. These measures included removal of taxes on manufacturing machinery and processes, incentive to import more modern equipment, and lowering of taxes on goods and services in EPZs. By December 2004, it was reported that there were 30 manufacturing plants in the EPZ employing 34,614 workers (Mutume, 2006).

Another recommendation to deal with the impending crisis will be to diversify the economy from overdependence on textiles and clothing. This calls for negotiating with China to trade in items other than textiles. This could be done by engaging in bilateral trade talks with China about potential commodities. However, this will require removal of subsidies on commodities and protectionism that still prevail in many countries in spite of WTO rules.

Clearly, it appears that the African textile and clothing industry has its work cut out. As Mutume (2006) indicates, it has either to adjust or perish. Adjustment will need upgrading of skills and retraining of workers who have lost their jobs. Another way is to reduce production cost, which in many African countries is in buildings, electricity, fabrics, and labor, and high transportation costs.

Apparels and garments Every African country has an apparel or garment industry, an offshoot of the textile industry, but the three top countries are South Africa, Egypt, and Nigeria. Traditionally, this subsector has been the domain of a large number of firms operating in the indigenous and small-scale production systems. Their low start-up cost in terms of capital, equipment, and locational flexibility allowed them to flourish in many settings. Thus, they range from small-scale custom tailors and seamstresses to medium-scale operators and cooperatives in isolated locations or in large and well-organized garment and clothing districts such as the Uhuru Market and the Kariobangi districts of Nairobi, Kenya, and the Johannesburg's Fashion District of South Africa.

Like textiles, the garment subsector is facing growing competition and the effect has been more dramatic not only in the top garment countries such as South Africa, Egypt, and Nigeria but also in Swaziland, Lesotho, and Botswana, especially. This competition is from modern production systems consisting of subsidiaries of multinational companies. In South Africa, they include Woolworth, Mr. Price, Edgars, Truthworths, and Foschini. In Egypt, international brands such as Gap, Guy Laroche, Pierre Cardin, and Tommy Hilfiger are producing for the domestic markets under licensing agreements (UNECA, 2013). In Nigeria, multinationals with subsidiaries from Hong Kong, India, the United Kingdom, the Netherlands, the United States, Japan, and China are doing the same thing (Eneji et al., 2012).

Another problem facing the garment industry is the mismatch between inputs due to inefficiencies and past policies. At one extreme are major cotton producing countries such as Mali, which exports all its cotton. At the other extreme is Egypt, which has the only fully vertically integrated textile industry on the continent, where from cultivation of cotton through production of yarns and cotton fabrics to garment are all controlled domestically by the large public sector. Yet due to ineffective technology, low capital utilization, production inefficiencies in the publicly owned textile facilities, the garment industry has to import some yarns and fabrics from India, Turkey, Bangladesh, and Pakistan. Some cotton has to be exported to other countries for processing before sending it back to Egypt to be used in the garment sector (UNECA, 2013). Other problems related to this include deficient facilities, unskilled workers, and cumbersome export process, all of which are making it difficult for foreign firm operations.

Africa's garment industry is also facing stiff competition from the second-hand clothing (SHC) industry and cheaper imports from East Asia. A report by Baden and Barber (2005) indicates that in the mid-1990s there were about 41 textiles and clothing manufacturing firms in West African Economic and Monetary Union (WAEMU), by 2004 there were only six companies that were operating at full capacity, and only three were performing at satisfactory level. Baden and Barber (2005) also report that Nigeria, the largest textile producer in West Africa, has lost over 80,000 jobs in the industry since the 1990s. Much of this loss was attributed to the SHC industry, For example, in 2003 Africa accounted for more than 26.8% of the global imports of SHC, and the ratio of SHC imports to all imports was highest in Africa than any other region—10.3%. Finally, due to the large numbers of jobs the apparel industry is able to create, African countries have put in place several incentives to attract foreign firm into this sector. However, this usually conflicts with the policy of protecting their domestic industries.

In spite of all these problems, local manufacturers have managed to survive due to the distance factor with Asian countries. In addition, African governments are taking actions to help support their domestic textile industries. For example, in Ethiopia a major overhaul of the textile sector was reported in 2012 that included increasing the volume of homegrown cotton, and expanding the garment subsector into women's fashion for international as well as domestic markets. In Mauritius, after severe job losses in 2006, the government launched a major comeback strategy estimated to be $100 million for the manufacturing sector in 2010, with particular focus on the textile industry. The textile industry has since recovered, become competitive, and has diversified into garment production to even hiring more foreign workers from India and China. To deal with the problem of SHC, Nigeria, Uganda, and Kenya are among the countries that have banned the importation of SHC, although implementation has been difficult. For example, in 2016, East African countries raised tariffs on SHC as an indirect way of banning SHC from their markets. However, the US SHC dealers lobbied the US government to intervene because a collapse of their business would cost 40,000 jobs and create a landfill nightmare. The US government responded with a threat to expel the East African countries from AGOA if they went ahead with the tariffs (Freytas-Tamura, 2017). Kenya pulled out and so did Tanzania and Uganda later on, but Rwanda did not. In April 2018, the United States issued a 60-day notice to Rwanda that if it did not remove its tariffs on second-hand clothing goods from the United States, it would lose its AGOA privileges with respect to clothing, and when Rwanda refused to do so, it lost its privileges in July 2018.

Problems and Prospects of Industrialization

The discussion of the select number of industries has already highlighted some if not all of the problems of industrialization in Africa. They include political instability, lack of sustained industrialization policy, low value addition, weaker inter- and intrasectoral linkages, ownership, control, and management characteristics of capital, shortage of skilled labor, and weak supporting infrastructure.

Political Instability and Leadership

Like all other aspects of economic development, industrialization cannot take place in the middle of chaotic political environments and the economic and social uncertainties that come with such environments. Over the past two decades, political situation has improved in most African countries but the instability that occurred in many countries from the early post-independence era through the 1980s took its toll on socioeconomic development policies. It robbed the continent of a strong and stable leadership that was dedicated to industrialization as a path to development. Political leadership in the early post-independence era looked strong but for all the wrong reasons. Most of the leaders wanted to be leaders for life, and were more interested in perpetuating themselves in power through autocratic rule and stamping out all forms of opposition than paying attention to economic development of their respective countries. As the high expectations of rapid economic development failed to materialize and the cost of rapid development began to mount, frustration and pressure also increased. African leaders reacted in many different ways. Some became more autocratic; others fell victim to the Cold War politics and were overthrown. In some countries, political leadership became a revolving door as several factions of the military took turns to rule the country. Many of these governments had no clue about how to navigate and manage the international political economy. Political leadership became more concerned with survival than economic development. Thus, unlike successful Asian countries, state involvement in industrialization only existed in the name of state-owned enterprises—that were not only mismanaged but state investment in capacity, R&D, and incentives virtually ceased causing many of the established industries to deteriorate.

Lack of Sustained Industrialization Policy

As it was discussed in the first sections of this chapter, the majority of African countries started with ISI and then tried export-based industrialization. However, these policies were not pursued with any sustained and consistent efforts. In spite of all of the criticisms of ISI, history shows that it has been the path of every industrialized economy. The problem is not with the policy but with the lack of commitment and the inability to transition from an ISI base to a competitive industrialization. In the majority of African countries, many of the import-substitution industries became dysfunctional, inoperable, or even abandoned within a decade. The export-led industrialization in most cases existed only on paper with empty or very sparsely populated EPZs as the only ground evidence. Indeed, during the period of SAPs implementation in Africa and a decade or so after that, the majority of African countries and their lending international institutions and donors took their eyes off industrialization as the path to development. Instead, there was an obsession with privatization and trade liberalization, and in some circles ICT, as panacea for Africa's economic development problem. Without a consistent and sustained industrialization policy for economic development, it is difficult to keep a focus on industrialization in the development process.

Low Value Addition

One of the results of the lack of a consistent policy to guide industrialization is that African countries have been satisfied with low value addition of industrial output. As Dr. Yumkella, the Director General for United Nations Industrial Development Organization has rightly observed:

> Prosperity is not due to resource endowment and poverty is not due to the lack of resources. Prosperity is the outcome of value addition. Resource-rich countries remain poor due to the lack of value addition.

> (Yumkella, 2010)

Yet because industrialization fell off the radar of most African countries, the push for value-added manufacturing also fell by the way side. Thus, Africa produces most of the world's cocoa, yet it is not competitive in the manufacturing of high-end cocoa products. The same can be said of other major agricultural crops and minerals in which Africa leads in production. In an article on manufacturing Harding (2011) quotes Rob Davies, South Africa Minister of Trade and Industry, as saying: "Titanium sand sells for US$440 a ton; processed into titanium sponge it fetches $4,000 a ton and as an alloy, used in the aircraft industry, the price goes up to $100,000 a ton." By not moving into value-added output, African countries lost and continue to lose the much-needed financial capital for further industrialization.

Weak inter- and Intrasectoral Linkages

With the exception of South Africa, industrialization policies for the most part have not been able to tap into intersectoral and intrasectoral linkages in African economies. This means that manufacturing activities have not been of the type that stimulate growth in both their input and output sectors. Most inputs including some raw materials are imported. Similarly, because not much effort have been devoted to high value addition, forward linkages have also been weak. Part of this situation could also be due to the neglect of indigenous and small-scale industries in Africa. As already pointed out, these activities play a major role in African economies. Yet they did not receive any public support for improvement and formalization. The result is that many remained stagnant and some even disappeared.

High Dependence of Foreign Capital

Industrialization involves capital and especially creating value-added products require substantial amount of capital. Owing to limited domestic resources that have for the most part been mismanaged, there has been a long-standing practice of relying on foreign sources in order to develop some of these industries. However, it is not the source of capital per se, but who owns and who controls it that are crucial. As evident from the past efforts of large-scale industrialization, foreign capital is at best precarious since that investment could be pulled anytime the terms do not live up to the expected bottom line. It also leads to projects that are often not in the interest of the country hosting the investment but for those who own and control the capital. It takes out the independence and freedom to direct funds into appropriate areas. In this case, the best alternative is generating enough domestic revenue or borrowing, but for some reason, African countries have struggled with both sources of revenue generation leaving foreign direct investment (FDI) as the most probable option.

Weak Supporting Infrastructure

Successful industrialization goes hand in hand with solid infrastructure. A fully developed infrastructure if ever attainable is not a prerequisite for industrialization, but at the minimum there should be cheap and efficient transportation and communication systems to move goods and transact business. There should also be cheap and reliable sources of energy to ensure continuous production; effective administrative, financial, and legal institutions to facilitate and protect business transactions; and a trained and productive workforce for goods production and effective demand. Absence of these increases the cost of doing business and discourages investments that could go into manufacturing, and makes manufacturing less competitive. The poor transportation networks, frequent power outages, archaic and bureaucratic structures that breed corruption in public offices, all make it difficult for industrialization to take root in Africa.

Prospects for Industrialization

In spite of these problems, the prospects for industrialization in Africa are still very good. For one thing, the continent still has enormous natural and human resources that can be harnessed to its advantage if appropriate policies are implemented.

Given the prominent role that agriculture plays in Africa's economy. many policy recommendations have focused attention on agribusiness, as a strategy to jump start industrialization of Africa. For Alemayehu (2000), such an agricultural-led strategy for industrialization should prioritize (1) industrial agricultural chemicals, agricultural equipment, and machinery; (2) equipment and machinery for preserving, storing, processing, and transporting agricultural inputs and products; (3) industries oriented to other basic needs; and (4) industries producing inputs for small-scale industries. Both AU's Comprehensive Africa Agricultural Development Program (CAADP) and UNIDO/UNCTAD (2011) have identified with most of these ideas, emphasizing (1) improving agricultural productivity through improved industrial inputs; (2) increasing industrial processing of agricultural products; (3) strengthening industrial production of processing machinery, equipment, tools, and packaging materials, and improving transportation and storage infrastructure, that all relate to agriculture. These will develop linkages to other sectors that are either directly or indirectly related to agriculture.

Dihn et al. (2012) also argue that Africa has comparative advantage in light manufacturing. These are manufacturing activities that are less capital-intensive or more labor-intensive, require less raw material, and produce items that are not only easily transported but also low cost. The report encourages African countries and their respective governments to follow the steps Asian countries took, which is a two-pronged strategy—first develop excellent trade logistics to support imports to make inputs ready available and second reform and support key input industries to become competitive. In a working paper on industrialization policy in Africa, Stiglitz et al. (2013) also suggest policies that will (1) transfer resources to high-productivity sectors including migrating the rural unskilled labor to unskilled labor-intensive industries and (2) increasing productivity through education and training.

Every successful industrialized country has achieved its status with the strong and active roles of their respective governments, and African countries cannot be different. African countries cannot industrialize without the active roles of their governments. These roles are not for governments to become directly engaged in the actual production and distribution of goods as they did in the 1960s and 1970s. Instead, the governments are to serve as regulators, facilitators, and investors in industrial promotion activities (Alemayehu, 2000). As regulators, governments have to ensure that the market system works and that price is fairly determined by the supply and demand forces. As facilitators, they should put in place policies and programs that encourage private sector and investments in relevant industrial activities that will advance development. For example, they should make it easy for formation of new industrial enterprises without unnecessary red tapes, cumbersome paperwork, and exorbitant registration fees; they should relax import duties on raw material, and industrial machinery; they should provide tax incentives for export activities, and they should ban imports of domestically produced items. As investors, they should take research and development seriously, invest in infrastructure—roads and power resources and they should invest in human resources development—in quality education and health of their citizens (Alemayehu, 2000).

Summary

Manufacturing is key to economic development of nations. However, as colonies of Europe, Africa missed out on all the benefits of the industrial revolution that transformed the economies of Europe and North America. Instead Africa was subject to production of primary products except the few enclaves of white settlements of South and North Africa. In a few cases, it was only during the late colonial period—specifically the period after World War II that some serious efforts were made toward some industrial activities. The result was that at the time of independence most African countries did not have any modern industrial sector. What existed were remnants of small-scale activities from the precolonial period that had stagnated due to neglect during the colonial period, producing items of local use and cultural value. For this reason, African countries embarked on industrialization in the early post-independence period with the import-substitution policy. Many state-owned large-scale industries were established to produce items that were previously imported. In addition, these industries provided jobs for thousands of people. However, these industries failed to live up to expectations due to a host of factors including balance of payments difficulties, recession, external competition, economic mismanagement, and political instability and high operation cost due to poor infrastructure. Continuous economic decline forced many countries to institute SAPs that led to divestiture and retrenchment in most of the large-scale industries. Privatization of large-scale industries had mixed results. In some countries, it led to disintegration of the manufacturing base of the economy, while for some it brought in private capital that resulted in energizing the economy. At any rate, manufacturing as a sector weakened leaving the small-scale production systems that had been ironically neglected by modern large-scale industrial policies to hold the fort. Throughout all these Africa's contribution to global manufacturing value added was negligible. Apart from this, low value addition, weak sectoral linkages, and high dependence on foreign capital characterized Africa's manufacturing.

Over the past decade, both the international development enterprise and African countries have rediscovered the role of manufacturing and policy papers, conferences, plans, and resolutions as to how African countries can industrialize is once again in vogue. Some suggest focusing on light industries rather than heavy industries because that is where African countries have comparative advantage. Others emphasize the need for value addition whether it is light or heavy industries. Most agree that agriculture-led industry will be the best way to go due again to comparative advantage and the dominant role that agriculture plays. However, this needs to go beyond the usual agro processing to include agricultural chemicals, agricultural equipment, and machinery; equipment and machinery for preserving, storing, processing, and transporting agricultural inputs and products; industries oriented to other basic needs; and industries producing inputs for small-scale industries. One factor that is constant in all these prescriptions is the role of African governments. Governments need to play the multiple roles of regulators, facilitators, and investors. African countries need to look at their industrialization policies more critically. They need to determine where their priorities are with regard to the future and which areas of industrial activity will hold promise for the future and position themselves in that direction.

In the current state of affairs, it is very difficult to tell if industrialization can take off without direct foreign investment. However, with emerging countries in East and South Asia, as well as Latin America, African countries will have a hard time attracting any such investments unless they create the enabling and inviting environment for such investments. Such enabling and inviting environment will need to emphasize solid and adequate transportation and telecommunication infrastructure, a large pool of skilled but cheap labor, a stable political climate in which there is rule of law and predictability, improved public health and sanitation, and shrewd bargaining with potential investment.

Postreading Assignments

A. Study the Following Concepts

export-led industrialization
policy
manufacturing production
system (MPS)

manufacturing value
added (MVA)
multifiber
arrangement

pharmaceutical
manufacturing plan for
Africa

B. Discussion Questions

1. Check your answers to the prereading questions and see if you would change anything.

2. Based on this chapter why do you think industrialization has failed to take root in Africa?

3. What do you think African countries should do to industrialize?

4. What are the main problems and prospects of African countries using foreign direct investments to industrialize?

5. Do you think it would be possible for African countries to industrialize given the current international environment? Why and Why not?

6. Should Africa concentrate on light or heavy industries?

References

Abdel-Khalek, G. 2001. *Stabilization and Adjustment in Egypt.* Cheltenham, UK: Edward Elgar.

Abegunde, A. A. 2011. "Community Development in Africa Through Indigenous Afro Allied Industries; A Recourse to Bottom-Up Strategy?" *International Journal of Business and social Science* 2(18): 253–260.

AfDB 2011. "Republic of Cameroon Lom-Pangar Hydroelectric Project: Summary of the Environmental and Social Impact Assessment (ESIA)."

African Development Bank Group 2012. "Mining Industry Prospects in Africa." http://www.afdb.org/en/blogs/afdb-championing-inclusive-growth-across-africa/post/mining-industry-prospects-in-africa-10177/

African Union 2012. Pharmaceutical Manufacturing Plan for Africa. Addis Ababa: African Union.

Agbu, O. 2007. "The Iron and Steel Industry and Nigeria's Industrialization: Exploring Cooperation with Japan." *Institute of Developing Economies, Japan External Trade Organization, Visiting Research Fellow Series N0. 418.*

Alemayehu, M. 2000. *Industrializing Africa: Development Options and Challenges for the 21st Century.* Trenton, NJ: Africa World Press Review.

Annan, K. 2000. "Africa Need to catapult Forward." *A Speech Delivered to CIPIA April.* https://www.globalpolicy.org/component/content/article/213/45663.html. Accessed September 12, 2015.

Aworh, O. C. 2008. "The Role of Traditional Food Processing Technologies in National Development: The West African Experience." In Robertson, G. L., and Lupien, J. R. (Eds.) *Using Food Science and Technology to Improve Nutrition and Promote National Development.*

Baden, S., and Barber, C. 2005. *The Impact on Second-hand Clothing Trade on Developing Countries.* London: Oxfam.

Castel-Branco, R. 2012. "The Dilemma of Growing Sugar Cane in KwaZulu-Natal." *The Africa Report August 2012.*

Coote, E., and Coetzee, K. ND. "The Scope of the Electronics Industry in the Western Cape." http://www.westerncape.gov.za/other/2005/11/final_first_paper_electronics_printing.pdf

Coupe, S. 1995. "Divisions of Labour: Racist Trade Unionism in the Iron, Steel, Engineering and Metallurgical Industries of Post-War South Africa." *Journal of Southern African Studies* 21(3): 451–471.

Dinh, H. T., Palmade, V., Chandra, V., and Cossar, F. 2012. *Light Manufacturing in Africa: Targeted Policies to Enhance Private Investments and Create Jobs.* Washington, DC: The World Bank.

Estefan, F. E. 1985. "The Economy." In Nelson. H. (Ed.) *Morocco: A Country Study.* Washington, DC: US Government, pp. 161–232.

Farge, E. 2013. "New Analysis: Africa's Oil-refining Ambitions Fade." *BusinessDay.* http://www.bdlive.co.za/africa/africanbusiness/2013/12/22/news-analysis-africas-oil-refining-ambitions-fade

Freytas-Tamura, K. 2017. "For Dignity and Development, East Africa Curbs Used Clothes Imports." *The New York Times, October 12.* https://www.nytimes.com/2017/10/12/world/africa/east-africa-rwanda-used-clothing.html. Accessed December 1, 2017.

Fry, M. 2012. "Under the Skin of Ethiopian Leather Industry." *Think Africa Press.* http://thinkafricapress.com/ethiopia/leather-asian-concern

Hamza, R., and Zaher, S. 2012. "Competitiveness Targeting: Automotive Industry in Egypt." *Paper Presented at the Cambridge Business & Economics Conference.* Cambridge, UK, June 27–28.

Harding, C. 2011. "Can Africa Become the Next China?" *How We Made It In Africa.* May 24.

Hasan, F., Soheim, M., and Farkouh, C. F. 2009. "Egypt Steel Sector." Safat, Kuwait: Global Investment House KSCC.

Hassan, S. F. 2008. "Development of Sugar Industry in Africa." *Sugar Tech* 10(3): 197–203.

Hathaway, T. 2007. "Aluminum in Africa: A Case Study for Earthlife Africa eThekwini and Friends of the Earth."

Hayter, R. 1997. *The Dynamics of Industrial Location: The Factory, the Firm, and the Production System.* Chichester: John Wiley.

Husband, C., McMahon, G., and van der Veen, P. 2009. *The Aluminum Industry of West and Central Africa: Lessons Learned and Prospects for the Future.* Washington, DC: The World Bank.

Ibrahim, F., and Ibrahim, B. 2003. *Egypt: An Economic Geography.* London: I. B. Tauris & Co. Ltd.

Jacobs, S. 2012. "Africa's Auto Industry Stuck in Second Gera?" *African Business Magazine* (October 22). http://africanbusiness magazine.com/sector-reports/industry/africas-auto-industry-stuck-in-second-gear/

Krassowski, A. 1974. *Development and the Debt Trap: Economic Planning and External Borrowing in Ghana.* London: Croom Helm and Overseas Development Institute.

Lorentzen, J., Robbins, G., and Barnes, J. 2007. *Industry Clusters and Innovation Systems in Africa: Institutions, Markets and Policy.* In Oyelaran-Oyeyinka, B., and McCormick, D. (Eds.) *Industrial Clusters and Innovation Systems in Africa: Institutions, markets and Policy.* Tokyo: United Nations University Press, pp. 189–201.

Mabogunje, A. L. 1973. "Manufacturing and the Geography of Development in Tropical Africa." *Economic Geography* 49(1): 1–30.

Mazumdar, R. 2014. "Africa Awakening Opportunities for Indian Chemical Industry in Africa." *Chemical Industry Digest*, 31 Jan. 2014. *Academic OneFile*, Web. 22 Sept. 2014.

Murtada, A. 2014. "Morocco Looks to Further Boost Automotive Investments." http://www.english.globalarabnetwork.com/2014 070813398/Industry/morocco-looks-to-further-boost-automotive-investments.html

Mutume, G. 2006. "Loss of Textile Market Costs African Jobs." *Africa Renewal* (April), p. 18.

Newman, H. R. 2012. "The Mineral Industries of Cameroon and Cape Verde." *2012 Minerals Yearbook. USGS.*

Nitschke, C. 2011. *A Model for Sustainability of Local Suppliers in the South African Automotive Value Chain.* A Dissertation Presented for the Degree of Doctor of Philosophy at the University of Stellenbosch Business School.

Nzau, M. 2010. "Africa's Industrialization Debate: A Critical Analysis." *The Journal of Language, Technology & Entrepreneurship in Africa* 2(1): 1998–1279.

Ohimain, E. I. 2013. "The Challenge of Domestic Iron and Steel Production in Nigeria." *Greener Journal of Business and Management Studies* 3(5): 231–240.

Oppong, J. R. 2003. "Medical Geography of Sub-Saharan Africa." In S. Aryeetey-Attoh (Ed.) Geography of Sub-Saharan Africa. 2nd Edition. Upper Saddle River, NJ: Prentice Hall, pp. 324–362.

Osei-Amponsah, C., Visser, L., Adjei-Nsiah, S., Struik, P. C., Sakyi-Dawson, O., and Stomph, T. J. 2012. "Processing Practices of Small-Scale Palm Oil Producers in the Kwaebibirem District,

Ghana: A Diagnostic Study." *NJAS - Wageningen Journal of Life Sciences* 60–63: 49–56.

Oyelaran-Oyeyinka, B. 2007. "Learning in Local Systems and Global Links: The Otigba Computer Hardware Cluster in Nigeria." In Oyelaran-Oyeyinka, B., and McCormick, D. (Eds.) *Industrial Clusters and Innovations Systems in Africa: Institutions, Markets and Policy.* Tokyo: United Nations University Press, pp. 100–132.

Peter, W., de Kuyper, J.-Q., and Candolle, B. 1995. Arbitration and Renegotiation of International Investment Agreements. The Hague: Kluwer Law International.

Pogue, T. E. 2008. "A Sectoral Analysis of Wood, Paper and Pulp Industries in South Africa." *Pretoria: Institute of Economic Research on Innovation.*

Rettig, M., Kimenyi, M. S., and Routman, B. 2013. "The Imperative of Boosting Africa's Oil Refinery Investments." *Africa in Focus Brookings.*

Rinehart, R. 1985. "Historical Setting." In Nelson. H. (Ed.) *Morocco: A Country Study.* Washington, DC: US Government, pp. 1–94.

Roberts, S. 2005. "A Big Steal? The South African Steel Industry and the Appropriate Industry Policy for Large-Scale Industry under Internationalization." *Briefing Paper 31-2005, School of Economics and Business Sciences, University of Witwatersrand.*

Rogerson, C.M. 1998. "Small-Scale Manufacturing in South Africa's Economic Heartland: Problems and Prospects." *Urban Forum* 9 (2): 279–300.

Rugumamu, S. 1989. "The Textile Industry of Tanzania." *Review of Radical Political Economics* 21(4): 54–72.

Schneider, G. E. 2000. "The Development of the Manufacturing Sector in South Africa." *Journal of Economic Issues* XXXIV(2): 413–444.

Scott, P. 1951. "The Iron and Steel Industry of South Africa." *Geography* 36(3): 137–149.

Selim, T. H. 2009. "The Egyptian Food Processing Industry: Formalization versus Informalization within the Nation's Food Security Policy." Paper Submitted to the *Alfred P. Sloan Industry Studies Association General Industry Studies Annual Conference*, Chicago.

Tumanjong, E. 2009. "DJ Cameroon's Only Smelter Stops Production." *FWN Financial News* (August 11).

UNECA 2013. "Economic Report on Africa 2013 Egypt Country Case Study." http://www.uneca.org/sites/default/files/uploaded-documents/era2013_casestudy_eng_egypt.pdf

UNIDO/UNCTAD 2011. *Economic Development in Africa: Fostering Industrial Development in Africa in a New Global Environment.* New York: United Nations.

US Department of Commerce. 1983. Computers and Peripheral Equipment Country Market Survey. Washington, DC.

Xiaoyang, T. 2014. "The Impact of Asian Investment on Africa's Textile Industries." Beijing: Carnegie–Tsinghua Center for Global Policy.

Yumkella, K. K. 2010. Agro-industry Strategy/Development of Agribusiness and Agro-industries in Africa. (Yumkella, K. 2010.htm).

CHAPTER 15

Trade and Tourism

Trade and tourism are two important components of Africa's service sector. Both economic activities have deep roots in the evolution and development of Africa's economy. Today, they both serve as sources of employment for millions of Africans, they generate substantial foreign exchange earnings for African countries, and they both have high potential contributions to Africa's current and future development. The first section of this chapter deals with trade, and the second section deals with tourism. Each section begins with a brief introductory review of some basic characteristics and concepts of the activity, followed by the activity's evolution and development in Africa, its contemporary geography, and current problems and issues. To start, complete the prereading assignments.

TRADE

Like elsewhere, trade, the process of buying and selling or exchanging of goods and services, occurs in different forms and at different levels in Africa. Thus, there is retail trade and wholesale trade, and there is internal or domestic trade and external or international trade. Retail trade involves selling to households while wholesale trade involves selling to intermediate distributors. Internal or domestic trade occurs within countries, while external or international trade occurs across national borders. Although all trade, whether retail, wholesale, internal, or external, is conducted by firms, trade statistics and discussion are done at the regional, national, or supra regional level.

PREREADING ASSIGNMENTS

1. Estimate the percentage of world trade that is due to Africa.
2. What do you think are the major exports and imports of African countries?
3. Do you think African countries trade more among themselves than with countries outside Africa?
4. What do you think will be some of the major barriers to trade by African countries?
5. What do you think are the main draw for tourism in Africa?
6. Where do you think most tourists to Africa go and why?
7. What do you think are the main obstacles to tourism in Africa?

Evolution and Development of Trade in Africa

Precolonial Africa

As an economic activity, trade in Africa predates the arrival of the first Europeans on the continent. Trade had been part of the evolution of African societies and cultures and was both a cause and outcome of empires, kingdoms, and city-states, beginning with Ancient Egypt. Initially, most trading activities were geographically confined to the local area, but the rise of kingdoms and empires expanded the trade beyond the locality. Some settlements, particularly the capital cities of these empires and kingdoms, became very important market centers. Trade was, however, not confined to established kingdoms and empires alone. Africans living beyond the realms of empires were also traders. For example, in the northern and eastern half of the Sahara and the Sahel regions, nomadic and semi-nomadic groups in the drier south traded with their settled or semi-nomadic counterparts in the north, exchanging products such as hides, skin, and dates for grains, oil, figs, and metal products.

The geographic expansion of trade produced new groups of traders—the itinerant merchants and the caravan traders. The first group traveled from place to place peddling assorted collections of products. In West Africa, these included the Dyula, the Fulbe, and the Hausa. The caravan traders traveled between Western Sudan and the Mediterranean Coast of Africa in the famous Trans-Saharan Trade (see Chapter 2).

In the eastern half of the continent, there was internal trade such as the salt trade of the Ankore district of Uganda and the fish trade further south of the Lakes Tanganyika and Nyasa (Malawi) regions. There was also long-distance trade between Africa and India in which gold from Southern Africa and ivory from the East Africa were exchanged for cotton cloth and beads from India. The coastal city-states from Mogadishu to Sofala were the points of contact between Indian merchants—the Muslim sultanate of Gujarat—and the interior lands of East and Southern Africa. Indeed, when the Portuguese arrived in the area in 1500, they saw Gujarat merchant ships from Cambay, the Gujarat capital city, in Malindi and Mombasa, trading in ivory, gold, cloth, and beads (Alpers, 1976).

The arrival of Europeans in Africa from the 15th century slowly but surely transformed Africa's internal and external trade. For the first 50 years of the 16th century, the Portuguese were the dominant European traders and they were mostly interested in gold. They built several forts along the coast of Africa for their trading activities. However, in 1520, a concession granted to a French merchant in Marseilles for fish trading in Ottoman North Africa made it possible for other interested merchants from Holland, Britain, Sweden, and Spain to eventually get concessions (Ruedy, 2005). From 17th to late 18th century, the Dutch, the British, the French, the Swedes, and the Danes became active traders with the rest of the continent, and many more forts or castles were built for their merchant companies most of them in West Africa.

The organization, composition, and direction of Africa's external trade changed. While keeping their internal trading activities, many African traders also became middlemen between the interior of the continent and the European trading posts on the coast. As Africa became the eastern anchor of the Atlantic Slave Trade (see Chapter 2), the land-based external trade across the Sahara and to Europe was slowly replaced by sea-borne route across the Atlantic.

The abolition of the Atlantic Slave Trade in 1807 and subsequent institution of legitimate trade brought another transformation in the organization, composition, and direction of Africa's trade. The second half of the 19th century was a particularly active period for new European firms' engagement, and West Africa, by virtue of its geographic proximity to Europe, became the hotbed of Africa's external trade (see Pedler, 1974). Composition of trade changed from slaves to palm oil, kola nuts, groundnuts, rubber, and timber from Africa, in exchange for manufactured goods from Europe. The development of the steamship eventually paved the way for Europeans to reach the interior of West Africa through the Senegal, the Gambia, and the Niger-Benue waterways. A number of inland towns such as Kayes and Bamako (Mali), and Lokoja, Onitsha, Bonny, and Burutu (Nigeria) became important commercial river ports and centers for European trading firms. For the first time, the itinerant merchants began to face competition from European traders. However, because most of the European trading firms at this period were only confined to the navigable rivers, African middlemen were still needed between the river ports and the rest of the interior. At the same time, competitive rivalries among the many European trading firms both strengthened and weakened the position of African traders. On the Niger River, for example, many African groups were caught up in armed conflicts sometimes due to their opposition and sometime due to treaty agreements they had reached with rival European trading firms (Pedler, 1974).

In Central Africa, Africans had battered with Portuguese traders on the coast as early as the 16th century. During the 19th century, as European missionaries, explorers, and hunters began to penetrate into the interior from South Africa, the direction of this trade shifted southward (Wild, 1992). A booming trade in ivory for guns ensued and by the 1880s, the elephant population had been decimated.

While chiefs and kings in West, Central, and Southern Africa were signing trade agreements and treaties with European firms, in Egypt, Mohammed Ali, the viceroy turned Pasha (see Chapter 2), saw an opportunity to generate revenue from trade for his economic development program in Egypt. His effort to restrict both imports and exports brought conflict between him and the Ottoman Sultan, which was exploited by Britain to secure the Anglo-Turkish Commercial Convention in 1838, which banned all monopolies (Issawi, 1982).

In the eastern and southeastern coast of the continent, the African trade was dominated during this time by Arabs and the Sultanate of Zanzibar, with an exception of a few towns in Mozambique (Ward and White, 1971). Trade routes from the coast reached the interior of the Great Lakes region and to independent kingdoms such as the Karagwe, Buganda, and Bunyoro. Along the trade routes emerged centers such as Mpwapwa, Tabora, and Ujiji in modern Tanzania. By the time of the Berlin Conference in 1884, concessions, treaties, and forced agreements between European trading firms and African chiefs and kings had already resulted in scattered European colonial enclaves that would form the basis of the partition of the continent.

Colonial Africa

The transformation of Africa's trade continued during the colonial period. First, the need to formalize exchange by way of a common currency on regional basis led to the introduction of European currencies. Second, improvements in transportation and communication by way of railroads and roads (see Chapter 10) opened up the interior of Africa to more commerce particularly in the areas that did not have navigable rivers (Laan, 1981). Third, the large European trading houses that were operating on the continent became more dominant actors after improvements in transportation and communication. Among these were the United African Company (UAC), John Holt Paterson Zochonis, for British West Africa, and *Societe Commerciale de l'Ouest Africain* (SCOA) and the *Compagnie Franciaise de l'Afrique Occidentale* (CFAO) in French West Africa, and GB Ollivant (Crowder, 1969), and the Susman Brothers and the Wulfsohn Group in Southern Africa (Miller et al., 2008).

Initially colonial governments had a laissez faire policy toward European traders. The British followed a free trade policy in their colonies, while the French adopted a mixed policy—protectionism in Senegal and Guinea, and free trade in other colonies (Crowder, 1969). In Senegal, the large French firms colluded against the Senegalese traders by supplying the Senegalese traders goods at the same price as the goods they sold from all their depots irrespective of geographic location. By 1925, many Senegalese traders had lost their ability to trade and had become employees of the French companies (Amin, 1981).

However, it was the small-scale Asian and European traders who became the most formidable competitors of African traders. Among these were the Lebanese and Syrian (Levantine) in West Africa, Indians in East and Southern Africa, and Greeks and Jews in North Africa. The only exceptions in West Africa were in the Gold Coast (Ghana) and western Nigeria, where the African traders held their own (Crowder, 1969).

Colonial racist practices also made the situation worse for African traders. In Central Africa, for example, laws were passed to confine African traders to African townships only (Chileshe, 1981). In East Africa, the British regarded Asians as more preferable business partners than native Africans thus making it more difficult for Africans to become active and equal competitors in local trade (Wild, 1992).

The establishment of the railroad in the early 20th century diverted much of the trade from the river ports to new railroad nodes and terminals (see Chapter 10). In Northern Nigeria, for example, the railroad precipitated the great "groundnut rush" of 1912–1913 that began the modern development of Kano, an old trading metropolis (Pedler, 1974). From the 1920s, some of the large European companies began establishing modern department stores in a number of African cities. Among these were UAC's Kingsway in Nigeria and Ghana; the Edgars Consolidated Limited (Edcon) store in Johannesburg in 1929, and the Woolworth Company in Cape Town in 1931. However, the advent of road transportation stopped the advance of the large trading firms in West Africa because Europeans did not want to drive on the mostly bad roads, and also road transportation did not come with revolutionary communication technology, and it was difficult for companies to establish buying stations and relay messages to them. All these gave the opportunity to the small intermediaries firms to operate more profitably. By the 1950s, many intermediary firms composed of Lebanese and African middlemen were able to acquire trucks that could go to more places than the railroads and water transportation would go (Van Der Laan, 1981). In spite of this, by the eve of the independence movement, trading and other business practices under colonialism had produced three classes of business people in most colonies. At the top were the Europeans and Americans who controlled the large trading houses. In the middle were Lebanese and other Asians who were in charge of the middle-level retail businesses. At the bottom were the Africans, who were still farming and engaged in market trading and rudimentary services. The only few exceptions were once again in Ghana and Nigeria, where Africans were more significant in the middle-level retail businesses (Adedeji, 1981).

Apart from the European trading firms in Africa, colonial governments did not put in place formal structures for international trade until during the late colonial period. One such formal structure was the establishment of produce marketing boards in some countries for products such as cocoa, palm oil, cotton, and groundnuts (peanuts). In addition, colonial Africa became part of bilateral and multilateral trade agreements signed among the colonial powers in Africa and elsewhere including the General Agreements on Tariff and Trade (GATT) Treaty of 1948. GATT's specific mission was to establish an International Trade Organization (ITO), with the ultimate goal of removing trade barriers through a series of multilateral trade negotiations that were referred to as Rounds. The only independent country in Africa that was an original signatory of GATT was South Africa, but by default, the rights and obligations of GATT were extended by the colonial powers to all the African colonies with an exception of Morocco, which France did not sponsor to be part of GATT (Mshomba, 2009). The ITO was never established, but GATT's ultimate goal to liberalize trade through removal of trade barriers in the form of tariffs was pursued. The first four rounds occurred when most African countries were still colonies. The formation of the European Economic Community (EEC) by six European nations including France, Belgium, and Italy in 1957 granted the respective African colonies of these countries associated states (AS) status of the EEC. The intent of this was to remove tariffs on commodities traded within the EEC and AS over a period of 12–15 years (Sissoko et al., 1998).

Postcolonial Africa

The postcolonial period has been characterized by the growth of internal and intracontinental trade, and the search for a better deal in international trade.

Growth of domestic trade Domestic trade has grown rapidly during the postcolonial period as a result of a number of factors. First, the discriminatory practices of colonialism that had relegated Africans to the bottom of the social ladder in their own homeland produced a backlash. African countries pursued two main policies—nationalization and indigenization. **Nationalization** involved the take-over of expatriate businesses for the most part through negotiation or in a few cases by forcible acquisition and compensation of previous owners by the new African governments. In contrast, **indigenization** involved barring expatriates from certain sectors of the economy to provide opportunities for indigenes to own and operate that sector. The extent to which these policies were adopted varied. Resource-rich countries such as Nigeria and DRC were very aggressive. The countries that pursued socialist ideologies such as Egypt, Algeria, Zambia, Tanzania, Ethiopia, Somalia, Guinea, and Benin nationalized foreign businesses, while countries such as Burundi, Cameroon, Chad, Gabon, Cote d'Ivoire, Liberia, Cameroon, Chad, and Niger did very little or nothing to interfere with foreign business (Uche, 2012). In Egypt, for example, all commercial agencies were given five years from 1956 to convert themselves into domestically owned join-stock companies (Hanafi, 1981). In July 1961, sectors of the Egyptian economy including banking, insurance, and cotton trade and foreign trading firms were nationalized. In Sierra Leone, the government passed laws to restrict foreigners from retailing a select list of products including cigarettes, sugar, canned tomato puree, salt, canned milk, matches, kerosene, and tobacco (Jalloh, 1999). In Ghana, the government passed an alien compliance order in 1969 to force all undocumented foreigners, mostly Nigerians, to leave the country (Owusu-Ansah, 1981). In Nigeria, the Indigenization Decree of 1972 barred foreigners from owning or being part owners of four commercial activities—department stores, and supermarkets; distribution of machines and technical equipment, distribution and servicing of motor vehicles, tractors, and spare parts, and wholesale distribution. Exemptions were granted to firms that made available up to 40% of their total equity shares to Nigerians (Ogbuagu, 1983). Zaire (DRC) nationalized land and mineral rights and banned all foreigners from petty trading in 1973. This affected small-scale Portuguese, Pakistani, and Greek retailers who were operating in the rural areas of the country (Segatti, ND). Tanzania also nationalized foreign businesses and real estate and established government-run cooperatives in the rural areas that eventually forced the Asian traders from the rural areas to the cities.

This led to the emigration of more than 40,000 Asian business groups in Tanzania (Aminzade, 2013). In Uganda, Idi Amin's government expelled about 25,000 Asians. As part of the nationalization and indigenization projects, the state became more involved in the distribution sector in many countries, establishing state-owned retail chains such as the Ghana National Trading Corporation (GNTC), the Kenya National Trading Corporation (KNTC), and Tanzania's State Trading Corporation. All these policies opened up the domestic trade sector to more native traders.

Second, population growth and improved economic conditions associated with more employment opportunities, income growth, and rapid infrastructure development, especially in improved transportation and communication, provided large domestic markets to be exploited. The fact that initial capital outlay for small-scale retail trade was not substantial made it possible for millions of Africans to become traders.

Third, the worsening economic conditions of the 1970s and 1980s that eventually led to trade liberalization and SAPs made retail trade the most logical employment avenue for the millions of people who were laid off from government establishments.

Growth of intracontinental trade Intra-African retail trade also expanded on the continent especially in the 1990s due to four main reasons. The first was the SAPs that liberalized trade policies in African countries. The second is the end of the apartheid regime in South Africa that opened Africa's strongest economy for cooperation and integration into the continental economy. The third is the establishment of new regional economic integrations, namely, UMA in 1989, SADC in 1992, and COMESA in 1994 (UNCTAD, 2009). The fourth is the expansion strategies of large retail firms on the continent, especially those based in South Africa. For example, as early as 1966–1969, Edgars of South Africa (Edcon) expanded into Swaziland, Lesotho, and Botswana. From the late 1990s and early 2000s, the firm expanded rapidly by diversifying into general merchandising and books and newsstand products moving into Zambia in 2011. Elsewhere on the continent, supermarkets and shopping malls grew rapidly from the 1990s. Beginning from South Africa and Egypt, supermarkets and shopping malls began to spread across the continent. In the sub-Saharan Africa, these were led mostly by South African companies such as McCormick Property Development and retailers such as Shoprite, Maasmart, Woolworth, and Pick'n Save. By 2012, most African cities had shopping malls with the largest cities such as Johannesburg, Cairo, and Lagos boasting of multiple malls, although some of the early malls in Cairo, for example, began to fail as a result of the expensive prices of their merchandise as well as bad store design (Abaza, 2006).

In search for a better intercontinental trade deal With respect to trade outside the continent, however, African countries realized that international trade rules and regulations were not favorable to them so they spent a better part of the postcolonial period searching for a better international trade deal. They did this either in collaboration with other developing countries or on their own.

GATT and the Yaoundé Convention The first step the majority of African countries took in their search for a better international trade deal was to join GATT. The first GATT negotiation that occurred in postcolonial Africa (i.e., during when the majority of African countries had returned to independence) was the Kennedy Round (1964–1967), which was also GATT's sixth round of negotiations. However, it was the next round, the Tokyo Round (1973–1979) that was more significant to African countries. In particular, special focus was given to agricultural and tropical products and the tariff and nontariff preferences that could be given to such goods.

For the African colonies that had been granted AS status of EEC, their new independent sovereign countries meant that a new form of agreement was needed. Thus, in July 1963, the EEC and former French colonies signed the **Yaoundé Convention** (Yaoundé I) in Yaoundé, Cameroon. The agreement eliminated custom duties on tropical products not covered by EEC common agricultural policy and tariffs on EEC exports by the African countries, except for those that generated revenues for development (Sissoko et al., 1998). Yaoundé I expired in May 1969 and was extended by Yaoundé II from January 1970 to January 1975.

In the meantime, African countries grew concerned about their **terms of trade**. Terms of trade is the rate at which a country's imports exchange for its exports. Most primary products are valued less than most manufactured products and because African countries were primary producers, the terms of trade were naturally against them. At the same time, foreign aid, which had been purported to be the fix for the problems, was not working, as it should. As a result, developing countries including African countries pushed for a forum for discussing trade and development issues.

Non-aligned movement and the United Nations Conference on Trade and Development In 1961, African countries joined a group of developing countries that claimed to be non-aligned to either the West or the East to form the **Non-Aligned Movement (NAM)**. In July 1962, the group issued the Cairo Declaration that (1) developing countries should focus on processing of raw materials and labor-intensive manufacturing; (2) developed countries focus on higher capital goods production that did not require resources from developing countries; (3) there was no need to form another economic bloc; (4) commodity price stabilization should be fixed; and (5) there was the need to convene an international conference on trade and development (Nesadurai, 2008).

The first **United Nations Conference on Trade and Development** (UNCTAD) convened in March 1964 in Geneva, Switzerland, but that conference as well as subsequent ones was wrecked by differences between developed and developing countries. At the end of the 1960s, there was a great deal of disappointment among developing countries in general, and African countries in particular. Yaoundé I and II agreements and efforts at securing individual commodity agreements had failed except for the International Coffee Agreement of 1962. In 1971, UNCTAD developed a list of least developed countries including 16 African countries to receive special treatment from developed countries. GATT adopted this system as the **Generalized System of Preferences** (GSP) in 1971, which consisted of preferential treatments that each developed country chose to give a particular developing country on a limited number of commodities. There was no general list, and the preferences were limited because none of the commodities involved was duty-free (Minta, 1984). Apart from this, reciprocity was often enforced in multilateral trade negotiations.

The New International Economic Order (NIEO) African countries next joined other developing regions in calling for a **New International Economic Order (NEIO)**. The Declaration on the Establishment of a New International Economic Order (NIEO) and a Program of Action for the Establishment of a New International Economic Order was adopted by the UN General Assembly on May 1, 1974 (Corea, 1977; Gwin, 1977; Sauvant, 1977; Streetem, 1982). The program contained seven proposals for change: (1) More stable prices for agricultural commodities and raw materials through the establishment of a Common Fund that would be used to stabilize prices similar to the buffer stock mechanism. (2) Transfer of resources from rich countries to poor countries through such mechanisms as generalized debt relief and increased aid that was less dependent on developed countries' politics and government. (3) Access to technology that would enable developing countries to industrialize and contribute about 25% of global manufacturing by 2000. (4) Stricter control of the activities of multinational corporations in developing countries so that the corporations would not only concern themselves with their bottom line but also take into consideration the well-being and development of their host countries. (5) More access to the market of developed countries by developing country manufactures through lowering of tariff and nontariff barriers. (6) Reform of the international monetary system. In particular, developing countries complained about the conditionality attached to loans received from the International Monetary Fund (IMF), as well as the dominance of the IMF by developed countries. (7) Developed countries should give more voice to the developing countries in international trade and investment matters (Sauvant, 1977; Gwin, 1977; Streeten, 1982).

Developed countries initially opposed the NIEO, especially the idea of a Common Fund, which was to serve as a buffer stock for commodities. However, by the next UN meeting in 1975, the positions of both developing countries and the United States, in particular, changed from confrontation to cooperation because of mutual interests. Some sort of compromise between the general position of developing countries and the US position was attempted at the meeting, but overall the meeting was a disappointment for developing countries. Subsequent conferences continued to discuss some elements of the NIEO, but by the 1980s, the NIEO idea was dead.

The Lomé Conventions In the meantime, African countries had entered into other trade deals on their own, while the NIEO dragged on. One of these trade deals was the International Cocoa Agreement of 1972 and the more comprehensive **Lomé Convention**. The convention was signed for the first time in 1975 between the European Economic Community (EEC) and African (excluding North African), Caribbean, and Pacific (ACP) states. It was negotiated after Britain was admitted into the EEC to allow its former colonies to have a relationship with the EEC. Essentially, the agreement gave preferential treatment to ACP countries to trade with the EEC. In particular, sugar, beef, banana, and rum received special treatment. Commodities that fell under the Common Agricultural Policy (CAP) of the EEC, however, did not get free access due to quality and health restrictions imposed by the EEC. An important piece of the Lomé agreement was the establishment of **Export Earning Stabilization System** (STABEX). This system provided funds from the EEC to ACP countries that fell short in export revenues (at least 7.5%) due to natural disasters. Initially, STABEX covered 34 commodities. The Lomé Convention was extended several times by Lomé II (1981–1985), Lomé III (1986–1990), and Lomé IV (1990–2000). Under Lomé II, STABEX was extended to cover 44 commodities, including mining, and the shortfall in export revenue that would make a country eligible for STABEX funds was reduced to 6.5% (Sissoko et al., 1998). Lomé III emphasized self-sufficiency in food production, while Lomé IV had a political dimension.

Analyzing the impact of these trade agreements on African countries, Sissoko et al. (1998) noted that the results were generally insignificant. Indeed, EEC imports from Associated States declined under both Yaoundé I and II, while exports from Associated States to others increased. Under Lomé I and II, however, African countries did better. Their exports to the EEC grew to 62.1% even though African countries in the British Commonwealth did better than their counterparts in Yaoundé I and II. Much of the growth was, however, limited to a few commodities and countries. For example, since oil and coffee accounted for 33.7% and 4.6% of imports, respectively, the countries that benefited the most were Nigeria, Angola, Gabon, and Cote d'Ivoire. Imports by the EEC grew more slowly in sub-Saharan African countries compared to North African countries (Sissoko et al., 1998). With respect to STABEX, Sissoko et al. (1998) reported that the impact was positive for West and East Africa, especially as it pertained to cotton production but was negative for Central and North African countries, especially Sudan because of political and social crises. Finally, effort to use GATT's GSP by the EEC within the framework of the Lomé Conventions was not successful because of too many restrictions. In the end, the Lomé Conventions failed to diversify exports of African countries.

Trade liberalization policies As mentioned in several of the preceding chapters, following the economic crises of the 1970s, African countries were from 1980 through late 1990s subjected to **trade liberalization policies** as part of the World Bank and the International Monetary Fund's **structural adjustment programs** (SAPs). These policies involved reduction of tariffs, conversion of nontariff barriers to tariffs, and devaluation of national currencies (UNCTAD, 2008). The argument was that such policies would encourage export trade through efficiency and production of tradable goods. The UNCTAD (2008) report revealed that between 1995 and 2006 tariffs in Africa went from 22% to 13%. Most of the nontariff barriers were removed, while national currencies fell from 200% overrated levels in 1981–1985 to 50% in the 1990s. These policies also did away with the agricultural commodity marketing boards in many African countries, except in Ghana, that were using the buffer stock mechanism to support price fluctuations.

World Trade Organization (WTO) and African countries The formation of the World Trade Organization (WTO) in January 1995 with the mandate to implement, administer, and manage all trade agreements reached under GATT impacted African trade in many significant ways. First, the preferential treatment regarding the EU banana trade within the Lomé Convention was challenged by the banana producers of Central and South America backed by the United States. WTO ruled that the EU banana regime, as the agreement was called, was inconsistent with WTO rules. After both an appeal and a revised proposal by the EU had failed, the EU agreed to phase out the ACP agreement by 2006. In its place a new agreement, the **Cotonou Agreement,** was signed for a period of 20 years (2000–2020). The Agreement allowed African countries to export goods to the EU duty-free and retain their tariffs on goods imported from the EU. However, this applied to only the countries that were classified as least developed countries, most of which were in Africa. The countries that were relatively well off had to negotiate their own trade agreements with the EU.

Second, the WTO also has the mandate to administer the agreement on **trade-related aspects of intellectual property rights (TRIPS)**. This agreement gives protection to inventors of new products and processes, especially in the pharmaceutical industry in developed countries for a period of 20 years before the product could be made by others or the process might be available to others. A test of this agreement arose when in 1998 the Pharmaceutical Association of South Africa filed a lawsuit against a South African law that allowed parallel importing and compulsory licensing of HIV/AIDS drugs to make them more accessible to HIV/AIDS patients.

Parallel importing is when a product is resold by a third party without the consent of the patent holder and **compulsory licensing** is where a government allows a third party to produce a product without authorization of the patent holder, a practice permitted under public health emergency (Mshomba, 2009). Although HIV/AIDS infection in South Africa had become a national public health emergency, both the United States and the EU sided with the Pharmaceutical Association. The law suit was however dropped in 2001 due to international public outcry and the intervention of the World Health Organization (WHO).

The third and definitely the area of most concern to African countries is the trade in agricultural products. The agreement that established the WTO had an **Agricultural Trade Agreement**, which called for increased access to market and reduction in domestic support and export subsidies to agricultural products. However, the agreement had no clear commitment so not much happened. The sticking point in the agreement was the farm and export subsidies that the EU, the United States, and China gave to their respective farmers. At its meeting in Doha, Qatar, in November 2001, WTO members agreed to initiate a new round that would focus on development and increase market access in agriculture, manufacturing, and service activities. However, what began with high hopes amidst fanfare has been a major disappointment after more than 15 years of negotiation due to the differences among developed countries on nontariff barriers and differences between developing and developed countries about agricultural subsidies.

In the meantime, the debate over the importance of the Doha Round to African countries seems to have focused more on the implications of the removal of subsidies on African countries. Some experts have argued that the removal of the subsidies would actually hurt African countries (Panagariya, 2005). This is because Africa has many countries, which are net importers of food. Agricultural subsidies in developed countries help lower the price of food on the world market. If those subsidies are removed, prices would go up and that will make it more expensive for the food imports. Others argue that the above view pertains only if one takes a short-term view, because in the long run, the subsidized foods from developed countries take away the incentive for African countries to become self-sufficient in food production and also to diversify their agricultural sector (Draper et al., 2013; Mshomba, 2009).

Fourth, the WTO launched a new initiative, called **Aid for Trade** in 2005, which had implications for African countries. The purpose of the initiative was to (1) develop trade strategies, negotiation, and implementation of outcomes; (2) build trade-supporting infrastructure such as roads, ports, and telecommunication networks; (3) improve productive capacities for export diversification; and (4) deal with the cost of trade due to loss of tariff revenue, preferential treatment, or declining terms of trade. A review of the Aid for Trade program in 2011 by the United Nations Economic Commission for Africa (UNECA) showed that from 2006 to 2009 African countries received more Aid for Trade commitments than years before, from $7.6 billion in 2002–2005 to $16.5 billion in 2006–2009. However, disbursements fell from 75% in 2006 to 62% in 2009 (UNECA, 2011a). Apart from this, a disproportionate share went to a few countries including Egypt, Ethiopia, Ghana, Kenya, Morocco, Mozambique, Tanzania, and Uganda. The largest proportion, more than 50%, of this aid went to economic infrastructure, followed by improvement in productive capacity particularly in agriculture and banking sectors. About 60% of the economic infrastructure projects were in road transportation and storage facilities. The remaining 40% went into the energy sector (30%) and telecommunication (10%). Subsequent biennial reviews of Aid for Trade by the WTO indicate that the program is working. However, the amount of commitment and disbursement to Africa has declined from a peak of $18.5 billion in 2010 to $13.1 billion in 2011, a drop of 29%. Under WTO, African countries have continued to receive preferential treatment but that too has limited their ability to participate fully in the dispute settlement understanding (DSU) process, which in itself is a very complicated and expensive process (Mshomba, 2005).

These developments show that African countries have expended a great deal of energy to get a better international trade deal either through the search for fair prices for their commodities or getting preferential treatment to trade with the rest of the world. Little effort has however been expended by African countries at product diversification and value addition that can make them competitive on the world market. In the absence of this, African countries' trade performance has continued to be relatively negligible at the international level and have therefore continued to be at the mercy of their trading partners.

Types and Organization of Trading Activities

Contemporary trading activities have not deviated much from the past. The two broad types of trade such as internal and external trade are well and alive in all African countries. Internal trade here refers to trade within individual African countries while external trade refers to trade between African countries and trade with the outside world.

Internal or Domestic Trade

Retail trade dominates internal trade of African countries. In large cities, retail is arguably the largest economic activity and seems ubiquitous throughout the entire urban landscape. The geography of these activities conforms to Berry's (1967) categorization of market centers and retail distribution. Thus, there are nucleations, specialized areas, and ribbons.

Nucleated retail centers Nucleated retail centers consist mostly of geographically demarcated market places within cities, towns, and villages across the continent where buyers and sellers meet to do retail business. The number and size of these centers vary by settlement size. In large cities and towns, these market places are numerous and are usually scattered around the city by community and neighborhoods. They therefore vary in sizes and exist in a hierarchy with the largest and the most complex usually in the downtown or city center. In Islamic cities, this may be also in the Medina or the Old City. The large market places have numerous stalls and stores for hundreds and thousands of traders. Such a market is usually segregated by product specialty. Thus, there are separate sections for fresh food vendors, vegetables, dried fish, fresh meat, and clothing and garment. These nucleated retail centers operate daily, however, beyond the large cities and towns some of them operate periodically. In this regard, the market is held on certain days of the week—sometimes, once a week, twice, or thrice a week. On those market days, traders converge from different parts of the region or country to buy and sell goods from fresh farm produce to manufactured goods. These markets also vary in size in their range and trade area. Depending on the size of the country, some have national trade areas, while others may only be regional. Since the 1990s, shopping malls have become part of nucleated retail centers in many African countries. These are similar to any modern mall elsewhere in terms of their layout, vendor organization, and merchandise. While both daily and periodic markets cater to all classes of society—low, middle, and high income—the shopping malls generally cater to the middle- and high-income population since the low-income population is usually priced out of that market.

Specialized retail areas The second geographic concentration of retail trade in Africa occurs in the form of specialized retail areas. These districts specialize in the buying and selling of single products such as building materials, consumer durables, furniture, or particular foodstuffs such as grain, cassava, banana, or cattle. Like nucleated centers, these occur in defined areas of the city and sometimes may be the only place in the whole city that a particular item can be purchased. The traders are usually small-scale enterprises, but they form clusters or agglomerations to draw customers. These often operate as both wholesale and retail traders and may consist of particular ethnic groups depending on the country and city.

Retail ribbons and corridors The third geographic concentration of retail activities in Africa are retail ribbons and corridors. These consist of major streets, central part of the city, and arterial roads that run through suburbs. They usually offer a wide range of goods. Retail trade in most regional and district capitals do conform to this type of concentration. A special type of this concentration is the street vendors that crowd major arterial roads and intersections or checkpoints in many sub-Saharan African cities. These street traders take advantage of the traffic stops at such intercession or checkpoints to sell their items to the drive-by passengers. These are also very common in small cities, towns, and villages.

External or International Trade

Africa's percentage share of world export and import trade has been very small. In the 1960s, it accounted for an estimated 5.6% of world export trade. In 2015, it was only 2.3% (Table 15.1). In comparison to other developing regions, the contribution of South and Central America and the Caribbean to World trade went from 7.5% of the world's export trade in 1960 to 5.5% in 2015, while that of developing countries in Asia went from 11.7% in 1960 to 32.4% in 2015.

Imports have followed a similar trend. Thus, in 1960, Africa's share of world imports was estimated at 6.2%. By 2015, it had dropped to 3.3%. However, unlike export trade, the steady decline in percentage of imports trade became more consistent from the late 1980s. Indeed, the period from mid-1980s through 2006 was the lowest performing years, during which Africa accounted for less than 3% of world import trade (Table 15.2). During the same period, the percentage share of Central and South America and the Caribbean in world import trade went from 7.3% in 1960 to 6.1% in 2015, after declining to 3.5 in 1990, decline, while the share of developing countries in Asia went from 11.7% in 1960 to 32.3% in 2015 (Table 15.2).

Composition of trade The composition of Africa's trade has changed but only slightly. Since the 1960s, the overwhelming majority of Africa's exports have been primary commodities broadly categorized as food and beverage, agricultural raw material, ores and metals, and fuels. In 1960, primary commodities accounted for about 82.8% of total export trade with manufactured goods accounting for only

TABLE 15.1												

Percentage Contribution of Africa and Other Developing Regions to World Export Trade, 1960-2015

Region	1960	1965	1970	1975	1980	1985	1990	1995	2000	2005	2010	2015
Developing Africa	5.6	5.4	5.1	5.1	5.9	4.3	3.0	2.2	2.3	3.0	3.4	2.3
Eastern Africa	1.2	1.1	0.9	0.5	0.3	0.3	0.2	0.2	0.2	0.2	0.2	0.2
Middle Africa	0.6	0.5	0.5	0.4	0.4	0.4	0.3	0.2	0.3	0.5	0.6	0.4
Northern Africa	1.3	1.5	1.6	1.8	2.1	1.7	1.1	0.7	0.9	1.1	1.2	0.6
Southern Africa	1.5	1.4	1.1	1.0	1.4	0.9	0.8	0.6	0.5	0.6	0.7	0.6
Western Africa	1.0	1.0	0.9	1.3	1.6	1.0	0.6	0.4	0.5	0.6	0.8	0.5
Developing America	7.5	6.5	5.4	5.2	5.4	5.6	4.2	4.5	5.7	5.6	5.8	5.6
Caribbean	1.5	1.1	0.9	1.4	1.1	0.7	0.4	0.3	0.3	0.3	0.2	0.2
Central America	0.9	1.0	0.8	0.6	1.1	1.6	1.3	1.7	2.8	2.3	2.2	2.6
South America	5.0	4.3	3.7	3.1	3.2	3.3	2.5	2.5	2.6	3.0	3.4	2.8
Developing Asia	11.2	9.7	8.4	14.0	18.2	15.8	16.9	21.0	23.8	27.6	32.8	36.5
Eastern Asia	2.7	2.3	2.2	2.7	3.8	6.2	8.0	10.9	12.1	14.7	17.8	21.8
Southern Asia	2.4	2.4	1.8	1.7	1.3	1.5	1.3	1.3	1.4	1.8	2.5	2.4
South-Eastern Asia	3.6	2.5	2.0	2.5	3.5	3.7	4.1	6.2	6.7	6.3	6.9	7.0
Western Asia	2.6	2.6	2.3	7.1	9.6	4.4	3.4	2.6	3.7	4.9	5.6	5.2
Developing Oceania	0.1	0.1	0.2	0.1	0.1	0.1	0.1	0.1	0.1	0.1	0.1	0.07

Source: World Trade Organization.

17.2%. In 2015, primary commodities accounted for 76.6% of the total export trade, while manufactured goods constituted the remaining 23.4%. Fuels was by far the largest group of the primary commodities exports, while machinery and transportation equipment were the most important manufactured goods exported. In terms of specific commodities fuels is the leading export of Africa as a whole accounting for 44.2% of the total export trade in 2015, followed by food (13.1%), ores and metals (10.1%), other manufactured goods (9.1%), and machinery and transportation equipment (8.8%) (Figure 15.1).

Imports have followed a similar pattern. Manufactured products have dominated Africa's imports trade since the 1960s. However, from the 1990s through 2015, the percentage of primary commodities of total imports grew slowly to over 30%. In 2015, manufactured products accounted for 67.7% of the total import trade, while primary commodities accounted for 32.3%. The main import commodities in 2015 were machinery and transportation equipment (32.6%), other manufactured goods (23.3%), food (14.5%), fuels (13.2%), chemical products (11.8%), ores and metals (2.4%), and agricultural raw materials (1.4%) (Figure 15.2).

Direction of trade Africa's international trade follows two main directions—one within Africa (intracontinental (African) trade) and the other outside Africa (intercontinental trade).

Intracontinental (African) trade African countries trade less among themselves than they do with countries or groups outside the continent. This in itself is not

TABLE **15.2**

Percentage Contribution of Africa and Other Developing Regions to World Import Trade, 1960–2015

Region	1960	1965	1970	1975	1980	1985	1990	1995	2000	2005	2010	2015
Developing Africa	6.2	5.2	4.4	5.0	4.6	3.7	2.6	2.4	2.0	2.4	3.1	3.3
Eastern Africa	1.2	1.1	0.9	0.6	0.5	0.4	0.4	0.3	0.3	0.3	0.4	0.5
Middle Africa	0.4	0.3	0.3	0.2	0.3	0.3	0.2	0.1	0.1	0.2	0.3	0.3
Northern Africa	2.1	1.4	1.2	2.0	1.5	1.6	1.0	0.9	0.7	0.8	1.2	1.2
Southern Africa	1.2	1.3	1.2	1.0	1.1	0.7	0.6	0.7	0.5	0.7	0.7	0.8
Western Africa	1.2	1.1	0.8	1.1	1.2	0.8	0.4	0.4	0.3	0.4	0.6	0.6
Developing America	7.3	5.9	5.5	6.2	5.9	4.1	3.5	4.7	5.8	5.0	5.8	6.1
Caribbean	1.7	1.4	1.3	1.5	1.3	0.9	0.5	0.4	0.5	0.4	0.3	0.3
Central America	1.3	1.3	1.2	1.2	1.4	1.3	1.4	1.7	3.1	2.5	2.4	2.9
South America	4.4	3.2	3.0	3.5	3.2	1.9	1.6	2.6	2.3	2.0	3.0	2.8
Developing Asia	11.7	9.8	8.4	11.0	13.3	15.4	15.9	21.5	20.9	24.3	30.0	32.3
Eastern Asia	3.1	2.4	2.7	3.1	4.2	6.3	7.4	10.9	11.2	13.1	16.4	17.6
Southern Asia	3.4	2.9	1.8	2.4	1.8	2.0	1.6	1.4	1.4	2.2	3.3	3.3
South-Eastern Asia	3.4	2.7	2.5	2.8	3.1	3.3	4.5	6.8	5.7	5.6	6.2	6.6
Western Asia	1.9	1.8	1.5	2.8	4.2	3.8	2.4	2.4	2.6	3.4	4.2	4.8
Developing Oceania	0.2	0.2	0.3	0.2	0.2	0.2	0.1	0.1	0.1	0.1	0.1	0.07

Source: World Trade Organization.

uncommon since Europe is the only continent with a higher percentage of its international trade within its borders. What is remarkable with Africa is that it has the lowest percentage of intracontinental trade in the world. Thus, from 1960 to 1962, only 5.6% of total export trade was intracontinental, compared to Latin America's 16%, Asia's 21.1%, North America's 26.6%, and Europe's 61.3% (UNCTAD, 2009). Recent data show that Africa's intracontinental export trade has increased a bit, but it is still low compared to other regions of the world. For example, in 2015, intracontinental trade was only $66.6 billion or 18.8% of Africa's export trade and 13.7% of import trade. In comparison, intracontinental trade accounted for 56.1% of America's exports and 42.3% of its imports. For Asia, it was 56% of exports and 63% of imports, while for Europe it was 67.2% of exports and 70.5% of imports (Table 15.3).

The low percentage of Africa's intracontinental trade may, however, be due in part to lack of data on the large informal sector. In spite of the low percentage of intracontinental trade, there were a number of countries that had considerable amount of trade within Africa. Indeed, data from the International Trade Center (ITC) Trade Map indicate that in 2001, 17 African countries conducted at least 20% of their export with other African countries. In 2015, the number was 24 (Table 15.4). Only nine countries registered a decline in the percentage of export trade with other African countries (Table 15.4). With respect to imports, 18 countries had at least 20% of their import trade with other African countries in 2001. In 2015, the number was 19. Only 17 countries registered a decline in the percentage of imports from other African countries in 2015 compared to

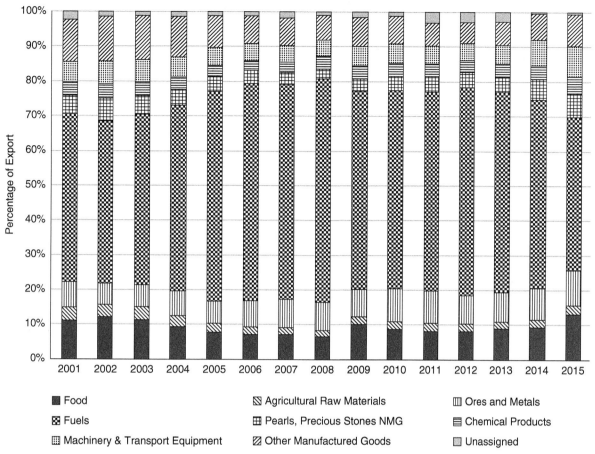

FIGURE 15.1 Composition of Africa's Export Trade, 2001–2015.
Source: Data from UNCTAD and International Trade Center Trade Map.

2001. Countries conducting more than 50% of their export trade within Africa in 2015 included Gambia, Namibia, Rwanda, Swaziland, Togo, and Zimbabwe. On the imports side they included Botswana, Lesotho, Namibia, Swaziland, Zambia, and Zimbabwe (Table 15.4).

As was discussed in Chapter 3, Africa has a large number of regional economic integrations that were established with trade promotion as one of their main goals. By volume of trade, the most export trade in 2015 occurred in the SADC (24.4%), followed by SACU (18.1%), CEN-SAD (17%), ECOWAS (10.3%), and COMESA (10%). Import trade followed a similar pattern with about 26% generating from SADC, followed by SACU (15.5%), COMESA (13.6%), CEN-SAD (15.7%), and ECOWAS (7.7%). Yet, these trading blocs conduct most of their export and import trade with countries outside their blocs than inside their blocs (Tables 15.5 and 15.6). There are several reasons why regional economic integration have not been very effective in Africa, but one that appears to be most pertinent regarding intraregional trade is the product mix of African countries. African countries are mostly primary producers and this limits the scope of trade among them. At the country level, the top exporter countries of Africa's intracontinental trade in recent years—from 2010 to 2015 include South Africa, Nigeria, Cote d'Ivoire, and Egypt, while the top importers include South Africa, Botswana, Namibia, and Zambia (Table 15.7).

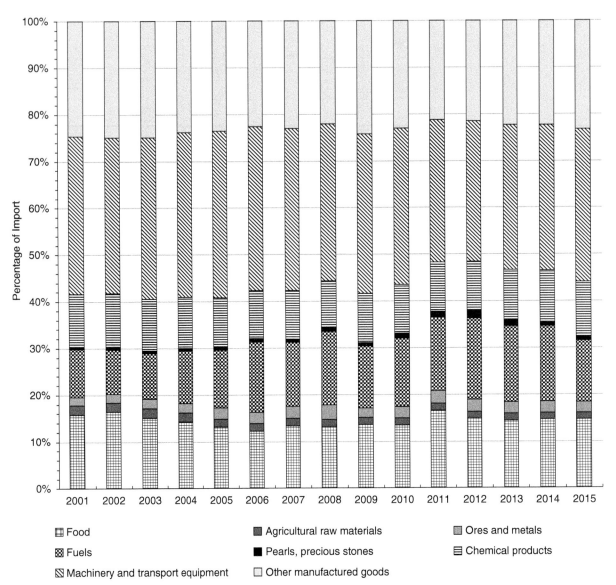

FIGURE 15.2 Composition of Africa's Import Trade, 2001–2015.
Source: Data from International Trade Center Trade Map.

Intercontinental trade According to 2015 data, intercontinental trade accounts for 82.4% of Africa's export trade and 86.3% of its imports trade. Africa's colonial roots committed much of its intercontinental trade to Europe, a commitment that has been maintained by such agreements as the Yaoundé Agreements and the Lomé Conventions. It is only in recent years about 2010 that the Europe's role in Africa's trade has been declining.

Figure 15.3 shows at least two main changes since 2001. The first is the gradual decline of the European share of Africa's intercontinental export trade from more than 56% before 2003 to 44% in 2015. The second change is the increasing importance of Asia as a trading partner of African countries. This is largely due to the rise of China as Africa's trading partner. From about only 18.1% of Africa's intercontinental export in 2001, Asia's importance as Africa's trade partner grew slowly and steadily until 2009 when it replaced North America (the United States and Canada)

TABLE **15.3**

Percent Share of Intraregional Trade to Total Trade of Selected Regions

Region	Export			Import		
	2001	2008	2015	2001	2008	2015
Africa	11.9	12.8	18.8	14.4	13.7	13.7
Americas	61.1	42.4	56.1	47.1	42.3	42.3
Asia	50.2	51.2	56.0	60.1	63.0	63.0
Europe	73.1	74.6	67.2	69.4	70.5	70.5
Oceania	10.5	8.0	8.0	10.4	9.6	7.5

Source: Author's calculation based on data from International Trade Center's Trade Map.

TABLE **15.4**

African Countries Shares of Intra-African Trade, 2001 and 2015

Country	Percentage of exports		Percentage of imports	
	2001	2015	2001	2015
Algeria	2.1	6.1	1.8	3.0
Angola		2.6		7.6
Benin	19.0	28.5	26.6	20.0
Botswana	1.0	29.2	81.4	74.9
Burkina Faso	24.6	17.2	28.2	24.7
Burundi	26.1	46.4	24.4	28.3
Cameroon	1.7	12.2	23.9	25.5
Cape Verde	14.3	5.5	2.2	2.2
Cent. African Rep.	5.0	21.4	19.2	29.0
Chad		0.1	0	20.8
Comoros	0.8		18.8	
Congo				
Cote d'Ivoire	30.8	27.9	25.2	23.5
DRC		19.3		41.1
Djibouti				
Egypt	5.2	12.7	2.7	2.4
Equatorial Guinea		3.9		7.8
Eritrea				
Ethiopia	23.2	18.2	6.2	3.7
Gabon	5.1		8.0	
Gambia	10.4	79.3	11.4	35.1
Ghana	11.6		23.2	
Guinea	6.6	26.7	18.4	

(*Continued*)

TABLE **15.4**

African Countries Shares of Intra-African Trade, 2001 and 2015 (Continued)

Country	Percentage of exports		Percentage of imports	
	2001	2015	2001	2015
Guinea-Bissau				
Kenya	35.9	37.7	10.2	9.4
Lesotho	53.5	29.1	97.0	76.8
Liberia				
Libya				
Madagascar	6.1	7.8	12.6	11.0
Malawi	35.9	39.0	58.4	33.6
Mali	44.4		40.1	
Mauritania	8.0	9.4	8.2	15.9
Mauritius	11.1	18.6	18.2	11.8
Morocco	4.2	9.8	5.5	5.0
Mozambique	22.8	24.8	38.2	33.6
Namibia	38.9	54.9	86.4	71.8
Niger	40.0	23.4	33.7	15.8
Nigeria	6.4	14.5	9.1	6.2
Rwanda	23.1	56.2	20.6	31.4
S. Tome & Principe	2.6	38.0	19.6	23.7
Senegal	30.0	46.5	17.8	15.8
Seychelles	2.8	1.1	8.5	16.6
Sierra Leone		16.4		29.9
Somalia				
South Africa	15.5	29.4	2.7	12.3
South Sudan				
Sudan	2.8	3.6	6.8	9.4
Swaziland	85.5	91.2	80.2	82.6
Tanzania	11.0	41.0	20.3	6.8
Togo	63.9	62.3	17.9	7.5
Tunisia	7.0	12.1	6.2	5.9
Uganda	34.5	42.5	37.5	18.3
Zambia	31.3	24.1	68.3	57.7
Zimbabwe	16.8	91.7	62.5	50.0

Source: Data from UNCTAD

as the second destination for Africa's exports after Europe and has since increased its share to about 40%. Africa's import trade has mirrored the export trade trends with only slight variations. Up to 2003, European share of Africa's imports averaged about 45%. Since then it has declined steadily below 40% to about 35% in 2015 (Figure 15.4). Indeed, in 2012, Asia overtook Europe as Africa's leading trading

TABLE **15.5**

Percentage Shares of Intra-African Export Trade by Regional Economic Integration (REI), 2001-2015

REI	Percentage of REI export trade in Bloc			Percentage of REI export trade with the rest of Africa			Percentage of REI export trade with rest of world		
	2001	2008	2015	2001	2008	2015	2001	2008	2015
AMU	2.4	2.7	4.1	3.6	4.2	7.5	94.1	93.1	92.5
CEN-SAD	8.1	6.9	9.3	10.6	11.3	14.1	81.3	81.9	85.9
CEPGL	0.4	2.0	3.5	10.8	20.0	22.7	88.7	78.0	77.3
COMESA	8.4	6.5	10.0	20.7	11.7	21.6	70.9	81.8	78.4
EAC	16.1	20.3	21.2	28.4	42.8	39.8	55.6	36.8	60.2
ECCAS	2.5	1.1	3.1	8.6	6.8	12.1	88.9	92.1	87.9
ECOWAS	9.2	10.4	11.7	12.8	17.6	19.1	78.0	72.0	80.9
IGAD	10.9	9.8	12.4	21.4	20.1	19.5	67.7	70.0	80.5
MRU	2.7	1.8	0.9	27.5	28.3	27.7	69.9	69.9	72.3
SACU	3.9	3.2	16.8	18.9	19.2	31.8	77.2	77.6	68.2
SADC	14.1	18.4	22.6	17.7	23.3	25.8	68.3	58.3	74.2
WAEMU	14.8	15.4	16.0	33.2	41.5	30.3	51.9	43.1	69.7

Source: Author's calculation based on data from International Trade Center Trade Map.
Notes: CEPGL=Economic Community of the Great Lakes Countries (in French). It includes Burundi, DRC, and Rwanda

TABLE **15.6**

Percentage Shares of Intra-African Import Trade by Regional Economic Integration (REI), 2001-2015

REI	Percentage of REI import trade in Bloc			Percentage of REI import trade with the rest of Africa			Percentage of REI import trade with rest of world		
	2001	2008	2015	2001	2008	2015	2001	2008	2015
AMU	2.8	3.3	3.0	4.5	5.1	3.4	92.7	91,6	91.6
CEN-SAD	7.5	6.0	6.1	10.5	9.3	8.8	82.0	84.6	85.2
CEPGL	0.4	1.6	2.8	31.2	51.2	38.2	68.4	47.2	59.0
COMESA	5.3	4.8	4.6	18.5	13.0	12.5	76.3	82.2	82.8
EAC	6.5	6.6	4.9	17.1	17.2	11.0	76.4	76.2	84.0
ECCAS	3.6	3.4	3.4	32.3	24.4	21.0	64.1	72.3	75.6
ECOWAS	13.6	12.5	8.8	18.0	17.3	12.7	68.4	70.2	78.5
IGAD	6.0	3.6	3.8	13.1	9.7	9.5	80.9	86.7	86.7
MRU	2.8	0.9	0.5	23.9	31.4	22.2	73.2	67.7	77.3
SACU	13.2	9.1	14.9	15.8	16.2	21.9	71.0	74.7	63.2
SADC	20.2	19.5	19.7	22.0	22.5	22.9	57.8	58.0	57.4
WAEMU	10.7	9.4	5.2	26.1	29.7	20.4	63.2	60.9	74.4

Source: Author's calculations based on data from International Trade Center Trade Map.

TABLE 15.7

Leading Exporting and Importing Countries in Intra-Africa, 2010–2015

Exporters				Importers			
2010		2015		2010		2015	
Country	Share (%)	Country	Share (%)	Country	Share (%)	Country	Share (%)
South Africa	30.7	South Africa	34.4	South Africa	12.4	South Africa	13.6
Nigeria	13.8	Nigeria	10.2	Namibia	6.7	Botswana	8.4
Egypt	5.4	Côte d'Ivoire	4.8	Botswana	6.3	Namibia	8.2
Ghana	4.3	Egypt	4.0	Zimbabwe	5.2	Zambia	7.2
Cote d'Ivoire	4.3	Namibia	3.7	Zambia	5.0	Zimbabwe	4.4
Namibia	3.3	Zimbabwe	3.6	Equat. Guinea	4.6	Mozambique	3.9
Kenya	3.1	Tanzania	3.3	Nigeria	4.3	DRC	3.8
Zimbabwe	2.7	Kenya	3.2	Cote d'Ivoire	3.9	Côte d'Ivoire	3.3
Tunisia	2.5	Morocco	3.2	DRC	3.5	Nigeria	3.1
Algeria	2.3	Algeria	3.1	Morocco	3.1	Ghana	2.9
Total	75.0	Total	73.6	Total	55.2	Total	58.7

Source: Author's calculation from Data from International Trade Center's Trade Map.

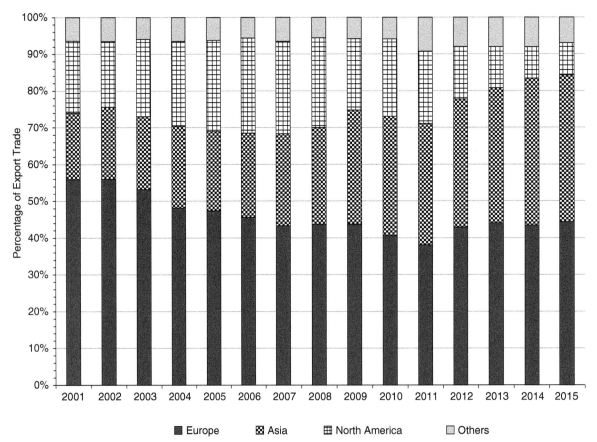

FIGURE 15.3 Direction of Africa's Export Trade, 2001–2015.
Source: Data from International Trade Center Trade Map.

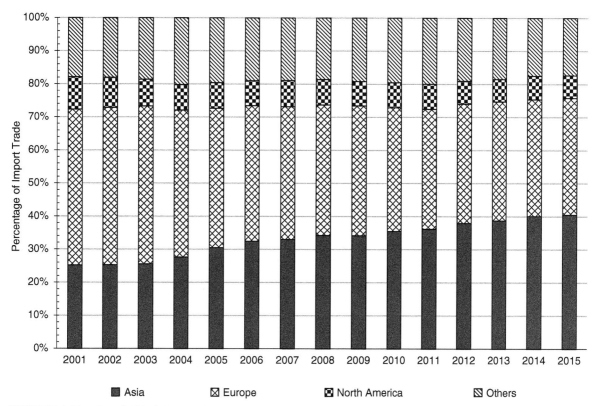

FIGURE 15.4 Direction of Africa's Import Trade, 2001–2015.
Source: Data from International Trade Center Trade Map.

partner in terms of imports. In contrast, the share of the United States has remained the same—about 10%.

Figures 15.5–15.7 also provide origins and destinations of Africa–Europe trade, Africa–Asia trade, and Africa–North America trade in 2015. With respect to Africa–Europe trade, the top European destinations for Africa's exports were Spain, Italy, France, Germany, the United Kingdom, and the Netherlands, while the top African importers of European goods were Algeria, South Africa, Egypt, Morocco, Nigeria, and Tunisia (Figure 15.5). The top Asian destinations for African exports in 2015 were China, India, United Arab Emirates, Japan, and South Korea, while the top African importers of Asian goods were South Africa, Egypt, Algeria, Nigeria, and Kenya (Figure 15.6). The United States dominate the Africa–North American trade. In 2015, it accounted for 81.5% of Africa's exports to North America and 89% of its imports. Major African exporters to the United States in 2015 were South Africa, Algeria, Angola, and Nigeria, while the importers included South Africa, Egypt, Nigeria, and Algeria (Figure 15.7).

Tables 15.8 shows the top exporting and importing countries in Africa's intercontinental trade in recent years, from 2010 to 2015. Africa's top exporting countries are Nigeria, South Africa, Algeria, Angola, Libya, and Egypt, while the top importers include South Africa, Egypt, Nigeria, Algeria, Morocco, and Tunisia. China is the largest trading partner of Africa. In 2015, it accounted for 16.5% of Africa's total export trade, a little more than France, Germany, and the United States, the next three trading partners combined. China was also the largest importer of African products, but it accounted for only 9.6% of the total imports, followed by India (6.9%), Spain (6.3%), France (6.2%), Italy (5.7%), and the United States (5%).

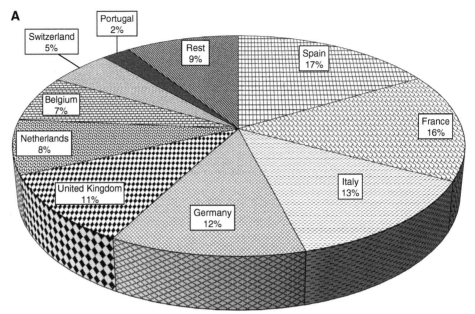

Destination of African Exports to Europe

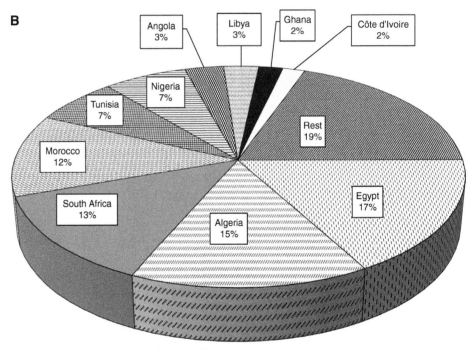

Destination of Europe's Exports to Africa, 2015

FIGURE 15.5 Africa's Trade with Europe, 2015. *Source:* Data from UNCTAD and International Trade Center Trade Map

Africa's Trade Issues

The UNCTAD (2013) report on intra-African trade discusses a number of challenges facing African countries in intracontinental trade and recommendations. Although these focus specifically on intracontinental trade, they seem relevant to trade in general, so this section draws on the report.

A

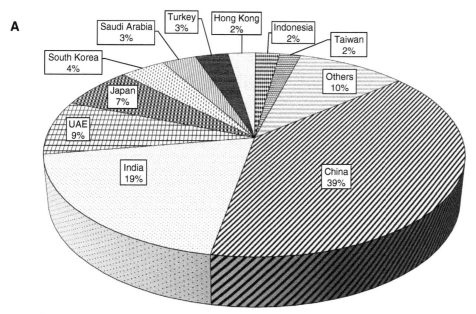

Destination for Africa's Export to Asia

B

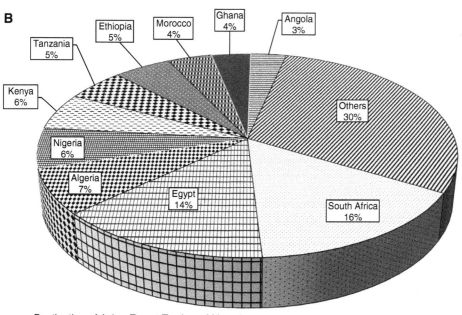

Destination of Asian Export Trade to Africa

FIGURE 15.6 Africa's Trade with Asia, 2015.
Source: Data from UNCTAD and International Trade Center Trade Map

Challenges

Lack of export and productive competitiveness First, the report observes that there is lack of export competiveness because of high production costs and high tariff and nontariff barriers. The high production costs arise from poor infrastructure—especially transportation and energy resources. The report points out that the tariff and nontariff barriers are actually higher than those of Africa's intercontinental trade.

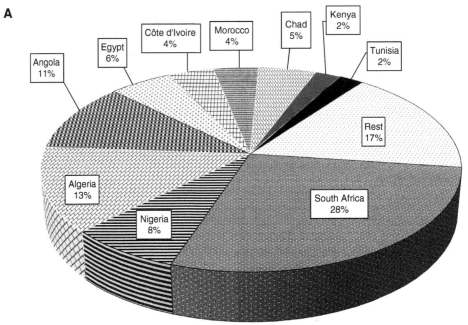

Origins of US Imports from Africa

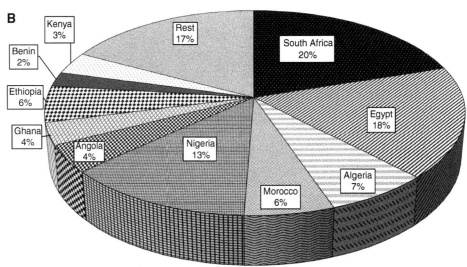

FIGURE 15.7 Africa's Trade
with the United States
of America, 2015.
Source: Data from UNCTAD
and International Trade
Center Trade Map

Destination of US Exports to Africa

Limited range of products Second, Africa's external trade is based on a limited range of products—mostly primary commodities—minerals and agricultural raw materials. These are not of interest to intracontinental trade, while for intercontinental trade, they are not value-added not to mention the competition from other countries.

Low productive capacities of African economies Third, the limited range of export products is due to low productive capacities in African economies. As discussed in several of the preceding chapters, African economies have more than

TABLE **15.8**

Major Exporters and Importers of Africa's Intercontinental Trade

Exporters				Importers			
2010		2015		2010		2015	
Country	Share (%)	Country	Share (%)	Country	Share (%)	Country	Share (%)
Nigeria	17.5	South Africa	19.2	South Africa	17.3	South Africa	15.6
South Africa	16.7	Nigeria	13.3	Egypt	11.1	Egypt	14.6
Algeria	11.5	Algeria	9.6	Nigeria	9.2	Algeria	10.2
Angola	10.8	Angola	9.1	Algeria	8.6	Morocco	7.4
Libya	7.4	Morocco	6.1	Morocco	7.4	Nigeria	6.6
Egypt	5.3	Egypt	6.0	Tunisia	4.6	Tunisia	4.0
Morocco	3.6	Tunisia	3.9	Libya	3.7	Ethiopia	3.2
Tunisia	3.3	C. d'Ivoire	3.3	Liberia	3.4	Kenya	3.8
Sudan	2.3	Libya	3.2	Angola	3.3	Angola	3.3
Cote d'Ivoire	2.1	Zambia	1.9	Kenya	2.5	Libya	2.5
Total	80.5	Total	75.6	Total	71.2	Total	71.1

Source: Data from International Trade Center Trade Map.

proportionate informal sectors. Firms operating in this sector lack access to basic infrastructure and credit. The sector also deprives the government tax revenues, which if properly managed can help the firms to boost their productivity. As a result, the majority of African firms are small and remain so with very weak inter-firm linkages. They also lack export competitiveness due to low labor productivity, low educated and technically skilled labor, low capital intensity, and lack of exporting experience as well as innovative capabilities. The small sizes of firms also hinder efficiency and the ability of those firms to export.

External factors Fourth, external factors such as globalization and certain aspects of multilateral and bilateral agreements also hurt Africa's capacity to trade. Globalization has converted regional and local markets to global markets, making cheaper alternative products available on African markets. While this may be good for consumers, it makes it difficult for local industries to compete. In addition, the "reciprocity principle" embedded in many economic partnership agreements has the potential of displacing trade in African countries. Also, African countries have been quick to sign agreements and very slow in implementing the terms of the agreements. An example of this is ECOWAS. The report says that it is more than 20 years ago that ECOWAS members signed agreement to remove trade and nontrade barriers. Yet, the agreement has not been fully implemented.

Recommendations

To deal with these, the report makes several recommendations. These include fostering entrepreneurship and building supply capacity; establishing a credible mechanism for dialog between state and business, building regional value chains;

enhancing implementation of existing trade agreements; rethinking approach to regional integration; and maintaining peace and stability.

Fostering entrepreneurship and build capacity These efforts must address structural problems of African enterprise, the high proportion of informal sector, the weak inter-firm linkages, and lack of competitiveness and innovation capacity. Governments must facilitate transition of firms from informal to formal sectors through simplifying the process of how to start a business and registration. Credit, information on opportunities in the productive sector as well as training should be made available to small firms. African governments must also address the infrastructure problem and seriously encourage research and development and support innovative activities from the R&D.

Establishing a credible mechanism for dialog between state and business The dialog between governments and business communities must be improved so that governments will know how various agreements—bilateral and multilateral—will impact the local economy. However, this must be done in a way that will be beneficial to the whole state rather than encouraging rent-seeking behavior.

Building regional value chains This calls on African governments to seize the opportunity they have in natural resources to build value-added products. This could be done on a regional basis, but it will also require enhancing the hardware and software of regional infrastructure.

Rethink regional economic integration and enhance implementation of existing regional trade agreements African countries need to rethink their approach to regional economic integration. In particular, removal of trade and nontrade barriers is not going to increase trade if productive capacities are neglected. Unfortunately, that has been the whole approach of African countries toward regional economic integration. In the meantime, the gap between signing agreements and implementing the terms of the agreement needs to be closed. For the most times, the lag in implementation is blamed on government bureaucrats who refuse to enforce agreements due to rent-seeking behaviors. However, this is a failure of leadership on the part of African governments.

Peace and security The importance of peace and security to trade cannot be overemphasized. Without peace and security, it is difficult to produce anything since people end up becoming fearful, anxious, and sometimes refugees. Thus, the productive sector suffers and that passes directly on to trade.

There is no argument with the UNCTAD (2013) report. Africa's trade issues have not changed much since the continent emerged from colonial domination. After more than five decades of postcolonization, the single most important trade issue facing African countries is its low capacity to trade. This in turn derives from Africa's low capacity to produce value-added goods that can be competitive on the world market. Africa has had a hard time shaking off the colonial legacy of producing basic raw materials, some of which are nonrenewable such as mineral resources. Those that do not depend on nonrenewable resources have remained stagnant due to technological inertia such that not enough is produced or what is produced is not of quality high enough to be competitive.

As we have seen, a great deal of effort has been expended by African countries to negotiate better terms of trade, commodity prices, and signing multilateral and bilateral trade agreements. While some of these have brought modest improvements in intracontinental trade, intercontinental trade within the global trade context has been disappointing. The lessons from all these are that improvement in trade performance cannot occur without a strong productive sector and accompanied supporting institutions.

TOURISM

Tourism, the traveling of people from one location to another for the purposes of leisure and or business over a period ranging from at least one night to less than one year, is another service activity that is becoming increasingly important in Africa. As a service activity, tourism is similar to all tradable commodities in one sense but also different in another sense. It is similar in the sense that it must be produced, promoted, and marketed like any other tradable commodity. However, it is different because it cannot be transported across national borders. Instead, the product must be consumed at site, so consumers have to travel to the location of the product in order to consume it.

According to the World Travel and Tourism Council (WTTC) in collaboration with its partner Oxford Economics, tourism accounted for $6.7 trillion or 9.8% of the world's GDP in 2014 and employed nearly 277 million people, which is 1 in 11 people employed in the world (WTTC, 2015). This makes tourism one of the largest and fastest growing economic activities in the world. Africa's tourism industry has also seen positive signs of growth, especially in recent times, having recorded an 8% in annual growth of international arrivals between 2009 and 2010 compared to 4-5% since 1950s. Given its rich history, abundant wildlife, expansive beaches, all-year round warm weather, and rich cultural diversity, African countries and their donor community see tourism as a potential source of economic development. In this section, we examine Africa's tourist trade. We begin with the evolution and development of tourism in Africa. This is followed by the contemporary features of the industry and problems and issues facing the industry. The terms tourism, tourist industry, and tourist trade are used interchangeably in the discussion.

The Evolution and Development of Tourism in Africa

Precolonial Africa

Defined in modern terms, it might be difficult to think that tourism existed in precolonial Africa. However, at least three types of tourism can be inferred from historical records. The first was trade or **business tourism,** which involved the participants of the Trans-Saharan trade, the East African trade, and the European trade, as well as regional traders within the continent.

The second type of tourism was religious tourism, which initially involved travelers to famous shrines, divinities, and deities of traditional African religions for spiritual renewal and sometimes for healing—a form of medical or health tourism. The geographic scope of **religious tourism** was widened during and after the introduction of Judaism, Christianity, and Islam to Africa. Christian and Islamic missionaries crisscrossed the continent, while devout African converts made pilgrimage to the Holy Land and Mecca. From the late 18th through the mid-19th century, European curiosity and interest in finding more about Africa's interior generated a third type of tourism—**adventure tourism**. The stories the missionaries, explorers, and traders sent back to Europe and to other parts of the world had two effects on tourism in Africa. First, it brought more adventure tourists to Africa. Egypt and big game hunting became the leading attractions that brought celebrities and professional hunters to the continent.

The second effect of the missionaries and explorers' stories was the development of stereotypical images of many African communities and ethnic groups that would be a mixed blessing for African tourism for more than a century. Such images included the warlike Maasai who often terrorized their peace-loving Kikuyu neighbors, and the view that the San and Khoikhoi people were much closer to apes than to human beings (Wels, 2000; Akama, 2000).

Colonial Africa

The colonial period laid the foundation of modern tourism in Africa. First, big game hunting continued to bring many adventure tourists to Africa during the early 1900s including Theodore Roosevelt, the 26th President of the United States. Second, the physical features of Africa sighted by Europeans during the period of exploration in Africa generated more curiosity in Europe and America. Private entrepreneurs began promoting some of these features in Europe through various publications and magazines to lure Europeans to visit those sites. Later on these efforts were supported by colonial governments through agencies such as chambers of commerce. Third, a number of Europeans wanted to walk in the footsteps of the early African explorers such as David Livingstone. Fourth, increasing concerns over wildlife led to an international environmental agreement, the first of its kind among the colonial powers. The Convention for the Protection of Animals, Birds, and Fish in Africa was signed by all the colonial powers—Britain, France, Germany, Italy, and Portugal—in 1900 (Hall and Frost, 2009). The goal of the Convention was to protect game, regulate trade, and suggest conservation measures, but the convention was never implemented, so each colonial power was left to figure out how best to deal with the problem. Britain introduced licensing and the institution of closed season. In contrast, Germany introduced game reserves. Back in 1894, the Pongola Game Reserve had been established in the Transvaal. Most of these reserves began with prohibition of hunting in designated areas, but were converted into national parks during the late colonial period. In 1925, following his extensive visit to the United States including the Yellowstone National Park, King Albert of Belgium established the Albert National Park in Belgian Congo. In 1926, South Africa established the Kruger National Park.

After World War II, the British government moved quickly to establish national parks in Kenya, Tanganyika, and Uganda. Among these were Nairobi in 1946, the Tsavo in 1948, and the Serengeti in 1951. It also began promoting tourism through slogans such as "the Tourists of Today would be Settlers or Investors Tomorrow" (Mogombo and Rogerson, 2012). A network of tourist sites in Southern African colonies were established for the affluent white population. These included South Africa's Kruger National Park, Rhodesia's Great Zimbabwe ruins, Wankie National Park, and Victoria Falls, and Nyasaland's Lake Nyasa (Teye, 1986).

In East Africa, the Kenyan-based East African Tourist and Travel Association (EATTA), formed in 1947, was particularly successful in persuading the colonial government for land grants, exchange control, loans, and infrastructure development for tourism. The Ministry of Tourism and Wildlife for East Africa was established in 1958.

Growing interest in tourism also led to transformation of African cultural groups from violent to "noble savages" with exotic cultures that were promoted and marketed by overseas tour operators (Ondicho, 2000). However, the selective nature of these marketing and promotion strategies also ignored the rich diversity of Africa's ethnicity.

In the French realm, Imperial France began organizing international expositions to showcase its vast overseas empire to promote the idea of Greater France. Following the successful world exposition in Paris in 1889, more expositions focusing specifically on French colonies—the Colonial Expositions of 1906, 1922, and 1931—were organized in Marseilles (Lucas, 2013). The idea of these exhibitions, however, was to bring the colonies home to the French public since most French people could not afford to travel to the colonies. Thus, the exhibitions showed selected aspects of life in the colonies choreographed and lived by selected families from the colonies for the French public to see. After the 1922 colonial exhibition, Andre Citroen, the French automobile pioneer, organized major road expeditions from Algeria through West and Central Africa to Cape Town and eventually to Madagascar, covering a distance of 12,500 miles (20,117 km) from October 1924 to June 1925 (Levine, 2005). Although Citroen's ultimate goal was to promote his automobile, his effort encouraged tourism in the French colonies. From the 1930s, tourism in French West Africa was vigorously promoted through publication of travel guides, legislation on terms of admission, and establishment of a Tourism Syndicate although destinations such as Senegal were better promoted than Mauritania and Niger (Lucas, 2013).

By the end of the colonial period, a tourist industry was beginning to emerge in Africa, but it was mostly limited to parts of the continent that had substantial European settler populations—North Africa (Algeria) and East and Southern Africa. Only few tourists came from outside the continent, including the United Kingdom, Saudi Arabia, North America, and Asia. Tourism infrastructure was scanty—small family hotels and hunting tourists used trails and camping (Ondicho, 2000).

Postcolonial Africa

With the exception of a few countries, tourism did not become an important economic sector for African countries in the early postcolonial period (1960s and 1970s) until decades later. This was partly due to the belief that industrialization and agricultural development were keys to Africa's development. Part of it was also due to radical development theories that dominated the political discourse in many African countries at the time. These theories saw tourism as somewhat detrimental to the masses in developing countries. The few countries that were exempt from these trends were South Africa, Egypt, Morocco, Tunisia, Gambia, Kenya, Tanzania, Uganda, Senegal, and Seychelles (Archer and Fletcher, 1996).

In South Africa, as a result of a large movement of people during World War II, the government saw the potential of tourism and established the South African Tourist Corporation (SATOUR) as part of the South African Railways and Harbors in 1947 (Grundlingh, 2006). However, the National Party that came to power in 1948 was more concerned with establishing the apartheid policy than promoting tourism. As a result, tourism remained restricted to the white population in the neighboring areas, until the return to majority rule in 1994.

In Egypt, while the socialist government of Nasser nationalized the Egyptian economy including tourism and Egypt Air following the 1952 revolution, certain subsectors of the tourist industry such as suppliers of tourist goods and foreign shipping and airlines remained in private hands (Gray, 1998). Efforts to reform the industry were minimal and were just limited to giving more freedom to the private business and removing restrictions on imports. The Arab-Israeli War disrupted the industry, but the Sadat government brought some reforms to the sector. The Ministry of Tourism was given the overall management of tourism, the power to set rules and regulations for the sector, and authority to designate areas for tourism development. Special exchange rates and duty-free shops that sold goods in foreign currencies were also established. Guaranteed property rights and ability to repatriate profits overseas by both foreign and Egyptian firms were also put in place. These allowed private companies to operate alongside the state-owned Msr Travel. From 1974, tourism began to recover until it was halted by the assassination of President Sadat in 1981. The Mubarak government continued to reform the sector including liberalization of airline rules, free operation of charter flights, and granting of more management autonomy to foreign hotels. These allowed more investments into development of beach tourism. However, throughout the decade, tourists numbers fluctuated widely due to such events as the Israeli invasion of Lebanon in 1982, the hijacking of the cruise ship Achille Lauro in 1985, and the US bombing of Libya in 1986 (Gray, 1998).

In Morocco, tourism was one of the three targets in the 1965–1967 Three-Year Plan. The other two were agriculture and management training (Berriane, 1999). The state established a number of agencies charged with public investments in tourism such as the Moroccan National Tourists Office, the Public Investment and Management Organization, and Homebuyers and Hoteliers Bank. The Public Investment and Management Organization set up tourist programs and gave them to others, while the Homebuyers and Hoteliers Bank granted loans to investors. The state also created the environment for tourism to thrive including hotel and tourism legislation, various tourism investment codes, training of management staff, organization of the travel agency sector, transportation infrastructure, hotel classification, and promotion abroad (Berriane, 1999). The three-year plan of 1978–1980 saw a gradual retreat of the State from the tourist sector.

Like Morocco, Tunisia identified tourism as an important economic sector in the early 1960s, which led to the establishment of the first hotel operations in the Hammamet region through the Tunisian Hoteliers and Tourist Company. In 1969, the Ministry for Land Use and Tourism was established. From then on, a combination of State and private sector parties started building tourist facilities first along the coast and later in major cities in the interior such as Kairouan, Tozeur, Kebili, and Gafsa (Poirier, 1995).

In East Africa, the work of the ETTA bequeathed a tourist industry that had relatively better infrastructure than in most African countries. The Kenyan government began promoting tourism in 1965 and made tourism as part of its 1965–1970 National Development Plan. It created its own Ministry of Tourism and Wildlife to set tourism and wildlife policies. It established the Kenya Tourist Development Corporation (KTDC) with a mandate to (1) provide finance and technical support to investors especially in the small- and medium-size hotel sector and (2) closely monitor the hotels and other forms of accommodation to ensure that the government fully participated in the tourist industry according to the state policy of African socialism (Ondicho, 2000). Laws requiring hunting license and laws banning hunting from all Game Reserves as well as nonpreservation activities from National Parks were passed. Formal training in hotel management was started in 1969, and in 1975, the Kenya Hotel Management and Training College was established to train personnel for the hotel and tourism industry. In Tanzania, the state established the Tanzania Tourist Corporation in 1971 to promote tourism inside and outside of Tanzania. The state also undertook an expansive hotel building program that led to increase in international visitors. However, this growth was interrupted by the drought in 1974, the Uganda War in 1979, and a national economic crisis in the late 1970s through the mid-1980s.

Both Gambia and Senegal considered tourism as a viable alternative in the mid-1960s when the world groundnut or peanut market became unstable. However, for Gambia, it was not until 1972 that the government paid more attention to the sector. In 1974, a 15-kilometer strip along the coast was designated as a Tourism Development Area (Sharpley, 2009). In Seychelles, tourism began to thrive when an international airport was completed in Port Victoria, its capital in 1972, followed by political independence in 1976 (Archer and Fletcher, 1996).

There were a few other countries, such as Zambia, Ethiopia, and Nigeria, that had tourism on their economic development radar, but as a result of political instability and prolonged civil war within them or in their region, they were not able to develop a viable tourism industry (Teye, 1986). Majority of African countries, however, ignored tourism as an engine of growth until late 1980s and 1990s (Rogerson, 2004). The economic crises that occurred in most African countries from the late 1970s through the 1980s followed by structural adjustment programs (SAPs) and political reform movement helped change the status of tourism as an economic sector in Africa. For the countries that already had viable tourism sectors, privatization and liberalization of their economies brought some efficiency into the sector. Government control of tourism assets passed on to private hands except for marketing, promotion, and monitoring. A number of other policy measures followed. In Tanzania, for example, a national tourism policy was promulgated in 1991 with the goal of maximizing the contribution of tourism to economic development through increased foreign exchange earnings, employment creation and human resources development, and sustainable tourism development through conservation of tourist attractions and preservation of the environment. The Tanzania Investment Act of 1997 and the revision of the Tourist Policy in 1999 brought more investments into the sector (Luvanga and Shitundi, 2003). In Egypt, the state lowered indirect tax on tourism and began to focus on promoting Arab tourism (Berriane, 1999; Gray, 1998).

For the countries that had not paid much attention to tourism, there was an opportunity to search for alternative economic sectors that would re-energize the economies and help meet the problem of unemployment. Boosted by the collapse of socialist and communist ideology, increasing globalization, and the enormous natural and cultural resources in their possession, as well as increasing social science research that focused on tourism and development these countries began to see the potential of tourism as an economic sector.

In 1997, the members of Southern Africa Development Community (SADC) signed the charter of the Regional Tourism Organization for Southern Africa (RETOSA) to cooperate in the development of tourism in the subregion. In 2002, RETOSA asked South Africa to develop an action plan on tourism for the subregion (Matlou, ND). SADC shared the plan with the other regional groups on the continent through the United Nations World Tourism Organization Commission for Africa (UNWTO-CAF), which include 46 countries in the sub-Saharan region. After adopting the plan in 2003, the group asked NEPAD Secretariat to fund a study that would convert the strategic document into Action Plan for the member countries. The Action Plan, which was adopted by the African Union at its summit in 2004, envisioned tourism to be a key mechanism in Africa's transformation and development. The goal was for tourism sector to contribute successfully to poverty eradication, economic growth, and diversification by 2020. To accomplish this, the plan targeted eight main focus areas including (1) promoting policy and regulatory environment, (2) strengthening institutional capacity, (3) promoting tourism marketing, (4) promoting research and development, (5) promoting investment in tourism infrastructure and products, (6) refinancing human resources development and quality assurance, (7) establishing and adopting a code of conduct and ethics for tourism, and (8) mobilizing financial resources (Fontabong, 2014; AU/ NEPAD, 2014).

After this, tourism became an integral part of national and regional economic development discussion, visioning, and plans. African countries with no tourism plans formulated one while those with plans revised or revamped them. Majority of these plans set long-term visions with three main objectives or targets: (1) to raise the number of tourists, (2) to increase the number of receipts, and (3) to create jobs. More tourism-enhancing policies were adopted in many African countries. For example, Kenya began a process toward a comprehensive tourism policy and legislation in 2002 under the leadership of the Ministry of Tourism and Wildlife (Njoya, ND). Morocco launched its Vision 2010 in 2001 aimed at attracting 10 million tourists by 2010 (Henkelman, ND). The vision focused on converting six regions of natural beauty with high potential tourist attraction into resorts. It also adopted Open Skies policy that allowed more airlines to come into the country, in 2004, while private capital was allowed into renovation of traditional houses and older buildings in the medinas (old parts of towns) of cities such as Marrakech, Casablanca, Rabat, Fez, Essaonira, and Tangier (Arriba, 2011). Even though Vision 2010 did not achieve all its objectives, it was extended to Vision 2020 with the goal of placing Morocco among the top 20 tourist destinations in the world (Henkelman, ND).

In addition to individual country plans, there were also a number of regional plans or assessment plans with similar objectives. For example, in 2004, UNESCO developed a program for cultural tourism development for six West African countries including Cape Verde, Senegal, Mali, Burkina Faso, Ghana, and Niger (UNESCO, 2004). Again, in 2012, ECOWAS ministers of tourism met in Banjul, Gambia, to develop a framework for tourism development in the region. The long period of neglect of tourism by many African countries meant that Africa with regard to international tourists' arrivals and receipts have been the lowest in the world. In the next section, we examine Africa's contemporary tourism trade.

Africa's Tourist Trade

The discussion in this section is based on the World Travel and Tourism Council (WTTC) and the United Nations World Tourism Organization (UNWTO) databases. These databases are not perfect so a word of caution is in order. First, the UNWTO classifies the world's regions and subregions differently and especially for Africa. Egypt and Libya are grouped under the Middle East, while North Africa consists of Morocco, Algeria, Tunisia, and Sudan. In addition, Zambia, Zimbabwe, Malawi, and Mozambique are all grouped under East Africa, while Angola is part of Central Africa. Second, the database is incomplete because it is based on country reports. Some country reports are complete per the categorization used by the UNWTO, others are incomplete. While the discussion here uses the UNWTO data, it does not use its regional grouping.

The Role of Tourism in African Economies

Tourism directly employed 8,570,790 people in Africa in 2015, which was 2.7% of Africa's total employment (WTTC, 2015). The percentage share of national employment varied from as high as 26% in Seychelles to as low as 0.5% in DRC (Table 15.9). When all indirectly related employment is taken into account, tourism employed 21.1 million people in Africa in 2015, which was 6% of Africa's total employment

Total Contribution of Tourism to Employment in Africa—2015

Country	Employment ('000)	Share of employment (%)
Algeria	327.31	2.96
Angola	79.47	1.63
Benin	91.62	1.99
Botswana	27.08	2.84
Burkina Faso	72.22	1.38
Burundi	43.62	2.21
Cameroon	283.31	3.11
Cape Verde	34.75	15.40
Central African Republic	16.62	1.91
Chad	21.81	0.98
Comoros	6.50	3.91
Cote d'Ivoire	163.39	3.09
DRC	144.20	0.53
Egypt	964.51	3.66
Ethiopia	540.15	2.30
Gabon	3.93	0.95
Gambia	49.57	6.95
Ghana	273.19	2.39
Guinea	51.07	1.90
Kenya	385.85	3.42
Lesotho	30.93	4.60
Libya	39.65	2.12
Madagascar	245.87	4.49
Malawi	213.42	2.91
Mali	83.96	2.52
Mauritius	42.62	7.74
Morocco	811.56	7.15
Mozambique	272.84	2.83
Namibia	24.49	3.25
Niger	19.74	1.86
Nigeria	634.88	1.51
Congo	8.98	1.00
Rwanda	112.82	4.00
S.T. & Principe	7.63	13.26
Senegal	240.47	4.12
Seychelles	11.75	25.94
Sierra Leone	14.40	1.26
South Africa	706.36	4.49

(Continued)

TABLE 15.9

Total Contribution of Tourism to Employment in Africa—2015 (*Continued*)

Country	Employment ('000)	Share of employment (%)
Sudan & S. Sudan	188.80	1.88
Swaziland	7.76	2.14
Tanzania	445.76	3.83
Togo	35.44	3.27
Tunisia	207.78	6.08
Uganda	2.15	2.15
Zambia	106.23	1.80
Zimbabwe	157.73	2.12
Total	8570.79	2.74

Source: Data from World Travel and Tourism Council (WTTC) 2015.

(WTTC, 2015). Once again, the highest contributions were in Seychelles (58.6%), Cape Verde (41.9%), and Namibia (21.3%).

In terms of direct contribution to GDP, tourism accounted for $66.8 billion or 3.2% of Africa's GDP in 2015 (WTTC, 2015). The contribution was substantial for several African countries—from 21.4% in Seychelles, 17.6% in Cape Verde, 14.0% in Sao Tome and Principe to 0.6% in DRC. With respect to total contribution (which includes direct, indirect, and induced contributions) to GDP, it was $164.6 billion or 7.9% of Africa's GDP. The share again was as high as 56.8% in Seychelles, 44.9% in Cape Verde, 29.3% in Sao Tome and Principe, 24.4% in Mauritius, 20.9% in Gambia, 18.2%% in Morocco, and to as low as 2.1% in Uganda (Table 15.10).

TABLE 15.10

Total Contribution of Tourism to GDP in Africa—2015

Country	Product US$ billion	Share of GDP (%)
Algeria	5.89	6.6
Angola	2.06	4.3
Benin	0.20	5.7
Botswana	0.56	11.1
Burkina Faso	0.19	4.0
Burundi	0.08	5.7
Cameroon	1.08	8.0
Cape Verde	0.28	44.9
Central African Rep.	0.05	6.4
Chad	0.14	4.3
Comoros	0.03	10.4

(*Continued*)

TABLE **15.10**

Total Contribution of Tourism to GDP in Africa—2015 (*Continued*)

Country	Product US$ billion	Share of GDP (%)
Congo	0.14	4.04
Cote d'Ivoire	1.16	7.48
DRC	0.24	4.0
Egypt	10.36	8.6
Ethiopia	1.58	6.5
Gabon	0.14	3.0
Gambia	0.07	20.9
Ghana	1.22	7.1
Guinea	0.18	5.4
Kenya	2.40	9.8
Lesotho	0.10	11.9
Libya	1.22	7.2
Madagascar	0.54	14.9
Malawi	0.19	7.4
Mali	0.49	10.1
Mauritius	0.92	24.4
Morocco	8.20	18.4
Mozambique	0.40	9.4
Namibia	0.31	15.4
Niger	0.17	4.8
Nigeria	7.08	4.5
Rwanda	0.38	11.6
S. T. & Principe	0.04	29.3
Senegal	0.65	11.0
Seychelles	0.34	56.9
Sierra Leone	0.05	3.5
South Africa	8.51	9.1
Sudan & South Sudan	2.34	5.7
Swaziland	0.10	5.9
Tanzania	1.90	13.0
Togo	0.17	8.6
Tunisia	2.73	13.9
Uganda	2.15	2.1
Zambia	0.61	6.9
Zimbabwe	0.48	7.9
Total	164.6	7.9

Source: World Travel and Tourism Council (WTTC), 2015.

Composition and Volume of Africa's Tourist Trade

Like elsewhere, Africa's tourist trade consists of two main components by origin. They are domestic, which occurs within individual countries, and international, which occurs inside and outside the continent.

Domestic tourism Domestic tourism occurs in every African country, yet it is difficult to know its size, volume, and characteristics because of lack of documentation. A few countries make the effort to collect data on domestic tourism. In 2015, for example, only 17 African countries reported domestic tourism data to the UNWTO database. The data show that there were more than 73 million domestic tourists in Africa in 2015. Most of them were in South Africa (33%), Nigeria (24%), Tunisia (10%), Algeria (9%), Kenya (4%), and Angola (4%). The activities of these tourists occurred for the same reasons as international tourism, which are discussed below, and they include adventure, medical, religious, festival, and leisure.

International tourism In 2015, international tourism data reported by 40 African countries show that more than 61.6 million international tourists visited Africa. In 2015, this was about 5.7% of the over 1.1 billion international tourists worldwide. In contrast, Europe, including Russia, accounted for 51%, Asia and the Pacific 24%, the Americas 16%, and the Middle East 3%. As already indicated, Africa's international tourism has grown at a considerable rate over the past decade. For example, UNWTO data indicate that in 2004, Africa received 39.7 million. Thus, between 2004 and 2015, the number of international tourists to Africa increased by 35.5%. It is very likely that this would have been more had all the countries reported data.

Direction of Africa's international tourist trade Africa's international tourist trade follows two main directions—intracontinental (intra-African) tourism and intercontinental tourism. The first occurs among African countries and regions and the second between Africa and the outside world. Of the 61.6 million international tourists recorded in 2015, 27.7 million (45%) were from Africa, 15.9 million (26%) were from Europe, 4.4 million (7.1%) from Asia and the Pacific, 2.1 million (3%) from North America, 0.7 million (1%) from South and Central America, 0.3 million (0.5%) from Australasia, about 10.4 million or 17% from unspecified countries or regions.

Intra-African tourism Intra-African tourism has been growing over the last decade. As late as 2009, Europe was the leading source of international tourists to Africa. By 2015, however, more international tourists to Africa were originating from within the continent. The reasons for this are complex. It could be improvement in data reporting by African countries; it could also be due to a growing middle-class Africans who are traveling more as well as safety and uncertainty concerns at some of the most popular destinations for international tourists, especially in North Africa. Whatever reason it is, this is a noteworthy positive trend. The leading countries of origin and destination have remained the same with only a slight change from 2010 to 2015 (Table 15.11). Among the originating countries include South Africa, Zimbabwe, Lesotho, Libya, and Mozambique, while the top destination countries were South Africa, Tunisia, Zimbabwe, Nigeria, and Mozambique.

The regional nature of the origin-destination pattern of this intra-African tourism demonstrates one of the fundamental laws of geography, namely, a **distance decay** function. Distance decay is the tendency for interactions between places to decline with increasing distances between them. Thus, most of the international tourists from Africa travel within their own regions than outside their regions. For

TABLE **15.11**

Origins and Destinations of International Tourists from Inside Africa in 2010 and 2015

| | Origin | | | | Destination | | | |
| | 2010 | | 2015 | | 2010 | | 2015 | |
Country	Tourist (000)	Country	Tourist (000)	Country	Tourist (000)	Country	Tourist (000)
South Africa	3,907	South Africa	4,545	South Africa	5,734	South Africa	7,501
Zimbabwe	2,639	Zimbabwe	2,658	Nigeria	4,185	Tunisia	3,032
Lesotho	2,635	Lesotho	1,778	Zimbabwe	1,951	Zimbabwe	1,854
Libya	2,331	Libya	1,427	Mozambique	1466	Nigeria	1,605
Mozambique	1,888	Mozambique	1,955	Swaziland	1,218	Mozambique	1,353
Niger	1,287	Algeria	1,951	Tunisia	1,136	Rwanda	1,155
Algeria	1,239	Swaziland	938	Namibia	714	Lesotho	1,132
Swaziland	1,091	Botswana	841,335	Uganda	676	Swaziland	1,111
Botswana	998	Zambia	755,785	Zambia	583	Namibia	1,083
Benin	862	DRC	753,546	Malawi	562	Uganda	1,047
Top 10	17,388	Top 10	17,603	Top 10	18,225	Top 10	20,873
Other		Other	10,1110	Other		Other	6,839
Total		**Total**	27,712	**Total**		Total	27,712

Source: Data from World Tourism Council (UNWTC)

example, about 70% of African tourists to East Africa in 2015 were from East Africa. Similarly, about 90% of African tourists to North Africa were from North Africa (Table 15.12). The only exception was Central Africa, where perhaps due to prolonged civil strife has made tourists from the region develop more diversified destinations beyond their region.

Intercontinental tourism The origins and destinations of Africa's intercontinental tourism are summarized in Table 15.13, which shows some changes from 2010 to 2015. In terms of the origins, it is clear that a shift from Europe's domination to a more diversified source occurred in 2015. Destinations did not change very

TABLE **15.12**

Interregional Travel in Africa in 2015 (Percentage of Travelers)

| | Destination | | | | |
Origin	Central Africa	East Africa	North Africa	Southern Africa	West Africa
Central Africa	5.6	48.9	2.7	15.2	27.7
East Africa	0.6	70.1	11.1	16.1	2.1
North Africa	0.6	0.5	97.0	0.5	1.4
Southern Africa	0.1	1.6	0.2	97.3	0.8
West Africa	3.2	3.9	13.1	6.6	73.2

Source: Data from World Travel and Tourism Council, 2015.

TABLE **15.13**

Origins and Destinations of International Tourists from Outside Africa in 2010 and 2015

Origin				Destination			
2010		2015		2010		2015	
Country	Tourist (000)	Country	Tourist (000)	Country	Tourist (000)	Country	Tourist (000)
France	4,905	France	3,599	Egypt	13,749	Morocco	9,792
UK	3,226	UK	2,232	Morocco	9,032	Egypt	4,602
Russian Fed.	3,181	Germany	1,976	Tunisia	5,766.	Nigeria	4.410
Germany	2,655	USA	1,648	Botswana	4,705	Tunisia	2,654
Italy	2,203	China	902	South Africa	2,340	South Africa	2,531
USA	1,252	Spain	859	Algeria	2,070	Mauritius	1,275
Spain	1,120	Italy	825	Nigeria	1,928	Algeria	957
Poland	832	Russian Fed	763	Kenya	1,330	Tanzania	598
Netherlands	761	Saudi Arabia	668	Mauritius	709	Ethiopia	548
Belgium	737	India	619	Sudan	4,460	Cape Verde	468
Top 10	20,873	Top 10	14,090	Top 10	42,074	Top 10	27,835
Other	9,170	Other	13,622	Other	4,553	Other	3,488
Total	30,043	Total	31,323	Total	46,627	Total	31,323

Source: Data from World Tourism Council (UNWTC)

much except for their relative importance and the lower attraction numbers in 2015 compared to 2010. The most important of these is the decline of Egypt as tourist destination from 2010 to 2015, and most of this could be attributed to the political developments in the past several years and growing concerns about safety.

Beyond these trends, Europe still was the leading source of tourists for Africa, and about 85% of these tourists originated from 10 countries, including France, the United Kingdom, and Germany (Table 15.13). For 67% of these tourists, the top destinations were Morocco, Egypt, South Africa, and Mauritius. Other less popular destinations were Nigeria, Kenya, and Cabo Verde.

The most important countries of origin of intercontinental tourists from Asia and the Pacific are China, Saudi Arabia, India, Israel, Jordan, Japan, United Arab Emirates, and South Korea. Egypt was the top destination country for these Asian tourists. It accounted for 42% of intercontinental tourists from Asia and the Pacific in 2015. The other important destinations were Nigeria, Uganda, South Africa, Morocco, and Mauritius. Of the reported 2.1 million North American tourists who visited Africa in 2015, 1.7 million or 78% were from the United States, 374,081 or 18% were from Canada, 43,251 or 2% were from the United States and Canada, while the remaining 32,771 or 1.5% were from Mexico. The most popular destinations for these tourists were South Africa, Nigeria, Morocco, Egypt, and Ethiopia.

Purpose and Types of International Tourism

UNWTO data show that international tourists visit Africa for two main reasons, namely, personal and professional reasons. By far, personal reasons drive most of the international tourists to Africa. They accounted for 86% of international arrivals in 2009 and 85% in 2015 (UNWTO, 2016). The proportion of tourists who attributed their visit to holidays and leisure out of personal reasons has also increased. For example, in 2011, 56% of the international tourists gave holidays and leisure as personal reason to visit. In 2015, it was 73%.

Whether personal or professional, Africa's international tourists participate in specific types of tourism products or activities. The Regional Infrastructure Development Master Plan for the SADC region (2012, p. 12) identifies seven types of tourism products provided by Africa. They include nature-based tourism, community-based tourism, cultural tourism, backpackers and youth tourism, volunteer and education tourism, adventure tourism, and medical tourism. To these, we may add beach tourism, sex tourism, and diaspora tourism.

Nature-based tourism including ecotourism This is the oldest, best known, and for that matter the largest sector of Africa's tourist industry. It accounts for 20–40% of international tourists, and it includes tourist, who visit for hiking, camping, wildlife viewing, snorkeling, and scuba diving. The most typical spots are national parks and other wildlife reserves, hilly and mountainous areas. For international tourists, it is usually important if these sites are listed as World Heritage Sites by the United Nations Scientific, Educational, and Cultural Organization (UNESCO). Africa has 40 (20%) of the world's 197 sites on the list based on physical features. Unfortunately, 35 (18%) of these sites, mostly national parks, wildlife reserves, are also in danger according to the UNESCO list.

Cultural and religious tourism This targets cultural monuments that have been recognized as World Heritage sites by UNESCO. In recent years, however, cultural tourism has also branched into community-based tourism, where the idea is to bring the benefits of tourism to the communities and people who live around the tourists' destinations. Like the nature-based tourism sites, Africa has 79 (10%) of the 779 world cultural heritage sites. Another form of cultural tourism is religious tourism, which takes place across the continent. Perhaps the most well-known religious tourism destination is Ethiopia whose rich tradition of Christianity and numerous churches and mosques make it a very attractive destination. A third form of cultural tourism that is beginning to get traction is food tourism. This is tourism with a focus on Africa's rich food traditions where food varieties are used as the main attractions.

Backpackers and youth tourism This involves young people ages 26–30 who are interested in exploring and learning more about other cultures. These usually travel light, and where possible will hop from one destination to another.

Volunteer and education tourism This involves unpaid participatory activities during vacations, for example, building schools and clinics. The participants in this tourism may span across all ages and are usually people who love to spend their free time doing charity and other volunteer work in Africa, while taking the opportunity to visit and enjoy the nature and cultures of their destination.

Adventure tourism This caters to people who love high-impact outdoor experience. Among the popular activities are mountain climbing, biking, whitewater rafting, hiking, kayaking, wildlife viewing, and bungee jumping. Some of Africa's highest mountains such as Mount Kilimanjaro (Tanzania), Atlas Mountains (Morocco), Mount Kenya (Kenya), Simien Mountains (Ethiopia), Mount Elgon (Uganda–Kenya), and the Drakensberg (South Africa-Lesotho) are the popular destinations for mountain climbers. Whitewater rafting destinations include the Zambezi (Zimbabwe), the Fish River Canyon (Windhoek, Namibia), Omo River and the Blue Nile (Ethiopia), the Doring and Orange Rivers (South Africa), the Albert Nile (Uganda), the Rufiji River (Tanzania), the Mangoky River (Madagascar), and the Ahansal River (Morocco).

Medical tourism This involves people who travel out of their home countries to other destinations to seek physical healing and or other forms of physical well-being. Although this is not new to Africans in modern terms, it is a much smaller component of the tourism sector. Generally, the most important destination in Africa for this type of tourism is South Africa, mainly because of the quality of its health-care system and its international reputation. In a landmark study of South Africa's medical tourism, Crush et al. (2012) found that from 2006 to 2010, medical tourism accounted for 5.8% of tourists visiting South Africa. These tourists were of two streams—the North-South and the South-South. The North-South stream consisted of tourists who come from Europe (mostly the United Kingdom and Germany) and North America for such procedures as hip replacement, rhinoplasty, breast augmentation, liposuction, facelifts, and tummy tucks. Trips for these services are usually packaged with safari. The South-South stream consists of Africans from South Africa's neighbors who go to South Africa for regular medical treatment because they do not have access to such treatment in their home countries. Leading the pack in this is Lesotho, followed by SADC countries and East and West African countries. Crush et al. (2012) found that this south-south stream accounted for 85% of all the medical tourists to South Africa from 2006 to 2010. The tourists in this stream are less likely to engage in other tourists activities compared to those in the North-South stream, although medical tourists from SADC countries may engage in business as part of their trips. They also go for medically needed procedures such as cancer treatment, cardiovascular, trauma, obstetrics and gynecology, HIV/AIDS, and reconstructive surgery.

Another destination for medical tourism is Tunisia. From 2007 to 2010, Tunisia received more than 515,931 medical tourists. Of these, 457,639 or 89% came from Tunisia's neighbors, with Libya alone accounting for more than 57%, followed by Algeria and Morocco. The rest of the tourists came from Europe with France, Italy, the United Kingdom, and Germany as the main countries (Lakhoua, 2012). Other African countries with emerging medical tourism sector in Africa include Kenya, Egypt, Mauritius, and Morocco (UNCTAD/ALDC/Africa, 2017).

Beach, diaspora, and sex tourism Beach tourism involves tourists who like to enjoy Africa's warm and sandy beaches, while diaspora tourism involves Africans in the diaspora who either do not want to lose their roots with the continent or like to trace their roots to specific places in Africa. In contrast, sex tourism involves tourists who visit Africa in search of sexual encounters with young African women and men. The tourists are usually old white men and women while their African mates are either working or unemployed youths. To the tourists it is for pleasure, while to the Africans it is for money and also for the hope that somehow such a relationship with the rich white customers will result in a lasting relationship that will help alleviate them from poverty. Some also feel a sense of prestige to have sexual relationship with rich white people, but generally speaking, African societies in which this kind of tourism occurs, usually shun such activities, and sometimes ostracize the people who engage in them. Hughes (2008) reports this type of tourism in Nairobi, Malinda, and Mombasa, Kenya, but it is found in other parts of the continent as well.

Tourism and Economic Development of Africa

Over the past 5 to 10 years, the status of tourism in Africa has been raised to new heights by a number of publications focusing on the potential of tourism to Africa's economic development, and why African countries should focus on tourism as a way to economic development (e.g., UNEP, 2006; UNECA, 2011; SADC, 2012; AfDB, 2013; and Christie et al., 2014). We will examine the prospects and problems of this proposition.

Prospects

Following Christie et al. (2014), we can summarize some of the prospects for African countries to use tourism as a means to economic development.

(1) Tourism will spur economic development. This is because tourism is vast and still growing. For example, in 2015, 935 million people traveled internationally, spending $399 billion in developing countries and contributing over $1 trillion to global trade. Africa could get a piece of this if it embraces tourism. In addition, tourism has a record of accomplishment around the world as an engine of economic growth as demonstrated by Thailand, Dominican Republic. Indonesia's Bali, Mexico's Cancun, and Egypt, where tourism has grown from very small to very substantial component of the domestic economies. (2) Tourism creates good jobs and this is important for Africa where unemployment and underemployment are both massive. Tourism, it is argued, has the potential of creating jobs exponentially and compares with other sectors in creating opportunities for small and medium enterprises. (3) Tourism has the ability to build remote and developing regions, because tourism is growing faster in emerging and developing regions than anywhere else. (4) Tourism can accelerate the pace of policy reforms, because as indicated by the experience of Cabo Verde and Rwanda, such reforms attract investors and more tourists. (5) Tourism has the potential of boosting infrastructure, because in order to attract visitors, tourist destination need quality infrastructure in terms transportation, communication, electricity, water, and health care. (6) Tourism increases domestic consumption and diversifies exports, because tourism creates demand and supply opportunities for goods and services that can send multiplier effects throughout the economy. (7) Tourism empowers women, young people, and marginalized populations. This is evidenced by the fact that majority of potential employees in the touristic sector are women, young, and marginalized. The learning curve of a lot of tourist jobs is not high and a good portion of them require only a short training. It is even better if the destination is in a remote or rural area since that will provide employment opportunities for people living in those areas. (8) Tourism preserves cultural heritage and conserves the environment since it is important to take care of the very things that attract tourists. (9) Tourism promotes public–private partnerships in planning, conservation, and infrastructure development. (10) Tourism if successful can change the external perceptions of a country, create cultural understanding, and create a positive internal frame.

The report recommends the Malaysian model to African countries because a few years ago Malaysia's tourism sector was very much like that of African countries. The Malaysian model is based on a larger domestic market than an international market. Next, it targets a regional market—for example, from Singapore. As a result, Malaysia's tourism is less affected by international shocks. The report argues that there is a growing middle class in Africa with purchasing power similar to their Western counterparts—about 32 million that needs to be targeted—as well as the emerging new markets in Asia, Eastern Europe, and South America.

The report recommends a regional approach. For East Africa—a tourism Master Plan is called for with destination management, harmonization of policies, and regulatory frameworks; selling of East Africa as a single destination—one visa requirement. These call for joint roles and responsibilities of both the public and private sectors. For the public sector, its most important role will be to ensure a climate conducive to tourism development by recognizing the potential of the tourism sector in national development strategies. It should also provide the broad framework and infrastructure support within which tourism could thrive. For the private sector, its role is to invest in tourism development that focuses not only on natural resources but also on cultural resources. Nongovernmental organizations should also play the role of facilitating broader conversation to ensure that all stakeholders are participating in the industry. They should also serve as industry watchdog.

Other arguments in favor of tourism include the fact that it is a product that is consumed at the spot, so it will bring benefit to the people in the area. In addition, it is seasonal and therefore go very well with other activities such as farming. Furthermore, it offers a lot of employment opportunities for people and requires multiple infrastructure such as roads and hotels, which tend to benefit rural areas (Uchegbu and Kanu, ND).

Constraints

There is no doubt that tourism could be an engine of economic development for some African countries. However, African countries should be careful not to see tourism as the new panacea that will solve all their development problems, because it is not. First, one can in fact make most of the above arguments on behalf of other economic sectors such as agriculture, manufacturing, or some service sector activity. Besides, in Tanzania, for example, Kweka et al. (2003) reports that while tourism plays an important role in the economy, its income-generating ability is weak due to low wages. Second, a viable tourism sector that can lift up whole economies in Africa requires solid infrastructure that include excellent transportation system, telecommunication, efficient and reliable sources of energy, excellent hotels, health-care facilities, environmental quality, and trained personnel in tourism and hospitality management that will ensure the well-being of tourists in both normal and emergency situations. As we saw in Chapters 10 and 13, the quality of infrastructure in most African countries will require major upgrades to meet and attract tourists. Indeed, with the current state of transportation and telecommunication infrastructure, it is much easier, safer, and more comfortable for Africa's growing middle class to travel to Europe, and North America than to neighboring African countries. Third, a vibrant tourist industry requires a good governance system devoid of bureaucratic red tape, bribery and corruption, and in which stability, predictability, and the rule of law are assured (see, e.g., Havi and Enu, 2013). These are needed to attract investments and assure smooth and continuous operations of tourists firms without fear of interruption. Fifth, and related to the governance system, a vibrant tourism industry requires a secure and safe environment that allows tourists to make the most out of their visit without any fear of what will happen to them.

All these imply that African countries will need a lot of resources to provide the necessary environment for tourism to be successful. It is possible to selectively develop the most important tourist areas as tourist enclaves with up-to-date facilities to attract tourists. However, this has its own problems. First, there is no guarantee that the benefits from tourism in those areas will spread to the rest of the country. In the Botswana's Okavango Delta, for example, Mbaiwa (2001) showed that all the resources in the tourist enclave belonged to foreigners, while the locals had very limited access to resources. Second, tourist enclaves themselves may be subject to attacks. Egypt, for example, has had several of its resort towns in the Sinai Peninsula attacked over the years. In 2004, a bomb blast killed 31 people and wounded 159 in Taba, a resort town near the border with Israel. Another bomb blast killed 34 people and wounded 12 in Ras al-Shitan campsite in the same year. In 2005, a car bomb killed 88 people and injured 200 in Shamir el-Sheikh another resort town in Sinai Peninsula. In 2006, a bomb killed 23 people and injured 80 in Dahab City. In 2008, 11 tourists were kidnapped near Aswan, Egypt. Other events include the murder of Coptic Christians in Naj Hammadi and Alexandria in 2010 and 2011, the killing of South Korean tourists in 2014 near Taba, and the downing of the Russian airline from Egypt's Shamir el-Sheikh Tourist resort in 2015. Eventually, such events take their toll on tourism. Thus, Lister (2015) reports that Dahab is declining into a ghost town following the death of the South Korean tourists in 2014, though it is 140 km away from Taba, the scene of the murder.

It is true that Africa has many natural assets that it can turn into a viable tourism sector. The landscape is beautiful and climate is good for travel all year round. It possesses an incredible abundance of game and wildlife that are unique in the world. It has a human landscape, which is rich in history and complex in culture. However, turning these into the sector that will lift entire economies is going to be no easier than transforming its other natural resources into value-added products to compete on the international stage. African countries and their donor supporters are quick to identify particular economic sectors as the panaceas for all of Africa's development problems only to find out later that that is not the case. Thus, the spotlight had been on agriculture, manufacturing, environment, women, ICTs, and now tourism. African countries that have the capacity to develop tourism as a vibrant economic sector should do so, but they should not neglect the other sectors that are needed to make their efforts at tourism worthwhile. The history of economic development in Africa is replete with too many of such actions, and it is hoped that the push to focus on tourism will not shortchange other sectors that need to be developed.

Postreading Assignments

A. Study the Following Key Concepts

Distance decay	Generalized System of Preferences	Terms of trade
Export Earning Stabilization System	Lomé Convention	

B. Discuss the Following Questions

Revisit the following questions again and check your initial answers with what you know now.

1. Estimate the percentage of world trade that is due to Africa.
2. What do you think are the major exports and imports of African countries?
3. Do you think African countries trade more among themselves than with countries outside Africa?
4. What do you think will be some of the major barriers to trade by African countries?
5. What do you think are the main draw for tourism in Africa?
6. Where do you think most tourists to Africa go and why?
7. What do you think are the main obstacles to tourism in Africa?
8. What have you learned about Africa's trade and tourism?

References

Abaza, M. 2006. *Changing Consumer Cultures of Modern Egypt: Cairo's Urban Reshaping.* Leiden: Brill Academic Publishers.

Adedeji, A. 1981. "Historical and Theoretical Background." In Adedeji, A. (Ed.) *Indigenization of African Economies.* London: Hutchinson University Library for Africa in Collaboration with African Association of Public Administration and Management, pp. 29–32.

Akama, J. 2000. "The creation of the Maasai image and tourism development in Kenya." In Akama, J., and Sterry, P. (Eds.) *Cultural Tourism in Africa: Strategies for the New Millennium Proceedings of the ATLAS Africa International Conference December 2000.* Mombasa, Kenya, pp. 43–53.

Alpers, E. A. 1976. "Gujarat and the Trade of East Africa, c. 1500–1800." *The International Journal of African Historical Studies* 9(1): 22–44.

Amin, S. 1981. "Senegal." In Adedeji, A. (Ed.) *Indigenization of African Economies.* London: Hutchinson University Library for Africa in Collaboration with African Association of Public Administration and Management, pp. 309–327.

Aminzade, R. 2013. *Race, Nation, and Citizenship in Post-Colonial Africa: The case of Tanzania.* Cambridge: Cambridge University Press.

Archer, B., and Fletcher, J. 1996. "The Economic Impact of Tourism in the Seychelles." *Annals of Tourism Research* 23(1): 32–47.

AU/NEPAD. 2014. "Progress of Implementation of the NEPAD Tourism Action Plan UNWTO Commission for Africa." *Fifty-sixth Meeting. Luanda, Angola,* April 28.

Berriane, M. 1999. *Tourism, Culture and Development in the Arab Region: Supporting Culture to Develop Tourism, Developing Tourism to Support Culture.* Paris: UNESCO.

Berry, B. J. L. 1967. *Geography of Market Centers and Retail Distribution.* Englewood Cliffs, New Jersey: Prentice Hall.

Bouzahzah, M., and El Menyari, Y. 2013. "The Relationship between International Tourism and Economic Growth: The Case of Morocco and Tunisia." *Munich Personal RePEc Archive.* http://mpra.ub.uni-muenchen.de/44102/

Chileshe, J. H. 1981. "Zambia." In Adedeji, A. (Ed.) *Indigenization of African Economies.* London: Hutchinson University Library for Africa in Collaboration with African Association of Public Administration and Management, pp. 81–132.

Christie, I., Fernandes, E., Masserli, H., and Twining-Ward, L. 2014. *Tourism in Africa: Harnessing Tourism for Growth and Improved Livelihoods.* Washington, DC: International Bank for Reconstruction and Development/The World Bank.

Corea, G. 1977. "UNCTAD and the New International Economic Order." *International Affairs* 53(2): 177–187.

Crowder, M. 1969. *West Africa under Colonial Rule.* London: Hutchinson.

Crush, J., Chikanda, A., and Maswika, B. 2012. *Patients without Borders: Medical Tourism and Medical Migration in Southern Africa.* Cape Town: Southern African Migration Programme (SAMP).

De Arriba, C. G. 2011. "From Hotel Accommodation to Residential Tourism in Morocco: Between Real Estate Business and Socio-spatial Remaking." *Cuadernos de Turismo* 27: 1091–1093.

Draper, P., Freytag, A., and Al Doyaili, S. 2013. "Why Should Sub-Saharan Africa care about the Doha Development Round?" *Economics: The Open-Access, Open-Assessment E-Journal* 7: 2013–2019. DOI:10.508/economics-ejournal.ja.2013-19.

Fontabong, E. 2014. "NEPAD Work on Sustainable Development." *Meeting of the Ministerial Working Group on the Tourism Sector Development Strategy for Africa: AU 2063.* Seychelles, March 13–14.

Gibbon, P., and Ponte, S. 2005. *Trading Down: Africa, Value Chains, and the Global Economy.* Philadelphia: Temple University Press.

Gray, M. 1998. "Economic Reform, Privatization, and Tourism in Egypt." *Middle Eastern Studies* 34(2): 91–112.

Grundlingh, A. 2006. "Revisiting the "old" South Africa: Excursions into South Africa's Tourist History under Apartheid, 1948–1990." *South African Historical Journal* 56: 103–122.

Gwin, C. B. 1977. "The Seventh Special Session: Towards a New Phase of Relations between Developed and Developing States." In Sauvant, K. P., and Hasenpflug, H. (Eds.) *The New International Economic Order: Confrontation or Cooperation between North and South?* Boulder, CO: Westview Press, pp. 97–117.

Hall, M., and Frost, W. 2009. "Introduction: The Making of National Parks Concept." In Frost, W., and Hall, C. M. (Eds.) *Tourism and National Parks: International Perspectives on Development, Histories and Change.* New York: Routledge, pp. 3–15.

Hanafi, M. N. 1981. "Egypt." In Adedeji, A. (Ed.) *Indigenization of African Economies.* London: Hutchinson University Library for Africa in Collaboration with African Association of Public Administration and Management, pp. 49–80.

Havi, E. D. K., and Enu, P. 2013. "The Impact of Tourism on Economic Performance in Ghana." *European Scientific Journal* 9(34): 242–257.

Henkleman, B. ND. "American Real Estate Firms' Failure to Buy-in to Morocco's Vision: Why American FDI in the Real Estate Sector will continue to Lag." Northwestern University: Kellogg School of Management.

Hughes, D. 2008. "Sun, Safaris, and Sex Tourism in Kenya." *ABC News,* October 7.

Issawi, C. P. 1982. *An Economic History of the Middle East and North Africa.* New York: Columbia University Press.

Jalloh, A. 1999. *African Entrepreneurship: Muslim Fula Merchants in Sierra Leone.* Athens, Ohio: Ohio University Press.

Kweka, J., Morrissey, O., and Blake, A. 2003. "The Economic Potential of Tourism in Tanzania." *Journal of International Development* 15: 335–351.

Lakhoua, C. 2012. "Medical Tourism Industry in Tunisia." *Paper presented at the Third EUNAM Meeting.* Hammamet, Tunisia, March 12–13.

Levine, A. M. 2005. "Film and Colonial Memory: La Croisiere Noire 1924–2004." In Hargreaves, A. (Ed.) *Memory, Empire, and Post colonialism: Legacies of French Colonialism.* Lanham, MD: Lexington Books, p. 81.

Lucas, J. 2013. "Orientalism and Imperialism in French West Africa. Considerations on Travel Literature, Colonial Tourism, and the Desert as 'Commodity' in Mauritania." In Sarmento, J., and Brito-Henriques, E. (Eds.) *Tourism in Global South: Heritages, Identities and Development.* Lisbon: Center for Geographical Studies, pp. 25–43.

Luvanga, N., and Shitundi, J. 2003. "The Role of Tourism in Poverty Alleviation in Tanzania." Dar es Salaam: University of Dar es Salaam Research Report No. 03.4.

Matlou, M. P. ND. *NEPAD Tourism Action Plan: Challenges and Opportunities for Africa and Turkey to Cooperate.*

Mbaiwa, J. E. 2001. "The Socio-economic and Environmental Impacts of Tourism Development on the Okavango Delta, Northwestern Botswana." *Journal of Arid Environments* 54: 447–467.

Miller, D., Nel, E., and Hampwaye, G. 2008. "Malls in Zambia: Racialised Retail Expansion and South African Foreign Investors in Zambia." *African Sociological Review* 12(1): 35–54.

Minta, I. K. 1984. "The Lome Convention and The New International Economic Order." *Howard Law Journal* 27: 953–974.

Mogombo, A., and Rogerson, C. M. 2012. "The Evolution of the Tourism Sector in Malawi." *Africa Insight* 42(2): 46–65.

Mshomba, R. E. 2009. *Africa and the World Trade Organization.* Cambridge: Cambridge University Press.

Nelson, F. 2010. "The Political Economy of Wildlife Management in East and Southern Africa." In Lead, D. R. (Ed.) *The Political Economy of Natural Resource Use: Lessons for Fisheries Reform.* Washington, DC: The International Bank for Reconstruction and Development/The World Bank, pp. 157–173.

Nesadurai, H. E. 2008. "Bandung and the Political Economy of North-South Relations: Sowing the Seeds for Re-visioning International Society." In Tan, S. S., and Acharya, A. (Eds.) *Bandung Revisited: The Legacy of the 1955 Asian-African Conference for International Order.* Singapore: National University of Singapore Press, pp. 68–104.

Ogbuagu, C. S. A. 1983. "The Nigerian Indigenization Policy: Nationalism or Pragmatism?" *African Affairs* 82(327): 241–266.

Ondicho, T. G. 2000. "International Tourism in Kenya: Development, Problems, and Challenges." *EASSRR* XVI(2): 49–69.

Owusu-Ansah, K. A. 1981. "Ghana." In Adedeji, A. (Ed.) *Indigenization of African Economies.* London: Hutchinson University Library for Africa in Collaboration with African Association of Public Administration and Management, pp. 132–163.

Panagariya, A. 2005. "Agricultural Liberalization and the Least Developed Countries: Six Fallacies." *The World Economy* 28(9): 1277–1299.

Pedler, F. 1974. *The Lion and the Unicorn: A History of the Origins of the United African Company 1787–1931.* London: Heinemann.

Poirier, R. A. 1995. "Tourism and Development in Tunisia." *Annals of Tourism Research* 22(1): 157–171.

Rogerson, C. M. 2004. "Adventure Tourism in Africa: The Case of Livingstone, Zambia." *Geography* 89(2): 183–188.

Ruedy, J. 2005. *Modern Algeria: The Origins and Development of a Nation.* Bloomington: Indiana University Press.

Sauvant, K. P. 1977. "Towards the New International Economic Order." In Sauvant, K. P., and Hasenpflug, H. (Eds.) *The New International Economic Order: Confrontation or Cooperation between North and South?* Boulder, CO: Westview Press, pp. 3–19.

St. Ange A. ND. *Growing Sustainable Tourism: The Seychelles Approach.*

Sharpley, R. 2009. "Tourism and Development Challenges in the Least Developed Countries: The Case of The Gambia." *Current Issues in Tourism* 12(4): 337–358.

Sissoko, M. M., Osuji, L. O., and Cheng, W. L. 1998. "Impact of the Yaounde and Alome Conventions on EC-ACP Trade." *The African Economic & Business Review* 1(1): 7–24.

Streeten, P. P. 1982. "The New International Economic Order." *International Review of Education* 28(4): 407–430.

Teye, V. B. 1986. "Liberation Wars and Tourism Development in Africa: The Case of Zambia." *Annals of Tourism Research* 13: 589–618.

Uche, C. U. 2012. "British Government, British Businesses, and the Indigenization Exercise in Post-Independence Nigeria." *Business History Review* 86: 745–771.

Uchegbu, S. N., and Kanu, E. J. ND. *The Impact of Climate Change on Tourism.*

UNCTAD. 2013. *Economic Development in Africa Report 2013: Intra-African Trade-Unlocking Private Sector Dynamism.* Geneva: United Nations.

UNCTAD. 2009. *Economic Development in Africa: Strengthening Regional Economic Integration for Africa's Development.* Geneva: United Nations Conference on Trade and Development.

UNCTAD. 2008. *Economic Development in Africa: Export Performance following Trade Liberalization: Some Patterns and Policy Perspectives.* Geneva: United Nations.

UNCTAD. 2003. *Economic Development in Africa: Trade Performance and Commodity Dependence.* New York and Geneva: United Nations.

UNCTAD/ALDC/. 2017. *Economic Development Report: Tourism for Transformative Inclusive Growth.* New York and Geneva: United Nations Publication.

UN World Tourism Organization (UNWTO). 2016. *Compendium of Tourism Statistics dataset [Electronic], UNWTO,* Madrid, data updated on 21/09/2016.

UNECA. 2013. *Building Trade Capacities for Africa's Transformation: A Critical Review of Aid for Trade.*

UNECA. 2011a. *Global Review of Aid for Trade 2011: Africa Case Stories.* Addis Ababa.

UNECA. 2011b. *Towards a Sustainable Tourism Industry in Eastern Africa: A Study on the Challenges and Opportunities for Tourism Development.*

UNESCO. 2004. *Tourism, Culture, and Development in West Africa.* Paris.

Van Der Laan, H. L. 1981. "Modern Transportation and the European Trading Firms in Colonial West Africa." *Cahiers d'Etudes Africaines* 21 (84): 547–575.

Ward, W. E. F., and White, L. W. 1971. *East Africa: A Century of Change.* London: George Allen & Unwin Ltd.

Wels, H. 2000. "A Reflection on Cultural Tourism in Africa: The Power of European Imagery." In Akama, J., and Sterry, P. (Eds.) *Cultural Tourism in Africa: Strategies for the New Millennium Proceedings of the ATLAS Africa International Conference December 2000.* Mombasa, Kenya, pp. 55–64.

Wild, V. 1992. "An Outline of African Business History in Colonial Zimbabwe." *Zambezia* XIX (1): 19–28.

World Travel and Tourism Council. 2015. *Economic Impact of Travel and Tourism 2015 Annual Update Summary.* London: WTTC.

World Travel and Tourism Council. 2014. *Travel and Tourism Economic Impact 2014 Africa.* London: WTTC.

CHAPTER 16

Education and Health Care

Education and health care are two other sectors of Africa's economy that are essential in two respects. The first is the ability of the two sectors to positively transform the physical and social well-being of Africa's most important resource—its people. The second is the two sectors' ability to provide employment. In this chapter, we examine the evolution and development of these sectors in Africa, their contemporary geographic characteristic and problems and issues associated with them. Besides the prereading assignments, the chapter is divided into two broad sections—the first section deals with education, and the second section deals with health sectors.

EDUCATION

"Do you have schools in Africa?" This is a question that I was asked years ago when I was in graduate college and had gone to talk to a community group. Given the role of education in a country's life, it is unconscionable for anyone to ask such a question, but this again talks about one of the images out there about Africa. This section is divided into three. The first section traces the evolution and development of Africa's education system. The second will discuss the geography of education system as it exists today, and the third will discuss the problems and issues facing the education system. Before we start a word about the data will be appropriate. Education statistics on Africa is very spotty. The leading source of data is the United Nations Education, Scientific, and Cultural Organization (UNESCO) Institute for Statistics (UIS). However, UIS relies on UNESCO member countries to report data on their educational indicators. Unfortunately, not every African country does this on a regular basis. The result is that the database has so many holes that it becomes very difficult to use, especially for purposes of comparison. The discussion in this section that is based on the above data source should therefore be interpreted with caution.

PREREADING ASSIGNMENTS

1. What pictures come to your mind when you think of education system in Africa?
2. How do you think this education system evolved?
3. What do you think are the main problems facing Africa's education system?
4. What mental pictures do you have about health care in Africa?
5. List any diseases that occur in Africa.
6. What do you think are the main problems facing Africa's health-care system?

Evolution and Development of Education in Africa

Precolonial Africa

Education was part of the socialization process in precolonial African societies. Various modes of instruction were used to educate young people as part of their growing up. These included learning by doing, observation, and demonstration. The instructors were parents, grandparents, siblings, and age groups, but there were also master teachers. While immediate family members helped in educating the young members of the family in the norms, beliefs, values and traditions of society, skill trades and other professions were taught by master tradesmen and women who were established in the various trades and professions, who had been trained by the generations before. These trades and professions covered a wide range of services that were needed by society and they included farming, fishing, manufacturing, medicine, administration, merchandise trading, building trades, tool making, pottery, wood works, hospitality, warfare, and story-telling.

As African societies became more organized into kingdoms and empires, the education system became more organized. The first of this organized system occurred in Ancient Egypt, where schools were established mostly for boys from wealthy families aged 9 and above. Initially, students were taught reading and writing, but as they grew older, they learned mathematics, medicine, geography, history, music, science, and ethics. Up in the Nile Valley, similar education institutions at the elementary to college levels developed in Axum, and subsequently in Ethiopia, most of which were located in monasteries (Lulat, 2005). This education system continued to evolve as North Africa came under the control of one external hegemonic power after another. One of those changes was the establishment of Bibliotheca Alexandrina, or the Museum and Library Complex of Alexandria in 288 BC during the Hellenistic period of Ancient Egypt. The Library Complex included both a place for worship, living quarters for scholars, lecture rooms, a school for the royalty, botanical gardens, a zoological park, an astronomy observatory, and a library (Lulat, 2005). With a mandate to acquire copies of all learning known to people at that time by all means, the library became a great center of learning attracting scholars from all over the world, who came there to pursue learning and acquire knowledge. Among its patrons were great scholars like Archimedes, the mathematician; Aristarchus, the astronomer; Eratosthenes, the geographer; Euclid, the mathematician; Herophilus, the physician; Masetho, the historian; Strabo, the geographer and historian; and Hypatia, the philosopher, astronomer, and mathematician. In the words of Lulat (2005, p. 50).

> The Bibliotheca Alexandrina was undoubtedly an institution of higher education, in fact one can go as far to say that it was among the world's earliest known prototype universities. It helped sustain a thriving publishing industry thereby assisting in the dissemination of knowledge that the library acquired and produced to the four corners of the ancient world. . . . the library was also indirectly responsible for helping to permanently preserve works that would have been lost forever.

The Arab conquest of North Africa from 640 AD brought Islamic education system to Africa. According to Lulat (2005), the Islamic education system consisted of four types of institutions. The first were the elementary schools or the *kuttab*, that were found in most mosques; the second were informal secondary schools or majlis; the third were formal secondary schools or the *halqas* that were located in principal or district mosques of large cities, and the fourth were the universities or the *madrasahs* that were either stand alone or attached to major urban mosques. At the elementary level, the curriculum focused on Arabic literacy and memorization of the Quran. The secondary level taught Arabic Language and Literature, Islamic Law, Theory and Logic, Quranic Exegesis, Traditions of Muhammed, and Islamic and Local History (Umar, 2001). The madrasahs offered more advanced, critical, and rigorous studies of the above. Astronomy, history, medicine, and mathematics were also taught, but these were often regarded as less important (Lulat, 2005). The Fatimid (Chapter 2) established the first madrasahs, the University of Al-Qarawiyyin in Fez, Morocco, the World's oldest university, in 859 AD, and the Al-Azhar University in Cairo, Egypt, between 970 and 972 AD. The rise of the Western Sudanese Empires of Ghana, Mali, and Songhai and the role Islamic religion and scholars played in the affairs of these empires brought Islamic education to West Africa. From about 13th to the 17th centuries, Timbuktu became the center of Islamic learning, with three universities, serving as a hub for scholars from the Islamic world and from West Africa (see Chapter 2). Islamic education declined in West Africa after the fall of the Songhai Empire, but it was restored by the Fulani Jihads of the 19th century West Africa and was introduced to East Africa by Arab traders.

The arrival of Europeans in Africa brought Western European education system to Africa. In 1644, the first school of this system was established in the Elmina Castle in the Gold Coast (Ghana) (Anonymous, ND). The school was established primarily for two reasons. The first was to educate the children that European merchants had fathered with African mothers, and the second was to train those children to take over the management of the trading posts because it was believed that they were better suited to the climatic and other environmental conditions (Anonymous, ND). Classes taught included Dutch, Dutch culture, and the Christian faith. In 1658, a school for African slaves captured from the Portuguese by the Dutch was established by the Dutch East India Company in the Cape region of South Africa. This was followed by a school for the children of the Cape colonists in 1663 and another one for slave children in 1685. In 1722, another castle school was opened in the Gold Coast in Christiansborg by the Danes. These castle and early schools did not get much help from their founders' respective governments, but they continued to operate and even sent some of their students for further studies in Europe. Thus, with the exception of South Africa, where education became state responsibility in 1785 in the Cape Colony, these schools ended when their founders departed from the African trade.

A major force in the establishment of Western education in Africa was Christian missionary activities. Christian missionaries had accompanied the explorers of Africa's coast, and in the Portuguese colonies of Angola and Mozambique, for example, Jesuits and Dominicans of the Roman Catholic Church had operated schools in the 16th and 17th centuries. However, it was in the 19th century that Christian missionary activity reached its peak in Africa. The catalyst was the formation of the Church Missionary Society (CMS) in London in 1799. Owing its foundation to the humanitarians that had pressed for abolition of slave trade in Britain, CMS embarked on evangelical mission to Africa beginning in 1804 in Guinea, West Africa. By the mid-19th century, they had opened missions across the continent—Sierra Leone (1816), Egypt (1825), Ethiopia (1827), Nigeria (1844), East Africa (1844), Mauritius (1854), and Madagascar (1863). More denomination-based missions—the Wesleyan,

Presbyterian, Lutheran, Roman Catholic, and Episcopalian—also followed operating in various parts of the continent.

Two main factors precipitated the need for these missions to establish schools. The first was the death rate among the early missionaries that was quite high, so it was thought that it would be more prudent to train African clergy to take over the work of evangelizing their own people. The second, and especially among the protestants, was to enable the African to read (the Bible) and write. A major expansion in elementary and secondary education occurred due to competition among the various missions.

In Egypt, however, Mohamed Ali's desire for people to run his western-style bureaucracy led him to make education a state responsibility and establish a western-style education system. A major reform began with higher education and the focus especially was on Al-Azhar University and its curriculum, moving it away from a typical madrassah to a more secular institution (Sayed, 2006).

By the eve of the official colonial period, a large network of elementary and secondary schools and a much smaller network of vocational and technical schools had been established across the continent, all of them run by missionaries with the exception of Egypt and South Africa, where mission schools existed side by side with state-sponsored schools. In addition, a small number of new colleges and universities had been established, especially in the European settlements and supported enclaves. Among these were Fourah Bay College in Freetown, Sierra Leone (1826); South African College at Cape Town (1829); Victoria College at Stellenbosch, South Africa (1829); Lovedale Institution in South Africa (1841); the University of Cape of Good Hope, South Africa (1873); and the Superior School of Medicine-Pharmacy at Algiers, Algeria (1879) (Lulat, 2005).

Colonial Africa

With the exception of the enclaves of significant European settlements such as South Africa, Algeria, and coastal Senegal, colonial governments had minimal role in education initially due to the dominance of mission schools. Besides, colonial governments were at odds with Christian missions about education. The missionaries wanted to protect their schools from government intervention, while the colonial governments did not like the biblical and evangelical focus of the mission schools. However, the situation changed because the missionaries needed the protection of colonial governments from unfriendly Africans, and colonial governments needed the missionaries to educate Africans in Western culture and become obedient to colonial rule.

Colonial governments' responses to education varied directly with their colonial philosophies. The British adopted a more liberal position accepting both Protestants and Roman Catholic missions, while the French and Portuguese were more supportive of Roman Catholic Missions. The French, however, transferred more control from missionaries to the state (Clignet and Forster, 1964). At any rate, mission schools continued to expand in all the colonies with a great deal of help from the Africans, who became the majority of the teachers in the schools (Frankema, 2012).

A catalyst for change in colonial education came in the 1920s, when the American Baptist Foreign Missionary Society asked the Trustees of the Phelps-Stokes Fund in the United States to conduct a study of education in Africa to help them determine how it might use its resources. The Fund authorized a Commission of experts from the United States, Britain, and the Gold Coast (Ghana) to evaluate the state of education in Africa. After an extensive tour of the continent, the Commission issued a two-volume report: *Education in Africa: A Study of West, South and Equatorial Africa* published in 1921, and *Education in East Africa: A Study of East, Central and South Africa* published in 1924. The report was critical of the education system in Africa. First, education policies were inadequate and not relevant to the needs of Africa. Second, education did not address the full development of the African native— either it was too much passing on of information or it was too much interested in teaching people to read the Bible and understand Christianity. Third, the curriculum was dominated by foreign content to the detriment of local content. These problems varied across the continent with the worst situations being identified in the Portuguese colonies. The Commission emphasized adaptation of education to the needs of Africa as well as organization and supervision. To this end, the Commission made recommendations covering all aspects of education including curriculum, buildings, organization, and supervision (Jones, 1921, 1925; Lewis, 1962).

The Commission's impact on education in Africa was significant, especially in the British colonies. The British government established an Advisory Committee on Education in the Colonies in 1923. Among other things the Committee recommended that the colonial government should (1) supplement the mission schools instead of competing with them; (2) extend literacy to as many people as allowed by financial resources; (3) train low-level government officials—clerical workers, interpreters; (4) emphasize vocational and technical training opportunities; and (5) allow some higher education training for such professionals as teachers, agriculturalist, and health workers. Implementation of this report led to establishment of Makerere Technical School in Uganda in 1922; Achimota College in Ghana in 1924; Kitchener Memorial School of Medicine in Sudan in 1924; Government College at Ibadan, Nigeria, in 1929; and the Higher College at Yaba, Nigeria, in 1934 (Lulat, 2005).

From the establishment of this first wave of higher education institutions through the end of the World War II in 1945, the question of higher education in British colonies became the subject of several commissions partly because of differences of opinion between colonialists and the small African elite as to the type of higher education Africa needed. Collectively, these Commissions recommended upgrading of existing colleges of higher education to universities through affiliation with British universities and incorporation of research into the college curriculum (Lulat, 2005). These recommendations led to the establishment of the University College of Ibadan, Nigeria, in 1947; University College of Gold Coast in 1948; Khartoum University College, Sudan, in 1949; Makerere University College, Uganda, in 1949; Royal Technical College in Nairobi, Kenya, in 1951; and University College of Salisbury (Zimbabwe) in 1953. All these were affiliated with the University of London, which awarded the degrees and diplomas to students in those institutions.

In the Portuguese colonies, the Colonial Act of 1930 was a turning point in how Portugal treated its African colonies. It placed all colonies directly under the Overseas Ministry of the central government in Lisbon. In addition, it created two classes of people—the indigenous group consisting of native Africans and the nonindigenous group consisting of whites, *mesticos* (mixed race), and *assimilados* (natives that become qualified as Portuguese citizens) (Fine, 2007). The Missionary Statute of 1941 entrusted the direction of elementary, secondary, and professional schools (mainly teacher training) for European and African children to the Catholic Mission, but after 1941, much of the education for Africans fell to the Catholic mission (Duffy, 1961). A two-tier school system, one for Europeans and *assimilados* and the other for Africans was established. The European system was a duplication of the system in Portugal, while the African system was mainly for indoctrination into the Portuguese world (Duffy, 1961). However, for a number of reasons, including poor quality of education, little access to government schools, and inability to afford the alternative mission schools, most of the African children dropped out of the education system. A few high schools were established, but they were for the European children and the *assimilados*, and they were found only in the cities. No efforts were made to establish universities, until 1962 when the General University Studies of both Angola and Mozambique were established. Until that time, the very few Africans who could qualify for university education had to go to Portugal (Langa, 2013).

In the French colonies, a decree passed in 1922 required government permission, government-certified teachers, government curriculum, and the use of French as a language of instruction for new schools (White, 1996). From then on, the education system became more centrally controlled compared to the missionary education system. Enrollment restrictions were also instituted to avoid unemployment of educated youth. Finally, a two-tier system of primary education was established—an European system aimed at training Europeans and a few African elites for the lower positions in the public service, and an African system aimed at educating the masses (White, 1996). In addition, there were three types of primary schools—village schools predominantly for Africans; regional schools, which were transitional; and urban schools for Europeans. Two developments of note were a Conference on African Education in Brazzaville in 1944 and the Commission on the Modernization of Overseas Territories' report in 1948. The Brazzaville Conference recommended expansion of education, use of French language, and recruitment of more African teachers, while the 1948 report elaborated the need for higher education in the overseas territories and a policy of bringing people from the territories to France to pursue higher education (White, 1996).

In contrast, education in Belgian colonies relied solely on the mission schools until 1954, when a secular school system was established in Belgian Congo (Bigawa, 2014; Yimam, 1990). Similarly, in the Spanish colonies, education of Africans was not a priority. As a result, missionary schools that were only interested in teaching reading and writing in Spanish and converting Africans to Christianity dominated the education system. It was only at the end of the colonial period—1959 that an effort was made by the colonial government to send young high school graduates to Spain for university education (Njlale, 2014).

So, by the eve of independence, Western European system of education had been introduced into every part of Africa. However, the quality of education was still contentious. Africans felt that the quality of education was both inferior and inappropriate in the sense that the content of education alienated the educated Africans from their societies and cultures. In contrast, colonial powers believed that Africans could not achieve the same level of education as Europeans. There was also the problem of quantity. Only a small proportion of African children were enrolled in the colonial education system. In Morocco, for example, only 13% of primary school age and 2.3% of secondary school age children attended school (Segalla, 2009). In Algeria, only 30% of secondary school and 10% of university students were Algerian (Metz, 1994). Indeed, the majority of African countries did not have university graduates at the time of independence. These were some of the challenges of the education system as African countries transitioned from colonies to independent sovereign countries.

Postcolonial Africa

The postcolonial period saw the greatest expansion of Western form of education at all levels—primary, secondary, and tertiary as African countries took the challenges of colonial education head-on (see Chapter 3). Yimam (1990) provides an excellent summary of how this major project was accomplished, and it all began with an historic meeting of African Ministers of Education at the Conference of African States on the Development of Education in Africa held in 1961 in Addis Ababa, Ethiopia.

The Addis Ababa Conference of 1961 The Conference was cosponsored by UNESCO and the United Nations Economic Commission for Africa (UNECA). The main charge was to "prepare an outline of educational plan that would provide economic growth and social progress in African countries" (Yimam, 1990). The Conference deliberated on a wide range of educational issues but the most important were (1) education that was relevant to the sociocultural factors of African countries, (2) a needs assessment of education for economic and social development, and (3) what it would take to deliver such an education. The conference made recommendations covering various areas of education including objectives, financing, planning, curricular changes, adult education, and the relationship between education and economies (UNESCO, 1961; Yimam, 1990). It also identified and set strategic targets for expansion of education in Africa from 1961 to 1980. Among these targets were (1) universal, free, and compulsory primary education; (2) thirty percent of the students completing primary education would be admitted to secondary schools; (3) twenty-three percent of the students completing secondary education would be admitted to higher education (UNESCO, 1961; Yimam, 1990). Subsequent meetings were held in 1962, 1968, and 1976 to review the progress being made, identify areas of challenges, and how best to address them. The 1962 conference encouraged member states to strengthen educational planning institutions, integrate educational plans into national development plans, improve and expand teacher training at primary and secondary education levels, relate curriculum to the environment, expand adult education, explore the use of mother tongue in instruction, and request aid from UNESCO (UNESCO, 1963).

Massive emphasis was placed on universal primary education and the need to train more teachers. However, the need for educated Africans to help fill administrative and technical positions tilted attention toward secondary and higher education. African governments supported education with full scholarships and sent their young scholars abroad for further studies, while expanding higher education at home to fulfill those functions in the future. As indicated in Chapter 3, expansion of higher education was rapid in most countries, especially in Nigeria, Ethiopia, and Egypt. The World Bank (1988) reported that between 1960 and 1983, the enrollment in Africa's educational institutions at all levels grew dramatically to 63 million. Enrollment grew at an annual rate of 6.5% from 1960 to 1970, and 8.9% from the 1970s to 1980s, while the general enrollment ratio (GER) of primary education went from 36% in 1960 to 75% in 1983. In 1983, students in tertiary education increased from 21,000 to 437,000.

However, there were some African countries such as Equatorial Guinea, where as a result of the rise of dictatorship of personal cult in the person of Francisco Macias Nguema, education generally deteriorated. In fact, education was seen as a threat to the stability of the dictatorship so rapid expansion was curbed and existing teacher education institutions were even closed in 1971 (Njlale, 2014).

Structural adjustment programs and the World Bank's education for Africa The economic crisis of the late 1970s and 1980s that has been mentioned several times in previous chapters, affected Africa's education system as well, leading to either a slow-down or complete halt of the expansion in education in many countries. The World Bank (1988) reported that public spending on education fell from $10 billion in 1980 to $8.9 billion in 1980–1983. Similarly, enrollment growth fell from 8.9% during 1970–1980 to 4.2% from 1980 to 1983, while primary enrollment rate dropped from 8.4% in 1970–1980 to 2.9% in the early 1980s. This was also the period when the majority of African countries were experiencing high population growth rates. Responding to these issues, the World Bank (1988) offered a three-pronged policy framework, which included adjustment, revitalization, and selective expansion, to countries in sub-Saharan Africa. For adjustment, the bank recommended diversification of funding sources and containing unit cost. This meant African governments had to pass on more of the cost of education to students, especially at the higher education level. For revitalization, the Bank recommended renewed commitment to academic standards, restoration of necessary input and material for schools such as textbooks. For selective expansion, the Bank recommended renewed commitment of universal primary education, distance education programs, training, and research and postgraduate education. African countries were invited to formulate national education policies within these broad guidelines.

SAPs impacted Africa's education system in several ways. First, the devaluation of national currencies led to rising cost of school supplies given that the majority of the countries that implemented SAPs imported those items. Second, teachers' salaries lost value and in some cases governments struggled to make payroll. The reduction in government spending meant reduction in the proportion of government expenditure that was allocated to education. This meant less funds per capita for students, and less support for physical infrastructure. Third, enrollments and completion rates dropped in the primary and secondary level education as governments tried to pass on the cost to students, but this helped higher education enrollment to go up (Babalola et al., 1999).

The 1990 World Conference on Education for All (EFA)—Jomtien The World Conference on Education for All (WCEA) came about, when the executive heads of the United Nations Children Fund (UNICEF), United Nations Development Program (UNDP), UNESCO, and the World Bank decided to organize a world conference in 1989 to "launch a renewed worldwide initiative to meet the basic learning needs of all children, youth and adults, and to reverse the serious decline in basic education services observed in many countries during recent years" (UNDP et al., 1990, p. 1). Specifically, the conference had three main objectives:

> (1) To highlight the importance and impact of basic education, and renew commitment to make it available to all; (2) To forge a global consensus on a framework for action to meet the basic learning needs of children, youth and adults; (3) To provide a forum for sharing experiences and research results to invigorate ongoing and planned programs. (UNDP et al., 1990, p. 2)

The original four sponsors were joined by 18 other governments and nongovernmental agencies from developed countries. The conference met at Jomtien, Thailand, from March 5 to March 9, 1990. The conference established six goals and adopted a framework of action to guide individual countries and their supporters to formulate their own plans of actions to implement the goals. The goals were to (1) expand and improve early childhood care and education, especially for the most vulnerable children; (2) ensure that by 2015, all children, particularly girls and the disadvantaged, have access to quality, free, and compulsory primary education; (3) eliminate gender disparities in primary and secondary education by 2005, and achieving gender equality in education by 2015; (4) ensure that the learning needs of all young people and adults are met through equitable access to appropriate learning and life skills programs; (5) achieve a 50% improvement in levels of adult literacy by 2015, especially for women, and offer equitable access to basic and continuing education to all adults; and (6) improve all aspects of the quality of education and ensure excellence. The framework also suggested two phases of implementation—the first phase from 1990 to 1995 and the second phase from 1996 to 2000. However, no agreed monitoring system was set up, and the implementation of the framework was all tentative (King, 2015).

African countries embarked on various programs of their own to achieve the goals set by the EFA conference in Jomtien. However, by the end of the 1999, only about 65% of children at school-going age were enrolled (Munene, 2015), and when it became clear that the EFA goals were not going to be met, another international conference on education was convened in Dakar, Senegal.

The Dakar EFA Conference—2000 and the Millennial Development Goals (MDG) The Dakar conference adopted the Dakar Framework for Action, which reaffirmed commitment to achieving the EFA goals by 2015, but with particular emphasis on education of girls (UNICEF, 2012). After the conference, the United Nations added the conference's Goal 2—Universal Primary Education and Goal 3—Gender Equality in Education by 2015 to its educational Millennium Development Goals.

Recent evaluation of EFA goals showed that no country in Africa reached all the EFA's global educational goals. Eleven countries achieved 80% or more enrollment for Goal 1, early childhood care and education. Seven countries achieved Goal 2 which is universal primary enrollment. For Goal 4, which required 50% reduction in adult literacy, only seven countries reached the goal. For Goal 5—gender parity, the report indicated that 25 countries achieved the goal in primary education but on the whole girls were still at a disadvantage compared with boys. For Goal 6—improved quality of education, the result was inconclusive since many children spend two or three years in primary school without acquiring reading and writing skills (Rose, 2014; EFA Global Monitoring Report, 2015).

A crucial shortcoming of the Dakar Declaration was financing. The Declaration contained a phrase that stated no country seriously committed to achieving the goals of EFA would be hampered by lack of resources. However, the Global Monitoring Report of 2015 indicated that donors failed to live up to their promises.

The Incheon World Education Forum—2015 In May 2015, the World Education Forum convened again in Incheon, South Korea, to extend the EFA goals through 2030. The declaration focused on important themes of inclusion, equity, gender equality, quality of education, and life-long leaning opportunities for all. To implement these goals, the declaration called on individual governments and nongovernmental agencies to collaborate. Already there are concerns about the implementation and financing of these new goals, but how these will turn out by 2030 is too soon to tell.

The crises in higher education While African governments and their donor supporters turned their attention to basic education, higher education in Africa was going through crises (Sawyer, ND). These crises were long in coming and had both internal and external underpinnings. Internally, African governments believed that higher education was so vital to the economic development of their countries that they should fully support higher education institutions. Unfortunately, this idea became unsustainable because of the severe economic downturn and the growing young population that demanded more education. In addition, political instability in majority of the countries and prolonged civil wars in a few others added to the problem. In particular, the impact of military dictatorships that dominated the majority of African countries on Africa's higher education system was mixed. In Nigeria and Ethiopia, for example, the military governments expanded higher education institutions without adequate funds. In Nigeria, most of them were polytechnic institutes that were ill-equipped to become universities. In other cases, authoritarian and military governments were too much concerned with their own security that the universities became one of the "enemies" of the state leading to their extensive closures. Externally, the collapse of the Soviet Union and socialism as an alternative vision of social development and the triumph of capitalism and neoliberal ideas that preached liberalization and limited government intervention in socioeconomic development forced African governments to cut back on their support for higher education during the structural adjustment period.

The results of these on the universities were devastating. Universities that were established for less than 5,000 students found themselves with student population that were four to five times the original size in most cases with the same physical infrastructure. Dormitories and classes became overcrowded, with very high student–teacher ratios. Library resources and use of modern technologies in the classrooms lagged behind. Faculty salaries stagnated, and in some cases were not paid causing a decline in morale. Frustrated, many of them left the continent, while those who stayed behind took up part-time teaching jobs in private colleges or other commercial ventures to supplement their income. Under these circumstances, research and scholarly productivity dwindled. In countries with more fragile economies such as Eritrea, the University of Asmara founded in 1991 closed down in 2002 to be replaced by a number of discipline-specific colleges (Rena, 2014). As universities struggled to survive these crises a number of measures were introduced, which in turn created their own new problems. For example, the introduction of tuition fee payments has brought more resources to the universities and helped to address many of the issues raised above, but it has also limited accessibility to only those students who could afford.

The resurgence of private education institutions

As we have already seen, Africa's education system was initiated by the private sector. However, during the latter part of the colonial period and especially in the first three decades of the postcolonial period, governments took central role of providing education to the people. However, the economic crisis in Africa over the last two decades of the 20th century paved the way for private sector to again enter the education provision sector. In addition to the speed with which this occurred, what was remarkable about this resurgence was that the private sector did not stop just at the pre-university, technical, and commercial schools as before. It entered the university sector. Thus, for the first time in the history of education in the majority of African countries private universities, most of them affiliated with African religious organizations— Christian and Islamic—appeared on the scene. This led to second wave of university growth in the postcolonial period. Today, private schools feature very prominently in the education systems of many African countries. In CAR, for example, the percentage of primary school enrollment in private schools went from 2% in 1998/1999 to 10% in 2004/2005 (Lambert and Wolhuter, 2014). In Congo Republic, Nordman and Kuepie (2014) report that private schools account for 35% of primary enrollment, 34% and 38% of first and second cycle secondary schools, respectively, in 2009. In Djibouti, they account for 15% of total enrollment and 34% of all secondary school enrollment (Tsehaye, 2014). In the former Portuguese colonies of Cape Verde, Guinea-Bissau, and Sao Tome and Principe, there are even more private universities than public universities (Langa, 2013). Rose (2014) also reports similar trends in North Africa. In Egypt, private schools account for the education of 7.7% of primary school children and 5.5% of secondary school students. In Morocco, they account for 91.6% of preschool education, 11.8% of primary, 6.6% of middle, 7.7% of secondary, and 7.8% of higher education students. Given the broad outlines of the evolution and development of education systems in Africa, we will now examine the geography of Africa's contemporary education system and some of the problems and issues facing the system.

Africa's Education System

Contemporary education in Africa consists of the same two broad systems—the traditional indigenous or informal and the formal system. Our discussion in this section will be limited to the formal education system, which like education systems elsewhere falls into the three usual levels of primary, secondary, and tertiary education.

Primary Education

As already pointed out, primary education in Africa varies across the continent in terms of length and structures. For the majority of countries, it is a six-year duration, for another nine countries, it is seven years, while in another three, it is five years (Table 16.1). The basic philosophy is universal and free. However, the implementation of this philosophy varies across the continent. Within each country, there is a wide variation in the physical and human resources. School buildings vary from standard brick buildings that are well designed and well equipped with modern facilities to the under-tree-shade, lacking the minimum facility that can make learning possible. However, the single most important variation is between rural and urban areas. Thus, rural schools are more likely to have inadequate physical structures and facilities than urban schools. The same goes for distribution of human resources and the performance of students. In Burundi, for example, the pupil–teacher ratio varies from 32 in Bujumbura City to 72 in Muyinga Province (Rwantabagu, 2014). In urban areas, however, the variation is along socioeconomic status. Thus, schools in

TABLE **16.1**

Expected Years of Primary, Secondary, and Post-secondary Nontertiary Education in African Countries, 2015

Country	Primary education	Secondary education	Post-secondary nontertiary
Algeria	5	7	..
Angola	6	6	..
Benin	6	7	2
Botswana	7	5	1
Burkina Faso	6	7	1
Burundi	6	7	..
Cameroon	6	7	2
Cape Verde	6	6	1
Central African Republic	6	7	..
Chad	6	7	1
Comoros	6	7	2
Congo	6	7	..
Côte d'Ivoire	6	7	2
DRC	6	6	..
Djibouti	5	7	2
Egypt	6	6	2
Equatorial Guinea	6	6	..

(Continued)

TABLE **16.1**

Expected Years of Primary, Secondary, and Post-secondary Nontertiary Education in African Countries (*Continued*)

Country	Primary education	Secondary education	Post-secondary nontertiary
Eritrea	5	7	1
Ethiopia	6	6	1
Gabon	5	7	1
Gambia	6	6	1
Ghana	6	6	2
Guinea	6	6	..
Guinea-Bissau	6	7	2
Kenya	6	6	2
Lesotho	7	6	1
Liberia	6	5	3
Libya	6	6	3
Madagascar	5	6	2
Malawi	6	7	2
Mali	6	6	2
Mauritania	6	6	..
Mauritius	6	7	2
Morocco	6	7	2
Mozambique	7	6	..
Namibia	7	5	2
Niger	6	5	1
Nigeria	6	7	2
Rwanda	6	6	..
Sao Tome and Principe	6	6	..
Senegal	6	6	1
Seychelles	6	7	3
Sierra Leone	6	7	3
Somalia	6	7	..
South Africa	7	6	2
South Sudan	6	5	3
Sudan	6	6	..
Tanzania	7	7	2
Togo	6	5	1
Tunisia	6	5	2
Uganda	7	7	..
Western Sahara	..	8	..
Zambia	7	6	..
Zimbabwe	7	6	2

Source: UNESCO-UIS.

middle-class and better neighborhoods tend to have better physical infrastructure than schools in low-income neighborhoods. In the case of the latter, some schools have either the same resources as rural schools or even less.

In general, there are two or three types of primary schools in African countries—they are the religious, public, and private. The religious schools take after the schools established by both Christian and Islamic missions. The public schools are the schools that were established by the governments with public funds, while the private schools were established with private funds most of which were during the wave of private institutions. Most of the latter have the word "international" or "preparatory" in their names. There is a general belief that these international schools are of better quality than most of the public schools and therefore in both urban and rural areas, parents prefer sending their children to international schools if they can afford it. Curriculum varies but they focus on basic education—reading, writing, elementary science, and social studies.

Secondary Education

Like primary education, secondary education in most African countries may be broadly classified into two—general secondary education and technical and vocational education.

The general secondary education The general secondary education prepares students primarily for tertiary education, namely, polytechnics and universities. Depending upon the country, they may also prepare students for teacher and other forms of technical education. Generally speaking, they range from six- to seven-year duration (Table 16.1), The schools are commonly divided into junior or lower secondary schools and senior or upper secondary schools. Transfer between the two is by successfully passing of a standardized test that is administered by governmental agencies of education. A smaller segment of secondary schools is the secondary technical schools, which combine some technical education with the normal secondary school curriculum. The technical curriculum usually includes technical drawing and draughtsmanship. Institutions providing secondary education are varied in their ownership and include public, private nonsecular, and private secular schools.

As with primary education, there is a sense that the quality of education in these schools vary with the type of school—specifically the oldest secondary schools established by Christian missions and governments during the colonial and in the early post-independence era are considered to offer better education than the rest of the schools, especially those established in rural areas. In addition to these top-tier high schools, private high schools, which offer international baccalaureate programs, are also held in higher esteem by parents and students than the other schools in the system. Such schools are therefore very popular with parents who want to give their children a leg up to pursue further studies overseas.

From their earliest histories, most of the high schools were also boarding schools because they were established in colonial enclaves. It was necessary therefore for the few African students who could be admitted into the schools to leave their homes to attend the schools. This tradition has continued in the post-independence era in many countries. The result is that most of the secondary schools provide full boarding facilities for all students.

Technical and vocational education Technical and vocational education is the "Cinderella" of the Africa's education system. It is crucial yet it is the least developed, understood, and appreciated education subsector. As a result of overemphasis on reading, writing, and arithmetic and the dire need for personnel in the civil service in the early post-independence period, vocational and technical education was not regarded as important. Thus, with the exception of a handful of polytechnic institutes, technical and vocational education were left to the private sector, which in the majority of African countries was financially weak and inexperienced in establishing and managing such institutes. As a result, most of the vocational and technical institutes were poorly equipped and did not have the training rigor to produce the badly needed middle-level skilled workers for economic development. This lack of recognition and investment gave vocational and technical institutions the unfortunate reputation as a haven for the intellectually weak and a last resort for high school dropouts. Similarly, vocational schools were seen as schools for young girls and women. The irony is that this deprived Africa of the very skills that were needed to stem off what would later become a massive youth unemployment problem.

In recent years, African governments and their donor supporters have emphasized technical and vocational education, especially as a way to address the youth unemployment problem. These have led to establishment of secondary technical schools, polytechnic institutes, commercial schools, and many compressed programs aimed at job creation even for university graduates and other unemployed youth, However, it will take a while to break the old notions about vocational and technical education.

Tertiary Education

Tertiary education consists of teacher training colleges, polytechnic institutes, and universities.

Teacher education Teacher education has gone through major transitions as Africa's need for teachers has changed. In the early post-independence era, because of the urgent need for teachers, African countries implemented fast track programs for teacher training. In most countries, these teachers had only primary and secondary school education. This was followed by establishment of two-year and four-year teacher training colleges. Overtime post-secondary teacher training colleges were established for high school graduates who wanted to be primary school teachers. In some countries, specialist teacher training colleges were also established for advanced training in specific fields—social sciences, humanities, and technical fields for secondary school and teacher training colleges. The final evolution in teacher education is universities that are devoted for teacher education for secondary schools. As we will see later, there is a big gap between the number of teachers Africa needs and what it can actually train. The result is a very high pupil–teacher ratio in African schools. The situation is even worse when it comes to teachers for technical and vocational education. In-service training was part of the function of Ministries of Education in African countries and was a way to provide quick and easy upgrade for teachers. However, due to dwindling resources, this important component of teacher training has dropped by the wayside.

Polytechnics and universities Polytechnics or polytechnical institutes are mostly post-secondary institutions that offer two- to four-year degrees in a wide range of technical, scientific, and applied mathematical fields as well as commercial trades. Most of them are government or publicly owned. Most of them also have the same problems as the vocational and technical education institutes. Thus, they are considered as second best institutions to universities. Only people who were not able to gain admission or could not afford university education go to these institutes. Some countries have moved to address this problem by making it possible for polytechnic graduates to pursue baccalaureate degrees in universities.

Universities occupy the top hierarchy of Africa's tertiary education system. As already mentioned, these saw their biggest expansion in the postcolonial period. For a long time in many countries, these were all public institutions. However, due to population growth and increasing demand for higher education and liberalization policies, private universities began to grow in many African countries. These consist of two main types—private entrepreneurs and church-affiliated universities. Majority of these private universities, however, offer a limited range of programs, the most popular being business administration. In contrast, Africa's public universities, especially the very large ones, offer a wide range of programs at both undergraduate and graduate levels in many fields including humanities, fine art, social sciences, mathematics and physical sciences, engineering, education, law, and medicine. African universities have changed in many respects. Majority of them started small and that made it possible for every student to be resident on the campus. However, with the growth in demand and facilities lagging behind, many students have become nonresidential. This situation became serious during the crisis that was discussed earlier and even though private universities have stepped to ease the pressure, many universities have not recovered fully from the overcrowding and limited physical infrastructure.

Educational Attainment and Participation

Education attainment refers to the level of education completed by a country's population while **education participation** refers to enrollment trends and patterns in educational institutions of country. Education attainment is usually measured by the percentage of a population that has completed primary, secondary, and tertiary education, while education participation is measured by enrollment, enrollment distribution and enrollment ratios.

Educational attainment Education attainment in 27 countries that reported the data is given in Table 16.2. The data were reported in different years, so it is difficult making any general comparisons. However, we can observe that majority of the countries had substantial segments of their population aged 25 years and above with no schooling. In particular, if the data are accurate, then Burkina Faso's 81% of its people 25 years of age in 2014, Mali's 77.9% in 2015, Ethiopia's 75.2% in 2011, and Senegal's 66% in 2013 raise a lot of concerns about the effectiveness of all the education policies and efforts in those countries since independence. In contrast, the Table shows a number of countries that have relatively smaller proportion of their population with no schooling. These include Mauritius (6.6%) in 2011, South Africa (6.1%) in 2014, Zambia (0.2%) in 2010, and Zimbabwe (0.7) in 2012. Primary education appears to be the highest education attainment in the majority of the countries, with the exception of Algeria, DRC, Ghana, South Africa, and Zimbabwe. In each of these countries, the percentage of the population with lower secondary school education was higher. However, only Algeria, DRC, Mauritius, and South Africa had a higher percentage of people with upper secondary school education compared to primary education. With respect to tertiary education, only two countries had 10% or more of their population attaining bachelor degrees—Tunisia (12.3%) and Zambia (14.5%).

TABLE 16.2

Education Attainment in African Countries Reporting Data in Various Years

Country	Year	Population 25 years and older (000)			No schooling (%)			Primary education (%)			Lower SS*	Upper SS	Bachelor	Not known
		MF	M	F	MF	M	F	MF	M	F	MF	MF	MF	MF
Algeria	2008	17,611	8,803	8,808	35.4	26.3	44.5	16.9	18.3	15.5	21.7	17.3	8.0	0.7
Benin	2002	2,631	1,261	1,371	69.6	57.1	80.3	16.0	21.6	11.3	5.7	12.2	2.2	-
Burkina Faso	2014	6,037	2,878	3,159	81.7	75.1	87.2	9.8	13.4	6.8		2.8	-	-
Cameroon	2010	7,393	3,649	3,744	39.1	28.1	49.4	0.1	0.1	0.0	18.1	4.7	1.4	0.0
Chad	2004	3,077	1,507	1,570	77.7	68.9	85.4	3.0	4.4	1.8		2.3	3.2	0.2
DRC	2013	24,903	12,192	12,711	18.3	7.7	27.8	14.3	14.9	13.8	22.6	14.4	1.7	0.2
Ethiopia	2011	32,047	15,638	16,409	75.2	62.4	85.7	12.1	19.0	6.4	3.7	2.9	1.1	-
Ghana	2010	9,895	4,706	5,189	35.3	26.6	43.0	10.4	8.7	11.8	33.8	9.2	3.1	-
Kenya	2010	14,738	7,298	7,440	26.0	27.0	24.9	21.5	21.6	21.5	6.9	13.9	-	1.7
Lesotho	2008	756	350	405	15.7	24.7	7.6	20.1	14.3	25.3	7.1	8.5	1.9	-
Malawi	1998	3,514	1,716	1,798	42.9	30.2	55.3	11.2	15.8	6.8	3.4	4.7	0.5	-
Mali	2015	5,853	2,892	2,961	77.9	71.3	83.9	10.5	12.5	8.7	5.5	4.0	1.7	-
Mauritius	2011	785	383	401	6.6	3.2	9.8	12.6	11.7	13.4	10.5	30.5	5.2	1.2
Mozambique	2011	8,691	4,000	4,691	30.1	22.2	35.2	5.4	9.4	2.8	8.0	2.4	1.7	15.2
Namibia	2001	759	361	397	22.9	21.8	23.8	20.9	20.0	21.6	10.6	11.7	2.2	3.0
Rwanda	2012	4,086	1,820	2,266	31.0	24.0	37.1	18.4	20.1	16.9	3.7	4.7	1.8	2.8
Sao Tome & Principe	2012	66	32	34	11.6	5.6	17.4	47.7	46.5	48.8		34.5	3.2	3.0
Senegal	2013	5,162	2,406	2,756	66.0	59.9	71.6	13.5	14.9	12.1	5.7	4.0	1.2	0.0
Seychelles	2002	46	22	23	5.6	5.6	5.6	23.5	22.3	24.7	22.6		7.4	4.1
South Africa	2014	27,452	12,872	14,580	6.1	4.5	7.5	5.1	4.8	5.4	12.1	48.5	6.2	2.2
South Sudan	2008	3,362	1,651	1,711	29.6	25.0	39.4	29.6	30.8	27.0	18.5	4.2	2.9	1.0
Togo	2011	2,442	1,171	1,271	48.7	32.7	60.9	12.1	15.5	9.6	9.0	3.8	5.4	0.2
Tunisia	2012	6,457	3,132	3,326	25.3	14.8	35.3	34.9	38.6	31.3		27.5	12.3	0.1
Uganda	2012	11,025	5,424	5,601	24.2	13.3	33.7	8.3	10.0	6.9	13.9	1.7	1.7	1.6
Tanzania	2012	17,258	8,487	8,771	25.8	18.6	32.3	53.8	57.5	50.4	7.6	0.8	1.9	-
Zambia	2010	4,587	2,256	2,331	0.4	0.2	0.5	47.8	39.7	56.9	20.2	17.1	14.5	-
Zimbabwe	2012	5,283	2,557	2,726	0.7	0.4	0.9	18.3	17.0	19.4	49.7	2.4	3.1	9.1

M = Male; F = Female; MF = Both Male and Female; SS = Secondary School.

Source: UNESCO-UIS

Participation The number of students enrolled in primary and secondary schools of African countries reporting data to the UIS database are shown in Table 16.3, which shows that for most of the countries, the number of children enrolled in primary schools has been growing since 1999. Total enrollment, however, does not give the full picture of participation since it does not indicate the school-age population that is enrolled. Two measures that deal with this are the **gross enrollment ratio** (GER) and the **net enrollment ratio** (NER). The GER is a ratio of all people enrolled in primary or secondary education to the population in the officially defined primary or secondary school-age group. Since it takes into consideration all people enrolled regardless of age, the GER can sometimes be higher than 100%. A high GER means a high participation in education, and

TABLE 16.3
Gross Enrollment Ratio—2014

Country	Preprimary % of relevant age group	Primary % of relevant age group	Secondary % of relevant age group	Tertiary % of relevant age group
Algeria	..	119	..	35
Angola	..	..	..	10
Benin	21	126	54	15
Botswana	18	109	84	28
Burkina Faso	4	87	30	5
Burundi	7	128	38	4
Cabo Verde	70	113	93	23
Cameroon	34	114	56	..
Cent. African Rep.	..	93	17	3
Chad	1	101	22	3
Comoros	23	105	59	9
Congo, Dem. Rep.	4	107	44	7
Congo, Rep.	14	111	55	10
Côte d'Ivoire	7	90	40	9
Djibouti	4	68	46	..
Egypt	25	106	86	30
Equatorial Guinea	68	84	..	..
Eritrea	15	51	36	3
Ethiopia	30	100	36	6
Gambia	34	86	..	..
Ghana	115	106	67	16
Guinea	..	89	39	11
Kenya	74	111	68	..
Lesotho	31	107	52	10
Liberia	..	96	38	12
Madagascar	14	147	38	4
Malawi	..	147	39	..

(Continued)

TABLE **16.3**

Gross Enrollment Ratio—2014 *(Continued)*

Country	Preprimary % of relevant age group	Primary % of relevant age group	Secondary % of relevant age group	Tertiary % of relevant age group
Mali	4	77	44	7
Mauritania	3	98	30	5
Mauritius	102	103	98	39
Morocco	60	116	69	25
Mozambique	..	104	25	6
Namibia	21	111	..	..
Niger	7	71	19	2
Rwanda	14	138	40	8
Sao Tome & Principe	42	112	77	10
Senegal	15	81	..	..
Seychelles	93	104	75	6
Sierra Leone	10	130	43	..
South Africa	77	100	98	20
Sudan	37	69	40	17
Swaziland	..	113	63	5
Tanzania	32	87	32	4
Togo	15	125	..	10
Tunisia	41	111	90	35
Uganda	11	110	28	..
Zambia	..	104	..	..
Zimbabwe	27	102	47	6

Source: UNESCO -UIS.

a GER greater than 100 says that the country is able to take care of all its primary or secondary school-age population. Table 16.3 indicates that of the 39 African countries that reported data in 2014, only 8 had GER of 60 or better for preprimary education, and only two countries theoretically could accommodate all their preprimary school-age population—Ghana (115%) and Mauritius (102%). The GERs were a lot better for primary education. Of the 47 countries that reported data, 32 or 68% had GER above 100% with Madagascar and Malawi scoring 147% each. With the exception of Eritrea that had 51%, the remaining 14 countries had below 60%. The GER for secondary education, however, show more room for improvement. Of the 40 countries that reported data, 28 or 70% had GER below 60%. For higher education, it was much lower across the board. The highest was 39% in Mauritius.

The NER, which is a ratio of the people in primary or secondary age group that is enrolled in primary or secondary education to the population officially defined in the primary or secondary age group, is more refined than the GER. From Table 16.4,

TABLE **16.4**

Net Enrollment and Children Out of School, 2014

Country	Net enrollment ratio				Children out of school	
	Primary % of relevant age group		Secondary % of relevant age group		Primary school-age children	
					Male	Female
	1999	2014	1999	2014	2014	2014
Algeria	88	..	53	..	..	..
Angola	50	..	..	..	..	..
Benin	62	96	17	42	..	..
Botswana	80	91	53	63	14,659	12,395
Burkina Faso	35	67	9	22	457,071	499,647
Burundi	41	95	..	25	41,906	27,340
Cabo Verde	97	98	..	69	578	463
Cameroon	..	92	..	43	8,536	184,714
Central African Rep	..	71	..	14	72,428	134,223
Chad	50	84	7	..	61,330	295,355
Comoros	60	83	..	44	7,257	9,563
Congo, Dem. Rep.	35	..	..	..	..	..
Congo, Rep.	..	91	..	..	36,678	10,671
Côte d'Ivoire	57	75	..	..	363,910	514,940
Djibouti	26	59	14	..	14,730	18,734
Egypt	86	100	..	..	28,048	145,352
Equatorial Guinea	66	57	24	..	23,079	22,806
Eritrea	31	41	16	29	199,447	205,607
Ethiopia	36	86	11	..	847,531	1,276,139
Gabon	91	..	..	..	..	..
Gambia	74	68	..	..	54,524	44,729
Ghana	61	89	34	55	214,072	199,242
Guinea	42	74	11	32	187,946	260,689
Guinea-Bissau	47	..	8	..	..	..
Kenya	62	85	33	57	542,666	413,319
Lesotho	59	80	18	35	36,174	29,707
Liberia	47	38	..	17	222,044	220,411
Madagascar	63	..	..	31	..	..
Malawi	96	..	29	33	..	..
Mali	44	59	..	35	476,301	553,371
Mauritania	60	74	14	22	81,624	69,010
Mauritius	93	96	66	..	2,338	1,201
Morocco	71	98	..	56	17,183	20,186
Mozambique	52	88	3	18	282,182	395,391
Namibia	87	90	39	54	20,727	14,935

(Continued)

TABLE **16.4**

Net Enrollment and Children Out of School, 2014 (*Continued*)

Country	Net enrollment ratio				Children out of school	
	Primary % of relevant age group		Secondary % of relevant age group		Primary school-age children	
					Male	Female
	1999	2014	1999	2014	2014	2014
Niger	27	61	6	16	553,081	680,251
Nigeria	62	..	..	..	..	..
Rwanda	79	96	..	..	44,784	22,858
Sao Tome & Principe	82	95	..	..	657	725
Senegal	55	71	..	..	355,723	278,394
Seychelles	85	95	67	75	253	196
Sierra Leone	..	98	..	37	121	6,479
South Africa	90	..	62	..	..	..
Sudan	..	54	..	..	1,413,736	1,298,832
Swaziland	70	79	32	34	22,510	22,729
Tanzania	49	81	..	..	874,055	841,324
Togo	85	91	20	..	21,243	57,537
Tunisia	94	99	..	..	..	..
Uganda	..	94	14	..	296,808	180,660
Zambia	65	87	..	..	178,008	147,141
Zimbabwe	83	89	40	43	153,068	130,366

Source: UNESCO-UIS.

we can see that all African countries that reported have shown improvements in their NER since 1999, with 13 countries either at or close to universal primary education (Table 16.4). Like primary education, the NER of secondary education of the reporting countries all improved in 2014 compared to 1999, but no country had NER of 60% or better except Seychelles (77%). As the table indicates, there are a lot of children that were not going to school in 2014.

Africa has come a long way from its precolonial, colonial and early postcolonial times with its education system. The number of education institutions has increased tremendously at all levels of the education system. There are more people formally educated and more in the system than any time before. In spite of these, the brief discussion on educational attainment and participation shows that Africa still lags behind all major regions of the world. There are still more adult population that have no schooling than in any other part of the world, and there are fewer university-educated people on the continent than any other part of the world. After many years and efforts put into the education system, the highest education attainment for the majority of Africans is primary education. These features are reflections of certain problems and issues that still confront the country's education system. We will address some of these issues in the next section.

Problems and Issues in Africa's Education System

Problems and issues facing Africa's education system are many and have been subject to numerous research and national and international conferences. The discussion in this section will focus on a select number of these including financing, accessibility, affordability, and quantity, quality, and relevance as it relates to the return on investment to the individual and to the state.

Financing and Education Policy

Financing of education continues to be a challenge to African countries. Generally speaking, the majority of African countries spend either a comparable or higher percentage of their GDP on education than other regions of the world. Available UIS data indicate that in 2014 it ranged from Madagascar's 2.1% to Malawi's 7.7%. Indeed as a percentage of government expenditure, Africa spends more on education, with a range of 10.3% in Gambia to 27% in Ethiopia. However, this is still not enough. The result is that education finance in Africa has increasingly come to rely on students and the donor community. This has its own downsides because it does not give the full freedom to African countries to develop and chart their own course of education. Samoff (1999) was particularly critical of the way Africa's dependence on external donors has created a plethora of education sector studies that were often alien to African governments because they do not participate in the most important decisions, namely, what studies were needed and why. At the university level, institutions have created various ways of getting additional funds but some of these have had the negative impact of restricting accessibility to only those who can afford.

Accessibility

Accessibility has become a pervasive issue in Africa's education system. It was the main reason behind the policies enacted in the early post-independence period in every African country. Initially this was more in terms of geographic accessibility—which fell broadly along the lines of urban and rural areas. The sweeping education policies that were adopted in the early postcolonial period in the majority of African countries were aimed at addressing this geographic accessibility. This was also the rationale behind the expansion of higher education system. In spite of these, accessibility is still a problem as these spatial strategies were not accompanied by resource allocation. Thus, differences in resources endowment have created different tiers of the education system. In this case, it appears that urban schools continue to attract more resources than rural schools.

Accessibility issues are much more pronounced at the tertiary institutions—universities in particular—as the oldest universities also command the highest prestige in their respective countries and for that reason have immense pressure to admit students they do not have facilities to support. The result is that the universities keep raising admission standards for those students who can be admitted on government scholarship, while fee-paying spots are filled by students who can afford to pay. The privates have stepped in to admit more of the students who do not gain admission into the top public universities, but they tend to be more expensive and limited in the scope of programs they offer—most of them business and computer-related programs only. This in turn exacerbates the accessibility problem.

Social Inequities

Africa's education system has serious social inequities and discrimination. Two groups of people that bear the brunt of these are the females and people with physical and learning disabilities. All across the continent there are fewer girls and women in the education system than boys and men. Of all the countries that reported data on educational attainment, only Kenya had a higher percentage of men than women with no schooling. Ghana, Lesotho, Mauritius, Namibia, Sao Tome & Principe, Seychelles, and South Africa also had a higher percentage of women than men with primary education (Table 16.2).

The situation for people with disabilities is even worse. In many countries, there is no accommodation for physical and learning disabilities. In a few countries, there are schools for the blind and the deaf, but until recently, students with learning disabilities were generally ridiculed and tormented for being dumb and academically inferior. In most cases, they were ruled out completely for doing any schoolwork and were humiliated until they dropped out. Other vulnerable groups include orphans, street children, and ethnic minority children (Wolhuter, 2014). In recent years, some movements have been made to accommodate this group of students through special education. However, the major hindrance to these efforts is the lack of trained teachers who can work with such students.

Affordability

Affordability is still an issue even in the face of fee-free education. There are some families that cannot afford to send their children to school because of the household conditions they live in or poverty. This again is much more common in rural areas of the continent. This was the rationale behind the early postcolonial policies of universal free primary education in the majority of African countries. Initially, government support made education more affordable, but with population growth and difficult economic conditions and demand for more education, it has increasingly become more expensive for governments to provide the same support they did years ago. As a result, households now have to bear more of the cost of education, especially at the higher level, and this has made it more difficult for poor households. The affordability problem is also being compounded by a growing trend in many African countries whereby primary and high school students have to take private lessons sometimes from the same teachers who teach them in regular hours. This practice has emerged because of either low teacher salaries and poor service conditions or teacher absenteeism. In Tunisia, for example, Rose (2014) reports that about 70% of all high school students had to take some private lessons in the course of their education while about 54% took such classes from their own teachers.

Resources, Quantity, and Quality Issues

The education expansion of the post-independence period may have addressed the inadequate number of schools and colleges, but it did not solve the problem of quality. In particular, the expansion did not come with adequate financial and human resources due to the economic downturn that hit many African countries in the late 1970s and 1980s. The result is that many of the schools lack proper and adequate physical infrastructure, equipment, textbooks, and more importantly trained and qualified teachers to staff the schools, develop, and implement relevant curriculum to the needs of African countries (see, for example, Akande, 2014; UNESCO Institute for Statistics (UIS), 2012).

As already pointed out at the primary level rural schools range from well-constructed buildings to tree shades and may be furnished with proper desks or nothing at all, except a chalkboard for the teachers. Closely associated with this is the problem of inadequate sanitation, including access to clean toilet, water, and electricity. Schools that lack proper buildings definitely do not have clean toilet and water facilities, but the UIS (2012) reported that in 1 out of 3 countries that provided data, more than half of the schools did not have toilets. In Chad, Côte d'Ivoire, Equatorial Guinea, and Madagascar, it was reported that more than 60% of the schools had no toilets. With respect to clean water and electricity, the report found that the majority of the schools on the continent were lacking. At the secondary school level, many schools lack laboratory facilities (see, for example, Akande, 2014; Nsiangengo et al., 2014; UIS, 2012).

There is also the problem of large classes and overcapacity. In 2013, only 6 out of 34 countries reporting data had pupil–teacher ratios in primary schools below or close to the global average of 24.2. These were Seychelles (13.1), Tunisia (17.4), Mauritius (19.8), Cabo Verde (22.9), and Algeria and Egypt (23.3). The remaining 28 countries reported pupil–teacher ratios ranging from 26 in Morocco to 69 in Malawi. In addition to Malawi, three other countries reported pupil–teacher ratios of above 50—Mozambique (54.5), Rwanda (59.8), and Chad (62.4). In the face of limited physical and human resources, the impact of these large classes on quality of education and student learning becomes particularly serious at the critical stages of education, namely, first grades. The problem with these large classes is compounded by the fact that most of them tend to be multigrade classes, with at least two grades on the average. A UIS (2012) study of 45 countries in sub-Saharan Africa reported that in Cape Verde, Chad, Congo, Guinea, Madagascar, Mali, and Niger, there were classes that covered three or more grades. These conditions impact student learning and cause significant dropout rates in primary education.

Several past and recent studies of education in Africa have particularly raised the issue of quality and relevance, especially as it relates to the human resource needs of the African continent (e.g., Majgaard and Mingat, 2012; Rose, 2014; Saheli-Isfahani, 2012; World Bank, 2008; Wolhuter, 2014). These studies have noted that in spite of the major investments and progress made in education in Africa, educational attainment among the adult population is still below other comparable regions, and among the reasons for this are both pedagogical and content issues. For example, Mulderig (2013) reports of serious pedagogical problems in North African schools that unfortunately can be found elsewhere on the continent as well. She writes

"students spend hours copying numbers and words off of blackboards, with eyes buried in textbooks or focused on a sole teacher addressing the entire class in oral repetitions of lists of facts" (Mulderig, 2013, p. 10).

This type of education encourages memorization and rote learning, instead of originality, group work, debate, and expression of opinion.

The relevance of Africa's education comes to sharp focus when we consider the fact that Africa as a whole has not made use of the accumulated human capital for economic growth. Instead, unemployment is very high among college and university graduates, and the products of the education system do not have the skills to compete globally. Thus, instead of enhancing employability, education seems to retard or limit it. Part of the reasons for this situation can be attributed to the policies pursued in the early post-independence era. Those policies guaranteed civil service jobs that required training mostly in the humanities and social sciences, with universities to provide them to boot. This social contract worked well until the economic crisis of the late 1970s and 1980s made the contract unsustainable. The private sector that could have filled the gap was unable to do so because it had been ignored, discarded, and in many cases harassed by government policies as being informal and backward. The result is that the sector has not been able to develop the types of jobs that meet the high expectations of university and college graduates. At the same time, Africa's tertiary education continue to overproduce graduates in the same old way without much regard to the changes that are occurring in the labor market. Lacking the skills to start their own jobs, these graduates still look for government jobs that are nonexistent (Mcauliffe, 2013). The irony is that the share of vocational and technical education in the entire education system remains relatively small because the general public continues to look down on these institutions.

Solutions offered to deal with these problems include providing or generating more financial resources for schools, curriculum reform, aligning education content with the needs of respective countries, emphasizing vocational and technical education, and providing more teacher training and improving the conditions of service for teachers. However, Africa's education policies have been too much dominated by external forces. As Samoff (1999) rightly argued, unless Africa gets control of its own educational policies, it will be difficult for it to address these issues because external supporters have their own agenda and their support and efforts do not have the sustaining power that most of these problems require. To do this, African countries need to find ways to generate more internal revenue that could be used to finance its education policies and programs. This is the first step to wean itself from the aid dependency and foreign control that it finds itself.

Summary

Education has always been present in African societies. Before colonialism, it was constituted within the socialization process through formal and informal instructions in the various traditions and norms as well as the technologies of society. As society became more organized in the form of kingdoms and empires, formal education institutions in the form of schools emerged. Beginning in Ancient Egypt, education institutions became transformed by various external forces—the Greeks, the Arabs, and finally the Western Europeans. By the end of the colonial period, Western type of education had been established in Africa, but very few Africans had received the education from the system. Recognizing the importance of education to the well-being of their citizens, African countries pursued education policies that focused on expanding and extending all levels of education to their citizens. The economic crises of the late 1970s and 1980s halted the expansion, but the shortfall in public spending was picked up by private investment in education at all levels—from the primary through university. Today, every African country has more educational institutions than they had in the early post-independence era. More Africans have received primary, secondary, and tertiary education than ever before. Yet, Africa's education system continues to grapple with several problems including accessibility, affordability, quality and relevance, financing, and inequity issues. Educating a country is an expensive investment, but it is an investment that is necessary. African countries cannot stop investing in education, but they must find ways to keep cost down and also make the return on investment worthwhile by reducing the unemployment among the educated youth through careful educational planning and human resource needs. To this they must first take control of their education policies and programs by becoming less dependent on external financial resources to get the leverage they need to address the issues and programs facing their respective systems and programs.

Health is the one of most important characteristics of a population as it has several implications for economic development of countries. At the very minimum, a healthy population lives longer, produce more, consume more, save more, and invest more in the national economy. Apart from this, health also constitutes an economic sector, which offers jobs to millions of people. Our study in this section will be in three parts. First, we will examine the evolution and development of health care in Africa. Second, we will discuss the contemporary geography of diseases and the health-care delivery systems in place to deal with those diseases. Third, we will discuss the issues and problems facing the system. The data used in the discussion come from the World Health Organization database, but they have the same issues as the education data. So as before, these must be interpreted with caution.

Evolution and Development of Africa's Health-Care Systems

Precolonial Africa

Precolonial African societies had several health-care systems for their physical, emotional, psychological, as well as spiritual well-being. The medicines used in these systems were herbs, plants, and animal parts, and the practitioners included herbalists, diviners, and spiritual doctors. The herbalists were skilled people in the art of healing with herbs, as well as plant and animal residues. The diviners and spiritual doctors, in addition to their knowledge of herbal healing, claimed special powers or insights that allowed them to address extraordinary events such as epidemic outbreak, prolonged drought, or diseases that could not be explained by existing knowledge. These special powers rested on the belief that diseases could be caused by witchcrafts, evil spirits, or breaking of taboos or committing an offence against the ancestors all of which required supernatural intervention before healing could occur (Abdalla, 1992; Flint, 2008; Keita, 2007; Waite, 1992). As Flint (2008) observes, these practitioner's understanding of disease was not based on the germ theory, but practices such as quarantine and the use of fire as cleaning agent provide a glimpse into the way they understood some of the diseases. Moreover, they all received training from master practitioners before they were allowed to practice.

As African societies became more organized, medical practitioners became more prominent with kings and emperors. In the highly successful empires and kingdoms, such as Ancient Egypt, health care became more advanced with formal training of physicians in different areas of specializations. Anatomy of the human body was studied and documented, while diseases were properly diagnosed, treated, and documented. This level of health care attracted scholars from the Ancient World—Greeks and Phoenicians to Egypt. The Phoenicians later on took the Egyptian medical practices to the Maghreb, where they founded Carthage as a colony (Keita, 2007).

The medical legacy of Ancient Egypt, maintained or improved by subsequent civilizations such as the Babylonians, Persians, Greek, and Romans, were adopted and enhanced by the Arabs, and reintroduced to Africa through the Arab Muslim Conquest of Egypt in the 7th century. Trained in Greek practice of medicine and philosophy, Muslim physicians managed to separate medicine from religion, eliminated the priest from healing and followed an empirical approach to health care (Abdalla, 1992). Hospitals and outpatient facilities were established (Keita, 2007). However, by the beginning of the modern era this practice of scientific medicine had reverted back to the role of the Imam and the supernatural. Abdalla (1992) attributes this to the decline of Islamic civilization and the rise of Christian Europe. Apart from this, there was also an ideological and philosophical shift from liberal to more conservative interpretation of the Koran and the Hadith, mostly due to the influential ideas of Malik Ibn Anas (711–795) and the rise of Shiasm. Medicine and religion became merged, with Malams and Imams assuming more prominent positions in health-care delivery. This was the type of medical practices that came with Islam to West Africa (Abdalla, 1992). Even so, records show that Sankore University of Mali was offering courses in anatomy, pharmacology, chemistry, and medicine in the 15th century. In addition, the Asante Empire in modern day Ghana had a well-organized system of healers that were registered under the chief doctor of the King (Gros, 2016).

The next major influence on precolonial health-care system came from Western Europe, and it began with the exposure of more Europeans to Africa's environment. Since the 15th century, Europeans had been trading with Africa. However, it was after the abolition of the Atlantic Slave Trade and the establishment of the new colonies for freed slaves as well as the desire to spread Christianity and establish legitimate trade that really exposed more Europeans to Africa's diseases. Curtin (1998) reports that 46% of the white settlers of the new colony of Sierra Leone died in the first year. The Sierra Leone Company, which took over the settlement in 1792–1793 lost 49% of its staff. Also from 1804 to 1825, the Church Missionary Society lost 54 of its 95 missionaries who went to West Africa. Among the military the death rate for British soldiers in Sierra Leone from 1819 to 1836 was 483 per 1,000, while that for French troops in 1839 was 573. The leading killer diseases of Europeans were malaria, gastrointestinal diseases, and yellow fever (Curtin, 1998), which gave West Africa the label of "the White Man's Grave."

Initially, Europeans did not understand tropical diseases and attributed them to the climate, wetness that produced chills, or lack of immunity from the disease. As a result, their approach to preventing or curing some of those diseases was also questionable. For example, malaria was treated through bloodletting and purging to balance bodily impurity and fluid. However, the isolation of quinine from the bark of the cinchona tree by two French chemist Joseph Pelletier and Joseph Caventou in 1820 provided some relief from the seriousness of malaria. By the 1860s, the death toll among the colonial soldiers had gone down considerably because of the use of quinine as prophylactic.

From the mid-1800s, medical mission increased greatly due to David Livingstone who pushed the idea that health care should be an integral part of missionary work. Many missionary societies such as the Church Missionary Society (CMS), the Church of Scotland, the American Congregational Church (ACC), the Finnish Missionary Society (FMS), the American Board of Commissioners for Foreign Missions, and the newly formed Universities Mission to Central Africa (UMCA) sent medical missionaries to various parts of Africa. Just as it was with education, biomedicine came to be seen as the way to win souls for God and to challenge Africa's indigenous medicine.

The only areas of the continent where government became involved in health care during this time were in South Africa, the British coastal enclaves of Sierra Leone and Gambia, and Egypt. In South Africa, the state became active in health matters after a smallpox epidemic with the building of two hospitals in 1755. In 1807, the first legislation to control the practice of medicine was passed (Delobelle, 2013). In Sierra Leone, Fyfe (1962) reports that a wooden hospital shipped from England was established in Sierra Leone in 1792–1794. After the coastal areas of Sierra Leone and Gambia became colonies in 1808 and 1816, respectively, a military hospital was built in Freetown in 1804, and in 1820, the Kissy Lunatic Asylum, which later became a hospital, was established for the new settlers. Another military hospital was built in Bathurst (Banjul) before 1825 and a colonial hospital (Victoria Hospital) in 1854 (Edy, 1983). In Egypt, Mohamed Ali built Cairo's Qasr al-Aini, a medical school and teaching hospital, as part of his Egyptian modernization project (Abugideiri, 2004).

Colonial Africa

From the late 1880s through the World War I, Christian missionary societies expanded their health-care activities by opening more hospitals, dispensaries, and asylums in many parts of Africa (Good, 1991). Among these were the (UCMA)'s hospitals in Zanzibar and Nyasaland (Malawi) in 1887 and 1899, respectively, the CMS' Mengo Hospital in 1897 in Uganda, and the Church of Scotland's hospital of the Kikuyu Mission in Kenya in 1907. In Zimbabwe, three medical facilities were opened in succession—the AMC's Mt Selinda Dispensary in 1893, the Dutch Reformed Church's Morgenster Hospital in 1894, and the American Board of Commissioners for Foreign Mission's Chikore Hospital in 1900 (Zvobgo, 1986). Others were the Catholic Mission's hospital in Abeokuta, Nigeria in 1895, the Finnish missionary's Onandjokwe Hospital in Namibia in 1911, and the Albert Schwietzer's Lamberene Hospital in French Equatorial Guinea in 1913.

Colonial governments also became more involved in health care. In South Africa, a legislation to train nurses was passed in 1877, and more hospitals were constructed in all major cities following the discovery of diamonds and gold in the second half of the 19th century (Delobelle, 2013). For the remaining British colonies, the first serious health-care plans were made after the appointment of Joseph Chamberlain as Secretary of State in 1895 and his subsequent appointment of Dr. Patrick Manson as the first Consulting Physician to the Colonial Office. The London and Liverpool Schools of Tropical Medicine were established in 1899 and formal training of medical officers to work in Africa began (Crozier, 2007). By the end of the first decade of British rule, hospitals had been built in Mombasa, Entebbe, and Nairobi all in British East Africa, and Tabora, Ocean Road, and Sewa Hajj in German East Africa. In 1902, a West African Medical Staff was established as a precursor to a unified Colonial Medical Service for all the British colonies in 1932.

In the French colonies, a Pasteur Institute was established in Tunis in 1893, but for decades, the French sent their sick, both Europeans and Africans, in their Algerian colony to Paris for treatment. In Belgian Congo, the Union Miniere, the Belgian mining company, created African villages for its mining operations from where men were selected according to strict medical guidelines. After 1920, spouses were selected for the men through strict medical examination to make sure that the couple would produce healthy children for the mining operations (Gros, 2016).

A parallel development during the early colonial period was the race to find curative or preventive measures to some of the deadly tropical diseases. In 1880, Karl Joseph Eberth described the bacteria that caused typhoid fever and confirmed that it was a waterborne disease. In 1881, Carlos Finlay traced the source of yellow fever to the mosquito. In 1882, the bacteria that causes tuberculosis-related pneumonia was isolated. In 1883, Robert Koch discovered the virus that causes cholera and confirmed that it was a waterborne disease. In 1897–1898 and 1899–1900 Ronald Ross and Robert Koch, respectively, traced the malaria parasite also to the mosquito. While these breakthroughs did not immediately lead to the development of effective vaccines, they helped put in place a number of preventive measures that reduced the death rates among Europeans and African natives as well. For example, in the case of malaria, four measures came to be widely adopted: mosquito eradication, the use of prophylactic quinine, segregation of victims, and personal protection from the mosquito (Curtin, 1989). For the waterborne diseases, preventive water purification and use of intravenous injection were adopted.

In Egypt, the British took over the Qasr Al-Aini and converted it to a British-type teaching hospital. They changed the curriculum to British-styled clinical studies, instituted fees, changed the medium of instruction from Arabic to English, and appointed British medical administrators (Abugideiri, 2009). After the 1919 Egyptian Revolution and the departure of British doctors, it became possible to train more Egyptian doctors.

Initially, these health-care facilities were open only to Europeans in Africa and the Africans who worked for them. However, after 1919, health care was extended to the wider African community in the urban centers, with the rural areas included only when there were major epidemics. From the 1920s, health-care delivery systems progressed very fast in the colonies. Colonial governments built hospitals to take care of both Europeans and the Africans in the major centers of colonial domination, but how health care was delivered varied even with colonies of the same imperial power. In Kenya, Hartwig (1979) reports that government facilities were for the European population, the missionary hospitals were for Africans, while the Asian population got care from sponsored wards in either the government or missionary hospitals, and other natives. In other areas such as Namibia, urban hospitals, both government and mission, were for the European population, while the rural mission hospitals were for Africans.

In South Africa, health care became more fragmented after the Union in 1910 and the Public Health Act of 1919 tried to resolve the discrepancies. Hospitals were placed under provincial governments while the central government was in charge of national health issues. However, differences in resource allocations resulted in uneven health-care delivery system. Hospitals received more resources at the expense of the poor segments of the population—the black majority. Disease incidence increased among the African migrant labor due to overcrowded conditions in the face of limited access to health care. The Land Act of 1913 that restricted the African majority population to 13% of the land made this situation worse. Delobelle (2013, p 166) argues that this law proved

> "deleterious for the health of the African population for the next eighty years by creating a perverse system of circulatory migrant labor, in which the capitalist mining sector, settlerfarms, and industrial complexes would increasingly attract black laborers from their 'reserves' in order to serve the economical interests of the white elite."

Delobelle (2013) continues that from 1928 through 1936 efforts to address the health of Africans were ignored, including a recommendation to train African doctors and another to provide sickness insurance to both black and white. At the same time, a recommendation to improve the health conditions of poor whites was taken up by the government. In 1935, the Public Health Amendment Act extended health care to the African natives but this resulted in a segregated health-care system for the Africans. A new report—the Gluckman Report—denounced the level of heath care in South Africa in 1945, and called for a National Health Care Service to provide primary health care for all citizens along with a major overhaul of the entire health-care system. Unfortunately, just when a plan incorporating most of the report's recommendations were about to be implemented, the Nationalist Party came to power in 1948 and formally instituted the Apartheid Policy in South Africa, from which point the health of the African majority population declined rapidly (Delobelle, 2013).

The doctors in all the colonies were expatriates from Europe or India as it was the case of East Africa, but the need for more medical personnel in the World War I and the performance of the East Africa Native Medical Corps during the War convinced the British that Africans were capable of higher medical training. In 1917, a training school was established at the Mengo Hospital that eventually evolved into the first medical school in East Africa. The training was extended to Kenya in 1920 and the colonial government entered into an agreement to provide some funding to the missionary hospitals in the training (Hartwig, 1979).

The administration of health care varied even among the colonies of the same imperial power. For example, while indirect rule was implemented in British East Africa, each colony was different. Kenya followed a decentralized system that included a few well-equipped central hospitals in Nairobi and Mombasa, and few more regional hospitals, and a number of dressing stations, health centers, or dispensaries in the rural areas. Local Native Councils ran the local government and had the authority to levy taxes that made it possible for Africans to receive free care. The emphasis of the care was more of preventive than curative. In contrast, Uganda adopted more centralized system of administration. Other programs that were introduced into the system were medical safaris, health surveys, immunization campaigns, and sanitation, vector control, and public health education (Chaiken, 1998).

Colonial health care in Africa had mixed effects. On the positive side, it brought more effective cure or prevention from some of Africa's deadliest diseases. It also introduced better sanitary conditions into the health-care system and enhanced the understanding of disease ecology in Africa. In very rare cases, colonial medicine used indigenous health-care system to improve health-care delivery. Hakansson (1998) reports how missionaries in German East Africa used the knowledge of indigenous medical practices to help reduce infant mortality in the South Pare district from 1909 to 1914. In South Africa, Flint (2008, p. 2) describes transformation of African healers from political activism to "venture capitalist who competed for turf and patients with white biomedical doctors and pharmacist" from about the 1820s. Perhaps because of this transformation, in 1891, the Natal government passed the Natal Native Code legalizing and licensing the practices of the African healers, making it possible for them to form an association in 1928 (Flint, 2008).

On the negative side, colonialism helped spread diseases such as the small pox and the plague around the continent due to increased migration. Apart from this, the vilification of Africa's indigenous health-care system as pagan, fetish, or unscientific truncated the evolution and development of indigenous medicine that would continue through the postcolonial era. In South Africa, the success of African healers in the colonial period referred to above was short-lived, because the white medical establishment used legislation to discredit the indigenous medical practices (Flint, 2008).

Also, the differences between Africa's cultural context and the one in which colonial health-care givers were trained resulted in the creation of an elitist group of health-care professionals in Africa that were condescending on their own society. In Egypt, Abugedeiri (2009) argues that Victorian values that were at the root of training medical doctors after the British took over Egypt produced a group of doctors whose ideas helped reinforce the domestication of Egyptian mothers.

Finally, colonial medicine also had a profound impact on planning of Africa's colonial cities. Curtin (1992) provides a fascinating account of how colonial African governments used the segregation of victims or sanitary segregation to create segregated colonial cities in Africa, a practice that began with the French in North Africa and the Dutch in South Africa.

Postcolonial Africa

At the return to independence, the health-care system of the majority of African countries consisted of a patchwork of central and regional government hospitals and a network of mission hospitals that were mostly urban based. A few countries had some locally trained health-care workers, while the rest did not. With the strong belief that a healthy country was necessary for economic development, African governments focused on a select number of guiding principles. First, health care should not be subject to cost control. Second, health care should be universally accessible to all, with emphasis on public health and preventive measures. Third, given the dearth of health-care professionals, training of health-care workers should be priority. Fourth, there was also the desire to build more hospitals in urban areas, and a hierarchy of clinics and health centers in rural areas. Guided by these principles, African countries built large medical schools and teaching hospitals for free medical education in a relatively short time using either their own individual or pooled resources (Gros, 2016). However, efforts to expand the health-care systems intertwined with a number of global initiatives that either helped or disrupted plans.

The Alma-Ata Declaration (AAD)—1978 One of the very first and perhaps the most important of these global initiatives was the **Alma-Ata Declaration (AAD)**. The AAD was the result of the International Conference on Primary Health Care held in Alma-Ata, Kazakhstan in 1978. The declaration saw primary health care as consisting of eight elements:

> (i) education concerning prevailing health problems and the methods of preventing and controlling them, (ii) promotion of food supply and proper nutrition, (iii) adequate supply of safe water and basic sanitation, (iv) maternal and child health care, including family planning, (v) immunization against major infectious diseases, (vi) prevention and control of locally endemic diseases, (vii) appropriate treatment of common diseases and injuries, and (viii) provision of essential drugs.

The Declaration called for decentralization of health-care delivery and called on all member states to achieve "health for all" by 2000. All African countries at that time signed on to the AAD and in some countries efforts were made to implement the decentralization system through a hierarchy of health centers—teaching hospitals at the top followed by regional and district hospitals and rural health centers (WHO, 2008). However, the prospects for achieving the goals of the AAD faded when the precarious financial positions of majority of African governments in the 1980s were made worse by the structural adjustment programs (SAPs).

Structural adjustment programs and health care The SAPs imposed on African countries by the World Bank and the International Monetary Fund (IMF) that has been discussed in previous chapters made the implementation of AAD difficult because of the health-care demands the programs made on African governments. According to Gros (2016), SAPs made four demands. First, there was the need for recovering the cost of health care. Second, governments were to provide incentives to the private sector to enter into health care and thereby relieve the government of the cost. This was to be done by reducing the retirement age of doctors in government service and giving them severance package to go into private practice. Third, there was the need for private sector insurance, and fourth was subcontracting health care to NGOs. For Gros (2016), the implementation of these measures had mixed results on the health-care system. The cost recovery measure priced people out of the market and threw the idea of universal primary health for all out of the window. The hope that a substantial number of doctors on government payroll would leave for private practice did not happen because the incentives were not big enough for doctors to leave their relatively well-paid government jobs vis-à-vis the risk of failure in the private sector. The health insurance system did not work properly due to the low purchasing power of the majority of Africans and immature private insurance market in the majority of African countries. Other critics have also argued that the austerity measures that came with SAPs made it very difficult for governments to support primary health care. This led to deterioration of health indicators in most countries. The government divestiture also led to high unemployment, which then affected household incomes. Institution of user fees in this case became more difficult; many people became unemployed and could not afford to pay the fees. In most of the agricultural countries, the emphasis on export crops removed incentives from food production, which in turn affected nutrition level of people, particularly children (Anyinam, 1989; Kanji et al., 1991). All these exacerbated the already crumbling health-care situation, culminating in the large-scale drug shortages, breakdown of facilities, and the flight of doctors and other health-care workers out of the continent (Anyinam, 1989; Alubo, 1990). At the same time, others have argued that the crisis was not necessarily due to the decline in government expenditures on health but more to the way the limited resources were allocated within the health sector (Sahn and Bernier, 1995). At any rate, it was just impossible to support universal primary health care when governments were forced to cut back their role in the health sector in times of economic crises.

The Bamako Initiative of 1987 By the mid-1980s, it was clear that the majority of African countries were not going to meet the goals of the AAD due to the severe economic crises they were facing. One solution to the growing problem was the **Bamako Initiative (BI)**. The Initiative was announced at the international Conference of African Health Ministers in Bamako, Mali, in 1987, and it essentially sought to increase primary health-care coverage by creating a revolving drug fund that would be managed by local communities. The drug fund would initially come from the sale of free generic drugs donated by the United Nations Children's Fund (UNICEF) to the dispensaries of local committees (Garner, 1989). The proceeds would then be used to restock the drugs and to improve access to health care as well as quality of service of health workers (Ridde, 2003). Critics immediately charged that the idea of asking poor people to pay for drugs would deny access to a lot of people the care they needed since they would not be able to pay. Also, the idea that local community would manage the funds assumed too much since most rural communities in Africa did not have the expertise to do that. Furthermore, the payment would be seen by people as their right to demand drugs and injections that were not appropriate (Garner, 1989). Since the adoption of the Initiative, a number of studies have been conducted to see how it has been working. For example, in an evaluative study of the Initiative in Burundi, Kenya, Nigeria, and Uganda, McPake et al. (1993) found mixed and variable results across the countries. They found that people were able to pay for the drugs and that the Initiative provided cheaper services. However, the quality of service was variable across the countries and so was the ability to raise funds. In another study, Knippenberg et al. (1997) found that the Initiative was working in Benin and Guinea. It had made drugs and other essentials available, increase contact between communities and community health providers, and improved efficiency and quality of care. Other studies in Ghana, Kenya, Lesotho, and Zambia showed that the Initiative reduced the use of health care since people could not afford (Ridde, 2003). On the whole, the BI has not been able to meet the goals of the primary health care promised by the AAD.

The Millennium Development Goals (MDG) of 2000 Another watershed moment in Africa's health-care policy occurred at the turn of the century in September 2000 when the United National General Assembly in New York adopted the Millennium Development Goals (MDG). The last two decades of the 20th century had, in particular, seen disturbing health trends, especially among some of the poorest regions of the world. The first was a resurgence of malaria parasites that had made longtime conventional preventive medicines ineffective. The second was the HIV/AIDS epidemic that was ravaging the African continent. The third was an increasing infant and maternal mortality again in poor economies. It was therefore not surprising that three of the eight MDGs were all focused on health: MDG 4—reduce by two-thirds between 1990 and 2015 under-five child mortality, MDG 5—improvement in maternal health; and MDG 6—combating HIV/AIDS, malaria, and other diseases. These three applied to Africa more than any other continent. Infant mortality for 0–5-year-olds was to be cut by 66% by 2015; universal access to treatment by all HIV/AIDS patients was to be achieved by 2010; and maternal death was to be cut by 75% by 2015. The rich countries would provide funds to the poor countries to help them achieve these health-related goals. As before, African countries adopted the MDGs and began working toward the achievements of the goals.

The Ouagadougou Declaration of 2008 In 2008, 30 years after AAD, participants at the International Conference on Primary Health Care and Health Systems in Africa, held in Ouagadougou, Burkina Faso, admitted that Africa had failed to meet the goals of the AAD. In particular, Dr. Luis Sambo, the WHO Regional Director for Africa, noted that despite the fact that Africa was home to just 11% of the world's population, it bore 25% of the world's disease burden. In addition, sub-Saharan Africa had more than 65% of the world's HIV/AIDS infection and accounted for 75% of all HIV/AIDS-related deaths. Furthermore, Africa had 90% of the world's malaria burden (WHO, 2008a).

Another WHO (2008b) review of primary health care showed that no country met the requirements of the declaration. For example, only 15 of the 37 African countries surveyed had health education. The rest had some sort of information and communication but not specifically on health education. In addition, the number of chronic undernourished people increased. While the percentage of good drinking water increased from 32% to 52%, the coverage of sanitation saw a slight decline. Maternal mortality rate (MMR) continued to be the highest in the world. While immunization rates had increased all across the board that against tetanus among women of child-bearing age was still below average. The review found that other elements such as prevention and control of locally endemic diseases, use of appropriate treatment, and access to drugs still posed serious challenges (WHO, 2008b). The Ouagadougou Declaration reaffirmed African countries' commitment to the Alma-Ata Declaration and expressed the need for accelerated action by African governments and their partners to improve health and achieve internationally-agreed health goals including the Millennium Development Goals by 2015.

Assessing the progress toward the MDGs, UN Economic Commission of Africa (2015) reported that for MDG 4, Africa on the whole reduced its under-5 child mortality by 55% between 1990 and 2012. It was 146 per 1,000 live birth in 1990 and 65 per 1,000 live birth in 2012. Egypt, Ethiopia, Liberia, Malawi, Tunisia, and Tanzania met the 2012 target. For MDG 5, only four countries were able to reduce their MMR by 75% between 1990 and 2013. These were Cape Verde, Equatorial Guinea, Eritrea, and Rwanda. Another four that were able to reduce their MMR by more than 60% were Ethiopia (70%), Angola (67%), Mozambique (63%), Egypt (62.5%), and Morocco (61.3%). For MDG 6, the evaluation showed that between 2001 and 2013 the number of new HIV/AIDS infection per 100 adults aged between 15 and 49 years was reduced by 50% in Southern, Central, and West Africa; it was reduced by 46% in East Africa and was constant at 0.01% in North Africa. It was also reported that all countries except Angola and Uganda registered declining trend in new infections. However, universal access to treatment by people living with HIV/AIDS was far from being achieved. The evaluation put the percentage at 37% in 2010 in sub-Sahara Africa. With respect to malaria and other diseases, the WHO (2014) reported that malaria cases had dropped by 34% since 2000 and death rate by 54% over the same period in sub-Saharan Africa. Tuberculosis control during the period was however slow.

Disease Ecology, Morbidity, and Mortality in Africa

Disease ecology refers to how people, given their physical, cultural, and socioeconomic environments, interact with disease pathogens to cause morbidity and mortality. **Morbidity** describes the state of illness, sickness, or injury. Intrinsic in morbidity is the scale of the disease, which in turn leads to several disease terminologies. A disease is an **epidemic** when it appears suddenly over an area (Oppong, 2003). A recent example is the Ebola outbreak in West Africa. If the outbreak becomes worldwide such as HIV/AIDS, the disease is a **pandemic**. A disease that is common in an area is an **endemic** disease to the area, and if the disease occurs over a long period of time it is **a chronic** disease (Oppong, 2003). Morbidity can be measured by disease incidence and disease prevalence. According to WHO, **disease incidence** refers to the number of new cases of a disease reported or diagnosed over a given period, while **disease prevalence** refers to the total number of people in a population sick with that disease. Mortality refers to the number of deaths in a given population at a particular time and place.

Endemic Diseases of Africa

Cardiovascular diseases Cardiovascular diseases (CVDs) refer to disorders of the heart and blood vessels that can lead to death. According to WHO (2016), there are various type of CVDs depending on the part of the body they affect. They include coronary heart disease—which affects blood vessel supplying the heart; cerebrovascular disease—which affects blood vessels supplying the brain; peripheral arterial diseases, which affect blood vessels supplying the arm and legs; rheumatic heart disease, which damages the heart muscle and valves; congenital heart disease, which is present at birth; and deep vein thrombosis or pulmonary embolism, which is blood clots in the leg vein. The severe form of any of these may lead to heart attack or stroke. Due to the fact that the most common cause of CVDs is the blockage of the blood vessels that supply the heart or brain by fatty deposits, WHO says unhealthy diet, tobacco use, excessive use of alcohol, and physical inactivity are risk factors. Changes in lifestyle—healthy eating, stopping smoking and drinking excessive, and increased physical activity—are therefore the top recommendation for prevention. In the past, it was generally thought that CVDs were the "rich man's" diseases and for that matter they should not be a problem in Africa. However, that is no longer the case. As we will see later, CVDs are now among the top causes of death in Africa.

Dracunculiasis or guinea-worm disease *Dracunculiasis* is a disease that can render its victims inactive for about three months (Oppong, 2003). It is contracted through drinking stagnant water, containing cyclops of infected parasites. The larvae are released in the stomach from where they penetrate the intestine walls into the body tissue. After 12–14 months, the matured and fertilized female worm travels under the skin tissue until it reaches its exit point, which is usually the leg. The worm comes out through a painful blister or abscess. When the abscess is submerged in water, the worm releases its embryo and the cycle begins again. The disease is not fatal, but it may afflict a person year after year, and each infection may incapacitate a person for about three months (Oppong, 2003). There is neither a vaccine to prevent guinea-worm disease nor a drug to treat it. However, because it is transmitted by drinking stagnant contaminated water, it can be prevented through the provision of safe drinking water, water filtering, education, and proper care of the wounds of infected persons to cut the transmission cycle. Indeed, WHO (2016) Factsheet reports that of the 20 countries in which the disease was endemic in mid-1980s, only four of the countries reported cases in 2015. The countries were Chad (9 cases), Mali (5), South Sudan (5), and Ethiopia (3). The disease could therefore be eradicated soon.

Ebola virus disease According to WHO (2016) Ebola Factsheet, the Ebola virus disease (EVD) is a very serious and deadly disease. The virus was first discovered in 1976 in two outbreaks, one in Nzara in South Sudan and the other in Yambuku, a village near the Ebola River in the DRC. Since then five species have been identified—Zaire, Bundibugyo, Sudan, Reston, and Tai Forest. The first three have been associated with large outbreaks. It is currently believed that fruit bats serve as hosts to the virus. People get the virus when they come into close contacts with infested animals such as Chimpanzees, monkeys, fruit bats, and other dead forest animals. After a person catches the virus, it takes 2–21 days for the symptoms to show. These include fever, fatigue, headache, and sore throat, which progress into vomiting, diarrhea, rash, kidney and liver malfunctioning, and internal and external bleeding. Once symptoms develop, the virus can be transmitted to another person through close contact with secretions, blood, organs, and other bodily fluid of the infected person (WHO, 2016).

The 2014 EVD outbreak is the largest outbreak since the disease first appeared in 1976. It was caused by the Zaire Ebolavirus, which is considered as the most fatal species (Oppong, 2003). It is believed to have started with the death of a two-year-old boy in December 2013 in Meliandou, small village in south-eastern Guinea. In March, hospital staff in the region reported of a strange disease that had killed 59 out of 86 infected people in three villages of Gueckedou, Macenta, and Kissidougou to the Guinea Ministry of Health. On March 23, 2014, WHO confirmed that the disease was Ebola and declared an outbreak. On March 29, Liberia confirmed its first case and by August the disease had reached the capital, Monrovia. From there the disease spread to a number of West African countries in rapid succession: Sierra Leone on May 25, Nigeria on July 25, Senegal on August 29, and Mali on October 23. The disease next appeared in the DRC on November 21. The outbreak brought a massive mobilization of domestic and external health workers and volunteers as well as foreign aid.

Nigeria, Senegal, Mali, and the DRC were able to contain the disease quickly, mainly due to either quick response, rapid tracking of contact persons as was the case of Nigeria, Senegal, and Mali, or previous experience with the disease as was the case of the DRC. In October 2014, WHO declared Senegal and Nigeria Ebola-free. Mali was declared Ebola-free on January 18, 2015; Guinea on February 16, 2015; and Liberia on January 13, 2016. Liberia was the hardest hit followed by Sierra Leone and then Guinea. BBC News Africa (2016) reports that of the 11,315 estimated Ebola deaths from the outbreak till January 2016, 4,809 (36%) were in Liberia,

3,955 (35%) were in Sierra Leone, and 2,536 (22%) were in Guinea. The reasons why these countries were hit the hardest are partly cultural, partly economic, and partly political. Culturally, the way the dead is handled in most African cultures can allow infectious diseases to spread easily. In particular, practices such as washing the dead body and getting it ready for viewing and then burial require close body contact especially from the closest relatives, instead of professionals. Second, funeral in many African cultures is a community rather than immediate family affair, which in turn involves a lot of body contact and an ideal environment for the spread of communicable diseases. Economically both Liberia and Sierra Leone had gone through a long period of civil war that had devastated the economy and dismantled the health-care infrastructure in both countries to fight such a deadly disease. Politically, like typical African countries, none of the three countries had the will and foresight in the past to plan for an effective public health-care system that is able to stem emergencies of any kind. Instead, planning in these countries for almost everything has been on ad-hoc basis and very aid-dependent. Under these conditions, all the three countries were at the mercy of the epidemic until external help arrived.

HIV/AIDS According to WHO (2016) Factsheet, the human immunodeficiency virus (HIV) attacks victims' immune system and makes them more susceptible to various kinds of diseases. The most advanced form of infection, the acquired immunodeficiency syndrome (AIDS), takes about 2–15 years to develop. Symptoms of initial infection include headache, fever, and sore throat. As the disease progresses, other symptoms may include swollen lymph nodes, weight loss, diarrhea, and cough. Left untreated, people may develop severe illness such as tuberculosis, meningitis, and lymphoma. The virus is transmitted through exchange of body fluids such as blood, breast milk, and semen. The use of condoms, HIV testing and counseling, medical circumcision, and use of antiretroviral drugs are the most effective ways to prevent the infection. HIV/AIDS is a pandemic that affect Africa the most. Although research now indicates that the HIV/AIDS virus may have been detected in the 1930s, the disease did not become a pandemic in Africa until the 1980s. Initial incidence was very high in East Africa, especially in Uganda, a development that has been attributed to sex workers along the truck routes that linked the East African countries. However, the rapid spread and the high death rates gave rise to several rumors and superstition as well as stigmatization of the disease's victims, which did not help to do something about the diseases. In 1987, the Ugandan government made HIV/AIDS prevention a priority and embarked on national education of AIDS prevention. Other governments slowly followed including South Africa, which became the epicenter of the disease in Africa in the 1990s. The development of the AZT drug and the subsequent successful negotiation with the drug companies and the US government to reduce the cost of the drugs and also to allow generic production of it by third parties finally made the drug accessible. By 2010, the infection rate of HIV/AIDS had been reduced in 22 African countries. Even so, in 2014, WHO estimated that there were 36.9 million people globally living with HIV, of which 25.8 million or 69.9% were living in Africa (mostly sub-Saharan Africa).

Malaria Malaria is the deadliest diseases in Africa after HIV/AIDS. It is especially deadliest among infants and juveniles. The disease is caused by a parasite that is carried by the *Anopheles gambiae* mosquito. The disease is passed on to humans through mosquito bites. Symptoms include chills and recurrent fever. Victims usually become deprived of energy and more vulnerable to other diseases. Transmission is intense in the forest and savannah regions, at altitudes up to 3,000 feet and an average rainfall of 200 cm (78 in.) per year. The disease is more prevalent in sub-Saharan Africa than in North Africa. About 80% of world malaria occurs in Africa, particularly in sub-Saharan Africa. In 2015, WHO estimated that 88% of the 214 million new cases globally were in sub-Saharan Africa, while 90% of deaths worldwide (384.2 million) occurred in sub-Saharan Africa (WHO, 2016). Of these an estimated 292 million or 76% were children. These figures actually show a decline in the incidence rate according to WHO estimates. Thus, between 2000 and 2015, the incidence rate in Africa decreased by 42% while mortality rate decreased by 66%. WHO also reports that over the same period the two most effective ways to prevent malaria—insecticide-treated mosquito net (ITN) and indoor residual spraying (IRS) have increased. However, the global burden of malaria in 2015 was still concentrated in 15 African countries. Together, these countries accounted for about 80% of all malaria cases and 77% of malaria deaths (WHO, 2016).

Respiratory tract diseases Respiratory tract diseases refer to a group of diseases that affect the respiratory tracts and the lungs. They include asthma, pneumonia, and chronic obstructive pulmonary diseases (COPD). Asthma is a chronic disease of the air passage that results in breathlessness and wheezing. It is not fatal but frequent attacks may cause inactivity, sleeplessness, and school and work absenteeism. Pneumonia is a disease of the lung that causes difficulty in breathing because the air sacs become filled with puss and fluid during breathing instead of air. Pneumonia is very deadly especially for children. COPD is also a lung disease that blocks airflow from the lungs. They include what used to be called bronchitis and emphysema (WHO, 2016). Like the CVDs these were not formerly thought to be diseases of Africa but that also has changed. Most of these diseases are attributed to smoking and indoor and outdoor pollution.

River blindness Also called onchocerciasis, river blindness is caused by a parasitic worm, *Onchocerca volvulus*, which is transmitted by the blackfly. The fly lives near swift-flowing streams and rivers. Infection begins when the fly lays its eggs on human skin. After hatching, the infant worm migrates to other parts of the human body eventually reaching the eye, where it dies causing the victim to become blind (Oppong, 2003). Symptoms include severe itching, disfiguring skin, visual impairment, and permanent blindness. WHO (2016) reports that in 2014, about 99% of the infected people globally lived in 31 African countries. There have been several past efforts to eliminate the disease. For example, between 1974 and 2002, a program was launched to bring the disease under control in West Africa. In 1995, the African Program for Onchocerciasis Control (APOC) was launched, and in 2009, it was switched to elimination of the disease. WHO reports that in 2014 a total 112 million people were treated by APOC.

Schistosomiasis Also called bilharziasis, schistosomiasis is "a parasitic worm disease that causes chronic ill health in people" (Oppong, 2003, p. 337). The disease is transmitted when infected people pass on the eggs containing the parasite through excrement into standing water. The eggs release the parasite which then finds a snail host and multiplies in thousands. The parasite reenters body openings during contact with the infected water and the cycle repeats itself. Since large bodies of standing water is ideal for the parasites, many irrigation and hydroelectricity development projects in Africa have inadvertently introduced the parasite to populations that did not have the disease (Oppong, 2003). According to WHO (2016), there are two types of schistosomiasis—intestinal and urogenital. The symptoms of intestinal schistosomiasis include abdominal pain, diarrhea, and liver enlargement, while the symptoms of urogenital type include blood in urine, fibrosis of the bladder and ureter, and kidney failure. The disease is not fatal, but in some cases, it can cause long-term damage including infertility. Both types are common in Africa, and it is estimated that about 90% of the 258 million people who needed treatment from the disease in 2014 lived in Africa (WHO, 2016).

Trypanosomiasis Also called sleeping sickness, this disease is transmitted by the tsetse fly, which serves as a carrier. The disease is passed on to humans or animals through tsetse fly bites. In humans, symptoms include fever, swelling of the lymph nodes, inflammation of the brain and spinal cord, lethargy, and listlessness (Oppong, 2003). Many affected people go undiagnosed. Killing the vector is the most effective line of attack. Although the tsetse fly is the vector of the disease, the existence of the tsetse fly does not necessarily coincide with the existence of the disease. According to WHO (2016), there are two types of human Trypanosomiasis. The *Trypanosomiasis brucei gambianse* occurs in 24 countries in West and Central Africa. This is the more common type, and it accounts for 98% of all the cases of the disease. In its advanced stage, this may affect the nervous system. The second type the *Tryponosomiasis brucei rhodesiene* is found in 13 countries in East and Southern Africa and accounts for less than 2% of reported cases. The disease burden is thus concentrated in the 26–27 countries in sub-Saharan Africa. However, according to WHO (2016) Factsheet, the DRC is the only country that reported 100–200 new cases in 2014. Another 14 countries reported less than 100 cases in 2014, while others have not reported any cases for over a decade.

Tuberculosis (TB) TB is a bacterial disease caused by the *Mycobacterium tuberculosis* that affects the lungs. It is an airborne disease, and it is spread from person to person when an infected person coughs or sneezes. The disease germs are released into the air and when that air is inhaled the person becomes infected. TB symptoms include cough, fever, and night sweat. TB is a worldwide disease that kills a lot of people and especially women as well as people who are HIV-positive. However, WHO (2016) estimated that in 2014, even though 58% of all new cases occurred in Southeast Asia and the Western Pacific Region, Africa bore the most severe burden of the disease with 281 cases per 100,000 population compared to the global average of 133 per 100,000 population. Of the six countries that had the highest incidence rates two were in Africa—Nigeria and South Africa. Oppong et al. (2014) show that the mega-slums of developing countries, including those of Africa, constitute potential incubators for re-emerging diseases such as TB.

Yellow fever This is a viral disease transmitted by the *Aedes* or *Haemogogus* mosquito. This is the disease that gave West Africa the infamous name of the "White Man's Grave" because it killed a lot of Europeans in the 18th and 19th centuries (Oppong, 2003). Symptoms include headaches, backaches, vomiting, and jaundice. People who develop severe symptoms can die within 7–10 days. The disease has no cure so once it is contracted, it must run its course, and survival will depend on treatment of such side effects as dehydration, kidney and liver failure, and fever. However, prevention of yellow fever by vaccination is very effective and can provide a life-long protection against the disease. Other measures including mosquito control and preparedness toward an outbreak are also effective. Yellow fever is a tropical disease and is thus confined to the tropical regions of Africa. It is endemic in 46 African countries. Other infectious diseases that are common in Africa are shown in Table 16.5.

TABLE 16.5

Incidence (Number of Reported Cases) of Selected Infectious Diseases in 2013

Country	Infectious disease							
	Cholera	Leprosy	Malaria	Measles	Meningitis	Rubella	Tetanus	Tuberculosis
Algeria	...	...	16	25	...	414	0	20,701
Angola	6,655	850	1,999,868	8,523	...	36	360	58,607
Benin	528	254	1,078,834	637	711	10	8	3,866
Botswana	...	...	456	1	...	121	0	6,834
Burkina Faso	...	253	3,769,051	375	3,476	27	27	5,326
Burundi	1,557	...	4,141,387	0	...	7	1	7,467
Cabo Verde	...	...	22	0	...	3	0	305
Cameroon	29	441	0	760	1,156	148	43	25,648
Central African Republic	...	99	116,300	596	169	31	68	8,590
Chad	...	391	754,565	226	235	...	176	11,237
Congo	1,624	53	43,232	124	...	107	5	10,699
Côte d'Ivoire	56	1,169	2,506,953	48	196	98	15	24,749
DRC	26,944	3,744	6,715,223	8,881	10,109	781	1,359	112,439
Djibouti	...	...	939	28	...	0	...	3,162
Egypt	...	...	0	405	...	34	9	7,876
Equatorial Guinea	...	...	13,129	321	...	0	0	...
Eritrea	...	...	21,317	45	...	19	0	2,860
Ethiopia	...	4,374	2,645,454	5,253	1,744	793	16	131,677
Gabon	...	...	28,982	122	...	5	0	5,179
Gambia	...	34	240,792	0	214	66	0	2,325
Ghana	50	...	1,639,451	319	448	168	1	15,043
Guinea	319	387	211,257	53	582	10	51	11,313
Guinea-Bissau	969	...	54,584	0	...	0	0	2,087
Kenya	...	...	2,335,286	190	...	299	1	89,796
Lesotho	...	...	...	516	...	516	0	9,555
Liberia	92	...	1,244,220	0	...	0	8	7,511
Libya	...	...	...	...	...	...	...	1,344
Madagascar	...	1,569	387,045	6	...	131	556	26,561

(Continued)

TABLE 16.5

Incidence (Number of Reported Cases) of Selected Infectious Diseases in 2013 (*Continued*)

Country	Cholera	Leprosy	Malaria	Measles	Meningitis	Rubella	Tetanus	Tuberculosis
Malawi	…	…	1,280,892	1	…	23	7	17,779
Mali	23	176	1,367,218	221	327	19	37	5,810
Mauritania	…	…	1,587	62	1	61	4	2,223
Morocco	…	38	0	92	…	1	29	126
Mozambique	1,869	…	2,998,874	8	…	127	59	53,272
Niger	585	424	1,431,798	1,224	327	6	71	11,251
Nigeria	6,600	3,385	0	52,852	1,175	88	556	94,825
Rwanda	…	…	962,618	17	…	50	0	5,702
Senegal	…	247	345,889	17	102	44	78	13,186
Sierra Leone	377	…	1,701,958	15	…	…	9	12,072
Somalia	6,864	…	43,317	3,173	…	…	321	12,994
South Africa	1	…	8,645	25	…	103	0	312,380
South Sudan	…	576	262,520	525	111	…	32	6,422
Sudan	…	677	592,383	2,813	207	291	88	19,056
Swaziland	…	…	402	0	…	110	0	6,641
Tanzania	270	2,005	1,552,444	185	…	116	…	64,053
Togo	166	…	882,430	564	351	38	26	2,600
Tunisia	…	0	…	16	…	15	8	3,035
Uganda	748	…	1,502,362	7,878	…	7,878	2,928	45,549
Zambia	…	…	0	35	…	183	0	40,638
Zimbabwe	…	…	422,633	0	…	130	4	32,899

Source: WHO.

Causes of Death

Africa's average life expectancy of 59 years is the lowest in the world. WHO compiles data on the causes of death globally using the convention communicable diseases, noncommunicable diseases, and injuries. According to the data, 52.3% of all the deaths in Africa in 2015 were due to communicable diseases, 37.8% were caused by noncommunicable diseases, while 9.9% were due to injuries. Of the communicable diseases, 55.5% were infectious and parasitic diseases, followed by respiratory diseases (18.8%), neonatal conditions (16.5%), nutritional deficiencies (6.1%), and maternal conditions (3%). For the noncommunicable diseases, 39% were cardiovascular diseases, followed by malignant neoplasms (cancers) (15%), digestive diseases (11.8%), respiratory diseases (6.4%), congenital anomalies (4.9), and genitourinary diseases (4.6%). Compared with 2000 data, there is an improvement in communicable disease which then accounted for 67.7% of total death. However, the share of both noncommunicable diseases and injuries was lower, being 24.9% and 7.9%, respectively. This could be due to the effectiveness of efforts to reduce HIV/AIDS as a cause of death. It could also be due to changing lifestyle of the growing middle class in Africa that are adopting new ways of living including diet and less physical activity.

Tables 16.6a and 16.6b show the top 10 diseases that caused death in Africa in 2000 and 2015, respectively, compared with that of the world. The tables reveal some interesting trends regarding the leading causes of death in Africa compared

---

TABLE **16.6a**

Top Ten Causes of Deaths in Africa and the World—2000

	Africa				The World		
Rank	Disease	Deaths (000)	Deaths (%)	Rank	Disease	Deaths (000)	Deaths (%)
1	HIV/AIDS	1,365	12.4	1	Ischemic heart disease	5,974	11.3
2	Lower respiratory infections	1,177	10.7	2	Stroke	5,662	10.7
3	Diarrheal diseases	905	8.3	3	Lower respiratory infections	3,491	6.6
4	Malaria	813	7.4	4	Chronic obstructive pulmonary disease	3,059	5.8
5	Measles	448	4.1	5	Diarrheal diseases	2,171	4.1
6	Stroke	435	4.0	6	HIV/AIDS	1,678	3.2
7	Preterm birth complications	428	3.9	7	Tuberculosis	1,343	2.5
8	Ischemic heart disease	362	3.3	8	Preterm birth complications	1,316	2.5
9	Birth asphyxia and birth trauma	360	3.3	9	Trachea, bronchus, lung cancers	1,164	2.2
10	Protein-energy malnutrition	332	3.0	10	Diabetes mellitus	1,046	2.0

Source: Global Health Estimates 2015: Deaths by Cause, Age, Sex, by Country and by Region, 2000-2015. Geneva, World Health Organization, 2016.

TABLE **16.6b**

Top Ten Causes of Deaths in Africa and the World—2015

	Africa				The World		
Rank	**Disease**	**Deaths (000)**	**Deaths (%)**	**Rank**	**Disease**	**Deaths (000)**	**Deaths (%)**
1	Lower respiratory infections	1,088	10.3	1	Ischemic heart disease	8,756	15.5
2	HIV/AIDS	766	7.3	2	Stroke	6,241	11.1
3	Diarrheal diseases	679	6.5	3	Lower respiratory infections	3,190	5.7
4	Ischemic heart disease	667	6.3	4	Chronic obstructive pulmonary disease	3,170	5.6
5	Stroke	575	5.5	5	Trachea, bronchus, lung cancers	1,695	3.0
6	Tuberculosis	447	4.3	6	Diabetes mellitus	1,586	2.8
7	Malaria	409	3.9	7	Alzheimer disease and other dementias	1,542	2.7
8	Preterm Birth Complications	382	3.6	8	Diarrheal diseases	1,389	2.5
9	Birth Asphyxia and Birth Trauma	351	3.3	9	Tuberculosis	1,373	2.4
10	Road Injury	305	2.9	10	Road Injury	1,342	2.4

Source: Global Health Estimates 2015: Deaths by Cause, Age, Sex, by Country and by Region, 2000-2015. Geneva, World Health Organization, 2016.

to the World. In 2000, HIV/AIDS was the leading cause of death in Africa followed by lower respiratory diseases, diarrheal diseases, malaria, measles, and stroke. In contrast, the leading cause of death globally was Ischemic heart disease, followed by stroke, lower respiratory infection, chronic obstructive pulmonary diseases, and diarrheal diseases. HIV/AIDS was only sixth on the world list, while malaria and measles were not among the world's top 10 killers. In 2015, lower respiratory infections slightly edged HIV/AIDS as the leading cause of death in Africa. The two were followed by diarrheal diseases, Ischemic heart disease, stroke, and tuberculosis (Table 16.6b). In contrast, Ischemic heart diseases, and stroke continued to be the top two killers globally with slight changes in the rest from 2000.

The rise of lower respiratory infections, Ischemic heart disease, and stroke as causes of death and the decline of malaria as well as the disappearance of measles from the top 10 causes of death in Africa are particularly important to note. This could be due to a number of reasons including changing lifestyle, declining environmental health quality, and effective prevention methods against such diseases

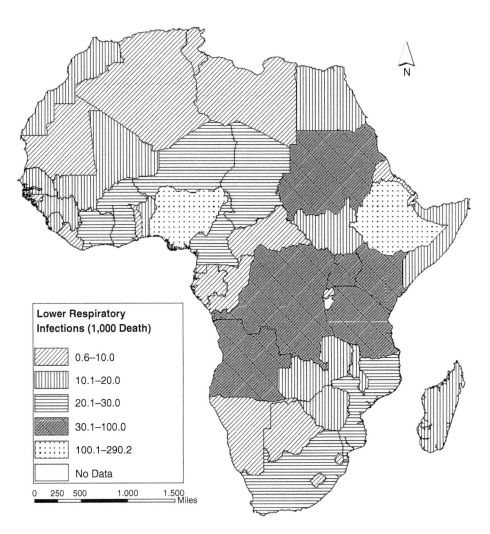

FIGURE 16.1 Death by Lower Respiratory Diseases, 2015. *Source:* WHO Estimates

Lower Respiratory Infections (1,000 Death)

- 0.6–10.0
- 10.1–20.0
- 20.1–30.0
- 30.1–100.0
- 100.1–290.2
- No Data

0   250 500   1.000   1.500
Miles

as malaria. The distribution of some of these leading causes of death are given by Figures 16.1–16.5.

Improved Drinking Water and Sanitation

Improved drinking water and improved sanitation are two other indicators that both depict and affect the well-being of people. Safe drinking water that can prevent a lot of water-borne diseases is still out of reach of millions of Africans, despite significant improvements made by African countries. In 2015, the coverage percentage of improved drinking water ranged from a high of 99% in Mauritius and Egypt to a low of 30% in Somalia (Figure 16.6). Nine countries including Egypt, Botswana, Comoros, Togo, Namibia, Djibouti, and South Africa had 90% or more coverage. Another 10 countries were in the range of 80% or more, while 6 countries had 71% or more coverage. However, there were 17 countries that had below 60% coverage.

The percentage coverage of improved sanitary conditions, however, was less impressive (Figure 16.7). Only four countries—Libya, Algeria, Egypt, and Mauritius—had 90% or more coverage. The only other countries with substantial improved

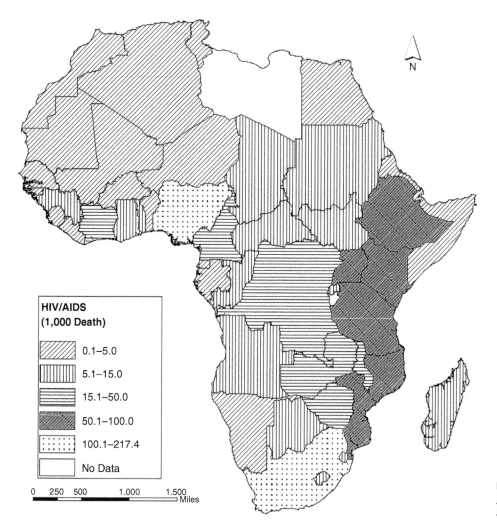

**HIV/AIDS
(1,000 Death)**

	0.1–5.0
	5.1–15.0
	15.1–50.0
	50.1–100.0
	100.1–217.4
	No Data

0   250   500   1.000   1.500
Miles

FIGURE 16.2 Death HIV/
AIDS, 2015.
Source: WHO Estimates

sanitation coverage were Togo (85%), South Africa (77%), Morocco (69%), Gambia (67%), and Botswana (60%). The remaining countries all had less than 60% coverage in improved sanitary conditions. The lowest coverage was 9% in Niger and Chad. Thus, in many countries, there is also no proper management of refuse and human waste. In the majority of countries, even urban areas lack adequate toilet facilities as well as proper landfills for garbage disposal. Instead, one sees open garbage dumps or pits often in the middle of low-income residential areas. Open sewer and sewage systems in most cases serve as dumps for garbage and human excreta. These garbage often block the water flow which then become good mosquito-breeding grounds.

Africa's Health-Care Delivery System

Africa's contemporary health-care system has remained almost the same in spite of all the reforms over the years. Broadly, there are three sectors—the modern medicine, the traditional medicine, and faith healing.

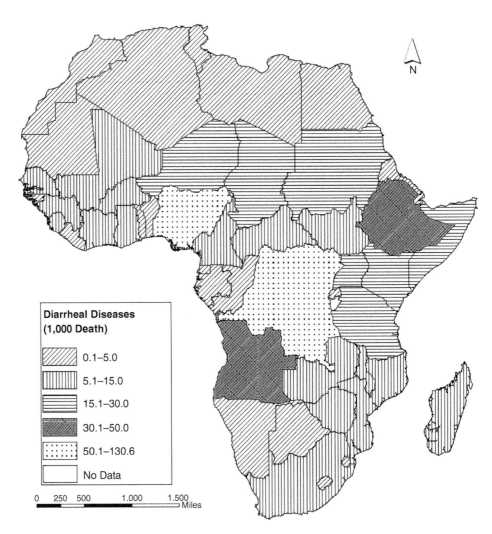

FIGURE 16.3 Death by Diarrheal Diseases, 2015.
Source: WHO Estimates

The Modern Medicine Sector

The modern sector consists of two subsectors—public and private. The public sector consists of a hierarchy of hospitals, developed as part of the AAD declaration. As mentioned before, facilities in this system include teaching, regional, and district hospitals as well as rural clinics or health centers. In addition, there are also specialty hospitals for mental health, leprosy, and tuberculosis (Oppong, 2003).

The private subsector of Africa's modern health-care system consists of mission or charitable hospitals most of which date back to the precolonial or colonial period. Unlike their public sector counterparts, these do not follow any particular geographic location pattern. The role they play in the health-care system varies from country to country. In some countries, they have very significant role, while in others they do not. In addition to the mission and charitable health providers, the private sector also includes a wide range of providers such as maternity clinics, small clinics to full blown hospitals that are run by individual or a group of medical practitioners. As Oppong (2003) points out, many African countries allow medical practitioners in public facilities to run their own private clinics or hospitals to supplement their income. This subsector has seen rapid growth over the

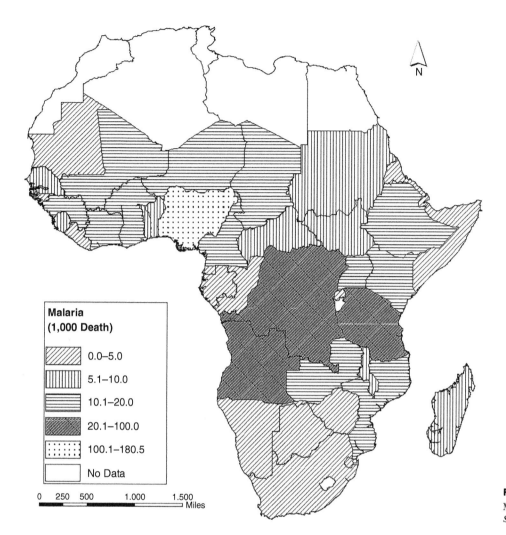

FIGURE 16.4 Death by Malaria, 2015.
Source: WHO Estimates

past few decades and have become popular with those who can afford to pay the relative higher user fees. This popularity is largely due to the fact that these private practitioners are becoming better in terms of equipment and medicine than even the public hospitals. Like their counterparts in the public sector, most of them are located in the urban centers.

A very important player that needs mention here is the thousands of nongovernmental organizations (NGOs) that focus on health care. Some of these are externally based with operations in African countries, but the majority are Africa-based. Some of these especially the religious-based ones such as the Muslim Brotherhoods of North Africa and West Africa had been around for a long time but the majority of the Africa-based ones emerged during the economic crisis of the 1980s and the effect of the SAPs. Examples are Partners In Health (PIH), which runs hospital facilities in Lesotho, Malawi, and Rwanda; Christian Health Association of Ghana (CHAG), which serves as the link between the Ministry of Health and the Ghana Health Service, whose member institutions provide about 42% of the health care in Ghana; and Treatment Action Campaign (TAC) of South Africa, which started as an advocate for funding of HIV/AIDS patients in South Africa, and was able to finally convince the government to fund AIDS treatment (Gros, 2016). Others

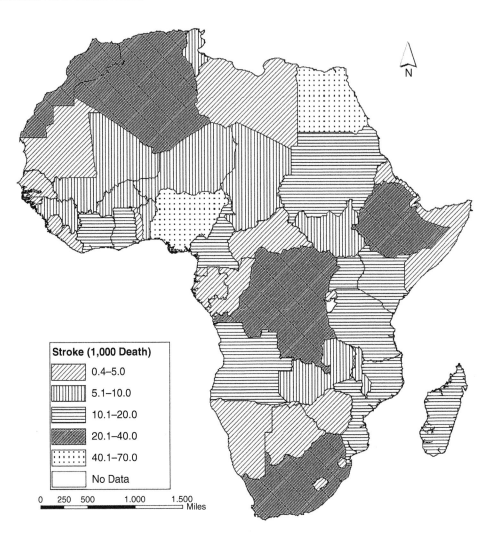

FIGURE 16.5 Death by
Stroke, 2015.
Source: WHO Estimates

include the Chandaria Foundation of Kenya, the Dongote Foundation on Nigeria, and the Well-Being Foundation of Nigeria. The Dongote Foundation recently broke ground for 1,000-bed hospital in the city of Kano in Nigeria and provided support for health professionals and medical equipment to Liberia in its fight against the Ebola outbreak. The Well-being Foundation is more devoted to maternal health in sub-Saharan Africa. Among the most well-known external-based organizations with big presence in Africa include Medicins Sans Frontieres (MSF) or Doctors Without Borders, the Carter Center, and the Bill and Melinda Gates Foundation. Gross (2016) reports that from 1999 to 2014 the Bill and Melinda Gates Foundation provided more than $1.1 billion to fund health care in Africa.

The Traditional Medicine Sector

The traditional sector consists of the herbalists, diviners, and religious or spiritual healers most of which came under assault during the colonial period and were neglected in the early postcolonial period. Today, it is the most widespread health-care delivery system in Africa. The survival of this system can be attributed to a number of factors. It is also more culturally acceptable to most Africans. It performs a

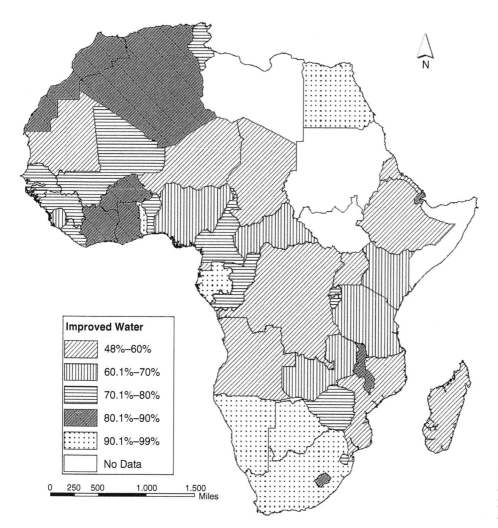

FIGURE 16.6 Percentage of Population with Good Drinking Water 2015. *Source:* WHO Estimates

wide range of psychological as well as social functions. It treats a broad spectrum of diseases. The only major weakness of this system is lack of standardized training and basic sanitation. In recent years, African countries have made efforts to incorporate traditional medicine into their health-care system. With the help of the WHO, African countries are now looking into collaboration between traditional and modern health-care systems. Among the possible areas of interests are regulation of herbal medicine, standardization of training and treatment methods, research into and establish safety standards and education of providers and users of traditional medicine.

The Faith Healing Sector

A third and a growing sector of Africa's health-care delivery system is faith healing, whereby members of both Christian and Muslim faiths seek healing through prayer and other religious rituals from charismatic leaders, most of whom claim to have the power of healing. This has resulted in a proliferation of churches and prayer camps where the sick flock to seek healing. Faith healing associated with Christian groups such as African Independent Churches occur in three main

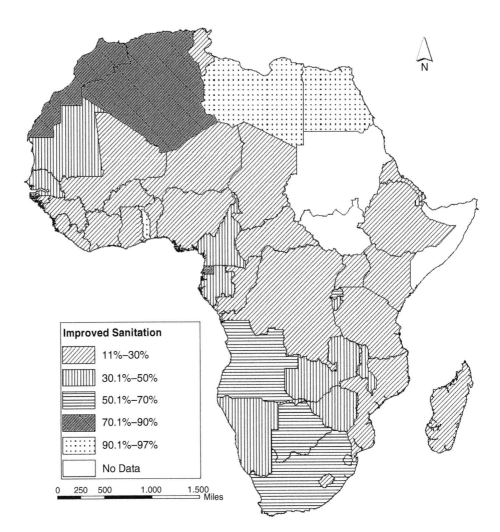

FIGURE 16.7 Percentage of
People with Improved Sanita-
tion Coverage 2015.
Source: WHO Estimates

forms—healing through public prayer, healing by water immersion, and healing through consultation of a prophet. All of these involve a call to self-examination and personal faith in the power of God over whichever force or cause of the disease. People seek this type of healing, especially when the causes of the disease is less understood, as a form of protection against a threatening epidemic, or as a last resort, when modern biomedicine has failed.

A recent study by WHO of 13 African countries selected from all the regions of the continent to document community perception of health care in Africa reported that 93.5% of the 10,315 respondents were aware of where to access health care (WHO, 2012). Of these, 85% reported that public sector health facilities were their main source of health care. This was followed by private sector facilities in urban areas (55.9%), peri-urban areas (46.7%), and rural areas (44.2%). Other sources were traditional healers (17.9%), faith-based facilities (14.7%), and informal drug dealers in urban areas (13.8%) (WHO, 2012).

The interesting thing about all these medical systems is that Africans use all these multiple sources of health-care systems to get well. Thus, it is common for a sick person to go to the hospital or see a doctor, consult with a traditional doctor, and at the same see a faith healer. This health-seeking behavior is deeply rooted in the African concept of disease and healing, which has both physical and spiritual dimensions.

Problems and Issues in Africa's Health-Care System

Africa's health-care system still faces a number of issues and problems that include policy, financing, inadequate facilities and resources, accessibility, affordability, and brain drain.

Financing

Financing is the number one problem facing Africa's health-care system. For the majority of African countries, health care accounts for between 3 and 6% of their GDP, except for countries such as Sierra Leone, Djibouti, Lesotho, and Liberia where it accounts for more (Table 16.7). WHO estimates show that Africa's average health-care expenditure in 2015 was 6.2% of GDP. This was below the global average of 6.3% but above 4.7% of South-east Asia and 5.3% of WHO's Eastern Mediterranean region excluding Egypt and Libya. In addition, African governments accounted for an average of 50.8% of all the health-care expenditures in 2015. Indeed, in Algeria, Cabo Verde, Equatorial Guinea, Ghana, Lesotho, Madagascar, and Seychelles government health expenditures were 60% or more of total health-care expenditures (Table 16.8). However, Africa's average was below the global average of 60%, and governments in all other major regions of the world except the Southeast Asia region accounted for higher share of health-care expenditures than the majority of African countries. The problem is with Africa's relatively lower GDP compared to the other major regions and with many competing demands, government health-care spending is on the average only 10% of the total government expenditure compared to the global average of 15.5%. The data actually show that the government's share of health-care expenditure declined in 23 countries over that past decade while it increased in 21 countries over the same period. The issue becomes more problematic when the sources of the funds are considered, because in 2015, 9.7% of the total health-care expenditure in Africa came from external sources. No other major world region came close given that the global average was 0.2% (Table 16.9). In nine of

TABLE **16.7**					
Total Health Expenditure as Percentage of Gross Domestic Product					
Countries	**1995**	**2000**	**2005**	**2010**	**2015**
Algeria	4	3	3	5	7
Angola	6	3	4	3	3
Benin	5	4	5	5	4
Botswana	4	5	6	6	6
Burundi					8
Burkina Faso	5	5	7	7	5
Cabo Verde	5	5	5	5	5
Cameroon	4	4	5	5	5
Central African Republic					5
Chad	6	6	4	3	4
Comoros	5	4	4	6	8

(Continued)

TABLE **16.7**

Total Health Expenditure as Percentage of Gross Domestic Product (*Continued*)

Countries	1995	2000	2005	2010	2015
Congo	3	2	2	2	3
Côte d'Ivoire	6	6	5	6	5
DRC	3	1	3	4	4
Djibouti	4	6	7	9	4
Egypt	4	6	5	5	4
Equatorial Guinea	5	3	2	4	3
Eritrea	5	4	3	3	3
Ethiopia	3	4	4	7	4
Gabon	3	3	3	3	3
Gambia	3	4	5	6	7
Ghana	3	3	5	5	6
Guinea	4	3	3	5	5
Guinea-Bissau	6	5	6	7	7
Kenya	4	5	4	4	5
Lesotho	7	7	6	11	8
Liberia	:	6	8	12	15
Libya	3	3	3	3	
Mali	5	6	6	6	6
Madagascar					5.2
Mauritania	5	5	4	3	5
Mauritius	4	4	4	5	5
Mozambique					5.4
Morocco	4	4	5	6	6
Namibia	6	6	7	8	9
Niger	7	6	7	6	7
Nigeria	3	3	4	3	4
Rwanda	4	4	7	8	8
Sao Tome and Principe	8	9	10	5	10
Senegal	4	5	5	5	5
Seychelles	5	5	4	4	3
Sierra Leone	11	14	12	10	18
South Africa	8	8	8	9	8
South Sudan	:	:	:	:	3
Sudan	4	3	3	8	6
Swaziland	5	5	7	8	7
Tanzania	3	3	5	5	6
Togo	4	4	5	5	6
Tunisia	6	5	6	7	7
Uganda	6	7	9	11	7
Zambia	5	7	8	4	5
Zimbabwe	:	7	6	5	10

TABLE **16.8**

Government Health Expenditure as Percentage of Total Health Expenditure, 1995-2015

Countries	1995	2000	2005	2010	2015
Algeria	72	73	70	70	71
Angola	72	60	49	61	48
Benin	45	44	50	54	20
Botswana	52	62	73	63	55
Burkina Faso	38	40	60	55	28
Burundi	31	28	30	62	38
Cabo Verde	80	73	75	71	68
Cameroon	23	21	24	29	15
Central African Republic	38	50	49	51	49
Chad	35	42	40	40	55
Comoros	62	43	53	25	33
Congo	59	58	59	60	82
Côte d'Ivoire	26	30	24	27	29
DRC	5	3	24	26	37
Djibouti	60	68	68	58	64
Egypt	47	40	39	39	38
Equatorial Guinea	72	79	56	80	77
Eritrea	48	36	37	44	46
Ethiopia	41	55	61	54	59
Gabon	36	40	40	72	68
Gambia	32	34	58	60	69
Ghana	53	50	65	72	60
Guinea	35	32	20	44	48
Guinea-Bissau	25	10	19	28	20
Kenya	46	46	42	36	61
Lesotho	48	50	53	74	76
Liberia	:	25	19	23	31
Libya	46	49	65	70	74
Madagascar	35	51	52	54	48
Malawi	37	46	74	63	53
Mali	52	33	48	44	23
Mauritania	48	53	48	46	50
Mauritius	55	52	50	49	49
Mozambique	64	70	63	56	56
Namibia	71	69	49	58	63
Niger	22	25	42	34	46
Nigeria	24	33	29	26	21
Rwanda	38	39	47	37	17

(Continued)

TABLE **16.8**

Government Health Expenditure as Percentage of Total Health Expenditure, 1995-2015 (*Continued*)

Countries	1995	2000	2005	2010	2015
Sao Tome and Principe	37	43	53	48	21
Senegal	33	41	56	51	37
Seychelles	85	82	93	89	97.0
Sierra Leone	21	26	22	23	9.0
South Africa	41	41	43	47	No data
South Sudan					53.6
Sudan	20	28	34	34	21.1
Swaziland	57	56	68	70	31.1
Tanzania	45	43	64	39	64.7
Togo	38	33	37	36	35.3
Tunisia	49	55	51	59	28.0
Uganda	25	27	25	28	56.3
Zambia	43	52	52	52	13.4
Zimbabwe	:	62	43	31	36.6

Source: WHO 2015 Estimates.

TABLE **16.9**

External Sources as Percentage of Total Health Expenditure in Africa

Countries	1995	2000	2005	2010	2015
Algeria	<	<	<	<	<
Angola	5	3	4	2	3
Benin	20	17	21	29	34
Botswana	1	<	5	8	8
Burkina Faso	16	14	36	36	30
Burundi	14	19	27	51	41
Cabo Verde	4	13	18	6	7
Cameroon	5	4	5	7	8
Central African Republic	9	19	35	25	44
Chad	23	25	13	9	15
Comoros	30	21	24	14	10
Congo	6	5	8	5	11
Côte d'Ivoire	2	4	4	10	26
DRC	6	2	21	45	39
Djibouti	49	33	12	19	23
Egypt	3	1	1	1	<
Equatorial Guinea	4	7	3	3	2

(*Continued*)

TABLE **16.9**

External Sources as Percentage of Total Health Expenditure in Africa (*Continued*)

Countries	1995	2000	2005	2010	2015
Eritrea	16	27	36	34	25
Ethiopia	12	16	37	50	15
Gabon	8	2	4	1	1
Gambia	3	19	48	34	29
Ghana	8	15	23	18	26
Guinea	8	23	17	36	25
Guinea-Bissau	3	30	26	32	32
Kenya	5	8	22	35	19
Lesotho	6	3	17	19	26
Liberia	:	9	31	48	71
Libya	-	-	-	1	<
Madagascar	6	15	27	17	27
Malawi	29	27	68	58	54
Mali	3	8	14	24	36
Mauritania	10	11	17	11	9
Mauritius	2	1	<	2	3
Mozambique	33	25	43	65	85
Namibia	3	4	17	18	9
Niger	14	23	29	15	26
Nigeria	<	16	4	8	10
Rwanda	5	52	53	64	44
Sao Tome and Principe	46	35	33	27	49
Senegal	9	16	22	22	12
Seychelles	1	5	1	6	1
Sierra Leone	1	7	13	13	53
South Africa	2	2	2	2	2
Sudan	<	4	4	3	2
Swaziland	2	6	3	14	16
Tanzania	9	28	24	40	37
Togo	1	7	24	13	15
Tunisia	1	1	<	<	<
Uganda	12	27	24	51	40
Zambia	12	13	38	50	24
Zimbabwe	:	:	:	:	24

Source: WHO 2015 Estimates.

the countries that had data on the subject in 2015, foreign sources accounted for between 10 and 20% of the health-care expenditure. In another 15 countries, the share was from 20% to 40%, while in yet another seven countries, the share of foreign sources exceeded 40%. The past initiatives including cost sharing and national health insurance systems have had some positive effects but funds to support these programs are still insufficient, which in turn cause long delays in paying health-care providers in many countries. In the case of Ghana for example, the delays in reimbursement have caused the health-care providers to refuse to participate in the system. Other problems facing the program include low enrollment, high level of poverty making premiums too expensive, perceptions that NHIS does not provide quality health-care service, distance and accessibility from health-care facilities, financial sustainability, and corruption and theft that leads to the loss in revenue (Dixon et al., 2011, 2013; Teye et al., 2015). All these are driving many people away from seeking health care until it is too late. In many cases, going to the hospital becomes last resort when it is usually too late. In the larger scheme of things, African countries would need stronger and more diversified economies and would also need to find ways to raise more internal revenue through taxation to support such important social programs.

Policy

The substantial dependence on foreign sources in the health-care expenditure of African countries has created a situation where African countries do not have a firm control on their health-care policies. Instead, much of the policy making and resulting policies are driven by external interests and agenda. The result is that the focus of the policies is somewhat out of sync with local needs. A case in point is the increasing importance of lower respiratory diseases and stroke as causes of death in African countries; yet, these diseases have not attracted donor attention in Africa as HIV/AIDS and malaria have. This is not to say that HIV/AIDS and malaria are not important, but the neglect of these emerging causes of death will eventually rise to epidemic situations. In the WHO (2012) study on community perceptions, less than 15% of the respondents mentioned HIV/AIDS as a major health problem. Instead, in all regions, malaria and fever were mentioned for children, while for adults, it was hypertension and diabetes. Apart from this, there is an overemphasis on curative medicine and less on public health (monitoring and containment of disease pathogens, public education of the physical and human environment that makes them thrive, plans to deal with them, and trained personnel to execute all these). The result is that the system is incapable of dealing with epidemics. This is what occurred in the HIV/AIDS epidemic in the 1990s and the 2014 Ebola outbreak. Finally, despite the proliferation of regional economic integration in Africa, and despite the strong role played by external agencies in the health-care systems of most African countries, there are no integrated health-care policies inside and outside the continent to deal with epidemics. As Gros (2016, p. 150) rightly points out:

> The sad fact is more than half a century after independence Africa as a whole remains woefully unprepared to deal with any major social and crises on its own and must resort to external help.

Inadequate Facilities, Human Resources, and Service

African health-care system is grossly inadequate in terms of physical facilities, human resources, and the technology to pursue cutting medical treatment. Few countries such as South Africa and Botswana have the physical facilities together with the human resources to meet the increasing demand for health care. For the most part, the physical facility is not adequate—not enough beds, drugs and medicines, as well as equipment. There is a shortage of health workers due in part to brain drain and in part to poor conditions of service, which make them pursue their own private interest for survival. Data are not only spotty but also old; so, it is difficult to make a definitive statement about the state of health-care personnel in Africa. However, from a collection of spotty data from 2007 to 2013, only three countries, all of them in North Africa, had physician density above 10 per 10,000 population (Table 16.10). These were Egypt (28.3), Tunisia (12.2), and Algeria (12.1). The number of nurses and midwives was relatively better in Egypt (35.2), Botswana (33.5), Tunisia (32.8), and Namibia (27.8). However, the number of dentists, pharmacists, and psychiatrists per 10,000 population as well as the number of hospitals per 100,000 population were woefully inadequate across the board. The health-care workers who stay at their posts tend to have a bad attitude toward patients. All these tend to create long queues and prolonged periods of waiting at health-care facilities. In addition to these, the WHO (2012) reported situations where priority in health care was given to relatives and friends or acquaintances of health-care workers in the public facilities. The fact that top government officials including the president are able to go outside for health care at the expense of the state does not seem to help the sorry state of health-care infrastructure in many African countries.

Spatial and Social Inequities in Health-Care Service

The overconcentration of health-care facilities in urban areas that began in the colonial period has continued in the postcolonial era, and African countries have not been able to get away from it. Thus, better health care is still inaccessible for the majority of people who live in rural areas. Rural health centers or clinics that were built in the postcolonial period have so far not helped because most of them are not well equipped and most have a hard time recruiting and retaining qualified health workers. A select sample of health-care services in Table 16.11 illustrates the

TABLE **16.10**

Density of Health Workforce per 10,000 Population, (2007–2013)

Country	Physicians	Nursing and midwifery personnel	Dentistry personnel	Pharmaceutical personnel	Psychiatrists	Hospitals per 100,000
Algeria	12.1	19.5	3.3	2.4	0.2	...
Angola	1.7	16.6	...	...	...	...
Benin	0.6	7.7	<0.05	<0.05	<0.05	0.4
Botswana	4	33.5	0.8	2.1	<0.05	1.3
Burkina Faso	0.5	5.7	<0.05	0.2	<0.05	0.3
Burundi	...	...	...	0.2	<0.05	0.5
Cabo Verde	3.1	5.6	0.1	0.1	...	1
Cameroon	0.8	4.4	<0.05	<0.05	...	0.8
Central African Rep.	0.5	2.6	<0.05	<0.05	<0.05	0.5
Chad	...	...	...	...	...	0.7
Congo	1	8.2	...	0.2	<0.05	...
Côte d'Ivoire	1.4	4.8	0.1	0.2	<0.05	1.7
DRC	...	...	...	<0.05	<0.05	0.4

(Continued)

TABLE **16.10**

Density of Health Workforce per 10,000 Population, (2007-2013) (*Continued*)

Country	Physicians	Nursing and midwifery personnel	Dentistry personnel	Pharmaceutical personnel	Psychiatrists	Hospitals per 100,000
Djibouti	...	8	1.2	3.2	<0.05	...
Egypt	28.3	35.2	4.2	16.7	0.1	0.6
Equatorial Guinea	...	...	...	...	...	...
Eritrea	...	...	...	...	0	0.4
Ethiopia	0.3	2.5	...	0.3	...	0.2
Gabon	...	...	...	...	...	3.5
Gambia	1.1	8.7	0.3	0.5	<0.05	0.7
Ghana	1	9.3	0.1	0.7	<0.05	1.4
Guinea	...	...	...	...	<0.05	0.4
Guinea-Bissau	0.7	5.9	0.1	0.1	...	56.4
Kenya	2	8.6	0.2	0.5	...	1.5
Lesotho	...	...	...	...	<0.05	...
Liberia	0.1	2.7	<0.05	0.8	...	0.4
Libya	19	68	6	3.6	0.1	2.6
Madagascar	1.6	...	<0.05	...	<0.05	0.5
Malawi	0.2	3.4	0.1	0.2	...	0.4
Mali	0.8	4.3	0.1	0.1	<0.05	0.5
Mauritania	1.3	6.7	0.3	0.4	...	1
Morocco	6.2	8.9	0.8	2.7	<0.05	...
Mozambique	0.4	4.1	...	0.6	<0.05	...
Namibia	3.7	27.8	0.4	1.8	<0.05	1.9
Niger	0.2	1.4	<0.05	<0.05	<0.05	0.5
Nigeria	4.1	16.1	0.2	1.1	<0.05	...
Rwanda	0.6	6.9	0.1	0.1	<0.05	...
Senegal	0.6	4.2	0.1	0.1	<0.05	0.2
Sierra Leone	0.2	1.7	<0.05	0.2	<0.05	...
Somalia	...	...	...	...	<0.05	...
South Africa	7.8	51.1	2	4.1	<0.05	0.7
South Sudan	...	...	...	...	<0.05	...
Sudan	2.8	8.4	0.2	0.1 I	<0.05	1.3
Swaziland	1.7	16	0.4	0.5	<0.05	0.8
Tanzania	0.3	4.4	0.1	0.1	...	...
Togo	0.5	2.7	<0.05	<0.05	<0.05	0.6
Tunisia	12.2	32.8	2.9 I	3	0.3	2.3
Uganda	...	...	...	0.3	<0.05	0.4
Zambia	1.7	7.8	0.3	0.9	<0.05	0.5
Zimbabwe	0.8	13.4	0.2	0.4	<0.05	0.5

Source: World Health Statistics 2015: Part II Global Health Indicators.

TABLE **16.11**

Rural – Urban Differences in Selected Women Reproductive Health Care Services

Country	Year of Estimate	Contraceptive prevalence - modern methods (%)		Contraceptive prevalence - modern and traditional methods (%)		Demand for family planning satisfied (%)	
		Rural	Urban	Rural	Urban	Rural	Urban
Benin	2011	6.8	9.5	11.5	15.0	27.8	32.1
Burkina Faso	2010	10.8	30.8	11.3	34.3	32.0	62.1
Burundi	2010	16.7	28.8	20.6	35.4	40.6	59.4
Cote d'Ivoire	2011	9.8	16.3	14.7	23.1	33.9	48.2
Cameroon	2011	8.7	20.8	14.4	33.4	37.2	59.5
Central African Rep.	2010	2.5	20.1	8.4	26.0	No data	No data
Chad	2004	0.4	7.1	1.2	9.9	5.6	29.0
Comoros	2012	11.0	20.6	14.4	29.6	29.2	55.1
Congo	2011	11.7	24.6	41.9	46.3	68.7	72.4
DRC	2013	4.6	14.6	15.4	31.1	37.0	52.6
Djibouti	2006	3.5	17.7	4.9	18.4	16.1	45.5
Egypt	2008	54.8	61.6	57.5	64.3	84.3	90.7
Ethiopia	2011	22.5	49.5	23.4	52.5	46.0	77.8
Gambia	2005	No data	No data	No data	No data	No data	No data
Ghana	2011	23.4	23.3	32.5	36.9	No data	No data
Guinea	2012	3.5	7.4	4.3	8.7	16.6	25.5
Guinea-Bissau	2006	2.4	15.2	6.8	19.0	20.9	45.6
Kenya	2008	37.2	46.6	43.1	53.1	61.3	72.4
Lesotho	2009	40.7	57.2	42.2	58.3	61.5	79.6
Liberia	2013	16.3	21.6	16.8	23.2	35.3	44.5
Madagascar	2008	28.0	35.6	37.2	54.3	66.1	75.6
Malawi	2010	40.7	49.6	44.5	53.7	62.5	69.5
Mali	2012	6.8	21.8	7.1	22.8	24.7	54.8
Mauritania	2007	3.3	13.8	4.0	15.8	15.5	37.3
Morocco	2003	53.2	56.0	59.7	65.5	85.4	87.5
Mozambique	2011	7.2	21.1	7.4	21.6	26.4	47.4
Namibia	2006	43.0	63.8	44.6	65.4	63.5	80.9
Niger	2012	9.7	27.0	11.3	29.0	42.3	63.2
Nigeria	2013	5.7	16.9	8.5	26.8	35.4	66.0
Rwanda	2010	44.9	47.0	51.4	53.1	73.2	78.2
Sao Tome & Principe	2008	40.1	28.0	44.1	33.3	57.9	44.5
Senegal	.2	9.2	27.3	10.7	29.3	25.9	53.2
Sierra Leone	13	12.3	24.7	13.0	26.6	36.6	52.0
Somalia	2006	0.2	3.0	13.4	16.9	No data	No data
South Africa	1998	43.7	62.8	45.1	63.7	68.2	85.4
Swaziland	2010	60.5	69.0	62.5	71.6	No data	No data

Rural – Urban Differences in Selected Women Reproductive Health Care Services (*Continued*)

Country	Year of Estimate	Contraceptive prevalence - modern methods (%)		Contraceptive prevalence - modern and traditional methods (%)		Demand for family planning satisfied (%)	
		Rural	Urban	Rural	Urban	Rural	Urban
Togo	2010	11.8	15.4	13.6	17.7	No data	No data
Uganda	2011	23.4	39.2	26.9	45.8	45.3	69.5
Tanzania	2010	25.2	34.1	30.5	45.9	52.9	70.2
Zambia	2007	27.6	42.0	36.7	48.4	56.5	67.5
Zimbabwe	2010	55.7	60.4	57.0	61.5	81.6	84.5

Source: WHO Estimates.

differences in health-care delivery services between rural and urban areas. The table shows that the access of modern contraceptive use in urban areas is better than that in the rural areas in almost every country, although the percentages are generally low. The same applies to the use of both traditional and modern methods of contraception as well as the demand for family planning that is satisfied. Similar inequities exist in access to health along educational background and income status. As a result oftentimes people who live near rural health centers tend to bypass the facilities to go to the district or regional hospitals for care (Oppong, 2003).

Drug Shortages and Fake Drugs

The rising cost of health care and competing priorities have led to acute shortages of drugs. Often patients cannot find prescribed medicine to buy even if they can afford it. In the WHO (2012) report, up to 73.5% of the respondent reported this situation. Reimbursements of medical expenses are limited. Only few countries such as Algeria and Cameroon have such programs. In most cases, there is health insurance, but it applies to only those in the formal sector with the vast majority of people in the informal sector not covered. In the absence of drugs at the health-care facilities, there has arisen a major problem of fake drugs and itinerant drug vendors that go through the countryside posing as quack physicians and giving medication that turn out to be rather harmful to human health (Oppong, 2003).

Summary

Health care has always been present in Africa. Precolonial Africans had their own ways of treating diseases. While this system was not based on the germ theory of diseases, it was developed on the African concept of health and well-being that had both physical and spiritual dimensions. Colonialism brought changes to this system, including institution of scientific or biomedicine, and curative and preventive measures of some of Africa's endemic diseases. However, competitive rivalry with traditional African medical practices led to vilification of Africa's traditional medicine as evil. At the same time, the differences in colonial philosophies left a patch work medical facilities on the continent after colonialism ended. Africa's new governments tried to expand their health-care system and became signatories of the Alma-Ata Declaration of 1978. However, political instability, economic misman-agement, collapse of primary commodity prices, and rising oil prices in the 1970s plunged many of these countries into economic crises. Rescue efforts by way of structural adjustment programs made the situation worse for many of these coun-tries. The majority of African countries have not fully recovered from the crisis as demonstrated by the recent Ebola outbreak. Africa still grapples with many of its endemic diseases and is becoming more and more dependent on external aid to meet its health-care obligations. This has subjected Africa to many global initiatives that are not able to meet its need, instead of having freedom to chart its own path. Africa needs to find ways to focus on public health since much of its health-care problems generate from basic sanitation and environmental health conditions. This could be done by public education. It also needs to find ways to generate internal revenue to develop an effective health-care delivery system.

Postreading Assignment

A. Study the Following concepts

Alma-Ata Declaration (AAD)	Bamako Initiative (BI) Disease ecology	Education attainment education participation	Morbidity

B. Discussion Questions

1. Go back to the answers you wrote down for the preread-ing assignment questions and compare your answers to what you know now. Is there any ones that you would like to change?

2. If you were to identify one problem facing Africa's edu-cation system what will it be?

3. What will you propose for African countries to do to resolve that problem?

4. What would you say is the leading problem facing Africa's health-care system?

5. What solutions can you offer to help African countries deal with the problem?

References

Abdalla, I. H. 1992. "Diffusion of Islamic Medicine into Hausa-land." In Fierman, S., and Janzen, J. M. (Eds.). *The Social Basis of Health and Healing in Africa.* Berkeley: University of California Press, pp. 177–199.

Abugideiri, H. 2004. "The Scientisation of Culture: Colonial Medi-cine's Construction of Egyptian Womanhood, 1893–1929." *Gender & History* 16(1): 83–98.

Akande, T. 2014. "Youth Unemployment in Nigeria: A Situation Analysis." https://www.brookings.edu/blog/africa-in-focus/2014/09/23/youth-unemployment-in-nigeria-a-situation-analysis/. Accessed December 9, 2018.

Alubo, S. O. 1990. "Debt Crisis, Health and Health Services in Africa." *Social Science & Medicine* 31(6): 639–648.

Anonymous (ND). Ghana. The Castle Schools. http://educa-tion.stateuniversity.com/pages/529/Ghana-HISTORY-BACK-GROUND.html, *History Background.*

Anyinam, C. A. 1989. "The Social Costs of the International Monetary Fund's Adjustment Programs for Poverty: The case of Healthcare Development in Ghana." *The International Journal of Health Services* 19(3): 531–547.

Babalola, J. B., Lungwangwa, G., and Adenyinka, A. A. 1999. "Edu-cation and Structural Adjustment in Nigeria and Zambia." *McGill Journal of Education* 39(1): 79–98.

Bigawa, R. N. 2014. "The Democratic Republic of the Congo: An Overview." In Wolhuter, C. (Ed.) *Education in East and Central Africa.* London: Bloomsbury Academic, pp 131–156.

Chaiken, M. S. 1998. "Primary Health care Initiatives in Colonial Kenya." *World Development* 26(9): 1701–1717.

Clignet, R. P., and Foster, P. J. 1964. "French and British Colonial Education in Africa." *Comparative Education Review* 8(2): 191–198.

Crozier, A. 2007. *Practicing Colonial Medicine: The Colonial Medical service in British East Africa.* New York: I. B. Tauris.

Curtin, P. D. 1998. *Disease and Empire: The Health of European Troops in the Conquest of Africa.* Cambridge, UK: Cambridge University Press.

Curtin, P. 1992. "Medical Knowledge and Urban Planning in Colonial Tropical Africa." In Fierman, S., and Janzen, J. M. (Eds.) *The Social basis of Health and Healing in Africa.* Berkeley: University of California Press, pp. 235–255.

Curtin, P. D. 1989. *Death by Migration: Europe's Encounter with the Tropical World in the Nineteenth Century.* Cambridge, UK: Cambridge University Press.

Delobelle, P. 2013. The Health System in South Africa. Historical Perspectives and Current Challenges." In Wolhuter, C. C. (Ed.). *South Africa in Focus: Economic, Political and Social Issues.* Hauppauge, N.Y: Nova Science Publishers, Inc. pp. 159–205.

Dixon, J., Tenkorang, E. Y., and Luginaah, I. 2013. "Ghana's National Health Insurance Scheme: A National Level Investigation of Members' Perceptions of Service Provision." *BMC International Health and Human Rights* 13(1): 35.

Dixon, J., Tenkorang, E. Y., and Luginaah, I. 2011. "Ghana's National Health Insurance Scheme: Helping the Poor or Leaving Them Behind?" *Environment and Planning C: Government and Policy* 29: 1102–1115.

Duffy, J. 1961. "Portuguese Africa (Angola and Mozambique): Some Critical Problems and the Role of Education in their Resolution." *The Journal of Negro Education* 30(3): 294–301.

Edy, T. P. 1983. "The Evolution of British Colonial Hospitals in West Africa." *Transactions of the Royal Society of Tropical Medicine and Hygiene* 77(4): 563–564.

EFA Global Monitoring Report, 2015. *Education For All: Achievements and Challenges.* Paris: UNESCO.

Fine, L. 2007. *Colorblind Colonialism Lusotropicalismo and Portugal's 20th Century Empire in Africa.* https://history.barnard.edu/sites/default/files/inline/fine-thesis.pdf. Accessed January 23, 2016.

Flint, K. E. 2008. *Healing Traditions: African Medicine, Cultural Exchange, and Competition in South Africa, 1820–1948.* Athens: Ohio University Press.

Frankema, E. P. 2012. "The origins of formal education in sub-Saharan Africa: Was British rule more benign?" *European Review of Economic History* (16): 335–355.

Garner, P. 1989. "The Bamako Initiative: Financing Health In Africa By Selling Drugs." *British Medical Journal* 299(6694): 277–278.

Good, C. M. 1991. "Pioneer Medical Missions in Colonial Africa." *Social Science & Medicine* 32(1): 1–10.

Gros, J. 2016. *Healthcare Policy in Africa.* Lanham, MD: Rowman & Littlefield.

Hakansson, N. T. 1998. "Pagan Practices and the Death of Children: German Colonial Missionaries and Child Health Care in South Pare, Tanzania." *World Development* 26(9): 1763–1772.

Hartwig, C. E. 1979. "Church-State Relations in Kenya: Health Issues. [1]" *Social Science and Medicine* 13C: 121–127.

Keita, M. 2007. *A Political Economy of Health Care in Senegal.* Leiden: Brill.

King, K. 2015. "The Global Targeting of Education and Skill: Policy, History and Comparative Perspectives." *NORRAG.*

Langa, P. V. 2013. *Higher Education in Portuguese Speaking African Countries.* Cape Town: African Minds.

Lulat, Y. G-M. 2005. *A History of Higher Education in Africa from Antiquity to the Present: A Critical Analysis.* Westport, CT: Praeger Publishers.

Majgaard, K., and Mingat, A. 2012. *Education in sub-Saharan Africa: A Comparative Analysis.* Washington, DC: The World Bank. DOI: 10.1596/978-0-8213-8889-1 (License: Creative Commons Attribution CC BY 3.0).

Mcauliffe, J. 2013. "Addressing the Youth Unemployment Crisis in the Middle East." https://archive.skoll.org/2013/04/09/addressing-the-youth-unemployment-crisis-in-the-middle-east/. Accessed November 22, 2018.

Metz, H. C. (Ed.) 1994. *Algeria: A Country Study.* Washington: GPO for the Library of Congress, http://countrystudies.us/algeria/. Accessed July 12, 2016.

Mulderig, M. C. 2013. *An Uncertain Future: Youth Frustration and the Arab Spring.* Boston, MA: Trustees of Boston University.

Munene, I. I. 2015. Providing Basic Education For All in Africa: What We Have Learned. *Africa Education Review* 12(1): 1–6.

Njlale, P. M. 2014. "Equatorial Guinea and Sao Tome and Principe: Context, Analysis and Comparison." In Wolhuter, C. (Ed.) *Education in East and Central Africa.* London: Bloomsbury Academic, pp. 176–190.

Nordman, C. J., and Kuepie, M. 2014. "Republic of Congo: Education and Labour Market." In Wolhuter, C. (Ed.) *Education in East and Central Africa.* London: Bloomsbury Academic, pp. 89–130.

Nsiangengo, P., Andre', D. J., and Wolhuter, C. C. 2014. "Angola: An Overview." In Wolhuter, C. (Ed.) *Education in East and Central Africa.* London: Bloomsbury Academic, pp. 15–36.

Oppong, J. R. 2003. "Medical Geography of sub-Saharan Africa." In Aryeetey-Attoh, S. (Ed.) *Geography of sub-Saharan Africa.* 2nd Edition. Upper Saddle River, NJ: Prentice Hall, pp. 324–362.

Oppong, J. R., Mayer, J., and Oren, R. 2014. "The Global Health Threat of African Urban Slums: The Example of Urban Tuberculosis." *African Geographical Review*, DOI: 10.1080/19376812. 2014.910815

Rena, R. 2014. "Eritrea: Educational Development Pre- and post-Independence." In Wolhuter, C. (Ed.) *Education in East and Central Africa.* London: Bloomsbury Academic, pp. 191–222.

Ridde, V. 2003. "Fees-for-services, Cost Recovery, and Equity in a District of Burkina Faso Operating the Bamako Initiative." *Bulletin of the World Health Organization* 81: 532–538.

Rose, M. 2014. *Education in North Africa: The Leadership Challenge Responding to Rapid Change in the 21st Century.* A Review Submitted to the Hammamet Conference. London: The British Council.

Rwantabagu, H. 2014. "Burundi: Trend and Challenges." In Wolhuter, C. (Ed.) *Education in East and Central Africa.* London: Bloomsbury Academic, pp. 37– 68.

Saheli-Isfahani, D. 2012. "Education, Jobs, and Equity in the Middle East and North Africa." *Comparative Economic Studies,* 54: 843–861.

Sahn, D., and Bernier, R. 1995. "Have Structural Adjustments Led to Health Sector Reform in Africa?" *Health Policy* 32: 193–214.

Samoff, J. 1999. "Education Sector Analysis in Africa: Limited National Control and Even Less National Ownership." *International Journal of Educational Development* 19: 249–272.

Sayed, F. 2006. *Transforming Education in Egypt: Western Influences and Domestic Reforms.* Cairo: American University Press.

Segalla, S. D. 2009. *The Moroccan Soul: French Education, Colonial Ethnology and Muslim Resistance 1912–1956.* Lincoln, Nebraska, p. 248.

Tsehaye, R. S. 2014. "Djibouti: Formal and Non-formal Education." In Wolhuter, C. (Ed.) *Education in East and Central Africa.* London: Bloomsbury Academic, pp. 157–174.

UIS. 2012. "School and Teaching Resources in sub-Saharan Africa." UIS Information Bulletin No. 9. UNESCO.

Umar. M. S. 2001. "Education and Islamic Trends in Northern Nigeria: 1970s–1990s." *Africa Today* 48(2): 127–150.

UNDP, UNESCO, UNICEF and World Bank. 1990. *World Conference for All: Education for All: Meeting Learning for Basic Needs Final Report.* Jomtien, Thailand, 5–9 March.

UNESCO. 1963. "Records of the General Conference." *Twelfth Session.* Paris: UNESCO.

UNESCO and UNECA. 1961. Final Report. Conference of African States on the Development of Education in Africa. Addis Ababa, 15–25 May.

UNICEF. 2012. "Basic Education and Gender Equality." http://www.unicef.org/education/index_44870.html. Accessed February 27, 2016.

Waite, G. M. 1992. *A History of Traditional Medicine and Health Care in Pre-Colonial East-Central Africa.* Lanham. MD: Edwin Mellen Press.

White, B. W. 1996. "Talk about School: Education and the Colonial Project in French and British Africa, (1860–1960)." *Comparative Education* 32(1): 9–25.

WHO. 2008a. "International Conference on Primary Health care and Health Systems in Africa." *Final Report.* Ouagadougou, Burkina Faso, 28–30 April.

WHO. 2008b. *Report on the Review of Primary Health in the African Region.* Brazzaville: WHO Regional Office for Africa.

WHO. 2012. *Health Systems in Africa: Community Perceptions and Perspectives. The Report of a Multi-Country Study.* Brazzaville: WHO Regional Office for Africa.

WHO. 2016. "Factsheets on various diseases." http://who.int/mediacentre/factsheets/

Wolhuter, C. (Ed.) 2014. *Education in East and Central Africa.* London: Bloomsbury Academic.

World Bank. 2008. *The Road Not Travelled: Education Reforms in the Middle East and Africa MENA Development Report.* Washington, DC: The International Bank for Reconstruction and Development/The World Bank.

Yimam, A. 1990. *Social Development in Africa 1950–1985.* Aldershot, UK: Avebury.

Zvobgo, C. J. 1986. "Medical Missions: A Neglected Theme in Zimbabwe's History, 1893–1957." *Zambezia* XIII(ii): 109–118.

INDEX